UNITED STATES, 1960

1000 MILES

NORTH DAKOTA 1889
Bismarck

SOUTH DAKOTA 1889
Pierre

NEBRASKA 1867
Lincoln

KANSAS 1861
Topeka

OKLAHOMA 1907
Oklahoma City

TEXAS 1845
Austin

MINNESOTA 1858
St. Paul

IOWA 1846
Des Moines

MISSOURI 1821
Jefferson City

ARKANSAS 1836
Little Rock

LOUISIANA 1812
Baton Rouge

WISCONSIN 1848
Madison

MICHIGAN 1837
Lansing

ILLINOIS 1818
Springfield

INDIANA 1816
Indianapolis

OHIO 1803
Columbus

KENTUCKY 1792
Frankfort

TENNESSEE 1796
Nashville

MISSISSIPPI 1817
Jackson

ALABAMA 1819
Montgomery

GEORGIA 1788
Atlanta

FLORIDA 1845
Tallahassee

VERMONT 1791
Montpelier

MAINE 1820
Augusta

NEW HAMPSHIRE 1788
Concord

MASSACHUSETTS 1788
Boston

NEW YORK 1788
Albany

RHODE ISLAND 1790
Providence

CONNECTICUT 1788
Hartford

PENNSYLVANIA 1787
Harrisburg

NEW JERSEY 1787
Trenton

WEST VIRGINIA 1863
Charleston

WASHINGTON
Dover

DELAWARE 1787

MARYLAND 1788
Annapolis

VIRGINIA 1788
Richmond

NORTH CAROLINA 1789
Raleigh

SOUTH CAROLINA 1788
Columbia

A HISTORY

of the

AMERICAN

PEOPLE

Volume II · *since* 1865

A HISTORY
of the
AMERICAN
PEOPLE

Volume II ❧ *since* 1865

BY

Harry J. Carman
Harold C. Syrett & Bernard W. Wishy

COLUMBIA UNIVERSITY

SECOND EDITION, REVISED

19 61

Alfred · A · Knopf   NEW YORK

L. C. catalog card number: 60–6023

© *Harry J. Carman, Harold C. Syrett, and Bernard W. Wishy,* 1961

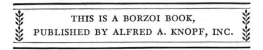

THIS IS A BORZOI BOOK,
PUBLISHED BY ALFRED A. KNOPF, INC.

PUBLISHED 1952, REPRINTED FIVE TIMES

SECOND EDITION, REVISED AND RESET, 1961

TO

M. M. C. & P. M. S.

To an Anxious Friend

You tell me that law is above freedom of utterance. And I reply that you can have no wise laws nor free enforcement of wise laws unless there is free expression of the wisdom of the people—and, alas, their folly with it. But if there is freedom, folly will die of its own poison, and the wisdom will survive. That is the history of the race. It is the proof of Man's kinship with God. You say that freedom of utterance is not for time of stress, and I reply with the sad truth that only in time of stress is freedom of utterance in danger. No one questions it in calm days, because it is not needed. And the reverse is true also; only when free utterance is suppressed is it needed and when it is needed, it is most vital to justice. Peace is good. But if you are interested in peace through force and without discussion, that is to say, free utterance decently and in order—your interest in justice is slight. And peace without justice is tyranny, no matter how you may sugar coat it with expediency. This state today is in more danger from suppression than from violence, because, in the end, suppression leads to violence. Violence, indeed, is the child of suppression. Whoever pleads for justice helps to keep the peace; and whoever tramples upon the plea for justice, temperately made in the name of peace, only outrages peace and kills something fine in the heart of man which God put there when we got our manhood. When that is killed, brute meets brute on each side of the line.

So, dear friend, put fear out of your heart. This nation will survive, this state will prosper, the orderly business of life will go forward if only men can speak in whatever way given them to utter what their hearts hold—by voice, by posted card, by letter or by press. Reason never has failed men. Only force and repression have made the wrecks in the world.

WILLIAM ALLEN WHITE
Emporia *Gazette*, July 27, 1922

A Note on the Revised Edition

IN THE YEARS since the first edition of this volume appeared there has been an impressive revaluation of much American history, and substantial scholarship has been published to support ideas that were largely suggestive and tentative at the end of the 1940's. This revision attempts to balance this newer scholarship against traditional interpretations but without, it is hoped, emphasizing what may turn out to be mere fashions in contemporary history. The book remains loyal to the original intention of providing a full analysis of American history that is true to the complexity of events and a fair test of the student's best possibilities as a serious scholar.

HARRY J. CARMAN

HAROLD C. SYRETT

BERNARD W. WISHY

Preface

J. B. Black in *The Art of History* contends that every age interprets "the record of the past in the light of its own ideas." We have preferred to take Black's words as a warning to historians rather than as a definition of written history, for we have made a conscious effort to judge the past in the light of the past and to avoid imposing the standards of our generation upon preceding generations. On the other hand, we have not renounced our right to interpret the past, for we have constantly tried to present the events of American history with a thesis in mind and to point out what we think is the significance of these events.

Our approach to history is eclectic. We do not think that the past should be studied from a single viewpoint or that it can be explained by one theory to the exclusion of all other theories. But, while rejecting any over-all thesis, we have not failed to take a stand on controversial issues. In each instance the nature of the issue has helped to determine our stand; and the fact that we have advanced a succession of different interpretations rather than used the same interpretations for a succession of events accurately reflects our conviction that every historical event is unique.

The organization of these volumes represents a compromise between the chronological and topical approaches to the material under consideration. We have divided American history into a number of comparatively large periods, and within each period we have dealt with a series of major topics. This method necessitates some repetition, but in a book that is designed for students repetition, in our view, is an asset rather than a defect. We have proceeded on the hypothesis that no part or period of American history is inherently more important than any other, and we have therefore sought to present in all its aspects the history of the American people.

HARRY J. CARMAN

HAROLD C. SYRETT

BERNARD W. WISHY

Acknowledgments

A HISTORY OF THE AMERICAN PEOPLE is an outgrowth
of Professor Carman's *Economic and Social History of
the United States*. We have used the earlier work,
which covers the period from the first settlements in
America to 1876, as a point of departure for our first
volume. At some points we have expanded Professor
Carman's material, and at others we have cut those portions of it that seemed unsuitable for a general text-
book, but in every instance we have subjected it to
extensive revisions. In addition, we have supplemented
it with a full account of American diplomatic and political history.

Throughout the preparation of these two volumes
we received considerable assistance from a number of
friends and colleagues. Professors Herman Ausubel,
Donald N. Bigelow, Henry F. Graff, and Cnilton Williamson of Columbia University, Professors Michael
Kraus and Oscar Zeichner of the College of the City
of New York, Professor Oscar Handlin of Harvard
University, Professors Frank Freidel and Fred A. Shannon of the University of Illinois, Professor James A.
Barnes of Temple University, Professor Joe L. Norris
of Wayne University, Professor R. J. Ferguson of the
University of Pittsburgh, Professor Burke M. Hermann
of Pennsylvania State College, and Mr. Thomas R.
Hay furnished us with invaluable criticisms and suggestions. Lois Green Clark of Alfred A. Knopf, Inc.
read the entire manuscript and showed unusual skill
and knowledge in criticizing both its form and content.
Mrs. Patricia Syrett typed most of the manuscript, and
both Mrs. Syrett and Miss Margaret Carscadden per-

formed a variety of generally unpleasant tasks associated with the work on this book. Both, moreover, treated its authors with remarkable tolerance and patience. Mr. James P. Shenton and Dr. Walter P. Metzger of Columbia University helped us in the preparation of the bibliography. We are also indebted to Professor Bigelow and Mr. Charles E. McCarthy for the assistance they gave us in checking the proof.

In the preparation of the revised edition our special thanks go to now Professor Shenton for help with the bibliography, to Mr. Morton Klevan for aid on research for the photographs and charts, and to Mrs. Frank Slater and Mr. Joseph Plut for their patience and precision in typing the manuscript. Along with Mrs. Slater, Barry Augenbraun and Stephen Lerner have our special thanks for their help in completing this second volume in its final stages. The fine craftsmanship of Theodore Miller is responsible for the new maps and charts in Volume II. The common sense and forebearance of Phyllis Sherman of Alfred A. Knopf, Inc. were indispensable in the preparation of the entire revised edition.

We are jointly responsible for whatever errors this book may contain.

HARRY J. CARMAN
HAROLD C. SYRETT
BERNARD W. WISHY

CONTENTS

Part III · War, Boom, and Bust

Part IV · The Welfare Republic

Part V · Shores Dimly Seen

Illustrations

Maps and Charts

BY THEODORE R. MILLER

PART I

THE PASSING
OF THE
OLD REPUBLIC

The Legacy of Civil War

THE CIVIL WAR, which was fought to preserve the Union, helped to undermine the economic and social foundations on which the antebellum Union had rested. After the war, the South was reduced to the status of a conquered province, and the North was transformed by a revolution that subordinated the farm to the factory and supplanted the standards of an agrarian society with the mores of an industrial civilization. By 1877, when the last northern troops were withdrawn from the defeated South, it was clear that the North had won more than a military victory. Although farmers still comprised the single largest element in the population, the United States had become an industrial nation for good or ill.

The Victorious North

In the years immediately following the Civil War, the North entered a period of unprecedented prosperity. Profits reached record levels, wages were higher than at any previous time in the nation's history, and farmers had little difficulty in disposing of their products at favorable prices. Turning their backs on the reforms that they had espoused before the war, northerners plunged wholeheartedly into the more prosaic—but equally serious—business of making money. Few doubted that the end justified the means, and most agreed that the end was the accumulation of wealth.

Proposed Arcade Railway, New York City, 1876

The postwar boom was sustained by the rapid development of northern industry. A friendly government, an expanding domestic market, and a seemingly limitless supply of natural resources combined to produce a spectacular growth in all forms of business activity. Men who had accumulated wartime profits invested their surplus funds in new and old enterprises, and Europeans poured money into the American economy. The government, which before the war had devoted its energies to promoting the interests of the farmers, now aided industrialists by raising tariffs, encouraging the immigration of cheap labor, depriving southern agrarians of a voice in national affairs, and turning over to private corporations extensive tracts of the public domain. Entrepreneurs were quick to take advantage of these opportunities, and for almost a decade after Appomattox the North steadily enlarged its manufacturing facilities, extended and improved its transportation system, and exploited its mineral resources.

Almost every branch of American industry grew with amazing rapidity during the war and postwar years. From 1860 to 1870, the number of factories in the United States increased by 80 per cent, railroad lines increased by 22,000 miles, oil refining developed into a major industry, and the United States became one of the world's leading producers of iron and steel. Comparable advances were made in the consumer goods industries. The output of shoes, for example, rose from 5,000,000 pairs in 1864 to 25,000,000 in 1870; the number of woolen mills increased from 1,559 in 1850 to 2,891 in 1870, the number of workers employed in the mills from 39,352 to 80,053, and the number of pounds of wool turned into cloth from 70,900,000 to 172,100,000. In many fields of manufacturing, moreover, there was a marked increase in the tempo of mechanization, in the subdivision of labor, in mass production, in industrial consolidation, and in the use of high pressure salesmanship to reach a national rather than local market.

The postwar boom gave speculators and freebooters unexampled opportunities for quick profits. The inexperience of a large part of the investing public and the absence of restrictive regulations made it comparatively easy for economic adventurers to water stock, turn security exchanges into gambling casinos, and sell stock in any one of a variety of bogus enterprises. In an age that was perhaps the most corrupt in the nation's history, Daniel Drew, Jay Gould, and Jim Fisk earned well-merited reputations as practitioners of the art of fraudulent manipulation. One of their most notorious exploits was the "Erie War" waged against Cornelius Vanderbilt in 1867.

When Vanderbilt, who was head of the New York Central, attempted to obtain control of the Erie from Drew, Gould, and Fisk, they prevented him from securing a majority of the stock and crippled him financially at the same time by issuing $10,000,000 of worthless Erie securities which they dumped on the market at just the moment when Vanderbilt's heavy purchases had pushed the price to record levels. In the legal quarrels that followed, Gould and Fisk more than matched the bribes that Vanderbilt had paid to both judges and legislators. In the summer of 1868, they issued still more Erie stock, sold it to a gullible public, and put their profits in New York City's leading national banks. Because the National Banking Act of 1863 required every national bank in New York to maintain a reserve in greenbacks or other legal tender equal to 25 per cent of its indebtedness, Drew, Gould, and Fisk were able to disrupt the money market by demanding that the banks repay them in greenbacks. To meet this demand the banks had to call in their loans, and the resulting money stringency produced a decline in both trade and security prices. The Erie triumvirate immediately capitalized on this situation by buying up large blocks of securities at a fraction of their former value. As gold had also fallen in price, they purchased it at bargain rates and pushed up its

"The Commodore" Cornelius Vanderbilt

price to record figures by withdrawing it from the market. In the fall of 1869, after inducing President Grant to refrain from any move that might lower the price of gold, Gould and Fisk again cornered the country's gold supply. On September 24, 1869—or "Black Friday"—gold, which had been quoted at 132* on September 2, had reached 160; and the country was saved from financial ruin only after Grant had belatedly authorized the government to place $4,000,000 in gold on the market.

Drew, Gould, and Fisk were the most notorious—but not the only —examples of business corruption in the postwar decade. In an age in which misrepresentation was often synonymous with "good business," a premium was placed on results regardless of how they were achieved.

* This figure represents the price of gold in relation to greenbacks.

"Gentleman Jim" James Fisk, Jr.

Convinced that there was no greater crime than to die poor, many businessmen felt that they were forced by circumstances to be ruthless, predatory, and dishonest. Ethically it is difficult to distinguish between a railroad-wrecker like Daniel Drew and a professional desperado like Jesse James, and perhaps all that is left for the social historian to record is that the first died in his bed and that the second was killed by a bullet in the back of his head.

The correct practices of some of the nation's businessmen were matched by the fraudulent activities of numerous officials in the local, state, and federal governments. The success of many of the business ventures undertaken during the Civil War depended in part on some form of governmental assistance, and after the war the politicians soon made it clear that they expected to be reimbursed for any aid that they provided. Judicial decisions more than once went to the highest bidder, and legislators at every level of government were paid for subsidies, utility franchises, contracts for public works, monopolistic grants, and the assurance that the authorities would neither investigate nor regulate certain business practices. Because the politician had favors to sell and the entrepreneur had the money to purchase them, bribery became an accepted way of doing business. In Mark Twain and Charles Dudley Warner's *The Gilded Age* (1873), one of the characters tells how to obtain a congressional appropriation for a "public improvement" company—a description that provides some indication (even after adequate allowance has been made for the satirist's right to exaggerate) of the techniques of political corruption:

> Why the matter is simple enough. A Congressional appropriation costs money. Just reflect, for instance. A majority of the House committee, say $10,000 apiece—$40,000; a majority of the Senate committee, the same each—say $40,000; a little extra to one or two chairmen of one or two such committees, say $10,000 each—$20,000; and there's $100,000 of the money gone, to begin with. Then, seven male lobbyists, at $3,000 each—$21,000; one female lobbyist, $10,000; a high moral Congressman or Senator here and there—the high moral ones cost more . . . ten of these at $3,000 each, is $30,000; then a lot of small-fry country members, who won't vote for anything whatever without pay—say twenty at $500 apiece is $10,000; a lot of dinners to members—say $10,000 altogether; lot of jim-cracks for Congressmen's wives and children—those go a long way—you can't spend too much . . . in that line—those . . . cost in a lump, say $10,000—along there somewhere;—and then comes your printed documents—your maps, your tinted engravings, your pamphlets, your illuminated show-cards, your advertisements in a hundred and fifty papers at ever so much a line—because you've got to keep the papers all right or you are gone up, you know. Oh, my dear sir, printing bills are destruction itself. Ours so far amount to—let me see—10; 52; 22; 13;—and then there's 11; 14; 33—well, never mind the details, the total in clean numbers foots up $118,254.42 thus far!

Although every major American city was looted by designing politicians during the postwar years, New York City enjoyed the dubious distinction of being the most corruptly governed municipality in the nation. A Tammany "ring," headed by William Marcy Tweed, a former chair-maker and volunteer fireman, robbed the city of millions of dollars annually. Under the direction of Boss Tweed, Mayor A. Oakey Hall, Peter B. Sweeny, and "Slippery Dick" Connolly, New York increased its debt tenfold within a decade. A county courthouse, worth approximately $25,000, cost the taxpayers $8,000,000, and the

"Boss" William Tweed

building's furnishings added another $3,000,000 to the total. Paving contracts, public printing, sewers, parks, and hospitals all provided profits for members of the ring, which had stolen more than $20,000,000 by 1871. Tweed, who boasted that he would soon be as rich as Vanderbilt, moved to a large mansion on Fifth Avenue, kept his blooded horses in mahogany stables, and replied to his critics by asking: "What are you going to do about it?" And for a time it seemed as though nothing could be done. With the support of his henchmen in the state legislature and a subservient governor, he secured a revision of the city charter that placed New York completely at his mercy. At the same time, a committee of prominent citizens, after investigating the city's finances, announced that they could discover no irregularities. Although Thomas Nast had waged a merciless campaign against Tweed in his cartoons in *Harper's*, it was not until an attempt was made to bribe both the *Times* and *Harper's* that public opinion turned against the boss. The chance installation of one of Tweed's enemies in the city comptroller's office led to a split in Tammany, a series of revelations, and the eventual prosecution of the machine leaders. Tweed, who was convicted of stealing $6,000,000, escaped to Spain; but he was subsequently extradited and returned to jail, where he died in 1878.

State governments were as corrupt as those of the nation's cities. Most New York state legislators—whether they were merchants, lawyers, up-state farmers, or members of Tammany Hall—had their price; and at the height of the Erie War, one New York senator accepted $75,000 from Vanderbilt and $100,000 from Gould, and then voted for Gould. At Harrisburg, the capital of Pennsylvania, Simon Cameron and Matthew S. Quay saw to it that almost no bill of importance could be put through unpurchased. For years the Illinois legislature was run by the state's corporations, contractors, and land speculators. In Wisconsin a powerful railway lobby crushed unfriendly measures, while in Kansas, Missouri, and a number of other western states the giving and taking of bribes was an accepted part of the legislative process.

Because the federal government could offer businessmen particularly favorable prizes, its members were able to make enormous sums of money from graft and bribery. Politics was converted into a business, and, like any good businessman, the politician sold his wares and services to the highest bidder. Vernon L. Parrington, in describing what he called "the great barbecue," has written:

> Congress had rich gifts to bestow—in lands, tariffs, subsidies, favors of all sorts; and when influential citizens made their wishes known to the reigning statesmen, the sympathetic politicians were quick to turn the government into the fairy godmother the voters wanted it to be. A huge barbecue was spread to which all presumably were invited. Not quite all, to be sure; inconspicuous persons, those who were at home on the farm or at work in the mills and offices, were overlooked; a good many indeed out of the total number of the American people. But all the important persons, leading bankers and promoters and business men, received invitations. There wasn't room for everybody and these were presumed to represent the whole. It was a splendid feast. If the waiters saw to it that the choicest portions were served to favored guests, they were not unmindful of their numerous homespun constituency and they loudly proclaimed the fine democratic principle that what belongs to the people should be enjoyed by the people—not with petty bureaucratic restrictions, not as a social body, but as in-

dividuals, each free citizen using what came to hand for his own private ends, with no questions asked.*

In aiding the businessman, the government also accelerated the postwar cycle of boom and bust. By the end of the 1860's, there was ample evidence of overexpansion in many areas of northern business enterprise. The number of business firms in the United States jumped from 431,000 in 1870 to 609,904 in 1871. The annual increase in railroad mileage, which averaged about 1,300 miles in 1860–67, rose to about 5,000 in 1869, and to about 5,700 in 1870; and during the next two years 13,000 miles were built. But of 364 railroads in 1872, only 104 paid dividends, and 69 of these paid less than 10 per cent. At the same time, American exports lagged behind imports, and in the early 1870's the United States had to export $130,000,000 annually to cover its trade deficit and interest payments on the capital it had borrowed abroad. The nation's credit structure also was top-heavy, for in the period from 1868 to 1873 the volume of bank loans increased seven times as fast as bank deposits. Perhaps most dangerous were the movements of capital from productive to speculative enterprises and the rise in the number of business failures from 2,915 in 1871 to 4,069 in 1872.

The crash came in 1873. On September 8, the New York Warehouse and Securities Company failed, followed within two weeks by Kenyon, Cox and Company and Jay Cooke and Company. On September 20, the New York Stock Exchange closed for ten days "to save the entire Street from utter ruin"; but nothing could prevent the cumulative effect of the collapse. By the end of 1873, there had been more than 5,000 commercial failures with liabilities totaling $228,500,000, and 89 railroads had defaulted on their bonds. For the next five years, there was little prospect of returning prosperity. In 1876–7, more than 18,000 business firms failed, at least half the nation's mills and factories closed, and unemployment steadily increased. It was not until 1878 that any signs of a business revival appeared, and it was not until 1880 that full recovery had been achieved.

The Defeated South

At the end of the Civil War, the South was bitter and exhausted. In five years the section's white population had declined from almost 5,500,000 to fewer than 5,000,000, and more than 250,000 Confederate

* Vernon L. Parrington: *Main Currents in American Thought*, Vol. III, *The Beginnings of Critical Realism, 1860–1920* (New York: Harcourt, Brace & Company, Inc., 1930), p. 23. Copyright 1930 by, and reprinted with permission of, Harcourt, Brace & Company, Inc.

soldiers had been killed during the war. To those who survived, the present seemed intolerable and the future hopeless, for the war had destroyed not only a large part of the South's physical assets, but also its way of life. With the northern victory, the southerners were left with little to cherish but their memories.

Few parts of the South had escaped the effects of the war. From Harper's Ferry to Newmarket, Virginia—a distance of about eighty miles—barns, mills, haystacks, and houses had been burned to the ground. Livestock, fences, and bridges had been destroyed. The region between Washington and Richmond was a wasteland of gutted villages and farm buildings. In Georgia and the Carolinas, Sherman's army had left a path of destruction that was "heart-sickening," while large parts of Arkansas and northern Alabama presented scenes of appalling ruin. The valley of the Tennessee was so devastated that six years after the war Robert Somers, an English traveler, reported that

> . . . it consists for the most part of plantations in a state of semi-ruin, and plantations of which the ruin is for the present total and complete. . . . The trial of war is visible throughout the valley in burnt-up gin-houses, ruined bridges, mills and factories . . . and in large tracts of once cultivated land stripped of every vestige of fencing.

The towns and cities of the South were almost as desolate as the countryside. Richmond, largely destroyed by fire when it was evacuated by the Confederate troops, was a mass of charred ruins. In Columbia, South Carolina, an area of eighty blocks containing 1,386 buildings had been converted into a dreary stretch of blackened chimneys and crumbling walls. Charleston, which had suffered from repeated bombardments and two disastrous fires, was described by a northern visitor as a city "of ruins, of desolation, of vacant houses, of widowed women, of rotting wharves, of deserted warehouses, of weed-wild gardens, of miles of grass-grown streets, of acres of pitiful and voiceless barrenness." Masses of fire-smoked brick and mortar, burned timber, twisted scraps of tin roofing, and thousands of tons of débris were evidence that Sherman had passed through Atlanta. "Hell has laid her egg," said a Georgian viewing Atlanta, "and right here it hatched." In Mobile, nine blocks had been destroyed by an explosion; a large part of the wharves had been torn up and used for firewood; half the warehouses and shops were closed; and an atmosphere of decay enveloped the narrow, dirty streets in which wretched men loafed dispiritedly. Galveston, according to a reporter, was "a city of dogs and desolation . . . utterly insignificant and Godforsaken." Even in New Orleans, where there was little physical damage, the spirit of the people seemed broken, and business was virtually at a standstill.

The South was devastated, but its people were not completely poverty-stricken. But much of their capital had disappeared in a sea of worthless Confederate stocks, bonds, and currency. Many banks and insurance companies were bankrupt. The property in slaves, estimated at almost two billion dollars, had been wiped out by the Thirteenth Amendment to the Constitution. Farmers and planters lacked tools, stock, seeds, and money. Land values were incredibly low, and many plantations were heavily mortgaged. Mills, factories, and mines that had not been destroyed were closed. All coin had disappeared long before 1865, and stocks of merchandise were practically exhausted. Whitelaw Reid, a New York journalist who visited the South just after the war, wrote:

> Everything has been mended, and generally in the rudest style. Window-glass has given way to thin boards in railway coaches and in the cities. Furniture is marred and broken, and none has been replaced for four years. Dishes are cemented in various styles and half the pitchers have tin handles. A complete set of crockery is never seen, and in very few families is there enough to set a table. . . . A set of forks with whole tines is a curiosity. Clocks and watches have nearly all stopped. . . . Hair brushes and tooth brushes have all worn out; combs are broken. . . . Pins, needles and thread, and a thousand such articles, which seem indispensable to housekeeping, are very scarce.

Despite the widespread destruction and the contemporary sense that the South had been ruined, the former Confederate states had not been fully impoverished. Much of the crudity, rudeness, and even some of the ruins seen by northern and foreign observers at the time had carried over from before 1860, when whole areas of the South had lived in crude conditions. Most of the war devastation and bankruptcy had taken place within the planter class who, whatever the economic facts, were convinced that the war had ruined them and their society. Nevertheless, after 1865, the rebuilding of southern cities, the early postwar expansion of cotton factories and the rebuilding of some railroads were southern financed. Even within the planter group, many men were still wealthy enough to apply for the special presidential pardon for rebellion necessary for ex-Confederates with wealth in excess of $20,000. Mounting evidence seems to indicate that, although there was probably a large shift in ownership, the plantation system did not break up but soon reverted to the prewar pattern of growing at the expense of the middle size and smaller farmers.

In the first year or two after the war, the available southern energy for reconstruction was hindered in several ways. The South's economic problems were aggravated by the almost complete lack of transportation facilities. Horses, mules, wagons, and carriages were scarce; country roads had become practically impassable through neglect; and bridges that had not been burned or washed away were in need of repair. Most of the river steamboats had been captured or destroyed, while the few that were intact were worn out. With the exception of the railroads that had been used by the federal government, southern rail facilities were either destroyed or useless. Two thirds of the railroad companies in the section were bankrupt. Virtually all the Virginia lines were out of commission. Every mile of railway in Georgia and South Carolina that could be used by the Confederacy had been destroyed by Sherman. Alabama's 800 miles of railway were practically worthless, and the New Orleans, Jackson, and Great Northern—Mississippi's leading railroad before the war—was a scrapheap.

With the defeat of the Confederate armies, the region's central, state, and local governments collapsed, and for some time there was little or no check placed on the more unruly elements in the population. Guerrilla and outlaw bands terrorized many parts of the South. In Texas alone, more than 5,000 men secured their livelihood by organized robbery and murder. Almost every neighborhood north of the Arkansas was pillaged by guerrillas, and in Alabama and Mississippi highwaymen made it practically impossible to carry on trade between towns.

Southern economic recovery was also impeded at first by the activities of federal treasury agents, who were paid a commission of approximately 25 per cent to discover and confiscate Confederate army stores. Left largely to their own devices, many of these agents seized and sold private property to which they had no legal claim. Horses, mules, wagons, tobacco, rice, sugar, and cotton were frequently taken in spite of the protests of their rightful owners. "I am sure I sent some honest cotton agents South," Secretary of the Treasury McCulloch wrote, "but it seems doubtful whether any of them remained honest very long." In his special report of 1866, McCulloch stated:

> . . . Residents and others in the districts where these peculations were going on took advantage of the unsettled conditions of the country, and representing themselves as agents of this department, went about robbing under such pretended au-

The Capture of Jefferson Davis, Disguised as a Woman

thority, and thus added to the difficulties of the situation by causing unjust opprobrium and suspicion to rest upon officers engaged in the faithful discharge of their duties. Agents . . . frequently received or collected property . . . which the law did not authorize them to take . . Lawless men, singly and in organized bands, engaged in general plunder; every species of intrigue and speculation and theft were resorted to.

While these agents turned over about $34,000,000 to the United States, it is impossible even to guess how much money they kept for themselves. In subsequent years, 40,000 southern claimants were indemnified for property that had been taken from them illegally. Many thousands of others, unable to prove that they had been defrauded, received nothing.

At the same time that the South was seeking to solve its economic problems, it was also forced to work out a new set of relationships between the region's white groups and the 3,500,000 newly liberated Negroes. The majority of the Negroes were at first too bewildered to appreciate the meaning of their new status. To some, freedom meant a change of name, a new job, and the right to go wherever they pleased. Many freedmen became migrants; some supported themselves by thievery; and still others died from hunger. Many, too, thought that freedom meant education, an opportunity to become the equals of the whites, and a gift from the government of "forty acres and a mule." A relatively large number of Negroes remained with their former masters until their role as freedmen had been clarified. Although freedom meant many different things to the Negroes, the white southerners, like most northerners, were almost unanimous in their agreement that it should not mean equality of the races.

The South started upon this critical period of readjustment without the political services of its former leaders, for the federal government at first barred most members of the planter class from politics in the years immediately following Appomattox. This policy, regardless of its merits, further antagonized a people who were already embittered by war and defeat. At the same time, a large part of the control over southern political affairs passed initially into the hands of northern military and civilian officials. For the white southerners, the hatred engendered by the war was compounded by its aftermath, and in 1866 a Virginia patrician, who had been robbed and pillaged by northern troops, in drawing up his will wrote:

> . . . I give and bequeath to my children and grandchildren, and their descendants throughout all generations, that bitter hatred and everlasting malignity of my heart and soul against the Yankees, including all the people north of Mason and Dixon's line, and I do hereby exhort and entreat my children and grandchildren, if they have any love or veneration for me, to instill in the hearts of their children and grandchildren, and all their future descendants, from their childhood, this bitter hatred and these malignant feelings, against the aforesaid people and their descendants throughout all future time and generations.

To some wealthy and influential southerners, defeat and the prospect of northern domination were so distasteful that they preferred emigration to remaining in America, while others moved to northern cities. But most southern leaders—including Robert E. Lee, Wade Hampton, and Jefferson Davis—believed that the South's difficulties were the very reason why its people should not abandon their homeland. Hampton urged his fellow citizens to "devote their whole energies to the restoration of law and order, the reestablishment of agriculture and commerce, the promotion of education and the rebuilding of our cities and dwellings which have been laid in ashes." And Lee, in arguing against emigration, maintained that all should "share in the fate of their respective states." "The thought of abandoning the country and all that must be left in it [he said] is abhorrent to my feelings . . . The South requires the aid of her sons now more than at any other period of her history."

For the mass of southerners who remained in their section, the most pressing problem was economic rehabilitation. Half a million farms and plantations, many of them bankrupt or on the verge of insolvency, had to be restored; gutted homes and a ruined transportation system had to be rebuilt; credit had to be re-established; and, perhaps most important of all, some substitute had to be found for slave labor. Neither the whites nor the Negroes had had much experience with the wage system, and after the war a number of conditions militated against its use. Because most farmers were penniless, they were unable to pay their hired help until they had marketed their crops. Many southern whites, moreover, were opposed on both social and economic grounds to employing free Negroes. Throughout these years, plans for transporting the freedmen to Africa or the West Indies and importing foreign white labor were seriously discussed in many parts of the South. But an impoverished South could offer few inducements to immigrants from the Old World, and few newcomers settled below Mason and Dixon's line. On the other hand, the Negro, who was reluctant to give up any part of his new freedom and was suspicious of white employers, showed no enthusiasm for hiring-out.

The wage system was tried in some parts of the rural South after the war, but in most instances it proved unworkable. The limitations of southern banking and the scarcity of money so reminiscent of prewar years, prevented all but a small number of planters and farmers from hiring help. The Negroes also generally objected to the terms on which they were employed. Frequently, they complained of low wages, and on numerous occasions—and often with much justification—they insisted that they were being cheated. As most freedmen soon refused to work for wages under these circumstances, and as most southerners had little money to pay out for wages anyway, southern landowners increasingly turned to the share, or cropping, system. Under this arrangement, the planter provided the croppers with land, seed, draft animals, and implements and arranged credit facilities for them at the local store. The croppers, in turn, agreed to plant, cultivate, and harvest the crop in return for a portion of it that usually ranged from one third to one half. The store, which was owned sometimes by a planter but usually by a local merchant, provided the tenant with credit in return for a mortgage on his share in the season's crop. Although the so-called crop-lien system provided the agrarian South with much needed credit facilities, it was also largely responsible for the section's concentration on cotton—a cash crop—to the exclusion of most other products, for the perpetuation of backward methods of farming in the region, and for the creation of a class of virtual peons—both Negro and white—in the rural areas of the South.

The hard times following the war were responsible not only for the growth of share cropping and the crop-lien system, but also for many changes on the section's large plantations. Many old planters were forced to dispose of their lands at a fraction of their prewar value, and the newspapers were filled with advertisements of plantations for sale at a "sacrifice." In 1865, it was possible to buy good land anywhere in the South at from three to five dollars an acre—or at a price that represented one fifth to one sixth of its value in 1860. With cotton prices high, men from all parts of the South took advantage of the unprecedented opportunity to acquire land in the first two years or so after the war. A Georgia editor wrote:

> Never perhaps was there a rural movement accomplished without revolution or exodus, that equalled in extent and swiftness the partition of the plantations of the ex-slaveholders into small farms. As remarkable as was the eagerness of the Negroes—who bought in Georgia alone 6,850 farms in three years—the earth-hunger of the poorer class of the whites, who had been under the slaveholding oligarchy to own land, was even more striking.

Northerners also invested heavily in southern land. A group of Ohioans, believing that they could revolutionize cotton production by introducing scientific methods of cultivation, settled in Noxubee and Lowndes counties, Mississippi; Whitelaw Reid moved to Louisiana; Colonel Henry Lee Higginson and others bought up large tracts of plantation land in Georgia; and John Hay put a considerable sum of money in Florida orange groves.

Census returns seemed to indicate that the plantation system had broken up. Tennessee, which in 1860 had only 82,368 farms, had 118,–141 in 1870. In South Carolina the number increased from 33,000 to 52,000; in Mississippi from 43,000 to 68,000; and in Louisiana from 17,000 to 28,000. At the same time, there was a corresponding decrease in the size of most southern farms. The area of the average Louisiana farm decreased from 536 acres in 1860 to 247 acres ten years later; and even in North Carolina, which before the Civil War had had more small farms than most southern states, the average farm fell from 316 acres to 212. These figures, however, are deceptive. A great number of men listed as landowners in the census returns after the war were actually tenants or even sharecroppers. Although many plantations in most states were divided into a smaller number of units, actual ownership remained with the old planter or the new rural business class that was drawn from wartime profiteers and merchants. New farms, furthermore, which were small at first, very soon were encompassed by neighboring farms or plantations or themselves became the nucleus of larger units. Very swiftly the South resumed the national tendencies to ever larger farms and more commercial farming.

By 1875, southern agriculture, although still relatively backward, had almost regained its prewar footing. Thousands of small growers acquired holdings either as tenants, croppers, or owners. Across the Mississippi, pioneer farmers opened up extensive new cotton lands in Arkansas and Texas. From 1865 to 1875, the area under cotton cultivation averaged 8,810,000 acres annually. With the exception of 1866 and 1867, when the South suffered from severe droughts, yields rose steadily and good prices prevailed. By 1878, the crop equaled that of the off year of 1860, and in 1880 the South surpassed the best prewar cotton year. Many farmers were making money for the first time since the war, and the South was gradually lightening its heavy burden of debt.

The reorganization of southern agriculture was accompanied by fundamental changes in the section's mercantile system. Before the war, the large planters had bought their supplies at wholesale rates in Mobile, Charleston, Richmond, New York, and other urban centers. In the postwar years, the southern farmer—both Negro and white—made his purchases at the village or crossroads store, which in turn obtained its goods from northern merchants. In similar fashion, the individual farmer, instead of consigning his crop directly to commission jobbers, as was the common practice before the war, sold it to a local dealer. As the character of the southern economy altered, both towns and townspeople assumed a position of unprecedented importance in the South's economy. Many planters, who during the antebellum period had devoted their major efforts to the management of their plantations, turned to business enterprise. "The higher planting class," P. A. Bruce has written, "so far as it has survived at all, has been concentrated in the cities. . . . The talent, the energy, the ambition, that formerly sought expression in the management of great estates and the control of hosts of slaves, now seeks a field of action in trade, manufacturing enterprises; or in the general enterprises of development." While the South remained overwhelmingly agrarian, both the mores and economy of the section were increasingly shaped by an ambitious growing middle class—an influence that indicated that the North had won more than a military victory at Appomattox.

Lincoln and Reconstruction

During the postwar years, almost every aspect of southern life was either directly or indirectly affected by the reconstruction policies of the federal government. The course of reconstruction, in turn, was in large part determined by the outcome of the struggle between the Republican factions for the control of the nation's government. Conservatives, who were led by Lincoln and probably composed the bulk of the party during the war, urged that the bitterness of the past be forgotten, that the southern states be restored to their antebellum status as rapidly as possible, and that following the abolition of slavery no further moves be made to alter the social and economic structure of the South.

Radicals were drawn from a number of diverse groups within the Republican party. Abolitionists, who had opposed slavery long before the war, demanded that the freedmen be granted political, social, and economic equality. The abolitionists, who distrusted both the southern whites and the northern conservatives, had a powerful ally in the growing industrial class. The Civil War had stimulated the growth of industry and had driven planter-spokesmen from Congress. If the former Confederates were now kept politically impotent, the way would be clear for the industrialists to push their schemes for transcontinental railroads, large-scale manufactures, high tariffs, and the exploitation of the nation's natural resources. Under the circumstances, they had every reason to desire that the Republican party—champion of free homesteads, unrestricted immigration, internal improvements, protective tariffs, shipping subsidies, and a national banking system—retain its control over the national government. Republican politicians, grown fat on wartime patronage and favors, realized that by giving the Negro the vote and by withholding it from large numbers of white southerners they could ensure the success of their party in the states of the former Confederacy. In these various groups within the Republican party the radicals found a basis for cooperation to break the power of the old white ruling class in the South.

During the postwar years, the leading men favoring a radical policy toward the South were Charles Sumner of Massachusetts, Thaddeus Stevens of Pennsylvania, Benjamin Butler of Massachusetts, Benjamin F. Wade of Ohio, Zachariah Chandler of Michigan, G. W. Julian of Indiana, Henry Wilson of Massachusetts, Richard Yates of Illinois, and James M. Ashley of Ohio. Stevens was pre-eminent in the House, while Sumner was perhaps the outstanding radical in the Senate. Stevens, born in New England, spent most of his life practicing law in Pennsylvania. He had been a member of the Anti-Masonic party, a champion of free public schools, an abolitionist, and a member of the House of Representatives. From the end of the Civil War until his death in 1868, Stevens repeatedly demanded that the southerners be deprived of their political rights, that they be compelled to pay the cost of the war, that their property be confiscated, and that the head of each Negro family in the South be given forty acres of land. Sumner was a Boston aristocrat and intellectual who had opposed slavery all his life. A lawyer, scholar, politician, and reformer, he was one of the ablest opponents of Lincoln's nonvindictive attitude and Johnson's lenient reconstruction program. In Sumner's view, the seceded states occupied the same status as territories, and the prerequisite for any reconstruction plan had to be Negro suffrage. To their enemies, Stevens and Sumner were fanatics; to their supporters, they were selfless crusaders. Both groups were right.

Both the conservatives and the radicals sought to reinforce their respective positions with constitutional arguments. During the war, northern officials had maintained that, since secession was illegal, the South in constitutional law had not withdrawn from the Union. It followed inevitably that there could be no question about readmitting the southern states to a Union that they had never left. The problem then was to restore to the citizens of the South the rights which they had temporarily renounced but to which they were still entitled. While adopting this line of reasoning, the conservatives did not think that constitutional questions should be emphasized at the expense of what they felt were practical considerations. On April 11, 1865, Lincoln spoke for many other conservatives when he said:

> We all agree that the seceded states, so-called, are out of their
> proper practical relation with the Union; and that the sole

Thaddeus Stevens

[NATIONAL ARCHIVES]

object of the government, civil and military, in regard to those States is to again get them into that proper practical relation. I believe it is not only possible, but in fact, easier to do this, without deciding, or even considering, whether these States have ever been out of the Union, than with it. Finding themselves safely at home, it would be utterly immaterial whether they had ever been abroad.

In opposing the conservative position, the radicals, some of whom had argued in 1860–1 that the Union was indissoluble, in effect now took over the original southern view of secession and maintained that the states of the Confederacy had actually withdrawn from the Union. By insisting that secession was a fact rather than an untenable constitutional theory, the radicals could conclude that the inhabitants of the seceded states had forfeited the rights and privileges guaranteed by the Constitution. This interpretation of secession left the defeated South completely at the mercy of the victorious North. The inconsistency of the radicals was matched by that of the southerners. Having maintained during the war that their states were irrevocably out of the Union, they proceeded to ask at the end of the war that they be treated as though they had never left the Union.

In their conflicts with the conservatives, the radicals were at first at a marked disadvantage, for Lincoln, as a wartime president, was able to put some generous reconstruction policies into effect even before the final defeat of the Confederacy. Lincoln's best known program, which was called the Ten Per Cent Plan, was first presented to the American people in December, 1863. According to its provisions, participation in the reconstructed state governments in the South was to be denied leading Confederate military, naval, diplomatic, and civil officials. Full pardon as well as restoration of property would be granted to any other Confederates who would take an oath to uphold the Constitution in the future and comply with all executive proclamations and acts of Congress concerning slavery. In any state, as soon as ten per cent of the population that had voted in 1860 had taken the oath, they could proceed to organize a new government loyal to the United States.

Even before the announcement of his Ten Per Cent Plan, Lincoln had taken steps to facilitate the re-establishment of Union governments in those southern states that were controlled at least in part by northern troops. In 1862, he had placed Tennessee, North Carolina, and Louisiana under the supervision of provisional military governors, and by 1864 Tennessee, Louisiana, and Arkansas had organized governments in accordance with the terms of the Ten Per Cent Plan. Lincoln had also recognized the loyal government that had been formed by the Unionists of western Virginia.

Although Lincoln had the authority to set up new governments in the southern states, no state could be restored to the Union without congressional approval. Congress could not only refuse to recognize the validity of the Lincoln governments, but it also had the right to prevent the senators or representatives of any state from being seated. It was through Congress, therefore, that the radicals sought to block the President's reconstruction program. In opposing Lincoln's plan, the radicals in Congress accurately reflected the widespread feeling that grew in the North as the war became more bitter that the southerners should be punished for both secession and the war. The radicals also obtained considerable support from several moderate congressmen who felt that the President, in assuming the initiative in restoring the states of the South to the Union, had encroached on the province of the legislative branch of the government.

The radicals made no attempt to conceal their hostility to the President's program. Largely because of radical opposition, Congress refused to recognize the Lincoln governments; the representatives from the reorganized states were not seated; the Union—or Republican—platform of 1864 contained a plank calling for congressional control of Reconstruction; and the electoral votes of the states with Lincoln governments were not counted in the election of 1864. The radicals spelled out their own reconstruction plan in the Wade-Davis Bill, which was adopted by Congress in July, 1864. This measure, which was based explicitly upon the premise that the seceded states had actually left the Union, put readmission entirely in the hands of Congress and made complete subjugation the first prerequisite to reinstatement. As soon as the military conquest of a state had been completed, a census was to be taken of all adult white males. When a majority of these—not a mere ten per cent as under Lincoln's plan—had taken an oath that they had been loyal to the Union and would be in the future, they would be permitted to elect delegates to a state constitutional convention. The new constitution would need the approval of half the eligible voters. To secure a state's readmission into the Union, its convention had to abolish slavery, repudiate the debts of the Confederate state government, and disfranchise practically all citizens who had held high civilian and military offices under the Confederacy. When Lincoln prevented the adoption of this bill by a pocket veto, the radicals replied with the Wade-Davis Manifesto warning the President to confine himself to his executive duties and to leave the problem of political reconstruction to Congress. In discussing reconstruction with Charles Sumner, however, Lincoln tried for a compromise between his plan and that of the radicals, thereby showing that, while his attitude was humane, he had no one policy to which he was unreservedly committed.

The Wade-Davis Bill and the Manifesto that followed it revealed that there was a strong faction in each house of Congress that opposed both presidential control over reconstruction and a lenient policy toward the defeated South. Although the exigencies of the military conflict prevented the radicals from pressing their views during the war, they did secure the passage of a bill creating a Bureau of Refugees, Freedmen, and Abandoned Lands in March, 1865. The Freedmen's Bureau, as the new agency was generally called, was set up to aid the Negroes in the South and to prevent any move to re-enslave them. Under the direction of General Oliver O. Howard, the bureau assigned "abandoned" and confiscated lands to the freedmen, distributed food and clothing, furnished medical aid, organized Negro schools, supervised Negro employment, and exercised certain judicial powers in cases involving freedmen. The Freedmen's Bureau saved thousands of destitute freedmen from starvation; in three years it distributed

Charles Sumner

nearly 21,000,000 rations, more than 15,000,000 of these to freedmen. In this and other work the agency also helped poorer whites.

The Freedmen's Bureau both antagonized the southern whites and helped to make actual the radical plans for the South. Within a short time, the bureau had also become a branch of the Republican party, and much of its relief work had political as well as humanitarian objectives. In aiding the freedmen, the bureau in effect purchased their votes. Many of the bureau's officials, moreover, were corrupt and on several occasions they misappropriated the agency's funds. To most southern whites, despite its achievements, the bureau was a symbol of all that they hated in reconstruction; to the radicals, on the other hand, it was a highly effective device for creating a social and political revolution in the South.

Johnson and the Radicals

Abraham Lincoln had shown himself remarkably adept at handling the political phases of reconstruction policy during the war. He alien-

Andrew Johnson

ated no group entirely and waited for a chance to make the best choice open to him. Although Lincoln had the most generous feelings toward the South, summed up in his famous words, "With malice toward none; with charity for all," he had not wedded himself irrevocably to any one program. Many radicals greeted Lincoln's assassination in April 1865 with unconcealed rejoicing, for they believed that his successor, Andrew Johnson, favored a harsh policy for the South. Andrew Johnson, born in 1808 in North Carolina, was a self-made man and a southern Democrat. Settling at an early age in Greeneville, Tennessee, he earned his living as a tailor and became a forthright spokesman for the more radical elements of the Democratic party in his state. For a decade after 1843, he was a member of the House of Representatives, and during the 1850's he served two terms as governor of Tennessee. Elected to the Senate, he did not secede with his state, in spite of the fact that he had voted for Breckinridge in 1860. During the war, he was named military governor of Tennessee by Lincoln, and repeatedly demonstrated his courage and devotion to the Union cause. His nomination as the Republican vice-presidential candidate in 1864 was largely the result of the desire of the party's leaders to win the support of the War Democrats and to create the impression that the party stood for the Union regardless of partisan considerations. Unfortunately, as a politician, Johnson the Democrat had no chance to acquire claims on Republican loyalties before he became President, only a month after the inauguration.

Despite Johnson's record as an antisecessionist Democrat and a Union military governor of Tennessee, the new President soon revealed that he had none of Lincoln's shrewdness and little sympathy for the radical program. Acting largely under the advice of General Grant and other military men, after a few months Johnson dropped his initial hostility to the defeated Southern elite and made a positive program of Lincoln's mere proposals, but he used much less tact than Lincoln. Consequently, Johnson's reconstruction policy was both mild and militant in character and brought the radicals together against him. Under the Johnson plan, which went into effect soon after he took office, the President granted a general amnesty to all participants in the rebellion who took an oath of allegiance to the United States. Southern states were to be readmitted to the Union as soon as their newly formed governments had repealed the ordinances of secession, abolished slavery by constitutional conventions and by legislative ratification of the Thirteenth Amendment, and had repudiated the debts incurred in the prosecution of the war. Although the radicals denounced the Johnson program, they were powerless to prevent its immediate adoption; for when Johnson became President, Congress was not in session, and it did not reconvene until December, 1865. Johnson gambled that he could present Congress with irreversible facts. By the end of the year, the seven Confederate states that had not been reconstructed under the Lincoln plan had established new governments in accordance with Johnson's proposals, and sent leading Confederates to Washington.

Following their reorganization under either the Lincoln or Johnson plans, the southern states, confronted with their economic and race problems, enacted the "Black Codes"—a series of laws that affected the status of the Negro in the South. This legislation granted the freedmen certain civil rights—to make contracts, to sue and be sued in regular state courts, to acquire and hold property (in most instances), and to be secure in person and estate. But at the same time the Black Codes imposed a number of restrictions on the freedom of the southern Negro. They forbade intermarriage of the races; in some states they forbade Negroes to carry weapons without a license; in several states they did not permit Negroes to be witnesses in court against white persons; and

Lincoln's Remains in New York, 1865 (The garish funeral was used to embitter the North against the South.)

in practically every state they severely circumscribed the freedman's right to work. The laws concerning vagrancy were discriminatory, and in many cases magistrates were given wide discretionary powers in ordering Negroes to be held as vagrants and in assigning them to the highest bidder to work out fines. The most drastic codes were enacted by Mississippi, Louisiana, and South Carolina, the states in which the Negroes outnumbered the whites. In Mississippi, for example, a freedman could not own or rent land except in incorporated towns and cities, while South Carolina forbade them to engage in any trade or business other than husbandry or domestic service except under a license requiring a substantial annual fee.

Although in part the Black Codes had been based on former northern laws to maintain white supremacy, many northerners now condemned them. Horace Greeley thought that they indicated that the South would not "stop short of the extermination of the black race," and the *Chicago Tribune* wrote "that the men of the North will convert the state of Mississippi into a frogpond before they will allow any such laws to disgrace one foot of soil in which the bones of our soldiers sleep and over which the flag of freedom waves." Although the majority of southern whites approved of the Black Codes, there were some who believed that they were both oppressive and politically inexpedient. The *Clarion,* one of the most influential papers in Mississippi, conceded that certain aspects of the Black Codes were "unfortunate," and the *Columbus Sentinel* stated that those responsible for the laws were a "shallow-headed majority more anxious to make capital at home than to propitiate the powers at Washington."

The Black Codes and the election of ex-Confederates aroused radicals against the South and the mild Johnson program. Convinced, as between former rebel leaders among the planters and rebel soldier "poor whites," that there was no other reliable group to deal with in the South, and that both Negro freedom and Republican supremacy depended on Negro political power, when Congress convened in December, 1865, the radicals were prepared to launch an all-out offensive against the President and his reconstruction policies. Their first move was to have the House and Senate establish the Joint Committee of Fifteen on Reconstruction—which the radicals dominated from the outset—to review Johnson's reconstruction program and to pass on questions concerning the admission to Congress of members from the seceded states. A tug of war between Congress and President now followed. Congress approved a measure that extended the life and enlarged the powers of the Freedmen's Bureau, but Johnson vetoed this measure in February, 1866. In the following month, the radicals returned to the attack with a concurrent resolution stating that no senator or representative could be seated until Congress had granted representation to the state in question. At the same time, Congress adopted over Johnson's veto the Civil Rights Bill, which forbade the states to discriminate against citizens because of their color or race and served as a warning to the southern legislatures that their plan to set the Negro apart under the Black Codes would not be tolerated by the federal government. If any doubt remained concerning either congressional or radical supremacy, it was dispelled in July, 1866, when Radical majorities in the House and Senate passed—and then repassed over Johnson's veto—the Second Freedmen's Bureau Bill.

Because the Civil Rights Bill was subject to repeal by any succeeding Congress and because there was always the possibility that the Supreme Court might declare it unconstitutional, the radicals decided to write it into the Constitution. Accordingly, in April, 1866, the Joint Committee on Reconstruction submitted to Congress a proposal that eventually became the Fourteenth Amendment. As finally submitted to the states, Section 1 of the Amendment made the Negro a citizen of the United States and of the state in which he resided, and said that no state could deprive "any person of life, liberty or property, without due process of law" or deny any person the equal protection of the laws.

Section 2 provided that representation among the several states should be now apportioned on the basis of total population instead of by counting only three fifths of the Negroes, but when the right to vote for national or state officials was denied by a state to any male inhabitants "being twenty one years of age, and citizens . . . except for participation in rebellion or other crime," the state's basis of representation should be proportionately reduced. The third section disqualified for either state or federal office all persons, "who, having previously taken an oath . . . to support the Constitution of the United States, shall have engaged in insurrection or rebellion against the same," until Congress by a two-thirds vote of each removed such a disability. Section 4 confirmed the validity of the debt of the United States, outlawed the Confederate debt in all its forms, and denied the legality of all claims arising from the emancipation of the slaves.

The Fourteenth Amendment proved of inestimable aid to the radicals. It enabled them to impose their program on the South and it also provided them with another opportunity to discredit both Johnson and his reconstruction policies. In submitting the amendment to the states for ratification, the President stated that he thought it unconstitutional and urged the eleven southern states to reject it. All but Tennessee, which was readmitted to the Union in July, 1866, followed his advice. In adopting this course, both the President and the southerners played into the hands of the radicals, who now had little difficulty in convincing the voters that Johnson was allied with the former enemies of the North and that the people of the South had shown that they were not fit to govern themselves. In discussing the refusal of the southern states to ratify the Fourteenth Amendment, James A. Garfield of Ohio said: "The last one of the sinful ten has at last with contempt and scorn flung back into our teeth the magnanimous offer of a generous nation. It is now our turn to act."

The conflict over the Fourteenth Amendment set the stage for the midterm elections of 1866. Instead of the traditional type of contest between the two major parties, the campaign quickly developed into a struggle between the President and the radicals. At the "National Union Convention," held by Johnson's followers at Philadelphia in August, in an attempt to rally moderate support behind the President, the Democrats overshadowed the Republicans. During the entire campaign, the President was handicapped by the fact that his program was more appealing to his one-time opponents than to the members of the party that had elected him. Johnson, moreover, was opposed not only by critics of his reconstruction policies but also by many businessmen who feared that he would attempt to deprive northern industry of the many favors that it had been granted by the Republicans. While the business class was still relatively small it provided radical campaigners with invaluable financial assistance.

Throughout the campaign of 1866, radical newspapers and stump speakers attacked Johnson's character as well as his views on reconstruction. On various occasions he was accused of being a drunkard, of maintaining a harem in the White House, and of having had a part in Lincoln's assassination. Although administration spokesmen sought to refute these preposterous charges,* the accusations invariably received more publicity than the denials. At the same time, the radicals gave extensive publicity to reports of floggings and murders in the South, and the race riots in Memphis (May, 1866) and New Orleans (July, 1866) were pictured as the inevitable results of the President's reconstruction program. In an effort to strike back at his detractors, Johnson made his famous—and, as it turned out, disastrous—"swing around the circle." A two-and-a-half week (August 28 to September 15) speaking tour that took Johnson as far west as Chicago, the swing around the circle undoubtedly cost him more votes than he gained. At every stop, heckling by radical groups either drowned out his words or goaded him into making foolhardy and intemperate rejoinders. The effectiveness of such tactics was revealed by the outcome of the election, for the radicals won overwhelming majorities in both houses of Congress.

Congress Takes the Reins

Strengthened by their victory in the congressional elections of 1866, the radicals forced through Congress the first Reconstruction Act of March 2, 1867. Under this act, the South was placed under comprehensive and rigorous military rule. The state governments set up under executive authority were abolished as illegal, and the entire region was divided into five districts, each under the jurisdiction of "an officer of the army not below the rank of brigadier-general and . . . a sufficient military force to enable him to perform his duties and enforce his authority . . ." To gain relief from military rule and to obtain representation in Congress, each state was required to call a convention consisting of delegates "elected by the male citizens . . . of whatever race, color or previous condition." This convention in turn was required to frame a new constitution giving Negroes the right to vote. When such

---

* Johnson was drunk at his inauguration. Being sick and weak at the time, he thought that a drink or two might sustain him during the ceremonies; but he took too much and became intoxicated. He was not, however, a drunkard.

a constitution had been ratified by the same electorate and approved by Congress and when the Fourteenth Amendment had been ratified, the state's congressional delegation could resume its seats in the capitol. Supplementary Reconstruction Acts of March 23 and July 19, 1867, further perfected the administrative machinery for carrying out the objectives of the radicals.

Frustrated in his appeal to the electorate, Johnson now tried to use his patronage and removal powers to undercut radical strength. In response, the radicals sponsored two measures, both of which were enacted on March 2, 1867. The first of these, the Tenure of Office Act, prohibited the President from removing officeholders except with the consent of the Senate. Congress overrode Johnson's veto of this act. The second—a rider to the Army Appropriation Act—forbade the executive to issue orders to the army except through General Grant, to relieve Grant of command, or to assign him to any command away from Washington except at the General's own request or with the previous approval of the Senate. Violation of either of these acts was a misdemeanor punishable by imprisonment. The first measure was designed to prevent Johnson from removing radical officeholders, and the second to prevent the President from exercising his constitutional command of the army.

Johnson soon played into the hands of the radicals again by removing Secretary of War Edwin Stanton from office. A member of Lincoln's cabinet, Stanton had remained in office in spite of his opposition to the President's reconstruction program and his close association with most of the leading radicals in Congress. After Stanton had refused to resign at the President's request in August, 1867, Johnson suspended him and named Grant as his temporary successor. When Congress convened in December, 1867, the Senate failed to approve the suspension of Stanton, and Grant—despite his earlier promise to stand by the President—withdrew and permitted Stanton to resume his duties as Secretary of War. Johnson countered by dismissing Stanton, but the Secretary of War refused to give up his office. In removing Stanton without the consent of the Senate, Johnson violated the Tenure of Office Act.

Stanton's dismissal provided the radicals with a golden opportunity, and, under the leadership of Stevens, the House on February 25, 1868, approved a resolution "That Andrew Johnson, President of the United States, be impeached of high crimes and misdemeanors in office." On March 2–3, the House adopted eleven charges against the President. The first nine charges were concerned with Johnson's violation of the Tenure of Office Act; the tenth charge accused him of attacking Congress with "inflammatory and scandalous harangues"; and the eleventh

Ulysses S. Grant, U. S. A.

charge, or "omnibus article," summed up the earlier accusations and added a few more for good measure.

The trial before the Senate was presided over by Chief Justice Salmon P. Chase and lasted from March 5 to May 26, 1868. The prosecution, under the direction of Stevens and Benjamin F. Butler of Massachusetts, sought by the use of innuendo and unsubstantiated accusations to create the impression that Johnson was no longer "fit to retain the office of President." Johnson's lawyers emphasized that he had committed neither crimes nor misdemeanors, and that he had violated the Tenure of Office Act so that the courts would have an opportunity to decide on the constitutionality of a measure that he had considered unconstitutional from the outset.*

When the vote was taken in the Senate, Johnson was saved by seven Republican senators who put principle above party and voted with twelve Democrats to acquit the President. The final vote was 35 to 19, or one vote short of the two-thirds majority required by the Constitution.

With the failure of the impeachment proceedings, the radicals turned their attention to the presidential campaign of 1868. At the Republican convention in Chicago every delegate voted for Grant on the first ballot, while Schuyler Colfax of Indiana, a radical and Speaker of the House, was nominated for the vice-presidency. From the Republican standpoint Grant, who as far as can be ascertained had no previous party affiliations, was an ideal candidate. He had cooperated with the radicals in the move to impeach Johnson, and his military career was a priceless asset in the North. The party's platform endorsed the radical record in the South, advocated measures to encourage immigration, and reflected the Republican alliance with the business-creditor class by demanding a "hard" rather than "soft" currency.† The leading candidates for the Democratic nomination were Johnson and Chief Justice Salmon Chase, who after his failure to be selected by the Republicans indicated his willingness to lead their opponents. Although Johnson received sixty-five votes on the first ballot and Chase also had considerable support in the convention, the nomination eventually went to Horatio Seymour, a Union Democrat and former governor of New York. As his running mate, the Democrats chose Francis P. Blair, Jr., of Missouri, a former Republican who had become an outspoken opponent of radical reconstruction. The platform, while attacking Congressional reconstruction for subjecting the South to "military despotism and Negro supremacy," had a "soft-money" plank calling for the payment of United States' bonds with greenbacks rather than with gold.

Throughout the campaign, the Republicans enjoyed certain obvious advantages. Because of their monetary plank and the assistance which they had given industry in the past, they could count on liberal financial support from the nation's business groups. In addition, their control over the South assured them of a large colored vote in that

---

* In 1926, the Supreme Court in *Myers vs. U. S.* ruled that the Tenure of Office Act was unconstitutional.

† Debtors were inflationists because they wished to pay their debts with a cheaper currency than they had borrowed. Creditors were deflationists because they wished to be paid in a dearer currency than that which they had loaned.

area, while Grant's candidacy took advantage of his status as the military savior of the Union. The Democrats' strategy lay in constantly exposing and attacking Republican corruption in both Washington and the South, and they were able to make an unexpectedly strong showing. Although Grant received 214 electoral votes to 80 for Seymour, his popular majority was only 305,458 in a total vote of 5,724,684.

The South Under the Radicals

Having gained control of Congress and with a more passive President at the head of the federal government in Washington, the radicals proceeded to carry out their reconstruction program in the South. With the establishment of a military administration in the South in accordance with the terms of the Reconstruction Act of 1867, control of the section's political affairs passed initially from the hands of the upper-class whites to groups that in the past had had little or no voice in the management of their states' governments. When the new registration of voters was completed under the direction of the district commanders in the South, there were 703,000 Negroes on the rolls and only 627,000 whites. In six of the ten unreconstructed states—Alabama, Louisiana—South Carolina, Florida, Mississippi, and Georgia—there were Negro majorities. In every part of the South, the white electorate was largely composed of "scalawags" and "carpetbaggers." The "scalawags" were native southern whites, sometimes former prewar wealthy Whigs, who in most instances had opposed secession and were now prepared to cooperate with the radicals. The "carpetbaggers" were drawn from every section and class of the North. At best they were humanitarians, and at worst they were adventurers. When the elected representatives of these groups met to draw up new state constitutions, they took as models the constitutions of the more progressive states of the North. Provision was accordingly made—on paper at least—for free public education, democratic local government, and complete civil and political equality regardless of race.

White southerners, who at the close of the war had hoped that the freedmen would look to their former masters for leadership, were at first disillusioned. The Negroes, who quite naturally attributed their changed status to the Republican party, saw no reason why they should now spurn their principal benefactors for an alliance with those who had fought to perpetuate slavery in the South. This view was reinforced by northern spokesmen—including Yankee soldiers, missionaries, school teachers and politicians—who traveled about the South denouncing the Democrats and praising the Republicans. At the same time, the Freedmen's Bureau and the Union, or Loyal, Leagues, which had been organized during the war to promote the northern cause, proved effective agencies for lining up the new Republican voters in the states of the ex-Confederacy.

Because of the undeviating loyalty of the Negroes to the radical Republicans, the leading whites of the South were unable to prevent the ratification of the new state constitutions. By the end of 1868, seven states—the two Carolinas, Georgia, Florida, Alabama, Louisiana, and Arkansas—had ratified the new instruments and had elected new governors and legislators. In 1870, Mississippi, Texas, and Virginia took similar action. In every state but Georgia, Republicans and their allies dominated every branch of the government. Ten of the fourteen United States senators and four of the seven governors were northerners who had moved to the South after the war. Although Negroes and scalawags filled most of the minor offices and every one of the new legislatures contained a substantial number of freedmen, only in South Carolina did the Negro members outnumber the whites, 88 to 67. Most of the new officials were men of little property. The members of the South Carolina legislature in 1868, for example, paid collectively less than $650 in taxes, and 91 of the 155 paid no taxes. In Alabama, the total taxes paid by members of the legislature were estimated at less than $100. In the same period, New York and the five New England states were the only northern states that even permitted the Negro to vote, and four other northern states—Minnesota, Michigan, Kansas, and Ohio—voted down proposals to extend the franchise to the Negroes.

Corruption, incompetence, and extravagance frequently characterized the Carpetbagger-Scalawag-Negro administration of the state governments. The worst experiences of South Carolina, which were not typical, still color the southern memory of "Black Reconstruction." More than $200,000 was spent for State House furniture that was actually worth less than $18,000; bills were submitted for $750 mirrors, $60 chairs, $650 chandeliers, $600 timepieces, and $60 imported china spittoons. Under the heading "Legislative Supplies" appeared such items as Westphalia hams, imported mushrooms, a side of bacon, feather beds, extra-long stockings, garters, chemises, gold watches, corsets, perfumes, three gallons of whisky, and a metal coffin. A barroom with forty different kinds of beverages was maintained in the State House at government expense. On one occasion, the legislature voted the speaker of the house $1,000 to reimburse him for a lost bet on a horse race. Public printing, which from 1790 to 1863 had totaled $609,000 amounted in the years 1868–76 to $1,326,589. In Louisiana the legislative session of 1871 averaged $113.50 a day for "travelling and other expenses for each

senator, representative, clerk, sergeant-at-arms, doorkeeper and page."
In Arkansas the auditor's clerk hire, which was $4,000 in 1866, cost
$92,000, or twenty-three times as much, in 1873.

Under radical control, public indebtedness in the South mounted
rapidly. In two years the public debt of North Carolina increased from
$16,000,000 to $32,000,000; South Carolina's rose from $7,000,000 in
1865 to $29,000,000 in 1873. The debt of New Orleans multiplied
twenty-five times and that of Vicksburg a thousandfold. As state debts
mounted, taxes also increased. In 1870, Louisiana levied $21.85 on every
$1000 worth of property compared with a rate of $7.47 in New York.
Similarly, Mississippi's rate was $17.86 contrasted with $6.44 for Pennsylvania. At the same time, property values declined sharply. The decrease in Alabama amounted to 65 per cent; in Florida 45 per cent; and
in Louisiana from 50 to 75 per cent.

While it is true that such extravagance and graft existed, it is also
true that there was a pressing need to spend large sums of money in the
postwar South. Not only did areas devastated during the war have to
be rebuilt, but for years previous to the war the southern states had
neglected to provide their citizens with many essential services. To
supply these deficiencies cost money, and, even though some legislatures
spent funds on trifles and luxuries, they all provided the South with
several much-needed improvements. The spending programs of the
radical governments were not opposed by all the members of the South's
former ruling class, who later helped distort the achievements of the
so-called black regions. State subsidies to railroads greatly contributed
to the South's debt, and the recipients of these grants found it easy
to place their desire for profits ahead of their loyalty to their section. There is abundant evidence that southern businessmen (regardless of what class they were drawn from) were as willing as those of
the North to accept whatever assistance any government would give
them.

Although the newly constituted southern governments were often
corrupt, no particular locality or party had a monopoly on thieving
politicians in the postwar period. While the carpetbaggers, scalawags,
and freedmen were holding forth in the South, Boss Tweed, a Democrat, was robbing millions in New York City; the state legislatures at
Harrisburg, Pennsylvania, and Albany, New York, were demonstrating
that they could be as corrupt as any south of Mason and Dixon's line;
and the federal government in Washington was being shaken by the
revelation of unprecedented scandals. Corruption was a national rather
than a sectional or racial phenomenon and cannot be attributed exclusively to radical or black misrule. Indeed, some radical governments

were remarkably honest and efficient and the Bourbon regimes that assumed power at the end of Reconstruction were often as corrupt as their predecessors had been. In Mississippi, for example, there were only three instances of official stealing under the Reconstruction government of the state. A Republican treasurer of a hospital stole $7,251; a Negro librarian took some books; and a native white Democratic treasurer stole $61,962. After the southern Democrats had regained control of the state government, they elected an official who stole $315,612.

Care should also be exercised in judging the personnel of the radical state governments. Although all the freedmen were inexperienced and most were illiterate, naive, and susceptible to the influence of designing men, the fact remains that some of them compiled excellent records in public office. Nor were all carpetbaggers rascals. Some went South to put into effect reforms that they had long advocated, others were un-doubtedly motivated by a desire to make money—a desire that in other instances Americans have often been prone to commend rather than condemn. Most scalawags, whom their fellow white southerners branded turncoats and traitors to their section, in reality never shifted their allegiance. With a long record of opposition to slavery, planter rule, and secession, they revealed an understandable wish to participate in governments from which they had always been excluded. Moreover, despite the many Negroes elected to the state legislatures, the vast ma-jority of chief state officers and of Representatives and Senators from the South at Washington were white men. Increasingly, as time passed these officials came from the old white elite whose political disabilities were gradually removed by the very "black regimes" against whom they later turned as the white Bourbons gained power and confidence and their resentment rose against high or progressive state taxes, debts, and the remaining limits on their political activity.

Any fair appraisal of the radical state governments of the South should include some mention of their positive accomplishments. Al-though there was considerable variation from state to state, the radical governments made a sustained—and sometimes successful—effort to provide educational facilities, revise tax laws on the basis of the ability to pay, reorganize voting districts so as to give adequate representation to the more populous but less wealthy regions, reform the judicial sys-tem, provide relief for the indigent, and build railroads, roads, schools, hospitals, orphan asylums, and insane asylums.

Of the various reforms advocated by the radicals, those affecting education perhaps provide the best guide to the character of the radical reconstruction program within the southern states. Before 1860, the South had only a semblance of a public-school system, and the war wiped out most of the hard-won gains of the antebellum years. Public and private schools were forced to close; students and teachers were dispersed; many school buildings were burned or converted into hospitals; and public libraries practically disappeared. When the radicals assumed control of the southern state governments, they were faced with the task of restoring the shattered school-system and of furnishing the Negroes with adequate educational facilities. Although their actual accomplishments always fell short of their aspirations, the radicals undoubtedly did more for southern primary education than previous southerners had done in two centuries. By 1876, the constitution of nearly every southern state contained provisions making tax-supported, free public schools for both whites and Negroes mandatory. While lack of funds, racial animosity, and public indifference made it impossible to enforce these constitutional provisions rigidly, considerable progress was made in a relatively short time. In South Carolina, which has been repeatedly cited by opponents of Reconstruction as an outstanding example of radical inefficiency and corruption, there were more than 50,000 white and 70,000 Negro children attending public schools in 1876. In 1860, the total figure had been 20,000.

In the eyes of most white southerners, any accomplishments of the radical state governments were largely, if not entirely, nullified by the means employed and by the grant to the freedmen of equal civil and political rights. Since they were unable to dislodge their opponents by the use of the ballot, many southerners resorted to such extralegal agencies as the Ku-Klux Klan, Knights of the White Camellia, Society of the White Rose, '76 Association, and similar secret societies. Of these the K.K.K. was the most powerful. Organized in 1865 before the Radical take-over, the Klan later spread over the South. Limited in membership to southern whites, the Klan refused admission to Union veterans, Republicans, and Union Leaguers. Its members were pledged to oppose equality of the races, to work for the restoration of the "rights" of the southern whites, and to "defend constitutional government." In 1876, just as the Reconstruction Acts were being put into operation, a grand convention in Nashville transformed the Klan into a sectional organization in which the former slave states, with the exception of Delaware, were erected into the "Invisible Empire." The administration of this empire was entrusted to a hierarchy of officials whose titles were calculated to frighten the ignorant and superstitious: Grand Wizard, Grand Dragons, Grand Titans, Grand Giants, and Grand Cyclops.

By nocturnal visits, warnings inscribed in blood, ghostly parades in white robes and weird-looking masks and other methods, the Klansmen terrified the freedmen. If "peaceful" intimidation failed, violence was used. The results achieved by the Klan and other similar orders were highly successful from the standpoint of the conservative whites. In addition to regulating the conduct of many Negroes, the vigilantes sharply scrutinized the activities and teachings of northern preachers and teachers, dispersed gatherings of freedmen, and forced some Reconstruction officials to leave the South. Above all, by frightening large numbers of Negro voters away from the polls, they substantially reduced the electoral support of the carpetbaggers.

The radicals, who were determined to save the Negro vote, struck back at the southern whites with the Fifteenth Amendment, which prohibited a state from denying any citizen the right to vote on account of race, color, or previous conditions of servitude. Its ratification was required of those southern states which had not at that time been readmitted to the Union, and the new amendment was proclaimed on March 30, 1870. It was immediately followed by the passage of an enforcement act imposing heavy penalties for infringement of either the Fourteenth or the Fifteenth Amendment. To circumvent the probability of loose interpretation in the South, the framers of this bill placed jurisdiction over all cases arising under it in the hands of the federal rather than the state courts. Democratic gains in the elections of 1870, as well as fraud and violence in elections in New York and other northern cities, stimulated the Republicans in Congress to push through another enforcement act (February, 1871) that extended rigorous federal control over congressional elections in the South. Less than two months later, Congress passed the Ku-Klux Act, which gave the federal courts jurisdiction over conspiracies against the freedmen and authorized the President to suspend the writ of *habeas corpus* and to declare martial law in any terrorized community. This measure was so effectively applied that by the fall of 1872 the military, when it chose to, had effective control over the South.

Grantism

While the radicals were attempting to impose their program on the South, Grant was demonstrating in Washington how inadequately his triumphs on the battle field had prepared him for the highest civilian office in the land. The Grant administration was distinctive for the incompetence of most of its officials and the uninhibited fashion in which it, in effect, turned over both the North and South to the country's special interests. Aside from Secretary of State Hamilton Fish, who held his position for the eight years that Grant served as President and for the short tenure of Attorney General E. R. Howe and Secretary of the Interior J. D. Cox, the cabinet was a way station for incompetents and mediocrities. During his two terms, Grant made twenty-four appointments to his seven-man cabinet. Without any experience in politics, Grant turned over the management of most of the government's affairs to hacks or old army cronies. Instead of attempting to check corruption, he stood by dishonest officials on the ground that it was not right to abandon a friend or subordinate in trouble. He had no interest in the reform of the tariff, currency, or civil service; he lacked either the knowledge or inclination to espouse a program for the regulation of business; and he thought that reconstruction could best be left in the hands of those who had controlled the South since 1866. The result was chaos; but it was a kind of chaos that permitted the politicians to get their graft, the businessmen to run the nation's economy with government aid rather than interference, and the radicals to continue their domination of the South.

During Grant's administration, the radical Republicans were able to continue their program of government assistance to the nation's businessmen. The railroads were granted huge tracts of the public domain; the federal land laws were administered in such a way as to aid the speculator rather than the settler; and Congress conducted what amounted to a bargain basement for the sale of subsidies. Although Congress lowered the tariff in 1872 to aid the Republicans in the presidential campaign of that year, in 1875 the old rates were restored. Perhaps most important was the fact that the government gave those northeastern businessmen who were creditors the type of currency that they desired.

The first postwar conflict over the currency issue centered on the question of whether the government's war bonds should be redeemed in gold or in the unsecured greenbacks that had been issued in accordance with the Currency Acts of 1862 and 1864. The inflationists and deflationists advanced the traditional arguments on both sides of the question, and the issue was further complicated by the fact that many of the bonds did not state specifically how they were to be redeemed. To the soft-money advocates, this omission seemed to indicate that greenbacks should be used. The hard-money groups, on the other hand, argued that, since federal bonds had always been redeemed in gold in the past, the government had a moral obligation to abide by this precedent. The question was finally decided in favor of the deflationists. The Republican platform of 1868 included a gold-payment plank, and following the party's victory, Grant announced that the Republicans would observe their pledge. Accordingly, on March 18, 1870, Congress passed a law stating that the government would pay all its debts in "coin or its equivalent"—a phrase that Grant and his successors interpreted to mean gold. While it can be argued that the government was morally committed to this step, the fact remains that this policy resulted in a substantial—and unearned—profit for all those who had purchased bonds with depreciated paper money during the war.

The same groups that argued over the redemption of the war bonds were unable to agree on what policy should be adopted toward the greenbacks. Issued during the war as part of the emergency financing program, the greenbacks were legal-tender notes whose value depended on government fiat rather than on their convertibility into specie. As soon as the war ended, creditors demanded that the government either destroy the greenbacks or make them convertible into specie. Debtors were equally insistent in their opposition to the resumption of specie payments. The first victory, however, went to the hard-money interests, for in 1866, Congress adopted a bill that provided for the gradual retirement of the greenbacks. But in 1868, after $44,000,000 in greenbacks had been withdrawn, Congress halted any further contraction of the currency, and thus helped create a Greenback party.

While Congress was attempting to discover a satisfactory solution to the greenback problem, the Supreme Court was seeking to determine whether or not the legal-tender notes were constitutional. In 1869, in *Hepburn v. Griswold* the Court ruled that the greenbacks were not legal tender. This case, however, concerned a debt that had been contracted before the Legal Tender Act of February 25, 1862, and therefore did not provide an adequate precedent; and in 1871, the Court in *Knox v. Lee* reversed its earlier decision. The majority opinion stated that "Congress has power to enact that the government's promises to pay money shall be, for the time being, equivalent in value to the representation of value determined by the coinage acts or to multiples thereof."

Although the Supreme Court's decision settled the legal status of the greenbacks, it neither precluded nor insured the resumption of specie payments. The soft-money groups were as determined as ever in their opposition to any plans for the contraction of the currency; and when the Panic of 1873 created a money shortage, they seized on this development to urge the government to increase rather than reduce the supply of paper money. Responding to these demands, Congress in April, 1873, adopted a bill authorizing an expansion of the greenbacks from $382,000,000 to $400,000,000. But Grant, to the chagrin of the nation's debtors, vetoed the bill. In his veto message, the President said: "I am not a believer in any artificial method of making paper

money equal to coin, when the coin is not owned or held ready to redeem the promises to pay, for paper money is nothing more than the
promise to pay, and is valuable exactly in proportion to the amount of
coin that it can be converted into."

The inflationists suffered their final defeat in the conflict over the
greenbacks in January, 1875, when Republican majorities in Congress
passed the Resumption Act, which provided that specie payments were
to be resumed on January 1, 1879. John Sherman, Secretary of the
Treasury in President Hayes' cabinet, was the individual most responsible for the successful fulfillment of the Resumption Act. By selling
bonds for gold, he was able to build up an adequate specie reserve; and
when the provisions of the Resumption Act went into effect, paper was
quoted at par. Many students of this subject have commended the government for its adoption of a "sound" monetary policy; but it must be
remembered that the Resumption Act took money from one group and
gave it to another. Resumption was a deflationary measure that increased the value of a debtor's obligations while awarding a bonus to
creditors.

Grant not only acceded to the demands of the businessmen and
politicians, but he also refused to interfere with radical plans for the
control of the South. Although each of the ten unadmitted states had
by 1870 established new governments in accordance with the terms of
the Reconstruction Act, federal interference in the South continued.
Congressional committees repeatedly investigated the new state governments; Southern anti-Republicans were forced to relinquish offices
to which they had been elected; and when the radicals felt that the
occasion warranted it, federal troops were employed. Moreover, the
radicalism of the 1870's had lost most of the idealism that had been a
distinguishing feature of the movement during the Civil War and in
the years immediately after the conflict. The radicals in Grant's administration paid less and less attention to the lot of the Negro, and they
increasingly used Reconstruction as a device to conceal their attempts
to promote the interests of northern businessmen and the Republican
party. Realizing that once the southerners had regained their political
rights, they might team up with other groups to repeal the government's favors to business and to vote the Republicans out of office, the
radicals used every conceivable means to prevent the participation of
the South in national affairs. Many of the radicals of the 1860's had
been reformers who wished to create a social revolution in the South;
their successors, on the other hand, more often than not were spoils
politicians who viewed Reconstruction simply as an instrument to aid
themselves and their allies among the business classes. And this change

in the attitude of the radicals, in turn, accurately reflected the change in the character of the Republican party, which within less than two decades had been transformed from a militant crusading movement to a staunch defender of the nation's leading business groups.

By 1872, a considerable number of northern Republicans were openly opposed to the administration's program in the South. Calling themselves Liberal Republicans, they maintained that the issues of the past were dead and that the government should concentrate on the many pressing problems of the present. As early as 1870, the Liberal Republicans in Missouri had split with the regular party and with the aid of the Democrats had elected B. Gratz Brown as governor. The movement soon spread to other states, and in 1872 the Liberal cause was being supported by such dismayed patricians as Charles Francis Adams, who had been minister to England during the Civil War; Carl Schurz, a German immigrant who represented Missouri in the Senate; Horace Greeley, editor of the New York *Tribune;* Chief Justice Salmon Chase and Justice David Davis of the Supreme Court; and Senator Lyman Trumbull of Illinois. While the Liberals placed their principal emphasis on their demand for the end of the radical recon-struction program, most of them also favored civil service reform. On the tariff and currency questions the group was without unity. As time passed, the movement attracted a number of maverick politi-cians who weakened whatever call to gentlemanly principle and old virtues the reformers intended making.

When it became clear that the regular Republicans intended to renominate Grant despite opposition within the party, the Liberals, now a rag-bag group, held their own convention at Cincinnati in May, 1872. Their platform called for civil service reform and reconciliation with the South, but the delegates were unable to agree on a tariff plank, and the convention sidestepped the issue by referring "the dis-cussion of the subject to the people in their Congressional Districts, and to the decision of Congress . . . wholly free of Executive inter-ference or dictation." The rift in the convention over the tariff ques-tion was further widened by the nomination of Greeley, who for years had advocated a high tariff in the columns of the *Tribune.* Despite Greeley's tariff views and his long association with the Republican party, the Democrats—more in desperation than from conviction—agreed at their convention to support both the platform and candidate of the Liberal Republicans. The combined parties, however, proved no match for the Republicans, and Grant, with 286 votes to 66 for Gree-ley, carried every state but Georgia, Kentucky, Maryland, Missouri, Tennessee, and Texas. The Republican victory can be attributed to the party's ability to control a large part of the southern electorate, Greeley's ineptitude as a candidate, the prosperous times that prevailed throughout the campaign, and the difficulties encountered by the Liberal Republicans in seeking low-tariff votes with a high-tariff candidate.

The Scandals Break

With the exception of the Resumption Act and the continued efforts of the radicals to retain their control over the South, the most significant developments of Grant's second term were a series of revelations of widespread corruption in practically every branch of the government. As exposure followed exposure, the alliance between business and politics became increasingly clear. It soon became apparent that politicians of every rank had participated in the "great barbecue." Robert Schenck used his post as Ambassador at the Court of St. James to foist bogus mining stock on English investors; Senator James G. Blaine of Maine accepted a thinly disguised bribe in return for his efforts to secure a land grant for a western railroad; General Daniel Butterfield, head of the New York subtreasury, helped Gould and Fisk corner the country's gold supply in 1869; and Secretary of the Treasury William A. Richardson had to resign when it was revealed that he had permitted one John A. Sanborn of Massachusetts to keep half of the $427,000 in back taxes that he had collected as a Federal agent. The internal revenue system was a center of corruption; taxes on tobacco, cigars, and, above all, on distilled liquors, were openly evaded. A "Whisky Ring," composed in part of high government officials, defrauded the treasury of enormous sums. Even General O. E. Babcock, President Grant's private secretary, was involved, and Grant himself was the recipient of many presents from members of the ring. The government practice of rewarding those who gave information about tax evaders encouraged blackmailing, and "hush-money" running into millions of dollars went into the pockets of government agents as the price of silence. The administration of the customs was equally lax and corrupt. When Secretary of War William W. Belknap was accused of selling an appointment to a position in the trading post at Fort Sill, Oklahoma, he hurriedly sent his resignation to the President, who accepted it with "great regret." Nevertheless, the House of Representatives drew up and passed articles of impeachment on which Belknap was duly tried by the Senate. No question existed as to Belknap's guilt, and only the lack of technical jurisdiction saved him from conviction.

Most sensational of all the national scandals of this period was the Crédit Mobilier affair. Following the authorization of the Union Pacific

Railway by Congress, a group of the controlling stockholders formed a construction company called the Crédit Mobilier, headed by Oakes Ames, Congressman from Massachusetts. In 1867, this concern obtained an award from the Union Pacific for building and equipping the railway. In payment, the construction company received nearly all the stock of the Union Pacific at about one third its face value plus the proceeds from its bonds. To keep Congress in a friendly mood, Ames induced the Crédit Mobilier directors to transfer to him as trustee Crédit Mobilier stock that he sold to various members of the House and Senate at par value. Inasmuch as the stock was worth twice its par value, Ames found ready purchasers among his colleagues. Soon after the shares had been distributed where they would "do the most good," the Crédit Mobilier "cut a melon" of nearly $3,500 for every thousand dollars invested. All went well until 1872, when a Crédit Mobilier stockholder, Colonel H. S. McComb of Delaware, after a quarrel with Ames, turned over to the New York *Sun* a series of letters that at once led to a congressional investigation. Ames was found "guilty of selling to members of Congress shares of stock in the Crédit Mobilier . . . with intent . . . to influence the votes and decisions of such members . . ." and his expulsion from the House was recommended. Vice-President Schuyler Colfax, Senator Patterson of New Hampshire, Representatives James Brooks, James A. Garfield, and others were implicated with Ames in varying degree, although they stoutly maintained that they were not "guilty of any impropriety or even indelicacy."

Although Grant did not "cause" the corruption that flourished during his administration, he made no apparent move to prevent or expose it, and his naive trust in a number of unscrupulous individuals undoubtedly helped to create an atmosphere in which official dishonesty seemed to be at least tacitly encouraged. To Grant the presidency was an honor that a grateful people had bestowed upon him for his outstanding record during the war. Under the circumstances, he usually preferred to stand by his friends—regardless of the crimes they committed—rather than to protect the honor of his administration or the interests of the taxpayers.

The Compromise of 1877

Throughout Grant's two terms as President the radicals steadily lost ground in the South. Neither constitutional amendments nor congressional "force acts" could hold the South for the Republicans, and the conservative southern whites gradually reestablished their power by making temporary common cause with the so-called black regimes.

The Republicans were ousted from control of Tennessee as early as 1869, and in Georgia, North Carolina, and Virginia in 1870. Four years later, the conservatives carried Alabama and Arkansas. The following year, Texas and Mississippi swung into the Democratic column. By 1875, only Florida, Louisiana, and South Carolina remained under radical control, and in these states the ruling groups were torn by internal dissension. Attracted by new issues and new interests, the northern electorate showed steadily smaller interest in the welfare of the freedmen. In the short session of the Forty-third Congress (1875) only one measure on the radical program was adopted—the "Supplementary Civil Rights Bill," long urged by Sumner, which prohibited discrimination against Negroes in hotels, theaters, and public conveyances. When President Hayes withdrew the federal armed forces from Louisiana and South Carolina in 1877, the radical governments in those states promptly collapsed. Political reconstruction was practically at an end.

The final collapse of radical rule in the South was the direct result of the disputed presidential election of 1876. The Republicans entered the campaign of 1876 with a number of serious handicaps. The Democrats had gained control of the House in 1874, and for two years a series of House committees had exposed Republican graft and corruption in the federal government; the radicals had been driven from all but three of the southern states; and the country was still suffering from the depression precipitated by the Panic of 1873. Largely because of these considerations, the delegates to the Republican convention passed over a number of prominent men in the party who had been affiliated with the Grant administration and gave the nomination to Rutherford B. Hayes, an advocate of civil service reform and the Governor of Ohio for three terms. To oppose Hayes, the Democrats selected Samuel J. Tilden, a New York corporation lawyer who had taken a prominent part in the destruction of the Tweed Ring and had been elected governor of his state in 1874.

Hayes and Tilden had much in common, for both advocated hard money, the restoration of conservative rule in the South, and civil service reform. But the similarity of the two candidates' views did not detract from the bitterness with which both parties waged their campaigns. While Democratic stump speakers sought to make political capital out of the depression, corruption in high places, and the abuses of radical Reconstruction, Republican orators warned the voters against entrusting the national government to a party that was still "the same in character and spirit as when it sympathized with treason." That Tilden received 4,300,590 popular votes to 4,036,298 for Hayes was due not only to the widespread disgust with the excesses of the Grant ad-

48

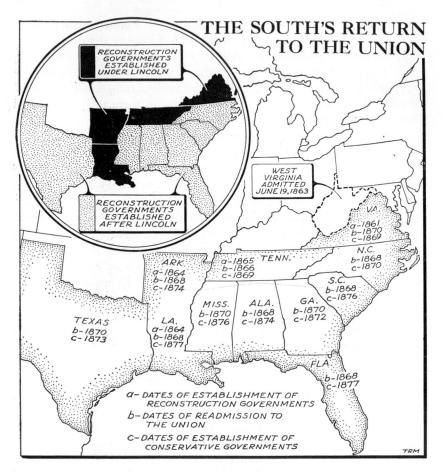

THE SOUTH'S RETURN TO THE UNION

RECONSTRUCTION GOVERNMENTS ESTABLISHED UNDER LINCOLN

RECONSTRUCTION GOVERNMENTS ESTABLISHED AFTER LINCOLN

WEST VIRGINIA ADMITTED JUNE 19, 1863

VA.
a-1861
b-1870
c-1869

N.C.
b-1868
c-1870

ARK.
a-1864
b-1868
c-1874

TENN.
a-1865
b-1866
c-1869

S.C.
b-1868
c-1876

MISS.
b-1870
c-1876

ALA.
b-1868
c-1874

GA.
b-1870
c-1872

TEXAS
b-1870
c-1873

LA.
a-1864
b-1868
c-1877

FLA.
b-1868
c-1877

a- DATES OF ESTABLISHMENT OF RECONSTRUCTION GOVERNMENTS

b- DATES OF READMISSION TO THE UNION

c- DATES OF ESTABLISHMENT OF CONSERVATIVE GOVERNMENTS

TRM

ministration, but also to the fact that the collapse of radical rule in the South permitted a majority of the states in the region to return to the Democratic column.

Despite Tilden's popular majority, the Republicans were able to prevent his election as President. On the day after the election, when the returns were still incomplete, it was clear that Tilden had 184 electoral votes—or one less than the necessary majority—and that the outcome of the contest would depend on the electoral votes of the three "unreconstructed states of South Carolina, Florida, and Louisiana. Although the Republicans probably had a majority in South Carolina, the Democrats led in Florida and Louisiana. But in all three states the returning boards were controlled by the Republicans, and in each instance they certified the Hayes rather than the Tilden electors. The Democrats, however, refused to accept this decision. The confusion

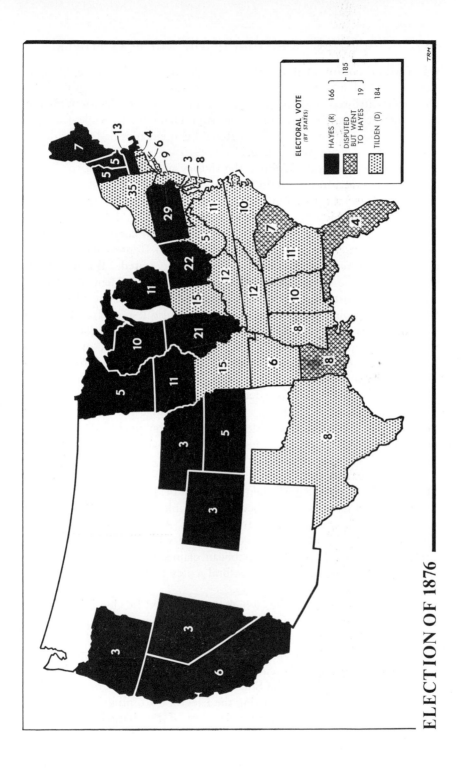

ELECTION OF 1876

was further confounded by the fact that one of the three Oregon electors (all of whom were Republicans) was declared ineligible. The Democrats insisted that the vacancy be filled by the elector with the next highest number of votes (that is, a Democrat), while the Republicans maintained that the two Republican electors had the right to name the third man on the slate.

Although both sides claimed the victory, it was apparent to all that the federal government would have to settle the contest by ruling on the outcome of the election in the disputed states. No one, however, was quite sure which branch of the government should assume this responsibility. The Constitution stated that "The President of the Senate shall, in the presence of the Senate and House of Representatives, open all the certificates and the votes shall then be counted." But it did not state whether the votes should be counted by the President of the Senate, by the House and Senate voting separately, or by the House and Senate voting jointly. And this was the central question, for the President of the Senate was a Republican, the House was Democratic, the Senate was Republican, and the Democrats had a majority of the combined Senate and House membership. Under the circumstances, a decision on who was to count the vote (and thus rule on the disputed returns) was tantamount to a decision on who was to win the election.

After months of haggling and maneuvering, the spokesmen for both parties in Congress decided to resolve the problem by the appointment of an electoral commission of five Senators, five Representatives, and five Supreme Court justices. The original plan for the commission called for the selection of seven Republicans and seven Democrats while the eighth member was to be Justice David Davis, an independent. Davis, however, became ineligible when he resigned from the Court to become a Senator from Illinois. A Republican Justice was appointed to fill his place on the commission which by a vote of 8 to 7 proceeded to uphold all the Republican claims. On March 2, 1877, the final count giving Hayes 185 electoral votes and Tilden 184 was approved by the Senate.

The Republican victory, which was achieved by depriving Tilden of electoral votes that were legitimately his, was made possible by southern Democrats. In return for Republican promises of the withdrawal of the federal troops from the South, of the appointment of at least one southerner to the cabinet, and of generous appropriations for internal improvements in the South, the southern Democrats agreed to join the Republicans in supporting the Electoral Commission's decision. Hayes, in turn, lived up to at least part of the bargain by making

"Another Such Victory and I Am Undone" (Harper's Weekly)

The Republicans' Trick Victory in 1876

David M. Key of Tennessee Postmaster General and by withdrawing the last federal soldiers from the South in April, 1877.

The compromise of 1877, which made possible Hayes' accession to the presidency, was in part the result of the activities of a lobby headed by Thomas A. Scott, president of the Pennsylvania Railroad, and by Grenville Dodge, who had served as chief engineer of the Union Pacific from 1866 to 1870. Both men were backers of the proposed Texas Pacific railroad to the coast and they were able to convince many southern congressmen, first, that such a line would aid the South and, second, that its completion was dependent in turn on a Republican victory.

In a larger sense, the southern support of Hayes in the disputed election of 1876–7 reflected the power of the business interests in the

"The Freed Slave": Philadelphia Centennial Exposition, 1876

new South. Realizing that the expansion of the southern economy depended in large measure on federal grants, they backed the Republican party in the hope that it would be as generous to their section as it had been to the North since the end of the war. While these southerners were Democratic in name, many were also ex-Whigs who did not find it difficult to support a party that espoused a program of internal improvements. In short, the only significant difference between the businessmen of the North and those of the South in 1877 was their party labels.

While the radicals had failed to achieve their major objectives in the South, they had been able to carry out their diverse programs in the rest of the nation. By 1877, industry was entrenched in the Northeast, growing in the South and, in both Democratic and Republican parties North and South, the allies of business interests froze out farmers and workingmen. There seemed little or no likelihood that the nation's farmers would ever again be powerful enough to thwart the country's businessmen. The new southern ruling class had quickly revealed that it had little interest in challenging the reign of business. Known collectively as Bourbons, the radicals' successors in the South consisted of remnants of the old planter-class and native whites who had been able to better their fortunes during the Reconstruction period. On the one hand, the Bourbons proclaimed the uniqueness of their section, while, on the other, they sought to make it over in the image of the North. Under the Bourbons and their friends in both parties, coal and iron mines were opened up in Alabama and Tennessee; textile factories were established in the Carolinas, Georgia, and Alabama; New Orleans became the center of a growing gambling empire and the sugar and molasses industry; and by the late 1870's more than 100 tobacco manufacturing establishments were operating in North Carolina alone.

While seeking to create what they referred to as the New South, the Bourbons systematically lessened the power of the Negro in their section's politics, largely by franchise provisions in the new constitutions that ingeniously sidestepped the Fifteenth Amendment. Although Negroes continued to vote in the South for a generation after 1877, it became increasingly difficult for them to do so. The most common new barriers were literacy and educational tests, poll taxes, or property qualifications for voting. Most useful of all was the "grandfather clause" by which any man who could not meet the educational and property qualifications could nevertheless be admitted to the suffrage if he had voted before 1867 or was the son or grandson of a person who had. Obviously, this device strengthened the conservatives, since it acted to disfranchise the Negroes. As for those Negroes who did vote, they were completely controlled by Bourbon leaders.

By 1890, the last physical—if not emotional—traces of Reconstruction rule in the South had been removed, and southern politics were dominated by native politicians who effectively prevented the solution of the grievous social and economic problems of the South. Despite the assumption that in 1877 the South had been "redeemed," political corruption continued, many social gains were cancelled, and the South's economy was controlled by northern capital; many of its Negro and white farmers lived in abject poverty; and its social life was torn by interracial tensions and conflicts. Reconstruction now became a memory that, along with the Civil War, served as a psychological safety valve for those southerners who preferred to think that their present difficulties could be attributed exclusively to their troubled past rather than to their own choices.

FOR SUPPLEMENTARY READING

No work has drawn together the last decade's exciting scholarship on reconstruction. Students should start with H. K. Beale, "On Rewriting Reconstruction History," *American Historical Review*, Vol. XLV (July 1940). Beale's *The Critical Year* (1930) states what is still probably the most accepted although increasingly challenged view of the forces at work during reconstruction.

Highlights in the writing of reconstruction history are W. A. Dunning, *Reconstruction, Political and Economic* (1907); W. L. Fleming, *The Sequel of Appomattox* (1919); and E. M. Coulter, *The South During Reconstruction* (1947). All of these reflect attitudes and biases considerably at variance with most recent research. Three good studies point out the newer paths: V. L. Wharton, *The Negro in Mississippi 1865–1890* (1947); F. B. Simkins and R. H. Woody, *South Carolina During Reconstruction* (1932); and G. B. Tindall, *South Carolina Negroes 1877–1900* (1952). An excellent retrospective look at the years 1865–77 is one of the many virtues of the fine general work by C. V. Woodward, *The Origins of the New South 1877–1913* (1951). R. Shugg, *Origins of Class Struggle in Louisiana* (1939), has important information on the postwar plantation system, and T. H. Williams, *Beauregard, Napoleon in Gray* (1955), has chastening views on the alleged return of sane, honest government in the South after 1877.

Social changes in the postwar years are the theme of A. Nevins, *The Emergence of Modern America 1865–1878* (1927). Nevins's *Hamilton Fish* (1936) is the leading study of the years under Grant. C. V. Woodward, *Reunion and Reaction* (1951) (Pb),* is the best analysis of the end of northern rule in the South and of the settlement of the election of 1876. M. Josephson, *The Politicos 1865–96* (1958), is the only full political history of the period.

On the special problems of the freed Negroes go first to R. W. Logan, *The Negro in American Life and Thought* (1954), and to J. H. Franklin, *From Slavery to Freedom* (1947).

On the liberal Republicans use E. D. Ross, *The Liberal Republican Movement* (1919).

---

* (Pb) following the date, in this and subsequent lists, means that the work cited also exists in a paperback reprint. Pb followed by a date means that only the paperback edition is available.

2

→>>-→>>-→>>-→>>-→>>-→>>-→>>-→>>

Creating an
Industrial Republic

T HE GROWTH of industry in the United States after 1865 brought an unparalleled increase in national power. Justified in the name of individualism and progress, industrialization actually made Americans more dependent on each other and aroused dreams of wealth incompatible with their ideals of equality. Although industrial progress seriously conflicted with America's traditional spiritual aspirations, the two generations of economic expansion after the war placed the nation among the leading manufacturing countries of the world.

The Background of Industrial Expansion

The United States had a long tradition of technological innovation before the start of the Civil War. "Yankee ingenuity" had often been applied to scores of industries. The sewing machine had revolutionized the manufacture of men's clothing, and the Hoe press had transformed the newspaper business. Colt revolvers were the best in the world; reapers had started their conquest of the prairies; vulcanized rubber was commonplace; and American iron manufacturers had experimented with the Bessemer process. Before Lincoln was elected, New Englanders were turning out guns and watches on a mass-production basis with standardized interchangeable parts, and Boston was the largest boot and shoe center in the world.

Years before southern canon fired on Fort Sumter, the pattern for the future development of the American factory system had also been set. In New England textile mills, for example, machinery was extensively used, the division of labor was ever more minute and more rationalized, and propertyless workers were hired for wages as a laboring force. The corporate device for raising large amounts of capital on the basis of limited liability, trained clerical staffs, and a distinct managerial class were all characteristic features of many of the mill towns in the Merrimac and Connecticut valleys in the 1850's.

The raw wealth of the American continent was still prodigious in 1860. Timber stands, which had supplied successive generations of pioneer homebuilders, were still abundant. Coal and iron ore, the sinews of industrialization, were seemingly limitless. The South produced more than enough cotton to supply New England's textile industry. Vast deposits of oil lighted the nation's lamps, and were later to drive its automobiles. Water power sites, which eventually were used for generating electricity, dotted the American landscape from the Atlantic to the Pacific and from Canada to Mexico. On the mining frontier there was found practically every metal—precious and base—known to man at the time. The United States, in short, owned in abundance most of the natural resources for which the industrialists of other nations had to search the world over.

To plentiful natural resources was added a favorable market. After England entered a period of rapid industrialization, it disposed of much of its goods abroad. Latecomers among the exporting industrial nations found the world market in large part pre-empted by the English. The American manufacturer, with the advantage of an expanding continental home market, could avoid international competition while he supplied the needs of American consumers. The population of the United States, which stood at 23,000,000 in 1850 and rose to 31,500,000 in 1860, totaled 76,000,000 by 1900. American industrialists did not have to look abroad for the sale of surpluses until the twentieth century.

The American market in 1860 consisted largely of farmers who needed manufactured goods. The United States was already a vast free-trade area whose parts were being bound ever closer together by iron rails. Practically every phase of the economy was favorably affected by the railroad boom. Railroads brought manufacturers into touch with hitherto unavailable consumers and raw materials, provided work for numerous laborers, increased the demand for coal, iron, and timber, and opened a world-wide market to the western farmer.

The marked increase in population after 1850 provided America with factory workers as well as customers. A growing stream of immi-

THE TYPE-WRITER.

WHAT "MARK TWAIN" SAYS ABOUT IT.
Hartford, March 19, 1875.

GENTLEMEN: Please do not use my name in any way. Please do not even divulge the fact that I own a machine. I have entirely stopped using the Type-Writer, for the reason that I never could write a letter with it to anybody without receiving a request by return mail that I would not only describe the machine, but state what progress I had made in the use of it, etc., etc. I don't like to write letters, and so I don't want people to know I own this curiosity-breeding little joker. Yours truly,

SAML. L. CLEMENS.

"Prestige Advertising" in the Seventies

grants supplied laborers for the nation's factory system. From 1860 to 1900, approximately fourteen million immigrants came to the United States. Unlike many of their predecessors of the antebellum period, they tended to settle in cities and become members of the industrial work force. Few of these new Americans possessed any industrial skills, and they were willing to toil long hours for little pay at menial and dangerous jobs. Labor leaders complained that the immigrant undermined standards built up by the native worker, but they could not deny that immigration was of major importance in the spectacular advance of American industry during the second half of the nineteenth century.

In one vital respect, however, America was deficient. The supply of American capital to finance industrial expansion was small. Before 1850 the shortage of capital was perhaps the principal deterrent to the growth of manufacturing, for most investors preferred to put their money into foreign trade, western land speculation, and internal improvements. But between 1850 and 1860, the amount of capital invested in industry nearly doubled. Part of this money came from California's gold mines; part of it was drawn from the profits of trade; and some portion was supplied by European investors. After the Civil War, American industrialists continued to have difficulty in raising money. But this was seldom an insuperable obstacle. Profits produced still more profits, and Europe poured unprecedented amounts of money into the American economy. It is impossible to estimate accurately how much financial aid Europe gave to American industry, but that it was considerable is beyond question.

Government Aid to Industry

Long-term changes in the European and American economies thus set the stage for the industrialization of the United States, but an immediate event—four years of Civil War in America—impressively altered the national economy. In the 1850's, most northern businessmen viewed the threat of sectional conflict with misgivings and foreboding. But the northern businessman did not then know his own best interests, for war-born prosperity after 1862 more than compensated for the loss of the economic advantage that had bound the two sections together. Government war orders for clothing, food, munitions, building equipment, and rolling stock for the Union armies created a national economic boom. The artificially stimulated prosperity of the war years gave northern industrialists both the incentive and the funds to expand and mechanize their plants in an unprecedentedly short period of time.

The government's policies during the war directly benefited American industry. Before 1861, the federal government had been controlled by a loose alliance of southern planters, western farmers, and northern commercial interests. These groups had frequently differed among themselves on a variety of issues, and the small number of industrialists among them tried to turn these disagreements to their advantage. With the election of 1860, however, there occurred a definite change in the attitude of the federal government toward the development of American industry. This change cannot be attributed entirely to the exigencies of war, for the Republican platform of 1860 had promised aid to business several months before the first southern state had seceded.

The Republican party of 1860, however, was not a businessman's party, but a free-labor, free-farmer, free-soil party, which hoped to pick up some additional votes among the nation's businessmen. The Republican platform promised businessmen a protective tariff, a national banking system, and improved transportation facilities. Still, although no adequate statistics are available, most evidence indicates that the majority of northern businessmen in 1860 preferred other parties to the seemingly intransigeant Republicans, whose victory might precipitate disunion. But when the Republicans repeatedly demonstrated during the war and postwar years that they planned to honor the promises that they had made in 1860, many industrialists and financiers quickly joined the party.

The new administration's attitude toward industry was made clear by its tariff policy during the war. On March 2, 1861, two days before Abraham Lincoln's inauguration, Congress adopted the Morrill Act. This measure, which could not have been passed if seven southern states had not already seceded, raised the tariff and proved a fitting prelude for wartime tariff policies. With the onset of war, all taxes, including tariffs, were increased. A series of tariff bills, culminating in an act of 1864, placed the average rate at 47 per cent. Republican high-tariff advocates defended the increase on the grounds that additional revenue was needed to finance the war and that manufacturers subjected to heavy internal revenue taxes could only be protected from foreign competition with a higher tariff barrier. When the war was over and government expenditures had declined, the excise taxes were drastically reduced. But the tariffs passed to raise wartime revenue remained, and protectionism for its own sake became an established policy of postwar administrations.

For more than half a century after Appomattox, both parties continued the tariff policies that had been inaugurated during the Civil War. In 1867, Congress rejected a measure for tariff reduction, and in subsequent years it passed a number of special bills to provide greater protection for particular industries. Fear of political repercussions impelled the Grant administration to enact a 10 per cent across-the-board reduction just prior to the election of 1872. But after a relatively short time, these cuts were restored. In 1882, a commission appointed by President Arthur proposed a 20 per cent tariff cut, but Congress in a bill passed in 1883 reduced the general average by only 4 per cent. In ensuing years, the Republicans raised the tariff with the passage of the

McKinley bill in 1890, the Dingley Tariff of 1897, and the Payne-Aldrich Act of 1909. Although the Democrats criticized Republican tariffs, they did not lower them substantially. Cleveland's appeal for tariff reduction in 1887 was checked by the Senate defeat of the Mills bill. The Wilson-Gorman Tariff, which became law without Cleveland's signature in 1894, carried only minor reductions in duties. It was not until 1913, with the passage of the Underwood-Simmons bill, that the Democrats under the leadership of Woodrow Wilson reversed the policy that had been established by the Morrill Tariff. In the fifty-two-year interval between these two measures, the consumers of the United States paid what was in effect an enormous subsidy to American industry.

Although the government provided immeasurable aid to American business, it did not do so on a uniform basis. Nor were all businessmen united on the merits of any specific government policy. Few industrialists, for example, agreed on what constituted an adequate tariff policy, and the competition for markets among steel, wool, and leather manufacturers was carried over into a bitter struggle for government tariff favors. In the 1860's and 70's, for example, many iron and steel manufacturers whose iron ore came from newer American mines were predominantly in favor of high tariffs on imported ores; yet some of them favored lower tariffs on certain imported machines or ores for alloys not produced in this country. On the other hand, an older iron-monger, such as the New Yorker, Peter Cooper, whose domestic supply of good ores was running low, favored lower rates on imported iron than his Pittsburgh competitors. The picture of over-all high tariffs after the Civil War obscures the deep divisions among many American producers and gives the false impression of a monolithic business community, united in its ideals and shrewdly clear-sighted in its conception of its interests.

In a society increasingly dominated by the ideals and methods of an industrial system, the position of the state was ambiguous. To refuse to give business support might seriously weaken the entire American economy—laborers and farmers as well as industrial owners. Yet to give such support the government had to select from a mass of proposals made by conflicting and squabbling interest groups those policies best suited to serve public as well as private interests. The possibility of a thoroughly disinterested government policy is usually so remote as to be nearly out of the question, but in a democratic society, with its pride in immediate satisfaction of commonly felt needs, how are men to choose what is the greatest good for the greatest number, however clear the choice may be to people fifty years or a century later? If, for example, a more flexible currency policy with less vigorous reliance on the gold standard would seem to have been in the public interest after 1865, how then cope with the fact that throughout most of the nineteenth century this country's privately owned business was part of a world-wide economy centered principally at London and based almost uniformly on the gold standard? However great the power of Wall Street over the American economy, Wall Street had to pay for needed foreign capital in gold. Wall Street's call for sound money based on the gold standard was the result of financial pressures it itself had to face, and bankers thus had little choice but to pass on the demand for gold to the American public—quite apart from the question of how advantageous a paper inflation or truly bimetal system might have been for our economic growth.

Such considerations about the complexities of American economic history must temper today's moralistic judgments about what government policy should or could have been. Of course, what is missing from the politics of post–Civil War industrialization is any sign of deference to a general notion of the public good. But, again, what was "the public good," and how, specifically, was it to be served? Most Americans in so far as they relied on general moral or political notions, equated the public good with the satisfaction of their private interests. For example, the financial policies of the Republican party that were inaugurated to win the Civil War ultimately redounded to the benefit of dominant business groups. The banking acts of 1863 and 1864 did provide a national banking system and a measure of wartime financial stability; but, by increasing the reserve requirements for rural banks, this legislation also accentuated the trend toward the concentration of financial control in the hands of larger, more conservative bankers in the northeastern cities. After the war, the government's financial policies continued to reflect the interests of these same groups. In 1869, Congress voted for the payment of all government obligations in gold; in 1873, it demonetized silver; and in 1875, it provided for the resumption of specie payments. These laws, favorable in the main to the gold standard, tended to benefit many large business interests at the expense of other parts of the population, yet the wishes of the less favored groups who desired more silver or paper money were no less selfish than those of the big bankers and considerably more risky in the eyes of the conservative London financiers.

The formation of a national financial policy may thus be difficult to judge as a moral issue but huge government grants of the national domain to business groups who were powerful enough to demand or extort them seems to be a different matter. But this too can be viewed

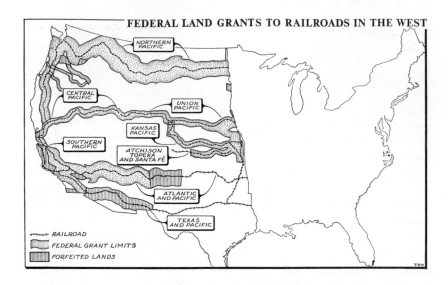

FEDERAL LAND GRANTS TO RAILROADS IN THE WEST

NORTHERN PACIFIC

CENTRAL PACIFIC

UNION PACIFIC

KANSAS PACIFIC

SOUTHERN PACIFIC

ATCHISON TOPEKA AND SANTA FÉ

ATLANTIC AND PACIFIC

TEXAS AND PACIFIC

RAILROAD
FEDERAL GRANT LIMITS
FORFEITED LANDS

as the triumph of the strong over the weak (rather than of right over wrong) in a nation in which most people felt little need to develop a continuing, informed, disinterested political consciousness and had a work-a-day ethos that was the same as that of the big railroad or land company that took the prizes. Behind the moral indignation of the oppressed post-Civil War landowner was often, though not entirely, the jealousy and sentimentality of the defeated men who, given power, would act just as voraciously as the victors had. The outcry against the government land grants to the large railroad companies was often that of people who had failed to be "cut in," as well as that of smaller farmers and commercial men who had to pay overheavily for choice lands for farms or town sites.

In the generation after the Civil War such government favors provided what was in effect a direct source of private profit and increasing capital for the American land business, a policy which, if condemned by farmers, merchants, or jealous railroads in one respect, was likely to be used by them in another. Most railroads, in fact, were the principal beneficiaries of the generous land policy. Counties, cities, and towns subscribed to railroad securities and awarded them terminal sites and rights of way. States turned over to railroads land that the federal government had transferred to them for this purpose. Congress lent money to the Union Pacific and Central Pacific companies and gave great tracts of the public domain to the transcontinental lines. In addition to these direct land grants, which amounted to a cash subsidy, by false entries and other frauds, the railroads obtained huge amounts of land that had been reserved for the nation's farmers under the Homestead Act.

Some of the nation's most valuable timber stands as well as farm lands thus passed into the hands of a few acquisitive and unscrupulous entrepreneurs. Although the Homestead Act of 1862 had been designed to apply only to farm areas, it was so loosely administered that this provision was frequently circumvented. Employees of large lumber concerns took over timber lands under either the Pre-emption or Homestead Acts only to turn them over to the companies for which they were working. Under the Timber Culture Act, which became law in 1873, any individual who planted and protected 40 acres of timber would be granted the quarter-section of 160 acres of which the 40 acres were a part. Although this law was ostensibly designed to "encourage the growth of timber on the western prairies," it served mainly as a device to promote further western real-estate speculation. The Timber and Stone Act of 1878, which applied to land "unfit for cultivation," offered land for as little as $2.50 an acre—or at a price that has been estimated as less than the value of one log from one tree standing on this land. Because the government was either unable or unwilling to prevent land transfers under the Timber and Stone Act, this law permitted the monopolization of large amounts of valuable timber by a few wealthy individuals and corporations. In 1901, the Commissioner of the General Land Office stated:

> Immense tracts of the most valuable timber land, which every consideration of public interest demanded should be preserved for public use, have become the property of a few individuals and corporations. In many instances whole townships have been entered under this law in the interest of one person or firm to whom the lands have been conveyed as soon as receipts for the purchase price were issued.

The government also disposed of large amounts of the nation's mineral wealth in much the same way that it distributed timber stands. People taking up land under either the Pre-emption or Homestead Acts, had to swear that their land did not contain valuable mineral deposits. The government frequently was unable to check these statements, and the use of dummy settlers enabled a few individuals and concerns to acquire valuable minerals under both laws. Other legislation was circumvented with equal ease. A law in 1873 stipulated that government land containing iron ore could not be sold for less than $1.25 per acre. Since the minimum price tended to become the maximum price, an untold number of acres with iron-ore deposits were disposed of at this ridiculously low figure. The government also did not intend to include iron-ore lands in its grants to railroads, but it frequently did so. Government lands containing minerals were also distributed through grants made under the Timber and Stone Act.

Roy M. Robbins, in his illuminating study of *Our Landed Heritage*, has furnished some revealing examples of the effect of these government land policies on the ownership of mineral deposits. The Minnesota Iron Company acquired 8,772 acres of iron-ore land through homestead and pre-emption entries. In 1882, at a public land sale at Duluth, one company paid only $14,000 for 11,000 acres. Fifty years later, much of this land because of its mineral deposits was valued at $50,000 an acre. The American businessman after the Civil War was doubly fortunate in his country's unparalleled resources and in the fact that his government was willing to dispose of its property to private operators for almost nothing.

By also refraining from thoroughgoing investigations of business practices, by not adopting legislation to protect labor, and by not establishing effective regulatory commissions, the federal government gave immeasurable aid to business pioneers, who knew that they could move ahead as they wished without fear of either restriction or punishment. Despite sporadic, superficial, and transitory "protests," most Americans, conditioned by successive frontier experiences and deeply committed to the value of private initiative and limitless accumulation saw little or no reason before 1890 for the government's supervision of business activity. The methods used to gain wealth were widely and simply judged "no concern" of government. Economic life, it was insisted, was a race in which the devil took the hindmost and the government had no right to deprive the winners of their prizes. This philosophy might result in waste, corruption, and injustice, but it also gave American businessmen greater opportunities than those of any other land. The results were the same as critics of American life had observed before the Civil War: a fantastic, even magnificent, energy most often finding its embodiment in the lowest and meanest forms of worship of money, power, and success. Whatever the pride of Americans in their individual achievement, rapid industrial growth after the Civil War was ambiguous in other ways. More than a product of the ingenuity, drive, and resourcefulness of the nation's business leaders, it was also a government-supported project. Without high tariffs, land grants, favorable labor and financial policies, and the absence of public regulation, American industrialization would have followed a course far different from the one it took after 1860.

The Continuing Transportation Revolution

Apart from government favors, basic to the success of the American industrialist was a growing network of railroads that gave him access to both a national market and seemingly limitless natural resources. In the decade before the Civil War, the railroad mileage of the United States had already increased from 9,021 to 30,625 miles. The war temporarily interrupted the expansion of the nation's rail system, but large-scale railroad construction was resumed almost as soon as the guns were silenced. Between 1868 and the Panic of 1873, 28,000 miles of new track were laid in the United States; and in 1869, when the recently consolidated New York Central first reached Chicago, the East Coast and California were also linked when a gold spike was driven into the railroad tie uniting the rails of the Central Pacific and Union Pacific 53 miles west of Ogden, Utah.

By 1874, major consolidations of railroad lines in the Northeast and Middle West had already taken place, but in the war-torn South railroads were being rebuilt and expanded. At the start of the Civil War, the South possessed 10,000 miles of railroad, most of which was either destroyed by the conflict or made worthless by constant use and neglect. Between the end of the war and the Panic of 1873, funds supplied by the Reconstruction governments, northern capitalists, and European investors enabled the South to rehabilitate its railroad network and lay an additional 8,000 miles of track. But this was only a beginning, for by 1890 the South had more than 50,000 miles of railway.

Railway construction in the Middle West exceeded that of any other section in the years immediately following the Civil War. Even before the east-west roads had crossed the Appalachian Mountains, midwestern railway lines were under construction everywhere. During the eight years after Appomattox, new track was laid in every part of the Middle West. By 1873, eight of the new states and territories had been provided with rail facilities for the first time, and Illinois alone had 5,000 miles.

The completion of a series of railroads in the Middle West cut down on the freight carried on the Great Lakes, on canals, and on the Mississippi by providing direct, all-season access to all parts of the country. When rivers and lakes were ice-free, the competition of boats might make rail costs drop nearly 50 per cent, but by 1872 the railroad trunk lines were carrying 70 per cent of the grain formerly sent east by boat, and only the growth of iron ore shipping in the midseventies helped revive Great Lakes commerce.

The railroads also deprived the Mississippi River of most of its traffic and destroyed its distinctive way of life. In a characteristically vivid passage, Mark Twain described the change that occurred on the river:

> Boat used to land . . . captain on hurricane roof . . . mighty stiff and straight . . . iron ramrod for a spine . . . kid gloves, plug tile, hair parted behind . . . man on shore takes off hat and says: "Got twenty-eight tons of wheat cap'n . . . be a great favor if you can take them." Captain says: "I'll take two of them . . ." and don't even condescend to look at him. But nowadays the captain takes off his old slouch, and smiles all the way around to the back of his ears, and gets off a bow which he hasn't got any ramrod to interfere with, and says: "Glad to see you, Smith, glad to see you—you're looking well— haven't seen you looking so well for years—what you got for us?" "Nuth'n" says Smith; and he keeps his hat on, and just turns his back and goes to talking with somebody else.

These economic and cultural changes in the Middle West did not capture the national imagination as much as did the completion of an Atlantic-to-Pacific rail line. For almost two decades before the firing on Sumter, Americans had been excited about a transcontinental railroad. Asa Whitney (1791–1874), a New York merchant who had made a fortune in the China trade, had long been convinced that a railroad to the Pacific would enable American businessmen to regain their earlier ascendancy in the Far East. In the 1840's, Whitney's lectures, pamphlets, addresses to state legislatures, and memorandums to the federal government led *Niles Weekly* to call him the "prince of all projectors," while *DeBow's Review* stated that he "perhaps more than any man in the country illustrated the importance of a connection to the Pacific." In 1845, Whitney asked Congress to grant a strip of the public domain sixty miles wide along the route of his proposed railway. Boards of trade and chambers of commerce, as well as sixteen state legislatures, sent resolutions to Congress in support of Whitney's plan.

Sectional rivalry, however, blocked adoption of the bills, and not until after the South's secession was the project approved. By an act of 1862 and an amendatory act of 1864, Congress authorized the Union Pacific Railroad Company to build a line west of Omaha, Nebraska, through Wyoming, Utah, and Nevada to the eastern boundary of California. The Central Pacific, a California corporation organized by a group of Sacramento businessmen, was to construct the western end of the line in California. Both companies received substantial aid from the federal government. Congress donated a 400-foot right of way across the public domain, furnished the stone, timber, and earth needed for the undertaking, and awarded land grants of 12,800 acres in alternate sections for every mile of road constructed. Both the Union Pacific and Central Pacific also obtained a thirty-year government loan of $16,000 a mile for track laid through level country, $48,000 a mile for the mountainous regions, and $32,000 a mile for those portions constructed between the mountain ranges. This loan was secured by a second mortgage on the completed system, and the builders were permitted to issue first mortgage bonds equal in amount to the government lien.

Both the Union Pacific and the Central Pacific were harassed by unforeseen problems. Because of the shortage of labor in the West, the Central Pacific had to import thousands of Chinese workers. Machinery and rolling stock, all of which came from the East, had to be shipped around Cape Horn or sent overland across the Isthmus of Panama. Iron, which sold for $62 a ton in New York, was worth $150 in San Francisco, and locomotives that cost $8000 in the East brought $32,500 in Sacramento. Mountains had to be scaled, tunnels bored, and snow often more than sixty feet deep had to be blasted away. Hundreds of workers lost their lives in snowslides and avalanches. Work was frequently interrupted by Indian raids. In spite of these handicaps, the two lines met in Utah in the spring of 1869, the Central Pacific having received permission to build eastward beyond the California boundary. In May, when the last spike joining East and West was driven, Asa Whitney's dream was at last realized, for the Chicago and Northwestern had already reached Omaha and made connection with the Union Pacific, and the Kansas Pacific had penetrated as far west as Denver and joined the Union Pacific at Cheyenne. For the first time, American manufacturers and merchants had an opportunity to distribute their goods to a nation-wide market. Businessmen interested in trade with the Orient and the Far West were placed in direct communication with their customers and with sources of essential raw materials. At the same time, western miners and farmers were no longer priced out of the eastern market by high costs of transportation.

Before the Panic of 1873 temporarily checked the expansion of the nation's rail system to the Pacific coast, work was in progress on several parallel trunk lines to the West coast: the Northern Pacific, Atlantic and Pacific, Texas and Pacific, and the Atchison, Topeka, and Santa Fé. These land-grant roads stimulated settlement west of the Mississippi. Built in advance of population and often heavily burdened with high construction costs and watered stock, many of the new trans-Mississippi railways could not meet current costs and dividends. Even the Union-Central Pacific, which initially enjoyed a regional monopoly, was soon in financial difficulties. The railroads thus had to make every effort to invite settlement on their wide holdings. They established land departments, subsidized advertising campaigns, sent recruiting agents to the eastern United States as well as to Europe, and carried homeseekers at reduced fares.

Despite the interlude of the depression of the midseventies, by the end of the decade the railroad boom was again in full swing. More than 40,000 miles of lines were built in the 1870's, and a record-breaking 73,000 during the 1880's. By 1900, the American railroad system measured 193,000 miles; and ten years later the total was 240,000 miles. In 1914, the United States had more miles of railroad track than all of Europe.

The expansion of the nation's transportation facilities affected almost every phase of American civilization. The revolution in transportation helped to produce a realignment in political parties, contributed to the decline in provincialism, and dramatically increased the government's concern with business enterprise. At the same time, the railroad made possible the rapid settlement of the trans-Mississippi West; the rise of great urban centers; the exploitation of mine, field, and forest; the regional concentration of agriculture and industry; and the distribution of the products of countless farms, mills, and factories to national and world markets. The construction of a country-wide transportation system was, in sum, essential to the emergence of modern America.

Creating the Essential Industrial Plant

In the United States from 1865 to 1915, there was a phenomenal increase in the production of durable and consumer goods, machinery was applied to virtually every part of the manufacturing process, and the factory system spread to the South and West. By World War I, advances in technology, mass-production methods, and assembly-line techniques had combined with the natural and political advantages enjoyed by American industry to make the United States the world's leading manufacturing nation. During this period, the index number of American industrial production rose from 13.3 in 1865 to 100 in 1899 and to 175.7 in 1914. This growth was not solely to the advantage of businessmen, for, despite periodic depressions and the harshness of the new industrial-urban life, the real wages of American workers doubled in the period 1865–1900.

It was coal that supplied most of the energy that drove the nation's thousands of railroad engines, turned the wheels in its new fac-

Carnegie's Partner Builds His Empire

tories, and made possible the spectacular development of the all-important steel industry. American coal production rose from a yearly average of 20,538,000 short tons in 1861–5 to more than 400,000,000 tons in 1914, an increase not based on significant technological innovations. Not until after 1900 did some mines begin to adopt automatic cutting tools and mechanical loaders; brute and brutalizing hand labor cut out the vital black rocks from the American earth. By 1915, bituminous coal was providing five times as much energy for the American economy as anthracite which, during the Civil War, fifty years earlier, had exceeded the soft-coal output of the nation. Throughout these years, Pennsylvania continued to mine the bulk of the nation's coal; but before World War I, twenty-three other states, led by West Virginia, Illinois, and Ohio, also produced considerable amounts of coal.

The combination of business energy and the vast coal supply of the nation made possible the prodigious growth of the basic industry of a modern society, iron and steel. Pig iron output in 1873 totaled more than 2,500,000 tons, or three times the output of 1865, and steel production increased from approximately 19,000 tons in 1865 to nearly

600,000 tons in 1876. But this growth was merely a beginning. By 1915, the production of pig iron and ferro-alloys had risen to nearly 30,000,000 tons, and the manufacture of steel ingots and castings increased over a hundredfold—from 389,799 tons in 1875 to 42,773,680 tons in 1916. By World War I, the United States was the leading steel- and iron-producing nation of the world.

Unlike the coal industry, expansion in iron and steel was facilitated by numerous technological improvements. Although the so-called Bessemer process for making steel had been invented in the 1850's almost simultaneously by the Englishman Henry Bessemer and the American William Kelly, the method was not used in the United States until the Civil War.* In 1864, a company at Wyandotte, Michigan, that had secured control of the Kelly patents produced the first Bessemer steel to be made in the United States. In the same year a concern at Troy, New York, acquired Bessemer's American patents. Since neither firm could use the new process without infringing upon the legal prerogatives of the other, the two companies agreed in 1866 to merge their patent rights. The business of making Bessemer steel then spread rapidly, and in the next ten years more than a dozen important Bessemer works were established. Another method of steel manufacture, the Siemens-Martin, or open-hearth, process,† was first introduced into this country in 1868 by Abram S. Hewitt, who, with his father-in-law, Peter Cooper, owned the New Jersey Steel and Iron Company at Trenton, New Jersey. While open-hearth steel was softer than Bessemer and therefore particularly suitable for locomotive boiler plates, it required more time and money to produce. The adoption of this method, therefore, advanced slowly at first, and only slightly more than 8,000 tons were manufactured in 1875. In the following year, the output of open-hearth steel rose to more than 19,000 tons, and by 1908 its output had surpassed that of Bessemer steel.

Improvements in blast furnaces were paralleled by advances in

---

* In the Bessemer process a blast of air is forced through a great converter partly filled with molten iron. The air rushing through the incandescent liquid mass oxidizes the silicon and carbon. Inasmuch as some carbon is always required to produce steel, Bessemer intended to stop the process at the point where just enough carbon would be left for that purpose. This idea, however, proved impracticable. In 1856, another Englishman, Robert F. Muchet, remedied this difficulty by adding to the decarbonized and desiliconized white hot metal a compound (spiegeleisen) of iron, carbon, and manganese.

† When first introduced in America the open-hearth method consisted in melting pig iron in a large dish-shaped vessel, or reverberatory furnace, and then decarbonizing it by adding wrought iron, steel scrap, or iron ore and spiegeleisen, of ferro-manganese. The materials used were melted by the union of atmospheric air and combustible gases.

rolling-mill techniques. Manual labor was almost entirely eliminated as the steel ingots were moved by huge cranes from the furnace to the rollers, where mechanical devices pushed them back and forth until they had been squeezed to the required size. The metal was then automatically cut into "blooms," which were transferred to other parts of the mill, where they were converted into rails, wire, structural steel, and a host of other products. By 1910, the output of rolled-steel products amounted to over 21,000,000 tons—more than a fourfold increase over the figure for the 1880's.

Into the growing variety of finished iron and steel products went ores from new western fields that were adaptable to improved mining techniques. The most important new deposits of iron ore were discovered in the Mesabi range in Minnesota. Large-scale operations were undertaken in the 1890's, and by 1913 approximately 35,000,000 tons, or more than one-half the nation's annual production of 62,000,000 tons, was being drawn from the Mesabi field. Lying close to the surface and being finely textured, the Mesabi ore could be mined by steam shovel and transported by cars that traveled on tracks laid in the open pits. The Mesabi iron became the mainstay of the economy of western Pennsylvania and eastern Ohio, the leading steel-producing region of the United States. With abundant supplies of coal and limestone and with easy access by water to the Lake Superior ore fields, this region's superiority was never seriously challenged. The development of the Alabama steel industry, which was centered at Birmingham and drew fully on local coal, limestone, and iron ores after the Civil War, was retarded for years by the unsuitability of the iron ore for the Bessemer process. The superior financial resources of its northern competitors and the growing competition of newer iron and steel centers in Illinois, Indiana, and Michigan also limited the sales and prestige of southern steel, but the Birmingham output still grew enormously.

Steel production was the key to the development of America's new industrial order. It formed the basis of many American fortunes. It furnished employment to thousands in the country's fast-growing population. Transportation and structural engineering were to a very large extent revolutionized by the use of steel. The growing steel industry also made possible the production of armor plate for the American navy, the construction of steel merchant ships, the building of bigger and stronger bridges, and the erection of skyscrapers, which were basically steel skeletons covered with sheathings of masonry and windows. Steel also played a key role in the development of American railroads after the Civil War. Iron rails gave way to a heavier and more durable steel product. Improvement in the quality of the tracks—

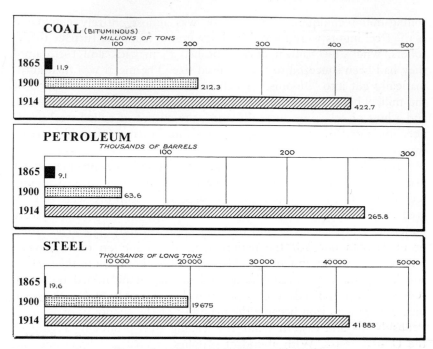

Growth of Basic Industries, 1865–1914

in conjunction with improvements in roadbed construction—enabled the railroad companies to use heavier rolling stock and to move their trains at higher speeds. Everywhere steel was used for an increasing variety of articles including locomotives, railway cars, farm machinery, castings, metalworking machinery, and almost every variety of tool.

Next in importance to coal and iron deposits in a modern industrial society is an adequate supply of crude oil, and, like coal and iron, crude oil existed in abundance in America. But to what uses might it be put, and how was it to be made useful? Petroleum had long been known to exist in the United States. The journals of many of the early explorers of the valley of the Allegheny and its tributaries record the presence of thick oil on the surface of the springs and streams. By 1850, rock oil, as petroleum was usually called, was being sold all over the United States as a cure-all patent medicine; but the remarkable extent of its commercial possibilities was not realized until 1855, when Professor Benjamin Silliman of Yale, after an analysis of a quantity of the fluid, announced that it would furnish as good an illuminant as any the world knew, and that it would also yield gas, paraffin, lubricating oil, and other valuable products. Four years later,

"Colonel" E. L. Drake, a former railway conductor, sank the first oil well near Titusville in western Pennsylvania. This well, not quite seventy feet in depth, began producing at the rate of 500 barrels a month. The news of Drake's success spread rapidly, and western Pennsylvania, whose frontier days were supposedly over, was again soon swarming with prospectors, speculators, and other adventurers. Land once considered worthless brought fabulous prices; towns came into being almost in a day; and millions of dollars were poured into dozens of hastily organized enterprises. By 1864, an area of more than 400 square miles about Titusville had been converted into a forest of derricks. Before half a dozen years had elapsed, the Pennsylvania field expanded to cover approximately 2,000 square miles, and wells were being sunk from West Virginia to Missouri in the hope of finding new fields. By 1872, nearly 40,000,000 barrels of petroleum had been produced in the United States, and oil had climbed to fourth place among the country's exports.

Despite rapid growth, the industry faced many difficulties in its early and most competitive years. Large sums invested in land, derricks, boring implements, and labor never yielded a cent in return. Adequate facilities for storing and transporting the crude product as it came from the ground were at first lacking, and the waste was enormous. The roads leading from the fields to the railroad terminals were quickly turned into quagmires of sticky mud by the weight of the loaded wagons dragged over ground soaked with rain and oil. Vehicles and teams were often ruined in a few days, but the freight rates were so high that teamsters seldom suffered losses. Much of the oil was floated to Pittsburgh in specially constructed barges that occasionally capsized or caught fire. These difficulties were largely overcome by the introduction in the middle sixties of the pipeline and the tank-car. By 1866, the heyday of the teamster was over. The leaky and inflammable wooden tank-car gave way to the tubular iron car, and these improvements, in turn, reduced the cost of oil transport by 60 per cent.

Shrewd businessmen near the oil fields, such as John D. Rockefeller, soon discovered that the oil-refining business was even more profitable than crude-oil production. Before 1865, refineries, large and small, were widely scattered. With the introduction of the pipeline and the tank-car, oil refining became concentrated in two principal inland centers, Pittsburgh and Cleveland. Although 200 miles from the oil region, Cleveland had taken the lead at the opening of the 1870's. It commanded practically the entire western market and was closely linked with the East by railroad line and by Lake Erie and the

Waiting for Rockefeller: Pennsylvania Oil Fields, 1865

Erie Canal. Pittsburgh, on the other hand, was completely dependent on the Pennsylvania Railroad for the transportation of its product to the eastern markets.

Rapid advances were made after the 1870's in every branch of the petroleum industry. Vast oil deposits discovered in the southern Plains states and California made a substantial contribution to the annual increase in petroleum production from 26,300,000 barrels in 1880 to 300,800,000 barrels in 1916. This immense output was carried through a network of pipelines across the country, and by 1900 more petroleum was transported by pipeline than by rail.

The principal petroleum product before 1900 was kerosene, which was used for heat and illumination, but the development of electric lighting, the increasing demand for industrial lubricants, and the widespread adoption of the gasoline motor, especially in automobiles, revolutionized the petroleum industry during the first two decades of the twentieth century. Earlier methods of refining, designed primarily to produce kerosene by applying heat to petroleum, were supplemented by the "cracking process," which made possible the extraction of larger quantities of gasoline from petroleum than in the past. Devices were also perfected to salvage gasoline from the natural gas that formerly had been permitted to escape from the wells. By 1918, American oil refineries were producing twice as much gas oil and fuel oils as kerosene.

In the first generation of this "oil revolution," however, another source of power was made available to Americans. Although Sir Humphry Davy had demonstrated an electric arc-lamp powered by batteries to the Royal Society in London in 1807, it was not until seventy years later that Charles F. Brush of Cleveland perfected an arc-lamp suitable for street illumination. Similar progress was made in electromagnetic induction. Michael Faraday made his pioneering discoveries in 1831, and by the 1870's the work of several scientists in a number of countries had made possible the construction of a dynamo that could generate a continuous supply of direct electric current. Electric power and electric lamps now existed, but arc-lights were too glaring for use in either home or office. In 1879, Thomas A. Edison perfected a practicable carbon-filament lamp in his Menlo Park laboratory in New Jersey. Three years later Edison, as successful a businessman as he was an inventor, built a power station in New York to supply current to eighty-five buildings. Within six years, the American people were using two million electric lights.

The Edison Electric Light Company, which had been formed in 1878, was merged with the Thomson-Houston Company in 1892 to form the General Electric Company. Its only important rival was the Westinghouse Electric and Manufacturing Company, which had been founded in 1886 by George Westinghouse, the inventor of the air brake, to supply power for industry and transportation. The Edison firm manufactured direct current, which could be transported only a relatively short distance, but Westinghouse understood the superior advantages of alternating current. Using transformers that had been developed in the 1880's and armed with the patent rights that he had purchased from a Serbian immigrant, Westinghouse soon demonstrated that alternating current could be carried great distances at comparatively low cost. While the range of direct current was limited to little more than a mile, by the end of the 1890's alternating current was being transported as far as twenty miles away from powerhouses run by steam or internal combustion engines or water power. As early as 1900, Niagara Falls was being used for a power plant, and by 1913 the Mississippi was giving its power to help electrify the nation from a great dam at Keokuk, Iowa. Electric motors came rapidly into factory use, and electric lights, streetcars, and trains spread with equal rapidity.

Almost as soon as the new sources of power became available, the revolutionary implications for common consumers became clear. The natural plenty of the continent could now be quickly converted into man-made plenty and deliver a nation of millions from the age-old threats of scarcity and taxing labor. Food, for example, could now be preserved for indefinite periods. The canning of vegetables was a major American industry as early as 1870, and by World War I every step in the canning process had been mechanized. The refrigerator car, whose practicality was demonstrated in the midseventies, similarly revolutionized the meat industry and enabled the packers of Chicago to take on the task of feeding a large part of the nation. In the shoe industry, machines eliminated a large amount of hand labor. By 1914, there was scarcely a consumer-goods industry that had not expanded its output by substituting machines for hand labor. Many of the inventions that made this revolution possible were put into practical form by Americans, but in many cases they were based upon the earlier work of Europeans. Americans did not have a unique genius for invention, but they did have unusual talent for applying inventions to the industrial process.

America's famed mass-production techniques were the result of uniting new sources of power, abundant raw materials and technical skills with a search for consumers for the products of the untiring machine. The large-scale production of a standardized item with uniform, interchangeable parts had already been carried to a high point of perfection by New England arms manufacturers in the decade before the Civil War. The Springfield arsenal, for example, took only 80 minutes to make a musket in a manufacturing operation that involved about 300 different machines and 500 separate mechanical processes. American pistols and guns, produced by such famous armsmakers as Colt, Whitney, Remington and Sharpe, had no machine-made superior throughout the world. Yankee gunmakers supplied not only the North during the Civil War, but also the European nations participating in the Crimean, Austro-Prussian, and Franco-Prussian Wars.

After the Civil War, as the all-important machine shops grew in number and increased the variety and efficiency of their products, automatic turret lathes, planers, gear-cutting machines, drills, and borers were produced in large quantities. Machines were equipped with jigs that could be attached and removed according to need, and tremendous advances were made in both the speed and accuracy of operation of all machine tools. Most American machine tools had been originally patterned on English models, but the Americans soon displayed their ingenuity at adapting these machines to many uses. In 1885, an Englishman wrote: "The tools and processes which we are inclined to consider unusual are the commonplaces of American shops, and the determina-

Early Days on the Ford Assembly Line

[BROWN BROTHERS]

tion to do by hand nothing which can be done by machinery is the chief characteristic."

The mass-production technique was made directly possible by the development of the machine tool industry and of its most important product, the interchangeable part. Sewing machines, watches, clocks, and agricultural machinery came early, but it was the automobile manufacturer who pushed mass production further than any other American industrialist. After the establishment of the industry in the 1890's, most automobiles were made of interchangeable parts, and during 1913–14, the firm headed by Henry Ford introduced the moving assembly line. Workers who had formerly moved around the plant to do their respective jobs now remained in one place while their job was brought to them. Each worker was assigned a simple, specific task, which he repeated on a never-ending series of cars-in-the-making that were dragged past him on a continuous belt. Mechanical conveyors had been used earlier in flour milling and meat processing, but to Ford's small group of associates and their imitators belongs the credit for developing this relatively simple device to an incredible degree of efficiency.

The Fabulous Grant-Corliss Engine at the Philadelphia Exposition of 1876

The machine, the factory, the assembly line put a new premium on technical knowledge. Graduates of the scientific schools established after the Civil War found numerous jobs waiting for them in American industry. Large corporations began to hire scientists to devise new products and new machines or processes to manufacture them. As early as 1879, the American Telephone & Telegraph Company established its own laboratories manned by skilled technicians and experienced scientists. Other corporations followed suit, and by World War I the individual inventor, like the small businessman laboring in his own improvised shop, had become little more than a hallowed figure in the folklore of American industry. Innovations were now the result of the collective efforts of specialists who had no other job than to produce the inventions that were needed by their corporations. Science, like the machine, had been adapted by the American industrialist to fit the pattern of mass production.

Relentlessly, this collective rationalization and standardization affected the worker as well as the employer and technician. As early as the 1880's, the American Society of Mechanical Engineers had begun to give its attention to increasing the productivity of labor as well as machinery. In 1895, Frederick W. Taylor, who was soon to become known as the "father of scientific management," addressed the society on "A Piece-Rate System." Taylor believed that the efficiency of factory workers could be increased by paying them according to their rate of production and by using time-and-motion studies to eliminate waste motions. Taylor's ideas received wide publicity and were adopted by a number of manufacturers. But to workers, "scientific management" was merely an old system under a new name. They preferred to call it the "speed-up."

Toward Western and Southern Industrialization

As American industry developed after the Civil War, there was a gradual shift of the nation's center of manufacturing westward. The Northeast, which had been the leading American industrial section since colonial times, managed to maintain its supremacy until about 1880, but then it steadily lost ground. The westward movement of population, better rail service east and west, and the desire of manufacturers to be near essential raw materials from the West stimulated the growth of midwestern industry. Sometimes, established eastern industries emigrated from the East; for instance, the McCormick reaper works moved in successive stages from Virginia to Chicago by way of Cincinnati. Cincinnati, on the other hand, was a machine-tool center in 1880 while this industry still flourished in New England. Some industries, however, such as the manufacture of automobiles, were founded in the Middle West and never had any serious eastern competitors.

According to the federal census of 1870, the nation's manufacturing establishments had increased by almost 80 per cent during the preceding decade. The gain was greatest in the states of the Old Northwest. Indiana, for instance, had twice as many establishments as in 1860, and Illinois three times as many. States in the upper Mississippi *centers of NW Industry*

Valley, which on the eve of the war had been little more than agrarian frontier regions, now contained flourishing factory towns. Chicago was already internationally known for its stockyards, Pullman cars, clothing factories, and agricultural machinery. Other towns and cities in Illinois and Ohio closely rivaled many of the industrial centers of the older eastern mill zones. In Indianapolis, metropolis of an extensive and fertile agricultural region, nearly one fifth of a population of about 100,000 was employed in factories manufacturing furniture, starch, textiles, vehicles, and farm tools. Detroit's ironware and stoves, Grand Rapids furniture, and St. Louis and Milwaukee beer already had national reputations. Meat packing and flour milling became great midwestern industries as Chicago took the lead in packing from Cincinnati, and Minneapolis already seemed destined to become the world's greatest milling center, producing, as it already did in 1870, nearly 90,000 barrels of flour a month.

At Chicago the meat barons of America—men with names like Armour, Morris, and Swift—revolutionized the meat industry by shrewd use of the refrigerator car, mass production, and the newer railroads to the cattle country. Washburn and Pillsbury did for the Minneapolis mills what Armour and Swift did for the Chicago stockyards. By the late 1870's thousands of cars were needed annually to carry Minneapolis flour to the Atlantic seaboard, where much of it was transshipped to the markets of the Old World. Minneapolis eventually lost its supremacy as millers in other cities adopted more advanced techniques, but in 1914 Minneapolis was still a leading flour-milling center.

As the nation's center of population moved westward, many industries followed—to be nearer their markets or raw materials. By the 1890's, barbed wire came from Illinois rather than Massachusetts, while the iron and steel industry moved from Philadelphia and Trenton to Pittsburgh and Youngstown, and later to Detroit, Chicago, and Cleveland. Michigan automobiles and Akron rubber, however, were introduced by inventive local citizens.

Far more dramatic changes took place in the South than in the northern Middle-West. Much of the South had been devastated by war and racked by Reconstruction. It lacked adequate capital, large cities, a trained laboring force, experienced business executives, and an industrial tradition. Many southerners, however, thought that the South's salvation lay in the development of industry and during Reconstruction the southern railroad system was rebuilt and expanded. But little was done to promote manufacturing until after the 1880's, when serious attempts were made to establish a textile industry in the South.

Southern cotton mills were first built by enterprising members of

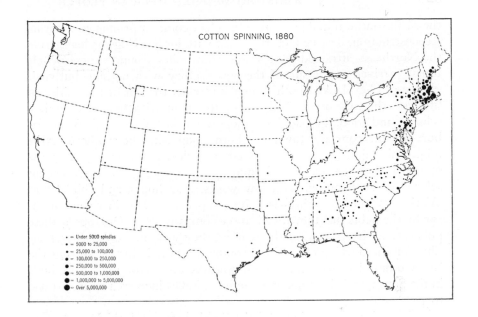

COTTON SPINNING, 1880

COTTON SPINNING, 1880 AND 1926

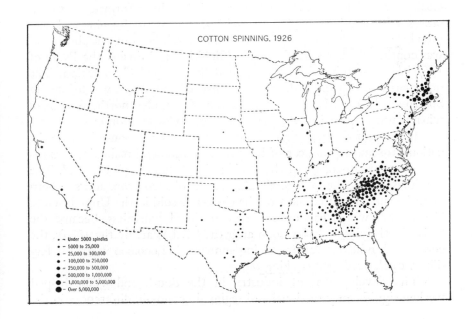

COTTON SPINNING, 1926

the small southern middle class, which had come to prominence during Reconstruction. Textile factories, built with local savings or loans from the Northeast, attracted poor whites from miles around. These people usually arrived at the site of the new factory with nothing but their clothing. They lacked both money and even the barest necessities of life, and the mill owner had to furnish them with homes, churches, schools, and food. To pay for these, the worker pledged his future labor; and the company town was born along with the southern textile mill. This labor system, originated as a device for overcoming the southern shortage of capital, quickly developed into a permanent scheme of exploitation, with low wages, long hours, and child labor. Workers who might otherwise have escaped were held in virtual bondage by the debts that they owed to the company store. Onerous as these policies may have been for the worker, they were in large part responsible for the development of the southern textile industry. During the last two decades of the nineteenth century, 340 cotton mills were built in the South, and the number of active spindles increased from 561,000 to 4,368,000.

Other leading products of the South before World War I were lumber, tobacco products, cottonseed oil, and iron and steel. The center of the southern iron and steel industry was Birmingham, Alabama; and by 1892 the Tennessee-Alabama district was producing approximately 25 per cent of the country's total output of iron ore. The Tennessee Coal, Iron and Railroad Company, which had been formed by southerners with southern capital, established a plant in Birmingham that soon became the South's largest steel producer. The company, however, was continually beset by financial difficulties, and during the Panic of 1907 it was purchased by the United States Steel Corporation. The other large steel plant in the South before World War I was located at Sparrow's Point, Maryland, but it, too, fell under northern control when it was acquired by the Bethlehem Steel Corporation in 1916.

Because of the depletion of northern forests, the South became the nation's foremost producer of lumber after 1900 and maintained its supremacy until 1930, when the Pacific Coast states took the lead. The South also grew the bulk of the American tobacco crop, and southern factories manufactured most of the cigarettes sold in the United States. Cottonseed, which had once been considered worthless, became the basis of a thriving industry soon after the Civil War. By the 1880's, the cottonseed industry was producing annually $12,000,000 worth of fertilizer, cattle feed, and cooking oil.

The development of industry in the South and West helped weaken significantly sectional and regional economic differences in the

United States. In contrast with the antebellum years, by 1914 every major section had its important manufacturing centers, and no industrial region dominated the rest of the nation as the Northeast had done before 1860. On the eve of World War I, Birmingham was a more important industrial center than any city in Massachusetts, and Chicago had long since outdistanced Philadelphia. In the new industrial republic the distinctive regional economies of an earlier era had given way to a division of labor in which every section of the nation produced its own manufactured specialties while all shared the common problems of industrial-urban life.

FOR SUPPLEMENTARY READING

For general background on industrialization read T. C. Cochran and W. Miller, *The Age of Enterprise* (1942); A. Nevins, *The Emergence of Modern America, 1865–1878* (1928); and I. M. Tarbell, *The Nationalizing of Business, 1878–1898* (1936). Joseph Dorfman, *The Economic Mind in American Civilization* (1949), analyzes economic theory during the period but also read on this E. C. Kirkland, *Dream and Thought in the Business Community, 1860–1900* (1956). Work on the growing railroads can begin with T. C. Cochran, *Railroad Leaders, 1845–1890* (1953); and G. R. Taylor and I. D. Neu, *The American Railroad Network* (1953). Studies of businessmen and industries are voluminous. A start can be made with W. Miller (ed.), *Men in Business* (1952); A. Nevins, *Study in Power: John D. Rockefeller* (2 vols., 1953); B. J. Hendrick, *Andrew Carnegie* (2 vols., 1932), an official biography; and M. Josephson, *The Robber Barons* (1934), strongly anticapitalist in bias. Roger Burlingame's *Engines of Democracy* (1940) is a worthwhile social history of inventions and technology. The problems of the South and West can be approached through B. Mitchell and G. S. Mitchell, *The Industrial Revolution in the South* (1930), and C. Goodrich and others, *Migration and Economic Opportunity* (1936).

3

Business Regulation: Private or Public

ALTHOUGH Americans have traditionally extolled the virtues of competition and economic individualism, after the Civil War they appeared to go out of their way to destroy their most cherished economic ideals. In industry after industry, competition was either eliminated or circumscribed, and in the process the independent individual steadily lost ground to the impersonal corporation. Moreover, competition was the villain of the piece, for, instead of being the life of trade, it proved to be the first step down the road toward monopoly. But this fact did not shake the faith of the American people, who continued to give their allegiance to the very economic theories they seemed bent on destroying. Although, generally speaking, large corporations had more to contribute to a steadily rising standard of living than did many small competing firms with their wasteful duplication of effort, Americans were stubbornly sentimental in their loyalty to the image of a small businessman's society. In sum, they refused either to practice what they preached or to preach what they practiced.

The role of the government in the economy also posed problems that the American people were unable to resolve. Most big businessmen complained that government regulation would stifle competition and individual initiative, but they did not hesitate to ask the government for a protective tariff or some other form of subsidy. Many reformers, agrarians, and small businessmen maintained that the government should assume responsibility for restoring competition by curbing or destroying the trusts, but they shrank from advocating policies drastic enough to achieve this goal, for such policies would have undoubtedly disrupted the nation's economic organization and impaired the efficiency of American industry. Few Americans seemed to understand that even if the government could destroy a steel or oil empire without disarranging the entire economy, its action would merely reinitiate the struggle for supplies, markets, and labor that had produced concentration in the first place. Once again tradition and reality were in conflict, but the Americans nevertheless found it difficult to abandon their ideals, however much they changed their practices.

The Coming of the Railroad Giants

The conflicting tendencies and the general problems of competition and control were first demonstrated on a wide scale in financing and managing the nation's railroads in the 1870's and 80's. Before the Civil War, railroad construction had been largely confined to relatively short, detached lines that supplemented water routes or connected nearby towns and cities. In the postwar years, many of these local roads were joined together. Railroad operators wanted to provide their customers with continuous rail travel over comparatively large distances and were determined to eliminate competition. Disastrous rate wars demonstrated that unrestricted competition reduced the revenues of all lines. Desperate to guarantee their profits, the railroad operators organized pools, but the rates fixed by the pools could not be enforced, and so-called gentlemen's agreements were broken almost as soon as they were made. The more powerful roads next tried to buy up their weaker rivals. Through merger or purchase, competition was systematically eliminated, and by World War I a few gigantic systems dominated the American railroad industry. This movement to nearly monopolistic control was brought on by shrewd and skillful businessmen who were unwilling to pay the price or to take the risks of wide open competition.

The first major rail consolidation was the New York Central system. As early as 1862, Cornelius Vanderbilt had started to piece together the links of an all-rail route between New York and Chicago. In 1869, he combined the New York Central and Hudson River railroads to establish a through route from New York City to Buffalo. In the following year, when he obtained control of the Lake Shore and Michigan Southern, the New York Central consisted of 965 miles of track connecting Chicago with the Atlantic seaboard. Agreements in 1870 with the Rock Island and the Chicago and Northwestern enabled him to provide uninterrupted service to as far west as Omaha. Before his death in 1877, he had secured the Michigan Central, which ran between Detroit and Toronto. A far-sighted railroad manager, Vanderbilt double-tracked the Central's lines with heavier rails, improved its roadbed, bridged streams and embankments with sturdier materials, bought new rolling stock, acquired the Grand Central Terminal in New York City, and shortened the running time for passenger service between New York and Chicago from fifty hours to twenty-four.

When Vanderbilt died, control of the New York Central passed to his son William and to the House of Morgan. But the change in administration did not prevent the road's continued expansion. By the turn of the century, the New York Central had gained entrance into Boston and Montreal, had penetrated the coal, iron, and oil regions of central and western Pennsylvania, and had terminals in Wheeling, Cincinnati, Louisville, Cairo, Peoria, St. Louis, and in Mackinaw City at the northern end of the lower peninsula of Michigan. Both the mileage and the capitalization of the Vanderbilt system were further increased when the younger Vanderbilt was practically blackmailed into acquiring the West Shore and the New York, Chicago, and St. Louis lines. The latter paralleled the Lake Shore and Michigan Southern and had been built by a group of railroad freebooters for no other purpose than to exact tribute from the owners of the New York Central. It was known as the "Nickel Plate," because when it was eventually purchased by Vanderbilt, the price was so high that he is said to have thought that the rails must be made of "nickel plate." The West Shore, going up the west bank of the Hudson to Albany and then westward, parallel to the original New York Central, was acquired under similar circumstances.

The development of trunk lines elsewhere in the nation involved similar practices to those used by or forced on Vanderbilt of the New York Central. At the price of public corruption, reckless financing, rate wars, wasteful building of rival parallel roads, and buying up of competitors, the national railroad network grew in size and, despite all, in quality of service. Two types of entrepreneurs emerged in the railroad empire, the buccaneer and the builder; these radically different types represented attitudes toward railroading usually found combined in most of the railroad barons.

For years, buccaneers like Daniel Drew, Jay Gould, and James Fisk used the Erie Railroad in New York as a financial plaything, giving no thought to improving service or to sound financing. Their fabulous stock manipulations threw Wall Street into small panics. They waged a great private war with Vanderbilt, who, after the Central was formed,

Grand Central Station Under Construction in New York

[CULVER SERVICE]

wanted to control all rail traffic into New York in order to become czar of American commerce. Although autocratic and crooked in many of his dealings, Vanderbilt as a railroad builder would have brought order and greater if not perfect honesty to Erie affairs, but from "the secret haunts of the Erie" came as much stock as Vanderbilt wanted to buy. Court injunction countered court injunction as the Erie robbers used their Democratic judge to oppose the orders of Vanderbilt's Republican judge. The "Erie War" became a comic opera when the Erie directors had to flee hastily from Wall Street in New York City to New Jersey across the Hudson River to avoid arrest. Absence of public regulation, lavish corruption of officials in both political parties, and the callous ruthlessness of these great manipulators left the Erie a shambles and fleeced many "sheep." By the midseventies the Erie was the most corruptly managed railroad in the land. When it finally escaped the clutches of Drew, Gould, and Fisk it was in bankruptcy. Following its reorganization in 1878, it resumed its policy of expansion until the Panic of 1893 forced it into the fourth receivership in its history. Reorganized once more—this time with the aid of the House of Morgan—the Erie's directors finally settled down to the mundane business of improving their line's facilities and of converting the road into one of the nation's most important carriers of anthracite and bituminous coal.

After doing his share to wreck the Erie, Gould became active in railroad speculation elsewhere, with new associates like Russell Sage and Sidney Dillon. He purchased a controlling interest in a number of weak railroads in the trans-Mississippi West, including the Kansas Pacific and the Denver Pacific, which together paralleled the Union Pacific as far as Cheyenne. By threatening to extend his line to Ogden and by cutting rates, he forced the Union Pacific to accept his terms for the consolidation of the three properties. Under this arrangement, Kansas Pacific and Denver Pacific stocks, quoted at 12, were exchanged for Union Pacific stock, quoted at 93. As a result of the bargain driven by Gould, the Union Pacific was saddled with two railroads that it did not need and was compelled to assume a burdensome financial responsibility. During the 1880's the Union Pacific, faced by increasing competition and compelled by Gould to purchase from him lines that he had bought for relatively little, rapidly expanded its mileage. At the same time, the road, which from the outset had been hampered by its heavy indebtedness, was plunged into financial difficulties by Gould's manipulations. The Panic of 1893 drove it into receivership, and in the next four years it had to relinquish 5,800 miles of line. In 1897, following a foreclosure sale, the Union Pacific was taken over by E. H. Harriman.

Harriman, unlike Gould, was primarily a builder of railroad systems for whom huge profits and stock manipulation were not incompatible with improvement of rail services. He was a leader of a group of second generation railroad men, who, if not models of virtue, were more conservative and more constructive than the buccaneers of the sixties and early seventies.

Harriman had begun his business career in 1862 as a fourteen-year-old office boy in Wall Street. Seven years later he owned a seat on the New York Stock Exchange, and in 1881 he entered the railroad industry with the purchase of a bankrupt railway that he immediately reorganized and sold at a profit to the Pennsylvania Railroad. After serving as a director of the Illinois Central, he calculated that the Union Pacific road, despite its financial difficulties, was potentially profitable. He participated in its reorganization in the midnineties, and became a member of its board in 1897, chairman of the board's executive committee in 1898, and president of the entire system in 1903. Soon after becoming chairman, Harriman spent $25,000,000 obtained from Kuhn, Loeb and Company, one of the largest Wall Street investment bankers, on improving the Union Pacific's roadbed, reducing grades, eliminating curves, purchasing new rolling stock, and buying up other railroads. In

1900, he assured the Union Pacific of access to the Southwest by purchasing a half-interest in the San Pedro, Los Angeles, and Salt Lake line. In the following year he acquired control of both the Southern Pacific and the Central Pacific. The Union Pacific now had direct connection with Sacramento and Oakland. Harriman became the dominant railroad figure of the Southwest.

His capture of the Southern Pacific took power from four western buccaneers, Leland Stanford, Collis P. Huntington, Mark Hopkins, and Charles Crocker. Setting out to monopolize California's railroads in 1872, like their more voracious eastern counterparts on the Erie board, these men had quickly learned how to use politics to get what they wanted. They bought congressmen and state legislators and made the Southern Pacific offices in San Francisco the capital of the state in all but name. Harriman's succession to their powers gave him a role in the Southwest similar to that played by Henry Villard and James J. Hill in the Northwest.

Although chartered by Congress in 1864 to build a railroad from some point on Lake Superior to Puget Sound, the Northern Pacific company did not begin construction until 1870, when it secured the financial support of the banking house of Jay Cooke and Company. The crash of 1873 forced both financier and railroad into bankruptcy; and construction was not resumed until the road was reorganized in 1875. But before the Northern Pacific reached the Pacific coast, it was acquired by Henry Villard, who feared that the new line would jeopardize his extensive holdings in the Willamette and Columbia valleys. Soon after assuming the presidency of the Northern Pacific in 1881, Villard completed its route to Portland and then north to Tacoma on Puget Sound.

Villard's management of his road was strikingly different from the practices of his chief rival, James J. Hill, who in 1878 purchased the virtually bankrupt St. Paul and Pacific Railroad. Despite its name, this short Minnesota line, formerly a feeder of the Northern Pacific, was little more than a connecting link for the steamboat lines operating on the Mississippi and Red rivers. Hill promptly changed its name to the St. Paul, Minneapolis, and Manitoba Railroad and, with the backing of Canadian and American capital, pushed its rails westward and northward with a view to capturing Canadian as well as American business. By 1887, the road extended across the Dakotas to Great Falls, Montana, and in 1890 Hill created the Great Northern Railway Company. Three years later the Hill lines reached Seattle. Although the main routes of Villard's Northern Pacific and the Great Northern paralleled each other, they were in many respects markedly different. The Hill lines were built without government aid, were better located, and were more efficiently constructed. Routes with favorable grades were selected and sharp curves avoided. Overcapitalization was shunned, financial storms were weathered, and an uninterrupted dividend record maintained. Hill never lost sight of his dictum: "Intelligent management of railroads must be based on exact knowledge of facts. Guesswork will not do." As a railroad manager and financier, Hill the builder was all that Jay Gould the buccaneer was not. Speaking of the development of the lands of the Northwest, Hill said: "Make it desirable for people to come here, make it easy for them to carry on their business, and we will get the freight. We consider ourselves and the people along our line as co-partners in the prosperity of the country we both occupy; and the prosperity of the one should mean the prosperity of both; and their adversity will be quickly followed by ours." Hill, like Villard, carried on a continuous campaign to induce settlers to migrate to the territory served by his railways and did everything in his power to make them prosperous and contented. He established banks, helped build schools and churches, ran agricultural demonstration trains over his lines, and distributed free to farmers of the Northwest blooded bulls imported from England. Throughout his career, he never lost sight of the fact that his success as a railroader was intimately bound up with the economic welfare of those who had settled in his empire.

The Sorry Tale of Railroad Financing

By the late eighties, despite exceptional roads created by men like Hill, the instability and predominant bungling of American railroad affairs had created growing public anger. But more important than indignation in bringing order and regularity, if not scrupulous honesty, into railroad life, was the role played by bankers like J. P. Morgan, who stabilized the American railroads after a generation of reckless manipulation and a seemingly endless cycle of mismanagement, bankruptcy, reorganization, mismanagement, and failure again.

All the postwar railway projects in the United States required large capital outlays. Money was needed for surveys, rights of way, grading, laying the rails, and the acquisition of rolling stock and other essential equipment. Railroad investments were inherently highly speculative, for many lines were built in advance of population, and high overhead costs inspired cut-throat competition. However piratical the intentions of some railroadmen, they did take risks, even if these were the risks of thieves. Despite these difficulties, the railroads were built; eager

American and European investors added funds to those advanced by local, state, and federal governments.

The capital needed for railroad construction was so great that American governments had to provide substantial assistance to the railroad builders. Towns, cities, and counties, wanting improved transportation, supplied railroad promoters with $300,000,000 while the states—at a conservative estimate—furnished an additional $228,000,000 as well as land grants totaling approximately the area of Texas. The federal government was even more generous. Congressional grants of public lands to states for railway purposes were first made in 1850, and during the next two decades this policy was steadily expanded. By 1871, the states of the Mississippi Valley had received eighty such grants. Several railroad corporations chartered by Congress during the sixties were also given great tracts of the national domain by the federal government. Approximately 131,000,000 acres of federal lands and 55,000,-000 acres of state lands were conditionally credited to railway promoters. But because of failure to meet all the conditions under which this land was granted, the railroad companies were eventually able to retain only about 116,000,000 acres. The federal government also made $65,000,000 in loans to six trans-Mississippi railroad companies. Failure to set aside earnings to retire this debt made it necessary in the late 1890's for the government to threaten foreclosure in order to secure payment. In the final settlements the government was a loser.

Whatever the rhetoric of private enterprise, in all probability 40 per cent of the cost of all railway construction before 1870—exclusive of land grants—was thus borne by public authority, but by the mid-seventies, the earlier enthusiasm for railroads had given way to indifference and often to open hostility. Labor leaders, antimonopolists, land reformers, homesteaders, and land speculators demanded that the policy of granting public lands to railroad companies be abandoned. Shippers, victimized by exorbitant rates, rebates, and other railroad abuses, also objected to government assistance to one group of businessmen at the expense of others. The activities of Drew, Fisk, and Gould, the Crédit Mobilier scandals of the Grant era, and increasing railroad bankruptcies suggested that railroad promoters did not deserve the assistance that they had received. In 1872, the Supreme Court ruled that counties, towns, and cities were fully liable for all debts that they had contracted to foster railroad construction. The program of public assistance then virtually ended; for many years to come, taxpayers had to pay out money to retire bonds that their governments had issued to finance railroads. There was no way, however, to prevent the railroads from defaulting on their obligations. During the seventies, after the damage had been done, several states forbade the extension of public credit to private corporations. Government aid had quickened the pace of railroad building, but it also encouraged the construction of roads before they were needed and induced investors to put their money into highly speculative railroad projects.

In the earliest years of the American railroad industry, farmers, workers, and businessmen as well as public authority had supplied a relatively large proportion of the necessary railroad capital. The depression of 1837 dried up many of the sources of this venture capital in the United States, but by the 1850's and 1860's railroads were again regarded as sound investments. Men and women of small means continued to invest in railway stocks and bonds, but much larger sums were supplied by individuals who had already acquired sizable fortunes from railroading, merchandizing, or some other enterprise.

Despite the growth of American venture capital, native finance, whether public or private, was unable to satisfy the railroads' needs for funds after the Civil War. Promoters were forced to turn to Europe for additional money. Europeans had helped to finance some of America's earliest railroads, but in the 1850's foreign capital began to play an important role in the American transportation industry. Large amounts of European capital also helped finance most of the nation's leading rail systems after 1865. The excesses of Jay Gould and his followers and the Panic of 1873 sharply checked foreign investment in American railroads, but foreign confidence soon revived and was not again seriously undermined until the depression of 1893. But the depression of the nineties, like that of the seventies, had only a temporary effect on the rate of European investment in the United States. By the

Distribution of American Railroad Securities in Europe
January 1, 1899 *

England	$2,500,000,000
Holland	240,000,000
Germany	200,000,000
Switzerland	75,000,000
France	50,000,000
Rest of Europe	35,000,000
TOTAL	$3,100,000,000

* Reprinted with permission from William Z. Ripley: *Railroads: Finance, and Organization* (New York: Longmans, Green and Company, 1915), p. 6.

turn of the century Europeans owned $3,100,000,000 worth of American railroad securities.

By the late eighties railroad history was predominantly a story of the violation of the confidence of public and private, foreign and domestic investors. Watered stock, security speculation, dummy construction companies, padded costs, and a host of other questionable devices were used by the buccaneers who had gutted the corporations that were unfortunate enough to fall under their control. The railroad executives were robbing both the investor and the taxpayer. The *Banker's Magazine* estimated that in the five years following 1874, European investors in American enterprises—mostly railroads—had lost $600,000,000 by bankruptcy or fraud, and that this had been "going on for more than a generation." By July, 1893, at the outset of the most severe financial crisis after the Civil War, 126 companies had been consigned to receiverships, and a year later the number had risen to 192. From 1893 to 1898, approximately 67,000 miles, or about one third of the country's total mileage, underwent foreclosure. The first prominent road to go under was the Philadelphia and Reading. Within a short time, it was followed by the Erie, the Northern Pacific, the Union Pacific, and the Atchison, Topeka, and Santa Fé. A year or two later the Norfolk and Western collapsed, followed by the Baltimore and Ohio. Innumerable lesser lines were added to the wreckage.

Cries for relief from the effects of overexpansion, overcapitalization, looting and inefficient management had been growing for nearly twenty years. In the early nineties, the London *Economist* wrote:

> The American railway world has afforded abundant scope in the past for all kinds of financial trickery and apparently the "smart" operators, who have reaped such a large harvest in the past, seem still disposed to look for further facilities for plunder in the future. The "crop of lambs" to be sheared, of course, varies from time to time, but, on the average, it would appear that the folly of investors may be regarded as a fixed quantity. . . . To us it appears that there has been an utter lack of all principle in dealing with the right of the Income Bond-holders, and their securities have been made to serve as first rate gambling counters for the benefit of the big financiers who are in a position either to pull the strings or to obtain all the inside information.

Even the Baltimore and Ohio, long regarded as one of the soundest and safest business enterprises in America, became a victim of mismanagement. By 1887, after three years of rapid expansion, the road

needed financial assistance. A syndicate arranged by the House of
Morgan and composed of the British banking firm of J. S. Morgan
& Son, Baring Brothers & Co., and Brown, Shipley & Co., together with
their American associates agreed to come to the relief of the embar-
rassed road on condition that the management of the company be
placed in responsible hands satisfactory to the syndicate. Although the
road accepted these terms, the arrangement soon broke down, and
debt piled up to such an extent that collapse was inevitable. During the
period of receivership, investigation indicated that malpractices had
been largely responsible for the road's failure. Again the London *Economist* warned British investors to avoid American railway securities:

> And when people here find that such malpractices as these
> have been carried on for a series of years, on what was believed
> to be one of the best-managed of the American railroads, and
> that, after they have been exposed, nobody seems to think of
> bringing those responsible for them to account, it cannot be
> wondered at if the small degree of confidence in American
> railroads that has been left them is still further impaired.

Morgan's attempt in the 1880's to force the Baltimore and Ohio
to adopt more rational policies so as to guarantee steady and safe, if less
spectacular, returns to the conservative investors whom he represented,
was a clue to the future history of railroads. Indeed, Morgan's role in
the railroad industry foreshadowed his power elsewhere.

Banker financing of the American railway system had begun on
a smaller scale as early as the 1850's when eastern bankers like J. E.
Thayer of Boston and Moses Taylor of New York and the Barings and
Rothschilds of England had funds invested in American railroads. Joining them before the rise of Morgan were Jay Cooke and Company,
closely associated with the Northern Pacific and eastern and Canadian
banks that backed Villard and Hill.

By the late eighties, firms like the House of Morgan, engaged primarily in investment banking, were practically compelled to become
even more interested in railroad finance and ever stricter in their controls. The railroad industry had become so chaotic and had so exploited
railway-security holders that the elder Morgan and others began to
fear for the safety of the investment business as a whole. Public confidence both at home and abroad had to be restored if the investment
banker was to survive and flourish.

With the House of Morgan in the lead, the bankers' penetration of
the railroads rapidly grew in the 1890's. The desire for power and profits
was not, however, subordinated to the wish for protection. Strategic

stockownership, interlocking directorates, voting trusts, and the community of interests were the major devices employed by the bankers to build up immense railway systems. By the end of the century, a large share of the railroad mileage was concentrated in six dominant systems:

Harriman	20,245 miles
Vanderbilt	19,317 miles
Morgan	19,073 miles
Pennsylvania	18,220 miles
Gould	16,074 miles
Hill	10,373 miles

Of these, only two—the Harriman and the Gould—were outside complete or partial domination by the House of Morgan, and both of these were not independent but considerably controlled by Kuhn, Loeb and Company. A battle of financial titans now developed that dwarfed earlier fights between the captains of the railroads. The dramatic fight between Morgan and Kuhn, Loeb and Company came to a climax through the competition between J. J. Hill and E. H. Harriman.

Hill had received his main financial support from the House of Morgan, which had obtained control over the Northern Pacific. Hill was soon in conflict with Harriman after the latter's rise to power in the nineties. The immediate cause of their rivalry was the Chicago, Burlington, and Quincy. Because its main lines from Minneapolis, Kansas City, St. Louis, Omaha, Denver, and Billings in Montana all entered Chicago, it would provide either Hill or Harriman with access to Chicago, and thus with a means of capturing the entire Mississippi Valley market, as well as securing connections with the cotton-carrying roads of the South and a route that covered the principal lumber-consuming states of the nation. In 1901, Harriman learned that the Hill-Morgan interests had acquired the Chicago, Burlington, and Quincy for the Northern Pacific and Great Northern. He then asked for permission to buy a one-third interest in the key line into Chicago. But Hill refused, and Harriman sought to obtain control of the Burlington by purchasing a majority of Northern Pacific stock in the open market. To forestall Harriman, the Hill-Morgan group also entered the market. Within a few days, shares of Northern Pacific stock rose from $110 to $1000; and because many brokers sold short (i.e., sold stock for future delivery that they then did not own in the hope they could in the interim buy it for themselves cheaply), 78,000 more shares of the stock were sold than actually existed. Harriman gained control of $78,000,000 out of a total capital stock of $155,000,000, but he still

James J. Hill (center) with Bankers Baker (left) and Steele

[BROWN BROTHERS]

did not have control of the company. He held less than half of the
line's common stock and the owners of the other part, being in a majority, could retire the preferred stock which Harriman owned. To
avert what in all probability would have been a severe panic, both
groups agreed to a truce. At Hill's suggestion they formed the Northern Securities Company with a capitalization of $400,000,000. The
shares of this corporation, which was a holding company, were exchanged for all the stock of the Northern Pacific, which Harriman and
Hill now jointly owned, and for the great majority of the stock of the
Great Northern. Three of the fifteen directors of the Northern Securities Company were also directors of Harriman's Union Pacific. Three
formerly independent roads—the Northern Pacific, the Great Northern,
and the Chicago, Burlington and Quincy—were united, and Harriman
shared in their control. Under this arrangement, a small group of railroad operators and Wall Street financiers had finally come to control

practically all the major railroad lines west of the Mississippi. By the 1920's, the foreign money behind these men had been bought out, and American financiers had taken full control of the nation's railroads.

The Businessman Rejects Laissez Faire

The evolution of the American railroads after the Civil War was similar to the history of other industries. Railroads also helped stimulate business consolidation generally, for the spread of the railroad network tended to break down regional monopolies and brought all the producers within a single industry into direct national competition with one another. As unprecedented opportunities for profits were opened up by the growth of the railroads and by the discovery of new sources of raw materials, new manufacturing techniques, and new products, businessmen made all-out efforts to outstrip rivals in the race for richer rewards and greater prizes than had ever before been offered on the American continent.

Theorists might view this wider competition as the life of trade, but, as in the railroads, a growing number of business leaders came to look upon it as inefficient and wasteful and, above all, as a threat to their profits. Price wars had become so intense in some industries that many firms were compelled to operate at a loss. Before the Civil War, some industrialists had already sought to check competition through combination; after the war, the trend toward concentration was accelerated. By 1914 the largest parts of American industry were in the hands of a few individuals and corporations.

As one method to check the "evils of competition" proved either unworkable or illegal, another was employed until that too had to be either modified or abandoned. The search for privately controlled, predictable markets proceeded on a trial-and-error basis, but the successive steps used by American businessmen fall into a rough pattern. Pools were used in many industries during the Civil War period but were generally abandoned by the end of the 1880's as unworkable. After the formation of the Standard Oil trust in 1879, several corporations made use of the trust, but adverse court decisions soon led to other means to control competition. By 1900, most of the large semi-monopolistic firms were organized as holding companies, and a few years later interlocking directorates were employed as a successful device for giving the appearance of competition to the reality of monopoly. Throughout these years many firms also rose to power within their industries by simply purchasing their rivals.

Pools were designed essentially to limit competition in industries with a relatively large number of firms, none of which was strong enough either to eliminate or dominate its rivals. Pools—or "gentlemen's agreements," as they were frequently called—have been described as "partnerships of corporations." A number of concerns pledged themselves to observe regulations for production quotas, price fixing, division of markets, maintenance of minimum standards of quality, and pooling of patents. Pools had marked defects: they were not sanctioned by law and unruly members could not be coerced through the courts. The success of a pool depended on the cooperation of all the firms within an industry; no company could be forced to join a pool; and a single member could destroy a pool's effectiveness by launching a price-war. In short, the gentlemen's agreement was no stronger than the word or honor of its members—a fact that often gave it a very short life indeed.

The difficulties in using the pool to regulate competition were illustrated by the experiences of the Michigan Salt Association. In 1866, after overproduction had caused numerous failures among Michigan salt manufacturers, they combined to establish a common selling-agency. Two years later they formed the Saginaw and Bay Salt Company, which lasted until it was destroyed by dissension among its members in 1871. Declining prices again forced the member firms back into cooperation. In 1876, they set up the Michigan Salt Association, which experienced a series of ups and downs for the next decade as it attempted to compel its members to abide by its regulations. Pools in other industries were usually even less successful. In general, they merely managed to postpone rather than eliminate price wars.

As pools repeatedly demonstrated that at best they could only give temporary relief from the effects of competition, a few far-seeing industrialists began to search for a more efficient means of regulating the policies of all the members within a single industry. Unlike the pool, the new device would have to include some method of coercion without violating established law. The problem was worthy of the talents of the man who did the most to solve it, for John D. Rockefeller was perhaps more generously endowed than any of his contemporaries with a combination of acquisitive instincts, leadership, ruthlessness, and organizing ability.

John D. Rockefeller received a thorough training in acquisitiveness from both his parents. His mother, a devout Baptist, taught him at an early age that it was his Christian duty to work hard, make as much money as possible, and give a tithe to the church. His father's approach to the problem of his son's education for life was more practical. On one occasion, he boasted to a friend: "I cheat my boys every time I get a chance. I want to make 'em sharp." As part of his program to keep his son "sharp," the elder Rockefeller would lend him money and then before the note was due, appear and say: "I shall have to have that money." The young Rockefeller always met his test. In his later life Rockefeller recalled with pride his father's labor policy:

> He would hire men to work for him; after a time tell them with a smile, "I don't need you any longer"; then in a few days hire them over again. His "policy of firing and hiring over" he called it. It kept the men on tiptoe—no stagnation among them.

In 1858, at the age of nineteen, Rockefeller had entered the produce-commission business in Cleveland. In the early sixties, he saw a great future for himself in the oil industry. At the end of the war, he sold his interest in the commission business and formed a company with Samuel Andrews, a Cleveland oil-refiner, to whom he had already lent money. Rockefeller understood at once that competition and small-scale production were unprofitable, and he decided to rid the refining industry of both. Rockefeller and Andrews enlarged their plant, took H. M. Flagler into partnership, established a New York office, and built a second refinery. Under Rockefeller's management, business expanded rapidly, and in 1870 the concern was transformed into the Standard Oil Company of Ohio with a capitalization of $1,000,000.

Powerful from the first, the Standard Oil Company proceeded methodically to eliminate its competitors. In 1872, Rockefeller joined with a group of Pittsburgh and Philadelphia refiners to form the South Improvement Company—a combination of "insiders" who wanted control of the entire refining industry. A secret agreement was made between the new corporation and the Pennsylvania, Erie, and New York Central Railroads. After considerably increasing freight rates on oil, these railroads were to grant rebates to the new syndicate not only on its own oil but on that of its competitors. For every barrel of oil shipped from the oil regions to New York at the published tariff of $2.56, the South Improvement Company was to receive a rebate of $1.06 regardless of what company produced it. The Pennsylvania legislature was forced by public opinion to annul the South Improvement Company's charter, but Rockefeller's business was too important for the railroads to disregard. He soon secured extensive private rebates for Standard Oil. One by one the independent refiners of Cleveland were forced to choose between selling out to Rockefeller or bankruptcy. In 1874, plants in Pittsburgh, Philadelphia, and New York were absorbed, and the following year the company's capital was increased to $3,000,000. By 1880, Standard produced more than 90 per cent of the nation's refined oil.

Rockefeller's hold on the nation's oil business was further strengthened by his control over the newer pipeline system for transporting petroleum. Despite generous rebates from the railroads, Rockefeller thought that his transportation costs were still too high. In the mid-seventies Standard Oil started construction of pipelines. By 1880 most of the pipelines in the Appalachian oil fields were controlled by the United Pipe-Line Company, a Standard subsidiary. Deciding to destroy this virtual monopoly, a group of independent producers formed the Tidewater Pipe-Line Company and built a pipeline to one of the railroads that did not grant rebates to Standard. Rockefeller built more pipelines, acquired the refineries that did business with the Tidewater Company, spread rumors that it was bankrupt, and placed one of his men on its board of directors. In 1883, Tidewater gave up the unequal struggle, and an agreement was reached: Standard's United Pipe-Line Company was to receive four fifths of the business while Tidewater was to have the remainder.

Rockefeller was also able to crush competition through a highly efficient and at times unscrupulous marketing organization. The United States was divided into a number of sales districts over each of which presided a Standard executive. He, in turn, was assisted by subordinates who sold Standard products and made regular reports on Standard's competitors. If a rival firm undersold Standard, its agent would visit retailers in his territory and warn them of the dangers of doing business with the competitors. If these threats failed, Standard would start a price war. Rockefeller never lost a fight. Standard owned its own marketing system and did not have to pay middlemen, and with a nationwide business, it could afford to sustain temporary losses in one district as long as it continued to make substantial profits in the rest of the country.

Standard Oil was not only able to destroy its leading competitors, but it was also the first company to discover a method for legalizing monopoly. By 1882, S. C. T. Dodd, a Standard lawyer, had worked out a plan for the use of the trust as a device for controlling Standard's properties. Under this arrangement, stockholders in seventy-seven companies transferred their stock certificates—that is, all their voting rights—to nine Standard trustees, who took over the management of the affairs of all the concerns. In return for their stock certificates, the stockholders received trust certificates that entitled their owners to dividends. As the earnings of all seventy-seven companies were placed in a single treasury, the holders of trust certificates were assured of dividend payments even if the particular company in which they had invested had lost money during the preceding year. In the 1880's, nine men (of whom Rockefeller was the most important) thus controlled virtually the entire petroleum business in the United States.

Behemoth Business

Once the feasibility of the trust had been proved, other industrialists—notably the whisky and sugar producers—used it. But the trust was vulnerable to attack from the courts. The sugar trust, organized by H. O. Havemeyer in 1887 as the American Sugar Company disbanded when New York State withdrew the charter of one of its member concerns. A temporary change in the structure of the trust proved unsatisfactory, and in 1891 the former participants in the trust established the American Sugar Refining Company in New Jersey as a fifty-million-dollar holding company.* The effect of this change has been described by Ida Tarbell in *The Nationalizing of Business*:

> Except for the change in legal structure, the business continued to be carried on as before. Under the new organization the management was further unified, since there was now but one board of directors and one set of officers.
>
> Controlling about eighty-five per cent of the total sugar output, the American Sugar Refining Company was able to raise prices at will. Representatives of the concern could offer no satisfactory reason why the price of sugar should rise in the face of economies claimed except that the company exercised a monopolistic control. From the beginning it adopted the policy of issuing no public statements. The only information it vouchsafed appeared in the annual reports required by the state of Massachusetts, and these were simply balance sheets which revealed little of its inside workings. According to H. O. Havemeyer, president of the company, even stockholders were not given information unless they demanded it as a body.†

Stung by the courts, Standard Oil also had to substitute the holding company for the trust. In March, 1892, the Supreme Court of Ohio

---

* A holding company produced no goods. Instead, it bought up and held a controlling interest in a number of concerns, most of which were usually in the same industry.

† Ida Tarbell: *The Nationalizing of Business, 1878–1898* (New York: The Macmillan Company, 1936), p. 206. Copyright 1936 by The Macmillan Company, and reprinted with their permission.

ordered the dissolution of the Standard trust on the ground that it was designed to "establish a virtual monopoly" and was "contrary to the policy of our state." Although the nine Standard trustees returned the stock to the stockholders, they continued to manage the member concerns as "liquidating trustees," a stratagem that was not abandoned until Standard was charged with evasion of the court order five years later. In 1899, Standard's officials finally formed a holding company in New Jersey. Under the liberal corporation laws of that state, the Standard Oil Company of New Jersey purchased the securities of the companies that had belonged to the trust, and Standard's control over the refining business was as complete as ever. In 1911, the Supreme Court ruled that Standard Oil of New Jersey had violated the Sherman Antitrust Act.* This decision, however, had little more effect than earlier state-court rulings. The Standard empire was broken up into its component parts, but only the techniques of monopoly were altered. Through interlocking directorates and unwritten agreements, the officials of the legally separate Standard Oil companies in the various states continued to conduct their respective business with remarkable unanimity.

New Jersey's liberal incorporation laws, which were adopted as a means for increasing the state's revenue, made it easy for consolidationists to eliminate competition in their industries. Holding companies incorporated under New Jersey law had no other function than to own a controlling share of the stock of other concerns regardless of where they were located or incorporated. The directors of a New Jersey corporation had to maintain a New Jersey office, which they generally used once a year when they went through the formalities of conducting their company's annual meeting. By 1901, the list of New Jersey corporations read like a Who's Who of American industry. In addition to Standard Oil and the American Sugar Refining Company, New Jersey was the headquarters of the Amalgamated Copper Company, American Smelting and Refining Company, Consolidated Tobacco Company, International Mercantile Marine Company, and United States Steel Corporation.

Most Americans referred to all large corporations as "trusts," a word that soon became synonymous in the public mind with monopoly, but only a few industrialists actually used the trust to attain concentration of control, and those who did were eventually forced to abandon it. Most monopolies were created through the merger of two or more companies or through the purchase of weaker firms by more powerful

* See pages 127–9.

rivals. The National Cordage Company, for example, was the product of a merger of the four largest members of the industry. The American Tobacco Company, which was formed in 1890 by the five leading cigarette manufacturers under the leadership of James B. Duke, purchased its leading competitors for the next decade. In 1898, the Continental Tobacco Company was formed as a sister firm to take over the production of plug tobacco, and three years later the Consolidated Tobacco Company was established as a holding company to control the Continental and American Tobacco Companies. Merger and acquisition were also the policies of companies producing matches, lead, nails, barbed wire, meat, and a host of other commodities.

The climax of mergers in the steel industry was the formation of the United States Steel Corporation in 1901. The consolidation movement in steel was started by Andrew Carnegie in the 1870's. Born in Scotland of poor parents and brought to this country by his mother, Carnegie went to work as a bobbin boy in a cotton mill. At the age of fourteen, he was a messenger for a Pittsburgh telegraph office. In 1853, he became private secretary to Thomas Scott of the Pennsylvania Railroad, who soon made him superintendent of the line's Pittsburgh division. During the Civil War, Carnegie invested his savings in iron making, and in 1865 he resigned from the Pennsylvania Railroad to enter the iron industry. In the early seventies, he turned to steel production. After completing the Edgar Thomson Steel Works at Braddocks Field on the Monongahela River, Carnegie outdistanced all other steel producers in western Pennsylvania. Like the master consolidationist of the oil business, Carnegie obtained rebates from railroads and took advantage of the depression of the seventies to buy out his less fortunate competitors. In 1877, Carnegie properties earned a profit of 42 per cent, and by 1880 Carnegie had become the undisputed leader of the eastern steel industry. But he was still not satisfied, and in the next years his company purchased more rivals, established its own fleet of ore boats on the Great Lakes, acquired a railroad, leased part of the Mesabi ore fields, and assured itself an adequate supply of coke by merging with the Frick Coke Company. In 1892, with the organization of the Carnegie Steel Company, Carnegie retired from active business affairs and left the management of his steel empire to Henry Clay Frick. By 1900, the concern had a capital stock of $160,000,000.

While Carnegie was building up his steel industry in the Pittsburgh district, steel-makers in other parts of the country were using similar methods to achieve comparable results. The major producer in the South was the Tennessee Coal, Iron, and Railroad Company, and the Colorado Fuel and Iron Company was the largest single producer in

Mr. Carnegie in Private and Before the Public at the University of California, 1913

the Rocky Mountain states. The Federal Steel Company, which was incorporated in 1898 and controlled the most important steel-producing facilities in the Middle West, had emulated Carnegie's policy of integration through its purchase of ore and coal fields, railroads, and ore ships on the Great Lakes. In 1901, a long step toward national monopoly in the steel industry was taken with the formation of the United States Steel Corporation. Organized as a New Jersey holding company, the new steel corporation was a "combination of combinations," that included not only the Carnegie and Federal Steel companies, but ten other giant steel concerns as well.

US Steel Corp.

By 1914, there were few other branches of American industry that had not been affected by the consolidation movement. In 1904, John Moody listed 318 industrial "trusts," which had a total capitalization of more than seven billion dollars built up by a series of mergers involving more than fifty-two hundred separate plants. Of the ninety-two largest corporations in 1904, seventy-eight controlled 50 per cent or more of their respective industries; fifty-seven controlled 60 per cent or more; and twenty-six controlled 80 per cent or more. The merger movement slackened perceptibly after 1905, for by then most of the major combinations had been formed. In the remaining years before World War I, the nation's industrial trusts steadily strengthened their hold over the American economy.

The trust-makers curbed or eliminated competition to assure their own profits, but they always insisted that the growth of monopoly aided the general public. They maintained that they were substituting order and stability for the chaos of unlimited competition and that the concentration of industrial control reduced inefficiency, waste, and duplicated effort and expense. Big business, they claimed, had brought an ever-growing increase in American industrial output and a greater variety of products. They often argued that the trend toward concentration was an inevitable development that neither they nor anyone else could obstruct.

Although monopoly may have been more efficient than competition and may have been responsible for the mass production of goods that might not otherwise have been manufactured, it had certain marked disadvantages. Under a competitive system, a decline in demand usually brought about a corresponding decrease in prices. Monopolists, however, responded to a reduction in demand by cutting production rather than prices. Consequently, profits were frequently preserved at the expense of satisfying the wants of consumers. As a result, even in times of prosperity there was idle productive capacity despite great consumer demand. As early as 1894, Henry Demarest Lloyd, in *Wealth Against*

"Robber Barons of the Middle Ages and Today" (Puck, *1889*)

Commonwealth, pointed out the contradictions produced within the American economy by the growth of industrial concentration.

> The world, enriched by thousands of generations of toilers and thinkers, has reached a fertility which can give every human being a plenty undreamed of even in the Utopias. But between this plenty . . . and the people hungering for it step the "cornerers," the syndicates, trusts, combinations, and with the cry of "overproduction"—too much of everything. Holding back the riches of earth, sea, and sky from their fellows who famish in the dark, they declare to them that there is too much light and warmth and food. They assert the right, for their private profit, to regulate the consumption by the people of the necessaries of life, and to control production, not by the needs of humanity, but by the desires of a few for dividends. The coal syndicate thinks there is too much coal. There is too much iron, too much lumber, too much flour—for this or that syndicate.*

Although critics of his work thought Lloyd's call to return to free competition no answer, they had other grounds on which to attack the

---

* Henry Demarest Lloyd: *Wealth Against Commonwealth* (New York: Harper & Brothers, 1894), p. 1.

trusts. Industrial concentration did not produce the coveted economic stability that had been predicted by monopolists. The business cycle turned as crazily as ever, despite the decline of competition. The economic revival that had followed the depression of the 1870's was interrupted by a slight recession in 1884. After recovering from this interlude, business boomed until it went into a full-scale depression in the midnineties—at the very time when with the growing power of trusts one might have anticipated increasing order and rationality in business life. Instead, in 1893, 573 bank and loan companies were forced out of business, and there were 15,242 commercial failures. In the next three years, unemployment increased, industrial production declined, wages fell, and farm income decreased. It was not until 1897–8 that the worst depression in the nation's history to date was over and business began to assume an upward course. If the industrialists helped create the boom times of America's Iron Age, they also failed to find the private controls that could have averted the widespread economic distress in the depressions of the seventies and the nineties.

The Bankers Enter Industry

Twenty-five years after the Civil War, American business was dominated by individuals like Rockefeller, Carnegie, Swift, and Havemeyer. These men had grown up with their industries and were skilled organizers. Energetic, shrewd, fact-minded, they were also often crude, ruthless, and immoral. Their successors, the great bankers, rose to power, not because they could contribute any special technical skills or knowledge to American industry, but because they controlled vast sums of money that could be used to purchase authority.

The triumph of bankers like J. P. Morgan, first in the railroads and then in industry, was preceded by the rise and fall of the speculative capitalist. In the years immediately after the Civil War, enterprising individuals in railroads and manufacturing frequently had more imagination than ready cash. To obtain capital for expansion and conquest, they issued securities which were sold to the general public. The clearinghouse for these transactions was the New York Stock Exchange, which then, as now, was the largest and most important security exchange in the United States. The stock market was then unregulated, and unscrupulous operators were in a position to take advantage of the ignorant and naïve investors. For nearly twenty years after the Civil War, men like Drew, Fisk, and Gould dominated the activities of the New York Stock Exchange. In contrast to the builders of industry, the buccaneers in industry as in the railroads made their profits by ruining corporations that had been built up by the skill, ingenuity, and hard work of others.

To the princes of speculation a corporation was a carcass, and they were its bloodsuckers. They would draw off the blood, leaving only the skin and bones, and then pump in new blood so that it could be drawn off again. While other men produced goods for profits, the buccaneer obtained his profits from stock watering and stock manipulation. If Drew, Gould, and Fisk, for example, wanted additional funds, they merely printed more Erie stock and sold it to gullible investors. Their expenses stopped with the cost of printing, for new stock issues were not backed by new money in the railroad's treasury. Once the new stock was issued, these stock jugglers could change the price of Erie stock whenever they wished. By dumping huge quantities of Erie stock on the market, they would force down its value. When it had reached a suitable low point, they would buy it back, trade in it furiously among themselves to force up the price, sell it profitably when it could be pushed no higher, and then be ready to begin the process all over again.

Yet even in the age of the Erie ring there were many financiers anxious for an orderly and steadily profitable financial system. Among these men was Jay Cooke, who had obtained wealth and fame by marketing the government's Civil War securities. Cooke was essentially a seller rather than a manipulator of stocks, and he was the first individual to introduce a semblance of order into a chaotic business. By combining shrewd appeals to patriotism with an over-all plan for the disposal of these issues, Cooke sold unprecedented amounts of bonds and was responsible for introducing into this country the system of underwriting securities. After the war, Cooke applied his techniques to the sale of corporate securities. When he marketed Northern Pacific stock, his firm employed a corps of trained salesmen and enlisted the support of local newspapers, postmasters, clergymen, lawyers, and shopkeepers.

Jay Cooke's banking firm collapsed with the crash of 1873; his financial career was brought to an abrupt end. But Cooke had already set the pattern for the subsequent growth of investment banking under men like J. P. Morgan. The very desire of the industrialist to expand his business made him dependent on powers other than himself. Continually hampered by a shortage of available capital, he turned to the investment banker for funds. In return for a commission, the investment banker marketed the industrialist's securities. Before long, the investment banker began to insist that he be given a share in the management of the concerns in which his customers had invested their money. Industrialists, hard pressed for capital, were frequently not in a position to refuse such a request; and during the last two decades of the nineteenth century, the names of prominent bankers appeared with increasing frequency on the directors' lists of some of the nation's most prominent manufacturing as well as railroad concerns.

The investment banker originally moved into industry, as he had into railroads, to protect his clients' funds. The bankers, however, did not remain mere watchdogs, and by the turn of the century many corporations had passed into their control.

After 1900, J. P. Morgan exerted more influence on the American economy than any other single individual. Unlike most American businessmen, Morgan had been born to wealth. He was English by birth, and his father was a great banker before him. The younger Morgan received a college education, and he thought for a time of becoming a mathematics teacher. He soon abandoned this idea and entered his father's banking house in London in 1856. Four years later, he opened a branch of the concern in New York. Morgan's firm was a typical private banking establishment and concentrated on the sale of American securities abroad. In 1873 it invaded Jay Cooke's special province when it marketed some government securities; but it was not until the 1880's, when it became involved in financing American railroads, that its impact on American industrial management and organization began to be felt.

J. P. Morgan's pre-eminence as an investment banker is simply explained. He had an excellent organization, great skill, and, above all, ample capital for investment in the securities issued by railroads and manufacturers. He knew that the leading commercial banks, trust companies, and insurance firms of the nation also had large sums of money available for investment, and that any individual who could determine their policies would be in a position to dominate the nation's security market. Largely through a system of interlocking directorates, the House of Morgan at the height of its power before World War I became the single most important influence in New York commercial banking. J. P. Morgan was a vice-president of the National Bank of Commerce; George F. Baker, a Morgan partner, was president of the First National Bank. Interlocking directorates and stock ownership gave the Morgan firm a powerful voice in the affairs of the Chase, Liberty, Hanover, and Astor National banks as well as several banks outside New York City. Morgan's influence over the management of the principal trust companies was equally great. J. P. Morgan & Company organized the Bankers' Trust Company; it was associated with the Manhattan Trust Company through its control over the First National Bank; it took over the management of the Guaranty Trust Company in 1909; and it had representatives on the boards of the Union, Commercial, and

Fidelity Trust Companies. Morgan's lines of power also reached into some of the United States' richest insurance companies. George W. Perkins, a vice-president of the New York Life Insurance Company, was made a Morgan partner; and stock ownership gave the Morgan firm a powerful voice in the management of the Mutual Life Insurance Company and the Equitable Life Assurance Company.

This control over many of the wealthiest banks, trust companies, and insurance concerns in the land gave Morgan few rivals in the use of what Louis D. Brandeis called "other people's money." Industrialists who wished to raise money through security issues were frequently at his mercy. When Morgan marketed their securities, he demanded, in addition to the usual commission, a share in management. From 1890 to 1914, the largest security issues in the nation came from the United States government, railroads, and manufacturing companies. All three at one time or another came to Morgan, and all three accepted his terms.

Morgan's immense power had no greater tribute paid to it than during the struggle to maintain the gold standard in the midnineties. After two bond sales had failed to relieve the Treasury's gold shortage, President Cleveland in 1895 was compelled to turn to the House of Morgan to market federal securities in such a way as to increase the government's supply of gold. It was J. P. Morgan—rather than the United States government—who possessed the financial power to preserve the gold standard!

Morgan's ascendency over American business was foreshadowed in his great coup against the railroads. Morgan's rise in railroading was made certain in 1889 at a meeting of rail executives over which he presided. At the conclusion of the conference, the following statement was released to the press by Morgan:

> I am authorized to say, I think, on behalf of the banking houses represented here that if an organization can be formed practically upon the basis submitted by the committee, upon which the bankers shall be represented, they are prepared to say that they will not negotiate, and will do everything in their power to prevent the negotiation of, any securities for the construction of parallel lines or the extension of lines not approved by that executive committee.

These problems of unregulated competition held no terror for the bankers. Morgan, as the nation's leading banker, informed the assembled railroad executives that an organization had been established to eliminate competition, and that he and his colleagues would run it. After his great victories in taking control of the Erie, Chesapeake and

Ohio, and most of the important railroads of the South and West, after 1900 the Morgan firm also moved into control of the shipping, rubber, and electrical supply "trusts"—in addition to its greatest industrial triumph, the steel "trust." At the time of its organization in 1901, the United States Steel Corporation included companies that produced approximately half the annual American supply of pig iron, coke, and steel rails, more than half of the output of structural steel, and virtually all the supply of barbed wire, wire nails, tin plate, and steel tubes. These companies also built nine tenths of the nation's bridges and owned a large proportion of Lake Superior ore fields and the ore vessels on the Great Lakes. At the head of this huge corporation was J. P. Morgan, a banker who never knew and never made any pretense of knowing the first thing about the techniques of manufacturing iron and steel.

Morgan was not quite the czar of the American economy, for he had to share power with several Standard Oil officials who had invested profits from the petroleum business in a wide variety of enterprises. The National City Bank, which had not fallen under Morgan's domination, was closely associated with Standard Oil and was known to Wall Street intimates as a "Rockefeller bank." Like the Morgan firm, the Rockefeller, or Standard Oil, group acquired control of valuable iron resources in the Lake Superior district and a number of large railroad corporations. This same small group formed powerful alliances with several public utilities and became dominant in the ice, smelting, and tobacco trusts. The Rockefeller and Morgan interests were not always competitors, for they frequently had heavy investments in the same corporations and often had representatives on the same board of directors.

The effect of the rise of these financiers on the control of the American economy was shown by Louis D. Brandeis shortly before World War I in *Other People's Money*, a book largely based on the Congressional Pujo Committee's revelations concerning the money trust. Using the New Haven Railroad as an illustration, Brandeis pointed out that its real managing directors were:

> . . . J. Pierpont Morgan, George F. Baker, and William Rockefeller. Mr. Morgan was, until his death in 1913, the head of perhaps the largest banking house in the world. Mr. Baker was, until 1909, President and then Chairman of the Board of Directors of one of America's leading banks (the First National of New York), and Mr. Rockefeller was, until 1911, President of the Standard Oil Company. Each was well advanced in years.

J. P. Morgan, Sr., with His Son and Daughter, Arriving to Testify Before the Pujo Committee

[BROWN BROTHERS]

Yet each of these men, besides the duties of his own vast business, and important private interests, undertook to "guide, superintend, govern and manage," not only the New Haven but also the following other corporations, some of which were similarly complex: Mr. Morgan, 48 corporations including 40 railroad corporations with at least 100 subsidiary companies, and 16,000 miles of line; 3 banks and trust or insurance companies; 5 industrial and public-service companies. Mr. Baker, 48 corporations, including 15 railroad corporations, with at least 158 subsidiaries, and 37,400 miles of track; 18 banks, and trust or insurance companies; 15 public-service corporations and industrial concerns. Mr. Rockefeller, 37 corporations, including 23 railroad corporations with at least 117 subsidiary companies, and 26,400 miles of line; 5 banks, trust or insurance companies; 9 public-service companies and industrial concerns.*

* Louis D. Brandeis: *Other People's Money; And How the Bankers Use It* (New York: Frederick A. Stokes Company, 1913), pp. 206–7. Copyright 1913 by Louis D. Brandeis and reprinted with the permission of his estate.

The triumph of the financiers created the greatest concentration of economic power in the nation's history. The industrialists had been able to dominate at most a single business, but finance capitalism cut across industries. Through interlocking directorates, community of interests, and stock purchases, investment firms like J. P. Morgan & Company, Kuhn, Loeb & Company, and Kidder, Peabody & Company could exercise a controlling influence over a host of unrelated industries. By 1912, the Morgan empire held 341 directorships in 112 corporations with total assets of more than $22,000,000,000. After examining the ramifications of the Money Trust, the Pujo Investigating Committee, which was dedicated to the ethos of the small competitive businessman, concluded:

> . . . The acts of this inner group, as here described, have . . . been more destructive of competition than anything accomplished by the trusts, for they strike at the very vitals of potential competition in every industry that is under their protection, a condition which if permitted to continue, will render impossible all attempts to restore normal competitive conditions in the industrial world.

Over and beyond their sound argument that it was impossible and unprofitable to go back to a more competitive system, the great bankers maintained that they had brought much-needed stability to American business conduct by instituting safe and sound banking practices for the exuberant recklessness of the industrialists. J. P. Morgan's solemn and austere conduct of his business bore no surface resemblance to the high jinks of a Gould, Drew, or Fisk, but he was as skillful at overcapitalization as the most flamboyant buccaneer. When the United States Steel Corporation was organized, it was capitalized at $1,400,000,000, or more than twice the value of its physical assets. The water pumped into the stock of such Morgan enterprises as the New Haven Railroad revealed that even the earlier princes of speculation could have taken some lessons from the self-professed conservative bankers.

Despite the bankers' insistence that they represented sanity and stability in business life, they were no more successful than the industrialists had been in flattening out the curves in the business cycle. The financiers were probably most responsible for the depressions of 1903 and 1907. Overcapitalization of the numerous "trusts" created between 1898 and 1902 started a stock boom that collapsed when the market became flooded with what James J. Hill called "indigestible securities." Recovery was well under way by the end of 1904, and business activity increased steadily until 1907, when the events of 1903 were repeated.

In March, 1907, stock quotations fell sharply, but a general collapse was averted until the following October, when the failure of the Knicker-bocker Trust Company precipitated a full-scale panic. Business did not revive until 1909; and minor recessions in 1910 and 1911 postponed full recovery until 1912–13. These depressions, however, strengthened rather than weakened the hold of the leading financiers on the Ameri-can economy. Hard times gave them the opportunity to buy out their less fortunate rivals. During the Panic of 1907, the Morgan firm ac-quired Charles W. Morse's shipping combination; and the United States Steel Corporation, after receiving permission from President Theodore Roosevelt, purchased the Tennessee Coal, Iron, and Railroad Company.

The conservatism of the bankers was better shown in other ways than control of the business cycle. In 1911, a memorandum written by the Investors' Guild stated:

> It is a well-known fact that modern trade combinations tend strongly toward constancy of process and products, and by their very nature are opposed to new processes and new products originated by independent inventors, and hence tend to restrain competition in the development and sale of patents and patent rights; and consequently tend to discourage inde-pendent inventive thought, to the great detriment of the na-tion. . . .

It was hardly an accident that the automobile industry, which de-veloped faster than any other branch of American manufacturing in the years just preceding World War I, received little or no assistance from the nation's financiers. In explaining the attitude of the bankers toward the early automobile manufacturers, Henry B. Joy, president of the Packard Motor Car Company, said:

> It is the observable facts of history, it is also my experi-ence of thirty years as a business man, banker, etc., that first the seer conceives an opportunity. He has faith in his almost second sight. He believes he can do something—develop a busi-ness—construct an industry—build a railroad—or Niagara Falls Power Company,—and make it pay! . . .
>
> The motor business was the same.
>
> When a few gentlemen followed me in my vision of the possibilities of the business, the banks and older business men (who in the main were the banks) said, "fools and their money soon to be parted"—etc., etc.
>
> Private capital at first establishes an industry, backs it

through its troubles, and, if possible, wins financial success when banks would not lend a dollar of aid.

The business once having proved to be practicable and financially successful, then do the banks lend aid to its needs.

Whether American industry would have grown faster, more soundly, and with greater innovations without banker control is debatable. Routinization and the decline of radical innovation in industry have sources within the structure of the industry itself, regardless of whether bankers or engineers control the business.

Despite waste, chaos, and questionable morality, the development of American industry in the decades immediately following the Civil War had had a lusty exuberance. During the first fifteen years of the twentieth century, signs of a more conservative, guarded, and rationalized growth became apparent as the "safe and sane" bankers took over the chairs around the directors' tables that had formerly been occupied by the last generation of industrialists who had worked their way "up from the bottom." If nothing else, the arrival of the finance capitalists signified that the American economy had come of age.

The Defense of Business

Americans have always been businessmen, but after the Civil War commercial values and business routines rapidly weakened the hold over the conscience of America's Christian and humane heritage. Business success also made the businessman what he had not been formerly, the social equal of the statesman or minister. By 1875, most of the antebellum orators and statesmen had passed from the political scene, and the merchant prince and great landowning family had lost much of their power and prestige. Their successors, the industrialist and the banker, were often brutal in their appetites and raw in manners, but they quickly developed an elaborate defense of their right to the nation's deference.

"These modern potentates," as Charles Francis Adams called them, enjoyed power as supreme as that of any absolute monarch. They dictated terms to their workers; when workers rebelled, they used private or public armies against them. They raised prices and, when consumers complained, joined with their competitors to raise them still higher. They bought legislatures, but when numerous scandals shocked the public into demanding reform, they abandoned such crass and costly methods to become political overlords in their own right. Living as they pleased, spending their fortunes on entertainment, city palaces, country estates, grand tours, old art, and favorite churches or colleges, they were as hungry for the trappings of "culture" and respectability as they were for the money that was the source of their power.

Occasional complaints against their methods of acquiring and spending their wealth could be ignored or passed off with William Vanderbilt's famous dictum, "the public be damned." The people could object, but they were not to interfere. Business leaders had nothing to hide, not because they were beyond reproach, but because they were beyond successful attack. H. O. Havemeyer boasted that he did not know enough about ethics to apply them to business; and J. P. Morgan did not hesitate to tell a newspaper reporter that he "owe[d] the public nothing."

Many successful businessmen who were less outspoken still acted as if they had adopted views of Vanderbilt, Havemeyer, and Morgan, but others made an effort to win popular support for their policies. As early as 1878, Abram S. Hewitt in an address to a meeting of the Church Congress on the "Mutual Relations of Capital and Labor" urged co-operation instead of conflict as a solution to the industrial disputes of the period; and in the 1880's Andrew Carnegie began to publish the first of his many articles in defense of the businessman. As opposition to business policies increased, numerous executives in a wide variety of industries came to the conclusion that they could no longer afford to ignore public opinion. In the language of the time, it was decided to "educate" the American people. In 1904, J. W. Van Cleave, president of the Buck Stove and Range Company, told the members of the Citizens' Industrial Association of America that it was their duty "as the employing classes of this country" to "crystallize public opinion." As there was nothing that could "resist the power of public opinion," Van Cleave concluded that there was "no reason why the employing classes, the intelligent classes, and the money classes, if you please, should not influence public opinion." Much the same advice was given a year later by Van Cleave's good friend, President David M. Parry of the National Association of Manufacturers.

During the first years of the new century, several other business leaders recognized the necessity for a favorable public opinion. In 1908, Colonel J. D. Powers, president of the American Bankers Association, urged the members of his organization to "begin a vigorous campaign of education." President Theodore Vail of the American Telephone and Telegraph Company ordered his corporation's officials to "educate the public." In a speech before the members of the American Electric Railway Association in 1916, the king of the nation's early public relations men, Ivy Lee, stated that "the greatest thing that could be done for . . . all the utilities of the United States, would be to do for them what Billy Sunday has done for religion."

The most convenient argument for the businessman's use was an old American idea, the notion of an immutable higher law, given to man by God or inherent in nature. The Puritans of Massachusetts Bay Colony, the Revolutionists of 1776, the founding fathers of 1789, the expansionists of the 1840's, and the antagonists on both sides of the slavery conflict had all insisted that they were living by a higher law that took precedence over mere man-made laws.

The most popular "higher law" adopted by the businessman after the Civil War was derived from Darwinian notions of evolution, especially as tailored by another Englishman, Herbert Spencer, to fit the needs of a competitive industrial society. According to Spencer, life would always be an unremitting struggle in which the weak fell by the wayside while the strong inevitably pushed forward. However unfortunate this process might appear to humanitarians, there was nothing that could be done to alter it, for it was a law of nature that only the fit survived, and that those who survived were fittest.

The patness and flattering implications to social leaders of Spencer's theories naturally appealed to a generation of businessmen wanting to put the best construction on their motives and ideals, and many soon became adept at using the clichés of Social Darwinism. To most of them Spencer was a man who had added a few valuable phrases to business's vocabulary of defense, but to Andrew Carnegie he was the man who had found the answer to all the world's mysteries. Carnegie knew Spencer intimately, visited him in England, was his host in America, and referred to him as "my teacher" and to himself as "one of his disciples." Carnegie's conversion to Social Darwinism was akin to St. Paul's experience on the road to Damascus. Going through the works of Darwin and Spencer, he came upon pages explaining "how man has absorbed such mental foods as were favorable to him, rejecting what was deleterious"; and then, wrote Carnegie "light came in as a flood and all was clear."

Social Darwinism was used by Andrew Carnegie and other American businessmen as a principal defense for their control of the American economy. Like Spencer, they argued that a society's economy and life in the jungle were both characterized by a fierce, never-ending struggle for survival and supremacy. Those who were best equipped by nature for this battle invariably emerged as victors. Carnegie thought that the "degree of success" was in direct proportion to the "degree of ability," and most business leaders of his generation agreed with this view. Volney W. Foster, former president of the Western Paving and

Supply Company, in 1902 attributed business success to a " 'divine ratio' between brains and capital, which if observed, brings rich rewards—violated it results in disaster." In the same year, Russell Sage, the railroad speculator, wrote: "So long as some men have more sense and more self-control than others, just so long will some men be wealthy."

The corollary to the survival of the fittest was the failure and eventual destruction of the unfit. To a young man complaining that he had not had the "opportunity to prove his ability and to rise to partnership," Carnegie could quote Shakespeare:

> The fault, dear Brutus, is not in our stars,
> But in ourselves, that we are underlings.

In 1893, S. C. T. Dodd, who devised the trust form for the Standard Oil, told the students of Syracuse University that there would "always be beggars on our streets, tramps on our roads, debauchery in our saloons, corruption in our politics, injustice and dishonesty in our business." Why was this so? "One reason is because nature or the devil has made some men weak and imbecile and others lazy and worthless, and neither man nor God can do much for one who will do nothing for himself." As long as some individuals "are content, or even consent, to work for wages barely sufficient to supply them with such barbarous needs, they will find the work and wages suited to their wants."

Carnegie conceded that nature's law at times seemed harsh, but he insisted that all progress depended on the elimination of the unfit. While admitting that the "price which society pays for the law of competition . . . is . . . great" and "may be hard on the individual," Carnegie concluded that it was "best for the race because it insures the survival of the fittest." Any attempt to circumvent the natural law by equalizing the rewards of the fit and unfit would defeat its own ends. "Abolish poverty," said Carnegie, "and what would become of the race? Progress, development would cease."

Despite Carnegie's admonition, workingmen, discontented with the operation of supposed natural laws, formed unions that would presumably aid the unfit as well as the fit. Social Darwinists among businessmen repeatedly pointed out that such organizations were futile, for they rested on the false assumption that economic life was controlled by man instead of by natural law. Henry Clews, a Wall Street broker, warned:

> The workingmen are taken care of by the natural laws of trade far more perfectly than they can be by any artificial arrangement; and trade unions are simply an intrusion upon the do-

main of these laws, without the power to supplant or perfect
their operation, and with a certainty of obstructing and preventing their tendency, with the inevitable result of mischief
to all parties.

Although it was true that "unions do occasionally get an advance in
wages," it was certain, nevertheless, that the advance "would have come
anyway by the natural laws of competition among the capitalists" and
"without the loss of wages and suffering entailed by the strike." Under
the circumstances, Clews concluded that "workmen would be safer in
the end to wait for the natural advance."

The Social Darwinists were far more doctrinaire than the earlier
classical economists in the belief that any government interference with
the economy would be just as ineffectual as the attempts of organized
labor to circumvent the natural law. Because business activity was controlled by a natural law that had been fixed for all time, man-made
legislation could have no permanent effect on economic life. "Oh, these
grand, immutable, all-wise laws of natural forces," exclaimed Carnegie
in 1886, "how perfectly they work if human legislators would only let
them alone! But no, they must be tinkering," and "so our governors,
all over the world are at Sisyphus' work—ever rolling the stone uphill
to see it roll back to its proper bed at the bottom."

Social Darwinism was easily combined with the teachings of the
classical economists in a defense of business freedom. Many Americans
in the years before Darwin already believed that a normal economy
was marked by a free competition that would automatically determine
prices, direct the flow of capital, fix wages, and justly govern the
quantity and quality of goods produced. If this system were permitted
to operate without interference, its advocates asserted, it would inevitably lead to maximum production at minimum prices. If an entrepreneur raised prices above the level dictated by the condition of the
market or if he produced inferior goods, another entrepreneur would
manufacture superior goods at the market price. If wages and hours
did not accurately reflect the available supply and demand of labor,
the workers concerned could shift to employers who observed the economic law. It was easy to combine Social Darwinism with these ideals,
for both stressed the virtues of competition and the inherent victory of
the most honest and skillful man in the market place. If a manufacturer
or merchant could not meet the price or higher standards of his competitors, he was forced out of business. This constant check on sloth
and dishonesty produced progress that was shared by society in the
form of better goods at lower prices.

The watchdog of the nation's economic health was thus the ever-alert, ever-calculating, ever-active economic man. At all times he was supposed to know the available supply and demand of any given commodity, his competitor's costs and profits, and his own best interests. As a consumer, he was clever enough to recognize shoddy goods when he saw them and to ascertain when prices had been artificially raised above the figure set by the supply-demand formula. As a worker, he was well enough informed to realize when his wages were below those fixed by a free labor-market, and he was mobile enough to shift and change employers at will. As a manufacturer or banker he knew which forms of investment were the soundest, and his assets were so flexible that they could readily be transferred from one enterprise to another. In fact, for a supposed mere creature of a great cosmic process he was called upon to use an extraordinary degree of conscious deliberation and choice.

The growth of industrial concentration after the Civil War had helped to destroy the very competitive conditions which the classical economists sought to defend, but leading American big businessmen continued to use older competitive and the newer Darwinian ideals to defend their practices. The greatest advantage of the economic law to the nation's industrial and finance capitalists was that it enabled them to claim credit for all material progress while shirking any responsibility for economic adversity. Businessmen usually explained depressions as resulting from violation of the economic law; in 1908, for example, the president of the American Bankers Association said that the panic of the preceding year had been beneficial, for it had punished those who had acted "so completely in contravention of the law of supply and demand." Economic law rather than the businessman was also held responsible for the depressed state of the workingman. "A laborer," said John D. Rockefeller from his retirement, "is worthy of his hire, no less, but no more. . . . You can't hold up conditions artificially, and you can't change the underlying laws of trade."

Far more than classical economic doctrines, however, Social Darwinism justified monopoly and left no room for government regulation of business. Prices, quality of goods, wages, hours, interest rates, and rents were all automatically fixed by the economic law for the common welfare. Businessmen argued that government interference in business affairs inevitably disrupted the operation of the economic law and injured the very people that it was designed to benefit. In 1900, the head of the sugar trust said: "Trade will always take care of itself. If it is left to pursue ordinary channels, A will see to it that B does not have any extraordinary advantages. It is only when the State interferes, that a situation is created of which advantage can be taken against the interest of the community."

The entrepreneurs responsible for these wonders of efficiency and practicality contributing to progressive evolution were also said to show the direct correlation between personal morality and worldly success. Andrew Carnegie, for instance, once wrote: "A great business is seldom if ever built up except on lines of strictest integrity. A reputation for 'cuteness' and sharp dealing is fatal in great affairs." John D. Rockefeller stated that "there can be no permanent success without fair dealing"; and Judge Elbert Gary, the chairman of the board of the United States Steel Corporation, said: "Moral principles . . . [are] the base of all business success."

The moral qualities of the ideal businessman were derived in part from America's Puritan heritage. Considerable emphasis was placed on the virtues of hard work, obedience, and thrift as means of acquiring wealth. Wealth was a sign of "fitness" in much the same way as it once was a sign of God's election for earlier Americans. The bankrupt or business failure was a marked man. "Most people who fail," wrote John Wanamaker, "only work half-time, take too many holidays, and are quitters." The businessman's philosophy of discipline was never more succinctly stated than when August Heckscher said: "You must learn to obey before you are fit to command." Like the Puritan rules of life, the businessman's moral law placed great emphasis on thrift. Solomon Guggenheim demonstrated that Judaism was as compatible with this modern business ethic as was Christianity. He thought the "wage earner more extravagant in proportion to his earnings than the millionaire"; and his brother Daniel said that the rich were rich because "they have been thrifty," while the poor were "poor because they did not save."

Farmers in bad times might protest against the effects of the businessman's ideology and workers at times might resort to violence against its effects, but most Americans envied rather than condemned successful businessmen. Clergymen, professors, and politicians generally agreed with business leaders that wealth came to those who deserved it. In an age of rapid material growth, the businessman alone seemed responsible for the nation's phenomenal industrial progress. Although many Americans by 1890 believed that some business practices should be outlawed as "unfair," they were equally determined that the government should do nothing that would interfere with the right of the individual to "get ahead" in life.

The State Violates the "Natural Order"

The railroads, again, were the first large American business to provoke any significant attempt at state and national regulation. However much financiers and reformers might oppose each other in other respects, both were unwilling to pay the price of laissez faire in railroading. The bankers wanted economic stability, steady dividends, and safer investment opportunities. Reformers wanted an end to poor service and public exploitation. Despite their professed loyalty to freedom of enterprise, reformer and financier brought public and private power to bear against what was inherently one of the nation's most competitive forms of business enterprise, for, with heavy fixed charges that continued regardless of the amount of freight carried, railroads had been compelled to resort to almost any expedient to lure customers from rival lines.

Soon after the Civil War, some railroads began to offer rebates to large shippers in return for a monopoly of their business. When this proved an insufficient attraction, favored customers were granted drawbacks—that is, rebates on the freight charges paid by their competitors. Those farmers and small businessmen who were served by only one railroad and who, unlike large shippers, had relatively little bargaining power were frequently charged prohibitive rates. Towns and cities as well as individual shippers suffered from discriminatory railroad practices. Communities served by competing lines could count on lower rail charges, but those with only one rail connection were charged all that the traffic would bear. Through the long- and short-haul freight clauses, customers in some areas had to pay higher rates to ship goods a short haul than others who were more favorably located paid for a long haul. On the Pennsylvania Railroad, freight rates from Pittsburgh to Philadelphia were higher than those on the same line from Cleveland to Philadelphia. Under the circumstances, the weight of goods and the number of miles they were carried frequently had little or no effect on freight rates.

The inability of the railroads to establish and maintain an equitable system of rate-making led many small shippers to demand that the government intervene to eliminate discriminatory railroad practices. In the Midwest, more substantial farmers and their allies among smaller shippers, grain storage men and merchants took the lead in urging some form of governmental regulation. From 1870 to 1874, the legislatures of Illinois, Wisconsin, Minnesota, and Iowa adopted laws fixing maximum and minimum rates for freight and passenger traffic and warehousing. The so-called Granger laws, named after the farmers' organization that agitated for them, also abolished passes and established state commissions to regulate rail transportation. The railroads sought to nullify the Granger laws in the courts, but they had little initial success. In 1876, in *Munn v. Illinois*, the railroad lawyers maintained before the U. S. Supreme Court that a state's right to fix rates was a violation of that part of the Fourteenth Amendment which stipulated that a state could not deprive a person of property without due process of law. But the Court rejected this contention and ruled that "when . . . one devotes his property to a use in which the public has an interest, he, in effect, grants to the public an interest in that use, and must submit to be controlled by the public for the common good. . . . He may withdraw his grant by discontinuing the use, but, so long as he maintains the use, he must submit to the control." In the same year, in *Peik v. Chicago and Northwestern Railroad*, the Court affirmed the right of a state to fix rail rates.

These decisions by the Court showed the full implications of the sixty-year-old doctrine of Chief Justice John Marshall that the political and judicial power of the state must be coextensive with the economic activity of the nation. Public power had to match a public problem; however, that national power might be used to block as well as advance reform was shown ten years after the Granger cases in *Wabash, St. Louis, and Pacific Railway Company v. Illinois*, when a majority of the justices stated that the determination of rates for interstate shipments was outside the province of a state legislature. The Wabash decision made it clear that under the Constitution only the federal government now had the authority to regulate the nation's major rail systems.

As early as 1872, Congress had passed a law designed to eliminate some of the abuses in the transportation of livestock. In the same year, President Grant in his annual message spoke of the need for "more certain and cheaper transportation of the rapidly increasing western and southern products, to the Atlantic seaboard," and the Senate established a committee under William Windom to investigate railroad practices. The Windom Committee report of 1874, advocated numerous changes in the organization and administration of railroads, but most emphasized the need to reduce rail rates. Although the House responded with a bill to lower rates, the Senate did not act on this measure. In subsequent years, Congress shifted its attention from the problem of rate reduction to proposals to prevent discriminatory practices injurious to small shippers. Measures designed to prevent various forms of discrimination were repeatedly introduced into Congress. After the Wabash decision in 1886, the need for major legislation became acute. Following the report of a committee headed by Senator Shelby Cullom of Illinois, Congress in 1887 adopted the Interstate Commerce Act.

The Interstate Commerce, or Cullom, Act stated that all charges for interstate "transportation of passengers, or property . . . , or for the receiving, delivering, storage, or handling of such property, shall be reasonable and just." Discriminatory practices such as rebates and drawbacks were declared unlawful, while the long- and short-haul abuse was made illegal under certain circumstances. Pooling agreements were specifically forbidden. Schedules of rates had to be published and filed with the government, and corporations and individuals who violated these provisions were subject to a fine of not more than $5,000; in 1889, provision was also made to send violators to jail. The regulatory provisions of the Cullom Act were the guides to action for a five-man Interstate Commerce Commission, which was granted the "authority to inquire into the management of the business of all common carriers" in interstate trade and the right to "obtain from such common carriers full and complete information" concerning their business practices. After hearing complaints from shippers, the commission was empowered to direct railroads to alter their policies. If the railroad refused to obey the commission's order, provision was made for recourse in the courts.

The Interstate Commerce Act was, as Professor William Z. Ripley remarked, "a compromise, entirely satisfactory to no one." * Senator Nelson Aldrich of Rhode Island, who was opposed to any form of federal regulation, thought the new law a "delusion and a sham . . . made to answer the clamor of the ignorant and the unreasoning." In the last analysis, its effectiveness rested with the courts. The Interstate Commerce Act did not permit the commission to fix rates, and the judiciary alone had the power to determine the measure's scope and enforceability. The law helped assuage public anger but was vague enough not to upset the railroad leaders; indeed, some of the leaders welcomed the act as a means of bringing pirate lines to order.

From the outset, shippers, who feared retaliation from the railroads, refused to lodge complaints with the commission. During the first five years of its existence, the commission received only thirty-nine formal complaints. The commission soon learned that it was unable to compel witnesses to testify, and appeals to the courts produced interminable delays. Even those cases that eventually reached the Supreme

---

* William Z. Ripley: *Railroads: Rates and Regulations* (New York: Longmans, Green and Company, 1912), p. 453.

Court generally resulted in decisions that upheld the railroad rather than the commission. From 1887 to 1905, the Supreme Court handed down sixteen decisions in cases appealed by the commission to the courts. In one of these the commission's ruling was partially reaffirmed; in the other fifteen its position was reversed. The most important effect of the Court's stand was to remove any remaining doubt about the inability of the commission to fix rates. In 1897 in the Maximum Freight Rate case, the Court ruled that "under the interstate commerce act the commission has no power to prescribe the tariff of rates which shall control in the future, and therefore cannot invoke a judgment in mandamus from the courts to enforce any such tariff by it prescribed." As Justice Harlan was to point out in a minority opinion a few months later, the Court's attitude meant that the commission had "been shorn, by judicial interpretation, of authority to do anything of an effective character." Not until the era of the Progressives was a successful effort made to give the government adequate authority over railroad rates.

Constantly mixed with the controversy over railroad rates was the larger question of monopoly itself, for where one line controlled a region the producer was helpless. No one seriously proposed reintroducing a competition among many small rail lines but in the growing debate over monopoly elsewhere in American industry it seemed as though most critics of the trusts believed that a return to vigorous competition was possible and desirable. The American antitrust movement, which emerged during the closing years of the nineteenth century and flourished during the heyday of Progressivism, was an attempt to recapture the past. While radicals in Europe at the time usually advocated government ownership of large businesses, American critics of monopoly on the whole looked back wistfully to an earlier age of individualism. They did not want to turn the monopolists' wealth over to the proletariat, or to the state, and they did not want to abolish private property; but they did want to prevent the monopolist from using his power to undermine the economic freedom of others. Although they lived in an age of bigness, they hoped to find some device for protecting the small producer. They had been nurtured on the American dream of rags to riches and log cabin to White House which they now saw menaced by the trusts. They did not demand economic equality, but they did demand equality of economic opportunity. Their creed was as old as their nation, for they believed that every one should be given the same chance to succeed.

The American opponents of monopoly feared big government even more than they feared big business. Like Jefferson, they viewed all governments with suspicion, as necessary evils that should be tol-

Wall Street, 1900

[BROWN BROTHERS]

erated rather than encouraged. Although they thought that the government should be permitted to regulate business, they insisted that it
confine its efforts to the restoration of competition. They viewed economic life as a race, and they looked on the government as a referee
who would make sure that the contestants were given an equal opportunity to win. They believed that the race could be made fair for all
if an umpire government would revive and enforce the rules of open
and fair competition that supposedly had been followed by the nation's
artisans and farmers in the halcyon days before large-scale industrialization. Only a negligible number of socialists believed that the government should abolish the race.

By 1890, resentment against the trusts was too great to be ignored
politically. Already, too, the fatalistic mood at first associated with So-

cial Darwinism was passing. Reformers like Henry George and sociologists like Lester Frank Ward were analyzing the role that man's moral ideals and wishes played in directing life to its proper goals of happiness and abundance. Many groups in the nation simply would not wait until the cosmic process righted all wrongs. Government, they insisted, had to help those unfairly discriminated against to compete more effectively than they could if they were automatically judged the weak and unfit who had fallen in the battle of life. Farmers and consumers complained of the high prices charged by trusts; workers objected to the labor policies of huge corporations; reformers pointed out the deleterious effects of industrial concentration on political democracy; and small entrepreneurs charged that they were being forced out of business by the "unfair" trade practices of monopolistic firms. Further impetus was given the antitrust movement by the facts turned up by Congressional investigations of railroad operations during the two years preceding the passage of the Interstate Commerce Act, by the revelations of other legislative committees, and by numerous newspaper accounts of the formation of trusts. Several states—particularly in the South and West —responded to these developments by adopting either laws or constitutional amendments that were designed to prevent any attempt to eliminate or restrict competition. By 1890, at least fifteen states had inserted antitrust provisions in their constitutions or had passed antitrust acts. These laws and amendments, however, had often been sufficiently influenced by the friends of monopoly and they usually did little more than repeat the existing common-law doctrines against monopoly and restraint of trade; they failed to check the development of industrial concentration in the United States. Many trusts were more powerful than the state governments that attempted to regulate them; and as soon as one device for creating monopoly was declared unconstitutional by a state court, the trust-makers merely resorted to another, equally effective technique. With the passage of the Sherman Antitrust Act on July 2, 1890, the federal government belatedly, but ineffectually, recognized that no state or combination of states could adequately cope with what was essentially a national problem.

The Sherman Antitrust Act was brought forward by the Republicans as a device for satisfying the farmers and small businessmen in the party without alienating the wealthy bankers and industrialists on whom the party depended for money. The presidential campaign of 1888 had been fought largely over the tariff question. The Republicans were victorious, and they redeemed their campaign pledge with the McKinley Tariff. This measure, which provided for a marked increase in most rates, was opposed by a substantial segment of the party's agrarian supporters in the Midwest, who looked upon it as a subsidy to industry. In an effort to appease these disgruntled farmers and other groups opposed to monopoly, Congress simply went on record as favoring competition over industrial concentration. Apparently only a small number of congressmen thought that the new law would provide an effective means for destroying monopoly, and Senator Orville H. Platt undoubtedly spoke for many of his less frank colleagues when he said:

> The conduct of the Senate for the past three days . . . has not been in the line of the honest preparation of a bill to prohibit and punish trusts. It has been in the line of getting some bill with that title that we might go to the country with. The questions of whether the bill would be operative, or how it would operate, or whether it was within the power of Congress to enact it, have been whistled down the wind in this Senate as idle talk, and the whole effort has been to get some bill headed: "A Bill to Punish Trusts" with which to go to the country.

The nature and scope of the Sherman Act, which was described in its preamble as "an act to protect trade and commerce against unlawful restraints and monopolies," was revealed by the first sections of the law.

> Sec. 1. Every contract, combination in the form of trust or otherwise, or conspiracy, in restraint of trade or commerce among the several States, or with foreign nations, is hereby declared to be illegal. Every person who shall make any such contract or engage in any such combination or conspiracy, shall be deemed guilty of a misdemeanor, and, on conviction thereof, shall be punished by fine not exceeding five thousand dollars, or by imprisonment not exceeding one year, or by both said punishments. . . .
> Sec. 2. Every person who shall monopolize, or attempt to monopolize or combine or conspire to combine with any other person or persons, to monopolize any part of the trade or commerce among the several States, or with foreign nations, shall be deemed guilty of a misdemeanor. . . .

Congress refused to define the terms employed in the Sherman Antitrust Act, and it was left to the courts to determine the meaning of such words as "restraint" and "monopoly." The law also required the cooperation of the Attorney General, who was authorized to direct proceedings against alleged violators of the act. For more than a decade after the passage of the Sherman Act, neither federal judges nor the Justice Department made any move that seriously jeopardized big business in the United States. Richard Olney, Attorney General during the second Cleveland Administration, thought the Sherman law "no good," and the majority of opinions of the Supreme Court indicate that its members did not have a much higher opinion of the measure.

From 1890 to 1901, the Justice Department instituted only eighteen antitrust suits, and four of these were directed against labor unions! Although the government obtained some convictions against industrial combinations, it failed to force the dissolution of the powerful trusts that dominated the whisky, sugar, and cash-register industries. Soon after the passage of the Sherman Act, W. H. H. Miller, President Harrison's Attorney General, started proceedings against the whisky trust. But when a district court ruled that the indictment against the whisky combine was "clearly insufficient according to the elementary rules of criminal pleading," the government abandoned the case and stopped similar proceedings against the cash-register trust. In 1895, the government's attempt to break up the sugar trust, which at the time controlled 98 per cent of the sugar refined and sold in the United States, was thwarted by the Supreme Court's decision in *United States v. E. C. Knight Co.* The majority of judges ruled that, although the sugar trust had a virtual monopoly over the manufacture of its product, the government had not been able to prove that the company had sought "to put a restraint upon trade or commerce." This decision, which was tantamount to a declaration that the Sherman Act was unenforceable, was considerably modified in 1899, when the Court in the Addystone Pipe case ruled that it was illegal for the members of a pool to enter into agreements for the sale and purchase of their product across state lines. The executive branch of the government, however, made little effort to take advantage of the Supreme Court's change of heart. During McKinley's administration, only three antitrust suits were instituted by the Attorney General. As in the case of the railroads, it was not until the advent of the Progressive movement that the federal government made a serious attempt to deal with the effects of economic concentration on American life.

Although most Americans continued to believe in the virtues of competition, they failed to understand how their competitive and acquisitive way of life led almost inevitably either to the massed economic power they deplored or to government strong and active enough to keep competition alive. It was not until the eve of the first World War that Americans began to awaken to the possibilities of public regulation rather than destruction of big business.

FOR SUPPLEMENTARY READING

Railroad plunder and chaos are themes of a famous tale by contemporaries, C. F. Adams and Henry Adams, *Chapters of Erie* (1886) (Pb). T. C. Cochran's work on railroad leaders and Taylor and Neu's volume on railroads, both previously cited, should also be used here. Most studies of the railroad chiefs and of the roads themselves either over-praise or damn their subjects; but of the laudatory volumes perhaps the best is J. G. Pyle, *The Life of James J. Hill* (2 vols., 1917). A recent study by Julius Grodinsky, *Jay Gould: His Business Career, 1867–1892* (1957), comes nearer a balanced view, although the subject makes moderation difficult. R. R. Riegel's *The Story of the Western Railroads* (1926) is a general chronicle of the growth of the railroad empires. W. Z. Ripley's two volumes, *Railroads: Rates and Regulation* (1912) and *Railroads: Finance and Organization* (1915), are first rate.

The growth of concentration in business has many students. Research should start with S. Daggett, *Railroad Reorganization* (1908), or a later work by E. G. Campbell, *The Reorganization of the American Railroad System, 1893–1900* (1938). John Moody's *The Masters of Capital* (1919) is a short sketch of highlights and key figures in industrial combination. R. W. and M. E. Hidy's *Pioneering in Business, 1882–1911* (1955), is an excellent study that both supplements and corrects Nevins's study of Rockefeller and Standard Oil. On regulating business, a reliable first book is E. Jones, *The Trust Problem in the United States* (1921). "Finance capitalism" primarily means J. P. Morgan and his work. Go initially to G. W. Edwards, *The Evolution of Finance Capitalism* (1938); F. L. Allen, *The Great Pierpont Morgan* (1949); and L. Corey, *The House of Morgan* (1930). E. P. Oberholtzer's *Jay Cooke, Financier of the Civil War* (2 vols., 1907) is on the earlier giant. The study of business rationale and ethics begins with R. Hofstadter, *Social Darwinism in American Thought* (1944) (Pb), and I. G. Wyllie, *The Self-Made Man in America* (1954). Two recent works, S. Fine, *Laissez-Faire and the Welfare State, 1865–1901* (1956), and S. P. Hays, *The Response to Industrialism 1885–1914* (1957), have many important fresh views on state intervention. On the regulatory agencies themselves use R. E. Cushman, *The Independent Regulatory Commissions* (1941), and H. B. Thorelli, *The Federal Antitrust Policy* (1955). Three important theoretical works are J. Schumpeter, *Capitalism, Socialism and Democracy* (2nd ed., 1947); S. Webb's essay in *Fabian Essays in Socialism* (1889); and T. Arnold, *The Folklore of Capitalism* (1937).

4

The Worker's World

A FUNDAMENTAL change in the status of the American workingman took place with the advances of industry. Former craftsmen now became urban factory workers with little control over wages and working conditions and little power to bargain effectively with employers. The hostility of the government and nonlaboring public to militant unionism made it difficult for the worker to improve his lot. From 1865 to 1914, American wage earners used strikes, political action, and occasional violence but won only limited victories, for before World War I the workingman's weapons were never as effective as those of his employer.

The Labor Force

Although it is easy to lapse into sentimentality about the era before the triumph of the factory system, it is true that the typical American worker was once a craftsman with a skill all his own. He usually owned his own tools, and frequently he did all the work on a single product. Often working in his own home or in the cottage of a neighboring employer, he was not chained to his job, and he was neither a wage slave nor a landless proletarian. However he depended on the risks of a competitive society, however hard times might press on him, he was an individualist in an age that believed that economic opportunities for the individual were limitless.

When the factory forced the craftsman to become a machine tender, he lost a measure of independence and "identity." In place of his tools, which had been his servants rather than his master, was a machine that left little scope for individual taste or touches. His former skills, instead of being an asset, were frequently a liability; his job now required him to follow a rigid routine. In theory, the man ran the machine, but this was no more than a theory. In industrial society, the average factory worker was forced to accept an unchanging discipline imposed by the relentless motions of the machine. The machine was responsible for changing many workers from craftsmen into automata.

The machine also robbed the worker of the bargaining power of special talents. As long as he had been a craftsman, the worker had possessed an asset when he bargained with his employer. Only a skilled and trained worker could perform certain operations, and he had undoubtedly been as essential to his employer as his employer was to him. But almost any man of average intelligence who desired to work could be hired to replace a machine tender who was dissatisfied with his job. And, with frequent depressions and a steady flow of immigrants to the United States, there was always a backlog of potential factory workers who were willing to accept factory jobs on the employer's terms.

When the craftsman became a machine worker, he also lost what little control he had once had over his working conditions. There had always been friction between artisan and employer, but the older type of artisan, when dealing with his employers about wages, hours, and working conditions, had a confidence in his craft and in his presumed future as an owner and boss. When industry was small-scale and labor markets local, whatever hardships bad times might bring—and there were many—the older worker did have an "identity." But, with the increasing rationalization and greater division of labor in the machine-dominated factory, the laborers in the basic work force and even the more skillful machinists and finishers became members of an increasingly anonymous mass. Wages, hours, and the physical environment of the factory were all determined by the employer. If a worker lost his job for any reason, he knew that finding another position depended more upon chance than upon ability. His ignorance of the labor market and his lack of mobility also prevented him from applying for jobs for which he might have been eligible.

Although the life of the artisan in contrast with that of the factory worker should not be glamorized, the factory did make many men feel that they had no worth beyond their brute strength and no dignity in a world of impersonal machines and assembly lines. As corporations became larger, furthermore, the former personal relationship between employer and employee disappeared. In the place of the owner of a small firm who had frequently worked alongside his employees, had known their personal problems intimately, and had often helped them through sickness and other hardships were thousands of stockholders who were scattered throughout the United States—and even in the world—and who neither knew nor cared about the fate of the workers employed by their corporations. The corporation officials knew the workers principally as statistical abstractions that, taken collectively, were entered in the accounts as "labor costs." Directors, meeting in a downtown office building in New York City, made decisions that affected the lives of thousands of workers to whom they usually felt neither financial nor moral obligations.

The Ethnic Revolution

The native American worker's problem after the Civil War was unique in the Western world. Like the worker in Europe, he knew the shock of the change from a predominantly agricultural society to the disciplines of an urban-factory civilization. Yet after 1880 in the United States, he also had to deal with the competition of millions of immigrants and, still later, of Negroes whom he regarded, rightly or wrongly, as aliens. Most Americans born before 1880 thought of the United States as a land of small-town, white, Anglo-Saxon, middle-class Protestants who believed in private property, a business of their own, and the Puritan and entrepreneurial virtues of thrift, diligence, and accumulation. The mass urban and factory world increasingly destroyed the viability of those ideals from within, but immigrants brought languages, customs, and beliefs that seemed even further at variance with the traditional national ethos.

Newcomers to the United States before 1914 have often been classified into two groups: "old immigrants" and "new immigrants." This distinction has traditionally implied that the old immigrants—largely pre-Civil War Irish or Germans—were easily assimilable (a notion belied by the experiences of the Irish in the nativist frenzy of the 1840's and 1850's). The immigrants after 1880, coming principally from eastern and southern rather than northern Europe, were said to be more reluctant to accept—as they were expected to accept—the dominant American mores. Defenders of the "new immigrants" were at pains to point out their contributions to American life. These defenders also claimed that after 1880 the immigrant had not changed as much as America had and that to assume that American mores dominant at any time were unvarying or perfect was ethnocentric arrogance. In the understandable desire to improve the lot of the later immigrants and to oppose snobbery against them, there developed a tendency to lump all immigrants together and thus to deny the very social differences that supposedly were to be maintained in the new diverse and complex American culture that emerged in the late nineteenth century.

However correct the desire that all Americans, regardless of national origin or religion, be treated as equals, morally and before the law, as a sociological or historical fact the immigrants after 1880 were different in religion, language, family life and in the many intangibles that make up the uniqueness, for example, of Greek or Italian or East European Jewish culture. The hostility against the more recent arrivals may have been a violation of the spirit of the Declaration of Independence and of other American ideals, but it was based on more than the superficial difference of the post-1880 immigrants. Surely, America at the end of the nineteenth century was different than it had been in the 1840's. It is also probable that the invitation, when it was offered, to become "real Americans—just like us" was often halfhearted at best, and that many immigrants or their children who sought to cross into the world of the old Americans were not welcomed. But even given the absence of these disabilities, the effect of European ways and ideas could probably not be obliterated quickly. Indeed, if one examined the vaunted homogeneity of the old American stock as of 1900 what would one make of the Amish of Pennsylvania, the German Lutherans and the Scandinavians of the Old Northwest and the Northern Plains states, the French Creoles of Louisiana, or of the "professional Irishman"?

His recent arrival and his cultural differences made the post-1880 immigrant more easily exploitable than English-speaking natives or already assimilated workers. It also gave the not yet fully assimilated on the upper rungs of the immigrant ladder someone to look down on and to blame for the nation's or his own ills—much as the lowliest white in the South could despise the still lower Negro. Together with the competition between skilled and unskilled, male and female, adult and child labor, the divisions along national, racial, and religious lines within the national work force severely limited the effectiveness of joint action to secure a better share of the rewards of American industry.

The foreign-born population of the United States increased from 4,138,697 in 1860 to 9,249,560 in 1890 and to 13,345,545 in 1910. The

Immigration Commission in 1909 revealed that in most of the nation's leading industries immigrant workers outnumbered native Americans. Many of the immigrant workers after 1865 lacked everything necessary for success except a willingness to work. Without even the skills and training needed for machine tending, they were compelled to accept menial jobs at low pay and poor working conditions. Arriving with only a few cents in their pockets and the clothes on their back, they had to take whatever work was offered them. Their inability to understand English made them easy victims of unscrupulous employers. The strangeness of a new land made them too timid to protest when they were victimized. Poverty and ignorance often drove them into the most hazardous jobs in American industry, and all available evidence points to the conclusion that immigrant status and the industrial accident rate were closely linked. In such dangerous occupations as coal mining and steelmaking, many immigrants who were unable to read the posted warning signs were prevented from achieving even a minimum of physical security on the job.

In the compact and isolated construction and railroad camps in the South and West, the exploitation of the immigrant was even more highly developed than in the cities. A tight system was maintained by company guards with the support of local authorities. With little knowledge of English and no conception of labor standards of their adopted land, immigrants in these camps were forced to work twelve or more hours a day for little more than board and room in crude barracks. On and off the job they were guarded by armed bosses. If an immigrant worker left a construction camp, he was pursued by guards or by local officials who were usually willing to help the company "preserve law and order." If an immigrant refused to work, he was confined to his barracks or sent to the county jail until he had changed his mind.

The difficulties of the immigrant were enhanced by the prejudices of American laborers. Native workers usually viewed the immigrant with suspicion and derision because of his different customs and language. Of course, they also looked on him as a threat to their security, and jobs that were thought beneath an American were considered good enough for an immigrant. In many industries the poorest paying and the most hazardous forms of work were known as "foreign jobs." In some industries different types of work were assigned to separate nationalities, the most recent arrivals occupying the least desirable positions. With every new wave of immigration, each national group moved a step up the ladder of occupations. Thus, the Irish, disdained as "mick ditchdiggers" before the Civil War, were supplanted in later years by new groups of foreigners whom other workers, including the once-despised Irish Americans, now referred to as "wops" and "hunkies."

Both their race and their much lower standard of living made the Chinese perhaps the most ill-treated immigrant group. Because they accepted lower wages than most native workers, they were the principal victims of the American labor's opposition to immigrant laborers. In 1862, Congress adopted legislation prohibiting the importation of Chinese contract labor, but this law was loosely enforced; and the Burlingame Treaty of 1868, which guaranteed the Chinese unrestricted immigration to the United States, did little to reassure American workers. In 1870, the hostility of organized labor to the Chinese was further aroused by the use of California Chinese as strikebreakers in Massachusetts. With the onset of the depression of the midseventies, native workers in California increasingly blamed the Chinese for their troubles. Led by the demagogic Denis Kearney of San Francisco and at times using mob action, California workers demanded that the state legislature impose severe restriction on Chinese laborers. In 1879, this campaign bore its first fruits. A new state constitution prohibited California corporations from hiring Chinese workers. Two years later, the national government, partly in response to pressure from frightened Chinese merchants in this country, concluded a new treaty with China that permitted the United States to regulate, restrict, or suspend Chinese immigration. In 1882, Congress gave weight to this treaty by suspending the immigration of Chinese laborers for ten years. This measure was re-enacted for successive periods and was made permanent from 1904 until after the end of the second World War. A similar policy was adopted toward Japanese immigrants in 1907, when the Japanese government agreed not to issue visas to Japanese laborers who wished to emigrate to the United States.

Despite numerous protests of organized labor against European as well as Asian immigrants, the federal government made little attempt to check or regulate the flow of immigration from Europe. After the Civil War, American employers imported gangs of workers as strikebreakers and manual laborers, and agents of American business firms toured southern and eastern Europe advertising the wonders of life in the New World. In 1885, Congress forbade the importation of contract labor to the United States, and in 1891, when labor's campaign against the immigrant blossomed along with a growing concern of older Americans about the immigrant's place in national life, Congress enacted a law to prevent American employers from advertising for workers in foreign lands and steamship companies from serving as recruiting agents for American industry. Before the twentieth century,

Americanizing Immigrant Children, at the Mott Street Industrial School, 1889
(photo by Jacob A. Riis)

the only other move to limit general immigration was made in 1882, when Congress excluded idiots, potential paupers, and criminals. The act of 1891 added immigrants with contagious diseases to the category of undesirables.

The immigrants in the cities at least were not completely powerless in their struggle for assimilation. Their understandable first tendency was to live together, almost helplessly, with people of their own background. This ghetto life was strengthened and maintained, however, by the refusal of most Americans outside of immigrant neighborhoods to be sincere about any invitation to the new arrivals to become full American citizens. But confusion, pain, and ambition among the immigrant groups soon bred politically exploitable resentment. Their own newspapers and fraternal societies and the knowledge of American ways learned by their predecessors and their children in the public schools helped the immigrants create their own tough and durable cultures within the dominant American ethos. Within a generation after the "new immigration" began, the city political bosses, using immigrant votes and anxious to keep the immigrant conscious of his special identity, were making a formidable challenge to the political power and social prestige of the old Americans.

On the whole, the multi-national nature of immigration after the Civil War further weakened attempts to organize effective workingmen's opposition to business. The long domination of a small businessman's ethos in America, the splits between skilled and unskilled labor, or between those who thought of themselves as potential shop owners and those who had accepted a permanent role as mill workers, were made even more difficult to overcome by the presence of the immigrants. The spread of the factory system, however, made for additional complications, given the increase of female and child labor and, eventually, the desire of Negroes for industrial jobs.

From 1865 to 1914, the number of gainfully employed American women and children steadily increased. According to the census of 1870, the work force included nearly 750,000 children of both sexes between the ages of ten and fifteen. By 1910, when every state but Nevada had adopted legislation either regulating or forbidding certain forms of child labor, nearly 2,000,000 children held jobs. In 1890, there were more than 3,700,000 women holding jobs; by 1910, there were more than 8,000,000, comprising 21.2 per cent of all the gainfully employed in the nation. Although many women worked as domestics (more than 2,400,000 in 1910), they were eligible for most other jobs, and by 1910 women were working in every type of industry listed by the federal census report, including paint factories, chemical works, rubber factories, and munition plants. Women and countless children who were not listed as gainfully employed by the federal census worked long hours in tenements on a piece-work basis or in obscure sweatshops that made no report to the federal authorities. As a rule,

Average Earnings of Factory Workers, for a Year of 300 Working Days, 1904 *

LOCATION	MEN	WOMEN	CHILDREN
Urban	$566	$307	$186
Rural	$479	$264	$158

* Isaac A. Hourwich: *Immigration and Labor; The Economic Aspects of European Immigration to the United States* (New York: G. P. Putnam's Sons, 1912), p. 298. Copyright 1912 by, and reprinted with the permission of, G. P. Putnam's Sons.

children in industry were paid less than women who in turn earned less than men.

This increasingly diverse work force did not include large numbers of Negroes in the first generation after the Civil War. Most freed Negroes at first remained in the South; it was not until World War I that they migrated in comparatively large numbers to northern cities to take jobs in industry. Those southern Negroes who were not farmers were employed as domestics or longshoremen or worked in the so-called "Negro-job" industries: coal mining, railroading, lumbering, and the building trades. The South's comparatively rapid industrial expansion after 1890 had little effect on the Negro, for most of the new jobs were reserved for white workers. Male Negroes in 1910 thus comprised only a small percentage of the industrial working class, but they disrupted labor life out of all proportion to their numbers. White workers considered Negroes a threat to their jobs and refused to admit them to their unions. Those Negroes who could get no other type of work and who served as strikebreakers tended to confirm the hostility of the white workers and to reinforce their traditional racial prejudice.

The Standards of Labor

Regardless of age, sex, color, or nationality, all American wage earners had to satisfy the demands of modern industrial society. Working conditions varied from industry to industry, and even from job to job within a single industry, but these were differences of degree rather than of kind. The wages of all workers were affected by the fluctuations in the business cycle over which they had little or no control. Some laborers had a shorter work week than others, but all had to devote long hours to their jobs. Even those wage earners in relatively safe occupations might be injured on the job; and no worker was free from the threat of unemployment.

Paradoxically, despite great discontent and widespread misery during the half-century before World War I, there was a marked overall increase in the money wages received by American workers. In 1860, artisans were paid approximately $12 a week. Twenty years later, their average weekly wage had risen to $15, and in 1915 it was $24; however, the wages of the common laborer in nonagricultural pursuits lagged far behind those of the artisan. The average weekly wages paid to a common laborer, approximately $6 a week in 1860, rose to only $7.50 in 1880 and to $12 in 1915. In the same fifty-five years the money wages received by male farm workers (who were paid in board as well as money) increased from $10 to $20 a month.

Real wages also rose as the cost of living declined and as money wages climbed after the Civil War. The index of real wages (1892 = 100) climbed from 49 in 1866 to 80 in 1873. Following the depression of the seventies, when real wages fell less than money wages, there was a steady increase in real wages until in 1892, on the eve of another depression, the index figure had reached 100, or more than double that for 1866. The sharp drop in prices in the depression of the 1890's sent real wages up to an index number of 110 in 1897, and during the next seventeen years it did not again fall below 100. But this was an over-all increase and did not reflect the times of unemployment, or the uncertainties and squalor of many workers' lives.

Despite the efforts of trade unions, the hours of labor in American industry remained long. In 1860, some workers labored fourteen hours a day, and only a small number in the more skilled occupations had achieved a ten-hour day. The standard work week was six days, but in many industries wage earners had to work every day of the week. Soon after the Civil War, organized labor established the goal of an eight-hour day, but throughout the nineteenth century this objective remained largely an ideal. However, federal legislation enacted in 1869, and amended in 1892 and 1912, established the eight-hour day for workers on government projects, and after 1900 numerous states passed laws regulating the hours of labor in industry. But a series of strikes in the mideighties, staged by organized workers in order to obtain the eight-hour day, were almost universally defeated. By 1900, most American laborers still worked a ten-hour day and a six-day week.

Wages and hours, however, provide an inadequate guide to the status of the wage earner during the years after the Civil War. Often workers were unable to obtain jobs for long periods of time. The major depressions of the 1870's and 1890's threw uncounted thousands out of work, while shorter panics and recessions in 1884, 1903, and 1907 also added to the ranks of the unemployed. Seasonal jobs, new machinery, and more efficient manufacturing processes, as well as changes in consuming habits, frequently created unemployment. When, for example, public taste changed, the number of wage earners in the bicycle and motorcycle industries declined approximately 75 per cent from 1899 to 1909.

Inadequate statistics preclude detailed study of the effect of increasing industrialization on the health of the worker. But long hours of monotonous labor in drafty, poorly illuminated, or dusty factories could not have produced a lively and happy work force. Few statistics on industrial accidents were compiled before the twentieth cen-

Powder Men at a Coal Mine

tury; but in 1913, Frederick L. Hoffman, a life insurance official who had made a close study of the available evidence, stated that the number of fatal industrial accidents "among American wage-earners, including both sexes, may be conservatively estimated at 25,000 for the year 1913, and the number of injuries involving a disability of more than four weeks . . . at approximately 700,000." Hoffman's study further revealed that the percentage of fatal industrial accidents was higher in mining than in any other single industry in the United States.

The Beginning of a National Labor Movement

Although the problems of wages and hours, the impersonal or authoritarian factory system, the lessened dignity of labor, technological unemployment and the heterogeneity of the working force all seemed to call for collective action, most workers found it difficult to abandon their ideal of economic individualism. To many laborers, union membership was a badge of defeat signifying that they could not fulfill the American dream of becoming independent and wealthy in their own right. Farmers, businessmen, professional people, and white-collar workers generally looked on unions as alien devices for encouraging the lazy and penalizing the industrious, and before World War I most of the nonlaboring public usually gave its moral support to employers in the war against unions. The nation's newspapers, which seldom sympathized with striking workers, frequently described labor leaders as anarchists and dangerous radicals who sought to undermine the American way of life. Most public officials shared the antipathy to unions and often sided with the employer, virtually never intervening to protect strikers.

Despite widespread opposition, many local craft-unions had been established in the United States during the first half of the nineteenth century. Before the spread of the railroad network, a worker's interest in his job was usually confined to his own plant or community. But as improved transportation facilities brought firms in widely separated parts of the country into competition with one another for the first time, the employees of these firms began to realize that working conditions were no longer an exclusively local concern. If the apprenticeship rules or the wage scale in one plant were lowered, it would not be long before competition would compel the managers of other plants to introduce similar changes. The national trade-union was the wage earner's response to the increasing nationwide scope of American industry.

Because artisans usually possess considerably more bargaining power than common laborers, the national unions founded before the Civil War were confined to groups who had some hopes of success: typesetters, iron molders, hat finishers, and machinists, for example. During the war, new national unions were established and old ones strengthened as skilled workers sought to combat the rapid increase in prices and to take advantage of the labor shortage created by the army's drain on the supply of manpower. From 1861 to 1865, approximately twenty unions were founded in the northern states, including the miners, railroad engineers, cigar makers, plasterers, carpenters, bricklayers, spinners, and shoe workers.

These trade-unionists of the Civil War era wanted to prevent their members from becoming proletarians and were more interested in restoring economic individualism for the workers than in developing class consciousness. Looking back longingly to a craft society in which each worker supposedly had a large measure of economic freedom, their goals were freedom from rather than victory within the wage system. A. C. Cameron, editor of the *Workingman's Advocate,* urged the government to issue more Greenbacks as the only way of preventing the financier from destroying completely the independence of small worker-producers. Ira Steward, a member of the Machinists' and Blacksmiths' Union, advocated an eight-hour day for all workers, but insisted that this reform be achieved by legislation rather than by the use of the strike. Virtually all the new national unions called for producers' cooperatives, through which, they believed, workers could avoid losing their independence and would return to the good old days when a skilled laborer was his own boss. In 1869, an official of the Knights of St. Crispin, the shoe workers' union, said: "The present demand of the Crispin is steady employment and fair wages, but his future is self-employment." But labor's faith in cooperatives was seldom rewarded; almost every one of the many cooperatives was unable to compete successfully with established private firms.

In 1866 came the first attempt to gather the various craft unions into a single, nationwide organization. The National Labor Union was founded by a group of humanitarian reformers and union leaders under William H. Sylvis, the head of the iron molders' union. Long-term reforms rather than militant trade-unionism was the keynote. The use of the strike was minimized, and National Labor Union platforms called for eight-hour legislation, abolition of alien contract-labor, the establishment of a federal department of labor, rights for women and Negroes equal to those of white men, land reform, and the elimination of monopoly. Wage earners primarily concerned with more pay and improved working conditions quickly lost whatever interest they may have initially had in the National Labor Union. As the workers withdrew, the leadership of the National Labor Union—in the words of Norman Ware—was taken over by "labor leaders without organizations, politicians without parties, women without husbands, and cranks, visionaries, and agitators without jobs." * In 1871, the National Labor Union entered politics and changed its name to the National Labor Party. Its poor showing in the election of 1872 lost it most of its remaining prestige, and it soon died. If it accomplished nothing else, the National Labor Union demonstrated that without a mass basis and a realistic program, a national labor movement was doomed.

The 1870's were dark years for organized labor. Many employers were determined to crush the union movement, and the depression so weakened the bargaining power of most unions that they were seldom able to hold their own. The violent tactics employed by a group of

* Norman J. Ware: *The Labor Movement in the United States: 1860–1895* (New York: D. Appleton and Company, 1929), p. 11.

Pennsylvania coal miners known as the Molly McGuires brought ig-
nominy on the entire labor movement in the United States. The Molly
McGuires were a secret organization among the members of the Ancient Order of Hibernians in the anthracite fields of Pennsylvania.
They committed a series of crimes, including murder, against the representatives of the coal operators. In 1876, James McParlan, a Pinkerton detective who had joined the group under an assumed name, made
public the role of the Mollies. As a result, ten of the Molly McGuires
were hanged and fourteen others received jail sentences. The Molly
McGuires were actually a limited and isolated phenomenon in the labor
history of the period, but many Americans considered them typical of
the extremes to which workers as a class would go.

In 1877, organized labor suffered a more severe defeat. On July 17,
spontaneous walkouts took place on the Baltimore and Ohio railroad
lines in response to wage reductions and the use of the blacklist. The
strike quickly spread to the important rail centers. State and federal
troops were sent out and battled the rail workers and groups of unemployed who joined in the struggle. Violence flared up in Baltimore,
Pittsburgh, Toledo, Chicago, St. Louis, and San Francisco. Millions of
dollars worth of property damage took place, but by August 3 the
strikes on the leading lines had been broken. The courts willingly
granted injunctions to the operators. State and federal troops, the poverty of the rail unions, and the refusal of the trainmen to go out with
the engineers had all frustrated the hopes of the workers.

Ever since 1869, however, the Noble and Holy Order of the
Knights of Labor was attempting to establish a workingman's organization that would cut across individual crafts and rest on such a broad
foundation that it would be invulnerable to attacks from employers.
Founded as a secret benefit society by nine Philadelphia garment cut-
ters, the Knights of Labor expanded rapidly under the leadership of
Uriah Stephens, and within four years eighty local assemblies had
been established. Workers who had been intimidated by the antilabor
drives of the period welcomed a secret organization that would conceal
the identity of union members from employers. The elaborate ritual
with which meetings were conducted undoubtedly also gave many
workingmen a sense of importance and a feeling of release from the
humdrum character of their jobs.

Membership in the Knights of Labor was open to "all who toiled."
True to its motto, an "injury to one is an injury to all," the Knights
accepted workers regardless of their sex, color, or degree of skill. Unlike most trade unions, no provision was made for an apprenticeship
for a craft, and the only "nontoilers" specifically excluded from the

Knights were liquor dealers, lawyers, bankers, stockbrokers, and professional gamblers. In some instances the local and district assemblies of the Knights included the workers in a single trade, and in other cases all wage earners in one locality regardless of their individual skills. Diversity in local organization enabled the Knights to enlist workers who wished to preserve their trade union affiliations as well as those who were joining a union for the first time.

Like the National Labor Union, the Knights of Labor wanted reforms to restore the worker's status as an individual producer. Opposing the use of the strike and announcing that its objective was to make "every man his own master—every man his own employer," it demanded the eight-hour day, compulsory arbitration of all labor disputes, equal pay for both sexes, abolition of child and prison labor, establishment of a bureau of labor statistics, and the formation of producer and consumer cooperatives by workers. At various times in its history, the Knights also took positions on leading public questions and advocated an income tax, abolition of national banks, paper money, public ownership of utilities, prohibition, and postal savings banks. When the rank and file used the strike to improve wages and working conditions, they received little encouragement from the officials of the organization who were dedicated to the Jacksonian ideal of the individual entrepreneur.

In the 1880's, the Knights of Labor moved to the height and then rapid downfall of their power. In 1878, the General Assembly was made the organization's ruling body; a year later Terrence Powderly was selected as Grand Master Workman, supplanting Uriah Stephens as the Knight's executive officer; and in 1882, secrecy was abandoned. In the next four years, especially during the depression of 1884-5, workers joined the Knights in large numbers and forced the leadership to adopt a slightly more militant attitude than it had held in the past. Nevertheless, Powderly frequently refused to give either moral or financial support to striking members, and many unauthorized strikes took place during the depression. The order's greatest success came in 1885-6. In strikes against the Gould railroad system, the workers not only attained their immediate objectives but also won recognition for their union from Gould. By January, 1886, the membership of the Knights of Labor approximated 700,000. The organization was then at top strength.

Suddenly, a completely unforeseen event brought disaster. Despite the express prohibition of Powderly, many members of the Knights of Labor joined with other workers on May Day, 1886, in a nationwide demonstration for an eight-hour day. Although Chicago was consid-

Chicago Anarchists in the Eighties

ered the center of radical labor in the United States, the May Day
celebrations in that city passed without incident. But two days later,
when pickets and scabs clashed outside the McCormick reaper plant,
the police intervened and killed four people. On the following night,
a protest meeting was held in Haymarket Square. When the police attempted to disperse the crowd, a bomb thrown into their ranks killed
seven persons and injured several others. The Haymarket affair sent a
wave of antilabor hysteria through the nation. Chicago officials arrested eight anarchists and charged them with inciting—but not actually committing—the crime. All were found guilty by the jury. Of the
eight, four were hanged, one committed suicide, and the remaining
three were sent to prison for life.*

Although the Knights of Labor had played little or no part in the
events in Chicago that led up to the Haymarket bombing, the national
sense of outrage left no room for careful discriminations. As the leading labor organization of the country, it was widely blamed for an
event that many people considered a typical labor tactic. Because
many members of the order had participated in the eight-hour demonstrations that had preceded the Haymarket affair, it was generally as-

* In 1893, they were pardoned by Governor John Peter Altgeld of Illinois.

sumed that they had resorted to violence to attain their objectives after other methods had failed. Unfortunately for the Knights, Albert Parsons, one of the men hanged by the Chicago authorities for allegedly inciting the bombing, was a dues-paying member. The Knights of Labor never recovered from this setback. An essentially conservative organization, whose leaders had urged reform and condemned violence, it was the principal victim of the public outcry against a crime committed by an individual whose identity is still unknown.

The Haymarket affair proved a turning point in the history of the Knights of Labor, but the rapid decline in its numerical strength after 1886 would be better interpreted as a result of its inability to achieve its announced objective of making every worker his own master. The Knights, for example, had great faith in cooperatives, and at one time they were operating more than 200 of them, but eventually they all went under, victims of the superior power of private enterprise. Leaders and grass-roots members, furthermore, were often at odds. Powderly's long-range reforms had relatively little appeal for workers who wanted higher wages and a shorter working day. The attempt to organize all workers on the same basis regardless of their individual skills also did not prove feasible. Because skilled laborers in times of industrial conflict ran the risk of blacklisting and other forms of employer retaliation that would deny them jobs, they withdrew from the Knights in increasing numbers to join trade-unions that afforded them a greater measure of protection. The unskilled and semiskilled who thus remained in the order generally lacked the bargaining power needed to cope with militant employers backed by public opinion and government officials who were willing to use armed force and the courts to suppress "labor disturbances."

By 1890, the membership of the Knights of Labor had declined to approximately 100,000. After a political alliance with the farmers in the 1890's, the order played no important role in national life. By the turn of the century, the assemblies were confined almost exclusively to small towns in which the Knights' creed of every man his own master still seemed to be viable and served as the basis for local fraternal societies with comparatively few members.

Bread-and-Butter Unionism

The Knights of Labor's principal appeal had been to the unskilled. Members of established craft-unions, with their pride in their work and fear of losing their identity, were antagonistic to the idea of one big union for all workers. The national trade-unions that survived the disasters of the 1870's sought to build up union organizations that differed markedly from that of the Knights. Looking neither backward to a golden age that had been nor forward to a Utopia they were to make, disdaining the Knights' program for reforming society as unrealistic, the craft-unions rigorously confined their efforts to obtaining increases in pay and a reduction in the work week of their own members. Relying on craft-unions whose membership was restricted to the skilled members of a single trade, they believed that collective bargaining and use of the strike as a last resort could compel employers to sign contracts that would guarantee union demands. The aims of the national trade-unions appeared narrow when contrasted with the Knights, but after a generation of larger schemes and failures they seemed a safe bed-rock for a program that was realizable within the near future.

The emerging trade-union philosophy of the 1870's was perhaps best exemplified by the International Cigar Makers' Union, which at the time consisted largely of skilled workers of foreign origin. They believed in a compact organization that would provide its members with tangible benefits. After an unsuccessful strike in the disastrous year 1877, the union was revived by Adolph Strasser and Samuel Gompers. Through regular collection of dues and by restricting membership to those with the same economic interests and demands, Strasser and Gompers were able to build a union that not only improved conditions within the industry but also furnished financial assistance to members suffering adversity. By 1880, the International Cigar Makers' Union had proved so effective that it was serving as a model for unions in several other industries.

In 1881, representatives of several craft-unions met in Pittsburgh and formed the Federation of Organized Trade and Labor Unions of the United States of America and Canada. This organization consisted of skilled craft-unions. In 1886, the organization's name was changed to the American Federation of Labor, and Samuel Gompers was elected to the presidency, a position that he held every year but one until his death in 1924. When several national unions seceded from the Knights of Labor, the success of the federation was assured. Within a decade after Gompers had assumed office, the American Federation of Labor had become the most important labor organization in the United States.

The A. F. of L. avoided most policies that brought other groups to grief. Recognizing the diversity of labor conditions, it was a loose alliance of national trade unions, each enjoying large autonomy. The national unions were made up of locals with representation in city centrals and state federations, and federal unions were established as catchalls for groups of workers who were not eligible for membership in the established craft-unions. Women, Negroes, and the unskilled were excluded by unions affiliated with the A. F. of L., and skilled workers were admitted only after they had served a long apprenticeship and paid a large initiation fee. Shunning political and economic reforms, the leaders worked almost exclusively for higher wages and shorter work weeks for the comparatively small number of members. They opposed third parties, although they paid lip service to the slogan that the ballot box should be used to reward labor's friends and punish its enemies.

Essentially a conservative organization that successfully resisted the few socialists in its ranks in the formative years, the A. F. of L. believed its job was to obtain a larger share of the fruits of American capitalism for the élite of the working class. Although assuming labor to be a class, the A. F. of L. considered class cooperation essential to the welfare of the workingman. If employers refused to sign collective-bargaining contracts that covered wages and hours, A. F. of L. unions believed that they had no alternative but to strike to compel cooperation. The strike was a class-conscious weapon, but its aim was class cooperation.

This bread-and-butter philosophy of the American Federation of Labor made it more acceptable to American employers than almost any other type of workingman's organization. By restricting its membership to highly skilled workers and by organizing them according to their trades, it divided rather than united the nation's laborers. By confining its objectives to wages and hours, it sought to control only the most immediate aspects of the job. Employers felt no real threat to their management of the economy. Forswearing politics and opposing all radicalism, the A. F. of L. underwrote American capitalism. It demanded only the right to get more for its own members within the existing American economy.

In 1890, the unions belonging to the American Federation of Labor had a total membership of 550,000. A decade later, the figure was 1,500,000; and in 1914, it was 2,000,000. Only the Railroad Brotherhoods of the major trade unions remained unaffiliated. By 1914, a few A. F. of L. unions had won the eight-hour day for their dues-payers, and others had established benefit programs to assist members who were unemployed. The National Civic Federation, which had been established to facilitate the peaceful settlement of industrial disputes, recognized the Federation as the outstanding spokesman for the American worker and frequently provided it with a forum for presenting labor's side of a case. But the accomplishments of the A. F. of L. during its first decades should not be exaggerated, for in reality it had little effect on the status of most American workingmen. The Federation included only a small percentage of the total laboring force, and it was able to win only minor victories for even this limited and select group. Before the outbreak of World War I, militant employers supported by public officials were both better organized and more powerful than any labor union; and, using the blacklist, lockout, yellow-dog contract, private and public troops, and injunctions, they repeatedly thwarted the larger efforts of American workers to improve their lot.

The Labor Sectarians

Before World War I, when the average American wage earner joined a union or went out on strike, he was not protesting against the profit system but was merely demanding a greater share of profits in the form of increased wages.

Despite the fundamental conservatism of most American workers, they occasionally took the law in their own hands to improve their economic status. The Molly McGuires murdered mine operators, and the railroad workers in the strike of 1877 destroyed millions of dollars worth of private property. In 1892, the striking workers of Andrew Carnegie's Homestead Steel plant in western Pennsylvania shot and killed the strikebreakers imported from the Pinkerton Detective Agency to take their jobs. Two years later, in the Pullman strike, the workers again met force with force. Such labor violence arose spontaneously out of a sense of desperation and hopelessness. When every other means had failed or when attacked by armed thugs or government troops, the average American workingman suddenly found himself using extralegal methods to defend his job. With no desire to overthrow the existing economic system and with no formal loyalty to violence, if driven far enough, he would occasionally use force to protect what he considered his right.

In the closing decades of the nineteenth century, some labor leaders asked whether the lot of the workingman could really be improved within the capitalist system, whether its competitiveness and acquisitiveness, even if profitable to workers in the short run, was not an intolerable basis for social life. The American socialists, anarchists, and communists derived all or part of their inspiration largely from Karl Marx's bitter indictment and allegedly scientific analysis of the nature of capitalist society. Observing the misery and poverty of early industrial England and contrasting its selfishness and degradation with the potentialities for freedom and happiness that seemed implicit in the growth of technology, Marx predicted the doom of capitalist society by violent revolution. Required to compete in a cutthroat world, employers would try to buy their labor as cheaply as possible and would use the state and church to keep the rebellious in line. Turning, however, with increasing frequency to machines because they were cheaper and more efficient and more reliable than human labor, in a world of dog-eat-dog, the capitalist would progressively debase and impoverish his society. Capable of producing abundance he would instead create increasingly worse and eventually uncontrollable crises. However, his very need to use science and technology to win his own game would require him to train a number of skilled technicians. Capable of reading and writing, finding common cause with dissatisfied intellectuals and defeated small entrepreneurs, the "vanguard of the proletariat" would come to understand the capitalist system for what it was. Mobilizing the overwhelming majority of the population at the moment when the capitalist market lost all capacity to absorb its own gluts, but compelled to use force against the hostile capitalist-controlled state, the enlightened communists, or "scientific socialists," would bring the ignominious and bankrupt bourgeois world to its end. The "inner contradictions" of capitalism would break the system and usher in a new socialist age of public ownership of the means of production and of popular political controls. Given, at last, control of the weapons of science and technology, mankind for the first time in history would be free to make its own destiny for good or ill.

Visionary, yet supposedly scientific, appealing to justice as well as to self-interest, Marx's basic analysis was presented in such works as *The Communist Manifesto* (1848), *The Critique of Political Economy* (1859), and *Capital* (first volume 1867). Wrong, however, in its analysis, and absolutist in its pretensions about the future, the Marxist faith nevertheless attracted many men and women of good will as well as fanatics to join in a crusade to free mankind from the cash nexus.

Despite the relative fluidity of American society and the absence of any significant developed class consciousness, the social and economic dislocations of the generations after the Civil War, especially during the severe depressions of 1873, 1884–6, and 1893 made Marxism seem to some a generally correct analysis of the tendencies of American industrial society. Declaring themselves the prophets of the future, foreign-born and native American radicals sought to rouse American workers to a revolution to overthrow capitalism in the United States.

For more than thirty years after Appomattox, Chicago was the center of left-wing labor agitation in the United States. German,

Marxism

Austrian, and French immigrants who had been forced to cross the Atlantic partly because of their radicalism settled in relatively large numbers in Chicago and attempted to develop a revolutionary spirit among the workers of their adopted land. Preaching either socialism or anarchism, they held secret meetings, printed pamphlets and papers, issued calls for all workingmen to "offer an armed resistance to the invasions by the capitalist class and capitalist legislatures," and urged wage earners to overthrow American capitalism by "energetic, relentless, revolutionary and international action." These appeals found only a small receptive audience among the masses of either native or foreign-born workers; and after the Haymarket bombing, the Chicago radicals lost what little influence they had possessed.

Among the leading critics of American capitalism in the years before World War I none was more outspoken and vitriolic than Daniel De Leon. Born on the island of Curaçao and educated in Germany, De Leon migrated in the midseventies to the United States, where he studied law and taught for a short time at Columbia College. De Leon soon abandoned both the law and teaching and devoted the remaining years of his life to propagating orthodox Marxism. In many pamphlets and speeches, he took a militant stand against traditional trade-unions, whose leaders he termed "labor fakers." He urged all workingmen to join an independent political movement that would win control of the government and establish a "socialist or co-operative commonwealth, whereby the instruments of production shall be made the property of the whole people." In 1892, De Leon joined the Socialist Labor party, and in the following year he was selected as the party's candidate for governor of New York. Meanwhile, as a member of the Knights of Labor, he made an unsuccessful attempt to capture control of that organization. In 1895, he withdrew from the Knights to form the Socialist Trade and Labor Alliance, whose principal work was to attack the conservative leadership of the American Federation of Labor and those socialists who supported the American trade-union movement. De Leon was both autocratic and doctrinaire. He alienated all but a small coterie of his most loyal followers and failed either to destroy "Gomperism" in the American Federation of Labor or to build an effective socialist organization outside the established trade unions.

Other socialists were more successful in formulating an anticapitalist creed with ideological roots in America rather than Europe. In 1897, Victor L. Berger and Eugene V. Debs, who had been converted to socialism during the prison term he received for contempt of court as leader in the Pullman strike, formed the Social Democratic party. Two years later they were joined by a splinter group from the

De Leon forces, and in 1901 they founded the Socialist Party of America. Although the Socialist party shared De Leon's distaste for Gompers's labor philosophy, its leaders were gradualists who believed that American society could be changed piecemeal by the democratic process. Their long-term aim was to destroy the capitalist system, but the immediate economic and political demands of the Socialist party often duplicated those of the non-socialist reform groups. By 1910 the Socialist party had approximately 125,000 members; it had elected Socialist mayors in Milwaukee, Schenectady, and a few other communities; and it had considerable influence in at least two national trade-unions. Eugene Debs, who had served as the party's presidential candidate in every election from 1900 to the outbreak of World War I, polled 420,793 votes in 1908 and 900,672 votes in 1912.

The mining frontier of the Rocky Mountain states produced a more militant and more desperately class-conscious working-force than Debs and De Leon found in the cities. During the 1890's, the western silver and lead mines were scenes of a class warfare of incredible brutality and viciousness. As Selig Perlman and Philip Taft have pointed out, western miners refused to:

> . . . remain passive while their jobs were being given to strikebreakers. They defended their jobs with Winchester[s]. . . . Employers, Westerners like their employees, were even "quicker on the trigger." Armed guards and armed strikebreakers were mustered in as armies. Civil processes and "due process of law" were ignored and were replaced by "bull pens" and forcible deportations—the paraphernalia of dictatorship.*

The opening guns in the class war on the mining frontier were fired in the Coeur d'Alene district of Idaho in the first years of the 1890's. After a three-month lockout, the operators reopened the mines, but the workers refused to return to work at the wages offered. A strike followed, and both sides used force to achieve their aims. Strikebreakers imported by the owners were driven from the mines by armed strikers. Many pitched battles between company guards and miners took place. Casualties were high on both sides, and on one occasion the strikers blew up a mill with 100 pounds of dynamite. After several futile attempts to restore order, the Governor of Idaho appealed to the Secretary of War for assistance, and soon after the

---

* Selig Perlman and Philip Taft: "Labor Movements," in John R. Commons (ed.): *History of Labor in the United States, 1896–1932* (New York: The Macmillan Company, 1935), Vol. IV, p. 169.

arrival of federal troops, the strike was completely crushed. Martial law was established. Union men were arrested and herded into bull pens, lost their jobs to strikebreakers, and the army rigorously enforced the open-shop. Thirty miners were accused of conspiracy and held for trial in the federal courts, and eighty-five others were charged with contempt of court. Those accused of conspiracy were eventually released, but twelve union men were found guilty of contempt and received sentences of from four to eight months.

The Coeur d'Alene strike was to become part of the legend of the modern American West. While serving their prison terms in the local county jail, the twelve men convicted of contempt discussed plans for the formation of a more effective metal miners' organization. Soon after their release from prison, arrangements were made for a miners' convention, and on May 15, 1893, delegates from Idaho, Montana, Colorado, and South Dakota gathered in Butte, Montana, to establish the Western Federation of Miners. Originally conceived only for improving the wages and working conditions of its members, the pressure of events quickly forced the new union into a more revolutionary position. In the decade after its organization the Western Federation of Miners waged a series of bitter and violent strikes in the mining camps of Cripple Creek and Telluride in Colorado and Coeur d'Alene in Idaho. The essential features and tactics of the Coeur d'Alene strike of 1892 were repeated over and over again, not only with arms but also with revolutionary doctrine. Although the Western Federation of Miners had originally been affiliated with the American Federation of Labor, it withdrew in 1896, and, along with the more militant eastern socialists, became an outspoken foe of "Gomperism" in the labor movement. In 1902, the Western Federation of Miners' convention approved a resolution to "adopt socialism without equivocation," and within a short time a provision was inserted in the preamble of its constitution stating that

> . . . there is a class struggle in society and that this struggle
> is caused by economic conditions; . . . the producer . . . is
> exploited by the wealth which he produces, being allowed to
> retain wages barely sufficient for his elementary necessities; . . .
> that the class struggle will continue until the producer is recog-
> nized as the sole master of his product; . . . that the working
> class, and it alone, can and must achieve its own emancipa-
> tion; . . . finally, that an industrial union and the concerted
> political action of all wage earners is the only method of attain-
> ing this end.

In January, 1905, representatives of the Western Federation of Miners attended a secret conference in Chicago called by radical labor leaders and journalists. At this meeting, plans were laid for a convention to organize "one great industrial union embracing all industries, . . . founded on the class struggle . . . and established as the economic organization of the working class, without affiliation with any political party." The convention, which met on June 27, 1905, was attended by two hundred radicals representing approximately forty different trades and occupations. The delegates, led by Eugene V. Debs, William (Big Bill) Haywood of the Western Federation of Miners, and Daniel De Leon, named the new organization the Industrial Workers of the World. Both the employers and the A. F. of L. were attacked with equal vehemence; and the delegates approved a preamble, stating:

I.W.W.

> The working class and the employing class have nothing in common. There can be no peace so long as hunger and want are found among the millions of working people, and the few, who make up the employing class, have all the good things of life.
>
> Between these two classes a struggle must go on until all the toilers come together on the political as well as on the industrial field, and take and hold that which they produce by their labor, through an economic organization of the working class, without affiliation with any political party.

During the first three years of its existence, the I.W.W. was torn by factional strife, the traditional trouble of sectarian groups. At the 1906 convention, an all-out struggle quickly developed between the so-called radicals and conservatives, who thought that the creation of an effective organization should take precedence over the revolutionary demands of their opponents. The radicals, led by De Leon and supported by the rank and file of the poorer unions, easily routed the conservatives, who in almost any other labor organization would have been considered extremists. Following the defeat of the conservatives, the Western Federation of Miners and the members of the Socialist party withdrew from the I.W.W. Now a new conflict arose between the more doctrinaire and moderate De Leonites and the representatives of the western migratory and unskilled workers, who favored direct action rather than De Leon's theoretical approach. In the 1908 convention, De Leon and his followers were defeated and forced out of the I.W.W. The "Wobblies," as the toughest members of the I.W.W. were called, were now firmly in control of the movement.

For more than a decade after the 1908 convention the I.W.W. stood for a down-to-earth radicalism, all-out class struggle, one big industrial union, and revolution. The ultimate aim of the movement was perhaps closer to syndicalism and anarchism than to socialism—"let the workers run the industries"—but its immediate objective was improved working conditions. Drawing its support largely from the itinerant agricultural, lumber, and construction laborers in the West and from unskilled foreign-speaking workers in eastern factories, the I.W.W. preached an authoritarian, uncompromising creed of class conflict in which the bosses were always wrong, the "wage-slaves" and "working stiffs" always right, and all other unions were "nothing more than parasites upon workingmen."

Poor and despised, the I.W.W. frequently used unusual tactics to attain its objectives. For example, Spokane, Washington, in 1909 adopted an ordinance that deprived the Wobblies of the use of the city's streets for meetings and organization drives. The I.W.W. replied with a militant and spectacular "free speech" campaign that attracted nation-wide attention. As soon as one street orator was arrested by the Spokane police, another took his place. Within ten days, 300 Wobblies had been arrested, the city jail was overflowing, taxpayers were complaining of the increased expense involved in feeding the prisoners and paying the salaries of the special police hired to enforce the ordinance, and each freight train that arrived in Spokane carried a fresh contingent of Wobblies, who were both ready and eager to mount a soap box and join their fellows in jail. Eventually the I.W.W. overwhelmed Spokane's officials and taxpayers by sheer numbers. The city and county jails were not large enough to hold all the offenders, and in March, 1910, the municipal authorities capitulated. I.W.W. speakers were granted the right to use the city streets, and arrangements were made for the release of the prisoners. Between 1909 and 1912, the I.W.W. repeated the techniques they had perfected in Spokane to win free-speech fights in Fresno, California; Victoria, British Columbia; Kansas City, Missouri; Aberdeen, Washington; and San Diego, California.

These free-speech fights were among the I.W.W.'s milder activities. The Wobblies also conducted militant strikes among the itinerant workers of the West and the unskilled factory workers of the East. An active organizing campaign among the lumber workers of Louisiana, Arkansas, and Texas culminated in 1912 in a seven-month strike in which the Wobblies were eventually defeated by state troops, company gunmen, the courts, and a Good Citizens' League. In 1913, the I.W.W. led 2,800 migratory workers, many of whom were women and

Violence at the Oil Refineries: 1915 Strike in Bayonne, N. J.

children, in a strike against the Durst hop ranch in Wheatland, California. The employers had help from private armies and state and local authorities; but the publicity given to the strike led to some improvement in the management of the labor camps maintained by the large commercial farms in the state. One of the most dramatic of I.W.W. strikes took place in 1912 in Lawrence, Massachusetts. The Wobblies assumed the management of a strike of 25,000 textile workers, most of whom were foreign born. They threw endless picket lines around the plants, established a relief system, and sent children of many of the strikers to workers' homes outside of Lawrence for the duration of the strike. Despite the assistance the employers received from local officials and 1400 soldiers, the I.W.W. was able to fight the strike to a successful conclusion. In 1913, the I.W.W. also led strikes of textile workers in Paterson, New Jersey, and rubber workers in Akron, Ohio. Attempts were made to repeat the tactics used at Lawrence, but after weeks both strikes ended in failure.

Every I.W.W. leader who entered a strike area risked his freedom and even his life. Two were sentenced to life imprisonment for their part in the Wheatland strike. Big Bill Haywood, who directed numerous I.W.W. strikes, was arrested in Lawrence, Paterson, and Akron. Another I.W.W. organizer, was lynched by vigilantes for his strike activities in Butte, Montana. Countless other Wobblies were often forced to flee for their lives, were herded into bull pens, or were beaten up by militiamen, police, company guards, or citizens' committees.

Although the Wobblies scorned the gradualists of the American Federation of Labor, they had little to show for their own militant tactics. Their repeated calls for direct action and their open radicalism antagonized the great majority of Americans, who were prepared to go to any extreme to crush the I.W.W. The result was that the mass of American workers received little large-scale assistance from labor organizations before World War I. The conservative unions risked little for their members and nothing for millions of unorganized workers, while the radical unions like the I.W.W. were so radical that they frequently risked and lost all.

Legislation Lightens Labors' Burdens

One of the tenets of classic Marxism was the insensitivity of the bourgeois capitalist state to the poverty of the working class. Yet in America and in Europe during the last part of the nineteenth century the state seemed increasingly willing to pass legislation easing the burdens and disabilities of the workingman. By 1890, some socialists had abandoned the notion that a violent revolution would be needed to bring industrial justice. Laws favorable to labor, the chance to participate in political life, the friendship of powerful middle-class reform leaders, and a slowly rising standard of living, all seemed to point to the inaccuracy of Marx's prediction that capitalist society would "polarize" and explode. More doctrinaire Marxists, particularly those who would later become known as Bolsheviks, insisted that these changes in the conditions of the workers were mere scraps thrown to

Saluting the Government's Eight-Hour Day, 1868

[LIBRARY OF CONGRESS]

the dogs and that capitalism would remain fundamentally exploitative, incapable of reform and of avoiding its own revolutionary doom.

Despite these predictions American labor won some of its most notable victories in the years before 1917 in the nation's legislatures rather than on the picket line. From the end of the Civil War until the turn of the century, several states adopted measures designed to protect workingmen on the job. After 1900, state and federal legislatures passed an amazing number and variety of labor statutes that provided certain minimum standards for men, women, and children in American industry. Organized labor frequently supported these measures, but the principal sponsors of labor legislation were mostly middle-class reformers, many of whom were determined to prevent the triumph of either big business or labor radicalism in America.

In 1884, the federal government created a Bureau of Labor Statistics and in 1913 a Department of Labor. These may have aided all workers, but other federal measures in the period were limited in application either to government workers or to those employed by firms engaged in interstate trade. Congress passed an act for an eight-hour day for laborers on public works in 1868, and in 1892 it extended the eight-hour provision to all federal workers. Under the La Follette Seamen's Act, which became law in 1915, seamen were guaranteed improved living conditions, a nine-hour day while in port, minimum standards of safety, and a measure of protection against tyrannical captains. In both 1916 and 1919, Congress passed bills designed to regulate the employment of children in interstate industries. Congress also improved working conditions on the interstate rail systems. In 1888, it set up a program for the arbitration of industrial disputes on interstate carriers; in 1908, it passed a statute that provided for employer's liability on railroads; and in 1916, it passed the Adamson Act, which established an eight-hour day for railroad employees.

This labor legislation enacted by Congress was negligible in comparison with the host of labor laws placed on the statute books of the various states during the same period. These measures covered almost every phase of working conditions in American industry. After 1900, and at the height of the Progressive movement, states seemed to vie with one another in attempts to improve working conditions, and by the outbreak of World War I many American workers were protected by a series of state statutes that fifty years earlier would have been considered unthinkable violations of the principles of laissez faire.

After the Civil War, the states first attempted to legislate minimum safety standards for various types of industrial workers. In 1877, Massachusetts, which pioneered in labor legislation, passed a bill requiring employers to set up protective devices to safeguard workers around elevators, machinery, and hoists. New York adopted similar legislation in 1887, and ten years later it provided for the enforcement of this measure by factory inspectors. By 1893, fourteen states and territories had adopted some form of safety legislation, and by 1917 most of the others had followed suit. Often, however, these laws had inadequate provisions and funds for enforcement.

The states were slower to establish systems for compensating disabled workers. In 1908, no state provided for compulsory compensation for workmen; but in 1909, Montana became the first state to pass a compensation law, and by 1917 thirty-two states and three territories had adopted such legislation. There was still, however, little attempt to protect the laborer and others against the hazards of old age and unemployment. The first old-age pension law, which was adopted by Arizona in 1915, was declared unconstitutional, and no other state followed Arizona's lead until the 1920's. Before World War I, no state

Coal Mine Boys

[BROWN BROTHERS]

made any attempt to assist its workers during periods of unemployment, and it was not until 1932 that Wisconsin became the first state to pass an unemployment-compensation bill.

No problem received greater legislative attention on the eve of World War I than child labor. In the first decade and a half of the twentieth century, the majority of the states adopted laws that raised the minimum age of children in industry, excluded children from occupations that were hazardous to either their physical or moral well-being, and limited their working hours. In 1900, twenty-four states and the District of Columbia had no minimum-age law for factory employees. Nine years later, all but six states had adopted such legislation. From 1902 to 1907, forty-three states either passed new child-labor laws or strengthened existing statutes.

After 1900, several states also passed laws to safeguard women in industry. As late as 1896, only thirteen states had attempted to limit the hours worked by women, and only three states had enacted laws that were capable of enforcement. One state established a weekly maximum of fifty-five hours for women; ten others provided a maximum of ten hours a day; the two remaining statutes, which called for an eight-hour day, could not be enforced. For some years, adverse court decisions retarded the adoption of further legislation, but after 1908, when the Supreme Court ruled favorably on an Oregon statute, progress was rapid and marked. From 1909 to 1917, nineteen states for the first time adopted legislation dealing with women in industry, and twenty states strengthened existing laws. These laws generally limited women's work day to eight hours, forbade night work for women, and sought to protect all women in industry regardless of occupation.

The American male worker did not share these benefits. Although by 1896, seventeen states had adopted maximum-hour laws for men in industry, these statutes were limited in scope, and few attempts were made to enforce them. Although some states followed the lead taken by Congress in 1868 and passed eight-hour laws for laborers on state projects, in 1913 twenty-one states still lacked legislation regulating the length of the work day on public works. Despite the efforts of the American Federation of Labor and other workingmen's organizations for a general eight-hour law, the best that they could obtain from the state legislatures were eight-hour bills for particular industries such as railroading, mining, and street transportation.

Understandably, laws covering minimum wages were most resisted by employers, since these most directly affected their profits. In 1913, Massachusetts became the first state to adopt a minimum-wage law. But this measure was enforceable only through publicity, and its rates were fixed according to the financial condition of the industries concerned as well as by the cost of living. In 1913, eight other state legislatures passed minimum-wage bills. Five of these statutes, unlike the Massachusetts law, provided for fines and imprisonment for employers who failed to abide by its provisions. From 1915 to 1917, three other states placed minimum-wage bills on their statute books. The effectiveness of the minimum-wage legislation of this period was, however, considerably reduced by adverse judicial decisions and by the fact that, with the exception of Massachusetts, these laws had been adopted by states that were not heavily industrialized. Given the smallness of labor's voice at the time, most of the first wage laws were indeed minimal, and after passage the minimum tended to be the maximum.

The great weakness of all early labor laws was the inadequacy of enforcement machinery. In 1896, seventeen states provided for fac-

Expenditures for Labor Law Administration in Eleven States
Combined, in Actual Dollars and in 1909 Dollars *

YEAR	TOTAL EXPENDED IN ACTUAL DOLLARS	TOTAL EXPENDED IN 1909 DOLLARS	ACTUAL DOLLARS EXPENDED PER WAGE EARNER	1909 DOLLARS EXPENDED PER WAGE EARNER
1889	$202,549	$235,796	10.4 cents	12.1 cents
1899	405,790	481,364	16.9	20.1
1909	809,232	809,232	24.0	24.0

tory inspection, but there were only 117 factory inspectors in all.
After 1900, however, several states did try to make the administration
of their labor statutes more effective. Additional inspectors were hired;
existing laws were amended in an effort to prevent evasions; and larger
sums of money were allotted for the enforcement of the statutory labor standards. But the extent of even these advances should not be
exaggerated. In 1912, there were still only 425 factory inspectors in the
United States, and the appropriations for the enforcement of state
labor laws was never sufficient to meet even minimum needs.

The Courts and the Unions

If legislatures after 1900 seemed more sensitive to the condition
of the workingman, reformers still faced more formidable obstacles in
the courts. Lax enforcement of labor laws at least left the laws, however inert, on the books, but many of the newer state regulations were
stricken from the state statute books by court nullification, principally
in the name of free competition and the right of the owner-employer
to set his own conditions for his workers. Although the child-labor
laws of 1916 and 1919 were the only important federal labor bills declared unconstitutional by the judiciary in this period, state laws were
repeatedly voided by the courts.

Brought up in an age of belief in laissez faire and armed with the
sweeping powers of the due-process clause of the Fourteenth Amendment, federal and state judges did not hesitate to restrain the state
legislatures from what they considered undue interference in the re-

* Elizabeth Brandeis: "Labor Legislation," in John R. Commons (ed.): *His-*
tory of Labor in the United States (New York: The Macmillan Company, 1935),
Vol. III, p. 636. Copyright 1935 by The Macmillan Company and used with their
permission. The eleven states are: California, Connecticut, Illinois, Kansas, Massachusetts, Mississippi, Missouri, New Jersey, New York, Virginia, and Wisconsin.

lations between employer and employee. In 1885, a New York court invalidated a state law forbidding the manufacture of cigars in tenement houses. An Illinois court in 1895 voided a law limiting the number of hours worked by women, although the Massachusetts Supreme Court had upheld a similar law almost twenty years earlier. In 1898, the Supreme Court upheld a Utah eight-hour law; but seven years later, it invalidated a New York ten-hour law for bakers. Some years later, this pattern was repeated by the Supreme Court when it approved an Oregon minimum wage bill in 1917, but reversed its decision when it was considering a similar bill for the District of Columbia in 1923.

Despite the opposition of many judges, the courts were unable to check the passage of state labor laws. Public opinion frequently compelled the courts to reverse earlier antilabor decisions, and, in general, judicial rulings succeeded at most in postponing rather than preventing the enactment of bills to provide essential safeguards for industrial workers. With a few notable exceptions, such as the invalidation of the federal child-labor law, the courts by the end of the second decade of the twentieth century had approved the main body of labor reforms that had been written into the federal and state statute books in the preceding half-century.

Even those courts that sanctioned laws designed to protect and benefit the worker seldom supported organized labor in its conflicts with organized capital. Repeatedly before World War I the judiciary ruled that both the strike and boycott, the unions' principal weapons, were illegal. Court injunctions frequently restricted union activity. Whenever an individual believed that any union policy was in any way destroying the value of his property, he was permitted to appeal to the courts for an order directing the union to abandon a strike or boycott. Since almost any attempt by a union to improve the lot of its members necessarily had an adverse effect on the property interests of someone, the courts were seldom at a loss to find a reason for issuing an injunction. Injunctions were used to restrain the workers in the railroad strikes of 1877, and subsequently there was hardly a major industrial conflict in which they were not used to check unions. Many militant workers came to view the injunction "to cease and desist" as little more than a thinly disguised legal device for strike breaking and boycott busting. Although the Clayton Act, which became law in 1914, specifically outlawed injunctions in labor disputes, judicial decisions largely nullified this provision in later years.

Anti-union decisions were based on either the common law or the federal statutes of the United States. Although as early as 1842, Judge Lemuel Shaw of Massachusetts in *Commonwealth v. Hunt* had exempted unions from some of the restrictions imposed by the common law, in later years the courts continued to rule that certain forms of union activity were violations of the common-law doctrines of unlawful conspiracy and illegal restraint of trade. The Sherman Antitrust Act of 1890 had as its first provision that "every contract, combination in the form of trust or otherwise, or conspiracy in restraint of trade or commerce among the several states, or with foreign nations, is hereby declared illegal." Although it had never been demonstrated that the authors of this measure intended it to apply to labor unions, members of the federal bench frequently used it against unions. Under the act the courts issued indictments, injunctions, and damage suits; and in the years after 1890, the Sherman Act was used more frequently against organized labor than against organized capital.

The Pullman strike of 1894 was the first major industrial dispute in which organized labor felt the full power of the courts. When the American Railway union under the leadership of Eugene V. Debs supported a strike against the Pullman Car Company in Chicago, the federal government requested an injunction under section 4 of the Sherman Act * to prevent the strikers from interfering with mail shipments on the railroads. In response to this demand, the court issued a preliminary order restraining any persons from

> . . . interfering with, hindering, obstructing, or stopping any mail train, express train or other trains, whether freight or passenger, engaged in interstate commerce . . . and from in any manner interfering with, injuring, or destroying any of the property of any of said railroads engaged in or for the purpose of, or in connection with, interstate commerce, or the carriage of the mails of the United States; . . . and from using threats, intimidation, force or violence to induce employees to quit the service of the railroad, or to prevent persons from entering the employ of the railroads.

When the workers ignored the court order, President Grover Cleveland, despite the protests of Governor John Altgeld of Illinois, who insisted that he had the situation well in hand, dispatched federal troops to Chicago, and, after considerable violence, the strike was

---

* Section 4 of the Sherman Act read: "The several circuit courts of the United States are hereby invested with jurisdiction to prevent and restrain violations of this act. . . . Such proceedings may be by way of petition setting forth the case and praying that such violation shall be enjoined or otherwise prohibited . . . ; and pending such petition and before final decrees the court may at any time make such temporary or restraining order or prohibition as shall be deemed just in the premises."

Cavalry Protecting Meat Shipments from Chicago During the Pullman Strike

[LIBRARY OF CONGRESS]

forcefully crushed. Debs and other union leaders were arrested and charged with contempt of court for their refusal to observe the injunction. The presiding judge of the Circuit Court for the District of Chicago ruled that the injunction was authorized by both the Sherman Act and the common-law prohibition against unlawful conspiracy, and the defendants were sentenced to six months in prison. The case was then carried to the Supreme Court, which sustained the lower court's ruling. The Supreme Court, refusing to pass on the applicability of the Sherman Act, based its decision on the grounds that the government had authority over the transportation of the mails and interstate commerce and that an injunction could be issued to prevent persons from jeopardizing this authority. In his opinion, Justice Brewer said:

> Every government, entrusted by the very terms of its being with powers and duties to be exercised and discharged for the general welfare, has a right to apply to its courts for any proper assistance in the exercise of the one and the discharge of the other. . . . While it is not the province of the government to interfere in the mere matter of private controversy between individuals, or to use its great powers to enforce the

rights of one as against another, yet, whenever the wrongs complained of are such as affect the public at large, and are in respect to matters which by the constitution are entrusted to the care of the nation, and concerning with the nation owes the duty to all the citizens of securing to them their common rights, then the mere fact that the government has no pecuniary interest in the controversy is not sufficient to exclude it from the courts.

The "Debs case" was an overwhelming defeat for organized labor. An unprecedentedly sweeping injunction had been issued to end a strike, and the judiciary had found a variety of reasons to substantiate its stand. The circuit court had stated that unions could be enjoined under both the common law and the Sherman Act. The Supreme Court had ruled that injunctions could be issued against any union that threatened the "general welfare." It is difficult to conceive of a strike that could not be construed to lie within at least one of these categories.

The judiciary restricted the use of the boycott as well as the strike in the famous Danbury Hatters' Case. When D. E. Loewe and Company of Danbury, Connecticut, refused to accede to the demand of the United Hatters of America, an A.F. of L. affiliate, that its plant be unionized, the American Federation of Labor retaliated by imposing a nation-wide boycott on all Loewe hats. The boycott was remarkably effective, and Loewe instituted a suit against the union in the circuit court in Hartford. The principal point at issue was whether or not the Sherman Act prohibited restraint of trade by a union. The circuit court answered this question in the affirmative, for it ruled: "The Act prohibits any combination whatever to secure action which essentially obstructs the flow of commerce between states, or restricts, in that regard, the liberty of a trader to engage in business." Because the union "aimed at compelling third parties and strangers involuntarily not to engage in the course of trade except on the conditions that the combination imposes," the court decided that the union's boycott was a violation of the Sherman Act. In 1908, the Supreme Court upheld the lower court's decision. The *American Federationist* wrote soon afterward: "Our industrial rights have been shorn from us and our liberties threatened."

This and other anti-union decisions of the federal courts deprived organized labor of many of its most powerful weapons. It was not until the passage of the Clayton Antitrust Act in 1914 that organized labor was provided with a small measure of protection against the judiciary.

Section 6 of the Clayton Act stated that the "labor of a human being is not a commodity or article of commerce. Nothing contained in the antitrust laws shall be construed to forbid the existence and operation of labor . . . organizations . . . nor shall such organizations or the members thereof, be held or construed to be illegal combinations or conspiracies in restraint of trade under the antitrust laws." Section 20 of the act restricted the issuing of injunctions in labor disputes. Samuel Gompers welcomed these two provisions as the Magna Carta of American labor, but his optimism proved premature, for the courts in subsequent years interpreted the labor sections in such a way that they were practically nullified. Unions had to wait until the adoption of the Norris-La Guardia Federal anti-injunction law in 1932 and the National Industrial Recovery Act in the following year before they received any substantial assistance or protection from the government.

Judicial curbs on organized labor reflected the opinions of the non-wage-earning public. Many Americans had reluctantly agreed that government should guarantee workers a certain measure of protection on the job, but they were not prepared to endorse either the methods or the objectives of workingmen who banded together to present a united front to their employers. The boycott, slowdown, picket line, and strike were viewed with hostility as weapons to subordinate the American entrepreneur and public to working-class or socialist rule. Such employer devices as the lockout, yellow-dog contract, private or public armies, and strikebreakers created no equivalent fears against business owners. Most Americans had been taught to accept and revere a theory of economic individualism that seemed amply substantiated by the nation's material progress and by countless "rags-to-riches" stories. Those more comfortable and secure Americans raised in this tradition considered unions both a violation of the American creed and a threat to their ideals. As long as the American people clung to these views, unions could obtain only a few limited victories in their struggles with the nation's employers.

FOR SUPPLEMENTARY READING

The classic work on American labor reflects the "bread-and-butter union" point of view. It is the multi-volumed *History of Labor in the United States* (1918–35), by J. R. Commons and others. More recent and less slanted is J. G. Rayback, *A History of American Labor* (1959).

N. J. Ware's two volumes, *The Labor Movement in the United States, 1860–1895* (1929) and *Labor in Modern Industrial Society* (1935), are well regarded general studies of labor organizations. See also the several works of Selig Perlman. A controversial subject is well treated by P. H. Douglas, *Real Wages in the United States 1890–1926* (1930). The leading laborite biographies and memoirs are: T. V. Powderly, *Thirty Years of Labor* (1889) and *The Path I Trod* (1940); S. Gompers, *Seventy Years of Life and Labor: An Autobiography* (2 vols., 1925); R. Ginger, *The Bending Cross* (1949), on Debs; and *Bill Haywood's Book* (1929). On individual unions and labor associations use L. L. Lorwin, *The American Federation of Labor* (1933); P. F. Brissenden, *The I.W.W.* (1919); and P. Taft, *The A. F. of L. in the Time of Gompers* (1957). Two works can introduce the study of strikes and industrial unrest: S. Yellin, *American Labor Struggles* (1936), and H. David, *The History of the Haymarket Affair* (1936). On women at work use J. A. Hill, *Women in Gainful Occupations, 1870–1920* (1929); on child labor, E. L. Otey, *The Beginnings of Child Labor Legislation in Certain States* (1911); J. Spargo, *The Bitter Cry of the Children* (1906); and U. S. Bureau of Labor Statistics *Bulletin No. 175* (1916), on children's (and women's) working conditions. The Negro worker is analyzed in C. H. Wesley, *Negro Labor in the United States, 1850–1925* (1927). Four works only introduce the complex problems of the immigrant: G. M. Stephenson, *A History of American Immigration, 1820–1924* (1926); C. Erickson, *American Industry and the European Immigrant, 1860–1885* (1957); O. Handlin, *The Uprooted* (1951) (Pb) and J. Higham, *Strangers in the Land* (1955). The easiest approach to labor legislation can be made through E. E. Witte, *The Government in Labor Disputes* (1932), and E. Lieberman, *Unions Before the Bar* (1950).

PART II

MAKING A
NEW REPUBLIC

5

===

-»->»->»->»->»->»->»->»->»

===

The Last Frontier

IN 1860, the broad expanse of territory between the Middle Border and the settlements on the Pacific Coast, a vast region of prairies, plains, deserts, and mountains, was occupied almost exclusively by Indians. Forty years later, the Indians had either been killed or forced onto reservations, much of the land had been taken up by easterners and immigrants, and a large part of the area had been carved into states. As miners, cattlemen, and farmers moved into the region, an era in the nation's history ended, and only the folk image of the pioneer remained to remind twentieth-century Americans of their forefathers' struggles with the wilderness.

The Lands and Resources of the West

The American West is not one but several regions. Extending westward to approximately the ninety-eighth meridian—or roughly to west central Texas, Oklahoma, Kansas, Nebraska, and the Dakotas— are the level, treeless, prairie plains of the Illinois country and the gulf plains of the South. Separated by the Ozark Mountains and plateaus, these two plains areas are barren of minerals but sufficient rainfall, suit- able temperatures, an absence of rocks and stones, and a rich soil make them ideally suited for agriculture. Eventually the southern part of this section became an extension of the cotton belt; the central part became the western half of the great corn- and winter-wheat region; and the northern part became the spring-wheat area.

West of the prairie and gulf plains are the semiarid High Plains. Embracing nearly all of western Texas, Oklahoma, Kansas, Nebraska,

PHYSICAL CHARACTERISTICS
OF THE LAST FRONTIER

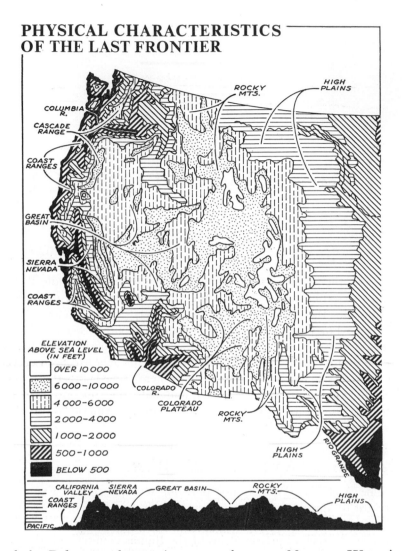

and the Dakotas and extensive areas of eastern Montana, Wyoming, Colorado, and New Mexico, this enormous tract was primarily a grassland region, where trees failed to develop because of unfavorable soil conditions, poor drainage and aeration, intense cold, high winds, deficiency of moisture, and repeated fires. The greater part of this territory was carpeted with a heavy, though not deep-rooted, sod and was the natural home of the short, or plains, grass. Nearer the slopes of the Rockies, where the climate was too dry to support continuous growth, the sod gave way to tuft or bunch grass and sage brush. The borderline between the short- and tuft-grass areas was determined by the seasons; in wet seasons the short grass encroached upon the bunch grass, while in dry seasons the bunch grass spread east.

Beyond the high plains lie the stretches of plateau plains that are bounded on the east by the Rockies and on the west by the Pacific Mountain system. This region—which includes eastern California, southeastern Oregon, southern Idaho, and all of Arizona and Nevada— is in turn divided by a height of land into two parts. The lower, or southern, portion is composed of the southwestern plateaus and what is familiarly known as "The Great American Desert." * Because this desert area has a rainfall of less than ten inches a year, it is useless for farming unless irrigated. The northern plateau, with a heavier rainfall than the desert and a number of small rivers along its eastern and western margins, can be used for grazing. On the other hand, much of it is so dry that without irrigation it will support neither man nor beast. The climate of the northern plateau is very changeable; in summer, temperatures range from blazing heat at noon to fifty degrees at night, and in winter, temperatures of twenty-five degrees below zero are common.

West of the Sierra Nevada Mountains and the Cascade range there is a wide diversity of both climate and topography. Central and southern California are subtropical, have virtually no rain in the summer, and possess stretches of some of the most fertile soil in the United States. Three hundred miles north of the great valley of California and separated from it by the Klamath Mountains is the long, fingerlike Willamette-Puget Sound Valley. Situated between the coastal range and the Cascades, this valley—with its rich soil, abundant rainfall, and favorable climate—attracted thousands of pioneer farmers during the 1840's and 1850's. North of the Columbia River the valley was heavily forested. Early settlers avoided this region, for clearing the land was an arduous and expensive task, and the heavy rains had long ago washed away the enriching potash and lime from the gravelly soil.

To the east of the Willamette-Puget Sound Valley and the Cascades is the Columbia River Basin. This plateau-basin of lava formation, which embraces the greater part of the central portions of the present states of Washington and Oregon, has a rich soil. Rainfall is so scanty that leaching—the washing away of minerals which is so ruinous

* The Great American Desert has many names. Northeast of Los Angeles it is called the Mohave Desert; northeast of Yuma, Arizona, the Colorado Desert; west of Yuma, the San Bernardino Desert; east of Yuma, the Arizona Desert; east of the Gulf of California, the Sonora Desert. Lower California is geographically part of this desert.

to soils of a similar character—does not occur. At the mouth of the
Snake River—the lower part of the basin—the rainfall averages only six
inches, and over much of the remainder of the area it is less than ten.
On the other hand, great storms blowing in from the Pacific during
the winter and spring months prevent the region from becoming a
desert. Despite these storms, much of the area does not get rain enough
even for wheat; unless irrigated, it is fit only for grazing and dry
farming.

In the mountainous and desert regions of the West were immensely valuable mineral resources, including vast stores of gold, silver,
copper, iron, lead, quicksilver, zinc, nickel, salt, coal, and petroleum.
Rarer metals, although possessing a more limited value, were also
plentiful, including platinum, osmium, iridium, arsenic, antimony, and
bismuth. In what is now Colorado and in adjoining states were great
stretches of oil-bearing shales capable of producing millions of barrels
of oil, and practically all of the mountain ranges contained large quantities of granite, sienite, and marble. Limestones, slates, and sandstones
of every shade were also plentiful.

A considerable portion of the trans-Mississippi West was treeless,
but certain parts of the region contained extremely valuable stands of
timber. Minnesota had extensive forests of white pine and a scattering
of harder woods. In the Northwest—western Montana, Idaho, Washington, and Oregon—were great forests of fir, spruce, cedar, and pine.
In northern California and on either side of the state's great central
valley grew unsurpassed forests of redwood, yellow pine, and Douglas
spruce. South of the Oregon Trail, the Osage Mountains, the plateau
region of northwestern Arkansas and southwestern Missouri, and a
narrow elongated strip in western Texas were the only important
forest areas, and these produced a great variety of hardwoods. The
mountains of Utah, Arizona, Colorado, and New Mexico were also
partially covered with pine and spruce.

Much of the West is either arid or semiarid, but some parts of it
have ample supplies of water. Because of the heavy rainfall and deep
snow fields of the Northwest, Oregon, Washington, and northern
California have water supplies that are exceeded only by those of the
Congo Basin in Africa. Without the water of the numerous streams of
the Sierras, all southern California would be barren; and without the
waters of the Colorado, the Gila, the Salt, the San Juan, and the Green,
all of the "Great American Desert" would be another Sahara. Similarly, the Arkansas, the North and South Platte, the Yellowstone, and
the Missouri furnish enough water to make life possible on the semi-
arid plains east of the Rockies.

Given this great diversity of soil and climate in the Far West, a region of numerous possibilities for exploitation awaited Americans after the guns of Civil War were stilled.

The Last Stand of the First Americans

Between the raw abundance of the last frontier and its successful exploitation there lay the resistance of nature and of the "redman." On the eve of the Civil War, there were approximately 320,000 Indians in the United States. About 50,000 lived on the Pacific coast proper, and from 225,000 to 240,000 inhabited either the plains or the inter-mountain valleys and plateaus between the Rockies and the Pacific coast ranges. The nearly 70,000 northern Plains Indians included four important nations: the Sioux, Crow, northern Cheyenne, and Arapaho. Of these, the Crow alone were friendly to the whites. The 90,000 Indians who belonged to the southern Plains tribes were members of either the pacific and semicivilized Cherokees, Creeks, and Choctaws— all of whom had been removed from the East before the Civil War— or the militant Kiowas, Comanches, southern Cheyenne, and southern Arapahoes. In the intermountain region between the Rockies and the Sierras were the Nez Percés, Utes, Bannocks, and Shoshones.

The Plains Indians—except for those transferred from the East— were nomads who did no farming and were almost wholly dependent on the buffalo for their food, shelter, and clothing. Given the white man's desire for buffalo hides, his discovery of the great buffalo herds of the West was to lead to a tragedy that was epic in its proportions. In the buffalo hunt and in other respects possession and complete mastery of the horse made the Plains Indians superior to all other tribes as hunters, warriors, and thieves. The equipment for the hunt and the warpath consisted of a spear, knife, bow, and quiver of arrows. A shield made of smoked buffalo-hide hardened with glue from the hoofs gave these Indians—the most formidable warriors on the American continent—effective protection in battle.

Intermittent warfare had characterized relations between the Plains tribesmen and the advancing whites in the decade before the Civil War. In 1862, 1,300 Sioux warriors went on the warpath and the great strug- gle between white men and Indians broke out again. Led by Little Crow, the Sioux raided the outlying settlements in the Minnesota River region, killing more than 700 men, women, and children and destroying homes and other buildings. To the south, the central group of Arapaho and Cheyenne had been crowded onto a small, barren tract of land in southeastern Colorado, and in vengeance made a series of sporadic at-

"The Scalped Hunter" (Harper's Weekly, *1869*)

tacks on scattered farms, ranches, and stagecoaches. Encouraged by the lack of opposition, the Cheyenne launched a full-scale offensive in 1864. They swooped down on Ben Holladay's stage and freight line east of Denver and soon left trails of blood and pillage from eastern Colorado to western Kansas and Nebraska. Within a short time, every ranch but one along 370 miles of Holladay's route was deserted.

The westerners' solution to what they called the "Indian problem" was simple—annihilation. In a proclamation to the citizens of Colorado, Governor John Evans stated that any man who killed a hostile Indian was a patriot; and the *Rocky Mountain News* undoubtedly spoke for most of its readers when it wrote that "a few months of active extermination against the red devils will bring quiet and nothing else will." The military leaders conducting campaigns against the Indians had similar ideas. In November, 1864, Colonel J. M. Chivington, a preacher and a former missionary among the Indians, led nearly a thousand Colorado volunteers against 500 or 600 sleeping Cheyenne and Arapaho Indians who had encamped on Sand Creek under the impression that they were under the protection of the United States. The Indians, mostly women and children, were slaughtered with sickening barbarities. Easterners were shocked by the news of the Sand Creek massacre and demanded a congressional investigation. But in the West Chivington was a hero.

Although there was a lull in hostilities after the Sand Creek massacre, even greater warfare soon followed. The Apache, Kiowa, Comanche, Arapaho, and Cheyenne, forced to give up their last bit of land in the Sand Creek reservation, spread terror over the region south of the Arkansas River. In the central and north Plains country the Indians went on the warpath. From Denver to the Missouri, they repeatedly raided the Platte route, cut telegraph lines, captured trains, and killed men and women. Hurried appeals to the federal government for protection brought additional troops fresh from the Civil War, and by the end of 1865, 25,000 soldiers were in the field patrolling every part of the frontier from Minnesota and Dakota to New Mexico and Arizona. They kept open the great central and southwestern routes, protected two thousand miles of the navigable Missouri above Kansas City, kept the overland telegraph from Omaha to Carson Valley uncut, and safeguarded the lives and property of the emigrants moving into the trans-Mississippi West.

Military protection for the West came at a high price. James Harlan, Secretary of the Interior, estimated that every regiment used against the Plains Indians cost the federal government $2,000,000 a year. Although by 1868 the soldiers had demonstrated that they could kill Indians, they were powerless to compel the tribes to abandon the warpath permanently. The prospect of endless slaughter at a cost of millions of dollars made the government give up temporarily its policy of extermination for peaceful negotiations. Some agreements were concluded with a few tribes, but no attempt was made to remove the causes of Indian hostility, and within a short time the tribes and the soldiers were again at war. For the next twenty years the Indians, led by such famous warriors as Sitting Bull, Geronimo, Red Cloud, Crazy Horse, and others, fought a courageous but losing campaign against American forces led by Generals Hancock, Miles, Custer, Sherman, and Sheridan.

The dreadful conflict to break the spirit of vigorous, if primitive, people lasted longer than it might have, not only because of the tenacity of the Indians, but also because of the incompetence of some army commanders and the friction that developed between the Departments of War and Interior. The Bureau of Indian Affairs, which had been placed under the War Department in 1832, was transferred to the Department of the Interior in 1849, and the two branches of the government were in constant conflict about their respective jurisdictions over the Indians. Officials of the Interior Department issued rifles and ammunition to Indians for hunting, but the weapons supplied to the tribesmen by the Department of the Interior after the Civil War were also used in fighting the armies sent out by the War Department. Frequently the equipment given the Indians was superior to that used by the soldiers.

What frontal military assault failed to do in pacifying the Plains Indians was accomplished by destruction of the basis of tribal economy, the buffalo. Buffalo meat, preserved by smoking, was the Indian's principal food. The buffalo also provided him with hides for clothing, shoes, tents, and blankets; its bones were fashioned into bows, knives, and hoes; its tendons supplied thread and bow strings; and its intestines were made into sausages and its lungs into water bags.

At the close of the Civil War, there were at least fifteen million buffalo in the trans-Mississippi West. Their range originally lay between the Canadian plains to the north and the Gulf of Mexico on the south, but the building of the Union Pacific, which was begun in 1865, separated them into northern and southern herds. As the demand for buffalo hides in the East increased, the westerners undertook the systematic destruction of the herds. The buffalo, slow in gait, clumsy in movements, and with poor eyesight, fell in droves before bullets from the long rifles used by the professional hunters, teamsters, construction workers, trappers, guides, and soldiers. Buffalo Bill (W. F. Cody) killed 4,280 buffalo in eighteen months, and Colonel R. I. Dodge estimated that 5,500,000 were shot from 1872 to 1874. By 1875, the southern herd had been practically annihilated, and buffalo skins were a glut on the market. Although the northern herd was smaller and more isolated, the opening of the Northern Pacific Railroad made its destruction merely a matter of time. Deprived of their means of subsistence and pursued by American soldiers, the Plains Indians were no longer able to resist the advance of white settlers, and by the late 1870's a pall of death and destruction hung over the once great hunting grounds.

While the Plains Indians were being compelled to relinquish their lands to the white settlers, the Pacific coast and Rocky Mountain Indians were being confined to small, isolated reservations. Within a year of the discovery of Sutter's gold in 1849, Californians were demanding that the coastal tribes be moved to the eastern slopes of the Cascade Mountains. Although the California legislature was opposed to granting any lands to the Indians, the federal government induced the tribes to emigrate to the interior. But the Indians found the region set aside for their use already occupied by miners and prospectors who refused to relinquish their claims. Treated at best as squatters on their own lands, thousands of Indians became mendicant hangers-on in the alleyways of a mushrooming civilization. Penniless, abused, and infected with diseases they had never known before, the coastal tribes were all but wiped out by the end of the 1850's.

The Indians of the plateaus were treated in much the same fashion as those on the coast. When settlers and miners entered Oregon in the decade before the Civil War, the principal tribes were forced onto reservations. In 1855, in return for a promise of annuities and supplies, they moved to a reservation in northern Idaho. In the early 1860's, miners entered this region, and the federal government now demanded that the Nez Percés, the most civilized of the tribes, sign a treaty providing for a reduction in the size of their reservation. When Chief Joseph refused to approve the government plan, the Indians had no alternative but to wage a war of self-preservation. Joseph was an extraordinarily able leader, but superior numbers finally forced him to yield. Eventually, he and his followers, who had dwindled pitifully to fewer than 500 were moved first to Fort Leavenworth, Kansas, and then to the Indian Territory (later Oklahoma), where more than half of them were killed by disease.

In the southern plateau region, the government met far less tractable opponents than the Plateau and Northwest Indians. The Apache offered particularly ruthless and stubborn resistance to white encroachment. The Apache were resourceful fighters who repeatedly demonstrated their determination to die rather than give up their lands. But in 1886, their great leader Geronimo and his entire band were captured and deported to Florida as prisoners of war. Subsequently, broken and abused, they were sent to Alabama and finally to Fort Sill, Oklahoma. With the exception of scattered uprisings in later years, the capture of Geronimo marked the end of the long series of Indian wars and the removal of the last sustained human resistance to the exploitation of the great West.

A National Indian Policy

While the Indian was engaged in a day-to-day struggle to maintain his way of life, his fate was being decided in Washington. For years the federal government had dealt with the tribes as independent nations, but in 1871, Congress abandoned this policy. Under the new program, the Indians were made pensioners of the government and were forced onto reservations where they were permitted to lead a modified tribal life. By 1885, practically the entire Indian population of the United States was confined within the boundaries of 171 reser-

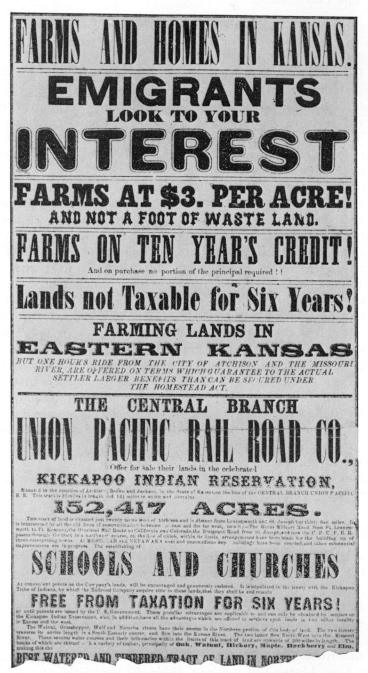

Pushing the Kickapoos Aside: The Union Pacific Sells Its Land Grant

[BAKER LIBRARY, HARVARD UNIVERSITY]

vations. Although, all told, these reservations covered an area as large as Texas, they were scattered in twenty-one states and territories, most of which were west of the Mississippi.

Life on the reservation brought the final degradation of the Indian. Contagious diseases impaired his health; government handouts undermined his self-reliance; and unscrupulous traders and agents often deprived him of what he had been guaranteed by law. There were only sporadic protests against these policies in the 1870's. In 1881, Helen Hunt Jackson published *A Century of Dishonor* and many Americans first learned the extent to which the Indian was being victimized. In the next year eastern humanitarians organized the Indian Rights Association and in 1883 founded the Lake Mohonk Conference of Friends of the Indians. Memorials demanding an improvement in conditions on the reservations were sent to Congress by the legislatures of Maine, Connecticut, New York, Pennsylvania, Delaware, and Michigan.

Some reform was obviously necessary, but there was little agreement on just what policy should be adopted. Should the old tribal organization be restored? Could an effort be made to make the Indian a full-fledged member of American society? The most prominent spokesman for the latter policy was Carl Schurz, who, after retiring from the Hayes cabinet, had become editor of the New York *Evening Post*. Arguing that the Indian question was a sociological rather than a military problem, and confident of the superiority of Anglo-Saxon institutions, Schurz recommended that the reservations be abandoned and that the Indian be taught to adopt the white man's civilization. Schurz's program, which was also advocated by E. A. Hoyt, Indian Commissioner under President Hayes, called for giving individual Indians tracts of land to cultivate and eventually making them citizens. The government showed little interest in these proposals and confined its efforts to providing minimal educational facilities for the Indians. By 1878, approximately 4,000 Indian children were attending government reservation schools. An attempt was also made to give the Indians instruction in the use of domestic animals and farm tools. In 1879, a young army officer, R. H. Pratt, obtained permission to open an Indian boarding school in the old army barracks at Carlisle, Pennsylvania, where he and his wife gave industrial training to Indian boys and girls and provided them with an opportunity to acquire the white man's technical standards.

In 1887, the Dawes General Allotment Act was the government's first serious attempt to translate Schurz's proposals into law. This measure, which was sponsored by Henry L. Dawes, a senator from

Massachusetts and a leading member of the Mohonk conference, authorized the president to end tribal government and to parcel out the lands of any reservation to individual owners. Each head of a family was to receive 160 acres, each single adult or orphan 80 acres, and each dependent 40 acres. The Indians who received land were to become American citizens, although they were denied the right to dispose of their holdings for twenty-five years. All reservation land not required for allotment to the Indians could be purchased by the government for sale to settlers, a provision that made the other proposals acceptable to many who were not directly concerned with the problems of the Indian. The money derived from these sales was to be held in a trust fund for educating the former tribesmen.

Those coveting even the reduced areas given the Indians under the old reservation policy were amply rewarded by the Dawes Act, for the division of lands under it added approximately four-fifths of the Indian soils to the public domain. The most popular territory released for settlement now comprises the state of Oklahoma. Even before this region was taken from the Indians, squatters had moved in and staked out their claims. Although these "sooners" or "boomers" were repeatedly driven off by army detachments, they invariably returned. In 1885—two years before the passage of the Dawes Act—President Arthur issued a proclamation opening up 500,000 acres of Creek and Winnebago territory in western Oklahoma, but Arthur's successor, President Cleveland, sent troops to drive out the settlers. Western Oklahoma was finally opened to homesteaders in 1889. Homeseekers and speculators rushed into the region to pre-empt farms, town sites, and water sites, and in a matter of weeks the prairies of Oklahoma had been staked out and settled. In the following year, Congress established the Territory of Oklahoma. 1890

The Dawes Act aided western homesteaders, but in practice it provided few benefits for the Indians. Allotments were sometimes made before the Indians were capable of assuming proper responsibility. On the other hand, the ambition of the more competent Indians was frequently blunted by the requirement that they could not sell for twenty-five years. The new citizens were often victimized by unscrupulous politicians, cattlemen, and land speculators. The Indian as a citizen now had the right to buy and drink hard liquor, and with his new right came a marked increase in drunkenness, crime, and immorality. In 1906, the Burke Act was passed to remedy what were considered the major defects of the earlier legislation. Citizenship was deferred until the end of the probationary twenty-five years except for those individuals who could demonstrate ability and competence.

The End of the Trail: Geromimo at the Wheel of a Pierce Arrow, 1907

[NATIONAL ARCHIVES]

But neither the Dawes nor the Burke Act solved the Indian problem. After thoughtlessly destroying the Indian's tribal life, the government, even with the best intentions, could not create an adequate new culture by fiat. Neither private property nor citizenship could compensate the Indian for the loss of his former way of life. The appointment of John Collier as Indian Commissioner during the first administration of President F. D. Roosevelt was an intelligent attempt to reverse traditional policy. Efforts to break up tribal culture were discontinued, and attention was directed to fostering tribal arts and handicrafts; but, whatever notable advances have been made since 1933, the Indian lingers on in American society as a marginal figure, a reminder of the price paid to secure the Far West for modern American life.

Some Americans looked on the final conquest of the Indians as the inevitable triumph of civilization over barbarism; others thought that it demonstrated nothing more than the ability of a powerful majority to destroy a weak minority. But, regardless of how contemporaries regarded the passing of the Indian, two facts remain: a culture that had existed for centuries had been wiped out in three decades, and the last frontier had been opened up to settlers.

The Mining Frontier: "Half Grab, Half Gamble"

Long before the final conquest of the Indians, the mining frontier had reached the Pacific coast. By 1880, more than 200,000 seekers of fortunes hidden in the earth had invaded the trans-Mississippi West. The California gold rush of 1849 had established a pattern that was to be repeated on countless occasions throughout the mountain regions of the Far West. With the announcement of each new discovery, thousands of prospectors rushed to the new diggings, claims were hurriedly staked out, towns were thrown together out of whatever material was at hand, and gamblers and prostitutes seemed to appear from nowhere. When the supply of metal in the region was exhausted, the cycle was completed: the miners and hangers-on moved to other camps, and only a ghost town remained to mark the advance of the mining frontier.

In the same year that gold was discovered in California—1849—a party of Georgians who were bound for the California fields found gold a short distance from the site of the present city of Denver, Colorado. But no move was made to exploit the Colorado deposits until 1858, when gold was again discovered in the Pikes Peak district. News of the new field spread rapidly throughout the East and the Mississippi Valley, and within a short time fortune hunters on foot, on horseback, or in prairie schooners marked "Pikes Peak or Bust" moved across the plains toward Colorado. Approximately 100,000 people passed through Nebraska in 1859 on their way to the Colorado gold fields, and in April of that year, William Tecumseh Sherman, who was living at Leavenworth, Kansas, described the great bustle of those leaving for the new fields, and then added: "Strange to say, even yet, although probably 25,000 people have actually gone, we are without authentic advices of gold."

As though to give substance to Sherman's foreboding, the Colorado mining boom ended almost before it began. Gold and other minerals were plentiful throughout the region, but they were imbedded in quartz rock and heavy machinery was required to reach and reduce them. Unable to afford equipment for this type of mining, the prospectors quickly became disillusioned. Some moved on to other camps; others settled on the fertile farming lands of the Platte Valley; and many returned home. As the would-be miners retraced their steps in wagons bearing the slogan "Busted by gosh" they met those on their way to the gold fields and quickly disabused them of their dreams of sudden wealth. The route far up the Platte to the Missouri was strewn with supplies that had been intended for use in the mining country, and it has been estimated that at least 50,000 prospective miners turned back before they reached Colorado. Before the Colorado fields could be exploited, new ways of working the refractory ore had to be discovered and sufficient corporate wealth had to be accumulated to make possible the large-scale investments that were needed. It was not until the mid-1880's, when the Guggenheim interests took over the Colorado mines, that the region was able to capitalize on its mineral resources. With the opening of the Cripple Creek district in the 1890's, Colorado finally became one of the nation's leading mining states.

Despite the early collapse of the mining boom in Colorado, several towns were established to provide for the needs of the new population. After four of the smaller villages had been combined to form Denver, the new town became the principal entrepot of the district. In 1860, it had a population of 5,000; five years later, the figure was 8,000, and Denver was doing an annual business of $10,000,000. In August, 1859, delegates from the Colorado mining camps organized the territory of Jefferson and set up a provisional government of "Rocky Mountain growth and manufacture." Two years later the name "Colorado" was substituted for "Jefferson." Although the number of miners in the territory declined, its farm population increased steadily, and in 1876 Colorado was admitted to the Union.

A few miners had worked further west than Colorado in the Washoe district of Nevada throughout the 1850's, but full-scale operations were not begun there until the closing years of the decade. The Comstock Lode in the Washoe area was one of the most famous and important "finds" in the history of the West. The lode was discovered by Ethan and Hosea Grosh and named after Henry Thomas Page Comstock, a visionary braggart known among his acquaintances as "a hell of a liar." As soon as news of the Comstock Lode reached the outer world, miners, gamblers, confidence men, and women "entertainers" converged on Nevada from all directions. By the fall of 1859, the mountain roads from California to the valley of the Carson were jammed with those bound for the Washoe. As during the California gold rush in 1849, people traveled in every way available—on horseback, by coach and wagon, and on foot; some trundled wheelbarrows before them; and one, Captain Richard Watkins, who had lost a leg in Nicaragua, went on crutches. More emigrants followed in 1860, and in a few months Washoe had more than 20,000 people. Carson City, just off the California trail, and Virginia City, on the site of the Comstock Lode, became the raw but vigorous centers of the new mining operations.

Despite its underground wealth, everything for daily life in the Washoe—food, clothes, drink, and machines—had to come over the Sierras from California. Salt was hauled in by camel; wood for buildings, fuel, flumes, shafts, drifts, and winches had to be freighted in from the outside; and the tree-lined shores of Lake Tahoe and the eastern slopes of the Sierras were quickly denuded. But these problems had little apparent effect on the region's prosperity, and Virginia City probably holds the all-time record for conspicuous consumption. The richest citizens lived in mansions costing as much as a half-million dollars. Ornate furniture, brick mansions, high-stepping horses, silver-trimmed coaches and harness were the hallmarks of the community's *nouveaux riches.* One social-climber had his horses shod with silver shoes and his bed equipped with a specially designed headboard that extended from the floor to the fourteen-foot ceiling of his bedroom. Like every self-respecting American community, Virginia City had a school, church, and theater; like every mining town, it also had its quota of iron-shuttered stores, hotels, restaurants, saloons, and gambling halls. Life in Virginia City was carried on in the midst of dense clouds of swirling smoke and alkali dust, while night and day background sound effects were provided by cursing teamsters, hissing steam, thundering machinery, and whining bullets.

The Nevada mines, like those of Colorado, required a large outlay of capital for successful operation. Prospectors, lacking both the equipment and capital to develop their claims, were compelled to sell out to huge corporations. Comstock, for example, sold his claim in the lode that bears his name for $11,000, or a fraction of its actual value. The firms that took over Nevada's mines both spent and made large sums of money on their operations. Enormous profits were also made from speculations in mining stocks. The shares of the California Company, for example, rose from $37 in September, 1874, to $780 in January, 1875, and those of the Sierra Nevada went from $4 to $275 in eight months. The Federal Commissioner of Mining Statistics, in describing the security manipulations of the companies in the Washoe district, wrote: "It would confirm the mischievous feeling that mining is half grab and half gamble; that the only way to make money at it is to dig out what rich ore you can get and then find a fool to buy the property; or failing that to make a fool of that collective individual, the public, and to 'unload' yourself of your stock." But Washoe's mineral supplies were not inexhaustible, and by 1880, the bonanza days were only a memory. In that year, Nevada's mining stocks, which had been valued at more than $393,000,000 in 1875, were worth less than $7,000,000.

Nevada attained statehood in 1864, but economically it was little more than a colony of California throughout the early years of its history. Its mining population came from California, and Californians organized and controlled most of its companies, financed its corporations, manipulated the corporation stocks, and pocketed the profits. Topography, mineral resources, and proximity to California all combined to prevent Nevada from developing into a stable community with a diversified and expanding economy.

As in Colorado and Nevada, the mining frontier conformed to the established pattern of discovery, boom, and bust in most places in the West where precious metals were found. In the 1850's and 1860's, there were "rushes" to what is now northeastern Washington, along the Fraser River in Canada, to the Boise district of Idaho, along the Great Divide between Idaho and Montana, and in New Mexico and Arizona. Largely because of the increased population from mining operations, the territories of Arizona (1863), Idaho (1863), Montana (1864), and Wyoming (1868) were organized by the federal government. Cities with familiar names like Coeur d'Alene, Virginia City, and Helena grew rapidly in size and corruption. In Montana by 1876, placer mines had yielded $150,000,000 in gold, and as late as 1884 a contractor who was excavating for the foundation of the Montana National Bank in Helena was willing to accept the gold-bearing gravel that he dug out of the site as payment for his services.

Gold was not the only valuable mineral in Montana; there were also rich deposits of silver, copper, antimony, arsenic, and manganese, and when the profits from placer mining began to decline in the mid-1870's, the first large-scale attempts were made to exploit the region's other mineral resources. Within a short time, a few big corporations monopolized mining in Montana. Prominent in the development of these new ores were Marcus Daly and William A. Clark. Daly, the founder of the famous Anaconda Copper Mining Company, also owned valuable coal mines and extensive timber stands. He organized banks, built power plants, started irrigation systems, and established Montana's leading newspaper. Clark controlled a number of mines in the vicinity of Butte and was the head of the Colorado and Montana Smelting Company.

The early Montana towns and the mining camps of Arizona and New Mexico, where gold and silver production soon gave way to copper mining, were as lawless as any in the United States. Raphael Pumpelly, who was the only one of five successive managers of a Tubac silver mine not to be killed by either Mexicans or Indians, left a description of life on the mining frontier that confirms the terrible tales about the opening of the Far West. He wrote:

Off to the Diggings in New Mexico

[LABORATORY OF ANTHROPOLOGY, MUSEUM OF NEW MEXICO]

Law was unknown and the nearest court was several hundred miles distant in New Mexico. Indeed, every man took the law into his own hands, and a man's life depended upon his own armed vigilance and prudence, and mainly on the fact that public opinion was the only code of laws, and a citizen's popularity the measure of his safety. In a society composed to a great extent of men guilty of murder and every other crime, popularity was not likely to attach to the better class of citizens. The immediate result of the condition of public opinion was to blunt ideas of right and wrong in the minds of newcomers, who, suddenly freed from the restraints of the East, soon learned to justify the taking of life on trifling pretexts, or even to destroy it for the sake of bravado. Murder was the order of the day; it was committed by Americans upon

Americans, Mexicans and Indians; by Mexicans upon Americans; and the hand of the Apache was, not without reason, against both of the intruding races.

The gold rush in the Black Hills of South Dakota, which began in the middle 1870's differed little from those that had preceded it in other parts of the West, but it did make a chapter of history that provided future generations with the vicarious thrill of reliving, with great safety and comfort, the most memorable days of American frontier individualism.

As in other areas, the individual miner in South Dakota soon gave way to the large corporation, and by 1880, the richest claims had been taken over by the Homestake Mining Company, a $10,000,000 corporation that dominated the economic life of the region. The character of the population was the same as that of the other mining camps, but the names of the folk heroes—in this instance, Wild Bill Hickok and Calamity Jane—were different. Deadwood was the area's leading community. Its dance halls, saloons, barrooms, gambling joints, prostitutes, and gunmen were in all essential respects replicas of Virginia City. Like its model, it was completely dependent on the outside world. Before the railroad, supplies were brought in by ox teams, and the output of the mines was sent out by stagecoach to either Cheyenne or Bismarck. The steel-lined, heavily guarded coach of Wells, Fargo and Company, which pulled out of Deadwood twice a month, transported $60,000,000 of gold without a loss. It was never even in apparent danger. But years later Buffalo Bill Cody made an attack on the Deadwood coach the most spectacular feature of his Wild West Show and thereby caught more of the essence of Deadwood and the Wild West than is implied in the fact that the Deadwood coach was never actually robbed.

The Rise of the Cattle Kingdom

Treeless, semiarid, and lacking navigable rivers, the Great Plains between the ninety-eighth meridian and the foothills of the Rockies were viewed by most Americans before the Civil War as a barren wasteland that could serve no other function than to provide a broad and level—although frequently hazardous—highway to the mining centers in the mountainous districts or the fertile and humid regions of the Pacific coast. As late as 1868, the Commissioner of the General Land Office wrote that "this belt of country is an obstacle to the progress of the nation's growth—or impediment to the prosperity of the new communities west of it, in not yielding that sustenance for increasing population." But the Plains, although offering few attractions to settlers, were ideally suited for grazing stock, and within a short time the entire area had become a cattle kingdom.

The cattle empire originated in southern Texas. Before the Texas revolution, Mexican rancheros maintained herds of Spanish stock, but when Texas gained its independence, the Mexicans were driven out and Americans took over both the land and the stock. Because of inadequate transportation, the Texans were unable to market the cattle, and in the ensuing years the stock ran wild and multiplied with amazing rapidity. From 1830 to 1860, the number of Texas longhorns increased 330 per cent, and in the next decade it rose 1,070 per cent. In the same period, herds were being formed in the northern range country to satisfy the demands of emigrants, freighters, miners, soldiers, and railroad workers. Horace Greeley, on his way to Salt Lake City in 1859, found "several old mountaineers, who have large herds of cattle which they are rapidly increasing by a lucrative trade with the emigrants, who are compelled to exchange their tired, gaunt oxen and steers for fresh ones on almost any terms."

By 1876, the cattle herds had spread over western Texas, Oklahoma, Kansas, Nebraska, Montana, Wyoming, the Dakotas, Colorado, and parts of Utah, Nevada, and New Mexico. The rapid expansion of the western cattle industry was made possible by the extension of the nation's railroad system to the Great Plains in order to nourish the growing industry and cities in the East which had created an enormous demand for meat products at record prices. At the end of the Civil War, the Texans controlled the largest herds in America and were the first to take advantage of these developments. In 1866, not realizing that they were creating one of America's most famous folk tales, they rounded up their long-neglected and semiwild stock and headed north. Crossing the Red River with approximately 260,000 head of cattle, they pushed on to Fort Worth and Denison and then proceeded either by way of Arkansas to Sedalia on the Missouri Pacific Railroad or through the Indian Territory into southeastern Kansas. From the outset, the Texans encountered unexpected difficulties. Because much of the country through which they drove their cattle was rough and timbered, the stock frequently became unmanageable. Farmers along the route sought to prevent the passage of the herds across their lands and complained bitterly that the longhorns were damaging their crops and infecting their own cattle with Texas or Spanish fever. In the Indian Territory, both Indians and outlaws were a constant menace. A contemporary wrote:

A . . . scheme of the milder-mannered of these scoundrels to plunder the cattlemen was that of stampeding a herd at night. This was easily done, and having been done the rogues next morning would collect as many of the scattered cattle as they could, secrete them in an out-of-way place,—much of the country being hilly and timbered—and then hunt up the owner and offer to help him, for an acceptable money consideration per head, in recovering his lost property. If the drover agreed to pay a price high enough to satisfy the pirates, they next day would return with many, if not all, of the missing cattle; but if not, the hold-ups would keep them, and later take them to the market and pocket the entire proceeds.

Although only a small proportion of the cattle driven north in 1866 ever reached market, the Texans realized that they had solved their principal problem and that the only question remaining was the selection of a more suitable route. At this point, the Texans were unexpectedly aided by J. G. McCoy, an Illinois livestock dealer, who for some years had sought to find a convenient entrepôt for the buyers and the cattlemen. "The plan," McCoy later wrote, "was to establish at some accessible point a depot or market to which a Texan drover could bring his stock unmolested, and there, failing to find a buyer, he could go upon the public highways to any market in the country he wished. In short, it was to establish a market whereat the Southern drover and Northern buyer would meet upon an equal footing, and both be undisturbed by mobs or swindling thieves." McCoy took his proposals to a number of western railroad executives, but they considered his plan impractical. Finally, the general freight agent of the Hannibal and St. Joe agreed to grant favorable rates from the Missouri River to Chicago. McCoy then selected Abilene, a frontier settlement on the Kansas Pacific, as his base of operations and sent out word to the drovers that there was a market place for their cattle. Abilene was the ideal cowtown. The surrounding country was unsettled, well watered, treeless, level, and covered with a rich growth of grass. From Abilene cattle could be shipped directly to Chicago by the Kansas Pacific and Hannibal and St. Joe railroads.

The selection of Abilene as a market revolutionized the western cattle industry. Crossing the Red River fifty miles to the west of the 1866 route, the now eager Texans were able to drive their cattle without difficulty along the Chisholm Trail to Abilene. As farmers moved into western Kansas, however, new trails to the West had to be developed. Of the other trails, the most important were the Dodge City route, which extended from the vicinity of Laredo, Texas, through Dodge City to Ogallala, a Nebraska town on the Union Pacific; and the Pecos, or Goodnight, Trail which ran from Central Texas to New Mexico and then on to Colorado and Wyoming. When east-west railroads—notably the Northern Pacific and the Canadian Pacific—were built in the Northwest, the western cattle trails were lengthened to Miles City and Glendive in Montana, and to Moosejaw in Sasketchewan. From 1860 to 1880, nearly 4,250,000 cattle went north over these trails to the meat-packing centers of the East and the upper range-country of the Great Plains. An even larger number went west to the ranges of New Mexico, Arizona, and other mountain states.

All the cattle reaching the cow towns did not go promptly to the slaughterhouses. Instead many were sold to Northern feeders who fattened them on the grasses of the public domain before shipping them to Omaha, Kansas City, or Chicago. As the cattle business developed, Texas growers found it to their advantage to give more attention to breeding. The more prolific females were sired with imported bulls; scrub bulls were weeded out; and eventually the original rangy, muscular longhorn was supplanted by an improved meat animal.

Although cattle had been raised in America from the time of the first settlements on the Atlantic seaboard, it was not until the development of the cattle kingdom that the industry assumed its modern economic and social organization. Since the cattle were permitted to roam the Plains at will, grass and water were shared by all on a communal basis. The age-old device of the brand that served to identify the cattle's owners was the only evidence that the business was conducted on a private rather than co-operative basis. Each year, spring and autumn roundups permitted the owners to reassert their property rights and to brand the calves that had been born during the preceding winter or summer. At the spring roundup, selections were made for the long drive to the north. Cowboys conducted every phase of these operations. Romanticized in song and fiction, they were in actuality skilled craftsmen who practiced an arduous and highly specialized trade. Most of their work was dull rather than colorful, and most of their tasks were monotonous rather than spectacular. The essential drabness of their lives was relieved by the dance halls, saloons, and gambling casinos of the nearest cow-town. Like the mining camp, the cow-town was distinguished by the rough and raucous life of its citizens and the numbers of them who met violent deaths. In Dodge City, the "Cowboy's Capital," twenty-five men were killed in the first year of the town's existence. Outlaws were known so well by nicknames that their real names were forgotten, and the town's citizens, who called their cemetery "Boot Hill," were the first people to use the word "stiff" as a noun.

Cattle raising, which was a highly speculative enterprise, was made even more hazardous by many conditions over which the cattlemen had relatively little control. In some areas large flocks of sheep destroyed the range grass and tainted the water. There was always the danger that Spanish or Mexican fever would infect the herds. As the size of the herds increased and as homesteaders, or "nesters," moved on to the Great Plains, the ranchers found it increasingly difficult to maintain the open range. Finally, the herds were always menaced by cattle thieves. Many Indians and professional bad men—among whom were Sam Bass, Billy the Kid, Bullwhack Jones, and Scarface Ike—were proficient rustlers, and the cowboys were constantly stealing from their employers.

Neither the federal government nor local authorities were able to enforce law and order on the public domain, and the cattlemen quickly learned that they would have to form their own quasi-official organizations to safeguard their interests. As early as 1868, small groups of Texas owners had established protective associations to be followed very soon after by similar societies throughout the cattle-lands. The very competitiveness and individualism of the West, paradoxically, thus forced westerners to adopt collective efforts to save their individual interests. The purposes of the various associations, in the words of the president of a Montana organization, were complex, but above all aimed

> . . . to establish a system that allows each individual stock grower to retain all the rights and privileges he now enjoys, and add to those privileges a system that will not only compel but encourage and even pay men to be honest; . . . a system that is more democratic in its broadest sense, not only doing the greatest good to the greatest number but one that will result in great benefits to every stock grower; . . . a system that resolves stock growers into a protective force and pays them to look after the interests of one another, inasmuch as our interests are identical.

The various stockmen's associations were able to produce a semblance of order in what was an essentially chaotic industry. They established range detective forces that put a careful watch on strangers —especially drifting cowboys—and cowboys with a bad record were blacklisted. They supervised roundups and investigated complaints immediately. They inspected brands at loading and marketing points, withheld cattle with altered brands from shipment, and returned them to their rightful owners. Those they accused of wrongdoing were prosecuted. The stockgrowers' associations were also responsible for both state and federal legislation to protect cattle from disease, and the creation of the Bureau of Animal Husbandry in the federal Department of Agriculture was the direct result of their agitation. But, with all these achievements and powers, the associations did not have the ability to save the cattle industry from the worst danger of all, the risks of an ever larger, ever more impersonal, ever more distant market.

Boom and Bust in the Cattle Industry

Because of its dependence on the eastern market, the cattle kingdom was particularly sensitive to fluctuations in the business cycle. Even before the depression of the mid-70's, the cattle industry on the western plains began to fall off. The Texas drive of 1871, which was the greatest in history, coincided with a decline in the demand for meat products and a rise in rail rates. Many drovers were unable to find buyers, and approximately half the cattle brought from Texas had to be wintered at a loss on the Kansas plains. During 1872, the situation grew steadily worse, and the panic of the following year forced many cattlemen into bankruptcy. But on the Plains, as in the rest of the country, the depression eventually gave way to good times. By 1878, the worst was over, and for the next seven years the cattle kingdom had its biggest—and last—boom. In 1883, steers on the Texas plains brought prices running from $35 to $50 a head, and beef cattle in the Chicago market sold for as high as $9.35 per hundredweight.

The boom of the early 1880's was in part the result of the extension of the cattle kingdom to the northern ranges and the consequent increase in demand for new stock for these areas. From 1881 to 1885, the demand for cattle for the northern ranges reached the limit of available supply, and the Texas producers could not fill the orders of the northern ranchmen. Colorado, with its ranges already overcrowded, sent thousands of cattle into the vacated Indian lands along the Yellowstone and the Big Horn rivers. Additional thousands of breeding stock and young steers came from the farms of Illinois, Wisconsin, Michigan, Iowa, and Missouri. Finally, carload after carload of "pilgrims," "states" cattle, or "barnyard" stock was brought in from the eastern states, and during 1882–4 as many cattle were shipped west as east. This influx of cattle transformed the northern range country. Granville Stuart, in *Forty Years on the Frontier*, wrote:

It would be impossible to make people not present on the Montana cattle ranges realize the rapid changes that took place on those ranges in two years. In 1880 the country was practically uninhabited. One could travel for miles without seeing so much as a trapper's bivouac. Thousands of buffalo darkened the rolling plains. There were deer, elk, wolves, and coyotes on every hill and in every ravine and thicket. In the whole territory of Montana there were but 250,000 head of cattle, including dairy cattle and work oxen.

In the fall of 1883 there was not a buffalo remaining on the range, and the antelope, elk, and deer were indeed scarce. In 1880 no one had heard tell of a cowboy in this "niche of the woods" and Charlie Russell had made no pictures of them; but in the fall of 1883 there were 600,000 head of cattle on the range. The cowboy . . . had become an institution.

The rapid growth of the cattle industry in these years can also be attributed to the extension of the nation's railroad system to the west and southwest. By the 1880's Texas had been linked to the North and East by several major railroad lines, which made it possible to ship cattle direct from the Texas range to the great Mississippi Valley slaughtering and packing centers. Texas cattle could also be sent by other rail routes to the northern ranges through Denver and Cheyenne.

The cattle boom was sustained by the willingness of easterners and Europeans to believe that the "boundless, gateless, fenceless pastures" of the Plains offered an easy and unprecedented opportunity to get rich quick. The land was apparently free; the initial capital outlay was relatively small; and the chances for profits presumably limitless. These views, while having some basis in fact, were also the products of an extensive propaganda campaign to publicize the cow country. Territorial legislatures voted large sums for pamphlets describing the grazing lands of the West. Newspapers in the East and in England and Scotland printed letters from stockgrowers, accounts of observers who had visited the cattle country, excerpts from the prospectuses of newly organized companies, and market reports on the movement, condition, and prices of range cattle. In the western press the cattle business was described exclusively in superlatives. The *Colorado Live Stock Record* wrote that cattle was "one of those investments which men cannot pay too much for, since, if left alone, they will multiply, replenish and grow out of a bad bargain." And an exchange from the *Breeders' Gazette* of September 1883 stated, "That is all there is of the problem and that is

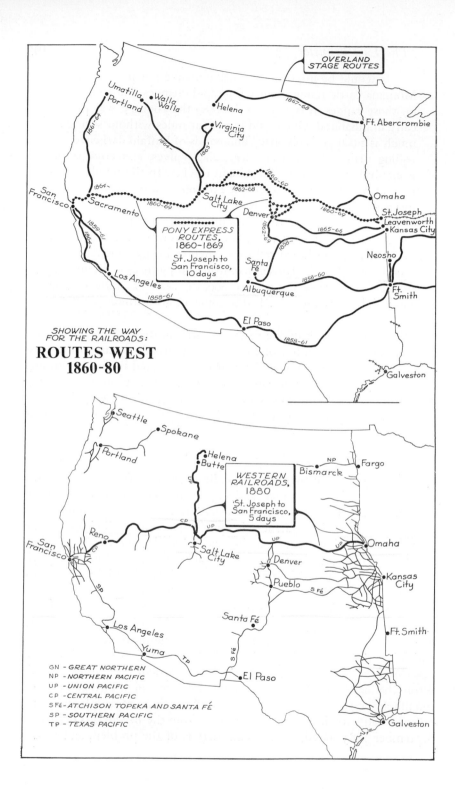

OVERLAND
STAGE ROUTES

PONY EXPRESS
ROUTES,
1860–1869

St. Joseph to
San Francisco,
10 days

SHOWING THE WAY
FOR THE RAILROADS:

ROUTES WEST
1860-80

WESTERN
RAILROADS,
1880

St. Joseph to
San Francisco,
5 days

GN – GREAT NORTHERN
NP – NORTHERN PACIFIC
UP – UNION PACIFIC
CP – CENTRAL PACIFIC
SFé – ATCHISON TOPEKA AND SANTA FÉ
SP – SOUTHERN PACIFIC
TP – TEXAS PACIFIC

why our cattlemen grow rich," after explaining how easily a $5,000 investment grew to a net profit of $35,000 to $40,000 in four years.

As tales of sudden riches on the Plains reached the East and Europe, capital flowed to the range country in unprecedented amounts. In 1883, twenty companies with a total capitalization of more than $12,000,000 were incorporated under the territorial laws of Wyoming. Many of these enterprises were backed by foreign capital; and in England, according to a contemporary observer, "drawing rooms buzzed with the stories of this last of bonanzas; staid old gentlemen, who scarcely knew the difference between a steer and a heifer, discussed it over their port and nuts." By 1882, there were almost a dozen English and Scottish cattle companies in the United States.

Newcomers from the East and Europe, who knew little or nothing about stock raising, flocked into the cattle country. Legitimate business gave way to speculation, and the cow-towns were converted into miniature Wall Streets. Many companies were overcapitalized. Paper corporations with nothing but well-written prospectuses sold attractive stock certificates to gullible buyers at outrageous prices. In August, 1882, the *Laramie Boomerang* wrote: "Millions are talked of as lightly as nickels and all kinds of people are dabbling in steers. . . . A Cheyenne man who don't pretend to know a maverick from a mandamus has made a neat little margin of $15,000 this summer in small transactions and hasn't seen a cow yet that he has bought and sold."

By the mideighties the ranges were overcrowded, the market was glutted, and the inflated price structure of the cattle industry had collapsed. The boom had turned into a bust, and before the cattlemen had a chance to recover from the depression, they were overwhelmed by a series of natural disasters. The winter of 1885–6 was unusually severe. Blizzards and low temperatures killed 85 per cent of the herds of western Kansas, Colorado, and the Texas Panhandle. A hot, dry summer, followed by a winter that was even more severe than that of 1885–6, completed the damage. In the spring of 1887 the coulees and aspen and cottonwood groves were filled with dead cattle, and all that was left of the great herds were some emaciated animals so weak that they were scarcely able to move.

The bad weather and the cycle of boom and bust marked the beginning of the end of the open range. From then on, pastures were fenced in, scrub stock was replaced with a better grade of beef cattle, ranchers began to grow hay and other forage crops to feed the cattle during the winter, and wells and windmills were used to secure an adequate supply of water for the animals. By careful management and scientific methods, the western cattle industry managed to survive—

although on a considerably reduced scale—but the passing of the open range signalized the downfall of the cattle kingdom.

The Farmers' Frontier

To many western cattlemen the greatest enemy was not a capricious nature or the uncertain business cycle but the westward advancing farmers. Even before the boom of the eighties, the homesteaders had driven most of the ranchers out of Kansas and staked out claims in many other parts of the cow country. Relentlessly pushing on to land that the cattleman had come to look upon as his own, the "nester" cut up the open range by fencing his land or by plowing a furrow around its margin. As the ranges became more crowded, the cattlemen made every effort to drive out or exclude the homesteaders. Stock growers' associations issued manifestoes and posted notices warning off newcomers. At the same time, many cattlemen illegally enclosed great tracts of the public domain or acquired vast stretches of land through the use of dummy entrymen and false swearing. Private wars, ruthless vigilantes, and deliberate murder, fire, and theft were not successful dissuaders; still the farmers came, and it was only a matter of time before the cattlemen were forced to admit defeat.

For some years the farmer was at a disadvantage in the fight with the cattleman because of his inability to find suitable fencing material. In the East the settler had used either stones or wood for fences, but on the Plains, where a homesteader's very livelihood depended on his ability to prevent the cattle from destroying his crops, both were lacking. Some farmers, thinking that the problem could be solved by importing wood from forested regions, soon found that the cost made this plan impractical. For a time it was believed that hedges would be a suitable substitute for fences, and throughout the West farmers experimented with them. But hedges in most instances were not strong enough to hold off the cattle.

In 1874, three Illinois farmers took out separate patents for barbed wire. Barbed-wire fences could not be broken down by cattle, did not shade the crops, and were relatively cheap to construct. Although barbed wire was at first looked on with suspicion by both middlemen and farmers, its advantages were so obvious that it was soon selling as fast as it could be manufactured. By 1880, American factories were producing 40,000 tons of barbed wire annually; a decade later, output had trebled and the cost to the consumer had dropped from $10 per 100 pounds to $3.45.

The introduction of barbed wire brought open warfare between

Keeping the Nebraska Range Open

the cattlemen and the farmer. The West was divided into "fence men" and "no-fence men." Ranchers cut the fences as quickly as the homesteaders built them, and on numerous occasions both sides tried to settle their differences with guns. But, however much the cattlemen might wish that the "man who invented barbed wire had it all around him in a ball and the ball rolled into hell," they were fighting a losing battle. Barbed wire had come to stay, and its triumph marked the end of the open range. More than anything else, barbed wire was responsible for the successful advance of the farmer's frontier on the Great Plains. Some years after the cattlemen had gone down to their final defeat, an old trail driver wrote:

> . . . These fellows from Ohio, Indiana, and other northern and western states—the "bone and sinew of the country," as politicians call them—have made farms, enclosed pastures, and fenced in water holes until you can't rest; and I say D——n such bone and sinew! They are the ruin of the country, and have everlastingly, eternally, now and forever, destroyed the best grazing-land in the world.

In their efforts to settle in the Plains country, farmers were frequently impeded rather than assisted by the federal Pre-emption and

Homestead Acts. Both of these were designed to meet the needs of the pioneer in the forested and humid areas, but they proved altogether inadequate on the Last Frontier. The settler on the treeless level prairies found that the 160 acres granted him by the government were not sufficient to permit him to practice the large-scale agriculture for which the region was ideally suited, while the homesteader in the arid and semi-arid sections was not even able to sustain life on the relatively small plot that he was allotted under the existing land laws. Irrigation might have made some of the arid lands productive, but in most instances the cost of irrigation was prohibitive. One authority on the history of public land policies has concluded that the "great weakness of the Homestead Act" was

> . . . its utter inadaptability to the parts of the country for which it was not designed. The idea of the farm small in acres within the semi-arid regions was tenacious but untenable. It was even vicious in its operation. Congress was converted to the homestead principle in the large, and instructed in detail, by the people on the Missouri River frontier, backed up by the experience of the whole country, not essentially different, between Ohio and the Missouri. The frontiersmen on the plains were too few in numbers, and too unlike the early frontiersmen to the East of them, to compel the working out of desirable modifications of the land laws.*

The provisions of the inadequate Homestead Law were frequently ignored by both cattlemen and farmers west of the ninety-eighth meridian. Repeated requests that its provisions be altered led Congress in 1873 to pass the Timber Culture Act. Under the terms of this act, any person receiving a homestead quarter-section could acquire an additional quarter-section by planting and maintaining forty acres of timber on it. The authors of the Timber Culture Act had assumed that if enough trees were planted, the arid West would have enough rainfall to permit its farmers to practice the same type of agriculture as in the humid sections of the country. But rain-making and tree-growing by legislative fiat proved farcical, and congressmen soon discovered that, like the Homestead Act, the law invited many abuses by men determined to gobble up most of the public domain. In 1891 the Timber Culture Act was repealed.

The Desert Land Act, passed by Congress in 1877, also failed to

---

* Benjamin Horace Hibbard: *A History of the Public Land Policies* (New York: The Macmillan Company, 1924), p. 409. Copyright 1924 by, and reprinted with the permission of, The Macmillan Company.

meet the needs of the westerners. This act, which applied to the Dakotas, Montana, Idaho, Wyoming, Utah, Nevada, Arizona, New Mexico, and the arid parts of California, Oregon, and Washington, permitted an individual to acquire 160 acres of desert land, not by homesteading, but by purchase at $1.25 an acre. Moreover, to hold his land the purchaser had to spend at least $3 an acre on improvements and to irrigate at least one eighth of it within three years. The bill's provisions for cash expenditures destroyed whatever effectiveness it might have had. Few settlers, except front men, could afford to buy these lands, and fewer still could afford to irrigate them. The sponsors of the measure also overlooked the fact that there were large areas in the West where irrigation was impossible. Congress's effort to legislate the farmers westward was no more successful in 1877 than it had been in 1873.

No attempt was made in federal land laws for the Plains settlers to take into account the difficulties inherent in farming in an arid or semiarid country. Cattlemen and farmers, both of whom had long recognized the problem, had sought to solve it by digging wells and erecting windmills. But water was so scarce and the obstacles so great that individuals could do little more than devise makeshift arrangements. Only a long-term plan, sponsored and executed by federal authorities, could make the Plains habitable. Moreover, many parts of the West were so lacking in moisture that there was no known way of making them capable of supporting either human or animal life. The first public official to recommend a comprehensive and integrated program for the arid areas of the West was Major John W. Powell, a government geologist. In his *Report on the Lands of the Arid Region of the United States*, which was submitted to the Secretary of the Interior in 1878, Powell proposed that these lands be classified into mineral, timber, coal, irrigable, and pasture lands, that rectangular surveys be abandoned, and that the homestead system be modified to fit the new environment. Although Powell's recommendations were incorporated into two bills that were presented to Congress, no action was ever taken on either measure. In 1894, the Carey Act turned the problem of irrigation over to the individual states. This plan, however, proved altogether unworkable, and in 1902, with the adoption of the Newlands, or Reclamation, Act, the federal government at last inaugurated a large-scale irrigation program. Although by 1920 approximately 20,000,000 acres of land were under irrigation, this represented a very small fraction of the arid regions.

The Census Bureau in its report for 1890 announced that it was no longer possible to determine the frontier line of population in the West; but this fact did not signify the end of free land in the area. By June of

1890, only 372,659 homestead entries—or an area less than that of the state of Nebraska—had been perfected. The amount of free homestead land deeded after 1890 was four times the amount deeded before that date, and an enormous acreage of untenanted lands was still in the hands of the railroads and land companies. As late as 1890, Ohio alone had more improved farm land and approximately half as many farms as the entire Far West.

Yet the comparatively slow advance of the farmers' frontier beyond the Mississippi should not obscure the fact that the West at the turn of the century bore little resemblance to the same region on the eve of the Civil War. In 1889, North and South Dakota, Montana, and Washington were admitted to the Union; the next year, Wyoming and Idaho became states; and within twenty years, the territories of Utah, Oklahoma, Arizona, and New Mexico were transformed into states. Between 1860 and 1900, the West lost its most distinctive features. The Indians and buffalo were driven from the Plains; the miner and prospector gave way to the giant corporation; open-range cattle were supplanted by breeded stock that were confined to fenced-in pastures; and the struggling homesteader was followed by the large-scale producer of grains. In the future, the West would be set off from the rest of the country, not so much by what it was, but by its memories of what it had been.

FOR SUPPLEMENTARY READING

Two general works on the Plains merit first attention. J. C. Malin's *The Grassland of North America* (1948) is a fine scholarly work, and W. P. Webb's *The Great Plains* (1931) is the classic attempt to define the special nature of the culture west of the ninety-eighth meridian. R. A. Billington, *Westward Expansion* (1949), treats most of the subjects covered in this chapter as part of the general history of the West. For a Turnerian view of the history of the Plains use F. L. Paxson, *The Last American Frontier* (1910). The region between the Rockies and the Pacific coast is studied in three books: O. O. Winther, *The Great Northwest* (1950); J. W. Caughey, *History of the Pacific Coast* (1933); and C. C. Rister, *The Greater Southwest* (1934).

Three works to start study on the Indians are J. C. Collier, *Indians of the Americas* (1947); A. Debo, *And Still the Waters Run* (1940);

and C. Wissler, *Indians of the United States* (1954). On the Indian Wars consult Stanley Vestal, *Warpath and Council Fire* (1948).

The exploitation of the western mines is the theme of the early work by W. J. Trimble, *The Mining Advance into the Inland Empire* (1914). The standard general history of mining is T. A. Rickard, *A History of American Mining* (2 vols., 1932). The most famous of the Western mines is the subject of G. D. Lyman, *The Saga of the Comstock Lode* (1934).

The cattle country is treated in various works. The most recent study is a generation old: L. Pelzer, *The Cattlemen's Frontier* (1936). E. S. Osgood, *The Day of the Cattleman* (1929), has a different interpretation. The best work on the cowboy is J. B. Frantz and J. E. Choate, Jr., *The American Cowboy* (1955). The classic original source on the cowboy is Andy Adams, *Log of a Cowboy* (1903). Two competitors of the cattlemen on the plains are described in E. N. Wentworth's *Shepherd's Empire* (1945) and F. A. Shannon's *The Farmer's Last Frontier* (1945). The control of crime and violence on the frontier has been treated in W. Gard, *Frontier Justice* (1949). On daily life on the farms of the great plains read E. Dick, *The Sod-House Frontier 1854–1890* (1937) and the novels of Ole Rölvaag, *Giants in the Earth* (1929), and Willa Cather, *O Pioneers* (1913). R. M. Robbins's *Our Landed Heritage* (1941) is a standard study of government land policies.

No book more effectively describes the conflicts between the various frontiers in one locale than J. K. Howard's *Montana High, Wide, and Handsome* (1943).

6

-≫≫-≫≫-≫≫-≫≫-≫≫-≫≫-≫≫-≫≫

The
Farming Business

T HE AMERICAN FARMER in the late nineteenth century was increasingly caught in a conflict between his ideal aims and the realities of commercial agriculture. Taking his inspiration from Thomas Jefferson and other writers who believed that America should be a society of yeomen farmers, the man of the soil drew a flattering portrait of himself. In comparison with the merchant, banker, and industrialist, he saw himself as a man who wished only to be permitted to make a living on the family farm and to be troubled by the larger world as little as possible. In fact, from the first generations of settlement in America, the American farmer had raised some crops for cash profit. Often he ruined his soil in his eagerness for money, and he was not above a little speculation in lands at the expense of his fellow farmers. As time passed, the gap widened between his wish to be considered a yeoman who was free of the taint of crass commercialism and the realities that gave him a market psychology and sharp acquisitive habits. Increasingly, as the demand for his produce grew when train and ship expanded the market available to him, he gave an ever larger part of his land and labor to raising commercial crops. He accumulated steadily rising debts, became more avid in his hopes for a "killing" as speculation in choice lands became more intense, and, in his haste for quick returns, failed to develop any techniques that would protect him against hard times brought on by nature or the vagaries of the market place to which he was tied.

During the years between the Civil War and World War I, the increasing use of machinery, the opening up of new agricultural areas, the changing character of the farmers' market, and the growth of specialization should have made agriculture a modern business enterprise. Instead, what remained of the self-sustaining farm community was destroyed, and the commercial farmer became ever more dependent on markets and suppliers beyond his control. His profits now were determined not only by the elements but also by freight rates, world supply and demand, and the state of the money market.

A World's Larder

During the second half of the nineteenth century, as western Europe—particularly England—turned from agriculture to manufacturing, the American farmer assumed more of the burden of feeding the Old World. At home, the growth in population and the rapid development of cities provided the farmer with a constantly expanding domestic market. There was, consequently, a spectacular rise in the number of American farms, the area of land under cultivation, the size of most of the major crops, and the application of machinery to agricultural production.

From 1860 to 1910, the number of farms in the United States trebled, going from approximately 2,000,000 to more than 6,000,000 units; the extent of cultivated land rose, in round numbers, from 163,000,000 to 347,000,000 acres; the 1,500,000 farm families increased to 6,123,610. The newer lands in the Middle and Far West had the most significant growth. The relatively cheap lands in the West attracted countless eastern farmers of some means and immigrant farmers. The population on farms and cities west of the Mississippi grew prodigiously. Although the immediate post-Civil War immigrant generally settled in eastern cities, large numbers also became farmers in the West. The census of 1880 revealed that from 50 to 75 per cent of the population of leading farm states had foreign parentage.

Only a relatively small percentage of these western settlers acquired their land under the Homestead Act. This law, enacted on May 20, 1862, awarded settlers in the public domain 160 acres of land if they had lived on their land for five years and had improved it. But the eastern laborer or tenant farmer who wished to take up land in the West received no help from the act. No provision was made for the cost of the trip or for the credit that the potential settler needed to

Nebraska Sod Dugout, 1892

[S. D. BUTCHER COLLECTION, NEBRASKA STATE HISTORICAL SOCIETY]

acquire draft animals and equipment. Moreover, in the arid and semi-arid lands between the 100th meridian and the Pacific coast, where after 1865 the great bulk of the area available for homesteading lay, the 160-acre unit was entirely too small for dry farming or grazing.

The Homestead Act, moreover, did not prevent land monopoly in the West. By making fraudulent entries or by taking advantage of the act's purchase and commutation clauses, foreign and domestic syndicates were able to purchase blocks of 100,000 acres or more. The greater part of the public domain thus went first to speculators, monopolists, and railroads and was then sold by these groups to actual settlers. Less than a sixth of the increased agricultural acreage between 1860 and 1900 was a direct gift from the government to homesteading farmers.

The best government lands had been pre-empted by the close of the century, but scattered public lands of inferior quality were still available. Despite allegations that the frontier had closed in 1890, more land was homesteaded in the decades after 1890 than in the years 1862–90. To facilitate the settlement of these remaining lands, Congress modified the Homestead Act. In 1904, the Kinkaid Act permitted the granting of 640-acre homesteads in western Nebraska, and in 1909 the Enlarged Homestead Act made it possible to acquire a 320-acre homestead in other states and territories. Finally, the Stock-Raising Homestead Act of 1916 authorized 640-acre homesteads in those areas classified as good only for grazing or forage.

Railroads and speculators, having acquired vast tracts of the public domain, made every effort to attract purchasers for their lands. Groups like the National Land Company conducted extensive advertising campaigns and established immigration centers in New York and other eastern cities. Western state governments, land companies, and railroad and steamship concerns used the same techniques in Europe. Many foreigners were thus lured to the American West in the hope of finding the new lease on life that generations before them had sought.

Machines, Men, and Markets

Before 1850, the American farmer used simple, inexpensive tools, many of which were manufactured at home. Despite innovations available to him, his land was turned with heavy and clumsy plows drawn by horses and oxen raised on the farm. The seed was sown by hand and harrowed into the ground by home-built drags or even by bushes. Cotton was picked by hand (much as it was to be until recently); grain was cut with a sickle or a cradle, bound by hand, threshed on the barn floor with wooden flails, and separated from the chaff by a manually operated fanning mill. The dairy producer did all his work by hand: he milked the cows by hand, strained the milk by hand into pans, skimmed the cream by hand, and worked and churned the butter by hand. His tasks were endless, the hours of labor long, and the opportunity for profit limited. On the eve of the Civil War, however, nearly $250,000,000 worth of farm tools and machinery were sold. As early as 1860, patents had been granted for the basic principles of many modern farm machines, but ignorance, poverty, and tradition prevented wide acceptance of these machines. By 1900, however, farmers spent $750,000,000 and by 1910 $1,265,000,000 on farm tools and machinery.

The new equipment aroused the farmers to a more reckless, more ambitious, and more rapid exploitation of the virgin soil of the West. In 1830, before the introduction of modern plows, harrows, planters, and cultivators, it took 32.8 minutes to prepare the soil for a bushel of wheat. In 1900, it took 2.2 minutes to perform the same operation. During the 1850's, McCormick agents had sold thousands of wheat reapers in the Middle West. By 1880, one man with a three-horse team or a tractor attached to a mechanical self-binder harvester that McCormick would have envied could accomplish as much as twenty men toiling and sweating with sickle or cradle. Before the end of the cen-

Steam Threshers at Work (Scribner's *Magazine, 1897*)

tury, the giant combine—a machine that cut, threshed, and bagged the grain—was in use in California.

As it was with wheat, so was it with other crops; corn, hay, potatoes, truck produce, and dairying all had their particular machines. Even in the South, where hand labor persisted longer than in other sections, mechanization made some progress. The cotton-gin was improved, and the cotton-seed planter, fertilizer distributor, and cotton-stalk cutter were introduced. But, as in other sections of the country, these machines continued to be powered or pulled by draft animals, or, here and there, by heavy steam tractors. By 1910, however, giving auguries of the future, a gasoline tractor occasionally startled the surrounding countryside.

These improved methods accounted for a saving of nearly 50 per cent in the time needed for the production of the nation's ten major crops. With the exception of cotton and tobacco, the costs of machine labor became fractional in comparison with the costs of hand labor. In 1900, for example, 10 minutes of human labor produced a bushel of wheat; in 1830 the same process took 183 minutes. In comparison with 1830, the nation in 1900 saved $523,000,000 in growing its corn crop, $79,000,000 in growing the wheat crop, and $52,000,000 in growing the oat crop.

Mechanization, when adopted, decreased the back-breaking and spirit-deadening toil of American farmers. Machines made it possible to feed and clothe the constantly growing urban population and to accumulate surpluses for export. Yet while the machine helped to relieve farm drudgery and helped feed the nation and world better, it also confirmed some of the worst habits of farm management. Paradoxically, the very machines that seemed destined to increase the power of the individual farmer added to his risks as a businessman, with disastrous results.

In the days when agricultural implements were few and often homemade and when land was relatively cheap, it was not difficult financially to become a farmer. But as the price of farm land advanced and costly machinery had to be bought, the farmer had to make a larger initial outlay. The new machines absorbed considerable money in repairs, wore out more rapidly than the simple tools they replaced, and often had to be discarded because they were outmoded by newer and improved models. As in industry, the price of any farm product was determined at least in part by the costs of the most efficient producers. Many farmers who could not afford to purchase new equipment had to give up their farms and work as machine tenders for their more prosperous colleagues. After 1865, all over the nation the middle-sized producers were increasingly squeezed between rising numbers of farm tenants and the growing power of large commercial farms. The harassed middle-sized farmers were not unlike the craftsmen who were compelled by the rise of industry to take jobs in factories.

Failing to develop, as industry had, a realistic market and political policy to protect his interests, but continuing on his path of ruinous individualism, the farmer failed to make his life more secure and prosperous. Machines only confirmed his old tendencies to overinvest, overexpand, and overborrow. The farmer gambled that the market forces over which, in fact, he had decreasing control would treat him kindly. New fertilizers (whose use increased thirty-five times over between 1860 and 1910), government sponsored irrigation projects, the advice of experts in the universities and government bureaus, including the U. S. Department of Agriculture (established in 1862, and given a cabinet rank in 1889)—all could have been used to develop a viable modern husbandry; instead, they were in the main used to expand production recklessly, always in the hope of that one big "killing" in the market place.

Agricultural Specialization

One way in which the farmer could have strengthened his chances for success would have been to attempt diversification of his crops. Al-

(sp.) crop-lien

though, nationally, American farm production became more diverse after the Civil War, in many sections of the country farmers continued to invest in traditional crops rather than to try new ones.

In the South, the war temporarily dethroned King Cotton. This change proved only an interlude. In 1866, the cotton crop was some two million bales, or less than half that of 1860; but five decades later, largely because of the increased use of fertilizers in the older cotton regions and the opening of new cotton-growing areas—especially in Texas and Oklahoma—it had risen to more than eleven million bales. With many parts of the South caught in the crop-lien, tenant, and sharecropping systems, many farmers could not break away from cotton even if they had wished to; their landlords or creditors would only give credit on familiar crops. Understandably, they would not risk their investments or capital on crops whose market chances they did not know at all. What expansion there was elsewhere in southern farming was along familiar lines: tobacco most of all, and rice, sugar, fruits, nuts, and garden truck.

Production of Cotton in Leading Cotton-Growing States in Bales
(one bale equals 500 pounds)

STATES	1859	1879	1899	1919
Mississippi	962,000	963,000	1,286,000	957,000
Alabama	791,000	699,000	1,093,000	718,000
Louisiana	622,000	508,000	699,000	306,000
Georgia	561,000	814,000	1,232,000	1,681,000
Texas	345,000	805,000	2,584,000	2,971,000
Arkansas	293,000	608,000	705,000	869,000
Tennessee	237,000	330,000	235,000	306,000
South Carolina	282,000	522,000	843,000	1,476,000
North Carolina	116,000	389,000	433,000	858,000
Oklahoma			227,000	1,006,000

What was true of cotton in the South was the case with wheat and corn in the North. Conditions for the wheat farmer's conquest of the Upper Mississippi were almost ideal. Nature had blessed the area with a soil unsurpassed anywhere in the world. Its level character fitted it admirably for mechanized agriculture, and most of the more important types of farm machinery were the inventions of Prairie-state people and were manufactured in Prairie-state factories. Growing transportation facilities and local great flour-milling and meat-packing centers stimulated Prairie agriculture. Despite natural hazards of grass fires,

Leading Wheat Producing States
(Figures in thousands of bushels)

1859		1879		1899	
Illinois	23,837	Illinois	51,110	Minnesota	95,278
Indiana	16,848	Indiana	47,284	North Dakota	59,884
Wisconsin	15,657	Ohio	46,014	Ohio	50,376
Ohio	15,119	Michigan	35,532	South Dakota	41,889
Virginia	13,130	Minnesota	34,601	Kansas	38,778
Pennsylvania	13,042	Iowa	31,154	California	36,534
New York	8,681	California	29,017	Indiana	34,986
Iowa	8,449	Missouri	24,966	Nebraska	24,924
Michigan	8,336	Wisconsin	24,884	Missouri	23,072
Kentucky	7,394	Pennsylvania	19,462	Iowa	22,769
Other States	42,611	Other States	105,159	Other States	226,940
Total	173,104		449,183		655,430

blizzards, floods, droughts, and grasshopper plagues, massive wheat production pushed steadily westward. In 1850, the center of wheat production was near Columbus, Ohio. Within another fifty years, it had moved much further west to the area beyond Des Moines, Iowa. After 1880, the East, though growing rapidly in population, was supplying a diminishing amount of wheat and other cereal breadstuffs. By World War I, specialized wheat regions extended from Maryland and eastern Pennsylvania to the states of Idaho, Washington, and Oregon.

The American corn crop exceeded in acreage and in production the combined quantities of wheat, oats, barley, rye, buckwheat, and rice, each of which in its own right had a huge and growing annual production. Although corn was grown to some extent in every state of the Union, corn production centered in the region of fertile prairie soils extending westward from Ohio to Kansas to the south and South Dakota to the north. Supplemented by the South's significant crop, by 1860 total corn production was about 839,000,000 bushels. During the last decade of the nineteenth century, more than two billion bushels of corn was grown annually.

Most American corn was used to feed or fatten millions of hogs, 61 per cent of which were raised in the Prairie states by 1900. Along with the 25,000,000 beef cattle and 61,500 sheep scattered across almost the entire trans-Mississippi West by 1900, the nation's meat production more than kept pace with its increased crop output.

Faced with the increase of specialized crops and of livestock production in the West, the East continued its pre-Civil War tendency to develop specialties of its own. The most dramatic changes in eastern farming came in production of cereals and livestock. In 1860, for exam-

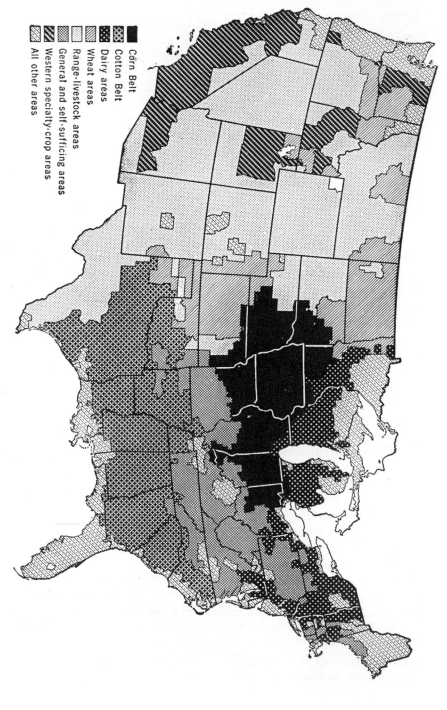

AGRICULTURAL REGIONS OF THE UNITED STATES

Corn Belt
Cotton Belt
Dairy areas
Wheat areas
Range-livestock areas
General and self-sufficing areas
Western specialty-crop areas
All other areas

ple, New England produced more than 1,000,000 bushels of wheat; in 1899, less than 137,000. Corn, beef cattle, and sheep production had similar if less dramatic falls in the Middle Atlantic states. Topography, industrialization, urbanization, and nearness to market stimulated instead the growth of dairy and truck products that could be quickly sped to the tables of nearby cities.

North

By 1900, New York and Pennsylvania each had more than 1,000,000 dairy cows, while New England as a whole had nearly reached that figure. Luckily, a great and growing demand and the easy and rapid spoilage of dairy products prevented the large dairy industry of the Middle West from wiping out dairying in the East, for even before 1860 farmers in the North Central states were turning to the production of milk, butter, and cheese. By 1900, Iowa, with 1,500,000 dairy cows led all other states, followed by New York, Illinois, and Pennsylvania, in that order. The next six states were all in the Prairie regions, and each had more than 500,000 dairy cows, or more than half of all New England's herds.

Truck and fruit farming, like the dairy industry, were closely related to population growth, urbanization, improvements in refrigeration, and rapid transportation. By 1910, almost every village or city in America had nearby truck gardens or farms producing a great variety of vegetables and fruits, both for the fresh-vegetable market and for the commercial canneries, which multiplied in number and in influence after the successful appearance in the 1870's of the tin can.

As in the case of grains and livestock specialization, truck farming made quick headway, especially where special soils or climates were needed. The midseason and late summer crops of celery, for example, were concentrated mainly on the muck soils of New York, Michigan, New Jersey, and Pennsylvania, with smaller acreages on the irrigated lands of Colorado, Oregon, and Washington. As the Far West and deep South went into the fruit-growing business before World War I, oranges, grapefruit, lemons, limes, kumquats, dates, and figs came by the trainloads from these hotter climates, but, at the same time, a large part of the nation's peach crop, three eighths of its plums, one third of its pears, nearly all the apricots, many walnuts, and the overwhelming tonnage of grapes were also now grown in California. Oregon and Washington produced great quantities of apples, berries, and other small fruit, and thus came into competition with older fruit-growing areas.

Markets Overseas

During the thirty years that preceded the Civil War, four fifths of American exports were farm products, consisting mostly of cotton, tobacco, cereals, and meat. In return for these commodities, Europe sent the United States a variety of manufactured products. But, although the export trade in agricultural goods declined proportionately as American industry expanded after 1865, farm products still constituted an important part of American foreign trade. European demand seemed insatiable. For forty years after 1860, approximately 76 per cent of the United States' export trade was in farm products, and the value of American agricultural exports rose from about $277,000,000 in 1870 to more than $840,000,000 in 1900.

After 1900, however, Europe was unable to continue to supply the United States with goods that could balance its own imports of American farm products. The United States was beginning to produce its own manufactures on a large scale, and high American protective tariffs helped keep out European goods. American imports of European manufactures dropped from more than 60 per cent of all imports in 1860 to about 30 per cent in 1900. American imports of raw materials for manufactures may have trebled, but the sources of these products were largely non-European. Europe itself increasingly turned to Canada, Argentina, and Russia for grains, to Argentina for meat, to India and Egypt for cotton, and to Australia and New Zealand for sheep and dairy products. Its own agricultural expansion and improved farming techniques lessened European dependence on important but more expensive agricultural commodities from America.

American exports of fresh beef fell from 352,000,000 pounds in 1901 to 6,000,000 in 1914; wheat, butter, and cheese exports fell off calamitously during the same period. Despite the growing competition of India and Egypt, however, American cotton shipments abroad increased between 1905 and 1914, with large consignments now going to Japan in exchange for silk. Like cotton, exports of leaf tobacco to America's principal customers (Great Britain, Germany, France, Italy, and China) rose from more than 300,000,000 pounds in 1899 to almost 450,000,000 in 1913. During these years the United States still produced approximately one third of the world's tobacco crop.

The Farmer: Businessman and Worker

A world-wide market, expensive machinery, and specialization made the farmer into a businessman and a capitalist, whose profit-and-loss ledger was affected by forces over which he had no control. The post-Civil War farmer needed money to acquire his land, to buy modern farm equipment, and to purchase products he had once raised for his own use. Rising land costs also accelerated the trend to capitalistic farming. Despite periodic depressions, land values rose steadily during the years after the Civil War, and in the decade 1910–1920 they almost doubled. The prosperity of the farmer had come to depend on domestic and world conditions that affected the business cycle, on credit facilities he did not own, on land systems he dimly understood, on communications, transportation he did not control, and on government policies, markets and marketing machinery, a labor supply, and a price structure he could not dictate.

Despite great variations among farmers, common trends in the response to increasing commercialization can be discerned. Although farm population after 1865 increased, the percentage of farmers decreased from three fifths of the total population in 1860 to approximately one third at the end of World War I. If a longer time span is considered, the proportionate decline in the popularity of agriculture becomes even more pronounced. As late as 1820, more than 90 per cent of the working population of the United States was engaged in agriculture. After that date, there was a persistent decline; in 1920, the figure was 29.9 per cent and was growing smaller.

Increasingly, the farm economy developed cyclical features. For eight years after the Civil War, most farmers shared in the general prosperity that prevailed throughout the United States. During the depression of the midseventies, the farmer's market shrank, and the prices that he received for his commodities declined sharply. During the industrial boom that followed the depression of 1873, the farmer did not regain his lost ground, and the depression of the 1890's made a bad situation even worse. By the end of the century, however, most farmers had again entered a period of prosperity. An expanded home market more than compensated for the declining foreign sales, and experiments with other crops brought some new sources of income. Sugar production was enlarged, the poultry and dairy industries were further developed, and new attention was given to the production of fruit and vegetables. From 1900 to 1914, agriculture was relatively prosperous, and the American farmer was better off than he had been at any time since the 1860's.

The most accurate barometer of the effect of the commercialization of agriculture upon the farmer was the extent of his mortgaged indebtedness. Before the Civil War, when suitable farm lands were still relatively cheap, it was not necessary to go heavily into debt to become a farmer. But after the war, the rising price of land and the need to acquire expensive machinery forced many farmers—particularly those taking up new lands in the West—to borrow large amounts of money at high interest rates. The prolonged agricultural distress during the last quarter of the nineteenth century generally prevented farmers from repaying the debts they had contracted during the postwar expansion and prosperity. Many farmers had difficulty in meeting even their interest payments, and many lost their farms through foreclosure.

For fifty years after the Civil War, free and clear ownership of farm property declined steadily. Farmers were inclined to mortgage their property in periods of prosperity, when they needed funds for expansion or speculation; they therefore borrowed money when it was cheapest but were often compelled to pay back the interest and principal during hard times, when money was dear. Statistics are lacking on the mortgaged indebtedness of American farmers for the twenty-five years after the Civil War, but the total undoubtedly represented a sizable percentage of the value of all farm property in the United States. By 1910, farm mortgages totaled more than $3,000,000,000, and within the next decade this figure had more than doubled. The average farm mortgage was $1,224 in 1890, $1,175 in 1910, and $3,356 in 1920. It has been estimated that in 1890 there were as many mortgages as there were farms in Kansas, Nebraska, the Dakotas, and Minnesota.

This greater use of the money market enabled the farmer to try to make his coveted profits by borrowing money to increase acreage or to buy a little uncultivated land in the hope that a rise in values would pay him for his speculative risk. Both these policies when combined with his inefficiency, old-fashioned marketing techniques, and the temptations of the machine, caused the disappearance of a large number of middle-income farmers who owned and operated their own farms. After the Civil War, this class, which had been idealized by Jefferson and had always served as a dignified folk-image of the American farmer was now regarded as the "hick" or hayseed and was increasingly supplanted by a relatively small group of wealthy large-scale farmers, on the one hand, and a constantly expanding landless rural proletariat, on the other.

Accelerating a trend already underway before 1860, big farms grew bigger and rich farmers became richer. Many more farmers now faced bankruptcy. Having lost their land, home, and equipment, they could move to the city and change their occupation. Many younger farmers chose this alternative, especially in the more industrialized East. But others, who preferred to follow the only trade that they or their fathers had ever known, were forced either to rent farms or to become farm employees.

At the bottom of the agricultural ladder by 1920 and with practically no chance of ever climbing it were a small but growing group of migratory workers. Consisting of dispossessed landholders, ruined farmers, and rural wage-earners, as well as ex-city dwellers who could find no other jobs, the migratory workers were first used as harvesting crews in the Middle West. Later they were employed on practically all farms that mass produced a cash crop on what has been called a "factory" basis. Many migrants drifted from South to North during the harvest season and spent the winter in the woods as lumberjacks. Wherever they worked, their jobs were highly routinized, they labored in gangs that were carefully supervised, their annual wages were among the lowest in the United States, and their jobs gave them no security and no future.

Before World War I, most tasks on the farm were not performed by such migrants but either by the members of the farmer's family or by hired hands. In 1900, there were more than 5,000,000 men and women agricultural laborers in the United States, of whom nearly 40 per cent were southern Negroes. The national average workday for these farm laborers was ten hours. Their wages were lowest in the South, and highest in some Far Western states. In 1895, for example, South Carolina paid $9.91 a month to farm workers, while Nevada paid $40.71. In the entire nation from 1866 to 1899, the average April-to-December wage-rate for male farm workers ranged from $15 to $20 a month. With such wages, few hired hands could save enough money to purchase their own farms; thus many hired hands left the farm for the city, but no record exists of a comparable exodus from the city to the farm.

Those farmers who lost their farms or farm workers who could arrange it often rented homes, land, and even equipment. By 1880, 25 per cent of all the farms in the United States were tilled by renters; twenty years later, the proportion had risen to 35 per cent; and in 1910, it was 37 per cent. Tenants by choice were understandably the exception. They constituted in 1910 only a small fraction of more than 2,000,000 American tenant families found predominantly in the southern states but growing in number in every section of the United States.

The tenant possessed a certain measure of economic independence, for he held a lease upon his land, he often had the right to select his own crops, and he paid a stipulated rent in either money or produce. The sharecropper, however, enjoyed none of these advantages. Sharecropping was that variation of tenancy that was developed in the post-Civil War years by southern landlords who invented a labor system that would require little capital and would help keep the former slaves on the land. Sharecropping rapidly became the dominant labor system in many parts of the South.* Together with the crop-lien system of pledging current crops to local merchants, sharecropping debased both Negroes and poor whites. These systems held back the diversification of southern agriculture, sapped the initiative of its victims, perpetuated backward farming techniques, and kept many Negroes close to serfdom.

At the other end of the scale from hired workers, tenants, and sharecroppers were a few large-scale farmers who ran mass-production enterprises. Not all giant farm experiments, however, worked well; for example, cattle farms of more than 25,000 acres were established in Illinois after the Civil War, but rising land values made them impractical, and by the 1880's most of them had been broken up into smaller units. The bonanza wheat farm, however, which in the meantime had appeared in the Dakotas and California, was highly profitable. The Northern Pacific established such a farm in the midseventies, and it soon became a model for others. The typical bonanza farm, which was often owned by eastern and foreign money, was between 75,000 and 100,000 acres. Most of the tasks were performed by machines operated by seasonal laborers whose jobs were not unlike those of eastern factory workers. One such "outdoor factory" used 200 pairs of harrows, 125 seeders, 155 binders, and 26 steam threshers. The administration of these farms was entrusted to managers, who were assisted by several superintendents, each of whom was responsible for the work on about 6,000 acres of land.

Such farms were few in number, but they pointed to the future. Like the eastern factory, the bonanza farm was characterized by the widespread application of machinery, absentee ownership, mass production, specialization, and the employment of landless workers to perform routine jobs.

Patterns of Agrarian Protest

The farmer had become a businessman, but he had little of the power that helped to make business leaders prosperous. Unable to eliminate competition, to control production, or to fix prices, he was victimized by those who could do all these things and by his own

* See Chapter 1 for details.

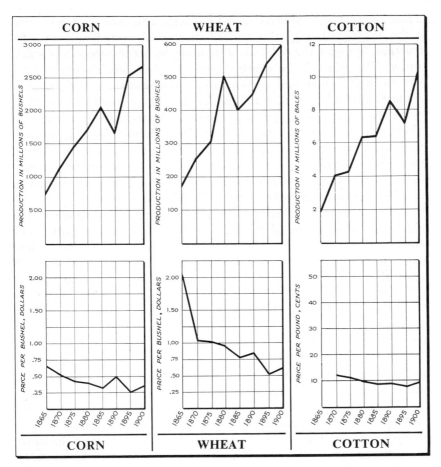

CORN	WHEAT	COTTON

Trends in Production and Prices of Basic Agricultural Commodities,
1865–1900

outmoded psychology and methods. The farmer dealt as an individual with monopolistic corporations whose strength lay in their proved ability to destroy individualism. The individual farmer was no match for the nation's organized business groups. Combined in cooperatives, using modern growing and marketing techniques, and operating his own lobbies at Washington, he could have been far better off, but these were methods he was not to discover or adopt until after 1900.

Farmers did not foresee the seriousness of their position during the post-Civil War boom, but during the period of agricultural distress that lasted from the early seventies until the end of the nineties they repeatedly complained that they were being defrauded by the railroad operators, middlemen, and bankers. The farmer—particularly in the West—had originally enthusiastically advocated railroad construction; but once the railroads were built, he became their implacable enemy. The railroads, he charged, bribed public officials, granted favors to businessmen, and monopolized grain elevators. Freight rates in the South and west of the Mississippi were invariably higher than in the Northeast. Such railroad abuses as long- and short-haul discriminations, rebates, and pools often hit the farmer hardest. In some rural areas, rates were so high that farmers sometimes destroyed their produce instead of shipping it. Where there were no competing alternative routes because of railroad monopolies, the farmer either had to pay the rates that were asked or not ship his goods.

Because farmers failed to develop marketing organizations, the middlemen who purchased the farmer's commodities frequently combined to fix prices. Most middlemen knew market conditions, owned major storage facilities, could buy when prices were low and sell when they were high. The farmer, on the other hand, competed with farmers in both the United States and the rest of the world; he had no means for storing his crop until there was a rise in prices; and he knew little or nothing about the world-wide market for his goods. Wheat prices, for example, were determined by supply and demand in Chicago, New York, and Liverpool, but the farmer on the plains or prairies had no way of knowing of—let alone capitalizing on—the price changes that occurred in the wheat pits of distant cities.

The farmer was open to exploitation by bankers as well as railroad operators and middlemen. If he took a mortgage either because of debts or because he wanted to speculate, he had to do it on the banker's terms or not at all. Farmers took out mortgages on which interest rates ranged from 8 to 24 per cent and in some instances were as high as 40 per cent. If they failed to meet these payments, they lost their property; while the farmer toiled from sunup to sundown only to end up in ruin, the banker seemed to do nothing but sit behind a desk and wait for the farmer to go bankrupt. Throughout the West and South, bankers and loan sharks were hated symbols of all that the farmer believed he was not.

In the early Republic the nation's farmers had enough power in the state or federal governments to protect their interests. But in the years after the Civil War, politicians increasingly responded to the demands of the businessman and largely ignored those of the farmer. The decline in the farmer's political strength represented far more than a loss in prestige, for the government in aiding the businessman often injured the farmer. Repeated tariff increases raised the prices of goods

that the farmer had to purchase and reduced the ability of foreign
countries to pay for American farm products. The government's postwar monetary policy forced farmers who had contracted debts during
inflation to repay them with dearer money. State and federal governments failed to carry out an effective program to regulate transportation, marketing, and finance.

Alone, the farmer was unable to solve his political and economic
problems. When the shoe pinched, however, he might temporarily
cooperate with his fellow farmers to improve his lot. The first important farmers' organization established after the Civil War was the National Grange of the Patrons of Husbandry. Formed in 1867 by Oliver
Hudson Kelley and some other clerks in the Bureau of Agriculture, the
Grange was conceived by its founders as primarily a social organization
that would relieve the drudgery and boredom of American rural life.
It would also offer members an opportunity to discuss their common
problems and to receive reliable information on improved agricultural
methods. In a declaration in 1874, the Grange stated that its objectives
were:

> . . . to develop a better and higher manhood and womanhood
> among ourselves. To enhance the comforts and attractions of
> our homes, and strengthen our attachments to our pursuits. To
> foster mutual understanding and co-operation. . . . To buy
> less and produce more, in order to make our farms self-sus-
> taining. To diversify our crops, and crop no more than we can
> cultivate. . . . To discountenance the credit system, the mort-
> gage system, the fashion system, and every other system tend-
> ing to prodigality and bankruptcy.

The Grange was established at the height of the post-Civil War
agricultural boom. True to their tradition of turning to cooperative
effort or reform programs only in hard times, many farmers ignored
the Grange during its early years. At the end of 1868, there were only
ten granges in the United States, and six of these were located in Minnesota; two years later only nine states had granges. But in 1872, 1,105
granges were founded, and with the onset of the depression the number increased rapidly. By 1875, there were approximately 20,000 local
granges, mostly in the Middle West or South, with a total membership of more than 800,000.

As Grangers in the 1870's began to understand that many of their
aims could be achieved only through political activity, farmers and
their allies among smaller businessmen in such states as Illinois, Minnesota, Kansas, Wisconsin, and Iowa elected several candidates to state

"The Leaky Connection": *Farmer's View of the Cause of Low Income*
(Judge)

legislatures and courts. There followed in some midwestern states the passage of the so-called Granger laws for the regulation of the railroads. The Grange also went into business. It established cooperative warehouses, grain elevators, and creameries, formed insurance companies, and set up factories to manufacture stoves, farm machines, and other necessities. Despite the promise of such enterprises to provide farmers with realistic weapons in a commercial competitive world, all the Grangers' business ventures proved short-lived. Unable to manage their own farms well, farmers were not prepared to carry on other businesses successfully. Many of the cooperatives overexpanded. Others were unable to meet the competition of their rivals.

By 1880, the Grange had little political influence, its attempts at business had failed, and its membership was down to 100,000. If later the Grange more than regained the ground it had lost, that Grange was a social-welfare organization that entered neither business nor politics.

Farm groups other than the Grange were organized within a number of southern and western states to agitate for measures that would give farmers a larger share of the national income. By the end of the 1880's, most of these state organizations had been swallowed up by either the Northern or Southern Alliance; and in the early nineties the Alliances, in turn, gave way to the Populist party. Although the Populists made articulate the widespread agrarian discontent in the United States, they were not able to dislodge the major parties, and William Jennings Bryan's defeat in 1896 marked a turning point in the history of the farmer's protest movements.* With the return of prosperity shortly after 1896, farmers tended to forget their earlier grievances and to rejoin the established parties.

The farmer did not use political action to solve his economic problems again until World War I. In 1915, the Farmers' Non-Partisan League was organized in North Dakota. Within a short time, it attracted the support of farmers in several midwestern states. The League's largest success was in North Dakota, where it helped pass laws that provided for state ownership of flour mills and grain elevators, the establishment of a state-owned bank, and state loans to finance home construction and land purchases. Unlike earlier farm reform groups, the Non-Partisan League was not merely a crisis party. It was a modern farm-pressure organization working in good times as well as bad to protest or speak for its members' interests. Still, the League had only local successes.

By 1920, the American farmer was still at the mercy of the busi-

---

* See Chapter 8, pages 257–65.

ness cycle, his fate was still determined by world supply and demand, and he was still competing blindly with his fellow farmers at home and abroad.

FOR SUPPLEMENTARY READING

Great knowledge in short compass is the special virtue of F. Shannon, *The Farmer's Last Frontier* (1945). For a longer view use U. S. Department of Agriculture, *Farmers in a Changing World* (1940). The perspective in both these volumes should be analyzed in the light of R. Hofstadter, *The Age of Reform* (1955). Two older "classics" are S. J. Buck, *The Agrarian Crusade* (1920), and J. Hicks, *The Populist Revolt* (1931). On the farmer's image of himself consult the recently re-issued I. Donnelly, *Caesar's Column* (1891, new ed. 1960), and W. J. Bryan, *Memoirs* (1925). A. Bogue, *Money at Interest* (1955) is a long-needed revised view of the farm credit situation. C. C. Taylor (ed.), *Rural Life in the United States* (1949), also has much new material. Various phases of "protest" including Greenbackism and the Grangers are the theme of C. M. Destler, *American Radicalism, 1865–1901* (1946). Careful note should be taken of regional differences as shown in C. Vann Woodward, *Origins of the New South, 1877–1913* (1951), and *Tom Watson: Agrarian Rebel* (1938); F. B. Simkins, *The Tillman Movement in South Carolina* (1926); P. R. Fossum, *The Agrarian Movement in North Dakota* (1925); and W. D. Sheldon, *Populism in the Old Dominion* (1935). Important biographies include: A. Nevins, *Grover Cleveland: A Study in Courage* (1932); F. B. Simkins, *Pitchfork Ben Tillman* (1944); M. R. Werner, *Bryan* (1929); and F. E. Haynes, *James B. Weaver* (1919).

7

The Politics
of Conformity
and Revolt

WITH THE RAPID GROWTH of American industry and the increasing public esteem given to businessmen, politics after the Civil War declined in prestige, and party strife appeared—on the surface at least—to be little more than a game. But, still, it was a game in which the stakes were high, for it often involved such prizes as lucrative contracts, grants of large tracts of western land, or increases in tariff schedules for favored industries. To the players, the game was an all-out struggle for the spoils of office; to the businessman, the outcome was largely irrelevant, for, regardless of the results of any election, the American economy remained virtually unaffected. Republicans and Democrats waged a relentless war with all the weapons at their command; but one party defeat and another's victory made no appreciable difference. Both parties existed to keep things as they were, and the advent of a new administration in Washington usually meant only that a new set of officeholders had taken power.

The Politics of Dead Center

In the years following Grant's two terms as President, the American Presidency was dominated by mediocrity. Rutherford B. Hayes, James A. Garfield, Chester A. Arthur, Grover Cleveland, and Benjamin Harrison were essentially colorless men who believed that the President was an executive agent rather than a vigorous leader. They displayed little sustained interest in reform, and even their most ardent supporters hesitated to picture them as crusaders. Few historians today would label any one of them a statesman. Honest but plodding, dull and unimaginative, they kept the rigging on the ship of state in adequate repair, but they seldom displayed any desire to sail into uncharted waters. While farmers complained of declining income, workers conducted militant strikes, and industrial leaders amassed huge fortunes, these Presidents performed the routine duties of their office and did little to disturb the status quo. From 1877 to 1893, American politics were in dead center, not because there were no issues, but because the politicians refused to recognize and act on the issues.

The postwar Republican party, like every major political party in American history, was a loose alliance of diverse groups that presumably had little in common. Geographically, the Republican party found its strength along an axis that extended from the Northeast to the upper Middle West. At one pole were most American businessmen, who had been attracted to the party during and after the Civil War by its tariff policies, banking and monetary programs, and the distribution of war contracts. At the other end of the axis were most of America's grain growers. They and their forefathers had helped to found the party in the 1850's and during the war they had been rewarded with the Homestead Act. Besides these two major groups, Negroes also supported the Republican party because it had given them their freedom. Northern war veterans viewed it as the party that had fought and won the war and had rewarded them with generous pensions. The memory of Lincoln, of the party's opposition to the spread of slavery, and of its successful preservation of the Union, and the belief that Republicanism was as much of a crusading doctrine as it had been in the antebellum years—all these enlisted the support of other Americans.

Because of its wide appeal and successful use of a smaller patronage, the Republican party was able to retain its control of the federal government throughout most of the postwar years. From James Buchanan to Woodrow Wilson (1861 to 1913), Grover Cleveland was the only Democrat to occupy the White House. While the Republicans at times lost one branch—and occasionally both branches—of Congress to the opposition, they were able to dominate the judiciary during the entire period. Still another measure of Republican success was the fashion in which the party repeatedly broke up into factions that fought for the fruits of repeated victories. As early as the midseventies, the party was split into the Half-Breeds, led by James G. Blaine of Maine, and the Stalwarts, led by Roscoe Conkling of New York. Although the members of one faction hated those of the other as much as, if not more than, they hated the opposition, they did not disagree on policy. Their major differences arose over the party division of the ever-increasing spoils of office. The Half-Breeds believed that all federal jobs should be occupied by Half-Breeds, and the Stalwarts contended that Stalwarts alone should staff government posts.

Angered by the insensitivity of the Republicans to such issues as tariff and civil service reform, in 1872 a group of men calling themselves Liberal Republicans sought to revive the crusading spirit that had once characterized Republicanism. The Liberal Republicans, like most third party movements, became a catchall for various discontents. They advocated a more moderate Reconstruction policy, a reversal of the trend toward the centralization of government, and a reduction in the tariff. This program was similar to that of the Democrats, with whom the Liberal Republicans allied in 1872 in an attempt to elect Horace Greeley to the presidency. But Greeley was easily defeated by Grant, ever the symbol of the Union's victory. In 1880, the reform groups within the party did successfully block the nomination of Grant, and four years later they sought to prevent the selection of Blaine as the party's standard-bearer. When, despite their protests, Blaine received the nomination they bolted the party and, under the name of Mugwumps, cast their votes for Cleveland.

As "the party of rebellion," bereft of either public esteem or government patronage, the Democrats could seldom afford the luxury of full-blown factionalism. As the party out of power, they were only infrequently troubled by the problems involved in the distribution of federal patronage. The Democratic party after 1876 had two principal sources of support—the Solid South and most of the big-city machines of the Northeast. Following Reconstruction, the South became a one-party section, and every Democratic presidential candidate began his campaign with the assurance that he would receive all the electoral votes of the states that had once comprised the Confederacy. Because the West was generally Republican and the South always Democratic, it was the Northeast that decided most national elections. Although the Democratic machines of the Northeast provided the party with consistent urban majorities, they usually lacked sufficient strength to prevent the Republicans in the rural areas from controlling the political machinery and electoral vote of their respective states. Neither northern city bosses nor southern politicians were as capable as leaders as the Democrats had been in antebellum years. From 1865 to 1896, the party's principal national spokesmen consisted of a small group of merchants and international bankers who were opposed to Republican high-tariff policies. But these businessmen, unlike those in the Republican party, could not furnish effective leadership for a party that drew its support from southern agrarians and the urban underprivileged.

From 1876 to 1892, few issues of any importance divided the Democrats and Republicans. Although the tariff made for never-ending debate, it nevertheless was not basically altered by either party. Currency questions—particularly the relation of silver to gold—frequently agitated the voters, but each party contained inflationist and deflationist wings. Neither party ever put forward a program for the control of business, and the Interstate Commerce Act of 1887 and the Sherman Antitrust Act of 1890 were passed by bipartisan majorities. When Congress voted on economic issues, party lines tended to blur as the agrarian forces of the South and West combined to oppose the business interests of the Northeast. The politicians of both parties always feared that a clear-cut stand on any major issue would reduce their chances of success by alienating substantial blocs of voters. Politics had become a big business in its own right. No party leader was prepared to adopt a policy that might jeopardize the chances of obtaining and holding public office. The party in power did not wish to alter a system that had been so profitable. The politicians of the minority party, looking forward to the day when they would take over the government, had no desire to destroy a system that would be fully as profitable to them as it had been to their opponents.

Hayes, Garfield, and Arthur

When Rutherford B. Hayes became President on March 4, 1877, many of his Republican supporters confidently expected that he would soon make the voters forget the excesses of "Grantism." Born and brought up in Ohio, Hayes had served as a volunteer officer with the Union Army during the Civil War and had made a notable record as the governor of his state. Throughout the campaign of 1876, he had repeatedly emphasized the need for reform, and his cabinet contained several men of undoubted ability and integrity. Despite these facts, his Administration could accomplish little.

Hayes lacked real drive and political acumen, but there were important circumstances over which he had no control. Throughout his four years in the White House, many people regarded him as a fluke, if not a fraudulent President, put in power in 1877 in a crooked settlement of the election dispute. The Democrats, who had probably won the election of 1876, were intransigent in their defeat; unfortunately for Hayes, during the first two years of his term, the Democrats controlled the House, and during the last two years, the opposition had majorities in both branches of Congress. Whatever Hayes did seemed to alienate either the people or the politicians. Although his decisions to end Reconstruction pleased the southerners, it did not make them Republicans, and it antagonized many northerners who were still unwilling to forgive and forget. Hayes's announcement, upon assuming office, that he did not plan to run for re-election made it difficult for him to deal with the Republican politicians who knew that within four years they would no longer be under obligation to him. His hard-money policies alienated the inflationist wing of the party in the West, but it did not prevent Congress in 1878 from repassing over his veto the Bland-Allison Act for government silver purchases.* He made no move to regulate the irresponsible leaders of industry, commerce, or finance, but he did not hesitate to call out federal troops to oppose the railroad strikers in 1877. All this might have been less important had his handling of the patronage not widened rather than narrowed the cleavage in the party between the Stalwarts and the Half-Breeds.

For more than a decade before Hayes became President, sporadic efforts had been made to eliminate the more glaring evils of the spoils system. The Civil War had greatly increased the size of the patronage available to the party that captured the presidency. By using government employees and their families as party workers and by tithing them for financial support, the national political leaders became relatively independent of the interest groups who sought their favors. Those who were "stalwart" in their notion that party loyalty and service must be the test for a government job became so secure that they could almost call their own tune. Civil-service reform thus seemed to cut at the heart of the system on which they depended, for it threatened to free government jobs from party political control. As early as 1864, Charles Sumner had proposed a plan for civil-service reform, and four years later Congress had considered and rejected a bill that provided for competitive examinations for applicants for certain government posts. Meanwhile, an educational campaign for civil-service

* See page 246.

reform was being conducted by such men as Senator Carl Schurz of Missouri, C. W. Curtis of *Harper's Weekly*, and E. L. Godkin of the *Nation*. In 1871, Grant responded to this pressure by appointing a civil-service commission with Curtis as its chairman, but three years later the commission's funds were cut off by Congress. Soon after Hayes assumed office, Carl Schurz, who was Secretary of the Interior, attempted to introduce a merit system in his department. At the same time, Secretary of the Treasury John Sherman sought to undercut the political power of the Stalwarts by reforming some of the most glaring abuses of the patronage system in the New York Custom House, patronage center of the nation's largest political machine. By making this move, Sherman openly defied Senator Roscoe Conkling, the party's leading Stalwart and the boss of the Republican machine in New York. Conkling not only wanted to keep control over the most important source of patronage in his state, but he also defended the spoils system as a positive good that alone made possible the existence of American political parties. To Conkling, parties were "not built up by deportment, or by ladies' magazines, or gush!" but by jobs for faithful political workers.

The struggle between the Administration and Conkling was precipitated by the report of a commission that stated that the workers in the New York Custom House accepted bribes and were compelled to make regular contributions to the Republican party in order to hold their jobs. Hayes in an executive order of June 22, 1877, prohibited political activity among government employees, and Sherman ordered Chester A. Arthur, Collector of the Port of New York, and Alonzo Cornell, the port's Naval Officer, to clear up the mess in the Custom House. But both men were Conkling's lieutenants, and they refused to follow the instructions of the Secretary of the Treasury. Conkling, for his part, lashed out at the Administration; and when Hayes in October, 1877, named Theodore Roosevelt, Sr., and L. B. Prince to succeed Arthur and Cornell, respectively, Conkling was able to win the support of enough senators to prevent the confirmation of the President's nominees. Hayes countered by making two new appointments following Congress' adjournment in July, 1878. When Congress reassembled, Conkling returned to the offensive, but he was so vitriolic in his attacks on the President that he alienated many Republicans, and in February, 1879, Hayes' appointees were finally confirmed by the Senate.

Conkling carried his fight with the Administration to the Republican convention of 1880, where he hoped to defeat the Half-Breeds by securing Grant's nomination for a third term. The two other leading candidates were Sherman and Blaine. Although Grant led all the other contenders for more than thirty ballots, he could not secure a majority, and the delegates finally settled upon James A. Garfield of Ohio as a compromise candidate. A Union veteran and senator who had also served in the House of a number of years, Garfield was a Half-Breed. To "balance" the ticket and to appease the Stalwarts, the Republicans therefore gave the vice-presidential nomination to Chester A. Arthur. The Democrats nominated General Winfield S. Hancock of Pennsylvania and William H. English of Indiana. Hancock, who had played a relatively important part in the Union victory at Gettysburg, had won the approval of the South by his conduct as military Governor of Louisiana. English was a nonentity who had supported the Buchanan Administration's pro-southern policies before the war. In the campaign both parties were careful to avoid the issues, and much was made of the military records of the two candidates. In reality, neither Hancock nor Garfield stood for much more than a desire to be president, and Garfield's victory can perhaps most accurately be attributed to the fact that his party controlled the national patronage and that it was only slightly less bankrupt politically than the Democratic party.

With Garfield's accession to the presidency, the intraparty squabble over the patronage was resumed. The new President left no doubt concerning his attitude by making Blaine Secretary of State, by refusing to appoint any Stalwarts to important positions in the Administration, and by giving the juiciest patronage plums in New York to the Half-Breeds. Conkling continued to fight back. In a dramatic gesture that was designed to prove that he had his state's support in his campaign against Garfield, Conkling resigned from the Senate. Then, he and Senator Thomas Platt of New York, who had also resigned, asked the New York state legislature to give them a vote of confidence by re-electing them to the Senate. But the plan backfired when the legislature refused to do their bidding. Vice-president Arthur lowered his own prestige and that of his office by going to Albany to lobby for the re-election of Conkling and Platt. This whole sorry spectacle was soon to be a national tragedy. On July 2, 1881, Charles J. Guiteau, a Stalwart and a disappointed officeseeker, shot and mortally wounded Garfield. As he stood over the President's body, Guiteau said: "I am a Stalwart and Arthur is President now."

Garfield died on September 19, 1881, and Chester A. Arthur, after a career as a spoils politician, became President. A former teacher and lawyer, he had worked his way up through the Republican organization and had earned the dubious distinction of being widely known as the "Gentleman Boss." As head of the New York Custom House he had made the customs service synonymous with political graft and cor-

"The President's Room": The Death of Garfield (Harper's Weekly)

ruption. "For twenty years," Matthew Josephson has written, "he had devoted himself to gathering and awarding the spoils of office; one saw him in smoky hotel rooms, where brandy and cigars were dispensed freely, . . . negotiating with committees, chairmen, [and] agents." * But on becoming President, Arthur turned on his past and provided the people of the United States with a constructive, although not outstanding, administration. If anything, Arthur's long experience with professional politicians admirably prepared him for a position in which he had to be constantly on guard against the pressures of the special interests. On taking office, he refrained from dismissing many of the Half-Breeds that had been appointed by Garfield, and throughout his term he repeatedly showed that he could not be controlled by either a faction or a party.

The most notable achievement of Arthur's Administration was the adoption of a law designed to mitigate the worst evils of the spoils system. Garfield's assassination had shocked the people into demanding some type of reform, and revelations before his death about corruption in Post Office contracts for "star routes" † had provided additional evidence of the need for ridding the government service of political appointees. In his first message to Congress, Arthur proposed that "appointments should be based upon ascertained fitness," and in January, 1883, the Pendleton Act, a Democratic bill sponsored by Senator George H. Pendleton of Ohio, was passed by bipartisan majorities in the House and Senate. This measure provided for the creation of the Civil Service Commission, the establishment of a classified service among certain groups of postal and custom-house workers, and competitive examinations for the positions that fell within the law. Although only 14,000 government employees in a force of more than 100,000 were placed under the jurisdiction of the law, the President was given the authority to extend the classified lists in the executive branch of the government. Dorman B. Eaton, the Secretary of the Civil Service Reform Association, was appointed the first chairman of the commission, and Arthur scrupulously observed both the spirit and the letter of the law during the remainder of his term as President.

* Matthew Josephson: *The Politicos; 1865–1896* (New York: Harcourt, Brace and Company, Inc., 1938), p. 323.

† The "star routes" were those routes on which mail was carried by either riders or stages. They received their name because the Post Office used a star to identify them on its lists. In the star-route frauds the principal culprits were Second Assistant Postmaster General Thomas J. Brady, who acted in collusion with star-route contractors, and Stephen W. Dorsey, who was grossly overpaid for the star routes that he operated. Dorsey was an ex-senator from Arkansas and the secretary of the Republican National Committee.

Arthur could claim little personal credit for the adoption of civil-service reform, but there were a number of cases in which he showed political independence. Despite the fact that the leading figures in the star-route frauds were important members of the Republican national machine, he vigorously backed their prosecution. In 1882, he pleased the taxpayers, if not their representatives, by vetoing a river and harbors bill. Congress soon repassed this pork-barrel measure over the President's veto. Arthur also vetoed an act of 1882 that excluded the entry of Chinese into the United States for twenty years. This time his opponents in Congress could not muster the necessary two-thirds majority to override his veto, and eventually a compromise measure that reduced the period of exclusion to ten years was approved by both President and Congress. Although Congress accepted Arthur's proposal for a tariff commission, it staffed the new board exclusively with protectionists. When the commission, to virtually everyone's surprise, recommended a tariff reduction, Congress ignored this proposal and adopted a bill that called for an increase in some rates and small cuts in others.

The Lone Democrat and the Last Old Republican

Arthur's record seemed too independent to many of the party's regulars, and not independent enough to make the reformers forget his earlier activities as a spoils politician. The Republican convention of 1884 passed over Arthur and gave the nomination to James G. Blaine of Maine. Blaine was the first Republican nominee since the Civil War without a military record, and the party named John A. Logan of Illinois, a Union veteran, to the second place on the ticket. In a famous speech at the Republican convention of 1876, Robert Ingersoll in a moment of aberration had referred to Blaine as a "plumed knight." The Republican candidate was in fact a veteran politician with a well-tarnished reputation. One of the most unsavory episodes in his long career had occurred when he had helped the Little Rock and Fort Smith Railroad to secure a land grant by selling the company's stock on a commission basis to his fellow Congressmen. The details of this exploit were contained in the so-called Mulligan Letters, which throughout the campaign were widely publicized by the Democrats.

The nomination of Blaine dramatized the change occurring in the relation of the parties to the business community. Tired of the high price of bribes and tribute and of the instability that came with factional wars within the parties, by 1880 important business leaders had decided that they would contribute to the parties' treasuries only if the

"The Plumed Knight" of the Republicans, James G. Blaine (Thomas Nast in Harper's Weekly)

politicians gave them what they wanted. With the increasing costs of political campaigns, particularly in the many close elections after 1876, and with the threatened loss of tithes from those government job-holders who had come under Civil Service protection, the politicians had to turn increasingly to the businessmen of the country for financial support.

Sometimes a Senator or Congressman would be controlled by a

KEY STATES

Popular and Electoral Vote for President, 1880–88

	1880			1884			1888		
	Popular Vote GARFIELD	Popular Vote HANCOCK	Electoral Vote	Popular Vote BLAINE	Popular Vote CLEVELAND	Electoral Vote	Popular Vote HARRISON	Popular Vote CLEVELAND	Electoral Vote
National Total	4,454,416	4,444,952	214G 155H	4,851,981	4,874,986	219C 182B	5,439,853	5,540,329	233H 168C
Key States									
Calif.	80,348	80,426	1G, 5H	102,416	89,288	8B	124,816	117,729	8H
Conn.	67,071	64,415	6G	65,923	67,119	6C	74,584	74,920	6C
Ind.	232,164	225,522	15G	238,463	244,990	15C	263,361	261,013	15H
Nev.	8,732	9,613	3H	7,193	5,578	3B	7,229	5,362	3H
N. H.	44,852	40,794	5G	43,249	39,183	4B	45,728	43,458	4H
N. J.	120,555	122,565	9H	123,440	127,798	9C	144,344	151,493	9C
N. Y.	555,544	534,511	35G	562,005	563,154	36C	648,759	635,757	36H
Ore.	30,619	19,948	3G	26,860	24,604	3B	33,291	26,522	3H
Va.							150,438	151,977	12C
W. Va.				63,096	67,317	6C	77,791	79,664	6C

(Weaver received 308,578 votes on the Greenback ticket)

(Butler received 175,370 votes on the Greenback ticket)

(Fisk received 249,506 votes on the Prohibitionist line)

group of businessmen, but not usually for matters beyond immediate interests in a specific government policy such as the tariff or land grants. More often politicians had themselves been businessmen or lawyer-associates of men in business and thus tended to have the "business point of view." A common outlook on business policies, strengthened by the fear that business would not pay for campaign expenses (which, in the case of underpaid Congressmen, came every two years) were enough to draw politicians closer to businessmen after 1880. As in the case of Blaine, this community of interest, although not in itself illegal, often led to outright bribes in money, stocks, expensive gifts, and inside information on lucrative business or stock-market opportunities.

Very often Half-Breeds like Blaine had accepted the need for some Civil Service reform as a means of placating important businessmen who were outraged at the tribute demanded by Stalwarts. Roscoe Conkling was shrewd when he recognized that the victory of Civil Service reform would tend to make previously independent politicians ever more reliant on the wealthy men of the nation. In 1880 and again in 1884, the Stalwarts had opposed the rising Half-Breeds at the party conventions for good cause.

At the 1884 convention the more vigorous reformers in the Republican party (the Mugwumps) had also opposed Blaine, and after they failed to block his nomination, they made it clear to the Democrats that they would support Grover Cleveland if he received the Democratic nomination. The Democrats had to attract independent votes to win and were in no position to argue; Cleveland was duly nominated. For Vice-President the Democrats selected Thomas A. Hendricks of Indiana. As Assistant District Attorney and Sheriff of Erie County, New York, Mayor of Buffalo, and Governor of New York, Cleveland had been an aggressive, uncorruptible Democrat who had antagonized the leaders of Tammany Hall and the other machine groups in the party while winning a nation-wide reputation as a reformer. In essentials, he was all that Blaine was not.

The Campaign of 1884 was one of personalities and vituperation. The Democrats rehashed the contents of the Mulligan Letters and the Republicans charged—and Cleveland made no attempt to hide the fact —that the Democratic candidate was the father of an illegitimate son. As election day approached, observers felt that New York, where the parties seemed evenly divided, held the key to the outcome of the contest and that the Irish voters in New York City probably held the balance of power in the state. In the closing days of the campaign, the Reverend Dr. Samuel Burchard, in a speech at the Fifth Avenue Hotel in New York, said the Democrats were the party of "Rum, Romanism, and Rebellion." The Irish, who perhaps needed no such inspiration, voted as usual for the Democrats. Cleveland with a variegated support carried New York; and New York's electoral votes provided him with a sufficient majority to insure victory. But Cleveland's plurality over Blaine was only 23,000, and the electoral vote was 219 to 182.

Grover Cleveland was the first Democrat—if Johnson is excepted—to occupy the White House since 1861, but his accession to office produced no major changes in government policies. Cleveland spent most of his first term in administrative reforms. The Navy Department eliminated a number of irregularities while continuing the expansion program that had been inaugurated under Garfield and Arthur. In the Department of the Interior, a concerted move was made to check the government's policy of giving away large areas of land to private corporations. Cleveland also tried to reverse the Republicans' generous pension policy. He vetoed a number of special pension measures and the Blair Dependent Pensions Act, which would have provided governmental assistance for any Civil War veteran who had served three or more months and was at present disabled. Cleveland also attempted to continue the civil-service program that had been established under the Pendleton Act; but at the end of his administration, most government jobs were occupied by loyal Democrats.

Once during his first term Cleveland did take a major step; in 1887, he urged Congress to reduce the tariff. The House responded with the Mills Bill, which included most of the President's suggestions. In the Senate, however, the Republicans introduced a protectionist measure. It was impossible to work out a satisfactory compromise bill, and the movement for tariff reduction ended with nothing accomplished.

Many historians have praised Cleveland for his courage, devotion to principle and his refusal to let his first Administration become the victim of special interests. Although Cleveland was obviously a man of integrity, none of the sweeping changes that were transforming the American economy were reflected in his acts and statements as President. He never indicated that he was aware of the widespread protests of the nation's farmers and workers. Aside from his tariff message, he acted on the assumption that the state must not interfere in the economy but was to remain strictly neutral. His pledge to impartiality meant that he failed to distinguish between wealthy industrialists seeking government favors and poor workingmen or small farmers who needed government aid. Even in his campaign for tariff reduction he failed to attain his objectives. It is possible to commend Cleveland's probity, but it is impossible to credit him with any major achievements. He failed as a presidential leader, and also as a party politician, for in 1889 the Democrats lost the government to the Republicans.

For the presidential campaign of 1888 the Democrats again nominated Cleveland for the presidency and made Allen C. Thurman their vice-presidential candidate. Although many Republicans thought that Blaine should be given another chance, the party's convention on the eighth ballot gave the necessary number of votes to Benjamin Harrison of Indiana and chose Levi Morton, a New York banker, as his running mate. Harrison, who was the grandson of William Henry Harrison, was a colorless man who had served one term in the Senate but had never been popularly identified with any particular cause or measure. In contrast to 1884, personalities were largely ignored during the campaign. The Democrats sought to make the tariff the sole issue, and the Republicans gladly accepted the challenge. But the enmity between England and Ireland also was involved in the election. When Sir Lionel Sackville-West, the British minister to the United States, received a letter asking him how he thought a naturalized American should vote, he replied that Cleveland's election would best serve the interests of Great Britain. Matthew Quay, Pennsylvania's Republican boss and chairman of the party's campaign committee, had Sackville-West's reply published. Whether enough Irish-Americans were alienated from their normally Democratic loyalty to vote Republican and to give Harrison the victory may never be known, but it is possible that many Irish-Americans, upon learning that Cleveland was regarded as a friend of Ireland's enemy, decided to vote for Harrison.

By 1888, many businessmen had become active in the day-to-day affairs of both parties. The likelihood of a close election and the availability of larger campaign funds than ever before made the election of 1888 probably the most corrupt in the nation's history. The Republican campaign chest overflowed with contributions from manufacturers who opposed the Democratic tariff plank, and much of the money was used to purchase votes in doubtful states. The election was very close, and the Republicans' fraudulent practices were probably important reasons for Harrison's victory. Although Cleveland polled approximately 100,000 more votes than Harrison, the Republicans won in the electoral college by a vote of 233 to 168. When Harrison learned of the outcome of the election, he said: "Providence has given us the victory." Matt Quay, who had borne him the glad tidings, was so aghast at this interpretation of the election that he is reported to have said: "Think of the man. He ought to know that Providence hadn't a damn thing to do with it. . . . [Harrison will] never know how close a number of men were compelled to approach the gates of the penitentiary to make him President." *

Cleveland had sought to keep the government impartial in the conflicts between the nation's interest groups, but Harrison went to the other extreme and in effect gave the government's hand to the most powerful pressure groups in the land. When Harrison became President, veterans wanted more pensions, Republican spoilsmen wanted jobs, manufacturers wanted higher tariffs, and westerners wanted more favorable silver legislation. Within a short time, all these groups had been satisfied. The Democrats were cleaned out of government office, and John Wanamaker, the Postmaster General, practically ignored civil-service regulations. The tariff was a more difficult problem, for the government had a surplus that presumably would have been augmented by an increase in duties. But was it not always possible to spend money on pensions and silver purchases? When Corporal James Tanner was appointed head of the Pension Bureau by Harrison, he said, "God help the surplus"; and within a short time he was busily at work getting an appropriation "for every old comrade who needs it." Harrison also approved the Dependent Pensions Act, which had been vetoed by Cleveland. Any remaining doubts about the problem of a surplus were removed by the passage of the Sherman Silver Purchase Act. With the way thus cleared for an increase in the tariff, Congress adopted the McKinley Tariff, which represented a new high in American protectionism.

The McKinley Tariff, which became law on October 1, 1890, was introduced into Congress by William McKinley, a representative from Ohio and chairman of the House Ways and Means Committee. McKinley had devoted his political career to extolling protectionism, and the McKinley Tariff was well-named. In some instances, rates on certain manufactured goods were so high that they were prohibitory, and in others provision was made for duties on products that were not even manufactured in the United States. Although American agriculture was not generally threatened by foreign competition, the McKinley Tariff placed duties upon butter, eggs, potatoes, and wheat. Another unusual feature of the new tariff was the intricate method used to take care of every segment of the sugar industry. To aid and protect the American refining industry—most of which was controlled by the Havemeyer Sugar Trust—the duty was removed from raw sugar, while a tariff of one-half cent a pound was placed on refined

* Quoted in Josephson, *op. cit.*, p. 433.

The Passage of the Tariff Bill

[THE BETTMANN ARCHIVE]

sugar. To safeguard the interests of native sugar-growers, the act called for the payment of a bounty of two cents a pound on all raw sugar produced in the United States. Finally, provision was made for a type of reciprocity designed to further Secretary of State James G. Blaine's plans for the increase of United States exports to Latin America. A number of Latin American products consumed in the United States were placed on the free list, with the stipulation that the President could put duties on them if the countries of their origin failed to reduce the rates on certain American exports before January 1, 1892.

The McKinley Tariff gave the most striking evidence of how the businessman had become the most powerful man in American politics. Whether he worked behind the scenes or openly participated in party affairs, he had ample reason to believe that his wishes would not be ignored. Regulatory measures such as the Interstate Commerce and Sherman Antitrust Acts did not disturb him deeply, for he knew that there was little prospect of their being rigidly enforced. If all else failed, there was always the Supreme Court, which throughout these years gave the businessman virtually free rein by interpreting the laws in an industrial economy of large-scale producers in accordance with the mores of a vanished society of small entrepreneurs. At times, the businessman had his way because of the prevailing belief that business expansion represented a desirable form of progress. At other times, he had to use extralegal or illegal devices to achieve his objectives in politics. But, regardless of his methods, he could count on the fact that the government would do relatively little to threaten his control over the American economy.

The Currency Issue

Despite the desire of Democratic and Republican politicians to play down any question that might threaten their continued control over the government, they were unable to keep the currency issue out of American politics.

Debates, even armed conflicts, over the nation's currency had played an important part in American political history since colonial times, and in the years after the Civil War the battles between the inflationists and deflationists were fought with growing intensity. As in the past, creditors demanded a stable currency, and the debtors advocated inflation. Leading business groups of the Northeast were proponents of "hard" money, whereas the mortgage-ridden farmers of the West and South asked for an expansion of the currency.

The nation's bankers had up to then faced an unprecedented problem of financing an enormous economic growth. Their general faith in the gold standard was partly strengthened by the nation's debtor relations to European financiers. Had there been enough gold for a larger currency, the whole of the nation might have enjoyed greater prosperity. But to insist on the gold standard when much of the country lacked adequate banking or credit facilities and had too little hard coin to finance all demands was sure to create great discontent and hardships that were bound to become festering political grievances. No one section nor any group in the nation was united on the currency question. Nearly everyone wanted more money, but where was it to come from and what form was it to take? Although the Republican party was thought by many contemporaries to be the champion of "sound" money and the Democrats were usually identified with "soft" money, neither party pursued a consistent currency policy during the last third of the nineteenth century. Both parties contained inflationist and deflationist blocs, and in congressional votes on the currency issue, party lines were frequently obliterated by sectional and economic interests.

Demo.

The Two-Headed Democratic Tiger of 1876, Tilden (left) and Hendricks

[THE BETTMANN ARCHIVE]

The Republican party, despite its strength among farm debtors in the West, had adopted a postwar currency policy designed to meet the needs of its eastern members, and, although the Democrats generally opposed the Republican's hard-money program, they were either unable or unwilling to prevent its adoption. Inflationists were virtually forced to turn to third-party movements to advance the cause of their first panacea, what came to be known as Greenbackism. Greenbackism arose out of the decision of the Treasury under Grant to reduce or retire the nearly half-billion dollars in paper money printed to help finance the Civil War. To retire or to devalue sharply what had become a vital part of the nation's currency for millions of people without providing an alternative created widespread fear of financial ruin. Both the National Labor Union and the National Labor party had demanded currency inflation, and in 1874 the Independent party—or Greenback party, as it was usually called by contemporaries —was organized to work for currency expansion. Consisting of a comparatively small number of labor leaders, farmers, and small businessmen, the Greenback party in 1876 nominated the wealthy iron manufacturer Peter Cooper for the presidency on a platform calling for the repeal of the Resumption Act. After the party's poor showing in the election of 1876—Cooper received less than 1 per cent of the total votes cast—the party was reorganized, and in 1878 it ran congressional candidates under the name of the Greenback Labor party. With pro-labor as well as soft-currency planks, it was able to poll approximately

1,000,000 votes, or more than ten times as many as Cooper had obtained two years earlier. But 1878 marked the high tide of Greenbackism, for its strength rapidly declined, and in 1880, James B. Weaver, the party's presidential candidate, received only a little more than 300,000 votes. Returning prosperity following the depression of the midseventies, failure of the resumption of specie payments in 1879 to produce the hard times that the inflationists had repeatedly predicted, and the growing prominence of the silver issue brought about the decline of the Greenbackers.

Although the place of silver in the nation's monetary system was eventually to become one of the most controversial issues in the entire history of American politics, it attracted comparatively little attention in the decade immediately after the Civil War. During these years, silver was not coined extensively, silver dollars were bulky and therefore little used, and, because silver was undervalued at the mint, only relatively small amounts of it were sold to the government. In 1873, when the silver dollar was dropped from the list of government coins, there was no concerted opposition to the move, and the Senate unanimously adopted a bill that authorized its abandonment. In later years, the silver interests were to refer to this step as the "Crime of '73," but there is no evidence that contemporaries made much of it at all.

Unforeseen developments in both Europe and the United States made the coinage of silver a controversial issue as the very time that the government was refusing to inflate the currency with paper money. The money stringency caused by the Panic of 1873 produced demands for silver coinage as well as paper inflation; and when Grant blocked a paper expansion of the currency, the addition of silver was viewed by many soft-money men as the only logical alternative. At the same time, a decline in the demand for silver in the world market placed the nation's silver-mining interests in a precarious position. In 1871, Germany demonetized silver, and three years later the countries of the Latin Union suspended the minting of silver coins. However, the opening up of new silver deposits in Nevada at this time led to a sharp increase in American silver supplies. The consequent drop in silver prices made the silver interests turn to the government for assistance, and Congress in 1878 responded to this pressure with the Bland-Allison Act. Enacted by a bipartisan coalition that drew its principal support from the mining states of the West and the farm states of the West and South, the Bland-Allison Act was repassed over President Hayes' veto. This measure required that the Secretary of the Treasury "purchase . . . silver bullion, at the market price thereof, not less than two million dollars worth per month, nor more than four million dollars per month, and cause the same to be coined monthly, as fast as so purchased," into silver dollars at the current ratio to gold.

Although many deflationists predicted that the Bland-Allison Act would drive gold from circulation by making so much silver money available, such forecasts were not borne out. The silver dollars proved as unpopular as they had before their demonetization in 1873, and they formed a relatively insignificant part of the country's monetary system. Furthermore, the government always purchased the minimum rather than maximum amount of silver called for by the Bland-Allison Act. Finally, the revival of the American export market after the depression of the 1870's caused an influx of gold and increased the nation's gold supply to such an extent that there seemed little likelihood that gold would be driven from circulation by silver. Despite these developments, both Republican and Democratic Treasury officials were disturbed by what they considered the potential dangers of the Bland-Allison Act. In 1884, Hugh McCulloch, Arthur's Secretary of the Treasury, declared that the continued coinage of silver would eventually force the government to abandon gold payments. In the following year, Daniel Manning, Secretary of the Treasury under Cleveland, demanded the repeal of the Bland-Allison Act on the grounds that gold was being hoarded in fear that inflation was coming and that the business community was losing confidence in the nation's currency system.

The Treasury Department's concern over the future of its reserves of gold was not shared by a comparatively large group of congressmen who were determined to expand rather than contract the currency. Representatives and senators from the western mining states formed an interparty alliance known as the "silver bloc." Pledged "to do something for silver," they could count on the cooperation of several farm-state congressmen whose constituents were demanding that inflationary measures be taken to lighten the burden of agrarian debt. To the farmer, silver seemed to offer the only solution to a problem that he thought could be largely solved by supplying more money to meet his demands. While the production of gold had declined from $129,614,000 in 1866 to $118,848,700 in 1890, the population of the United States had steadily increased. There was, as the farmer saw it, simply not enough money for all. But as the output of gold decreased, that of silver rose from $11,000,000 in 1865 to $57,000,000 in 1890. The farmer believed that the obvious solution was to coin more silver.

In a bid for the votes of both the mining and farm states the Republicans in the campaign of 1888 promised to aid the silver interests. And, with the adoption in 1890 of the Sherman Silver Purchase Act, they redeemed their campaign promise. The Sherman Act was made possible by a deal that called for western Republican votes for the McKinley Tariff Act in return for eastern Republican votes for silver; it was generally opposed by the Democratic inflationists, most of whom felt that it did not go far enough.

The Sherman Silver Purchase Act directed the Secretary of the Treasury to buy 4,500,000 ounces of silver each month and to pay for these purchases with treasury notes. The act further stated that it was the "established policy of the United States to maintain the two metals [silver and gold] on a parity with each other upon the present legal ratio"; and the Secretary of the Treasury was authorized to redeem the treasury notes "in gold or silver coin, at his discretion"; but, as long as the Sherman Silver Purchase Act was in effect, the Treasury Department interpreted this provision to mean that the "notes shall always be redeemed in gold or its equivalent."

Checking the Drain on Gold

When the Sherman Silver Purchase Act was adopted, the United States treasury had a surplus; but within four years, the surplus was converted into a deficit by the Harrison Administration's generous pension program, a drop in tariff receipts under the McKinley Tariff, and the silver purchases required by the law of 1890. As the surplus declined, the pressure on gold increased. Fearing the effect of the silver purchase program on the nation's monetary system, people hurriedly converted their assets into gold. At the same time, the flow of gold from the United States to Europe was accelerated by the decline of American exports in 1892.

Although the currency question was the most important issue facing the voters in 1892, it was largely ignored by both major parties, and only the Populists, a newly formed agrarian party, came out for the free coinage of silver. The Democrats, hoping to capitalize on the widespread dissatisfaction with the McKinley Tariff, again nominated Cleveland and ran him on a low-tariff platform. The Republicans, who had been overwhelmingly defeated in the midterm elections of 1890, once more chose Harrison, and the Populists nominated James B. Weaver of Iowa. The outcome of the election was an accurate indication of the voters' disgust with Harrison's submission to the pressure groups that had played such an important role under his administration. The Democrats gained control of both houses of Congress, and Cleveland received 227 electoral votes to 145 for Harrison and 22 for Weaver.

Cleveland at once inherited Harrison's financial problems and in a few months faced the Panic of 1893. The hardest times since the Civil War followed, attended by numerous business failures, widespread unemployment, severe suffering, and a deterioration in the government's financial position. Federal revenue fell off sharply, and many people, fearing that their gold and silver certificates would not continue to be redeemable in gold, hastened to present them to the treasury before it was too late. The net gold reserve declined from $190,232,405 in 1890 to $114,342,367 in 1892 and $64,873,025 in 1894. It seemed to be only a matter of time before the United States would be forced to abandon gold payments.

Despite the strength of the silver interests in the Democratic party, Cleveland was determined to maintain the gold reserves, and soon after taking office in 1893, he demanded the repeal of the Sherman Silver Purchase Act. Congress, however, was reluctant to take this step, and only after Cleveland had used the patronage to win over a number of doubtful representatives and senators was the bill for the repeal adopted. This measure ended silver purchases by the government, but the government's problem remained, for gold was still flowing from the treasury at an alarming rate. The basic difficulty was that the government had to pay out gold to citizens who presented either silver or gold certificates to the treasury; but it was also compelled by law to put these notes back into circulation as currency; and they could then be resubmitted to the treasury for more gold. This "endless chain," as it was called, could only be broken by convincing the people that the country was not about to be forced to end gold payments. In short, if individuals were confident that the government had an adequate supply of gold, they would no longer seek to redeem their notes.

By 1894, the government's gold stocks were so low that the Cleveland Administration decided that they could only be replenished by a sale of bonds for gold. But the first two bond issues in January and November, 1894, which were subscribed to by banking syndicates, were purchased by gold obtained from the treasury in exchange for notes. This operation left the government's gold supply in no better shape than before the bonds had been issued. Cleveland was forced to turn to a syndicate led by J. P. Morgan. In February, 1895, Morgan agreed to buy bonds with gold, half of which would be obtained from Europe and none of which would be drawn from the treasury of the United States. Morgan further agreed to use his influence to check the flow of American gold to Europe. Although Morgan received the bonds at 104½, they subsequently rose to 119. Historians have used much paper and printer's ink in debates over whether or not Morgan's terms were extortionate; most think that they were, but the Cleveland Administration nevertheless attained its objective. Morgan fulfilled his part of the bargain, confidence in the nation's monetary system was restored, and payments in gold were continued. Contemporaries—particularly representatives of the farm and silver groups—complained that Cleveland had subordinated the welfare of the nation to the interests of the money power, but despite such charges, the arrangement with Morgan was so successful that in 1896 the government was able to by-pass the bankers and offer its fourth bond issue of $100,000,000 directly to the public.

The split in the Democratic party created by the repeal of the Sherman Silver Purchase Act made it practically impossible for the Administration to carry out its program of tariff reduction. The advocates of inflation in the western wing of the party were no longer prepared to recognize Cleveland as their leader, and eastern Democrats proved as willing to cooperate with the Republicans on the tariff as they had on the currency question. As a result, Cleveland's plans for tariff reform were blocked by party factionalism and the pressure of the special interests. Although the Wilson Bill, which was introduced by Representative William L. Wilson of West Virginia and adopted by the House, was a low-tariff measure that resembled the Mills Bill, its character was completely altered by more than six hundred increases that were added to it by Senate amendments. The sugar bounty was ended, but duties were imposed on raw as well as refined sugar. Although the new act also made provision for an income tax, in 1895 the Supreme Court ruled it unconstitutional. While generally lower than the McKinley Tariff, the Wilson Tariff, which was approved by the House and Senate in 1894, was blatantly protectionist, and Cleveland allowed it to become law without his signature.

By the end of his second administration, Cleveland had alienated large blocs of voters. His tariff policy had satisfied no one completely; his use of federal troops in the Pullman strike had antagonized the workers; and his stand on the silver question had convinced the farmers and western miners that the Democrats as well as the Republicans were controlled by Wall Street. His positive accomplishment, continuing gold payments, had also split his party into two irreconcilable groups and had given the United States its most controversial issue since Reconstruction. Cleveland gave the farmers the final evidence they needed to prove to themselves that the government of the United States was owned and run by the moneyed interests of the seaboard cities. Measuring their distress only by their lack of money and thus convinced that only expansion of the currency by printing paper money or by the free coinage of silver could solve their major economic problems, farm leaders in the West and South eventually resolved to join forces with the western silver miners to wrest control of the government from the "bloated bondholders" of the East.

Waves of Farm Protest

By the late 1880's, many American farmers had already decided that only political action could save them. They had played a dominant rôle in the nation's life before the Civil War, and they found it difficult to accept their subordinate position in the postwar decades. The farmer's principal grievances were caused largely by his own ruinous individualism and by his inability to control the conditions upon which his profits depended. The farmer who had developed no modern marketing techniques on any significant scale complained that he had little or no say over the prices of the products that he bought and sold, his credit terms, the value of his currency, and his shipping rates to market. The prewar farmer had had no more control than the postwar farmer over market prices for his produce; but he had not been at the mercy of railroads in a position to charge what seemed to be exorbitant rates, and his representatives in the government had been able to limit or prevent the enactment of tariff, credit, and currency laws detrimental to his interest. The farmers' lack of economic power seemed merely a manifestation of their loss of political power and social prestige. Reasoning that those who controlled the government were in conspiracy against them, they concluded that they could improve their lot only by voting the businessmen and their representatives out of office and capturing the government again for themselves, "the people." This kind of struggle was as old as the American nation; and, in launching the campaigns, the farmers of the 1890's were convinced that they were refighting the battles that Jefferson and his agrarian allies had fought and won in the 1790's.

In the 1870's the Grange won a number of notable political victories in several midwestern farm states. But the Grange represented mainly larger farmers and their commercial allies, and once they had obtained the railroad regulation they desired, the Grangers tended to lose interest in politics. As it declined, there arose other farm organizations in the South and West. As early as 1878, a Grand State Alliance was formed in Texas, and within a decade it had combined with the Farmers' Union of Louisiana to organize the National Farmers' Alliance and Co-operative Union of America. By 1887, the Alliance had spread to nine southern states. In the same years, the Agricultural Wheel, founded in Arkansas in 1882, soon attracted the support of many southern farmers. In 1888, the two organizations joined forces to form the Farmers' and Laborers' Union of America. Although the union had a number of political planks in its platform, its principal objectives were social, and its economic program emphasized agricultural improvement through the use of more efficient farm techniques and the establishment of cooperatives.

In the old Northwest the National Farmers' Alliance—or the Northwest Alliance, as it was more generally known—was first established in Illinois, and in 1880 it established itself as a national organization. The Northwest Alliance encouraged the formation of cooperatives, but it also gave considerably more attention to political action than did the southern farm groups. In its platform of 1887, the Northwest Alliance demanded the free coinage of silver, paper-money issues, the direct election of senators, and the nationalization of the railroad and telegraph systems. Although the alliance made no attempt to form a third party, it proposed that "farmers throughout the country . . . aid in the work of immediate organization, that we may act in concert for our own and the common good." In December, 1889, both the Northwest Alliance and the Farmers' and Laborers' Union—which was renamed the National Farmers' Alliance and Industrial Union—held their conventions in St. Louis. Although representatives of both groups sought to devise a formula on which they could unite, the negotiations broke down, and the two organizations continued to go their separate ways.

Despite the reluctance of both Alliances to form a third party, the platforms adopted at St. Louis had numerous demands that could be obtained only by political action. The Southern Alliance—as the National Farmers' Alliance and Industrial Union was generally called—advocated the free coinage of silver, abolition of national banks, government ownership of the railroads and telegraph, and the prevention of trading in grain futures. They also proposed an imaginative system of commodity credit that would be financed and administered by the federal government. Under this plan, the government would set up a series of subtreasury offices and grain elevators in which a farmer could deposit his nonperishable staples. In return for his crops, the farmer would receive a certificate of deposit that could be used to obtain a loan that was worth 80 per cent of the current price of the commodities stored. Produce not reclaimed at the end of the year was to be sold at auction. The Northwest Alliance did not adopt the subtreasury plan, but its platform in all other essentials was similar to that of the Southern Alliance.

The regular Democratic and Republican parties refused to accept the program of the Alliances. This forced the farmers to enter their own candidates in the election campaigns of 1890. In the southern states,

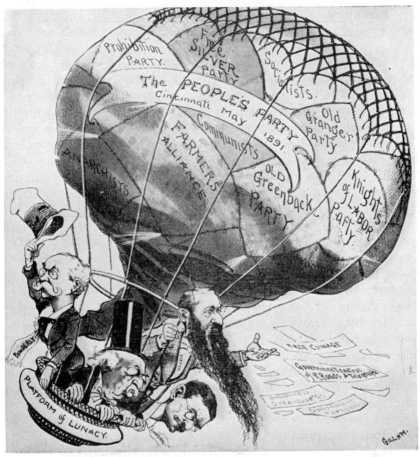

"A Party of Patches": *The Populists* (Judge)

the Alliance sought to gain control of the Democratic party machinery. In the West, the farmers drew up their own tickets and formed third parties—which were variously named People's, or Independent, or Industrial parties—to challenge the dominant Republicans. Despite the lack of a national political organization, the farmers won notable victories. In the South, they gained majorities in five state legislatures and elected three Governors, one senator, and forty-four representatives. In the West, the farmers made their most impressive showing in Kansas, where the People's party secured control of the lower house of the legislature and elected five congressmen and one senator. In Nebraska, they obtained a majority in the legislature, while the Independent candidate won the senatorial race in South Dakota.

The outcome of the election of 1890 strongly encouraged the farmers to form a national party. But the successes also alarmed the regular parties and enticed dissident politicians looking for a popular issue with which to associate themselves. Both of these groups, from this time forward, began to infiltrate the ranks of the reformers and to weaken them from within. In May, 1891, representatives of various farm groups met at Cincinnati with delegates from the Knights of Labor. Their convention voted overwhelmingly for the organization of a third party. More than a year later—in July, 1892—the Populists held their first national convention in Omaha. After stating that "wealth belongs to him who creates it," the party's first platform demanded "free and unlimited coinage of silver and gold at the present legal ratio of sixteen to one," a graduated income tax, the nationalization of railroads, telephones, and telegraphs, a reform of the nation's land system, and the establishment of postal savings banks. The Populists also attempted to appeal to a wider electorate than the farm sections. The currency plank was designed to attract farmers as well as the voters in the silver-mining states. Labor's interests were revealed in planks calling for immigration restriction, abolition of detective—that is to say, strikebreaking—agencies, and the enforcement of the eight-hour day in all federal projects. War veterans were promised pensions; and the support of political reformers was sought with demands for a single term for the President of the United States, the direct election of senators, and the initiative, referendum, and recall. For their candidates, the Populists nominated General James B. Weaver, a Union veteran, for president and General James G. Field, a Confederate veteran, for vice-president.

In the election of 1892, Weaver and Field polled 1,041,600 popular votes and 22 electoral votes. In the West, the Populists carried North Dakota, Colorado, Idaho, Kansas, and Nevada, and showed considerable strength in both Oregon and Nebraska. The southern Populists, while less successful than those of the West, for the first time since the end of the Reconstruction weakened, if they did not break, the Democratic party's monopoly in the South's political affairs. Two years later, in the midterm elections of 1894, the Populists polled 1,471,600 votes and elected six senators and seven representatives.

In the campaigns of 1892 and 1894, the Populists received the support of the silver miners—and to a lesser extent, that of the workers and reformers—but the party was essentially agrarian. In down-to-earth language, the party's spokesmen preached a type of agrarian radicalism that shocked and appalled "respectable" groups in the East. They urged their supporters to "rob the plutocrat who puts chains and shackles

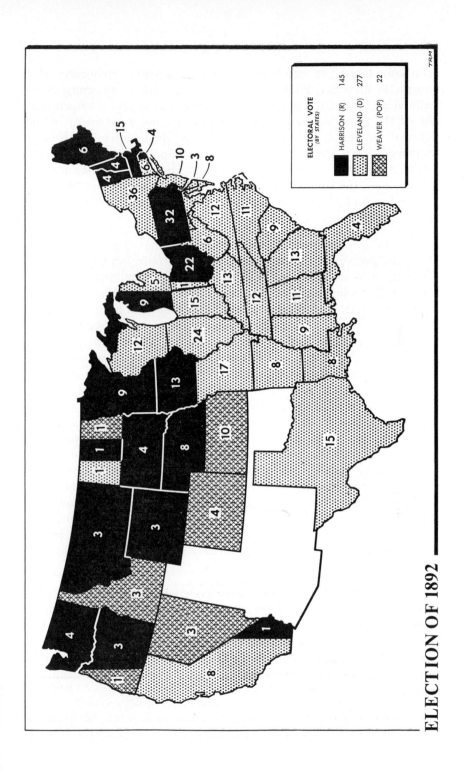

ELECTION OF 1892

ELECTORAL VOTE
(BY STATES)

HARRISON (R)   145

CLEVELAND (D)   277

WEAVER (POP)   22

upon your limbs." In attacking their opponents, they frequently used remarkable invective. Pitchfork Ben Tillman, while campaigning nominally as a Democrat, denounced Cleveland's candidacy as "a prostitution of the principles of the Democracy . . . and a surrender of the rights of the people to the financial kings of the country." In Kansas, "Sockless" Jerry Simpson, referring to his opponent as "Prince Hal," ridiculed him for wearing silk stockings. Mrs. Mary Lease, another Kansan, took the stump to urge the farmers of the state to "raise less corn and more hell." In a speech typical of Populist campaign oratory, Mrs. Lease said:

> Wall Street owns the country. It is no longer a government of the people, by the people and for the people, but a government of Wall Street, by Wall Street and for Wall Street. The great common people of this country are slaves, and monopoly is the master. The West and South are bound and prostrate before the manufacturing East. Money rules, and our Vice President is a London banker. Our laws are the output of a system which clothes rascals in robes and honesty in rags. The parties lie to us and the political speakers mislead us. . . . The common people are robbed to enrich their masters. . . . There are thirty men in the United States whose aggregate wealth is over one and one-half billion dollars. There are a half a million looking for work. . . . We want money, land and transportation. We want the abolition of the National Banks, and we want the power to make loans direct from the government. We want the accursed foreclosure system wiped out. . . . We will stand by our homes and stay by our firesides by force if necessary, and we will not pay our debts to the loan-shark companies until the government pays its debts to us. The people are at bay, let the bloodhounds of money who have dogged us thus far beware.

Despite the wide range of issues covered by the Populists' platforms, after 1892 the party increasingly subordinated all other questions to that of silver. The simple formula of the free coinage of silver had the greatest appeal to dissatisfied groups inside and outside farm ranks, but it was also an issue on which the Democratic and Republican parties seemed unwilling to compromise. In 1895 a Populist party manifesto stated:

> As early as 1865–66 a conspiracy was entered into between the gold gamblers of Europe and America . . . [for] the fol-

lowing purposes: to fasten upon the people of the United States the burdens of perpetual debt; to destroy the greenbacks which had safely brought us through the perils of war; to strike down silver as a money metal; to deny to the people the use of Federal paper and silver—the two independent sources of money guaranteed by the Constitution; to fasten upon the country the single gold standard of Britain, and to delegate to thousands of banking corporations, organized for private gain, the sovereign control, for all time, over the issue and volume of all supplemental paper currency.

By 1894, the Populists were convinced that the future of their party rested with the silver issue. Party speakers subordinated other planks in the Populist platform to silver; rural papers carried countless editorials on the advantages of the free coinage of silver; and books and pamphlets on the subject became best sellers. None of this literature was as influential or as popular as W. H. Harvey's *Coin's Financial School*. Issued in 1894, this book described how a "Professor Coin" won over a number of widely known advocates of the gold standard to silver by the clarity of his exposition and the skill with which he refuted their arguments. *Coin's Financial School* was read by perhaps a half-million Americans, many of whom undoubtedly agreed with Harvey that silver was the "money of the people, and gold the money of the rich." The year after the appearance of *Coin's Financial School*, Ignatius Donnelly, a Minnesota Populist, published *The American People's Money*, in which a farmer repeatedly scored in an argument with a businessman. Although less popular than *Coin's Financial School*, Donnelly's book, by going beyond the demand for silver to other planks of the Populist program, provided a more reliable explanation of farm discontent.

The Campaign of 1896 and Its Aftermath

By the midnineties, conditions strongly militated against greater successes for the farmers than they had already achieved. The diversity of American farm production in which, for example, southern farmers selling cottonseed oil were actually in competition with corn-and-hog men who sold lard, a varied rather than uniform national pattern of shipping and credit costs, weakness within the reform ranks caused by the presence of opportunists and traitors, and the concentration on one issue—silver—all these presaged a scattered rather than strong national election appeal. In the tradition of American politics, any party taking

"Taking the Gold Cure"

a strong stand on one issue, such as silver, stood to lose votes in areas of the country where that issue had little appeal. By the late 1890's also, the rhetoric of the reformers, essentially an appeal to distressed native Protestant small businessmen had little attraction for the most populated and politically powerful areas of the country, since these were increasingly dominated by an urban, immigrant, and industrial wage earner's outlook.

Despite these weaknesses, the Populists based their hopes for success in the election of 1896 on the conviction that both the Democrats and Republicans would refuse to advocate the free coinage of silver. With the gold vote thus split between the two major parties, the Populists were confident that they could capture both the Presidency and Congress. The Republicans did not disappoint the Populists. Their convention was dominated at all times by Mark Hanna and his supporters from the gold wing of the party. Hanna who had once proclaimed that "no man in public life owes the public anything," was the archetype of the businessman who had now directly entered politics. Having gained control of the Republican party in Cleveland and then in Ohio, he was now ready to take over the party's national organization. Hanna's plans called for the nomination of his fellow Ohioan, William McKinley, whose assets as a candidate were undeniable. A handsome man of commanding appearance, he looked like an artist's stereotype of a "statesman"; William Allen White has written that he "walked among men [like] a bronze statue . . . determinedly looking for his pedestal." * Despite an extensive career in state and national politics, he had seldom taken a clear-cut stand on any controversial issue except for the high tariff for which Eastern businessmen respected him. Yet westerners were reminded that he had voted for the Bland-Allison Act and that he favored some form—precisely what form was never made clear—of bimetallism. To the voters of every section he was announced by Hanna simply as "Bill McKinley, the advance agent of prosperity."

In the months preceding the Republican convention, Hanna had secured the support of almost all the southern and western delegates for McKinley. Easterners, who were worried about McKinley's vague remarks on bimetallism † and who resented Hanna's plans to seize control of the party, were faced by a *fait accompli*. McKinley was nominated on the first ballot, and the party's currency plank opposed the free coinage of silver (except by international agreement) and "every measure calculated to debase our currency." Following the adoption of the gold-standard plank, thirty-four delegates, led by Senator Teller of Colorado, withdrew from the convention amidst cries from the majority of "Go! Go! . . . Go to Chicago [the site of the Democratic convention]! Take the Democratic train!"

The Democratic convention differed radically from that of the Republicans. From the outset the party's rebels were in the ascendency, and rebellion and silver were synonymous. The platform, was an itemized repudiation of the Cleveland Administration. It demanded the

---

* William Allen White, *Masks in a Pageant* (New York: The Macmillan Company, 1928), p. 155.

† Hanna, who favored the gold standard as much as the eastern Republicans, refused to commit himself until the last moment. When Henry Cabot Lodge told Hanna that he would have to put a gold plank in the platform, the following exchange took place:

Hanna: "Who in hell are you?"

Lodge: "Senator Henry Cabot Lodge, of Massachusetts."

Hanna: "Well, Senator Henry Cabot Lodge, of Massachusetts, you can go plumb to hell. You have nothing to say about it."

"free and unlimited coinage of both silver and gold at the present legal ratio of 16 to 1." It advocated federal regulation of the trusts and railroads and condemned the government's sale of the bonds to the banks and the use of the injunction in labor disputes. But it was silver—and silver alone—that brought the delegates to the point of hysteria and provided William Jennings Bryan with an opportunity that has seldom been granted to any other American politician. As the final speaker representing the silver faction in the debate over the platform, Bryan found an overwhelmingly sympathetic audience that did not need to be convinced but asked only to be aroused. And Bryan did not disappoint his listeners.

He had a speech in hand which he had delivered with great success countless times before in the West. Now he had a national audience. Opening his speech in a seemingly moderate and even conciliatory tone, he gradually developed a simple but vivid thesis, which he presented with mounting fervor. Drawing a line between the "struggling masses" and the "idle hoarders of idle capital," he hammered away at the single theme that the producing classes had been made prisoners of a system from which they could be released only by the free coinage of silver. As he developed the agrarian indictment of the financial classes, he identified himself and his party with the sons of the soil, who had made possible America's growth and success but who were now forced to fight in "defense of our homes, our families, and posterity." Once more, the Jeffersonians were asked to overthrow the New Federalism, right the balance between city and country, and return the country and its economy to their rightful rulers. The issues were clear and the time for action had arrived. In his concluding passages, Bryan contrasted the contending forces and called on his supporters to launch a crusade:

> [The advocates of gold] come to us and tell us that the great cities are in favor of the gold standard; we reply that the great cities rest upon our broad and fertile prairies. Burn down your cities and leave our farms, and your cities will spring up again as if by magic; but destroy our farms and the grass will grow in the streets of every city in the country.
> . . . If they [the gold interests] dare to come out in the open field and defend the gold standard as a good thing, we will fight them to the uttermost. Having behind us the producing masses of this nation and the world, supported by the commercial interests, the laboring interests and the toilers every-

where, we will answer their demand for a gold standard by saying to them: You shall not press down upon the brow of labor this crown of thorns, you shall not crucify mankind upon a cross of gold.

Bryan's speech, which had been repeatedly interrupted by bursts of sustained applause, was followed by an hour-long ovation. The convention had found both its issue and its leader; and on the following day, Bryan was nominated on the fifth ballot and Arthur Sewall of Maine was chosen as his running mate. To eastern business groups, the Democratic convention was a "political debauch" and Bryan was a class-conscious radical demanding a revolution. But if Bryan's opponents had taken the trouble to read carefully the speech of this hitherto obscure Nebraskan politician, they would have discovered that he was asking only for a return to an America of an earlier day. He was not urging the proletariat on to the barricades, but asking only that the nation's small producers—whether in factory, shop, or farm—be restored to the place that they had once occupied in the American economy. In a significant section of his speech that was addressed to the convention's gold delegates he said:

> When you come before us and tell us that we are about to disturb your business interests, we reply that you have disturbed our business interests by your course.
>
> We say to you that you have made the definition of a business man too limited in its application. The man who is employed for wages is as much a business man as his employer; the attorney in a country town is as much a business man as the corporation counsel in a great metropolis; the merchant at the cross-roads store is as much a business man as the merchant of New York; the farmer who goes forth in the morning and toils all day, who begins in the spring and toils all summer, and who by the application of brain and muscle to the natural resources of the country creates wealth, is as much a business man as the man who goes upon the Board of Trade and bets upon the price of grain; the miners who go down a thousand feet into the earth, or climb two thousand feet upon the cliffs, and bring forth from their hiding places the precious metals to be poured into the channels of trade are as much business men as the few financial magnates who, in a back room, corner the money of the world. We come to speak of this broader class of business men.

The Democratic party's stand on the currency question upset the plans of the Populist leaders and forced them into a position where they could do little but choose between the lesser of two evils. If they nominated their own candidates, they would split the silver vote and give the election to the Republicans. If, on the other hand, they supported Bryan, they would be signing their own party's death warrant. Meeting three weeks after the Democrats, the delegates to the Populist convention finally concluded that the pressure of events compelled them to abandon Populism for silver and Bryan. In nominating Bryan, they staked everything on a panacea rather than a realistic program; and Henry Demarest Lloyd, a Chicago reformer who had sympathized with the Populists' social and economic reforms, wrote:

> The Free Silver movement is a fake. Free Silver is a cowbird of the Reform movement. It waited until the nest had been built by sacrifices and labour of others, and then it laid its eggs in it. . . . The People's party has been betrayed.

While the Populists were willing—however reluctantly—to vote for Bryan, they could not accept Sewall, who was a banker, railroad director, and shipbuilder. The southern delegates, bitterly opposed to a coalition with the Democrats, demanded that the party make at least a show of independence. With these considerations in mind, the convention selected Tom Watson, a veteran agrarian leader in Georgia, as the party's candidate for vice-president.

Although the Gold Democrats nominated their own ticket, they played a relatively insignificant role in the campaign of 1896, for to most voters the choice was between Bryan and silver, on the one hand, and McKinley and gold, on the other. The Democratic-Populist candidate conducted a strenuous campaign in which he concentrated on the silver issue, and he traveled 18,000 miles and made countless speeches. (John Hay said that Bryan made only one speech, but that he made it twice a day.) The Republicans under Mark Hanna's direction kept their candidate at home, where he waged a decorous "front-porch" campaign. Almost daily, large crowds of loyal Republicans visited McKinley at what the silver groups nicknamed the "shrine of the golden calf." McKinley's statements, which were carried in the nation's leading newspapers, harped on the single theme that the Republicans alone were capable of providing the country with prosperity and stability. As the campaign drew to a close, the Republicans revealed both their fear of the election's outcome and their determination to win the contest. Many businessmen, drawing up contracts, inserted in them a clause making their validity contingent on Bryan's defeat; workingmen's pay

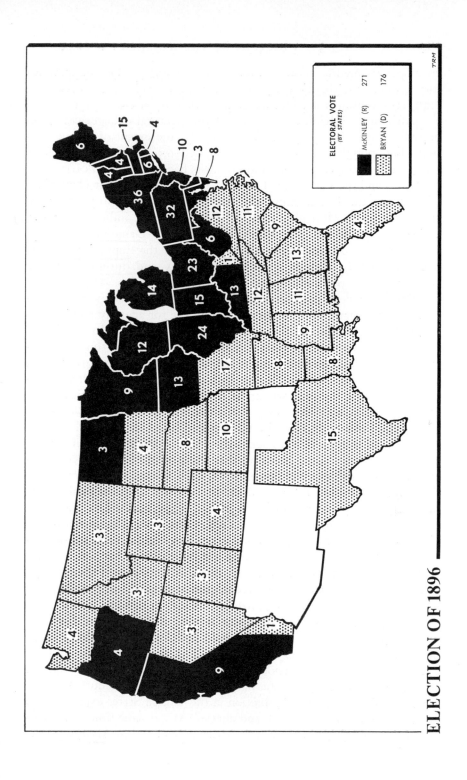

ELECTION OF 1896

ELECTORAL VOTE
(BY STATES)

McKINLEY (R)   271

BRYAN (D)   176

envelopes frequently contained notices warning that a Democratic victory would cost them their jobs; and some farmers were threatened with foreclosure if the silver interests carried the election.

Although McKinley's majority in the electoral college was unexpectedly large—271 to 176—it did not reflect the extent of Bryan's appeal. The popular vote for Bryan totaled 6,509,925 to McKinley's 7,104,779; but the Democrats and Populists had been able to carry only the South and the Far West. The efficient organization that Hanna had created for the Republicans, the party's almost inexhaustible funds, and the support McKinley received from the most influential people immeasurably helped the Republican victory. Democratic-Populist campaign expenditures were only $300,000, but the Republicans in the last weeks of the contest spent $25,000 a day and during the entire campaign they probably spent more than $7,000,000. The repeated warnings of college presidents, clergymen, business leaders, and newspaper editors that a vote for Bryan was a vote for anarchy and revolution presumably affected the decisions of many voters. Most members of the nonagrarian middle class considered Bryan a threat to their property, savings, and income; and urban workers and labor groups had very little in common with the Jacksonian traditions Bryan represented. Without the support of the large but unorganized middle and working classes, no party could win a national election.

In the years after 1890 the farmers had based their appeal on class and sectional issues and were accused by their opponents of being radical revolutionaries. But, knowing that those who controlled the government were its principal beneficiaries, they wished not to overthrow the government, but to capture it and make it work for the small rather than large entrepreneurs. Their effort had really reached its peak even before their loss in 1896. A hundred years after the inception of the struggle between Jefferson and Hamilton, the farmers, still deluding themselves that they really were not businessmen but simple innocent yeomen, went down to defeat. But their loss caused them to develop, at last, modern political techniques that have since made them one of the most powerful organized minorities in national politics.

The Populists lost the argument as well as the election, for their predictions about the effect of the gold policies on the nation's economy were not substantiated by events. The upswing of the business cycle following the depression of the midnineties benefited the farmer as well as other groups in the nation. European crop failures in 1897 and increasing industrial production in the United States expanded the farmer's market both at home and abroad. At the same time, the opening of the gold fields in the South African Rand and in Alaska and the introduction of the cyanide process for refining gold combined to disprove the farmers' contention that there could never be an adequate supply of gold.

On assuming office, one of McKinley's first acts was to call Congress into special session to consider an upward revision of the tariff. The Dingley Tariff, which was introduced by Representative Nelson Dingley, Jr., of Maine and adopted by Congress in 1897, marked a new high in American protectionism. Duties were placed on raw wool, hides, and other products that had been on the free list since 1890; the McKinley Tariff rates on metals, which had been removed by the Wilson Tariff, were restored; special care was again taken to safeguard the interests of sugar refiners; and the reciprocity provisions of the McKinley Tariff were revived. Rates were so high under the Dingley Tariff that imports declined despite returning prosperity; and during the first year that the tariff was in operation, the revenue collected from it was $27,000,000 less than that produced by the Wilson Tariff during a similar period. If there remained any doubt in contemporary minds about the significance of the election of 1896, it was removed by the Dingley Tariff.

Because of many western inflationists in his party, McKinley approached the currency issue with far more caution that he had the tariff. A month after his inauguration, he appointed a three-man commission to investigate the status of international bimetallism in Europe. But when Great Britain, which throughout the century had called the tune in international finance, made it clear that it had no interest in silver coinage in any form, the President was able to tell the soft-money groups in his party that the Administration's only alternative was the gold standard. At the same time the upswing in the business cycle and the marked increase in world gold production deprived the inflationists of their two most effective points. Accordingly, in March, 1900, the Currency Act which legalized the gold standard, was adopted. Under this measure, a gold dollar of 25.8 grains nine-tenths fine was made the unit of value; all other forms of the currency were to be kept at parity with the gold dollar; and parity was to be maintained through a special gold fund of $150,000,000.

The Currency Act of 1900 stands as an epitaph to the farm protest movement. Mark Hanna had promised the voters prosperity; and American business—if not the Republicans—had fulfilled this promise. Good times blunted the old reform impulses, and farmers tended to forget their earlier grievances, return to the traditional parties, and take their stand with the defenders of the status quo.

FOR SUPPLEMENTARY READING

There exists no really superior general work on American politics for this period. One colorful study to be used with caution is M. Josephson, *The Politicos, 1865–1869* (1938). The more recent L. D. White, *The Republican Era, 1869–1901* (1958), is decent on administrative history. Regional studies and biographies are the principal works to be consulted, however. To Woodward's fine study *Origins of the New South*, add H. S. Merrill, *The Bourbon Democracy of the Middle West* (1953). Merrill's *Grover Cleveland and the Democratic Party* (1957) is shorter and less adulatory than Nevins's *Grover Cleveland*, still, however, a basic work. The latter should be preceded by a better work by Nevins, *Hamilton Fish* (1936). The standard, but not exemplary, biographies of the Presidents are, in order: H. Barnard, *Rutherford B. Hayes and His America* (1955); R. G. Caldwell, *James A. Garfield, Party Chieftain* (1931); G. F. Howe, *Chester A. Arthur* (1934); the aforementioned studies on Cleveland; A. Sievers, *Benjamin Harrison* (2 vols., 1952, 1959); and C. S. Olcott, *The Life of William McKinley* (2 vols., 1916). D. S. Muzzey has written *James G. Blaine* (1934); D. B. Chidsey has presented *The Gentleman from New York: A Life of Roscoe Conkling* (1935); and Herbert Croly memorializes *Marcus Alonzo Hanna* (1912). Third parties are surveyed in Destler's book, *American Radicalism;* W. E. Binkley, *American Political Parties: Their Natural History* (1943); and F. E. Haynes, *Third Party Movements Since the Civil War* (1916). Radicalism in the 1890's is covered in the previously cited books of Solon Buck, John Hicks, and Richard Hofstadter. On the tariff read the classic F. W. Taussig, *The Tariff History of the United States* (1931). On the money question use W. J. Schultz and M. B. Caine, *Financial Development of the United States* (1937). On the Supreme Court consult C. B. Swisher, *American Constitutional Development* (1943). Civil service reform has its standard analysis in C. R. Fish, *The Civil Service and the Patronage* (1904); a more recent work is A. B. Sageser, *The First Two Decades of the Pendleton Act* (1935). Two famous contemporary studies of American politics are W. Wilson, *Congressional Government* (1885) (Pb) and J. Bryce, *The American Commonwealth* (2 vols., 1888) (Pb).

8

-≫≫-≫≫-≫≫-≫≫-≫≫-≫≫-≫≫-≫≫

Expansion Overseas

ROM ITS EARLIEST DAYS, America seemed "destined" for expansion. Founded as outposts of religious faith and of growing empires, the American colonies pushed ever westward, lured by the richness of the continent. Between 1789 and 1861, the United States moved steadily into the unsettled lands of the North American continent. Federalist or Republican, Jacksonian or Whig, every President accepted expansion on the continent as a fundamental tenet of American foreign policy. The purchase of Louisiana, the acquisition of Florida, the annexation of Texas, the conquest of New Mexico and California, and the division of Oregon, all showed the willingness of political leaders to satisfy the American desire for new territory. Although certain commercial groups looked avidly on such overseas outposts as Samoa and Hawaii and slave interests clamored for Cuba, the government held steadfast to a policy of continental expansion.

In the years between Appomattox and Versailles, the United States became an industrial nation and a world power. The old lure of continental expansion gave way to the new magic of expansion overseas into the Pacific and Caribbean. The character and direction of expansion had changed as the United States, now filling the continent, planted outposts overseas to protect its growing world-wide interests.

Imperialists without a Mandate

Immediately after the Civil War, Americans temporarily abandoned their traditional interest in expansion. Worn out by civil conflict, they were inclined to shun foreign adventures that might lead to further bloodletting and misery. Not the acquisition of weak neighbors or distant islands, but the reconstruction of the South, the conquest of the last frontier, and the development of industry claimed their energy and interest.

What postbellum expansionists there were, were both voices of the past and portents of the future. Although continually urging the continental expansion of the United States, they argued even more strongly that America's destiny lay on the high seas. William H. Seward, Secretary of State under Presidents Lincoln and Johnson, in many ways bridged the gap between the pre-Civil War spirit of Manifest Destiny and the spread-eagle Americanism of the 1890's. Seward was convinced that American continental domination and American sea power were intimately related, and that the increased strength with which the United States had emerged from the Civil War could permit it to assume a more important role in world politics, particularly in the Caribbean, the Pacific, and eastern Asia.

For Seward, the purchase of Alaska in 1867 was part of a larger program for the extension of American political and economic control across the Pacific. As early as 1860, he had predicted that the Alaskan "outposts of St. Petersburg" would eventually "become outposts of my own country—monuments of the civilization of the United States in the Northwest." Despite Seward's interest in the acquisition of Alaska, the impetus for its transfer originated in Russia rather than the United States. During the Crimean War, Russia had considered disposing of its North American possession as a strategic liability, and in 1860 Baron de Stoeckl, the Russian ambassador to the United States, discussed the possibility of American purchase of Alaska with Washington officials. By the conclusion of the Civil War, the Russian plans for the sale of Alaska had crystalized, and in December, 1866, the Tsar directed Stoeckl to offer Alaska to the United States for not less than $5,000,000. Behind the Tsar's decision was the fact that the Russian American Company in Alaska was close to bankruptcy, and the Tsarist government was not disposed to subsidize it. Many Russian officials were also convinced that Alaska should be abandoned so that the government could concentrate on the economic development of the Amur region in Siberia. Finally, it was thought that the sale of Alaska would rid Russia of a region that was considered a potential source of conflict with the United States.

In March, 1867, Baron de Stoeckl made his offer to the American Secretary of State. Seward referred the matter to the President and cabinet, and the purchase of Alaska for $7,200,000 was approved. As soon as these terms were accepted by the Tsar's government, a treaty embodying them was drawn up and signed on March 30, 1867. Al-

"The Big Thing": Thomas Nast sees Alaska as Seward's Salve for Johnson's Troubles (Harper's Weekly)

though not informed of these negotiations until they were completed, Americans greeted the treaty with surprised approval. Few Americans, aside from some fishermen and traders on the Pacific coast, had displayed any previous concern with Alaska, but most of them were delighted with what they considered a good bargain. Seward's principal problem was not the American people, but the United States Senate.

To overcome the opposition of many senators who suspected any project of the unpopular Johnson Administration, Seward launched a campaign of education. Reports concerning Alaska's salubrious climate and limitless resources were given to the press; letters of prominent

Americans favoring annexation appeared in leading newspapers; senators were wined and dined; and the need for promoting Russian-American friendship was emphasized to such an extent that opposition to the treaty became tantamount to an expression of hostility toward a generous and friendly Tsar. Most important was the support of Charles Sumner, senator from Massachusetts and the chairman of the Senate Foreign Relations Committee. The turning point in the Senate debate was a three-hour speech by Sumner, who urged the acquisition Alaska on the grounds that it would cement Russo-American friendship, insure American fishing and hunting privileges, prevent England from extending its domain in North America, increase United States trade with the Orient, and spread American institutions by removing "one more monarch from this continent." On April 9, the Senate ratified the treaty by a vote of thirty-seven to two. The House showed some reluctance to approve the appropriation for the purchase and did not act until July, 1868. But the Administration had made it almost impossible for the House to do otherwise than pay. The United States took formal possession of Alaska in October, 1867, and a subsequent withdrawal would have been interpreted as a rebuke to Russia. As a further inducement, Stoeckl promised some of the recalcitrant representatives part of the purchase price as a reward for an affirmative vote. On July 14, 1861, the appropriation was approved by a vote of 113 to 43.

The American people were inclined to look on the purchase of Alaska as an accident, but Seward considered it just one part of a much larger program for strengthening and expanding the American position in the Pacific. In 1867, he proposed that the United States cooperate with the French in a punitive expedition against Korea, and in the same year, he annexed the Midway Islands. Meanwhile, he continued to urge that the United States acquire the Hawaiian Islands. During the 1870's, American traders and naval officers were casting covetous eyes on the Hawaiian Islands and Samoa. A commercial treaty brought the Hawaiian Islands within the American sphere of influence in 1875, and an agreement was reached with Samoa three years later. Imperialists would have liked a more aggressive policy in the Pacific, but they had to be content with these limited advances. Politicians were usually willing to take up these issues only when they could distract the public from domestic problems. Try as they might, the small number of expansionists in the government could not stir the same depth of feeling as did Reconstruction issues.

The growth of American interests in the Pacific came with demands that the United States extend its sovereignty over all of North

America. Canada, squeezed between the United States and an American Alaska, was considered by Seward and imperialists to be a ripening fruit that would eventually fall into the hands of a patient United States. On the other hand, expansionists were not averse to speeding up nature. Bellicose politicians warned Britain that it could only atone for its assistance to the Confederacy during the Civil War by ceding Canada to the United States. Aggressive Americans also welcomed the notorious but ineffective Fenian raids, in which Irish nationalists in the United States gathered at a few points along the Canadian border from 1866 to 1871 with the avowed purpose of attacking Canada. Although American imperialists gave the Fenians their blessing and the United States government made little attempt to interfere with their plans, inadequate numbers and resources turned the projected invasions of Canada into a fiasco.

The widespread belief that Canada would eventually become a part of the United States took into consideration everything but the Canadian people. The very ardor of the Americans for annexation so stimulated Canadian nationalism that the maintenance of an autonomous Canada became one of the cardinal points of its government's foreign policy; and by the end of the 1890's, when American expansionism had reached flood tide, Canadian patriotism had removed Canada from the "active list" of American imperialism.

Another unfulfilled dream of the post-Civil War expansionists was in the Caribbean. Seward, anxious to extend American influence to this region, sought to promote American canal interests in Nicaragua, negotiated a treaty that was never ratified for the purchase of the Danish West Indies, and attempted to secure an American toehold in Santo Domingo. On a cruise of the Caribbean in 1866, Seward was impressed by the desirability of Samaná Bay in Santo Domingo as a naval base. A year later, his son Frederick was sent to Santo Domingo to to secure a leasehold or cession of Samaná Bay, but the mission proved a failure.

Seward's interest in Santo Domingo had been based on strategic considerations, but there were some speculators who were agitating for American intervention to promote their own fortunes. William L. Cazneau and Joseph Warren Fabens were two New England adventurers who had concocted a host of dubious ventures in Dominican minerals, cotton, banking, harbor improvements, a steamship line to New York, and a fantastic arrangement that permitted them and their associates to obtain one fifth of the republic's land in return for what was called a geological survey. Joined in these enterprises were politicians like Ben Butler, industrialists like Cyrus McCormick, old cronies of President Grant like Ben Holladay, and financial firms like the New York investment house of Spofford, Tileston & Company. Because the value of their projects would be vastly enhanced by American annexation of Santo Domingo, the speculators appealed to President Grant, who was easily convinced of the necessity for obtaining a naval base on Samaná Bay. In 1869, Orville Babcock, the President's secretary, was sent to Santo Domingo, where he was conducted through the maze of Dominican politics by a representative of the speculators. According to the terms of the agreement that Babcock reached with the local officials, the United States was given the right to purchase Samaná Bay for $2,000,000 or to buy all of Santo Domingo by also assuming its public debt of $1,500,000. As evidence of American sincerity, President Grant advanced $150,000 to the island government, and American warships soon appeared in Dominican waters. When a treaty of annexation was presented to the Senate in 1870, Grant did not overlook a single argument in urging its ratification. Strategic advantages, the Monroe Doctrine, and the stimulus to the merchant marine, to industry, and to lower debts were all mentioned. Most ringing were the words:

> The people of San[to] Domingo are not capable of maintaining themselves in their present condition, and must look for outside support. They yearn for the protection of our free institutions . . . , our progress and civilization. Shall we refuse them?

Grant's message stands as an impressive summary of the rationale of American imperialism. Within thirty years, the American people would use every one of Grant's arguments to justify overseas expansion, but in 1870, they held little or no appeal, and the Senate rejected the treaty.

Similar lack of interest prevented intervention in Cuba after the Civil War. There were numerous pretexts that could have been used, but the rebellion against Spain that broke out in Cuba in 1868 and ended a decade later with a Spanish victory elicited the sympathies of many Americans, but not their active support. Emerging from the Civil War as the undisputed leader of the Western hemisphere, the United States could easily have taken advantage of Spain's distress. But, despite traditional appeals to American humanitarianism, Secretary of State Hamilton Fish steered the United States along a course of strict neutrality.

From 1865 to 1880, the United States possessed all the prerequisites of expansionism but one. It had the power, the arguments to rationalize imperial moves, and a few key figures in American life who were willing to lead their country into overseas adventures. Only a popular mandate was lacking.

The Will to Expand

The willingness of the American people in the 1890's to sanction a type of imperialism that they had rejected in the 1870's can be attributed to the changing mood of the Republic. Between the Civil and Spanish American wars the United States became a world power with vital interests in two oceans. The Mexican War and the Oregon settlement had brought the United States to the Pacific Ocean, but it was not until after 1865 that the Far West was linked with the East by rail, and it was not until 1890 that most of the territory acquired before the war was declared settled. By the 1880's developments in the Pacific required a Pacific policy whose ultimate success was predicated on the expansion of the American navy, the construction of an isthmus canal, and the acquisition of Caribbean bases to guard its approaches. As the American economy shifted from agriculture to industry, the demands for the acquisition of overseas bases to protect and stimulate American commerce also exercised a proportionately greater influence upon the direction of American foreign policy, but the principal impetus for expansion did not come from merchants or industrialists who needed overseas possessions to avoid collapse at home.

The prelude to the expansion of the 1890's was the vigorous diplomacy of James G. Blaine, who served as Secretary of State under Presidents Garfield and Harrison. In many respects Blaine's objectives were similar to those of Seward. The main difference between the two men lay in the times in which they lived rather than their aims. Aside from Alaska, Seward's program of expansion had elicited little popular response. Blaine's aggressive moves in the Pacific and Latin America, however, ushered in a new era in United States relations with the rest of the world.

James G. Blaine's foreign policy was the product of his determination to find future markets for American industry and to insure his country against foreign attack. Blaine was principally interested in areas that had been coveted by leading American imperialists of the past. He was convinced that economic and strategic considerations demanded the annexation of Hawaii by the United States. He thought that Canada also fell within the American sphere of influence, and in 1891 he predicted that Canada would "ultimately . . . seek admission to the union." Blaine sought unsuccessfully to obtain naval bases in

Haiti and Santo Domingo and worked assiduously to recapture for the United States the exclusive right to build a canal across the Central American isthmus.

Blaine's preoccupation with American overseas commerce was most clearly revealed in his Latin American policy. Because he believed that Latin America would never be a profitable market for American goods until it was freed from war and strife, he set out to establish the United States as the arbiter of all disputes among the nations south of the Rio Grande. During his two terms as Secretary of State, Blaine attempted to settle differences between Mexico and Guatemala, Costa Rica and Colombia, British Guiana and Venezuela, and Chile and Peru. These interventions, however, had no appreciable effect upon the volume of American exports to Central and South America. It resolved none of the disputes in question and increased the traditional antagonism of the Latin Americans toward "gringos" to the north. Equally unsuccessful were Blaine's efforts to increase hemispheric trade through conferences on tariff reductions. His proposal of a Pan-American conference in 1881 was abandoned when he was forced to resign after Garfield's death, but eight years later he was able to preside over the first Pan-American Conference, which convened in Washington during Harrison's administration. Despite Blaine's prestige as the representative of the conference's most powerful member nation, the Latin American delegates had no desire to give up their highly profitable trade with Europe for what were at best dubious commercial ties with the United States, and they rejected Blaine's plans for either a customs union or tariff reciprocity.

Blaine had little to show for his vigorous foreign policy, but his ideas were gaining increasing popularity among Americans. Other politicians began to proclaim their belief in what came to be known as a "large policy." By 1886, Theodore Roosevelt was anticipating the "day when not a foot of American soil will be held by any European power." Roosevelt's good friend, Senator Henry Cabot Lodge of Massachusetts, thought that "from the Rio Grande to the Arctic Ocean there should be but one flag and one country," and that the United States should control the Hawaiian Islands, Samoa, an isthmus canal, and Cuba. Even the anti-imperialist Cleveland at the time of the Venezuelan crisis of 1895 was to employ the language of this muscular nationalism with such vigor that the United States and Great Britain were brought closer to war than at any time since 1815.

The politicians and political writers who recommended imperial ventures after the 1880's were not, as a common argument supposes, representatives of industrial groups needing cheap raw materials and markets for surpluses. American expansion overseas in the late 1880's and 1890's was not an attempt to avoid an impending domestic economic crisis. In fact, many of the leaders of the imperialist groups were by background and training hostile to the rising commercialism of American culture and fearful of the directions industrial America was taking. Empire suggested a manly heroism and national activism to counter the pettiness and greed of the moneyed round of life of industrial society. The political corruption of the 1870's and 1880's, the growing power of crass industrial potentates, the "threats" of labor unions, immigrants, and political bosses seemed to be undermining America's national character. The ideals of sacrifice, discipline, courage, of spiritual mission, and of a life delivered from humdrum materialism were invoked to save America from Mammon and from rule by vulgar businessmen.

The demands for a glorious foreign policy were reinforced by many writers who argued that Charles Darwin's evolutionary theories applied to nations as well as to living creatures. According to these apostles of the new imperialism, no nation could remain static without dying. Struggle for survival was the law of life, and the stronger nations were destined by a higher law to assimilate their weaker and less fortunate neighbors. "The survival of the fittest" applied to international society as well as to biology. Among the most ardent spokesmen for such views was Alfred Thayer Mahan, a navy captain, whose book *The Influence of Sea Power upon History* was first published in 1890. In his many articles and books, Mahan maintained that, since international relations were based on "dog-eat-dog" attitudes, it behooved the United States to eat rather than to be eaten. Mahan believed that history proved that a nation's ability to survive was determined by its "seapower," a broad concept that referred not only to fighting ships and costal defenses, but to overseas bases, a merchant marine, and coaling stations. Seapower and commercial supremacy were inseparable, and both could be promoted by a large navy, an extensive merchant marine, and a far-flung colonial system. Specifically, Mahan insisted that the American people construct a canal across the isthmus and seize commercial and military outposts among the islands of both the Pacific and the Caribbean.

Other followers of Darwin maintained that the "racial superiority" of the American people had already rendered inevitable the expansion of the United States over large portions of the globe. John Fiske, one of Darwin's earliest and most ardent disciples in the United States, argued in 1885 in a magazine article entitled "Manifest Destiny" that the English race was destined to take over the whole world. In the same year,

Josiah Strong, a Congregational clergyman, published a book entitled *Our Country: Its Possible Future and Its Present Crisis*. Strong wrote that the Anglo-Saxon was "divinely commissioned to be in a peculiar sense his brother's keeper" and that the United States was to "become the home of this race, the principal seat of his power, the great center of his influence." Strong concluded that the racial superiority of the American people ordained that there could be no limit to the territorial expansion of the United States. In similar vein, Senator Albert J. Beveridge stated that overseas conquests were inevitable, for the "American Republic is part of the movement of a race,—the most masterful race of history—and race movements are not to be stayed by the hand of man." Paradoxically, however, as we shall see, a similar racism inspired American critics of imperialism in the late 1890's.

It is impossible to measure the effect of these advocates of imperialism on the thoughts of the American people, but their articles were published in popular magazines; their lecture tours included most of the major cities and many smaller towns; and their direct influences on those in power were many and varied. Moreover, many politicians with visions of imperial grandeur occupied strategic positions in the government. Theodore Roosevelt was the Assistant Secretary of Navy who planned Dewey's attack on Manila; and Lodge and Beveridge were both influential members of the Senate. On many occasions, then, politicians were able to use their official positions to make real their dream that it was the United States' destiny to become a world power. From 1880 to 1900, the traditional intense nationalism of the United States became increasingly imperialistic, and the preachers of expansionism—admirals, clergymen, politicians, or professors—promoted the growth of an American overseas empire.

The emergence of this more vigorous nationalism was revealed in the changed attitude of the American people toward their navy. Although the Union government had used steam and armor plate on its warships during the Civil War, during the years that followed the conflict the American navy fell far behind those of the European powers. Domestic problems forced concern about the navy into the background, and by 1880 the United States Navy consisted of only 140 ships, most of which were wooden and almost all of which were unfit for service.

With the inauguration of James A. Garfield, Reconstruction as a political issue had been liquidated, and the depression of the seventies had passed. With a surplus in the treasury and no pressing domestic concerns, the way was clear for "navalists" to make their case. They asked that the nation build a navy commensurate with its status, as a

A Plea in the Seventies for a Larger Navy (Thomas Nast in Harper's Weekly)

rising world power. It soon became clear that it was pointless to plan for an isthmus canal and island bases in two oceans while the United States remained the naval inferior of several South American countries.

In 1881, Congress created the Naval Advisory Board, which made incessant requests for larger and ever larger naval appropriations. The big-navy enthusiasts now had an official lobby financed by the taxpayers of the United States. This system soon brought results, and in 1883, Congress authorized the Secretary of Navy to build four steel ships equipped with steam as well as sails. The implications of the new naval policy did not become clear until after 1890, when a Navy Policy Board created by Secretary of the Navy Benjamin Tracy made a report that reflected the changed position of the United States as a world power. While the board conceded that the United States had "no colonies nor any apparent desire to acquire them," that its overseas trade was largely "carried in foreign vessels," that its manufactured products were competing "with those of other nations in but few markets," and that the United States was not threatened by any foreign power, it nevertheless requested Congress to authorize the construction of more than 200 warships of all classes. The board's recommendation was based on the assumption that the United States would soon find itself in commercial rivalry with the major powers of the world and that it also would need more ships to protect the proposed isthmus canal.

The Naval Act of 1890, which came as a direct result of this report, did not go as far as the policy board had recommended, but it did mark the beginnings of the change from the conception of the navy as a defensive force to that of a navy designed to meet a potential enemy on the high seas. The strategic implications of this legislation were also indicated by the report of the House Naval Affairs Committee, which visualized the bill as a measure for establishing battleship fleets in the western Atlantic, the Caribbean, and the Pacific. Despite the depression of the 1890's the new naval policy was consistently pushed by both Democratic and Republican administrations. Inspired by the new sense of America's power and "destiny," the United States moved from twelfth to third place among the world's naval powers during the last two decades of the nineteenth century.

The "Case History" of Samoa

Twenty years after the Senate had rejected President Grant's comprehensive list of arguments for expansion, the United States was ready for imperial ventures overseas. An industrial nation with strategic and commercial interests in both the Atlantic and Pacific, it also possessed both the seapower and aggressive nationalism essential to any people who wished to take growing control of distant lands.

The relations of the United States with Samoa before 1890 were an augury of the future. Samoa occupies an important niche in the history of American imperialism. The peaceful invasion of the Samoan Islands by the United States after the Civil War was one of the earliest examples of the effect of new economic and strategic interests upon the nation's foreign policy. The ease with which a comparatively small and unrepresentative group of Americans, despite public apathy, involved the United States with Samoa revealed the key role that naval and commercial groups could play in the development of American expansionism. The rivalry among the American, German, and British interests in these islands was a specific illustration of the way that the extension of American influence into the Pacific brought the United States into conflict with the major powers of Europe.

Before the Civil War, New Englanders had engaged in the China trade and the United States Navy had displayed some interest in Samoa. The completion of the first transcontinental railroad in 1869 again focused the attention of some commercial groups on a future lucrative Pacific trade. A New York shipbuilder drew up plans for a steamship line between San Francisco, New Zealand, and Australia with way stations at Hawaii and Samoa, and a group of San Francisco businessmen formed the Polynesian Land Company to speculate in Samoan real estate. Because the success of these ventures largely depended on the extension of American political control to Samoa, their authors urged that the United States establish a naval base at Pago Pago, Samoa's principal harbor, and take over control of the island government. As a direct result of the agitation of these businessmen, Commander Richard W. Meade visited Samoa on an American warship in 1872 and negotiated a treaty that granted naval rights in the islands to the United States. The Senate, reflecting again the popular aversion of the time to foreign adventures, never acted on the treaty.

The Senate's failure to ratify the Samoan treaty delayed rather than halted the American advance into the Pacific. In 1873, President Grant selected as his special agent in Samoa Colonel A. B. Steinberger, a former employee of one of the leading San Francisco speculators in Samoan land. Steinberger is one of the most unusual figures in the diplomatic history of the United States or any other country. He treated the natives with so much consideration and understanding that they permitted him to reorganize their government and selected him as their premier. The same policies that made Steinberger attractive to the natives rendered him unpopular with the British and German traders in the islands, and in 1875 he was deported on a British man-of-war. But the memory of his enlightened regime remained in the island after his departure. In 1877, La Mamea, a Samoan prince, was escorted by a United States vice-consul to Washington, where he proposed an American protectorate over Samoa. In the following year, a treaty between the United States and Samoa was ratified by the United States Senate. The American people were irrevocably committed to a major role in Samoa.

The Samoan treaty of 1878 granted the United States the right to establish a naval base at Pago Pago and provided that if "any differences should have arisen, or shall hereafter arise, between the Samoan government and any other government in amity with the United States, the government of the latter will employ its good offices for the purpose of adjusting these differences upon a satisfactory . . . foundation." Although this provision did not convert Samoa into an American protectorate, if was sufficient to embroil the United States in the island's politics for more than two decades. Samoa in 1879 signed treaties with Britain and Germany awarding them commercial privileges. The United States thus found itself in conflict with two of the world's most powerful nations. Samoa became the center of an imperial free-for-all in which the diplomatic, commercial and military representatives of the three rival nations maneuvered, threatened, and intrigued with the natives. An attempt by Secretary of State Thomas Bayard in 1887 to reach a *modus vivendi* with the British and German ministers in Washington ended in a stalemate that was followed by an intensified struggle for power in Samoa. The Germans, making an undisguised bid for control, deposed the native King, replaced him with one of their own supporters, and waged an undeclared war against bands of Samoan guerillas. When British, American, and German warships appeared in the Samoan harbor of Apia, the possibility of open conflict was only averted by a hurricane that disabled all but one of the vessels.

The United States' efforts to hold its own against the European imperialists in Samoa made the nationalism of the American people more aggressive, and suddenly forced them to take greater interest in the possibilities of American possessions overseas. Congress voted funds for the protection of American lives and property in Samoa, and the press criticized the forceful policy of the Germans. The American people were determined to uphold what they considered their country's national honor in the face of Germany's highhanded behavior. The popular support of the government's policy in Samoa did not arise from a desire to acquire some remote tropical islands, but was based on the conviction that the United States could not retreat in Samoa without loss of national honor. The professional expansionists wanted the United States to become a major power, and its critizens demanded that it behave like one when its interests came into conflict with those of the imperialist nations of Europe. The nationalists and imperialists quickly pointed out that a nation had to prepare to be a major power if it wanted to act like one.

Bismarck, the German Chancellor, was unwilling to permit a possible conflict in the Pacific to upset the delicately balanced system of alliances that he was constructing in Europe. He invited Britain and the United States to send delegates to Berlin to settle their differences over Samoa. The agreement that emerged from the Berlin conference of 1889 provided for a tripartite protectorate over Samoa—a plan that changed the form rather than the substance of the earlier arrangement. The old pattern of deceit, distrust, recrimination, and open warfare was soon resumed to the mounting disgust of the American people. The more moderate Samoan policy pursued by the anti-imperialist Cleveland Administration in the midnineties served only as an interlude. By 1899, the Americans, having overrun Cuba, Puerto Rico, and the Philippines, had tasted the power that empire could bring. They now could see no reason for refusing to add Samoa to their list; the largest share of the islands was ceded to Germany, but the United States acquired Tutuila, which included the harbor of Pago Pago.

The history of American intervention in Samoa thus illustrates the transformation of the American attitude toward overseas expansion during a period of approximately thirty years. The American entered the task of empire building through the back door and almost accidentally. A few traders accompanied by some naval officers involved the United States government in the politics of islands also coveted by Germany and Great Britain. German and American nationalism did the rest. The American people originally had no desire to acquire any part of Samoa, but they soon discovered that the question had become much bigger than the problem of controlling a few islands in the South Pacific. It was a matter of national honor in which the prestige of the United States was pitted against that of two of the most powerful nations of the Old World.

Hawaii Annexed

Many of the same circumstances that brought Samoa under partial American control operated with equal force in Hawaii. In both instances the desire of naval and commercial groups for a Pacific base furnished the original impetus for American intervention. The attempt to check Germany in Samoa was paralleled by a similar wish to prevent Hawaii from falling under the control of either England or Japan. As in Samoa, Grover Cleveland temporarily checked the tide of American expansionism in the Hawaiian Islands only to have them engulfed by the wave of imperialism that accompanied the Spanish American War. There was, however, differences in the case of Hawaii. American missionaries played an important role in stimulating an early American interest in Hawaii; the growth of the native sugar industry conditioned the moves and attitudes that culminated in American annexation; and the State Department generally employed a more aggressive diplomacy in Hawaii than in Samoa.

New England missionaries had reached Hawaii in 1819, and during the first half of the nineteenth century, American traders in China and whalers had employed it as a base for their operations in the Pacific. Responding to the demands of their commercial constituents, on more than one occasion before the Civil War politicians had insisted that Hawaii belonged within the American sphere of interest. The Democrats, swept along by the heightened spirit of Manifest Destiny in the 1850's, made a futile attempt to annex Hawaii in 1854, and Whig leaders had also called for annexation. Every rumor that Hawaii might be taken over by some rival power only added to the general American conviction that the islands should either remain independent or be acquired by the United States.

The American missionaries, traders, and sugar planters who by 1850 dominated Hawaii's political and economic life believed that increased trade with the United States would promote Hawaiian prosperity without threatening its sovereignty. Commercial treaties negotiated with the United States in 1855 and 1867 were rejected by American senators who wished to protect the Louisiana sugar growers and feared that a strengthened Hawaiian prosperity would lessen rather than promote the changes for eventual American annexation of the islands. It was not until 1875 that these objections were overcome and a reciprocity treaty with Hawaii ratified by the United States Senate. By permitting Hawaiian sugar to enter the United States duty free, the treaty of 1875 produced unprecedented prosperity for Hawaii's largest industry and bound its economy firmly to that of the United States. During the first ten years of the treaty's operation, Hawaii's annual sugar exports to the United States increased nearly tenfold, from 17,909,000 to 169,653,000 pounds.

The treaty of 1875 was more than a commercial agreement, for exclusive American control over Hawaii was insured by a provision that forbade the native ruler to "lease or otherwise dispose of or create a lien upon any port, harbor, or other territory in his dominions, or grant any special privilege or rights or use therein to any Power, State or Government, . . . [or] make any treaty by which any other nation should obtain the same privileges relative to the admission of articles free of duty, thereby secured to the United States." Hawaii's bonds with the United States were further strengthened in 1887, when the United States was granted the right to construct a naval base at Pearl Harbor.

The treaty of 1875 almost exclusively benefited a comparatively small group of Hawaiian sugar producers. With a large share of Hawaiian wealth in their hands, an expanding market for their sugar in the United States, a docile native government, and a guarantee against foreign intervention, they considered their position ideal in every respect. But the power of the islands' white oligarchs, while extensive, was based entirely on outside forces over which they had little or no control, and the events early in the 1890's clearly revealed their vulnerability. The McKinley Tariff of 1890 removed the duty on foreign raw sugar and gave a bounty of two cents a pound to the producers within the United States. Deprived of their privileged position in the American market and confronted by the chance of economic ruin, the Hawaiian sugar interests were easily converted to the belief that their only salvation lay in annexation to the United States. Although a few of the islands' largest growers opposed annexation for a time, on the ground that United States' laws prohibiting the import of contract labor would deprive them of their supply of cheap Oriental workers, the effects of the McKinley Tariff eventually convinced all but a few that there was no alternative to union with their erstwhile benefactor.

Hawaiian politics precipitated the movement for annexation after 1890. The pronounced antiforeign views of Queen Liliuokalani, who ascended the Hawaiian throne in 1891, indicated that it would only be a matter of time before the white oligarchy lost its hold over the native government. The Queen in 1893 made good her boast of "Hawaii for the Hawaiians" by transferring the political power formerly held by the sugar growers to her own hands. The Americans in the islands decided that it was time to act. They hastily organized a revolution and asked the United States to intervene to protect the lives and property of its nationals in Hawaii. This appeal did not go unheeded. John L. Stevens, the American minister to Hawaii, in his dispatches to the State Department had repeatedly advocated that the United States take a more active role in Hawaiian affairs. He repeatedly predicted a revolt against the Queen and warned his home government that it would have to act with dispatch if it wished to anticipate British intervention or prevent the islands' native population from being swamped in the mounting wave of Oriental immigration. Stevens' attitude toward Hawaii was shared by his friend and superior, Secretary of State James G. Blaine, and the revolution engineered by the small but powerful group of American annexationists on January 16, 1893, received the moral and physical support of the United States government.

Although Stevens was absent from Honolulu during the ten days that preceded the *coup d'état,* he returned in time to insure the revolution's success by landing 160 marines from an American warship in the harbor. The temporary government set up by the revolutionists was granted immediate American recognition by Stevens, and a delegation was hastily bundled off to the United States to negotiate a treaty of annexation. On February 1, Stevens announced an American protectorate over Hawaii and cabled the State Department, "The Hawaiian pear is now fully ripe, and this is the golden hour for the United States to pluck it."

wasn't accepted

Despite the dispatch with which the annexationists had acted, they had not moved fast enough to prevent the new President, Grover Cleveland, from balking their plans. He withdrew the treaty of annexation, which had been submitted to the Senate on February 15, soon after his inauguration on March 4. James H. Blount, who shared the President's anti-imperialist views, was sent to Hawaii as Cleveland's special representative. After a comprehensive but one-sided study of recent developments in the islands, Blount reported that the Hawaiian people were opposed to annexation and that the revolt would have collapsed if Stevens had not employed the power and prestige of the United States. Although Cleveland withdrew American support from the new government, he was not able to effect the restoration of Queen Liliuokalani, and the white oligarchy continued to rule the islands until Dewey's victory at Manila helped to convince the American people that they had a date with destiny in Hawaii as well as in the Philippines.

Cleveland was praised as a man of principle by his supporters and accused for pig-headedness by his opponents. In any event he never permitted the popular will to interfere with his own concept of right and wrong. McKinley, his successor in 1897, was not burdened with scruples like Cleveland's about Hawaii. Soon after McKinley assumed office in 1897, a new treaty of annexation was submitted to the Senate. When it appeared that the annexationists would not be able to command the necessary two-thirds vote, the treaty was supplanted by a joint resolution for annexation which required only a simple majority in both houses.

Annexationists both in and out of Congress who urged the acceptance of the joint resolution appealed to history—that bargain basement of all special pleaders. They cited the long list of prominent Americans who had advocated the acquisition of Hawaii in the past. Hawaii was pictured by the annexationists as a strategic necessity for the navy, a source of inestimable wealth to American economic interests, a moral obligation upon the American people, and an obvious opportunity for the nation to fulfill its Manifest Destiny. Each of these arguments was reinforced by the imperialist insistence that if the United States did

Formal Ceremony of Hawaii's Annexation (Leslie's Illustrated)

not take Hawaii, some other nation would. England had already announced its intentions with the request for a cable station in Hawaii, and a Senate committee warned against the "silent but rapid invasion of the pagan races from Asia."

The anti-imperialists, who, largely for partisan rather than moral reasons, found their principal strength among the Democrats, sought to refute each of the annexationists' points. They too could appeal to history by stating that there was no American precedent for overseas expansion. They predicted that the acquisition of Hawaii was only the first of many projected steps toward the creation of an American empire that would undermine the country's democracy at home and mongrelize the white race by bringing colored and backward people under the American flag. To the promise of commercial prosperity, they replied that annexation was a plot of the islands' few powerful sugar growers. Talk of moral obligation was ridiculed, and Champ Clark termed Manifest Destiny the "specious plea of every robber and freebooter since the world began." The anti-imperialists may have won the argument but they lost the vote, and on July 7, 1898, Hawaii became a territory of the United States.

As in the case of Samoa, small groups of Americans in Hawaii with special interests only had had to wait for events to take their course. By sitting tight, they were able to see their aims achieved as successive diplomatic incidents and fundamental changes in the American economy and strategic position combined to convince the mass of Americans that it was both their duty and their destiny to acquire these islands.

The Martial Spirit

Much of the territory that the United States acquired before the Civil War consisted of the remnants of Spain's once great American empire. Louisiana, Florida, Texas, New Mexico, and California had all at one time or another belonged to the King of Spain. These territories, many times the size of the original states of the Union, had been obtained at what were considered bargain prices in American money and blood.

Although the antebellum United States was ready to serve as the receiver of Spain's bankrupt North American empire, it was unable to extend its control to Spain's most valuable Caribbean possession. This failure did not occur for want of trying, for throughout these years the potential value of Cuba to the United States was widely recognized. It was the strategic key to the Caribbean, and from 1820 to 1860 American trade with Cuba was exceeded only by that with the United Kingdom and France. Many times before the Civil War, prominent American expansionists displayed a marked interest in Cuba's future. Thomas Jefferson and John Quincy Adams stated that Cuba was destined eventually to become a part of the United States, and partly in response to the demands of those southern supporters who wanted additional slave territory, Presidents Polk and Pierce made unsuccessful attempts to wrest the island from Spain. The failure of the United States to acquire Cuba before 1860 revealed, not a fear of Spain or a lack of expansionist enthusiasm, but the North's aversion to increasing southern power and extending the South's peculiar institution, and the general conviction that Cuba posed no threat to American security so long as it remained in such weak hands.

Immediately after the Civil War, the United States had both the opportunity and the power to intervene in Cuba. The Ten Years' War, as the revolution that broke out in Cuba in 1868 was called, brought much Spanish cruelty and oppression. But, despite a tradition of sympathy for those fighting for their freedom against European oppression, Americans made no overt move to take advantage of Spain's distress.

The *Virginius* affair, in which fifty-three passengers and crew members on a ship flying the American flag were taken and executed by the Spanish, was a more provocative incident than any that had preceded the Mexican War, the United States was willing to accept apologies and an indemnity from the Spanish government and to remain at peace.

Although Spain was able to end the Cuban rebellion in 1878, it had learned little from a decade of bloodletting. Spanish imperial rule was reimposed. The corruption and favoritism that had characterized the administration before the rebellion continued. Forced into the straitjacket of Spanish mercantilism, the Cubans were again subjected to an inequitable tax system and a tariff that compelled them to obtain most of their imports from Spain while sending approximately 75 per cent of their exports to the United States. After 1890, the United States as well as Spain contributed to Cuba's misfortunes. A large part of Cuba's sugar crop, which represented four fifths of the island's wealth, had been sold in the United States through a preferential tariff agreement; but the Wilson-Gorman Tariff of 1894 deprived the Cubans of this free market by imposing a duty on their sugar. By 1895, the Cuban people had had enough, and once again they revolted against their Spanish rulers.

At the start of the Cuban revolt, General Martínez Campos, who had induced the rebels to lay down their arms in 1878, was placed in charge of Spanish forces in Cuba. When his policy of "conciliation backed by the sword" produced neither victories nor any diminution in the revolutionary ardor of the Cubans, he was supplanted by the more aggressive General Valeriano Weyler. Nicknamed the "Butcher" by the American press, Weyler proclaimed martial law, systematically destroyed any property that might be of value to the rebels, and herded the island's noncombatants into concentration camps, or *reconcentrados*, where they died by the thousands. Weyler's policies were duplicated by the insurgent leader, Máximo Gómez. Knowing that his forces were no match for the Spanish troops, Gómez set out to wreck Cuba's productive capacity so thoroughly that the Spanish would have no alternative but to evacuate the island. Although American sympathies were overwhelmingly on the side of the rebels and American sensibilities were shocked by Weyler's (not Gómez's) tactics, there was little difference in the conduct of the two belligerents. The Cubans were determined that this revolt would not repeat their earlier failure. They were willing to use almost any device to rid the island of its hated rulers. The Spanish were equally insistent that the rebellious spirit of their Cuban subjects be crushed once and for all.

The mounting enthusiasm of the American people for the Cuban

cause was equaled by President Cleveland's determination to prevent
the United States from being drawn into the conflict. In the face of a
steady stream of atrocity stories, a flood of releases from the propaganda mills of the Cuban "junta" in this country, and frequent demands for a firmer attitude toward Spain, the Cleveland Administration refused to intervene. A congressional resolution urging American
recognition of Cuban belligerency was ignored by the President. The
American navy and revenue service made valiant, if not always successful, efforts to intercept filibustering expeditions to Cuba, and American diplomacy was employed to protect American lives and property
in Cuba, rather than to promote the cause of the insurgents. Cleveland
would make only one concession to the interventionists. In April, 1896,
his Administration made an offer of American mediation, only to have
the proposal promptly rejected by the government in Madrid. There
was little immediate change in American policy when McKinley succeeded Cleveland to the Presidency. The earlier attempts to prevent
filibustering and to protect American lives and property in Cuba were
continued, and McKinley's offer of American mediation in September,
1897, was refused as Cleveland's had been.

　The United States went to war against Spain in 1898 with the
overwhelming support of the American people. Seldom, if ever in
American history, has there been a more genuinely popular war. Most
American newspapers became megaphones for Cuban independence,
but only a few were able to approach the extremes of jingoism attained by New York's yellow journals—Joseph Pulitzer's *World* and
William Randolph Hearst's *Journal*. Both papers colored the news in
favor of the insurgents, announced the most trivial Cuban news incidents in spectacular and provocative headlines, and occasionally fabri-
cated stories that would appeal to their readers' sympathies for the
Cubans. Examples of Spanish cruelty, which the *Journal* compared to
the "Spanish inquisition of the sixteenth century," were described in
purple prose and lurid pictures. Running through every Cuban news
report, editorial, and illustration in the *World* and the *Journal* was the
theme that the American people should come to the assistance of their
oppressed and stricken neighbors.

　The newspaper publishers who played up the bloody and spectacular aspects of the war in Cuba wanted greater circulation and profits. Hearst and Pulitzer knew that murder sold papers, and the conflict
in Cuba could be reported as mass murder. Their descriptions of the
suffering of the Cubans played on the traditional American sympathy
for the underdog fighting for his liberty against European despotism.
The appeal to interest in blood and ideas almost tripled the *Journal's*

circulation during the excitement over the destruction of the *Maine*. Certainly the press did not create American opinion, for most Americans had favored the Cuban cause from the first day of the rebellion, but the more bellicose papers went far toward crystallizing and reinforcing the views already held by their readers.

Pulpit joined press in stirring the martial spirit. In the months that preceded the intervention of the United States in Cuba, many Protestant ministers argued that the United States was impelled by moral and religious duty to aid the long-suffering Cubans. A Methodist paper stated that American participation would be "just" and that in the event of war "Methodism will be ready to do its full duty," and "every Methodist preacher will be a recruiting officer." Other Protestant groups, with the exception of the Quakers and Unitarians, were equally bellicose. A Presbyterian journal asked: "Shall thousands of starving and dying Cubans appeal to the humane people of this republic in vain?" An Episcopal bishop said that the only way to make effective President McKinley's "humane and righteous determination was by force of arms; and that means war." The Catholics, however, saw no religious justification for a war to free Catholic Cuba; and one Catholic paper suggested the warlike intentions of Protestant clergymen be satisfied by organizing them into a regiment and shipping them off to Cuba in a body.

Many professional politicians looking for a popular issue after the fright they had received from William Jennings Bryan in 1896 were more than receptive to a glorious foreign adventure with which to divert their constituents from the troublesome silver question and the other issues of the nineties left unsettled by McKinley's victory. Besides the party hacks who were looking for a safe issue, there were those key political figures who had long advocated United States expansion and who welcomed the rising tide of nationalism. A few weeks after the outbreak of the revolt in Cuba, Senator Shelby M. Cullom stated that "we certainly ought to have that island in order to round out possessions as they should be, and if we cannot buy it, I for one should like to have an opportunity to acquire it by conquest." Theodore Roosevelt made no attempt to hide his desire for war, and his friend John Hay asserted that a war would be "as necessary as it was righteous." These men whipped up the popular enthusiasm for intervention, and their positions of power at times enabled them to take specific steps that hastened the coming war.

In February, 1898, the demands of the American interventionists were strengthened by two "incidents"—the word applied in the language of diplomacy to those minor crises that precede and frequently lead to the major crisis of war. On February 9, 1898, William Randolph Hearst's New York *Journal* published a letter written to a friend in Cuba by Enrique Dupuy deLôme, the Spanish minister to the United States. DeLôme suggested establishing a lobby to influence the United States Senate and criticized President McKinley's annual message of the previous December for its "ingrained and inevitable coarseness." He described the President as "weak and a bidder for the admiration of the crowd, besides being a common politician who tries to leave a door open behind himself while keeping on good terms with the jingoes of his party." DeLôme's immediate resignation after publication of the offending letter did not lessen the enthusiasm of the American people for a war that they now considered inevitable. The jingoism stimulated by the publication of the DeLôme letter was only exceeded by the popular outcry that greeted the announcement of the sinking of the *Maine* after an explosion in Havana harbor on February 15, 1898. The question of who sank the *Maine*—a question that has remained unanswered—was no mystery to the American people in 1898. "Remember the *Maine*" became the national war whoop as most Americans shouted their agreement with Theodore Roosevelt's announcement that the "*Maine* was sunk by an act of dirty treachery on the part of the Spaniards."

The only significant check upon the popular demand for war after the sinking of the *Maine* came from the nation's business groups. In 1895, American trade with Cuba was valued at $65,000,000, and American capital invested in the island totaled $50,000,000, but most American businessmen had no financial stake in a war to drive Spain out of Cuba, and they looked on the possibility of armed conflict with considerable trepidation and hostility. After the depression of the mid-nineties, American business leaders were convinced that the signs of returning prosperity would quickly be dispersed by a war against Spain. Throughout the winter of 1897–8, every threat of war provoked antiwar editorials in the financial press and sharp declines in stock prices. Theodore Roosevelt became so incensed at the attitude of the business groups that he said, "We will have this war for the freedom of Cuba in spite of the timidity of the commercial interests."

Whatever the public attitude, the decision about war lay in the hands of the President. In the spring of 1898, the President conducted negotiations with Spain while warning of the possibilities of war. McKinley himself shared the aversion of America's business leaders to war. A gentle man with kindly impulses, he had no desire to lead his country into war, and, as a businessman's President, he had no wish to offend his strongest supporters. But McKinley was a politician who

Front Page of the New York Journal after the Explosion of the Maine

was not willing to run the risk of defying public opinion indefinitely, and he was also an intensely pious man who, under appropriate circumstances, was sensitive to broad moralistic and humanitarian appeals like those that deluged the White House in the months before war began. McKinley at first tried peaceful means. On March 27, he asked Spain to abolish its concentration camps in Cuba and to announce a six-months armistice. Spain's immediate refusal to consider McKinley's proposals was reversed under pressure from the Vatican. By April 9, the Madrid government had signified its willingness to comply with both of the American President's demands. By properly publicizing Spain's retreat, a stronger president could at once have thrown the full prestige of his office against the tides of jingoism. He could then have continued negotiations with Spain and have lined up world opinion behind his peacemaking efforts. But, instead, Spain's concession proved to be too late. Two days after the Spanish retreat, McKinley nevertheless sent a war message to Congress. After reviewing the course of the revolution in Cuba and the attempts of the United States to terminate it, he gave the reasons for his fateful decision:

> In the name of humanity, in the name of civilization, in behalf of endangered American interests which give us the right and the duty to speak and to act, the war in Cuba must stop. In view of these . . . considerations, I ask Congress to authorize and empower the President to take measures to secure a full

and final termination of hostilities between the government of
Spain and the people of Cuba, and to secure in the island the
establishment of a stable government, . . . and to use the military and naval forces of the United States as may be necessary
for these purposes.

Spain's capitulation to McKinley's ultimatum of March 27 was
mentioned by the President in a single sentence on the last of the nine
closely printed pages that made up his war message. But Congress
knew a mandate when it saw one. It had abandoned all thought of
further negotiation with Spain. A joint resolution, which was passed
on April 19, authorized the President to use force to drive Spain from
Cuba and to insure the island's freedom. The Teller Amendment,
which was adopted on the same day, renounced American claims to
Cuba. The Teller Amendment has been variously interpreted as an indication of American altruism and as a device employed by the American sugar interests for denying their Cuban competitors free access to
the American market.

The End of the Spanish Empire

The Americans at last had their war. It seemed to most of them
the natural outcome of their moral indignation over what they considered an intolerable situation in Cuba. Their feeling of revulsion had
originally been spontaneous, but it had also been nurtured by the yellow press, which wanted a larger circulation, by professional imperialists who thought that the United States should undertake a "large policy," by clergymen inspired by humanitarian considerations, and by
politicians who wished to bury the issues of 1896.

Most Americans approved of Congress' decision to free Cuba, but
they had not bothered to prepare for the war that they entered with
such enthusiasm. The army consisted of only 28,183 regulars with
military experiences largely confined to Indian fighting in the West
and patrol work in Alaska. Even the recently strengthened navy debated just how the war should be fought. Admiral Mahan, the acknowledged authority on such matters, had taught that seapower should be
employed, primarily, in maintaining a blockade, and for a short time a
naval blockade of Cuba was contemplated. But Congress was determined to give the American people a shooting war. On April 22, the
President was empowered to call on the states for volunteers. The next
day, McKinley asked for 125,000 men.

Comic-opera confusion marked the American war effort. Either

American Troops Go Ashore in Cuba

[NATIONAL ARCHIVES]

the wisdom or good fortune of the United States had made a weak and decadent Spain the guinea pig on which it vented its hypernationalism. The Administration repeated all the mistakes of the Civil War and used none of its lessons. State governments, rather than the national government, were responsible for recruiting. Political appointments to military posts were insured by permitting governors to select all lower officers. Despite its inadequate rail facilities, Tampa, Florida, was made the port of embarkation and became the center of some of the government's more spectacular blunders. Only the resourcefulness of a Theodore Roosevelt was equal to the problems posed by the confusion in Tampa in the early summer of 1898. Roosevelt had barnstormed down the East Coast picking up his devoted band of liberators. On arriving in Tampa, he discovered that two other regiments were about to board the transport that had been assigned to his Rough Riders. He acted with characteristic dispatch and described his actions afterwards:

> I ran at full speed to our train; and leaving a strong guard with the baggage I double-quicked the rest of the regiment up to

the boat to board her as she came into the quay and then to hold her against the 2d . . . and the 71st, who had arrived a little late, being a shade less ready than we in the matter of individual initiative. There was a good deal of expostulation, but we had possession.

The War Department's supply system for the troops broke down completely. On June 4, Major-General Miles wrote from Tampa, "Several of the volunteer regiments came here without uniforms; several came without arms, and some without blankets, tents or camp equipage." Winter uniforms were issued for a summer campaign in the tropics. Because of the shortage of modern rifles, the volunteers had to use old-fashioned Springfields. The Rough Riders, whose Lieutenant-Colonel had friends in Washington, were the only volunteer regiment with smokeless powder. Medical supplies remained inadequate throughout the war. The food was wretched, and the soldiers called their canned meat "embalmed beef."

Most Americans fought the Spanish American War in their front-porch rockers instead of in the swamps and jungles of Cuba and were willing to overlook the lapses of the War Department. To them, as to John Hay, it was a "splendid little war." It was a short war, as all wars should be. It was a colorful war, supplying in two and a half months as many slogans and heroes as subsequent wars would produce in five years. Best of all, it was a glorious war, for the American victories were unrelieved by a single piece of bad news from the front. Dewey's destruction of the Spanish fleet at Manila was matched by the annihilation of its counterpart at Santiago Bay. The land fighting consisted of three minor engagements in Cuba and followed a most acceptable pattern. The battles were not struggles of attrition between huge conglomerates of nameless automatons, but story-book intimate conflicts that permitted cavalry charges and deeds of individual heroism. Ten weeks passed without a single Spanish success. On August 12 Spain accepted an armistice that granted Cuba its freedom and the United States Puerto Rico and any island that it might select in the Ladrones.

The fighting was over in Cuba, but it had just begun in the Philippines. On the day after the signing of the armistice, 11,000 American soldiers entered the city of Manila as occupiers rather than liberators. The Filipinos had been led by the American commander to believe that they would share in the city's occupation. They interpreted the American move as a breach of faith. Filipino insurgents had been fighting for their independence rather than to exchange one set of rulers for another. As soon as they realized that the American troops had no

THE SPANISH-AMERICAN WAR

intention of withdrawing, they turned on their new conquerors. The Philippine rebellion, which was ably led by Emilio Aguinaldo, was to last more than two years. Before it was finally suppressed, Americans in the Philippines found themselves using the same hideous tactics—even the once despised concentration camps—that they had found so revolting in Cuba.

With the rebellion in the Philippines still raging, delegates con-

vened in Paris on October 1, 1898, for the peace conference. The preliminary problems were handled with dispatch. The United States had
already selected Guam in the Ladrone Islands, and Spain reluctantly
agreed to assume Cuba's debt of approximately $400,000,000. Only the
fate of the Philippine Islands remained to be settled. They could be
returned to Spain, granted their independence, or retained in whole or
part by the United States. Although the average American before the
Spanish-American War was as little acquainted with the Philippines
as his grand child before World War II was with the Marshalls, there
was little doubt in his mind by war's end that it was both the duty
and the destiny of the United States to acquire the Philippines. The appearance of a powerful German fleet in Manila Bay soon after Dewey's
victory seemed sufficient evidence that a Spanish-controlled or independent Philippine government would immediately fall prey to one of
Europe's imperialist powers. On the other hand, under American control, expansionists argued, the Philippines would give the United States
a strategic and economic base in the Far East. Businessmen who had
opposed American intervention in Cuba had been converted to expansionism by the easy successes of the Spanish-American War. They were
now convinced that the Philippines would give American producers
access to Oriental markets. Humanitarians also joined the chorus, insisting that the United States had an obligation to uplift the benighted
but obstinate Filipinos. They had support from abroad when Rudyard
Kipling wrote "The White Man's Burden" to urge the United States
to take the Philippines. But most Americans wanted the Philippines
simply because their acquisition seemed a fitting climax to the glorious
adventure of 1898.

The anti-imperialists, while in a definite minority, made up for
their lack of numbers by their prestige and industry. Bound together
by the Anti-Imperialist League, they included Democratic and Republican politicians like Grover Cleveland, William Jennings Bryan, Carl
Schurz, and George F. Hoar; philanthropists like Andrew Carnegie;
editors like E. L. Godkin of the *Nation* and Samuel Bowles of the
Springfield *Republican*; clergymen like Bishop Henry Godman Potter,
Henry Van Dyke, and Charles Parkhurst; college professors like William James, Felix Adler, and William Graham Sumner; and a notable
group of literary figures, among whom were Mark Twain, William
Dean Howells, William Vaughn Moody, and Thomas Bailey Aldrich.
The anti-imperialists devoted some attention to refuting the economic,
strategic, and humanitarian claims of their opponents, but their central
political themes were a curious mixture of democratic and illiberal
ideas. They insisted that the acquisition of the Philippines would be

McKinley Measures Uncle Sam for His "Expansion Suit" as Schurz's Reducing Medicine Is Declined (Puck)

a complete denial of the fundamental American concept that all government rested on the consent of the governed, but they also warned that the admission of nonwhite natives to American privileges would debase the old Anglo-Saxon stock that had made America great and that alone of all races showed fitness for self-government. Moreover, the so-called anti-imperialists showed little hostility to the idea of annexing racially pure and democratic Canada. Andrew Carnegie even dreamed of reunion with England.

Despite the luster of their leaders' names and the power of their arguments, the anti-imperialists were fighting a losing battle. McKinley had already made up his mind. After some soul-searching, he ordered the American commissioners in Paris to take all of the Philippine Islands. On a later occasion, McKinley, an intensely pious man, told a group of clergymen that it had not been an easy decision:

> I walked the floor of the White House night after night until midnight; and I am not ashamed to tell you, gentlemen, that I went down on my knees and prayed Almighty God for light and guidance more than one night. And one night late it came to me this way—I don't know how it was but it came: (1) that we could not give them back to Spain—that would be cowardly and dishonorable; (2) that we could not turn them over to France and Germany—our commercial rivals in the Orient—that would be bad business and discreditable; (3) that we could not leave them to themselves—they were unfit for self-government—and they would soon have anarchy and misrule over there worse than Spain's was; and (4) that there was nothing left for us to do but to take them all, and to educate the Filipinos, and uplift and civilize and Christianize them, and by God's grace do the very best we could by them, as our fellowmen for whom Christ also died. And then I went to bed, and went to sleep and slept soundly.

When Spain, not knowing McKinley's high intentions, showed an understandable reluctance to part with the Philippines, the United States agreed to pay $20,000,000. The Treaty of Paris was signed on December 10, 1898, and ratified by the United States Senate two months later.

There is no accurate way of assessing the public response to America's taking an overseas empire. All the available evidence suggests the approval of the mass of people. Imperialism was one of the major issues of the election of 1900. McKinley was renominated by the Republicans, and Theodore Roosevelt was selected as his running mate.

The Democrats again chose Bryan, while Adlai E. Stevenson of Illinois, who had served as Vice-President under Cleveland from 1893 to 1897, was given second place on the ticket. Bryan insisted that imperialism was the "paramount issue," but Democratic campaign speakers also repeated their earlier demands for free silver and a reduction in the tariff. The Republicans campaigned on their party's record. While defending expansion abroad, they pointed with pride to prosperity at home. The depression of the early nineties had given way to a boom. Republican orators and editorial writers did their best to convince the voters that the "full dinner pail" could be attributed to McKinley, the gold standard, and the Dingley Tariff. In winning the election, McKinley had a larger majority than in 1896. He carried every state outside the solid South except the silver states of Colorado, Idaho, Montana, and Nevada. The popular vote was 7,207,923 to 6,358,133, and the electoral vote 292 to 155. The election was understood as a mandate for empire.

The last two years of the nineteenth century were a major turning point in American history. In a few months the United States had acquired Hawaii by legislative act, secured a part of Samoa through negotiation, obtained Puerto Rico, Guam, and the Philippine Islands by conquest, and taken possession of Wake (in 1899). Before 1898 many Americans had believed that the United States was a world power. In 1900 they knew it. What they did not recognize was that empire building entailed responsibilities as well as glory.

FOR SUPPLEMENTARY READING

Three general works on imperialism should be read: Lenin's *Imperialism, the Last Stage of Capitalism* (1917); J. Schumpeter, *The Sociology of Imperialism* (Pb, 1955); and P. T. Moon, *Imperialism and World Politics* (1926). The "will to expand" can be studied more deeply in Hofstadter's *Social Darwinism*; A. K. Weinberg, *Manifest Destiny* (1935); W. D. Puleston, *Mahan* (1939); and E. Morison (ed.), *The Letters of Theodore Roosevelt* (vols. I and II, 1951). On "navalism" read H. and M. Sprout, *The Rise of American Naval Power* (1939); D. Perkins, *A History of the Monroe Doctrine* (1950), is obviously pertinent. See also his *The United States and the Caribbean* (1947). On the early attempts at expansion after Appomattox use C. C. Tansill, *The United States and Santo Domingo* (1938), and the indispensable

Nevins, *Hamilton Fish*. Samoan policy is studied in G. H. Ryden, *Foreign Policy of the United States in Relation to Samoa* (1933). The Hawaii episode has its closest scholar in S. K. Stevens, *American Expansion in Hawaii, 1842–1898* (1945). The general story of expansion in the 1890's begins with J. W. Pratt, *Expansionists of 1898* (1936). The role of yellow journalism is overstressed in W. Millis's popular study of the 1898 War, *The Martial Spirit* (1931). A delightful work to start with on the Spanish-American War is F. Freidel, *The Splendid Little War* (1958). On the debate about the spoils of war read the exploratory essay by R. Hofstadter, "Manifest Destiny and the Philippines," in D. Aaron (ed.), *America in Crisis* (1952).

9

The American Empire

W HETHER justified or not in taking an empire, once the stars and stripes flew over distant possessions the United States had to accept the painful responsibilities of an imperial power. It had to learn that even decisions based on the noblest intentions toward a subject people would breed resentment and misunderstanding and that hatred would far outweigh gratitude for the best accomplishments of American administration. The responsibilities of American authorities often required many decisions to uphold law and order that were brutal or violated native customs. Even when the American tried to understand certain native habits, he simply could not condone or tolerate them. Those who thought that the work of empire would bring glory or welcome release from the home country's restrictions would learn that in the end empire traps and degrades the conqueror as well as the conquered.

The acquisition of islands in the Caribbean and Pacific forced the United States to devise a colonial policy and to revise its foreign policy. Both tasks proved more complex and onerous than the imperialists had anticipated. Not only was it difficult—and at times impossible—to reconcile the interests of colony and mother country, but the people of the United States repeatedly indicated that they were unwilling to make the sacrifices needed to defend their newly won interests in two hemispheres. Both the financial and psychological costs of the empire

Aguinaldo Surrenders

[NATIONAL ARCHIVES]

for a liberal society were terribly high. In 1898, many Americans had looked on imperialism as a glorious adventure, but in subsequent years they were to learn that the maintenance of an overseas empire involved burdens as well as prestige and expenditures as well as profits. It was a hard lesson, and the Americans learned it the hard way.

Problems of Administration

In suppressing the Philippine rebellion, the American people seemed to forget many of the ideals for which they had professedly fought in Cuba. As soon as their empire had been secured, as if tormented by guilt for their violations of the creed of their fathers, they set to work to furnish the inhabitants of the newly acquired islands with schools, hospitals, roads, partial democracy, and the miracle of American plumbing. Whenever possible and profitable, the American

"Our Foreign Missions—An Embarrassment of Riches" (Puck)

dollar marched side by side with humanitarianism into the farthest reaches of the new American empire.

Although an uneasy conscience—or perhaps, as some contemporaries preferred to put it, a sense of justice—drove the American people to "uplift" the "backward peoples" who had come under their control, they did not feel equally obliged to extend to their new subjects all the blessings of American liberty. In the first years of the new century, the Supreme Court in a series of controversial and confusing rulings known as the Insular Decisions announced that all the provisions of the Constitution did not necessarily apply to those Americans who lived under the flag, but beyond the continental borders, of the United States. It made a distinction between incorporated and unincorporated territories. Residents of the unincorporated territories were denied the "fundamental" rights of the Constitution and were excluded from the American tariff system unless Congress specifically ruled otherwise. Stripped of legal verbiage, the Insular Decisions were the Supreme Court's statement that the American administration could do whatever it wished with the new colonies.

A preview of American colonial policy was furnished by the occupation forces in Cuba before their withdrawal in 1902. Under the leadership of General Leonard Wood, the Americans sought to impose a new way of life upon the Cuban masses. The island's administrative machinery was overhauled, and its financial system was reorganized. Schools were set up on the American model. The moribund University of Havana was revived, modernized, and given a new faculty. Physical rehabilitation was undertaken with the construction of roads, railroads, bridges, schools, and hospitals. All these activities were overshadowed, however, by the conquest of Cuba's most dreaded disease, yellow fever. Under the direction of Dr. Walter Reed, a group of American doctors proceeded on the then novel assumption that yellow fever was carried by the stegomyia mosquito rather than produced by filthy living conditions. They permitted themselves to be bitten and infected, and within a relatively short period, they were able to substantiate this hypothesis. Once the source of the disease had been ascertained, the army cleaned up the breeding grounds of the mosquitoes, and by the conclusion of the occupation, American military forces had won a battle of more lasting glory than any of the victories over the Spanish a few years earlier.

Cuba's nominal independence was preserved, while its continued subservience to the United States was insured by the Platt Amendment, which was passed as a rider to an army appropriation bill in 1901. The island's independence was guaranteed against outside interference other

than that of the United States; a limit was set on the Cuban debt; and
Cuba was compelled to grant the United States land for coaling stations and the right to intervene for the maintenance of Cuban independence and domestic tranquillity. For almost three decades the Platt
Amendment served as a pretense for the protection of American strategic and economic interests in Cuba. Changes in political conditions in
the United States had little effect upon Cuban policy. Between 1901
and 1921 Presidents Roosevelt, Taft, and Wilson all sent troops to occupy the island. Although Americans insisted that they were intervening to insure the stability of government in Cuba, the presence of
American troops served only to perpetuate reactionary and autocratic
native regimes. The Cuban masses had no chance to change their governments by ballots or bullets, for their larger neighbor used force to
maintain stability, and that usually meant preservation of the economic
and strategic status quo. It was not until 1934 and the advent of the
New Deal's Good Neighbor policy that the Platt Amendment was
abrogated.

Cuba's experience as an independent nation revealed that economic
imperialism did not necessarily have to be preceded by formal territorial acquisition. After the withdrawal of American troops from Cuba
in 1902 and the lapse of the Foraker Amendment, which prohibited the
award of economic concessions to Americans during the occupation,
American economic interests steadily penetrated the island. American
investments in Cuba, which in 1898 approximated fifty million dollars,
were estimated by the United States Department of Commerce at
more than one billion dollars in 1924. Some of this capital went into
Cuban railroads, tobacco plantations, public utilities, government securities, and mineral resources, but the bulk of American funds in
Cuba was in sugar production. Before 1910, the ownership of the
island's sugar industry was divided almost equally among European,
American, and Cuban capitalists; by 1920, however, American-owned
mills were producing almost half the Cuban sugar supply, and eight
years later, American mills accounted for nearly two thirds of the total.
The Cuban and United States economies were linked by commercial
ties as well as capital outlay. In 1921, Cuban exports to the United
States amounted to about $230,000,000 out of a total of about
$278,000,000. In the same year, American products accounted for about
$264,000,000 of Cuba's total import bill of more than $354,000,000.
Nominally independent Cuba was the United States' most successful
experiment in economic imperialism.

Although Cuba was never formally incorporated into the American colonial system, in most other respects it can be seen as a model of

the treatment of the United States' newly acquired empire elsewhere. The details might vary from possession to possession, but in every instance humanitarianism and a measure of self-government came with policies designed to promote the strategic interests of the United States and American economic expansion. The results of the program were far from uniform. The Philippines turned out to be an economic liability and during World War II failed the only strategic tests to which they were submitted under American rule. Hawaii, on the other hand, developed into an asset of immeasurable strategic and economic value. Puerto Rico, although never playing a major role in American power politics, became a major asset to small but powerful groups of American businessmen who, in recent years, have provided the capital for a remarkable social transformation in the island's life.

The Philippine Islands were to be viewed by many Americans as a showcase of a new and enlightened type of imperialism. The United States spent millions on physical improvements, health and educational programs, administrative reforms, and the purchase of land owned by the Catholic orders in the islands. The Filipinos were promised their independence as soon as they had successfully completed a probationary period. In 1900, William Howard Taft headed a commission to establish a civil government in the islands. A year later, Taft became the first civil governor of the Philippines. The other members of the commission also stayed in the islands and with the assistance of three Filipinos served as the legislature of the government. After 1907, the Filipinos were permitted to elect their own assembly, while the United States continued to retain its control over the upper house and the executive. Taft and the four governors who followed him from 1903 to 1913 instituted public-works programs, improved educational facilities and strengthened the government's finances.

The mass of Filipinos approved of good roads and public schools, but they were not satisfied; they demanded independence rather than paternalism. With this object in mind, Woodrow Wilson named Francis Burton Harrison as governor in 1913. Under Harrison's administration, Filipinos were given a larger share in the government, and native business enterprise and agriculture were encouraged. In 1916, Congress, with the support of the Wilson Administration, passed the Jones Act, which substituted an elective senate for the commission and promised the Filipinos independence as soon as they had established a "stable government." Both Wilson and Harrison assumed that the requirement had been fulfilled, but when the Republicans returned to power in 1921, they ruled otherwise. New commissions were sent out to investigate the islands, and Harrison's major policies were reversed by Governor Leonard Wood and his successors. It was not until 1932 that the Hawes Act, passed over President Hoover's veto, provided for Philippine independence by the end of a decade. The Filipinos rejected this offer but they accepted a somewhat similar one in the Tydings-McDuffie Act of 1934.

Although American financial and commercial interests exercised a predominant influence over the Philippine economy, the islands never produced the returns envisioned by the imperialists at the turn of the century. The total American investment in the Philippines of approximately $166,000,000 in 1930 and the $78,000,000 in American exports to the Philippines in the same year accounted for only a small fraction of the sum that the United States spent annually on the administration and defense of the islands. On the other hand, the United States annually bought approximately 99 per cent of the Philippines' total sugar exports, 96 per cent of its coconut oil exports, and 62 per cent of its cordage exports. These and other commodities entered the United States duty free, to the obvious economic disadvantage of the American producers of the same or comparable products. Despite American control, the Philippine Islands were an outstanding failure as a venture in economic imperialism.

For most of World War II, large parts of the islands were under Japanese occupation after the collapse of a brave joint American-Filipino defense in the spring of 1942. Despite the extensive damage to cities like Manila and to parts of its economy, the Philippines made a rapid recovery after the defeat of the Japanese. On July 4, 1946, the Filipinos proclaimed their independence—almost a half-century after Admiral Dewey had sailed into Manila Bay. Although the honesty of the new nation's governments has not always been as complete as it might be, in an Asia beset by revolutions since 1945, the Philippines have remained a stable and democratic society. Through outstanding leaders such as the reform President Ramon Magsaysay (who was tragically killed in an accident) and Ambassador to the United States and United Nations Carlos P. Romulo, Philippine democracy and diplomacy have played a remarkable role in Asian and world affairs. The islands since 1946 have remained good friends of the United States and continue to provide us with bases. In 1959, a new treaty negotiated by American Ambassador Charles Bohlen put relations on an even firmer footing of equality than theretofore.

The effects of empire on Puerto Rico were less fortunate. In April, 1900, the end of the military occupation of Puerto Rico came with the passage of the Foraker Act, which provided for a government of an executive council and a governor, both of which were to be selected by the President of the United States, and a house of delegates to be elected by the Puerto Ricans. In 1917, the Jones Act made Puerto Ricans citizens of the United States and replaced the executive council with an elective upper house of the legislature. American political control, however, was assured: the President of the United States was to appoint the governor, and he had the right to veto the acts of the Puerto Rican legislature. No other important changes were made in the administration of Puerto Rico until 1946, when Jesus T. Piñero became the island's first native governor. In 1947, the United States Congress adopted a bill that provided for the popular election of the governor, and in 1948, Luis Muñoz Marin, the leader of the Popular Democratic party, was elected governor for a four-year term.

The Puerto Rican economy was never able to provide the population with an adequate standard of living. Many natives had hookworm, malaria, tuberculosis, and other diseases; unemployment was a constant problem; and most of the rural families suffered from chronic undernourishment. Puerto Rico's population expanded from 953,243 in 1899 to 2,113,058 in 1947. Without any comparable over-all economic growth, and with sugar cultivation so overshadowing the economy, the island was unable to produce most of life's necessities. Because Puerto Rico was within the American tariff wall, most of its sugar was exported to the United States, and approximately half of its output of sugar was produced by American-owned mills.

For the past half-century, the United States has tried to improve conditions in Puerto Rico. Attempts have been made to expand educational facilities, and the federal government has financed a number of internal improvements. During the depression of the 1930's, federal relief and land-reform programs were introduced, and during Rexford Tugwell's term as governor (1941-6), the Puerto Rican government took over the operation of some public utilities. In recent years, Puerto Rico has sought to attract industry by offers of tax exemptions and assurances of cheap labor. Recently, under Governor Marin, the island's economic growth has at last begun and promises to transform the stricken land. A large Puerto Rican emigration to the United States has helped relieve population pressures. The wealth brought by new factories during "operation bootstrap," as Governor Marin's extensive campaign to attract capital and industry is called, has favorably affected the standard of living. The advent of swift air transportation to the island from the United States has made the island a favorite vacationland where tourists now spend millions of dollars yearly.

The Virgin Islands, which were purchased from Denmark by the United States in 1917, have proved to be the least profitable of the

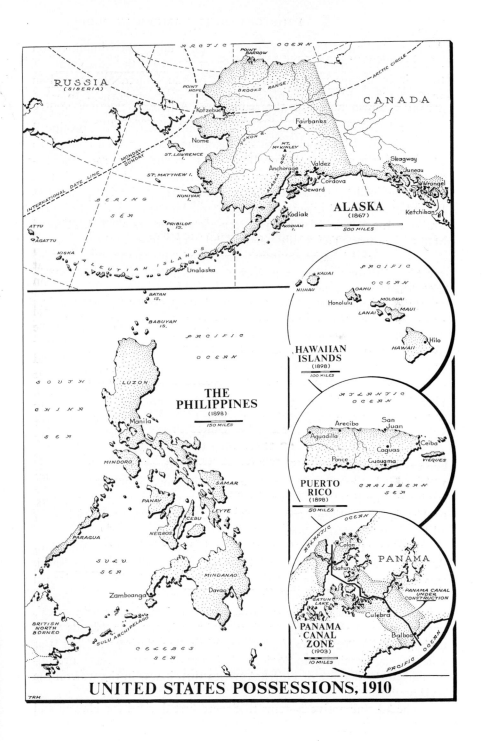

UNITED STATES POSSESSIONS, 1910

American colonies. They were placed at once under the administration of a governor appointed by the president. In 1927, the inhabitants of the Virgin Islands were made citizens of the United States, and in 1936, the islands' two municipal councils were authorized to meet jointly as the "Legislative Assembly of the Virgin Islands." Although the islands enjoyed free trade with the United States, they produced little that could be exported to the mainland and not even enough to provide for the needs of the inhabitants. As a result, the Virgin Islands— as Herbert Hoover said in 1931—were an "effective poorhouse" that was maintained by the United States. Since 1917, federal expenditures for internal improvements, economic rehabilitation, and relief programs in the Virgin Islands have been a constant drain on the United States Treasury. The United States, however, has not been able to solve the islands' basic economic problems, and, despite the recent great growth in tourism, a majority of the inhabitants do not attain more than a bare subsistence.

Hawaii and Alaska have been the United States' most successful ventures in empire building. Hawaii, which was brought within the American free-trade area, developed an economy tied closely with that of the United States. Concentrating on the production of sugar and pineapples, it sent almost all of its output to the United States, while more than 90 per cent of its imports came from the mainland. In 1939, Hawaii's imports from the United States were valued at nearly $102,000,000, while its exports to the United States totaled over $113,000,000. Alaska was also a valuable asset to the United States. By 1937, its mines had produced minerals worth $750,000,000. In 1947, its exports of fish, furs, gold, and other products to the United States were valued at more than $80,000,000. Even more important were the territory's undeveloped assets, for its unexploited mineral deposits, timber stands, and hydroelectric sites made it potentially the richest of all the American possessions.

During World War II, both Hawaii and Alaska were important American bases and experienced Japanese assaults. The Japanese "sneak attack" on Pearl Harbor on December 7, 1941, precipitated our formal entry into the war. Throughout the next four years Hawaiians served handsomely in the American forces, and the islands were America's greatest base in the Pacific. A few of Alaska's Aleutian Islands were under Japanese occupation for a time. After 1945, during the Cold War with Russia, proximity to Soviet Asia has made Alaska even more important to the defense of North America than it was in the war on the Axis powers.

The administrative systems that were first devised for Hawaii and

Alaska had many points in common. Under the terms of an act of
1884, provision was made for the appointment of a governor and judicial officials for Alaska, and in 1912, the territory was granted the right
to have a bicameral legislature. After 1900, Hawaii's government consisted of a governor appointed by the president, an elective legislature
of two houses, and a judicial system whose top officials have been
federal appointees. After 1945, their status as incorporated territories
helped the attempts of both Hawaii and Alaska to gain admission to the
Union as states. The demand was supported by President Truman and
the two major parties in their 1948 platforms. Repeatedly, statehood
bills for Alaska and Hawaii were presented to Congress, and finally,
with great rejoicing, in 1959 Hawaii and Alaska became the forty-ninth
and fiftieth states, the first two members of the Union not physically
joined to the others.

Power Politics in the Far East

The creation of an American empire in the Pacific marked the end
of an era in American diplomacy. For more than a century, the relations of the United States with Europe had centered on American efforts to prevent the leading nations of the Old World from extending
their influence to the Western hemisphere. After 1815, America lacked
any sustained significant interest in European affairs, despite our great
stake in European peace and common cultural ties. Interest in Asia,
however, far exceeded our actual investments or political stake in the
area. The source of that interest is still not clear. Much emphasis has
been placed on continuing hopes for a future "great China trade" and
on the role of American missionaries in the Far East, but scholars cannot yet agree on these or other causes for our involvement with China,
Japan and Korea before the 1890's. With the acquisition of actual Asian
possessions in the Philippines, however, mere continental domination as
exemplified by the Monroe Doctrine was no longer enough. If American diplomats wished to protect their newly won outpost in the Pacific,
they would have to take an active part in Far Eastern power politics.

When the United States entered the Philippines, international relations in the Far East were rapidly changing. Imperial China appeared
to be on the verge of disintegration, and the world's major nations
were closing in for the kill. Following its easy victory in the Sino-
Japanese War of 1894–5, Japan moved into Formosa and strengthened
its hold over Korea. Japan's lead was quickly followed by several
European powers. England, France, Germany, and Russia began a
frantic scramble in China for greater spheres of influence, leaseholds,

and railroad concessions. The United States for more than half a century had enjoyed the same commercial privileges in China as other nations. In 1898 America's new economic and strategic base in the Philippines was threatened even before it was firmly established. England was equally disturbed by developments in the Orient during the 1890's. While France, Russia, and Germany juggled alliances, England's diplomatic isolation weakened its chances in any war that might grow out of imperialistic rivalries in the Far East. With the largest commercial stake in China, England would be the greatest loser if Chinese independence were destroyed. In an effort to rebuild its fences in the Far East, England turned to the United States. In 1898, Sir Julian Pauncefote, the British ambassador in Washington, suggested to Secretary of State John Sherman that England and the United States undertake a joint Far Eastern policy to guarantee equality of commercial opportunity for all foreign nations in China. The British proposal was rejected by Sherman; but within two years it had become the cornerstone of American Far Eastern policy under John Hay.

When John Hay became Secretary of State in September, 1898, he selected as his principal adviser on the Far East W. W. Rockhill, who had spent many years in China and had formed a lasting friendship there with Alfred Hippisley, another "old China hand" and a British subject. In 1899, Hippisley outlined a course of action for the United States in China and sent it to Rockhill in the form of a written memorandum. Rockhill submitted Hippisley's proposals to Hay, who, after making some minor revisions, dispatched them as a circular note to Germany, Japan, Italy, Russia, France, and England. What came to be known as the Open Door Note asked each nation to pledge itself not to interfere with the commercial rights of other nations in its leaseholds or spheres of influence. Although most of the powers in replying to the Open Door Note used language ambiguous enough to be meaningless, Hay announced that the principle of commercial equality had been accepted by all the nations, with interests in China.

Within a year after its promulgation, the Open Door policy was seriously threatened by the Boxer Rebellion, an armed anti-foreign protest by Chinese fanatics that was suppressed by the combined military forces of all the powers, including the United States, with concessions from China. Hay was fearful that the foreign troops in China might be used to shut the Open Door. On July 3, 1900, he sent another circular note to the powers, which stated that the United States intended to "preserve Chinese territorial integrity and administrative entity." China escaped dismemberment after the Boxer Rebellion, but not because of the American note. Each nation with a stake in China was so afraid that any overt move would precipitate a general world war for which it was not prepared that it was willing to settle, however reluctantly, for the maintenance of the uneasy balance of power in the Far East. There is no reason to believe that John Hay's efforts had any effect upon either the economic or territorial situation in the Far East. With the Open Door policy, however, the United States had assumed obligations beyond concrete American interests in China. Without willingness to make available the military force that might be necessary to maintain this policy, as the future was to show, America would merely encourage expectations among the Chinese that were not to be fulfilled.

The Open Door policy was not the product of American investments, but of our commercial aspirations and strategic necessity. American trade with the Far East represented in 1899 only 2 per cent of the United States' total foreign trade, but several American politicians and businessmen thought that the acquisition of the Philippines had provided the United States with an ideal opportunity for increasing its commerce with the Orient. John Hay's notes were designed to prevent this potential market from being pre-empted by the European powers. As important as these economic considerations was the strategic problem posed by the Philippine Islands. The American people, with a one-ocean navy and little inclination to sacrifice their lives in the defense of the Philippines, nevertheless were committed to hold the islands against all comers. As force was out, only diplomacy remained. John Hay based his policy on the hypothesis that the Philippines could only be saved from foreign aggression by the maintenance of the balance of power in the Far East and that this in turn could be achieved by preserving Chinese territorial integrity. Hay's successors never challenged this analysis, and future Presidents all made an independent China the keystone of their Far Eastern policy.

John Hay tried to save China and the Philippines by writing notes; Theodore Roosevelt sought the same ends by pursuing a spirited and often spectacular diplomacy—a technique that he once somewhat inaccurately described by saying that he preferred to "speak softly and carry a big stick." In one respect Roosevelt's problem differed from Hay's, for before the conclusion of his administration, Japan had emerged as a major power in the Orient. Therefore, while Hay's policy of necessity had been directed primarily toward checking the advances of the European nations in China, Roosevelt had to concentrate upon curbing the expansion of Japan.

Roosevelt's Far Eastern policies were first revealed by his part in the Russo-Japanese War. At the outset of the war, Roosevelt and most other Americans gave their moral support to what they considered a weak Japan struggling against a mighty, autocratic, reactionary enemy. Russia, however, proved to be a hollow shell. Nevertheless, Japanese leaders feared that the drain of successive victories on the meager resources of Japan would result in ultimate defeat if the conflict turned into a war of attrition. With this in mind, after their initial great victories, they requested the American President to intervene as peacemaker in the Far East. Roosevelt, well aware of the dangers involved in such a role, was at first reluctant to accept, but the logic of the American position in the Orient eventually convinced him that he could not afford to refuse. A clear-cut victory for either Russia or Japan would have threatened the territorial integrity of China and jeopardized the American position in the Philippines. Like John Hay, Theodore Roosevelt assumed that an independent China was the keystone of American Far Eastern policy.

A treaty of peace ending the Russo-Japanese War and sponsored by Theodore Roosevelt was concluded at Portsmouth, New Hampshire, in 1905. It represented a victory for the Japanese. They obtained the southern half of the island of Sakhalin, the Liaotung leasehold in Manchuria, the South Manchurian Railway, and further recognition of their power over Korea. Despite these advantageous terms, the treaty fell short of Japan's war aims, for Roosevelt backed Russia's refusal to accede to the Japanese demand for a huge indemnity from Russia. While this tactic successfully maintained the precarious balance of power in the Far East, it also produced considerable anti-American feeling among the Japanese, who had hoped the indemnity would relieve them of the high taxes necessary to maintain a wartime economy.

After the Russo-Japanese War there was a marked increase in anti-Japanese sentiment in California. This attitude was not primarily a reaction to the Japanese military successes in the recent war; it arose largely from racial prejudice, fear of the effect of cheap Oriental labor upon California's standard of living, and an irresponsible press led by William Randolph Hearst's San Francisco *Examiner*, with its repeated warnings against the "yellow peril." The San Francisco school board in October, 1906, ruled that the ninety-three Japanese children in the city would have to attend a separate school, and the Japanese government objected strenuously. Although Theodore Roosevelt had no jurisdiction over San Francisco's schools, he sent a special deputy and numerous threats to San Francisco in an attempt to prevent a few municipal officials from involving the United States in an international incident. When bluster failed to move the members of the school board, Roosevelt reversed his tactics and invited them to Washington,

The Peacemaker of Portsmouth, with Russian and Japanese Representatives

[BROWN BROTHERS]

where they speedily succumbed to the famous Roosevelt personality. The school board's rule was rescinded, and Roosevelt in 1907–8 reassured the jittery Californians by negotiating the Gentlemen's Agreement by which Japan promised to prohibit the emigration of Japanese workers to the United States. Roosevelt had been able to settle a disagreeable dispute through tact, ingenuity, and genuine statesmanship, but he was afraid that the Japanese would assume that he had been truckling to them. To convince Japan that the United States had acted out of generosity rather than timidity, he sent the United States' fleet on a round-the-world trip that included a long and impressive visit to Japan. Since the American people were unwilling to die for the Philippines, Theodore Roosevelt would save them by bluff and bravado.

Roosevelt also sought to maintain the American position in the

Orient by exacting pledges from Japan to support the status quo in the
Far East. In an executive agreement negotiated by Secretary of War
Taft in 1905, American recognition of Japanese control over Korea
was balanced by Japan's acceptance of the American position in the
Philippines. Three years later, in the Root-Takahira Agreement, both
countries pledged themselves to uphold the existing territorial settlements in the Far East, the Open Door, and Chinese territorial integrity.
Both agreements were based on the same hypothesis. Although Theodore Roosevelt could not stop the advance of Japan in the Far East, he
could blunt it and demand a *quid pro quo*—the continued inviolability
of the Philippines. He would have preferred to have had it otherwise,
but there was no alternative. While Roosevelt's Far Eastern policy undoubtedly represented a retreat from the position taken by Hay, his
active diplomacy at all times prevented it from developing into a rout.

William Howard Taft, who became President in 1909, changed
the techniques, but not the objectives, of his predecessors' Far Eastern
foreign policy. For John Hay's note writing and Theodore Roosevelt's
big stick Taft substituted what was popularly known as dollar diplomacy. The immediate origins of dollar diplomacy in Asia go back to
Willard Straight, who had served in the American consular service in
the Far East and convinced Secretary of State Philander Knox that
there were limitless opportunities for the investment of American capital in China. Dollar diplomacy, as conceived and promulgated by the
Taft Administration, was designed not only to promote American
business abroad, but also to enlist the support of the nation's leading
financiers in the government's struggle to maintain the balance of
power in the Orient. As in the past, the American stake in the Far East
was to be preserved by saving China from foreign aggressors. Just how
the dollar would buttress diplomacy was explained by a State Department memorandum of 1909:

> The nations that finance the great Chinese railways and other
> enterprises will be foremost in the affairs of China and the
> participation of American capital in these investments will give
> the voice of the U. S. more authority in political controversies
> in that country which will go far toward guaranteeing the
> preservation of the administrative entity of China. . . . So
> long as the U. S. holds the Philippines, the domination of China
> by other nations to our exclusion would be fraught with
> danger and it is unthinkable that this country should be
> squeezed out of any combination exercising an influence at
> Peking. The balancing of power in China is essential to peace

in the Orient. . . . Our interests in Asiatic waters require the
prevention of the establishment of predominant interests and
influences at Peking on the part of other powers and that
American prestige in China be undiminished.

In 1909 the State Department induced some of the leading financiers of the United States to join a consortium of British, German, and
French bankers who planned to construct a major railroad in China.
The British were opposed to American participation in the project, but
China was prevailed upon to withhold permission for the undertaking
until the American financiers had been included in the consortium.
But American investment in the railroad had little appreciable effect
on the United States' long-term objectives in the Orient. Even more
unfortunate was Taft's attempt to apply dollar diplomacy in Manchuria. On the assumption that continued Russian and Japanese control of Manchuria's two principal rail systems represented a threat to
the Open Door, Knox suggested that China borrow enough money
from private investors abroad to purchase the two railways. Neither
Russia nor Japan wished to relinquish their hold over Manchuria, and
they rejected the American proposal.

The election of Woodrow Wilson to the presidency in 1912
seemed to promise a new era in the United States' Far Eastern relations.
Wilson was the first Democrat to occupy the White House since
Cleveland's administration in the midnineties. His speeches were constant calls to justice and morality, while Roosevelt and Taft had posed
as more practical men in foreign affairs. He had campaigned as an opponent of unregulated business, and there seemed no reason to believe
that he would encourage irresponsible practices by American business
abroad while curbing them at home. On the other hand, the situation
in the Far East during Wilson's administration was in many respects
similar to that under Taft and Roosevelt. This fact, more than Wilson's
personal wishes, in the long run forced him to adopt much the same
course that his predecessors had followed in the Orient from 1899 to
1912.

For a short time Woodrow Wilson was able to curb dollar diplomacy in Far Eastern policy. Before Wilson became President, Taft
and Knox had urged the participation of American bankers in a six-
power loan to China. One of the new President's first moves was to
announce that his Administration was withdrawing the government's
support from a project that it considered a threat to the continued independence of China. Wilson was also able to limit the resurgence of
anti-Japanese feeling in California. When the California legislature an-

nounced that it intended to pass a law forbidding the ownership of land by Japanese in that state, Wilson exerted considerable moral pressure to block this legislation, and sent Secretary of State Bryan to California. Although the California lawmakers eventually had their way, the law they enacted was milder than had been originally anticipated.

But these were minor changes. Like Roosevelt, Wilson soon understood that American policy in the Far East depended more upon Japan's moves than upon ideals that were not backed by force. In 1914, Japan, in accordance with a treaty of alliance signed with Great Britain in 1902, declared war on Germany and then seized several German islands in the Pacific and assumed the German economic and political rights in the Shantung peninsula. A year later she made her boldest bid for Asiatic domination and presented China with the famous Twenty-One Demands. China was asked to give Japan full control over Shantung, to agree to an increase in Japanese power in Manchuria, and to grant Japan special economic privileges in China proper and a predominant role in the Chinese government. Although the United States objected vigorously to this new growth of Japanese imperialism, it could not prevent continued Japanese expansion. Under diplomatic pressure Japan modified but did not renounce her claims in China. Strangely, the United States soon sanctioned the new Japanese position on the mainland. The Lansing-Ishii agreement of 1917, although reiterating both nations' earlier pledges to uphold the Open Door and the territorial integrity of China, also contained a formal American recognition of Japan's "special interests in China."

Soon after the conclusion of the Lansing-Ishii agreement, the Wilson Administration took more forceful measures to check Japanese expansion. The first American countermove revealed a sharp clash between Wilsonian ideals and the facts of the Far Eastern situation. In 1918, Wilson insisted that American bankers participate in a new loan to the Chinese government. The wheel had turned full circle, and the realities of Far Eastern politics had forced Wilson to use the same dollar diplomacy that he had so heartily condemned in Taft. But Wilson was to go much further than either of his immediate predecessors, for he dispatched soldiers as well as dollars to the Orient. In 1918, the Allied nations, including the United States, sent troops to various parts of Russia, which under its new Bolshevik government had concluded a separate peace with Germany. Nine thousand American soldiers arrived in Siberia in August, 1918, and remained until April, 1920. Although Wilson's military moves prevented the Japanese from acquiring any territory in Russian Asia at the Versailles peace conference, he was compelled to agree to Japan's control over the former German islands in the Pacific and the German interests in the Shantung peninsula.

By the end of Wilson's second term in the White House, it was clear that the United States had continued to lose ground in the Far East. Roosevelt, Taft and Wilson had sought to preserve the existing balance of power by curbing Japan. Despite Wilson's initial protest, he was forced to use his predecessors' methods. Following Japan's Twenty-One Demands, he had, like Roosevelt, recognized the inevitable, and in 1918, he had championed a much maligned dollar diplomacy. And to these steps he had added a third—armed intervention. Despite all efforts during Wilson's Administration, the United States had retreated in the Far East; Japan had advanced.

The Struggle for the Panama Canal

After 1895, diplomatic maneuver, military occupation, and economic pressure were all used at various times to force Latin Americans to do the will of the United States while permitting them to maintain the fiction of political independence. Whenever American leaders felt the need for intervention, they invoked some interpretation of the Monroe Doctrine. In his message of 1823, Monroe had stated that the United States would oppose European interference in the internal affairs of any nation in this hemisphere. After 1900, American officials redefined Monroe's words. European intervention would now be prevented, if necessary, by the intervention of the United States.

Many American businessmen may have profited from the aggressive Latin American policy of the United States from 1890 to 1920, but the primary purpose of our policy was not economic. The country's moves in Latin America were to protect the United States strategic interests rather than to enrich American investors, manufacturers, and merchants. America's determination to dominate Central and South America was also just one more sign of the heightened nationalism that came with the United States' emergence as a world power at the beginning of the twentieth century.

At the center of the strategic problem raised by relations with Latin America was an isthmus canal. America's first policy was to revive their plans and hopes for a canal. After the canal had been built, American foreign policy south of the Rio Grande was oriented toward protecting it. As early as 1846 the United States had negotiated a treaty with New Granada (later Colombia) that granted the United States the right of transit across Panama in return for an American guarantee of New Granada's sovereignty over the isthmus. Four years later the extensive British interests in Central America were recognized by the United States in the Clayton-Bulwer Treaty. Both nations agreed that any future canal would be a joint undertaking and would remain unfortified. The Clayton-Bulwer Treaty did not eliminate Anglo-American rivalry in Central America, and throughout the 1850's there was a growing feeling in the United States that an isthmus canal should be an exclusively American project. The outbreak of the Civil War, however, temporarily ended plans of the American canal enthusiasts.

Canal diplomacy after the Civil War was complicated by financial obstacles and international rivalries. As the only possible canal routes lay through Nicaragua or Colombia, and as neither of these countries could finance such a large undertaking, capital would have to be obtained from outside sources. In 1878 a French company under Ferdinand de Lesseps, the builder of the Suez Canal, received a concession from Colombia to build a canal across the Isthmus of Panama. The possibility that an important commercial route and vital naval link might come under the control of a foreign power convinced many Americans that the United States would have to build and own the canal alone. Secretary of State Blaine in 1881 protested to the British that the Garfield Administration considered the Clayton-Bulwer Treaty a violation of the Monroe Doctrine and a threat to American supremacy in the Western hemisphere. Britain, however, had no intention of altering its Central American policies to suit the whim of the American Secretary of State, and the British foreign minister informed Blaine that the canal "question had already been settled by the engagements of the Clayton-Bulwer Treaty and that Her Majesty's government relied with confidence upon the observation of all the obligations of that treaty." There followed a more devious, if not more subtle, American attempt to nullify the effect of the treaty. In 1884, Frederick Frelinghuysen, President Arthur's Secretary of State, concluded a treaty with Nicaragua that provided for the joint ownership of a Nicaraguan canal and a United States' guarantee of protection to Nicaragua against outside aggression. The Frelinghuysen-Zavala Treaty did not obtain the necessary votes for ratification during Arthur's Administration, however, and was withdrawn from the Senate by Grover Cleveland soon after he became President in 1855.

By 1889, however, the French threat had been removed by the failure of the De Lesseps company after it had spent approximately $300,000,000. The Maritime Canal Company, an American corporation with a concession in Nicaragua, had abandoned efforts in 1893, after three years of preliminary work. With no immediate foreign threat

Mementos of the French Failure in Panama

[LIBRARY OF CONGRESS]

and with one American failure on the record the canal fever died down. Suddenly, in 1898, the United States had to turn its attention to a canal again. The U.S.S. *Oregon*'s race from Puget Sound around the tip of South America to beat the Spanish fleet to Cuba pointed an obvious strategic lesson. The United States had become a two-ocean power with a one-ocean navy. After the war, to protect its new acquisitions in the Caribbean and the Pacific, the isthmus seemed essential. Admiral Mahan had urged the United States to obtain Caribbean and Pacific bases to safeguard a future canal. Now that they had the bases, Americans turned the argument around: they needed a canal to protect the bases. Added to strategic considerations was the renewed demand for a shorter commercial route between the United States' Atlantic and Pacific ports. Fortunately, by the end of the 1890's, England was ready to reverse its earlier stand on the Clayton-Bulwer Treaty. Harassed by the vexatious problems of the Boer War and alarmed by the system of alliances being built up by its European rivals, England considered a retreat in Central America a small price to pay for the continued friendship of the most powerful nation in the Western hemisphere. In 1899, Sir Julian Pauncefote and John Hay negotiated a treaty that was rejected by the Senate because it did not allow the

United States to fortify the proposed canal. Two years later, the second Hay-Pauncefote Treaty, which permitted the United States to construct and maintain a fortified canal, was ratified by the Senate by a vote of 72 to 6.

With the Clayton-Bulwer Treaty eliminated, the principal question became the location of the future canal. Theodore Roosevelt, who became President in September, 1901, favored Nicaragua, and a group of engineers known as the Walker Commission reported that construction costs would be cheaper in Nicaragua than in Panama. However, the matter could not be settled on its merits alone, for it soon became hopelessly complicated by the machinations of backers of the reorganized French canal company.

All pretense of canal building had really been abandoned, and the only reason for the new concern's existence was the desire to sell its concession to the United States. As soon as the Walker Commission indicated its preference for the Nicaraguan route, any doubt about the objectives of the French company was removed, for it reduced the price of its concession to the United States from $109,141,500 to $40,000,000. This made the Panama route no more expensive than its rival. The company took particular care to point out to America's leading politicians the advantages of Panama over Nicaragua, and it chose William N. Cromwell, a prominent New York attorney, as its Washington lobbyist. Cromwell, who was later to charge his employers $800,000 for services rendered, induced the Republicans to drop the word "Nicaragua" from the canal plank of their 1900 platform and contributed $60,000 of his client's money to the Republican National Committee. His activities were supplemented by those of Philippe Bunau-Varilla, an engineer in the original company, who arrived in the United States to point out the dangers of Nicaragua's volcanos to such influential politicians as McKinley, Roosevelt, and Mark Hanna.

What was the effect of the tactics of the New Panama Canal Company upon the American decision to build a canal in Panama instead of Nicaragua? We cannot know precisely, but in June, 1902, Congress passed the Spooner Act authorizing the President to secure a right of way across the Isthmus of Panama. If Colombia were to prove recalcitrant or unreasonable the President was to undertake negotiations with Nicaragua. By constantly threatening to turn to Nicaragua, the United States was able to exact favorable terms from Herrán, the Colombian representative in Washington. The Hay-Herrán Treaty, signed in 1903, granted the United States a six-mile-wide canal zone across the Isthmus of Panama for $10,000,000 and annual payments of $250,000. Although the treaty was speedily accepted by the United

States Senate, it was rejected by Colombia, which wanted a higher price, part of the fee promised to the French company, and a guarantee against possible American infringement of its sovereignty.

Colombia's refusal to accept the American offer infuriated Roosevelt, who wrote to Mark Hanna on October 5, 1903, that the United States was "certainly justified in morals, and therefore . . . in law . . . in interfering summarily [in Panama] and saying that the canal is to be built and that they must not stop it." The supporters of the canal project were determined that if Colombia was not amenable to diplomatic reason, they would resort to force. Convinced that Roosevelt would look with favor on a popular uprising in Panama, Bunau-Varilla set to work to plan a Panamanian revolution. From his headquarters in a New York hotel room, which he described as the "cradle of the Panama Republic," Bunau-Varilla supplied the "revolutionaries" in Panama with a proclamation of independence, a new constitution, a "flag of liberation" made by the "agile and discreet fingers" of his wife, and orders that the revolution begin on November 3. Despite Bunau-Varilla's elaborate preparations, his representatives in Panama were able to gather only slightly less than 1,000 rebels—including 287 members of the Panama City fire department, 300 section hands of the Panama Railroad, and any Colombian soldiers who were willing to transfer their allegiance for fifty dollars. When this valiant band seemed reluctant to take on the Colombian Army, Bunau-Varilla learned enough from American officials to cable his adherents that the U.S.S. *Nashville* would arrive at Colón, Panama on November 2, 1903.

Events in Panama now followed closely the timetable laid down by Bunau-Varilla. The *Nashville* reached Colón on November 2. The revolution began and ended the following day as American forces prevented the landing of Colombian troops at the Isthmus. On November 4 the new Republic of Panama was announced to the world, and two days later it was recognized by the United States. Within a week Bunau-Varilla was accepted as the Panamanian envoy to the United States, and on November 18, he signed the Hay–Bunau-Varilla Treaty, which gave Panama the terms that Colombia had rejected. On February 23, 1904, the Senate ratified the treaty. The United States had at last obtained its canal route, and the French Company had its forty million dollars.

Theodore Roosevelt then remarked that "no one connected with this government had any part in preparing, inciting, or encouraging the revolution" in Panama, but in 1911 he put the matter more accurately when he stated that he "took the Canal Zone and let Congress debate."

Canal Diplomacy

As soon as the United States was committed to construct a canal in Panama, it had to insure its defense. Although neighboring Latin American countries were too weak to threaten the American position, their very weakness would make them inviting targets for any European nation with designs on the Panama Canal. Presidents Roosevelt, Taft, and Wilson were all aware that European intervention in Central America and the Caribbean would endanger the canal, and their Latin American policy was designed to maintain and increase American influence in these regions. From 1903 to 1921 the United States added to its holdings in the Caribbean, pumped American capital into shaky regimes in Latin America, used the Monroe Doctrine in a fashion that had never been anticipated by its author, and on several occasions sent American troops to countries threatened by financial or political instability.

The first challenge to canal diplomacy occurred before the Panama Revolution. In 1902 Great Britain, Germany, and Italy decided to use force to collect the debts that Venezuela owed their nationals. When they had blockaded Venezuela and bombarded one of its towns, Roosevelt announced his disapproval of such vigorous measures and warned against any violations of the Monroe Doctrine. The possibility of armed intervention in Venezuela was removed when the blockading powers agreed to submit their claims to the Hague Tribunal. A by-product of the Venezuelan debt question was the Drago Doctrine. In December, 1902, Luis M. Drago, the Argentine foreign minister, proposed in a note to the United States "that the public debt cannot occasion armed intervention nor even actual occupation of the territory of American nations" by European powers. Five years later, the Drago Doctrine was incorporated into international law by the Hague Conference.

Roosevelt's casual attitude toward the blockade of Venezuela gave no sign of the determination with which he tried to prevent European intervention in the Dominican Republic. By 1904 Roosevelt had decided that the United States had better do the spanking. In his annual message, he described the United States' new duties as a stern parent under what is now known as the Roosevelt Corollary to the Monroe Doctrine:

> Chronic wrong-doing, or an impotence which results in a general loosening of the ties of civilized society, may in America, as elsewhere, ultimately require intervention by some civilized

nation, and in the Western Hemisphere the adherence of the United States to the Monroe Doctrine may force the United States, however reluctantly, in flagrant cases of such wrongdoing or impotence, to the exercise of an international police power.

Although Roosevelt's statement was couched in moral terms, he was not interested in improving the character of the Dominican people. Nor did the Roosevelt Corollary imply either economic or territorial aggression. If a potentially hostile power were situated at the gateway to the future canal, the United States' most vital interests would be in continual jeopardy. In Roosevelt's mind it was therefore necessary to anticipate the moves of any European rival. The strategic implications of the Roosevelt Corollary to the Monroe Doctrine were clear enough to the United States; to Latin Americans, who had another point of view, it was a policy that forced them to arrange their lives according to the dictates of the United States.

Secure in his sense of the righteousness of this new doctrine, Roosevelt in 1905 concluded an agreement with the Dominican Republic that placed the Dominican customs system under the jurisdiction of a United States citizen who would impound 55 per cent of its revenues to be applied to the European debts. When the Senate refused to accept this agreement, Roosevelt induced the Dominicans, who knew that he had superior force on his side, to appoint an unofficial American collector. Under his administration, customs receipts were doubled, the European creditors accepted an almost 50 per cent reduction in the debts, and the accounts were settled.

In 1912 the scope of the Monroe Doctrine was again expanded with the announcement of the so-called Lodge Corollary. In 1911 a Japanese fishing company had attempted to lease a large tract of land from Mexico in Magdalena Bay. When the State Department indicated its disapproval of the project, the Japanese concern had abandoned its plans. A year later a resolution introduced by Henry Cabot Lodge and adopted by the Senate revealed the continuing concern of the United States with its canal defenses. According to the Lodge Resolution, the United States would view with "grave concern" the acquisition by a foreign corporation of "any harbor or other place in the American continents . . . so situated that the occupation thereof for naval or military purposes might threaten the communications or the safety of the United States."

Although the methods of Taft's dollar diplomacy might differ, the objectives remained fixed. The heart of the United States' Latin

Invoking the Monroe Doctrine (*McCutcheon in the* Chicago Tribune)

American policy was still the defense of the Panama Canal. To prevent rival imperialist nations from intervening in the neighborhood of the canal, Taft proposed to supplant European investments in this strategic area with American private capital. If the Caribbean and Central American republics had to rely on American rather than European financial resources, all pretext for European intervention in this area would be removed, and the continued safety of the canal would be assured.

President Taft and Secretary of State Knox continually attempted to use dollar diplomacy with financially weak regimes in Latin America. In 1909, when British bondholders began to move for the collection of their debts in Honduras, the Administration requested American financiers to assume the country's debt. A year later a group of New York bankers were induced to take over the assets of the National Bank of Haiti. When a revolution occurred in Nicaragua, Taft refused to accord diplomatic recognition to the new regime until it accepted large credits from American bankers for the liquidation of its debts to the British. Nicaraguan opposition to the plan was overcome by a visit from an American warship, and in 1911 a United States citizen took over the control of the country's customs revenues. In practice dollar diplomacy meant first the big dollar; if the country in question was not amenable to economic pressure, the big stick could always be employed.

Shortly after Woodrow Wilson became President of the United States, he delivered a speech at Mobile, Alabama, in which he stated that the United States' Latin American policy would no longer be concerned with the "pursuit of material interest," but would be devoted to the promotion of "human rights" and "national integrity." Although Wilson's words may have heartened the anti-imperialists in the United States, Latin Americans were to find little evidence that his words meant any fundamental change in American foreign policy. The marines did not leave Nicaragua, and the Bryan-Chamorro Treaty provided for exclusive American canal rights in Nicaragua, the leasing of the Great Corn and Little Corn Islands and the Gulf of Fonseca to the United States, and a new American loan to Nicaragua. A revolution in Haiti in 1915 brought the American marines as quickly as they had come under either Taft or Roosevelt.

It should be pointed out that Wilson was confronted by a strategic problem more pressing and more difficult than the problems faced by either of his immediate predecessors. During World War I, Germany's designs upon the Caribbean were part of the strategy of an enemy power; they could not be conjured away by expressions of Wilsonian idealism. More than ever before the United States had to look to its canal defenses. To counteract the possibility of European intervention in the Caribbean, earlier attempts to acquire the Virgin Islands were revived, and in 1917 the United States strengthened its Caribbean position with the purchase of the Danish West Indies for 25 million dollars.

Whenever the security of the United States was not at stake, Wilson's Latin American policy was more likely to accord with his ideals. When the question of the United States's responsibility for the revolution in Panama was reopened, the Wilson Administration agreed to a treaty that provided for an apology to Colombia and the payment of an indemnity of 25 million dollars. At the time Theodore Roosevelt stated: "An administration that will conclude such a treaty as this treaty for the payment of blackmail to Colombia has forfeited all right to the respect of the people of the United States." More than one third of the Senate may have agreed with this estimate; although the treaty was submitted to the Senate in June, 1914, it was not ratified until seven years later, when Harding was President—and then only after the deletion of the apology from the treaty, and the discovery of valuable petroleum deposits in Colombia.

Woodrow Wilson's Mexican policy started as an attempt to stand by principles and forego material benefits in the conduct of American foreign affairs. Shortly before Wilson became President, Francisco Madero, President of Mexico, was deposed and subsequently murdered by his successor, Victoriano Huerta. In the normal course of events, the United States would have recognized the Huerta regime as soon as it had demonstrated its ability to maintain its control over the Mexican government and people. This policy was in line with the tradition of *de facto* recognition established by Thomas Jefferson as Secretary of State in 1793, when he extended American recognition to the revolutionary regime in France. But Wilson, deciding to break with precedents that went back to the beginning of the American Republic, announced that he would not recognize as legal (*de jure*) a government that rested upon force rather than the popular will. If the Mexican people wished to enter into diplomatic relations with the United States, they would have to supplant the Huerta dictatorship with a constitutional democracy. On the other hand, the United States pledged itself not to intervene in Mexico's domestic affairs. Wilson was determined to stick to his policy of "watchful waiting" despite the continued loss of American life in Mexico, the jibes of his Republican opponents, the speed with which the European nations recognized the Huerta government, and the laments of American investors in Mexican oil, land, and railroads.

Wilson's Mexican policy may have represented a triumph of ideals over *Realpolitik*, but it also revealed considerable confusion in its author's mind. In the first place, Wilson's policy can hardly be characterized as "waiting," for diplomatic pressure was being put upon Huerta to resign, and after February, 1914, the United States permitted the export of arms to Venustiano Carranza and Pancho Villa, Huerta's principal rivals in Mexico. Wilson's Mexican policy was also self-contradictory. Opposing American intervention in Mexico, he demanded at the same time that the Mexicans change their form of government; but Mexico could not be transformed into a constitutional democracy without pressure from the United States. Finally, Wilson's criticism of

Pershing in Mexico

[NATIONAL ARCHIVES]

Huerta strengthened rather than weakened the latter's popularity among Mexicans who suspected and hated the "Yanquis."

The deadlock between Mexico and the United States was broken by the events that followed the arrest of some American sailors by the Mexican authorities in Tampico on April 9, 1914. Although the men were immediately released and the Mexican officer responsible for the arrest apologized, Admiral Mayo, the commander of the American fleet, demanded a twenty-one gun salute to the American flag and a "formal disavowal of and apology for the act, together with . . . assurance that the officer responsible for it will receive severe punishment." Although Wilson thought the terms of Mayo's ultimatum too harsh, it was virtually impossible for him to repudiate the American commander. Wilson's refusal to support Mayo's stand would have been interpreted as an American retreat by the Mexicans and a sacrifice of national honor by the Americans. Huerta, well aware of Wilson's dilemma, resolutely refused to order the salute to the American flag. By April 20, Wilson's patience was exhausted, and he asked Congress for authority to intervene by force in a move that—as he carefully pointed out—would be directed against the Mexican ruler rather than the Mexican people. The following day American naval forces shelled and captured the Mexican city of Vera Cruz. A full scale war between Mexico and the United States was averted, however, by a timely offer of mediation on the part of Argentina, Brazil, and Chile. Under the terms of the settlement worked out by the A.B.C. powers in June, 1914, the United States waived an indemnity and recognized a provisional Mexican government that had risen against Huerta. Huerta fled Mexico in July; Carranza took over the presidency; and a disappointed Pancho Villa went on the warpath and attacked *Carranzistas* and American citizens indiscriminately. When Villa raided towns in Texas and New Mexico, American troops under General John Pershing invaded Mexico in a futile attempt to capture the rebel leader. The American forces were not withdrawn from Mexico until February, 1917; then, as the American people turned to the much larger conflict in Europe, the Mexicans settled down to working out their revolution in their own way.

Woodrow Wilson's attempt to substitute ideals for force in Latin America produced only meager results. He had to resort to the tactics of his predecessors to maintain the position of the United States in the Caribbean, and his sympathy for the plight of the Mexican people did not prevent the bombardment of Vera Cruz and the occupation of Mexican soil by American troops. Wilson's use of conventional imperial techniques in Latin America, as in the Far East, revealed that the United States' foreign policy was determined, not by the high moral purpose of its President, but by geography, economics, "national honor," and the moves of its rivals. When the noble sentiments of Wilson's state papers and the minor liberal details of Wilson's Latin American policy are stripped away, little remains to differentiate it from the hardboiled programs of Roosevelt and Taft.

U. S. Intervention in Latin America 1898–1915

NATION	YEAR	FORM OF INTERVENTION	DURATION
Cuba	1898	Military occupation	1898–1902
Panama	1903	Naval aid to revolutionaries	1903
Santo Domingo (Dominican Republic)	1905	U. S. administration of customs	1905–1907
Honduras	1909	U. S. bankers assume national debt	
Haiti	1910	U. S. bankers assume assets of Bank of Haiti	
Nicaragua	1912	U. S. military occupation	1912–1925; 1926–1933
Mexico	1914	Bombardment and occupation of Vera Cruz	1914
Haiti	1915	U. S. military occupation	1915–1934
Santo Domingo (Dominican Republic)	1915	U. S. military occupation	1915–1924
Mexico	1916	U. S. army expedition	1916–1917

Business and Imperialism

It is impossible to ignore the economic pressures on American foreign policy in the years between the Civil War and World War I. Foreign relations, of course, had been influenced by American economic development from the early years of the republic. From the days of Hamilton's *Report on Manufactures* to the Civil War the primary foreign economic interest of the United States was in overseas markets for the surplus products of the American soil. Southern cotton and western grains made up the bulk of American exports in the two decades before 1860, with their principal buyers in England and Europe. After the Civil War, the United States continued to ship large amounts of agricultural goods abroad, but the products of our expanding industrial system soon went to overseas buyers too. Foreign trade continued to increase, but for the first time American capital also began to be invested in large enterprises overseas. America's foreign economic interests were still essentially commercial before 1914, but in the years between the Spanish-American War and World War I, the United States began to include great investments as well as commerce in its international economic dealings.

In the half-century after the Civil War there came an extraordinary increase in foreign trade. The yearly average value of American exports from 1866 to 1870 amounted to less than $400,000,000; from 1896 to 1900, it was well over $1,000,000,000; and between 1911 and 1915, it was more than $2,500,000,000. Imports, however, increased in a comparable fashion. From 1865 on, American manufacturers strengthened their hold upon the home market so that imports of manufactured goods declined slightly but imports of raw materials for industry increased from a yearly average of about 12 per cent of the total goods imported each year between 1866 and 1870 to about 35 per cent of the goods imported yearly between 1911 and 1915. Among the exports, agricultural products and raw materials declined from a yearly average of about 80 per cent of the total between 1866 and 1870, to about 70 per cent between 1896 and 1900, and to about 54 per cent from 1911 to 1915. The amount of manufactured exports remained almost constant at about 20 per cent of the total from 1865 to 1900. When American industry began to realize fully its potentialities in the first decade of the twentieth century, the volume of manufactured exports rose precipitously, and between 1910 and 1915 they amounted to about 46 per cent of the total American foreign shipments.

Despite these figures, most American industries were not involved in the competition for world markets. Most of the increase in manufactured exports was represented by the foreign sales of a few highly concentrated industries. For example, the United States Steel Corporation in 1913 had 268 selling agencies in sixty different countries and exported 1,800,000 tons of steel annually. Standard Oil, the first large-scale trust, was also one of the first American industrial firms to make a concerted effort to dominate the foreign market. It purchased petroleum fields in the Middle East and Latin America; its salesmen invaded Europe and Asia; and eventually it worked out a cartel arrangement with its English and Dutch rivals for the division of the world market. Standard Oil's pattern of foreign expansion was duplicated by James B. Duke's American Tobacco Company, which had important sales outlets in Asia and Germany and an agreement with the Imperial Tobacco Company for apportioning the British and American markets. These overseas activities were, however, the exception rather than the rule for most of American industry before 1914.

The sources of imports remained relatively constant during the years 1871 to 1921, but American exports found new destinations. Although exports to Europe declined from about 80 per cent of the total between 1871 and 1875 to about 60 per cent between 1911 and 1915, those to Canada and Nova Scotia rose from about 6 per cent to about 14 per cent. On the other hand, there was little change in the proportion of American products shipped to South America, and American exports to Asia between 1911 and 1915 still accounted for less than 6 per cent of the total.

Surprisingly, the amount of this increased international trade carried by our own merchant marine declined precipitously. In 1860, American ships in foreign trade totaled nearly 2,400,000 tons and 66 per cent of the nation's waterborne foreign commerce was carried in American vessels. During the Civil War many American ships were destroyed, however, and approximately 1,000,000 tons were transferred to foreign registry. After the war, partly because of cheaper foreign cargo rates, no effort was made to revive the American merchant fleet, and by 1910 it had shrunk to less than 800,000 tons and less than 9 per cent of American waterborne foreign commerce was carried in American bottoms. It was only after the outbreak of World War I that the United States regained its place as a leading maritime nation.

With the advent of the twentieth century, America's traditional dependence on European capital to supplement native finance began to end. The growth of domestic industry and banking in the previous forty years had made possible a future free of dependence on European bankers. However, foreign capital invested in the United States continued to exceed American investments abroad before World War I, and still reached between $4,500,000,000 and $5,000,000,000 in 1914. In 1900, however, the direct investments of the United States overseas already amounted to $455,000,000, and twelve years later the total was $1,740,000,000. The bulk of this increase was represented by the accelerated flow of capital to Canada, Mexico, Central America, and the Caribbean Islands. In 1914, two years later, American foreign investments approximated $2,500,000,000.

In its growth to industrial maturity the United States differed from other nations in ways that profoundly influenced the conduct of foreign policy before World War I. As a debtor nation with no large investments abroad, the government was not troubled with the need to protect the foreign investments of its nationals. Debtor status, however, did not produce American subservience to the world's powerful creditor nations. A firmly established government, a continent with apparently limitless resources, and a tradition of political isolation convinced the average American that his country was not the servant of the great powers of the world even when they were America's bankers. Before 1914, American prosperity did not require foreign adventures, because the nation was not dependent upon either foreign raw materials of foreign markets for its manufactured goods. Lavish supplies of coal and iron—the sinews of nineteenth-century industrialization— existed in the United States, and ample quantities of practically every other natural resource needed to develop manufacturing could be found within the country. The United States was never in a position to practice economic isolation, but it was more generously endowed with essential raw materials than any other industrial nation in the world. Moreover, the manufactured goods produced in the United States were consumed almost entirely at home. The midwestern grain grower might have had to export to live, but the American industrialist still made the bulk of his sales in an expanding home market. Finally, the United States was unique among industrial nations in that it did not have to support a surplus population.

Relatively self-sufficient, the American Republic was not under pressure to undertake a program of what some historians have described as investment imperialism—that is, the export of capital and manufactured goods to the so-called backward regions of the world, the establishment of exclusive control over foreign supplies of essential raw materials, and the construction abroad with exported capital of railroads and factories, all aimed at developing to the highest point possible the wealth and industries of the imperial nation. Instead, post-Appomattox America did develop further what can be termed commercial or trading imperialism—that is, the expansion of foreign trade rather than exploitation of the "backward" areas of the world.

There was nothing novel about "commercial imperialism" in American history. It had been used by certain mercantile groups in the American Revolution, and had been endorsed by the Federalists under Alexander Hamilton and by prominent Whigs like Daniel Webster and Henry Clay. Under the policy of expanding our foreign trade, however, only small amounts of capital were sent abroad, and these were usually invested in raw materials and agriculture, rather than industry. After the Republican party came to power in 1861, there was an increasing emphasis upon commercial imperialism. During the Civil War, United States warships twice bombarded the Japanese, who were reluctant to enter into commerce with this country, and in 1871, the same tactics were employed unsuccessfully against Korea. James G. Blaine's Latin American policies and John Hay's Open Door notes are further indications of the Republican party's preoccupation with foreign trade, and dollar diplomacy had as a subsidiary purpose what was described by President Taft as "an effort frankly directed to the increase of American trade."

The increased flow abroad before World War I of American investments did not necessarily mean American political control over foreign areas. The growth of American capital invested in Canada was at no time a threat to that country's sovereignty or self-rule. The funds pumped into Latin America and the Far East under Taft's program of dollar diplomacy primarily represented the government's attempt to enlist private finance to secure political ends rather than the traditional aim of governments to protect the foreign interests of its businessmen.

There were, however, a few instances of American economic penetration abroad essentially identical with the economic imperialism of European powers. As early as the 1880's, United States' consular agents were actively engaged in promoting the sales of Standard Oil's products in China; and extensive American economic control over Cuba had made that island an economic vassal of the United States by 1920. The United States' armed intervention in the Caribbean and Central America, although motivated primarily by strategic considerations, nevertheless also served as a guarantee to American investors that they would not be jeopardized by internal upheavals.

One noteworthy private colonial empire came into being overseas as a creation of adventurous American capitalists and an interventionist United States government. It eventually rivaled or surpassed the imperial accomplishments of the older European nations. As early as 1900, the United Fruit Company had extensive holdings in both Cuba and the so-called banana republics of Central America. It owned more than 250,000 acres of plantation, 112 miles of railroad, and investments of approximately $17,000,000. Twenty-eight years later its possessions in the Caribbean area were valued at $111,300,000 and included nearly 2,500,000 acres of land, more than 1600 miles of railways, and about 700 miles of tramways.

Despite these scattered examples of classic economic imperialism, between 1865 and 1914 American foreign policy never became the plaything of the nation's businessmen. Government officials may have been extraordinarily receptive to the wishes of the merchant, manufacturer, and financier in domestic affairs, but in foreign policy they subordinated these economic interests to political and strategic considerations necessary to protect their nation in an international society in which force and power rather than law and justice were ultimate arbiters of a nation's destiny.

FOR SUPPLEMENTARY READING

The American empire is generally treated in J. Pratt, *America's Colonial Experiment* (1950). On Cuba and the Virgin Islands and Puerto Rico use Perkins, *The United States and the Caribbean*. On the Philippine administration read J. R. Hayden, *The Philippines: A Study in National Development* (1942); G. Kirk, *Philippine Independence* (1936); and H. Pringle, *The Life and Times of William Howard Taft* (2 vols., 1939). Closer study of the Far East since 1898 begins with A. W. Griswold, *The Far Eastern Policy of the United States* (1938), and T. Dennett, *John Hay* (1933). The Panama Canal story is analyzed by D. C. Miner, *The Fight for the Panama Route* (1940), and the subsequent complexities in Latin America by S. F. Bemis, *The Latin American Policy of the United States* (1943). The imperial diplomacy of Roosevelt, Taft, and Wilson has three introductory works: H. K. Beale, *Theodore Roosevelt and the Rise of America to World Power* (1956); Pringle's life of Taft; and A. Link, *Wilson the Diplomatist* (1957). A once esteemed but openly biased indictment of American imperialism is S. Nearing and J. Freeman, *Dollar Diplomacy* (1925). On foreign trade before World War I read the National Industrial Conference Board's *Trends in the Foreign Trade of the United States* (1930).

10

Old Ideals
and New Ideas

LTHOUGH THEIR IDEALS seemed increasingly at variance with
the drift of the age, most native-born citizens of 1900 believed
in private property and free competition and favored as little
government as possible, except when their interests were
threatened. In the days of McKinley, however, many Americans were
increasingly troubled by the surrender of traditional ideals; yet they
were reluctant to forego the money and leisure that big industry and
the city were bringing them. Their sense of difficulty was as old as the
nation and reminiscent of the long battle between America's moral
and religious aspirations (drawn from Calvinist and Revolutionary
heritages) and the temptations of money and success. But in the generation after the Civil War, ideal aspirations seemed weak or beside the
point in a world in which the individual was increasingly subordinated
to ever larger organizations in business and politics, and equality seemed
mocked by a growing gap between rich and poor.

The Loss of Innocence

Not long after the Civil War, Americans sensed that with the
silencing of the guns something worthwhile had gone out of American
life. The feeling that all was not well with the Republic was expressed
in many ways. Reformers, poets, and philosophers spoke of their

anxiety; a sense of malaise even found its way into story-books for children, and after 1880, into the enthusiasm for what was called the "new education," the attempt to use more enlightened pedagogy to save the child for what Americans called "character" and "faith." Writers of the age as different from each other as Mark Twain, William Dean Howells, and Henry James, all sensed that a sweetness and innocence had disappeared from American life. Like the general public, they followed a persistent American tendency to idealize some part of the past, and in this case they made pre-Sumter America into a golden age which was quickly receding. Americans forgot that their ancestors of the Jacksonian period were equally concerned about "threats to the republic," that venality and coarseness had been criticized by the Transcendentalists and other reformers before the Civil War. Those who did recall the older troubles and reform enthusiasms nevertheless insisted that after 1865 there was a new brashness about wealth; Americans felt less need to cover the search for success with a pretense of morality. In his last prose work, *Democratic Vistas* (1871), Walt Whitman, who had once spoken so exultantly about the power and possibilities of American life, warned about the threat of America's growing materialism to the ideals of 1776. Herman Melville, who lived on until the 1890's, became increasingly dismayed. The postwar faith in money seemed to have replaced the older hunger for spiritual nostrums and panaceas that Melville had criticized in *Moby Dick* and other earlier works. Now, however, the threat to America came from a deficiency of idealism rather than from an excess of it. Melville's late work, *Billy Budd* (published posthumously in 1924) was an allegory of a virtuous young American sailor who, trapped by the necessities of power and law, is hanged for a murder he accidentally committed; the story was symptomatic of a fear that was increasingly widespread by the 1880's: innocent Americans seemed caught in a world in which their idealism did not work.

Two authors who wrote most effectively about the conflict between innocence and experience in American life were Mark Twain and Henry James. Their novels and stories have had profound influences on modern American writers, for both of them were, in radically different ways, masters of style and superb moralists.

When Ernest Hemingway remarked that all modern American writing came out of one book, *Huckleberry Finn*, he meant that Twain was the first important author to break the hold on American writers of a traditional genteel belles-lettristic style and to use the American vernacular—direct, vigorous, simple, and concrete—in a form worthy of the respect of serious novelists and critics. When one remembers the

The Author of Huckleberry Finn

flowery and "fancy" prose in even so great an earlier writer as Hawthorne and when one recalls Melville's constant but not too successful
struggle to break with the style of what was later called the genteel
tradition, Twain's achievement seems great indeed. Yet in its own time
Twain's masterpiece *The Adventures of Huckleberry Finn* (1885) was
often less noticed for its style than for its offense to polite taste and the
ideals of the "nice" American home. Although Twain, like Henry
James, was aware of the troubling changes taking place in America
after the war, his works should not be conceived primarily as being
directly inspired by the widely felt cultural malaise. Nevertheless, a
book like *Huckleberry Finn* was an important analysis of American
character and a shrewd assessment of American life.

   Huckleberry Finn is the story of a resourceful boy's rebellion
against a world in which every conceivable fraud, knavery, and corruption have managed to pass themselves off as "civilization." Thinking
that he has murdered his drunkard father and having connived at the
escape of a slave, "Nigger Jim," Huck knows that he has violated two
of the strongest taboos of his society—the killing of the father and making common cause with the black man. Huck runs away from his home
town in Missouri. Although he has tried to be a good boy, he cannot

take being "sivilised." Unlike his friend Tom Sawyer—who cannot break laws, rules, and customs without elaborate fantasies and absurd rationalizations—Huck feels no need to make peace with the conventions and proprieties of American life. His energy and directness strike at the heart of the false civilization along the banks of the Mississippi. Exemplifying as he does humane ideals of life, he is a constant rebuke to the adult world of compromise, evasion, and "the law." Although cut adrift from the certainties and security of society, Huck is not beaten by life. He may seem an innocent, but he has the weapons of energy, cleverness, and truth. In repudiation of civilization, he devises his own moral code, one that brings no social advantages, no guarantees that "character" will bring success or salvation, and none of the promises of the Christian faith that justice and God's word will be victorious. Yet, opposed as Huck is to "sivilisation," and much as he seems to drift through life, he shows that with bravery and by using his wits man does have the ability to resist wickedness and to become virtuous in defiance of the pat certainties that so marked and so marred American life.

No other work by Twain matched the power of *Huckleberry Finn*. Among his other best works, however, were *Life on the Mississippi* (1883) a long reverie about pre-Civil War America. It contrasts a golden age when the river was teeming and sprawling with life, was uncharted, tricky, and challenging, with the era after the war when the calculable and sluggish routines of commercial life and the seedy captains and pilots had ended the days of vitality and heroism. In *The Tragedy of Pudd'nhead Wilson* (1894), Twain attempted to deal with the sorest spot in American history, the relation between the black and white races. The recent exacerbation of the race question has helped revive interest in this story of mixed blood and of the white man's arrogance and the Negro's fear and shame. Although there are superb passages in the book and evidence of an imaginative use of irony, the story is not carefully enough controlled. Twain's attempt to expose the complexity of the psychologies of white and Negro often leaves the impression that the author has become lost in the thick complications of his plot.

Despite deep differences in temperament, in style, and in assessment of American life, Henry James shared with Mark Twain a continuous interest in the fate of the American innocent in a world that constantly tests the adequacy of his finer moral sensibilities. Like Twain, James could remember nostalgically America before the Civil War. Twain's style and outlook, however, are reminiscent of the frontier's energy and capacity for a direct confrontation of life, while James, born a New Yorker, used an increasingly fine-spun complex style, whose irony, innuendo, and carefully controlled slow revelations about motive and character are suggestive of the more mannered and tradition-conscious society of the American East and of Europe.

For much of his life and for a generation after his death in 1916, James's reputation suffered. He lived in England almost continuously after the 1870's and became an English subject shortly before he died. His deliberate expatriation, his increasingly demanding style, his love of ambiguity, and his interest in the culture of rich and aristocratic Americans and Europeans have led to charges that he was "remote from life," snobbish, and insensitive to American virtues. In the last twenty years, however, James's works have achieved the critical success and esteem that he himself so missed in his lifetime. It is now clear that he always had a deep love and lively affection for America and that his expatriate years gave him, as he thought they would, a capacity for finer insight into American life and character than he could obtain by living in the midst of what was then a culture with relatively uniform manners and morals. James anticipated, however, that as America became a more mature civilization it would offer the artist at home an equally rich stock of human "types" and of social "situations" as two thousand years of complex history had given Europe.

One of the continuous themes in James' novels and stories—perhaps his major concern—was the conflict between the American's honor, probity, energy, and "appetite for life" and those conditions that threaten him with betrayal, defeat, or death. Lacking fullness of moral knowledge that is forced upon men who live in societies with limited opportunities for "escape," and untouched by the developed nuances of a high civilization—the virtuous Americans in James's novels from Christopher Newman in *The American* (1876) through Isabel Archer in *The Portrait of a Lady* (1880) and Milly Theale in *The Wings of the Dove* (1902) are all frustrated in achieving their ideals. Newman is a young American millionaire, full of the future and of confidence in himself, who comes to Europe to find a wife who will be the best product of that esthetically rich but morally hopeless old world. He finds his girl but cannot win her as a wife because of her family's snobbishness about his being a "commercial person." Newman, nevertheless, refuses to revenge himself on the family when he has the chance to, and he returns to America, still superior in character to the corrupt Europeans but without the love he wanted to complete his "American dream" of life made perfect.

Isabel Archer in *The Portrait of a Lady* is a girl from Albany, New York, who, like Newman, has all the "American qualities"—

enthusiasm, open-mindedness, and supreme faith in the possibility of her ideal destiny. She too travels to Europe and visits her expatriate aunt's great country house in England, where she so impresses her uncle that he wills her a sizeable bequest to enable her to fulfill her ideal of making her life into a work of art. Isabel is spiritually a descendant of the American Transcendentalists; her idealism blinds her to harsh facts, especially to the moral defects of the man she marries. Gilbert Osmond, her husband, has himself fulfilled Isabel's ideal. He has made his life completely subservient to aesthetic considerations, but his manners and taste mask a cold monstrous conceit and moral baseness. He has married Isabel for her money and her worship of his style. Gradually, Isabel learns with increasing horror and helplessness the truth about Osmond's character. She is so trapped, however, by judging things only theoretically that when she has the chance, at the end of the story, to leave him she is powerless to do so. Despite her admirable spontaneity and charm, her wrong-headed idealism has led, not as she hoped, to the triumph of art over experience, but to a living death.

The Wings of the Dove (1902) is one of three masterpieces that James published within two years (1902–4). In it and in the other two long novels, The Ambassadors and The Golden Bowl, his famous "international theme" came to full flower. By 1902, James's image of Europe had changed. It is still the world of experience by which American innocence can either be brought to maturity or defeated, but his sense of Europe's moral corruption and exhaustion is at least as strong as—if not stronger than—his earlier belief that Europe's stability and art combined with American energy and probity could produce an ideally civilized man. In The Ambassadors, the hero, Strether, a middle-aged American writer, and in The Golden Bowl the millionairess American heroine, Maggie Verver, do manage to come to terms with Europe, but at a price. In Strether's case, the cost is semi-alienation from American life and loss of a wealthy fiancée. Maggie's victory over Europe comes by telling a lie, a sacrifice of virtue. In The Wings of the Dove, however, Milly Theale, the dove of the title, becomes the prey of two brilliantly conceived penniless Europeans, Kate Croy and her suitor, Merton Densher. Learning that Milly is soon to die of a fatal disease, Kate hatches a scheme by which Merton can marry Milly, inherit her great wealth and thus win the approval of Kate's aunt and mentor. Milly learns of their plot before Densher can bring off the engagement. Before Milly dies, however, her love for Densher is strong enough to overcome the awful knowledge of his duplicity. She leaves him a small fortune so that he can win Kate's hand. In the ironic ending, Milly's magnanimous act awakens Densher's sense of honor, stifled until then.

He will marry Kate only if she will agree to his renouncing the money and he puts this choice to her as the story closes. Milly's American innocence has opened her to exploitation and brings on her death, but in death her money, so beautifully offered, affords the Europeans—Densher and Kate Croy—some possibility of redemption.

The Search for the Real

Between the peaks of achievement represented by James and the small cluster of Twain's best works, the American scene in letters between 1865 and 1914 was bewildering in its variety. One theme, however, can be persistently discovered. Sharing with James and Twain the sense that something had shut America off from its promise, novelists were deeply troubled by the changes in American life. They contrasted the Gilded Age with an ever dimmer golden past, or they wrote picturesque stories and sentimental verse that tried to obscure or wipe away contemporary sordidness and venality.

After the war, new writers with large national audiences exploited the idiom and characters of their particular section of the country. The "local color" of the Far West was used most famously by Bret Harte. In such stories as *The Outcasts of Poker Flat* and *The Luck of Roaring Camp*, Harte revealed the persistent general weakness of the new regional writers—their sentimentality. He wrote about the mining camps of the West with a melodramatic pseudo-romanticism that concealed their sordidness and converted brutal and lustful men and women into lovable and playful characters with rough manners but hearts of gold. Mark Twain soon joined the new school of Far Western writers with *Roughing It* (1872); but, of course, he achieved greatest fame for his exploitation of themes connected with life along the banks of the Mississippi. Edward Eggleston's *The Hoosier Schoolmaster* (1871) is the most remembered of a large number of sentimental portraits of the old Middle West. In his day, Eggleston shared fame with now forgotten writers like Alice French and Mary H. Catherwood.

No region of the country had more cause to become aware of its local traditions than the South during and after Reconstruction. An entire generation of southern writers explored themes that have continued to preoccupy the region's novelists and poets to the present day. George Washington Cable, the most distinguished southern novelist of the time, had a special interest in social and cultural conflicts in southern Louisiana with its diverse heritage of nationalities and long history. With a fine ear for Creole dialect, he wrote about the effect of misleading ideals on families like the Grandissimes and on individuals living in the shadows of an aristocratic culture challenged by parvenus and enduring principally as a political fantasy of reactionaries. A far less skillful but more popular exploitation of southern themes was undertaken by Thomas Nelson Page in stories that romanticized Virginia's crumbling aristocracy and by Joel Chandler Harris, whose beloved Uncle Remus stories helped perpetuate misleading and sentimental ideas about Negroes and the South. In New England, a group of women writers were specially noteworthy for using regional themes. Their best talent was Sarah Orne Jewett, who depicted the daily lives of the descendants of a once vigorous people reduced to a "colorful and quaint" existence.

Taken as a group, although meagre or modest in their talents, the new regionalists did deal with American themes for a national audience. If they mourned over or sentimentalized the way of life of their part of the country, they did point to possible American subjects and "situations" that escaped the eye or interest of a Henry James, who, at the time, thought that America had little to interest the morally serious novelist. Had the talent of the local colorists been equal to their material—and Mark Twain showed that talent and local color could be brilliantly combined—the regional literature after the Civil War might have achieved greater distinction than it did with the passing of the years.

As it was, these works came too close to the best-selling romantic fiction of the day. A noble hero, a base villain, an improbable plot, and a trite morality were almost guarantees of success. Sticky love stories, historical romances, and adventure tales had sales in tens and hundreds of thousands. At the turn of the century, Americans most often found agreeable images of themselves or "escape" in books like Charles Major's *When Knigthood Was in Flower*, S. Weir Mitchell's revolutionary war tale *Hugh Wynne*, Maurice Thompson's *Alice of Old Vincennes*, Paul Leicester Ford's *Janice Meredith*, Winston Churchill's *The Crisis* and *Coniston*, and many other works that now gather dust on public library shelves. Nostalgia was often the dominant note, as it was in stories about the folksy wisdom and shrewdness of "by gosh" rural and small-town characters. Works like E. N. Westcott's *David Harum* and Irving Bacheller's *Eben Holden* enabled Americans to hold onto belief in the old and simple virtues that were in fact losing the battles to the real city-slickers in business and politics during the Gilded Age and after.

American children thrived on much the same type of literary fare as their parents. Horatio Alger, Jr., and William T. Adams, who wrote under the name of Oliver Optic, turned out a stream of books that were

all variations on the single theme of how a poor but noble boy overcame repeated buffetings to achieve success without sacrificing virtue
and honor. Girls, who liked their heroines pure in heart, could follow
the trials and triumphs of Elsie Dinsmore in the *Elsie* books ground out
year after year by Martha F. Finley. Dime novels, which were read
by millions of children and semiliterate adults, were one of the most
important single cultural influences of the age. Usually set against a
western background, they told tales of derring-do and made glamorous
folk heroes of Indian fighters, rangers, cowboys, hunters, and prospectors. Crammed with exciting adventures strung together into a plot
that hardly gave the reader—let alone the characters—a chance to catch
his breath, the dime novel stuck faithfully to the old American middle-
class morality. By the time that the posse had closed in on the cattle
rustlers in the last chapter, the reader had learned that hard work rather
than crime paid dividends, that justice always triumphed, that idleness
and evilness were synonymous, that the home and mother were
sacred, and that bravery could surmount any adversity.

Between the dominant demand for elegant writing and the genteel
tradition of morally uplifting stories fit for young ladies to read, those
writers trying to depict and deal with the problems of the new industrial and urban American were hard pressed. It was the gentlemanly
editor of the *Atlantic Monthly*, William Dean Howells (1837–1920),
who did most to help those writers trying to turn the attention of polite
readers to the great and grim battles that were being fought in America
after the Civil War, thereby rebelling against the falseness to life and
corruption of taste implicit in the sentimental romanticism of the day.
It was Howells, however, who also helped establish an equally restricting view that colored American literature for generations—that "the
real" in America was as commonplace as possible, as sordid and vulgarly materialistic as a writer could make it, and as hidden under some
piety or hypocritical creed as one could imagine. Howells' talent made
him, at his best, a decent practitioner of his creed of "fidelity . . . to
the probable and ordinary course of man's experience," but he gave
a great push to a style and to subjects that less skillful writers with
more partisan purposes were to fail to carry beyond dreary portraits
of people and events that were, despite their alleged realism, not true
to life at all. It is significant, for example, that as the life of the workingman was increasingly assumed to be more "real" than that of the
intellectual or artist, no major American writer created a workingman
character in any adequate complexity or actual "truth to life."

In 1885, when Howells came to New York from Boston, the nation was about to enter a series of grave social crises that were to last

William Dean Howells

until the defeat of Bryan in 1896. In New York, Howells saw the rawness and injustice of city life on a large scale. In *The Rise of Silas Lapham* (1885) Howells used a classic theme, that of the young man without advantages who comes to the city to win his fortune and forces himself on polite society as he climbs to wealth and status. *A Hazard of New Fortunes* (1890) takes place in New York and uses a gallery of types that were to become familiar in the American novel: the parvenu capitalist, the foolish society woman, the son with a social conscience in rebellion against his rich father, and the old humane Socialist. The book is about the class war, about poverty in the slums and plenty in the mansion houses. But as in most of Howells' work, the author hung back from indelicacy. His tendency was to mourn over what the American dream had become and to suggest the need for understanding and compassion.

There were three notable effects of the initiative taken by a realist such as Howells. The polite public read more than they had about the new America of the urban poor. "Local color" writers took off rose-colored glasses and went deeper under the surface of life. The disciple of Henry James, Edith Wharton, wrote novels about New

York and New England, and Ellen Glasgow published stories of Virginia during and after the Civil War that were, despite severe limitations, far superior to the work of the older local colorists. As early as the eve of Populism, Hamlin Garland had also demonstrated that "local color" did not require sentimentality. Garland's stories and essays helped set the stage for the "revolt against the village" that came to flower in American writers such as Sherwood Anderson and Sinclair Lewis in the 1920's. Born on the middle border but educated at Harvard, Garland took a hard look at his native culture of the Middle West in his essays *Crumbling Idols* (1894). In *Main-Traveled Roads* (1891), in contrast with the rising tide of reform sentiment about the yeoman farmer, he described the mud, monotony, sweat, manure, and isolation of rural life.

The third and most important result of the work of Howells was to prepare the way for the transformation of the realistic into the naturalistic novel. Realism was a relative term that depended on the author's sense of reality; almost anything could be called real. Even the workers' world could be treated with effective realistic insight, as Henry James himself had shown in his novel about the class struggle in London, *The Princess Casamassima* (1885). Naturalism differed from realism, however, in adopting a fatalistic philosophy. By the middle of the 1890's, American novelists could write for a large audience about life on the other side of the tracks. The naturalists were inspired by French writers like Emile Zola, who claimed he had analyzed the laws of life and society impersonally like a natural scientist. They were convinced that the individual was a plaything of irresistible impersonal forces and that moral influences were of no importance in a world governed by chance. Summing up his philosophy of naturalism, Frank Norris wrote: "Nature was, then, a gigantic engine, a vast cyclopean power, huge, terrible, a leviathan with a heart of steel, knowing no compunction, no forgiveness, no tolerance; crushing out the human atom standing in its way, with nirvanic calm, the agony of destruction sending never a jar, never the faintest tremour through all that prodigious mechanism of wheels and cogs." In *The Octopus* and *The Pit*, Norris, who seemed to delight in the largest possible display of power and force, made men puppets of an all powerful nature that was represented by the "vast Titanic flood" of wheat "along its predetermined courses from East to West."

Naturalism also differed from earlier realism in that it rejected the quickly recognized situation and reached out to the margins of life. It pulled far fewer punches in its pictures of the victimization of man by fate. The plight of the city's poor, for example, was described with unprecedented frankness in Stephen Crane's *Maggie: A Girl of the Streets*. Although the characters were wooden and Crane all but hit the reader over the head to make his point, *Maggie* showed a determination to tell all that had to be said about a poor city girl's seduction and suicide. If anything, the book suffered from the calculated assault on the type of reader for whom the only real events were those everyone has known. Crane's *The Red Badge of Courage*, which was far more successful as a work of art, was, however, only in part a naturalistic analysis of the responses of a rookie Union soldier to his first battle. Much has been made of the fact Crane had never seen a battle when he wrote this book; the book, however, gains its effect, not from Crane's naturalistic portrait or knowledge of war, but from his ability to bring out, by use of the symbols in the soldier's mind, the emotions of an individual in a crisis that was not of his own making.

By far the most influential and acclaimed naturalist writer was Theodore Dreiser (1871–1945). Dreiser first attracted attention through his frank discussion of sex in *Sister Carrie* (1900), which had to be withdrawn because of public objection. In *The Financier* (1912) and *The Titan* (1914), he described in awkward prose the career of a traction magnate who was a prisoner of his environment. Dreiser made little effort to conceal the fact that the central character of both books was modeled after Charles T. Yerkes, who had gained notoriety and wealth from the street railway business. Dreiser's relation to his protagonist Frank Cowperwood was, however, an ambiguous one. The hero has enormous if stormy success in the great American pursuits—money and women. Dreiser disliked his greed and ruthlessness, but he viewed these as inherent qualities of the struggle for existence, and, like Norris, he seemed covertly to like the raw energy and ruthless drive of his hero. Dreiser's thinly disguised worship of vulgar success and recurrent anti-Semitism made his eventual position as a literary hero of liberals and reformers difficult to understand. His most famous later work, *An American Tragedy* (1925), raised further questions about the philosophy of life and art underlying the naturalistic novel as it developed in America after 1914. In *An American Tragedy* Dreiser took a newspaper report of a murder trial and tried to show that society rather than his hero, Clyde Griffiths, was responsible for the crime. Aside from the philosophical crudity of his view of determinism and free will, on Dreiser's own reckoning—that all men are trapped by fate—how could society in general as well as any one man be held responsible for crime, or, for that matter, goodness?

The greatest limitation of Dreiser was that he lacked the talent as a writer to make his characters truly believable. Zola at his best and a few later naturalists who were primarily great writers were able to use the naturalistic technique to create memorable characters and insightful observations of life. They could conceive men and women with a rich complexity and describe the individual's motives and effects on the world with a power that Dreiser never matched. What Dreiser and other early naturalists did achieve was to establish a genre that had enormous influence on subsequent generations. But these writers also demonstrated that what counts first in the novel, as in the other arts, is not so much the genre as the genius that uses it.

Decay and Liberation

Whether Americans read the new novelists or stuck to old favorites, they caught a common concern about the adequacy of simple virtuousness in an urban and monied world that worshipped coarse power, vulgar success, and mediocrity. Henry Adams (1838–1918) mourned the passing of the old republic but combined his observations on what he called "the degradation of the democratic dogma" with speculations about "laws" of the growth and decay of civilization in general. Born into one of America's most famous families, Adams believed in the aristocratic republican ideals of his presidential ancestors. Like them also he believed he had been called to serve the nation. But from the day in 1869 when he heard Grant's first Cabinet choices announced, he became increasingly convinced that America no longer had places for men like the Adamses. The coming of Darwinism strengthened his belief that modern life had been unhinged. If materialistic democracy had debased a great ideal, Darwinism had destroyed the philosophic certainty of any ideal that might take its place. Mindless bursting energy seemed to him the great characteristic of his world, and Adams sensed that America's ultimate destiny was decay and death in a great explosion. The dynamo seemed to symbolize the impersonal force and energy running toward "multiplicity" that his world now worshipped. He contrasted the dynamo with what he imagined to be the spiritually purposeful high Middle Ages. In *Mont Saint-Michel and Chartres* (1904), he argued that the medieval cult of the Virgin had given men an inner sense of unity, peace, and order that modern man, worshipping nature and science, had permanently and tragically lost. In his autobiography, *The Education of Henry Adams* (finished in 1907, published in 1917), he traced the effects of modern American life on a man "born for failure" and further elucidated his dubious theory that a fixed sum of energy in the world was being constantly dissipated so that our civilization would thus run out of power and faith in the

1930's. Adams too often seemed to take pleasure in depicting himself as a morally significant victim of history in whose defeat was symbolized all that was wrong with mankind. In fact, he had received acclaim for several fine histories and biographies long before he wrote his *Education* and his critique of modern culture. But even in his brilliant long study of the presidencies of Jefferson and Madison, published in the 1880's, the hostility of the New England Federalist to the rising forces of equality and laissez faire can be discerned.

In some respects Henry's brother, Brooks Adams, was a more brilliant, if equally misguided, student of contemporary society. In *The Law of Civilization and Decay* (1895), Brooks tried to work out in detail a scientific account of the course of modern society and to establish the precise rate at which its accumulation of energy would reach its maximum. A generation later, after trying free silver and imperialism as remedies for America's troubles, Brooks was so overwhelmed by a sense of the sickness of civilization that he seemed close to adopting belief in original sin as an explanation of why democracy had failed to make good on its promises.

Both Henry and Brooks Adams represented the kind of men, their contemporary, William James (1842–1910), called "tender-minded." Appalled by the evolutionary spectacle of a world in which even the most enlightened order and highest ideals constantly had to yield their place, in which there seemed to be no inherent guarantees or certainties, in which all life, on the contrary, involved risk and chance, such men, said James, retreat into a debilitating scepticism and abjure, as Henry Adams did, active involvement in worldly affairs. In contrast with the "tough-minded," who recognize the possibilities, even the prevalence, of defeat and death but remain vigorous and confident in their own powers, the tender-minded often turn to idealist philosophies or dogmatic faiths which deny that change and uncertainty are man's basic expectations.

Like other philosophers in the generation after Darwin, James understood that the theory of human evolution was a shattering blow to closed systems of thought and fixed beliefs of all types. Unlike Adams and Mark Twain, who also retreated into a pessimistic fatalism, James accepted the theory of evolution as an invitation to see the world as it probably was and to make it what one willed. In the years before James's major works appeared, however, the predominant version of Darwinism was as closed a system of thought as the Calvinism it helped to dethrone. In Herbert Spencer's version of social evolution, the most popular early version of Darwinism in America, a simplistic account of the biological struggle for life was used to suggest that progress was inevitable if men would be content for "nature" to select the fit and dispose of the unfit. Although the key words—"nature," "progress," "fit," and "unfit"—in the new cosmology were essentially ambiguous, socially, Spencer's theory turned out to be a defense of the status quo; philosophically, it was a denial of the "openness" of the present and future; psychologically, it neglected the role of purposeful thinking and intelligent choice in directing life to the ends men desired.

Those evolutionists, like James, who wished to replace Spencer with a more sophisticated evolutionary philosophy had to struggle against other opponents as well as the Spencerians. A powerful group of university philosophers called "common-sense realists" maintained, before the coming of Spencer, that the human mind had a God-given ability or "faculty" to arrive at final truths in morals and politics; the mind as well as the truth it discovered were thus judged capable of transcending the ceaseless spectacle of trial and error that was implied in Darwin's view of man. Between 1860 and 1880, these realists believed they had successfully adjusted their formalistic psychology and system of values to the doctrines of evolution. At the same time, however, there arose a group of American Hegelians who, while accepting an evolutionary scheme of life and working for reforms in certain fields, notably in education, nevertheless believed that there was a progressive pattern inherent in the unfolding historical process. History, these optimists maintained, was working toward the triumph of reason, and its ultimate political expression would be a government guaranteeing the fullest possible development of man's rational powers. Common, therefore, to the devotees of Spencer, to the common-sense school, and to the Hegelians, was a mood of certainty that life was already what it had to be or that it would inevitably become better. These philosophies were either apologies for the status quo or optimistic assurances that all that seemed noxious in life was a necessary stage in evolution and would eventually, by itself, pass away.

By the 1870's, two philosophers, Charles Peirce and Chauncey Wright, had already challenged the mood of determinism by emphasizing that if evolution was universal, mind was a natural, not a divine power, that it itself was subject to evolution, and that there was nothing inevitable or certain about any system of values or claim of intellect. In sociology Lester Frank Ward in the early 1880's rejected the Spencerian connection of social with biological evolution and attacked the notion that laissez faire should be justified as a struggle for the survival of the fittest. Ward maintained that as man's mind evolves it sets him apart from the animal struggle for survival. Mind gave society the power and choice to lift life above the spectacle of mean conflict, poverty, and despair that the first generation of Social Darwinists had proclaimed both inevitable and progressive.

Such thinkers and ideas set the stage for William James' work. At the heart of James' thought was hostility to absolutes and closed systems of thought. In his theory of knowledge, James called himself a "radical empiricist," refusing to slice the universe into two parts, with one amenable to empirical investigation and the other beyond the tests of compatability with facts. But James differed from important scientists and positivists in his day by refusing to deny the reality of those aspects of experience that were not material or tangible. Dreams, religious beliefs, mystic feelings were as "real" for James as the most inert piece of matter. There was, he maintained, a "will to believe" in men that could not be satisfied with the cold and impersonal world projected by mechanistic scientists and by cosmologists like Spencer. Because of the logical limitations of its method and judged by its narrow views of reality, science, James asserted, could not speak as authoritatively as it claimed to. Where there was or could be no final scientific proof to the contrary, man was entitled to believe what made him feel most at home in the universe.

Although James's theory thus opened a place for religious belief in an age of increasing irreligion and validated a wide variety of faiths, it has been challenged for several errors. From the point of view of religious orthodoxy, it implies that there are many religious faiths, not one true faith. Any one of these, furthermore, by James's reasoning, is made dependent on man's needs and on the extent of his scientific knowledge; in other words, James makes the divine contingent on the natural. Although James correctly stressed the important roles of desire, will, and feeling in our choice of ideas and in our sense of their truthfulness, his theory tended to an extreme subjectivism and confused that which one needed to believe with what was true.

James's book *The Varieties of Religious Experience* (1902) spelled out in fullest detail his insistence that a faith must offer comfort and solace for it to be true for the believer. In that work and in others, James' belief in the diversity of an unfinished rather than a once-and-for-all given universe was generally consistent with his theory of the mind and his theory of truth. James rejected the classic empirical notion that the human mind merely passively received impressions from the world which then associated themselves with each other to produce ideas. In his masterly study *The Principles of Psychology* (1890), he stressed the degree to which man actively chose from those impressions flowing in chaotically on the mind those that best suited his needs. Thinking, in other words, was purposeful, and our choice of ideas in large part was controlled by our will and our desires. From this assertion it was an easy step for James to deny Spencer's claim that men must let nature take its course. The social environment men know at any time is the evolutionary result of choices to live one way or another; consequently, the genius as well as the common laborer was as much at liberty as the banker to use his ideas to make the future. Unlike the Social Darwinists or Hegelians, however, James found no inherently beneficent or ultimate purpose at work in history. Man's only fate was to be free and to run the risks as well as win the rewards of his freedom.

In choosing ideas James asked men to test them against facts; the abstract and the *a priori*, he believed, are at odds with life. In the pluralistic universe, there are no absolutes, final answers, or perfect minds. Men choose those ideas that help them come to terms with the reality that they are constantly creating. In choosing ideas, men proceed best when they think *pragmatically*. The "pragmatic method" of taking the world problem by problem and of adjusting the new to the old and the old to the new, piecemeal, is the method by which the mind and culture work and which best assures accuracy, fairness, and absence of crippling dogmatism. On the other hand, this method for gaining truth is different from the actual test of truth. An idea is true, says James, when it works. "True ideas are those that we can assimilate, validate, corroborate, and verify. . . . The truth of an idea is not a stagnant property inherent in it. Truth *happens* to an idea. It *becomes* true, is *made* true by events. Its verity *is* in fact an event, a process, the process namely of its verifying itself, its *verification*. Its validity is the process of its *validation*." Although his conception of truth has often been attacked as sheer expediency, in James' own mind the test of "works" was to take into account what is best in the past as well as what is most hopeful for the future, the highest purposes we have in mind as well as immediate practical needs. But, as James warned, "What meets expediently all the experience in sight won't necessarily meet all farther experiences equally satisfactorily." As a theory of truth, however, pragmatism was less vulgarly expedient than ultimately ambiguous. Its criteria of "does it work" had to be traced back to some ultimate rationalist or intuitive good-in-itself, be it man's desire for happiness or demand for consistency and logic.

In the 1890's, a young American Hegelian, John Dewey (1859–1952), read James and was converted to pragmatism. James once said that he advanced pragmatism as "a method of settling metaphysical disputes that might otherwise be interminable." Dewey understood that pragmatism might also be used as a basis for social reform, and under his influence it became a "method of understanding and rectifying specific social ills." Institutions (e.g., the corporation) and social theories (e.g., laissez faire) should be tested, Dewey asserted, by their consequences rather than by their appeal to logicians or to minds seeking certainty. Like all human contrivances, institutions and social ideals were instruments to be used for well-defined goals; if they failed to achieve their proclaimed purpose, they should be altered intelligently.

Dewey's "instrumentalism" thus represented a broadening of the application of pragmatism and a spreading of the experimental attitude to all thinking about society. As time passed, instrumentalism made closer alliances with scientific method than it had in James and the early Dewey. The scientific ideals of dispassionate inquiry, of responsibility to facts and expert information, and of retesting and recasting basic hypotheses seemed admirably suited to satisfy the demands of pragmatists to look on all life as an experiment and to be ready to revaluate the most cherished beliefs in the light of new or dissenting opinions.

Stressing the role of ideas in changing society, it was logical that Dewey continually gave close attention to the problems of the school and society, of the child and the curriculum. Actually, Dewey's interest in reforming American education came after twenty years of debate about the "failure of the schools to do their job," a recurrent theme in every generation of modern American history. A host of critics and commentators after 1880 had sketched out much of what was then called "the new education" before Dewey published *The School and Society* in 1899. Dewey, however, put more clearly than most critics before him the need to abandon rote learning and formal, lifeless pedagogy, and to draw on the child's imagination, natural activism, and curiosity in teaching him both how to think and what he had to know in order to think. Dewey wanted to free the child's powers of awareness and criticism from cram and useless facts, and while he was still at school, to teach him concern for democratic ideals of give and take, of rational and enlightened discussion. The child was not to be adjusted to the status quo but was to be encouraged to find those interests and ideals that best fulfilled his distinctive needs. Within a generation after Dewey's classic study, the "new education" had become known as progressive education and was revolutionizing the relations of teachers, parents, and children. More than anything else, Dewey's educational theories dissociated early modern pedagogy from its original purpose of saving the old republican virtues. Dewey united them instead with newer ideals of social diversity and cultural pluralism.

New Law, New Economics, New History

A transformation in American thought equally as profound as that in philosophy and education came about through the impact of latter-day Darwinism on the study of law, economics, and history. Inspired by the harmful social consequences as well as by the intellectual inadequacy of older ideals and concepts, a generation of young scholars and jurists grasped the deeper significance of what Dewey called "the influence of Darwinism on philosophy." "Formalism" was the enemy. In law, it had made sanctity of contract an abstract ideal that disregarded the facts of the disproportionate power of the industrialist and the working man in negotiating for wages and hours or in accepting responsibility for social welfare. In economics, formalists of the classical school, using Spencer's rhetoric of survival of the fittest, had obscured the facts of what "free competition" had come to mean in a world dominated by the big corporation and a social ethos of dog eat dog. The leading older historians had written largely political history and, ignoring the role of a wide variety of social and economic interests in the past, had tended to stifle debate of vital contemporary issues by implying that the men of 1776 created a perfect American Republic.

In the generation before 1900, an older tradition of so-called filio-pietistic history had already made its alliances with science and evolutionary doctrine, but the resulting studies, although heavily documented in the German scholarly style, often used evolution to justify hard money, Anglo-Saxon supremacy, extreme American nationalism, and other doctrines favorable to respectable and powerful groups in American society.

The revolt against the first generation of modern American historians like Herbert Baxter Adams of Johns Hopkins University and John Fiske was, however, often tied too closely to the views of progressive political reformers to permit disinterested scholarship. When after 1900 James Harvey Robinson called for a "new history" using the "genetic method," he implied that a full account of the past would expose unpleasant truths about what the American public had accepted as glorious achievements. History, in other words, was the weapon of reformers. "The one thing it [the new history] ought to do, and has not yet effectively done," said Robinson, "is to help us to understand our fellows and the problems and prospects of mankind."

In *The Frontier in American History* (1893), Frederick Jackson Turner denied earlier evolutionists' claims that the origins of American democracy were European and that they could be found in seeds planted in the Teutonic forests. Turner asserted that, on the contrary, democracy was native to this continent and that the true story of its development would be found not by studying early Europe but the American West. The alleged passing of the frontier in 1890 had brought Turner's research into focus. His frontier theory was in many respects an attempt to give prestige to the old Northwest, his own section of the country, and to its frontier virtues now threatened by the disappearance of free land and the rise of an urban and industrial America.

The partisan interests at work behind the new history were most dramatically revealed in the furor that greeted the publication in 1913 of Charles A. Beard's *An Economic Interpretation of the Constitution*. Writing at the height of Progressivism (yet, as subsequent research has shown, inaccurate in some major assertions and at times faulty in method), Beard asserted that the fathers of the Constitution of 1787 were not disinterested patriots but were among the wealthiest and most powerful figures in the new nation. They created a Constitution to protect interests, not, as Americans were taught to believe, to enshrine the word of Providence. Beard's implication was that the nation's great charter was a realistic answer to particular problems and had to be adjusted and amended when new problems arose. The Constitution, in the language of pragmatism, was thus an instrument to secure certain definite political and economic goals, not a final truth for all time.

What was at stake for Americans in the rise of the new history and in the pragmatic revolt in general was suggested by an editorial which appeared in *The New York Times* a few years after Beard's book appeared. Commenting on Beard's resignation at Columbia University in protest over a violation of academic freedom, the *Times* considered the University well rid of a man who had dared to question the high motives of the founding fathers. Could the Republic long endure, it asked, if men like Beard taught the young? Despite the fact that the new history had its own marked limitations, to the younger scholars of the period before World War I it did bring a sense of liberation from parochialism, and it created an atmosphere in which appraisals of the American past more accurate than those of both the new historians and their predecessors might be made. Insisting, as the new historians did, that no aspect of the record could be ignored in understanding both past and present, they greatly expanded the intellectual interests and scope of study of American historians.

An ambiguity similar to that in the work of the new historians can be found in the work of younger economists between 1885 and 1914. Justifying their studies in the name of realism, opposing the formalism of the older laissez-faire economists, and concerned with the concrete purposes rather than the final truth of economic doctrine, young men like Richard T. Ely, John R. Commons, and, most notably, Thorstein Veblen combined exciting breakthroughs in economics with an assault on laissez faire and the prestige of the millionaire. In 1885, led by Ely, a group of economists and liberal ministers founded the American Economic Association, which at once declared that laissez faire was "unsafe in politics and unsound in morals." Although these men laid the basis for modern American economic theory, most of them concentrated on technical economic analysis. Their tendency, however, to become programmatic and to fall into moralism was constantly apparent in the works of Veblen (1857–1929). Born on a poor Wisconsin farm, Veblen inherited a deep puritanical suspicion of waste and luxury which constantly distorted and colored his iconoclastic analysis of American institutions.

At the center of Veblen's economic essays was the vision of what an efficient and aesthetically oriented machine civilization could bring mankind. What was wrong with America was that the sense of craftsmanship and of prideful entrepreneurship that had evolved from a premachine culture had been subordinated to the "pecuniary interests" of businessmen. Call them what he would—captains of industry, the "leisure class," the manipulators of the "price system"—Veblen's indictment was constant. Efficiency, order, harmony, and beauty had been denied America by selfish industrialists who used their money for personal display and foolish extravagances. In *The Theory of the Leisure Class* (1899), Veblen used evolutionary evidence from ethnology and other social studies to depict the owning classes not as the fittest products of the struggle for survival but as wasteful drones and survivors of a tribal age whom modern society could not afford.

For the future Veblen envisioned a struggle between "the engineers and the price system." He believed that the modern technologist had inherited a pride in craftsmanship and a sense of what the machine might do for man. However, as long as industry was run for the good of the price system, the beauty and abundance promised by the machine would be frustrated. Veblen hoped that the time would come when the technicians would replace the businessmen and lead a reorganized society to efficiency and order.

Of all the leading figures who participated in the revolt against formalism, none was as genuinely free of a program and more ambiguous in his sense of life as an experiment than the jurist Oliver Wendell Holmes (1841–1935). Raised in an atmosphere of New England wealth and high-mindedness, Holmes's youthful optimism was shattered by his Civil War service. From that time on doubt, anxiety, and pain seemed to him the unavoidable price of life. Holmes was hostile to fixed concepts in law that the courts applied without close inquiry into the causes or consequences of the case at hand. Philosophically, the dominant formalistic tradition in American law irked him because it was so at odds with the actual complexity and variety of life. Practically, the law as construed by most jurists before World War I worked to the advantage of a minority, the new vulgar rich for whom the old New England aristocrat had little use. Holmes was convinced that the Constitution of 1787 had committed the nation for better or worse to majority rule, and he believed that the judges of his time were thwarting the wishes and undermining the well-being of most citizens for the advantage of a minority.

For twenty years Holmes served on the Massachusetts Supreme Court. In 1902, Theodore Roosevelt brought him to the United States Supreme Court. It was from that bench that he handed down his famous dissenting opinions in favor of minimal social welfare legislation and civil liberties. Holmes, in books like *The Common Law* (1881) and in his classic decisions, showed himself an enemy of abstraction and excessive deference to precedents in the law; yet, although he supported reform legislation, he had no deep faith in mankind or in the virtue of democratic man. He was sceptical, even cynical at times, about human nature but was so committed to his belief that life was a hazardous race and that the majority had the right under the Constitution to vote itself into hell if it chose to, that he went along with reforms provided that they observed due process.

If Holmes made any persistent demand on the laws, it was that debate and discussion be kept open in order to prevent the imposition of dogma. Although no man had a right falsely to shout "fire" in a crowd, he believed that American society was committed to a "free marketplace for ideas," that the best test of truth was its ability to get itself accepted in the marketplace, and that only a "clear and present danger" could ever warrant interference with freedom of speech. Through this creed, expressed in eloquent prose, Holmes became one of the nation's most honored men and, despite evidences of his conservatism and his persistent scepticism, an idol of a generation of liberals and reformers. Through his work and that of his colleague Justice Louis D. Brandeis, who wrote many trailbreaking briefs giving documentary evidence of what the laws were in fact doing or failing to do in American society, both the education and the courtroom practice of American lawyers were gradually transformed. "Legal realism" replaced judicial argument based on deductions from precedents, general rules, or "natural laws," and became increasingly the style of American law schools and judges.

Old-Time and New-Time Religion

If the hold of orthodox Christianity on the mass of Americans weakened steadily after 1865, it was not so much a result of the advent of Darwin or the pragmatists as of the continuing American battle between the world and the Word. Although it is impossible to make a precise correlation between the growth of wealth and leisure and the decline of strong Christian belief, most American churchmen were hardest pressed by the temptations offered their flock by money and success. This, coming with the challenge of evolution and other sciences, meant that by 1880, orthodoxy was on the defensive, religious groups were increasingly fragmented, and many churches had to make peace with the spirit of the age.

The rise of industry and an industrial proletariat, the growth of cities, the widespread popularity of science, and the galloping rate of material progress presented problems to the churches that were unprecedented in scope and complexity. Many Americans continued to attend church as regularly as they had in the past. Many still believed in a literal interpretation of the Bible. But even in the back-country sections of the South and Middle West, where the new America was least felt and traditional religious practices and beliefs were most strongly entrenched, some observers noted a diminution of the old-time zeal. In the cities, it was everywhere apparent that the position of the church was undergoing a radical transformation.

Among the better educated ministers in American religious circles, nothing was more disruptive than the advent of Darwinism. The immediate assumption of most religious leaders was that if Darwin was right the Bible had to be wrong. The first response of clergymen to the challenge was almost unanimous rejection of evolution out of hand as atheistic materialism. But Darwinism could not be talked out of existence, and an increasing number of clergymen thought it merited something beyond indignant condemnation. By the 1880's they were making a genuine effort to come to terms with the once-despised theory. Some ministers maintained that science and religion were distinct, and that developments in one had no effect upon the other; others argued that evolution complemented rather than controverted the accepted religious belief on the development of man. By the end of the decade, a workable thesis for reconciling the Bible and *The Origin of Species* had been made by such outstanding ministers as Henry Ward

Beecher, Washington Gladden, and Lyman Abbott. Beecher told his Brooklyn congregation that evolution was the "deciphering of God's thought as revealed in the structure of the world"; Lyman Abbott wrote that "God is not merely a 'Great First Cause,' but the one Great Cause from whom all forms of nature and of life continuously proceed." In short, evolution, like everything else, provided evidence of the infinite wisdom of the Divinity.

As disturbing as Darwinism were the problems raised by the development of what was called the higher criticism—an attempt, originally undertaken in Germany, to ascertain the historical validity of the Bible by subjecting it to scholarly examination. Students in Europe and America demonstrated that if taken literally the Bible contained factual errors, and some of their discoveries were incorporated in a revised version of the King James Bible that appeared in 1881 and 1885 and was primarily designed to "adapt the King James version to the present state of the English language without changing the idiom and vocabulary." The higher criticism was vigorously opposed by fundamentalists. Many denominations were torn by bitter controversy over the interpretation of the Bible as a whole or the exact meaning of specific passages within it. Despite a vehement defense, the orthodox were generally compelled to retreat as an increasing number of Americans—particularly in the urban centers—came to view Holy Writ less as an infallible record of a past era and more as a moral guide and literary masterpiece.

A direct effect on religion of America's growing wealth came with the huge fortunes of leading church members. Virtually every important industrialist of the period, with the exception of Andrew Carnegie, took an active part in church affairs; and even Carnegie, though presumably an agnostic, gave millions of dollars for the purchase of church organs. Successful businessmen donated large sums of money to religious institutions, and they increasingly occupied important lay positions within church organizations. Many ministers of wealthier churches became more conservative in their outlook. Church life grew more "respectable" than in the past, new and more costly church buildings were erected, and in the cities there was a steady emigration of church parishes from slum areas to middle- and upper-class neighborhoods. Of the major religious groups, the Roman Catholics, with poorer working class parishioners, remained relatively unaffected by such developments.

Wealthier and more respectable churches, however, frequently lost much of their former appeal for Americans accustomed to a more vigorous and emotional form of religious experience. A number of new, more emotional sects thus found a following in the rural areas, where the tradition of the old-time religion remained strongest. In the cities, new mystical and intuitive groups such as the Theosophists and Christian Scientists became popular. Huge audiences might flock to hear the noted agnostic Robert Ingersoll attack organized religion, but far greater throngs in the cities were attracted by Dwight L. Moody's revivals. A man of commanding presence and considerable oratorical powers, Moody preached thunderous sermons; and the singing of Ira D. Sankey, who accompanied Moody on all his principal tours, helped make a Moody visit a great event. After the turn of the century, the leading evangelist was William A. ("Billy") Sunday, an ex-baseball player, who harangued his audiences with all the finesse of a circus barker at a sideshow. Moody and Sunday were merely the most famous of a large band of revivalists whose fiery sermons gave countless Americans a few hours of the religion of their fathers.

The increasing wealth and exclusiveness of the established Protestant sects tended to alienate many workingmen who had formerly been church members. If they were welcomed at all, laborers often felt ill at ease in the rich surroundings of the more elaborate churches. Pews were filled with well-dressed families from the upper and middle classes, and working people learned that Protestant clerics often sided with employers rather than workers during strikes. Henry Ward Beecher probably spoke for many—though certainly not all—of his fellow ministers in 1877, when he said: "God has intended the great to be great and the little to be little. . . . I do not say that a dollar a day is enough to support a workingman. But it is enough to support a man! Not enough to support a man and five children if a man insists on smoking and drinking beer. . . . But the man who cannot live on bread and water is not fit to live."

Sensing the dangers of alienating working men from religion and church life, members of the clergy who did not share Beecher's views on economic questions began to preach either the Social Gospel or Christian Socialism. Outstanding advocates of the Social Gospel, like Josiah Strong and Washington Gladden, maintained that the problems created by the rise of industrial capitalism could only be solved by the universal application of the teachings of Jesus. Gladden's writings and sermons defended labor's right to organize and proposed that employer-employee strife be eliminated by an "industrial partnership" that would enable workingmen to receive "a fixed share" of industry's profits. The Christian Socialists went even further and proposed a collective society, to be achieved not by the class struggle, but by observing the law of love and adopting the precepts of Christ. The Christian So-

Christian Socialist cialists found little support outside their own immediate circles; and Walter Rauschenbusch, who was one of the movement's staunchest supporters, later wrote, "We were few and we shouted in the wilderness." Nevertheless, the little band did much practical work in labor and reform movements and in fights between labor and management. Few parishioners followed the examples set by such clergymen, but the immense popularity of *In His Steps* (1897), a novel by the Reverend Charles Sheldon, seems to indicate that a large number of people wished to hear their message. Describing a community in which all church members agreed to live just as Jesus would presumably have done under similar circumstances, *In His Steps* became an immediate best seller, and by 1925, when it was still going strong, its sales in the United States and Great Britain had exceeded 20,000,000 copies.

Many churches that adopted neither the Social Gospel nor Christian Socialism tried to meet the great problems of the industrial city by providing educational opportunities, recreational facilities, and a measure of financial assistance to underprivileged city dwellers. Gymnasiums, libraries, social clubs, sewing classes, and night schools tried to bring the so-called "institutional church" to the people and the people back to the churches. Such facilities saved many urban churches from extinction. St. George's Episcopal Church of New York was an outstanding example. When it became an institutional church in 1882, it had seventy-five members; fifteen years later, its membership exceeded four thousand. No institutional church, however, could rival the work of the Salvation Army among the poor and distressed. General Booth's organization became almost a society within American society, feeding, housing, and comforting hundreds of thousands of the poor.

Its long tradition of religious work among the poor put the Catholic Church in an excellent position to take advantage of the very conditions that had proved so perplexing to many of the Protestant denominations. American Catholics were fortunate that Catholic leadership was entrusted to such an able and farseeing religious leader as James Cardinal Gibbons. Appointed Archbishop of Baltimore in 1877, Gibbons in 1886 became the second American Cardinal. Thoroughly American in his outlook, he repeatedly urged the rapid assimilation of immigrants and upheld the separation of church and state. He was a life-long friend of labor and was instrumental in preventing papal condemnation of the Knights of Labor. A man of broad humanitarian instincts, he did all within his power to prevent the Catholic Church from "being represented as the friend of the powerful rich and the enemy of the helpless poor." Had the Church been less sensitive to poverty and misery, its growth in America might have been less dramatic. The Catholic population of the United States, which was more than 6,000,000 in 1880, rose to approximately 12,000,000 in 1900 and to more than 16,000,000 in 1910. Almost half of this increase was accounted for by immigration; nearly 5,000,000 immigrants became members of Catholic parishes in the United States during the three decades following 1880.

The mounting tide of Catholic immigration was largely responsible for the revival of antiforeign sentiment. The leading anti-Catholic group, the American Protective Association, was founded in 1887. It drew its chief support from the rural areas of the Middle West and appealed not only to anti-Catholic and antiforeign feeling but also to the traditional suspicion of the city. It used forged documents that purported to show the allegiance of American Catholics to Rome rather than Washington and compelled all its members to swear to do whatever they could to "strike the shackles and chains of blind obedience to the Roman Catholic Church from the hampered and bound consciences of a priest-ridden and church-oppressed people." The A.P.A. entered politics and enjoyed some success in local and state elections. By 1894, when it had approximately 1,000,000 members, it had reached the high point of its influence, and in the campaign of 1896, most Americans forgot their anti-Catholicism in the heated arguments over Bryan and free silver.

A number of Catholic priests, however, had become fearful for the future of the Church in America. They were convinced that Catholicism as a creed, as well as an organization, had to come to terms with the liberalism and growing secularism of American life. From the 1880's on, led by men like Archbishop Ireland and Bishop Keen, these priests sponsored a movement for the Americanization of the Catholic Church that went so far as to propose the surrender of parochial schools, the dropping of certain sacraments, and greater use of English in the Mass. In 1899, this modern American Catholicism was suppressed by Pope Leo XIII, but it left behind, as its principal monument, the Catholic University of America at Washington, D.C.

The struggles among Roman Catholics to adjust theology as well as churches to new conditions had their counterparts among Protestants. Members of almost every important Protestant group were attacked for unorthodox views after the Civil War. In 1879 the Southern Baptist Seminary dismissed a professor for using scientific methods in the study of the Old Testament. The Newton Theological Institution in Massachusetts compelled a Baptist teacher to resign under somewhat similar circumstances. Congregationalists, Episcopalians, Methodists, and Presbyterians also brought charges of heresy against ministers and teachers and had them removed from their posts.

The bitterness displayed in these cases was not a sign of strength or confidence. On the contrary, such actions represented the rear-guard actions of orthodoxy in retreat. Some complained that American religion had lost much of its older character and indeed, the growth of humanitarianism and a social conscience among the churches, the broadening of their interests, their partial acceptance of the scientific point of view, and the perceptible—although irregular—increase in re-ligious tolerance all pointed by 1910 to the general transformation of American religion. It became increasingly liberal when it was theologi-cal, and more concerned with spiritual comfort and the brotherhood of man than with the disturbing truths of the Calvinist or other older orthodox notions of God.

The Lower and Higher Learning in America

Before the common-school revolution of the Jacksonian period, most Americans relied on the family and the church to give the young moral guidance and patriotic ideals. As American churches lost their moral authority and as Americans after 1865 sensed growing dangers and threats to the republic, citizens became increasingly convinced that the schools could save the nation if the nation created the right kind of school system. Concurrently, however, the same American ma-terialism and demand for what was practical that had made such trouble for religious leaders tended to undermine the authority of the school-teacher who tried to teach young people to resist the "easy way." Para-doxically, the teacher after the Civil War was charged with an increas-ingly larger mission, but at the same time he was often regarded as an ineffectual man of ideas who had become a teacher because he could do little else.

Between 1865 and 1910, a classic pattern in American education was established: perpetual debate about the aims of education, a grow-ing financial investment in schools, and constant indictment of the school system for failing to do what schools should do.

By 1860, a minimal elementary education had become the birth-right of American children, and, in many parts of the country, it was available to boys and girls. Between 1870 and 1910, elementary educa-tional opportunities rapidly increased. After about 1880, the high-school revolution also began to make quick advances. In 1870, there were only 500 secondary schools in the United States; by 1910, there were more than 10,000. Over-all, in forty years the number of public-

A High School Class of 1900

school pupils almost tripled, reaching nearly 18,000,000, and the per capita expenditure for education went from $1.64 to $4.64.

A number of important novelties were also introduced after 1870. In 1873, St. Louis became the first American city to establish a kindergarten; a quarter of a century later, there were approximately 3,000 kindergartens in the United States. A concerted effort was also made to enforce school attendance, and by 1898, thirty-one state and territorial legislatures had adopted compulsory attendance statutes. Although these laws were loosely enforced, the amount of formal education received by the average American rose from less than four years in 1880 to five years in 1900 and six years in 1914. More notable was the decline of national illiteracy from 17 per cent in 1880 to 11 per cent in 1900 and to 7.7 per cent in 1910.

Improvements in pedagogy, however, generally lagged far behind the expansion of school facilities. Corporal punishment, although increasingly attacked by educators, remained a standard method for enforcing classroom discipline. The curriculum in most elementary schools was limited to reading, writing, and arithmetic. Textbooks, which had to be purchased by the pupils, were generally the same as those that their grandparents had used. McGuffey's readers, with their lessons in morality and exhortations to patriotism, were an important part of many boys' and girls' grammar-school training right down to the end of the century. A premium was placed on the pupil's ability to commit material to memory, and teachers were usually judged by their success in maintaining classroom discipline and cramming the heads of their charges with an inordinate number of unrelated facts. Teachers were notoriously underpaid; the average annual salary was $189 in 1870 and only $325 in 1900. Under the circumstances, few able women and even smaller numbers of men were attracted to teaching, and those who were seldom chose to make it a lifetime career.

The traditional mold of public-school education was first broken in the 1880's with the adoption of improved textbooks and the expansion of the curriculum to include work in the sciences and such applied courses as drawing, manual training, cooking, sewing, and commercial subjects. Meanwhile, the "new education" was emerging to supplant the widely accepted emphasis on "drill and review." Friedrich W. A. Froebel's ideas, imported from Germany, had already exerted a profound influence on kindergarten teaching, and after 1890, the ideas of another German, Johann Friedrich Herbart, emphasizing the need for arousing the student's interest, attracted considerable attention among leading American educators. The most important of the innovators, however, was John Dewey, who became head of the School of Education at the University of Chicago. Dewey's educational theories were to have the most profound influence on the nation's public schools in subsequent years. Education, for Dewey, was not only a preparation for life but a way of life that could develop the pupil both as a creative individual and an intelligent member of a democratic society.

Much of the ferment in education after 1880 centered in the cities, especially in the Northeast. Sparsely settled rural regions generally still had to be content with ungraded grammar schools and poorly trained teachers. The South lagged far behind other sections. During Reconstruction, Radical state governments provided for free tax-supported schools, and for the first time in its history the South was provided with an elementary school system comparable in organization to that of the North and West. Further impetus was provided to southern education by such northern philanthropists as George Peabody, who furnished $3,500,000 for the improvement of the southern public schools. Building on the foundations erected during the Reconstruction period, the southern school system advanced rapidly; enrollment doubled during the last quarter of the nineteenth century, and school revenues were steadily increased. On the other hand, as Arthur M. Schlesinger has pointed out in discussing the years 1878–98: "At most, education was regarded in the South as an opportunity for the individual child and not as a civic obligation, for not one of the states of the former Confederacy applied the principle of compulsion to attendance." *

The interest in adult was well as children's education was demonstrated by the popular response to the Chautauqua movement. Organized in 1874 on the shores of Lake Chautauqua, New York, and soon imitated by many communities in other parts of the country, Chautauqua was essentially an informal summer school for adults. Visitors to Chautauqua heard prominent speakers participate in "Round Tables" on Milton, Temperance, Geology, the American Constitution, the Relations of Science and Religion, and the Doctrine of Rent, and attended the Cooking School, the Prayer Meeting, the Concert, and the Gymnastic Drill. If the thirst for culture was not slaked during the summer months at Chautauqua, there were lectures and concerts throughout the winter in many towns and cities. Evening schools taught English to foreigners, and university extension divisions offered numerous courses covering all the important fields of learning. With funds supplied by taxpayers and private benefactors, of whom Andrew Carnegie was by far the most generous, urban and rural communities also established free circulating libraries that by the end of the century numbered more than 9,000.

In education beyond the high school, an equally impressive expansion and many innovations were made after 1870, but, in this case, there were great improvements in the quality as well as the quantity of college and university training. The two generations after 1870 were in many ways a golden age for the older American universities and exciting formative years for the great state universities and for many new excellent private institutions. With the assistance provided by the Morrill Act of 1862, the University of Wisconsin was reorganized in 1866, and new universities were established by Kansas in 1864 and Minnesota and California in 1868. The Morrill Act was also responsible for the founding of state agricultural colleges and, with a gift of $500,000 from Ezra Cornell, made possible the opening of Cornell University in 1868. Although the new state universities conducted courses in the liberal arts, they placed greatest emphasis on training in agriculture and engineering.

The establishment of publicly supported institutions of higher learning provided new opportunities for women as well as men, for the state universities either admitted women from the outset or became coeducational soon after their founding. Coeducational colleges never

* A. M. Schlesinger, *The Rise of the City, 1878–1898* (New York: The Macmillan Company, 1933), pp. 165–6. Copyright 1933 by The Macmillan Company and used with their permission.

enjoyed the popularity in other sections that they did in the West. In the East, however, many famous women's colleges were established. Within a decade after Appomattox, Vassar, Smith, and Wellesley opened their doors to students, to be followed by Bryn Mawr and Mount Holyoke shortly thereafter. Meanwhile Harvard, Columbia, and Tulane—among others—had formed separate, but allied, women's colleges. By the end of the century, 80 per cent of the nation's universities and professional schools admitted female students.

By 1865, reforms were long overdue in American university training. Most colleges were still ostensibly organized for preparing students for the ministry. Heavy emphasis was placed on instruction in mathematics, Greek, and Latin, but almost no work was given in modern languages, economics, politics, and government. Libraries and laboratory facilities were unbelievably inadequate; sectarian colleges refused to hire instructors of another denomination; and professors were compelled to teach courses in as many as four or five different fields of learning.

President Charles W. Eliot of Harvard deserves the principal credit for reforming collegiate instruction after the Civil War. Under his direction, Harvard College raised its entrance requirements and abandoned its rigid program of required courses for an elective system that enabled the student to exercise considerable discretion in planning his studies. Undergraduates were also granted more personal freedom and were placed under the supervision of a dean of students. Most important of all, the curriculum was expanded to include courses in physics, international law, political economy, fine arts, music, and advanced work in modern languages. Many of the changes introduced by Eliot at Harvard were soon adopted by other leading colleges under the direction of such able educators and executives as James McCosh of Princeton, James B. Angell of Michigan, Andrew D. White of Cornell, and Frederick A. P. Barnard of Columbia.

Professional training kept pace with notable advances initiated by Eliot at the Harvard medical and law schools. Technical institutes improved their offerings, and engineering education was refined into specialties. Normal schools increased in number, raised their requirements, and eventually developed as leaders in new theories of education. Several universities established schools of architecture, and following the turn of the century, university business schools began to gain a new academic respectability. In the South important training schools for Negroes were founded, most notably the Hampton Normal and Agricultural Institute and the Tuskegee Institute under Booker T. Washington, a graduate of Hampton.

Although Harvard and Yale had reorganized their programs of graduate study in the early 1870's, Johns Hopkins, which was founded in 1876, soon became the most notable center of graduate studies in America. Daniel Coit Gilman, Johns Hopkins' first president, used the funds at his disposal, not to construct buildings and create a collegiate atmosphere shrouded in ivy, but to buy books and to secure an outstanding faculty. Most of the members of the new staff had studied in Germany; in fact, Johns Hopkins was patterned after German universities. Specialization was encouraged, and the "scientific" approach to research was held up as the ideal of scholarship. Within less than a decade, earnest young men—Woodrow Wilson among them—armed with Doctor of Philosophy degrees from Johns Hopkins, had gone forth to spread the new gospel among the other universities and colleges of the land. They were aided in this work by other Americans who had done graduate work in Germany. The impact upon American higher learning of the German approach to scholarship cannot be overemphasized. All the major universities soon accepted Johns Hopkins or such famed German institutions as Heidelberg, Berlin, Jena, and Leipzig as their models. There was little room left for the dilettante or the man of broad interests, for the pursuit of knowledge became so arduous a business that only the specialist could hope to master even a small part of a particular subject.

New scientific theories stimulated by the inroads of Darwinism, combined with the painstaking techniques taught by the German universities, were a great incentive to American scientists. Americans contributed little to the world's knowledge of either chemistry or pure mathematics, but their accomplishments in astronomy, physics, and geology were notable. In a generation that produced major work by Clarence King and Major J. W. Powell in geology and O. C. Marsh in paleontology and T. C. Chamberlin's studies in glaciation, no man was more illustrious than J. Willard Gibbs of Yale. Henry Adams called Gibbs the "greatest of Americans," and his far-reaching discoveries in thermodynamics helped make possible Einstein's formulation of the theory of relativity.

These accomplishments of the physical scientists convinced many scholars that scientific method would prove equally fruitful in the study of man. About 1870, it was generally believed that man's mind was a more or less static entity. But, under the influence of Darwinism, psychologists began to view the mind as a means by which the human organism adjusted to its environment or created a new environment to replace one that it found unsatisfactory. Psychologists increasingly used laboratory techniques to test their hypotheses, and psychology was transformed into a natural science. G. Stanley Hall, Edward L. Thorndike, and William James all made notable contributions to the new psychology, and James' work *The Principles of Psychology* (1890) was easily its greatest achievement. The revolutionary impact of evolution and natural science also prepared the way at the universities for the fundamental transformations in philosophy, law, economics, education, and other social studies.

In reviewing this golden age of the universities after 1870, it may be said that both the best and worst tendencies of the future had been established. The ideals of painstaking scholarship and of inspired teaching had been firmly planted. Concurrently, however, the universities embarked on a program of expanded offerings and preparation for a variety of careers that would in many places eventually burden higher education in America with a host of "practical courses" that denigrated the scholarly ideals of the university. In financing the expansion of universities, private philanthropy played an enormous and worthy role; but this brought to university boards of trustees many industrialists and financiers who, as the future would show, did not always see eye to eye with their scholars on what subjects should be taught and what standards of teaching and conduct ought to be enforced.

Newspapers and Magazines for the Millions

In marked contrast to the sobriety and responsibility of the university's search for truth after the Civil War were the tone and techniques of the nation's newspapers. During the war, Americans increasingly read the papers for news accounts, and by 1880, the editorial views of the successors of a Horace Greeley or William Cullen Bryant had lost the national importance they once had. Papers became increasingly spectacular and more colorful in seeking readers. One notable change in editorial policy, the severing of formal ties with political parties, did not, however, banish open political bias in editorials or in the declining day-to-day reportage of national politics. Cartoons, humor and poetry "corners," "man bites dog" stories, scandals, and sensational stunts were all used to attract or hold readers. The younger James Gordon Bennett of *The New York Herald* sent Henry Stanley to find Dr. Livingstone in the heart of Africa and thus created one of the greatest "scoops" of the age.

It remained for Joseph Pulitzer to realize that the growth of cities and the expansion of literacy called for a new kind of newspaper for semiliterate urban masses, who, he believed, wanted a paper that was cheap, accurate, vivid, and simple. Under Pulitzer's management, the *New York World* quickly became noted for its sensational, but honest, reporting and its crusades, backed by exposures in its news columns. Its price was dropped to two cents, and in less than four years Pulitzer had built the *World* into a paper with a larger circulation than that of any other journal in the country. Pulitzer was responsible for two important innovations in American journalism—mass appeal and crusading zeal. To attract readers, he filled the *World* with woodcuts, placed enormous cartoons on the first page, gave extensive coverage to crime and murders, with accompanying diagrams, and introduced the comic strip.

Pulitzer was never content with mere sensationalism. When he took over the control of the *World*, he announced that it would be a paper that was "dedicated to the cause of the people rather than to that of purse-potentates" and that it would "expose all fraud and sham, fight all public evils and abuses" and "battle for the people with earnest sincerity." Pulitzer always strove to live up to this pledge, and the *World* fought Tammany Hall, exposed railroad graft, took the lead in the attack against the trusts, opposed the machinations of financiers, and courageously supported countless other causes. Many of Pulitzer's crusades were obviously undertaken to boost circulation; nevertheless, there were few major reforms of the period that did not have his unstinted support.

In 1895, William Randolph Hearst of California invaded Pulitzer's empire by purchasing the New York *Morning Journal*. He immediately began a circulation war with the *World* and cut the price of the *Journal* to one cent. By offering fabulous salaries to reporters, he was able to assemble one of the most brilliant staffs in American newspaper history. Stephen Crane worked for a time as a Hearst reporter; Richard Harding Davis reported the coronation of the Tsar in Russia for the *Journal*; and Mark Twain kept its readers informed on Queen Victoria's golden jubilee in London. Hearst, like Pulitzer, reached the masses; but, unlike his preceptor, Hearst soon gave up all but the pretense of being a crusading journalist.

With the excitement provided by the approach of the Spanish-American War, the daily circulation of each paper exceeded 1,000,000. During the war, the *Journal* topped 1,500,000, with the *World* right behind it. Despite the success formula of the two "yellow journals," many publishers refused to employ sensational techniques. When Adolph Ochs took over the management of the *New York Times* in 1896, he pointedly announced that it would be a paper that would not

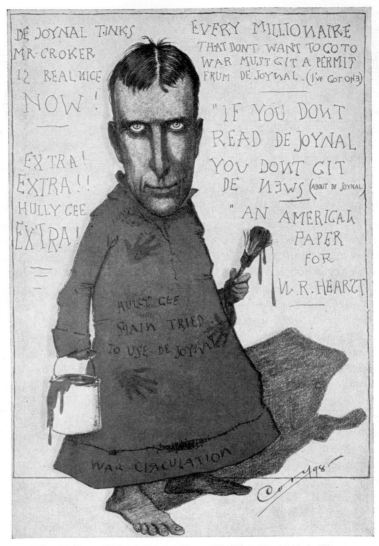

The Yellow Kid of Journalism—William Randolph Hearst
(The Bee, *1898*)

soil the breakfast table. The *Christian Science Monitor*, founded by
the Christian Science Church in 1908, shunned crime and disaster news
and conscientiously avoided the methods of the yellow press.

Despite important exceptions, as the larger papers became big business, a growing conservative outlook in editorial columns became noticeable. Arthur Brisbane, a Hearst employee, analyzed the change suc-

cinctly: "Journalistic success brings money. The editor has become a money man. 'Where your treasure is, there your heart will be also.' " As with other big businesses, there was also a marked development toward standardization. Press services supplied the same news to all their customers, and syndicates furnished many papers with the same cartoons, comic strips, photographs, and feature stories. Equally striking evidence of the trend toward standardization was the formation of newspaper chains in several cities under a single management. By 1912, Hearst, in addition to the San Francisco *Examiner* and the New York *Journal*, owned papers in Chicago, Boston, Atlanta, and Los Angeles. In the same year, Frank A. Munsey controlled papers in five eastern cities, and by 1908, there were some twenty papers in the Scripps-McRae chain.

The transformation of the American magazine proceeded at a more leisurely pace than that of the nation's newspapers. In the decade and a half after Appomattox, the leading American literary monthlies were *Harper's*, the *Atlantic*, and *Scribner's Monthly* (which became the *Century* in 1881); and the most influential news weekly was the *Nation*, under E. L. Godkin. Together with the principal religious periodical, the *Independent*, these leading magazines supported various nonradical reforms such as civil service, tenement-house improvement, and the establishment of kindergartens. Despite some innovations and improvements, while the newspapers were altering both their policies and material to fit the mass tastes of an industrial, urbanized America, the editors of *Harper's*, *Scribner's*, and the *Atlantic* continued to publish magazines designed for a relatively small audience of gentlemen-scholars and a small portion of the upper-middle class; they made little or no attempt to reach a wider public.

The general indifference of the older monthlies to current events was partially responsible for the establishment after 1885 of a number of magazines that concentrated upon news and reformism. But none of these newer magazines, like the *Literary Digest* or the *Forum*, reached a mass audience, and it remained for Edward W. Bok, a Dutch immigrant, to apply some of the lessons of mass journalism to periodical publishing. Bok became editor of the *Ladies' Home Journal* in 1889 and immediately set out to broaden its appeal. Like Pulitzer, he campaigned for various reforms, but understandably placed greatest emphasis on demands for women's rights. Much of the magazine's fiction was written by well-known authors. For safe sensation, on one occasion Bok published an issue written entirely by the daughters of famous men, and a special column provided advice to young girls in love. Considerable attention was always given, however, to everyday housekeeping problems. By 1892, the *Ladies' Home Journal* had a monthly circulation of 700,000, far ahead of its nearest rival, and nearly double the daily circulation of Pulitzer's two New York papers.

Such methods were further developed by Frank A. Munsey, a businessman who founded *Munsey's Weekly* in 1889 and shortly changed it to a monthly. From the outset, Munsey knew that the largest profits lay in mass production and a small return on each item sold. In 1893, he lowered the price of *Munsey's* to ten cents, and before the end of the century, the magazine's circulation had reached 650,000. New printing techniques also made it possible for Munsey to produce a magazine that was physically attractive to a wide range of people, and the growing use of advertising enabled him to sell his magazine at a cost that the average consumer could afford.

By 1900, the stage was thus set for Samuel S. McClure, the first publisher to realize the possibility of using the mass-circulation magazine to expose social abuses. *McClure's*, established in 1893, was distinguished by its excellent writing and well-known contributors. After 1902, it rapidly became the most famous crusading magazine of the time. Ida Tarbell set a pattern in 1902–4 in her series of articles on the Standard Oil corporation; muckraking accounts of political and corporate corruption then appeared with increasing frequency in the pages of *McClure's* and *Everybody's, Cosmopolitan,* and *Collier's.*

Neither Munsey's big business methods nor McClure's exposés, however, captured leadership of the American magazine market. The *Saturday Evening Post* never attempted to challenge the status quo, but, crammed with profitable advertising, it had a circulation of close to 2,000,000 by 1914 and was easily the most popular magazine of the age. Highly patriotic, abounding in old-fashioned morality, and pledged to keeping things as they were, in many respects it accurately reflected the attitudes of its large middle-class audience. *Post* readers might peek at sensations and scandal elsewhere or dally with reform, but fundamentally they preferred to see their own day-to-day conventional images of themselves held up before them and their families.

The Arts in a Business Age

America's new millionaires of the post-bellum years—an aristocracy of pork, oil, steel, railroads, and coke—tried to corner the world's supply of art in much the same way that they had set out to monopolize industries. These men could afford "the best"; and they hired professional collectors to buy up Europe's art treasures regardless of cost and commissioned architects to build them sumptuous town houses and country castles that duplicated as closely as possible the homes of the titled nobility of Europe. The obsession of many of the well-to-do with European art provided little work or encouragement for American artists, but it was responsible for the establishment of most of the nation's important art museums. In 1865, there was not a single American art gallery comparable to those in Europe. Within thirty-five years, every large city had at least one important museum of fine arts. Private gifts of money and art treasures established the Corcoran Art Gallery in Washington in 1869, the Boston Museum of Fine Arts in 1870, and Metropolitan Museum of Art in New York City in 1879, and most of the great collections amassed by the postwar generation of millionaires were also eventually turned over to museums and thus made available to the public.

Americans during the Gilded Age—as in most other ages—liked to think of themselves as a practical people. Hard working and moralistic, they disdained the aesthete and had little patience with the artist who insisted on being "arty"; they approved of "sensible" art, pictures that were "pretty," pointed a moral, or told a story that they could understand. This widely held attitude militated against the growth of a native school of art, but it proved a boon to American illustrators. The rapid expansion of the magazine and book-publishing industries provided a growing market for a number of proficient illustrators during the postwar decades. Howard Pyle, Edwin A. Abbey, and Joseph Pennell won the most enduring reputations as illustrators, but there were many others of marked ability. By the turn of the century, countless Americans were familiar with M. A. Woolf's pictures of immigrants, Frederic Remington's Indian and cowboy paintings, and E. W. Kemble's studies of Negroes.

Lacking both a receptive audience at home and an established national tradition worthy of their respect, many American painters turned to Europe for inspiration and training. Several Americans studied at either Munich or Düsseldorf, but the center of American artists abroad remained France, where they either enrolled at the conservative *École des Beaux Arts* or joined the ranks of the rebels. Traditionalists, however, always outnumbered the innovators, and the *Beaux Arts* was responsible for a whole generation of American artists who reflected the dominant trends in French academic painting and, at their most daring, portrayed the nude against an idealized background and in the neoclassical style of the academy. Despite the prestige of the *École des Beaux Arts*, several Americans rejected it for France's Barbizon school of landscape painting, which in going outdoors into the sunshine and away from Paris came to emphasize the creation of a mood rather than exactness of detail and stressed the use of color rather than precision of line.

Of the many American painters who fell under the influence of the Barbizon school, special mention should be made of William Morris Hunt, George Inness, and Homer Martin. Hunt returned to the United States in 1855 to take the lead in the revolt against the academy. He was a remarkably influential teacher and a painter whose versatility enabled him to produce not only outstanding landscapes but murals and portraits as well. Inness was probably the ablest American landscape painter of his day and perhaps the greatest landscape artist the nation has ever known. Martin—who, like Inness, never ceased to experiment—eventually became a convert to Impressionism, and in his later years he was an ardent disciple of Corot.

As an increasing number of artists returned from abroad with new and exciting ideas, there developed a sharp cleavage between the younger and older generations of American painters. When the progressives were rebuffed by the National Academy of Design, they formed the Society of American Artists in 1877. Championing the cause of the younger men and serving as the first president of the Society of American Artists was John La Farge, who was considerably older than most of the insurgents. With many interests, a dynamic personality, and a broad background in several subjects, La Farge was both the most versatile and eclectic of the American artists of his time. Painting landscapes as well as portraits, he was also this country's first authentic muralist, and through his pioneer work in opalescence, he made a major contribution to the art of designing stained-glass windows. He was also well versed in Japanese art, the Old Masters, and the Pre-Raphaelites, but his fascination with the effect of light on color put him in the advance guard of Impressionism. Although he encouraged the new generation of painters who had been trained in France, he himself belonged to no school, and in 1877 he wrote: "I should mistrust the French ambitions anyhow. It is by nobody's taste you must go, unless you find a mind just at sympathy with yours, and unless they can give you reasons, and the reasons should always be big ones."

Thomas Eakins and Winslow Homer provided additional evidence that American painting was not wholly dependent on European influences. Both men found their subjects in the everyday scenes and life of their fellow Americans; yet Eakins, who undertook a one-man crusade against respectability in art, had a monumental scorn for pictures that were merely pretty. In such fine studies as "The Gross Clinic" and "The Thinker," he portrayed his subjects with an integrity of

"The Gross Clinic" by Thomas Eakins

purpose and a precise—even harsh—objectivity that precluded even a hint of flattery. Trained as a lithographer, Homer served as an artist-correspondent for *Harper's Weekly* during the Civil War. When he turned to painting, he won immediate recognition with his "Prisoners from the Front," which was shown by the New York Academy of Design in 1866. During the next forty years, Homer, with almost fanatical intensity and singleness of purpose, devoted his energies to the production of powerful and forthright studies of scenes in the Caribbean, Adirondacks, and along the coast of his native Maine.

In contrast to such American-oriented painters as La Farge, Eakins, and Homer was a group of well-known expatriates that included Mary Cassatt, John Singer Sargent, and James McNeill Whistler. Miss Cassatt, after extensive study in America and Europe, settled in Paris, where she became one of the most popular secondary Impressionists. Sargent, whose studio was in London, won renown on both sides of the Atlantic for his highly stylized, and sometimes idealized portraits of wealthy leaders of English and American society. Whistler, after being expelled from West Point and serving a short term in the offices of the Coast and Geodetic Survey, studied in Paris and then spent the remainder of his years in England. Egotistical, belligerent, and unconventional in manner and dress, he relentlessly battled the Philistines and championed art for art's sake. Always more interested in the total effect of colors than in creating a likeness, he constantly drew parallels between his painting and music. On one occasion he wrote that it was the function of the artist to view nature, "not with the enlarging lens, that he may gather facts for the botanist, but with the light of the one who sees in her choice . . . of brilliant tones and delicate tints, suggestion of future harmonies." Equally at home with oil, watercolor, etching, or lithography, he turned out a prodigious amount of work between fights with critics and lawsuits against detractors. Best known for his "Study in Black and White," (commonly mistitled "Whistler's Mother") he was most effective in portraits and his innumerable "Harmonies," "Symphonies," and "Arrangements."

Despite the versatility and skill of these individual artists, American painting as a whole lacked the vitality and originality of European painting during the closing decades of the nineteenth century. No significant school of painting had emerged in the United States, and the bulk of the American work seemed trite and pedestrian when compared to the exciting developments in France. But in the midst of apparent indifference and complacency, new forces were shaping the rising generation of American painters. After 1900, a group of young New Yorkers turned their backs on both Europe and their own national past to produce a series of stark studies of contemporary urban life. Depicting elevated railroads, hall bedrooms, saloons, dance halls, prize fights, bums, and floozies, the "Ashcan School," men like George Bellows, Robert Henri, John Sloan, George Luks, and William Glackens, shocked the complacent and genteel by their determination to paint what they saw as they saw it.

As fully important a development as the advent of the hard-boiled

The Armory Show of 1913

[THE MUSEUM OF MODERN ART, NEW YORK]

school was the opening in 1913 of the New York Armory Show. Concentrating largely on the work of contemporary French painters, it provided America with its first real taste of Post-Impressionism, Modernism, and Cubism. Its impact was immediate and pronounced: conservatives rushed to the defense of the old ways and thereby publicized the new; the radicals replied in kind; and painting became front-page news. The Armory Show was a turning point in the history of modern American painting, for it marked the beginning of the end of the long years of provincialism of the American painter and his public.

The history of American sculpture roughly paralleled that of painting. Sculptors as well as painters were dependent upon European training and were confronted by public indifference and the calls of industrialized and urbanized America for the prosaic and sentimental. But in sculpture as in painting, innumerable obstacles proved only temporary barriers, and the achievements of a few individuals eventually compensated somewhat for years of mediocrity.

In the decade that followed the Civil War, American sculpture was characterized by a banality and triteness that have seldom, if ever, been equaled in the history of American art. The nationalism engendered by the war was reflected in such a plethora of statutes of military heroes that it was said that the foundries were turning them out on a mass-production basis. Middle-class homes were cluttered with highly romanticized plaster versions of figures from antiquity and the American past. Iron deer were considered the last word in lawn decoration, and few cities possessed a public monument of artistic merit. The Italians were the most important foreign influence, and the neoclassical school of sculpture had no serious rival. Typical of the period was the work of William Wetmore Story, who had a predilection for mournful females and noble males, all of whom he clad in the flowing robes of Greece and Rome.

The impetus for the break with the Italian tradition was provided by the Centennial Exposition of 1876, which furnished many Americans with their first view of the work of the leading French sculptors of the day. In the ensuing years, Paris supplanted Rome as the mecca of American sculptors, and the neoclassicists steadily lost ground to a group of artists who had received most of their training in France. With their emphasis on naturalism, skillful use of broken surfaces, undoubted technical ability, and originality of approach, these younger men gave American sculpture a distinct character that, although revealing foreign influences, was nevertheless unmistakably American. Of the new generation of sculptors, none won more fame than Augustus Saint-Gaudens, creator of the Farragut and Sherman monuments in New York, the Lincoln statue in Chicago, and the nameless figure that marks the grave of Mrs. Henry Adams in Washington—to mention only his most noted works. Among others, George Grey Barnard, a student of Rodin in Paris, produced a series of massive figures that conveyed a sense of raw strength reminiscent of some of his master's work. Daniel Chester French, one of the most prolific sculptors, produced a number of popular statues of prominent Americans including his "Lincoln" at Lincoln, Nebraska, his "Washington" at Paris, and his "Grant" at Philadelphia.

Architecture, far more than either painting or sculpture, reflected the vulgarity and materialism that typified so much of American life during the Gilded Age. Architecture gave the wealthy an opportunity for conspicuous consumption that few were able to resist. Apparently determined to make every building look like a wedding cake, American architects developed a style that managed to conceal any hint of functionalism beneath a myriad of scrolls, brackets, railings, cupolas, balconies, gables, and turrets. At best a corruption, this Victorian Gothic was used not only in churches, but in banks, homes, art museums, college halls, and government buildings. Despite its enormous popularity, Victorian Gothic did not have the field to itself; Fiske Kimball, in describing what he termed the "Battle of Styles," mentioned "Italian villas," "chalets," "Moorish cottages," and a number of public buildings that revealed the French influence of the Second Empire. In the Northeast, meanwhile, there was a Colonial revival, and in Florida there was an attempt to return to the earlier architecture of Spanish America. The half-timbered Queen Anne house topped by bunched chimneys gained an increasing vogue among middle- and upper-class homeowners, while the Fifth Avenue mansions and country palaces designed by Richard Morris Hunt furnished unbelievably luxurious settings for the American industrial and finance aristocracy.

The first indication that American architecture was beginning to emerge from the depths to which it had sunk after the war was provided by the work of Henry Hobson Richardson, who was the leading member of a new group of younger architects who had received their training at the *École des Beaux Arts*. Richardson, who, as Lewis Mumford has pointed out, was "not a decorator, but a builder," quickly rejected the Victorian Gothic for the more forthright Romanesque of southern France and Spain. His outstanding buildings were all distinguished by their heavy stonework, broad arches, squat pillars, and an over-all air of massed—even ponderous—strength that induced one critic to suggest that they were defensible only in a military sense. Although Richardson's name is usually associated with church architecture and his first notable building was Trinity Church in Boston, he was equally successful in his designs of railroad stations, town halls, jails, libraries, and college buildings. Until his death in 1886, Richardson had no serious rivals among American architects, and his buildings continue to stand as monuments to his emphasis on the purpose of a building rather than its decoration. In the midst of an age when building was shifting from masonry to steel-frame construction, Richardson used a dying tradition of stonework and a historic style to good advantage, but he founded no schools and his art died soon after him.

Richardson was a craftsman who experimented with old techniques rather than devised new ones, but several of his contemporaries realized that the Industrial Revolution had presented them with both the need and opportunity for a novel and indigenous form of architectural expression. Believing that the architectural forms that had been developed to meet the demands of ancient and medieval Europe were ludicrous when applied to a factory or commercial building, they sought to perfect a type of building that would satisfy without sham

The Modern Gothic of Brooklyn Bridge (Print by Currier & Ives)

the requirements of modern American economic life. Steel and glass were their distinctive materials. As early as 1851, the Crystal Palace in London had demonstrated the possibilities inherent in the use of broad areas of glass; for years, engineers had shown in bridge construction that iron and steel had tremendous structural potentialities. It was in every way fitting that the Brooklyn Bridge, which was completed in 1883, was the age's finest example of the daring but simple fashion in which the matter-of-fact employment of new materials could solve problems of design as well as of engineering.

Modern architecture—as it was called to distinguish it from the traditional styles—centered from the outset in Chicago, where convention seemed somewhat less oppressive than in the East and the fire of 1876 had presented builders with a clean slate. Although at first influenced by Richardson, western architects soon evolved a style of their own that quickly became identified with the multi-storied, steel-framed office building. The elevator, which had been perfected in the seventies, had little effect on commercial architecture as long as a building's height was limited by the masonry of its supporting walls; but when the elevator was hung in a steel frame, restrictions on upward growth were removed. As early as 1883, William Le Baron Jenney's design for the Home Insurance Building in Chicago had called for the use of iron uprights and crossbeams to serve as supports for the structure's walls and floors, and a few years later the same device was employed in the Tacoma Building. It was only a matter of time before steel was substituted for iron, and the modern office building emerged as a continuous steel frame sheathed in masonry that was broken at regular intervals by strips of windows. The leading exponents of the new style were Daniel Burnham, John Root, and Louis Sullivan; and of the three, Sullivan was easily pre-eminent. An artist as well as a builder, Sullivan brought to his work crusading zeal, a thorough mastery of his craft, and a philosophy of functionalism that emphasized the harmony between art and nature. Sullivan was at his best in the Wainwright Building in St. Louis, which more clearly than any other structure revealed his deep-seated conviction that "whether it be the sweeping eagle in his flight, or the open apple-blossom, the toiling work-horse, the blithe swan, the branching oak, the winding stream at its base, the drifting clouds over all the coursing sun, form ever follows function, and this is law."

Sullivan's work received little immediate recognition in the East, where a classical revival was reaching its high point in the numerous buildings of the New York architectural firm of McKim, Mead, and White. Emphasizing form rather than function and employing the classical façade, McKim, Mead, and White raised an ancient tradition to new summits of perfection. But their technical proficiency could not obscure the sterility of the style they had adopted. Very quickly what had been effective in their early work yielded to a safe conservatism.

The architectural forms of Greece, Rome, and the Renaissance could not meet the needs of a nation of farmers, factory hands, and office workers, and the firm's most noteworthy buildings gave little indication of the age in which they had been built. The classical revival achieved its greatest triumph at the Chicago World's Fair of 1893. Sullivan happily designed the fair's Transportation Building and western architects were to have set the tone for the exposition, but, in the end, the over-all theme was uncompromising classicism. Although much was made of the architectural splendor of the World's Fair, its outstanding feature was really its almost complete absence of originality. But it did have the worth-while effect of showing what a well-planned, carefully cleaned, and courteously policed "White City"—as it was called—could bring to the still raw and ugly American urban landscape.

Despite the triumph of the traditionalists at the World's Fair, they were soon forced to give ground. As urban concentration increased, ground rents rose proportionately. Under the cirumstances, the lesson seemed obvious: the taller the building, the greater the profits. Economic rather than aesthetic considerations thus forced the adoption of the steel-framed office building, for it alone could be pushed skyward beyond the seven or eight stories that all-masonry walls could sustain. Because of the extraordinary pressure of population and the limits imposed on horizontal growth by its island location, Manhattan was destined to provide the setting for the nation's first modern skyscrapers. The Flatiron Building, which was designed by Daniel Burnham and reached twenty stories at its completion in 1902, was followed within a decade by the much taller Metropolitan Tower, Municipal Building, and Singer and Woolworth buildings. These early New York skyscrapers and their counterparts in other cities generally represented an unhappy compromise between the old and new, for their towering steel frames were covered with a mass of decorative material that tended to obscure the clean and essentially beautiful upward sweep of their lines. Not until the next generation did architects come to realize that the attractiveness of the skyscraper was enhanced by emphasizing rather than concealing the fundamental simplicity of its design.

The skyscraper was neither derivative nor imitative, but uniquely American, and no other product of American artistic development so accurately reflected the age and land that created it. City planners could complain that it robbed its neighbors of air and sunlight and that it increased urban congestion, but to millions of people throughout the United States and the rest of the world the skyscraper stood as a symbol of American aspirations for power and wealth.

FOR SUPPLEMENTARY READING

Two general works that contrast vividly with each other on American culture after 1865 are V. L. Parrington, *Main Currents in American Thought* (1930), and R. Chase, *The American Novel and Its Tradition* (Pb, 1957). P. Miller's *American Thought: Civil War to World War I* (Pb, 1954) has an excellent introduction. See also H. S. Commager, *The American Mind* (Pb, 1960) for several essays. American writers since 1890 are studied by A. Kazin in *On Native Grounds* (1942) (Pb), stressing the rise of realism. Two famous works on Mark Twain are Van Wyck Brooks, *The Ordeal of Mark Twain* (Pb, 1955), and B. de Voto, *Mark Twain's America* (rev. ed., 1951). On Henry James there are two books to start with: F. O. Matthiessen and K. B.

Murdock (eds.), *The Notebooks of Henry James* (1947); and F. Dupee, *Henry James* (Pb, 1956). General and specific studies of other writers between 1865 and 1914 include the works cited above and: Van Wyck Brooks, *New England: Indian Summer* (1940) and *The Confident Years, 1885–1915* (1952); R. E. Spiller and others, *Literary History of the United States* (3 vols., 1948); E. Carter, *Howells and the Age of Realism* (1954); J. Berryman, *Stephen Crane* (1950); A. Kazin and C. Shapiro (eds.), *The Stature of Dreiser* (1955); F. O. Matthiessen, *Theodore Dreiser* (1951), demonstrating the ambiguous feelings of a sensitive critic and American progressive toward Dreiser. F. Lynn's *Dream of Success* (1955) has little piety about the first naturalistic novelists. Students of William James have an excellent work in R. B. Perry, *The Thought and Character of William James* (2 vols., 1935). Henry Adams's latest biographer is E. Stevenson, *Henry Adams* (1955). John Dewey's most famous student is his best biographer: S. Hook, *John Dewey* (1939). Holmes is best revealed in his own words in M. Lerner (ed.), *The Mind and Faith of Justice Holmes* (1943). J. Dorfman's scholarly *Thorstein Veblen and His America* (1934) needs the perspective supplied by D. Riesman, *Thorstein Veblen: A Critical Interpretation* (1953). M. White, *Social Thought in America* (1949) (Pb), analyzes the chief leaders of the "revolt against formalism," including Charles A. Beard. H. W. Schneider has two works relevant to this chapter: *A History of American Philosophy* (1946) and *Religion in Twentieth Century America* (1952). Church history still awaits a major analysis; a standard authority is W. W. Sweet, *The Story of Religions in America* (1930). On education use E. P. Cubberley, *Public Education in the United States* (rev. ed., 1934), and R. Hofstadter and W. P. Metzger, *The Development of Academic Freedom in the United States* (2 vols., 1955). On newspapers and magazines the works of F. L. Mott are foremost: *American Journalism* (rev. ed., 1950) and *A History of American Magazines* (4 vols., 1930–57). An exciting general history of American art is O. W. Larkin, *Art and Life in America* (1949).

Progressive Movements

T HE PROGRESSIVE MOVEMENTS at the beginning of the twentieth century were many-sided attacks on various glaring abuses of the decades following the Civil War. The Progressives never established a national organization to direct and coordinate their campaigns. Nevertheless, they were bound together by a contagious enthusiasm for reform and an all-pervading crusading optimism that at times approached naïveté. Working through local, state, and national legislatures and moving in and out of the established national parties as the occasion demanded, they were influential in virtually every part of American life from the end of the century until the outbreak of World War I. The activities of the Progressives ranged over the entire spectrum of reform, but all their reforms had a common objective. The growth of industrial and finance capitalism and of the cities with their millions of immigrants had disrupted the American civilization of an earlier day, and most Progressives, with a few notable exceptions, were bent on restoring or restating the ideals of the past without sacrificing the material gains of the present.

The Progressive Spirit

The Progressive movements were predominantly middle-class attempts to recapture an earlier age when single individuals rather than the corporation, union, or political machine had made the important decisions in American life. Far from being revolutionaries, the Progressives wished to conserve traditional American values, which they felt were being undermined by recent tendencies in business and government. They believed in political democracy, individual initiative, competitive capitalism, and property rights. Although many of their reforms called for an extension of government control, they were enemies of socialism. In their minds, a moderate increase in the power of the government provided the only means for preserving individual freedom and preventing the growth of those abuses that might eventually induce workingmen to turn to socialism. To most Progressives, the growth of governmental authority was only meant to restore freedom and was deeply feared as an end in itself.

Like the reformers of the pre-Civil War era, the Progressives were convinced that man was a rational creature who knew his own best interests. If given all pertinent information concerning any problem, he was capable of weighing the facts, arriving at the correct conclusion, and pursuing a course of action that would benefit himself and society. Man, in short, was inherently progressive. It was true that certain barriers to progress had appeared in recent years, but these were man-made obstacles that man could remove. The Progressives, of course, were not alone in their belief in the inevitability of both individual and collective improvement. What set them off from other Americans was their enthusiastic determination and specific programs to speed up the process.

The Progressives' faith in the judgment of the individual led them to reaffirm the principles of political democracy. Every man was thought capable of governing himself, and the alleged defects of democratic government were considered corruptions rather than inherent weaknesses of the democratic process. If representative government had broken down, the Progressives reasoned, its collapse was due to its failure to be genuinely representative. Because of their confidence in the ability of the individual to vote in his own best interest, the Progressives urged that citizens be permitted to participate more directly in government and that the gap that separated the government from the people be eliminated so that the two groups could work together effectively. Specifically, they recommended such reforms as the direct election of senators, and the initiative, referendum, and recall. Better political institutions, the Progressives believed, would insure a popular government in which the influence of either monopolies or boss-ridden machines would be reduced to a minimum. There was nothing novel in the political philosophy of the Progressives, for their principal tenets—if not their methods—could be traced to Thomas Jefferson at least a century earlier.

The Progressives' principal concern about the economy was to guarantee opportunity for the individual. They wished, not to destroy competitive capitalism, but to revive it by checking the growth of monopoly and promoting fair competition. In the American race for success, some contestants had gained such pronounced advantages that many of the less favored runners stood little or no chance of winning. Unlike the socialists, most Progressives did not wish to abolish the race, but to make certain that everyone began at roughly the same starting line and that all the competitors observed certain elementary rules of fairness. The government was to be called on to serve as referee to enforce the rules and punish the violators. No attempt would be made to make every person run as fast as every other person, but each individual would be assured of the chance to run as fast as he possibly could. Most Progressives were always strong advocates of competition; it was only "unfair" competition to which they were opposed. Those among them who were resigned to regulated big business were in a distinct, if influential, minority.

The Progressives' criticism of monopoly could lay little claim to originality. Most of their general principles and specific proposals had been advanced earlier by reform groups during the Gilded Age. The Greenback-Labor party, aside from its demands for cheap paper money, had advocated a program that in many respects was similar to that put forward by the Progressives a quarter of a century later. Several farm and labor organizations, as well as many small businessmen, had sought to curb the power of the trusts. Many urban groups had fought corruption in municipal government and tried to improve the lot of the urban poor through humanitarian reforms. Finally, the Populists, in addition to their advocacy of free silver, had adopted a series of platforms many of whose planks were taken over by the Progressives with little or no change.

The Progressives were also indebted to many social critics of the last quarter of the nineteenth century who repeatedly opposed several features of the growth of American industry. Special mention should be made of Henry George and Henry Demarest Lloyd.

Henry George, when living in California in the 1860's, had been struck by the fashion in which the movement of population into an area forced up property values and provided land speculators with an unearned profit. During a visit to New York City in 1869, he had been further impressed by the contrast between the city's astonishing material progress, on the one hand, and the poverty in its slum sections, on the other. After extensive reading and research, he concluded that the explanation for this paradox lay in the nation's land system, and in 1879, he published a fully developed version of this theory in *Progress and Poverty*. Although the manuscript of *Progress and Poverty* aroused no enthusiasm among commercial publishers and had to be privately printed, it soon reached a remarkably wide audience. George's theories on rent, which made up an important part of *Progress and Poverty*, were generally similar to those of the classical economist Ricardo. But the book, which revealed a characteristic faith in progress, was much more than an economic treatise in the classical tradition; it also contained an attractive simple analysis of the American economy. According to George, the expropriation of land by a few wealthy individuals and groups had created the gross inequities of nineteenth-century America. His cure was the single tax—a tax upon the unearned profit obtained from land through the rise in its value, which he believed was caused, not by its improvement, but by the increased demand for it as population increased. Such a tax, which George thought would yield enough to pay all the costs of government and thus make a tax on land improvements unnecessary, would cause speculators to sell their lands at reasonable prices and would eliminate land monopoly and with it the main obstacles to individual progress—all without eliminating the essential features of the capitalist system. Although his analysis was unsound, his answer overly simple, and his whole outlook only indirectly related to the problems of an industrial rather than farming society, George did dramatize and analyze the growing sense of malaise of his time. It was not the single tax that attracted men as much as his suggestion that there might exist a simple unambiguous nonsocialist solution to what were enormously complex problems. As against the fatalism of social Darwinism, George's demand for action to change the course of American society seemed a tonic. Few Progressives supported the single tax as a solution, but many of them were either directly or indirectly influenced by George's analysis of why wealth was unequally distributed in the United States.

Henry Demarest Lloyd, like George, set a pattern for many of the Progressives of the next generation. A newspaperman assigned to the Chicago financial district, Lloyd soon became critical of many of the business practices that he had to report. As early as 1881, he wrote an exposé of Standard Oil for the *Atlantic Monthly*, entitled "The Story of a Great Monopoly." This article provided Lloyd with the formula that he used in 1894 in *Wealth Against Commonwealth*. In contrast to *Progress and Poverty*, *Wealth Against Commonwealth* offered no panaceas. Instead, it contained a mass of facts dealing with the growth, techniques, and effects of monopoly in the United States. Gathering his information from court records and legislative reports, Lloyd ignored or deprecated the achievements of big business. Essentially a believer in the Jacksonian ideal of free competition, he, like many of his successors, did not appreciate the cost to the economy of breaking up monopolies; nor did he understand that any return to free competition, even if possible or desirable, would merely reintroduce the struggle from which business concentration almost inevitably emerged. Lloyd's indictment supplied his readers with names, dates, statistics, and countless examples to substantiate the thesis of his title. His book was to be a model for most of the muckraking exposés of the Progressive era.

Starting with observations about the contrast between American ideal aspirations and the facts about business or city life, reform writers like Lloyd went on to isolate the causes of disease and then usually either to suggest some specific cure or at least to urge a search for some therapy. Underneath their analyses was generally the assumption that the American Republic had once been or was intended to be a society of freedom and justice for all and that, with good will and proper tinkering with machinery, all could still be put right. Whether fired by religious or secular idealism, the reform writers and the diverse reform movements often had a sense of mission, a feeling that they were engaged in redeeming the nation from sin or wickedness, and the conviction that this or that remedy would restore the world to those conditions in which character and faith would again work. The golden age could either be restored or still realized.

Henry George and Henry Demarest Lloyd were probably the most influential precursors of the Progressives, but there were many others who helped to prepare the way for the general upsurge of reform after 1900. The importance of these forerunners of Progressivism should not, however, be overemphasized. While the Progressives borrowed heavily, they were more than mere imitators. In contrast to many of their predecessors, they were able to make reform an exciting—and even a fashionable—adventure. Within ten years after Bryan's defeat in 1896, many of the things that he and the Populists had advocated had been taken up by the same respectable people who had rejected Bryan for his radicalism. The Progressives were able to generate a nation-wide demand for change that bore little resemblance to Bryan's special pleading for a particular group.

The Muckrakers

It was the good fortune of the Progressives that they articulated their reform program at a time when the American people were both willing and able to listen to their message. The depression of the

1890's had raised many doubts about the unmitigated blessings of industrial and finance capitalism, while the cynicism that often accompanied the get-rich-quick mania of the Gilded Age had begun to wear thin even before the appearance of the Progressives. Recent developments in education and publishing made it possible for the Progressives to present their ideas to a nation-wide audience. Because of the rapid expansion of the school system, more Americans than ever could read and consider the proposals of the Progressives in the popular magazines and newspapers for which they wrote. A number of able writers took advantage of these opportunities to dramatize the Progressives' complaints against the status quo. Theodore Roosevelt compared them to the character in *Pilgrim's Progress* "who could look no way but downward with the muckrake in his hands." Shortly after Roosevelt became president in 1901, the "muckrakers," as they were called, began to expose what they thought were the outstanding evils of American life.

Henry Demarest Lloyd and others had written exposés as early as the 1880's, but the muckraking technique was not fully developed until the end of the century. S. S. McClure was the first publisher to see the possibilities of the muckraking article. In 1893, he sent a writer to the Chicago World's Fair to gather material on the Armour Institute of Technology. When the reporter included some information on the meat-packing industry, McClure was struck by the potential appeal to American readers of factual surveys of the practices of the nation's leading business firms. McClure mulled over this idea for several years, and in 1897, he asked Ida Tarbell to prepare a study of the Standard Oil Corporation. After extensive and painstaking research, Miss Tarbell published the first of a series of articles on Standard Oil in *McClure's* in November, 1902. Miss Tarbell's reports were notable both for their sensational revelations and for their high standards of scholarship. McClure had not misjudged his audience; there was a sharp increase in the circulation of his magazine after the publication of the first installments of the Standard Oil series.

Ida M. Tarbell's "History of the Standard Oil," which ran in *McClure's* during 1902–4, quickly became a model for other contributors to the same magazine. Lincoln Steffens studied municipal corruption in a series of articles that later appeared in book form as *The Shame of the Cities*. Ray Stannard Baker uncovered the malpractices of the railroads, and Burton J. Hendrick used the facts obtained by Charles Evans Hughes' investigation in New York for an exposé of the life insurance companies. The muckraking articles in *McClure's* had a number of notable features. They were based on extensive, time-consuming research. A premium was placed on the facts, and an at-

A CITY OF 35,000-BARREL TANKS, OWNED BY THE STANDARD OIL COMPANY
AT OLEAN, N. Y.

THE HISTORY OF THE STANDARD OIL COMPANY

BY

IDA M. TARBELL

AUTHOR OF "THE LIFE OF LINCOLN"

ILLUSTRATED BY GEORGE VARIAN AND WITH PHOTOGRAPHS

CHAPTER SEVEN

The Crisis of 1878

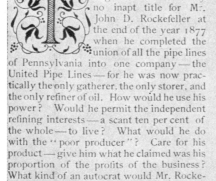

"THE Lord of the Oil Regions" was certainly no inapt title for Mr. John D. Rockefeller at the end of the year 1877 when he completed the union of all the pipe lines of Pennsylvania into one company — the United Pipe Lines — for he was now practically the only gatherer, the only storer, and the only refiner of oil. How would he use his power? Would he permit the independent refining interests — a scant ten per cent of the whole — to live? What would he do with the "poor producer"? Care for his product — give him what he claimed was his proportion of the profits of the business? What kind of an autocrat would Mr. Rockefeller show himself?

Serious Situation in the Oil Fields

The answer came sooner than was anticipated. It was hurried on by an unfore-seen and difficult situation — a great out-pouring of oil in a new field — the Bradford or Northern Field in McKean County, Pennsylvania. About the time that Mr. Rockefeller's lordship was realized it became certain that a deposit of oil had been discovered which was going to lead soon to a production vastly in excess of the consumption, as well as in excess of the then existing facilities for gathering and storing oil. If Mr. Rockefeller wished to keep his monopoly, he must, it was evident, enter upon a campaign of expansion calling for an immense expenditure of energy and money. He must lay pipes in a hundred directions to get the output of new wells; he must build tanks holding thousands of barrels to receive the oil. And all of this must be done quickly if rivals were to be kept out of the way.

There was no hesitation on the part of the United Pipe Lines. One of the greatest construction feats the country has ever

Muckraking Made Respectable: McClure's Conservative Format for Ida Tarbell's Exposé

tempt was made to eliminate, or at least subordinate, editorial comment or a moralistic bias. Although the articles were serious, the startling nature of their material and their lively prose made them interesting to the average reader.

McClure's success with muckraking prompted other magazine publishers to follow his lead. By 1905, *Munsey's*, *Everybody's*, the *Cosmopolitan*, *Collier's*, and the *American* were all carrying accounts of political and economic malfeasance and double-dealing. Thomas W. Lawson's "Frenzied Finance" was largely responsible for increasing *Everybody's* circulation from 197,000 to 735,000, while other notable muckraking jobs included such articles as David Graham Phillips' "Treason of the Senate" in the *Cosmopolitan*, Samuel Hopkins Adams' studies of dishonest advertising and the patent-medicine business in *Collier's*, Ray Stannard Baker's examination of the position of the Negro in American society in the *American*, Upton Sinclair's exposés of the meat-packing industry in *Collier's* and *Everybody's*, and Charles Edward Russell's description of the "beef trust" in *Everybody's*. Despite the effort of these reporters to maintain high standards, muckraking became increasingly sensational, and by 1910 it had lost much of its early objectivity. As readers tired of the constant stream of exposures, some publishers sought to hold their attention with articles that emphasized the spectacular while ignoring those features of the muckraking study that had made it valuable.

The muckrakers were always more adept at calling attention to abuses than at explaining them. There was a strong moral overtone in much of their work, for they generally attributed corruption or wrong-doing to the presence of "bad" men in positions of power. Reform was thus little more than a matter of replacing "bad" men with "good" men. Only a few muckrakers went beyond this point to ask why "bad" men had gained important offices in business and government in the first place, but the question was raised most notably by Lincoln Steffens. When he first began to investigate municipal administration, he assumed that "bad" men made "bad" governments. But he often observed that when reformers "drove the rascals out of office," the change had little or no effect on government. When "good" men assumed office, they somehow became "bad." Steffens believed that the system rather than the individual was at fault; the officeholder—whether good or bad—had favors (such as street railway franchises) to bestow, and the businessman had money with which to purchase these favors. The very public that condemned corruption in others had a hand in it for themselves. When a clergyman asked Steffens if he thought Adam was to blame, Steffens replied: "No, it was the apple." As time passed, Steffens saw

"The Recent Flurry in the Senate" (Puck)

no delivery from corruption except by abandoning the free-enterprise system that made private businesses dependent on government favors.

The muckraking, or reform, novel used a technique similar to that of the magazine articles and followed a pattern as rigid as that of the dime novel. In each case, an individual was pitted against a corrupt and powerful "system," usually either in business or government. Despite seemingly hopeless odds, the hero battled on until the last chapter, when his efforts were rewarded with the collapse of the forces of evil. By the final page, the "bad" man, who represented the system and who might be a machine politician or the head of a trust, had been routed, and the reader knew that the "good" man, who had done the routing, would live happily ever after. Of the many writers who used this formula, none typified it better than the American novelist Winston Churchill. After achieving considerable success with historical fiction, Churchill turned to accounts of New Hampshire politics with the publication of *Coniston* (1906) and *Mr. Crewe's Career* (1908). In both novels, the characters were essentially symbolic, and the corrupt bosses in the long run were always defeated by the virtuous reformers. David Graham Phillips, in *The Plum Tree* (1905) and *Light-Fingered Gentry* (1907), Booth Tarkington, in *The Gentleman from Indiana* (1899), and virtually every other author who used fiction to promote reform used the same successful formula.

The muckraking novel about economic abuses frequently became

"Knocking" Cattle in a Chicago Slaughterhouse, 1900

[BROWN BROTHERS]

a tract for a specific reform program. The numerous novels written by Upton Sinclair during the Progressive era were all cases for socialism. In *The Jungle* (1906), Sinclair's best-known book, the central character suffers almost indescribable hardships in the Chicago meat-packing industry. Eventually—that is, in the last chapter—he solves his problems by becoming a socialist. Although Sinclair wrote *The Jungle* to promote socialism, the book had a quite different effect. Because of its vivid accounts of the unsanitary methods used in the preparation of meat, it contributed greatly to demands for pure-food legislation. Other novelists, such as Jack London, used the muckraking novel to propagandize for Marxism. By mixing communist theory and criticism of capitalism with adventure and an exaggerated individualism that was often brutally authoritarian, London won a large audience of readers, most of whom had little or no interest in his economic theories but who may have found vicarious pleasure in the lives of his supermen-heroes.

The muckraking spirit also affected the writing of history. Against a tradition of patriotic and pietistic scholarship, many historians began to assume an irreverent attitude toward the American past, and students of sociology, economics, and government increasingly emphasized what they considered the defects of American society. Gustavus Myers' *History of Tammany Hall* (1901) and *History of the Great American Fortunes* (1909–10) were both muckraking exposés. Van Wyck Brooks in *The Wine of the Puritans* (1909) demonstrated his thesis that the much vaunted Puritan tradition was largely responsible for the poverty of contemporary American culture. In *The Spirit of American Government*, which appeared in 1907, J. Allen Smith shocked conservatives by attacking the Constitution as a reactionary and antidemocratic document. Six years later, Charles A. Beard's *An Economic Interpretation of the Constitution of the United States* reconsidered the Constitution in the light of the economic interests of its authors. Louis Brandeis exposed the power and depredations of finance capitalism in *Other People's Money* (1914), and Thorstein Veblen's numerous articles and books pointed out the contrasts between the existing economic practices of monopoly and the accepted economic theories of competition. The businessman was depicted by Veblen not as a hero but as a wasteful member of a leisure class preventing the machine and factory from fulfilling their possibilities of excellence and abundance, and giving prestige to an unworthy ethos of money-making.

These scholarly accounts reached only a relatively small audience, but there were also books designed to provide the general reader with both a summary of current abuses and a blueprint for a brighter future. The most important of these was Herbert Croly's *The Promise of American Life* (1909). It reflected the author's indebtedness to his Harvard teachers—the pragmatist William James and the idealist philosopher Josiah Royce—who had stressed the need for a common loyalty to a transcendent standard of justice as the basis of an acceptable social life. Croly was also influenced by the so-called "religion of humanity"—a secular faith of man's responsibility to his fellow man, dating back to St. Simon, the French reformer of the 1820's—which had flowered in post-Appomattox America under the leadership of men like Robert Ingersoll and Francis Ellingwood Abbot. *The Promise of American Life* was an exceptional book in that it criticized rather than accepted the Jeffersonian-Jacksonian traditions of a free competitive capitalism. Covertly attracted by power, efficiency, and service of the state—albeit a humane state—Croly tried to resuscitate the Hamiltonian tradition as a guide to modern public policy. Croly believed that "bigness" in America was here to stay and offered more advantages to Americans than the outmoded and wasteful ideals of free competition that many of his contemporaries were trying to save or revive. Croly outlined a reform program that was a curious mixture of twentieth-century Progressivism and eighteenth-century Federalism. He agreed with Hamilton that the government should be granted extensive authority over the lives of its citizens, but he thought that such authority could be used to fulfill the American ideals of freedom and abundance for all, rather than merely to accumulate wealth for the nation. Regulation, not destruction, of monopoly was the center of Croly's economic policy. His friend Walter Weyl also wanted to draw up a guide for a better America, but he made more of Jefferson than of Hamilton. In *The New Democracy* (1912), Weyl argued more strongly than Croly had that economic equality was a prerequisite of an effective political democracy. Much the same idea appeared in Walter Lippmann's *Preface to Politics* (1913), which repeatedly emphasized the intimate connection between economic power and government policy. In his next book, *Drift and Mastery* (1914), Lippmann wrote a brilliant analysis of the American sense of malaise. He argued for the abandonment of absolutes as guides for political life, and suggested the need for periodic reassessments of American beliefs and policies to test them for their pragmatic worth. To provide a continuing forum for the points of view represented in these books, Croly founded the *New Republic* in 1914. Although its circulation was always insignificant when compared to that of the "slick" magazines, the *New Republic* continued as a magazine of political and social criticism long after the collapse of the muckrakers and the Progressive movements.

By 1914, the muckraking era had ended. Readers had had a surfeit of sensational exposures. Some evidence also exists that the pressure of advertisers, on whom the muckraking periodicals were dependent, was partially responsible for halting the magazines' attacks on business. Most of all, the reforms of the Wilson Administration and the outbreak of World War I made muckrakers and their audience shift attention from abuses at home to problems abroad. For over ten years, the muckrakers had poked into almost every corner of American life. Although frequently simplistic in their analysis and limited in their scope, they often helped set in motion campaigns to eliminate abuses. If self-criticism is one of the measures of the health of a democracy, the success of the muckraking magazines indicates that, despite many problems, American democracy was flourishing.

The Struggle against Boss Rule

Progressivism was in many ways an urban counterpart of Populism, and many of the earliest Progressive reforms were directed against

New York City's Lower East Side Slums . . .

abuses that had come with the growth of cities. The rapid rise of industry had produced dislocations virtually everywhere in America, but it was the city rather than the country that suffered from unprecedented extremes of progress and poverty, degrading living conditions, and corrupt political machines. In their efforts to meet the many problems created by the new urban-industrial culture of the United States, the Progressives began the struggle for political reform at the end of the nineteenth century on the local level.

Municipal reformers had been battling the professional politicians since the 1870's and 1880's, but it was not until the 1890's that a concerted effort was made to overhaul the government of American cities. By 1900, every major city had at least one reform group that was trying to find a formula for destroying the alliance between wealth and politics. The task was never easy, for the success of the local political bosses rested on what appeared to be an unbeatable system. In return for the votes of the poor, the machine distributed favors that ranged from an occasional bag of coal to an annual outing in the country, while it obtained its funds from selling street railway and lighting franchises, building contracts, police protection, and countless other privileges to businessmen who were both willing and able to pay the price.

. . . And Brooklyn's Clinton Avenue, at the Same Time

[LIBRARY OF CONGRESS]

Despite the strength of the opposition, the Progressives attacked the machine politicians on many fronts, and they often won some noteworthy, if limited, victories.

Local differences at first precluded the formation of an effective national organization for municipal reform, but many of the Progressive mayors had a common indebtedness to Henry George. The author of *Progress and Poverty* had not been particularly concerned with city administration, but he had given what seemed to many observers to be a lucid analysis of the central problem of American civilization in the Gilded Age. Typical of the so-called Henry George mayors was Samuel Jones, who served as mayor of Toledo, Ohio, from 1897 to 1904. Known as Golden Rule Jones, because of his repeated attempts to apply the Golden Rule to public life, he fought the professional politicians and their allies among the business groups throughout his administration. When the Republican organization turned against him, he campaigned successfully for re-election without funds or formal party endorsement. When the utilities objected to his methods for awarding franchises, he came out for municipal ownership of the street railway and lighting facilities. When he antagonized the former rulers of Toledo, he went directly to the people and won them over to his idea that municipal government should be conducted on a nonpartisan basis. Following no apparent system and often giving the impression of extreme naïveté, Jones understood that there was an alliance between politics and business and that all vested interests had profited from the arrangement. Although there were obvious limits to Jones' idea that good will and sympathy with the underdog could solve the complex problems of urban society, he did grasp the fact that city life bred a perilous rootlessness and alienation of man from his neighbors. Unless some means could be found of creating common feelings of civic pride and of fraternity in the urban populace, all the positive possibilities of the city as a way of life would be squandered. Urban industrial society promised greater wealth and leisure for millions than men had ever enjoyed, but if it failed to give the city dweller and factory worker a sense of identity and of pleasure in his environment, it would leave behind deep and dangerous dissatisfactions that the enemies of the city from the time of Jefferson had recognized as the source of authoritarian and demagogic political movements.

Golden Rule Jones was only one of the many outstanding municipal reformers of the Progressive era who were striving to make the city a more humane place to live. Brand Whitlock, who succeeded Jones as chief executive of Toledo, was as successful a reform mayor as Jones. Tom Johnson, who became a single taxer after reading one of Henry George's books during a train trip, abandoned a successful business career to enter municipal politics. As mayor of Cleveland from 1901 to 1909, he won a national reputation for his campaign for home rule, the municipal ownership of utilities, and the single tax. Much the same pattern was repeated in several other cities. Mayor Hazen S. Pingree attacked the street railways in Detroit; reformers smashed the political rings that had formerly ruled St. Louis and Minneapolis; Emil Seidel, a socialist, became mayor of Milwaukee in 1910;

and New York City voters elected John Purroy Mitchel as mayor on a reform ticket in 1913.

No generalizations can adequately describe the accomplishments of the municipal reformers during the Progressive period. Many of their victories were short-lived, but they were also responsible for important changes in both the institutions and spirit of local government. In several instances they were able to gain an increased measure of home rule, although most state legislatures still had excessive control over the city governments. As a result of Progressive agitation, many cities experimented with the commission form of government, which had been first tried by Galveston, Texas, in 1900 after a disastrous tidal wave. The city-manager plan, which turned the government of a city over to a paid manager, also attracted wide attention after it had been successfully adopted by Dayton, Ohio, in 1914. Several cities sought to increase the power of their elective officials by decreasing their number. An attempt was also made to achieve greater efficiency in administration through up-to-date bookkeeping systems, executive budgets, the public purchase of supplies, expansion of the civil-service system, and training schools for firemen, policemen, and teachers.

Yet, despite the rationality and order that such "scientific management" introduced into urban administration, city manager plans and similar innovations often tended to be too rationalistic. Although they made city government more honest and gave the taxpayer his money's worth, they tended to be either short-lived, as Lincoln Steffens had complained, or they failed to get at the problems of social maladjustment toward whose solution Jones and others were groping. The very rationality of the new administrations made them seem cold and impersonal. The millions of poor immigrant factory workers suffered most from the confusion, anonymity, and heartlessness of the city, and the boss, whose cost to wealthier taxpayers may have been too high, did offer help to poorer citizens through "fixes" and winking at the law on behalf of the small shopkeeper or slum boy or girl who had had trouble with the police. In exchange for the boss's kindnesses, and with no taxes to pay, the urban masses thought a vote for the boss on election day a small price for the many little favors throughout the year that made city life more tolerable.

Partly because of their failure to build a bridge between the socially respectable old American families and the ghettos and poorer homes of the cities, and partly because corruption was always in the wings while reform enthusiasm petered out, the Progressives were repeatedly thwarted in their attempts to reform municipal politics. In many instances, the utilities that the Progressives wished to regulate were parts of powerful economic empires covering several states and exerting widespread political and financial influence. Lack of home rule frequently made city officials little more than puppets of the state legislatures and limited their power over large local-interest groups. Municipal reformers often sought to overcome these obstacles by transferring their attention to state politics. Tom Johnson, for example, campaigned unsuccessfully for the governorship of Ohio; Hazen S. Pingree's opposition to Detroit's utilities was at least partially responsible for his election to the governorship of Michigan; and Joseph Folk became Governor of Missouri in 1904 after smashing the political "ring" in St. Louis. Reform movements originating in the cities thus moved up to the state level.

The most famous of the Progressives in state politics was Robert M. La Follette. Born and educated in Wisconsin, he began his political career as a regular Republican. When he was defeated for election to a fourth term in the House of Representatives, he returned to Wisconsin and campaigned against the state Republican machine and its allies among the lumber and railroad interests. Despite the opposition of the regular organization, he was elected Governor in 1900 and re-elected in 1902 and 1904. By 1906, when La Follette entered the United States Senate, he had helped to place on the books statutes that became known as the "Wisconsin Idea." While La Follette was Governor, Wisconsin adopted the direct primary, passed laws to conserve the state's natural resources, developed an equitable tax system, and passed a body of labor legislation that included safety regulations, a workman's compensation act, and a child-labor law. Equally notable innovations were made in public administration. Women were appointed to numerous positions; professors from the University of Wisconsin served in various divisions of the state government in an advisory capacity; and nonpartisan commissions were established to regulate various economic activities. Although the state of Massachusetts had many of these reforms on its statute books long before the rise of Progressivism, at the time the "Wisconsin Idea" seemed a complete and hopeful novelty. La Follette's accomplishments gave a great boost to the Progressive movements throughout the nation. Wisconsin, which had been one of the most boss-ridden, interest-dominated states in the Union, within a few short years had been converted by La Follette into both a symbol and model for Progressives throughout the nation.

No other Progressive working to reform the state government achieved either the prominence or success of La Follette, but many others made notable contributions to the movement. William S. U'Ren, although elected only once, was largely responsible for Oregon's adop-

New York's Bosses: Thomas Platt, Republican, and Richard Croker of Tammany Hall, Democrat

tion of the Australian, or secret, ballot, direct primary, and initiative, referendum, and recall. In New Jersey, Republicans Everett Colby and George L. Record first proposed many of the reforms that were later put into effect by Woodrow Wilson and the Democrats after 1910. In fact, every section of the Union had its reform Governors. Albert B. Cummins served as a Progressive governor of Iowa from 1902 to 1908; Charles Evans Hughes was elected as a reform governor of New York in 1906; Hiram S. Johnson won the governorship of California in 1910 following his repeated assertions that "the Southern Pacific Railroad must be kicked out of state politics"; and Charles B. Aycock of North Carolina and "Alfalfa Bill" Murray of Oklahoma emerged as the leading reform governors of the South. Despite differences in approach and personality, the state Progressives had one common concern.

Without exception, they were out to destroy the alliance between organized big business and organized politics.

Throughout the Progressive era, the state reformers backed a number of plans for destroying machine rule by increasing both the power and opportunities of the voter. To enable the people rather than the bosses to select candidates, for example, the Progressives advocated the direct primary. In 1903, Wisconsin became the first state to adopt the direct primary for all nominations. Two years later, Oregon adopted a similar reform, and by 1915 some form of the direct primary was in use in approximately two thirds of the states. Yet, despite the enthusiasm with which the Progressives backed the direct primary, it, like the initiative, referendum, and recall, failed to weaken appreciably the power of the professional politicians. Frequently the machine was able to control the direct primary just as effectively as it had controlled the convention. And even with the direct primary and other reforms, it would be difficult to say that the quality of candidates or public officials improved so dramatically as to justify the high hopes that the Progressives had for changes in political machinery. Equally disappointing were the results of a more notable reform, the substitution of the direct election of senators for their selection by the state legislatures. Even before the Progressive era, several states, instead of waiting for a national constitutional amendment, introduced a system of preferential ballot that compelled the state legislature to choose the senatorial candidate desired by a majority of the voters. By 1912, twenty-nine states had provided some method to permit the voters to exercise considerable control over the selection of senators. The Seventeenth Amendment of 1913, which provided for the popular choice of senators, merely gave national recognition to a reform long underway; but, like the direct primary, it brought neither permanent nor dramatic change in the nature of the United States Senate.

In their efforts to strengthen democratic government within the states, the Progressives also had great confidence in the initiative, referendum, and recall. Through the initiative, a small percentage of voters could by petition compel the legislature to consider a measure; the referendum permitted the people to vote on a bill that was before the legislature. South Dakota introduced the initiative and referendum in 1898, and Utah followed in 1900 and Oregon in 1902. By 1918, twenty-one states from every section of the country had provided for the use of both the initiative and referendum. The recall, which enabled the voters to pass on the fitness of an official or his policies in a special election, was first adopted by the cities of Los Angeles and Seattle. After Oregon approved the recall in 1908, ten other states followed

"*The New Ringmaster*" *Tames All the Parties* (The Saturday Evening Post, *1916*)

suit within the next six years. The recall aroused greatest interest when it was applied to the judiciary. When Arizona in 1911 applied for statehood with a constitution containing a clause calling for the recall of judges, President Taft vetoed Congress' resolution granting admission. Arizona deleted the offending clause, gained admission to the Union in 1912, and readopted the recall the following year.

The Progressive era also had the effect of bringing to fruition other reform movements that had made only slow headway for generations. The campaign for women's suffrage, for example, which had had a long and hectic history throughout the nineteenth century, was given a marked impetus by the spirit of reform generated during the Progressive era and by the busy competition for votes that the intensified political activity of the age had stimulated. By 1900, only Wyoming, Colorado, Utah, and Idaho had given women full voting rights. During the next decade, women's rights made little progress, but between 1910 and 1912 five states amended their constitutions to include provisions for women's suffrage. By 1914, women enjoyed the same political rights as men in eleven states. Progress, however, still seemed disappointingly slow to the suffragettes, and such leaders as Mrs. Carrie Chapman Catt and Dr. Anna Howard Shaw decided on a campaign for the adoption of a national constitutional amendment. Through petitions, mass demonstrations, parades, pamphlets, and picketing, women's organizations aroused widespread interest in the demand for an amendment. This propaganda, joined with the belief that those women already with the vote held the key to victory in future elections, compelled the Wilson administration to come out in favor of women's suffrage. When the United States entered World War I and many women began to fill jobs formerly occupied only by men, the suffragettes were able to add one more argument to an already imposing list. In June, 1919, Congress approved an amendment that stated, "The right of citizens of the United States to vote shall not be denied or abridged by the United States or by any states on account of sex." By August, 1920, it had been ratified by the required number of states and became the Nineteenth Amendment to the Constitution.

When the Progressive era drew to a close after the outbreak of World War I, the reformers could point to a long list of impressive accomplishments in municipal and state politics. Still the basic tendencies of the Republic that Progressives had tried to check or reverse remained unaltered. Many Progressives thought that they had routed the bosses once and for all and that they had broken the arrogance of the corporation. Whether the reform enthusiasm of the usually non-political American public could have been kept up long enough to strengthen existing reforms and so to control the nation's drift to the big urban-industrial multinational society in which Americans now live can never be known. By 1914, the Progressive enthusiasm seemed spent or satisfied by the reforms of President Wilson. Most middle-class reform voters returned to their comfortable private lives. Some reformers moved into the prohibition campaign, which promised, like other reform movements, to make Americans moral by legislative fiat. Other reformers were silenced by the entry of the country into the World War in 1917. By the war's end, they had either made their peace with Main Street or awaited another round of reform after the war.

Despite the national revivalism that came with the Progressive movements, despite the money, time, and energy given by dedicated men and women to remaking America, events demonstrated that the Progressives had won a battle instead of a war. Critics have charged that the Progressive approach to politics was both naïve and superficial, but this judgment is not altogether fair. The Progressives had supplied the American voter with the machinery for self-government. If the people did not wish to avail themselves of the privileges won by Progressivism, they, and not the Progressives, were to blame.

Aid for the Underprivileged

The Progressives were aware that even improved political institutions could not work well in a sick society. They understood that many of the most distressing features of American life could be attributed to ignorance and poverty in the midst of plenty, and they advanced a broad program of humanitarian reform that was pragmatic in approach. Convinced of both the sanctity of private property and the right of the individual to manage his own affairs, they asked only that the poor be given a helping hand. They feared socialism and labor unions as much as they resented big business, but they insisted that the weak be afforded some protection against the strong, that the state assume a measure of responsibility for those who were unable to care for themselves, and that the poor be provided with at least minimum living standards and recreational facilities. If Progressives had a general ideal to justify this work, it was to keep as many citizens as possible loyal to traditional Jacksonian virtues by eliminating the poverty, ignorance, and immigrant's loyalty to the "old country" that bred disaffection from "true Americanism."

Within the individual states, Progressives sponsored a variety of laws to protect men, women, and children at work. Largely because of the agitation of the Progressives, several states took the first steps toward modern welfare legislation by adopting workmen's compensation statutes, safety and health codes, prohibitions against child labor, minimum-wage and maximum-hour provisions, and laws designed to safeguard women in industry. Toward the end of the Progressive era, a few states even undertook to furnish assistance to those who were unable to earn their own living. Arizona in 1914 became the first state to enact an old-age pension law. This measure was, however, invalidated by the state's supreme court, but by 1931, thirteen states had passed minimal old-age pension laws. Programs to aid mothers with dependent children were inaugurated by Illinois and Missouri in 1911 with the adoption of legislation providing for regular payments to women who, for whatever reason, received no other assistance in the support of their children. The pioneering efforts of the Progressives

Mrs. Astor's Drawing Room . . .

[BROWN BROTHERS]

to obtain social security legislation were limited in scope, but they
established a pattern that was to be widely emulated by the next generation of reformers in both state and national governments.

In their efforts to lighten, if not eliminate, the burden of poverty,
the Progressives considered no problem more pressing than the
wretched housing facilities available to the poor in the largest cities.
Jacob Riis and many others waged a valiant but unsuccessful campaign against the slums before 1900. Not until the new century was
any noticeable progress made in the battle against the slums. It was in
New York City, where the living conditions of the poor were as de-
plorable as those of any other American city, that the first significant
efforts to improve them were undertaken. In 1898, the Charity Organization of New York proposed legislation that would outlaw the most
blatant abuses, and two years later, it sponsored a widely noticed competition for the design of a model tenement. The state legislature in
1900 authorized a survey of New York City's and Buffalo's slums, and
in the following year, it adopted a law regulating housing facilities in
cities of more than 250,000. Under the provisions of this statute, all

. . . And an Immigrant Family's Home

[JACOB A. RIIS COLLECTION, MUSEUM OF THE CITY OF NEW YORK]

rooms and halls had to be ventilated, and certain minimum safety and health requirements were made mandatory. Although the new law outlawed the worst kind of tenement, it was another decade before there was any noticeable improvement in the slums of New York City.

Other states adopted legislation similar to New York's. In 1905, New Jersey passed a tenement-house law that applied to every city of the state, and similar measures were approved by the legislatures of Connecticut in 1905 and Pennsylvania in 1907. Most of the larger cities also raised their minimum housing requirements through revision of their building codes. By 1908, Baltimore, Boston, Chicago, Cleveland, and San Francisco, as well as New York City, had tightened up the regulations governing the construction of tenements. But new laws did not necessarily mean improved living conditions, for the Progressives were always far more successful at obtaining laws than having them enforced. Even in those cities in which the letter of the law was observed, overcrowding, filth, and disease remained the principal features of life in the tenements. A trip through the slum areas of any American city on the eve of World War I would have provided ample proof of the extent to which the reformers had failed. The Progressives, as in so many other instances, had called attention to the problem, but they had not been able to solve it.

The Progressives also attempted to provide slum dwellers with opportunities for recreation and self-improvement. No single institution played a more important role in this effort than the settlement house. In 1886, Dr. Stanton Coit established the nation's first settlement house, founding the Neighborhood Guild in New York City. In succeeding years, the American settlement-house movement, which was profoundly influenced by the work done at Toynbee Hall in London, developed with remarkable rapidity. In 1889, Hull House, probably the best known American settlement house, was opened in Chicago by Jane Addams and Ellen G. Starr; and at about the same time the Henry Street Settlement in New York and the South End House in Boston were founded. By 1895, there were approximately fifty settlement houses in the United States, and within the next five years this number doubled. Situated in slum and factory areas, settlement houses offered a wide variety of constructive activities to children and adults who possessed virtually no other means of escape from the stultifying and frustrating influences of their environment. Behind the projects, classes, games, and entertainments conducted by the settlement houses was a philosophy of reform that was admirably summarized by Jane Addams when she wrote:

> The Settlement, then, is an experimental effort to aid in the solution of the social and industrial problems which are engendered by the modern conditions of life in a great city. It insists that these problems are not confined to any one portion of a city. It is an attempt to relieve, at the same time, the overaccumulation at one end of society and the destitution at the other; but it assumes that this overaccumulation and destitution is most sorely felt in the things that pertain to social and educational advantages. From its very nature it can stand for no political or social propaganda. It must, in a sense, give the warm welcome of an inn to all such propaganda, if perchance one of them be found an angel. The one thing to be dreaded in the Settlement is that it lose its flexibility, its power of quick adaptation, its readiness to change its methods as its environment may demand. It must be open to conviction and have a deep and abiding sense of tolerance. It must be hospitable and ready for experiment. It should demand from its residents a

scientific patience in the accumulation of facts and the steady holding of their sympathies as one of the best instruments for that accumulation. It must be grounded in a philosophy whose foundation is on the solidarity of the human race, a philosophy which will not waver when the race happens to be represented by a drunken woman or an idiot boy.*

The growing concern over the need for adequate recreational facilities for city children was further revealed by the rapid increase in the number of municipally owned and operated playgrounds in the United States. With urban real estate at a premium, this problem of city living had long been neglected. As early as 1885, a group of philanthropic Bostonians had provided sand gardens for children, but not until 1899, when New York City opened thirty-one playgrounds, was the problem squarely faced by other cities. By 1915, when 432 cities were maintaining 3,294 play areas, the playground had become a commonplace feature of the American urban scene. With adequate facilities and supervision, playgrounds offered city children not only enjoyment, but also lessons in common action that were largely unavailable in other sectors of city life. The increasing number of fresh-air camps also gave a few city youngsters a brief chance at life in the country, while the Boy Scouts of America, organized in 1910, offered boys from town and country alike experience in camping and woodcraft. The establishment in 1912 of both the Girl Scouts and Campfire Girls opened up similar opportunities to young girls.

Additional recreational facilities in congested urban areas undoubtedly helped to reduce juvenile delinquency, but an equally significant contribution to the campaign to check criminal activity among the young was made by the juvenile courts. Recognizing that the judicial process used for adult lawbreakers was in many respects unsuitable for children, Illinois in 1899 became the first state to establish special courts for youthful offenders. By 1910, every major American city had followed Illinois' example. The juvenile court emphasized rehabilitation rather than retribution, and every effort was made to convert potential criminals into useful citizens. Although many selfless individuals devoted their lives to work among juvenile delinquents, few did as much as Judge Ben Lindsey of Denver. In addition to conducting a model children's court that won a justly earned national reputation, Judge Lindsey lectured and wrote widely on the most ad-

---

* Jane Addams: *Twenty Years at Hull House* (New York: The Macmillan Company, 1910), pp. 125–6. Copyright 1910 by The Macmillan Company, and reprinted with their permission.

vanced methods for handling young people who had run afoul of the law. What was wanted, Lindsey maintained, was not to instill fear of the law but to create a conscience and "character" that would shrink from crime.

The Progressive campaigns to make the city less dangerous to American ideals included an extensive health program for the underprivileged. At the turn of the century, a few cities undertook the medical and dental inspection of all school children, and within a decade and a half a city without such a service was the exception rather than the rule. Most major cities adopted milk codes to enforce pasteurization and prevent dilution, and milk stations in many urban centers distributed milk at cost to the poor. Baby clinics and visiting nurses assured infants of expert medical supervision and provided mothers with instructions on the most advanced methods in the care of their children. Many cities also established nurseries that assumed responsibility during the day for the children of working mothers. Most of these benefits were enjoyed almost exclusively by urban dwellers, but the establishment by the federal government of the Public Health Service in 1912 and the organization of such private institutions as the Rockefeller Foundation in 1913 indicated an increasing awareness that ill-health was a national rather than an urban problem.

During the Progressive era, as in earlier reform periods in American history, there was a marked upsurge in the century old crusade against alcoholic beverages. A militant prohibition movement had existed in the United States throughout most of the nineteenth century, but it had little to show for its efforts; by 1900, only five states—Kansas, Maine, North Dakota, New Hampshire, and Vermont—were legally dry. But the long years of failure and frustration were almost over for the prohibitionists. The enthusiasm for all manner of reforms generated by the Progressives provided the foes of the "demon rum" with a more receptive audience than in any other age in American history. Prohibitionism continued to be most popular among religious groups in rural sections, but the determination of the Progressives to root out every variety of private and public evil won the movement many new adherents who previously had little or no interest in the problem of strong drink. Important support was also furnished by employers, many of whom were willing to back any movement that seemed capable of enforcing sobriety among their workers.

The spearheads of the prohibitionist campaign were the Anti-Saloon League, which was loosely affiliated with a number of Protestant sects, the Women's Christian Temperance Union, and the Temperance Society of the Methodist Episcopal Church. All three organizations

Carrie Nation Took Her Ax
And Smashed Saloons with Mighty Whacks

[BROWN BROTHERS]

carried on an extensive propaganda designed to convince the voters of the need for outlawing the liquor trade. Under the leadership of Wayne B. Wheeler and William H. Anderson, the prohibitionists showed their skill at pressure politics. They established lobbies at the state capitals and at Washington; they organized drives for funds; and they injected prohibition into virtually every major political dispute. The success of these tactics was soon apparent. In the South, where it was claimed that the use of alcoholic beverages contributed to racial tensions, seven states went dry in the years between 1907 and 1915, and four others in the Middle and Far West quickly followed suit. By April, 1917, when the United States entered World War I, twenty-six states had adopted prohibition laws.

Despite repeated victories in rural America, the prohibitionists were still unable to rout the "wets" in the large cities. In 1914, for example, Chicago had more saloons than the entire South. Eventually it became apparent to the leaders of the movement that only an amendment to the federal Constitution could topple these last strongholds of the opposition. The United States' participation in World War I gave the prohibitionists their golden opportunity to save the Republic from the evils of drink. If Americans had to conserve food to win the war, the use of grains for the manufacture of alcoholic beverages was a drag on the war effort that could not be tolerated by patriotic citizens. Before the end of the war, Congress prohibited the manufacture or sale of intoxicants, and in 1917, both the House and Senate approved the Eighteenth Amendment, which forbade the "manufacture, sale, or transportation of intoxicating liquors." Ratification by the states followed speedily. By January, 1919, thirty-six state legislatures had acted favorably, and the Eighteenth Amendment went into effect a year later. The Volstead Act, providing the machinery for the enforcement of national prohibition, was adopted by Congress over President Wilson's veto in October, 1919, and the United States entered the "dry decade."

Although few leading Progressives played a prominent role in the prohibition crusade, the two movements had many points in common. The members of both groups were moralistic in their approach, eclectic in their methods, adept at dramatizing evil, and convinced that their own version of "do-goodism" held the answer to what ailed the nation. Like the Progressives, the prohibitionists were often willing to settle for a law that would control the symptoms rather than cure the diseases. As the history of prohibition was to show, the nation, for better or worse and despite the fears of reformers, was abandoning its old republican ideals and stern Christian sense of right and wrong for the wealth, comforts, and perils of an urban industrial society.

FOR SUPPLEMENTARY READING

The most recent general assessment of the Progressive outlook is Richard Hofstadter, *The Age of Reform* (1955). It can be profitably compared with the older study of H. U. Faulkner, *The Quest for Social Justice, 1898–1914* (1931). A. M. Schlesinger, *The American as Reformer* (1950), discusses progressivism in the general context of American reform movements. C. A. Barber's *Henry George* (1955) is now the standard biography. H. D. Lloyd, *Wealth Against Commonwealth* (1894), is better than any work on Lloyd. The muckrakers need new study but C. C. Regier, *The Era of the Muckrakers* (1932), can still be used. The impressive intellectual group associated with progressivism can best be studied directly. Read H. Croly, *The Promise of American Life* (1909); W. Weyl, *The New Democracy* (1912); and, best of all, W. Lippmann, *Drift and Mastery* (1914). There is a large and varied literature on bossism and civic reform. The famous work is L. Steffens, *The Shame of the Cities* (1904). Another contemporary account worth reading is J. Strong, *The Twentieth Century City* (1898). Few "case studies" are as good as C. McL. Green, *Holyoke, Massachusetts* (1939). A. Mann's *Yankee Reformers in the Urban Age* (1954) is excellent on Boston reformers. Of the many civic reform leaders Brand Whitlock's memoirs, *Forty Years of It* (1913), are outstanding and should be read with A. Nevins (ed.), *The Letters of Brand Whitlock* (1936). The various techniques of the urban reformers are surveyed in C. W. Patton, *The Battle for Municipal Reform* (1940). No one work does justice to the great upsurge of humanitarian work after 1885. Two "classics" that show radically contrasting attitudes toward the poor and the immigrant are J. Riis, *How The Other Half Lives* (1890), and Jane Addams, *Twenty Years at Hull House* (1910). R. H. Bremner, *From the Depths: The Discovery of Poverty in the United States* (1957), is excellent on its subject. On the prohibition forces, P. H. Odegard's *Pressure Politics* (1928) still has more to offer than any other work.

1 2

T. R., Taft, and Wilson

THE NATIONAL FLOWERING of Progressivism came shortly after the accession of Theodore Roosevelt to the presidency in 1901. Most of Roosevelt's domestic policies had been suggested by Bryan and other reformers in the nineties, and his record as a reformer never equaled that of such men as Robert La Follette in the Senate and George W. Norris in the House. But to many Americans, Theodore Roosevelt and Progressivism were synonymous. When he left the White House in 1909, he was succeeded by William Howard Taft, who, despite his recurring cooperation with conservatives, carried forward many parts of the program that had been inaugurated by Roosevelt. By the time of Woodrow Wilson's first administration (1913–17), the Progressive movements came to full maturity and long-sought Progressive measures were translated into law. Roosevelt, Taft, and Wilson used different methods to achieve their objectives, but they all believed that the nation needed and wanted reform.

The Strenuous Life

Theodore Roosevelt was born in 1858 of well-to-do parents in New York City. A sickly boy, he had a sheltered childhood and was educated by tutors until his family sent him to boarding school. After graduating from Harvard in 1880, he served for three years as a Republican assemblyman in the New York state legislature; as a member of

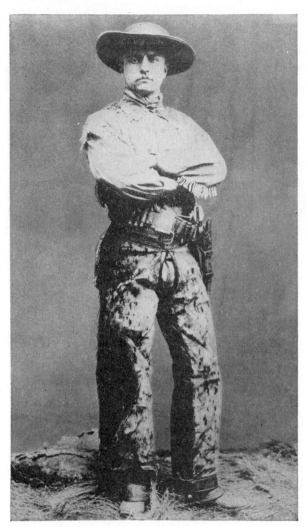

Roosevelt the Young Rancher

[THEODORE ROOSEVELT ASSOCIATION]

the New York delegation to the Republican convention of 1884, he opposed Blaine's nomination. For the next two years, he abandoned the East and politics for life as a rancher in the Dakotas, but in 1886 he was back in New York, where he waged an unsuccessful campaign as the Republican candidate for mayor. As a reward for his work in the Harrison campaign in 1888, he was made a member of the Civil Service Commission, and in 1895 he was appointed to the presidency of the

New York City police board. Two years later he became the Assistant Secretary of the Navy in the McKinley Administration.

Although Roosevelt was a nationally known figure before 1898, it was his spectacular role in the Spanish-American War that first gave him a unique place in American politics. When he returned home from Cuba a conquering hero, he was elected Governor of New York. Although his administration was a popular one, Roosevelt's independence satisfied neither the New York Republican machine nor its boss, Tom Platt. Consequently, Platt in 1900 decided to "kick Roosevelt upstairs" into the vice-presidency. Although Roosevelt at first announced that "under no circumstances" would he accept the nomination, and although Mark Hanna warned that Roosevelt's selection would mean that there was "only one life between this madman and the White House," the former Rough Rider was offered and accepted second place on the McKinley ticket. His nomination was due not only to Platt's desire to rid New York of its unruly Governor, but also to Roosevelt's tremendous popularity among the rank-and-file voters. In addition, his candidacy was backed by Boise Penrose and Matthew Quay, the Republican bosses of Pennsylvania. They had no use for Roosevelt's political views, but their objections to Mark Hanna's control of the party made them willing to support any candidate who was opposed by the Republican national leader.

Six months after McKinley's second inauguration, Roosevelt was President. On September 6, 1901, McKinley was shot by an anarchist in Buffalo, New York, and eight days later he died. Mark Hanna's worst fears were realized, and at McKinley's funeral he said to a friend, "Now . . . that damned cowboy is President."

During Roosevelt's Administration, more reform bills were adopted than in any other administration since the Civil War, but it was the President's personality rather than his program that most impressed the American people. The most versatile President since Jefferson, he was among other things an explorer, naturalist, politician, soldier, big-game hunter, historian, literary critic, naval administrator, and athlete. His critics often accused him of superficiality; although not a profound person, he felt at home with scholars and specialists and dispensed literary and moral judgments with gusto. Soon after graduating from Harvard, he published *The Naval War of 1812* (1882), which for years was the outstanding work on the subject. In subsequent years, he wrote *Hunting Trips of a Ranchman* (1885), *Thomas Hart Benton* (1886), *Gouverneur Morris* (1888), *Ranch Life and the Hunting Trail* (1888), and the four-volumed *The Winning of the West* (1889–96) as well as numerous articles, reviews, and editorials. Roosevelt, furthermore, had an extraordinary diversity of friends and acquaintances, being on good terms with kings, politicians, cowboys, writers, professional prize fighters, soldiers, and diplomats.

Roosevelt's versatility was matched by his spirited dedication to what he called the strenuous life. A man who often confused action with accomplishment, he frequently gave the impression that the ideal society was one in which all citizens were in constant motion. He exhorted the American people to "hit the line and hit it hard," and he made a conscious effort to live up to his theories. He killed a Spanish soldier in Cuba; he took his friends and associates on hikes that exhausted them; and a special messenger had to climb a mountain to inform him of McKinley's death. One critic thought Roosevelt "pure act," and an Englishman called him "an interesting combination of St. Vitus and St. Paul." It is impossible to doubt his physical fortitude; still, he repeatedly demonstrated that he lacked the staying power or interest required to stick by a principle that had proved overwhelmingly unpopular or that had lost its dramatic appeal for him.

Among Roosevelt's outstanding characteristics was a highly developed self-righteousness and a penchant for preaching to the people of the United States and the rest of the world. Confident of his own rectitude, he delivered innumerable sermons on any subject that happened to take his fancy. On a tour of Europe in 1910, he urged the French to have larger families, told a London audience how Great Britain should manage its affairs in Egypt, and informed the Germans that "one of the prime dangers of civilization" was "the loss of the virile fighting virtues, of the fighting edge." In America, he frequently lectured to audiences of one or more on the evils of being a dilettante, responsibilities of wealth, fruits of hard work, joys of family life, advantages of "strenuosity," disadvantages of cynicism, and the need for spelling reform.

Like most aggressive and imaginative people, Roosevelt enjoyed attention and acclaim. When he went west for the first time, he dressed in chaps and a ten-gallon hat for the ferryboat ride across the Hudson to his train. As New York police commissioner, he prowled the city streets at night to catch policemen derelict in their duty. In 1912, after being shot by a fanatic he insisted on making a scheduled speech in which he said: "I am going to ask you to be very quiet and please excuse me from making a long speech. I'll do the best I can, but there is a bullet in my body. It is nothing." His writing seldom left any doubt concerning the author's identity, and Harry Thurston Peck, a

Columbia professor of classics, said, "In writing one of his . . . books he used . . . 'I' so frequently that his publishers were compelled to order from a type foundry a fresh supply of that particular letter."

Roosevelt's enthusiasm and impetuousness frequently involved him in embarrassing scrapes while he was President. In 1906, for example, he became so convinced of the advantages of simplified spelling that he ordered the government printer to adopt it. But when the public refused to take the project seriously and Congress objected to the proposed changes, Roosevelt dropped the whole idea. On another occasion he joined with John Burroughs, the naturalist, in attacking the "nature fakers," which was the name Roosevelt gave to the authors of children's books whose descriptions of animals were more fanciful than accurate. This campaign also backfired; William J. Long, a Congregational minister who had been singled out by the President as "perhaps the worst of the offenders," challenged his critic's qualifications as an authority on wild life and maintained that Roosevelt's knowledge of animals was largely limited to the methods of killing them. While such incidents were trivial and tended to amuse rather than annoy most Americans, there were other times when the President's impetuosity produced unfortunate, or even tragic, results. For example, he ordered the dishonorable discharge of all the members of three companies of Negro troops stationed in Brownsville, Texas, after some of them had been accused—unjustly, as it later developed—of murder. This was the same Roosevelt who, in October, 1901, had shattered precedents and aroused southerners by inviting Booker T. Washington, the outstanding Negro educator, to have dinner with him at the White House, but Washington was not invited again.

Whatever the defects of Roosevelt's character—and it is easy for the historian to concentrate on bizarre episodes in Roosevelt's life—many of his contemporaries considered him the greatest man of his own or any other age. Lord Morley thought that the two "great wonders of nature" in the United States were Niagara Falls and Roosevelt. Rudyard Kipling, who had known Roosevelt in Washington when both were young men, wrote that when Roosevelt talked, "I curled up on the seat opposite and listened and wondered until the universe seemed to be spinning around and Theodore was the spinner." To countless others, Theodore was the spinner, for most people who came in touch with him—as well as many who knew him only through the newspapers—were completely captivated by his vibrant personality.

Roosevelt's critics have pointed out that he often preferred words to acts and that he would subordinate his principles to the main chance. Roosevelt may have been in some respects a "pseudo-progressive" but charges against his philistinism, lack of reasoned convictions, and authoritarian qualities still cannot detract from his contribution to Progressivism. With a flair for dramatizing the issues of the day, apparently inexhaustible energy, and almost boyish enthusiasm for every manner of project, Roosevelt became a symbol of the Progressive spirit to millions of Americans. He was not an original thinker; he possessed at best only a rudimentary knowledge of economics; and the lessons in morality that he delighted in expounding were commonplace. But these were irrelevancies. To countless reformers struggling against seemingly hopeless odds, Roosevelt made Progressivism a noble and exhilarating adventure. Frances Perkins, in recalling her early experiences in the Progressive movement, has written:

> . . . It was the era of Theodore Roosevelt, and we were all . . . under his spell. . . .
> Like many young people, I was an ardent admirer of Theodore Roosevelt. He had been a vigorous and educative President. He had recommended to the people Jacob Riis's book *How the Other Half Lives*. I had read it, and Theodore Roosevelt's inaugural address of 1905, and had straightaway felt that the pursuit of social justice would be my vocation.*

T. R. and the Trusts

When Roosevelt became President in 1901, he was distrusted by many Old Guard Republicans who viewed him as an erratic young man uncontrollable by the party's leaders. Roosevelt recognized that he had no party organization loyal to him as yet, and in his first term he used his patronage powers to try to make the Republican party closer to his own image. On the surface he seemed ready to conciliate the Hannaites. On taking office, he not only retained all of McKinley's cabinet, but he also announced that he intended "to continue, absolutely unbroken," his predecessor's policies. Behind Roosevelt's conciliatory attitude were two considerations. First, he realized that because an accident rather than the people had made him President he would have to proceed with considerable caution until the next presidential election. Secondly, he was a consummate politician who always knew that his ultimate success in office depended on the strength of his party. Under the circumstances, he could not afford to offend those who had to be his most powerful allies. Throughout his administra-

* Frances Perkins: *The Roosevelt I Knew* (New York: The Viking Press, 1946), pp. 9–10.

Waiting for Coal During the Strike of 1902

[CULVER SERVICE]

tion, he repeatedly employed the tactics that he had used immediately after McKinley's death, and he soon showed that his political genius lay in his ability to retain the backing of those that he presumably opposed. Even though he often castigated the "interests," the Republicans never lost the support of big-business groups during his presidency. He posed as an enemy of the conservatives and the professional politicians, but both groups stood by him as long as he was in the White House. Frequently he gave the impression of being an extremist, but in reality he never strayed far from the middle of the road, and in discussions of public questions he was usually careful to balance his "on-the-one-hands" with an equal number of "on-the-other-hands."

Roosevelt's ability to steer a middle course was illustrated by his handling of the coal strike during his first term. In May, 1902, 150,000 anthracite coal miners went on strike and, under the leadership of John Mitchell of the United Mine Workers, demanded a 20 per cent increase in wages, a nine-hour day, and union recognition. The operators, however, refused to make any concessions. After the strike had dragged on for five months and the approach of winter made a resumption of coal production imperative, Roosevelt called a meeting in Washington of representatives of both the employers and employees. When the operators refused to give any ground, Roosevelt announced that he planned to appoint an investigating commission and indicated that he might use the army to run the mines. At the same time, Secretary of War Elihu Root impressed on J. P. Morgan the seriousness of the situation. Morgan, in turn, induced the operators to agree to arbitration, and on October 13, they requested the President to name a commission. The miners then returned to work, and in March of the following year, the commission's report led to the establishment of a nine-hour day, the creation of arbitration machinery for the settlement of disputes in the industry, and a 10 per cent wage increase. The settlement of the dispute was a notable triumph for Roosevelt. Without permitting himself to be identified in the public mind with either management or labor, he had convinced the mass of Americans that he was working in their interests and that the government would see that they had coal regardless of who won the strike.

Roosevelt's middle-of-the-road policy—as well as his determination to move with caution during his first term—was also revealed by his attitude toward the trusts. By 1901, the trusts had few public defenders in the United States, and the question in most people's minds was not whether monopoly should be curbed, but just how the government should curb it. Mark Hanna and a few others still believed that the growth of monopoly was no concern of the government, but the vast majority of Americans believed that something should be done to preserve *laissez faire* and to compel businessmen to observe the rules of what had come to be known as "fair competition." The early muckraking articles and state and federal investigations of big business had convinced all but a small segment of the population that the trusts used "unfair" business practices, raised prices to artificial levels, and crushed the small businessman. Theodore Roosevelt was never an admirer of merely moneyed men and was not inclined to ignore a popular mandate. He quickly put himself in the forefront of the antitrust movement and enshrined himself in the public mind as "Teddy, the Trustbuster."

To Roosevelt, the problem of monopoly could only be solved by distinguishing between "good" and "bad" trusts. Although he never made clear the criteria of goodness or badness, he believed that industrial concentration was an accomplished fact that would have to be accepted even by its opponents. He therefore demanded regulation rather than extermination of trusts. Although he frequently gave the impression of impetuosity, he did not think that governmental action against the trusts should be precipitate or drastic, but he did think that certain minimum standards of business behavior should be enforced by the government. At times it was difficult to tell just where Roosevelt did stand on the trusts, a fact that was satirically expressed by Finley Peter Dunne's Mr. Dooley when he said:

> "Th' thrusts" says he [Roosevelt], "are heejous monsthers built up by th' inlightened intherprise iv th' men that have done so much to advance progress in our beloved counthry," he says. "On wan hand I wud stamp thim undher fut; on th' other hand not so fast. What I want more thin th' bustin' iv th' thrusts is to see me fellow counthrymen happy an' continted. I wudden't have thim hate th' thrusts. Th' haggard face, th' droopin' eye, th' pallid complexion that marks th' inimy iv thrusts is not to me taste. Lave us be merry about it an' jovial an' affectionate. Lave us laugh an' sing th' octopus out iv ixistence."

In 1903, Congress, at Roosevelt's suggestion, established the Bureau of Corporations under the Department of Commerce and Labor. The bureau did little regulatory work, but it gathered and disseminated information about unfair corporate practices. Through the use of what James R. Garfield, the bureau's first head, called "efficient publicity," it provided the Justice Department with the material needed for the prosecution of "bad" trusts, and it was able to arouse public opinion sufficiently to induce some corporations to alter their business methods. Most of the bureau's limited accomplishments, however, occurred during Roosevelt's second term. George B. Cortelyou, who was head of the Department of Commerce and Labor, was also Republican national chairman. Naturally, he did not favor any disclosures that would make industrialists refuse contributions to Roosevelt's 1904 campaign chest. A month before the election, Joseph Pulitzer in a signed editorial in the *World* charged that the Bureau of Corporations had done nothing during the 583 days that it had been in existence. He then added:

> Supposing, Mr. President, even at this late day, you were to give the country a little of that real publicity you once favored by telling it— 1, how much has the beef trust contributed to Mr. Cortelyou? 2, how much has the paper trust contributed to Mr. Cortelyou? 3, how much has the coal trust contributed to Mr. Cortelyou? 4, how much has the sugar trust contributed to Mr. Cortelyou? 5, how much has the oil trust contributed to Mr. Cortelyou? 6, how much has the

tobacco trust contributed to Mr. Cortelyou? 7, how much has
the steel trust contributed to Mr. Cortelyou? 8, how much
have the national banks contributed to Mr. Cortelyou? 9, how
much has the insurance trust contributed to Mr. Cortelyou?
10, how much have the . . . railroads contributed to Mr. Cortelyou?

For those "bad" trusts that could not be reformed by publicity,
Roosevelt resorted to court proceedings under the Sherman Act. The
first and greatest success in his antitrust campaign came in 1904, when
the Supreme Court ordered the dissolution of the Northern Securities
Company, the holding company that controlled the Hill, Morgan, and
Harriman railway systems. In a five-to-four decision, the Court ruled:

> It is manifest that if the Anti-Trust Act is held not to
> embrace a case such as is now before us, the . . . intention of
> the legislative branch of the Government will be defeated. If
> Congress has not, by the words used in the act, described this
> and like cases, it would, we apprehend, be impossible to find
> words that would describe them.

Although the Northern Securities decision was almost universally
condemned by members of the business community, it had little apparent effect upon their willingness to support Roosevelt for a second
term in 1904. Although some members of the party favored Hanna's
candidacy, he died before the convention met, and Roosevelt received
the nomination by acclamation. The Democrats, hoping to appeal to
the business vote, nominated Alton B. Parker, a conservative New
York judge who favored the gold standard. This strategy, however,
failed completely, and as election day approached, one prominent businessman after another urged Roosevelt's election. When the final returns were in, Roosevelt had won by 336 electoral votes to 140 for
Parker and a popular vote of 7,623,486 to Parker's 5,077,911. In a post-
election statement that he was later to regret, Roosevelt announced that
"under no circumstances" would he be a "candidate for or accept
another nomination" for the presidency. But his real interest was in
the present rather than the future, and he knew that the election meant
that he was now President in his "own right." For the first time he
felt free to carry out what he liked to call "my policies" and to give
the people of the United States a "square deal."

Four years of rebuilding the Republican party had also given
Roosevelt the controls over party machinery necessary to strengthen
the full use of the powers of the presidency. Roosevelt recognized that

justice for all groups in population

neither the American political party nor the Congress could provide forthright national leadership; only the President seemed able to claim to speak for all the people. In Roosevelt's view, he was put in office to lead the country and to bring Congress and his party into line behind him. When he thought that checks and balances or party or special interests were holding up some legislation he favored, he used the prestige of his office to appeal in the press to the people as a whole over the heads of party and legislative leaders. Such vigorous leadership marked the beginnings of what is now called the "modern presidency." Roosevelt gave the office of chief executive a prestige and power it had not known since the days of Andrew Jackson. But, with a national press, the telegraph, and the telephone, Roosevelt had more potential authority than Jackson could have had.

Much as Roosevelt relished power, he had come to understand some of the dangers of the concentration of power he was creating in the presidency. He was undoubtedly high-handed in handling the Panama Canal negotiations and in the so-called "Brownsville incident," but in theory at least Roosevelt thought two checks necessary on a modern president: "high-mindedness" and guaranteed periodic elections. The president's own self-discipline, capacity for a larger view of national well-being, and responsibility to his electorate—the nation— were the principal means he envisioned to prevent abuses of the people's trust and of the Constitution. Whatever Roosevelt's own failings in using the powers of the presidency, he did establish precedents on which Woodrow Wilson and Franklin D. Roosevelt were to build.

Following his election in 1904, Roosevelt pushed his antitrust program with renewed vigor. Suits were instituted against the beef, oil, powder, and tobacco trusts, among others, and attempts were also made to break up such railroad combinations as the Reading Company, the Union Pacific Railroad Company, and the New York, New Haven, and Hartford Railroad Company. While Roosevelt was President, the Department of Justice obtained twenty-five antitrust indictments. Roosevelt's accomplishments as a trust-buster, however, were more apparent than real, for only a few trusts were busted—and those that were soon reappeared in another guise, with their control over their particular parts of the American economy unimpaired. If nothing else, the Roosevelt Administration revealed that a government armed with nothing more powerful than the Sherman Act could not destroy monopoly as fast as the monopolists were able to destroy competition.

On at least one occasion, Roosevelt, who enjoyed denouncing the "malefactors of great wealth," was forced to acknowledge—and even sanction—the control of the trustmakers over the American economy.

At the height of the Panic of 1907, Henry Clay Frick and Elbert Gary made an early morning call at the White House as emissaries of J. P. Morgan. Informing the President that the complete collapse of the stock market could only be averted by permitting Morgan to buy Tennessee Coal, Iron, and Railroad Company securities from a brokerage company that was about to fail, they demanded assurances that such a purchase would not lead to the government's prosecution of the Morgan-dominated United States Steel Corporation as a trust. Roosevelt could not put off his decision, for Gary and Frick insisted that they had to have an answer before the stock exchange opened for the day. Roosevelt gave his assent, word was relayed to Morgan in New York, and the market was saved. Roosevelt later said of his interview with Gary and Frick, "I answered that, while of course I could not advise them to take the action proposed, I felt it no public duty of mine to interpose any objections."

How can one account for the failure of Roosevelt and his successors to check the growth of industrial concentration in the United States? Many trusts were old, respected, and powerful corporations with widely distributed securities. Although the American people enjoyed hearing their Presidents denounce the "interests," few were prepared to face the economic chaos that would have followed any wholesale and thoroughgoing application of the Sherman Act. Moreover, many trusts appeared to enjoy their advantageous position because of patent rights, and it was generally thought that patent monopolies did not fall within the jurisdiction of the antitrust law. Finally, whatever the President's wishes, the courts showed no disposition to use the Sherman Act to either preserve or restore competition. The Supreme Court was not inclined to consider mere size a violation of the antitrust legislation. Defendants were not held guilty for past violations of the law if they had abandoned illegal practices before being brought to trial. In a number of decisions the Court indicated that its rulings were based on the methods rather than the extent of concentration. In general, the Justices appeared willing to accept the elimination of competition if the monopolists refrained from using methods that were blatantly predatory. This view, which came to be known as the "rule of reason," was advanced by Justice White in 1911 in the opinion he wrote for the Standard Oil case; the authors of the Sherman Act, he stated, intended that "the standard of reason [should] . . . be the measure used for the purpose of determining whether in a given case a particular act had or had not brought about the wrong against which the statute provided." The rule of reason, which was closely akin to Roosevelt's distinction between good and bad trusts, set up a vague standard that permitted the Court to pursue whatever course it desired in subsequent antitrust suits.

Safeguarding the People's Interests

Closely related to Roosevelt's antitrust campaigns were his efforts to control the discriminatory rail practices that aided the growth of monopoly. The failure of the Interstate Commerce Act to check even the most flagrant abuses of the railroads had resulted in an increasing demand that greater authority over carriers be vested in the Interstate Commerce Commission. Despite repeated protests, the Act was not amended until 1903, when Congress responded to the pressure of the railroads rather than the public for changes in the law. Many rail executives whose lines had suffered severe losses because of rebating and other forms of rate cutting demanded that the government grant them further protection against cutthroat competition. Congress responded to these requests with the passage of the Elkins Act, which was designed to make the railroads adhere to their published rates. The Elkins Act, which was not concerned with the reasonableness of the rates charged by the railroads, consisted of little more than a list of penalties that could be imposed upon those rail corporations that did not play the competitive game according to established rules.

Roosevelt himself had little or nothing to do with the adoption of the Elkins Act, and no concerted effort was made to carry out its provisions until after the election of 1904. Between October, 1905, and March, 1907, the beef packers, the tin-plate combination, and the American Sugar Refining Company were convicted of accepting rebates. The American Sugar Refining Company's infractions resulted in a $300,000 fine, while a lower court decision that was subsequently reversed imposed a $29,240,000 fine on the Standard Oil Company. In these and many other cases, there was ample evidence of the widespread use of the hidden, or "smokeless," rebate. In an attempt to conceal their evasion of the law, carriers granted shippers rebates in the form of rental for a spur track, an allowance for fictitious damage in transit, a "refund of terminal charges," and "lighterage demurrage." Through these and similar devices, many railroads continued to violate the Elkins Act, and most students of the subject are inclined to agree with the commission's statement in 1908 that "many shippers still enjoy[ed] illegal advantages."

The Elkins Act, which was passed by Congress to prevent competing lines from destroying each other, left unanswered the problem of protecting shippers against excessive rate changes. Bills introduced into Congress in 1894, 1899, and 1902 provided for increased authority for the commission, but they all failed to be enacted. In 1904, at President Roosevelt's urging, the House passed the Esch-Townsend Bill, but the Senate, dominated by Nelson Aldrich and the Old Guard of the Republican party, refused to approve it. In the following year, after the President had renewed his demands, the House enacted the modest Hepburn Bill, and the Senate followed suit in 1906. The Hepburn Act broadened the powers of the Interstate Commerce Commission by granting it authority over pipelines, express and sleeping-car companies, and "all services in connection with the receipt, delivery, elevation, and transfer in transit, ventilation, refrigeration or icing, storage, and handling of property transported." On complaint of shippers, the commission was empowered to establish maximum rates, but these could be either altered or suspended by the courts.

Although Roosevelt had repeatedly urged greater federal control over the railroads, his stand during the debates on the Hepburn Bill disappointed many reformers. Following the bill's adoption in the House, it went to the Senate, where it was opposed by Nelson Aldrich and soon became bogged down in a controversy about the extent of judicial authority over the regulation of the railroads. The reformers favored a "narrow judicial review" in which the courts would merely decide the jurisdiction of the law. Conservatives advocated a "broad review," which would give the courts an opportunity to pass on the reasonableness of rates. Senator Benjamin ("Pitchfork Ben") Tillman, who was in charge of the bill in the Senate, introduced an amendment calling for the "narrow review" after learning that Roosevelt was prepared to back such a proposal. But when it appeared that the amendment would lose by one vote, Roosevelt withdrew his support, and the "narrow review" was defeated. Roosevelt, who did not wish to split the Republicans by defying the Old Guard, had surrendered to the conservatives in the party; and Progressives such as Robert La Follette never forgave him for what they believed was an act of pure expediency.

One immediate result of the Hepburn Act was an increase in the number of complaints filed with the Interstate Commerce Commission. From July, 1906, to August, 1908, more than 1,500 formal complaints were lodged with the commission, in contrast to the 878 complaints filed in the eighteen years preceding the enactment of the new law. The increase in the commission's business did not, however, foretell a corresponding increase in its effectiveness. The Hepburn Act did not permit the commission to pass on the reasonableness of new rate schedules; its authority was limited to the regulation of rates against which individual shippers had complained. As a result, the railroads were still able to raise rates at will, and the judiciary still continued to block any attempt to transform the commission into a genuine rate-making body.

Roosevelt's efforts to curb the trusts and railroads were paralleled by the first federal attempts to regulate the food and drug industries. For some years, Dr. Harvey W. Wiley, chief chemist of the Department of Agriculture, had been conducting studies on the effects of adulterated foods and drugs, and as early as 1902, Congress had considered a bill calling for accurate labels on drugs and commercially prepared foods. In 1905, Roosevelt recommended the passage of a pure-food law, and Senator Albert Beveridge of Indiana urged the government to set up a system for the inspection of meats. Meanwhile, patent medicines had been muckraked in both *Collier's* and the *Ladies' Home Journal*, and Upton Sinclair's *Jungle* had made countless Americans aware of the revolting conditions in Chicago's packing houses. All of these developments were responsible in some degree for the adoption of the Pure Food and Drug Act (June 23, 1906) and the Meat Inspection Act (July 1, 1906). The first of these measures eliminated some of the most glaring abuses in the processed-food and patent-medicine industries; the second provided for the federal inspection of all meat in interstate commerce.

Throughout his Administration, Roosevelt demonstrated greater concern over the lot of the workingman than had any of his predecessors in the White House. His role in the coal strike in 1902 made him the first President to view federal intervention in a labor dispute as a device that was not designed exclusively to aid the employers. In 1905, he recommended an investigation of child labor and the adoption of an employers' liability law; a year later, he warned against the "grave abuses" caused by the use of the injunction in strikes; and in his message of January 31, 1908, he reviewed the points that he had made on earlier occasions and then urged Congress to adopt a workmen's compensation law for government employees. Congress responded to the President's demands in 1906 by enacting an employers' liability act that covered accidents on common carriers, and when the Supreme Court declared this law unconstitutional, Congress passed a new law in 1908 that overcame the Court's objections. In the same year, Congress adopted a bill regulating the hours worked by trainmen and telegraph operators on interstate railroads.

Roosevelt's pioneering work in the conservation of natural resources was his most enduring contribution. Roosevelt had his roots in older pre-industrial families that were often hostile to *nouveaux riches* industrialists. It was not as difficult for him as for a factory owner to take a paternalistic interest in the rights of labor and to look with some scepticism on the claims of employers. So too did he regard the ruthless exploitation of the nation's resources as an irresponsible use of private advantage that the president as keeper of the commonweal had to check. In 1902, Congress adopted, with his support, the Newlands Act, which provided that the money obtained from the sale of public lands was to be used to reclaim through irrigation the arid regions of the West. Under this measure, approximately three million acres were irrigated within four years. Roosevelt also deserves a large share of the credit for checking the destruction of American forests by the lumber interests. While he was President, the national forests were increased from 43 to 194 million acres; reforestation was undertaken; publicity was given to the need for saving the country's timber resources; and the United States Forest Service was established to coordinate and direct the government's varied conservation activities. All these accomplishments were made possible in large part by the invaluable assistance given to Roosevelt by Gifford Pinchot, the director of the United States Forest Service. Equally important was the way in which Roosevelt publicized the need for preserving America's other natural resources. He sponsored a number of conferences that aroused the interest of many local, state, and territorial officials in coordinating all conservation activities, protecting valuable mineral resources and water-power sites, improving navigable streams, and making an inventory of the nation's physical resources. Even Roosevelt's most vehement detractors have found little to criticize in his work as a conservationist.

Some months before the election of 1908, Roosevelt had picked Secretary of War William Howard Taft of Ohio as his successor. The Republican convention, meeting at Chicago in June, duly nominated Taft on the first ballot, and Representative James S. Sherman of New York was selected for the vice-presidency. The Republican platform called for the continuation of Roosevelt's policies, tariff revision, and increased federal control over the trusts and railroads. The attempt by a group of western delegates led by La Follette to make the convention adopt a more radical program was overwhelmingly rejected and branded as "socialistic and Democratic." When the Democrats convened at Denver on July 7, they nominated Bryan on the first ballot and chose John W. Kern of Indiana as his running mate. In addition to a strong antitrust plank, the Democratic platform included demands for an income tax and the prohibition of the use of injunction in labor disputes. Taft, with 7,678,908 votes to 6,409,104 for Bryan, carried all the states outside the Solid South except Nebraska, Colorado, and Ne-

"Taft" at the Nickelodeon, Campaign of 1908

[BROWN BROTHERS]

vada. The electoral vote was 321 for Taft and 162 for Bryan. The election was in reality an endorsement of Roosevelt and his policies.

Having completed both his term as President and his task as President-maker, Roosevelt sailed for Africa to hunt big game. President Taft wrote ex-President Roosevelt, "I can never forget that the power I now exercise was voluntarily transferred from you to me, and that I am under obligation to you to see that your judgment in selecting me as your successor and bringing about the succession shall be vindicated according to the standards which you and I . . . have always formulated." J. P. Morgan, on the other hand, on learning of Roosevelt's trip, is reported to have said: "Let every lion do his duty."

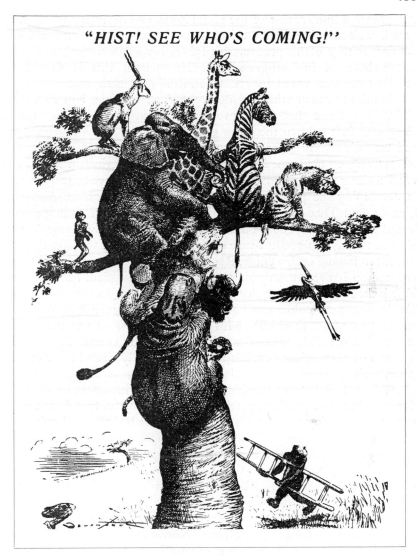

"HIST! SEE WHO'S COMING!"

Africa Awaits T. R. (Davenport, in the New York Evening Mail)

The New Presidency and an Old-Fashioned President

William Howard Taft, born in Ohio and educated at Yale, had practiced law in Cincinnati. Throughout most of his adult life he had held public office. Before becoming President, he had been Solicitor General under Harrison, a circuit court judge, civil Governor of the

Philippines, administrator of the Canal Zone, and Secretary of War. A genial, well-meaning man, he lacked both the political skill and the limitless energy of his predecessor. Inherently conservative, he nevertheless believed in "progress," but he thought that it should be achieved cautiously and by strict constitutional methods.

Unlike the man who had done the most to make him President and who believed that as the executive he had an obligation to lead Congress, Taft held to the more traditional belief that the legislature and executive were separate, though equal, branches of the government; Congress made the laws, and the president carried them out. Beyond making recommendations to Congress, he showed little interest in developing the presidential powers as Andrew Jackson, Abraham Lincoln, and Theodore Roosevelt had before him. An ex-judge who hoped that some day he would be a member of the Supreme Court, Taft was always painfully aware of the limitations that the Constitution seemed to impose on his office; Roosevelt, on the other hand, had often assumed an irreverent attitude toward the Constitution. Most of all— Taft lacked Roosevelt's ability to arouse the enthusiasm of Americans. To Roosevelt the public was his ward; he knew their likes and dislikes, and he knew how to publicize his ideas to them. Taft was never able to establish the same kind of an alliance with the voters, although his personal correspondence reveals that he frequently shared the views of the majority.

When Taft became President, the so-called insurgent or Progressive bloc in the Republican party was more powerful than it had been at any time during Roosevelt's Administration. Roosevelt, despite displays of independence, had cooperated with such Old Guard Republicans as Nelson Aldrich in the Senate and Speaker Joe Cannon in the House. By 1909, however, the Republican insurgents in Congress, who were mainly from the Middle West and had inherited some of the principles and much of the militancy of the Populists, were prepared to take over the control of the party. Under the leadership of Robert La Follette in the Senate and George Norris in the House, they were particularly keen on plans to overthrow both Aldrich and Cannon. Taft was in a position where he had to take sides, and he soon made it clear that he stood with the Old Guard. Although Roosevelt had adopted a similar policy when the issue was not as clearly drawn, he was nevertheless considered the nation's outstanding Progressive by many contemporaries; but Taft, by following the pattern set by his mentor, was branded a conservative. The Progressives were also disturbed by Taft's cabinet, for, although it contained three holdovers

La Follette Campaigning in Wisconsin

from the Roosevelt regime, it was also heavily weighted with corporation lawyers.

At the very outset of Taft's administration, the battle over the Payne-Aldrich Tariff revealed both the cleavage in the Republican party and the strength of the Old Guard in Congress. Roosevelt had managed to avoid the tariff issue, but for years the insurgents, the party's western agrarians, who looked on the tariff as a tax on the consumer to benefit the manufacturer, had been demanding a cut in the rates that had been established under the Dingley Act of 1897. The Republican platform of 1908 had advocated a revision of the tariff, and during the campaign Taft made it clear that he interpreted revision to mean reduction. On March 15, 1909, the President called a special session of Congress to consider a new tariff bill. Within a short time, the House had adopted the Payne bill, which provided for a moderate, but not drastic, reduction of the duties on a number of articles; but in the Senate, the Committee on Finance, of which Aldrich was chairman, substituted increases for most of the decreases and killed the

House plan for an inheritance tax. In its final form, the Payne-Aldrich Tariff Act established a higher level of rates than the Dingley Act. Many of its schedules showed the influence of various "interests" in Congress; it contained a number of "jokers" (such as providing protection for an industry in which there was only one firm); and the only duties lowered were those affecting industries that could not conceivably be threatened by foreign competition. It was an eastern bill that had been fashioned by Old Guard Republicans to satisfy the party's industrialists.

During the debate in the Senate over the Payne-Aldrich bill, a group of midwestern insurgents—among them La Follette of Wisconsin, Jonathan Dolliver and Albert Cummins of Iowa, Moses Clapp of Minnesota, and Albert Beveridge of Indiana—repeatedly criticized those features of the measure that they thought ignored the interests of the nation's farmers, small businessmen, and workers. Aldrich refused even to reply to these charges; and, although his opponents won the argument by default, he won the fight, for both the Senate and House approved the bill. Throughout the controversy Taft made no move to aid the opponents of the tariff, and when he signed the Payne-Aldrich Act on August 5, 1909, he was bitterly denounced by spokesmen for the small man in both the Republican West and the Democratic South. A series of speeches that Taft made in the West in September compounded the damage. When he spoke of carrying out Roosevelt's policies, he seemed a hypocrite to westerners; and in a speech at Winona, Minnesota, when he referred to the Payne-Aldrich Act as the best tariff act in the history of the Republican party, he convinced them that he neither understood nor cared about their problems. The result of the Payne-Aldrich Act and Taft's support of it was an East-West split in the Republican party; but this division was more than geographical, for among the bill's opponents in the West were some of the party's outstanding Progressives, while its eastern supporters included many leading conservatives.

The western opponents of Taft soon included the critics of Secretary of the Interior R. A. Ballinger's conservation policies. A Seattle lawyer who seemed to his critics at worst a thief, at best excessively legalistic in supervising the nation's natural resources, Ballinger was condemned by conservationists who claimed that he knowingly permitted private groups to take over federal water-power sites in Montana and Wyoming and wrongly supported the Guggenheim claims to valuable coal lands in Alaska. When Gifford Pinchot, the chief of the Forest Service, and Louis Glavis, the head of the Field Division of the Interior Department, attacked Ballinger's policies in print and public statements, both men were dismissed by Taft. However justified their removal—and by attempting to discredit their superior in public they gave the President no alternative—it shocked conservationists and convinced countless followers of Roosevelt that Taft was deliberately sabotaging his predecessor's program. Pinchot, for his part, hurried abroad to report to Roosevelt, who, after his trip to Africa, was making a triumphant tour of Europe's capitals.

The cleavage within the Republican party was further widened by the attempt of a group of Republican insurgents in the House to curb the extensive powers of Speaker Joe Cannon. Because the Speaker had the right to appoint all committees, he was in a position to name his allies to the most important posts in the House, while his rôle as the leading member of the Ways and Means Committee enabled him to determine in large part which bills should be considered by the lower branch of the legislature. Cannon, by using his authority to advance the cause of conservatism in the House, had turned his office into a symbol not only of Old Guard rule, but also of autocracy. In 1909, twelve Republican representatives indicated their objections to Cannon's rule by voting against his re-election as Speaker. A year later a coalition of Democrats and insurgent Republicans, led by George Norris of Nebraska, was successful in pushing through an amendment to the House rules that weakened the power of the Speaker by giving the House the power to elect the Rules Committee. In the following session, the same groups were able to strip the Speaker of much of his remaining authority. Under the new rules, all committees were made elective, and the Speaker's power was limited to that of a presiding officer.

By 1910, Taft had alienated all the major factions in the Republican party except the eastern conservatives, and the midterm elections resulted in an overwhelming victory for the Democrats. The new House contained 229 Democrats to 161 Republicans, and the small Republican majority in the Senate was largely nullified by the tendency of the insurgents to join forces with the Democrats. Roosevelt had bequeathed to Taft one of the most successful political organizations in the nation's history, but in two years Taft had reduced it to a shambles. Rightly or wrongly, the voters were convinced that Taft had turned his back on reform and surrendered to the conservatives.

Despite the Progressives' dissatisfaction with Taft, during his Administration several reforms that they endorsed were adopted. Roosevelt won fame as a trust-buster, but Taft attacked more powerful monopolies than had his predecessor, won more convictions, and collected larger fines. Under the direction of George W. Wickersham,

"Once clothed with power, now almost bare
He's lost his pull, but saved his chair."

The Fall of Cannon (Harper's Weekly)

Taft's Attorney General, antitrust proceedings were instituted against the United States Steel Corporation, the American Sugar Refining Company, the International Harvester Company, the General Electric Company, and the National Cash Register Company. Over-all, during Taft's four years in office, the Department of Justice prosecuted twice as many cases as it had during the seven years that Roosevelt had served as President. Other Progressive measures made law by Taft's signature included the Mann-Elkins Act for the regulation of railroads, the division of the Department of Labor and Commerce into two departments, the establishment of the Children's Bureau, the adoption of a parcel post law and a postal savings law, the creation of a tariff commission, and the enactment of legislation requiring publicity for campaign expenditures. During Taft's presidency, the Sixteenth and Seventeenth Amendments, both dear to the hearts of the Progressives, were also first proposed. Taft not only became the first President to withdraw oil lands from public sale, but he also created a Bureau of Mines, purchased a vast area of forest land in the Appalachians, and promoted legislation that permitted the government to conserve underground mineral as well as surface resources.

These reforms of the Taft Administration, however, do not provide an accurate index of the President's progressivism. While he continued—and even expanded—Roosevelt's antitrust and conservation programs, there were other problems on which he actively opposed the Progressives' objectives. For example, the bill that he himself had first proposed for the control of the railroads and that was introduced into Congress by Stephen B. Elkins actually deprived the government of some of its existing regulatory powers over the railroads. But the Progressive block virtually amended the original Elkins bill out of existence and the Mann-Elkins Act, which became law on June 18, 1910, bore little resemblance to the measure that had been advocated by Taft. The Mann-Elkins Act gave the Interstate Commerce Commission the authority to suspend new rates until they had been examined for their reasonableness; it outlawed unequivocally the long-and-short-haul abuse; and it established a Commerce Court to review the commission's decisions.* Like previous legislation, the Mann-Elkins Act fell short of the expectations of its authors, and its effective operation was soon impeded by the advent of war. On the other hand, it marked an important victory for the advocates of federal regulation. After a long and bitter struggle, the government had won the undisputed right to fix the rates charged by the carriers.

Teddy Takes on Taft

Regardless of Taft's status as a Progressive—and historians are generally inclined to view him as more of a Progressive than did his contemporaries—the fact remains that his effectiveness as a reformer was largely nullified by his ineptitude as a politician. Instead of attempting

---

* The Commerce Court was abolished in 1913.

to appease dissident groups within his party, he often gave the impression that he was going out of his way to antagonize them. In 1911, for example, when he returned to the tariff problem with a plan for reciprocity with Canada, he advocated a measure that once again was objectionable to the party's western farmers. The Taft program called for free trade in many agricultural commodities, on the one hand, and imposed identical rates in both countries upon a number of manufactured articles, on the other. To the western farmer this arrangement seemed grossly unfair, for it provided for a type of reciprocity that exposed him to Canadian competition while it assured industrialists adequate protection. Despite western opposition, Taft, with the aid of the Democrats, was able to get Congress to adopt his measure. Meanwhile, in Canada the Liberals, who had endorsed reciprocity, had fallen from power, and the Conservatives rejected the proposed treaty on the ground that it was a threat to Canadian independence. The upshot of the whole affair was that once more Taft had failed to achieve his objective and had further aroused the hostility of a powerful wing of the Republican party.

Granting that Taft lacked all the attributes that had made Roosevelt popular with the electorate, if his policies had been different, his prestige during his Administration might not have declined as it did. His friendship with the leading conservatives in the House and Senate displeased Progressives in both parties. His sponsorship of the Payne-Aldrich Act and the reciprocity program with Canada antagonized Republican farmers in the West; his record as an anti-union judge during his years on the bench had already deprived him of the backing of organized labor even before his accession to the presidency; and his willingness to advocate legislation favorable to the railroads seemed to offer convincing proof that he was not a genuine Progressive. Taft, in short, was satisfactory to no one but the Republican Old Guard, and by 1911 a large number of Republicans were openly opposed to his nomination for a second term. In January of that year, some of the party's insurgents organized the National Progressive Republican League to work for the nomination of a Progressive at the next Republican national convention. Its choice to lead the Republican party in 1912 was Robert La Follette. In December, 1911, La Follette began his campaign for the Republican nomination with a series of speeches in which he called for an effective antitrust program, the establishment of a federal commission to regulate business, the reduction of the tariff by a nonpartisan board, the direct primary, and initiative, referendum, and recall. But on February 12, 1912, after a savage attack against the "money trust" in a speech at Philadelphia, La Follette suffered a nervous and physical breakdown that forced him to withdraw from the campaign.

La Follette's collapse cleared the way for Roosevelt, who, after returning from his triumphs over the lions of Africa and the crowned heads of Europe, soon showed that he was ready to capitalize on the enthusiasm that the Wisconsin senator had aroused for progressivism within the Republican party. Roosevelt's decision to seek the Republican nomination in 1912 can be attributed to a number of diverse circumstances. One consideration was his undoubted disgust with Taft's record. Even before Taft's inauguration, there had been rumors that he had misgivings about his successor; and when Roosevelt returned to America in the spring of 1910, he informed some of his friends that he was dissatisfied with Taft's conduct of the government and that reading Herbert Croly's *The Promise of American Life* (1909) had made a powerful impression on him. Taft's refusal to reappoint several officials who had served under Roosevelt, his stand in the Ballinger-Pinchot controversy, and his decision to prosecute the United States Steel Corporation despite Roosevelt's promise to the Morgan firm, all contributed to the former President's willingness first to suspect and then to oppose his one-time protégé. Nor should Roosevelt's temperament be overlooked. He was still in his early fifties and, as always, ambitious; he had greatly enjoyed his years in the White House; and he had presumably learned to his distress that the life of an ex-President was little more than a series of anticlimaxes. Finally, Roosevelt was aware that his candidacy would be backed not only by many of the party's rank and file, but also by several prominent business leaders. Among the latter were George Perkins, a former Morgan partner; Frank Munsey, a millionaire newspaper publisher; H. H. Wilkinson, president of Crucible Steel; T. Coleman Du Pont of the Powder Trust; and Alexander T. Cochran, who had made a fortune in the carpet business. All these men were political realists who, knowing that Taft could not win in 1912, supported Roosevelt because of his popularity rather than because of his program, which, indeed, was still not clear.

After seven Progressive Governors—acting with Roosevelt's knowledge—requested him to be a candidate, he announced on February 24, 1912, that his hat was "in the ring." The Roosevelt supporters first based their hopes on their ability to capture the Republican convention when it met in Chicago in June, but this plan was forestalled by the party's regulars, who through the use of the patronage were able to control the convention's proceedings. The struggle between the two groups centered on a number of contested seats, and in almost every instance the Taft rather than Roosevelt delegates were seated. It was

Latest Arrival at the Political Zoo (Harper's Weekly)

no surprise that Taft was nominated on the first ballot, and James S. Sherman of New York, who had served as Taft's Vice-President, was again given second place on the ticket.

After an all-night session in the traditional smoke-filled hotel room, the Roosevelt high command decided to bolt the party and run an independent ticket. The convention of the Progressive party was held in Chicago on August 5. Roosevelt, having repeatedly announced that he was as strong as a bull moose, was the star, and the Bull Moose became the party's nickname. The convention was the national climax of the reform enthusiasms that had been building up all over the nation from as far back as the 1880's. It was attended by reformers, social workers, professors, members of what Roosevelt on other occasions had called the "lunatic fringe," businessmen, and some Republican politicians who recognized the hopelessness of Taft's candidacy. It was an enthusiastic and naïve gathering, manipulated behind the scenes by shrewd, professional politicians temporarily on the outs with the regular parties. Donald Richberg, who was one of the delegates, wrote that there "was room on that platform for anyone who had seen Peter Pan and believed in fairies." At the Republican convention, Roosevelt had said, "We stand at Armageddon and we battle for the Lord," and his supporters now took him at his word. The New York delegation entered the convention hall singing "Onward, Christian Soldiers," and throughout the proceedings most of the delegates acted as though they were attending a revival meeting rather than a political convention.

The Progressive platform, in addition to antitrust and tariff-reduction planks, called for female suffrage, the direct primary, increased federal control over railroads, governmental aid to agriculture, legislation to protect women in industry, minimum-wage and maximum-hour laws, and the prevention of child labor. Following the adoption of the platform, Roosevelt was duly and enthusiastically nominated, and Hiram Johnson of California was chosen as his running mate.

In the period between the Republican and Progressive conventions, the Democrats met at Baltimore. Many thought that Bryan would again dominate the convention, but it soon became clear that the contest was between several conservatives and Woodrow Wilson, a former Princeton University professor and president, who had won a national reputation as a reformer during his term as Governor of New Jersey. The leading conservative candidates were Oscar W. Underwood, a congressman from Alabama, and Champ Clark of Missouri, who had become Speaker of the House after the Democratic "off-year" victory in 1910. On the early ballots, Clark was in the lead, but, despite the efforts of his managers, he was unable to win over the supporters of either Underwood or Wilson. Even before the fourteenth ballot, when Bryan dramatically announced that he was shifting from Clark to Wilson, it was clear that Clark could not secure a two-thirds

ELECTION OF 1912

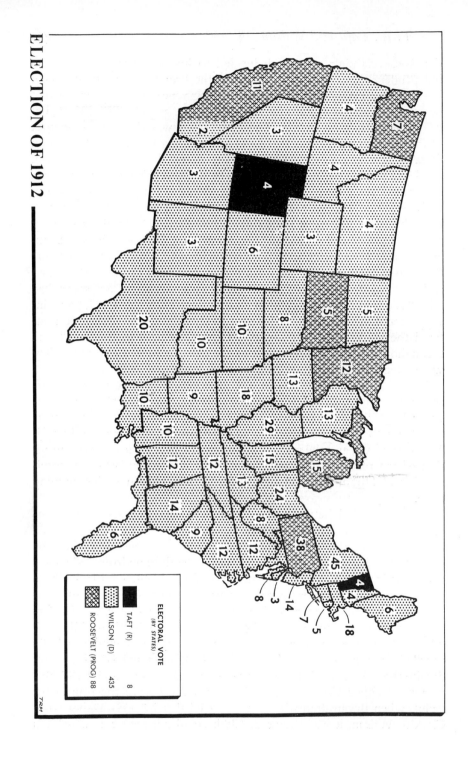

ELECTORAL VOTE
(BY STATES)

▮	TAFT (R)	8
▒	WILSON (D)	435
▓	ROOSEVELT (PROG)	88

TRM

majority in the convention. In the ballots that followed, the vote for Wilson gradually increased, and his ultimate victory was assured by a number of deals negotiated by his managers with some of the leaders of the party's state machines. It was not, however, until the forty-sixth ballot that Wilson obtained the nomination. Governor Thomas R. Marshall of Indiana was selected as the party's vice-presidential candidate.

Since Taft was supported primarily by the nation's conservatives, the election of 1912 was essentially a contest between Roosevelt and Wilson. Both men were Progressives, and, despite initial differences that marked Roosevelt as favoring regulation of big business and Wilson as a devotee of a return to *laissez faire*, by the time the campaign neared its end, their early differences had been qualified away; on the eve of the election, both men advanced roughly similar programs in their campaign speeches. Roosevelt called his brand of progressivism the New Nationalism, and Wilson appealed for what he entitled the New Freedom. Wilson's victory was the direct result of the split in the Republican party, for he polled less than 42 per cent of the popular vote, or less than Bryan had obtained in losing the elections of 1896, 1900, and 1908. Wilson received 6,286,124 votes, Roosevelt 4,126,020, Taft 3,483,922, and Eugene Debs, the Socialist candidate, 897,000. The electoral vote was 435 for Wilson, 88 for Roosevelt, and 8 for Taft. The Democrats also carried the House of Representatives by 290 to 145 and the Senate by 51 to 45. The election of 1912 was a clear-cut defeat for the Old Guard and its policies, for the Progressives, voting for either Wilson or Roosevelt, had overwhelmed those who had stood by Taft and the status quo. Wilson's victory signalized the national victory of the Progressive movement.

A Scholar in Politics

Woodrow Wilson was a skillful politician, a remarkably effective public speaker, an acknowledged authority on American government, and a moralist whose belief in his own righteousness sometimes resembled that of a Calvinist divine. Repeatedly he was able to beat the professional politicians at their own game. His public addresses were both models of clarity and moving appeals to the emotions of his listeners. He had spent most of his mature years studying the theory and practice of American government, and his books on this subject included *Congressional Government* (1885) and *Constitutional Government in the United States* (1908). He possessed a deep-seated sense of right and wrong that seemed particularly appropriate in a president

Wilson the Academic

who had assumed office at the height of the Progressive movement. Wilson was both the product and the maker of his times, and during his first Administration, the Progressives won their most noteworthy— as well as their last—victories in national politics.

Born in 1856 in Virginia, Wilson received his education at Princeton and Johns Hopkins. After dabbling in the law, he turned to college teaching and served on the faculties of Bryn Mawr, Wesleyan, and Princeton. In 1902, he became president of Princeton, where he introduced a number of notable reforms but was unable to work effectively with a majority of the university's trustees and alumni. When his position at Princeton became untenable, he entered politics and in 1910 was elected Governor of New Jersey. He had been a life-long conservative, had opposed the Progressives in New Jersey, and had thus greatly impressed several influential business leaders and the New Jersey Democratic machine who together sponsored the candidacy of this ideal man for a time of reform enthusiasm. Wilson seemed guaranteed to answer the revulsion against machines and "bad men" running through the electorate. Pressed, however, by the New Jersey reformers, he repudiated his former ideas and supporters soon after taking office. As New Jersey's chief executive, Wilson pushed through the state legislature a series of political and economic reforms that won him a national reputation as an outstanding Progressive. During the 1912 campaign, he put forward in numerous speeches a program that outlined the principal features of the New Freedom.

Wilson's conversion to Progressivism had come comparatively late in life. A southern Democrat whose position as president of Princeton had brought him in touch with wealthy trustees and alumni, he had shared most of the political and economic opinions of his associates. While still at Princeton, he had criticized trust-busting on the ground that it destroyed "individual liberty" and had announced his opposition to the "hostile" program of the "radical" Roosevelt. In 1908, he had stated that Bryan's ideas should be "knocked once and for all into a cocked hat" and that the Democratic party should again stand for the "conservative principles which it once represented." These views had made Wilson acceptable to George Harvey, the head of the publishing concern of Harper and Brothers, an associate of Morgan, and a wealthy man in his own right. As early as 1906, Harvey had begun to call Wilson to the attention of Democratic party leaders, and he had become the Princeton president's first political mentor. It was Harvey, moreover, who had been most responsible for convincing James Smith, the Democratic boss of New Jersey, that Wilson should be given the party's gubernatorial nomination in 1910. Smith, who had once referred to Wilson as a "Presbyterian priest," soon had had reason to regret his decision. The new governor had not only turned his back on the machine that had helped to elect him, but he had also deposed its boss in a victory that was so complete that he could write, "I pitied Smith at the last." Harvey, too, had soon been jettisoned. After Wilson had abandoned his conservative views, within a short time he had placed himself at the forefront of the Progressive movement. Under the circumstances, Harvey's outspoken support had become a liability, and on December 7, 1911, Wilson had told him as much. For the rest of his life, Harvey remained Wilson's implacable enemy.

When Wilson entered the White House, he had a definite attitude toward the presidency. He wanted to be a "strong" president who would provide the country with leadership, but he did not want to assume the rôle of an autocrat in his dealings with Congress. A close student of the English ministerial system, he considered it superior to the American plan of checks and balances. In Wilson's mind, the principal defect of the United States form of government was the separation of powers and the consequent rivalry between the president and Congress. To prevent such a rivalry from developing in his own Administration, he not only sought to dramatize the issues to the public as Roosevelt did but tried to work in close harmony with such Democratic congressmen as Carter Glass, Oscar Underwood, and Champ Clark. These men, as well as most of the other Democratic leaders in Congress, were southern conservatives and professional politicians. This, however, did not prevent them from pushing Wilson's reform program through Congress. In part they supported him because a large part of his program was similar to the one that the southerners had been demanding for years, and in part because he made no effort to interfere with the "bread and butter" side of the party. Throughout his Administration, Wilson gave little attention to the distribution of the patronage, and the task of rewarding loyal Democrats with jobs was left to Colonel Edward House, Wilson's close friend and adviser, Postmaster General Albert S. Burleson, and Joseph Tumulty, the President's private secretary.

During his first Administration, Wilson repeatedly demonstrated his skill as a politician and his ability as a presidential leader. By becoming the first president since John Adams to deliver his messages in person to Congress, he both symbolized and dramatized his sense of the need to build a bridge between the executive and legislative branches of the government. When it appeared that the Federal Reserve bill might become bogged down in Congress because of disagreements among Secretary of the Treasury William G. McAdoo, Representative Carter Glass, and Senator Robert L. Owen, Wilson was able to effect a compromise that was satisfactory to all three men. On still another occasion, when the Underwood tariff bill was jeopardized by pressure from various special interests, he successfully exposed the lobbyists in a public statement that referred to "great bodies of astute men [who] seek to create an artificial opinion . . . for their private profit."

The New Freedom

Wilson's views on social and economic questions were neither radical nor novel, and many parts of the New Freedom were as old as the United States. Some of Wilson's ideas went back at least to Jefferson, and his economic ideas were not unlike those of a nineteenth-century liberal. He believed that competition was the life of trade and that it was the function of the government not only to enforce competition on behalf of what he called the "man on the make," but also to see to it that competitors observed certain elementary rules of fairness. It was Wilson's conviction that a free capitalism was inherently beneficial but that within recent years its development had been

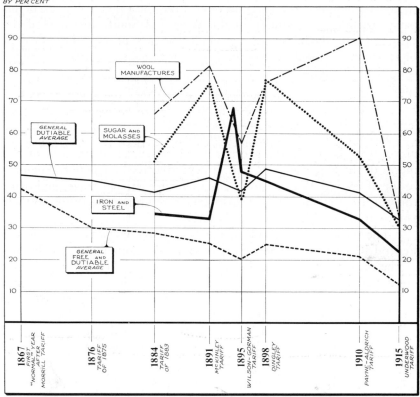

AVERAGE
AD VALOREM RATE
BY PER CENT

WOOL MANUFACTURES

GENERAL DUTIABLE AVERAGE

SUGAR AND MOLASSES

IRON AND STEEL

GENERAL FREE AND DUTIABLE AVERAGE

1867 FIRST "NORMAL" YEAR AFTER MORRILL TARIFF

1876 TARIFF OF 1875

1884 TARIFF OF 1883

1891 MCKINLEY TARIFF

1895 WILSON–GORMAN TARIFF

1898 DINGLEY TARIFF

1910 PAYNE–ALDRICH TARIFF

1915 UNDERWOOD TARIFF

The Tariff, 1867–1915

obstructed by the special privileges that had been won by the few at the expense of many. He wanted to return the nation to a heritage of freedom that had been circumscribed by high tariffs, industrial and financial monopolies, and the almost unlimited power of the employer over his employees. Even though any attempt to remove these drags on a free economy would necessarily entail considerable government intervention, Wilson believed that only in this fashion could the "unnatural" restraints on freedom of competition and equality of opportunity be eliminated. The system was essentially sound; it should not be destroyed, but cleansed. To achieve this objective, he successfully sponsored legislation that reduced the tariff, regulated credit and banking facilities, and curbed the trusts.

The Underwood Tariff, adopted by Congress in 1913, was the first part of the Wilson program to be placed on the statute books.

Although Wilson was not a free-trader, he believed that the tariff should be designed for revenue only. Like the other members of his party—particularly those from the West and South—he opposed the existing tariff schedules on the grounds that they prompted the growth of trusts and enabled favored businessmen to gain an unfair advantage over their foreign competitors at the expense of the American consumer. The Underwood Tariff lowered duties on more than 900 articles and provided for only 86 increases. Ad valorem duties were substituted for specific rates; many raw materials were placed on the free list; and the duties on most manufactured goods were reduced. Provision was also made for a graduated income tax. Regardless of the merits of the Underwood Tariff, it never received a fair test. The outbreak of World War I soon disrupted international trade, and after the war, the Republicans lost little time in returning the nation to their party's traditional high-tariff policy.

The second major plank of the New Freedom became law in the Federal Reserve Act. The report of the Pujo Committee in February of the same year had revealed the existence of a "money trust" that controlled a number of the nation's leading industries. There were, moreover, two inherent defects in the national banking system that had long been recognized by reformers and businessmen alike. It provided the country with an inelastic currency that did not expand and contract in accordance with the needs of the business community, and it contained no method by which healthy banks could come to the assistance of hard-pressed institutions during a financial panic. In 1908, Congress attempted to insure against a repetition of the events of the Panic of 1907 with the passage of the Aldrich-Vreeland Act, which permitted banks during a financial crisis to issue bank notes against government securities and some types of commercial paper. This measure, however, was admittedly only a palliative, and the bill also called for the creation of a commission to recommend reforms in the banking system. The commission's report, which appeared in 1912, recommended a plan that would have placed the sole control of American banking in the hands of the nation's bankers. In rejecting the suggestions of the commission, Wilson proposed the establishment of a banking system that would provide an elastic currency based on commercial and agricultural assets rather than government bonds, decentralized public control, and some means for the rapid mobilization of bank reserves during a period of crisis. All of Wilson's suggestions were incorporated in the Federal Reserve Act of December, 1913. This measure provided for the establishment of from eight to twelve Federal Reserve banks, which would serve as central banks in their respective districts. The policies of the Reserve banks were to be formulated and supervised by the Federal Reserve Board. Membership in the system was to include all national banks as well as those state banks and trust companies that met certain specified requirements. The regional Reserve banks were authorized to hold deposits for member banks, clear their checks, discount the paper of member banks and fix discount rates, and issue Federal Reserve notes and bank notes. Under the new system, the country was provided with a more elastic currency, a more equitable distribution of the nation's financial resources, an added curb on speculation, and a form of federal administration that was characterized by a skillful blend of centralized and regional control. The measure still did not, however, meet the historic needs of the farmers for long-term, readily available credit.

In asking Congress for antitrust legislation, Wilson repeated his belief in competition and stated that the government had an obligation to "make men in a small way of business as free to succeed as men in a big way." Unlike Roosevelt, Wilson did not differentiate between good and bad trusts, for he considered any form of industrial concentration an obnoxious deviation from the desired norm of competition. Wilson's first instinct about big business was that the only way to handle the trust problem was "to kill monopoly in the seed." On the other hand, he was not opposed to mere size, and on one occasion he said: "I am for big business and I am against the trusts. Any man who can survive by his brains, any man who can put the others out of business by making the thing cheaper to the consumer at the same time that he is increasing its intrinsic value and quality, I take my hat off to."

In an effort to create an environment favorable to a competitive economy, Congress in 1914 went beyond some of Wilson's intentions and adopted the Federal Trade Commission Act and the Clayton Antitrust Act. The Federal Trade Commission Act provided for a five-man group to be appointed by the president and approved by the Senate. The commission, which supplanted the Bureau of Corporations, was empowered to "gather and compile information concerning . . . the organization, business, conduct, practices, and management of any corporation engaged in commerce" and to "prevent persons, partnerships, or corporations . . . from using unfair methods of competition." To enforce its decisions, the commission was authorized to issue "cease and desist" orders. Corporations engaged in interstate commerce were required to "file with the commission . . . annual or special [reports] . . . or answers in writing to specific questions, furnishing to the commission such information as it may require as to the organization, business, conduct, practices, management, and relation to other corporations, partnerships, and individuals of the respective corporations filing such reports."

The Clayton Antitrust Act, apart from its sections dealing exclusively with freedom of labor to organize, was an attempt to reduce the generalizations of the Sherman Act by providing an itemized list of those corporate activities that constituted restraint of trade. Among the practices forbidden by the act were price discrimination among purchasers, exclusive or tying clauses in contracts, intercorporate stockholdings, and interlocking directorates. These practices, however, were not entirely proscribed, for the Clayton Act specifically stated that they were to be considered illegal only when they tended to eliminate competition. In an effort to increase the possibility of enforcing the antitrust laws, the Act further provided that whenever a corporation violated an antitrust statute, its responsible officers were to be punished by a fine of not more than $5,000 or by imprisonment for not more than one year, or by both.

The Federal Trade Commission and Clayton Acts did not live up to the expectations of their authors. Soon after their enactment, the Wilson Administration, confronted by the task of preparing for war, realized that the success of industrial mobilization depended upon the same monopolies that it had once hoped to destroy, and no attempt was made to enforce the antitrust laws during the war years. After the war, successive Republican administrations showed no disposition to revive the antitrust crusade. The Federal Trade Commission, originally conceived as a government watchdog that would ferret out and eliminate specific restrictions or destruction of competition, developed into a routine investigating agency. Like so many other government bureaus set up to regulate business, the commission soon assumed many of the ideals of the very groups it was seeking to regulate. The Clayton Act proved to be no more effective than the Sherman Act. Judges, who were given wide discretion in determining whether corporate practices listed in the measure actually lessened competition, handed down a series of decisions during the 1920's that in effect nullified most of its provisions.

The failure of the federal government to eliminate monopoly was largely the result of a dilemma that the American people could not resolve. Most Americans in the decades preceding World War I opposed big business, but, like Wilson, they were even more hostile to big government. Monopoly could have been destroyed by an all-powerful state, but the cure was feared more than the disease. Consequently, no course remained open for the government but to make solemn gestures toward the restoration of competition, while at the same time it made no move to alter the structure of American industry in any of its fundamentals. Like pronouncements against sin, the government's anti-trust campaign appealed to the popular conscience without damaging anyone's interests.

Although the tariff, banking, and antitrust laws were the corner-stones of the New Freedom, they comprised only a partial list of the reform measures that Wilson sponsored. At first convinced that his three major laws had finished the job he had been elected to do, Wilson then faced a rising tide of hostility from still dissatisfied reform groups. Democratic setbacks in the "off year" elections of 1914 and threats from the reformers pushed Wilson further along the road of Progressivism. Particularly notable were numerous measures to safe-guard and strengthen the position of workingmen and farmers. In ad-dition to the labor provisions in the Clayton Act, Wilson had to dem-onstrate in other ways his friendly attitude toward the workers. As his Secretary of Labor, he had selected William B. Wilson, a member of the United Mine Workers who had been proposed for the post by the American Federation of Labor. As the election of 1916 neared, Con-gress adopted the Adamson Act (1916), which established an eight-hour day for workers on interstate railways; a Workmen's Compensa-tion Act that covered Federal employees; the Keating-Owen Child Labor Act (1916),* which prohibited the employment of children under fourteen years of age in industries that produced goods for in-terstate trade; and the La Follette Seamen's Act (1915), which marked the first attempt by Congress to establish minimum standards for the working conditions of seamen in the merchant marine.

The first Wilson Administration was also forced to give assistance to the farmers. To furnish farmers with long-sought credit facilities comparable to those enjoyed by businessmen, Congress in 1916 ap-proved the Federal Farm Loan Act. Under this measure, twelve Fed-eral land banks were established to make loans at easy rates to individ-ual farmers. The farmers were also assisted by the Grain Standards and Bonded Warehouse Acts; the Smith-Lever Act of 1914, which made possible farm demonstration work in rural communities; and the Smith-Hughes Act of 1917, which provided further funds for agricultural education.

Woodrow Wilson's first Administration marked the culmination, if not the end, of the Progressive movement. Either out of conviction or fear of real radicalism and loss of political power, Wilson had trans-formed the aspirations of the Progressives into a national program of

* This measure was subsequently declared unconstitutional by the Supreme Court.

"The Eight-Hour Glass": Would the Adamson Act Bring Votes?
(The Saturday Evening Post, *1916*)

reform that had been adopted by Congress with only minor changes. Never a radical, he had not sought to change the pattern of American political or economic life in any of its fundamentals. Indeed, national life was not substantially altered by Wilson. He had given the going system needed safety valves and adjustments. Many businessmen looked on him as almost a revolutionary, but in reality he had done little that threatened either their income or power. What he had done was to show some concern for the hitherto forgotten men of the American economy. The small entrepreneur, importer, worker, and farmer had for the first time since the Civil War received some benefits from a government that had formerly bestowed its principal favors on big business.

In 1912, Wilson had campaigned for the New Freedom; four years later his party's slogan was: "He Kept Us Out of War." The election of 1916 marked the end of one of the most notable reform eras in American history. The New Freedom was dead, and the American people had grown tired of reform; certainly the war left little time for domestic issues. In any event, by 1916, Wilson had completed his program. To complain, as many critics have, that the Progressives left much work still to be done ignores their major accomplishments. Despite doctrinaire and utopian tendencies, they had attacked the outstanding abuses of their society with vigor and enthusiasm and had driven a few sizable wedges into the ranks of the nation's privileged. One measure of their success is gained by comparing the administrations of Harrison and McKinley with those of Roosevelt, Taft, and Wilson.

FOR SUPPLEMENTARY READING

Great interest in Theodore Roosevelt and Woodrow Wilson in recent years has produced a number of studies. The best full biography of T. R. is still an older book, H. F. Pringle's *Theodore Roosevelt* (1931) (Pb), but on Wilson use the fresh A. C. Walworth, *Woodrow Wilson* (2 vols., 1958). Pringle is also the author of *The Life and Times of William Howard Taft* (2 vols., 1939). First introductions to the politics of the reform presidents are both by J. M. Blum, *The Republican Roosevelt* (1954) and *Woodrow Wilson and the Politics of Morality* (1956) .The progressivism of 1912 is highlighted in Wilson's *The New Freedom* (1913) and Roosevelt's *The New Nationalism* (1913). LaFollette has two affectionate biographers in Belle Case and Fola LaFollette, *Robert M. LaFollette* (2 vols., 1953). K. Hechler, *Insurgency* (1940), and R. Nye, *Midwestern Progressive Politics* (1951), have much on LaFollette's reformism. Two fine general syntheses on the Progressive years are G. Mowry, *The Era of Theodore Roosevelt* (1953), and A. S. Link, *Woodrow Wilson and the Progressive Era* (1954). Both Link and Mowry have other important books on the period that should be read. On the trusts use H. B. Thorelli, *The Federal Antitrust Policy* (1955), and on conservation, S. P. Hays's *Conservation and the Gospel of Efficiency* (1959).

PART III

WAR, BOOM, AND BUST

[BROWN BROTHERS]

13

The Profits and Price of Peace

INETEENTH-CENTURY AMERICANS tended to view the Atlantic Ocean as both a barrier and a highway. It prevented European wars from reaching the Western hemisphere, and it also carried trade between the Old World and the New. American isolationism, based on the dual conception of the Atlantic as a defensive wall and a commercial highway, was impossible during the Napoleonic Wars. The Atlantic trade was disrupted, and Europe's war spread to North America. But between the Treaty of Ghent and World War I, American isolation proved to be highly effective. For a hundred years, Americans were able to keep out of Europe's conflicts, while their overseas trade increased. Fortunately for America, no general European war occurred during that century. In 1917, however, the American people were again forced to the conclusions of 1812. Once more the Atlantic had become a military as well as an economic highway. With the return of peace, the United States Senate ignored the lessons of 1917 in a futile attempt to apply a nineteenth-century policy in a twentieth-century world.

The United States and England, 1870–1914

World War I was precipitated by the assassination of the Austrian Archduke at Sarajevo on June 28, 1914, but it was the culmination of decades of economic rivalry, armament races, balance-of-power politics, heightened nationalism, and chaos resulting from the absence of either international law or morality. The precise responsibility of any particular country for the collapse of international peace in 1914 is impossible to ascertain. Germany hoped that a system of alliances and an aggressive foreign policy would enable it to obtain colonies and hold on to or increase the gains of the Franco-German War; Russia and Austria-Hungary were both prepared to counter any threat to their influence in the Slavic world; France was seeking Alsace-Lorraine and revenge for the defeat of 1870–1; England was determined to maintain the balance of power on the continent and to protect its great empire; Italy was ready to embark on any adventure that might transform it from a minor to a major power. For more than half a century, these ambitions had tended to cancel each other out as the European balance of power managed to survive a series of nerve-wracking crises. But in 1914 the delicate equilibrium produced by mutual stresses and strains broke down completely, and, for the first time since the end of the struggle against Napoleon in 1815, a small conflict developed into a general European war.

Although most Americans had little or no interest in the rivalries of the European nations during the half-century that preceded the outbreak of war in 1914, American diplomats in the same period became increasingly aware that their country could no longer afford to play the role of an aloof bystander in the struggle among the world's leading powers. The American policy of overseas expansion and American diplomatic isolation from Europe were not always compatible, for the American advance across the Pacific had brought the United States face-to-face with the most powerful nations of Europe. A decision on the future of Samoa, for example, was not an exclusively American problem, but merely a part of a much larger problem involving the world-wide interests of both Germany and England. If the United States wanted to play the part of a world power, it could no longer ignore the policies of other great powers. Despite traditional American attitudes, the United States was compelled by its policy of overseas imperialism to join in balance-of-power politics. Since the whole game was maintained by pitting one group of nations against another, there could be no such thing as a lone wolf. Once the United States left its continental borders, it had to take sides, and the evidence suggests that American diplomats had selected England as their country's partner some years before World War I.

The retreat from isolationism did not come easily for the United States government, and before 1900 England, rather than the United

States, took the initiative in the development of an Anglo-American *rapprochement*. Some indication that England was willing to revise its traditional policy toward the United States occurred during the Civil War. At the outset of war, the Union government established a blockade of the Confederacy's ports. England, as the South's largest customer and the world's leading naval power, had both the motive and wherewithal to challenge the North's blockade. Although it permitted southern privateers to be outfitted in its ports, unlike the United States during the Napoleonic Wars, England scrupulously observed the blockade regulations and cooperated with the United States in their enforcement. England thus indicated that it might be ready to treat the United States as an equal.

Further evidence of England's new attitude toward the United States was its willingness to accept the Treaty of Washington in 1871. During the Civil War, the English-outfitted southern commerce raiders—the most notable being the *Alabama*—had preyed on northern shipping with remarkable success. Following the war, any attempt to reach an understanding with England was made more difficult by the activities of the Fenians and the American Anglophobes who were determined to use the *Alabama* claims as a pretense for humiliating England and for expanding the territory of the United States. Charles Sumner, the chairman of the Senate Foreign Relations Committee, estimated that English aid to the Confederacy had cost the United States $2,125,000,000, while American jingoists urged that England atone for its lack of neutrality by relinquishing its North American possessions. The controversy over the *Alabama* claims was further complicated by the inability of the two countries to agree on the location of the Canadian-American boundary in the San Juan Islands in Puget Sound and the extent of American fishing privileges in Canadian waters.

The success with which the Washington conference overcame these obstacles to Anglo-American friendship was testimony to far-seeing statesmanship on both sides of the Atlantic. Hamilton Fish, the American Secretary of State under Grant, had no sympathy with Sumner's preposterous demands and was willing to deal with England on a realistic basis. The English, for their part, were so convinced of the need for peaceful cooperation with the United States that they were willing to place it ahead of Canada's demands for reparations for the Fenian raids, for more stringent control over Americans fishing in Canadian waters, and for commercial reciprocity with the United States. The Treaty of Washington selected the German Emperor as arbitrator for the San Juan boundary dispute, expanded American fishing privileges in Canadian waters, and referred the *Alabama* claims to a five-man commission that was to be guided in its decision by a set of rules that insured in advance a victory for the American claims. Meeting in Geneva in 1872, the commissioners, after lengthy debate and bitter opposition from the English representative, awarded the United States $15,500,000 for the *Alabama* claims. In the same year, the Kaiser decided in favor of the United States in the San Juan boundary dispute.

The Treaty of Washington demonstrated that both countries could settle even their most vexatious disputes peacefully. It revealed England's recognition of the increasing power of the United States and the understanding of both countries that they had much to gain and little to lose by cooperation. On the other hand, it did not preclude future controversies between England and the United States. There was a long legacy of hatred and suspicion between the two countries that could not be dispelled by a single treaty, and the robust tradition of Anglophobia in the United States persisted well into the period after the Civil War. The Irish vote in America was an especially formidable obstacle to friendlier relations, for the almost even balance between the Republican and Democratic parties that persisted for many years made it far more influential in American politics than its actual numerical strength seemed to warrant.

The desire of many American politicians to make political capital out of anti-English sentiment in the United States prevented any genuine understanding between the two countries during the quarter-century that followed the Treaty of Washington. Secretaries of State Blaine and Frelinghuysen both needlessly antagonized the British by their stand on the Clayton-Bulwer Treaty, and the fisheries question continued to plague the diplomats of both nations. When the United States in 1888 terminated the fisheries clauses in the Treaty of Washington, Canada replied by seizing American ships in Canadian waters. In 1888, Secretary of State Thomas F. Bayard and Joseph Chamberlain of England headed a commission that worked out a compromise plan providing for substantial concessions by both countries. But 1888 was an election year, and the Republican-controlled Senate, in a bid for the Irish vote, rejected the treaty in August. Similar difficulties were encountered in an attempt to resolve the dispute that arose from the American protest over pelagic sealing by Canadian schooners off the Pribiloff Islands in the Bering Sea. The Cleveland Administration, ignoring the traditional American policy of freedom of the seas, began to seize Canadian ships on the ground that the Bering Sea was a closed American preserve. When Harrison succeeded Cleveland as President, Blaine had to retreat from this untenable position, and in 1892, he agreed to submit the question to arbitration. A year later an international tribunal in Paris ruled against the American claims and made the United States liable for $473,000 for past seizures.

The climax of anti-British sentiment in the United States was reached in 1895 with Secretary of State Olney's belligerent note to England concerning Venezuela. For more than half a century Britain and Venezuela had engaged in a desultory dispute over the location of the boundary line of British Guiana. When the British landed troops in Venezuela in 1895, American jingoists professed to see a British plot in Latin America, and the Cleveland Administration concluded that the United States would have to save Venezuela from British imperialism. On July 20, 1895, Olney wrote to the British government requesting that it observe the Monroe Doctrine and submit its boundary dispute with Venezuela to arbitration. Olney's words were extraordinary:

> Today the United States is practically sovereign on this continent, and its fiat is law upon the subjects to which it confines its interposition. Why? It is not because of the pure friendship or good will felt for it. It is not simply by reason of its high character as a civilized state, nor because . . . justice and equity are the invariable characteristics of the dealings of the United States. It is because, in addition to all other grounds, its infinite resources combined with its isolated position render it master of the situation, and practically invulnerable as against any or all other powers.

Although the British had often indicated that they were ready to go more than half way to secure American friendship and cooperation, they were not prepared to be bullied into joining a partnership as the junior member. Lord Salisbury waited four months before he replied to what Cleveland called Olney's "twenty-inch gun"; and, when he did reply, he announced:

> The disputed frontier of Venezuela has nothing to do with any of the questions dealt with by President Monroe. It is not a question of the colonization by a European Power of any portion of America. It is not a question of the imposition upon the communities of South America of any system of government devised in Europe. It is simply the determination of the frontier of a British possession which belonged to the Throne of England long before the Republic of Venezuela came into existence.

Salisbury's blunt refusal to tolerate what he obviously considered American meddling made Cleveland "mad clear through," and on December 17, 1895, he requested Congress to appoint a commission to determine the boundary and to be prepared to authorize the use of force to uphold the commission's decision. Although the United States was in no position to take on the British fleet, Cleveland's message produced a war scare. But at the height of the crisis, English public opinion asserted itself, and numerous organizations and groups representing various English interests made it clear that they were opposed to a war with the United States. After a frenzy of uninhibited jingoism, the American people also awoke to the realization that armed conflict with England would be unthinkable. Responding to these unexpected displays of friendly sentiment in both countries, British and American diplomats were able to reach a face-saving compromise. England agreed to accept the good offices of the United States through an arbitration treaty that assured it in advance of its principal contentions. In 1899, a tribunal established under the terms of the treaty of arbitration upheld most of the British claims but gave Venezuela continued control of the mouth of the Orinoco River.

The peaceful settlement of the Venezuela dispute marked another important advance along the road to Anglo-American friendship. In rejecting war as an instrument for settling their differences, both countries had been motivated by considerations of national interest. Great Britain, diplomatically isolated and disturbed by the rising power of Germany, could not afford to alienate a potential ally. The United States, on the threshold of its overseas adventures, also needed powerful friends if it was going to hold its own in the free-for-all of imperialist competition.

When the United States embarked on its imperial ventures at the end of the 1890's, the foreign policies of both countries were closely coordinated. The British government gave moral support to the United States during the Spanish-American War and bestowed its unofficial blessing on the acquisition of bases in the Pacific and Caribbean. After the establishment of the American colonial empire, the two nations frequently cooperated in those parts of the world where they had joint interests. The Open Door notes, for instance, were an American policy with an English author. In 1901, the British gave way on the isthmian canal question, and five years later the British fleet was withdrawn from the Caribbean. For its part, the United States, with new responsibilities in the Pacific and the Caribbean, was more than willing to continue to entrust the Atlantic to British naval power, as it had in effect done throughout the nineteenth century. Furthermore, during Wilson's Administration, the United States demonstrated that it could grant as well as demand concessions. In 1912, Congress ex-

"And Peace Shall Rule": Uncle Sam and John Bull Become Friends, 1899
(Puck)

empted American coastal shipping from the payment of Panama Canal tolls. When Great Britain protested that the act violated the terms of the Hay-Pauncefote Treaty, Woodrow Wilson, who had previously supported the measure, reversed his stand and, by exerting pressure on Congress, was able to effect the repeal of the favors to American ships.

To some extent, the growing diplomatic cooperation between the United States and Great Britain was achieved at the expense of Canada, for Great Britain was willing to sacrifice the immediate interests of its North American possessions for the continued friendship of the United States. In 1903, a commission of three Americans, two Canadians, and one Englishman was appointed to settle a Canadian-Alaskan boundary dispute. After some not too subtle threats by Theodore Roosevelt, the English representative on the commission joined the three Americans to outvote the Canadians on practically every point under consideration. Canadians, enraged at what they considered the mother country's perfidy, were not solaced by the recognition that their country was little more than a pawn in an Anglo-American chess game that included the Atlantic, Pacific, Caribbean, and Far East as well as North America. A new world power had appeared, and Great Britain was determined to readjust its policies to take advantage of this development. Canada was not always the loser under this arrangement, for the Anglo-American understanding was accompanied by a corresponding shift in Canadian-American relations. The United States was at last ready to acknowledge that Canada was here to stay and was prepared to treat it as a fellow nation rather than as a future American colony. In 1909, Canada and the United States ratified the Boundary Waters Treaty, which governed the use of the waters of the rivers and lakes shared by the two countries, and three years later, the vexatious fisheries dispute was finally liquidated when a decision handed down by the Hague Court was confirmed by the Anglo-American Convention of July 20, 1912. Canada, in turn, reveled in its new status, and in 1911, it rejected President Taft's proposal for reciprocity on the ground that it threatened Canadian independence.

At the outbreak of World War I, Anglophobia was still a popular pastime for some Americans, and there were still congressmen who had gained office by twisting the British lion's tail for their constituents, but these facts had little or no effect upon the conduct of Anglo-American diplomacy. During the past half-century, the numerous disputes between the two nations had always been settled amicably, and each succeeding crisis served only to accentuate a growing solidarity. Great Britain, with interests in every corner of the globe, had encouraged the friendship of its fellow Atlantic power. The United States, with a new overseas empire to defend, had turned, however reluctantly, toward the nation with the world's strongest navy. As powers with limited political objectives, both countries had a stake in the maintenance of the international status quo and were inclined to look with distrust and hostility upon any nation that threatened to upset the precarious balance of power.

The United States and Germany, 1870–1914

The development of an informal Anglo-American entente during the half-century that preceded World War I was paralleled by a growing American suspicion of Germany. To many Americans, Germany became synonymous with ruthlessness, arrogance, and militarism, qualities of national character frequently summed up by Americans in the single word "Prussianism." Especially after Wilhelm II came to the throne in 1888, the Kaiser was thought by many Americans to be a typical Prussian, and occasionally the German ruler seemed to go out of his way to substantiate this conclusion. When German troops were departing for China in 1900, the Kaiser was reported to have ordered them to "give no quarter, spare nobody, make no prisoners. Use your weapons so that for a thousand years hence no Chinaman will dare look askance at any German. . . . Be terrible as Attila's Huns."

In the American mind Germany was more than a land of unpleasant people; it was also a potential menace to the security of the United States. Although the German navy was considerably smaller than the British fleet, American officials were generally convinced that it represented the single greatest threat to the Monroe Doctrine. Presidents Grant and Theodore Roosevelt and Secretaries of State Fish, Bayard, Hay, and Root all intimated or openly expressed their fear of the effect of Germany's foreign policy upon the United States. Behind the American distrust of Germany lay the fact that the two countries were rivals in many ways. Both nations were intent on developing their own industrial systems, and both were determined to obtain overseas possessions. Great Britain could afford to take a lenient view toward American imperialism, for it had its empire. But Germany and the United States, however, as latecomers to the scramble for empire, knew that this was their last chance to obtain colonies; and, because only the crumbs of the imperial banquet were left, both countries struggled vigorously to get their share of the remaining scraps.

Often German and American expansionism clashed in the Caribbean and the Pacific. When the Grant Administration attempted to obtain all or part of Santo Domingo, both official and unofficial American observers stated that Germany was also determined to annex the island. It was Germany, rather than Great Britain, that aroused the hostility of the United States in Samoa. During the Spanish-American

T. R. Lecturing the Kaiser, 1910

[BROWN BROTHERS]

War, German friendship for Spain was as pronounced as that of Great Britain for the United States, and the appearance of a German fleet in Manila Bay after Dewey's victory seemed additional proof to many Americans that Germany was attempting to thwart American colonial ambitions. The German bombardment of Fort San Carlos in Venezuela in January, 1903, was considered by many Americans a characteristic display of German militarism. When the Danish parliament refused to ratify a treaty for the purchase of the Danish West Indies by the United States, Americans incorrectly attributed the defeat of the treaty to pressure from Germany. Finally, the only instance of American intervention in a European dispute resulted in a triumph for France and a setback for Germany. In the Moroccan crisis of 1905, Theodore Roosevelt was primarily responsible for calling the Algeciras Conference (1906), which, while preserving peace, checked Germany in North Africa.

The Kaiser, although aware of the anti-German sentiment in the United States, made only ineffectual attempts to counteract it. A statue of Frederick the Great that the Kaiser presented to the United States reinforced the belief of many Americans that the donor was bent on following the military career of his illustrious predecessor. In 1901, he conferred a medal upon Theodore Roosevelt. A year later, Prince Henry was sent to the United States on a good-will mission, and Alice Roosevelt was asked to christen the yacht that was being built for the Kaiser in the United States. When she asked her father for assistance in the preparation of a speech for the occasion, the "only motto sufficiently epigrammatic," that came to the President's mind "was 'Damn the Dutch.' " *

At the outbreak of World War I few Americans were prepared to fight Germany or die for England. On the other hand, many American diplomats had come to believe that a German victory and an English defeat would constitute a major disaster for the United States.

The War of Words

Europe had been on the brink of war for more than a decade, but when the conflict began in the summer of 1914, most Americans were psychologically unprepared for it. The initial response of the American people to the news of war was shock and revulsion; and Senator John Sharp Williams of Mississippi undoubtedly expressed the general American disgust when he stated that he was "mad all over, down to the very bottom of my shoes, and somewhat sick and irritable, too," at this "outbreak of senseless war, setting all Europe aflame." Americans could not help feeling that it was altogether unreasonable of Europeans to start killing one another at a time so inconvenient to the United States.

At the start of the war, the United States government proclaimed its neutrality, and two weeks later, President Wilson asked his countrymen to be "impartial in thought as well as in action." The American people were united in their determination to prevent the United States from being drawn into the war. They at once found it difficult, if not impossible, to refrain from giving their moral support to one side or the other. Some Americans for a short while made a sincere but futile effort to comply with the President's request; others refused even to go through the motions of pretending that they were neutral in

* Henry F. Pringle: *Theodore Roosevelt: A Biography* (New York: Harcourt, Brace and Company, Inc., 1931), p. 282.

thought. From the very first day of hostilities, Americans were divided into two camps, and those who favored the Allies far outnumbered the friends of Germany. Few newspapers made even a pretense of being neutral, and many American papers announced the outbreak of the war by attributing it to the Central Powers in general and the Kaiser in particular.

The pro-Allied sentiment that dominated American public opinion from 1914 to 1917 was determined in part by the American response to the first weeks of the war. American sympathy for Belgium was easily converted into hostility for Belgium's invaders. France's valiant and successful resistance to an unexpected attack elicited the respect and support of many Americans. The stories of German atrocities in Belgium and the accounts of the German destruction of some of Europe's most famous cathedrals and centers of learning seemed to substantiate the Allied contention that Germany was waging a war against Western civilization. Anti-German sentiment in some quarters in the United States was also based on considerations of national and personal interest. Those Americans who recognized the importance of Anglo-American understanding to their country's security thought that an Allied defeat would leave the United States an island of democracy in a hostile and militaristic world. Other Americans, who had developed close economic ties with England, saw their prosperity threatened by a German victory. Regardless of motives, Americans supporting the Allies had one belief in common. They all agreed that the United States would be better off in a world dominated by the Anglo-French Entente than by Germany.

Those Americans who did not sympathize with the Allies were drawn from diverse walks in American life. A good number of German-Americans were convinced of the righteousness of Germany's cause, and thousands actually left the United States to fight for the Kaiser. Some people of Jewish faith, remembering the persecution of fellow Jews by the Tsarist government, hoped that Russia's enemy would be victorious. The Irish-Americans, with a long legacy of hatred for the English, were overwhelmingly on the side of the nations that were fighting Ireland's oppressors. Many Americans were equally opposed to both belligerents. In certain parts of the Middle West, where isolationism was particularly strong, many people tried to ignore the war on the assumption that its outcome did not concern the United States. Socialists and members of the I.W.W. considered the struggle in Europe an imperialist war and predicted that a victory for either side would be a defeat for the workingmen of the world. Pacifists refused to take sides as a matter of principle. Throughout the war, both the friends of Germany and the advocates of neutrality of thought remained a minority. Rightly or wrongly, most Americans believed that the Allies were fighting on the side of democracy and humanity.

American views on both sides were strengthened by the one-sided accounts of the events in Europe that were sent by the belligerents to the United States from 1914 to 1917. Germany and Great Britain were assiduous in efforts to cultivate American public opinion. Soon after the start of the war, they launched large-scale propaganda campaigns in the United States. Despite the spending of huge sums and the use of practically every conceivable publicity technique, it is doubtful if either German or British propaganda induced many Americans to change their minds about the war in Europe. Propaganda served largely to substantiate opinions that were already held, rather than to form new ones. Americans did not have to be told what to think about the various belligerents in Europe, but they did enjoy having their conclusions corroborated by either British or German spokesmen.

Like all successful propagandists, the British permitted no neutral colors to soften the black-and-white picture they painted for their American audience. According to British propaganda, the Prussian military clique that ruled Germany had been preparing for war since 1870. The Sarajevo crisis was not an historical accident, but the pretext employed by the German leaders to inaugurate their program of world conquest. France, Russia, and Great Britain had devoted all their efforts to the preservation of peace, but they at last had been forced into a position where they had no alternative but to resort to arms to save themselves and civilization. British propagandists not only made Germany solely responsible for the war but described German soldiers as little better than brutal automatons who were prepared to resort to any cruelty to further their country's program for enslaving the world. Some Americans might question the validity of some of the charges against Germany, but they could not disprove them; and Germany's invasion of Belgium, her use of poison gas, and her destruction of innocent lives at sea convinced some of the most dubious that the British had not overstated their case.

English propaganda techniques in the United States were subtle and persuaded many Americans that the Allied cause was the worthy one. Only established news channels and, whenever possible, American citizens were knowingly or unknowingly used to spread the British version of the war among their fellow Americans. A year after the United States had entered the war, Sir Gilbert Parker, a Canadian novelist in charge of British propaganda in the United States, revealed the scope and methods of his organization. After mentioning the extensive use made of American newspapers, magazines, clubs, libraries, and movies, he went on to say:

> We had reports from important Americans constantly, and established association, by personal correspondence, with influential and eminent people of every profession in the United States, beginning with university and college presidents, professors and scientific men and running through all the ranges of the population. We asked our friends and correspondents to arrange for speeches, debates, and lectures by American citizens, but we did not encourage Britishers to go to America and preach the doctrine of entrance into the war.

The German propagandists were no match for the British. German press releases were distributed directly to American newspapers; speakers were sent on lecture tours across the country; and on August 10, 1914, George Sylvester Viereck established *The Fatherland*, a newspaper that presented the German version of the war. The English made their appeal to American emotions. The Germans sought to convince the Americans by learned, but often obtuse, legal arguments. But, even with better techniques, the main advantages would have lain with the British. With control over the Atlantic cables and the chance to censor all the war news emanating from Europe, the British had easier access to the American public than the Germans. An even greater asset enjoyed by the British but denied to the Germans was the assurance of an overwhelmingly receptive audience in the United States. Prominent Americans willingly cooperated with the British publicists in the United States, and from 1914 to 1917, well-known British authors like H. G. Wells, G. K. Chesterton, and Rudyard Kipling were as popular as propagandists with the Americans as they had been as writers before the war.

It is possible that some Americans were deceived by the English and Allied description of the extent of Germany's war guilt, but no foreign spokesmen had to tell them the significance of the invasion of Belgium. Here as elsewhere, the German cause was weakened by German actions. Here was a fact: a neutral, inoffensive country had been invaded by an aggressor nation whose foreign minister referred to the treaty guaranteeing Belgium's neutrality as a "scrap of paper." From the German standpoint, the invasion of Belgium may have been a military necessity and a cardinal point in German strategic thinking for over a generation, but to Americans it was an inexcusable breach of international law. David Starr Jordan spoke for many Americans when he stated: ". . . the invasion of Belgium changed the whole face of affairs. As by a lightning-flash the issue was made plain: the issue of the sacredness of law; the rule of the soldier or the rule of the citizen; the rule of fear or the rule of law."

After the invasion of Belgium, many Americans were prepared to believe anything of the Germans. Count von Bernstorff, the German ambassador in Washington, said that the "Belgian question was the one which interested Americans most and which was most effective in working up American opinion against us," and the readiness with which Americans accepted reports of German rape, plunder, and oppression in Belgium seems to substantiate Bernstorff's impression. Despite the fact that a group of American journalists who were permitted to visit Belgium reported that in their opinion the so-called atrocity stories were groundless, most Americans preferred to think otherwise. Even some of the more sceptical were converted in May, 1915, by the publication of the esteemed Lord Bryce's *Report of the Committee on the Alleged German Atrocities*, which corroborated many of the earlier reports concerning the behavior of German troops in Belgium.

If the Americans were taken in by the atrocity stories, they did not have to be told by the British what to think about other aspects of Germany's conduct of the war. Submarine warfare was not a rumor, and neither German explanations nor apologies could convince most Americans that Germany was justified in killing their fellow citizens on the high seas. The destruction of the town of Louvain and the cathedral of Rheims may have been a by-product of war, but to the average American it represented a wanton disregard for two of the greatest cultural landmarks of western Europe. Even if Americans were willing to make allowances for Germany's conduct of the war, they found it difficult to excuse those agents of the Central Powers who fomented strikes in American munition plants and along the water-front, took a leading part in the American peace movement, and destroyed with explosives American factories, bridges, and cargoes bound for the Allies. Germany made few converts among those Americans who were not pro-German in 1914.

No amount of German propaganda could have induced the United States to fight on the side of the Central Powers. German propagandists, well aware of this fact, hoped to secure nothing more than the maintenance of American neutrality. On the other hand, the British propagandists, assured of a friendly reception, set their sights on American intervention as their maximum aim. From the first day of the war, the British had the great advantage that was never shared by the Germans—they could tell the mass of Americans what they wanted to be told.

A Bankers' Plot?

Following the failure of Germany's bid for a quick victory in 1914, the war became a struggle of attrition that severely taxed the resources of the combatants. As the troops of both sides dug into their trenches, questions of strategy and tactics often had to be subordinated to the problem of how to obtain adequate supplies for the armies at the front. As the European neutrals had imposed embargoes on the export of war matériel, only the United States remained to make up the deficiencies of the Allies. Germany may have wanted to tap American resources, but the effectiveness of the British blockade prevented all but a trickle of American goods from reaching the Central Powers. Once the war began to drag on, the enormous wealth of America, whether committed or withheld, would have held the balance of financial and material power.

American trade with the Allies soon reached enormous proportions. Exports to England, France, Italy, and Russia rose from about $825,000,000 in 1914 to nearly $3,215,000,000 in 1916, while direct exports to Germany and Austria-Hungary declined from approximately $169,300,000, to about $1,150,000 in the same years. But there was considerable American opposition to the continued export of this war matériel. Pacifists complained that it prolonged the war; pro-German groups considered it unfair to the Central Powers; and isolationists thought that it jeopardized American neutrality. Although resolutions condemning the war shipments were often introduced into Congress, none was ever adopted, and the Wilson Administration never made any move to prevent the trade. In October, 1914, the State department announced that "a citizen of the United States can sell to a belligerent government or its agent any article of commerce which he chooses." Under accepted international law, Americans were permitted to ship war supplies to the belligerents; and on December 15, 1914, Count von Bernstorff, the German ambassador to the United States, wrote to Secretary of State Bryan about American shipments of war matériel to the Allies: "According to the principles of international law above cited, a neutral state need not prevent furnishing supplies of this character. . . . Our enemies draw from the United States contraband of war, especially arms. . . . This in itself they are authorized to do."

The fact that Germany recognized the legality of the American export of war matériel to the Allies did not make the practice any more acceptable in German eyes. The Germans could not escape the conclusion that many of their soldiers were being killed by American bullets, and in 1917 a German author complained:

Germany finds herself in the position of a warrior, hemmed in on all sides, whose enemies are aiming at his heart. Every time this warrior succeeds in disarming the foe most harmful to him, every time the warrior strikes the sword from the hand of the enemy, a so-called neutral comes running from behind and places a new weapon in the hand of the defeated foe.

To repeated requests from the Central Powers that it place an embargo on arms shipments, the United States government always replied that any restriction on this trade would violate an established American policy and undermine the principle of strict neutrality. The official American position on the munitions trade was given by Secretary of State Robert Lansing in a note to Austria in August, 1915. As all the belligerents had known that international law permitted the export of war matériel by a neutral country, and as some of them had presumably entered the war with that fact in mind, Lansing concluded that it would be unjust for the United States to change the rules governing the conduct of neutrals after the war had started. Lansing further stated that the United States wished to establish a precedent, for with a small peacetime military establishment the United States would be unable to "repel invasion by a well-equipped and powerful enemy," unless it could in any emergency anticipate receiving the same type of assistance that it was now giving to the Allies.

Lansing, of course, thought that American interests would be threatened by a German victory and refused to take any step that might weaken the Allied war effort. But others shared in his opposition to an arms embargo. The United States did not stop the trade in contraband of war, because the American people did not want to stop it. In August, 1914, the United States was in the midst of a depression. Allied war orders placed with American manufacturers in the winter of 1914–15 only partially alleviated business conditions in the United States, but by the following summer the corner was turned. Within a few months the war trade had converted the depression into a boom, and few Americans wished to exchange prosperity for an economic neutrality that would benefit only the Central Powers. Practically every American business firm benefited from the war trade with Europe. Those supplying war equipment to the Allies made unprecedented profits. The earnings of American steel and iron companies increased fivefold: from about $203,000,000 in 1915 to nearly $1,035,000,000 in 1917. The wartime profits of E. I. du Pont de Nemours, which supplied an estimated 40 per cent of all the ammunition used by the Allies, amounted to $266,000,000; and J. P. Morgan & Company, which served as the American commercial agent for the French and British, collected commissions exceeding $30,000,000 for the purchases it made for both governments in the United States. Workers and farmers who shared in the good times based on sales to the Allies, were no more disposed to sacrifice higher incomes for neutrality than were the nation's industrialists and financiers. To those Americans hopeful of an Allied victory, the export of arms, ammunition, and foodstuffs was a double boon; it satisfied their consciences and lined their pockets. The Wilson Administration, with an overwhelming sympathy for the Allied cause to begin with, was more than willing to make its official stand on war trade conform to the popular mandate.

The most disturbing feature of the shift from depression to a war-born prosperity was the prospect that European customers would run out of money. American bankers were prepared, however, to finance the Allies if the government was willing. During the first week of hostilities, J. P. Morgan & Company had asked the Wilson Administration's approval of a loan to France. Although no law forbade private financial assistance to the belligerents, Secretary of State Bryan rejected the Morgan proposal on the ground that "loans by American bankers to any foreign nation which is at war are inconsistent with the true spirit of neutrality." Bryan, as a pacifist, thought that a refusal to lend money to either side would shorten the war and that American neutrality required that any loans to the Allies be matched by loans to Germany. If some American citizens and banks acquired a direct economic stake in the outcome of the war, Bryan feared, the American people would be divided and the nation's most powerful financial institutions would exert tremendous interventionist pressure on the government's conduct of foreign policy.

In late October, 1914, the Administration partially amended the earlier stand taken by Bryan. The government did not state that it would sanction war loans, but it did indicate that it was powerless to prevent them and that it would not object to short-term credits to the belligerents. Robert Lansing, counselor for the State Department, was the individual most responsible for the change in policy. When the National City Bank asked for permission to grant short-term credits to the Allies, Lansing submitted the bank's request with minor revisions as a memorandum to the President. Wilson was convinced by the bankers' arguments that there was a "decided difference between an issue of government bonds which are sold in open market to investors" and "credits which will avoid the clumsy and impracticable method of cash payments." With the President's consent, the National City Bank on

November 4 announced the completion of the arrangements for a $10,000,000 special credit to the French Government.

Such credits were at best a stopgap, for they postponed rather than solved the problem of the Allies' inability to pay for purchases in the United States. By August, 1915, leading American bankers were insisting that the government would have to permit long-term loans if it wished to save the Allies and maintain American war trade. The bankers' fears were shared by some of the most important officials in the Wilson Administration. Lansing, who had succeeded Bryan as Secretary of State, wrote to Wilson that the Administration should not permit its earlier opposition to loans to "stand in the way of our national interests which seem to be seriously threatened." Secretary of the Treasury McAdoo favored "anything that would help to finance export trade" and stated that if Americans did not finance that trade, it would stop and "that would be disastrous." Wilson, however reluctantly, was won over by his advisers to the need for a loan, and on September 25, 1915, a group of American bankers completed negotiations for a loan of $500,000,000 to the French and British governments. The Anglo-French loan was the first of many to the Allies, and by April, 1917, American investors had purchased $2,300,000,000 of bonds from the enemies of Germany.

The war trade and war loans certainly strengthened economic ties between the United States and the Allies, but they were not primarily responsible for America's entering the war. The insistence of the isolationists of the twenties and thirties that the United States went to war to save the bankers' loans is without foundation in fact. All but the first loan were backed by collateral deposited in the United States, and the American investors stood to lose nothing by an Allied defeat. Moreover, some businessmen making the greatest profits from trade with the Allies were most worried by the economic implications of an American declaration of war. Direct intervention would undoubtedly mean larger war orders, but it would also mean higher taxes and increased government regulation. Businessmen as a class no more wanted war in 1917 than any other economic group.

"Neutral" Diplomacy with England

Economic and sentimental ties may have bound the United States to the Allies, but they did not weaken the determination of most Americans to stay out of the war in Europe. Many Americans felt free to criticize the belligerents and to extract profits from Europe's distress, but they heartily opposed entering the conflict. From 1914 to 1917, the United States' policy was formally neutral, while its acts showed that its sympathies lay with the Allies.

Wilson's policy during the period of American neutrality was a compromise between two extremes of American opinion. As the war progressed, Wilson was bitterly attacked by pacifists and extreme isolationists, on the one hand, and the advocates of American intervention on the Allied side, on the other. William Jennings Bryan, as the leading spokesman of the former group, had strong support in the rural regions of the Middle West, with their heritage of isolationism and Populist hatred for "money bags England." Bryan thought that the United States should have nothing to do with the war except to serve as a mediator. To Bryan and his followers, there seemed to be little difference between the belligerents, and the Wilson Administration's obvious friendship for the Allies was a violation of American neutrality that would lead to war. Another group of Americans—largely drawn from the Northeast—opposed Bryan and believed that the United States had a vital stake in the outcome of the war. Maintaining that a German victory would threaten world democracy and American security, they urged intervention and criticized Wilson's devotion to neutrality as shortsighted and even cowardly. This small but powerful minority included such prominent Americans as Theodore Roosevelt, Charles W. Eliot, former president of Harvard, and the New York publisher George H. Putnam. They predicted that an Allied defeat would be followed by a German attack on the United States. The majority of Americans, recognizing some validity in the arguments of both groups of extremists, preferred a middle ground that permitted them to endorse neutrality while acknowledging the possibility that they might eventually be compelled to abandon it.

Before he became President, Wilson himself had condemned war as an ineffective and immoral device for settling international disputes. During his first months in office, he had supported Bryan's "cooling-off" treaties, and after the sinking of the *Lusitania*, he asserted that there was "such a thing as a man being too proud to fight" and "such a thing as a nation being so right that it does not need to convince others by force that it is right." But there was another side to Wilson. In 1911, in a speech that foreshadowed his stand in April, 1917, he stated that there were "times in the history of nations when they must take up the crude instruments of bloodshed in order to vindicate spiritual conceptions" and that "when men take up arms to set other men free, there is something sacred and holy in the warfare." Wilson had also long studied and admired British politics and literature. He had come to believe that there was an essential unity among the "English-speaking peoples" and that it should be encouraged by diplomacy. For his graduation address at Princeton in 1878, Wilson had chosen the subject "Our Kinship With England." Twenty-two years later, while a professor at the same institution, he had referred to "our happy alliance of sentiment and purpose with Great Britain." The war strengthened rather than weakened Wilson's sympathies for England, and in the first days of 1915, he told his secretary that "England was fighting our fight."

American neutrality was thus beset by contradictions and ambiguities. Not wanting war, but seeking profits from supplying the belligerents, the policy, in effect, aided the Allies. The English controlled the seas, and only Allied war orders could be placed in America. This left the Germans no alternative but to construe American neutrality as a cloak to cover aid to England. Even if America had refused to trade with either side, its financial and industrial wealth was so great that, pledged or withheld, it might hold the balance of power for one side or the other in a prolonged war. Real neutrality for the United States might well mean victory for Germany, and American neutrality in fact was always based on the hypothesis that Germany would be defeated. What attempts America did make to steer a truly neutral course were always complicated by the lack of any accepted international standards for the conduct of nonbelligerents during a war. In 1909, an effort had been made to arrive at a series of rules for neutrals in the Declaration of London, which forbade paper blockades, denied the continuous voyage, and stated that only war materials could be seized as contraband by the belligerents. From the standpoint of international law as expressed by the Declaration of London, the United States was as free to trade in noncontraband with the Central Powers as with the Allies. But the British government had never ratified the Declaration of London, and during the war, of course, it could not realistically live up to its provisions. England, fighting for its very existence, was determined that its seapower would not be weakened by any theoretical considerations of how it should employ its strongest weapon.

Throughout the period of American neutrality, the British interference with American trade made freedom of the seas little more than a meaningless slogan. At the start of the war, England established a long-range blockade that enabled it to intercept neutral vessels on the high seas. By a series of Orders in Council, it then widened the blockade's scope until it covered virtually all neutral commerce with the Continent. The contraband list was extended to include goods that had not previously been considered war matériel; the doctrine of continuous voyage was invoked to permit the seizure of goods bound for neutral countries that traded with Germany; and the North Sea was declared a military area, so that every neutral ship entering it was first funneled through an English port. Many Americans became convinced that England was as interested in destroying American commerce as in defeating Germany. English inspection of mail between the United States and Europe was interpreted by many American businessmen as a device of English competitors for learning trade secrets. American ships bound for neutral countries were detained in England for months, while English trade with the Continental neutrals increased. The publication of a British blacklist of American firms and individuals suspected of trading with Germany antagonized even the strongest pro-Allied supporters in the United States and moved Woodrow Wilson to state that it was the "last straw" and that he had almost reached the end of "his patience with Great Britain and the Allies."

Wilson, of course, never reached the end of his patience with Great Britain and the Allies; but his Administration, impelled by the need to uphold American rights and under the heaviest pressure from outraged American citizens, protested repeatedly to the British about violations of American neutrality. The British met the American protests with delay, long and involved legal arguments, the implication that Germany's behavior on the high seas was even more objectionable—and no change in policy. England had no alternative but to hope that the United States would not resort to force to uphold its position; or, as Sir Edward Grey, the British Foreign Minister, later expressed it, "British action preceded British argument; the risk was that action might follow the American argument." Action never did follow American argument, for Wilson and his advisers, with the exception of Bryan, would not take any steps that might seriously lessen the Allied chances of victory. Key Administration leaders like Colonel E. M. House, Robert Lansing, and Walter Hines Page, the American ambassador in London, subordinated practically every consideration to their desire for an Allied victory. House, as Wilson's personal representative, became an intimate of the leaders of France and England and shared their views on Germany and the war. Lansing, from the first days of the war, believed that it would only be a matter of time before the United States would have to join the Allies to insure Germany's defeat. Page was so wholehearted a supporter of the English cause that some of his critics complained that he had become more English than American.

American officials might make frequent protests to the British government regarding violations of American neutrality, but they never even suggested that the United States planned to take any drastic steps to uphold its position. Typical of the American attitude was a note sent to England in December, 1914, which asked the English not to interfere with American trade "unless such interference is manifestly an imperative necessity to protect their national safety, and then only to the extent that it is a necessity." Although their own government had sent the protests, Page and House were willing to assist English officials in replying to the American notes. After the war, Sir Edward Grey wrote that Page's advice and suggestions "were of the greatest value in warning us when to be careful or encouraging us when we could safely be firm." The American diplomatic protests were, of course, largely designed for home consumption rather than to bring England to heel. After the war, Lansing wrote that the notes

> . . . were long and exhaustive treatises which opened up new subjects of discussion rather than closing those in controversy. Short and emphatic notes were dangerous. Everything was submerged in verbosity. It was done with deliberate purpose. It insured continuance of the controversies and left the questions unsettled.

"Neutral" Diplomacy with Germany

The Wilson Administration made mild protests at British violations of American neutral rights, but it insisted that Germany scrupulously observe the letter of international law. German-American relations were without serious controversy until February 4, 1915, when Germany announced that all the waters "surrounding Great Britain and Ireland including the whole English Channel are hereby declared to be comprised within the seat of war and that all enemy merchant vessels found in those waters after the eighteenth instant will be destroyed." Six days later, the United States government contended American citizens traveling on belligerent ships in a war zone were protected by the United States and insisted that the Germans conform to the rules that covered surface raiders by refraining from sinking any merchant ship until they had searched it and provided for the safety of its passengers and crew. The Germans, however, understood that accepting the American arguments would destroy the effectiveness of the U-boat. They refused to alter their original plan beyond assuring the United States that it was "very far indeed from the intention of the German Government . . . to destroy neutral lives and neutral property."

Had the Germans subsequently at least permitted passengers and crews of merchant ships to enter lifeboats, they would have seemed far less inhumane. But the Germans had no reason to refrain from killing Allied merchant crews, and the time needed to lower lifeboats might have permitted radio messages for help to nearby Allied warships. To some extent the Germans also counted on total surprise and terror to help disrupt shipping in aid of the Allied cause.

The refusal of either the American or German governments to retreat from their original stands on the question of submarine warfare soon produced a series of incidents that brought relations between the two countries to the breaking point. On March 28, 1915, Leon C. Thrasher, an American citizen, lost his life when the British ship *Falaba* was torpedoed. On April 28, the *Cushing*, an American ship, was attacked by a German seaplane; and on May 1, the American tanker *Gulflight* was torpedoed, with the loss of its captain and two of its crew members. The American people hardly had time to recover from the shock of these events when news was received that on May 7 the British liner *Lusitania* had been torpedoed off the Irish coast and that the 1,198 drowned included 128 Americans. German protests that the ship was carrying munitions and that German advertisements in the press had warned Americans not to travel on the *Lusitania* could not obscure the fact that Germany had committed a colossal blunder. The American people were horrified at the ruthlessness of the German attack, and the American papers referred to the disaster as "slaughter," "wholesale murder," and "piracy." Colonel House predicted that the United States would be "at war with Germany within a month," and Walter Hines Page wrote from London, "We live in hope that America will come in. . . ." Bryan alone among prominent government officials protested with some justice that England was "using our citizens to protect her ammunition."

With the sinking of the *Lusitania*, the Wilson Administration had to decide whether to follow a course of impartial neutrality as advocated by Bryan or to accept Lansing's view that there should be one kind of neutrality for the Allies and another for Germany. Wilson was not prepared to lead the country into war against Germany in May, 1915, but there was no doubt in his mind that Lansing was right and Bryan wrong. In his protest to the German government, he stated that American citizens had the right to travel "on lawful errands as passengers on merchant ships of belligerent nationality," and that submarine attacks on passenger ships violated all the accepted principles of humanity. Bryan, certain that the President's policy would lead to war, argued that the United States should either put off the day of

The Sailing and the Warning

reckoning with Germany, as it had already done with England, or remove the cause of the controversy by refusing to accept responsibility for Americans traveling on belligerent ships. When Wilson rejected both these alternatives, Bryan resigned from the cabinet to work outside the government for his conception of American neutrality.

Wilson's decision to accept Lansing's rather than Bryan's views of submarine warfare was the turning point in the history of American neutrality. Wilson based his stand on the principle that the United States could not stand by while Germany violated the laws of civilization by murdering innocent American citizens. But Bryan, too, relied on principles and stated that Wilson's policy endangered American lives and neutrality. Wilson insisted that Germany was destroying American rights; Bryan replied that England was doing the same. There were, however, certain problems that Bryan refused to face. While it was true that Great Britain interfered with American commerce, it was also a fact that British policies never resulted in the loss of a single American life. Bryan could argue that Britain was merely in a more fortunate position than Germany in this respect, but the fact remained that the Germans killed Americans on the high seas without warning and the British did not. Bryan also refused to recognize the importance of strategic considerations in American neutrality. Bryan's solution of the submarine problem would have aided Germany and jeopardized the Allied chances of success. Bryan was willing to ignore this result, but Wilson, strengthened by Lansing, was not. German victory would represent a threat not only to democracy, but to the future security and independence of the United States. To Wilson and his principal advisers from the time of Bryan's resignation in June, 1915, until the American declaration of war in April, 1917, the possibility of a German victory became increasingly important in determining the United States' policy toward the war in Europe. To Bryan it was an irrelevancy.

In the months following the sinking of the *Lusitania*, Wilson refused to retreat from his original stand on the question of submarine warfare. On August 19, the British liner *Arabic* was torpedoed and sunk by a German submarine. Two Americans went down with the *Arabic*, and a complete diplomatic break between the United States and Germany was averted only when Bernstorff exceeded his instructions to inform the State Department that "liners will not be sunk by our submarines without warning and without safety of the lives of noncombatants, provided that the liners do not try to escape or offer resistance." After reprimanding Bernstorff for his unauthorized statement, the German government understood that it would have to support him, and on October 5 it assured the United States that the "orders issued by His Majesty the Emperor to the commanders of the German submarines . . . have been made so stringent that the recurrence of incidents similar to the *Arabic* case is considered out of the question." Despite the unequivocal language of these guarantees, German submarines continued to attack passenger vessels. On November 7, 1915, several Americans lost their lives when the Italian liner *Anconia* was sent to the bottom of the Mediterranean by an Austrian submarine, and on March 24, 1916, when the *Sussex*, a French Channel steamer, was torpedoed, some of its American passengers were injured. The attack on the *Sussex*, which was a violation of the German government's assurances to the United States and its orders to its own submarine commanders, produced a diplomatic crisis comparable to the one that had followed the sinking of the *Lusitania*. On April 18, Lansing warned Germany that unless it abandoned its "relentless and indiscriminate warfare against vessels of commerce by the use of submarines," the United States could "have no choice but to sever diplomatic relations." Germany was not yet prepared to convert the United States into a full enemy; and on May 4, 1916, it gave in to American pressure and announced that merchant vessels would not be sunk without warning and without saving human lives, but it added an escape clause that the "United States will now demand and insist that the British Government shall forthwith observe the rules of international law." After May, 1916, Germany lived up to what came to be known as the *Sussex* pledge until the inauguration of unrestricted submarine warfare in February of the following year.

The decline of German aggressiveness made the growing intensity and frequency of British interference with American neutrality more irritating than it had been while the Germans were killing American citizens and sinking American ships. Throughout 1916, most American protests were directed against the Allies. At the same time, although Wilson had rejected Bryan's demand for strict neutrality and had adopted Lansing's firm policy toward Germany, he continued to share with his former Secretary of State the belief that it was the duty of the United States to attempt to end the war by peaceful mediation. In 1915 and again in the early part of 1916, he sent Colonel House on a peace mission, but House's efforts did little more than indicate the unwillingness of either set of belligerents to end the war on the other's terms. Wilson, however, still clung to the idea that peace without victory was as possible as it was desirable, and in December, 1916, he asked the belligerents to state the conditions on which they would conclude peace.

A Fine Balance Is Required To Avoid Trouble
(*McCutcheon, in the* Chicago Tribune)

Unknown to Wilson, the German high command had decided to play up to his desire for a negotiated peace. Their plan was to appear as tractable as possible, thus putting the Allies in a bad light. They hoped that Wilson would be able to force the Allies to the peace table, at which time world longing for peace and an all-out German offensive would force the British and French to yield. Wilson, unfortunately, played into German hands in 1916 with his peace missions and angry notes to the Allies. The final replies to Wilson's December request for negotiations made it clear that neither the Allies nor Germany planned to end the war until they had won it. The failure of the German plot, German victories on the Eastern front, and the continued flow of American aid to the Allies made the Kaiser decide to risk American armed intervention at the start of 1917. He gambled that unrestricted submarine warfare and a massive blow in the West could end the war before American troops and mobilization could turn the tide. His gamble almost worked.

The End of Neutrality

Wilson's neutrality policy played a major part in the campaign of 1916. The Democrats maintained that prosperity and Wilson's proved ability to keep the United States out of war made it imperative that he be elected to a second term. To oppose Wilson, the Republicans selected Charles Evans Hughes, an Associate Justice of the Supreme Court and a former reform Governor of New York. Roosevelt, who had been furiously anti-Wilson and an outspoken advocate of "preparedness," was back in the Republican fold. Hughes was acceptable to both the party's conservative and liberal factions, and the Republicans at first appeared capable of winning the election. But as the campaign progressed, Hughes' position became increasingly difficult, for criticisms of American foreign policy were liable to be interpreted as disloyalty, while little could be gained by attacking Wilson's reform program, especially since in 1915 and 1916 Wilson had been forced by political reverses to request many reforms that progressive Republicans had long urged. Wilson, in other words, could stand on his record in both domestic and foreign affairs. The election was exceedingly close, and, until the final returns were in, it was thought that Hughes had won. But Wilson made an unexpectedly strong showing west of the Mississippi and was re-elected by a poplar vote of 9,129,606 to 8,538,221 and an electoral vote of 277 to 254. The balance was probably held by newly enfranchised women, who voted for Wilson and peace, and by workers, who favored prosperity and were pleased by Wilson's recent labor legislation. The Democrats also retained their control over both branches of Congress.

While Wilson was campaigning for peace, he could not ignore the argument of Roosevelt and others that a prolonged conflict might eventually lead to American participation. With considerable fanfare, he launched a limited preparedness campaign in the summer of 1916. Despite marked opposition from the South and West, Congress passed

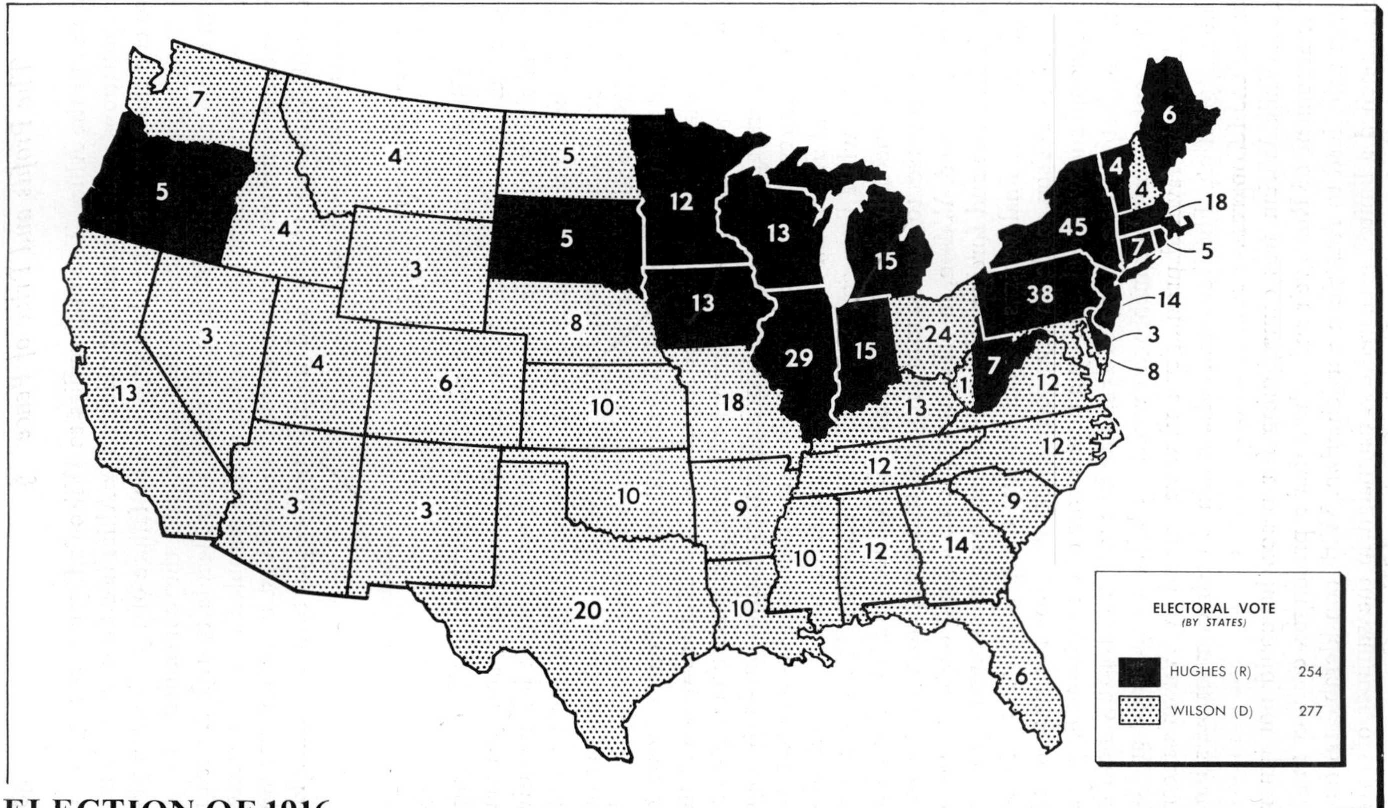

ELECTION OF 1916

ELECTORAL VOTE
(BY STATES)

HUGHES (R)   254

WILSON (D)   277

TRM

bills providing for an increase in the size of the army and navy, an expansion of the merchant marine, and the establishment of a skeletal organization for the mobilization of American industry. Preparedness could not be avoided after our *Sussex* warning of that spring, for the question of whether the United States would remain at peace or go to war was now left to the Germans rather than to the Americans. By his firm stand on German submarine warfare against merchant shipping, Wilson had placed the United States in a position where it could not avoid war if the Central Powers decided to break the rules he had laid down.

The German high command, however, had decided as early as August, 1916, that unrestricted submarine warfare alone could prevent Germany from being defeated by the British blockade. The U-boat fleet was steadily built up during the next months until Germany had completed its arrangements for a knockout blow. On January 31, 1917, the German government informed the United States that its submarines would attack all merchant vessels within prescribed zones in the Atlantic and the Mediterranean.

The German announcement of unrestricted submarine warfare left Wilson with no choice but to invoke the threat made after the *Sussex* was sunk and on February 3, he announced to a cheering Congress that the United States had severed diplomatic relations with Germany. Hoping that war could still be averted and that the United States might be able to ride out the crisis with a policy of armed neutrality, Wilson on February 26, 1917, asked Congress for the power to arm American merchant ships. When a Senate filibuster killed the bill, Wilson decided to act without congressional authorization. But neither Wilson nor any other American could now guide the course of American foreign policy, for after January, 1917, the German government alone could determine if and when the United States would go to war. And Germany soon left little doubt as to how the issue would be resolved. On March 1, 1917, the American press carried the news, already known to Wilson, that the British had intercepted the so-called Zimmermann note, in which the German foreign minister had urged Mexico to take advantage of an American declaration of war by joining with Japan in an attack on the United States in order to recover the territory lost in the Mexican War of 1848. The American people at last were being forced to the conclusion held by the interventionists since the outbreak of the war—that Germany was determined to destroy American independence. Only an incident was now needed to drive the United States into war, and during March it was supplied five times over as five American merchant vessels were tor-

Front Page of the NEW YORK TIMES, *April 3, 1917*

pedoed by German submarines. Wilson, concluding that Germany was waging an undeclared war against the United States, delivered his war message to Congress on April 2. Four days later, after overwhelming congressional approval, the United States was at war with Germany.

To the very last, Wilson had hoped that circumstances would not force him to lead the American people into war. Like many progressives, he was worried that the crusading fever of war would strengthen reactionary groups in the country and make for a wave of illiberalism. A notable debate among American progressive intellectuals had been taking place the previous year between the reform philosopher, John Dewey, and his former student, the brilliant young writer Randolph Bourne. It dramatized publicly what seems to have been Wilson's private dilemma. In leading journals, Bourne had maintained that the war was essentially a struggle between the same kinds of corporate interests that progressives had been attacking for a generation. To prepare for or to enter the war would be to abandon all hope of carrying reform further. Preparedness and war would replace reform fervor with jingoist intolerance. Dewey agreed that the war had thus far been a struggle among illiberal interest groups. Unless, however, liberals joined the fight and transformed it into a fight for justice, they would run the risk that either German militarism or Allied big business and imperialism would win. Without liberal participation, the war would end, one way or the other, with vindictiveness and without social justice. Wilson seems to have had fears like Bourne's, but he had conquered them with hopes like Dewey's. In any case, by March, 1917, circumstances were beyond his control. The only alternatives were peace and national degradation, on the one hand, and war, on the other. It was not an easy choice for a man with an intense conscience, but Wilson consoled himself with the thought that the United States was joining the forces of democracy and humanity against those of evil and autocracy.

Wilson did not ask if what he said in 1917 about the nature of the struggle had not been just as true from 1914 to 1917, when he seemed to regard neutrality as being as holy a duty as the war was to become. Perhaps the news of the deposition of the autocratic Russian Czar by Russian democrats in March, 1917, made him less uneasy about enlisting fully on the Allied side. Following his propensity to sanctify his major decisions, especially those distasteful to him or at variance with his previous policies, Wilson at the very beginning of the war succumbed to what one critic then described as the "temptation to feel holy." The United States was not fighting for its vital interests or a restoration of the balance of power, he said, but for the democratic redemption of the world, for the rights of all mankind. In his address to Congress on April 2 he closed with an appeal for an armed crusade for

> . . . democracy, for the right of those who submit to authority to have a voice in their own Governments, for the rights and liberties of small nations, for a universal dominion of right by such a concert of free peoples as shall bring peace and safety to all nations and make the world itself at last free. To such a task we can dedicate our lives and our fortunes, everything that we are and everything that we have, with the pride of those who know that the day has come when America is privileged to spend her blood and her might for the principles that gave her birth and happiness and the peace which she has treasured. God helping her, she can do no other.

FOR SUPPLEMENTARY READING

The leading work on the years 1914–17 is still C. Seymour, *American Neutrality, 1914–1917* (1935). For a different view read C. C. Tansill, *America Goes to War* (1938), and then E. R. May, *World War and American Isolation* (1959). An admirable analysis concentrating on the President's role is A. S. Link, *Wilson the Diplomatist* (1957). For general background on American relations with England read R. H. Heindel, *The American Impact on Great Britain 1898–1914* (1940). George Kennan, *American Diplomacy, 1900–1950* (1951) has provocative observations on the rationale of American neutrality after 1914. On propaganda during the period read H. C. Peterson, *Propaganda for War* (1939). A. S. Link's *Woodrow Wilson and the Progressive Era* (1954) ties foreign policy and domestic affairs together well. Excellent on social mood and political changes during the neutrality years is W. E. Leuchtenberg, *The Perils of Prosperity* (1958) (Pb).

14

"Over There"

T HE AMERICAN PEOPLE went to war in April, 1917, buoyed up by
a patriotic fervor that permitted them to ignore the scope and
difficulties of the task before them. But if the Americans were
naïve, they learned fast; and by the end of the war they had
raised, equipped, and transported a modern army, paid higher taxes
than ever before, and accepted a degree of control over industry, agriculture, and labor that a few years earlier they would have branded as
socialistic. On the other hand, although American democracy was able
to survive the new stresses and strains to which it was subjected during
the war, the number of political prisoners in American jails in 1918 revealed that victory abroad had been attained by a retreat, if not a defeat, at home.

The Allies Demand Manpower

For a short time after April 6, 1917, many Americans still thought
that belligerency would prove no more burdensome than friendly neutrality. These dreams of a soft war were dispelled by the early arrival
in Washington of the Allied War Missions with the news that without
immediate and unprecedented American aid their countries would be
defeated. Most disturbing of all to President Wilson was the Allied
insistence that the United States send an army as well as supplies to
Europe. General Joffre, the French representative, announced that he
had come to the United States to "discuss the sending of an American
expeditionary force to France" and urged that "the American soldier
come now." The suggestion that they might have to fight and die for

victory was a great shock to those Americans who had planned to contribute their country's resources rather than their lives to the Allied cause. The National Defense Act of June, 1916, had provided for a regular army of only 175,000, and the government understood even before the arrival of the Allied Missions that the United States would have to resort to a draft if called on to build an effective fighting force. When the Administration's conscription bill was introduced into Congress, opponents of the measure protested that it was unrealistic, for the United States did not have the ships to transport an army to France even if it could raise one. Others argued that compulsory military service was un-American. Champ Clark complained that his constituents in Missouri could see "precious little difference between a conscript and a convict," and Theodore Roosevelt, while supporting a draft for others, thought that he should be permitted to raise a volunteer unit as he had done in 1898. But this was no war for cavalry charges and adventurous amateurs, and on May 18, 1917, the Selective Service Act became law. By the end of the war, 2,810,296 of the 24,234,021 men between the ages of 18 and 45 who had registered at their local draft boards had been inducted into service; through the draft and enlistments, the United States was able to increase the combined strength of its army, navy, and the National Guard from 378,619 on April 2, 1917 to 4,791,127 on November 11, 1918. The draft met little popular resistance. Only 3,989 inductees claimed exemption as conscientious objectors, and of this number only 450 preferred jail to "some form of service satisfactory to the Government."

By the end of the war, the United States had shipped 2,079,880 men—not all of whom were fighting men—and more than 5,000,000 tons of supplies to Europe. The ships that transported these goods and men were organized in convoys that sailed under the protection of the United States Navy. The success of the convoy system, which was directed by Admiral Albert Gleaves, is revealed by the fact that German submarines did not sink a single American troopship on the eastward passage. Furthermore, by November, 1918, the United States Navy had approximately 300 ships manned by 75,000 men in European waters, all under the command of Admiral William S. Sims, whose headquarters were at London. The work of the fleet was supplemented by about 500 Navy planes stationed in Europe. In addition to its convoy duties, the Navy helped the British fleet maintain the blockade and played an important role in the relentless warfare against German U-boats. American warships also laid antisubmarine mines, attacked submarines with depth charges, engaged in mine-sweeping, and participated in assaults on submarine bases. It was, moreover, largely because of the insistent demands of the United States that a mine barrage was laid across the northern outlet of the North Sea. The Navy's air arm assisted convoys, took an active part in the antisubmarine campaign, and joined the Army Air Force in raids on Germany.

General John J. Pershing, who was made commander in chief of the American Expeditionary Force, reached Paris in June, 1917. Active American participation in the European fighting first occurred in October, 1917, when a small detachment of United States troops took up positions in the vicinity of Toul at the southern end of the Western Front. Five months later (March 21, 1918), when the Germans launched the first of their giant offensives that were designed to win the war, there were approximately 300,000 American soldiers in France. In the next four months, the Germans undertook five major assaults, each one of which seriously imperiled the Allied armies. The American force, at Foch's insistence, was split up and used piecemeal to help stem the German attack. Soon after, Americans saw action at Aisne (May 27–June 5), Noyon-Montdidier (June 9–15), and Champagne-Marne (July 15–18). In the last of these engagements, American troops made a notable contribution to the ultimate defeat of Germany. These forces had arrived in the nick of time, for in checking the German advance at the Marne they prevented the enemy from taking Paris, and at Chateau-Thierry they successfully resisted one of the heaviest German assaults of the entire war. General Walther Reinhardt, German chief of staff, attributed his army's repulse at the Marne to "the unexpectedly stubborn and active resistance of fresh American troops."

Largely because of the fighting qualities that the Americans displayed on this occasion, Marshal Foch, who was in supreme command of the Allied armies, consented to the demand that Pershing had made from the outset—that an independent American command be created. Foch had been determined to have the relatively untrained American troops used as reserves and replacements for the exhausted and decimated British and French, but Pershing insisted that Foch's plan would undermine the morale of the American troops and produce an adverse effect on the war effort at home. Finally, in August, 1918, the First American Army was formed and assumed the responsibility for holding part of the Allied line; and by the end of the war, the Americans were occupying about one fourth of the front, or more than the British. Pershing had to rely on the Allies for much of his matériel, however. The procurement of adequate supplies for his troops was always one of Pershing's most pressing problems, and throughout the war the Americans were hampered by the comparative lack of tanks, airplanes, and artillery. It was American blood, not guns, tanks, or planes

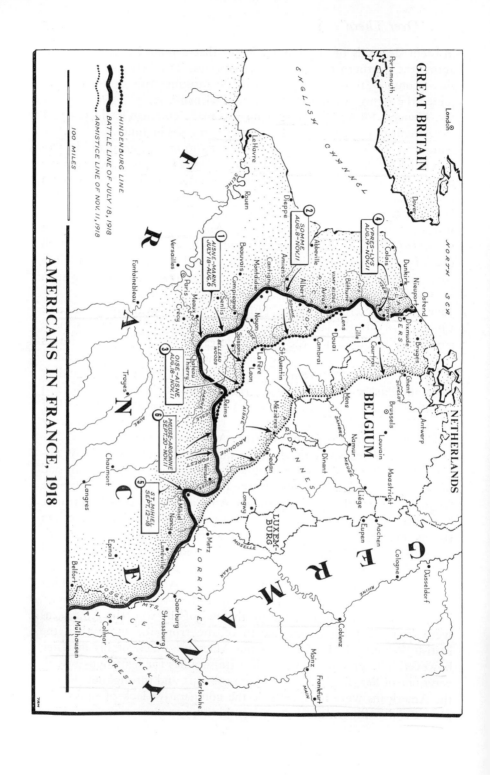

AMERICANS IN FRANCE, 1918

that prevented the Germans from winning their gamble that they could end the war before American power could be felt.

Following the German defeat at Champagne-Marne, the Allies began a series of coordinated counterattacks that were to last until the end of the war. The first assignment given the American Army in the Allied offensive was the reduction of the St. Mihiel salient, a 16-mile-wide wedge that extended across the Meuse River southeast of Verdun and that had been held by the Germans for four years. On September 12, 500,000 Americans, assisted by French and British planes and using French artillery, began their attack. Within four days—with the help of some French colonial troops—they had driven back the German forces and straightened out the front in the sector. Pershing now prepared to push forward and conquer Metz, but this project was vetoed by Foch, who had other plans for the American Army. During the battle, the Americans suffered 7,000 casualties, captured more than 400 guns, and took 1,600 prisoners.

After its victory at St. Mihiel, the American Army was shifted to the west and began an advance down the Meuse River and through the Argonne Forest with Sedan as its ultimate objective. The Meuse-Argonne campaign, which began on September 26, was part of the general Allied attack that included the Somme offensive (August 8–November 11), the Oise-Aisne offensive (August 18–November 11), and the Ypres-Lys offensive (August 19–November 11). The American and French forces that participated in the 40-day Meuse-Argonne battle captured more than 25,000 prisoners, 874 cannon, and 3,000 machine guns. Of the 1,200,000 Americans engaged in the fighting, 117,000 became casualties. Although the war ended before the capture of Sedan, the American forces advanced steadily throughout the campaign, and the progress of the Meuse-Argonne attack along with the successful offensives on the other sectors of the front led directly to the German decision to ask for an armistice.

Although the major American military effort was confined to France, an American regiment was dispatched to Italy in July, 1918, and two American divisions fought with the French in Belgium during the last month of the war. In addition, after the Bolshevik Revolution of November, 1917, and Lenin's *coup d'état* in 1918, a limited number of American troops joined the European Allies in widely separated attacks on Soviet Russia. In the Archangel-Murmansk campaign in 1918–19, 5,000 American soldiers fought, and 9,000 Americans participated in the attacks on Vladivostock and eastern Siberia. It was not until January, 1920, that the last American troops were withdrawn from Russia's eastern-most possessions.

During World War I, the American soldiers overseas captured 1,400 guns, took 44,000 prisoners, and destroyed 755 enemy airplanes. At the same time, 48,909 Americans were killed in battle, 237,135 were wounded, 2,913 were reported missing in action, 4,434 were captured, and 56,991 died of disease. This total of approximately 350,000 casualties in one year should be compared with four years of Allied losses. By 1918, Russian battle deaths were 1,700,000, German 1,600,000, French 1,385,000, British 900,000, and Austro-Hungarian 800,000.

Mobilizing American Industry and Transportation

Although comparatively few Americans had to fight in the war, every American had to help pay for it. The Department of the Treasury put the direct cost of the war to the United States up to October, 1919, at $32,830,000,000. Of this amount, approximately one third was contributed by American taxpayers, while $21,326,777,000 was raised by four Liberty Loans in 1917–18 and a Victory Loan in 1919. Profiting from the experiences of the European belligerents earlier in the war and Jay Cooke's spectacular success in the Civil War the Administration decided to sell its bonds directly to individual buyers and to attempt to reach small as well as large investors. All five bond sales, each of which was oversubscribed, were put across by the modern sales methods of American business enterprise. States were assigned quotas and encouraged to compete with one another; volunteers of all kinds, from Wall Street bankers to Boy Scouts, aided in the work; rallies were held in public squares; captured war trophies were exhibited with appropriate slogans; full-page advertisements were inserted in the press; ministers preached "Liberty loan sermons"; stage stars sold bonds to their audiences; prominent Americans toured the country urging greater contributions; and the manufacture and distribution of "Liberty Loan posters" became a major industry. The pressure was nearly irresistible, but a German-sounding name, a guilty conscience about a draft exemption, or a desire to keep up with the Joneses were probably as effective methods of bond selling as all the stratagems of the American advertising industry.

The difference between the total cost of the war and the proceeds from bond sales was made up by taxation. New duties were imposed on every form of luxury from chewing gum to Pullman berths, but the bulk of the additional revenue during the war was produced by increased taxes on incomes and business profits. When the United States entered the war, the basic income-tax rate was 2 per cent and the maximum surtax 13 per cent. Under the War Revenue Act of October, 1917,

JOSEPH PENNELL DEL.

THAT LIBERTY SHALL NOT
PERISH FROM THE EARTH
BUY LIBERTY BONDS
FOURTH LIBERTY LOAN

Liberty Bond Poster of World War I

the basic rate was raised to 4 per cent and the maximum surtax to 50 per cent. Provision was also made for a 6 per cent tax on corporations and an excess profits tax of 20 to 60 per cent on the business earnings of individuals and corporations. Increased expenditures during the second year of American fighting and protests about war profiteering necessitated a further upward revision; and in September, 1918, the basic income tax was raised to 12 per cent, the highest surtax to 65 per cent, and the excess profits tax to a range of 35 to 70 per cent. More than

$32,000,000,000 was thus raised by the government for the prosecution of the war. Of this, $10,338,000,000 was advanced to the Allies as loans, and the remainder paid for the American war effort.

When the United States entered the war, the task of organizing the American economy for victory was undertaken by the Council of National Defense, which had been established by Congress in 1916 as part of the preparedness campaign. In the months that followed the American declaration of war, the council, which consisted of six cabinet members and advisers from labor and industry, assigned the management of the American war economy to a series of specially created agencies, such as the War Industries Board, the Food Administration, the War Trade Board, the Railroad Administration, the War Shipping Administration, and a host of others that covered practically every phase of American wartime life. As the war progressed, it became increasingly apparent that the efficiency of the Council of National Defense and its subordinate agencies was being impaired by the failure to provide for centralized authority and responsibility. By the spring of 1918, the war in Europe was approaching its climax, but the hodge-podge of conflicting wartime bureaus was seriously threatening the United States' ability to supply the troops at the front. The government was forced to overhaul its entire wartime organization. On March 18, 1918, the War Industries Board was made an autonomous agency with almost limitless authority over American industrial life and was placed under the chairmanship of Bernard Baruch, who was responsible only to the President. Two months later, Congress passed the Overman Act, which granted the President the power to abolish old agencies and create new ones, to use money for whatever purposes he thought necessary and "to utilize, co-ordinate, or consolidate any executive or administrative commissions, bureaus, agencies, offices, or officers now existing by law."

The reorganization of the War Industries Board converted Bernard Baruch into a virtual czar over the American economy for the duration of the war. Under his direction, the War Industries Board fixed the prices of military and civilian goods, standardized industrial products, granted priorities to some firms and withheld them from others, compelled "nonessential" industries to convert to war production, assumed charge of all the government's purchases, and undertook a program for the conservation of the country's resources. These measures were strong medicine to a people bred on economic individualism, but critics could be silenced by appeals to patriotism. The efficacy of a planned economy was soon demonstrated by the results, for during

A Day's Production at the Ford Plant

[BROWN BROTHERS]

the last months of the war American factories poured forth an uninterrupted stream of goods for the armies of the United States and its allies.

To insure the continued production of American industry, the government had to take unprecedented steps to conserve and allocate the American fuel supply. Soon after the United States entered the war, increased demand for coal, a shortage of freight cars, and the flow of miners to the armed services and higher-paying jobs produced a serious fuel shortage. To meet the crisis the President in August, 1917, established the Fuel Administration, which, under the chairmanship of President Harry A. Garfield of Williams College, assumed responsibility for the production and distribution of coal and petroleum products. Fuel consumption was reduced by introducing daylight saving time, the temporary closing of nonessential industrial plants, and an informal but effective rationing system that included "fuelless Mondays" and "gasless Sundays" for the nation's automobile users. Under the supervision of the Fuel Administration, drastic methods increased coal production during the war. Submarginal mines were brought into operation; more efficient mining methods were introduced; and the relations between miners and mine owners were placed under government supervision.

Mere regulation assured industrial production, but the need for haste in delivering American soldiers and goods to Europe compelled the government to take over entirely the operation of the country's transportation and communication facilities. Five days after the American declaration of war, railroad officials representing 631 lines set up the Railroads' War Board as a voluntary association to eliminate competition for the duration of the war; but within eight months, the private administration of American railroads had become so chaotic that the Atlantic ports were receiving practically no shipments from the West. The railroad executives begged the government for assistance, and a member of the Interstate Commerce Commission complained that the "element of self-interest . . . is a persistent factor in postponing and resisting measures that seek . . . to secure transportation results as a whole." By the end of 1917, the situation was menacing the entire American war effort, and Woodrow Wilson announced—to the joy of the owners, who had been losing money despite the tremendous increase in traffic—that the government would take over the nation's railroads. Under the direction of Secretary of the Treasury McAdoo, the railroads were operated as a unified system, were compensated on the basis of their earnings for the three years preceding June 30, 1917, and came under the most efficient form of administration in their entire history. Before the end of the war, the Treasury Department also assumed responsibility for the management of express companies and inland water transportation, while the telephone, telegraph, and cable services became adjuncts of the Post Office Department.

Although in October, 1917, the control of American exports was also placed under a single agency, the War Trade Board, a far more difficult problem than regulating American overseas trade was to find additional ships to carry it. Woodrow Wilson had recommended as early as 1914 that the government build and operate its own fleet of merchant vessels, but Congress had refused to act, despite the ability of the German submarines to sink ships faster than the Allies could build them. Not until September 7, 1916, did Congress establish the United States Shipping Board, with an appropriation of $50,000,000 to purchase or build merchant ships. Following the American entry into the war, the Shipping Board set up an Emergency Fleet Corporation to build, buy, and commandeer an American merchant marine. Under the successive administrations of General George W. Goethals and Charles M. Schwab, the Emergency Fleet Corporation seized en-

Hog Island Shipyard, 1918

[BROWN BROTHERS]

emy vessels in American ports, bought neutral vessels, took over the operation of American private shipping, and built four enormous ship-yards using ninety-four different methods for the construction of new ships. By September 1, 1918, the Shipping Board controlled nearly 8,700,000 tons of merchant shipping—a figure, however, that showed the Fleet Corporation's ability to lay its hands on practically every-thing that would float rather than the speed with which it built new ships. A month before the end of the war, only slightly more than 464,000 tons of shipping had been completed. The fabulous Hog Island shipyard, with its 80 miles of railroad and 250 buildings, did not deliver its first ship to the government until three weeks after the armistice had been signed.

Despite life and death powers over American business enterprise during the war, few firms suffered; in fact, most of them enjoyed the most prosperous years of their existence. Even with the increase in taxes and government attempts at price fixing, several corporations made unprecedented profits during the war. In 1918, ten steel com-panies had profits ranging from 30 to 319 per cent of their investments. The profits of the four leading meat-packing concerns rose from an average of $19,000,000 during 1912–14 to $68,000,000 after the United States entered the war. In 1917, twenty-one copper companies earned 24 per cent on their investment, while in the same year, the profits after taxes of forty-eight lumber companies were 17 per cent and those of 106 refining companies 21 per cent.

A buyers' market during the war years partly accounted for swollen profits, but official laxity also helped. Several key positions in the wartime organizations controlling the American economy were held by dollar-a-year men. They served the government for virtually nothing while continuing to receive large salaries from private corporations for which they formerly had worked and with which they frequently had to deal as government representatives. Some dollar-a-year men occasionally revealed that their loyalties were with their private employers rather than the taxpayers; and in at least one industry—aircraft production—the American war effort was seriously impeded by maladministration of a dollar-a-year man. War profiteering was also helped by the government's device for granting contracts. Because the War Industries Board did not want production delayed by prolonged negotiations over terms with contractors, it abandoned the traditional practice of competitive bidding for the "cost-plus" contract, which guaranteed the firm in question a flat profit ranging from $2\frac{1}{2}$ to 15 per cent of the cost of production. By padding their costs, several contractors were able to obtain proportionately larger profits. Businessmen as a class were as patriotic as any other group of Americans, but some of them were willing to put a price on their patriotism.

The huge wartime profits of American industry convinced many workers that they should use their strategic position under war conditions to gain advantages that had been denied them in peace. Although the Wilson Administration had won the support of a large segment of organized labor with the passage of the Clayton and Adamson Acts, American workers were far from satisfied with their lot during the period of American neutrality. Wages in 1916 were 6 per cent higher than in 1913, but prices had risen approximately 50 per cent during the same period. Left-wing or direct-action labor organizations such as the Industrial Workers of the World, which condemned the war as an imperialist struggle fought for the benefit of the nation's financiers and industrialists, refused to give the government their support, and their propaganda put an edge on the demands of more conservative laborers.

On March 9, 1917, Samuel Gompers announced that the nonradical American workingman was ready to stand behind his government in a war against Germany. But Gompers, who was an advisory member of the Council of National Defense, did not give the Wilson Administration a blank check. In return for labor's cooperation, he demanded that the government curb war profiteering among businessmen, prevent employers from crushing the labor movement under the guise of patriotism, and set up some machinery that would enable the workers to preserve their rights without strikes. The government made an effort to fulfill these conditions. In March, 1918, the War Labor Conference Board, which had been set up as an advisory body by the Secretary of Labor two months earlier, drew up a set of principles that guided the Administration for the remainder of the war. In return for a no-strike pledge, labor was assured of the right to "organize in trade-unions and to bargain collectively through chosen representatives"; the maintenance of existing standards in union shops; "safeguards and regulations for the protection of the health and safety of workers"; "the basic eight hour day in all cases in which existing law requires it"; and in all other cases the settlement of the question of hours "with due regard to governmental necessities and the welfare, health, and proper comfort of the workers"; and a "living wage" with "minimum rates of pay . . . to insure the subsistence of the worker and his family in health and comfort." A National War Labor Board was established under the chairmanship of former President Taft and Frank P. Walsh to "settle by mediation and conciliation controversies arising between employers and workers," while "questions involving the distribution of labor, wages, hours, and working conditions" were handled by a War Labor Policies Board headed by Professor Felix Frankfurter of Harvard University.

The government's wartime labor program paid dividends. Most American workingmen made gains, but not in wages. Although by the end of the war, wages were 30 per cent above the 1913 level, real wages only approximated those of 1916. The length of the working day however was whittled down, and by 1918, 48.6 per cent of all American workers were employed on a forty-eight-hour week. The most dramatic change in labor conditions came in the growth of unionized workers. The American Federation of Labor with the support of the government increased its membership from 1,996,004 in 1913 to 2,726,478 in 1918. These labor advances, however, proved to be only an interlude made possible by a friendly government. Few of the wartime gains had come as a result of labor's own efforts, superior organization, or class solidarity; and when the war ended, the Wilson Administration and its successor became hostile to organized labor. Right-wing labor, with few resources of its own, fell an easy prey to militant employers who were bent on destroying the American labor movement. Radical labor suffered severe setbacks during the war as well as afterwards. In June, 1917, for example, 1,186 striking members of the

I.W.W. at the Bisbie, Arizona, copper mines were deported by the owners to Columbus, New Mexico, where they were interned; and for the remainder of the war the I.W.W.'s leaders were hounded and thrown into jail by the Department of Justice.

Making Farm and Home Militant

Farmers and housewives, as well as workers and businessmen, were mobilized for victory by the government, for the need to increase agricultural production and reduce domestic food consumption soon became one of the most pressing problems of the war. Since Russian food supplies were shut off and a large part of the most fertile regions of France were devastated, unprecedented demands were placed on the United States for foodstuffs for the Allies and the American armed forces. Under the slogan "Food Will Win the War," the government set to work to increase the output of the nation's farms and to cut down the consumption of those essentials most needed abroad. As early as May, 1917, Herbert Hoover, who had been widely acclaimed for his work as chairman of the Commission for Belgian Relief, was named Food Administrator, and three months later he was given as much authority over the production and distribution of American agricultural products as was eventually exercised by Bernard Baruch over industry. By the end of the war, the Food Administrator had assumed control over the shipments of all American foodstuffs, taken over and resold the supply of imported raw sugar, licensed approximately 250,000 food distributors, and established a Grain Corporation that purchased the entire wheat crops of 1917 and 1918 at fixed prices.

The American farmer did not have to be urged to increase production. Assurance of high prices and the demands of patriotism provided all the incentive that was necessary. During the war years, American agricultural production increased 24 per cent, while the annual wheat crop rose from 636,655,000 to 967,790,000 bushels from 1917 to 1919, and wheat acreage increased from 45,000,000 to 75,000,000 acres. This phenomenal rise in production was obtained, however, at a considerable price to the farmers, for in the postwar years they were to discover that they had mortgaged their future for wartime prosperity. With the easy credit facilities provided by the government, many staple producers expanded their holdings and assumed an inflated debt burden that they were unable to carry after European demand fell off. By hastening the trend toward one-crop specialization, the war also lessened the farmer's flexibility and made it that much more difficult for him to meet the needs of a changing peacetime market. Plowing up millions of acres of the Great Plains also prepared the way for a harvest of dust a few years later. By the 1920's, when the European market had collapsed, the American farmer, who had boasted during the war that he had fed the Allies, frequently found it difficult to feed himself.

In his program to reduce the domestic consumption of food, Hoover preferred to rely on exhortation rather than compulsion. European rationing systems were rejected for "wheatless Mondays" and "meatless Tuesdays." Propaganda campaigns preached the "gospel of the clean plate" and urged Americans to eat "whales, porpoises, and dolphins" and "less wheat, meat, milk, fats, sugar." Consumers were also asked to increase the supply of foodstuffs, and with government encouragement suburbanites and city children planted war gardens, and women volunteered for a land army to relieve the farm labor shortage. The mass of Americans willingly supported the whole of the government's program for food administration, and the steady increase in American food shipments to Europe showed the effectiveness of supplementing close government supervision over some details of the program with appeals for voluntary cooperation.

The morale-boosting effect of this home-front mobilization still fell short of the Administration's expectations. The local elections of the fall of 1917 seemed to show pockets of serious resistance to Wilson's call for all-out effort. The returns were most disturbing in cities with large foreign-born groups. Socialist candidates with pacifist leanings ran surprisingly strong. Clearly, the nation had to be stirred to greater patriotic fervor. On April 14, 1917, ten days after the American declaration of war, the Committee of Public Information had been established with George Creel, a former newspaperman, as its chairman, and it was this body that had the responsibility for building civilian morale and guarding against loss of vital secrets. Creel always maintained that his committee was in "no degree . . . an agency of censorship, a machinery of concealment or repression," but that it was waging a battle of words in a "fight for the *minds* of men, for 'the conquest of their convictions' " and that the "battle-line ran through every home in the country." Creel's audience was not, however, confined to the United States, for "every conceivable means was used to reach the foreign mind with America's message"; and in 1920, Creel stated that "before this flood of publicity the German misrepresentations were swept away in Switzerland, the Scandinavian countries, Italy, Spain, the Far East, Mexico, and Central and South America."

Creel enlisted the support of businessmen, politicians, professors, college presidents, poets, novelists, artists, photographers, essayists, and numerous others in every walk of life. The prediction that war would capture the enthusiasm of many intellectuals was borne out. Creel's assertion that there was "no medium of appeal that we did not employ" was not an exaggeration. The committee published more than fifty pamphlets in English and other languages and distributed them to more than 75,000,000 people in the United States; issued the *Official Bulletin of the United States*, a daily newspaper for government employees, with a circulation of 100,000; distributed "news" to more than 1,600 newspapers, including the foreign-language press; organized the Four Minute Men, with 75,000 speakers who made 755,190 speeches, "every one having the carry of shrapnel"; used 1,438 different drawings in its campaign of "pictorial publicity"; established the Division of Women's War Work, which "prepared and issued the information of peculiar interest to the women of the United States"; distributed movies bearing titles such as "Pershing's Crusaders" and "America's Answer"; and issued more than 200,000 stereopticon slides. Creel always insisted that he was interested only in publicizing the truth; but the line between education and indoctrination was a thin one, and Creel's office was responsible for more than one fabrication. Furthermore, the tendency of the Committee on Information, like all propaganda agencies, to attribute nothing but evil to the enemy and nothing but good to its own cause heightened the feelings of hate and distrust that permeated American society during the war years and that ill prepared Americans for the realistic tasks of peace-making that lay ahead.

Those that the government could not convince it often arrested. While every nation at war must take certain precautions to insure its internal security, there is no evidence that the government's program of wartime thought control contributed in any appreciable measure to the safety of the United States. Such puerile measures as banning pretzels or not playing Wagner operas or, more seriously, arresting pacifists or beating up German-American citizens put a premium on conformity, destroyed the civil rights of many citizens, and created a mass hysteria that could have become as serious a threat to American democracy as Germany's military forces. President Wilson urged freedom for the world, but his own government systematically hacked away at freedom in the United States.

The government's campaign to punish those who refused to accept its views or who obstructed the war effort was carried out under two statutes enacted during the war. The Espionage Act of June 15, 1917, provided:

> Whoever, when the United States is at war, shall . . . convey false reports or false statements with intent to interfere with

Aliens Are Sent to Jail, 1918

the operation or success of the military or naval forces of the United States, or to promote the success of its enemies, or . . . cause . . . insubordination, disloyalty, mutiny, or refusal of duty, in the military or naval forces of the United States or shall willfully obstruct . . . the recruiting or enlistment service of the United States . . . shall be punished by a fine of not more than $10,000 or imprisonment for not more than twenty years, or both.

Under the terms of the Sedition Act, which became law on May 16, 1918, Americans were forbidden to "willfully utter, print, write, or publish any disloyal, profane, scurrilous or abusive language about the form of government of the United States, or the military or naval forces of the United States" or to "urge, incite or advocate any curtailment of production in this country of any thing or things, product or products, necessary or essential to the prosecution of the war."

Armed with the sweeping powers provided by national and state legislation, federal and local officials undertook to purge the country of its disloyal elements. The Post Office Department banned from the mails the *Masses*, the socialist *Milwaukee Leader*, Thorstein Veblen's *Imperial Germany and the Industrial Revolution*, the *Nation*, and a magazine that quoted Jefferson on Irish independence. The Justice Department, however, outdid every other branch of the government in its determination to rid the country of what it considered subversive and traitorous persons and groups. Its Bureau of Investigation made illegal arrests, confiscated private papers, raided newspaper offices, destroyed private property, and held prisoners without bail. People were sent to jail, not for overt acts, but for opinions uttered "in the heat of private altercation, on a railroad train, in a hotel lobby, or at that battle ground of disputation, a boarding-house table." * Men and women were imprisoned for saying that the war should be financed by higher taxes instead of bond sales and for criticising the Red Cross or Y.M.C.A. One woman was sentenced to ten years in jail for stating, "I am for the people, and the government is for the profiteers." A movie producer received a similar sentence for releasing a film that depicted English soldiers killing women and children in the American Revolution. The Justice Department also enlisted the support of "hundreds of thousands" of Americans in a hunt for German spies. John Lord O'Brian, assistant to the Attorney General during the war, stated in 1919 that these amateur spy-chasers did little but add to the "war hysteria and war excitement" and that "no other cause contributed so much to the oppression of innocent men as the systematic and indiscriminate agitation against what was claimed to be an all-pervasive system of German espionage."

During the war and the years immediately following it, left-wing labor groups and other radicals were the principal targets of the government's loyalty program, and the claims of patriotism were used to destroy unpopular reform groups as well as genuine spy-rings. On September 5, 1917, agents of the Department of Justice made simultaneous raids on I.W.W. headquarters throughout the nation. In the trials that followed, 100 Wobblies, including "Big Bill" Haywood, were given prison sentences that ranged from one to twenty years and were fined a total of $2,300,000. By February, 1918, Haywood estimated that there were 2,000 members of the I.W.W. in jail. The democratic Socialists fared little better. Eugene V. Debs, Victor Berger, and several others were sent to prison because of their refusal to give the war their moral support. If no other evidence were available, the number of men and women who lost their freedom because of the unpopularity of their

---

* Zechariah Chafee, Jr., *Free Speech in the United States* (Cambridge, Mass.: Harvard University Press, 1941), p. 53.

ideas was sufficient proof that the New Freedom was dead and that the war had killed it.

However cruel and mindless it often was, the crusading spirit helped do the job. Within sixteen months a peace-loving, heterogeneous people had raised, shipped, and supplied an army that proved decisive in the final German defeat. But the price paid for the failure to give Americans a realistic view of the war, especially for Wilson's failure to educate them for what would be really needed to make the world safe for democracy, soon became apparent. Within a few months after the armistice, the American people were to learn that winning the peace could be even more difficult than winning the war.

The Fight for a Just Peace

Throughout the war, Wilson never permitted the people of the world to forget the ideals for which he thought the United States and its allies were fighting. In many speeches, which George Creel's Committee on Public Information distributed to Allied and neutral countries and even behind the enemy's lines, the American President proclaimed that the United States was waging war against the German government rather than the German people and that peace would mean neither annexations by the victors nor the payment of reparations by the losers. But Wilson went beyond the immediate question of the fate of the Central Powers, for he insisted that following the war, international anarchy would have to give way to international order and that the nations of the world would have to set up and join an organization to maintain peace. Wilson's peace proposals proved an invaluable Allied weapon, for they doubtless lessened the will of the Germans to continue the war. They were not, however, an accurate summary of Allied war aims, and no steps were taken during the war to force the European Allies who did not share Wilson's idealism to change their objectives. When the war was over and American aid was no longer needed, Wilson had no major weapon to force the Allies to change.

Even before the American entrance into the war, Wilson in a speech to the Senate on January 22, 1917 announced his opposition to a "peace forced upon the loser, a victor's terms imposed upon the vanquished," for it "would be accepted in humiliation, under duress, at an intolerable sacrifice, and would leave a sting, a resentment, a bitter memory upon which terms of peace would rest, not permanently, but only as upon quicksand." For a punitive peace Wilson would substitute a "peace without victory" and "a peace between equals." Approximately a year later, Wilson was ready to fill in the details of his proposals for an enduring peace, and on January 8, 1918, he announced his Fourteen Points:

I. Open covenants of peace, openly arrived at. . . .

II. Absolute freedom of . . . the seas . . . in peace and in war. . . .

III. The removal, so far as possible, of all economic barriers and the establishment of an equality of trade conditions among all the nations consenting to the peace and associating themselves for its maintenance.

IV. Adequate guarantees given and taken that national armaments will be reduced to the lowest point consistent with domestic safety.

V. A free, open-minded, and absolutely impartial adjustment of all colonial claims, based upon a strict observance of the principle that in determining all such questions of sovereignty the interests of the populations concerned must have equal weight with the equitable claims of the government whose title is to be determined.

VI. The evacuation of all Russian territory. . . .

VII. Belgium . . . must be evacuated and restored, without any attempt to limit the sovereignty which she enjoys in common with all other free nations.

VIII. All French territory should be freed and the invaded portions restored, and the wrong done to France by Prussia in 1871 in the matter of Alsace-Lorraine . . . should be righted. . . .

IX. A readjustment of the frontiers of Italy should be effected along clearly recognizable lines of nationality.

X. The peoples of Austria-Hungary, whose place among the nations we wish to see safeguarded and assured, should be accorded the freest opportunity of autonomous development.

XI. Rumania, Serbia, and Montenegro should be evacuated, occupied territories restored . . . and the relations of the several Balkan states to one another determined by friendly counsel along lines of allegiance and nationality. . . .

XII. The Turkish portions of the present Ottoman Empire should be assured a secure sovereignty, but the other nationalities which are now under Turkish rule should be assured an undoubted security of life, an absolutely unmolested opportunity of autonomous development, and the Dardanelles should be permanently opened as a free passage to the ships and commerce of all nations under international guarantees.

XIII. An independent Polish state should be erected which should include the territories inhabited by indisputably Polish populations, which should be assured a free and secure access to the sea. . . .

XIV. A general association of nations must be formed under specific covenants for the purpose of affording mutual guarantees of political independence and territorial integrity to great and small states alike.

Self-determination

League of Nations

Wilson and many of his supporters in both Europe and the United States assumed that in his pronouncements on the settlements that would follow the war he was speaking for both the Allied governments and the American people; but although Wilson's prestige was enormous during the last stages of the war, he had neither an Allied nor an American mandate as a peacemaker. The Allies never accepted the Fourteen Points as the basis for peacemaking. At best, they took Wilson's ideals as mere wartime propaganda. If Wilson's peace plans were to succeed, he had to win the Allied leaders over to his program and to convince the voters of his own country that his proposals would not jeopardize what many considered the national interests of the United States. Both tasks proved far more arduous than Wilson had anticipated.

The struggle over Wilson's proposals at the Paris Peace Conference has frequently been described as a clash of personalities. According to this view, Wilson, a noble idealist, was pitted against the wily, pragmatic Clemenceau, while Lloyd George played the part of the clever politician, and Orlando went home in a huff. In reality, the contest at Paris was as much a conflict of national aspirations as an argument among four high-spirited men. Italy entered the war for loot, and as soon as it became apparent that all its demands would not be met, the Italian representatives withdrew from the conference. Clemenceau and Lloyd George were the spokesmen of democracies, and the electorates of both countries had clearly indicated that they favored a harsh peace. The French and English people had been through more than four years of death, misery, and destruction, while Germany had emerged from the war starving but physically intact. Although the French and English masses might admire Wilson's peace aims in the abstract, they could not accept them as a substitute for the punishment of the enemy and a guarantee against future German aggression. Wilson offered them world order and international good will; they demanded revenge and security. Lloyd George had received the overwhelming support of England's voters when he promised to hang the Kaiser, and Clemenceau was undoubtedly speaking for most Frenchmen when he demanded that Germany give up the Rhineland and be forced to pay reparations.

Prior commitments, as well as the wishes of their countrymen, accounted for the opposition of the Allied leaders to the Fourteen Points. During the first years of the war, England, France, Italy, Rumania, and Japan had negotiated a series of secret treaties that provided for the partition of the German and Austrian empires. Wilson undoubtedly knew of the existence of these treaties, but he had made no effort to induce the Allies to renounce them when the United States entered the war. And when the war was over, neither the Allied statesmen nor their constituents were prepared to abandon these prospective territorial gains for the American President's version of a peace without victory.

Wilson was placed at a further disadvantage in his negotiations with the Allied leaders because he arrived in Paris without the full support of the American voters. Wilson, who had proved himself a master politician when he pushed his domestic reform program through Congress, failed to keep his political fences in repair after the United States entered the war. Overcome with a notion of his own moral superiority and a sense of mission, and convinced of the manifest advantages of his own peace proposals, he preferred to ignore rather than to recognize any domestic opposition. On the surface, at least, his task should not have been impossible. During the early years of the war in Europe, Republican leaders had apparently favored some form of world organization. The League to Enforce Peace, which had been founded in 1915 and had soon become the most prominent of the private societies established to promote peace through international cooperation and control, had received strong Republican support. William Howard Taft served as its president, and in 1916, Henry Cabot Lodge had publicly endorsed its objectives. But in 1918, the chances of a Republican victory in the midterm elections took precedence over the demand for international planning, and the party's high command decided to capitalize on the traditional isolationism of its midwestern supporters and the general war weariness of all voters by attacking the President's foreign policy. Wilson replied on October 24, 1918, by requesting the election of a Democratic Congress as proof of American loyalty. The Republicans, quick to recognize the extent of Wilson's blunder, pointed out that they as well as the Democrats had demonstrated their loyalty with their lives and their money, and on election day enough American voters ignored the President's request to give the Republicans control of both the House and Senate. Despite the success of these tactics, Wilson made no move to blunt or deflect the Republican offensive. He called on no prominent Republicans for assistance in the formulation of America's peace proposals, took no leading Republican politicians with him to Paris, and invited no member of the Senate to join the American delegation to the peace conference.

The Paris Peace Conference, which convened on January 18, 1919, fell far short of the ideal envisioned by Wilson. The legacy of centuries of hyper-nationalism, imperialism, and balance-of-power politics could not be uprooted by appeals to reason, and in the end the very forces in international society that Wilson had hoped to destroy wrecked his plans for a just peace. The threat of both national and international chaos in many parts of the world put a premium on speed. Complex problems that had perplexed statesmen for generations had to be resolved in a matter of days or hours. Sometimes the extraordinary size of the conference militated against its efficiency and made it so unwieldy that there seemed no alternative but to substitute secret for open diplomacy. Long before the Germans were called in to sign the completed treaty at Versailles on June 28, 1919, the plenary conference of the twenty-seven Allied and Associated Powers had become little more than a rubber stamp for decisions reached in advance by France, Great Britain, the United States, and Italy in either the Council of Ten or the Council of Four. The fear of communism also conditioned many of the conference's most important decisions. Russia, in addition to the Central Powers, had been excluded from the deliberations at Paris, and in the minds of many delegates the need to thwart Soviet plans for a world revolution took precedence over any desire to draw up a program for lasting peace.

Despite the obstacles that confronted him at Paris, Wilson was able to have some of his ideas for the reorganization of world society incorporated into the peace treaty. Germany's former colonies were not annexed by the Allied powers, but held as mandates under the general supervision of the League of Nations. An attempt was made to apply the principle of self-determination to the formation of the new states in eastern Europe, although a new federation of those many nations might have been a more realistic device for creating a viable central European economy and for assuring peace along the Danube and in the Balkans. Wilson could not prevent the territorial aggrandisement of the victors, but he did succeed in forestalling the Italian an-

Covenant

nexation of Fiume and the Japanese acquisition of the Shantung peninsula in China. Clemenceau abandoned French claims to the Rhineland
in return for Wilson's promise of a treaty that stated that the United
States would "come immediately" to the aid of France if there were
"an unprovoked movement of aggression" by Germany. Most important for Wilson was winning the approval of the other delegates for
the League of Nations and the inclusion of the League Covenant in the
Treaty of Versailles, for Wilson believed that the League would eventually right the major wrongs of the Versailles settlement.

Although the Covenant of the League of Nations was made an
integral part of the Treaty of Versailles, the settlements reached at
Paris remained in almost all other respects a victors' peace. Germany
was compelled to accept full responsibility for the war, pay reparations to the victors, abolish its fleet and army, relinquish its colonies,
transfer Alsace-Lorraine to France and part of Silesia and Posen to
Poland, consent to the French occupation of the Saar until 1935, and
turn over the control of a large portion of its economy to the Allies.
Germany's losses were the Allies' gains, for the provisions of the secret
treaties that divided the spoils of war were in many cases incorporated
into the Treaty of Versailles.

The Battle Lines for Peace

The concessions that were wrung from Wilson in return for support for the League produced a peace settlement that bore little resemblance to the program outlined in the Fourteen Points. The treaty
contained a section on reparations that heightened rather than reduced
international tensions and rivalries. It did not solve the problem of national boundaries in eastern Europe, and self-determination created as
many minority problems as it solved. The League was designed to preserve world peace, but the Covenant furnished no workable formula
for the reduction of national armaments or for defining or preventing
aggression. Although political peace depended on economic cooperation, no provision was made at Paris for the removal of trade barriers
that separated the nations of the world. Despite these defects of the
treaty, it remained the best that Wilson could obtain under existing
circumstances, and many of his critics in the United States objected
to the agreements reached at Paris for far less statesmanlike reasons.

The opposition that developed within the United States to the
Treaty of Versailles included various groups of Americans who had
little in common. Friends of Germany thought the terms of the treaty
too harsh. Irish-Americans feared that the Covenant would insure

Ireland's continued subservience to England. Italian-Americans complained that the treaty deprived Italy of the fruits of victory. Some Republicans disliked a peace framed by Democrats. Many isolationists thought that the League would destroy American sovereignty by creating a world superstate. Some liberals who had supported the war at the urging of men like John Dewey, and who had been prepared for a just peace by Wilson's speeches, blanched at what came back from Paris. They regretted the price America had paid in the suppression of liberties at home to win a victory for "power politics" abroad.

Within the Senate, there were four distinct groups involved in the struggle over the ratification of the Paris agreements. Many, but not all, Democratic senators thought that the Treaty and Covenant should be adopted without either major or minor changes. At the other extreme were a few "bitter enders," who were led by Senators William E. Borah of Idaho and Hiram Johnson of California and who were unalterably opposed to any kind of American participation in a world organization. Several Republicans who joined Henry Cabot Lodge as "strict reservationists," although unable to accept Borah's and Johnson's isolationist views, were equally determined to defeat any peace proposals presented to the Senate by Woodrow Wilson. A larger number of Republicans and a few Democrats who became known as the "mild reservationists," supported the Covenant in principle but favored certain changes that they believed necessary to insure the rights of the United States. But in the summer of 1919, Wilson had overwhelming press support for "his" treaty and resolutions of approval from nearly all state legislatures.

In most accounts of the defeat of the League of Nations in the Senate, Henry Cabot Lodge has been cast as the villain of the piece—a role that he may or may not deserve—but that does not explain the drama enacted in Washington during 1919–20. Lodge beyond doubt loathed Woodrow Wilson with all the malevolence that some other Republicans were to reserve for the next Democratic occupant of the White House. Although Lodge was determined to use the League as a lever for partisan advantage, his criticism was not altogether negative. Lodge, who had resigned from the League to Enforce Peace, advocated the same kind of punitive peace that had been advanced by Clemenceau at Paris. He supported an American alliance with France, thought that the League and the Treaty should be considered separately, and approved of German reparations. Both Wilson and Lodge wished to prevent another war. While Wilson insisted that the way to preserve peace was to eliminate the causes of war, Lodge maintained that the threat of war could be removed only by making the victors so strong and the defeated so weak that Germany would neither dare nor be able to become an aggressor nation in the future. Both men could agree that Germany should never be permitted to start another war and that the United States should support a system of collective security, but they could not agree on the means for attaining these objectives. Wilson was an internationalist, Lodge, an interventionist; neither was an isolationist.

Since Borah, Johnson, and the other "bitter enders" were opposed to any type of American participation in European affairs, they were outside the main struggle in the Senate. The real contest lay between the Wilson Democrats and the Lodge Republicans. Neither side would compromise, and Lodge was prepared to resort to any tactics to block Senate approval of the League of Nations. In the summer and fall of 1919, he set out to change the country's mind and to obstruct Wilson's plan. He joined forces with the "bitter enders," who, although opposed to Lodge's interventionism, considered it a less immediate threat to American isolation than Wilson's internationalism. He directed a propaganda campaign against the President's foreign policy with funds supplied by Henry Clay Frick and Andrew Mellon, two Republican millionaires from Pennsylvania who were so hostile to Wilson's domestic reforms that they welcomed the opportunity to finance plans for his downfall. In the Senate itself, Lodge skillfully employed parliamentary tactics to defeat the League with a flanking movement rather than a frontal attack.

Throughout the summer of 1919, the Senate Foreign Relations Committee, which had fallen under the control of the strict reservationists after the congressional elections of the preceding autumn, aroused considerable hostility to the President's peace program by conducting hearings that emphasized the divisive forces within the United States and erroneously created the impression of overwhelming American opposition to the League. In early September, Wilson, after urging the Senate to act on the treaty, undertook a grueling speaking tour of the West in a final attempt to rally public opinion. On September 25, 1919, after a speech at Boulder, Colorado, he suffered a stroke and returned to Washington a crippled and helpless man. He was confined to his room in the White House, where he was guarded and held incommunicado by his wife and physician. The United States was virtually without a chief executive; Wilson lost touch with the Democratic leadership in the Senate; and Henry Cabot Lodge put the finishing touches on his plans for defeating the Versailles Treaty by indirection.

The balance of power in the conflict between the Administration Senators and the strict reservationists lay with the mild reservationists.

As the Administration Democrats and the mild reservationists between them had enough votes to ratify the treaty, Lodge's strategy was designed to prevent the two factions from joining forces. Lodge's original plan had been to mutilate the Covenant beyond recognition, but the forty-five amendments that he proposed were easily defeated by a coalition of the Democratic supporters of Wilson and the moderate Republicans. When this strategem failed, Lodge abandoned the amendments, which would have changed the actual content of the treaty and required the approval of the other signatory powers, for fourteen reservations that were American interpretations of the Covenant. Since the fourteen reservations were acceptable to the mild reservationists, the success of Lodge's policy rested on his assumption that Wilson would not permit his Democratic followers to accept a treaty that included any reservations.

The famous fourteen reservations, which soon became the focal point of the struggle over the treaty in the Senate, did not change the meaning of the Covenant or relieve the United States of any of its fundamental obligations to the League of Nations. They were, however, phrased in such a way as to create the impression that the United States would never give more than reluctant cooperation to the League. The reservations concerning the Monroe Doctrine and the American right to withdraw from the League merely repeated provisions in the Covenant. The reservation for Article X—a reservation responsible for more controversy than any other—stated that the United States would refuse to come to the aid of a League member attacked by another nation "unless in any particular case the Congress, which, under the Constitution, has the sole power to declare war . . . shall, in the exercise of full liberty of action, by act or joint resolution so provide." This reservation proved especially obnoxious to Wilson; but it was a simple statement of fact, for under the Constitution, Congress alone had the right to declare war.

The Lodge reservations were acceptable to all but the "bitter enders," who were opposed to the League with or without changes, and the Wilson Democrats. The mild reservationists did not consider the reservations a threat to American participation in the League. Several prominent Republicans outside the Senate held a similar view, and the League to Enforce Peace endorsed the reservations. Before the Senate's final rejection of the treaty, even the British government let it be known that it did not consider the reservations detrimental to the League. But Woodrow Wilson, as Lodge had anticipated, thought differently. He looked on the reservations as a denial of all that the League represented and a challenge to his own moral leadership. He had made all the compromises he thought he could at Paris and now to compromise further at home seemed treason to his mission. Sick and politically isolated, he ordered the Democratic senators to vote against the reservations. Party regularity did the rest, for by taking this stand Wilson ruled out compromise, missed his last chance for an alliance with the mild reservationists, and gave the victory to his arch-antagonist. To the very end Wilson persisted in believing that the choice lay between the treaty as he had presented it to the Senate and a treaty with the Lodge reservations. The votes in the Senate revealed the extent of Wilson's miscalculations. The alternatives were the treaty with mild reservations or no treaty at all.

The Lost Peace

On November 19, 1919, the Senate failed to ratify the treaty with the fourteen reservations by a vote of 39 to 55. The fifty-five Senators who voted in the negative comprised the Administration Democrats and the "bitter enders." (Although Borah and Johnson had helped Lodge draft the fourteen reservations, they had also informed him that they planned to vote against them.) The thirty-nine Senators who voted in favor of the treaty with reservations consisted of the mild reservationists and the Lodge group. In a second vote on the same day, on the treaty without reservations, thirty-eight Democrats were defeated by a combination of the mild reservationists, the strict reservationists, and the "bitter enders."

The public's response to the debacle of November 19 was immediate and pronounced. The American people had expected some form of peace settlement to be approved by the Senate; and church groups, civic organizations, labor unions, and such prominent Republicans as Elihu Root, William Howard Taft, and Herbert Hoover all urged the Senate to reconsider its decision. On March 19, 1920, the Senate yielded to this pressure and voted for the last time on the Versailles Treaty with reservations. Once again Woodrow Wilson played the role that Lodge had assigned him, for he stated that the reservations destroyed the meaning of the original peace settlement and implied that he would veto a resolution of ratification of the treaty with reservations. Despite Wilson's warning, twenty-one Administration Democrats from the Northern states joined twenty-eight Republicans in voting for ratification. But twenty-three Democrats, mostly from the South, combined with twelve Republicans to vote against it. Of the eighty-four Senators present, only forty-nine—seven less than the two-thirds majority needed—had voted for the treaty with reservations. It was not until the

"*Teaching Him What To Say*"
(*Rollin Kirby in the New York* World)

summer of 1921 that Congress passed a joint resolution stating that the war between the United States and Germany was ended.

Henry Cabot Lodge, as has been so frequently stated, may have murdered the peace treaty and the Covenant, but he received assistance from both willing and unwilling accomplices. The clash of two domineering personalities should not obscure the deeper forces behind the League's defeat in the United States. In 1917, the United States had forsaken isolation to join in a collective action to curb an aggressor nation. Two years later, the United States was asked to participate in a peacetime program of collective security. But this break with the past was too sharp for most Americans, and they reverted to the isolationist policy that they had honored and cherished for more than a century before 1917.

Even after the vote of March 19, Wilson refused to accept defeat. Once again he decided to appeal to the people, and he proclaimed that the presidential election of 1920 would be a solemn referendum on the League. But the election of 1920 was neither solemn nor a referendum. Warren G. Harding, who made a farce of the campaign, either knowingly or unknowingly confused the League issue, while, at the same time, one group of prominent Republicans proclaimed that a vote for Harding was a vote for the League and another announced that it was a vote for American isolation. The American people themselves in 1920 voted on many other issues besides the League. Many working people were angered by administration policies after 1918. The middle classes were probably voting to get back to the pursuit of comfort and money, or, as Harding preferred to put it, a "return to normalcy." After two decades of "uplift," striving, and noble aspirations both at home and abroad, citizens were tired of reform as represented by either the Progressive movement or a crusade to make the world safe for democracy. In 1920, middle class America did not vote against the League; it voted for a return to the days of President McKinley.

FOR SUPPLEMENTARY READING

Many of the books cited for Chapter 13 carry over into the war years. On military and naval history use J. G. Harbord, *The American Army in France, 1917–1919* (1936) and D. W. Mitchell, *History of the Modern American Navy,* (1946). C. Seymour covers the history of wartime diplomacy in *American Diplomacy During the World War* (1934). Mobilization of the economy is analyzed in Bernard Baruch's own account, *American Industry in War* (1941). Wartime intolerance and indoctrination can be gauged well from H. C. Peterson and G. C. Fite, *Opponents of War, 1917–1918* (1957) and Z. Chafee, Jr., *Free Speech in the United States* (1941).

All strands are woven together in F. L. Paxson's comprehensive three volumes, *American Democracy and the World War* (1936–1948). On the armistice, the Paris Conference, and Wilson's defeat, use, in order, H. Rudin, *Armistice, 1919* (1944), and T. A. Bailey, *Woodrow Wilson and the Lost Peace* (1944) and *Woodrow Wilson and the Great Betrayal* (1945). Herbert Hoover has recently written a touching memoir of Wilson in *The Ordeal of Woodrow Wilson* (1958); together with Link's *Wilson the Diplomatist* it corrects Bailey's excessive severity with Wilson.

15

America During Normalcy

T HE ERA from Harding to Hoover was one of paradoxes and contrasts. For many Americans the "roaring twenties" were years of boom, yet millions of farmers and laborers did not share in prosperity. It was the time when the nation rejected Wilsonian internationalism, yet after 1920 America's economic and political ties with Europe steadily increased. With a new frankness and ease in relations between the sexes and the popularity of evading prohibition, the twenties became a time for "making whoopee," but in many parts of the nation a resurgent puritanism warred vigorously against liquor, lechery, and "liberalism." In some respects, the "prosperity decade" was an age of disillusion for artists and intellectuals, of a splurge of materialism for the Babbitts on main street, and of mediocrity in public life at Washington and elsewhere. In other ways, however, the age brought a notable flowering of American letters, a naïve idealism about money and the machine, and the increasing dependence of the nation on scientific and expert management in industry and in government departments.

From Bust to Boom

With the exhaustion and defeat of Wilsonian progressivism, Americans turned from political reforms largely inspired by Main Street's idealism to settle back with relief into Main Street's other tradition of Yankeeism: sharp bargaining, chasing the dollar, and searching for new gadgets. Progressivism, for all its high moral tone; was partly an attempt to save America for what Wilson called "the man on the make." In the 1920's, however, the man on the make decided to pile up his money without looking too deeply into the moral and political consequences of his actions. The conscience that had erupted in progressivism became quiet, if it did not die, but the progressive dream of success for every man endured—indeed became stronger and more open than when it appeared in 1912 in its ideal guise of "giving America back to the people."

In the months after the armistice of November, 1918, the country scrambled back to peace time production and started a carefree junking of irritating wartime controls. After some economic dislocation, by the end of 1919 the "boys" were home from France and business was again booming. The boom was helped by the government's post-Armistice boost to purchasing power in the form of final payments on war contracts, loans to Europe that were in turn used to pay for American farm products, the building of more ships under the Emergency Fleet Corporation than during the war, and the easy credit policy of the Federal Reserve Board. But as soon as the government retrenched on spending in 1920, tightened credit, and ended loans to Europe, domestic purchasing power shrank, businessmen liquidated inventories, and the short boom turned into a bust. In the year 1920–21 the wholesale price index (1926 = 100) dropped from 154.4 to 97.6, unemployment increased from 1,305,000 to 4,225,000, bankruptcies more than doubled, and average farm prices were nearly halved.

Fortunately for those workers who held their jobs, prices fell faster than wages. Most big corporations had such large reserves on hand from war profits that they continued to pay dividends, and they often cut output rather than prices. The farmer, however, was trapped in a familiar impasse. He faced much lower prices but uncontrollable high overhead in mortgages and the costs of credit and manufactured goods. The farmer's answer to his distress was traditional: continue to produce, especially for European markets, and hope that drastically fallen farm prices will rise and that competing European agriculture will not revive too soon.

Because inventories and prices had fallen faster than purchasing power, when prices and demand came closer into line with each other, the depression in the cities ended without renewed government spending or fresh demands from European markets. A building boom, during which Americans spent twice as much on housing in 1922 as they had in 1919, also gave the economy a great spurt forward. After 1921, except for minor recessions in 1924 and 1927 and continuous soft spots in agriculture, mining, textiles, and railroading, American industry expanded steadily until after the crash of 1929. Prices were relatively constant; consumer and durable goods had remarkably increased sales; and investments, especially after 1927, zoomed spectacularly. From 1921 to 1929, national income mounted from 50.7 to 81.1 billion dollars, and the index of industrial production (1899 = 100) went up from 177.9 in 1921 to 319.4 in 1929. In the same period corporate capital funds rose from 184 billion to 228 billion dollars.

In the 1920's, the machine, the factory, and standardized mass production came into their own in America. Building on the base laid down before 1914 and on the expansion brought by the war, technology and efficiency seemed to be making good on their promise to provide abundant goods, services, and new capital. By 1929, fifty-one laborers in manufacturing and sixty-seven farm workers could produce as much as eighty-four workers on the farm or in the factory only ten years earlier. Technology increased wages, and higher wages brought a demand for more products and thus more machines. Electric power was especially helpful in satisfying new demand. Only 30 per cent of American industry used electricity in 1914; 70 per cent did so by 1929. Electricity simplified and rationalized factory layout. Factories could now be built closer to sources of raw materials and bring in their energy from distant powerhouses over high-tension lines. Factories were increasingly built out instead of up and had to move to the outskirts of cities because of high real-estate costs "downtown."

Dramatic expansion came first in the building business. Pent-up wartime and postwar demand increased the total value of all construction from 6 billion dollars in 1929 to over 10 billion dollars in every year from 1924 to 1929 and created major markets for steel, glass, brick, cement, lumber, and electrical and plumbing supplies. In the 1920's, over 4 per cent of the nation's employees and 7.5 per cent of its wages and salaries went into the construction industry.

The automobile business had the most remarkable growth and most dramatic effects of all American industries after the war. Increasing efficiency and productivity gave Americans 23,000,000 passenger cars and millions of trucks and other vehicles by 1929. By then one out of every five or six Americans owned a car, but of the 200 firms originally established to supply the demand only 44 remained in business by 1927. Ford (with annual profits of 100 per cent) and General Motors (making over $200,000,000 a year from 1927 to 1929) were dominant in the industry.

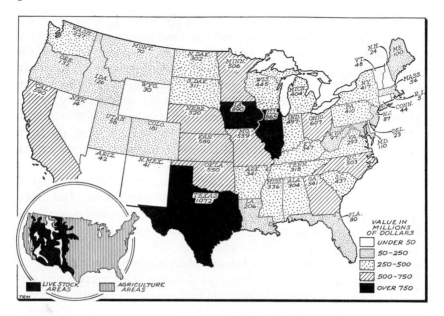

AMERICAN PRODUCTIVE CAPACITY, 1920

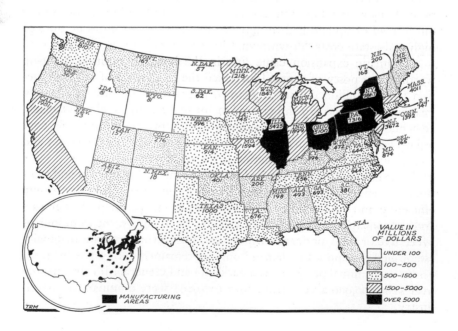

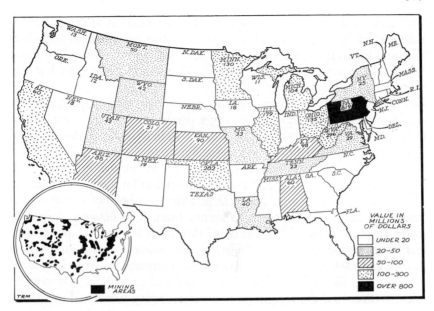

The automobile was not merely a convenience but brought many changes in American culture. It strengthened the growing American addiction to comfort, leisure, and what Thorstein Veblen called "pecuniary emulation" and "conspicuous consumption." The family car brought home the consciousness of what mass production could do for millions. The country went "car-crazy." For customers without cash there was installment buying; for owners enticed by the latest models there were trade-ins; and for everyone there was the expanding influence of advertising. In speakeasies, drugstores, and Pullman cars, on front porches, in small-town streets, and in crowded city apartment houses, millions argued the relative merits of this year's different "makes" and speculated on the lines of "next year's models." The man or boy who couldn't distinguish a Maxwell from a Franklin was marked as an eccentric. The arguments of the public about "cars" were not entirely realistic, for within the various groupings of automobiles by size and cylinders there was no great variety in quality; and manufacturers offered little chance for the public to buy at truly competitive prices. Nevertheless, the public bought and "traded in" and bought again. By 1929, automobile manufacturing accounted for 12.7 per cent of American industrial production, employed 7.1 per cent of factory wage earners, paid 8.7 per cent of manufacturing wages, and took 15 per cent of national steel production and much of the country's output of rubber, plate glass, nickel, and lead. With the automobile boom there also came extensive modern highway programs. The production of cement, macadam, electric lamps and cables, and the labor necessary to manufacture and install them, were thus increased by the automobile. And along the new highways appeared the service station and garage, the hot-dog stand, and the blight of the billboard.

The spectacular effects of the automobile were approached by other industries. Electrical appliances produced in 1899 were valued at $92,000,000; in 1927 their total worth was in excess of $1,600,000,000. Chemicals, which, like many other businesses, took giant strides forward during the war, had grown by 1929 to an annual output worth $3,750,000,000 and the giant Du Pont corporation alone was turning out more than a thousand different products. Radios became almost as necessary to being American as automobiles. The country manufactured 190,000 "receivers" in 1923, and this figure leaped 2500 per cent to 5,000,000 sets in 1929. The "movies" also played a part in the new leisure and took their place as a powerful influence on American manners and morals. By 1930, after three decades of growth, 22,000 motion-picture theatres drew 100,000,000 customers every week, and the movie industry employed 325,000 people on an investment of 2 billion dollars.

These enormous changes in productivity and taste both stimulated and came from the growth of American advertising. Installment buying might consume part of the mountain of goods piled up by mass production, but advertising helped create still bigger appetites and temptations. By 1929, it is estimated that America's annual advertising bill was nearing 2 billion dollars. All the techniques that were to become so familiar were tried on a massive national scale for the first time. Gewgaws and doodads were hawked as vigorously as articles that made life more comfortable and leisure more pleasant. Shrewdly playing on the American's fears of not being "modern" or as good as the Joneses, the advertising industry helped to introduce new products but also helped to destroy stability of taste and the capacity for discrimination. Producers continually changed styles to attract buyers, and the "latest thing" soon became synonymous with "the best."

One price paid for the changing nature of America's markets was the growing standardization of goods, but in many cases standardization did bring better-quality products. Another equally ambiguous result of market changes arose when many industries had to cut costs in order to compete more successfully for the ever larger consuming public. Much of New England's textile industry, which did not share in the prosperity of the twenties, moved to the South. Paper manufacturers also went south from Maine, and Massachusetts shoe producers went west, especially to St. Louis. In the South labor costs were 25 to 60 per

Genesee Isles

"Florida's Venice DeLuxe"

DISTINCTLY different from anything yet developed in this land of amazing developments is Genesee Isles. Here are blended the romance and mysticism 'of the colorful Riviera, the subtle witchery of old-world Venice and the brilliancy and gayety of Florida at its best. Overlooking the ocean at Picturesque Pompano, the beauty spot of the famous Florida East Coast. Midway between fashionable Palm Beach and merry Miami, Genesee Isles is destined to become the outstanding exclusive community of the year. A delight to the home-builder. Attractive to the investor.

GENESIS IMPROVEMENT CO
DOUGLAS J. LUCKHURST
Vice-Pres. and General Manager

MIAMI   WEST PALM BEACH
FORT LAUDERDALE   MIAMI BEACH

Advertising the Florida Real Estate Boom, 1925

[TOWN AND COUNTRY]

cent lower than in New England, but the South's partial gain was New England's loss. Severe depression in New England mill towns came with the departure of old established local factories. Wage earners in Massachusetts' shoe factories alone declined from 80,000 to 57,000 between 1919 and 1925.

With the shifts of old industries and the growth of others, new areas in the nation received the benefits of urban industrial life. Expansion in automobile and rubber production made Detroit and Akron major industrial centers. Canning significantly expanded industry in California, and southern steel and coal production jumped forward to supply regional as well as national needs. But with greater local wealth and leisure there came serious social dislocations in communities that previously knew a slower pace of life and only the small-town small-businessman's ethos. Moreover, now the final decisions about the future of many American towns were not made locally. New factories might be built near Atlanta or elsewhere in the South and steel production may have become further decentralized, but the direction and control of American industry continued their pre-war trends of centralization under boards of directors meeting a thousand or more miles away in New York, Boston, or Wilmington, Delaware.

Ever Bigger Business

Significant concentration of control over American business went back at least fifty years before 1920. World War I may have expanded production, but it also increased the power of small groups over industry and finance. Government controls showed what private monopolists had long contended: great profits and planning were not incompatible. After the Armistice, the merger, holding company, interlocking directorate, "community of interest," trade association, patent monopoly, and "gentlemen's agreement" were all used to prevent the return of the "evils of competition." Instead of predominantly trying to destroy all rivals, the new consolidationists now tended to take measures to see that all leading firms in an industry would be assured profits. The united front was now less often one of businessmen in one firm against all others than of the chief producers against the consumer. Stabilization of prices, allocation of production, and sharing of markets were as much the marks of business operations in the twenties as the cornering of sources of raw materials and the killing off of rivals had been a generation earlier.

The older forms of reducing competition also continued throughout the period, however, despite the existence on the books of the once much acclaimed Clayton Anti-Trust Act and the Federal Trade Commission Act. From the Armistice to the crash in 1929, more than 8,000 manufacturing and mining concerns, about 1,800 banking firms, and more than 4,000 public utilities were destroyed by mergers, and by 1929, 20 per cent of all the nation's merchandising was carried on by chain stores. In public utilities, however, through the use of the holding company, there occurred the most startling results. By 1930,

72 per cent of the nation's electric business was controlled by ten groups of holding companies which not only restricted competition but often used various illegal means such as watered stock and tax dodging to enrich their principal officers.

The buying up and pooling of patent rights, another favorite technique of the time, enabled manufacturers of vacuum cleaners, washing machines, and automobiles to control much of their markets without serious challenge and to raise prices almost at will. One famous patent pool created by the General Electric Company, after it established the Radio Corporation of America in 1919, involved agreements with the American Telephone and Telegraph Company, the International Radio Company, and Westinghouse. By 1930, R.C.A.—i.e., General Electric and Westinghouse—controlled about 3,500 patents, owned the National Broadcasting Company, had substantial interests in the movie and gramophone industries, and produced nearly 95 per cent in value of the nation's radio equipment. Branching out overseas, as did other industries, R.C.A. also entered a cartel to control world markets with the British Marconi Company. Similarly, America's Du Pont corporation and Germany's I. G. Farben controlled an international cartel in dyes. General Electric and the Krupp interests, also German, determined the world price and sale of tungsten carbide. Other international groups with American members closely regulated the sale and price throughout the world of matches, zinc, copper, glass, lead, titanium, and electric bulbs.

Formal or unwritten agreements in some cases preserved the façade of competition by establishing variations in sales methods, but for nearly identical products at identical prices. The justification for these private controls was allegedly a stable economy, but investigations after the panic of 1929 revealed that stability had often meant rigidity, huge profits for producers, and few advantages for consumers.

American businessmen in the 1920's also became particularly fond of trade associations. Like other devices for eliminating or regulating competition, trade associations had flourished before the war, but they came into their own after peace was restored. By 1925, approximately 1,000 American trade associations attempted to insure members' profits through price agreements, standardized products, and restricted output. "Price leadership" by the largest firm in an industry was another technique to avoid the risks of a competitive market. In the 1920's, for example, none of the nation's smaller steel producers dared to challenge the price leadership of United States Steel, which, supported by the American Iron and Steel Institute, pegged the price of steel rails at $43 a ton from 1922 to 1929.

When just a few giant corporations dominated an industry, a mere tacit understanding was often enough to avoid price wars. Sales techniques and advertising campaigns might differ, but the public bought practically the same products at virtually the same prices. With the exception of Ford, automobile manufacturers worked with such tacit understanding throughout the 1920's, and six major cigarette producers, without many formal agreements, gave the public cigarettes indistinguishable in shape, size, and price—although billboards and advertising pages tried to convince Americans that there were substantial differences among the competing brands.

By 1930, these many techniques to eliminate competition had made a small group of men and corporations the managers of the American economy. Of eight leading "lords of creation" on the eve of the depression, Charles E. Mitchell of the National City Bank, eighth in the group, served on thirty-two boards of directors; and Samuel Insull, the Utilities magnate, later indicted for his operations, was the nation's foremost business director, serving on more than eighty boards. Such interlocking directorates were not confined to single industries. The Du Ponts, for example, had family representatives on the boards of General Motors and many banks. Thomas W. Lamont of J. P. Morgan had directorships in railroad, coal, farm equipment, and publishing companies, as well as in various banks. The chairman of the board of the Chase National Bank, Albert H. Wiggin, was a director of almost fifty assorted corporations.

During the palmy days of the great Wall Street bull market, stock salesmen urged Americans to become owners by buying shares in American industry. In fact, thousands of shareholders in huge corporations were so scattered throughout the world that the traditional meaning of private property had become a fiction. Diffusion of ownership gave the individual no power over property except to sell the stock he had bought. Tens of thousands of security owners had no effective way of influencing the annual meetings of corporations, let alone day-to-day decisions. What counted was not ownership but management, and the directors of the corporations had no real interference from the owners. In 1929, for instance, the largest stockholder in the American Telephone and Telegraph group of 469,801 owners held only 0.6 per cent of the total stock. On the other hand, if an individual owned as little as 10 to 20 per cent of a corporation's stock and all the other shares were widely held in small amounts, it was not difficult for him to control policy; geographic distance, lack of interest, and inadequate knowledge prevented other stockholders from voting as a block. In other instances actual control of a business could be kept in a few hands by issuing stock without voting rights for public sale and by selling stock with voting rights only to "insiders."

The evidence about the separation of ownership and management presented in 1932 in the classic study of A. A. Berle and G. C. Means in *The Modern Corporation and Private Property* showed that half of the American economy in 1930 was controlled by 200 giant nonbanking corporations that were managed by less than 2,000 men. The implications of their study and of other evidence that the American economy was now controlled by managers rather than owners were clear.

There was by 1929, however, little chance that bigness could be undone. Even if the giant corporations could be broken up without precipitating a grave national economic crisis, competition would almost inevitably lead, as it had, to concentration. Bigness, furthermore, had great advantages. It could eliminate waste and provide limitless abundance and ever better products and services, although in most industries experience demonstrated that there was a limit to which monopoly could be carried without backfiring by introducing inflexibility and other dangers to business operations. But, aside from such internal threats, the question that the concentration of economic control really presented was whether any great conglomeration of private power could be trusted to serve the public well without government supervision or more private discipline and probity than many American economic leaders seem to have possessed.

The Cult of Business

As businessmen continued to pile up profits, many Americans began to look on business enterprise—and particularly business success—as the *summum bonum* of American civilization. America had always been a business civilization, but by the midtwenties the popular devotion to business standards and ideals as guides to daily living had approached the proportions of a national religion. Like most other religions, business worship had its clergy, and until the depression few Americans challenged the right of businessmen to serve as the high priests of the nation's largest cult.

Business worship rested upon the widely held belief that private business enterprise without state controls was the principal source of the remarkable material progress of the postwar decade. Intellectuals and radicals who questioned the values of America's business civilization were viewed by contemporaries as frustrated critics who had not been able to "make good" on their own and were taking out their disappointment by attacking the system which they could not master. Sceptics or heretics, moreover, could always be refuted by referring to such tangible evidence of the beneficent effects of business enterprise as new cars, radios, refrigerators, and a host of other products. In short, business represented the ideal way of life because business was booming, and to the average American business prosperity and progress had become interchangeable and synonymous terms.

To most Americans, businessmen were authorities not only on business matters but on practically every other subject. Henry Ford's remark that history was "bunk" gained wider currency than any comment by a contemporary historian. *The Man Nobody Knows*, which was written by a prosperous advertising executive to demonstrate that Christ was the world's most successful salesman, had a larger circulation than any book by a contemporary clergyman. The worth of Mussolini's fascist regime in Italy was fixed in many Americans minds by the statements of businessmen who visited Italy and returned to the United States to report that the trains ran on time.

The prestige enjoyed by the businessman during the postwar decade was not altogether accidental. Organized business groups made a concerted effort to demonstrate to the rest of the population that their members deserved power and prestige. Employing every medium of communication, businessmen's associations and individual industrialists and financiers sought to sell their ideas as well as their products to the American consumer. The propaganda mills of the United States Chamber of Commerce, the National Association of Manufacturers, and individual trade associations ground out an endless stream of releases; many teachers, politicians, authors, and clergymen either volunteered or were enlisted as defenders of American business enterprise; and once a week small businessmen in towns throughout the land gathered at luncheon as Rotarians, Lions, or Kiwanians to sing songs about serving their fellow man and to hear a speaker give a "booster" talk.

Like many of his products, the businessman's message was standardized. It extolled the "American Way" of unrestricted business enterprise and branded as un-American those who wished to regulate the freedom of the nation's financiers and industrialists. In the businessman's catalogue, the un-American Americans included militant trade-unionists; "radicals," a term broad enough to include liberals, socialists, and communists; and anyone else who advocated the extension of the government's regulatory power over business practices. The businessman's creed stressed that business' principal function was to serve the people, that only the able and industrious gained wealth and authority in the business world, and that unhampered business enterprise had made the United States the richest, freest, and most powerful nation in the world. Business leaders with large budgets for propaganda and with their own success to use as illustrations had little trouble in convincing the mass of Americans that the businessman's philosophy was indeed the American philosophy.

Business in the White House

The 1920's may have witnessed a retreat from reformism, but the idealism of Main Street, its faith in the dollar, the machine, and "the little woman" were unshaken. Given its motto by Coolidge, that "the business of America was business," the nation could not have asked for more appropriate presidents than the three occupants of the White House between 1921 and 1933. Warren G. Harding of Marion, Ohio, was a small-town businessman himself. Calvin Coolidge was the personification of Yankeeism—laconic, yet encouraging Americans to take the main chance. And Herbert Hoover, wealthy engineer, stood for efficiency, rationalization, and limitless production for private profit.

The political climate of postwar America was fully revealed in the presidential campaign of 1920. When the Republican delegates gathered at Chicago in June, 1920, the conservatives were in control of the party's machinery, and the convention's proceedings were largely dominated by a Senate cabal headed by Henry Cabot Lodge. The platform adopted by the Republicans not only failed to advocate any program of social legislation but called for a reduction in income taxes, a cut in the public debt, "constitutional government," the repeal of the excess profits tax, and an increase in the tariff. On the critical question of the League of Nations the platform was suitably vague. In the opening ballots, none of the leading candidates could obtain a majority, and at the end of the sixth ballot the convention recessed to give the party's leaders a chance to arrange for a compromise choice. They made it clear that they favored the selection of Senator Warren Gamaliel Harding of Ohio, and on the tenth ballot he was nominated. Governor Calvin Coolidge of Massachusetts was named as his running mate.

When the Democrats convened at San Francisco at the end of June, their party was disorganized and without adequate leadership. Wilson was too sick, Bryan too isolated, the crusaders too exhausted, and the liberals too disgusted to have any effect on the meeting. The representatives of the Solid South and the northern city machines which were in control had little to offer in the way of a constructive program. The Democratic platform was almost as conservative as that of the Republicans. On foreign policy, however, the Democrats took a clear-cut stand. Their platform endorsed Wilson's policy in Mexico, advocated independence for Puerto Rico and the Philippines, and stood firmly behind the League of Nations. The Democrats, however, did "not oppose the acceptance of any reservations making clearer or more specific any of the obligations of the United States to the League associates." Not until the forty-fourth ballot did Governor James M. Cox of Ohio receive the necessary two-thirds majority. Franklin D. Roosevelt, who had served as Assistant Secretary of the Navy during both Wilson Administrations, was nominated for the vice-presidency.

Cox waged a vigorous campaign that took him to every section of the country, but Harding remained at his home in Marion, Ohio, and made only a few formal speeches that were so extraordinarily vague that W. G. McAdoo did not overly exaggerate when he said that Harding's speeches left "the impression of an army of pompous phrases moving over the landscape in search of an idea; sometimes these meandering words would actually capture a straggling thought and bear it triumphantly, a prisoner in their midst, until it died of servitude and overwork." Cox placed greatest emphasis on his party's demand for American participation in the League of Nations. The Republicans, who had done the most to prevent the acceptance of Wilson's proposals for a postwar settlement, hedged on the League issue. Harding talked on every side of the question; Republican isolationists told isolationist audiences that Harding was unalterably opposed to the League; and Republican internationalists announced that a vote for Harding was a vote for the League.

Wilson had asked that the election be made a "solemn referendum" on the League, but Harding had demanded a return to "normalcy." And "normalcy" was apparently what the voters wanted, for Harding carried thirty-seven states and received 16,152,220 votes to 9,147,353 for Cox. The electoral vote was 404 to 127, and the Republicans also won impressive majorities in both the Senate and the House. The Republican victory—Joseph Tumulty, Wilson's former secretary, called it an "earthquake"—can be attributed, not to the Republicans' stand on either foreign or domestic policy, but to the desire of the voters to forget reform both at home and abroad and to get back to private "getting and spending."

The presidential choice, Warren G. Harding, was born in Ohio in 1865. He was a small-town politician and newspaperman, who—as some of his contemporaries liked to remark—"looked like a President." Always a Republican regular, Harding had climbed the political lad-

The President (front left) and Friends at a Ball Game, 1922

[NATIONAL ARCHIVES]

der to the United States Senate in 1914. During his term in the Senate, he had never been associated with an important bill, had been frequently absent, and had always voted as the party leaders dictated. A jovial, easygoing, shallow man, whose principal friends were in the Capital's poker-playing set, Harding brought to the White House the moral code of the hangers-on around a rural county courthouse.

Harding's cabinet did have three talented men, Secretary of State Charles Evans Hughes, Secretary of Commerce Herbert Hoover, and Secretary of Agriculture Henry C. Wallace. The other cabinet members, however, were either big businessmen like Secretary of the Treasury Andrew Mellon, head of the aluminum trust, or cronies, political hacks, and mediocrities. The heads of the various departments were practically autonomous. While Harding took care of the loyal party workers and his friends from Ohio, he let Congress alone.

The Harding Administration did produce a Washington conference for naval reduction under the direction of Secretary of State Hughes, but it also was responsible for the worst national scandals since the days of Grant. Yet Harding so captured the affection of the voters, so mirrored a fast-dying but sentimentally strong common idea of America, that his death caused deep national mourning. The first statements that his Administration was tainted were greeted with charges of "character assassination" against the investigators. It was months after his death in 1923 before scandal and Harding became virtually synonymous to many people or that people agreed with William Allen White, who wrote that "the story of Babylon is a Sunday school story compared with the story of Washington from June, 1920, until July, 1923."

The first evidence of corruption in the Harding Administration occurred in March, 1923, when it was found that Charles R. Forbes, the director of the Veterans' Bureau, had squandered or stolen approximately $200,000,000. When it became clear that the graft and fraud in the Veterans' Bureau could no longer be concealed, Forbes in February, 1923, fled to Europe and resigned his office. Forbes was eventually tried, found guilty, fined $10,000, and went to jail for one year and nine months at Leavenworth.

Another Senate investigating committee accused Harding's close friend, Attorney General Daugherty, of permitting the withdrawal of alcohol from government warehouses. When Daugherty, who had earned an illegal profit from these transactions, refused to cooperate with the investigation, he was forced out of office by President Coolidge in 1924. Also implicated in the charges against Daugherty was Jess Smith, another member of the "Ohio gang." Smith committed suicide before the expiration of Harding's unfulfilled term, and it was later discovered that he had accepted $50,000 to obtain a favorable decision in a case before Alien Property Custodian Thomas W. Miller. Miller, in 1927, was found guilty of conspiring to defraud the government and was sentenced to eighteen months' imprisonment and the payment of a fine of $5,000; but Daugherty, who was brought to trial on the same charge, escaped because the jury disagreed.

The Harding scandals came to fullest flower in the revelations concerning Secretary of the Interior Fall's handling of government oil reserves. After persuading Secretary of the Navy Denby to transfer the government's reserves at Elks Hill, California, and Teapot Dome, Wyoming, to the Interior Department, Fall then leased the first of these to E. L. Doheny and the second to Harry F. Sinclair. Both leases were made without competitive bidding, and in both instances Fall received large bribes in return for facilitating the transfers. In October, 1923, a Senate investigation conducted by Thomas Walsh, a Montana Democrat, showed that Doheny had paid Fall $100,000, and that Sinclair had paid him $223,000 in Liberty Bonds and $85,000 in cash. Following these revelations, Fall and Denby were forced to resign from the cabinet, and in 1927 the government was able to recover its oil reserves.

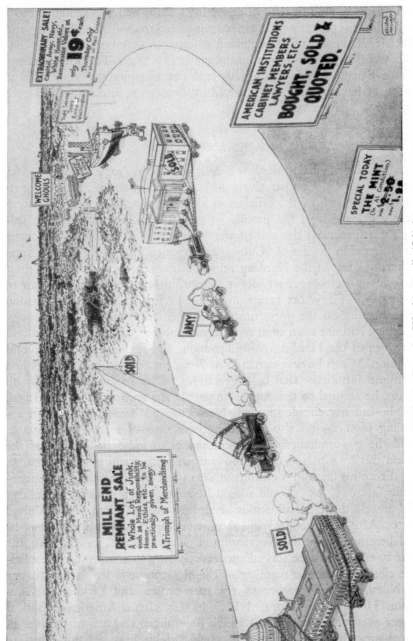

"Bargain Day in Washington" (Life)

Fall was convicted in 1929 of accepting a bribe and was sentenced to a year's imprisonment and the payment of a $100,000 fine. Doheny and Sinclair, however, were acquitted of charges of conspiracy, but Sinclair went to jail for three months and paid a $1,000 fine for contempt of the Senate. Later, during his trial for conspiracy, he was found guilty of having the jury followed by detectives, and he was given a six-months' jail term.

The Yankee and the Engineer

President Harding died in San Francisco on August 2, 1923, after a trip to Alaska. Comparatively little was then known about the corruption of many of the officials in his Administration, and the nation deeply grieved over the passing of the affable chief executive. Harding's death marked the end of the "Ohio gang's" rule in Washington and ushered in the era of "Coolidge prosperity." Despite repeated revelations of graft in the Harding regime during the next five years, most Americans were eager to forget the sordid features of the "return to normalcy." The short recession of 1924 soon ended, and the nation concentrated on the opportunities for profits provided by the boom. Coolidge had not been even remotely connected with any of the illegal activities of the Harding Administration, and his honesty was beyond question. When he was sworn in as President of the United States in a Vermont farmhouse that belonged to his father and was lighted by oil lamps, he seemed to the American people the archetype of the frugal, simple—but not simple-minded—New England Yankee. It was an appealing picture—and also an incongruous one—of a man who was to head the government of the most powerful industrial nation of the world during a period of flamboyant prosperity and extravagance.

From his birth in Vermont in 1872 until his accession to the presidency in 1923, few people would have guessed that Calvin Coolidge had possessed the qualifications needed by the President of the United States. After graduating from Amherst College and studying law, he had begun practice in Northampton, Massachusetts, in 1897. In the next twenty years, he served successively as a councilman, city solicitor, clerk of courts, a member of the Massachusetts legislature, mayor of Northampton, member of the state senate, and Lieutenant Governor. He had demonstrated little in this classic American political career except that he was a staunch Republican and a firm believer in the theory that the government could aid business but not interfere with it. In 1919, however, Coolidge became Governor of Massachusetts,

President Coolidge and His Team in Vermont

[CULVER SERVICE]

and within a short time the Boston police strike had made him a national figure.

On September 9, 1919, the Boston police went on strike after the police commissioners refused to recognize the A.F. of L. union that the policemen had organized; some of the force had been dismissed for union activity. Following the outbreak of the strike, disorder occurred in many parts of the city. The mayor transferred some state militia companies in the city to police duty. Within two days, order had been restored; but on the afternoon of September 11, when the situation was already well in hand, Coolidge, who had refused to respond to earlier demands of the municipal officials for assistance, ordered the state militia to Boston and wired President Gompers of the American Federation of Labor: "There is no right to strike against the public safety by anybody, anywhere, any time." Few outside Boston knew how tardily Coolidge had acted, but his stand caught the public imagination and was directly responsible for his selection as the Republican party's vice-presidential candidate in 1920.

Although Coolidge took over the Harding cabinet, he gradually forced the corrupt officials out of their posts. His own honesty was so unquestioned that it was widely believed that his assumption of office represented a clean break with the immediate past. A large part of the public willingly passed over the graft and corruption. Instead, in *The New York Times* and other papers across the nation, citizens read about the "Democratic lynching-bee" and "poison-tongued partisanship, pure malice, and twittering hysteria." The Senate's investigations were called "in plain words, contemptible and disgusting."

When the Republican convention met at Cleveland on June 10, 1924, Coolidge had been in office less than a year. Since becoming President, he had initiated no policies. In Congress his party's program had been blocked by a combination of Democrats and a small group of Republican insurgents, who were led by the older Progressive spokesmen, Robert La Follette in the Senate and George Norris in the House. Nevertheless, Coolidge was the inevitable Republican choice. Many Americans found his simple ways, his taciturnity, and his unassuming appearance and manner a refreshing change from the almost austere idealism of a Wilson. Coolidge was nominated on the first ballot, and Charles G. Dawes, a Chicago banker, received the vice-presidential nomination. The party's platform differed little in essentials from that of 1920. The Republicans still opposed American participation in the League (although they advocated American membership in the World Court), and they still favored high tariffs and low taxes.

The Democrats gathered for their convention on June 24 in New York with a divided party. In the past, the two factions of the Solid South and northern city machines had usually been able to maintain an uneasy, but none the less effective, alliance, but in 1924 they were split by both prohibition and Ku Klux Klan issues. The South was militantly dry, but the northern urban wing of the party was overwhelmingly wet. The Klan had been revived after the war as an anti-Negro, antiforeign, anti-Semitic, anti-Catholic organization. Such nativist doctrines held a strong appeal for many southerners and for many small-town people in the Middle West and other parts of the country. The Klan's postwar membership reached well into the millions, and it had to be reckoned with, but many of the Democratic party's northern rank and file as well as their leaders were drawn from the groups attacked by the Klan as "un-American." At the outset of the convention, any possibility of party harmony was destroyed by the introduction of a resolution that specifically denounced the Klan. But this resolution was defeated by 4.3 votes, and in its place the convention adopted a plank that read: "We insist at all times upon obedience to the orderly processes of the law and deplore and condemn any effort to arouse religious or racial dissension." In other planks the Democrats advocated lower taxes, a scientific approach to the tariff, a child-labor amendment, Philippine independence, and a referendum on the League question.

The sectional split in the Democratic party was carried over to the contest for the presidential nomination. W. G. McAdoo was the candidate of the South, while the northerners gave their votes to Alfred E. Smith, who was a native of New York City, a wet, a Catholic, a member of Tammany Hall, and an outstanding Governor of New York State who had sponsored some social reforms. These two men were so evenly matched that for 102 ballots neither could obtain a two-thirds majority. Finally, the deadlock was broken with the nomination of John W. Davis of West Virginia and New York. Because he was a corporation lawyer—one of his clients was the House of Morgan—the Democrats sought to balance their ticket with Charles W. Bryan of Nebraska, whose only claim to recognition was that he was William Jennings Bryan's brother. When the convention finally broke up on July 10, the Democrats were even more divided than when they had met.

The most significant aspect of the campaign of 1924 was not the split in the Democratic party, which had auguries for the future, but in the last national bid for power by reform groups whose roots were in prewar Progressivism and who now spoke for the complaints of farmers, workers, and liberals against the drift of "normalcy." The immediate origins of the new third party went back to 1922, when the Railroad Brotherhoods had called a Conference for Progressive Political Action. In the next two years the C.P.P.A. sought to win the support of the American Federation of Labor, the Socialist party, and dissatisfied farmers. By 1924, it had the nucleus of a genuine farmer-labor party. At its first nominating convention in July, 1924, the C.P.P.A. selected the famous insurgent leader Robert La Follette as its candidate and authorized him to pick his own running mate and draw up his own platform. La Follette chose Senator Burton K. Wheeler, a Democrat from Montana, for second place on the ticket and wrote a platform that blended socialism with midwestern progressivism. La Follette's program called for a reduction in taxes on small incomes and an increase in the levies on well-to-do individuals and corporations, public ownership of the railroads and of a number of the nation's natural resources, a lower tariff, abolition of judicial review, popular election of federal judges, federal protection of the rights of labor, and federal aid for distressed farmers. Although La Follette's candidacy was subsequently endorsed by both the Socialist party and the American Federation of Labor, he was handicapped

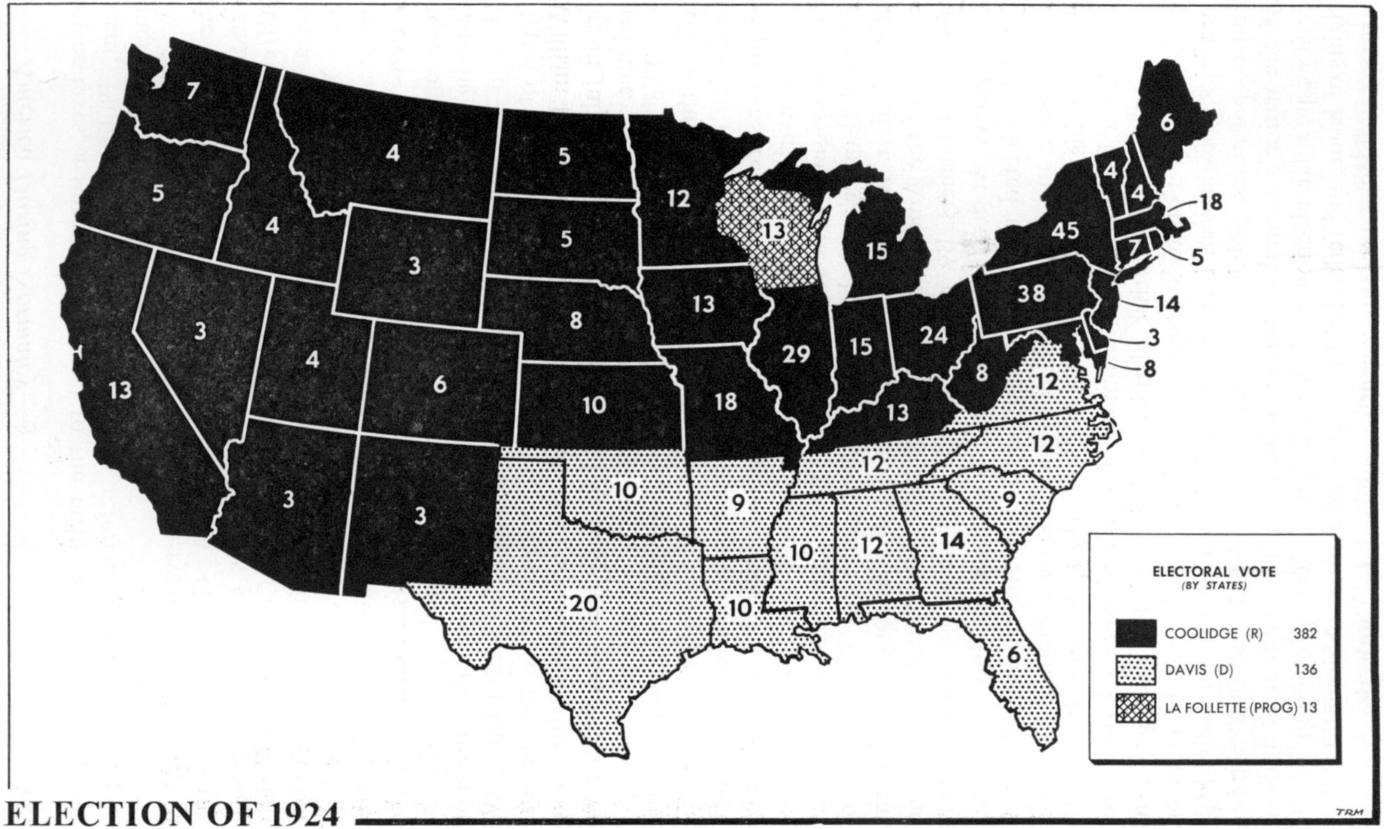

ELECTION OF 1924

ELECTORAL VOTE
(BY STATES)

COOLIDGE (R) 382

DAVIS (D) 136

LA FOLLETTE (PROG) 13

throughout the campaign by lack of both money and a national political organization.

In 1924, Coolidge received 54.1 per cent of the popular vote, compared to the 61.02 per cent obtained by Harding in 1920. Still, Coolidge won an overwhelming victory. With 15,725,016 votes to 8,386,503 for Davis and 4,822,856 for La Follette, Coolidge had a plurality of more than 7,000,000 over Davis and an over-all majority of 2,500,000. Coolidge carried all but the Solid South and Oklahoma (which voted for Davis) and Wisconsin (which voted for La Follette). The electoral vote was Coolidge 382, Davis 136, and La Follette 13. The Republicans also won large majorities in both the House and Senate. The conclusions that could be drawn from the outcome of the election of 1924 were that the urban world of the North was pulling up to equal the political power of rural and small-town America in the Democratic party, that neither major party was receptive to reform influences, and that, although the nation hoped for more prosperity, there were deep discontents across the country with the policies of the government and the unevenness of "good times." Despite its poor organization, the Progressives had gained nearly 5,000,000 votes, but with this brave showing old-style Progressivism died.

Coolidge's second term showed that he had no interest in what had caused the third party revolt in 1924. He let Congress go its own way. In fact, there is reason to believe that he believed that a recess in lawmaking would have been a good thing for everyone. He had no comprehension of the problems of either the farmers or the workers, and on two occasions he vetoed farm-relief bills without offering any alternative. As long as he was President, he was generally satisfied to sit by and watch the wheels of government turn; he wanted no new wheels, and he did not want the tempo of the old ones altered. He thought that the government should maintain law and order, aid business, refrain from any regulation of the nation's economic life, and practice economy.

Coolidge's thrift fitted in admirably with the temper of the times. As long as business boomed, many Americans preferred to have the government relatively passive. Consequently, Coolidge was widely credited with aiding, if not causing, prosperity; and millions of Americans thought that the country was safe as long as he was in the White House. But Coolidge did not press his luck, and on August 2, 1927, while on a vacation in the Black Hills of the Dakotas, he surprised almost everyone by announcing: "I do not choose to run for President in 1928." Although his supporters argued that his statement did not exclude him from running if he was drafted, no draft developed. On the eve of the convention, it was a foregone conclusion that Secretary of Commerce Herbert Hoover would be the party's choice. Hoover was nominated on the first ballot, and in an attempt to appease the dissatisfied farm groups in the party, Senator Charles Curtis of Kansas was named for the vice-presidency. The Democrats convened at Houston and selected Alfred E. Smith on the first ballot. Their vice-presidential nomination went to Senator Joseph T. Robinson of Arkansas, who was a dry and a Protestant. Both parties shunned reform proposals in their platforms. The Republicans praised the Coolidge Administration, and the Democrats condemned it; but on most points the two parties seemed in essential agreement. The Democrats even abandoned their traditional low-tariff position to advocate rates that would equal the "actual difference between the cost of production at home and abroad."

Smith and Hoover had little in common socially aside from their humble origins. Hoover was a classic case of the small-town American boy risen to national prestige. But, indicative of the trends of the twenties, his career had been as an engineer working for business firms. He had been born of Quaker parents in 1874 in Iowa and had been left an orphan at an early age. After graduating with an engineering degree from Leland Stanford University, he acquired a fortune as a mining promoter in Asia, Europe, and North America. Following his service as head of Belgian Relief, he had become Food Administrator during the war, chairman of the American Relief Administration in the period immediately after the war, and Secretary of Commerce under Harding and Coolidge. Hoover admirably combined many of the ideals of the twenties: he was an engineer who stood for efficiency, a businessman who had made a private fortune, and a humanitarian who believed that private enterprise and voluntary effort could take care of any human distress.

Alfred E. Smith was the first American nominated for the presidency by a major party to come out of the newer culture of the big city. Smith had been born in the slums of the East Side of New York in 1873. He had attended parochial school, had tried a variety of manual jobs, and at an early age had become a member of Tammany Hall. Working up through the ranks of the machine, he had eventually been elected governor of New York, and in all he had served four terms in Albany. As governor he had compiled an outstanding record as a vote-getter who combined orthodoxy in economics with some gestures toward humanitarian reform. Nevertheless, Smith seemed a threat to many Americans. He was the first real "city boy" to try to win the White House. As a wet, a Catholic, and a Tammanyite, he

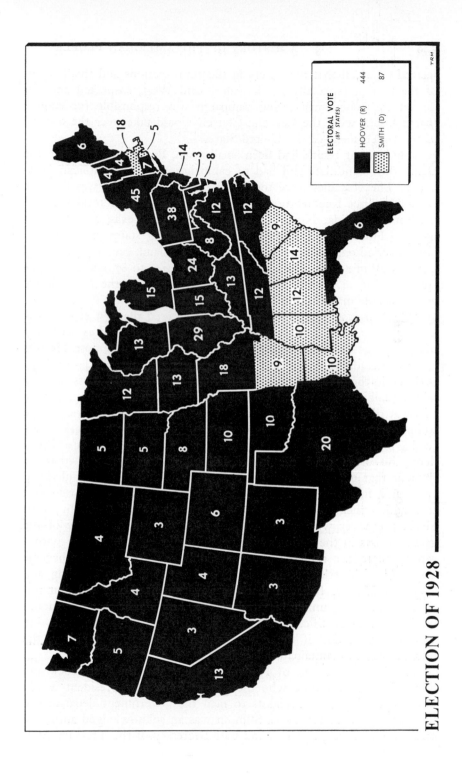

ELECTION OF 1928

ELECTORAL VOTE
(BY STATES)

HOOVER (R) 444

SMITH (D) 87

seemed to be all that the voters in the rural sections and small towns of the nation, especially in the South and West, suspected and abhorred. A vicious whispering campaign was responsible for rumors that if Smith won, the Catholic Church would take over the control of the government of the United States.

But even if Smith had been small-town, Protestant, and dry, the Democratic candidate still had to campaign against Republican prosperity. The obstacles were too much for Smith, and he was the first Democrat since Reconstruction to lose some of the electoral votes of the South. Florida, North Carolina, Tennessee, Texas, and Virginia went to Hoover; and, aside from the remaining states in the South, Smith carried only Massachusetts and Rhode Island, each of which had a large Catholic vote. The electoral vote was 444 to 87, and the popular vote was 21,391,381 to 15,016,443. Once again the Republicans gained sizable majorities in both branches of Congress.

On March 4, 1929, Herbert Hoover entered the first elective office he had ever held. His work as a mining engineer and as Secretary of Commerce had done little to prepare him for his new post. He was an efficient administrator and able organizer, but he had had no experience in the give and take of American politics. He possessed many of the qualifications needed by a successful President, but he had none of the attributes of a party leader. He was a rigid man who was unable to improvise; he lacked the "human touch" that is the hallmark of effective political leaders, whether they serve as ward leaders or as Presidents; he often gave the impression—rightly or wrongly—that he thought that general principles were more important than individual cases; and, finally, he was so wedded to theories that he was reluctant to abandon them when day-to-day events disproved them. In short, Herbert Hoover was not a politician. Had he not faced one of the gravest crises in the nation's history, he might have left office with a reputation at least no less shiny than Coolidge's. As it was, he became a symbol of heartlessness, stupidity, and inaction. Like Harding and Coolidge, Hoover believed that the government should aid, but not regulate, business; unlike his predecessors, he thought that this should be done on a scientific, rather than on a catch-as-catch-can, basis. He was convinced that if the government followed such a policy, the boom could be maintained indefinitely.

The announcement of Hoover's cabinet was the first shock and disappointment to those who thought that the new President would utilize the talents of specialists to man the government departments. Secretary of State Henry L. Stimson was an acknowledged authority on American foreign policy, and both Secretary of the Treasury Mellon and Secretary of Labor Davis had served under Harding and Coolidge, but the remaining cabinet posts were filled by virtual unknowns. The make-up of Hoover's cabinet marked the President's first defeat at the hands of the politicians. Instead of being able to surround himself by experts as he had wished, he was forced to appoint men whose only visible qualification was their loyalty and service to the Republican party.

From the outset, Hoover had difficulty in carrying out his policies and in working harmoniously with Congress. The Senate objected to many of his appointments. It refused to confirm John J. Parker's nomination to the Supreme Court and approved his selection of Charles E. Hughes as Chief Justice of the Court over the objections of many Senators. Many conflicts between President and Congress arose over specific measures. Hoover objected vigorously to congressional plans for the development of the Tennessee Valley; he had to stand by helplessly while his own party drew up a tariff measure of which he disapproved; and, although he prevailed upon Congress to adopt his proposal for farm relief, the measure failed to achieve its objectives.

Hoover's misfortunes were climaxed by the Panic of 1929 and the ensuing depression. As a man who had entered office as the advertised guardian of prosperity, he was lamentably unprepared to cope with the most severe economic crisis in the history of the nation. In the 1930 elections, the Democrats obtained a clear-cut majority of the House, and two years later they gained control of the presidency and both branches of the legislature.

The Government and Business Enterprise

For twelve years after the inauguration of Warren G. Harding on March 4, 1921, the United States government strengthened rather than circumscribed the economic power of the country's business executives. The mass of Americans and their Republican officials believed that the government's primary function was to encourage and assist— but not to regulate—American business enterprise. Because the three Republican Presidents of this period believed in government aid to business, they pursued only superficially different policies. Despite the change of actors, the script remained the same. Harding spoke not only for himself but his two successors when he asked for "less government in business and more business in government."

In some respects government aid to business after World War I followed earlier methods but carried them to extremes. The high-

"Selling Him Another Gold Brick" (*Rollin Kirby in The New York* World)

tariff policy, which had been a cornerstone of the Republican program since the Civil War, was revived by the party after 1920 to rectify what the party's leaders considered to be the mistakes of the Underwood-Simmons Tariff of 1913. Their midwestern farm supporters were crying for relief, and business constituents were voicing their perennial demand for more protection; Republican leaders concluded that a new tariff would not only carry on their traditional program but would also please the party's two largest groups of supporters.

Less than three months after Harding's inauguration, a special session of Congress passed an "emergency" tariff bill that placed duties on wool, sugar, meat, wheat, and corn. In 1922, the emergency tariff was superseded by the Fordney-McCumber Act, which in general either restored or raised the rates that had prevailed during the Taft Administration. Critics of the bill were assured that it furnished a scientific approach to protectionism, for it established a tariff commission that was to recommend revisions to the President when necessary—a provision that would both eliminate needless increases in duties and prevent American wage standards from being undermined by cheap European competition. The President was empowered to make rate changes that did not deviate more than 50 per cent from those of the Fordney-McCumber Act. In practice this system produced thirty-two increases in specific tariff rates and reductions in the duties on mill feed, bobwhite quail, paintbrush handles, cresylic acid, and phenol.

Agriculture showed no noticeable improvement under the Fordney-McCumber Act, and large segments of the business community demanded even more protection. In 1928, the Republicans announced that a further increase in tariff schedules was desirable. Lobbyists representing every conceivable economic group rushed to Washington to tell receptive House and Senate committees why their particular tariff schedules should be raised. The Hawley-Smoot Tariff, which was passed in 1930, provided for even higher rates than those of the Fordney-McCumber Act. Described by the Republican party as measures that benefited the entire nation, the tariff was in fact little more than a government-enforced subsidy that every American consumer had to pay to American business enterprise.

During the twenties, Secretary of the Treasury Andrew Mellon repeatedly stated that high taxes on personal and corporation incomes were detrimental to business development. By draining off surplus capital into the nonproductive government, steep taxes, in Mellon's view, forestalled the use of funds for building new industries and expanding old ones. In response to his demands, Congress in 1921 repealed the excess-profits tax, and within the next five years it reduced the rates on income taxes. The Treasury Department supplemented this aid to business by making no attempt to check the evasion of taxes by individuals and corporations in the upper brackets. During the twelve years of the Republican reign, tax returns were never made public, and the Treasury Department looked the other way as millionaires cut down on their tax bills by illegal transfers of their securities and the formation of somewhat fictitious nonprofit (and hence nontaxable) institutions.

Governmental policy not only increased opportunities for profits but also supported the businessman's drive to eliminate competition. While Herbert Hoover was Secretary of Commerce during the Harding and Coolidge administrations, his department urged industries to adopt self-imposed "codes of fair practice," to standardize products, and to promote the exchange of information among competitors. The Federal Trade Commission, which had been created at the high tide of the New Freedom to ferret out violations of the antitrust laws, had

SURTAX RATES FOR 1927

Amount of net income	Rate per cent	Surtax	Total surtax on each amount	Amount of net income	Rate per cent	Surtax	Total surtax on each amount
A	B	C	D	A	B	C	D
$10,000	------	------	------	$44,000	11	$440	$2,240
14,000	1	$40	$40	48,000	12	480	2,720
16,000	2	40	80	52,000	13	520	3,240
18,000	3	60	140	56,000	14	560	3,800
20,000	4	80	220	60,000	15	600	4,400
22,000	5	100	320	64,000	16	640	5,040
24,000	6	120	440	70,000	17	1,020	6,060
28,000	7	280	720	80,000	18	1,800	7,860
32,000	8	320	1,040	100,000	19	3,800	11,660
36,000	9	360	1,400	100,000+	20	------	------
40,000	10	400	1,800				

What Made the "Good Old Days" Good

passed under the control of the Republican friends of big business by the midtwenties. Instead of seeking to preserve competition, the new commissioners frequently gave the impression that they were attempting to minimize it. Comparatively few cease-and-desist orders were issued, charges of unfair business practices were kept secret, and various industries were given governmental sanction and support when they made informal attempts to regulate competition.

The Supreme Court also helped to reduce competition. In 1925, four years after the Court had ruled against trade associations, it reversed itself and stated in essence that trade associations could limit competition if they were careful to disguise their real intentions. The Court also sanctioned the consolidation movement. In the Court's decision in the antitrust suit against the United States Steel Corporation (1920), it ruled that neither size nor the possession of unused power to restrain competition provided sufficient grounds for ordering the dissolution of the corporation or for requiring it to give up any of its subsidiaries.

Throughout the 1920's, the government also granted special privileges to a number of different industries. The billions that national and local governments spent on highway construction from 1920 through 1930 amounted to an indirect subsidy to the automobile industry. To the nation's private shipping interests the government sold much of the large government-built war merchant fleet at give-away prices and granted a huge loan and thinly disguised subsidy to encourage expansion of the American merchant marine. The airlines also received direct financial assistance from the government in the form of mail contracts that were the equivalent of outright subsidies, and air-mail routes were awarded in such a way as to strengthen the large concerns. During the Hoover Administration, Postmaster General Brown went even further and forced the smaller airline companies to join forces with their more powerful rivals.

Although the nation's railroads had been government-run for most of the war, after the war, plans for an experiment in public ownership and rehabilitation or for joint government-industry-labor management under government ownership were dropped, and the railroads were given back to private owners. Under the Esch-Cummins Transportation Act of 1920, the domain and powers of the I.C.C. were enlarged, and provisions were made to eliminate competition, guarantee a "fair rate of return," and assure long-term funding for maturing railroad securities and capital for rehabilitation of needy roads. The new act failed in almost every way to achieve its objectives. Instead, private interests gained greater control over the nation's rail lines without any of the safeguards planned under the Esch-Cummins Act.

The failure of the I.C.C. with the railroads was matched by the inability of the Federal Power Commission to curb the public utilities. Established in 1920, with the right to grant licenses to power corporations on public lands and navigable rivers and to regulate rates charged by such licensed companies, the new regulatory agency awarded many licenses—449 between 1920 and 1930—but did little to regulate rates. The private holding companies in public utilities increased in number and powers and many utilities continued to water stock, maintain high rates, and practice other abuses. When President Hoover vetoed, as Coolidge had before him, Congress' measure to convert the Muscle Shoals, Alabama, facilities into government-owned-and-operated nitrate and power plants, he said that such a federal project would "break down the initiative and enterprise of the American people," would destroy equality of opportunity, and would negate "the ideals upon which our civilization has been based."

Hoover's words on this occasion could well describe the general justification for government refusal to limit business in any significant way in the twenties. Hoover's premise was shared by many Americans; the businessman knew what was best for business.

The Continuing Decline of Agriculture

The farmer, unlike other businessmen, never recovered from the deflation of 1920–1. Indeed, it took another world war to bring American farm prices out of the doldrums. Throughout the 1920's, although prices slowly rose again, annual farm income and the total value of farm property fell. As usual, the farmer's fixed charges remained high or mounted steadily.

The revival of competitive agriculture in Europe and elsewhere abroad and America's high tariff barriers helped drop farm exports from $3,861,000,000 for 1919–20 to $1,915,000,000 for 1921–2, and to even lower levels for the next ten years. Neither domestic food nor industrial consumption could take up the slack.

The farmers' answer to his "plight" was traditional. Lower prices due to a shrinking world market over which he had no control were met by increasing production in hopes of adding to sales. Instead, this greater production forced prices further down. The farm depression

Index of Farm Prices and Purchasing Power of Farm Products, 1913–29 *

YEAR	FARM PRICES	PRICES PAID BY FARMERS	PURCHASING POWER OF FARM PRODUCTS
1913	100	100	100
1917	176	150	118
1920	205	206	99
1921	116	156	75
1922	124	152	81
1929	138	155	89

also accentuated long-established tendencies to amalgamation of large farms on the one hand and the rise of tenancy on the other. In 1929, 11 per cent of all farmers received about half of all farm income, half of the nation's farm families produced individually less than $1,000 worth of products a year; and 750,000 farm families—two thirds of them in the South—each marketed annual crops worth less than $400. By 1930, 42.4 per cent of American farms were operated by tenants; a few of these graduated to full ownership and good times, but most remained not much more than rural slum dwellers, enemies to themselves and to the land.

In contrast, the small group of big-business farmers with large and efficient mechanized establishments could prosper. In 1929, each of about 25,000 farms, accounting for a little under 10 per cent of na-

* Reprinted with permission from Frederick C. Mills: *Economic Tendencies in the United States; Aspects of Pre-War and Post-War Changes* (New York: The National Bureau of Economic Research, Inc., 1932), p. 348.

The following text appears within the advertisement image:

For A Bigger Yield *The* SUPERIOR

BIGGER yields—more bushels per acre! Of course, that's what you want—every farmer does. And there's no better way to get them than good seeding—even seeding at an even depth with the right grain drill.

Superior Drills do not skip, bunch or clog. Fifty years of performance backs the fact that they actually do boost your total of bushels per acre.

For Team or Tractor

Superior Grain Drills for team or tractor are simple in construction, light draft, yet built so well that they give years and years of perfect seeding service. They leave no patches of idle soil, nor waste your seed.

Superior Tractor Drills have a special power lift and adjustable hitch for use with any tractor. Driver can raise or lower discs while in motion, without leaving his seat. Saves time and labor. Your dealer will show and explain all special features. See him now. Make sure of better seeding—a bigger yield.

The American Seeding-Machine Company
INCORPORATED
Springfield, Ohio

Inviting Trouble, 1920 (The Country Gentleman)

tional agricultural production, grossed at least $20,000. Dairy, truck, and fruit farmers especially, not being as dependent on overseas markets, did much better than the mass of farmers, and those farmers in any line who formed cooperatives to sell products and to purchase supplies also made more money than the more individualistic small farmer.

Efficient business methods and cooperatives had been two techniques more widely but slowly adopted by farmers after their political debacle in the 1890's under Bryan. In politics, too, the farmer's methods had begun to change. Broad ideological third party movements in times of crisis with relative inaction in good times were abandoned, and by the 1920's the more realistic "farm bloc" had come into being.

Working constantly at Washington, a bipartisan coalition of southern Democrats and midwestern Republicans used their votes as the balance of power in the House and Senate to block unfavorable legislation or to gain advantages for the farmer out of all proportion to the size and political strength of farm population. Before Bryan, the farmer's rhetoric had been that only the farm could save democracy; in the 1920's, despite the persistence of the so-called "yeoman myth," the farmers' representatives acted as though only democratic processes could save the farm.

The farmer was helped not only by America's responsiveness to sentimental claims about "the man with the hoe," but also by the equality of the states in the Senate and a failure to redistribute seats in the House according to the latest census returns. Although the country was increasingly urban, farm votes were still many, and they were shrewdly used. The farm bloc was spurred on and helped by another technique the farmers had learned to use—the full-time pressure group and lobby at Washington. Throughout the twenties, the three most important farm-pressure groups were the Farm Bureau Federation, the National Grange, and the Farmers' Educational and Co-operative Union, generally known as the Farmers' Union. The Farm Bureau Federation in general represented the largest, most prosperous, and conservative farmers. The Grange, which had stemmed from the agrarian discontent in the decade after the Civil War, had forsaken its radical past and also spoke for conservative commercial agriculture. Only the Farmers' Union professed to speak for the small farmer. Unlike the other two farm-pressure groups, it advocated inflation, government price fixing, and cooperation with the less radical labor organizations of the day.

The basis of the farmer's plight was that he had exportable surpluses that sold at low prices in the world market and that forced down farm prices at home also. As soon as the farm problem was recognized for what it was, farm politicians searched for a remedy. One of the most popular ideas was to separate the domestic and foreign markets. The McNary-Haugen Bill was passed with the support of the Farm Bureau in 1927 and 1928 and was on both occasions vetoed by President Coolidge on the ground that it provided for "unsound" price fixing. Under this bill, the government was to purchase the leading agricultural staples at a price that would assure the farmer a profit. The farmer would actually receive from the government the fixed price minus a fee he would have to pay for the government's losses in selling the balance of his surpluses abroad. If the farmer limited production, he would get only guaranteed profits on domestic sales; if he produced surpluses, his profits would be cut into by the fees. Other plans included guaranteed prices to be paid for by export bounties on major crops and livestock and crop-planting quotas. All plans, however, involved a retreat from the risks of the free market and at least hopes for better planned production. Both the division of opinion among the farm organizations and farm politicians and the coolness or opposition of Republican leaders blocked all these plans. The farm problem, however, was too desperate to be ignored entirely, and in June, 1929, the Agricultural Marketing Act became law. The new law set up a Federal Farm Board with a fund of $500,000,000 to be used to establish national cooperatives for every major farm product and to make loans to cooperative members against the security of their crops. The cooperatives were not to control production but to hold products off the market until prices were favorable.

Unfortunately, the market prices on major crops continued to fall, and often they went below the price at which the cooperatives had made loans to the farmers. Speculators at one point could thus buy wheat or cotton in the open market at $1.10 a bushel or $.145 a pound and sell back to the cooperatives at $1.25 a bushel or $.16 a pound. Government "stabilization corporations" were next set up to buy the surplus wheat and cotton on the open market. But this further guarantee of prices made production shoot up again. By the summer of 1931, the wheat board, which had bought a quarter of a billion bushels, could take no more. It abandoned the market, and prices plummeted. Clearly, without the production controls that the New Deal program was soon to try, the Hoover policy of only regulating prices could not work. Indeed, the Hoover board itself proposed in August, 1931, that every third row of cotton be "plowed under" and that Congress permit controls over farm output.

The complexity of the general problem of farm production in the 1920's can only be suggested by these changes in devising wheat and cotton policies. Cattle raisers, for another example, were to be helped by forbidding combinations and price fixing agreements among meatpackers; agricultural cooperatives were exempted from the antitrust laws; federal banks were set up exclusively for farm loans; and the already extensive and long-established government information and education services for farmers were expanded. Yet, after all was done, the farmer won battles in Congress and gained more government services, but he lost the war. Without expanding international and domestic markets or the elimination or serious decrease in the numbers of producers of surpluses, the nation had to anticipate more farm products than it could use. Without accepting more extensive planning of production and more serious steps to take unneeded farmers off the land than our traditions seemed to permit, the farmers would remain a public charge. Expansion in the demand for industrial labor combined with farm production controls and inducements to marginal or surplus farmers to leave the land might bring supply and demand closer into line, but since the 1920's no national politician has dared to advocate any such bold broad program.

Unions in Decline

Unlike most farmers, the real income of American workers in the twenties increased over-all, but job insecurity, the spottiness of employment, and successful attacks on trade unions made for continuing instabilities in the workingman's life.

Gross earnings, on a scale of 1914 = 100, had moved from 218 in 1920 to only 224 by 1928, but real wages increased from 106 to 132 for those years. During 1920–3, despite the short depression, workers profited from declining prices, and real wages went up 13 per cent. They rose another 11 per cent from 1926–8 because of relatively stable prices. There was, however, no significant reduction in the average work week of about forty-eight hours.

Earnings of Workers, 1919–28 *

YEAR	AVERAGE ANNUAL EARNINGS IN DOLLARS	MONEY EARNINGS INDEX (1914 = 100)	REAL EARNINGS INDEX (1914 = 100)
1919	1,144	187	105
1920	1,337	218	106
1921	1,171	191	108
1922	1,144	187	113
1923	1,228	200	119
1924	1,225	200	118
1925	1,255	205	119
1926	1,375	219	126
1927	1,375	219	128
1928	1,405	224	132

* By permission from *Recent Social Trends; Report of the President's Research Committee on Social Trends*, Vol. II, p. 820. Copyright 1933. McGraw-Hill Book Company, Inc.

These average figures for wages and hours thus depict a working class sharing in prosperity, but averages are misleading; in southern textile mills and mines, for example, many workers gave more than sixty hours of labor for about ten dollars a week, and in 1928 blast furnace workers were still hired for a sixty-hour week. Child labor, although declining, was still legally available for at least fifty-four hours a week in seven states by 1930. A constant backlog of at least 1,000,000 unemployed, partly traceable to the growth of technology, and the devitalizing effects of the machine-factory round of life brought little feeling of permanent prosperity to many workers.

American unions could do little to correct these conditions. In 1918, the American labor movement had unprecedented strength: nearly full employment, decent real wages, greater membership than ever before, and government support for minimum wages, maximum hours, and collective bargaining—seemingly an impregnable position, but not one without weaknesses. Heavy-goods industries were not strongly unionized, and many workers had joined unions without developing deep loyalty to them. When men lost jobs in war industries after the Armistice, they usually lost enthusiasm for the unions. Government support for right-wing unions not only declined but was reversed as the nation returned to peacetime conditions. The radical labor movement had been assaulted even during the war, and until he left office in March, 1921, Attorney General A. Mitchell Palmer kept up that attack. In January, 1920, during the so-called "red raids" he arrested about 2,500 assorted radicals. In two years, about 5,000 "suspicious" aliens were served deportation warrants. The remnant of the I.W.W., or "wobbly," leadership was thus arrested nearly out of existence, and New York State imprisoned Communist labor leaders and expelled five Socialists from the legislature at Albany.

Wartime government support for more conservative unions gave way to the use of federal injunctions against these same unions in 1919. With the war over, however, the unions' oldest weapon, the strike, was available again. In 1919, when many employers refused to raise wages to match price increases, workers in industries from coast to coast participated in more than 3,600 strikes involving well over 4,000,000 workers. Many strikes in 1919 were won by the workers, but not as many as contemporaries thought and not enough to outweigh union setbacks in the steel and coal industries.

Despite limited, if long-sought, wartime gains by the National Committee for the Organizing of the Iron and Steel Industry, Judge Elbert Gary, head of the United States Steel Corporation, had repeatedly stated that he would not deal with the union leaders; a general

A Contribution to the "Red Scare"—Bombing in Wall Street, 1920

[BROWN BROTHERS]

steel strike was finally called; and on September 22, 1919, more than 300,000 steel workers—under the leadership of William Z. Foster, a former syndicalist (and a future Communist)—left their jobs. The employers fought the strike with private guards, strikebreakers, state and federal troops, martial law, and a vigorous propaganda campaign that emphasized Foster's views on racial tolerance. Other unions and some nonlaboring groups gave aid, but the strikers lacked the weapons to overcome the employers' advantages. In November and December, many workers began to return to their jobs, and on January 8, 1920, the union leaders announced the end of the strike. Twenty men—eighteen of them strikers—lost their lives in the conflict. The steel workers had to wait until 1937, for the C.I.O. and the New Deal, before they could win the struggle that they had lost in 1919–20.

The coal miners' strike was little more successful. On November 1, 1919, the miners in the bituminous fields struck for higher wages and a shorter work week. On the motion of Attorney General Palmer, a federal district court issued an injunction against the striking miners, and the union leaders capitulated. But the strikers refused to return to

Even the Actors Went On Strike (1919)

work, and the strike dragged on until a federal commission granted
the miners part of their wage demands but refused to make any change
in basic hours. In 1922, both the anthracite and bituminous miners
struck against proposed lower wages and smaller union powers. Union
leaders, however, were unable to obtain more than a temporary agreement that reimposed the previous scale. After 1922, the United Mine
Workers steadily lost ground, and by 1929, the union's membership
had dwindled to a fraction of its former strength.

Decline in union strength also came elsewhere in the 1920's
after the burst of militancy in 1919–20. Union membership fell from
5,110,000 in 1920 to 4,330,000 in 1929. The statistics reveal an even
more dramatic drop in strikes. More income and shorter work weeks,
weakened loyalties to unions from within working ranks, and anti-
union drives with the tacit or real support of federal and state governments cut union strength.

An open-shop drive, stepped up during the postwar depression,
maintained its momentum for years. By the autumn of 1920, there were

Number of Strikes and Number of Workers
Involved in Strikes, 1919–29 *

YEAR	NUMBER OF STRIKES	WORKERS STRIKING (IN THOUSANDS)
1919	3,630	4,160
1920	3,411	1,463
1921	2,385	1,099
1922	1,112	1,613
1923	1,553	757
1924	1,249	655
1925	1,301	428
1926	1,035	330
1927	707	330
1928	604	314
1929	921	289

about 250 open-shop associations in the United States, and more than 50 in New York State alone. Union and closed shops were denounced as "un-American" devices for denying American individualism by prohibiting a man from working wherever he pleased. Propaganda for the "American Plan," as the open-shop program was called, was supplemented by using the old antiunion weapons: injunctions, lockouts, yellow-dog contracts, strikebreakers, labor spies, and armed thugs.

Old established craft-unions that had monopolized jobs for their members—especially in the printing, clothing, and building trades—resisted the employer attacks, but the over-all strength of organized labor declined, and by 1930 all that remained of the American labor movement was a small group of craft-unions in the A.F. of L. and the Railroad Brotherhoods.

The employers' proclaimed alternative to independent unions was "welfare capitalism," which promised to grant unorganized workers all the benefits that unions might bring, from higher wages to fancy rest rooms. Welfare capitalism, however, also meant company unions, organized under employer auspices and limited to one company or factory. Although they gave workers some benefits, their main objective was at best paternalistic, at worst to split, devitalize, and undercut a union movement that might seriously threaten employer interests.

* Reprinted with permission from John Ignatius Griffin: *Strikes; A Study in Quantitative Economics* (New York: Columbia University Press, 1939), pp. 38, 44.

The reversal of friendly attitudes towards labor in the last two years of the Wilson Administration was followed in the 1920's by federal and state judicial and executive decisions predominantly hostile to union labor. The use of the Sherman Act against unions, antistrike injunctions, yellow-dog contracts, union boycotts, peaceful picketing, as well as basic social legislation were all tested in the federal courts, and the decisions were almost always against labor. The general record of the states was more mixed than that of the federal government. The upholding of wage and hour laws and exemption of unions from antitrust prosecution came with laws against picketing, boycotts, and union interference with operations in mines and railroads and with legislation requiring compulsory arbitration of labor disputes.

The labor conflict which foreshadowed most clearly, perhaps, how union labor was to be on the defensive was the railroad dispute of 1921–22. A Railroad Labor Board with equal representation from labor, management, and the public was set up by the Transportation Act of 1920. It could only recommend decisions in railroad labor disputes, and in April, 1921, it approved reduced wages for workers. In July, 1922, it authorized another wage cut, and 400,000 rail shop workers went on strike. President Harding tried mediation, but he failed when the operators refused to restore seniority rights to the strikers. On September 1, Attorney General Daugherty obtained one of the most sweeping antistrike injunctions in American history. Only a few strikers heeded the court and went back to work; several companies with trump cards now in their hands settled with unions controlling 225,000 workers, but the remaining 175,000 strikers eventually had to accept total defeat from obdurate railroad executives who, backed by the Harding Administration, had little reason to grant the workers any of their demands.

In the 1920's the government's refusal to aid unions was justified, as it had traditionally been, in the name of free enterprise and freedom of contract. But without government support unions were too weak to compete with employer tactics that ranged from brutal "union busting" to paternalistic undermining. By 1929, effective unions were limited to a small minority of the working class and lacked popular support or public prestige. The unions had no general philosophy about what role they might play in industrial America other than their insistence, where and when they could insist, on more money, shorter hours, and better conditions. Their aggressive leadership had been almost completely cowed or destroyed. Labor was as ill prepared as business to meet the approaching cataclysm of depression.

The Creativeness of Alienation

Government hostility to unions and friendship for big business might have been enough to convince sensitive observers that the humane and cosmopolitan reform spirit that seemed so strong in 1914 was dead in the twenties. When, however, official illiberalism helped strengthen a vulgar and simplistic American faith in the power of money, standardization, efficiency, and machines to solve all human problems, many intellectuals concluded that American culture was hopeless.

Intellectuals in politics often find it difficult to reconcile themselves to the inability of workers and business people to remain militantly reformist for any length of time, but many American intellectuals on the eve of the war had suddenly found faith in reform through the Progressive movements. It seemed that a democratic public could respond effectively and enthusiastically to reform, and that a political life for the intellectual was an attractive possibility.

The sources of the so-called alienation or disillusion of America's intellectuals in the 1920's go back beyond that decade to the war years, after the Progressive movements when, true to the predictions of some writers at the time, nationalist and jingo fervor helped kill reformism. Other sources of disillusion were the war itself and the failure to make "peace with justice." In America, as in Europe, the "experience of the trenches"—battles, for example, in which 50,000 casualties brought a few yards of territory—made it impossible for many men to have the faith in human nature or the love of life that had so influenced reform thinking before the war. The hideousness and senselessness of war for the common soldier had already been portrayed several times in American literature—most notably in Stephen Crane's Civil War novel, The Red Badge of Courage (1895)—but the slaughter in France and the discovery, however naïve, that war and army life put a premium on conformity, force, and brutal leadership made it impossible for many intellectuals to have the optimism they once had. Such American war novels of the twenties as E. E. Cummings' The Enormous Room (1922), John Dos Passos' Three Soldiers (1921) and Ernest Hemingway's A Farewell to Arms (1929) were not, however, written during the war, but some years later, when peacetime disillusion helped strengthen the more painful memories of what war did to men. Despite the bleak picture of army life in these books, they did not reveal a loss of faith so much as the anger and dismay of youths forced quickly to become men and to discover that honor and decency did not rule the world.

Many liberal intellectuals who had not fought in France but who had supported the war and the Wilsonian peace program turned sour either at the treaty Wilson brought back from Paris or at the country's failure to accept the Paris pact. They became distrustful of high-sounding reformers and the general public. Many also had intense feelings of guilt for having contributed to American deaths overseas and to wartime illiberalism at home in what turned out to be vain hopes for a peacetime world safe for democracy.

The "hopeless materialism" of the twenties that did not seem worth these sacrifices, in fact, had its immediate source in profits and buying during the war. Critics of American materialism in the 1920's often forgot that America's business civilization had a long history and that as the nation's Christian and humane ideals were rapidly weakened after the Civil War, the stage had already been set for the Babbitts of the 1920's. Of course, Main Street's higher concerns with "character" and "faith" never seemed stronger than in the reform crusades that reached their height about 1912. But the more noble aspects of the creed of 1912 were strongly allied with materialistic desires, and in the twenties these gained predominance and the former progressive concerns about character and faith became mere sentimentalities, however often invoked.

The most ironic portrait of what was happening to American ideals in the 1920's was F. Scott Fitzgerald's *The Great Gatsby* (1925). Fitzgerald's hero was an idealistic young poor boy from the Midwest who becomes a fabulously rich racketeer in order to win back the girl he loves from the society millionaire she has married. Money, for Gatsby, is only a means to gain ideal love; for Daisy's husband money means crude power. The latter's America—the world of the twenties—is too much for Gatsby. Despite his gallant gesture to save Daisy from a hit-and-run charge, she decides to stay with her husband, who tells a lie that brings about Gatsby's murder. Gatsby is killed on the edge of the swimming pool on his "gorgeous" Long Island estate from which he used to look longingly across the bay to Daisy's dock, dreaming of the "orgiastic future" that finally eluded and killed him but that ceaselessly lures on other Americans.

The scenes in *The Great Gatsby* of lavish parties, drinking bouts in expensive hotel suites, wild rides in flashy automobiles, and sleazy liaisons with "dames in Washington Heights" who get "fox fur-pieces" from their lovers were all part of the "roar" of the twenties. In either childishly exaggerated forms or in long-needed release, the energy that exploded in the twenties has been characterized as a rebellion against America's puritanical traditions and as a "revolt against the village" or against the small-town code of life. The old Jacksonian–Protestant codes had, of course, been weakening for generations; indeed, part of American reform agitation after 1885 was inspired by fears of their passing, but after 1918, jazz, "booze," cars, and "sex appeal" built on their prewar prestige and convinced many people—although millions of Americans merely heard of the new morality—that liberation was at hand. The flush of postwar interest in the psychoanalytic ideas of Freud resulted in the conclusion that "science" had proved that suppressing desires was bad. Although Americans had started making whoopee before Freud's influence, it was convenient to enlist him, despite his protests, on the side of an overly optimistic breakaway from the past or in support of a debauch in alcohol, adultery, and automobiles.

The "Jazz Age," however, was largely a big-city phenomenon. It had limited or only occasional effects on America's small towns and rural areas. Liquor and "petting," the movies and the "daring novel," had new fans everywhere, but from rural America, especially in the South, came wide-swinging attacks on the new urban ethos of leisure and pleasure. Whatever hideousness accompanied the rebirth of the Klan and whatever the inanities of the prohibition forces (which were assuredly matched by the antics of some practicing "wets"), the wave of puritanism that swept out of the war years should be understood as desperate attempts by a dying old America to uphold ideals which in nobler forms had once dominated national life. The puritan code and Jacksonian faith now seemed to be ignored or, worse, despised by the followers of a new culture, one of whose "smartest" magazines, *The New Yorker*, declared smugly that it was not written for the "old lady in Dubuque."

The "revolt against the village" in literature grew out of best-selling works like Edgar Lee Masters' *Spoon River Anthology* (1915), Sherwood Anderson's *Winesburg, Ohio* (1919), and Sinclair Lewis' *Main Street* (1920) and *Babbitt* (1922). These works depicted the frustrating or crippling effects of small-town life on various men and women. The mood of these writers, however, was often nostalgic and sentimental rather than resentful. Despite Sinclair Lewis' skillful eye for the weak spots in Babbitt's "boosterism," his affection for him and Zenith takes much of the bite out of the satire. The really strong attacks on the small-town American came in magazines like *Smart Set*, and especially from one of its editors, H. L. Mencken. Unfortunately, the rural and small-town forces behind the Klan, prohibition, and the trial at Dayton, Tennessee, of John Scopes, a young teacher of Darwinian ideas, gave critics like Mencken all the ammunition they needed. The limitations of his opponents made Mencken's "sophisti-

Sinclair Lewis

[NATIONAL ARCHIVES]

cated" quips and barbs well placed but obscured Mencken's own
limitations as an enlightened satirist. His attack on the "boobocracy,"
the "cowtowns," and on passing American heroes like William Jennings Bryan, Theodore Roosevelt, and Woodrow Wilson were brutal,
even malevolent. Mencken's implication that a civilized way of life
was represented by quick-witted city writers and journalists who
smoked, drank, and had all-night poker sessions after Lucullan meals
perhaps did not entitle him to the status of seer that he enjoyed among
many people at the time. His literary criticism was equally shallow.

Not all the criticism of "boosterism" and small-town life was based
on urban chic or liberal hopes for freeing intellect and energy from
traditional illegitimate restraints. Two little-noted, but symptomatic,
groups of critics in the twenties were the so-called Southern Agrarians,
or "Twelve Southerners," a group which included the poet-critics Allen
Tate and John Crowe Ransom and the "new humanists" led by Professor Irving Babbitt and Paul Elmer More. In 1930, the southerners
published a manifesto, *I'll Take My Stand*, in which they called attention to the curse that had settled on the post-Civil War South as it

adopted the ideals and values of modern commercial society. Mixed with a well-founded protest against the ruthless commercial exploitation of southern lands was the hostility of some of the agrarians to egalitarianism and liberal democracy. Badly informed about the prewar history of their own section, the more conservative of these writers asked their audience to consider the advantages of antebellum artistocratic ideals as antidotes to the poisons of modernity.

Babbitt and More were critics with an even smaller but more influential following—T. S. Eliot, for example, had been a student of Babbitt's at Harvard. Babbitt and More argued that modern, mindless, crass America was the final outcome of a revolt against God and reason that dated back for centuries in the West. Babbitt contended that only classical and rationalist standards in art as well as in morals and politics could save modern civilization. Liberalism and democracy were said to be inspired by what Babbitt claimed were Rousseauian ideals of the superiority of instinct and appetite to reason and a self-imposed intelligent restraint—or the "inner check," as he called it. More's argument was essentially the same, but, unlike Babbitt, he eventually accepted orthodox Christianity and then claimed that only Christian faith could give man an effective alternative to the debasing creeds of modern society.

The writers' criticisms of American life in the twenties thus had various intellectual sources and different emotional biases. Many major writers and artists with differing points of view tried to escape from a philistine culture by going abroad or by creating small colonies of intellectuals in areas in New York City, Chicago, and San Francisco. Such art colonies as Greenwich Village were outgrowths of a bohemian movement in American arts that caught on after the 1870's. Both the expatriates and the bohemians at home were trying to find some place where they could, in the words of a Greenwich Village favorite, Edna St. Vincent Millay, "burn the candle at both ends," and ignore the vulgar world outside. It is difficult, however, to generalize about the bohemians or expatriates except to note that they all shared a sense of being isolated and alienated from their culture by a philistine public and barbarian leaders. However, what they lamented as alienation from one point of view was a condition of freedom and creativeness from another. Many writers, giving up on America, spoke glowingly of Europe's greater receptivity to the arts. In fact, ever since at least 1848 European writers and artists had also been fighting bourgeois and philistine forces similar to those that seemed rampant in the America of the 1920's; furthermore, the very idea of alienation as a mark of modern life had been first explored by the Europeans. Nevertheless, however naïve their view of Europe, as foreigners in new surroundings the expatriates *felt* free and, most important, could come directly into touch with the exciting modern movements in painting, music, sculpture, and poetry that had begun to flower in Europe in the generation before the war. Indeed, the influence of study and talk with European masters was the most valuable experience the expatriates brought home with them.

Of all the expatriates Ernest Hemingway achieved a reputation as a spokesman. His novel *The Sun Also Rises* (1926) was a touching, sentimental story about a group of rootless young men and women, many of them Americans, living in Paris immediately after the war, who found all "causes" sour except the pleasures of personal relationships, and of food, drink, snatches of love, and good sportmanship. In Hemingway's stories the skillful bullfighter, hunter, fisherman, or boxer who masters his style earns through his art a dignity and grace that are personal moral victories in an otherwise bleak struggle of life against death.

Hemingway and his fellow expatriates were described as a "lost generation" by Gertrude Stein, an American author experimenting with writing who had lived in France since before the war. She encouraged the attempts of many young men and women to work out new styles in the arts. As news from America reached Europe of such events as the trial and execution of Sacco and Vanzetti, two minor radicals who were probably innocent of the charges of murder lodged against them, the expatriates were convinced that America was lost to all hope and that only the arts, as Miss Stein and others claimed, offered sensitive people some vision of an order in which the creative intellectual might find pleasure and enlightenment.

Much of American intellectual life abroad and at home in the 1920's centered around the so-called "little magazines," periodicals with a very small circulation, run on shoestring budgets, and founded to give writers and artists the chance to ignore the philistines and to communicate with each other in their own language. Like other features of American culture in the twenties, the history of the little magazines went back at least a generation. The main link between the prewar and postwar American reviews was the magazine *Poetry*, founded in 1912 in Chicago. Among the poems it published before the war were early works of the two most talked about and influential poets of the 1920's, Ezra Pound and T. S. Eliot.

Pound was already living abroad in 1912, and he became *Poetry*'s European agent in the second issue. He did more than any man to tie American letters to the new international movements in the arts and, in the words of another contributor to *Poetry*, Carl Sandburg, "most of living men to incite new impulses in poetry." Besides Eliot and Pound, practically every major American and European poet of our time published in the early issues of *Poetry*. It was also at a dinner *Poetry* sponsored for the visit of the Irish poet William Butler Yeats in 1914 that American poets heard this master strike a theme of the future —that the American artist was too far from Paris, for it was from Paris "that nearly all the great influences in art and literature have come. . . . In France is the great critical mind."

The variety of poems published in *Poetry* precludes generalizations about the styles and "schools," but from its pages Eliot and Pound and other poets moved into the various little magazines of the 1920's. Aside from their great gifts as poetic innovators and as leaders in the discovery of Provençal, Far Eastern, and seventeenth-century English writers as new sources of poetic inspiration, Eliot's and Pound's view of life did much to strengthen the postwar mood of disgust with politics, reform, and public life in general. As early as 1908, when Pound expatriated himself, he already said that "there was no one in America whose work was of the slightest interest for a serious artist."

Pound's use of Japanese, Chinese, and Provençal sources was often pedantic and his "philosophy" thin. But his and Eliot's knowledge of languages and use of a wide range of cultural references in their works were important illustrations of what critics have stressed about Western intellectual life in the twentieth century, its deep sense of inheriting the culture and art forms of all ages, and thus, potentially, the capacity to take an even more cosmopolitan view of man than the Italian Renaissance humanists. However, in their own views of life, Pound and Eliot became increasingly parochial and dogmatic in their condemnation of modern culture. Pound's thought, unlike Eliot's, was much less impressive than his technique. Eventually he became a supporter of Mussolini's Fascism and virulently anti-Semitic. During World War II, he went insane, broadcast for the Fascists, and was, subsequently, indicted for treason in 1945. In the early twenties, however, Pound, like Eliot, was regarded as a revolutionary liberator in the arts.

Eliot's most famous and influential poem, published in 1922, was *The Waste Land*, which was both an expression of the desiccation and futility of modern life as caught in images of city life and an attempt to discover in primitive myth and folklore and in the cultures of the East some revivifying tradition by which the creative life might still be sustained. Three years later, however, Eliot published *The Hollow Men*, more frightening in its images than *The Waste Land*, and concluding with the now famous line that the world will end, "Not with a bang but a whimper." Eliot's early feelings of personal suffering, decay, and emptiness, of the need for, yet the difficulty of finding a tradition, eventually led him to announce in 1927 that he had become a classicist in literature, a royalist in politics, and an Anglo-Catholic in religion. Still, Christianity made little change in his sense of life, for the faith that he spoke of in his later poems, from *Ash Wednesday* (1930) on, was almost entirely dominated by the image of the crucifixion, and had little sense of the liberation offered the Christian from the spectacle of worldly death in this life by the birth and resurrection of a Savior.

Many of Eliot's contemporaries who were liberals and secularists were dismayed by his conversion. As Eliot increasingly attacked the liberal humanism that had become so influential in intellectual life in western Europe and America by 1910, and as anti-Semitic, snobbish, and snide remarks appeared in his notable critical essays, the great liberator of the early twenties became known as a reactionary, even a Fascist. In fact, Eliot's politics, despite vicious side comments, had only the most limited influence from reactionaries and owed far greater debts to his Harvard teacher, Irving Babbitt, to the traditions of English, Christian conservatism, and to the little-noted sorrows of his private life.

For many of the nation's intellectuals, liberals as well as conservatives, only a radical change in the political and cultural atmosphere of the 1920's would smash the seemingly unbreakable hold of the Babbitts and the bankers over American life. A few intellectuals, however, had managed to combine complete alienation from America with an intense activist, enlivening political faith. The Great Depression that started in 1929 was to test whether the future lay with the ideas of these Americans—radicals like John Reed and Lincoln Steffens, who early accepted Communism as the only answer to the sickness and futility of capitalist culture—or with those who would, on the very edge of disaster, just manage to patch up the old system. In the 1920's, as the Wall Street stock-market index, to the dismay of the intellectuals and small groups of reformers, climbed ever higher, Lenin and Stalin, as well as Hitler and Mussolini, were already building their tyrannies in Europe.

FOR SUPPLEMENTARY READING

The best work on the economy of the 1920's is G. Soule, *Prosperity Decade* (1947). The drama of 1929 is well studied in J. K. Galbraith,

The Great Crash (1955). On business thought in the 1920's use J. W. Prothro, *Dollar Decade* (1954). W. E. Leuchtenberg's *The Perils of Prosperity* (1958) (Pb) is an excellent general social and political history. There are a number of entertaining books on American manners and morals in the twenties. Of the older books of this type the favorite is F. L. Allan, *Only Yesterday* (1931) (Pb), and a more recent work of the same genre is P. Sann, *The Lawless Decade* (1957). Politics under Harding and Coolidge have many analysts. There is no biography of Harding but M. Moos in *The Republicans* (1956) avoids both nostalgia and finger-shaking. W. A. White has written an excellent biography of Coolidge, *A Puritan in Babylon* (1938). Al Smith still awaits a biographer but a start can be made with O. Handlin's sometimes sentimental *Al Smith and His America* (1958). Smith's defeat in 1928 is the subject of E. A. Moore, *A Catholic Runs for President* (1956). Perhaps the best works on the politics of the 1920's are F. Freidel, *Franklin D. Roosevelt: The Ordeal* (1954) and *The Triumph* (1956). Three works by experts throw much light on the decade: A. A. Berle and G. F. Means, *The Modern Corporation and Private Property* (1932); R. S. and H. M. Lynd, *Middletown* (1929); and the President's Research Committee on Social Trends, *Recent Social Trends in the United States* (2 vols., 1933). There is no one general work on the writers of the lost generation that is fully reliable. A famous expression of the sense of disillusion is J. W. Krutch, *The Modern Temper* (1929) (Pb). Other than reading the novelists directly try H. May, *The End of American Innocence* (1959), for background immediately before the period, and F. J. Hoffman, *The Twenties* (1958). Best of all are E. Wilson's essays of the time collected in *The Shores of Light* (1952) and *The American Earthquake* (1958).

PART IV

THE
WELFARE
REPUBLIC

[BROWN BROTHERS]

⫸⫸⫸-⫸⫸-⫸⫸-⫸⫸-⫸⫸-⫸⫸-⫸⫸-⫸⫸

American Capitalism in Crisis

O N OCTOBER 29, 1929, after several serious earlier breaks, stock prices on the New York exchanges dropped disastrously from inflated heights. Although Americans at the time did not realize it, the stock-market crash signaled the advent of the most prolonged and severe depression in their nation's history. Initially, politicians in both parties, large and small businessmen, organized and nonunion labor had neither the ideas nor techniques to deal with the Great Depression. The traditions of private initiative, voluntary relief schemes, and, at most, limited government aid to the distressed were widely accepted by most American leaders as the best remedies. Turning first to the businessman and then reluctantly to increased federal aid, President Hoover was unable to halt the downward plunge of the economy. His successor, Franklin D. Roosevelt, also adhering closely at first to dependence on the businessman to cure the nation's illness, eventually had to improvise policies that revolutionized the government's relation to the citizen; but even these did not end the crisis.

Amber Caution Lights

After a short recession in 1926, the nation's economy began a final zoom upward before the crash in 1929. Continuing soft spots from the earlier twenties in farming, mining, and textiles and a backlog of unemployment were present to remind those who watched only the stock-market quotations that many American homes had no chicken in the pot, let alone the two chickens that Republicans had promised the voters. The president of the National Industrial Conference Board stated in 1927 that there was "no reason why there should be any more panics," and a year later a New York business executive announced that the United States was "only at the beginning of a period that will go down in history as the golden age." Ex-Secretary of State Charles Evans Hughes saw little cause for alarm in the economic situation in 1928, for "prosperity feeds upon itself"; and Secretary of the Treasury Andrew Mellon assured the American people that the "high tide of prosperity will continue." In the presidential campaign of 1928, Herbert Hoover said: "The poor-house is vanishing from among us. We have not yet reached the goal, but given a chance to go forward with the policies of the last eight years, and we shall soon with the help of God be in sight of the day when poverty will be banished from this nation." Within eight months of Hoover's inauguration, the United States had entered upon the worst depression in its history.

Historians have not yet fully agreed on what was wrong with the economy, but most accept the idea that immense profits that might have made possible higher wages, sounder credit, lower prices, more employment, and imaginative relief schemes to increase the purchasing power of distressed farmers and miners instead were used for speculation and a shaky inflation of consumer and stock-market credit. The inability of consumption to keep pace with production would not have presented an insoluble problem if the American economic system had been flexible enough to adapt itself to changing conditions. As technology improved and production increased, consumers needed more real income to satisfy their desire for a higher standard of living. As new techniques created new industries and eliminated old ones, both capital and labor had to be sufficiently mobile to shift from industry to industry and even from firm to firm within a single industry. Farmers needed purchasing power, and workers suffering from technological unemployment needed new job opportunities. Investors had to be prevented from putting their capital into those enterprises that were already turning out more products than the market could absorb or into stock-market speculation at prices unrelated to the real strengths and weaknesses of industries.

As price competition—particularly in the heavy-goods industries—declined or disappeared, prices frequently bore little relation to supply and demand. Price rigidity in many industries made it difficult for a manufacturer to discover when his market was approaching the saturation point and made it highly improbable that prices would fall in response to a decline in demand. Profits went into increased production rather than higher wages leading to greater purchasing power; indeed, wages rose too slowly or were too sticky to help reduce growing inventories in the stores. Instead, a vast growth in installment buying maintained the illusion that solid purchasing power was matching increased production. Because industry as well as agriculture had come to rely on foreign sales for part of its profits, any shrinkage in the foreign market also necessitated drastic readjustments within the United States, but as more money went into production or the stock market at home instead of foreign investments, overseas demand previously financed by American loans began to fall off.

Two obvious signs of danger in the boom were declines after 1927 in the rate of growth of both the automobile and building industries. New registrations for passenger cars totaled almost 2,000,000 in 1924 but declined to less than half that figure in 1927, and increased to only slightly more than 1,000,000 in 1928. For each successive year from 1921 through 1926, more dwellings had been constructed than in the preceding years; but with 1927 the trend was reversed. Since both the automobile and housing industries had made major contributions to the expansion of the midtwenties, their relative decline was bound to have an adverse effect on the entire economy, but these danger signals were ignored.

Wall Street Follies

The stage was set for the collapse of American prosperity in 1929 by the increasingly intense Wall Street boom after 1927. As more investors put their money into securities in the hope of making a quick profit on a speculative rise in stocks, the New York Stock Exchange became an even greater betting ring than it had been. People gambled on stocks as though they were wagering on roulette or horse races. Security prices were forced up by competitive bidding rather than by any fundamental improvement in American corporate strength. There was little correlation between actual conditions in American industry and stock-market quotations.

Part of the money that flowed to the New York Stock Exchange in the last two years of the 1920's was supplied by corporations with unexpended and apparently unexpendable cash reserves. Instead of cutting prices and increasing wages, the pattern of a competitive economy, corporate officials placed surplus funds in the investment market. The traditional function of the stock market was thus reversed. Instead of being used to gather funds for corporate expansion, it swallowed the profits of corporations threatened by overexpansion and unwilling to cut prices.

Speculation in the security market was positively encouraged by brokers and bankers. High-pressure sales techniques, nation-wide advertising campaigns, and specially trained security salesmen recruited from the graduating classes of large eastern universities were all used to attract additional funds to the stock market. Investment trusts for small investors, from the taxicab driver to shop owner, were set up for cooperative stock purchases under banker direction, and liberal margin requirements permitted the investor to enter the market on a shoestring. By buying on margin, the investor had to pay only a fraction of the quoted price of a security. The additional money needed to cover the purchase was supplied by the broker, who obtained these funds from a bank with which he had deposited his customer's stock as collateral.

The margin buyer was particularly vulnerable to even a small decline in stock quotations. With any decrease in security values, he would have to pay the broker additional money to cover the corresponding decrease in his collateral. If he should be unable to supply this money—and usually was—the broker would be compelled to sell the stock to protect himself at the bank. Once this process had started, there was always the danger that it could not be stopped. If brokers had to dispose of their customers' holdings and investors were to sell part of their securities to increase their collateral, prices would be further depressed, and more margin buyers would be compelled to dump more stocks on the market. The circle would then be complete, for there was no apparent way of checking this downward spiral after it had been set in motion.

The stock-market boom was at first largely financed by money obtained at low interest rates. The Federal Reserve Board might have been able to retard speculation by raising the price of loans. But there was the risk that the brake would be applied prematurely or that the decision would have political repercussions for the party in power. At least three times between 1927 and 1929 when the Board wanted to tighten credit, foreign and American bankers successfully pleaded for continued credit expansion. By 1929, however, with or without easy credit, corporations had large enough cash reserves to pour them into the stock market, and there was little that the Federal Reserve Board could do to check these nonbank sources of the speculative rise in stocks. Nevertheless, in August, 1929, the board belatedly increased the rediscount rate from 5 to 6 per cent.

In the summer of 1929, some observers began to predict that a serious decline in security prices would inevitably pave the way for a full-scale crash. During the last two weeks of October, these fears were confirmed. On October 19, stocks took their first serious tumble. After a brief rally, they went down again on October 24, when almost 13,000,000 shares were traded. A group of bankers tried to check the collapse by entering the market to purchase securities at a point above their quoted prices. Once more there was a short rally, but it was followed by a complete collapse, and on October 29, the bottom dropped out of the stock market. Approximately 16,500,000 shares were traded, and some stocks dropped as much as 80 per cent. The crash had come, and the great boom was on its way to becoming the greatest depression in American history.

Some contemporaries, however, believed that the sharp decline in security prices was a healthy development. It seemed to have checked speculation while leaving American productive capacity intact. On October 26, 1929, *The Wall Street Journal* undoubtedly spoke for many Americans when it stated that "suggestions that the wiping out of paper profits will reduce the country's real purchasing power seem far-fetched." During November, Julius Rosenwald, the head of Sears Roebuck & Co., announced that "comparatively few people are reached by this crash"; and President Herbert Hoover stated that "any lack of confidence in the economic future or the basic strength of the business of the United States is foolish." These optimistic views were all based on the belief that the stock-market crash had not destroyed any real wealth—an idea expressed by Charles M. Schwab in December when he said:

> This great speculative era in Wall Street, in which stocks have crashed, means nothing in the welfare of business. The same factories have the same wheels turning. Values are unchanged. Wealth is beyond the quotations of Wall Street. Wealth is founded in the industries of the nation, and while they are sound, stocks may go up and stocks may go down, but the nation will prosper.

But by November, 1929, Americans had already begun to limit their purchases, and business leaders who were not sure of what was coming next also started to retrench. Orders for heavy goods were first canceled, new investments dried up, and the very thing that business-

TRANSACTIONS ON THE NEW YORK STOCK EXCHANGE

TUESDAY, OCTOBER 29, 1929.

Day's Sales.	Monday.	Saturday.	A Year Ago.	Two Years Ago.
16,410,030	9,212,800	2,087,660	3,483,770	1,676,570

Year to Date.

	1929.	1927.	1926.	1925.
350,797,190	708,649,607	464,944,575	376,924,360	365,084,123

The Breakfast News, October 30, 1929

men feared most was promoted by their fear. Business fears and business stagnation complemented one another to accelerate the descent into depression. Increasing unemployment and a falling wage scale were accompanied by a corresponding decrease in purchasing power.

The American economy went steadily downward until the first months of 1931, when there was a slight revival of business activity. But this proved only a flurry, for the earlier downward trends quickly reappeared. Another partial recovery in the early autumn of 1932 was equally deceptive, and the depression rapidly reached its all-time low in March, 1933. The national income, which had been $83,326,000,000 in 1929, decreased to $39,963,000,000 in 1932; and the number of unemployed in the first months of 1933 was in the neighborhood of 12,000,000. Between 1929 and 1932 the index number (1935–9 average = 100) of the physical volume of industrial production declined from 110 to 58; the industrial wage bill declined from $10,909,000,000 to $4,608,000,000; farm income, already depressed by 1929, fell further from $12,791,000,000 to $5,562,000,000; the Dow-Jones average of stock prices declined from $125.43 to $26.82; and the wholesale-price index (1926 = 100) declined from 95.3 to 68.3.

Hoover and the Depression

In every depression before 1929, forces at work within the economy—or else a war—had eventually checked the deflationary spiral and cleared the way for a new cycle of prosperity. Through price and wage slashes, foreclosures, bankruptcies, and the exhaustion of inventories, the economy had been forced down to a bedrock base from which it could once again begin the long, hard climb toward prosperity. But from 1929 to 1933, the American economy seemed bottomless, and many of the tendencies that had produced the economic inflexibility of the 1920's militated against a self-correcting recovery.

Price rigidity was maintained in the heavy-goods industries, many of which reduced production and payrolls while maintaining prices. Throughout the depression, nickel remained at $.35 a pound, sulphur at $18 a ton, and aluminum dropped from $.24 a pound in 1929 only to $.23 in 1932. Aside from the railroads, most big corporations showed profits—although not as large as in the twenties—during the depression. On the other hand, in agriculture and in many consumer-goods industries, competition forced producers to adopt just the opposite policy. Prices were slashed and production was increased in order to make up by volume what was lost by lower prices.

The price policies of the durable-goods industries forced the man-

"*It Works Both Ways*" (*Knott in the Dallas* News)

ufacturer of consumer goods to pay abnormally high prices for everything he bought while selling his own products at prevailing low prices. By keeping prices at fixed levels, instead of permitting them to fall with the decline in demand, the directors of many of the nation's basic industries prolonged the depression and virtually eliminated any possibility of a self-generating recovery.

The depression was also intensified by decline in the European demand for American products, the depressed condition of the United States' farm population, and the large debt burden that had to be carried during a period of deflation. American exports declined in value from $5,241,000,000 in 1929 to $1,611,000,000 in 1932. Since American foreign trade had been largely financed by loans abroad, there was little chance that this trade could be revived in the near future. What trade remained from Europe after 1931 was seriously restricted by the high rates of the new Hawley-Smoot Tariff. The farmer, for whom the depression in many instances had merely meant a transition from bad to worse, had no purchasing power to check the deflationary trends. Finally, private debts that had been contracted during the boom had become an almost intolerable burden. As individuals and business firms defaulted on their obligations, the number of foreclosures and bank-ruptcies mounted and threatened to drag the entire economy down with them into chaos and ruin.

At the outset of the depression, Herbert Hoover, along with most other Americans, assumed that government intervention would not be needed to prevent human suffering and check the deflationary spiral. When it became evident that the depression was more than a tempo-rary phenomenon, Hoover issued statements to reassure the American people that their problems were mainly psychological and that a re-turn of confidence would be accompanied by a return of prosperity. But the President's repeated pleas for a change of attitude had no appre-ciable effect on the course of the depression. By 1931, economic distress had turned into a social crisis of momentous proportions. To the home-less, unemployed, and hungry, Hoover's analysis of the causes of their plight seemed not only naïve but heartless. The resident of a Hoover-ville—as the makeshift shanty towns that were occupied by jobless wanderers were called—knew that the government would have to do more than change his outlook to change his status.

Hoover was criticized by many contemporaries for attempting to end the depression with words, but he also initiated several practical programs. In the winter following the crash, the Federal Reserve Board attempted to expand credit by lowering the rediscount rate, and the Farm Board made an heroic, but unsuccessful, effort to sustain agricul-tural prices by preventing farm surpluses from glutting the market. Primarily, however, Hoover depended on the businessmen to put the economy right as they had in earlier depressions. Since he had had notable successes with voluntary methods as a relief administrator, it was natural that he should again seek voluntary cooperation and the aid of the business community for a program to sustain purchasing power. In 1930, Colonel Arthur Woods was selected by Hoover to head a committee to collect money for relief. At the same time, at a series of conferences sponsored by the government, leading business-men assured the President that they would not cut wages. Nevertheless, although businessmen in general observed this pledge until the middle of 1931, they did not hesitate to reduce their working force.

The government was urged to take more vigorous steps to relieve suffering and hardship and to recognize that the social crisis was be-yond the funds and power of private and local relief agencies. Hoover, however, held firm to his belief that the American people would have to depend on their "character" and self-reliance, their traditional ideals, to pull themselves out of the depression. When some congressmen urged direct relief for victims of the Arkansas drought in 1931, the

General MacArthur and Aide at the Bonus Army "Battlefield," 1932

[UNITED PRESS INTERNATIONAL]

President insisted that the congressional appropriation be advanced to the farmers as a loan rather than as direct relief. He was equally adamant a year later, when World War I veterans demanded the payment in full of their bonuses. The "bonus army," which consisted of approximately 15,000 veterans who were asking for the immediate payment of their bonuses, descended on Washington in the summer of 1932. Steps were taken to guard the White House and the Capitol building, but the veterans, urged to do so by the few radicals among them, refused to take the law into their own hands. They also refused to leave. Hoover finally called on the army under the direction of General Douglas MacArthur to drive them from the capital. No event more confirmed Hoover's reputation for insensitivity than the tear-gassing, bayoneting, and firing of the tents and shacks of the patriotic veterans and their families who were reviled as a mutinous, insurrectionary mob.

With some justification, Hoover believed that American recovery was being retarded by developments abroad and that the depression was a world-wide rather than an American phenomenon. He therefore made a valiant attempt to shore up the European economy. On June 21, 1931, he proposed a moratorium on intergovernmental debts. France, which interpreted the American President's suggestion as a pro-Ger-

man move, withheld its approval until July 23. But by then it was too
late, for the German and Austrian economies had already collapsed,
with disastrous effects upon all the central European nations. As the
repercussions of the European debacle began to aggravate conditions in
the United States, the government concluded that decisive action was
necessary. In December, 1931, the National Credit Corporation was
established as a device to enable large banks to use their combined
funds to save small banks from failure. In January, 1932, Congress set
up the Reconstruction Finance Corporation and provided it with 2 billion dollars to be loaned to banks, railroads, and mortgage companies
threatened by bankruptcy. A month later, the Glass-Steagall Act made
it possible for the Federal Reserve System to offer an even more liberal
rediscount rate. Most of these measures, however, were designed to
rescue big business and depended, as had previous policies, on business'
ability to evolve its own policies to end the depression. Nevertheless,
the government did pump some money into the bottom as well as the
top of the economy. The Federal Land Banks lent approximately
$125,000,000 to help save some farm mortgages; expenditures on pub-
lic works were increased; and the Federal Home Loan Bank Act was
passed by Congress in July, 1932, to aid home owners who were in
danger of losing their property through foreclosure.

   In the three years after the stock-market crash of 1929, Herbert
Hoover had to move a long way from his original position on the nature of the depression and the role of the government in the American
economy. But as unemployment mounted, business failures increased,
banks closed their doors, farmers lost their property, and workers lost
their jobs, the American people demanded that the government go even
further in its efforts to relieve distress and end the depression. But
Hoover would go no further, for he believed that to do so would be to
turn his back on the nation's traditions of individualism and private
initiative. Rightly or wrongly, Hoover was held responsible for the
hard times. Still, the Republicans' only alternative seemed to be to
nominate him for a second term, and at the party's convention on June
14, 1932, both Hoover and Curtis were again chosen as the party's standard bearers. The Republican platform reaffirmed the Hoover Administration's policies. When the Democrats met in Chicago in July, the
leading aspirants for the nomination were John Nance Garner, the
Speaker of the House; Governor Albert Ritchie of Maryland; Alfred E.
Smith; Newton D. Baker, who had served as Secretary of War under
Wilson; and Franklin D. Roosevelt of New York. Of these, Roosevelt
had the strongest backing among the delegates; and on the third ballot,
following Garner's withdrawal, he was nominated. Garner was given

second place on the ticket. In addition to condemning the Republican foreign and domestic policies, the Democratic platform advocated reciprocal trade agreements, federal farm relief, a reduction in government expenditures, aid for the unemployed, repeal of prohibition, an increase in the government's control over banking, and the regulation of the security market. But there was little in it to suggest that the Democrats understood any better than the Republicans what was wrong with the economy, and even less than a hint at what was about to begin.

Although Roosevelt's election was a foregone conclusion, he waged an intensive campaign that took him to every section of the country and that contained appeals to virtually every interest group in the nation. Roosevelt displayed vigorous confidence in his powers to set the nation on its feet, and he attacked every feature of the Republican administration. The Republicans had already lost control of Congress in the "off-year" elections of 1930, and Hoover had had grudging cooperation from the Democrats in what relief and recovery measures he had proposed. A far less impressive speaker than Roosevelt, seemingly aloof and stiff, he waged a tepid campaign and received a cool, at times, even hostile, reception. Hoover could not dispel the impression that judged even by his own ideals of initiative and enterprise he had failed and that his cause was doomed. In winning the election, Roosevelt polled 22,821,857 votes to 15,761,841 for Hoover. The electoral vote was 472 to 59, and Hoover carried only Connecticut, Delaware, Maine, New Hampshire, Pennsylvania, and Vermont. The Democrats also substantially improved their majorities in both houses of Congress. The outcome of the election should be attributed not only to Roosevelt's popularity (and to his famous name), but also to the voters' disgust with the Hoover Administration's response to the depression. The Republicans had once taken credit for the boom; they were now held responsible for the bust.

It was not then clear that the election of 1932 marked anything other than the single fact that Hoover and the Republicans had been rejected. The new chief executive, who took office on March 4, 1933, had been described in the campaign as an affable young man who, though without any visible specific qualifications for the job, wanted very much to be president. Franklin D. Roosevelt did have great energy, was a supremely imaginative politician, and, unlike Hoover, was not wed to theory or principles. The country thus sensed, correctly, that the bleak months of inaction or fruitless cautious steps were over, but few men, least of all the new President, suspected what lay ahead. The election of 1932 marked the end of an era in the history of the

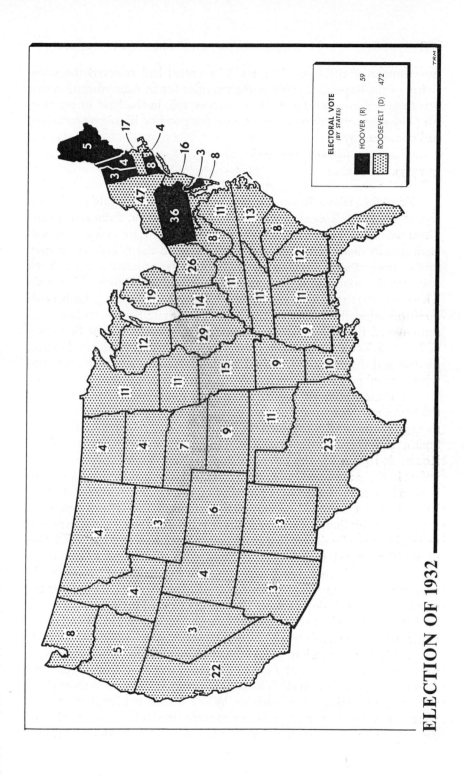

ELECTION OF 1932

ELECTORAL VOTE
(BY STATES)

HOOVER (R)   59

ROOSEVELT (D)   472

government of the United States. The voters had rejected the nega-
tivism of the Republican rule of the twenties for an Administration that
was to give the government an ever larger role in the lives of the people. The age of inaction was over, and, for good or ill, big government
had come to stay.

F.D.R.

Franklin Delano Roosevelt was born in 1882 to wealth and prestige at his family's estate in Hyde Park, New York. Educated at the
Groton School, Harvard College, and Columbia Law School, he was
equipped by both birth and training to assume the role of a country
squire or successful businessman. Although he entered a New York
law firm, he soon showed an aptitude for politics. Despite his cousin
Theodore's party affiliations, he was a Democrat. In 1910, he became
a reform-minded member of the New York State Senate. When Wilson entered the White House, Roosevelt became Assistant Secretary
of Navy. Selected as the Democrats' vice-presidential candidate in 1920,
he stumped the country for the League of Nations and was retired to
what seemed political obscurity by the Harding landslide.

In 1921, Roosevelt was stricken with poliomyelitis, and he spent
the next seven years waging a successful enough battle to permit him—
though permanently crippled in both legs—to re-enter politics. Al
Smith, the Democratic presidential nominee in 1928, prevailed on
Roosevelt to run for the governorship of New York. Despite Smith's
defeat in the nation and in his own state, Roosevelt was victorious, and
in 1930 he was re-elected by a plurality of 725,000. As governor of New
York, Roosevelt pushed to completion some of the reform programs
inaugurated by Smith, furnished direct relief for the state's needy, advocated the public development of power resources and the regulation
of utilities, urged repeal of the Eighteenth Amendment, supported
organized labor's traditional demands, and maintained an uneasy alliance with Tammany Hall. As a result of his gubernatorial record, the
careful spadework done by his lieutenants Louis Howe and James A.
Farley, and the alignment of the various factions within the Democratic party, Roosevelt was chosen the party's standard bearer in 1932.

With the exception of Abraham Lincoln, no other American
president assumed office at a time of crisis graver than that which confronted Franklin Roosevelt. The banking system had ceased to operate,
and bankers, businessmen, and the White House confessed that they
were at the end of the rope; factories were producing at a fraction of
capacity; idle workers numbered millions; and once-docile farmers

F. D. R., Al Smith (second row, fourth from right), and New York Politicians on Election Night, 1928

[WIDE WORLD]

were prepared to take the law in their own hands to save their homes and fields. Even more threatening than the state of the economy was the state of people's minds. A sense of hopelessness mingled with an undercurrent of panic, and signs were not lacking of a mass hysteria that could sweep the country into chaos and ruin. On March 4, 1933, the American people were beaten, confused, and frightened.

Franklin Roosevelt's inaugural address was a forecast of his leadership. In solemn but buoyant words, he promised new hope to the American people:

> This great Nation will endure as it has endured, will revive and will prosper. So . . . let me assert my firm belief that the only thing we have to fear is fear itself—nameless, unreasoning, unjustified terror which paralyzes needed efforts to convert retreat into advance. . . . The people of the United States have not failed. In their need they have registered a mandate that they want direct, vigorous action. They have asked for

discipline and direction under leadership. They have made me
the present instrument of their wishes. In the spirit of the gift
I take it.

The New Deal Agenda

During its life, the New Deal was all things to all men. Depending
on the standards of the observer, the New Deal was either capitalistic
or socialistic, progressive or reactionary, ruthless or humanitarian. Nor
was there any agreement about its leadership. To some the New Dealers were a gang of hardheaded, opportunistic politicians; to others they
were starry-eyed, impractical professors; and to still others they were
reformers and selfless idealists. In truth, the New Deal and the New
Dealers were none and all of these, for there were many New Deals.

The New Deal lived up to the promise of the inaugural, for Roosevelt soon provided both leadership and action. The New Deal has justly
been accused of inefficiency. It undoubtedly made countless mistakes,
and it lacked consistency; but it never stood still. In this fact lay its
strength with the American people, for, rightly or wrongly, the people
were convinced that the national government was actively trying to
solve their desperate economic problems. The New Deal was an experimental government that lived from one domestic crisis to another until
it was finally swallowed up in the world-shattering crisis of war. Its
long tenure was due, not so much to its ability to solve the problems
that arose out of successive crises, as to Roosevelt's ability to convince
the American people that democratic government could eventually
solve them. The lasting contribution of the New Deal to American life
was not its bridges, roads, buildings, or dams, but its rescue of the nation from the brink of disaster and the strengthening of belief in the
vitality of the democratic process.

The New Deal came into being because of a major depression, and
it did not escape the shadow of this crisis until the outbreak of war in
Europe and Asia. Although methods might change and the emphasis
might shift, the restoration of prosperity always remained the end-all
and be-all of the New Deal throughout its history. At times, frankly
stopgap methods were employed to check the hard tide of disaster, and
at other times, what were conceived of as long-term reforms were introduced. No amount of emphasis on reform aspects of the New Deal
can obscure the fact that its conscious purpose was not to revolutionize American society, American government, or the economic system,
but to change the course of the business cycle and to reverse the train

of events that had been set in motion by the stock-market crash of October, 1929.

The New Deal's opponents frequently accused it of socialism and even Communism, but its chief architects aspired only to preserve and reinvigorate American capitalism. Although the Roosevelt Administration advocated an increase in government control over business, it did not propose nationalization or direct government control. Businessmen were asked to observe certain rules that they had not observed in the past, but businessmen were never compelled to conduct their businesses as servants of an all-powerful state. Even when the government became an entrepreneur, as in the Tennessee Valley Authority, its avowed and achieved purpose was to stimulate private enterprise. When Franklin Roosevelt was asked by a reporter if he was a Communist, he was dumbfounded and replied: "I am a Christian and a Democrat—that's all."

In its attitude toward business enterprise, the New Deal was a conglomerate. It had affinities with Woodrow Wilson's New Freedom, Theodore Roosevelt's New Nationalism, the system of government controls used in World War I, even with the trade-association ideal of its Republican predecessors. On the assumption that certain practices militated against the efficient operation of capitalism and cut down the chances of economic advancement for the general public, the New Deal set about to create greater flexibility in the economy and to achieve equality of economic opportunity rather than economic equality. After initial enthusiasm for Roosevelt many businessmen became virulent about the New Deal's methods and accused it of socialism; yet the New Deal was designed to save capitalism in spite of the capitalists whose practices during the 1920's had almost destroyed it.

Roosevelt graphically explained his willingness to use many techniques to save capitalism when he described the shifting policies of his Administration as though they were the strategy of a game:

> It is a little bit like a football team that has a general plan of game against the other side. Now, the captain and the quarterback of that team know pretty well what the next play is going to be and they know the general strategy of the team; but they cannot tell you what the play after the next play is going to be until the next play is run off. If the play makes ten yards, the succeeding play will be different from what it would have been if they had been thrown for a loss. I think that is the easiest way to explain it.

Bailing out Banks and Saving Stock Markets

American banks were totally unprepared to meet the cataclysm at home and abroad after the stock-market crash. The United States had been the world's banker during the post-Armistice decade but was unable to shore up international finance after the panic of 1929. President Hoover was overwhelmed by forces beyond his control in efforts to restore stability. The financial structure of central Europe collapsed in 1931 and dragged down the rest of the Continent with it. One nation after another abandoned the time-honored gold standard. Everywhere, the century-old control of world finance by private bankers came under more direct supervision and manipulation by the state. So-called neo-mercantilist policies by which government programs tried to encompass all aspects of national economic life, withdrew much initiative, but not all influence, from the financiers. Inevitably, these changes had repercussions on American banking.

At home there had been an alarming increase in bank failures; from 1921 through 1929 more than 5,700 banks shut down. Thereafter, the number of bank failures mounted precipitously. From 1930 through 1932, 5,102 banks with deposits in excess of $3,250,000,000 closed their doors. A full-scale bank panic occurred during the early months of 1933. Gold was being drained from banks into private hoards or to Europe, while distraught depositors tried to rescue what was left of their savings. Runs on and failures of one bank after another bred rumors of impending disaster elsewhere, until it seemed that the entire American banking system was about to pass into oblivion. During the last week of the Hoover Administration, almost every bank in the country was either closed or besieged by a line of frightened but determined depositors.

This final crisis of the Hoover regime brought the country to its deepest despair. Those middle-class families and minor businessmen who had thus far not felt the full force of the depression now lost their small cushion of savings or could not finance their already shaky businesses. After three and a half years of pleas to the nation to trust them, leading bankers and White House spokesmen confessed that they were without ideas of what to do next.

Between October, 1932, and March 3, 1933, twenty-three state governors had declared bank holidays, suspending banking activity while bank officials tried to shore up and consolidate their operations before reopening. On the morning of the new President's inauguration, most of the remaining state governments, under pressure from the incoming Administration, also ordered bank holidays.

After the Holiday: Returning to the Banks, 1933

[WIDE WORLD]

Within a week after taking office, President Roosevelt declared a national bank holiday, took steps to restore confidence, and called a special session of Congress which, after only four hours of debate, passed an Emergency Banking Act validating the President's earlier moves and providing for the reopening of sound banks. On March 12, the President delivered his first "fireside chat" to American radio listeners. After explaining what had been "done in the last few days, why it was done, and what the next steps are going to be," he assured the American people, "We shall be engaged not merely in reopening sound banks but in the creation of sound banks through reorganization."

Authorized by the Emergency Banking Act, the President announced policies to control gold and foreign exchange, finance distressed banks, and create additional currency. Three days after the banking holiday, 76 per cent of the member banks of the Federal Reserve System had been reopened, and within two months more than 12,000 banks, with 90 per cent of the nation's bank deposits, were again in business. By a combination of shrewd psychological maneuvers and bold executive moves, Roosevelt had led the American people through the banking crisis.

When the New Deal turned from stopgap measures to a long-range banking program, it was faced by two alternatives. It could nationalize the banking system or return it to the now discredited inept private bankers. President Roosevelt, who was soon to earn the undying hatred of the bankers, rejected all suggestions for nationalizing the American banking system. In his first inaugural, he criticized the money-changers who "have fled from their high seats in the temple of our civilization," but he made no move to deprive them of their seats. He merely asked them to move over.

New Deal plans for the reform of American private banking were incorporated in the Banking Act of June, 1933. Provision was made for insuring bank deposits under the new Federal Deposit Insurance Corporation. Commercial banks could no longer use depositors' funds to purchase securities. Among other changes, more banks were admitted to the Federal Reserve System, whose powers of control were expanded.

A more thorough overhauling of the Federal Reserve System was later undertaken in the Banking Act of 1935. The Federal Reserve Board was then reorganized and given still greater controls over members' reserves and credit operations. In effect, by 1935 the Federal Reserve System was less an appendage of private enterprise than a branch of the government with powers that Administration leaders believed could end the current depression and avert future economic crises.

The New Deal also extended and tightened up government control of the security markets to avert the speculation and malpractices that had helped bring on the 1929 crash. With the investigations and disclosures of the Senate Committee on Banking and Currency as its guide, Congress enacted a series of laws that provided for increased government control over stock exchanges, holding companies, investment trusts, and bankruptcy proceedings.

Under the Securities Act of 1933 and the Securities Exchange Act of 1934, the issue and marketing of securities were placed under the supervision of a five-man Securities and Exchange Commission selected by the president. The commission was to furnish the public with accurate information on security offerings and to prevent those abuses that had characterized the stock exchanges of the twenties. All listed stocks and pertinent facts about them and their issuing corporations had to be registered with the commission. Stock exchanges had to be licensed by the commission, had to give full publicity to their practices, and had to conduct their business according to certain prescribed rules. The commission also could compel individuals and corporations to alter or cease certain practices that violated the laws of 1933 and 1934 or its own administrative rulings.

The Public Utility Holding Company Act of 1935 placed the management of holding companies almost completely under the supervision of the Securities and Exchange Commission. Although the measure disappointed many liberals, who had demanded the abolition of holding companies, it included the famous "death sentence," which provided for the dissolution of any holding company that failed to demonstrate its usefulness within a period of five years. Finally, in 1939–40, another series of laws broadened the commission's authority over investment trusts.

These laws gave adequate protection to the American investor for the first time. It is worth pointing out, however, that increased government control was accompanied by a marked decrease in the buying and selling of stocks. On the New York Stock Exchange, 120,000,000 shares were traded in July, 1933, but only 7,000,000 or so during the same month in 1940. Those who suffered most from these changes were those who had profited most under the old regime. Although bitterly critical of the New Deal for its innovations, they had no alternative to offer but a return to the practices of the past.

Money and Its Control

New Deal banking and security laws were generally conceived by their authors as moves to reform American capitalism, but the Administration's manipulation of the currency was an undisguised attempt to restore prosperity by a government-generated inflation. During the first months of the New Deal, President Roosevelt experimented unsuccessfully with several theories to lower the value of the dollar and to raise prices.

To carry out its program for stimulating recovery by depreciating the dollar, the executive branch of the government, through a series of congressional enactments and special executive orders, took control of all gold in the United States, imposed an embargo on gold exports, and nullified the payment in gold clauses in public and private contracts. Authority over gold was now firmly in government hands, and in May, 1933, the government received wide powers to use a variety of devices to induce inflation.

The Administration's attempt to restore prosperity by currency manipulation brought it into direct conflict with the nations at the London Economic Conference of 1933, which was seeking an international solution to such world-wide economic problems as the reduction of trade barriers, the establishment of sound currencies, and monetary stabilization. Hoover had accepted the League of Nations' invitation to the United States to attend the conference before the expiration of his term of office, and Roosevelt had appointed a delegation headed by Secretary of State Hull. But soon after the conference opened, the new President also made it clear that he placed American recovery ahead of world recovery and that the United States was going to substitute economic nationalism for an international cooperative experiment to stabilize currencies. In his message to the conference on July 3, Roosevelt said, "The sound internal economic system of a Nation is a greater factor in its well-being than the price of its currency in changing terms of the currencies of other nations."

The government started a gold-buying program in October, 1933, and by January, 1934, the government price for gold had climbed from $20.67 to $34.45 an ounce. This gold-buying program aroused the hostility of the business community but had no noticeable effect upon the general price level. In January, 1934, the Administration abandoned the policy and changed its tactics (but not its objective) with the passage of the Gold Reserve Act. Among other things, this measure permitted the President to alter the gold content of the dollar by as much as 60 per cent, withdrew all gold from circulation, and forbade the redemption of currency in gold. The Gold Reserve Act was, in effect, the final step taken to remove the United States from the gold standard. At the same time, an attempt was made to maintain the illusion that the country still operated on a gold standard. In theory, the currency was backed by gold, but in fact, no private person could own, use, or trade in gold coins. For good or ill, the Gold Reserve Act substituted a managed currency for the gold standard—a shift that forty years earlier would have been considered earthshaking and that in 1934 was still greeted by many bankers as the end of the world, though the decision was reaffirmed by the Supreme Court in 1935 in the so-called gold cases.

Following the passage of the Gold Reserve Act, the President revalued the dollar at 59.06 cents, and the treasury, which had been granted sole authority over gold purchases, fixed the price of gold at $35 an ounce. Neither action seemingly had any more effect upon the general price level than the program that they superseded. These New Deal gold policies produced one notable result, however: they undoubtedly accelerated the flow of the world's gold supply to the United States. By July, 1940, the federal government controlled approximately 80 per cent of the monetary gold in the world. This vast hoard was buried in Fort Knox, Kentucky, where it was guarded by the Army

Delivering the First Gold to Fort Knox

[WIDE WORLD]

and served as an expensive monument to the privately managed world economy based on gold that had been vanquished by the Great Depression.

The government also sought to stimulate inflation by a similar program in silver. A series of measures starting in 1933 permitted the free coinage of silver, large purchases of silver, the issuing of paper money backed by silver ("silver certificates") and nationalization of silver. All these devices were tried by the President. By 1940, the treasury had purchased well over two billion ounces of silver and had issued more than one billion dollars in silver certificates and silver dollars. The desired goal of higher price levels was not appreciably affected by these silver policies, but the nation's silver producers had received a handsome subsidy. Internationally, a flow of silver to America for the high prices paid there disrupted silver-standard currency systems in nations like China and Mexico, but countries that exchanged their silver for dollars did not use them to increase purchase of American products.

After 1934, the New Deal switched from emphasizing currency manipulation to other measures to stimulate inflation. Under the new banking laws, credit terms were eased but businessmen fearful of new debts and of expansion while consumers were weak did not significantly use the easier credit available. Despite Roosevelt's campaign pledge to balance the budget, the eventual government policy of direct aid to business created steadily growing deficits. From 1919 until after the Crash, the preceding Republican administrations had steadily reduced the high national debt created by the war. After 1930, Hoover had to abandon hopes for a balance of government income and expenditure. Relief funds granted to business were largely responsible for a deficit of federal outlays over income of nearly 3 billion dollars by June, 1932. This "extravagance" was a Roosevelt theme in the election of 1932. After taking office, he set about cutting federal salaries, pensions, and benefits, but relief for the needy and for shaky business firms forced emergency spending on the New Dealers. The emergency policy soon became a permanent program and eventually an established theory for ending the depression. After "deficit spending," as it came to be called, was well underway, the New Dealers learned of its theoretical possibilities from the works of John Maynard Keynes, the prominent English economist. For Keynes the tendencies of private capitalism to pile up idle savings and to encourage a *rentier* caution among businessmen were responsible for the business stagnation that marked the Great Depression. New Dealers proposed to free these savings and place them in the hands of consumers, whose purchases would stimulate industrial output. Where private savings were not enough, government expenditures would be expanded beyond present income. This "deficit financing" was an anathema to the orthodox, who hated debt, expensive and "meddling" government, and living beyond income. The New Dealers argued that the cure was less painful than the malady and that the government would abandon its spending program as soon as the patient was restored to health. In his 1940 budget message, the President explained the theory on which much New Deal spending rested:

> Following 1933 the fiscal policy of the Government was more realistically adapted to the needs of the people. All about were idle men, idle factories, and idle funds, and yet the people were in desperate need of more goods than they had the purchasing power to acquire. The Government deliberately set itself to correct these conditions by borrowing idle funds to put idle men and idle factories to work.

Throughout its history, the New Deal failed to balance the budget, and from the fiscal year of 1932 to 1940, the national debt increased from $19,487,010,000 to $42,967,000,000.

The New Deal obtained the bulk of the funds for its spending program by borrowing (that is, by increasing the national debt), but it also increased the supply of currency and raised taxes. The amount of money in circulation rose from $5,720,000,000 in 1933 to more than $8,000,000,000 in 1940, and the annual internal revenue of the federal government in the same period went up from $1,619,839,000 to $5,340,452,000. Businessmen objected to heavier taxes and warned of the dangers of unrelieved heavy spending. Partly as a result of this criticism and partly because of increasing signs of a business revival, the government reduced its expenditures in 1937; a depression followed (the Administration called it a "recession") and lasted until the government resumed its spending program in the middle of 1938.

The developments of 1937–8 seemed to indicate that there was a close connection between government fiscal policies and the course of the business cycle during the 1930's; but even if this point is conceded, the fact remains that the Administration was still no closer to a solution of its problem. On the one hand, even the most ardent New Dealers granted that continued deficit financing would eventually produce a runaway inflation and economic chaos worse than depression. On the other hand, a reduction in government expenditures was accompanied by still further descent into the depths of depression. This was the dilemma that was raised by New Deal spending—and it was a dilemma that the war rather than the New Deal resolved.

Curbing Competition

By adopting drastic measures at the height of the banking crisis, the New Deal saved American finance—and American capitalism as well. By pumping money into the American economy, the New Deal sustained the very capitalism that businessmen claimed it destroyed. When the New Deal turned from the banking and currency crisis to the industrial crisis in the spring of 1933, it created in the National Industrial Recovery Administration, or the N.R.A. as it came to be known, a plan that initially also had the support of practically all important businessmen. The plan did not attempt to reverse those tendencies in American business life that had helped precipitate the depression but to tame them and make them serve the public interest.

Essentially the N.R.A. was a program to revive American industry by promoting further integration and private planning of markets. Its origins went back at least to World War I. The War Industries Board had subjected the businessman to outside controls over production that he had considered onerous but that had guaranteed his profits. The War Industries Board had relied heavily on trade associations for the regulation of industry, and during the 1920's, trade associations had been further encouraged to dull the edge of competition in a number of industries.

As long as business boomed, there seemed little need to go further and inaugurate an all-encompassing government-enforced plan for controlling prices and production. The depression, however, revived earlier demands for such over-all planning. In 1930, Bernard Baruch demanded "industrial self-government under governmental sanction"; the next year Gerard Swope, president of General Electric, proposed a detailed program to mitigate or eliminate competition; the United States Chamber of Commerce approved a report calling for the relaxation of the antitrust laws and the creation of a "National Economic Council" to deal with the "tendency of productive capacity to outrun the ability to buy"; and the National Association of Manufacturers took a similar stand.

The National Industrial Recovery Act, which became law in June, 1933, incorporated many of these proposals. Industries were permitted to ignore the antitrust laws and to draw up codes of fair practice that would now be enforced by the government—but the government could reject a code, and labor was guaranteed the right of collective bargaining and provisions for maximum hours and minimum wages. The National Recovery Administration, established to supervise and enforce the provisions of the law, was headed by a chief administrator assisted by advisory boards for industry, labor, and agriculture. The specific object was to raise prices to the 1926 level; the general aim was to revive industry and end unemployment by the cooperative efforts of businessmen. The government thus accepted the fact that the American economy had already attained a high degree of integration. The N.R.A. sought to expand and control existing collective effort by businessmen for what it considered the good of the entire nation. It represented, in short, a long step toward a planned economy. In many respects the game was unchanged, but now the rules were out in the open for all to see. The government would enforce these rules and serve as referee, but business would still furnish the players.

Under the N.R.A., each industry submitted a tentative code for government approval after a public hearing. The corrected and completed code, when approved by the President, became law for the industry. Firms observing N.R.A. regulations were permitted to display posters bearing a Blue Eagle, which was the official symbol of the Recovery Administration. Of the 746 basic and supplementary codes eventually approved, each contained the required labor guarantees and rules of "fair competition," including provisions for minimum prices;

"That Ought To Jolt Him": The N.R.A. Blue Eagle Stings Old Man Depression (Talburt in the New York World Telegram, *1933*)

standardization of products, services, and business practices; the registration of prices; and regulation of production. Among the practices outlawed by many codes as "unfair competition" were false advertising and branding, breach of contract, price discrimination, tie-in sales, attacks upon the reputation of competitors, combinations to fix prices, and the pirating of a competitor's employees.

Fanfares of government publicity marked the start of the National Recovery Administration under the direction of General Hugh S. Johnson. There followed a fervid scramble for privileges by every vested-interest group in the United States. Code-making had been conceived of as a cooperative effort among government, business, labor, and consumer. It generally developed into an enterprise in which big business played the leading role. Labor leaders had to fight for enlarged rights for their members. The government sought to serve as mediator, but the consumer, despite provisions for his protection, was left out in the cold. Some codes were simple statements of objectives, others incredibly detailed; but all were drawn up and approved so hastily that they contained many inequities, contradictions, and violations of the spirit and the letter of the law.

Most businessmen quickly lost their first enthusiasm for the N.R.A. because of its labor provisions and the extent of government "interference" permitted by the act. Signs of returning prosperity convinced others that they could dispense with government assistance. Late in 1934, the president of the United States Chamber of Commerce, saying that "we are no longer pressed by the tide of disaster," suggested that the N.R.A. be supplanted by legislation that would "place upon industry the sole responsibility for formulating codes of unfair competition." Under his plan, the government would only be able to suggest code changes and each industry would then decide whether it would "accept the changes requested or go on without a code."

More serious than growing business opposition to the N.R.A. was evidence that the program was failing to achieve its objectives. Powerful interest groups set prices too high, made inordinate profits, kept inefficient or dishonest producers going, pushed small businessmen to the wall, and violated the codes despite repeated government threats to "crack down." Labor-union officials complained bitterly that their guaranteed rights were ignored. Socialists and other anti-New Deal reformers said that the N.R.A. was creating an American fascism. Others called the N.R.A. "the National Run-Around." The N.R.A. officials were eventually swamped with protests but were uncertain about their authority or afraid to antagonize the businessmen on whom the program's success depended. Only the courts could enforce rulings, and their decisions took too long to permit quick effective controls over the economy; of course, intrastate businesses were not subject to federal court orders except that they could not display the Blue Eagle posters.

By the spring of 1935, the N.R.A. was becoming a Frankenstein's monster that had turned on its creator. In simplest terms, when trusted by the government, major business interests had shown no more restraint or sense of the general welfare than they had in the preceding Republican era. Fortunately for the Administration, on May 27, 1935, in Schechter Poultry Corp. vs. United States, the Supreme Court unanimously declared the National Industrial Recovery Act unconstitutional. The Court reasoned that the federal act illegally regulated intrastate trade and permitted Congress to delegate legislative functions—i.e., the making of codes—to the President. The Supreme Court's decision received wide publicity and seemed to close forever any possibility of a revival of the N.R.A. In one sense, however, it was an anticlimax. After two years in action, the act had so little popular support, was so losely enforced, and had been so flagrantly violated that it was already in its death throes. The Court merely applied the *coup de grâce.*

The National Recovery Administration had been hastily conceived and haphazardly organized. It had placed the government squarely behind industry's drive toward monopoly and had bred conflict and confusion rather than the hoped-for cooperation and order. But in an hour of crisis, it had given industry the leadership that private enterprise had been unable to supply and the shot in the arm that was needed to lift it out of the economic doldrums. Unfortunately, like Hoover, but in their own way, the New Dealers in their early days had put too much faith in the businessman and in voluntary cooperation.

After the death of the N.R.A., New Deal regulation of business practices was confined largely to supervising specific industries in which the public interest seemed to require federal control. Established or new commissions, modeled on the Interstate Commerce Commission, were used to supervise rather than revive certain industries. The Federal Communications Commission, formed under the Communications Act of June, 1934, was given powers over the radio, telegraph, and cable industries comparable to the powers of the Interstate Commerce Commission. The Motor Carrier and Air Mail Acts of August, 1935, extended the authority of the Interstate Commerce Commission over interstate bus, truck, and airplane companies; and in 1938, the Civil Aeronautics Authority was set up to regulate the nation's airlines.

Curbing Monopoly

In its early stages the New Deal gave greater support to the integration of business enterprise than any other single administration in American history, but by the last years of the 1930's, it had become a stalwart champion of economic competition. The shift in New Deal emphasis from a planned to a competitive economy showed the influence of antimonopolists in the Administration and in friendly university circles who, as the N.R.A. showed its weaknesses, gained greater sympathy from the President. The antimonopoly drive did not get fully under way until the Administration adopted the belief that the recession of 1937–8 had been caused by high prices established by monopolists. In April, 1938, Roosevelt delivered a message to Congress assailing monopoly, and in June, Congress set up the Temporary National Economic Committee to "make a full and complete study and investigation with respect to the concentration of economic power in, and financial control over, production and distribution of goods and services." Manned by government experts and congressmen, the T.N.E.C. hearings and researchers tried to prove that the absence of competition was responsible for many of America's economic ills. In thirty-seven volumes of testimony, forty-three monographs, and a *Final Report and Recommendations*, the T.N.E.C. presented a comprehensive and documented history of the decline of competition in the United States. In industry after industry, the committee gave facts, dates, and figures on price fixing, patent monopolies, holding companies, trade associations, interlocking directorates, and international cartels.

In 1938, the New Deal also launched a large-scale trust-busting program reminiscent of the brave, dead days of an earlier Roosevelt. Thurman Arnold, a Yale professor of law, who in 1937 had written a book in which he referred to antitrust laws as "the great myth," was made Assistant Attorney General in charge of the Justice Department's antitrust division. Arnold sharpened up his spear, saddled his snow-white charger, hired bright young law-school graduates as fellow warriors, and set out to defeat an enemy that had lost many battles but never a war.

Under Thurman Arnold's energetic direction, the Justice Department prosecuted entire industries as well as individual firms and labor unions as well as corporations. The basic test was whether or not prices had been held at an artificial level through collusion. Those groups that showed willingness to abandon such practices escaped penalty. Suits were filed against both unions and contractors in the building industry. The motion-picture industry was also prosecuted. In 1939, General Motors was convicted of a violation of the Sherman Act and fined $20,000, and in the next year twelve oil companies were found guilty of conspiracy.

But the New Deal was no more effective in restoring competition than earlier administrations had been. Economic concentration seemed to proceed at a steady rate regardless of Thurman Arnold's program. In 1942, in industries that produced one third in value of all American manufactures, the four largest firms in each industry turned out more than three quarters of the industry's product. Two hundred and five manufacturing corporations, each possessing in 1942 more than

$50,000,000 in assets, owned 49 per cent of the nation's manufacturing assets; these same firms had owned only 37 per cent in 1934. On the other hand, manufacturing corporations with incomes of less than $250,000, which had received 19.1 per cent of the total income in 1929, had only 11.6 per cent in 1942. In contrast to earlier periods, this increased concentration in American industry during the 1930's was the result, in general, not of mergers but of an increase in the size and power of existing concerns.

Although the New Deal swung from support for big business to antitrust action, it never relaxed efforts to stimulate business enterprise. Future New Dealers in 1932 had complained that Hoover had subsidized business, but the New Deal in power expanded the Hoover program of business aid. The Reconstruction Finance Corporation's activities were greatly enlarged under the New Deal. From its start in 1932 through 1941, it spent more than $9,000,000,000, largely to aid farmers, banks, and governmental agencies. But from 1932 to 1939, it also lent more than $400,000,000 to American industry while the Federal Reserve banks from 1934 to 1939 made about $123,000,000 in loans to industry. Equally valuable—although less direct aid—to American industrialists, wholesalers, and retailers came in federal funds spent on relief programs and public works. Social security payments also increased the effective purchasing power of the nation's consumers. Many businessmen delighted in condemning the New Deal for its heavy expenditures, but it is difficult to see how the average businessman could have lived without its loans to business and boosts to the consumer's income.

Businessmen opposed to the New Deal also cited its invasions of the sacred precincts of free enterprise to prove that the Roosevelt Administration had an anticapitalist bias; but, although the New Deal did enter many fields that had formerly been restricted to private business, it assumed tasks that businessmen had failed or refused to undertake. The New Deal's slum-clearance and housing program, which aided the producers of building materials, was undertaken only after it was clear that the construction industry was either unwilling or unable to do as much. The Rural Electrification Administration was established because the power industry had neglected the American countryside, and the Administration's success was demonstrated by the increased sales of electric power. The Tennessee Valley Authority, which marked the most significant New Deal departure from the traditional notion of the government's role in the American economy, was intended not only to promote reforestation, flood control, the national defense, and agriculture but also to "provide for the . . . industrial development of said valley." There can be little doubt that this last objective was fulfilled. In 1944, David Lilienthal, who at the time was chairman of T.V.A., wrote:

> What of business in the industrial sense? That too is developing, and at a rapid rate. Even before the war the valley saw the addition or expansion of several large industries devoted to the basic materials of modern industry, such as aluminum, ferro-silicon, heavy chemicals; these included two of the largest phosphate chemical works in the country. . . .
>
> At least as important as these heavy industries is the rise of new light industries and the expansion of plants that existed before 1933.*

The New Deal also undertook to stimulate business activity through a revival of foreign markets. Export-Import banks made loans to foreign customers. The Roosevelt Administration's recognition of the Soviet Union in November, 1933, and the Russian-American trade treaty of 1935 were prompted in part by a desire to increase American exports. The New Deal also sought to widen the opportunities open to American exporters and to lower the growing international threats of economic nationalism by a reciprocal trade program.

A Trade Agreements Act of 1934, renewed every three years during the New Deal era, was the basis by 1941 for twenty-six reciprocal trade treaties negotiated by the Secretary of State, Cordell Hull, who deserves major credit for their success. Tariff-making was no longer left to Congress but was given to the executive. Tariff rates were proposed by special committees after public hearings. The Secretary of State then bargained with foreign governments for reciprocal reductions in tariffs. The executive could make changes in rates up to 50 per cent but could not alter the free list.

Despite difficulties in testing the exact effect of this trade program on the American economy, from 1934 to 1940 the United States did export twice as much to treaty countries as to nontreaty nations. Complaints that the treaties generally deprived American manufacturers of their traditional protection are not borne out by facts, for from 1934 to 1940 exports from treaty countries increased by 35 per cent, while imports from nontreaty nations, subject to higher protective American imposts, rose by 37 per cent.

* David E. Lilienthal: *TVA; Democracy on the March* (New York: Harper & Brothers, 1944), p. 35.

Effects of the Depression and New Deal on the Economy

	1929	1932	1937	1938	1939
National Income *	82.3	40	71.5	64.2	70.8
Volume of Industrial Production					
(1935–9 average = 100)	110	58	113	88	
Capital Issues *	11.6	6.3 (high point for 1930's)			
Corporate Dividends *	9.8	3.2		5.1	5.8
Value of Exports *	5.2	1.6			3.2
Value of Imports *	4.4	1.3			2.3

New Deal Capitalism in Retrospect

At various times in its career the New Deal both supported and attacked business consolidation and collective action, subsidized industry, financed purchasing power, regulated certain key industries, aided exporters, and went into businesses that in the past had been reserved for private enterprise. These policies showed energy, confidence, flexibility, and a frank willingness to experiment, but they were not able to restore prosperity to previous levels. Instead of regaining prosperity, business experienced a series of cyclical movements within a continuing over-all depression. Soon after Roosevelt entered office, there was a minor boom that lasted into the fall of 1933. Although the tempo of this upsurge was not sustained, it was followed by a gradual but steady recovery that lasted until August, 1937, when the recession began. When government spending resumed, the recession was halted, and business once again began to climb slowly and unsteadily upward until war production produced a boom that New Deal ingenuity had not been able to promote.

Before the outbreak of World War II business activity, as measured by *The New York Times's* weekly index, did not once equal (although it almost did on two occasions) the high point reached in June, 1929; and it was not until mid-1940 that the earlier mark was surpassed. The statistics in the chart above, if they reveal nothing else, demonstrate that the New Deal did not end the depression. Without the crutch supplied by the New Deal, American industrial capitalism might well have perished, but New Deal experimentation did not make the cripple a healthy man.

* In approximate billions of dollars.

FOR SUPPLEMENTARY READING

Continue to use those works cited after Chapter 15 that carry on beyond 1929. No one quite captures the desperation brought by the Depression as well as A. M. Schlesinger. Jr., in his otherwise too partisan, *The Crisis of the Old Order* (1957). T. C. Cochran, *The American Business System: A Historical Perspective, 1900–1955* (1957) is a most valuable general analysis. Hoover's own defense is in *The Memoirs of Herbert Hoover: The Great Depression 1929–41* (1952). The best analysis of the post-crash economy is B. Mitchell, *Depression Decade* (1947). The full length study of F. D. Roosevelt is J. M. Burns, *Roosevelt: The Lion and The Fox* (1956). The scholarly biography, still in process, is by F. Freidel (3 vols., 1952–56). Volume III reaches 1932. A. M. Schlesinger, Jr.'s *The Coming of the New Deal* (1959) underestimates the extent to which New Deal proposals were radical breaks with the past at the time, but the book is an exciting recreation of the period. Of the voluminous memoirs and biographical studies of the New Deal days few are as good as R. E. Sherwood, *Roosevelt and Hopkins* (1948) (Pb). Two different kinds of critics of the New Deal and F. D. R. are R. Moley, *After Seven Years* (1939), and *Jim Farley's Story* (1948). Both for their intrinsic worth and the light they throw on historians' changing attitudes towards the New Deal read the chapters on Hoover and Roosevelt in R. Hofstadter *The American Political Tradition* and compare with the view of F. D. R. in his later work, *The Age of Reform*. New Deal business and banking policies are analyzed in N. H. Jacoby and R. Saulnier, *Business, Finance and Banking* (1948); M. Fainsod and L. Gordon, *Government and the American Economy* (1941); J. Jones, *Fifty Billion Dollars* (1951), on the R.F.C.; T. Arnold, *The Bottlenecks of Business* (1940), on antitrust policies; and W. O. Douglas, *Democracy and Finance* (1940). A well-known contemporary indictment of business leadership before 1933 is F. T. Pecora *Wall Street Under Oath* (1939). On economic theory in the 1930's use A. Hansen, *Full Recovery or Stagnation* (1938), inspired by the recession of 1937 and written by America's leading Keynesian.

17

-->>>-->>>-->>>-->>>-->>>-->>>-->>>-->>>

Creating a National Welfare State

F OR AT LEAST forty years before the New Deal, individual states had been slowly and reluctantly accepting minimal responsibilities for the security of workingmen and their families suffering from the adverse effects of the industrial system. Although weakened by the courts, by inadequate inspection and enforcement, and by political hostility, many social welfare laws were on the books of the states by 1929. Practically none, however, had been passed by the federal government. The Great Depression showed that the welfare of tens of millions was beyond the power or resources of localities and states, and that only national social legislation could protect the great majority of Americans from the crueler uncertainties and inequities of the private-enterprise system. However loyal they were to the old virtues of self-reliance and individual initiative, politicians after 1932 also began to understand that the mass of voters would no longer accept the risks of private enterprise without some guarantees against sickness, unemployment, and old age. Out of genuine compassion and political necessity, the New Deal and individual states encouraged workers to organize and assured them of certain minimal standards. The New Deal also subsidized farmers, and it gave the unemployed either relief grants or jobs on projects financed by the government. Critics of the New Deal frequently complained that aid to the worker, farmer, and unemployed was used to purchase their votes. Whether or not this charge was fair (and the New Dealers vehemently denied that it was), the fact remained that the government was not only helping those most in need of assistance, but it was also attempting to end the depression by increasing purchasing power.

Labor's Basic Rights

As the prosperity of the twenties gave way to the depression of the thirties, many American workers learned for the first time that they lacked the ideas, organization, and economic weapons for life in twentieth-century America. Layoffs, wage cuts, and bread lines made the average worker frightened rather than angry, disheartened rather than militant. In March, 1933, he wanted neither charity nor revolution; but he did want hope, leadership, and an adequate standard of living. Soon after taking office, the Roosevelt Administration started to fulfill these demands.

The New Deal's labor program may have arisen, as many of its friends have contended, from the humanitarian impulses of its authors, but it was also based on a desire to restore American prosperity and to enhance the strength of the Democratic party. Higher wages and full employment would create mass purchasing-power that would in turn stimulate industrial production and prevent the disparity between wages and profits that had helped to destroy the prosperity of the twenties. And Democratic leaders understood that the United States now had a large industrial labor force that would probably vote in a bloc if it received suitable favors from the party in power. Organized labor's overwhelming support of Franklin Roosevelt in successive presidential elections conclusively demonstrated the soundness of this reasoning.

The New Deal labor policy employed three methods: (1) It supported collective bargaining by giving both moral and legal aid to workers who wanted to unionize their industries. (2) It provided relief for those who could not work. Direct relief and jobs on public works and in make-work programs were furnished to the unemployed as emergency measures. Social security and unemployment compensation were advanced as long-term safeguards. (3) Finally, the New Deal imposed and enforced certain minimum standards for workers who were employed.

Aside from relief and social-security measures, there were only three major New Deal labor laws. The N.R.A. gave labor certain formal guarantees that lasted until the act was invalidated by the Supreme Court in 1935. In that year, Congress passed the National Labor

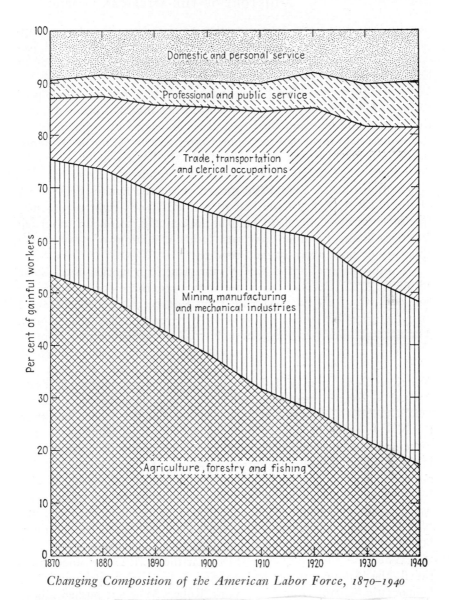

100

Domestic and personal service

90

Professional and public service

80

Trade, transportation
and clerical occupations

70

60

Per cent of gainful workers

50

Mining, manufacturing
and mechanical industries

40

30

20

Agriculture, forestry and fishing

10

0
1870   1880   1890   1900   1910   1920   1930   1940

Changing Composition of the American Labor Force, 1870–1940

Relations Act, and three years later, the Fair Labor Standards Act
became law.

Soon after Roosevelt entered office, he was forced by the pressure
of events to take a stand on the question of government aid to labor.
In April, 1933, Congress was on the verge of passing a law limiting
factory work to thirty hours a week. Large-scale protests from busi-

ness leaders caused the Administration to withdraw its tentative support from the measure and offer instead the National Industrial Recovery Act as an alternative program that would meet the needs of both industry and labor.

There were important reasons why the N.R.A. had to include provisions for improving the status of labor. Price increases planned under the codes could be maintained only if accompanied by wage increases that would help to sustain mass purchasing power. Also, the Administration was not in a position to antagonize the labor vote by aiding industrialists while it ignored workers. As a result, the Roosevelt Administration offered labor basic guarantees in the famous Section 7A of the N.I.R.A. Every code had to include labor's right to unionize free of company control, to bargain collectively, to obtain stipulated maximum hours, minimum pay and "other conditions of employment approved or prescribed by the President."

During the life of the N.R.A., the American worker made some advances. From October, 1933, to May, 1935, the index of industrial employment (1923–5 = 100) rose from 84.6 to 90, and the index of manufacturing payrolls (1923–5 = 100) increased from 61.1 to 61.7. The average hourly earnings of industrial workers mounted from an average of 44 cents in 1933 to 52 cents in May, 1935, while the length of the average work week fell from 42 to 36 hours. By 1935, the American Federation of Labor was claiming (undoubtedly it exaggerated) 4,500,000 members, and at the same time the independent-union membership totaled at least 300,000. On the whole, however, the N.R.A. failed to achieve many of its stipulated labor goals. The wage-and-hour provisions of many codes frequently duplicated existing standards and brought improvements only to those workers in less advanced firms. Section 7A was bitterly attacked and openly evaded by many employers, who either refused to recognize unions or established company unions in open violation of the law. Nor did the N.R.A. produce cooperation between capital and labor, for the number of strikes increased from 841 in 1932 to 1,856 in 1934.

When the Supreme Court ruled that the N.R.A. was unconstitutional, the Administration had to find a new labor program. The Democratic Senator from New York, Robert Wagner, pushed a hesitant Administration to support his proposals, and Congress in July, 1935, passed the National Labor Relations Act. The Wagner Act, as it was more commonly called, guaranteed anew the labor rights included in N.I.R.A.'s Section 7A, but the administration of this new act was entrusted to a three-man National Labor Relations Board empowered to summon employers to appear before it, issue cease-and-desist orders, hold elections to determine what collective-bargaining agency a particular group of workers wanted, and hear complaints from workers concerning violations of the law. Workers who appealed to the board were guaranteed against retaliation by their employers, and the board's rulings were enforceable through the courts.

Employers, assured by some of the most prominent lawyers in the United States that the Wagner Act was unconstitutional, ignored it and tried to block and undercut the law by court proceedings. The Supreme Court, however, upset the predictions of "the experts." A series of decisions in 1937–8 upheld every feature of the act. Despite employer opposition, the National Labor Relations Board became one of the most efficient and effective New Deal agencies. From 1935 through 1940, the board handled approximately 30,000 cases, most of which were settled by agreement. It prevented nearly 900 strikes, settled more than 2,100 strikes that had already been called, and reinstated more than 21,000 workers dismissed for union activities.

Having guaranteed an effective organized labor movement, the New Deal next tried by law to raise wages and reduce the work week. After 1936, businesses with federal contracts had to observe wage, hour, and child-labor regulations. The Fair Labor Standards Act of 1938 established maximum hours and minimum wages for all workers in interstate industries. Minimum wages were set at twenty-five cents an hour but were to be increased to forty cents within the next seven years. Maximum hours, limited to forty-four, were to be reduced to forty within two years. Wage committees were empowered to fix flexible minimum wages for specific industries. Goods produced by child labor (except in agriculture) could not be shipped in interstate trade. Employers who violated the law were liable to a fine of $10,000 and a jail sentence of six months.

Despite these New Deals aids to workers, unemployment was never less than 7,000,000 from 1933 to 1940. The new labor legislation did not cover domestic servants, many white-collar workers, and those employed in intrastate industries. In many cases, guaranteed minimum wages became a ceiling rather than a base. Nevertheless, the New Deal did more for American labor than had any previous Administration. It raised the wages and improved the working conditions of a large share of American workers, and, most important of all, it set off the greatest organizing drive in the history of American unionism.

The Flowering of American Unionism

The rapid development of industrial unionism grew out of the opportunities presented by the National Industrial Recovery Act. To the N.R.A. advisory board the President appointed John L. Lewis of the United Mine Workers, Sidney Hillman of the Amalgamated Clothing Workers, George L. Berry of the Printing Pressmen, and President William F. Green of the American Federation of Labor. Lewis and Hillman believed that the labor movement should invoke Section 7A's guarantees and campaign to organize the relatively unskilled workers in the mass-production industries. Green gave lip service to this proposal but feared that a flood of new members would destroy the exclusive craft-union character of the A. F. of L. From June to October, 1933, the A. F. of L. organized fewer than half a million workers and placed them in individual plant unions until they could be transferred to the federation's established craft-unions.

The leaders of the coal and clothing unions moved vigorously in other directions. When the N.R.A. coal code went into effect in October, 1933, a series of strikes and an intensive organizing drive led by Lewis had already almost completely organized the miners. Similar campaigns were waged by Hillman in the men's clothing industry and by David Dubinsky, president of the International Ladies Garment Workers, in the women's clothing industry. Between 1933 and 1935, the membership of industrial and semi-industrial unions increased by 132 per cent, while there was only a 13 per cent increase in the membership of craft-unions. Growing labor militancy increased the number of strikes. Between 1930 and 1932, 2,288 strikes involving 849,002 workers occurred. From 1933 to 1935, 3,752,180 workers waged 5,565 strikes, among them a general strike in San Francisco and a nation-wide textile strike; only presidential intervention averted an automobile strike.

Between 1934 and 1936, a struggle took place in the A.F. of L. between the new leaders of industrial unionism and the controlling chiefs loyal to the A. F. of L.'s traditional craft-unionism. In 1934, John L. Lewis was able to ram through the A. F. of L. convention a compromise resolution that called for an organizing campaign in the iron and steel industry and the granting of provisional charters to the automobile, cement, and aluminum industries. Within a year, Lewis was bitter over what he considered a betrayal and told the 1935 convention that the old guard "seduced me with fair words. Now, of course, having learned that I was seduced, I am enraged and I am ready to rend my seducers limb from limb."

A two-to-one vote against Lewis, name calling, and Lewis' fist

"*Who Caught It?*" (*Seibel in the Richmond* Times Despatch)

fight with the carpenters' union chief were the highlights of the 1935 convention. Three weeks later, the Committee on Industrial Organization was formed by Lewis and other A. F. of L. supporters of industrial unionism; and on November 23, 1935, Lewis wrote William Green: "Dear Sir and Brother: Effective this date I resign as vice-president of the American Federation of Labor." The break between the two organizations became irrevocable on August 4, 1936, when the Executive Council of the American Federation of Labor voted to suspend the C.I.O. unions unless they disbanded within a month. The A. F. of L. thus deprived itself of approximately one third of its membership and practically all of its militant leadership.

The C.I.O. consisted initially of almost a million members drawn largely from the mine and clothing workers. It won its first major victory when it organized the steel industry, long the citadel of anti-unionism in American industry. On March 2, 1937, the C.I.O.'s Philip Murray achieved what most observers considered the impossible by concluding a contract with the United States Steel Corporation for an eight-hour day, forty-hour week, increased wages, and vacations with pay. The fall of "Big Steel" was a signal, and within two months, more than 250 independent steel companies and U. S. Steel subsidiaries had followed suit. Only "Little Steel" (the name applied collectively to Republic, Bethlehem, Inland, and Youngstown Sheet and Tube steel companies) held out, and the violent Little Steel strike, which began in May, 1937, was eventually smashed by the energetic and often ruthless tactics of Tom Girdler, president of the Republic Steel Corporation. It was not until 1941 that the Little Steel companies were compelled by the N.L.R.B. to recognize the Steel Workers Organizing Committee as the collective-bargaining agency in its plants.

The automobile makers, like the steel firms, had successfully resisted attempts to unionize their plants. With the advent of the N.R.A. the workers in several Detroit automobile factories formed independent unions which by late 1934 had more than 100,000 members and a special status within a wary A. F. of L. By August, 1935, these so-called "federal local unions" became the United Automobile Workers. In 1936, the U.A.W. rebelled against the A. F. of L.'s conservative leaders and joined the C.I.O.

Several U.A.W. locals called unauthorized strikes late in 1936 while the C.I.O. was still organizing the steel industry. These "sit-down" strikes introduced a successful technique; workers refused to either work or leave their plants. By the middle of January, a full-scale strike was in progress against General Motors. The workers used the sit-down strategy, and the company replied with propaganda and violence. Largely because of the intervention of Governor Frank Murphy of Michigan, General Motors capitulated on February 11. The company recognized the union and signed a union contract, and the U.A.W. won all its demands except the closed shop. Within a month, workers at the Chrysler plants had struck, and on April 6, Walter Chrysler agreed to a contract similar to the General Motors agreement. After these initial victories, the C.I.O. moved against Ford in a drawn-out faction-ridden struggle with numerous outbreaks of violence on both sides, and, finally, a strike. After N.L.R.B. intervention in 1940, Ford signed a contract that granted the union virtually all its demands. By 1941, five years after its affiliation with the C.I.O., the U.A.W. had 392,000 members.

At the end of 1940, the C.I.O. had a membership of approximately 4,000,000. Strongest in the automobile, steel, textile, rubber, and maritime industries, it had profoundly influenced the American labor movement and improved the standards of living for its own members and for countless other workers whose employers raised wages, reduced the work week, and granted other concessions to their employees to forestall a C.I.O. invasion. The A. F. of L. was also goaded into action by the gains of its rival. The Federation increased its membership from approximately 3,500,000 in 1935 to 4,247,443 in 1941. In politics, Labor's Non-Partisan League, formed by the C.I.O. in 1936, worked for Roosevelt's re-election in that year, and a similar group did the same, although without a disgruntled John L. Lewis' support, in 1940. The American Labor party, organized in New York by the C.I.O. and independent liberals, supported New Deal and progressive candidates in both national and local contests. Similar policies were pursued by the C.I.O.'s Non-Partisan Leagues in Michigan and Pennsylvania.

In climbing to power, the C.I.O. had to overcome formidable obstacles placed in its path by employers. A Congressional investigation in the 1930's confirmed that unparalleled force, brutality, and deception had been used to combat unionism. Vigilantes, propaganda, threats to workers and their families, armed thugs, the National Guard, private detectives, strikebreakers and spies—all these were employed to halt or sabotage the unions. Among the great American corporations using such tactics, Ford's antiunion work was most shocking. Instead of hired outside detectives, the Ford service men, a group of about 800 thugs, intimidated and beat up workers suspected of union activity. The Ford empire had police-state tendencies; crimes ranged from talking on the job to joining a union.

The C.I.O. received government support that strengthened its determination to break with traditional union practices. The C.I.O. introduced new organizing and strike techniques in appealing to workers who had previously been unorganized. Most of its leaders were young, militant men who had not been discouraged by labor's past failures and who were able to count on a growing willingness to act as a class among factory as well as middle-class white-collar workers.

The new union members and most of their leaders did not want to overthrow either the government or American private enterprise. Like the A. F. of L., the C.I.O. demanded above all more money and less work for its members and agreed with the A. F. of L. that these goals could best be attained through the strike and collective bargaining. The difference was a matter of emphasis. The C.I.O. believed that no worker could advance without the solid cooperation of all workers, whatever their degree of skill or traditional position in the labor movement.

Like all organizations contending for power, however, the C.I.O. and its member unions were constantly troubled by internal fights and dangers. Leaders fought over offices as well as over tactics and strategy. Communists, gangsters, and opportunists were constantly at work to capture the new powerful group in the nation's life for their own purposes. Like big business and the big state, the big union also had to find some means by which leaders could be free and powerful and experienced enough to fight for their programs, without becoming dangerously entrenched or too remote from the public they served. The very success of the big union brought with it the problem of how to maintain democratic controls and a sense of brotherhood within the new organizations.

Experimenting with American Agriculture

The depression began for most American farmers not in 1929 but in 1921; the crash only made already existing difficulties worse. Between 1929 and 1932, farm income shrank from $12,791,000,000 to $5,562,000,000; the index of prices received by farmers (1910–14 = 100) fell from 147 to 65; and the total value of American farm property declined disastrously. Confused, discouraged, and without adequate leadership, farmers as usual tried to increase production to compensate for the decline in prices, thus forcing prices even lower. As farm income decreased, bankruptcies and foreclosures mounted. From 1930 to 1933, the number of farms that changed ownership as a result of forced sales and related defaults more than doubled. Faced with losing their homes, otherwise law-abiding farmers resorted to force. Potential bidders at sheriffs' sales were frightened into silence by armed farmers as owners bought back their farms at a fraction of their value. Iowa farmers went on strike, dumped milk on the roadside, and prevented a judge from proceeding with foreclosures by dragging him from the bench and threatening to hang him. Overwhelmed by forces that they neither controlled nor understood, many American farmers abandoned their traditional resignation and gave way to blind, unreasoning anger.

As in the banking and unemployment crises, the New Deal checked rising panic with bold action. In the long run, the New Deal probably came no closer to a solution of the farm problem than had the Republicans in the 1920's; it did, however, succeed in restoring some of the farmer's confidence in himself and in his way of life. Like many of its other policies, the New Deal's farm programs were often hastily conceived, inefficiently administered, and poorly coordinated; but no one —including the farmer—ever accused the New Deal of indifference.

The key to its farm program can be found, not in what it did for the farmer, but in the fact that it always did something.

New Deal aid to the farmer fell into four major categories: (1) financial aid to farmers threatened by bankruptcy, (2) attempts to reduce farm surpluses, (3) assistance to marginal and submarginal farmers, and (4) the conservation of the nation's agricultural resources.

When Franklin Roosevelt entered office on March 4, 1933, he was at once confronted with the epidemic of farm foreclosures. On March 27, by executive order he established the Farm Credit Administration and placed all existing farm-credit agencies under its control. Mortgage and credit acts passed in May and June authorized land banks to use $2,000,000,000 to pay off farm creditors and take over farm mortgages. Congress appropriated an additional $200,000,000 for special small loans to farmers with the lowest credit ratings. So grave was the foreclosure crisis that the officials were immediately swamped with applications. Unable to keep pace with the rate of foreclosures, they asked farmers faced with immediate loss of their property to wire the President "collect" for help.

These emergency measures saved a large part of the farm population from bankruptcy. Even a year later, from May through December, 1934, 550,000 applicants secured loans and the government assumed mortgages amounting to $1,500,000,000, or approximately one fifth of the nation's total farm mortgage debt of $8,000,000,000. In response to pressure for a national mortgage moratorium, Congress passed the Frazier-Lemke Farm Bankruptcy Act in the spring of 1934. Farmers threatened by foreclosure were granted a five-year moratorium on mortgage payments and the right to buy back their farms from creditors at a price set by a federal district court. When this measure was invalidated by the Supreme Court, it was replaced in 1935 by a law that was upheld by the Court. These federal farm-relief measures were supplemented by mortgage moratoriums put into effect by a number of state governments.

In addition to its emergency-aid program, the federal government took responsibility for supplying credit for normal farm operations. The Farm Credit Act of 1933 had provided for loans to farmers for financing a crop and established credit agencies to encourage both marketing and purchasing cooperatives. Congress also authorized, as it had in previous administrations, special loans to farmers who suffered from droughts, floods, or other natural disasters. Through this extension of federal aid, by the end of the 1930's the government instead of private bankers was providing a large share of the nation's farm loans.

The New Deal's farm-credit policies were only a minor, although essential, part of its farm program; the government's major efforts centered on plans for raising farm prices by reducing agricultural surpluses. Government control over surplus agricultural production had been advocated by some Populists in the 1890's, and the Federal Farm Board had urged farmers to curtail production during the Hoover Administration. But the board could not enforce its recommendations, and American farmers answered its requests with bumper crops. New Dealers concluded that controlled production could only be attained if the government had authority to require it. Many critics of the New Deal justly protested that this policy would only lead to scarcity in time of want, but they failed to recall that American industry had adopted similar policies for years and that the government had already endorsed them in the National Industrial Recovery Act—with the businessman's support.

The first Agricultural Adjustment Act, which was passed on May 12, 1933, was designed to give the farmer an income that would equal his products' purchasing power in 1914, a peacetime high. To attain what came to be known as "parity prices," the Secretary of Agriculture was empowered to make cash "benefit payments" to farmers who contracted to reduce the acreage formerly allotted to certain "basic crops." The land taken out of production was to be left idle or used for soil-conserving crops and kitchen gardens. Eventually the list of "basic crops" included practically every major familiar American crop, as well as hogs and cattle. Funds to finance this program were to be raised by an excise tax on food processors. The Agricultural Adjustment Administration was set up within the Department of Agriculture to manage general policy, but the day-to-day supervision of the program was placed in the hands of county associations of local producers affiliated with the A.A.A.

The Agricultural Adjustment Act went into effect in 1933 after most farmers had finished their spring planting. Overproduction, in cotton and hogs especially, threatened to have a ruinous effect upon prices, and the A.A.A. paid farmers who would destroy a portion of these commodities. In 1933, cotton planters plowed under approximately one fourth of the potential cotton crop, and the government paid farmers $9,000,000 for more than 6,000,000 slaughtered pigs. These drastic measures raised prices a little, but cotton farmers and corn-hog producers clamored for further assistance. The Administration then established the Commodity Credit Corporation in the fall of 1933 to make loans to any corn and cotton growers who agreed to deposit their crops as collateral and to sign A.A.A. restriction contracts for two years. Under this arrangement, the farmer could not lose. If the market price of his product fell below the price at which the government had granted the loan, he could cancel his debt by letting the government take over his collateral, the crop. If the market price went above the loan rate, he could sell his crop in the open market, pay back the government, and pocket his profit. In short, the Commodity Credit Corporation put a floor under cotton and corn prices (originally $.10 a pound for cotton and $.45 a bushel for corn) beneath which their producers' income could not fall. In later years, a similar arrangement covered other commodities as well.

The attempt of the A.A.A. to control production could be partially circumvented by more intensive cultivation of the restricted acreage and by increased production on farms outside the program. Congress, therefore, in 1934 and 1935 enacted laws to curtail all production of certain crops. Cotton, tobacco, and potato growers were threatened with special taxes if they failed to restrict production. Since no farmer could afford to pay the taxes, cooperation was now virtually mandatory. The farmer had refused to decrease production until the New Deal, however reluctantly, resorted to coercion.

It is difficult to judge the effects of the A.A.A. By 1935, more than 30,000,000 acres were withdrawn from production and government payments to farmers totaled $1,151,000,000, but drought rather than A.A.A. contracts was responsible for the drastic reduction in the corn and wheat crops. The 1935 peanut crop was larger than that of any preceding year, and curtailed cotton and tobacco production was largely due to the threat of special tax penalties. Still, the economic status of the farmer improved considerably. His total cash income rose by about one-half between 1932 and 1935, and the index of prices he received (August, 1909–July, 1914 = 100) increased from 65 in 1932 to 114 in 1936. Whether the A.A.A., the New Deal's other inflationary schemes, or drought was primarily responsible for these gains cannot, of course, be determined with accuracy.

On January 6, 1936, the Supreme Court in the Hoosac Mills case ruled that the A.A.A.'s methods for the control of production were unconstitutional because of the excise tax on food processors for financing the program. Other features of the act were not questioned, and they were re-enacted. The Administration, however, had no intention of permitting unregulated surpluses, and in February, 1936, Congress passed the Soil Conservation and Domestic Allotment Act, which, despite its title, was essentially another device for crop restriction. Under this law, the A.A.A. was authorized to pay farmers who adopted such soil-conserving measures as contour plowing and terracing, reduced the acreage of soil-depleting crops, and increased the area planted in soil-building crops. Since the principal soil-depleting crops were also the main cash crops (such as wheat, corn, cotton, and tobacco), the government could still reduce surpluses by subsidizing cooperating farmers. This program, however, was to be financed by congressional appropriations rather than by the now illegal processing taxes.

Under the new act, the government continued to pump cash into the farm economy, but without solving the problem of farm surpluses. A serious drought cut farm output in 1936, prices rose, and in 1937 the profit-hungry farmers made record plantings and better use of restricted acreage. The inevitable occurred: the 1937 crops were the largest since World War I; farm prices declined, and in 1938, gross farm income fell for the first time since 1933.

A second Agricultural Adjustment Act was thus passed in February, 1938. Its purpose was, again, good income for farmers without the production of surpluses. Soil-conservation programs were continued, but now national acreage quotas based on immediate "normal" and estimated emergency demand were established for cotton, wheat, rice, corn and tobacco. Cooperating farmers received so-called "soil conservation payments," but farmers exceeding quotas were permitted to store their surpluses for future sales and received loans on these crop deposits. With the producers' consent, the government imposed sales quotas and taxed sales in excess of the quotas. If market prices fell, the government would make up part or all of the difference between prices actually received and the prices needed to maintain purchasing power for farmers. If his crops failed, the wheat farmer was now to have insurance from a Federal Crop Insurance Corporation.

Again, however, despite the government's elaborate and extensive authority under this new "ever normal granary" program, the farmer's cash income climbed only slightly. The government paid farmers $807,000,000 in 1939 and $766,000,000 in 1940. When in 1941 the United States entered World War II, the American farmer had his first boom in twenty years.

For eight years, the New Deal had tried to solve the farm income and surplus production problems by all measures short of full socialist planning. In addition to its crop and acreage controls and various payments to farmers, the government had also, in the case of the N.R.A., encouraged marketing restriction agreements aimed at holding prices high. Surplus farm products were sold abroad under the Reciprocal Trade treaties; even subsidies, though sparingly used, were paid to stimulate agricultural exports. From 1933 on, under various plans, surpluses were distributed at home as direct relief or under widely used stamp plans for people on relief. Free school-lunch programs were also used. But, as in the case of industry and finance, New Deal energy and experiment revived faith in the doctor but failed to cure the disease.

Aiding the Marginal Farmer

The most justified complaint against the New Deal farm program was that, with millions of unemployed and millions more living on a shoestring, food production was being restricted. Plenty was being destroyed in the midst of poverty. Another well-taken criticism was that the price support and guaranteed-income programs did little or nothing for the great number of the nation's sharecroppers, tenant farmers, and hired farm laborers. The two A.A.A.'s and associated programs helped independent commercial farmers almost exclusively. The nonowning farmers, however, had no powerful lobbies and few congressmen to speak for their needs. In the 1930's, there were at least 5,000,000 underprivileged rural folk whose distress had developed not after the crash of 1929, or even after the farm decline of 1921–2, but had been constant for a lifetime.

New Deal general relief laws gave about 3,500,000 poor rural families cash and government construction jobs and in 1934, by special provision, even tools and seeds. But it was apparent that these later gifts were useless to farmers who lived on exhausted lands.

In 1934 the administration decided to undertake a resettlement program and began to purchase submarginal lands on a limited scale. Farmers living on these lands were granted loans and transferred to productive areas. A few agricultural communities were also established near cities to enable urban workers to increase their income by part-time farming. Administrative difficulties and lack of sufficient government support impeded these programs. To coordinate the work, in April, 1935, President Roosevelt created the Resettlement Administration, with jurisdiction over the whole problem of rural rehabilitation.

From the outset, the Resettlement Administration confronted almost insurmountable obstacles. Its chief, Rexford G. Tugwell, was unjustly accused of being an ultraradical collectivist, and a suspicious Congress never provided the agency with adequate funds. Surveys revealed that only a comparatively small amount of land was both suitable and available for resettlement. Some marginal farmers refused to

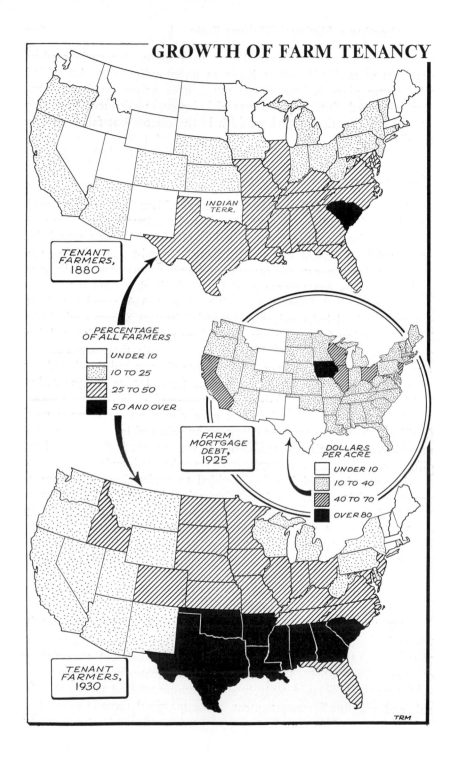

GROWTH OF FARM TENANCY

TENANT FARMERS, 1880

INDIAN TERR.

PERCENTAGE OF ALL FARMERS

UNDER 10
10 TO 25
25 TO 50
50 AND OVER

FARM MORTGAGE DEBT, 1925

DOLLARS PER ACRE

UNDER 10
10 TO 40
40 TO 70
OVER 80

TENANT FARMERS, 1930

TRM

be resettled, and many occupants of submarginal lands could not be transformed into self-supporting farmers, being farmers only in the sense that they lived on the land—they did not live off it. Few had even the rudiments of formal education, and many were so old that there was little chance that they would ever again be self-supporting or gainfully employed.

Despite these difficulties, the Resettlement Administration removed 9,000,000 acres of submarginal land from cultivation, erected new communities in resettled areas, extended loans to farmers unable to obtain credit elsewhere, and instructed some of the most backward farmers in the basic techniques of scientific agriculture. Whenever possible, the agency tried to stimulate cooperative efforts by farmers. Loans were extended to groups of farmers to enable them to buy and share supplies, machinery, and other equipment that they could not have afforded as individuals.

The Resettlement Administration's program convinced Roosevelt that an even broader approach to the problem of rural poverty was necessary. Largely as a result of the findings of a special committee of inquiry he appointed, Congress in 1937 passed the Farm Tenancy Act. It provided for loans to tenant farmers, sharecroppers, and farm laborers to assist them in the purchase of farms, livestock, equipment, and supplies. It reorganized the Resettlement Administration as the Farm Security Administration and gave the new agency all the functions of its predecessor except the purchase of submarginal lands, which was turned over to the Soil Conservation Service.

By June, 1940, the F.S.A. had given 1,400,000 families some form of financial assistance, and 120,000 loans had already been paid back. Of 360,000 families that participated in the program in 1939, the net income per family increased 43 per cent. The diet and health of the rural poor improved; education was made available to their children; and their mortgaged indebtedness decreased. By June, 1940, the agency also had established fifty-three camps in California, Florida, and Texas for "Okies" and other migrant rural workers. These were violently opposed by nearby residents because they attracted "undesirable" citizens who put an additional burden on local relief agencies.

The Federal Security Administration also inaugurated an openly experimental program to enable the rural dispossessed to become independent farmers. It advanced low cost forty-year small loans to those agreeing to run farms by F.S.A. rules and established a novel program for cooperative and subsistence homesteads. Some of the 164 experimental communities or "Greenbelt towns" thus set up followed the lines laid down in the earlier plans for rural homes for urban

The Dust Bowl in Oklahoma . . .

[LIBRARY OF CONGRESS]

workers. Others were genuinely cooperative and communal farming communities.

The New Deal also attempted to deal with some of the problems created by abused and neglected lands. It conducted a nation-wide survey of land resources, set up experimental stations to study various types of soil depletion, and created demonstration areas in which farmers were shown the most advanced methods for combatting erosion. A conservation program was conducted jointly by the federal and state governments. By 1940, under the Soil Conservation Act of 1935, 359 soil conservation districts in 34 states had adopted erosion control regulations enforceable by law, and the cooperating states received federal benefits. Land-use planning committees made up of government experts and local farmers, analyzed and prescribed for poor soils. The reforestation work of the Civilian Conservation Corps reduced, however slightly, the menace of floods. The T.V.A. conducted a remarkably successful conservation program among the farmers in the Tennessee Valley. Both the Resettlement and Farm Security Adminis-

. . . And the Dust Bowl's Legacy

[LIBRARY OF CONGRESS]

trations furnished clients with information on soil-building methods. And the government undertook to plant a hundred-mile-wide band of trees on the Great Plains from Canada to Mexico to break the force of the winds that blew across the "dust bowl." By mid-1940, approximately 190,000,000 trees had been planted on about 210,000 acres of "shelter belt."

The Balance Sheet on New Deal Agriculture

Between 1933 and the United States' entrance into World War II, the New Deal did more for the farmer than for any other single group in the population. It extended him credit, paid him not to produce, taught him how to be more productive, and instructed him in the most advanced methods of soil conservation. But, by forcing up the prices of farm products during a period of widespread want, it imposed a heavy burden on already hard-pressed American consumers. By try-

Strip and Contour Plowing in Georgia

[U. S. DEPARTMENT OF AGRICULTURE]

ing to save American agriculture, the New Deal made the farmer a privileged member of American society.

To be entirely successful, a modern farm program had to insure high prices both for farm goods consumed at home and for the farmer's exportable surplus. However, parity prices and a healthy export market were incompatible. Farmers could not export their surplus products unless other nations lowered their tariffs—a step such nations refused to take unless the United States did the same. But the American farmer was opposed to a reduction in the duties on agricultural goods, for he would then risk losing his domestic market to foreign competitors. He needed both parity and the foreign market to prosper, but he could not increase his exports without losing parity. There remained one alternative that no major politician dared to advocate— full-scale national planning of agricultural production that eliminated or minimized surpluses and took millions of farmers off lands that were abused or contributed to surpluses. Such planning would have its own dangers and drawbacks, but by trying to save capitalistic farming, the New Deal was left with the risks, vagaries, and costs of private enterprise.

Confronted by what seemed to be an insoluble problem, the New

Deal abandoned the foreign market (with the exception of its reciprocity program) and concentrated on the domestic. Nevertheless, the American farm remained an international rather than a national problem—a problem that could be solved temporarily by periods of war and postwar scarcity, or permanently by such unlikely developments as the end of economic nationalism and an expanding world economy in which American farm products could flow freely to the most active and best-priced markets.

Helping the Unemployed

The New Deal had a more direct effect on the lives of poorer Americans than any other administration in the history of the United States. In March, 1933, the unemployed numbered many millions, and, with the collapse and exhaustion of local and private relief, these people were often unable to obtain food, clothing, or shelter. On the eve of the crash, most Americans believed that the national government had no right to help the needy and that government aid sapped character and initiative. Ten years later, all but a few die-hards agreed that the federal government had to assist those unable to support themselves. The New Deal may not have revolutionized the American economy, but it helped to revolutionize the American attitude toward poverty. In the 1920's, a man without a job was considered lazy; under the New Deal, he became a victim of economic forces over which he had no control.

The unemployed never fell below 1,000,000 during the boom of the golden twenties, but the federal government made no move to provide the jobless with either work or relief. In October, 1930, with the unemployed now numbering almost 5,000,000, Hoover announced that the "sense of voluntary organization and community service . . . has been strong enough to cope with the problem [of unemployment] for the past year." Reassuring statements, governmental committees, "spread the work" campaigns, pleas by public officials, and re-employment drives conducted by civic organizations could be balanced against the harsh fact that the unemployed had grown to approximately 9,000,000. Private and local relief agencies, despite heroic efforts, lacked both the coordination and the resources to cope with the extraordinary demands placed upon them.

In the last year of Hoover's term, the federal government gave surplus farm products to the Red Cross for distribution among the unemployed, appropriated funds for a federal construction program, and authorized loans to state and local governments for public works and relief and to building and loan companies, savings banks, and insurance concerns. The faults of these programs were that their aid was too small and was to be administered through nonfederal authorities. Proposals that the federal government expand its public-works program and provide direct relief for the unemployed were steadfastly rejected by President Hoover, who alternately branded them as "inflationary" plans, "pork-barrel" bills, and pleas for "a cold and distant charity" at variance with American tradition.

During the first two Roosevelt Administrations, the government conducted a many-sided attack upon unemployment and poverty. No single theory can explain these policies, for they were the products of a complex mixture of political, economic, and humanitarian considerations. The New Dealers did not intend to let people starve, but they also believed that federal aid to the needy had to tie in with a program to stimulate industrial recovery. As in the banking, currency, farm, and labor programs, trial and error was the rule; relief was furnished through cash payments, loans, food and clothing allotments, make-work projects, and public works. Early relief policies under Roosevelt often followed patterns established by the preceding Administration; however, these were so expanded that they bore slight resemblance to Hoover's reluctant measures.

Roosevelt indicated the broad outlines of an unemployment program in an address to Congress in March, 1933. He suggested "three types of legislation":

> The first is the enrollment of workers now by the Federal government for such public employment as can be quickly started and will not interfere with the demand for or the proper standards of normal employment.
>
> The second is grants to States for relief work.
>
> The third extends to a broad public works labor-creating program.

Congress acted quickly. On March 31, it approved "an Act for the relief of unemployment through the performance of useful public works and other purposes"; and five days later, the President followed suit and established the Civilian Conservation Corps. In mid-May, Congress created the Federal Emergency Relief Administration, which was authorized to distribute aid to the needy—but in the Hoover pattern—through state and municipal agencies; and in mid-June, Congress set up the Public Works Administration, which established a program of public works.

The young members of the C.C.C. were drawn mostly from cities and were stationed in camps throughout the country. Paid small monthly wages they worked on reforestation and fire-prevention projects and built roads, recreational facilities, woodland trails, and bridges. By the end of 1941, 2,750,000 young men had been on the C.C.C. rolls. They increased and conserved the country's natural resources and found productive work, new interests, and higher morale to replace their previous discouragement and defeat. It was undoubtedly the most popular of the New Deal relief agencies.

The Federal Emergency Relief Administration, Congress's response to the President's request for "grants to States for relief work," was directed by Harry Hopkins, a former social worker, who had supervised New York state relief while Roosevelt was governor. Although similar in some respects to Hoover's policy of state-aid, the F. E. R. A. provided for outright grants rather than loans to affiliated agencies. As early as the summer of 1933, however, the agency began to experiment with federal work-relief projects. In 1935, when it was disbanded, almost half the people receiving its aid were on work relief. During its lifetime, the F.E.R.A. spent approximately 4 billion dollars, 71 per cent of which was contributed by the federal government and the remainder by states and municipalities. At its high point in February, 1934, almost 8,000,000 families were "on relief."

The F.E.R.A. was limited by the provision that it work through local agencies. In November, 1933, the President established the Civil Works Administration, administered directly from Washington. During the few months of its life, the C.W.A. started 180,000 projects such as road, school, park, and playground building on which considerably more than 4,000,000 individuals were employed. The C.W.A. did what its critics could not do: it provided work for those who did not have it. When the agency was disbanded in the spring of 1934, most of its projects were taken over by the F.E.R.A.

The Public Works Administration, established in the summer of 1933 and placed under the direction of Secretary of the Interior Harold L. Ickes, was viewed by New Dealers as essentially a pump-priming device. Its funds were used primarily to stimulate private enterprise, but it did hire 500,000 workers directly from the pool of unemployed in 1934. Ickes insisted that all P.W.A. projects be "useful" and in the national interest. Contracts were made with private companies, and the agency either financed projects itself or made loans or grants to states and cities to cover part of the cost of approved projects. Its methods were frequently criticized by opponents of economic planning, but no one could justly accuse it of "boondoggling" (unproductive make-work projects). The P.W.A. built bridges, dams, sewage systems, school and college buildings, recreational facilities, airports, low-income housing, roads, hospitals, and did much reclamation work.

These first New Deal relief and public-works programs were launched at a time of national emergency with little opportunity for long-term planning or a study of over-all objectives. Agencies frequently worked at cross purposes or duplicated each other's efforts; relief methods were changed with confusing frequency; and no attempt was made to distinguish between relief clients who had been forced out of work by the depression and the "unemployables" who could not have found jobs even in prosperous times. By the end of 1934, the government's entire relief program had to be overhauled. In January, 1935, the President proposed a new policy: federal aid was to be restricted to "employables," and the care of "unemployables" was to be turned over entirely to state and local agencies. Any semblance of a federal dole would then be removed, for federal assistance would be confined to people at work.

The new program was put into effect in May, 1935. The C.C.C. and the P.W.A. were left untouched, but all other work relief was put under the Works Progress Administration (later the Works Projects Administration). The new agency, headed by Harry Hopkins until he became Secretary of Commerce in 1939, had its own projects, and did not work through intermediaries.

The W.P.A. quickly became the largest single employer in the United States; by December, 1935, 2,600,000 workers were on W.P.A. jobs. The revival of private business and mounting criticism of the spending and relief programs made the government cut work-relief rolls in 1937. But the business recession of 1937-8 brought increased unemployment; and by November, 1938, more than 3,270,000 people were on W.P.A. rolls. The work-relief projects affected almost every phase of American life. During its lifetime the agency built airports, bridges, parks, schools, post-office buildings, public golf courses, roads, auditoriums, hospitals, libraries, sewers, levees, and drainage ditches. It conducted classes in sewing, art, vocational training, and naturalization; it distributed free lunches to school children, renovated clothing and books, taught illiterates to read, staged plays and symphonies, constructed and maintained conservation projects, gave inoculations against contagious diseases, inspected teeth, killed rats, and stuffed birds. In short, there was little that the W.P.A. did not do as it attempted not only to create jobs but to place the unemployed in the jobs for which they were best suited. Between 1935 and 1941, the W.P.A.

spent more than 11 billion dollars, hired more than 8,000,000 different individuals, and started more than 250,000 projects.

A striking feature of the W.P.A. was its subsidies to musicians, artists, actors, and writers, who had lost their jobs and were ill-equipped to take work in other occupations. The Federal Music Project, the Federal Arts Project, the Federal Writers Project, and the Historical Records Survey gave the nation's intellectuals, scholars, and artists sympathy and help. The W.P.A. was severely criticized for these cultural programs, but the fact remains that the New Deal was the first Administration in American history to recognize that the nation had a stake in supporting the creative arts as well as agriculture, manufacturing, and transportation.

The W.P.A.'s work-relief program was supplemented by that of the National Youth Administration, which gave assistance to young men and women between the ages of sixteen and twenty-five. The N.Y.A. aided boys and girls who had left school, and it furnished part-time clerical work in academic laboratories, libraries, and administrative offices to young people who needed financial assistance to continue their studies. The N.Y.A. never received the popular support given the C.C.C., however, and it was continually hampered by inadequate funds, inept local administrators, and serious inroads by Communists seeking to use the program for their own purposes.

Soon after the start of the New Deal, relief projects critics charged that the Administration spent too much money on frills and follies. A large number of stories and jokes sprang up criticizing New Deal bumbling and poking fun at minor aspects of the programs. People received the impression that lazy men and women were being paid only to pick up leaves or to carry stones from one pile to another. In some cases New Deal relief was poorly or foolishly administered. But, aside from the intangibles of hopes restored and lives renewed, thousands of public buildings and miles of highways in practically every part of the nation today testify to solid New Deal accomplishments. The biggest limit on more extensive productive relief work in the 1930's was the determination of the nation's businessmen and Administration leaders that the government not take over and run factories and farms; in other words, the essential parts of the American economy on which regular jobs depended were to remain under a system of private capitalism.

By 1940, the assets produced by New Deal relief measures were millions of people who, although living close to the margin, still had faith in the democratic system. How much longer Roosevelt could have continued to improvise in reviving prosperity can never be known, but in 1939, the nation still had 9,000,000 unemployed.

National Social Security and Federal Housing

For the first two years of its existence, the New Deal did little to provide long-range protection against the risks of a private economy for working people. But in 1935, it set up a social security program for the care of dependent children, the aged, the handicapped, and the temporarily unemployed. This move was long overdue. Most of the nations of western Europe had long had social security acts on their statute books, but only a few American states had passed similar laws—all of which were inadequate—and the federal government had done nothing. During the depression, this situation became a disaster for Americans.

Throughout the 1930's, but especially during the first years under the New Deal, the bitterness and frustration built up by the depression provided fertile grounds for demagogic movements and quackery of various sorts. Indeed, in the 1930's, there was a constant contrast between a lively rational purposefulness among many New Deal administrators and a continuing sense of despair and resentment among certain groups whom New Deal programs passed by or could not dissuade from hating fellow Americans.

Some of the panaceas hawked for the illnesses of depression were harmless, but others were dangerous because of both their simplification of complex issues and their openly antidemocratic bias. Upton Sinclair, a respectable Socialist, had nearly won a majority of California's voters in the state's 1934 gubernatorial election with his promise to "End Poverty in California"; Senator Huey Long, dictator of Louisiana and self-styled "Kingfish," had promised to make "every man a king"; Dr. F. G. Townsend had assured his aged followers that his plan would give them $200 a month; and demagogues like Father Coughlin and Gerald L. K. Smith had outlined programs that were startlingly similar to those of Nazi Germany and Fascist Italy. The popularity of these and similar proposals among the poor, as well as humanitarian considerations, convinced Roosevelt that the national government could no longer put off the adoption of social-security legislation.

The Social Security Act, which became law in August, 1935, provided for various types of assistance to the aged, the infirm, widows, dependent children, and the unemployed. Annuities ranging from $10 to $85 a month were paid to workers who retired at the age of 65 and who had participated in the program before their retirement. Funds to finance these benefits were raised by a payroll tax that was shared equally by employer and employee. By 1940, more than 50,000,000 workers had Social Security cards; but casual laborers, merchant seamen, civil serv-

Huey Long, the Louisiana "Kingfish"

ants, and the employees of nonprofit institutions were not covered. To provide for the old age of members of these groups, for workers who were older than 65 at the time that the law was passed, and for other dependents, the government helped the individual states to finance pensions.

The Social Security Act also provided for unemployment compensation through a collaborative plan between national and state governments. Benefits to unemployed workers ranged between $5 and $15 a week but were to last in most states for only approximately fifteen weeks. Money to maintain the various state systems was furnished by a 3 per cent payroll tax on employers. By June, 1940, more than 28,000,000 workers were covered by unemployment insurance, but many workers in the nation's smallest firms were excluded.

Two of the great disasters of the depression were the threatened loss of millions of private homes by foreclosure and the further degradation of life in urban slums. The New Deal attempted to assist families facing the loss of their homes and to furnish better housing for the underprivileged. The Home Owners Loan Corporation, established in

1933, assumed the mortgages of impoverished homeowners close to foreclosure proceedings. Between 1933 and 1936, this agency lent more than 3 billion dollars to more than 1,000,000 householders. By consolidating the homeowners' mortgaged indebtedness, reducing the principal, lowering the interest rate, and extending the period for repayment, it prevented countless American families from being forced out of their homes by their creditors. Householders were further aided by the Federal Housing Authority, created in June, 1934, to lend money at low rates of interest to owners who wished to repair, enlarge, or renovate their homes.

After at least fifty years of complaints and crusades against slums, under the New Deal the federal government took the lead in slum clearance and public housing. As with most New Deal welfare legislation, the first steps were timid and groping; but these gave way to bolder, better administered programs. In June, 1933, the P.W.A. established a division to plan and finance low-cost urban housing projects to be constructed by private contractors. By 1937, when it was terminated, the P.W.A. Housing Division had subsidized more than fifty public-housing developments, but the average rent for an apartment was $26 per month, a figure beyond the means of almost all American slum dwellers.

In 1937, the Administration's low-cost housing program was reorganized, and a United States Housing Authority took over the housing program and loaned or granted money to local housing authorities for slum clearance and federally planned public housing. By 1941, the U.S.H.A. had eliminated more than 78,000 unsafe and unsanitary residential buildings and had provided new dwellings for almost 200,000 families. Rentals in these projects averaged $12.64 a month, and the average annual income of families occupying them (late in 1941) was $837. The accomplishments of the U.S.H.A. are impressive, however, only when compared to past efforts to house the poor; and when the agency was liquidated because of the war, slums were still a most noticeable and disheartening feature of every large American city.

National relief, security, and housing programs were often conceived in haste, diluted by political expediency, and hampered by an inefficient bureaucracy and administrative confusion. The plan for the rehabilitation of the Tennessee Valley, on the other hand, was a long-term project in which recovery, industrial growth, the conservation of human and natural resources, and the revival of agriculture were all viewed as interrelated parts of a common regional problem.

The Tennessee River, which with its tributaries flows through seven states, had been subject for years to repeated and devastating

Senator George Norris at a T.V.A. Dam

[UNITED PRESS INTERNATIONAL]

floods. On its shores at Muscle Shoals, Alabama, the government in 1918 had constructed a dam and two nitrate plants that had produced vast quantities of explosives during the last months of World War I. After the war, the government had attempted to sell its facilities at Muscle Shoals, but potential buyers had offered to pay only a fraction of the plant's original cost. As a result, the installations, which were capable of producing fertilizer and electric power for peacetime uses, remained idle, while congressional moves for government operation were blocked by Presidents Coolidge and Hoover. But soon after Roosevelt entered office, Senator George W. Norris, with Administration support, revived his earlier proposals for a government program for the Tennessee Valley; and in the spring of 1933, Congress established the Tennessee Valley Authority to produce cheap power, promote conservation, improve navigation, and advance the "economic and social well-being of the people."

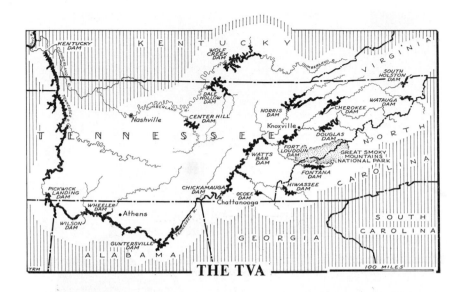

THE TVA

The Tennessee Valley Authority was created as an independent federal agency and given considerable latitude in making and executing policy in the area under its control. Despite their extensive powers, its officials preferred to help people to help themselves rather than to impose from above programs that had little popular support or understanding. Whenever possible, "demonstration units" were used to convince residents of the valley of the advantages of new techniques in farming and conservation. Valley residents were urged to cooperate in solving their common problems, while the T.V.A. furnished them with the necessary information, guidance, and encouragement. A close alliance was developed between the Authority and state and local governments, state universities, and business and civic organizations in the valley. Virtually every T.V.A. program was a joint undertaking relying heavily on a wide variety of experts and specialists to provide the facts that could be used to develop a better way of life for all people in the region.

During its early years, the T.V.A. was vigorously opposed by local power concerns and by conservative critics of the New Deal throughout the nation. In their campaign, the private power companies were led by Wendell Willkie of Commonwealth and Southern, which eventually sold its interests in the valley to the government at a high price. Other private utilities followed Commonwealth and Southern's example. By the end of the 1930's, the accomplishments of the T.V.A. had made it generally popular throughout the United States and, indeed, famous all over the world. Its staunchest supporters, however, were the people who lived in the region. The residents of the valley acquired cheap power, protection against floods, instruction in soil conservation and improved farming techniques, a connected series of navigable rivers and lakes, fertilizer, new conveniences for their homes, libraries, jobs, medical assistance, adult-education classes, and recreational facilities. These benefits were not bestowed on a subservient people by an all-powerful, paternalistic ruler, but were the direct results of intelligent planning, genuine cooperation between the citizen and his government, a regional approach to regional problems, and a reawakened vitality and optimism.

The Politics of the New Deal Coalition

The New Deal was a political organization as well as a crisis government. Like every major American political movement, the Democratic party of the 1930's was a hodgepodge of conflicting interests and groups. The core of party strength was supplied by the alliance that Jefferson had established between southern agrarians and northern city machines, and both the Solid South and the northern cities remained consistently Democratic, although with varying degrees of enthusiasm, in every election from 1932 through 1944.

The political genius of the New Deal's leaders lay in their ability to attract additional blocs of voters to the Democratic party. Before 1932, the American labor movement had dissipated its political strength by refusing to identify its interests with any party. After 1933, the average workingman became an ardent and steadfast New Dealer, although a few labor leaders (notably John L. Lewis after 1940) turned against the Roosevelt Administration.

Another major political triumph of the New Deal was its successful appeal to northern Negro voters. Since the Civil War, the Negro had looked on the party of Lincoln as its liberator and staunchest political ally. But Republicans had come to take the Negro vote for granted and had made no move to improve the lot of this underprivileged minority for more than fifty years. Republican negligence proved to be the Democrats' opportunity. New Dealers permitted the Negro (if he did not live below the Mason-Dixon Line) to share equally with his fellow white citizens in most of the government's social and economic programs, and the Roosevelt Administration also supported labor organizations that forbade racial restrictions in their membership. During World War II, the government went further and established the Fair Employment Practices Committee in an attempt to guarantee the

Negro as well as other minority groups equality of economic opportunity. Northern Negroes repaid the New Deal with their votes.

The New Deal for many years also gained votes in the traditionally Republican states of the grain-growing Middle West. In 1932 and 1936, none of these states gave their electoral votes to the Republicans. Hard times for the farmer, disgust with the Republicans' inability to relieve his plight, and the New Deal's obvious willingness to spend time and money on attempts to better his economic status paid political dividends. As conditions improved, however, Democratic strength in the farm states declined. In 1940, the Republicans recaptured North and South Dakota, Nebraska, Kansas, Colorado, Iowa, and Indiana. Four years later, the Republicans carried ten Middle West states.

Many middle-class reformers and progressives, who belonged to the tradition of Theodore Roosevelt's New Nationalism, Woodrow Wilson's New Freedom, and Robert La Follette's Progressive party of the twenties were also New Dealers for a time, although some, like Burton Wheeler and Hiram Johnson, later became bitter critics of Roosevelt. Young people were swept up by the idealism that characterized much of the New Deal. Professors saw for the first time some of the lessons that they had taught in the classroom being applied to the nation. Clergymen and social workers were attracted by New Deal social reforms. The New Deal also had the loyalty of a few members of the same upper-class aristocracy of landed and mercantile wealth that had produced Franklin D. Roosevelt, a group which disliked the newer aristocracy of industry and finance.

As in other administrations, the Cabinet was a guide to the groups the President counted on. Negroes and labor leaders never achieved Cabinet rank, but their allies or friends did. Secretary of the Treasury Henry Morgenthau, Jr., was a friend and neighbor of the President at Hyde Park and a Wall Street financier. He represented the old ties of many bankers to the Democratic party. Secretary of Agriculture Henry Wallace, whose father had held the same position in the Harding and Coolidge cabinets, represented the dissatisfied Republican farmers of the Middle West and drew on the traditions of Populism and insurgency. Postmaster James Farley was the spokesman of northern city machines; Secretary of State Cordell Hull was an old-line Wilsonian southern Democrat; Secretary of the Interior Harold Ickes and Secretary of Labor Frances Perkins, the first woman to hold a cabinet position, had both been staunch Progressives when the first Roosevelt was in the White House; Secretary of Commerce Harry Hopkins had spent his years before the New Deal as a social worker. Professors comprised almost all of the "Brain Trust," as the President's early circle of advisers was called. One professor, Felix Frankfurter, eventually became a member of the Supreme Court, and former college and university teachers were liberally sprinkled throughout most of the famous alphabetical agencies and the three branches of the government.

At almost every step in its piecemeal creation of a national welfare state, the Roosevelt Administration was sensitive to the distress and disasters it believed it had a mandate to halt and repair. But it also watched carefully for the political repercussions of its programs. The gradual shift to ever greater federal intervention in the nation's economic life helped create a Democratic party whose appeal was directly and openly to the nation's working classes. Although the control of the Democratic party continued to be shared by southerners and northern city machines, the rhetoric of the party and its programs implied the acceptance of a workingman's America as a permanent fact. The Democrats played down or abandoned the old theme that the worker or poorer farmer would graduate to property ownership and membership in a middle-class society. Although the century-old Jacksonian theme of equality of opportunity was used as much as ever, it was clear that most Americans would not grow up to become independent businessmen. The New Deal, instead, encouraged factory workers or nonowning farmers to look forward to the pleasures of decent homes, a family car, assured income during old age, and adequate education for their children.

The first programs of the New Deal, however, were tuned to a national emergency that affected millionaires as well as the urban unemployed and poor farmers. In the first weeks of its existence, the New Deal tried to shock and jolt the American people out of their lethargy and defeatism. The country demanded action, and the Administration provided leadership that soon revived popular confidence in the nation's destiny. By closing the banks, juggling the currency, establishing the Civilian Conservation Corps, and other such moves, the Administration, with the aid of a docile Congress, fulfilled its first objective—that of convincing most Americans that the government was capable of meeting the emergency.

As soon as the crisis had passed, the New Deal launched its first major program to restore prosperity. Following the Hoover precedent, although with greater energy and scope of aid, it turned to the nation's business leaders in the hope that revived prosperity and confidence among them would seep down and eventually aid all classes. From 1933 to 1935, the New Deal measures conferred more substantial favors upon the businessman than upon any other group. But the New Deal distributed favors to groups other than the businessman. Labor was granted certain rights; the unemployed were given relief payments; and the farmer was paid to restrict production under the first Agricultural Adjustment Act. By 1934, however, many businessmen had concluded that the advantages of government aid were outweighed by the disadvantages of government regulation and by favors to their opponents.

In 1933, Roosevelt had asked "our industry" for a "great spontaneous co-operation." Three years later he referred to some businessmen as "economic royalists." With the establishment of the Works Progress Administration in April, 1935, the New Deal set about in earnest to build prosperity from the bottom up. It curtailed aid to business but continued to support the farmer with a crop allotment program and the worker with the enactment in July, 1935, of the National Labor Relations Act.

The New Deal's early policies were endorsed by the nation's voters in 1934 and again in 1936. In the midterm elections, the Democrats obtained large majorities in both the House and Senate, and in 1936, their candidates were once more Roosevelt and Garner. The party's platform was an unqualified endorsement of the Roosevelt policies. When the Republicans convened in June, 1936, in Cleveland, they were hampered by the lack of a clear-cut program or a ready-made candidate. They knew what they were against, but they did not seem sure of what they would like to put in its place; they promised to attain the New Deal's objectives without using its methods. Like the Democrats, they planned to end unemployment, restore prosperity, and aid the needy; but they also assured the voters that in carrying out this program they would preserve states' rights, uphold the Constitution, and safeguard the "American system of free enterprise." For their candidates, the Republicans chose Governor Alfred M. Landon of Kansas and Frank Knox, the owner-publisher of the Chicago *Daily News*.

Throughout the campaign of 1936, the Republicans maintained that the New Deal was destroying the American way of life and depriving individuals of their freedom. This theme was repeatedly emphasized by an overwhelming majority of newspapers and by the American Liberty League, which had been formed in 1934 by Republican business groups and was joined by such well-known Democrats as Alfred E. Smith, ex-Governor Joseph B. Ely of Massachusetts, and former Secretary of State Bainbridge Colby. The Republicans also took care to present Landon to the voters as a man who understood the problems of both the businessman and the farmer. On the one hand, he was pictured as a hardheaded executive who had had a successful career in the oil business; on the other, he was put forward as a typical Kansan who knew at first hand the needs and aspirations of the farmers.

Governor Landon of Kansas

[NATIONAL ARCHIVES]

The Democrats campaigned on their record and asked for a mandate to carry their program to completion. Making no effort to attract support from the big-business community, the New Dealers sought votes among the workers, farmers, and people on relief. As never before, the Democratic party courted the votes of Catholic, Jewish, and Negro voters. The *Literary Digest* on the basis of a straw poll predicted a Republican victory. Democratic campaign manager James A. Farley, however, declared that Roosevelt would carry all states but Maine and Vermont, and the election returns proved him right. Roosevelt had 523 electoral votes to 8 for Landon, and the popular vote was 27,751,579 to 16,679,583. In the new House, there were 328 Democrats to 107 Republicans, and in the Senate, 77 Democrats to 19 Republicans.

After this electoral triumph, President Roosevelt felt strong enough to overcome the judicial barrier to the progress of the New Deal. The Supreme Court, to which he had had no opportunity to make a single appointment during his first four years in Office, had declared unconstitutional a long series of New Deal measures that included the N.I.R.A., A.A.A., the Railroad Pensions Act, the Bituminous Coal Act, the Municipal Bankruptcy Act, and the Frazier-Lemke Farm Bankruptcy Act. Faced by judicial opposition such as had plagued and stumped other strong Presidents, Roosevelt decided on a bold course, and on February 5, 1937, he announced to Congress a plan for what his enemies called "packing" and his supporters termed "democratizing" the Supreme Court.

The Court bill introduced into Congress provided that Supreme Court justices be permitted to retire at the age of seventy; that the president be allowed to appoint an additional justice for each one who at seventy refused to retire; and that the Court's maximum size be increased from nine to fifteen justices. Aside from the merits of this bill (and many students of constitutional law debated the proposals as avidly as the politicians did), its immediate effect was to disrupt the loosely organized alliance of groups that had endorsed Democratic policies in the 1936 election. Republicans took new hope, and—with the aid of newspaper editors and columnists, radio commentators, and many lawyers—their propaganda depicted the bill as a threat to the fundamental rights of every American citizen. Southern Democrats, whose conservatism had been shocked by New Deal "radicalism," joined forces with the Republican opponents of the President's Court plan. Some reform Democrats (led by Burton K. Wheeler of Montana) who had formerly given their allegiance to the Administration's domestic measures also fought the reorganization. Although Congress, after bitter debate, eventually rejected his proposals, the President nevertheless achieved his immediate objective. Even before the end of Congressional debate on judicial reform, the Court handed down several pro-New Deal decisions, and a series of retirements soon permitted the President to fill the Court with a New Deal majority that generally endorsed his program. But the President's indirect victory had seriously impaired the political strength of the Democratic party.

Opposition to the Court program helped convince the President and his closest advisers that the objectives of the New Deal could not be attained until the Democratic party had been rid of its more conservative members. In the 1938 primaries, Roosevelt singled out as unwanted conservatives several Democratic candidates for Congress (all but one of whom came from the South) and asked the voters to defeat them. Only one of the candidates (the non-Southerner) on what the President's opponents called his "purge list" was rejected by the voters, who resented Roosevelt's interference and who were also upset about the "recession." After the "off-year" election, the party was no closer to unity than before, and the Republicans had gained new seats in Congress for the first time since 1928.

Just Before the Fight—the Judges at the Inauguration, 1937

The New Deal, slowed down by the fight over the Court and the President's intervention in the 1938 campaign, was brought to a full halt by events abroad. Confronted by a divided party at home and a world about to go to war, Roosevelt in the winter of 1938–9 switched his emphasis to foreign policy. Southern conservatives, who a short time before had been threatened with expulsion from the party, received the Administration's blessing as they gave their wholehearted support to its foreign policy. Midwestern liberals from both parties, who combined the traditions of insurgency with those of isolationism and who had backed the government's domestic reforms, more often than not turned against the New Deal when the President abandoned or curtailed his plans for social betterment at home to concentrate on events in Europe and the Far East. Only the New Dealers in the cities of the Northeast and Far West remained loyal to the Roosevelt Administration from beginning to end. They had special reason to approve both New Deal domestic and foreign policies, for as New Deal relief programs had grown, they had helped undermine the local aid that had been so large a source of the city bosses' power. Without the new federal patronage and without playing to the city masses near-adoration of Roosevelt, the old-line bosses might lose what power they still had.

The New Deal as a reform movement was dead by 1939. As such, it had lived a comparatively short life. It had not come into existence until 1934–5, when it had turned from what was essentially a businessman's program to reform. It had reached its high-water mark with the election of 1936, after which it had disintegrated rapidly under successive political setbacks. By 1939, only the wishful thinkers among diehards continued to believe that the New Deal of the midthirties would be revived. The New Deal's formal interment did not take place until a press conference on December 28, 1943, when the President recognized the fact:

> The net of it is this—how did the New Deal come into existence? It was because there was an awfully sick patient called the United States of America, and it was suffering from a grave internal disorder—awfully sick—all kinds of things had happened to this patient, all internal things. And they sent for the doctor. And it was a long, long process—took several years before those ills, in that particular illness of ten years ago were remedied. But after a while they were remedied. And on all those ills of 1933, things had to be done to cure the patient internally. And it was done; it took a number of years.
>
> And there were certain specific remedies that the old doctor gave the patient. . . . [The patient is] all right now—it's all right internally now—if they just leave him alone.
>
> But since then, two years ago, the patient had a very bad accident—not an internal trouble. Two years ago, on the seventh of December, he was in a pretty bad smashup—broke his hip, broke his leg in two or three places, broke a wrist and an arm, and some ribs; and they didn't think he would live, for a while. And then he began to "come to"; and he has been in charge of a partner of the old doctor. Old Dr. New Deal didn't know "nothing" about legs and arms. He knew a great deal about internal medicine, but nothing about surgery. So he got his partner, who was an orthopedic surgeon, Dr. Win-the-War,

to take care of this fellow who had been in this bad accident. And the result is that the patient is back on his feet. He has given up his crutches. He isn't wholly well yet, and he won't be until he wins the war.

For all its varied activities, the large sums of money it spent, and its willingness to use almost any technique, the New Deal did not succeed in attaining its long-term objective. The war, not the New Deal, restored American prosperity. The fact that the New Deal failed to end the depression should not, however, obscure its major accomplishments. It saved American capitalism, and it preserved many other valuable national assets. It saved untold lives, and—perhaps equally important—it saved the self-respect of countless American citizens. It added to the nation's physical assets, and it broadened the educational and social opportunities of many Americans who hitherto had been what Roosevelt called "forgotten men." Finally, it awakened the American people to a new interest in their government and their way of life. The lasting contribution of the New Deal to its age and to posterity was this revitalizing of American democracy at a time when the democracies around the world were at their nadir.

FOR SUPPLEMENTARY READING

On labor in the 1930's consult M. Derber and others, *Labor Under the New Deal* (1957); H. Harris, *Labor's Civil War* (1940); and S. Perlman, *Labor in the New Deal Decade* (1945). On the farm problems use H. Barger and H. H. Landsberg, *American Agriculture, 1899–1939* (1942), and J. D. Black, *Parity, Parity, Parity* (1942). E. Ginzberg and associates, *Unemployed* (1943), has much useful information. On relief programs use G. Abbott, *From Relief to Social Security* (1941); R. E. Sherwood, *Roosevelt and Hopkins*; and A. E. Burns and E. A. Williams, *Federal Work, Security, and Relief Programs* (1941). A. Epstein, *Insecurity, a Challenge to America* (rev. ed., 1938) and P. H. Douglas, *Social Security in the United States* (rev. ed., 1939) are first books on the subject. Housing has a good study in C. Aronovici, *Housing the Masses* (1939), and N. Strauss, *The Seven Myths of Housing* (1944). The best volume on the T.V.A. is D. Lilienthal, *TVA: Democracy on the March* (1945) (Pb). New Deal politics are covered in the books cited at the end of Chapter 16, but add the following: H. F. Gosnell, *Champion*

Campaigner: Franklin D. Roosevelt (1952); R. G. Tugwell, *The Democratic Roosevelt* (1958); J. Farley, *Behind the Ballots* (1938); E. E. Robinson, *They Voted for Roosevelt* (1947); R. H. Jackson, *The Struggle for Judicial Supremacy* (1941); and E. S. Corwin, *Constitutional Revolution* (1941), the last two on the Supreme Court fight.

18

-»»-»»-»»-»»-»»-»»-»»-»»

From Isolation to Intervention

IN 1917, the United States embarked on what many Americans believed was a crusade to make the world safe for democracy. Three years later, most Americans were convinced that the rest of the world was beyond saving and that the United States would do well to ignore it. During the next two decades, the increasing efforts of Republican and Democratic officials to promote international cooperation and collective security always encountered the overwhelmingly isolationist spirit of the American people. Only in Latin American affairs was the government able to abandon traditional foreign policy.

After 1939, the American people were compelled to learn again the lessons of 1812 and 1917. Once more they were forced step by step to understand that isolation had made them the victims rather than the masters of events. Once more the American people debated while the rest of the world fought. The Japanese ended this debate at Pearl Harbor and the ensuing war and its aftermath put the citizens of the United States in a position of responsibility from which they could not retreat even if they had wanted to.

Peace at Bargain Rates

Convinced that the peace settlements were a failure and that their decision to participate in the war had been a mistake, Americans in

1920 seemed intent on forgetting their recent part in world events. They overlooked their enthusiasm for war in 1917 and soon convinced themselves that they had been tricked into fighting by the skill of English propagandists, the machinations of wily Continental diplomats, the naïveté of their own officials, the desire of the bankers to "save their loans," and the greed of the munition makers (or "merchants of death"). In the popular view, the peace conference demonstrated beyond doubt the folly of the decision of 1917, for it was generally believed that the meeting in Paris had shown that a noble, disinterested America would always be duped when it tried to reform the decadent, corrupt Old World.

The American people emerged from World War I overwhelmingly determined to avoid future wars. Having refused to join the League of Nations, they were equally opposed to the participation of the United States in any general plans for collective security that might require the use of force. They had crossed the Atlantic once to prevent Europe from destroying itself, and they now decided that neither they nor their children would ever recross it on a similar mission. As the current expression had it, Europe could "stew in its own juice." The average American believed that the United States could avoid future wars if it refused to fight and if it refused to participate in any diplomatic negotiations that might eventually lead to war. Maintaining peace seemed a matter of will power. War, like alcohol, was strong stuff, but Americans could swear off of it if they really wanted to.

Unfortunately for these wishes, the United States government was never again in a position after 1920 to ignore, as it once had, developments in the outside world. American businessmen had growing interests in every corner of the globe, and the State Department accepted the obligation to protect the American dollar in foreign lands. The hope of collecting war debts that former allies owed the United States required constant attention to European economics and politics. American possessions in the Caribbean and Pacific could be safeguarded only by an active diplomacy. Any attempt to pursue a policy of outright isolation was thus out of the question. The American people had repudiated Wilsonian internationalism and Theodore Roosevelt's interventionism, but their officials frequently had to use both techniques to maintain the traditional position of the United States in world affairs.

The American people would not give up overseas economic interests, sign "entangling alliances," surrender their small empire, or pay for an adequate defense in case of attack. In short, they wanted a cheap peace requiring little or no sacrifice in money or individual and national responsibility.

The conflict between America's interests and her aspirations became apparent soon after Harding took office. A host of so-called "non-political questions," American security in the Pacific and overseas business interests soon had the Administration busy in diplomatic negotiation of every sort. Once safely in office, Harding cleared up the ambiguity of the campaign of 1920 about where he and his party stood on joining the League of Nations; he had no intention of taking the United States into the League. But as early as 1922, the United States sent unofficial observers to League of Nations meetings on the opium and white-slave trade, and within a short time, American representatives were also attending conferences about trade in arms and munitions. By 1931, 212 Americans had served as United States delegates to League conferences, and five Americans were stationed permanently at Geneva to look out for United States' interests in the League. But these cautious moves did not lead the United States to take the next logical step and join the League.

Although the United States was wary of political commitments that might involve war or the use of force, it was at least susceptible to appeals for substituting law for power as an instrument of national policy. In 1923, President Harding advocated that the United States join the World Court (established the previous year), and similar recommendations were made by both parties in their platforms of 1924. The Senate, however, waited until 1926 before adopting a resolution that favored American participation in the Court, and even then made its approval contingent upon five reservations, one of which provided that the Court would not hear any disputes that involved the interests of the United States without first obtaining American consent. The League in 1929 agreed to the conditions, but the Senate refused to act until 1935, when by a narrow margin it blocked American participation in the Court. If nothing else, the Senate vote revealed that even when extraordinary precautions were taken to safeguard the interests of the United States, the representatives of the American people hesitated to approve any step that might be interpreted as a surrender of American sovereignty.

Refusal to limit the nation's sovereignty did not blind American leaders to the threat of war. To the naïve belief that the world might be ready to settle major political disputes by law, there was a parallel belief among Americans that armaments caused wars. Not understanding that political ambitions or insecurity had led to armament races and that unless diplomacy first created political security, nations would continue to arm, many prominent Americans demanded that the United States take the lead in planning to reduce the size of the world's navies.

*The American Delegates at the Washington Conference
with Mr. Hughes (center), 1921*

[WIDE WORLD]

When Senator William E. Borah introduced in February, 1921, a resolution that advocated a disarmament conference, it was almost universally approved by the American people. The Harding Administration, accordingly, in 1921 invited Great Britain, France, Japan, Italy, Belgium, Portugal, Holland, and China to such a conference. At the first plenary session of the Washington Naval Conference in November, 1921, Secretary of State Hughes not only proposed disarmament as a vague principle to be achieved in some distant day but specifically recommended a ratio of 5:5:3 for the navies of the United States, Great Britain, and Japan, respectively. As Hughes pointed out, this program meant that the United States would be compelled to scrap thirty capital ships, "with an aggregate tonnage (including that of ships in construction, if completed) of 845,740 tons," and that the three powers together would have to destroy a total of 1,878,043 tons. These proposals, while still leaving the United States and Britain the supreme naval powers, would also cut government expenses and taxes.

Three important treaties were adopted by the nations attending the Washington Conference. The Four-Power and Nine-Power treaties provided for the maintenance of the status quo in the Pacific and in eastern Asia; they represented an effort to support international co-operation in the Far East. The Washington Treaty established a ratio of 5:5:3:1.75:1.75 for the capital ships of the navies of the United States, Great Britain, Japan, France, and Italy, respectively. Ships in excess of the stipulated quotas were to be destroyed, and a ten-year moratorium on the construction of new naval craft was declared. The Geneva Disarmament Conference of 1927 failed to extend this agreement to smaller vessels, largely because of the lobbying activities of American shipbuilders. Three years later, a conference in London adopted some restrictions on the construction of smaller ships, provided a more liberal quota for the Japanese navy, and extended the ban on the construction of new ships to 1936.

Despite high American hopes, the agreements reached at the Washington and London conferences did little to guarantee the peace of the world. Because the Four-Power and Nine-Power pacts included no enforcement machinery, they remained little more than noble declarations of principle. Disarmament programs reduced the size of fleets but did not reduce the dangers of war. In 1934, Japan, having gobbled up Manchuria and being ready for further aggression, announced that it would not be bound by restrictive naval agreements after 1936. In that year, all naval powers of the world openly resumed the competition for supremacy that they had partly renounced in 1922. Instead of promoting peace, American disarmament had promoted nothing but the welfare of the American taxpayer, who was no longer required to support a large naval establishment.

The United States had thus refused to accept even the responsibilities of isolation by preparing for any eventuality through an extensive armament program. Military preparedness cost money. The American people, having no aggressive intentions, preferred a kind of disarmament that not only benefited their pocketbooks but also salved their consciences by leading them to believe that they had made a genuine—although painless—contribution to world peace.

The United States' desire to prevent war by pious works without making the necessary political and military commitments to preserve peace reached its height in the Pact of Paris. Many Americans thought that peace could be achieved simply by inducing the leaders of the nations of the world to renounce war as an instrument of national policy. In response to this widespread belief, Secretary of State Kellogg in 1928 negotiated an agreement outlawing war with Aristide Briand, the French foreign minister. The Kellogg-Briand Pact, or Pact of Paris, was eventually ratified by some sixty other nations, but it did nothing to remove the economic and political causes of war or, as the 1930's were to show, to curb aggressor nations. Most of the participating nations, including the United States, insisted on a series of qualifications that largely destroyed whatever effectiveness the pact might have had. The Treaty's only result was that several nations avoided being branded as aggressors by going to war, in the 1930's, without bothering to issue a formal declaration of war. The principal value of the Pact of Paris to the American people was not that it reduced the possibility of their going to war but that it persuaded them that they had made a noble contribution to the cause of peace without any risk or cost to themselves.

American Capital and Foreign Policy

World War I transformed the United States into a creditor nation and fundamentally altered its status in the world economy. Because of the Allies' demand for American products, exports mounted precipitously and foreign investments in the United States were liquidated to pay for American goods. American exports more than trebled between 1914 and 1919, and in the same period its international deficit of $3,686,000,000 had become a credit of $12,562,000,000. For ten years after the signing of the peace treaty, American investments abroad increased, and the value and volume of American exports remained at relatively high levels. American business and governmental leaders sought to dispose of surplus capital and goods in foreign countries. It was not until after the crash of 1929 that many Americans realized for the first time that the prosperity of the United States and the prosperity of the world were indivisible and that it was no longer possible to view international economic relations as a one-way street along which profits always traveled to rather than from the United States.

During the postwar decade, large segments of the European economy that had been destroyed during the war could be rebuilt only with outside financial assistance. American capitalists were quick to take advantage of these opportunities and to expand on their large earlier investments in Canada and Latin America. The balance of American private investments grew from nearly 3 billion dollars in 1919 to more than 8 billion in 1929.

Although Americans after the war continued their policy of direct investments in foreign raw materials such as Cuban sugar and Canadian mines, they sent considerably more money abroad to establish foreign factories than they had previously. By 1915 Americans had invested in about 250 foreign manufacturing enterprises. By the end of the twenties, such American private investments abroad totaled $7,553,300,000, nearly triple the figures for 1914 and more than ten times larger than in 1895. By 1929, in fact, American-owned factories abroad were producing many of the same kinds of goods manufactured in the United States.

An equally dramatic growth came in private American investments in foreign government and industrial securities. Between 1919 and 1929, these so-called portfolio investments were more than tripled and had reached well over 7 billion dollars. In part this growth was stimulated by an intense search for "good buys" by American bankers and stock agents eager for commissions. The careless practices that characterized the sale of domestic issues within the United States were even more apparent in dealing in international issues, for government regulations were even fewer and thinner in international finance than in the domestic economy. Literally dozens of American investment houses competed for business in such places as Bogotá, Colombia; Budapest, Hungary; and Belgrade, Yugoslavia. Scandals arising from deals to get business for American firms involved relations of the Presidents of Peru and Cuba; a small Bavarian town that needed $125,000 was persuaded by American agents looking for business to borrow $3,000,000 on Wall Street.

Despite the accelerated pace and dubious practices marking the push of American capital overseas, it cannot be said that the pattern that emerged confirmed the opinions of Lenin and other students of imperialism that such overseas expansion represented an attempt of advanced capitalist powers to postpone the final crisis of capitalism. According to Lenin, the capitalist markets at home would not be able to reabsorb profits, and financiers would be unable to make further profits on what they had already milked from their own nations; instead, capital would be sent abroad to the most backward nations in a desperate search for investment opportunities. In fact, although the rate of expansion overseas increased remarkably, the total sum involved by 1929, the year in which a major capitalist crisis started, represented a very small part—well under 10 per cent—of total American capital available for investment. The great bulk of American money stayed at home. It did not produce a further search for territorial possessions or much greater use of the small empire America already owned. Furthermore, when money did go overseas, it did not seek politically unstable or impoverished "backward areas" but overwhelmingly the most economically advanced and politically safe nations. It was Canada, not remote Asian or African villages, that took the largest share of direct investments abroad. By 1929, for example, United States firms owned about one third of the capital in Canadian industry. The location of an American factory in such other places as central Europe, while perhaps involving scandalous "kickbacks" and "payoffs" at times, helped create jobs and a higher standard of living for overseas workers, although also contributing to the social unrest common to all nations experiencing industrialization. A similar pattern can be discerned in the export of American goods after 1919—a marked increase in volume and total worth of products shipped abroad, which, however, found their outlets in the wealthier and politically more secure nations.

American Direct Investments, by Geographic Areas *
(in millions of dollars)

AREAS	1919	1929
Europe	693.5	1,340.3
Canada and Newfoundland	814.3	1,675.4
Cuba and other West Indies	567.3	1,025.5
Mexico	643.6	709.2
Central America	112.5	250.9
South America	664.6	1,719.7
Africa	31.0	117.0
Asia	174.7	446.5
Oceania	53.0	116.8

Increased productive capacity at home was stimulated by the war, and farmers and factory owners after 1918, while selling the bulk of their products at home, increasingly looked overseas for sales. Many overseas markets owned previously by Europeans had fallen into American hands during the war, and after peace returned nations like Germany and England were unable to recoup all their losses because of the effects of the war, the provisions of the peace treaties, and continuing depressions at home. Despite the growth of tariffs and other protective devices after 1920, Europe was still America's best customer and leading source of imports. By 1929, the United States had more than doubled the 1900 percentage of exports in finished manufactures, while the ratio of its imports of raw materials remained relatively fixed. Canada, again, bought more from and sold more to the United States than any other nation.

The net effect of the export of capital after the war was to con-

* Reprinted with permission from Cleona Lewis: *America's Stake in International Investments* (Washington, D. C.: The Brookings Institution, 1938), p. 606.

tribute significantly to America's favorable balance of trade throughout the 1920's. The war, however, had so weakened European economies that a large part of purchases of American goods had to be financed with American loans. The return of higher American tariff rates after 1921 also decreased the ability of Europeans to earn dollars directly in the American market. By 1919, Europe owed the United States $9,982,000,000, but by 1929, largely because of credits for postwar reconstruction, the sum had increased to $11,685,000,000. Reluctance to repay America for her contribution to what was, after all, a joint effort to defeat the Central Powers was compounded by European economic weakness and American tariff barriers. Increasingly in the 1920's Americans became irritated at Europe's slowness to meet its obligations and took its failure as further proof of the untrustworthiness of foreigners. Calvin Coolidge spoke for many Americans when he said: "They hired the money, didn't they?"

One source that the former Allies could have drawn on to meet their obligations to the United States was the reparations expected from Germany. In May, 1921, the Reparations Commissions established by the Paris Peace Conference put Germany's total reparations bill at 33 billion dollars. When Germany defaulted on its reparations transfers within a year after the commission had drawn up its schedule, the French occupied the Ruhr; and the Allies stopped payment on their war debts to the United States, despite the American insistence that there was no connection between reparations and war debts. As a result, in spite of its wish to have as little to do with Europe as possible, the United States had to take a leading part in revising the postwar international debt structure. In the years after 1923, the United States negotiated a series of agreements with the debtor nations to fund the war debts on a basis that would eventually reduce their total by approximately 50 per cent. The Dawes and Young plans, both of which were prepared by commissions headed by Americans, showed conclusively that the United States could not afford to ignore the financial relations of Germany and its principal creditors if it wanted to get its own money back.

The Dawes Plan, which went into effect in 1924, called for an annual reduction—but not in the total—of German reparations, a loan to sustain the German currency in the face of runaway inflation, and French evacuation of the Ruhr. Under the Dawes Plan, Germany resumed its payments to the Allies, who in turn resumed their payments to the United States. As the German reparations were in large part financed by American loans and as the Allied debt payments were taken out of German reparations, the whole operation amounted to a series of maneuvers by which money exported from the United States traveled through Germany to the European Allies and then back to the United States.

American private investments abroad began to decline in 1928–9, and Germany again defaulted. The Young Plan, which was inaugurated in 1929 to meet this development, reduced Germany's total reparations to $26,800,000,000 to be paid in fifty-nine annual installments. At the same time, the connection between war debts and reparations was recognized by a provision stating that any reduction in war debts would be accompanied by a proportionate cut in Germany's reparations bill. In 1931, after the world economic collapse, the Young Plan went the way of its predecessor. Germany abandoned even the pretense of meeting its obligations, and the other European nations except Finland either stopped their payments or made only insignificant payments on their war debts. By 1933, when Hitler came to power, Germany had paid approximately $4,500,000,000 in reparations and had borrowed almost $2,500,000,000 from the United States. The Allies, who had always insisted that reparations and war debts were intimately related, had paid only slightly more than $2,500,000,000 to the United States.

The Dawes and Young plans may be viewed as American attempts to resolve Europe's postwar economic problems; but neither proposed that the United States accept any responsibility for a long-term program for the economic reconstruction of Europe, and both were soon swept away by the forces that they were designed to control. After 1929, President Hoover thought that the United States should take the lead in a world-wide move to combat the depression, but his efforts were thwarted by circumstances beyond his control. In all other respects, the economic foreign policy of the United States during the postwar years was narrowly nationalistic. The United States had emerged from World War I as the world's largest creditor nation, but its businessmen continued to seek new markets abroad for their surplus goods, while at the same time the American government repeatedly raised tariff barriers to prevent the entrance of foreign goods into the United States.

The Democratic victory at the polls in 1930 and 1932 had no appreciable effect upon the conduct of American economic policy abroad. Throughout the 1930's, most Americans were engrossed in their own economic troubles. But as the decade progressed, and while the various dictator nations grew stronger, the American people—however reluctantly—were driven to the conclusion that whatever their economic relations with the world might be, the political threats of fascism overrode these. By 1940, with France defeated and Britain

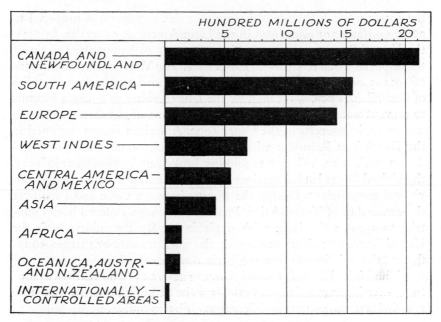

	HUNDRED MILLIONS OF DOLLARS			
	5	10	15	20
CANADA AND NEWFOUNDLAND				
SOUTH AMERICA				
EUROPE				
WEST INDIES				
CENTRAL AMERICA AND MEXICO				
ASIA				
AFRICA				
OCEANICA, AUSTR. AND N. ZEALAND				
INTERNATIONALLY CONTROLLED AREAS				

American Investments Abroad, 1940

nearly prostrate, their choice no longer lay between isolation and international cooperation but between isolation and war.

Marine Diplomacy

Although American capital had been exported to Latin America on a large scale before 1914, United States intervention in the affairs of nations south of the Rio Grande had been dictated primarily by strategic and political considerations. During the administrations of Harding and Coolidge, there was no fundamental change in the Latin American diplomacy of the United States. The Caribbean remained an American lake, and the Big Stick was used whenever it seemed necessary. But with the accession of Herbert Hoover to the presidency, these tactics were largely abandoned, and the United States undertook a program of hemispheric cooperation that provided the groundwork for Franklin D. Roosevelt's Good Neighbor Policy.

In a speech at Rio de Janeiro in 1922, Secretary of State Charles Evans Hughes declared that the United States desired the "independence, the unimpaired sovereignty and political integrity, and the constantly increasing prosperity of the peoples of Latin America." Despite the disinterested tone of this statement, the United States during the 1920's made it abundantly clear that this country was prepared to act as godfather or policeman in the Latin American countries. In 1921, the United States sent a battleship to Panama to hasten the cession of the disputed Toco territory to Costa Rica. The Washington Conference of 1922–3 on Central American Affairs, attended by the five republics of Central America, was called by the United States to devise a formula to prevent wars or revolutionary upheavals that might threaten American strategic interests in the Canal Zone. American troops stationed in the Dominican Republic when Harding took office were not withdrawn until 1924. When a revolution broke out in Honduras in 1923, the United States landed marines and took the lead in setting up a provisional government. During the dispute between Chile and Peru over the ownership of Tacna-Arica, President Coolidge ordered both countries to resolve the issue with a plebiscite. By the midtwenties the United States was either employing financial pressure or marines to influence the policies of some ten Latin American nations.

The United States' determination to resort to "marine diplomacy" to protect its economic and strategic stake in Latin America was fully revealed by its policy in Nicaragua. The withdrawal of American troops from Nicaragua in 1925 was followed by a revolution, and in the next year American forces reoccupied the country. By 1927, when 5,000 American marines were in Nicaragua, President Coolidge stated: "There is no question that if the revolution continues, American investments and . . . interests in Nicaragua will be very seriously affected, if not destroyed. . . . American as well as foreign bondholders will undoubtedly look to the United States for the protection of their interests." Americans, in Coolidge's opinion, had a "moral responsibility" in Nicaragua and were "not making war on Nicaragua any more than a policeman on the street is making war on passersby."

To restore order in Nicaragua, the United States recognized the Adolfo Diaz regime and permitted it to obtain arms from American arsenals while imposing an embargo on arms shipments to Diaz's rival, who had been recognized as Nicaragua's president by Mexico. In 1927, Henry L. Stimson, President Coolidge's special envoy to Nicaragua, induced the contending factions to accept a truce that provided for disarming the rebels, supervising new elections, and reorganizing the police force, all under American supervision. The Nicaraguan elections of 1928 and 1932 were managed to the apparent satisfaction of the country's different factions except for General Sandino, who took to the hills and waged a guerrilla campaign until he was assassinated in 1934.

The Coolidge Administration did prefer diplomatic negotiation to

Dwight Morrow Greeted in Mexico, 1927

[WIDE WORLD]

intervention in Latin America in one notable case—Mexico. The Mexican Constitution of 1917, which provided for the nationalization of her oil and mineral deposits, had aroused the fears of American investors and was largely responsible for the refusal of the United States to recognize President Obregón until 1923, when he exempted from nationalization any property acquired before the adoption of this constitution. In 1924, however, he was succeeded by President Calles, who thought the nationalization clause was retroactive. A diplomatic crisis soon developed. Some American newspapers, supported by Roman Catholics opposed to Calles' anticlerical program and by Americans with oil interests in Mexico, editorialized on the possibility of war. But President Coolidge sent Dwight W. Morrow, a Morgan partner, as ambassador to Mexico in 1927, telling him: "My only instructions are to keep us out of war with Mexico." Through a display of genuine friendship for the Mexican people, Morrow was able to win enormous popularity for himself and to reduce markedly the widespread suspicion of American motives. Through skillful and informal diplomacy, he succeeded in resolving—for the time being, at least—the vexatious dispute over nationalization. Mexico agreed to leave undisturbed the American oil rights obtained before 1917, and the Mexican Supreme Court reversed the Calles' government's earlier stand on this matter.

The Good Neighbor Policy

Dwight Morrow's successful mission to Mexico foreshadowed a fundamental shift in American relations with Latin America. At the Havana Inter-American Conference in January, 1928, some Latin American delegates criticized the interventionist policies of the United States and supported a resolution that no nation had the right to "intervene in the affairs of another." Secretary of State Hughes, who protested that any government—meaning the United States—was "fully justified in taking action . . . for the purpose of protecting the lives and property of its nationals" in any country in which they were threatened, was able to block this resolution. His victory was in reality little more than a delaying action. Latin Americans were making it increasingly clear that if this country continued to intervene in their affairs, it would have to face war and could no longer disguise its moves by posing as a benevolent but stern parent. Few nations elsewhere in the world would take seriously America's attempts to outlaw force while it repeatedly landed troops in Central America. In the face of these considerations, the Hoover Administration saw no alternative but to rely on hemispheric cooperation rather than the Big Stick.

In December, 1928, in accordance with a resolution adopted at the earlier Havana Conference, the Washington Conference on Conciliation and Arbitration drew up treaties signed by the United States which provided for the compulsory arbitration of legal disputes and the conciliatory settlement of all other disputes. The United States indicated that it would support the Washington Conference treaties when, in 1930, it published a detailed revision of its traditional interpretation of the Monroe Doctrine. Composed by J. Reuben Clark in December, 1928, the *Memorandum on the Monroe Doctrine* stated that the Theodore Roosevelt Corollary was not "justified by the terms of the Monroe Doctrine":

> So far as Latin America is concerned, the doctrine is now, and always has been, not an instrument of violence and oppression, but an un-bought and freely bestowed and wholly effective guarantee of their freedom, independence and territorial integrity against the imperialistic designs of Europe.

Between his election and his inauguration Herbert Hoover took a goodwill tour in Latin America, during which he stated that the "fear of

some persons concerning supposed intervention is . . . unfounded."
While he was President, Hoover and his advisers were able to dispel
some of the accumulated suspicion of the United States in the Central
and South American republics. Although American forces remained in
Haiti and the Hoover Administration displayed little enthusiasm for
the League of Nations' attempt to end the Chaco War between Bolivia
and Paraguay, Hoover abandoned Wilson's policy of nonrecognition
by accepting without question new governments in the Dominican
Republic, Panama, and six other nations. When El Salvador in 1932 defaulted on a bond issue, the United States refused to assist American
bankers to recover their losses. United States troops were withdrawn
from Nicaragua in 1932, and American opposition to intervention by
the League of Nations in Latin American affairs was partially abandoned when Secretary of State Stimson in February, 1933, announced
his approval of the League's proposed settlement of the dispute between
Peru and Colombia over the territory of Leticia.

Franklin D. Roosevelt broadened these policies and made them an
integral part of his conduct of foreign relations. Upon taking office on
March 4, 1933, the President stated that he planned to "dedicate this
Nation to the policy of the good neighbor—the neighbor who resolutely respects himself and, because he does so, respects the rights of
others—the neighbor who respects his obligations and respects the sanctity of his agreements in . . . a world of neighbors." President Roosevelt soon made it clear that this general policy had particular relevance
for the Latin American republics.

The Good Neighbor Policy was incorporated into a larger program of hemispheric cooperation in a series of inter-American conferences at which the United States formally abandoned the last vestiges
of interventionism. In 1933, Secretary of State Hull joined with the
other delegates at the Montevideo Conference of American States in
approving a pact one part of which stated that "no state has the right
to intervene in the internal or external affairs of another." Three years
later, at the Buenos Aires Inter-American Conference, the United
States' delegation accepted a proposal stipulating that the participating
nations would refrain from intervening "directly or indirectly, and for
whatever reason, in the internal or external affairs of any of the other
parties."

The Good Neighbor Policy received its first test in Cuba, and at
first it seemed that the old dollar diplomacy would again prevail. When
the reactionary regime of President Machado was overthrown in 1933,
the United States refused to recognize his successor, Ramón Grau San
Martín, on the ground that because American property in Cuba was

jeopardized he was not able to preserve order. President Roosevelt ordered warships to Cuban waters and withheld recognition from the new government until Carlos Mendieta, an avowed conservative acceptable to American business interests and the Cuban army, assumed the presidency in January, 1934. These strong-arm tactics, however, soon gave way to a cooperative program. In May, 1934, the Senate ratified a treaty that abrogated the American right to intervene in Cuba under the Platt Amendment. In the following year, the reciprocity treaty of 1902 was altered to permit lower duties on goods in Cuban-American trade, and the Jones-Costigan Act made possible increased imports of Cuban sugar.

Traditional police tactics were abandoned elsewhere. The recognition in 1934 of the Martinez regime in El Salvador, established by a *coup d'état*, indicated that the United States was at last prepared to accept Latin American governments regardless of how they gained office. In the same year, the American occupation of Haiti was ended; the marines withdrew, and the National City Bank sold its interests to the Haitian government. Under the terms of an agreement signed in 1936 and ratified in 1939, the United States gave up its right to intervene in Panama, renounced its unilateral guarantee of Panama's independence, and increased its annual payments for canal rights from $250,000 to $430,000.

The Roosevelt Administration also repudiated dollar diplomacy in its relations with Mexico. The Mexican government refused to compensate foreign owners of expropriated lands, and in 1938, President Cardenas decreed the seizure of all foreign-owned properties in petroleum. Although the Mexican government put the value of these holdings at a fraction of their true worth, the United States never even hinted that it planned to intervene to uphold the economic interests of its nationals. After protracted negotiations, the two countries reached a settlement on November 19, 1941. The amount of compensation for expropriated oil properties was to be fixed by a commission composed of representatives of Mexico and the United States, and Mexico agreed to satisfy all other property claims with the payment of $40,000,000 over a period of seventeen years.

The Good Neighbor Policy also involved a program of economic cooperation that emphasized the advent of a new era. Trade between the United States and other nations of the hemisphere was promoted by the reciprocity treaties that Secretary of State Hull negotiated with fifteen different Latin American states before 1943. The export of United States capital to the Central and South American countries, which before the New Deal had been largely restricted to private investments, was increasingly taken over by the federal government. By December 31, 1941, the Export-Import Bank had authorized over 3 billion dollars in government loans to Latin America, and Mexico, Brazil, and Argentina had obtained from the United States large loans that might prove mutually beneficial to the United States and the borrowing nations.

These dramatic shifts in economic and political policy, accompanied after 1938 by a large program of education and "cultural interchange," bore excellent fruit. The more intelligent and tactful pursuit of self-interest that inspired the Good Neighbor Policy prepared the way for a system of hemispheric security to safeguard the Western hemisphere. European and Asian aggressors increasingly impelled the American republics to cooperate for collective defense. The Inter-American conferences at Montevideo and Buenos Aires had been incidentally concerned with the defense of the Americas, but the Lima Conference in 1938 recognized hemispheric security as the paramount problem because of Hitler's diplomatic victory at Munich. The Declaration of Lima reaffirmed "continental solidarity," the principles established at earlier conferences, and the sovereignty of the American republics "against all foreign intervention or activity that may threaten them." Less than a month after the outbreak of war in Europe in 1939, the American and Latin-American foreign ministers assembled at Panama and put teeth in the Declaration of Lima by adopting detailed proposals for safeguarding the neutrality and independence of the American nations. Again at Havana, in July, 1940, they approved a declaration that "any attempt on the part of a non-American state against the integrity or inviolability of the territory, the sovereignty or the political independence of an American state shall be considered an act of aggression against the states which sign this declaration." Plans were also drawn up for establishing the machinery to make this declaration effective.

When the Japanese attacked Pearl Harbor on December 7, 1941, the United States knew that its southern neighbors would stand as partners in a common enterprise to safeguard the future of the Western hemisphere.

Retreat in the Far East

In the 1930's, United States prestige and power in Latin America were strengthened as the nation gave up former policies and tried to become a good neighbor. In the Far East, an equally dramatic change in policy took place, but in this case American fortunes suffered a disastrous decline.

Both the Big Stick and Open Door in China policies rested on the same assumption: stronger nations were responsible for the stability or well-being of weaker nations. The Open Door policy had been intended to preserve the territorial integrity of China, but at the same time it permitted the economic exploitation of China by outside nations. Should any of these nations come to believe that it was entitled to paramount privileges in East Asia and decide that it would risk war to gain these objectives, the United States would be faced with the painful choice of abandoning the Open Door or of going to war to save it.

After 1900, the United States wished to maintain the status quo in the Pacific and Eastern Asia. Because Japan had greater opportunity than any other nation to upset existing territorial arrangements in the Orient, American diplomacy in the Far East became essentially anti-Japanese. To check Japan, the United States sought to shore up China, which American officials regarded as the keystone in the shaky arch of Far Eastern relations.

Although the American people endorsed their government's objectives in the Far East, they were not prepared to use force to achieve them; and for the first two decades of the twentieth century, Japan steadily extended its influence beyond the borders of its home islands. After five years of occupation, Japan formally annexed Korea in 1910. During World War I, when the attention of other major powers was concentrated on Europe, Japan extorted a number of far-reaching concessions from China. Although compelled to abandon some of these in the postwar settlements of 1919–20, she still retained her economic interests in Shantung and obtained mandates over the former German islands in the Carolines, Marshalls, and Marianas. Although Japan under the terms of the League Covenant was not allowed to fortify her mandated islands, no machinery existed to enforce this provision. By 1921, Japan had become the most powerful nation in the Far East and was in a position to threaten not only the independence of China, but even American interests in the Philippines.

In the past, dollar diplomacy, occasional displays of power, and solemn pronouncements unsupported by force had only temporarily checked the Japanese advance. In attempting to maintain the status quo in the Far East by balance-of-power politics, the United States learned after repeated setbacks that there was no nation in the Orient strong or trustworthy enough to serve as a counterbalance to Japan. Although the Harding Administration turned its back on the League of Nations, a system of collective security in the Far East seemed to be the only alternative for the United States.

Harding's collective-security program for the Far East was inaugurated at the Washington Conference of 1922 with the adoption of the Four-Power and Nine-Power treaties. In the Four-Power Treaty, the United States, Great Britain, France, and Japan agreed to respect one another's rights in the Pacific and to discuss any conflicts in a joint conference. If their rights were threatened by the aggression of any other power, each was to communicate with the others before taking action.

The Nine-Power Treaty, signed by all the nations attending the conference, was designed to make more effective the "principles of the Open Door or equality of opportunity in China" and to preserve China's independence. The powers agreed to respect China's "sovereignty, independence, and . . . territorial and administrative integrity," and to maintain "the principle of equal opportunity for the commerce . . . of all nations" throughout China. All were to refrain from seeking special privileges in China that might interfere with the existing rights of subjects of friendly states.

American adherence to the Four-Power and Nine-Power pacts imposed no obligations on the United States and did not alter its foreign policy in the Far East in any fundamental respect. Neither agreement contained any provision for enforcement. Nor was an attempt made to erect an effective balance-of-power system to hold Japan in check. Russia was the only nation with interests in the Far East that could have served as a counterpoise to Japan in such a balance, but the widespread fear of Communism kept the Soviet Union outside any system of collective security. When the conference adjourned, Japan was still the most powerful nation in the Far East, and no effective steps had been taken to prevent its continued advance. In the language of power politics, the Four-Power and Nine-Power pacts were "scraps of paper."

For almost a decade after 1922, Japan sought to achieve what it considered its legitimate objectives in the Far East by ostensible cooperation and friendship with the United States. A constant tug of war in Japanese politics between those friendly to America and jingo militarists believing in Japan's mission to dominate East Asia gradually gave the jingoes the upper hand. When diplomacy and peaceful economic penetration failed to answer Japan's need to find raw materials, markets, and outlets for excess population, the Japanese authorities embarked on a program of undisguised aggression in Manchuria. For some years, Japanese privileges there had included jurisdiction over all her nationals and the right to maintain troops along the South Manchurian

Railway. In 1931, Japan used an incident along this railway as a pretext for a full-scale invasion of Manchuria. Since no nation was willing to stop the Japanese armies, they quickly overran the entire province. In 1932, Japan transformed Manchuria into the puppet state of Manchukuo.

The Japanese invasion of Manchuria was a flagrant violation of both the Kellogg-Briand Pact and the Nine-Power Treaty. At the outset of the conflict, Secretary of State Stimson informed the Japanese that they were not living up to their treaty obligations. When his protest produced no visible effect, Stimson sent an American representative to the League Council as an "observer and auditor" during its sessions on the Manchurian crisis. The League Council invoked the Kellogg-Briand Pact against the Japanese in October, 1931, and appointed a commission under the chairmanship of Lord Lytton to investigate the situation in Manchuria. The Japanese, however, continued their advance. The United States, Secretary Stimson concluded, could "not condone the tearing up of the treaties, and if it would not take any military or economic action to defend them," it must refuse to recognize the Japanese conquests. Accordingly, on January 7, 1932, Stimson stated in a note to China and Japan that the United States "does not intend to recognize any situation, treaty or agreement which may be brought about by means contrary to the covenants and obligations of the Pact of Paris of August 27, 1928, to which Treaty both China and Japan, as well as the United States, are parties."

When Stimson announced this policy of nonrecognition, he understood that it was nothing more than "a moral weapon, a moral sanction." Japan could be stopped only by force, and the American people had no intention of fighting or even of threatening to fight Japan in order to free Manchuria. Overwhelmed by problems arising out of the depression and opposed to intervention in a remote and little-known corner of the globe, most Americans viewed Stimson's stand with either lack of interest or hostility. The effectiveness of his note to Japan was further reduced by the refusal of any other major power to adopt a similar policy. Stimson had hoped for British cooperation, but it was announced that "His Majesty's Government have not considered it necessary to address any formal note to the Japanese Government on the lines of the American Government's note." Nor did the League give any assistance, for the Lytton Commission's report, though critical of the Japanese attack, led to no action.

When the Chinese protested the invasion of Manchuria by boycotting Japanese goods, Japan in January, 1932, attacked Shanghai. Stimson, unable to win the major powers over to a protest against Japan's violation of the Nine-Power Treaty, was again the only important statesman to condemn Japanese aggression. He did not send another formal note to the Japanese, but in a widely publicized letter to Senator *Stimson* Borah, he reiterated the United States government's opposition to Japanese aggression.

The Japanese conquest of Manchuria and the attack on Shanghai brought into the open the deficiencies of the collective-security system fashioned by the United States. No nation with interests in the Far East was either willing or able to resort to force to stop the Japanese advance. The United States, which took the firmest stand in 1931-2, was no more prepared than any other country to take positive steps to check Japanese expansion. Protests unsupported by force were a language that the officials of Japan could both understand and ignore. Japan's invasion of Manchuria posed a problem for the United States that could not be postponed indefinitely. Eventually the American people would be forced to decide whether they wished to abandon their traditional objectives in the Far East or to uphold them by force of arms.

The Quest for Neutrality

If anything, the Great Depression reinforced the widely held American view that the United States should concentrate on its own problems and ignore those beyond its borders. Events abroad seemed to most Americans to demonstrate that the rest of the world was no longer worth saving. Japan's victory in Manchuria, Mussolini's blatant nationalism, and the rise to power of the Nazis in Germany all contributed to the American conviction that the United States had better—as the current expression went—"put its own house in order" without wasting its energy on attempts to support an international order that was obviously collapsing.

Some liberal supporters of Franklin Roosevelt's New Deal, as well as many of the Administration's conservative critics, believed that the United States should refuse to assume even a limited responsibility for the fate of the rest of the world. A few years earlier, many of these same New Dealers had been among the most enthusiastic supporters of Woodrow Wilson's plans for the League. By 1933, however, they were arguing that international cooperation was no longer feasible. In their minds, the problems of the rest of the world were beyond American strength; "save America first" was the wisest motto. Committed to the idea that governmental planning could restore American prosperity, they thought that international planning for peace was, for the time being, incompatible with domestic programs for recovery. With the conversion of these liberals to isolationism, all but a handful of Americans abandoned the view that the United States had any obligations to the other nations of the world.

Roosevelt himself was, at first, in sympathy with the views of the liberal isolationists. Although he had campaigned for the League as the Democratic vice-presidential candidate in 1920, in the preconvention contest for the Democratic nomination, he made it clear that he did not intend to revive the issue. Before the New York State Grange in 1932, he stated his new position:

> American participation in the League would not serve the highest purpose of the prevention of war and a settlement of international difficulties in accordance with fundamental American ideals. Because of these facts, therefore, I do not favor American participation.
>
> What the world needs most today is a national policy which will make us an example of national honor to other nations.

Once in power, like the Republicans before them, the New Dealers often wavered without any apparent pattern between isolationist and internationalist policies. In 1934, the United States joined the International Labor Office of the League of Nations, and in the following year, the Administration made a futile effort to induce the Senate to permit America to join the World Court. Recognition of the Soviet Union by the United States in 1933 reflected the desire of the Administration to increase American overseas trade and the awareness of the American people that the Communist dictatorship was not going to be overthrown by the Russian people. These tentative moves toward a greater measure of international cooperation were more than offset, however, by the economic policies of the New Deal. Soon after taking office, President Roosevelt withdrew American support from the London Economic Conference. Unlike Hoover, Roosevelt was apparently convinced that domestic recovery took precedence over world recovery, and throughout most of the depression years, the United States was committed to a form of economic nationalism that was only slightly mitigated by the Hull reciprocal trade treaties. The same spirit of economic nationalism was revealed in Congress with the passage of the Johnson Act in 1934, outlawing private American loans to nations that had not paid their "war debts."

The isolationism of the early 1930's was predicated in large part on the assumption that the United States could remain at peace by simply

"Galley Slaves" (*Doyle in the Philadelphia* Record)

refusing to fight and by maintaining peace by statute. A prevailing belief was that business and political leaders were responsible for wars
in general and for the last war in particular. Several popular books appeared in the decade and a half after Versailles suggesting that the
United States had gone to war in 1917 because of the machinations of
its bankers and munitions-makers, the gullibility of its public officials,
and the ease with which its citizens had been taken in by Allied propaganda. Many Americans found their prejudices about the role of businessmen in war confirmed by the Nye Committee hearings in 1934,
which revealed that many citizens had made a great deal of money during World War I, although they did not prove that businessmen were
responsible for American participation in the conflict.

The general feeling that a nation's leaders rather than its people were responsible for war led directly to the adoption by Congress of measures designed to prevent American officials from bringing the country to the brink of war. By the midthirties events in Europe seemed to demonstrate the need for such legislation. In 1935, Italy invaded Ethiopia, Hitler began to rearm in violation of the Versailles Treaty, and Japan abandoned any pretense of abiding by the agreed ratios for naval limitation. In the following year, Germany remilitarized the Rhineland, civil war divided Spain into two armed camps, and Hitler and Mussolini announced the formation of the Rome-Berlin Axis. In 1937, Japan began its undeclared war against China. Fearful that these events in Europe, Asia, and Africa would involve the United States in war, Congress sought to keep the United States at peace by neutrality acts forbidding any economic or political commitments to belligerent nations.

The Neutrality Act of 1935 was a response to the crisis precipitated by Mussolini's attack on Ethiopia. Congress imposed an embargo upon the export of war matériel to belligerents and warned American citizens traveling on belligerent ships not to expect American protection. Following Italy's invasion of Ethiopia, the President announced an embargo on arms shipments to Italy, and two days later, the League Council agreed to apply sanctions against Italy. The United States government decided to cooperate with the League and asked American exporters to halt shipments of war matériel to Italy. But when Mussolini made it clear to Britain and France that sanctions might mean war, the League program broke down, and the Roosevelt Administration was left in the embarrassing position of asking Americans to uphold voluntarily a program that had been rejected by its authors.

The events of 1935 convinced many Americans that the United States should exercise even greater vigilance to maintain its neutrality, and in February, 1936, the original act was expanded to prohibit loans to belligerents. Because the existing laws did not apply to civil wars, Congress in January, 1937, adopted a joint resolution forbidding the export of munitions "for the use of either of the opposing forces in Spain." Finally, in May, 1937, Congress passed still another neutrality act. This measure not only included essential features of the earlier bills, but also provided that no belligerent nation could obtain raw materials from the United States unless it paid for them on delivery and imported them in its own vessels. The so-called "cash-and-carry" clause of the Neutrality Act of 1937 indicated that Americans wished to stay out of war, but not to renounce the profits of war. By 1938 American money and matériel were again for sale, as they had been after 1914.

Neutrality Legislation of the 1930's

YEAR	TITLE	PURPOSE
1934	Johnson Debt Default Act	Prohibited loans to any foreign government in default to the United States.
1935	Neutrality Act of 1935 (Duration: 6 months)	Authorized President to prohibit all arms shipments and U. S. citizens from traveling on belligerent vessels except at their own risks.
1936	Neutrality Act of 1936 (Duration: 1 year)	Extended Neutrality Act of 1935 to May, 1937. Forbade loans or credits to belligerents.
1937	Neutrality Acts of 1937 (Duration: 2 years)	(1) Applied Neutrality Act of 1936 to Spanish Civil War. (2) Authorized President to list commodities, other than munitions, for cash and carry exports. Made travel on belligerent ships unlawful.
1939	Neutrality Act of 1939	Repealed arms embargo and authorized "cash and carry" exports of arms and munitions to belligerents.

Isolationists and Interventionists

Although the neutrality legislation imposed certain restrictions on the nation's officials, it did not—and could not—curb people's loyalties. The dilemma that confronted the American people was clearly revealed by the Spanish Civil War. Soon after the Nationalist revolutionaries—led by General Francisco Franco and supported by large groups of the Spanish clergy, army, and aristocracy—started the war, Americans found that it was almost impossible not to take sides. The intensity of the conflict in Spain and its effect upon American public opinion were heightened by the brutality displayed by the contending forces, the aid that Communist Russia dispatched to the Loyalists, or Republicans, and the military assistance—including troops—that Fascist Italy and Nazi Germany sent to the Nationalists. Many American liberals, who a short time before had been outspoken isolationists, began to demand that the United States provide some form of active support for the Loyalists. Joined by American Communists and Communist sympathizers, these groups formed numerous organizations to aid the Loyalists, and by the end of the Spanish Civil War, millions of American dollars and approximately 3,000 American men had crossed the Atlantic to aid the enemies of Franco. At the same time, many—but not all—American Catholics, who believed that Russian intervention in Spain had converted the war into an unholy crusade against Roman Catholic Christianity, were equally determined in their support of the Nationalists.

American Volunteers Returning from Spain

[WIDE WORLD]

Although Americans could congratulate themselves on their success in maintaining strict neutrality, many of them were aghast at the results of this policy. When Guernica was razed by Fascist bombs in 1937, prominent Americans condemned this display of brutality; even Senator William E. Borah, who for years had been considered one of the nation's leading isolationists, said:

> So long as men and women may be interested in searching out from the pages of history outstanding acts of cruelty and instances of needless destruction of human life they will linger longest and with the greatest horror over the . . . story of the fascist war in Spain. . . . Guernica was not a single instance; it was merely the culmination of a long line of unspeakable atrocities.

Events in Germany, like those in Spain, horrified many Americans. They were alarmed by Hitler's imperialistic rantings and revolted by the Nazi persecution of the Jews, the repeated pronouncements of Nordic supremacy, and the systematic destruction of German democ-

U. S. Marine Guarding Americans in Shanghai, 1937

[BROWN BROTHERS]

racy and trade-unionism. Equally disturbing was the fashion in which the German-American Bund and demagogues like Father Coughlin, a Michigan priest, accepted and preached Nazi and fascist doctrines. In response to these developments, some Americans acted in a thoroughly unneutral manner. When demonstrators were arrested in 1935 for ripping down the Nazi flag from the German liner Bremen in New York harbor, the judge hearing the case denounced the Nazis in such violent terms that the German government lodged an official protest in Washington. In 1937, Mayor Fiorello La Guardia of New York proposed the erection of a chamber of horrors at the city's World's Fair for "that brown-shirted fanatic who is now menacing the peace of the world."

The outbreak of war between Japan and China in 1937 produced further confusion among Americans. They were indignant and horrified over Japanese aggression, but this attitude did not preclude them from leaving China to fend for itself. Newspapers and public speakers condemned the Japanese, but the United States did little to assist China or to check Japan.

As the dictator nations accelerated their tempo of aggression, the Roosevelt Administration began a cautious attempt to abandon economic nationalism and political isolation for a positive program of strengthening America's moral and military defenses. The President made no move to have the Neutrality Acts repealed, but he indicated that he thought that American security was imperiled by developments abroad. On October 5, 1937, in what came to be known as the "quarantine" speech, Roosevelt said:

> It seems to be unfortunately true that the epidemic of world lawlessness is spreading.
>
> When an epidemic of physical disease starts to spread, the community . . . joins in a quarantine of the patients in order to protect the health of the community against the spread of the disease. . . .
>
> War is a contagion, whether it be declared or undeclared. It can engulf states and peoples remote from the original scene of hostilities. We are determined to keep out of war, yet we cannot insure ourselves against the disastrous effects of war and the dangers of involvement. We are adopting such measures as will minimize our risk of involvement, but we cannot have complete protection in a world of disorder in which confidence and security have broken down. . . .

In the following year, on October 18, 1938, the President assured a Canadian audience at Kingston, Ontario, that the "United States will not stand idly by if Canada . . . [ever] is threatened by any other nation." Although the President did little to back up his words with political measures designed to strengthen the democracies in Europe, he was at least determined to repair American defenses. As early as January, 1938, he asked Congress to appropriate a billion dollars for the construction of a two-ocean navy. Twelve months later, when it was decided to re-establish a permanent Atlantic squadron, the United States was fully committed to the concept, if not the reality, of a two-ocean navy.

No amount of isolationist arguments or moral condemnation of aggressors by the President could change the course of events in Europe. In 1936, Hitler announced the remilitarization of the Rhineland; and in March, 1938, Austria was incorporated into the Third Reich. Prime Minister Neville Chamberlain, on returning to England in 1938 from Munich, where he and Premier Daladier of France had permitted Hitler to acquire the Sudetenland, announced that he had achieved "peace in our time." Eight months later, Germany occupied all of Czechoslovakia. The capstone in Hitler's preparations for world conquest was put in place with the signing of the Russian-German Pact in

August, 1939. Two weeks later, on September 1, Hitler's armies marched into Poland. England and France declared war on Germany. World War II had begun.

The outbreak of war in Europe widened rather than narrowed the split in American public opinion over the nation's foreign policy. The President at first lagged behind what public opinion might have supported in the way of measures to help England and France. The vociferousness of isolationists, their influential, although minority, position in Congress, the Neutrality Act provisions, and the fear of alienating blocs of voters of Italian or German ancestry held Roosevelt back. Very soon, however, the war demonstrated the need for strengthening American defenses, for asserting the moral leadership of the United States, and for aiding the enemies of the Axis countries. To opponents of the President's increasing interventionism, the war offered further proof of the necessity for isolating America from conflicts in Europe and Asia. After September, 1939, the isolationists included many midwesterners who still adhered to a once respected tradition, some native fascists, the members of the German-American Bund, conservatives who feared Russia more than Germany, and the remnants of the American pacifist movement. They were in many ways a strange crew, for within their ranks could be found rabble rousers like Gerald L. K. Smith, publishers like Robert McCormick of the Chicago *Tribune*, businessmen like Robert E. Wood of Sears, Roebuck, German-Americans like Fritz Kuhn of the Bund, politicians like Senator Burton K. Wheeler of Montana and Representative Hamilton Fish of New York, and an indeterminate number of sincere idealists whose aversion to war overrode all other considerations. American Communists were enthusiastic isolationists as long as the Soviet-German Pact lasted. As soon as Germany invaded Russia, they became equally enthusiastic interventionists.

Many of the isolationist groups in the United States eventually joined forces in the America First Committee and sought through speeches, pamphlets, and articles to win a majority of the American people over to isolationism and to prevent Congress from adopting measures that might jeopardize peace. Charles A. Lindbergh—who had won fame because of his solo flight across the Atlantic in 1927 and whose father, as a member of the House of Representatives, had voted against war in 1917—was the committee's most famous member and one of its principal spokesmen. From September, 1939, until the Japanese attack on Pearl Harbor, the isolationists tried to reconcile the irreconcilable. Maintaining that the Axis powers could not be beaten, they concluded that the United States should come to terms with the

The "Lone Eagle" (center right) at an America First Rally (Senator Wheeler at his right)

dictators. They saw no inconsistency in also stating that the United States was capable of defending itself without allies against a hostile world. The Atlantic and Pacific oceans seemed to isolationists as formidable barriers as they had been in the days of the sailing ship. On the one hand, they thought air power had made Germany invincible. On the other, they apparently did not consider air power a threat to the security of the United States.

The more isolationists talked about American interests, the more they seemed to be defending Germany's interests. Although most America Firsters were not Nazi sympathizers, they were wholeheartedly supported by the native Nazis, and several isolationist congressmen permitted the German-American Bund to use their franking privilege to distribute pro-Nazi propaganda free of charge throughout the United States.

The most convincing answer to isolationist arguments was supplied by events in Europe. Following six months of inaction in the "phony war," Hitler's armies in the spring of 1940 overran Denmark, Norway, Belgium, Holland, and then France. To Americans who did not subscribe to the doctrines of the America First Committee, the fall of France was an overwhelming catastrophe that marked the end of an era in Western civilization. The disaster was only partly mitigated by the evacuation of the British Expeditionary Force from Dunkirk. In subsequent months, when Britain stood alone, freedom-loving people took heart from the valiant defense put up by the Royal Air Force against the Nazi bombers and admired the courage of the English people, who refused to be terrorized into submission. Only extreme isolationists seemed unmoved by the struggle. They had always been inclined to blame "perfidious Albion" for many of America's ills, and they now believed that England was certain to fall and that the United States must stand alone.

The Roosevelt Administration viewed the German advance as conclusive evidence of the need for bold and forthright action by the United States. In the months that followed, the President dropped all pretense of being neutral in thought or action. On June 10, 1940, when Italy invaded southern France after the Germans had overpowered the French armies, Roosevelt in a memorable speech at the University of Virginia said that the "hand that held the dagger has struck it into the back of its neighbor," and he added:

> In our American unity we will pursue two obvious and simultaneous courses; we will extend to the opponents of force the material resources of this nation, and, at the same time, we will harness and speed up the use of those resources in order that we ourselves in the Americas may have equipment and training equal to the task of any emergency and every defense.

President Roosevelt's program to strengthen the defenses of both Britain and the United States was supported by a large proportion of the city dwellers on the Atlantic and Pacific coasts, and by most of the southern members of his party. A Committee to Defend America by Aiding the Allies, led by William Allen White and endorsed by prominent Americans from every walk of life, undertook a full-scale—and generally successful—campaign to educate their fellow citizens to the necessity for rushing supplies to beleaguered Britain.

By 1940, Roosevelt and most of his supporters had reached the conclusion that the world situation made it imperative that he break the two-term tradition for presidents. The Democratic convention was completely dominated by Administration forces, and Roosevelt was nominated for a third term. Largely because of Roosevelt's insistence, Secretary of Agriculture Henry Wallace was given second place on the ticket. The party's platform reaffirmed the Administration's domestic and foreign policies. When the Republicans met at Philadelphia, the leading candidates of the party professionals were Senator Arthur

Wendell Willkie

Vandenberg of Michigan, Senator Robert Taft of Ohio, and District Attorney Thomas Dewey of New York. At the grass-roots level of the party, Wendell Willkie, a former Democrat and president of a public utility company, was easily the most popular candidate. The division among the party leaders and Willkie's well-organized show of popularity determined the result. Although Dewey led on the first three ballots, Willkie was ahead on the fourth, and two ballots later he was nominated. The Republican platform criticized, but did not repudiate, virtually all of the New Deal's domestic program, and on the great foreign issue of the day it stated: "We favor the extension to all peoples fighting for liberty, or whose liberty is threatened, of such aid as shall not be in violation of international law or inconsistent with the requirements of our own national defense."

Roosevelt made only a few campaign speeches, but the energetic and personable Willkie traveled extensively, spoke often, and discussed the major questions before the voters in a forthright fashion. A firm believer in the need for American preparedness and assistance to the Allies, he refused to make foreign policy a campaign issue. At the same time, his approval (despite certain qualifications) of most of the New Deal's social and economic objectives left him in a position where he could do little more than promise to carry out the Democratic program more efficiently than the Democrats had done. In going down to defeat (by a popular vote of 27,244,160 to 22,305,198 and an electoral vote of 449 to 82), Willkie at least had the satisfaction of knowing that he had conducted his campaign on a high level and that he had helped to demonstrate that American democracy had retained its vitality in a period of crisis and in a world at war.

Measures Short of War

Soon after the outbreak of war in Europe, Congress at the President's request repealed the provisions for an arms embargo in the neutrality legislation. Not, however, until the Nazi "blitzkrieg" against France did the government undertake a broad program to promote national security and assist the enemies of Hitler. Following the President's request on May 16, 1940, for "at least 50,000 planes a year," Congress passed a series of appropriation bills that provided for a spectacular increase in American military expenditures. Plans to build up the Atlantic fleet to equal the strength of the Pacific squadrons were accelerated. In the summer of 1940, the National Guard was made a part of the regular army, and the United States adopted its first peacetime conscription act. Of defense measures, only the fight for a draft was strongly opposed by the critics of the President's foreign policy. The isolationists and pacifists were unable to prevent the passage of the conscription act, but they limited its effectiveness through an amendment that prohibited drafted men from being sent outside the United States and its possessions.

The Roosevelt Administration ran head on into the isolationists when it sought to find ways and means to assist Britain. One by one the provisions of the Neutrality Acts of the 1930's had to be repealed or by-passed in order to help England after the fall of France. In June, 1940, the United States made available to England a large supply of guns and ammunition that had been manufactured during World War I. Two months later, the President concluded an agreement providing for the transfer to the British of more than fifty "over-age" destroyers (which had been used in World War I) in exchange for a ninety-nine-year rent-free lease on sites for naval bases in the British West Indies, British Guiana, Bermuda, and Newfoundland. The bargain was drawn up in secrecy, and the President presented it to Congress as a *fait accompli*. Although the isolationists were bitter in denouncing both the agreement and Roosevelt's methods of obtaining it, Congress in essence ratified the arrangement by appropriating the funds to carry out its provisions. In the months that followed the announcement of the destroyer-bases agreement, the United States transferred bombing planes and revenue-cutters to the British, and more American factories began to produce war matériel for both the United States and England.

Despite these extraordinary measures taken by the President to convert the United States into what he called the "arsenal of democracy," it soon became apparent that England was unable to continue to pay for the war goods produced by American industry. The same problem had been solved in 1914–17 through private loans, but Roosevelt proposed a far more sweeping and statesmanlike solution. In his annual message to Congress on January 6, 1941, the President said:

> I . . . ask this Congress for authority and . . . funds sufficient to manufacture additional munitions and war supplies of many kinds, to be turned over to those nations which are now in actual war with aggressor nations.
>
> Our most useful and immediate role is to act as an arsenal for them as well as for ourselves. They do not need man power. They do need billions of dollars worth of the weapons of defense. . . .
>
> For what we send abroad, we shall be repaid, within a reasonable time following the close of hostilities, in similar materials, or at our option, in other goods of many kinds which they can produce and which we need.

The Lend-Lease bill, which was introduced into Congress in January, 1941, authorized the President to sell, exchange or lease any "defense article" to any anti-Axis country in return for "payment in kind or property, or any other direct or indirect benefit which the President deems satisfactory." An extended debate followed. Over the objections of the isolationists, the Lend-Lease bill was adopted on March 11, 1941, and Congress made an initial appropriation of 7 billion dollars to carry out its provisions. It is impossible to overestimate the significance of Lend-Lease. It provided for the transfer of military goods with maximum flexibility and a minimum of red tape and told the world that the United States was prepared to use its vast productive—if not its military—resources to check the advance of the dictators. The bulk of the early shipments under Lend-Lease went to the British Isles, but after the Soviet Union was invaded by Germany in June, 1941, it received an increasingly large supply of such goods. By September, 1942, thirty-five countries, as well as the British Commonwealth of Nations, had obtained assistance from the United States under the Lend-Lease Act.

Although the Roosevelt Administration had provided the goods for the anti-Axis coalition, German submarines were sending them to the bottom of the Atlantic. Direct American intervention in the war in the North Atlantic became imperative. The Soviet Union was not equipped to wage antisubmarine warfare, and the British were unable to spare additional planes and ships for U-boat work. Under the circumstances, the President concluded that the United States would have to increase its merchant tonnage and use its warships to assist the British and Canadians in convoy work. Participation in convoying would obviously move the United States closer to full-scale participation in the war, and the American people were reluctant to make what was tantamount to an act of war against the Axis. The President, sensing the need for convoy work and fearing public resistance to it, was never altogether frank in his public discussions of the growing role of the United States Navy in the early stages of the war in the North Atlantic.

In April, 1941, American troops established a base in Greenland, and three months later American troops began to replace the British forces in Northern Ireland. American planes and war vessels were also used to guard shipments across the Atlantic. The President originally stated that the American navy was only being used for patrol duty in the North Atlantic, but neither the Germans nor the mass of Americans were able to discover the difference between patrol and convoy duties. In May, 1941, in proclaiming an unlimited national emergency, the President told the American people that the Atlantic patrol was "helping . . . to insure the delivery of needed supplies to Britain" and that "all additional measures necessary to deliver the goods will be taken." Roosevelt justified his acts by an appeal to the traditional doctrine of "freedom of the seas," but a more frank appraisal of events would have emphasized strategic necessity. If the control of the Atlantic were to pass into the hands of the Axis, the security of the United States would be jeopardized.

As the Americans extended their naval arm over the Atlantic and the Germans pushed the war zone closer to the United States, incidents were inevitable. In May, 1941, an American merchantman, the *Robin Moor*, was sunk by a German submarine, which left the ship's crew and passengers to their own devices in small boats on the open sea. Some four months later, the President announced that the American destroyer *Greer* had been "attacked" while on "patrol" by a German submarine. With the torpedoing of the *U.S.S. Kearny* on October 17 and the sinking of the *U.S.S. Reuben James* two weeks later, all pretense of patrol was abandoned. On October 27, the President said: "We Americans have cleared our decks and taken our battle stations." The line between all aid short of war and a shooting war was becoming thinner every day. Despite the protests and delaying tactics of the isolationists, Congress made the law conform to the reality by repealing on November 13 the remainder of the neutrality legislation.

While seeking to reinforce the enemies of Hitler, President Roosevelt also sought to impress on the world the extent of American hostility toward the Axis countries. He repeatedly denounced the rulers of Germany, and he repeatedly made clear his conviction that Britain (and after June, 1941, Russia) were fighting American battles. On May 27, 1941, he pointed out what he considered the inevitable peace terms under a German victory would be:

> . . . under those terms Germany would literally parcel out the world—hoisting the swastika itself over vast territories and populations, and setting up puppet governments of its own choosing, wholly subject to the will and policy of a conqueror. . . .
>
> No, I am not speculating about this. I merely repeat what is already in the Nazi book of world conquest. They plan to treat the Latin American nations as they are now treating the Balkans. They plan to strangle the United States of America and the Dominion of Canada.

In August, 1941, a secret dramatic meeting between President Roosevelt and Prime Minister Churchill was held in the North Atlantic. From this meeting there emerged the Atlantic Charter. In eight sections, the Atlantic Charter stated the two leaders' objectives and aspirations in a world at war in language strongly reminiscent of Woodrow Wilson's Fourteen Points. Roosevelt and Churchill pledged their countries to policies of democratic self-determination for nations, economic well-being and social security for all peoples, and postwar collective action against aggressors.

Although directed primarily against Germany and Italy and seemingly unaware of what the Soviet Union would say to these proposals, the ideals of the Atlantic Charter were soon tested by Japan as well as the European Axis powers.

The Day of Infamy

The Roosevelt Administration's preoccupation with the war in Europe and the North Atlantic did not blind it to the Japanese threat to American security in the Far East and the Pacific. As early as 1934, Joseph C. Grew, United States ambassador to Japan, had forecast in a cable to his superiors in Washington that Japan planned to:

> obtain trade control and eventually predominant political in-
> fluence in China, the Philippines, the Straits Settlements, Siam
> and the Dutch East Indies, the Maritime Provinces and Vlad-
> ivostock, one step at a time, as in Korea and Manchuria, paus-
> ing intermittently to consolidate and then continuing as soon
> as the intervening obstacles can be overcome by diplomacy
> or force.

If any doubt remained concerning Japan's expansionist policies, it was removed by the "China incident." After fighting broke out between Japanese and Chinese troops near Peiping in July, 1937, Japan launched a full-scale war against China. Japan's attack on China was denounced by a conference of nineteen nations meeting at Brussels (November 3–24, 1937), but the Japanese ignored world opinion and continued their offensive. American citizens in China were killed or injured as a result of the war, and reports of Japanese atrocities appeared in the American press. When the *Panay*, an American gunboat on the Yangtze River, was bombed and sunk by Japanese planes on December 12, 1937, some alarmists thought war unavoidable; but most Americans had no desire to fight a war in China, and the incident was passed over after Japan had apologized and paid reparations to the United States.

Following the outbreak of hostilities in Asia, the President did not invoke the Neutrality Act on the technical ground that, since Japan had not declared war on China, a state of war did not exist. The President did not wish to take any step that might preclude assistance to China; however, his decision increased the effectiveness of the Japanese military machine, for in 1938 the United States, it is estimated, supplied Japan with 90 per cent of its scrap iron and steel, 91 per cent of its copper, 66 per cent of its oil, 45 per cent of its lead, and 67 per cent of its metal-working machinery. In the same period, American aid to China was negligible for the simple reason that Japan had the money and fleets to buy and ship from America, while China had no comparable power or opportunity.

By the end of the decade, Japan was prepared to establish what its leaders called the "Co-Prosperity Sphere of Greater East Asia" or the "New Order in East Asia." In the spring of 1940, Japanese officials, who were presumably seeking to divert public opinion at home from the stalemate in China, made it clear that they were contemplating an attack on French Indo-China and the Netherlands East Indies. By September, the Japanese forced the French government to grant them bases in northern Indo-China. In the same month, representatives of Japan, Germany, and Italy met in Berlin and concluded a treaty which provided that the three nations would "assist one another with all political, economic, and military means when one of the powers was attacked by a power not then involved in the European war or in the Chinese-Japanese conflict." Because the Soviet Union was exempted by name from the Berlin Treaty's provisions, there could be no doubt that the pact was aimed at the United States. With the signing of a Russo-Japanese treaty of neutrality on April 13, 1941, Japan had completed its diplomatic offensive and was prepared to launch its assault against southern Asia. The Japanese high command had already drawn its plans for a surprise attack on Pearl Harbor, and in May the Japanese navy began its preparations for the attack.

American officials continued the tradition of issuing formal protests condemning Japanese aggression, but Japan had long ago demonstrated that it understood no language but force. But even if the United States was prepared to use force, there was presumably no quick way of converting a one-ocean navy into a weapon that could both aid Britain and check Japan. The Roosevelt Administration could only apply economic pressure to Japan while it sought to build up its naval strength. In July, 1940, the President prohibited the export of oil and scrap metal without license and restricted the sale of aviation gasoline to the Western Hemisphere. Two months later, the United States granted the Chinese government a loan of $25,000,000 and placed an embargo on scrap iron and steel shipments to all countries except Great Britain and the nations of North and South America. In December of the same year, the United States provided China with $50,000,000 to stabilize its currency.

By the summer of 1941, both nations had taken positions from which they could not retreat without a serious loss of national prestige. In Japan, the jingoes were consolidating their political power and were determined to carry out their program of expansion. The United States, on the other hand, could not stand by while the Japanese completed plans for the conquest of southern Asia. On July 23, 1941, when Japan compelled France to grant it strategic bases in southern Indo-China, the Roosevelt Administration reinforced its diplomatic protests by announcing that it was freezing all Japanese assets in the United States. Japan countered immediately by freezing American assets in Japan.

Throughout the spring and summer of 1941, Kichisaburo Nomura, the Japanese ambassador to the United States, who was allied with the

The Japanese Envoys, 1941

[WIDE WORLD]

Japanese moderates, made repeated suggestions to Secretary of State Hull for settling the two countries' differences in the Far East. But as all the Japanese proposals provided in effect for American approval of Japan's expansionist program, they were rejected by the United States. The American proposals were equally unacceptable to Japan, for they called for the end of Japanese aggression and the withdrawal of Japanese forces from China. Relations between the two countries remained in uneasy equilibrium throughout the remainder of the summer, but a crisis developed soon after General Hideki Tojo took control of the Japanese cabinet on October 16.

The United States' opposition to further Japanese aggression played into Tojo's hands, for he claimed that Japan had been forced into a position where it had either to retreat or fight. In early November, Saburo Kurusu arrived in Washington as a special envoy to assist Nomura in discussions with Secretary of State Hull. On November 20, the Japanese representatives presented proposals to Hull that asked the United States to approve Japanese expansion in southeast Asia, to restore normal Japanese-American trade, and to give Japan a free hand in China.

The End of Isolation: Pearl Harbor, December 7, 1941

[U. S. NAVY PHOTO]

The Japanese note, in other words, was tantamount to a request for American approval of Japan's conquests in Asia. The United States rejected the note and on November 26 made a series of counterproposals calling for international political and economic cooperation and proposing Japanese withdrawal from China and French Indo-China, with guarantees of their future integrity, and a nonaggression pact among nations with Far Eastern interests. If Japan was willing to accept this program the United States was prepared to negotiate a trade treaty with Japan, to have the freezing of assets in both countries removed, and to agree upon a plan for the stabilization of the dollar-yen rate.

The American proposals were as unacceptable to the Japanese as Japan's proposals had been to the United States. Each nation, in effect, had served the other with an ultimatum. Japan rejected the American note of November 26 but kept the discussions open long enough to carry out the plans that its military leaders had perfected months earlier. For the next ten days, Kurusu and Nomura continued to play at negotiation while the Japanese task force advanced across the Pacific toward Hawaii. On December 7, 1941, the Japanese attacked Pearl Harbor. Striking at dawn with submarines and ship-based planes, the Japanese completely surprised the American defenders and practically destroyed the United States Pacific fleet. Both negotiations and American neutrality were now ended.

The Japanese attack ended almost a decade of debate on American foreign policy. On December 8, 1941, Congress responded to the President's request, and a resolution recognizing a state of war with Japan was unanimously approved by the Senate and received all but one vote in the House. Three days later, after Germany and Italy had declared war on the United States, both branches of Congress unanimously approved resolutions recognizing the existence of a state of war between the United States and the European Axis nations. The United States had entered its second world war within a quarter of a century.

FOR SUPPLEMENTARY READING

On European politics after 1918 read H. Holborn's essay *The Political Collapse of Europe* (1951). To George Kennan's work, *American Diplomacy, 1900–1950* (1951), add R. E. Osgood, *Ideals and Self-Interest in America's Foreign Relations* (1953). For the Harding and Coolidge years use J. C. Vinson, *The Parchment Peace* (1950), on the Washington conference; and R. H. Ferrell, *Peace in Their Time* (1952), on the Kellogg-Briand Treaty. On foreign policy under Hoover and the early Roosevelt, another recent volume by Ferrell, *American Diplomacy In the Great Depression* (1957), has great merit.

On the period from Versailles to Roosevelt also use H. Feis, *The Diplomacy of the Dollar: First Phase, 1919–1932* (1950). There are as yet no single commanding studies of the Good Neighbor Policy or of American involvements in Asia between 1918 and 1941. Besides the previously cited Bemis, *Latin American Policy of the United States,* and Griswold, *The Far Eastern Policy of the United States,* use Hoover's *Memoirs;* A. de Conde, *Herbert Hoover's Latin American Policy* (1951); and R. N. Current's irreverent *Secretary Stimson* (1954). E. O. Guerrant has studied *Roosevelt's Good Neighbor Policy* (1950). Cordell Hull's *Memoirs* (2 vols., 1948) are important sources. The great debate over isolation and intervention in the late 1930's has not yet died down. Highlights include C. A. Beard, *American Foreign Policy 1932–1940* (1946) and *President Roosevelt and the Coming of the War* (1948). These should be contrasted with W. L. Langer and S. E. Gleason, *The Challenge to Isolation, 1937–1940* (1952) and *Undeclared War, 1940–41* (1953). See also W. Cole, *America First* (1953) and S. Adler, *The Isolationist Impulse* (1957). H. Feis, *The Road to Pearl Harbor* (1950), is properly cautious on a touchy issue.

World War II: Triumph and Tragedy

THE SECOND WORLD WAR made unprecedented demands on the American people, requiring total mobilization of the home front and putting more than 13,000,000 Americans into uniform. Almost from the beginning of the war, it was apparent that the United States would never again be isolationist. As the defeat of the Axis powers came nearer, it was also clear to some Americans that, unintentionally, the war against Fascism had strengthened the hand of a third totalitarian power, the Soviet Union. Although America took the lead in planning for a postwar international organization, within a year after the defeat of the Fascists, Soviet-American relations had so deteriorated that the United Nations organization became incapable of settling political disputes in which the major powers were directly involved, and the hopes for a world ruled by the principles of the Atlantic Charter came to little.

Retreat and Return in Asia

American strategy during World War II was always based on the conviction of the Roosevelt Administration that Germany was a more important enemy than Japan and that the war in Europe should take precedence over the conflict in the Pacific and Asia. Many Americans who wished to obtain immediate revenge for the attack on Pearl Harbor resented the priority given to the European theatre and were appalled by the ease with which Japan enlarged its empire in the weeks following America's entry into the war. In rapid succession the Japanese occupied the Aleutian Islands, and conquered Malaya, the city of Singapore, the Dutch East Indies, Burma, New Guinea, and New Britain. These victories enabled the Japanese to menace both India and Australia, to cut the Burma Road, on which China depended for its supplies from the Allies, and to gain almost complete control over the sea lanes of the western and southern Pacific. But to Americans the most stunning Japanese victory occurred in the Philippines, where some 15,000 American and 40,000 Filipino troops under the command of General Douglas MacArthur waged a valiant but losing struggle against 200,000 Japanese. Cut off from supplies and reinforcements and compelled to retreat to the Bataan Peninsula on the island of Luzon, the American and Filipino forces found their position hopeless. On May 6, 1942, after MacArthur had been transferred to Australia, the small group of defenders on the island fortress of Corregidor surrendered to the Japanese.

Although the Allies in the months that followed Pearl Harbor were unable to stem Japanese expansion in the Far East, the United States was soon in a position to undertake limited, but effective, counterattacks. In May, 1942, American vessels inflicted heavy damage on an enemy flotilla in the Coral Sea, and a month later American planes scattered and repulsed a formation of advancing Japanese warships off Midway Island. At the same time, American submarines and planes undertook what proved to be an increasingly successful campaign of attrition against Japanese sea and air power. American ground forces launched their first offensive in the Pacific war in August, 1942, when marines landed on Florida Island in the Solomons and then moved on to Guadalcanal. In the subsequent months of bitter struggle, the Japanese proved themselves resourceful jungle fighters who preferred death to surrender. While the fighting continued on Guadalcanal, Australian and American troops under MacArthur's command launched a campaign to drive the Japanese out of New Guinea. MacArthur's plan was to use the Pacific Islands as steppingstones, to be taken one by one, on the road to the liberation of the Philippines and the invasion of the Japanese homeland.

The year 1943 marked the turning point of the war in the Pacific. By September, the United States had regained control over all the

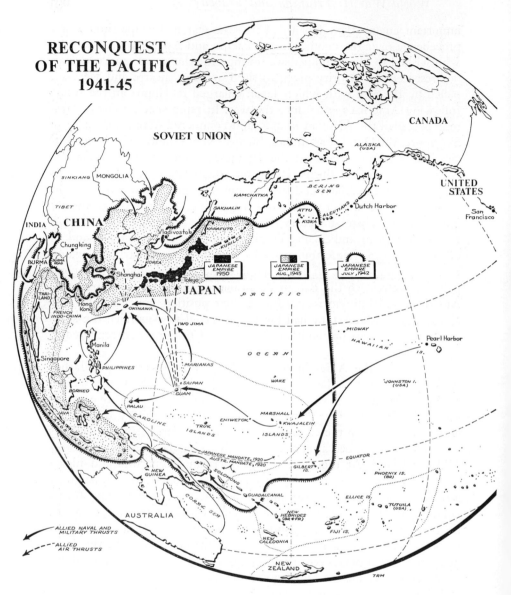

RECONQUEST
OF THE PACIFIC
1941-45

CANADA

SOVIET UNION

SINKIANG MONGOLIA

TIBET

INDIA CHINA

Chungking

BURMA BURMA
ROAD

THAI-
LAND

FRENCH
INDO-CHINA

Singapore

BORNEO

JAVA

Shanghai

KOREA

Tokyo

JAPAN

Hong
Kong

OKINAWA

Manila

PHILIPPINES

PALAU

CAROLINE

NEW
GUINEA

AUSTRALIA

ALLIED NAVAL AND
MILITARY THRUSTS

ALLIED
AIR THRUSTS

Vladivostok

KARAFUTO

KURILES

SAKHALIN

KAMCHATKA

BERING
SEA

ALASKA
(USA)

ATTU

KISKA

ALEUTIANS Dutch Harbor

UNITED
STATES

San
Francisco

JAPANESE
EMPIRE
1950

JAPANESE
EMPIRE
AUG., 1945

JAPANESE
EMPIRE
JULY, 1942

PACIFIC

IWO JIMA

MARIANAS

SAIPAN

GUAM

TRUK
ISLANDS

MARSHALL

ENIWETOK

KWAJALEIN

ISLANDS

JAPANESE MANDATE, 1920
AUSTR. MANDATE, 1920

SOLOMONS

CORAL SEA

GUADALCANAL

NEW
CALEDONIA

NEW
HEBRIDES
(BR & FR)

FIJI IS.

OCEAN

MIDWAY

HAWAIIAN

Pearl Harbor

IS.

WAKE

JOHNSTON I.
(USA)

EQUATOR

GILBERT
IS.

PHOENIX IS.
(BR.)

ELLICE IS.

TUTUILA
(USA)

NEW
ZEALAND

TRM

Aleutians, and in November, American marines and soldiers began a bloody but successful invasion of the Gilbert Islands in the mid-Pacific. The neighboring Marshalls were the next American objective, and Kwajalein was captured in the opening months of 1944. Within six months, the United States had taken Saipan in the Marianas and Guam and Tinian as well, and for the first time it was in a position to begin systematic air attacks on the enemy's home islands. Meanwhile Mac-Arthur's troops had landed on Leyte in the Philippines on October 20, 1944. When the Japanese fleet attempted to isolate the American invaders from their bases of support, it was decisively defeated in the Philippine Sea. Within three months, the Americans were on Luzon, and on February 3, 1945, they entered Manila. American forces in the Pacific still had a long road to travel to reach Tokyo, but no one doubted that they were on their way.

The progress of the war in Asia contrasted markedly with Allied successes in the Pacific. Logistic problems and the determination of the Allies to concentrate their major efforts on the war in Europe precluded any large-scale material or military assistance to the hopelessly outclassed Chinese. Brigadier General Claire Chennault's "Flying Tigers," a small American air group stationed in China, achieved a series of spectacular victories against enormous odds, but they were always hampered by a shortage of equipment and personnel. For a time it was thought that British and American troops in India under Lord Louis Mountbatten would drive back the Japanese, but Mountbatten's Burma campaign in 1944 made little headway against a stubborn enemy army that was superbly trained in the techniques of jungle warfare. The completion of the war in the Orient had to wait on Allied victory in Europe.

The War in the West

Both Britain and the Soviet Union, having borne the full brunt of the Nazi attack, considered Germany rather than Japan the principal enemy, and President Roosevelt accepted this view. For some months after Pearl Harbor, the United States could only assist its European allies with supplies, but American troops and equipment were also shipped in increasing numbers to bases in Northern Ireland, and American planes soon joined the British in raids on the Continent.

The United States struck its first major blow against Hitler's empire in the Mediterranean. For two years, British troops had been fighting a seesaw battle with the Germans and Italians for the control of North Africa. Then, on November 7, 1942, after General Bernard Montgomery's Eighth Army had routed the Axis troops at El Alamein, American and British soldiers under the command of General Dwight D. Eisenhower landed in French Morocco and Algeria. Although this region was controlled by Marshal Henri Pétain's pro-Axis government, the success of the invasion was assured with an armistice arranged by Vichy's Admiral François Darlan. Despite the saving in

"Pack Trains to Cassino": The Frustrating Italian Campaign, 1944
(painting by A. Reep)

lives and bloodshed, the so-called Darlan deal was in some ways unfortunate. American liberals bitterly resented an agreement with a high official of the Vichy regime. Moreover, when Darlan was assassinated on December 24, the appointment of General Henri Giraud to succeed him further confused the already complex French political situation. General Charles de Gaulle, as the leader of the Free French, objected vehemently to Giraud's selection. But the United States consistently refused to grant De Gaulle formal recognition, for Roosevelt insisted that only a liberated France had the right to choose its own leaders.

Following the initial success of the Allied landings, British and American military progress was slow. The Germans fought tenaciously for every foot of soil, and it was not until May, 1943, that all of North Africa was in the possession of the Anglo-American armies. Sicily, which was invaded on July 9, fell within six weeks under the three-pronged attack of the British Eighth Army, Canadian troops, and Americans led by General George S. Patton, Jr. When the fighting moved on to the Italian mainland, the Germans once more put up a stubborn resistance and consistently took advantage of the peninsula's mountainous terrain to check the Allied advance. Meanwhile, Mussolini, who had been overthrown by the Italians and rescued by the Germans, was succeeded by Marshal Pietro Badoglio, whose government in September, 1943, signed an armistice that made Italy a co-belligerent of the Allies. This surrender, however, had no appreciable effect upon Germany's determination to continue the struggle for Italy, and it was not until June 4, 1944, that General Mark Clark was able to lead his troops into Rome.

Soon after the United States entered the war, the Russian government began a propaganda campaign designed to hasten the day when the Western Allies would invade Europe. While the British and Americans were slogging north in Italy in 1944, Soviet troops were advancing with giant strides across eastern Europe, and leaders in the Kremlin let hardly a day pass without renewing their demands for the creation of a second front. Throughout this period, British and American planes continued around the clock to hammer at German military and industrial establishments, while staff officers of both countries, under the command of General Eisenhower, labored over plans for the impending invasion of Hitler's Europe.

By the spring of 1944, millions of highly trained British and American soldiers were stationed in England, enough equipment for the war's major campaign had been accumulated, and the invasion plans were completed. On June 6, designated as "D Day," the first Canadian, British, and American troops were ferried across the English Channel and successfully stormed the Nazi fortifications on the beaches of Normandy. After some weeks of intensive fighting at St. Lô and Caen, the Americans under command of General Omar Bradley broke through the German lines and conducted a lightning advance that equaled or surpassed the speed of the Nazi *blitzkrieg* in the opening months of the war. On August 15, British, French, and American armies landed on the southern coast of France and moved rapidly inland, and Bradley's troops made their triumphal entry into Paris ten days later.

In the autumn of 1944, when the Western Allies were fighting on German soil and the Russians were advancing rapidly from the East, many Allied observers thought that Germany would fall before the end of the year. But the Germans dug in, and in December, General Karl von Rundstedt launched a surprise counteroffensive that opened a wide gap in the Allied lines in the Ardennes area. In the Battle of the Bulge, the American troops first checked and then drove back the German advance, but it was not until February that the Allies were ready for their final assault against Hitler's Germany. By

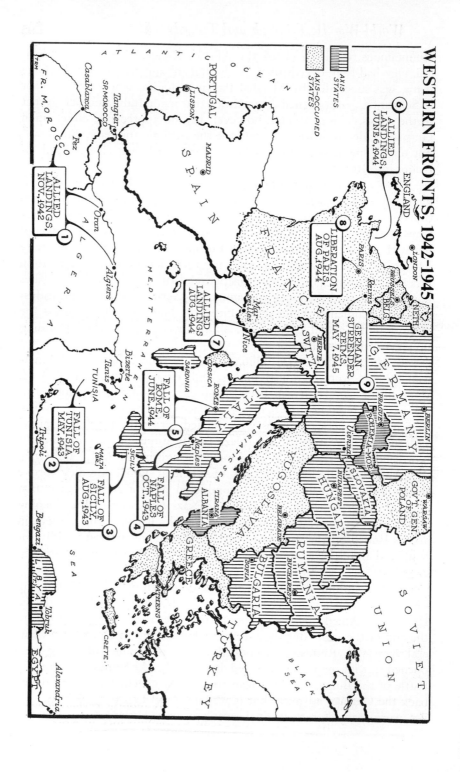

WESTERN FRONTS, 1942-1945

AXIS
STATES

AXIS-OCCUPIED
STATES

⑥ ALLIED LANDINGS, JUNE 6, 1944

① ALLIED LANDINGS, NOV. 1942

⑧ LIBERATION OF PARIS, AUG. 1944

⑦ ALLIED LANDINGS AUG. 1944

② FALL OF TUNISIA, MAY, 1943

⑤ FALL OF ROME, JUNE, 1944

⑨ GERMAN SURRENDER REIMS, MAY 7, 1945

③ FALL OF SICILY, AUG. 1943

④ FALL OF NAPLES OCT. 1943

March, British and American soldiers were across the Rhine, the Russians had taken Poland and were well into eastern Germany, and the Anglo-American army in Italy was driving the Nazi troops up the Po Valley. In the following weeks, German resistance on all fronts disintegrated before the blows of the Allied forces. On May 2, three days after Mussolini had been executed by Italian partisans, hostilities in Italy ended. When the Russians entered Berlin at the end of April, Hitler committed suicide, and Admiral Karl Doenitz, his successor, sued for peace. On May 7, Allied leaders met with General Alfred Jodl at Rheims and accepted Germany's unconditional surrender.

The Setting Sun of Japan

Following the defeat of Germany, the Allies were free for the first time to concentrate on the war in the Far East. The Japanese, although forced on the defensive by successive defeats in the Pacific in 1943–4, gave every indication that they were prepared to fight to the last man before capitulating. As the Americans drew nearer to the enemy's homeland, they found that each island was more heavily fortified and more tenaciously defended. Iwo Jima, a 3-by-5-mile island 750 miles from Tokyo, was assaulted by American troops in February, 1945, but it took a month to capture and cost the Americans 20,000 men in casualties. In April, Americans landed on Okinawa in the Ryukyus, and once again the enemy made them pay dearly for every foot of ground they gained. Before the Japanese surrendered all of Okinawa in June, they had killed more than 11,000 Americans and wounded some 33,000. Throughout the battle, Japanese suicide pilots in *Kamikaze* planes had inflicted severe damage on the United States' supporting fleet.

Although the fighting on Iwo Jima and Okinawa seemed to indicate that the Japanese were in no mood to end the war on American terms, President Truman on July 26, 1945, announced that Japan could only avoid total destruction by an immediate and unconditional surrender. No mention of the newly perfected, but still secret, atom bomb was made in the President's announcement; and when the Japanese ignored the ultimatum, an atom bomb was dropped on Hiroshima on August 5. The bomb left the city a shambles, and either killed or injured almost every one of its 343,000 inhabitants. When this event produced no response from the Japanese government, a second atom bomb was dropped four days later on the city of Nagasaki. On August 9, fulfilling a secret agreement made six months earlier, Russia entered the war against Japan and began a rapid advance in Korea and

Hiroshima, 1945: Near This Bridge the Atomic Age Began

Manchuria. Within a week, the Allies had the unconditional surrender of Japan. The war in the Pacific was officially terminated on September 1, when Japan's war leaders signed the terms of surrender on the battleship *Missouri* in Tokyo Bay.

American jubilation over the end of the war was tempered by thoughts of how the final victory had been achieved. The atom bomb, which had been developed during the war by American, British, and Canadian scientists at a cost of approximately 2 billion dollars, was acclaimed on all sides as a marvel of scientific achievement. But no amount of pride over the accomplishments of Allied scientists could obscure the fact that the atom bomb was the most destructive weapon ever invented by man. While Americans talked hopefully of the peacetime uses of atomic energy, all knew that its use in another war could lead to the annihilation of mankind.

Wartime Diplomacy

The victories achieved by American fighting forces in both the Pacific and Europe were made possible in part by a relentless diplomatic offensive. The United States not only had to anticipate and counter the diplomatic moves of the enemy, but also, as one member of a gigantic coalition, it was constantly compelled to maintain the closest possible liaison with the leaders of its allies. The problems of war could not exclude those of peace, and during the conflict, representatives of what came to be known as the United Nations repeatedly discussed their countries' plans for the postwar world. The ultimate responsibility for the conduct of America's wartime diplomacy rested with President Roosevelt, but the carrying out of various policies was often entrusted to Secretary of State Cordell Hull, Harry Hopkins, the President's close friend and adviser, and a host of other loyal, but often unsung, civil servants.

Throughout the war, a particular effort was made to maintain amicable relations with neutral nations in vital war areas and to ensure the cooperation of the other governments of this hemisphere. Relations were maintained with the Vichy government as long as it could affect the course of the war, and then it was abandoned to its well-merited fate, a complete German occupation. Sweden's and Eire's neutrality was always scrupulously respected, while diplomatic pressure was directed against Spain to prevent it from throwing in its lot with Germany. Although many Americans objected to a policy of ostensible friendship with Franco's Fascist regime, the Roosevelt Administration refused to make any move that might have driven Spain further into the camp of the enemy. In this hemisphere, the Good Neighbor Policy of the preceding decade provided an excellent foundation for a program of wartime cooperation. Relations with Canada were cordial during the entire war, while the ties that bound the United States to all the Latin American nations except Argentina were consistently strengthened. At the conference of foreign ministers at Rio de Janeiro in 1942, plans were developed for economic assistance to the Latin American countries and for the elimination of Axis agents below the Rio Grande. For the remainder of the war, the United States bolstered the economies of its Latin American neighbors, while they supplied the United States with raw materials and various types of military equipment.

Economic cooperation among the United Nations was an important part of the joint war effort. Throughout the war, Lend-Lease provided the principal material aid that the United States gave its allies. Lend-Lease exports increased from some $740,000,000 in 1941 to $11,297,500,000 in 1944. In 1944, the high point of war production, slightly less than one half of the Lend-Lease exports was sent to the United Kingdom, and more than one third was shipped to the Soviet Union, principally in machinery, vehicles and food supplies. President Roosevelt repeatedly pointed out that Lend-Lease was a two-way

Unloading Lend-Lease Shipments in Persia, 1943

[NATIONAL ARCHIVES]

street, but the value of reverse Lend-Lease, or the transfer of goods to the United States by its allies, totaled only $7,800,000,000 for the entire war.

World War II, in contrast with the first World War, was characterized by marked cooperation and interchange of views among the leaders of the Allied Nations. Soon after the attack on Pearl Harbor, Prime Minister Winston Churchill visited President Roosevelt in Washington, and until the latter's death, the two men remained in almost daily communication through radio-telephone or trusted intermediaries. Despite large differences of opinion, each understood and appreciated the other's ability; both placed victory above all other considerations; and both shared a strong belief in the essential unity of the Anglo-American peoples.

The most important question dividing Churchill and Roosevelt concerned the war's political objectives. Churchill made it clear that he did not regard the war as a prelude to the breakup of the British empire, despite the growing restlessness during the war in such possessions as India. Roosevelt himself was convinced that the major obstacle in the postwar years would be resurgent British and French imperialism. Underestimating Stalin's ambitions and the nature of Soviet

*At War's End: Secretary Forrestal Congratulates U. S. Top Admirals
(left to right) King, Halsey, Nimitz*

[NATIONAL ARCHIVES]

totalitarianism, Roosevelt believed that Russia would be satisfied with guarantees of its security against Germany and some territorial gains in eastern Europe. In fact, throughout the war Stalin was intent on gaining as much territory as possible to be used after the war as a basis for further world-wide advances by Communist troops and agents.

As the war neared its end, Churchill insisted that the Allies make every effort to drive as deeply eastward in Europe as possible so that, by the war's end, Western rather than Soviet armies would be in control of Berlin, Prague, and Vienna. These political objectives were to be supplemented by the most stringent guarantees to be extracted from Stalin for the independence of Poland. Americans, on the other hand, including the Western Commander-in-Chief General Eisenhower, were most intent on winning the military campaigns as quickly and as cheaply as possible, and it seemed logical to allow the onrushing Soviet armies to liberate central as well as eastern Europe from the Nazis. Allied troops were stopped about 100 miles from Berlin, and American advance units were pulled back from Czechoslovakia and Austria. As a result, the war in Europe ended with a totalitarian Soviet Union

The Big Three at Teheran: Stalin, Roosevelt, Churchill

[NATIONAL ARCHIVES]

in control of the very areas in Europe that England and France had gone to war to save from another totalitarian country.

Throughout the war years, the Western democracies always made the greatest effort to maintain cordial and intimate contacts with the Russian rulers. In August, 1942, Churchill visited Stalin in Moscow, and the American ambassador to the Soviet Union represented the United States at the talks that took place. In October of the following year, foreign ministers of Britain, the Soviet Union, and the United States, meeting in Moscow, arrived at an understanding on the second front, and after they had been joined by the Chinese foreign minister, they drafted tentative proposals for a postwar organization to preserve peace. Meanwhile, Churchill and Roosevelt had conferred at Casablanca in January, 1943, and had announced to the world that the Axis powers could obtain peace only through "unconditional surrender." In November of the same year, at Cairo the President, Churchill, and Generalissimo Chiang Kai-shek of China agreed on the dismemberment of the Japanese Empire following the war's successful conclusion, while a subsequent conference attended by Roosevelt, Churchill, and Stalin at Teheran resolved the principal problems concerning the prosecution of the war in Europe. No further meeting proved necessary until January, 1945, when the leaders of the Big Three met at Yalta, where problems of the impending peace overshadowed military discussions.

As the war progressed, the various inter-Allied conferences of necessity had to devote an increasing amount of time and attention to postwar planning. The Moscow Declaration, promulgated by the principal foreign ministers in 1943, had pledged their countries to the formation of a "general international organization" to prevent war. On November 5, the Senate overwhelmingly approved the Moscow Declaration, and the planning of the United Nations organization was underway.

Manpower, Finances, and Factories

While the war in Europe and Asia brought intolerable suffering and misery to millions of noncombatants, it was at most an inconvenience to American civilians. Global warfare required the widest government controls over the activities of the individual, but at no time was life in the United States regimented as in other belligerent nations. Most Americans enjoyed unprecedented prosperity, and, with minor deprivations, the nation produced both guns and butter.

Nearly every American had at least one relative in military or naval service, and that fact provided the civilian population with its most immediate association with the war. From 1941 to 1945, the size of the armed forces increased from fewer than 2,000,000 to more than 11,000,000 men and women. The army alone enrolled 10,800,000 men during the war. Every branch of the service permitted women to enlist for noncombatant work, and in 1945 the Army's Wacs, the Navy's Waves, the Coast Guard's Spars, and the Marines' Women's Auxiliary totaled 258,000. Civilian Americans in every community throughout the land served in many volunteer services, including the air-raid wardens under the Office of Civilian Defense.

No clear-cut basis was ever established for the selection of men to serve in the armed forces. The rules that governed exemptions changed with the shifting political winds in Washington. Each of the nation's 6500 local draft boards enjoyed considerable autonomy and was able to modify or ignore orders issued by federal authorities. As a result of pressure from farm politicians, agricultural workers were virtually exempted from military service by a congressional act of November, 1942. Although essential workers in industry were also eligible for deferment, they were called up in large numbers by their local boards. In the first years of the draft, fathers were automatically deferred, but as the war progressed, it became apparent that this policy could not be continued indefinitely. Nevertheless, many boards, sensitive to public opinion in their communities, refused to order the induction of fathers. By 1944–5, when the army was insisting on the need for young men, those who were of lowest age, regardless of their jobs or family needs, were taken ahead of all others. At the end of 1943, many Americans—including the President—urged the adoption of national manpower legislation that would permit the government to draft individuals for essential work as well as for the armed services. Industrial, agricultural, and labor leaders, however, opposed this proposal, and Congress refused to make the proposal law.

To raise, equip, and maintain a fighting force of unprecedented size put extraordinary demands on the government's financial resources. By the summer of 1943, the government was spending 8 billion dollars per month, and from 1941 to 1945 the national debt rose from less than 48 billion dollars to 247 billion. The Treasury Department used mass borrowing, and Congress passed new and higher taxes. An attempt was made to sell bonds to rich and poor alike, and all Americans were urged by press, radio, movie, sound trucks, and door-to-door canvasses to put their savings into war bonds. Many workers bought bonds regularly through payroll deduction plans. In addition to round-the-year advertising campaigns, the government conducted eight special drives to increase bond sales. From May, 1941 through 1946, government bond sales amounted to more than 61 billion dollars.

Tax receipts covered approximately two fifths of the cost of the war to the United States. Approximately 7 billion dollars in tax income in 1941 had swelled to more than 42 billion in 1945. Only single persons with incomes under $500 and married couples with less than $1,200 were not compelled to file income-tax returns. A new schedule of surtaxes went as high as 98 per cent. Stepped-up corporate taxes, excess-profit taxes on corporate income, and a widely expanded schedule of excise taxes brought additional revenue. After July 1, 1943, taxes on the income of salaried workers and wage earners were withheld at the source in order to facilitate payments and assure the government of the revenues to pay for the immense costs of the war.

Not until well into 1942 were the nation's factories devoting practically all their facilities to the manufacture of military equipment. Shortly after the United States went to war, the War Production Board, under the chairmanship of Donald Nelson, was given general authority over the "war procurement and production program." A number of other government agencies were also set up to handle special production problems. Among these were the Office of Rubber Director, Smaller War Plants Corporation, and the Petroleum Administrator for War.

The government was frequently accused of impeding production with bureaucratic controls and with administrative inefficiency, but, despite the plethora of red tape, American factories broke all previous records for industrial output in the war years. From 1940 to 1944, the index of industrial production (1935–9 = 100) rose from 125 to 235. Some civilian industries, of course, had to suspend operation in order for the nation to produce its astonishing volume of war goods. By the middle of 1945, the United States had produced 297,000 airplanes, 6,500 naval vessels (as well as 64,500 landing vessels), more than 17,000,000 rifles, and 5,400 cargo ships, 315,000 pieces of field artillery, 4,200,000 tons of artillery shells and 41,400,000,000 rounds of ammunition. Although businessmen chafed at government controls on their output, American industry as a whole earned enormous profits during the war. The net income of American corporations rose from 17 billion dollars in 1940 to 28 billion in 1943 and climbed even higher in the next two years.

The End of the Great Depression

The rapid expansion of American industry ended ten years of chronic mass unemployment in the nation. The 1940 census reported approximately 8,000,000 unemployed workers in a total labor force of more than 55,000,000. Shortly after the United States had entered the war, unemployment all but disappeared. Women joined the labor force in increasing numbers and often took jobs that had formerly been held almost exclusively by men. Many boys of high-school age, men over sixty-five, and individuals who were physically handicapped were also able to obtain employment. Increased wages and longer work weeks raised the average weekly earnings of all workers in manufacturing industries from $25.20 in 1940 to $46.08 in 1944. In the same period, the length of the average work-week increased from 38.1 to 45.2 hours.

Both the C.I.O. and the A. F. of L. made a no-strike pledge soon after the Japanese attack on Pearl Harbor, but many unions struck for wage increases to match the rise in prices. In response to public demands for a check on wartime strikes, Congress in June, 1943, passed the Smith-Connally Act over the President's veto. This measure empowered the President to seize any plant or firm that was threatened by a strike and provided penalties for leaders or instigators of strikes against companies working on government contracts. When John L. Lewis's United Mine Workers threatened to strike in November, 1943, Secretary of the Interior Ickes, at the President's direction, took control of the mines. A month later, under similar circumstances, the railroads were seized by the government and placed under the army's authority. Strikes and the menace of strikes received much unfavorable publicity in the nation's press, but a review of the record reveals that such work stoppages had comparatively little effect on wartime industrial production.

Strikes, 1941 to 1944				
	1941	1942	1943	1944
Number of strikes	4,288	2,968	3,752	4,956
Number of workers involved	2,362,620	839,961	1,981,279	2,115,637
Number of man-days idle	23,047,556	4,182,557	13,500,529	8,721,079

Meanwhile, the National War Labor Board, established in January, 1942, was unsuccessfully attempting to stabilize wages. The first major break in the wage line occurred in the summer of 1942, when the board approved a 15 per cent increase for the members of the C.I.O. United Steel Workers in the nation's smaller steel plants. What came to be known as the Little Steel Formula was soon extended to cover workers in other industries. From that time forward, wages and prices edged upward constantly, bringing an ever higher standard of living but with the constant threat of inflation.

During the war years, the farmer's income, like that of the worker and industrialist, steadily increased. Farmers might have preferred to have had prices fixed by supply and demand, but the government imposed price ceilings on most food products and guaranteed agricultural profits through an expanded program of parity payments. Because parity prices applied to only a few basic crops, however, other crops needed by the war economy were neglected. Despite the creation of a War Food Administration, the government had little control over agricultural production in the war years.

The high wartime level of industrial salaries and wages and of farm income, taken with the concurrent shortage of consumer goods, produced an increase in the cost of living that threatened to jeopardize the successful prosecution of the war. It was hoped that heavier taxation and bond sales would siphon off some surplus purchasing power, but the principal effort to check the inflationary spiral was made by the Office of Price Administration under the chairmanship of Leon Henderson. Price ceilings were imposed on many consumer goods in short supply, and a rationing system was set up to insure equitable distribution of scarce, essential commodities. Despite the growth of so-called black and grey markets in all sorts of products, the O.P.A., in view of the difficult task that confronted it, achieved considerable success. The index (1935–9 = 100) of consumers' prices rose from 105.2 in 1941 to 116.5 in 1942, 123.6 in 1943, and leveled off at 125.5 in 1944. Rents, which were frozen in 1942, did not vary appreciably for the remainder of the war.

The Social Effects of War

World War II gave rise to little of the hysteria that had blemished the war record of the United States in 1917–18. The Roosevelt Administration made a concerted effort to prevent the war from being used as an excuse for fomenting suspicion, intolerance, and hatred on the home front. Pacifists and conscientious objectors were treated much better than in World War I. The Department of Justice methodically and without fanfare checked on people of questionable loyalty and quietly moved against those suspected of supporting the enemy. Pro-Fascist organizations such as the German-American Bund and the Silver Shirts were disbanded; enemy-owned businesses in the United States were confiscated; and more than 3,000 enemy aliens were interned—a remarkably small number, for the Alien Registration of 1940 had revealed that there were some 5,000,000 aliens in the country. The Justice Department's most spectacular coup was the capture of eight German agents who had been landed on the east coast by submarine. Following a military trial, six were put to death and two sentenced to life imprisonment. An otherwise laudable record on civil rights in wartime was marred, however, by the treatment of 110,000 west-coast Japanese-Americans, the majority of whom were loyal and had been born in the United States. Taken *en masse* from their homes by the army, they were "relocated" at some distance from the west coast in camps unfit for American citizens. Not until the end of the war were they permitted to return to their former homes.

Unlike the relative sanity marking the problems of subversion and disloyalty during the war, racial and religious tensions worsened. Negroes found the armed services' policy of segregation especially distasteful in a war that was being fought against an enemy that had made a national religion of the myth of racial supremacy. On the other hand, white southerners, who had moved out of their section to take

West Coast Americans Awaiting Internment, 1942

[NATIONAL ARCHIVES]

jobs in industry, resented the economic and social position of the Negro in the North. Many southern whites despised and distrusted the Fair Employment Practices Committee, which had been appointed by the President in 1941 to prevent racial discrimination in employment. These stresses and strains, aggravated by agitators, produced a number of anti-Negro riots, the most serious of which occurred in Detroit. Detroit had for many years received a steady influx of Negro and white workers from the South. The good wages coming from the converted automobile plants worsened the problem of social mobility in the community. In June, 1943, a battle raged in Detroit's streets which did not end until federal troops had intervened and more than forty Negroes and whites had lost their lives. Although Negroes were the principal victims of racial prejudice during the war, other minority groups were subjected to abuse, indignities, and even assault. In 1943, a mob of young men attacked Mexican boys in Los Angeles, and in the same year there were demonstrations of anti-Semitism in both Boston and New York.

The government's attempt to control public opinion was designed to promote the successful prosecution of the war rather than to police the American mind. A system of voluntary press and radio censorship, started in the winter of 1941–2, was placed under the supervision of Byron Price, who, as Director of Censorship, was also authorized to censor all information that passed in or out of the United States. But no attempt was made to conduct domestic propaganda on a scale comparable to that undertaken by George Creel in World War I. Each branch of the government at first released its own information. After June, 1942, the information programs of these government agencies were coordinated by the Office of War Information, headed by Elmer Davis. Through a series of overseas broadcasts, the O.W.I. also conducted a campaign of psychological warfare that was designed to undermine enemy morale.

Politics as Usual

Politics was one of the few traditional American pastimes that the war did not seriously modify. The Republicans, as the minority party, often found it difficult to criticize the conduct of the war without also seeming to criticize the United States' war objectives, but they were quick to accuse the Roosevelt Administration of inefficiency and to complain of restrictions on civilian activity. In the 1942 congressional elections, they were able to capture thirty-four additional seats in the House and eight in the Senate. By 1944, the Republican chances of a presidential victory seemed better than at any time since the advent of the New Deal. The Republican convention recognized Governor Thomas E. Dewey of New York as the party's standard bearer, and he was nominated on the first ballot. At the Democratic convention, where Roosevelt's renomination was assured, a contest developed over the selection of a vice-presidential candidate. Although Henry Wallace entered the convention with strong hopes that he would again be given second place on the Democratic ticket, he was defeated by the city machines and southern delegates. The convention finally settled upon Senator Harry S. Truman of Missouri, a former stalwart of Kansas City's Pendergast machine, who had attracted favorable attention by his conduct of a Senate committee that investigated war production. Many of the New Dealers who had been complaining that the war had revived the influence of big business in American politics greeted the failure of Wallace's nomination as a setback for their cause.

The 1944 campaign revealed the dilemma of the Republicans. In most of his public statements Dewey accepted much of the New Deal's foreign and domestic policies. He struck repeatedly at the confusion and conflicts within the Administration, but he could promise the voters little more than that the Republicans would carry out the Democratic program more effectively than the Democrats themselves had been able to do. In meeting the Republican challenge, Roosevelt attacked the G.O.P.'s isolationist record, pointed to his party's achievements during the war, and promised Americans an "economic bill of rights." Both candidates favored the establishment of an international organization to preserve peace, but this issue played a minor part in the campaign.

On election day, the voters endorsed the Roosevelt Administration for the fourth successive time. With 432 votes to 99 for Dewey, Roosevelt won a smashing victory in the electoral college, but his popular majority of only 3,260,000 was less than that received by any successful presidential candidate since World War I. The Democrats also won a majority of the gubernatorial contests, held their own in the Senate, and picked up twenty-one seats in the House. Among other notable features of the election were the defeat of several prominent isolationists, the all-out campaign conducted for Roosevelt by the C.I.O.'s Political Action Committee, and the continued strength of the Democrats in urban areas.

Within six months of his re-election to a fourth term as President, Roosevelt was dead. His exuberant personality had seemed capable of carrying him through any crisis; he had thrived on conflict and had thoroughly enjoyed his job. But more than twelve years of unprecedented responsibility had undermined his physical stamina. When he returned from the Yalta Conference early in 1945 he was badly run-down, and he had not fully recovered when he went to Warm Springs, Georgia, to recuperate. There he died from a cerebral hemorrhage on April 12, 1945. On the same day, Harry S. Truman was sworn in as the thirty-third President of the United States.

The death of Roosevelt on the eve of victory over the Axis stunned the American people. Since Lincoln, no president's death in office produced such intense grief. F. D. R. had died, however, at the beginning of an era in American history for which even his brilliant methods of running his party and the nation might not have been an adequate preparation. Up to the end of World War II, Americans had assumed that democracy and belief in the individual were norms for the world; Fascism had been a temporary insane interlude, at most an aberration. After 1945, Americans confronted a world in which deeply held illiberal ideologies required new notions of politics and political life. The rise of the Soviet Union to the ranks of the major powers brought with it struggles in which men trained for limited, pragmatic political battles would have to learn to cope with the fact that totalitarian enemies would not be satisfied with anything less than the revolutionary transformation of the world.

The most sobering assessment of the results of the second World War was made by Winston Churchill who, keeping in mind the growth of Soviet power, gave as the theme of his final volume of war memoirs, "How the great democracies triumphed, and so were able to resume the follies which had so nearly cost them their life."

FOR SUPPLEMENTARY READING

Memoirs and apologies still dominate the scholarship of the years 1939–45. Consult the works by Eisenhower, Bradley, Montgomery, Byrnes, Hull, *et al.* Economic mobilization at Washington is surveyed in E. Janeway, *The Struggle for Survival* (1951). An official document by the Bureau of the Budget, *The United States at War* (1946), is perhaps most reliable on the home front. R. Young, *Congressional Politics in the Second World War* (1955), is safe to begin with on wartime politics. On the battles, F. Pratt's *War for the World* (1950) is a short survey. Three works establish major points at issue on grand strategy: C. Wilmot, *The Struggle for Europe* (1952); H. Feis, *Churchill, Roosevelt, Stalin* (1957); and S. E. Morison, *Strategy and Compromise* (1958). On the inner history of the Presidency use Sherwood, *Roosevelt and Hopkins*. The greatest work to come out of the war is undoubtedly W. S. Churchill, *The Second World War* (6 vols., 1948–53), also available in a one-volume condensation.

PART V

SHORES
DIMLY SEEN

[COURTESY OF THE UNITED NATIONS]

20

❯❯❯-❯❯❯-❯❯❯-❯❯❯-❯❯❯-❯❯❯-❯❯❯

The
Truman Legacy

THE EIGHT YEARS that Harry S. Truman served as President of the United States were as momentous in the history of the American people as the New Deal years before them. Truman's Fair Deal, while an extension of Roosevelt's New Deal, marked the slackening rather than the rebirth of the reform impulse in American life. The change in foreign policy was equally significant. At the end of the war, the American people thought themselves entering a world in which American and Soviet cooperation would bring peace and justice to millions of people everywhere. When Truman left the White House, all but the most obtuse among them were resigned to survival in a divided world in which two giant blocs feared and hated each other.

Toward a Peacetime Economy

Americans in all walks of life viewed the end of the war abroad as a signal for the immediate restoration of a peacetime economy at home. For almost four years, the enormous productivity of American industry and higher wages had given them dreams of the fruits of peace, and they were now determined to make their dreams come true. Servicemen clamored to be discharged; businessmen and farmers wanted prices raised and taxes lowered; workers believed that they deserved wage increases; landlords demanded the removal of ceilings on rents; and consumers wanted new automobiles, homes, and the countless gadgets denied them during the war. Those who warned that a speedy and unplanned return to a peacetime economy would create more problems than it would solve were helpless before the unrelenting pressure of practically every special-interest group in the country. Despite the pleas of the Truman Administration for an orderly and gradual transition from war to peace, the American people had their way, and within a year after the Japanese surrender, most of the government's wartime restrictions and controls had been removed.

Because of pressure by servicemen and their families, demobilization proceeded at a much more rapid rate than either military or civilian leaders thought advisable. By January, 1947, the armed forces, which at their peak in 1944–5 had numbered over 11,000,000, had declined to about 1,000,000 men, half of whom were stationed abroad in American armies of occupation. Officials responsible for national defense deplored this policy of wholesale discharges and urged the establishment of universal military training. But, despite mounting tension between the Soviet Union and the United States, Congress balked at this proposal and voted instead to continue the draft. The peacetime selective-service law imposed drastic limitations on the maximum size of the nation's armed services and provided for the exemption of fathers, eighteen-year-olds, and most veterans of World War II. But it also introduced, for the foreseeable future, a society in which most young men woud have to anticipate a period of military service.

During the war, there had been frequent predictions that returning servicemen would find it very difficult to adjust themselves to civilian life, yet the great majority of veterans made the transition with little or no trouble. Veterans were granted a number of special privileges in postwar America. Under the "G. I. Bill of Rights," which became law in June, 1944, they were assured educational opportunities and economic and medical assistance that were not available to civilians. Unemployed veterans were entitled to draw twenty dollars a week for not more than a year, and veterans who wished to purchase a house or start a small business were granted liberal credit facilities. The government also paid for the tuition and books of veterans in colleges and vocational institutions and made monthly subsistence payments to veterans who were students. Such government aid to veterans helped increase the impression that a college education was now a normal expectation for young Americans.

The comparative ease with which most veterans resumed civilian life was helped by a boom that eliminated all predicted threats of wide-

"Weather Clear, Track Fast" (*Fitzpatrick in the*
St. Louis Post-Dispatch, *1946*)

spread postwar unemployment. The backlog of consumer demand and
savings that had been built up during the war created a sellers' market
in which buyers seldom bothered to quibble over either price or quality. Continued heavy government expenditures on European recovery,
veterans' pensions, and the largest peacetime military establishment in
the nation's history also contributed to American prosperity. By 1947,
when industry had completed its reconversion to peacetime production, the number of employed reached a record 60,000,000, and the
annual value of goods and services produced amounted to the unprecedented total of 225 billion dollars.

The boom, however, brought a spectacular increase in prices, and
throughout the postwar years, inflation remained a constant threat to
American prosperity. In the months that followed the Japanese surrender, farmers and businessmen, anxious to take full advantage of
great public demand, conducted extensive propaganda for the immediate removal of all government restrictions on prices. The National

Association of Manufacturers, the principal spokesman for the advocates of decontrol, maintained that in a free market production would increase and prices would automatically reach an equitable level. The Truman Administration disagreed and urged that price ceilings and rationing be continued until supply had had an opportunity to catch up with demand. Congress, however, proved more susceptible to the pleas of the inflationists than to the logic of the President, and in June, 1946, it merely extended the life of the O.P.A. with little promise of effectively checking the upward spiral of prices. When Truman vetoed this measure, Congress responded with an almost identical bill. As the only alternative to runaway inflation, the President reluctantly accepted it. By autumn, prices under the new law had risen precipitously, and the government was being condemned both for permitting inflation and retaining controls. Truman then decided to abandon the struggle. In October, he announced the removal of all controls except those on rents. Although the President lost the battle over prices, he won the argument, for by December, 1946, prices were almost 32 per cent higher than in the preceding year.

Workers, as well as farmers and businessmen, were responsible for the postwar inflationary spiral. Labor leaders opposed the lifting of price ceilings, but they did not hesitate to call a series of strikes to obtain wage increases, which in turn pushed prices still higher and aggravated the problem that workers were attempting to solve. In the winter of 1945–6, there were strikes in the automobile, steel, and electrical industries. In April, 1946, the United Mine Workers went on strike and were joined by the railroad employees a month later; but when President Truman threatened to turn the roads over to the army to operate, the strikers returned to work. The first round of postwar strikes resulted in wage increases of approximately $.18 an hour. Subsequent strikes added still more to the nation's wage bill, and from 1945 to 1948 average hourly wage rates rose from $1.02 to $1.33. But, like Alice in Wonderland, no matter how hard labor ran, it seemed to stay in the same place, for in the same period the cost of living index (1935–9 = 100) increased from 128.4 to 171.1.

The most far-reaching labor crisis of the postwar years was set off by the United Mine Workers strike on April 1, 1946. The President then seized the mines, and when the operators refused to accept a contract that had been negotiated by federal authorities, the government retained its control over the industry. In November of the same year, John L. Lewis issued a second strike call, and the government replied with injunction proceedings. When Lewis ignored the injunction, he was ruled in contempt of court by a federal district judge, who fined him $10,000 and the United Mine Workers $3,500,000. On March 6, 1947, the lower court's decision was sustained by the Supreme Court, although the union's fine was subsequently reduced to $700,000. Three months after the Supreme Court's decision, a Republican-controlled Congress adopted the Taft-Hartley Act over the President's veto. This law, which its authors asserted was designed to redress the Wagner Act's alleged wrongs to employers, permitted management to sue unions that did not abide by their contracts, outlawed the closed shop, restricted the union shop, forbade campaign contributions by unions, gave employers the right to refuse to institute the check-off, required union leaders to sign a non-Communist affidavit, and made a sixty-day "cooling-off" period prerequisite to all strikes. Labor leaders unable to agree on almost anything else were all but unanimous in condemning what they called the "Taft-Hartley slave labor law," but subsequent events showed that the act did not cripple or seriously interfere with the growing power of unions in American life.

The Politics of the Fair Deal

Postwar politics were as confused as national economic trends. In the months that followed Japan's surrender, high prices, black markets, the housing shortage, and strikes were all indiscriminately attributed to the party in power, and in the 1946 congressional elections the Republicans gained control of both the Senate and House for the first time since the advent of the New Deal. Confident of victory in 1948, the Republican majorities in the eightieth Congress not only adopted the Taft-Hartley Act, but also consistently refused to heed the President's repeated demands for social and economic legislation.

The Republican convention, held in Philadelphia in June, 1948, nominated Governor Thomas E. Dewey of New York a second time for the presidency and Governor Earl Warren of California for the vice-presidency. Less than a month later, the Democrats convened in the same city to make the formal gestures in what most observers agreed was a lost cause. Many delegates hoped that they could induce either General Dwight D. Eisenhower or Supreme Court Justice William O. Douglas to accept the nomination, but when both announced that they were not candidates, Truman's selection was assured. As his running mate, the Democrats chose Senator Alben Barkley of Kentucky. Many southern Democrats, objecting to their party's strong stand in favor of civil-rights legislation, formed the States' Rights, or Dixiecrat, party. The Dixiecrats nominated Governor J. Strom Thurmond of South Carolina and Governor Fielding Wright of Mississippi and adopted a white supremacy and states rights platform. At the other end of the political spectrum was the Progressive party, whose standard bearers were Henry Wallace—who had broken with the Truman Administration over foreign policy—and Senator Glen Taylor of Idaho. Advocating cooperation with the Soviet Union and championing—but not defining—the "common man," the Progressives attempted to convince voters that Henry Wallace had inherited the mantle of Franklin D. Roosevelt. As the campaign developed, Communists and fellow-travelers played an increasingly large role in the Progressive party.

Throughout the campaign the so-called—and often self-styled—experts, the newspapers, and the professional poll-takers were almost unanimous in their predictions of a sweeping Republican victory. Dewey, convinced that he was riding an irresistible wave of popular sentiment, made cautious and sedate speeches in which he buried the issues beneath generalizations about the need for national unity. President Truman, who alone refused to concede his own defeat, waged an aggressive campaign. In countless prepared and off-the-cuff speeches, he charged that the eightieth or "do-nothing"—as he called it—Congress had consistently ignored the wishes of the people. Advocating civil-rights legislation, an expansion of public-power facilities, continued aid to agriculture, a firm policy toward the Soviet Union, and an increase in social-security benefits, the President made clear to the voters exactly where he stood on every major issue in the campaign.

On the day after the election, Truman could take almost sole credit for engineering the most stunning upset in the history of American presidential elections. With 49.5 per cent of the popular vote, Truman had won 303 electoral votes, Dewey 189, Thurmond 39, and Wallace none. The Democrats also regained control of both branches of the Congress and won impressive victories in state gubernatorial contests. Since both major parties had been in substantial agreement on foreign policy, the Democratic victory represented a reaffirmation by the voters of the domestic policies that had first been espoused by the New Deal. The Republicans, as in the past, had gone down to defeat before a farmer-labor alliance. While it was generally conceded before the election that the Democrats would receive labor's vote, their remarkably strong showing in the agricultural Middle West surprised almost everyone but President Truman.

When Franklin Roosevelt died in 1945, Harry Truman entered the Presidency with a profound sense of his own inadequacy. Appalled at having to follow a man of Roosevelt's stature, he made no attempt to conceal the trepidation with which he assumed his new unexpected responsibilities. But in the course of the next three years each new and

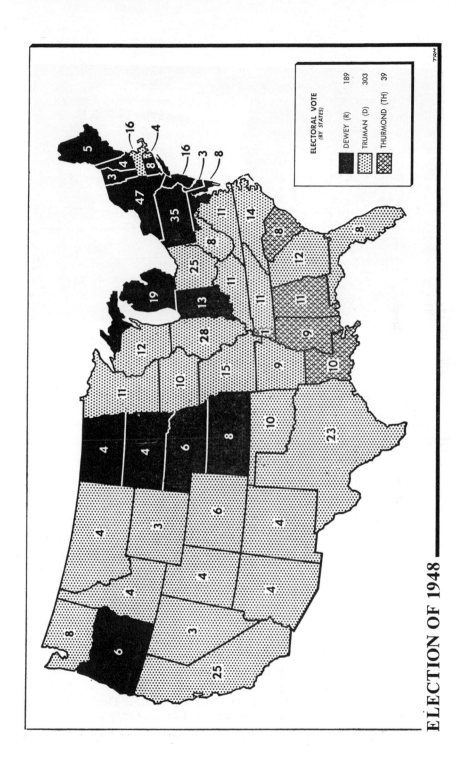

ELECTORAL VOTE
(BY STATES)

DEWEY (R)   189
TRUMAN (D)   303
THURMOND (TH)   39

ELECTION OF 1948

President in His Own Right, 1948

momentous decision increased his self-confidence, and his seemingly miraculous victory in 1948 removed any of his remaining doubts about his fitness for the Presidency. He began his first Administration as a weak president; he ended his second term as a strong executive and the recognized leader of his party and nation. The Presidency did not so much transform Harry Truman as enable him to recognize his potentialities.

The Fair Deal, as Truman called his domestic program in his State of the Union Message of 1949, contained little that was new to the American people. It was, as he said, "an extension of the New Deal." As such, it differed from its predecessor in degree rather than in kind. Truman asked for the application of the TVA idea to other river systems, an agricultural policy that would protect the consumer as well as the farmer, expansion of public-housing programs, added social-security coverage and benefits, new guarantees of civil rights, and an increase in minimum wages. In other instances—most notably in the demand for the repeal of the Taft-Hartley Act—the Fair Deal stood for nothing more than a return to the situation that had prevailed before the Republicans had gained control of Congress in 1946.

What distinguished the Fair Deal from the New Deal was not so much its program as its setting. Roosevelt had made his proposals to a people who were desperate enough to accept almost any suggestion that showed the remotest promise of relieving their economic problems. Truman, on the other hand, advocated an expansion of Roosevelt's depression-born policies in an era of unprecedented prosperity when the individual's major concern was no longer his next meal but his next car. Truman also placed major emphasis on some New Deal policies that Roosevelt had advanced in only the most tentative fashion. A case in point is provided by the civil-rights issue. The New Deal did enough for the Negro—if he lived in the North—to ensure his political support, but it did nothing to guarantee him his rights as a citizen if he lived in the South. The Fair Deal civil-rights program, in contrast, was an attempt to secure equality before the law for the Negro, regardless of where he lived; the Fair Deal actively advocated a program which the Roosevelt Administration had debated but made little effort to implement. Much the same generalization applies to the Fair Deal's proposals for medical insurance. In these and other instances, a difference in degree became a difference in kind.

The political setting of the Fair Deal also differed from that of its predecessor. During much of Roosevelt's first two terms as President, he could count on an overwhelming majority in Congress that made it relatively easy for him to win acceptance for his program. After Pearl Harbor, the overriding demands of war gave the President a degree of congressional support that would have been unthinkable in peacetime. With the defeat of the Axis, relations between the President and Congress—if nothing else—returned to the American norm of squabble. A coalition of northern Republicans and southern Democrats emerged as the most powerful bloc in Congress. This alliance of the most conservative groups in both parties favored governmental economy, freedom for business, strict regulation of labor, and states' rights. Its policies, in short, were diametrically opposed to those of the Fair Deal, and, despite Truman's upset victory in the 1948 election, the coalition's control over Congress remained unshaken and an insuperable obstacle to the Fair Deal.

The President, fully aware of the strength of the opposition, expounded and defended his program in messages to Congress, at press conferences, and in speeches. The results, however, were often disappointing. Some of his recommendations became law, but many others did not. In the last analysis, he lost—when he did lose—because he did not have the votes. Some observers thought that he tried to do too much too quickly, and others that he did not really press his program behind the scenes in Congress. Regardless of the tactics he employed, he could not change the facts of political life in Congress. The northern Democrats, who comprised the only bloc in the House and Senate that consistently supported his policies, remained a minority throughout his Administration. It is to Truman's credit as a politician and executive leader that Congress approved even part of his program.

The Fair Deal victories in Congress were won before the outbreak of war in Korea in 1950 and were largely confined to expanding programs inaugurated by the New Deal. Congress adopted two measures liberalizing the provisions of New Deal laws benefiting workers. In 1949, minimum wages, originally set at $.40 an hour by the Fair Labor Standards Act of 1938, were increased to $.75. In the following year, Congress approved a bill that increased Social Security payments and added some 10,000,000 individuals to those eligible for Social Security benefits. Bipartisan public and private housing bills were also adopted. The extension of rent control by Congress saved countless families— particularly those in city apartments—from eviction. The Housing Act of 1949 provided for slum clearance and the rapid construction of large-scale low-rent housing projects. In providing continued assistance for the farmer, Congress again adhered to principles established by the New Deal. The Agricultural Act of 1949 extended price supports at 90 per cent of parity for a year, with provisions for flexible price supports ranging from 75 to 90 per cent of parity for the year following.

Congress, however, rejected more of the Fair Deal program than it accepted. Despite the requests of the President and the pressure of union leaders, the Taft-Hartley Act was not repealed. The propaganda and lobbying campaign waged by the American Medical Association stiffened Congress's unwillingness to adopt the Administration proposal for a federal program of health insurance. Congress also failed to approve the Fair Deal plan for handling agricultural surpluses. Proposed by Secretary of Agriculture Charles Brannan, the so-called Brannan Plan, while retaining the essentials of the price-support program for nonperishable commodities, called for the sale of perishable commodities at the market price with the government paying the farmer the difference between that price and the support price. The Brannan Plan had obvious advantages for the consumer, but it was opposed by the large commercial farmers who influenced congressmen from the South and West to reject the proposal.

The President's shifting fortunes with Congress were particularly illustrated by the succession of immigration laws passed during his administration. In 1948, the Republican Congress adopted a bill admitting to the United States 205,000 "displaced persons"—the term used to describe Europeans made homeless by the war and its aftermath. Although Truman signed the bill, he did so with reluctance, for, as he pointed out, it plainly discriminated against Jews and Catholics. Two years later, the President appeared vindicated, for in a new measure the discriminatory provisions were eliminated and the number of displaced persons to be admitted to the United States was increased to 415,000. But in 1952, Congress approved an immigration bill that favored "Nordic" immigrants over those from southern and eastern Europe. When Truman vetoed this McCarran-Walter Immigration and Nationality Act, Congress passed it over his veto. This catch-all bill dealing with virtually every feature of immigration used the quota system established in 1924 to discriminate in favor of immigrants from northern Europe. Although it righted an old wrong by ending the total exclusion of Asians, its over-all effect was to tighten rather than liberalize the rules governing the admission of immigrants to the United States.

The Truman Administration's civil-rights program was the most controversial feature of the Fair Deal. It was the first full-scale effort made by the federal government since Reconstruction to eliminate some of the inequalities arising from racial prejudice. The program's sponsor was, moreover, a President who headed a party that was strongest in the region where prejudice against the Negro was most pronounced. The President himself came from a border state with a predominantly discriminatory attitude toward the Negro. In spite of these considerations, Truman in 1946 appointed a Committee on Civil Rights consisting of prominent Negro and white citizens from the South and other sections. In its report issued in 1947, the Committee not only condemned racial prejudice and its effects, but it also proposed anti-poll-tax and anti-lynching legislation, stricter enforcement of existing statutes to uphold minority rights, and the establishment of a permanent Fair Employment Practices Commission. Congress, however, acted on none of these proposals. A southern minority in the Senate either by filibustering or threatening to filibuster was always in a position to thwart the President's proposals. But the President through appointments and executive orders at least advanced parts of his program. He appointed Negroes to several important positions in the government, took steps to eliminate segregation in the federal bureaucracy, and had the Justice Department enforce strictly those laws that did protect the rights of minority groups.

Truman's efforts to carry out his Fair Deal program were also hampered by the mediocre quality of the Administration leaders around the President and a series of minor scandals, both of which lost the President much of the prestige he needed to make Congress follow his lead. Many of his appointments to Cabinet posts and to the Supreme Court, when taken with the "influence peddling" during his

Administration, deeply disturbed many citizens who otherwise admired the President's courage and strong leadership. Many friendly critics of Truman at the time wished that he would rise above narrow party concerns and loyalties on smaller matters of state as effectively as he did on what were called the "major decisions."

The Great National Debate about Communism

No issue more colored Truman's years in the White House than the threat of domestic Communism. The Communist issue, like the reforms sought by the Fair Deal, was a legacy of the New Deal. During the 1930's, Communists held responsible positions in the second rank of government officialdom, and several Communist cells of government employees were active in the nation's capital. At the time, these facts were generally either ignored or unknown. During the war years, when great stress was laid on the role played by the Soviet Union as a major ally, Communists were occasionally given places of considerable importance in the government's wartime agencies. But as the war drew to a close, the attitude toward Communist penetration of the government began to change from one of either criminal negligence or naïve acceptance to a feeling of alarm and consternation at the power that had been entrusted to individuals who if loyal Communist party members were likely to be secret agents of a foreign power.

Once started, the shift in public opinion moved with astonishing rapidity. Besides the genuine threat of their subversion and obfuscation, the Communists offered a convenient out for the frustrations of the period. After 1945, the nation found democratic ideals increasingly on the defensive in large parts of the world, and it was easy to believe that all the baffling problems Americans faced could be vanquished simply by getting rid of Communist subversives. Soon after the war had ended, a hunt was started to root out and expose Communists in American public life. Although this attack never reached the proportions that some American liberals and foreign observers thought it did— for they insisted that America was being swept by a reign of terror—in their more extreme and hysterical forms some security measures posed a dangerous threat to American institutions and ideals.

In the years immediately following the war, revelations of Communist duplicity and espionage made clear for those who looked at the facts the extent to which agents of the Soviet Union had infiltrated the governments of the United States and its allies. In 1945, the Justice Department prosecuted the editor of *Amerasia*, a magazine on Far Eastern Affairs sponsored by Communists, on the charge that he had illegally obtained secret government documents. In 1946, a spy ring consisting of domestic Communists and Soviet diplomatic officials was uncovered in Canada. In 1948, Whittaker Chambers, a senior editor of *Time* magazine, told a House Committee that Alger Hiss, while a government official, had stolen State Department documents in the 1930's as a secret member of a Soviet spy ring. In 1949, Judith Coplon, an employee of the Justice Department, was arrested in the act of handing over restricted government documents to a Soviet agent. In 1950, with the arrest of Klaus Fuchs, a British scientist, it was revealed that a group of British and American agents of the Soviet Union had several years earlier turned over to the Russian government the complete details on the construction of the atomic bomb.

Of all the cases connected with the Communist conspiracy in the United States, none aroused as much interest or produced as much acrimony as that of Alger Hiss. A graduate of Johns Hopkins and Harvard Law School and a government official during the New Deal and war years, Hiss resigned from the State Department in 1947 to become President of the Carnegie Endowment for International Peace. In the following year, Chambers, an admitted ex-Communist, testified before the House Committee on Un-American Activities that before the war he had received from Hiss stolen government documents for transmission to Soviet authorities. Hiss denied the charge and sued Chambers for libel. A grand jury in New York indicted Hiss for perjury. (The statute of limitations precluded an indictment for espionage.) In the ensuing trial, the jury was unable to agree, but in a second trial in 1951, Hiss was found guilty of perjury and sentenced to prison.

The bare facts of the Hiss case give no indication of the passions it engendered among Americans. In the first place, the drama of events was heightened by the contrast between Chambers and Hiss. The former, an ex-Communist who had led a Bohemian life, made no attempt to hide his past. Hiss, on the other hand, gave every outward appearance of being a model citizen and a typical product of a well-to-do eastern upbringing. His conservative, well-cut clothes and sensitive face made him look like anything but the stereotype of a secret agent in the Communist underground. This impression of Hiss was reinforced by the fact that several respected high public officials were willing to serve as character witnesses for him and that no less a person than the President of the United States in 1948 had referred to the House Committee's investigation of his past as a "red herring." But this apparent reversal in the roles of accuser and accused was not the only unusual feature of the Hiss case. To many liberals, Hiss seemed the epitome of the New Deal, and their wish to uphold the memory of the movement of which he had seemingly been a loyal member made it almost automatic to judge him innocent. With some justification, Alistair Cooke entitled his book on the Hiss case *A Generation on Trial*. Several critics of the New Deal, like many liberals, believed that the New Deal as well as Hiss was on trial; but, unlike liberals, they were certain that both were guilty. Long before Hiss was sent to prison, he had become a symbol to the American people of much that they considered good or bad in their recent past.

Regardless of how any individual viewed the Hiss case, the facts of Communist infiltration in the government remained. The government and people of the United States were threatened by a foreign power, and they had to take steps to defend themselves while exercising considerable care that anti-Communist measures did not destroy the basic liberties which its citizens enjoyed and to which they were entitled. No policy could have matched all shades of opinion in the United States; and when Truman's Administration drew up a loyalty program, it was almost inevitable that some liberals should think it a violation of civil liberties and some anti-Communists should think that it was not rigorous enough. In 1947, or a year before Chambers made his initial charges against Hiss before the House Committee on Un-American Activities, the President issued an executive order requiring a loyalty check of all federal employees. The investigation was conducted by both the Civil Service Commission and the Federal Bureau of Investigation and took four years to complete. It led to the dismissal of more than 200 individuals and was at least indirectly responsible for the resignation of more than 2,000 others. The loyalty program was modified in 1950 when provision was made for the dismissal of employees in certain key branches of the government who were charged with being "security risks" rather than with being disloyal. It was more difficult to define a security risk, but, despite certain egregious and even ludicrous errors, the revised program did not get out of hand.

The Administration did not confine its anti-Communist drive to the members of the federal service. Through the courts, it made a frontal assault against the Communist party of the United States. In 1948, eleven leading members of the party were arrested and indicted for violating the Smith Act of 1940. Specifically, they were charged with conspiracy to teach that the government of the United States should be overthrown by violent means. Following a nine-month trial in New York City, all eleven were found guilty in a decision that was reaffirmed by the Court of Appeals and the Supreme Court. Lesser party officials, who were subsequently arrested, were also tried and convicted under the Smith Act. By the end of Truman's second term,

the Communist party's foremost leadership—if not the party itself—
had been greatly weakened; and if any Communist still remained in the
government, he or she was unknown to even the Administration's Republican opponents.

In carrying out its anti-Communist program, the Truman Administration almost inevitably exposed itself to the charge that in seeking
to strengthen the nation it was undermining the freedom of the individual. Critics of the government's policies who accepted this view
charged that the loyalty and security program at times violated rights
guaranteed to the individual by the Constitution and that the courts
were entering on dangerous ground when they ruled that the measure
of guilt was the teaching of unpopular doctrines, even—some liberals
contended—if the doctrine was that the government should be violently overthrown.

Whether these opinions were right or wrong, the nation faced the
difficulty that the Communist conspiracy was one for which traditional security methods were in many ways inadequate. Communists
were so well organized and so well schooled that to wait for their
overt act to overthrow the government might be too late to save the
nation. Strict civil-libertarians claimed that that was the risk a free
society took. Others—not all of them illiberal—maintained that the history of thirty years of Communism throughout the world had shown
what Soviet intentions were; that a free society could not grant
freedom to any group powerful enough and, on the record, likely to
deny freedom to others if it came to power. These anti-Communists
insisted that if the nation's best legal minds established careful procedures and helped staff the security boards, the constitutional right
of both Communists and other citizens could be protected while the
nation was protected.

The absence of clear and careful procedures was especially obvious
in some of the actions of Congressional committees investigating Communism and Communists in the United States. Eager and uninstructed
congressmen intimidated witnesses, relied too uncritically on information supplied by professional informers, permitted names to be be-
smirched and careers to be disrupted by unsubstantiated rumors, and
used "guilt by association" as a device for judging the innocent as well
as the guilty.

The temper of Congress was revealed in the McCarran Internal
Security Act of 1950, which mixed together legitimate and illegitimate, careful and careless procedures. Communist and Communist-
front organizations, as well as individuals belonging to them, were
required to register with the Attorney General as foreign agents; aliens

who had once been Communists were denied entry into the United States as visitors as well as immigrants; the government was authorized to intern Communists in the event of war; Communists were denied passports and employment in either the government or defense industries; and a Subversive Activities Control Board was established to cooperate with the Attorney General in the campaign against Communism. In vetoing this measure, the President said: "In a free country, we punish men for the crimes they commit, but never for the opinions they have." But Congress disagreed, and the bill was repassed over the President's veto and became law.

Behind this bill were the two "Communist issues" of the postwar years. The first was concerned with the very real threat to American security posed by the Communist conspiracy. The second centered on the attempt of some Americans to build on a legitimate fear in order to limit the power of non-Communist radicals and liberals. The lack of clarity in the whole debate and the well-founded national fear of Communism enabled unscrupulous or unthinking individuals to promote either their own careers or programs. The advantages for those with questionable motives were undeniable. It gave some reactionaries a club with which to beat liberals; it enabled dubious organizations to wrap their causes and themselves in the American flag; but it also permitted some liberals to play the role of martyrs. Otherwise obscure politicians could obtain publicity by exploiting the anti-Communist issue. Some Republicans thought that a charge of being "soft on Communism" could defeat the Democrats. Anti-Communism, in short, opened up a whole new range of political possibilities, including the distortion of a serious question of momentous import for personal advantage.

No demagogue had a greater or more dramatic success than Senator Joseph R. McCarthy of Wisconsin. He combined ruthless cunning and astonishing audacity with a brazen disregard of truth to demoralize his opponents, enrapture his followers, turn American against American, and disrupt the orderly processes of government. He first achieved notoriety as an anti-Communist in February, 1950, when, searching for an issue to repair his political fortunes, he announced that there were 57 or 205 (no one, including McCarthy, could agree on just what the figure was) Communists in the Department of State. Although he failed to substantiate this charge with the name of a single Communist, this had no apparent effect on his subsequent career. With many Republican and Democratic leaders giving him tacit support, open encouragement, or insufficient challenge, and with the backing of practically every reactionary organization in the United States, he indiscriminately accused any one who aroused his displeasure, or challenged the validity of his charges, either of being a Communist or of having Communistic sympathies. When asked for proof, he merely moved on to fresh accusations, and his victims and dupes included not only professors and obscure civil servants but also such prominent Americans as George C. Marshall and Dwight D. Eisenhower. A new word coined to describe his methods, "McCarthyism," soon became all too prominent in American vocabulary. The most disquieting aspects of McCarthyism were not the man and his deeds, but the hearty support they received from many Americans who at least credited him with arousing the nation to the dangers of Communism.

The U.S. and the U.N.

During the war, Allied leaders had increasingly devoted much time and energy to postwar planning. The failure of the League of Nations served as a constant reminder of the need for action, and they were determined to work out plans for a postwar association of nations while the wartime spirit of unity was still strong. At the conference of foreign ministers at Moscow in 1944, no attempt was made to devise a detailed plan, but the Moscow Declaration pledged the Soviet Union, China, the United States, and Great Britain to establish a "general international organization" to preserve peace. The Senate overwhelmingly approved the Moscow Declaration. The possibility of actual Allied willingness to cooperate on nonmilitary problems seemed strengthened by the creation of the United Nations Relief and Rehabilitation Administration of more than forty nations. U.N.R.R.A. was designed to help feed, clothe, and shelter the millions who had lost their homes and means of support because of the war. Equally significant was the formation of the International Bank for Reconstruction and Development and the International Monetary Fund to promote international economic cooperation and stability.

President Roosevelt had made public his plans for a postwar organization to preserve the peace in June, 1944. Making it clear that he did not favor a world superstate, he said: "We are seeking effective agreement and arrangements through which the Nations would maintain, according to their capacities, adequate forces to meet the needs of preventing war and of making impossible deliberate preparation for war, and to have such forces available for joint action when necessary." Two months later, representatives of the Big Four attended the Dumbarton Oaks Conference to work out preliminary plans for the United Nations. The delegates agreed that the new organization should con-

Around the Table at Yalta: Stalin (upper left), Roosevelt (upper right), Churchill (lower right)

[NATIONAL ARCHIVES]

sist of a security council, to be controlled by the major powers with authority to determine and enforce United Nations' policies; a general assembly, in which every state was to be represented, but with only advisory functions; a court of justice; and an economic and social council.

Before any action had been taken on these proposals, Roosevelt, Stalin, and Churchill met at Yalta, in the Crimea, in February, 1945. The Yalta discussions covered a wide variety of topics and revealed a potentially serious cleavage of views between the Soviet Union and the Western Allies. Roosevelt went to the Yalta Conference determined to win Russian backing for a postwar international organization. He was less skeptical than Churchill about Soviet intentions. If these had been honorable—and some Americans had been warning the President they were not—the Yalta arrangements might have helped stabilize European peace. Instead, the Yalta agreements were used by the Soviet Union as the basis for hegemony over eastern and central Europe, and this seemed to some Americans a betrayal of the principles of the Atlantic Charter and of American interests. At Yalta, Stalin was preoccupied with increasing Soviet power and assuring Russian security. At Stalin's insistence, Churchill and Roosevelt agreed that two member republics of the U.S.S.R. would be granted separate representation in the United Nations; that each member of the United Nations Security Council would have the right to veto substantive decisions of the other members; that the Soviet Union could annex the eastern portion of Poland, which in turn would be compensated with a comparable amount of German territory; and that southern Sakhalin and the Kuriles as well as a preferential position in Manchuria should be granted to the Soviet Union. In return, Stalin pledged that Russia would support the United Nations, work for the establishment of democratic governments in Poland and Yugoslavia, and join in the war against Japan after Germany's defeat. The problem of the postwar occupation of Germany was resolved by a decision to divide it into four zones, which would be assigned to Great Britain, France, the Soviet Union, and the United States, respectively.

Four months after the Yalta meeting, the preliminary plans for a postwar international organization were transformed into the United Nations Charter at the San Francisco Conference of fifty nations that had declared war against the Axis. The Charter was drawn up on the hypothesis that the strongest nations were best suited to serve as guardians of world peace. Final authority was vested in the Security Council, which in turn was dominated by its permanent members—China, France, the Soviet Union, Great Britain, and the United States—and six other members elected by the Assembly for two-year terms; but each of the Big Five possessed the right of veto, and all Security Council decisions required a majority of seven votes. Despite the limits on their powers, the smaller nations accepted the Charter in the hope that the Big Five would be able to reconcile their differences. In the United States, there was practically no organized opposition to the Charter, and it was ratified by the Senate on July 28, 1945.

In accordance with the terms of the Charter, a number of other United Nations agencies were also established, including the Economic and Social Council and the Trusteeship Council with supervisory powers over certain "colonial areas." An International Court of Justice with fifteen judges was modeled on the World Court. The Military Staff Committee, composed of the Chiefs of Staff of the Big Five, was set up to plan the military enforcement of United Nations policies.

Had the Soviet Union and its allies been able to settle all outstanding political problems, the United Nations might have been able to work as originally intended. Instead, the new association was to be called upon to make a postwar security system instead of enforcing it. This it was incapable of doing. In the early years of its existence, the

THE UNITED NATIONS SYSTEM

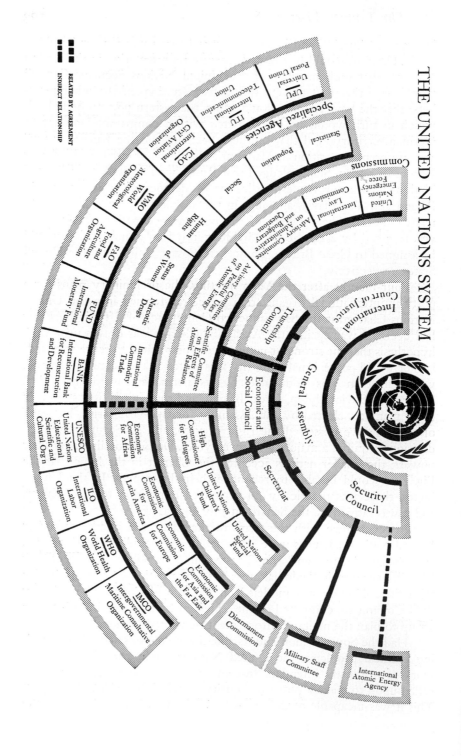

RELATED BY AGREEMENT

INDIRECT RELATIONSHIP

Specialized Agencies

UPU Universal Postal Union

ITU International Telecommunication Union

ICAO International Civil Aviation Organization

WMO World Meteorological Organization

FAO Food and Agriculture Organization

FUND International Monetary Fund

BANK International Bank for Reconstruction and Development

UNESCO United Nations Educational Scientific and Cultural Org n

ILO International Labor Organization

WHO World Health Organization

IMCO Intergovernmental Maritime Consultative Organization

Commissions

Statistical

Population

Social

Human Rights

Status of Women

Narcotic Drugs

International Commodity Trade

Economic Commission for Africa

Economic Commission for Latin America

Economic Commission for Europe

Economic Commission for Asia and the Far East

United Nations Emergency Force

International Law Commission

Advisory Committee on Administrative and Budgetary Questions

Advisory Committee on Peaceful Uses of Atomic Energy

Scientific Committee on Effects of Atomic Radiation

High Commissioner for Refugees

United Nations Children's Fund

United Nations Special Fund

International Court of Justice

Trusteeship Council

Economic and Social Council

General Assembly

Secretariat

Security Council

Disarmament Commission

Military Staff Committee

International Atomic Energy Agency

United Nations intervened in a number of disputes that jeopardized world peace. Soon after the U.N. began to function in January, 1946, Iran protested to the United Nations about the continued presence of Russian troops on Iranian soil. The Security Council took no action, but the subsequent withdrawal of Russian troops was caused in part by the publicity after the incident had been referred to the United Nations. In the fighting in Indonesia between the natives and the Dutch, a mission appointed by the Security Council was able to effect a temporary truce. The United Nations took a much more active part during the upheaval of the birth of the new state of Israel. Before the British withdrawal, a commission appointed by the General Assembly proposed a tripartite partition of Palestine, which the Arabs and Jews rejected. Then fighting between Arabs and Jews followed the establishment of the government of Israel. Count Bernadotte of Sweden and Ralph Bunche of the United States, as successive United Nations mediators in Palestine, helped to devise a formula for an armistice in the Holy Land.

United Nations intervention in Indonesia and Palestine proved the exception rather than the rule, for on virtually all other issues Russian intransigence effectively thwarted the will of a majority group that was usually led by the United States. In 1947, the Soviet Union used its veto to prevent the Security Council from attempting to halt the Greek civil war. Another Russian veto overrode the majority resolution on the proposed United Nations policy toward Spain, and Russian obstructionism made impossible the appointment by the Security Council of a governor for Trieste. In the first three years of its existence, Russia used the veto thirty times to block Security Council action. At the same time, the Soviet Union and the United States were unable to agree on the control of atomic energy. The United States had proposed the establishment of an International Atomic Energy Commission with complete authority over the manufacture and use of atomic energy in every nation; the Russians countered with a plan calling for every nation first to renounce atomic warfare. Since both countries refused to give way, there the matter stood. When President Truman announced on September 23, 1949, that the Russians had exploded an atom bomb, Americans knew that they were in the most deadly armaments race in the history of mankind.

The World Divided

The "cold war" between the Soviet Union and the United States developed in Europe soon after the surrender of Germany. In July,

1945, the leaders of the Big Three had met for the last time at Potsdam to discuss the policies that they would adopt toward Germany and her allies. Although all were agreed on the desirability of concluding peace treaties with Bulgaria, Finland, Hungary, Italy, and Rumania as soon as possible, the obstructionist tactics of the Soviet Union delayed the pacts, and it was not until February, 1947, that this work was finally completed. The treaties deprived Germany's wartime satellites of their power to make war, levied heavy reparations on them, and arranged a number of territorial changes. After ten years of negotiation, an agreement was reached about Austria, which regained its independence. In 1955, both Allied and Russian troops were withdrawn from that country.

The conflict between the Soviet Union and the Western democracies postponed indefinitely any final agreement about the future of Germany. Divided into four zones of occupation, Germany became the key to a political settlement in Europe, and, with the stakes set high by both sides, no solution for the reunification and independence of Germany could be found. Each occupying nation in Germany had complete authority over its own zone, but any policy that affected all of Germany required unanimous approval of the American, British, French, and Russian commanders in Germany, who collectively comprised the Allied Control Council. The area of possible disagreement was broadened by placing the city of Berlin, which was surrounded by the Russian Zone, under four-power control.

Initially, the wartime Allies were in complete agreement about the need for punishing Germany and destroying its war potential. Drastic restrictions were placed on heavy industry, and each power was permitted to obtain its reparations from Germany in the form of industrial equipment needed to rebuild its own war-torn areas. The victors were also free to use German prisoners of war in their reconstruction programs. The leading Nazis were placed on trial at Nuremburg in November, 1945, before a four-power tribunal. Their trial records fully documented the horrors of the Nazi regime. Of more than twenty defendants, three were acquitted, eight were sentenced to prison, and ten were hanged. Herman Göring escaped hanging by committing suicide. Meanwhile, the "smaller fish" were turned over to "denazification" courts, which undertook the almost impossible task of attempting to determine which Germans had supported the Hitler regime actively enough to be barred from political life.

Although the Western Allies and the Soviet Union were fully agreed that the war guilt was Germany's, there was little else on which they could reach a common understanding. Reparations provided an

Berliners Watching the Airlift, 1948

[U. S. AIR FORCE PHOTO]

endless source of conflict, although the Soviets practically denuded eastern Germany of its industrial power while systematically making it a Communist society under a puppet regime. Constant and interminable disputes between the Western commanders and the Russian authorities convinced the West that the Soviet Union was aiming at the control of all Germany. Starting in December, 1946, western Germany gradually was united, and in 1949 it was granted virtual political independence under the Bonn regime of Chancellor Konrad Adenauer. The new German chief led his nation in a remarkable economic revival, ended its ancient enmity with France, and made it a bulwark of Western power. American troops, however, remained in Germany under new treaty arrangements.

The conflict between East and West in Germany produced a major crisis in 1948. In the spring, the Soviet Union withdrew from the Allied Control Council, and Great Britain, France, and the United States made tentative plans for the political union of their zones. When the Western Allies in the summer of 1948 announced a new currency for use in their zones and in the portion of Berlin under their control, the Russians imposed a blockade upon all Western rail and water shipments into the German capital. Rather than evacuate Berlin, the Allies used British and American planes to fly supplies into the beleaguered city.

Within a few weeks, the extraordinary "air-lift" was operating around the clock and supplying western Berlin with enough food, fuel, and raw materials to keep its economy functioning. For several months neither side would give way; the Russians set up a separate police force and civil government for their sector of Berlin, and the Allies established a counterblockade to prevent shipments from the western to the eastern sectors of Germany. Finally, in the spring of 1949 the Russians let it be known that they were willing to end their blockade if the Western powers would end theirs, and in May both blockades were lifted. The Russian blockade helped convince the Allies of the need to create the Bonn regime. For their part, the Russians tightened totalitarian and military controls over their zone and made it clear that any German peace treaty would have to guarantee the continuation of the "Socialist achievements" in East Germany.

The "cold war" between the Soviet Union and the West quickly spread beyond Germany to the rest of Europe. Russian troops had occupied countries along the Soviet border, and, with the aid of native Communists, they converted Hungary, Poland, Yugoslavia, Bulgaria, and Rumania into totalitarian societies that were Russian satellites. Czechoslovakia was added to this list in 1948, following a successful Communist coup. At the same time, Communist parties in Italy and France resorted to sabotage and obstructionism in their efforts to gain power.

The Western powers were unable and unwilling to prevent any of these developments; but when the withdrawal of British troops from Greece seemed to leave the way open for the Communists to overthrow the Greek government, the United States assumed the diplomatic offensive. On March 12, 1947, President Truman asked Congress for $300,000,000 to aid Greece and an additional $100,000,000 for Turkey, which stood alone between the Soviet Union and the Dardanelles. What soon became known as the Truman Doctrine was approved in Congress by a coalition of Democrats and Republicans who agreed on a bipartisan foreign policy to check further Russian expansion.

Rebuilding Europe's Economy

The Truman Doctrine was at best a stopgap arrangement that successfully met a specific emergency. It soon became apparent, however, that a long-range program of assistance was needed both to revive the European economy and to prevent the Communists from adding to their gains. U.N.R.R.A., to which the United States contributed much the largest share of money and supplies, had no way of preventing the Communist rulers in eastern Europe from using its relief shipments for political purposes, while a large 1945 loan to Great Britain had proved a palliative rather than a cure.

Secretary Marshall at Harvard, June, 1947

The first high Western official to propose publicly a constructive general plan for Europe's economic problems was Secretary of State George C. Marshall. In an address at Harvard University in June, 1947, he suggested that if Europe's leaders would actively investigate what their countries could achieve through economic cooperation and what their principal needs were, the United States would be prepared to provide them with the necessary financial assistance. Marshall's proposal met with an overwhelmingly favorable response in western Europe, and in September, 1947, the representatives of sixteen European nations, including those from the combined British and American zones in Germany, met in Paris to work out the details of the program. Because Russia considered the Marshall Plan an instrument of American imperialism, none of the invited Soviet Union's satellite nations was permitted to attend the conference. When the delegates had completed the laborious task of drawing up a balance sheet for western Europe's economy, it was decided that $21,780,000,000 in loans and credits would be needed through 1951. After reviewing the conference's finding, the United States agreed to underwrite Europe's recovery with $17,000,000,000 for a four-year period.

Despite repeated demands in and out of Congress for a reduction in government expenditures, the Marshall Plan—or European Recovery Program—met with little opposition in the United States. Most American leaders were convinced that it provided the only feasible method for preventing the hard times and chaos on which Communism flourished. In December, 1947, Congress made a stopgap E.R.P. appropriation of $597,000,000, and in the following April, it voted an appropriation of $5,300,000,000 to cover the first year of the plan's operation. To administer the foreign-aid program, the Economic Cooperation Administration was established, and Paul G. Hoffman was made its director.

The effects of the E.R.P. upon western Europe were almost immediately apparent. It not only made possible a marked improvement in the European economy, but enabled democratic political leaders to adopt a stronger line toward the Communist opposition within their countries. The plan did not, however, cure the political sickness of France and Italy, for their governments continued to rise and fall with regularity, and the hard core of Communist voting strength of about twenty per cent of the ballots remained unbroken. But economic revival did awaken the European masses to the possibilities of a society of abundance. By 1950 a so-called Americanization of European society had started, to the dismay and even hatred of many European intellectuals who claimed that Europe was being threatened as much by American vulgarity and mechanization as by Soviet power.

In the ten years following the inauguration of E.R.P., Europe took many steps to coordinate and unify its economies. By 1949, the Benelux states (Belgium, the Netherlands, and Luxemburg) had worked out the first of European plans for a customs union, and in the next years, other formal economic blocs were formed and tried to work out their differences. The most conclusive evidence of the effectiveness of E.R.P. was provided by the Soviet Union's determination to speed up its diplomatic offensive. In September, 1947, while the Marshall Plan delegates were conferring in Paris, the Soviet Union and its satellites formed the Cominform to chastise the Communist chief of Yugoslavia, Marshal Tito, for his alleged "deviationism" and to reaffirm a single propaganda line for Communist parties throughout the world. The Cominform was merely the Comintern of the 1930's under another name, and Moscow had once again become the capital of the world revolutionary movement. The creation of the Cominform was followed in February, 1948, by the Communist coup in Czechoslovakia, and in the summer of the same year the Russians imposed their blockade upon Berlin.

By 1948, the aggressive character of Russian foreign policy had convinced the Western powers that military as well as economic unity was needed to insure their security. When Great Britain and the countries of northwestern Europe began to confer about mutual defense, they received the active encouragement of the United States, which soon became a full partner in the discussions. In March, 1949, ten European nations as well as Canada and the United States signed the North Atlantic Treaty. Under the terms of this pact, each nation agreed to come to the assistance of any of the others that might be attacked. By 1950, the United States was shipping arms to its European allies, and military staffs were discussing joint defenses of the West.

Victories and Defeats in the Far East

Throughout the postwar years, Far Eastern problems were fully as serious and complex as those in Europe. Only in Japan did American policy proceed more or less according to plan. Unlike occupied Germany, Japan in defeat was almost exclusively under the control of the United States. Although a Far Eastern Commission consisting of eleven Pacific powers had been established in Washington, and although there was an Allied Control Commission in Tokyo made up of the United States, the Soviet Union, China, and the British Commonwealth, these bodies had little effect on day-to-day policies in Japan. General Douglas MacArthur, as commander of the American occupying forces, exercised practically dictatorial powers over the Japanese, who for their part docilely obeyed his orders. As in Germany, drastic curbs were imposed initially upon all forms of heavy industry. Twenty-eight Japanese leaders were placed on trial for war crimes; seven were executed. The Japanese, meanwhile, seemed as intent on pleasing the Americans as they once had been on killing them.

MacArthur's policies resulted in a number of sweeping changes, at least on the surface of Japanese life. To break the economic power of the old ruling class and to improve the common lot of the people, large estates were broken up, and the major industrial and financial monopolies were dissolved. Although the Emperor was retained in order to facilitate the occupation, he was divested of both his power and his claim to divinity. Under a new constitution that went into effect in 1946, provision was made for a democratically elected legislature of two houses, and all Japanese were guaranteed certain basic civil rights. Women were given the right to vote; labor was encouraged to develop a trade-union program; and children were provided with a school system that emphasized democratic ideals rather than militarism.

The Philippine Islands, which also played an important role in American Far Eastern policy in the postwar years, were granted their independence by the United States on July 4, 1946. Unable to defend itself against potential aggressors or to rebuild its war-torn economy without outside assistance, the new nation was reluctant to have the United States withdraw completely. It was to the strategic advantage of both countries for the United States to take an active interest in Philippine affairs. Through the Military Assistance Act, the United States agreed to aid the new country in the establishment of an effective military force, while the Philippines in return granted the Americans the right to maintain naval and military bases in the islands. The Philippine Trade Act of 1946 provided for free trade between the islands and the United States for eight years, and the Philippine Rehabilitation Act appropriated $720,000,000 to repay Filipinos for property damage incurred during the war.

On the Asiatic mainland, American diplomacy suffered its most diastrous reverses in the years after the war. In China, the Communists swept all before them. The civil war, which had been interrupted by the Japanese invasion, was resumed by Mao Tse-tung's army; at the same time, there was little evidence that Chiang Kai-shek's Nationalists could provide China with either an honest or efficient government. Despite several American diplomatic missions to try to stabilize Chinese affairs, the United States had to stand by while the Communists overran China, and Chiang Kai-shek was forced to transfer what remained of his government to the island of Formosa. Although some Americans, during the earlier stages of the civil war, had believed that the Chinese Communists were merely agrarian reformers without Russian ties, this illusion was completely shattered in 1950, when Mao Tse-tung, the Chinese Communist leader, paid a state visit to Moscow. After that, the two countries became close allies. China, meanwhile, embarked on a ruthless conversion of its society to totalitarianism, sent agents into most Asian countries to do subversive work, and proclaimed itself the leader of the Asian movements to overthrow what remained of Western controls and influences in the Far East. Mao claimed the island of Formosa and entered on a continuous campaign of threats and military preparations to occupy it, while Chiang, having at last cleaned house in his government and having brought prosperity and stability to the island, periodically announced his readiness to liberate the mainland. The first country that provided Mao with an opportunity to translate words into action was not Formosa but Korea.

Three Frustrating Years in Korea

Although promised eventual independence by the Cairo Conference of 1943, Korea was occupied at the end of the war by both the Soviet Union and the United States, with the thirty-eighth parallel dividing the Russian zone in the north from the American zone in the south. Under the Russian administration the land in the northern zone was redistributed among the peasants, and a "Democratic People's Republic," patterned on the Soviet model, was established early in 1948. American occupation officials, while making few changes in the organization of the Korean economy, set up a provisional government that was viewed as the first step toward the creation of a united, democratic Korea. But when the United Nations General Assembly authorized an election for the establishment of a single government in Korea, the Soviet Union refused to allow the Koreans in its zone to vote and blocked the Security Council's intervention in Korean affairs by its use of the veto.

Despite constant friction and numerous incidents, the two zones maintained an uneasy peace until June 25, 1950, when North Korean troops launched a full-scale invasion of the southern half of the country. The South Koreans were no match for the invaders, who had been trained and equipped by the Soviet Union, and in the initial stages of the fighting the North Koreans captured the capital city of Seoul and continued to push southward.

Within twenty-four hours of the outbreak of fighting, the Security Council—in a meeting that was not attended by the Soviet Union—accused the North Korean Communists of a "breach of the peace" and demanded that they withdraw from the territory south of the thirty-eighth parallel. In addition, the nations belonging to the United Nations were asked to do all within their power to restore the status quo. On June 27, President Truman announced that American military forces

The Dreadful Hills of Korea

[U. S. ARMY PHOTO]

would be used to assist the South Koreans. On the same day, the Security Council requested the members of the United Nations to "repel the armed attack in Korea." Within a short time, Americans comprised the largest element in the twelve-nation U.N. force on the peninsula, and General Douglas MacArthur was made commander-in-chief of the U.N. forces.

During the first month of the war, the U.N. armies were repeatedly defeated by the numerically superior North Koreans, and by the first week in August, they held only a beachhead (approximately the size of Connecticut) located in the southeast corner of the Korean peninsula. Despite repeated attacks, the Americans and South Koreans were able to hold their ground, and on September 15 they took the offensive. While ground troops drove north from the beachhead, brilliantly executed amphibious landings at Inchon on the west coast of Korea near the capital of Seoul enabled the U.N. forces to outflank a large part of the Communist invaders. Within two weeks, U.N. troops had fought their way across the thirty-eighth parallel, and on November 21, advance units reached the Yalu River. The war seemed practically over, and MacArthur informed his soldiers that they would be home for Christmas. But on November 26, more than 200,000 Chinese Communists joined the North Koreans in a full-scale counterattack against the U.N. armies. Taken by surprise and overwhelmed by superior numbers, the U.N. forces retreated on every sector of the front, and it was not until mid-January that they were able to stabilize their lines some seventy-five miles south of the thirty-eighth parallel. In the following months, the U.N. troops were able to advance some miles beyond the parallel in the west.

During the first nine months of the war in Korea, General MacArthur and the Truman Administration had increasingly disagreed over the conduct of military aspects of American policy in Korea. After China intervened, the U.N. commander-in-chief believed that the China coast should be completely blockaded, that the United States should give all possible assistance to Chiang Kai-shek on Formosa, and that planes should be permitted to bomb enemy bases in what he referred to as the "privileged sanctuary" of Manchuria. A dramatic debate took place in America and Europe over MacArthur's proposals. The General and his supporters held that there was no substitute for total victory and that the risk of a world war would have to be taken in order to defeat the Chinese. President Truman, with the approval of Europeans and many Americans, opposed all these moves on the ground that they might convert the local war in Korea into a global war. After MacArthur issued repeated public statements that both implicitly and explicitly criticized the Administration policy in the Far East, President Truman in April, 1951, dismissed him for insubordination. Lieutenant General Matthew B. Ridgway, former commander of operations in the field, took over MacArthur's duties in both Japan and Korea. MacArthur retired from active service and received a hero's welcome on his return to the United States. Although many Americans thought that MacArthur had been shabbily treated, others, who agreed with the President, maintained that civilian rather than military authority should determine American policies and that the United States might have to be content with limited objectives in smaller wars such as in Korea in order to prevent a third world war.

Having extracted as much from the Korean "incident" as they were likely to get and given the ability of the U.N. forces to check Communist troops, the Russians proposed in June, 1951, that "discussions be started between the belligerents for a cease fire." Both sides welcomed the chance to end the war without apparent loss of face, but in the ensuing drawn-out and taxing truce talks the Communist and

U.N. representatives had difficulty in finding any area of substantial agreement. Neither side was in a position to dictate terms to the other, and negotiations were reduced to a form of diplomatic chess in which constructive efforts to reach a settlement were subordinated to the desire to anticipate and check the other side's moves. During the prolonged stalemate at the conference table, fighting continued sporadically under what reporters described as a tacit agreement to "ease" rather than "cease" fire.

The intervention of the United States in Korea served as a constant reminder to all Americans of their country's new role in world affairs. Americans were fighting and dying for a system of collective security that the United States had taken the lead in building. The defense of western Europe and Asia and the use of economic, diplomatic, and military power to control the course of events in every part of the globe free of Communist dictatorship were, for the foreseeable future, primary American responsibilities.

FOR SUPPLEMENTARY READING

Truman's *Memoirs* (2 vols., 1955) give the President's own views. Also use L. W. Koenig (ed.), *The Truman Administration* (1956). The later parts of T. C. Cochran, *The American Business System, A Historical Perspective, 1900–1955* (1957) has special value and should be used with W. N. Peach and W. Krause, *Basic Data of the American Economy* (1955), a statistical study, and A. F. Burns, *Prosperity Without Inflation* (1957). Compare also, however, the two editions of J. Dewhurst and associates, *America's Needs and Resources* (1947; revised 1955). On foreign policy a good analysis is W. Reitzel and others, *United States Foreign Policy, 1945–1955* (1956). Also use R. F. Mikesell, *United States Economic Policy and International Relations* (1952). On the U.N. read E. P. Chase, *The United Nations in Action* (1950). Walter Lippmann's *The Cold War* (1947) assessed the balance of power shortly after the American-Russian struggle began. The Yalta controversy is surveyed in J. Snell (ed.), *The Meaning of Yalta* (1956), and the uproar over China is made clearer by H. Feis, *The China Tangle* (1953). On Germany and Japan use E. H. Litchfield (ed.), *Governing Postwar Germany* (1953), and R. A. Fearey, *Occupation of Japan* (1950). On Korea start with J. C. Caldwell and L. Frost, *The Korea Story* (1952), and use as good journalism R. Rovere and A. M. Schlesinger, *The General and the President* (1951). On repercussions of Communism at home consult M. Decter and J. Rorty, *McCarthy and the Communists* (1954); S. Hook, *Heresy, Yes-Conspiracy, No* (1953); C. H. Pritchett, *Civil Liberties and the Vinson Court* (1954); and A. Cooke, *A Generation on Trial* (1950), on Hiss and Chambers.

21

>>>->>>->>>->>>->>>->>>->>>->>>

America at Bay

T HE DEMOCRATS ENTERED the campaign of 1952 with five straight
presidential victories over their Republican rivals. Their party's
greatest triumphs had been achieved by uniting the farmer
and worker, appealing to the underprivileged, and emphasizing
economic issues in domestic affairs. The Depression had provided the
party's leaders with the winning issues and the formula for successive
victories, but it had also left them unprepared for the politics of prosperity and reluctant to abandon the appeals that had proved so successful in the past. But times had changed and so had the American
electorate. Having lived through more than a decade of prosperity,
Americans were no longer interested in refighting the battles the New
Deal had won in the Depression. The old issues were dead, and the
political alliances that had carried the Democrats to victory for more
than two decades were wrecked beyond repair.

Escape from Frustration

If there was a prevailing mood in America in 1952, it was one of
frustration. World War II had been followed, not by peace, but by a
cold war in Europe and a shooting war in Asia. The United States had
spent billions and lost hundreds of thousands of men in both wars, but
the best it could expect from either was a long stalemate. At home,
despite prosperity, Americans increasingly felt that they had unwit-
tingly worked their way into a series of traps from which there was no
escape. They worried over inflation, but they did not know how to stop
it without jeopardizing prosperity. They wanted an end to Communist

infiltration in Washington, but each fresh newspaper allegation of disloyalty and subversion made them wonder if McCarthy's alarms were not justified. Americans were divided into two hostile camps over the question of equality for the Negro, but each side claimed that the unreasonableness of the other made an equitable settlement of the dispute impossible. Each of these problems seemed insoluble, and for each the Truman Administration was in some measure held responsible.

The Korean War especially imposed a severe strain on the patience of the American people and exposed the Truman Administration to the criticisms of all those who were unwilling to recognize the new responsibilities undertaken by the United States as a major power. Some Americans complained that it was unfair for the United States to have to assume a larger financial and military burden than its allies did in Korea. Others, agreeing with General MacArthur, condemned the Administration for waging a limited war on terms set down by the enemy. Still others considered American intervention a mistake and thought the original error compounded by the failure of the United States to withdraw all its forces from Korea. Those Americans who believed that the United States was pursuing the only feasible policy in an admittedly difficult situation found that they were unable to make their voices heard over a cacophony of complaints.

The truce negotiations were, if anything, more frustrating than the war itself. The Communists seemed to go out of their way to show their bad faith, and there was no reason to believe that the enemy would live up to the terms of any settlement accepted by the United States. The best the Americans could hope for was a prolongation of the stalemate, and to a people who had always considered war a prelude to victory, this was another frustration, if not a bitter and degrading lesson.

The dissatisfaction with the conduct of the war in Korea was matched by an unwillingness to accept even the minor sacrifices and adjustments necessitated by a limited war effort. Although the taxes enacted by Congress to finance the war were much lower than those demanded by the President, they were high enough to enable the Republicans to charge the Democrats with extravagance.

No one seemed satisfied with the Administration's attempts to check the inflation produced by the increased expenditures for the Korean War. In January, 1951, the government established wage and price ceilings; but in the following July, Congress largely nullified their effectiveness with a bill containing many inflationary loopholes and which Truman described as the "worst I have ever had to sign." The law pleased no one; while giving the Administration's critics an opportunity to accuse Truman of undermining the "free enterprise system," the law was not rigorous enough to curb inflation. Consumers complained of high prices, organized labor protested that prices rose faster than wages, and businessmen maintained that price controls cut profits and stifled initiative.

As the party in power, the Democrats were also held responsible by many Americans for Communist infiltration of the government. It was true that Truman had done much to check the spread of Communism in Europe and Asia and that he had taken steps to drive Communists out of the United States Government. But it was also true that the President had blundered when he called the investigation of Alger Hiss "a red herring." Truman also could not escape the fact that the Democrats rather than the Republicans had appointed Communists to government positions during the Depression and war years. The Republicans did not hesitate to convict the Truman Administration for the acts of its predecessor, and the charge that the Democrats had "coddled" Communists was made by virtually every prominent Republican spokesman. It is impossible to estimate accurately the effect of the Communist issue on the voters, but there is considerable evidence that large numbers of Catholics and descendants of immigrants from countries overrun by the Soviet Union shifted their allegiance from the Democratic to the Republican party because of the former's real and alleged record on Communism.

No charge leveled against the Democrats by the Republicans was more difficult to refute than the assertion that certain members of the Truman Administration had been either lax or corrupt in the conduct of their offices. Unfortunately for the Democrats, all the evidence to substantiate the charges was provided by the investigating committees of a Democratic Congress. In 1951, businessmen testified before a Senate subcommittee that they had been unable to obtain government contracts until they had hired middlemen who made a business of influencing government officials and who were variously known as "influence peddlers" or "five per-centers." Another Senate subcommittee, investigating the Reconstruction Finance Corporation, learned that after rejecting a company's application for a loan on three different occasions, the R.F.C. approved the application soon after the chairman of the Democratic National Committee had been hired as the company's attorney. The Republican chance to make political capital out of this information was short-lived, for the same committee soon discovered that the chairman of the Republican National Committee had intervened with the R.F.C. to secure more liberal terms for a loan to a company of which he was president. In 1952, additional corruption was uncovered in the Bureau of Internal Revenue. An investigation revealed that an Assistant Attorney General had accepted bribes from individuals accused of either income-tax evasion or fraud. Corruption, furthermore, was not confined to the federal government. Senator Estes Kefauver led a Senate committee in an investigation of organized crime in 1950, and demonstrated the existence of collusion and alliances between notorious criminals and urban political bosses, almost all of whom were Democrats. The melodramatic hearings of the Kefauver committee, which were televised to an enthralled audience, were easily the most popular daytime program in the brief history of American television.

The President's response to revelations of wrong-doing among Democrats played into the hands of his opponents. Truman created the impression that he considered Kefauver a renegade who was willing to further his own political ambitions by discrediting his party. The President also seemed unduly reluctant to move against any officials in his Administration who had been charged with malfeasance. He may have been stubborn, or he may have been moved by a sense of loyalty to his subordinates; but, whatever his motives, many Americans were convinced that he was not interested in cleaning up what the Republicans called "the mess in Washington."

The difficulties confronting the Democrats in 1952 were compounded by the split in their party over civil rights. The President's demands for greater equality for the Negro served only to alienate the majority of the southern white population without adding to the party's voting strength in the North and West. The South and the northern city machines had provided the Democratic party with the bulk of its votes since Reconstruction, but by 1952, the South was ready for political rebellion. Southern senators and governors vied with one another in announcing their hostility to the Democratic regime in Washington. In 1948, southern die-hards had fought the Democrats with a third party, but in 1952, many of the section's voters were prepared to support any Republican candidate who was not outspokenly in favor of equality for the Negro.

Widespread dissatisfaction with the Democrats did not guarantee that the Republicans would win the election of 1952 by default. The Republicans, like the Democrats, were split into two hostile camps, and the party's leaders were faced with the formidable task of finding a candidate acceptable not only to the Republican factions but also to the dissident Democrats. The spokesmen for the neo-isolationist, conservative wing of the party, which had its principal strength in the Middle West, maintained that the Republicans should avoid the "me-too-ism" that had presumably contributed to Dewey's defeat in 1948. The conservatives claimed that the voters were clearly disgusted with New Deal–Fair Deal liberalism and that Senator Robert A. Taft of Ohio, the acknowledged champion of Republican conservatism, was the party's only hope for victory. The midwestern conservatives were opposed by most eastern Republicans and many on the West Coast who rejected isolationism in foreign affairs and favored a middle-of-the-road liberalism in domestic policy. The leaders of this wing of the party were Governor Thomas Dewey of New York, Senator Henry Cabot Lodge, Jr., of Massachusetts, and Senator James H. Duff of Pennsylvania. They argued that the Republican party's chances of success depended on selecting a candidate who had an appeal that transcended classes and sections, who was above party squabbles, and who had not been directly involved in any recent unsavory events. There was only one such man, Dwight D. Eisenhower.

The anti-Taft forces in the Republican party scored their first victory in January, 1951. Eisenhower, who was stationed in Paris as commander of the North Atlantic Treaty Organization forces, agreed to be the Republican candidate if he were drafted. His willingness to run coupled with his enormous popularity seemed to make his nomination by the Republicans a foregone conclusion. But Taft, who was the choice of most of the party's professional politicians as well as the conservatives, refused to withdraw from the contest. While Eisenhower swept the primaries in several states, Taft was equally successful in securing delegates in the South and Middle West. When the Republican convention met, both men had approximately the same number of delegates pledged to their support. The outcome of the contest thus would be influenced by whether the convention would seat the contested delegates pledged to Taft or those pledged to Eisenhower. Because Taft and his followers controlled the Republican National Committee, Eisenhower's backers, led by Dewey and Lodge, carried the fight over the disputed delegates to the convention floor. This strategy led to one of the most bitter convention debates in Republican history, but it proved successful; Eisenhower was nominated on the first ballot. Richard M. Nixon, a young Senator from California who had played a prominent part in the investigation of Alger Hiss by the House Committee on Un-American Activities, was selected as Eisenhower's running mate.

The Democrats, unlike the Republicans, began their convention with several contenders for their party's nomination. Truman announced in March that he was not a candidate to succeed himself and the contest was thrown wide open. His choice was Adlai E.

Adlai E. Stevenson, 1952

Stevenson, an Illinois lawyer and grandson and namesake of Grover Cleveland's Vice-President, who had been elected governor of his state in 1948 after serving the New Deal and Fair Deal in various administrative posts. But when Stevenson made it clear that he was reluctant to be a candidate, the President shifted his support to Vice-President Alben W. Barkley. Although almost all the southern delegates were pledged to Senator Richard Russell, the most popular candidate with the party's rank and file was another southerner, Kefauver, who had gained nation-wide attention through the televised hearing on organized crime and who had piled up a succession of victories in the preconvention primary elections.

Stevenson was the only leading contender—albeit a very reluctant one—whose candidacy was not marred by serious drawbacks, for he alone was unopposed by any major interest-groups in the Democratic party. Such considerations outweighed his unwillingness to be a candidate, and he was nominated on the third ballot. In an effort to balance the ticket and insure the support of the South, Senator John J. Sparkman of Alabama was chosen for second place.

The Republicans made the Truman Administration the central issue of the campaign. In newspaper advertisements, television and radio programs, and speeches, Republican candidates linked the Democrats with Communism, charged them with corruption in Washington, and blamed them for the "blunders" in Korea. But as the campaign progressed, the Republicans discovered that the Korean War was an even more effective issue than either Communism or corruption. While carefully avoiding the more reckless charges made by some Republicans, Eisenhower was fully cognizant of the widespread dissatisfaction created by the Korean War, and on October 24, in a speech in Detroit, he promised, if elected, to go to Korea to bring the war to "an early and honorable end."

Forced to take the defensive at the outset, the Democrats were never able to seize the initiative. Stevenson entered the campaign determined to make it a high-level debate of the issues, but, despite his wishes, he was compelled to run on the record made by the Truman Administration.

The personalities of the candidates provided a study in contrasts. Eisenhower went out of his way to appease the dissidents in his party by announcing that he would support all Republican candidates—including Senator McCarthy—and by emphasizing the importance of Taft's role in the party and campaign. Stevenson knowingly alienated the leadership of the Democratic party in Texas when he stated his opposition to the transfer of off-shore oil rights from the federal government to the states. Eisenhower's speeches, while impressing audiences with his sincerity, were confined largely to generalities and appeals for a moral crusade to solve the problems facing Americans at home and abroad. Stevenson's speeches were distinguished by their wit, insight, and urbanity. The candidates, however, were substantially agreed on issues. Eisenhower, as well as Stevenson, did not propose to repeal the New Deal, and neither candidate had an alternative to the foreign policy that had evolved under the Democrats since 1945.

The outcome of the election was a sweeping victory for Eisenhower. Polling 33,824,351 popular votes to 27,314,987 for Stevenson, he amassed a total of 442 electoral votes from 39 states. Stevenson's 89 electoral votes all came from either southern or border states, but even

The President-elect, 1953

[UNITED PRESS INTERNATIONAL]

in this region Eisenhower carried Florida, Tennessee, Texas, and Virginia. Throughout the nation, Eisenhower consistently ran ahead of his party. Despite the landslide proportions of his victory, the Republicans ended up with only a majority of eight in the House of Representatives and a tie in the Senate.

Eisenhower's election was one of the greatest personal triumphs in the history of American politics. The dissatisfaction with the Truman Administration and the divisive forces at work within the Democratic party provide only a partial explanation of the Republican victory. Essentially, it was the triumph of a man rather than a party. With no background in politics, Eisenhower caught the mood of a people who wanted to be assured that simple goodness, decency, and honesty could solve all the problems that had baffled the American people and professional politicians. The voters liked him because of his modesty and sincerity; they admired him because he had succeeded; but most of all they trusted him.

The Eisenhower Way

Eisenhower entered the presidency as a symbol of stability. He seemed an obvious contrast to the flamboyant leadership provided by Democratic executives during the preceding twenty years. Appearing to be above politics, he seemed to many voters the only man in the nation who was capable of ending partisan strife and the atmosphere of crisis that had surrounded the government for two decades. He promised moderation at home and peace abroad, but to his opponents moderation became a euphemism for an abdication of leadership.

Dwight D. Eisenhower was born in 1890 in Denison, Texas, but when he was a year old his family moved to Abilene, Kansas, where he spent his youth. Following high school, he attended the United States Military Academy at West Point, from which he was graduated in 1915. After serving in Europe in World War I, he settled down to the routine of life in the regular Army, in which promotions were slow and moves to new bases and assignments were frequent. His peacetime career was distinguished without being spectacular, but after the outbreak of World War II his rise was meteoric. In 1942, he was made Commander of Allied Forces landing in North Africa; the following year, he was appointed Supreme Commander, Allied Expeditionary Forces; in 1944, he led the Normandy invasion; and in May, 1945, he received the German surrender at Rheims. He served briefly as Commander of the United States Occupation Forces in Germany and then returned to the United States to become Chief of Staff. In 1948, he accepted the presidency of Columbia University, but in 1950, he took a leave of absence to be Supreme Allied Commander in Europe to organize the forces of the North Atlantic Treaty Organization. In June 1952, he left the Army, and a month later he was nominated for President of the United States by the Republicans.

Eisenhower emerged from World War II with enormous prestige. In the years immediately following the war, his prestige reached such heights that in 1948 many leading Democrats hoped that he would be their party's candidate for President. Four years later, many Democrats helped to elect him President and provided new evidence of his popularity with the American people. In one sense, it was his misfortune that, unlike Lincoln, he had become a folk hero even before he became President.

Although Eisenhower had spent most of his life in the regular Army, as President he proved to be the very antithesis of the stereotype of the professional soldier. Instead of issuing commands, he made requests. Instead of attacking his opponents, he sought to conciliate them. Instead of being domineering, he was kind, modest, and considerate. The paradox of a military man who refused a fight completely confounded his critics, for the more they attacked him the more his prestige increased. The politicians often considered him naïve, but it was Eisenhower rather than the politicians who accurately gauged the public temper. After two decades of crisis and strife in Washington, the American people welcomed a leader who refused to turn every political skirmish into a major war. To his more demanding critics he seemed to lack forthright convictions, but to a majority of the American voters he was a symbol of national unity transcending both factional and partisan politics.

When Eisenhower entered the White House his philosophy of government was Jeffersonian. He thought that the functions of government should be reduced rather than expanded, that powers assumed by the federal government should be returned to the states, and that the costs of government should be drastically cut. Six months after his inauguration, he stated that his Administration had "instituted what amounts to a revolution in the Federal Government as we have known it in our time, trying to make it smaller rather than bigger and finding things it can stop doing instead of seeking new things for it to do." But the talk of revolution was premature. Big government was not the result of a Democratic plot, but a product of circumstances that neither Republicans nor Democrats could resist. There is no evidence that Eisenhower as President changed his ideas about the functions of the government, but there is also no evidence that he succeeded in carrying out his announced ideals.

While Roosevelt had sought to dominate Congress and Truman had frequently used it as a whipping boy, Eisenhower attempted to pursue a policy of peaceful coexistence with the legislature. On several occasions he went out of his way to announce that Congress had every right to dispose of his legislative proposals as its members saw fit. Eisenhower's attitude led to an increase in the power of Congress and a decline in that of the executive. The most remarkable feature of this shift in the balance of power within the government was that it had no discernible effect on the popularity of the President.

Eisenhower's relatively modest view of the powers of the Presidency made his repeated illnesses less serious than might have been the case if a strong executive had been in the White House. In September, 1955, while vacationing in Colorado, he suffered a heart attack. In the following June he became seriously ill with ileitis, and in 1957 he had a mild stroke. On each of these occasions, the executive branch of the government was administered by the President's closest advisers, and the American people were repeatedly assured that the President's "team" was capable of performing almost all his duties during his enforced absences from office. During each illness, Democratic leaders maintained that the President was much sicker than either his doctors or Republican officials were willing to admit, but the American people did not seem unduly alarmed by "team government" substituting for personal leadership by the President.

As a party leader, Eisenhower not only tolerated opposition within Republican ranks, but he often gave the impression that it did not exist. In successive elections, he supported all Republican candidates, including those who had repeatedly attacked his policies. He refused to discipline or even to criticize Republican congressmen who voted against measures that he had advocated, and he remained unperturbed —at least in public—when Cabinet officials openly disagreed with his policies. Privately, during his first term, he became so disgusted with the opposition of the right-wing Republicans that he contemplated the formation of a third party, but he soon abandoned the idea and resumed his laissez-faire attitude toward his Republican opponents. At times, therefore, the President might say one thing, a Republican leader in Congress another, and a Cabinet member still another. It is doubtful that these tactics converted many right-wingers to what came to be known as either "modern Republicanism" or "Eisenhower Republicanism." What the President did do was to lift himself above his party in the minds of the American voters. The extent to which the electorate refused to associate him with his party was revealed at the polls. Although in the 1954 campaign for Congress the President went to unusual lengths to support Republican candidates, the Democrats regained control of both the House and Senate.

The results of the presidential election of 1956 further revealed Eisenhower's strength and his party's weakness. Despite his two major illnesses in the preceding year, Eisenhower was renominated by the Republicans. Nixon was again chosen as the President's running mate. The Democrats, following a hard-fought preconvention campaign between Stevenson and Kefauver, chose Stevenson for the Presidency, and gave second place on the ticket to Kefauver. The campaign was a listless affair. Stevenson, hit by charges of undue levity in 1952, conducted a serious—and even solemn—campaign that lacked much of the sting and color of his earlier effort. The results, moreover, were a foregone conclusion, for Eisenhower appeared to be at the height of his popularity with the voters. Eisenhower's victory was even more decisive than in 1952. Gaining 58 per cent of the popular vote, he carried 41 states and won 457 electoral votes to 74 for Stevenson. But, although they lost the presidential elections, the Democrats captured the Senate (by the barest margin) and the House. Ironically, Eisenhower's efforts to strengthen the Republicans seemed only to convince the voters that he was superior to his party.

Eisenhower was, as he often said, "basically conservative." As president of Columbia University he had stated that individuals seeking security could find good examples of it in men in prisons. Soon after becoming President, he cited the TVA as an example of "creeping socialism" in the United States. He thought businessmen ideally suited to run the government, and his views on government economy, lowered taxes, and states' rights were, of course, all cardinal tenets in the businessman's dogma of the day. But Eisenhower's acts were often more liberal than his words. He was essentially pragmatic. He liked to settle individual cases on their merits, and when he did so, he frequently forgot his conservative sentiments. Being more responsive to fact than to theory, the longer he remained in the White House, the more liberal he became in his social and economic views; and remarks that he made at the outset of his Administration little resembled the policies he suggested in later years. What America had become conquered his wishes of what it might be.

Thunder on the Right

When the Eisenhower Administration first took office, there was no doubt concerning the conservative cast of the new government. Eisenhower had promised to enlist the "best minds" to lead his "crusade," but when he announced his cabinet, it was apparent that he thought the best minds belonged almost exclusively to successful big businessmen. A liberal critic in the *New Republic* described the Cabinet as "eight millionaires and a plumber." Martin Durkin, a Democrat and president of the United Association of Journeymen, Plumbers and Steamfitters, was the plumber, but he resigned as Secretary of Labor after six months, to be succeeded by still another businessman.

For the first time in twenty years, the United States government was staffed by men who wished to aid business. Charles Wilson, who resigned as president of General Motors to become Secretary of De-

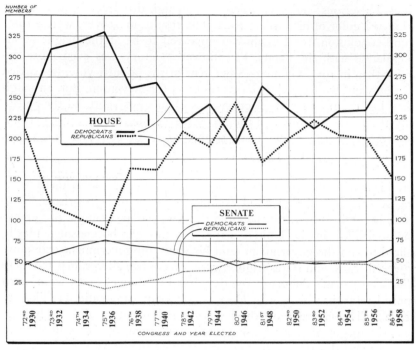

HOUSE

DEMOCRATS
REPUBLICANS

SENATE

DEMOCRATS
REPUBLICANS

CONGRESS AND YEAR ELECTED

Varying Distribution of Congressional Seats between Democrats and Republicans, 1930–1958

fense, told a Senate committee that he believed "what was good for the country was good for General Motors, and vice versa." Sinclair Weeks, a Massachusetts industrialist and Secretary of Commerce, attacked the Bureau of Standards because it lacked "the business point of view." Secretary of the Treasury George Humphrey, who had served his apprenticeship for government service as the head of one of the nation's largest holding companies, entered office determined to reverse Democratic fiscal policies. Douglas McKay, an Oregon automobile dealer and Secretary of the Interior, advocated a "partnership" policy that was designed to give private utilities a much greater opportunity to develop power resources than had been possible under the Democrats. Ezra Taft Benson, Secretary of Agriculture and the most consistent exponent of economic individualism in the New Administration, proposed that price supports for agricultural products be abandoned and that the farmer be forced to compete in a free market.

The members of the Administration went to work with a will. Within a few months after it had taken office, the new government had abolished wage and price controls, reduced the size of the federal bureaucracy, and cut expenditures on public works. At the same time, Congress, while ignoring most of the President's other requests, fulfilled a Republican campaign pledge by passing a bill transferring most of the nation's tidelands oil resources from federal to state jurisdiction. In 1954, the conservative trend of the Eisenhower Administration became, if anything, more pronounced. In that year, Congress not only approved tax cuts that favored corporations and stockholders, but it also adopted the Administration's farm program in modified form. The new farm bill replaced rigid price supports with a system of flexible supports that ranged from $82\frac{1}{2}$ to 90 per cent of parity on the so-called basic commodities (corn, cotton, peanuts, rice, tobacco, and wheat) and authorized the Secretary of Agriculture to fix the level of support for other farm products as he saw fit. An effort was also made to carry out the "partnership" program in public utilities by contracting with a private company for the construction and operation of new power facilities in the Tennessee Valley. This proposal, however, met with widespread opposition from the defenders of the TVA, and it was eventually abandoned by the government.

Despite the pro-business policies of the Eisenhower Administration during its first two years in office, it was not conservative enough to satisfy the right wing of the Republican party. Although Senator Taft supported most of the Administration's policies until his death in July, 1953, many of his less moderate followers found it difficult, if not impossible, to abandon the role that they had played so consistently during twenty years of Democratic rule. When, for example, the President nominated Charles E. Bohlen, an acknowledged authority on Russian affairs, as ambassador to the Soviet Union, his confirmation was bitterly fought in the Senate by conservative Republicans who objected to the fact that he had served in the State Department during the Roosevelt and Truman presidencies. Again, when Eisenhower insisted that the budget should be balanced before taxes were cut, it was Daniel Reed, a New York Republican and chairman of the House Ways and Means Committee, who headed the opposition to the President.

The determination of the Republican Old Guard and some Democrats of the same stamp to resist "modern Republicanism" was clearly revealed during the protracted struggle over the Bricker Amendment. Drawn up by Senator John Bricker of Ohio, the proposed amendment was ostensibly designed to prevent the United States from accepting treaties that would deprive the people of their constitutional rights or prevent the states from exercising the powers reserved to them under the Constitution. The political implications of the Bricker Amendment,

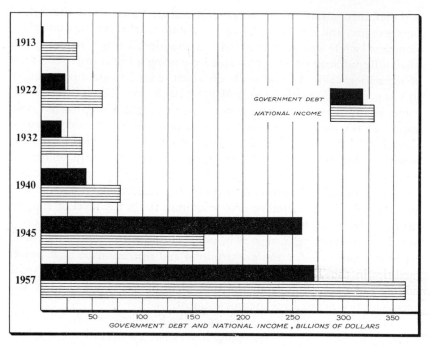

Government Debt and National Income, 1913–1957

however, were unmistakable, for it quickly became the rallying point for isolationists and extreme right-wingers wishing to impose a permanent check on the powers of the chief executive. The fight for the Bricker Amendment, in reality, was an assault on Roosevelt's (rather than Eisenhower's) internationalism and executive leadership; as such, it represented still another example of the Old Guard's determination to refight battles that had already been lost. Although the Bricker Amendment was opposed by Eisenhower, this did not prevent it from becoming a major source of debate and controversy thoughout the 1953 session of Congress. When Congress reconvened in the following year, the amendment's supporters returned to the attack. On February 25, the Bricker Amendment was rejected by the Senate by a vote of 50 to 42. On the next day, a modified version of the same amendment failed to secure a two-thirds majority in the Senate by 60 to 31. The Administration had defeated the Old Guard, but it had won its victory by the narrowest possible margin.

Before Eisenhower had been in office a year, Senator Joseph McCarthy's strident and vituperative denunciations of the government's policy toward Communists had drowned out all other right-wing opposition to the Administration. McCarthyism, in short, was to prove as big a problem for Eisenhower as it had been for Truman. Eisenhower began his first term with the announcement that he favored an anti-Communist program that would be "fair to the rights of the individual and effective to the safety of the nation," and would "clear the atmosphere of that unseasonal suspicion that accepts rumor and gossip as a substitute for evidence." He then proceeded to overhaul the Truman loyalty program. The Loyalty Review Board was abolished, and security boards were established for each federal department and agency. Agencies were given the right to remove any employee for reasons of "security" (a word that was so loosely defined that it could cover much more than basic loyalty to the United States government), and no opportunity was provided for a dismissed worker to appeal beyond his agency or department head.

The results of the Eisenhower security program soon became a subject of partisan controversy. The Democrats repeatedly accused Administration spokesmen of inflating the actual number of subversives dismissed from government service. The figures supplied by both Republicans and Democrats were often misleading and confusing. Available evidence indicates that by July 1, 1954, approximately 7,000 government workers had been dismissed or had resigned as a result of the Eisenhower security program, but of this number, a very small percentage had been discharged because the government had demonstrated either that they were subversives or that they had subversive associations.

McCarthy had nothing but disdain for the Administration's security program. He resented what he considered executive interference in his specialty of Communist-hunting, and he refused to abandon his role as America's anti-Communist conscience merely because his own party had taken control of the government. As chairman of the Senate Committee on Government Operations and of the Permanent Subcommittee on Investigations, he laid about with renewed vigor, spreading confusion, fear, and dissension throughout the government. During Eisenhower's first year in office, McCarthy condemned the Administration for its timidity and hesitation on the Communist issue. He assailed the Voice of America for harboring subversives; appointed as director of his subcommittee a man who had accused the Protestant clergy of sympathizing with Communism; questioned the reliability of the Director of the Central Intelligence Agency; charged the State Department's overseas libraries with circulating subversive books; and started—with the usual fanfares of publicity—a search for spies in the Army Signal Corps laboratory at Fort Monmouth, New Jersey. When

Joseph E. McCarthy of Wisconsin

[BROWN BROTHERS]

the President stated that Communism would not be an issue in the 1954 congressional campaign, McCarthy replied: "The now, harsh, unpleasant fact is that Communism . . . will be an issue in 1954 . . . Republican control of the Senate determines whether I shall continue as chairman of the investigating committee."

The series of events that eventually led to McCarthy's downfall began in January, 1954, during an investigation of the Army by the Senate Permanent Subcommittee on Investigations. When Captain Irving Peress, an Army dentist, refused on the ground of self-incrimination to answer questions concerning his loyalty, McCarthy demanded he be court-martialed. Instead of a court-martial, Peress was given a promotion and an honorable discharge. There then followed a period of mutual recrimination. McCarthy attacked the Army for its handling of the Peress case and its lack of cooperation with the subcommittee. The Army countered, first, with the charge that McCarthy had abused and insulted a brigadier general testifying in an executive session of the subcommittee and, second, with the accusation that McCarthy and his counsel, Roy M. Cohn, had used improper methods to obtain preferred treatment in the Army for a former subcommittee consultant. In March, the Senate voted that the subcommittee (with Senator Karl Mundt serving as acting chairman) hold open hearings on the activities of McCarthy and his staff. During the hearings, which dragged on for weeks, McCarthy repeatedly demonstrated his skill at vituperation and invective to a nation-wide television audience. The results, however, were inconclusive. Although the report of the Democratic minority on the Committee condemned both McCarthy and Cohn, the Republican majority, while criticizing Cohn, let McCarthy off with little more than a mild rebuke. The willingness of the Republican majority of the subcommittee to stand by McCarthy postponed, but did not prevent, the eclipse of the Wisconsin Senator. In August, the Senate appointed a special committee under the chairmanship of Senator Arthur Watkins of Utah to consider charges against McCarthy's behavior as a senator. The following month, the Watkins committee recommended the censure of McCarthy, and on December 2, the Senate voted 67 to 22 to "condemn" him for behavior unbecoming a senator.

Throughout the bitter and protracted struggle over McCarthy, the President steadfastly refused to become embroiled publicly in the dispute. Although he despised McCarthy and his methods, he thought that an open fight between the President of the United States and McCarthy would be a disgraceful and degrading spectacle. Many of Eisenhower's supporters, as well as his critics, considered his refusal to put himself openly at the head of the anti-McCarthy forces an abdication of leadership. But in the end his policy of public aloofness paid off, for the Senator from Wisconsin finally managed to destroy himself. Although McCarthy remained a senator until his death in 1957, he exerted no discernible influence over the Senate or his party.

The Supreme Court and Subversion

The decline and fall of McCarthyism coincided with a series of Supreme Court decisions that reinforced the rights of individuals in a wide variety of fields. In its 1956-7 term, the Court ruled on a number of cases involving Communism and civil rights, and in almost every instance it manifested what *The New York Times* described as a "trend toward liberalism." In granting a new trial to nine California Communist leaders and in directing the acquittal of five others accused of violating the Smith Act, the Court ruled that it was not a crime to advocate overthrow of the government if such advocacy did not lead to violent action. In the Watkins case, the Court reversed the conviction of a labor leader for contempt in refusing to give information concerning his associates to the House Committee on Un-American Activities. In this decision, the Court held that the questions asked John T. Watkins were so lacking in pertinency and the purposes of the inquiry were so vague that the defendant had no way of knowing that his refusal to answer the Committee's questions had been either constitutional or unconstitutional. The Court also reversed the conviction of Paul M. Sweezy, a college professor who had been convicted of contempt of a state court because of his refusal to answer questions in the course of an investigation of alleged subversive activities. In the Jencks case, the Court ruled that when reports of the Federal Bureau of Investigation were used in oral testimony by a government witness in a criminal trial, they also had to be made available to defendants for the preparation of their cases. The Court also made possible the granting of passports to Communists and fellow-travelers.

The Court's decisions protecting the rights of Communists and other unpopular individuals seemed to some critics an unjustified invasion of the authority of the President and Congress. Many others believed that the Court's stand in such cases deprived the nation of needed safeguards against the dangers posed by domestic Communism. Civil-libertarians who had been most disturbed by the excesses of McCarthyism viewed the Court's defense of civil rights as an overdue clarification and strengthening of basic rights of citizens. Fortunately, by 1956, even the new strict construction of civil rights did not protect subversives in any important way, for all known subversives had been removed from any positions of power and influence.

The Negro and His Rights

Long before Eisenhower became President, the denial of the Negro's rights as a citizen had created issues that most white Americans preferred to ignore. Reconstruction had raised questions concerning the status of the Negro, but it had not solved them; and in the years after 1877 the South, left more or less to its own devices, had largely eliminated the Negro from any prominent role in southern life. After the 1890's, when a Jim Crow culture was institutionalized in the South, the Negro had virtually no opportunity to vote; he was not allowed to use public facilities available to whites; he was refused equal economic opportunities; and he was constantly made to feel his inferiority. If he migrated to the North—as southern Negroes did in increasing numbers in the twentieth century—more often than not he ended up in an urban ghetto. In the North, he could vote, ride on nonsegregated buses and trains, and send his children to nonsegregated schools. But he lived in a slum and could work at only the most menial tasks. He remained, moreover, a social inferior, for he was forbidden to enter most hotels and restaurants except as a servant. He was, in effect, forbidden to expand his opportunities beyond the limits set for him by the white majority.

The New Deal, however, marked a turning point in the history of the American Negro. Northern Negroes were permitted to participate on an equal basis in the various federal relief and work programs, and they also acquired a new sense of their political power. World War II accelerated these trends by providing Negroes with greater and more diverse economic opportunities than they had ever enjoyed in the past and by permitting a few Negroes in the armed forces to obtain at least a measure of equality. Following the war, the Negro continued to make slow, but obvious advances on many fronts. Several states, with New York taking the lead, passed laws forbidding discriminatory practices in employment. Further progress was made in the elimination of discrimination in the armed services, and the Supreme Court steadily limited southern attempts to prevent Negroes from voting. An important lesson was also given to the nation when Negroes became leading players in professional baseball. After Jackie Robinson became a member of the Brooklyn Dodgers in 1946, he did far more than break down one more color barrier, for countless Negroes vicariously shared his triumphs and were reassured by his example of what a Negro could do when given the chance. Within a few years, the Negro had become an accepted part of American baseball, and millions of fans had painlessly learned to admire a man's ability whatever his color.

The progress of the Negro in the postwar years occurred in a period of unprecedented prosperity. A continuing scarcity of labor opened up new jobs for the Negro, raised his pay, and brought him associations with white society that had been denied him in the past. Increased purchasing power provided Negroes with an economic weapon that American business firms increasingly acknowledged and respected. White businessmen were forced, however reluctantly, to learn that it was good business to hire Negroes, to sell to Negroes, and to employ Negroes from the small but growing group of colored people in the professions.

The Eisenhower Administration entered office with no clean-cut program on civil rights. As a military leader, Eisenhower had given some support to integration in the army; but as a Republican candidate who had won the votes of many white southerners, he was presumably under considerable pressure not to alienate a group whose members generally opposed any break in the color line. Although the President, as in most other matters, opposed compulsion to enforce a policy, he did believe that Federal funds should not be used to finance segregated facilities. This view was soon put to the test, for in the summer of 1953, Representative Adam Clayton Powell, Jr., a New York Democrat and Negro, sent an open telegram to the President charging that the Administration had done nothing to eliminate segregation in government offices and installations. The Administration did not ignore this challenge, and in subsequent months segregation was abolished in the armed services, in schools on military posts, in all institutions maintained by the Veterans Administration, and on many projects for which private firms held government contracts. It was also largely as a result of pressure exerted by the Administration that the telephone and transit companies as well as various municipal agencies in the Capital began to hire Negroes on an equal basis with whites and that Washington's hotels and theatres formally abandoned the color line.

The Administration's efforts on behalf of the Negro were overshadowed by a series of historic Supreme Court decisions on civil rights. Segregation was a national phenomenon, but in the South mere attitudes were reinforced by the Jim Crow laws that required separate facilities for Negroes in most public places and in all schools. These laws, in turn, had been upheld by the Supreme Court in 1896 in its famous decision in Plessy vs. Ferguson. Although at the time Justice Harlan in a minority opinion had stated that the Constitution was color-blind, the majority had ruled that segregation did not violate the Fourteenth Amendment if the separate facilities for Negroes were equal to those provided for the whites. It was this "separate but equal" doctrine that the Court repeatedly rejected in its civil rights decisions in the 1950's.

The lawyers of the National Association for the Advancement of Colored People, in initiating cases in the lower courts to challenge the constitutionality of Jim Crow laws, maintained that separate facilities were by their very nature unequal. When these cases reached the Supreme Court the NAACP's view was invariably upheld by a majority of the Justices. The Court, accordingly, ruled that Negroes could not be excluded from the postgraduate schools of state universities, that Negroes could not be excluded from primary elections, and that interstate trains and buses could no longer maintain separate facilities for Negro customers. Each of these rulings helped to prepare the way for the Court's epoch-making decision desegregating the nation's public schools.

On May 17, 1954, the Supreme Court, in a unanimous decision written by Chief Justice Earl Warren ruled that racial segregation in public schools was unconstitutional in that it denied citizens equal protection under the law as guaranteed by the Fourteenth Amendment. The Court declared that to separate Negro school children "from others of similar age and qualifications solely because of their race generates a feeling of inferiority as to their status in the community that may affect their hearts and minds in a way unlikely ever to be undone." Before this decision, segregation had been mandatory in the District of Columbia and seventeen states with a population of approximately 10,500,000 Negroes and almost four times as many whites. The Court recognizing that it was impossible to change the mores of an entire region overnight, emphasized a gradualist approach for carrying out its decision. In May, 1955, the Supreme Court ordered the states to make "a prompt and reasonable start" toward complying with the 1954 decision, and local authorities were directed to establish nonsegregated school systems "with all deliberate speed." In November, 1955, the Court struck still another blow at segregation when it ruled against segregation in public parks and playgrounds and on public beaches and golf courses.

The Court's decisions produced a varied response throughout the South. Many southerners—particularly in the Deep South—were determined to resist integration at all costs. They formed White Citizens Councils to propagandize for white supremacy and terrify the Negroes, while in some areas the Ku Klux Klan was reactivated. Other white southerners, many of whom lived in the Border States, disapproved of the desegregation decision while stating that they were prepared to obey it as the law of the land. Finally, there was a tiny minority, including leading churchmen, who welcomed the Court's ruling. By the end of 1955, Virginia had joined the Deep South states of Georgia, Mississippi, Louisiana, and South Carolina in adopting legislation that was designed to provide for the eventual dissolution of the state's public school systems and for the payment of money to children who chose to go to segregated private schools. On the other hand, prompt action was taken to desegregate the schools in the District of Columbia, Maryland, Missouri and in other parts of the upper South.

The Supreme Court decision helped to turn every September into a month of crisis and tension for the South and the nation. As each new school term was about to begin, nation-wide attention would be given to a hitherto insignificant school district where desegregation was being attempted and the opposing forces met in head-on conflict. In 1956, Clinton, Tennessee, was on the front page of every major newspaper in the United States because of the extreme measures adopted by the segregationists to prevent the integration of the town's schools. In the following year, Little Rock, Arkansas, earned even greater notoriety. But Clinton and Little Rock were the exceptions. Other towns and cities integrated their schools with no fanfare and little trouble, while throughout the South still other towns and entire states made no move to follow the Supreme Court's decision.

Racial friction in the South did not always center on the public schools. In 1956, the nation and the world watched with dismay the events which followed the admission of Miss Autherine Lucy, a Negro, to the University of Alabama. Although she had a legal right to attend the University, her appearance there set off a series of riots and racist demonstrations that made it virtually impossible for her to attend classes or for the university to conduct its classes. Although a federal judge upheld her right to enter the university, she was expelled by the trustees because of charges that she made against them. In the same year, the Negroes of Montgomery, Alabama, led by Dr. Martin Luther King, a minister, won a major victory by using a boycott as a form of passive resistance to end segregation on the city's buses.

The conflict over integration in Little Rock in the fall of 1957 precipitated a constitutional crisis of major proportions. Shortly after the Supreme Court's ruling against segregation in 1954, the local school board adopted a plan for the admission of Negroes to the City's Central High School in September, 1957. Governor Orval Faubus, maintaining that school integration would make impossible the maintenance of law and order in Little Rock, had members of the National Guard stationed at the school. When nine Negro students attempted to enroll in the school, they were barred by the National Guard, acting on the Governor's orders. Following the withdrawal of the National Guard, as the result of a federal court injunction, violence broke out and the lives of the Negro students seemed to be threatened by mob action. At this point, President Eisenhower issued a "Proclamation and Statement" calling for the peaceful carrying out in Little Rock of the Supreme Court's decision. The President's pronouncement, however, had no effect on either the Governor of Arkansas or the antisegregationists of Little Rock, for the mob continued to dominate the area in the vicinity

Federal Troops at Little Rock, 1957

of the school. The President, accordingly, ordered federal troops into Little Rock and called the Arkansas National Guard into federal service, thus removing it from the Governor's control. By October 1, the nine Negro students were able to attend Central High School under the protection of federal bayonets. Many southern spokesmen denounced the President for what they considered a blatant violation of states' rights. Others throughout the nation applauded his willingness to enforce the Supreme Court decision while condemning his failure to endorse it as morally justified.

Although the Supreme Court did more than any other branch of the government to destroy the barriers erected by racial prejudice, Congress also contributed to greater equality for minority groups. In 1957, Congress for the first time in eighty-two years enacted a bill designed to protect the voting rights of the Negro. Since 1933, similar measures on nine different occasions had passed the House only to be defeated in the Senate by filibusters by Senators from the South. But in 1957, Senate Republicans, who had apparently abandoned any hopes they once had of winning the votes of white southerners, joined forces with liberal Democrats from the North to enact a civil-rights bill. When southern Democrats in the Senate realized that they could not block such a measure, they sought to reduce its effectiveness by proposing that violations of civil rights be tried before juries. As southern white juries had repeatedly displayed their prejudice against the Negro, the proposal for juries would have immeasurably weakened the bill. In the end, the jury issue was resolved by a compromise; and after months of haggling and recrimination that culminated in an unsuccessful filibuster, the bill became law in September, 1957.

The Civil Rights bill created a bipartisan Commission on Civil Rights, which was to be appointed by the President and have the power to investigate the denial of either voting rights or equal protection of the law because of race, color, national origin, or religion. An additional Assistant Attorney General was provided for and given the power to initiate injunction proceedings in federal district courts in cases in which there was evidence of interference with the right to vote. In such cases, the federal district courts were authorized to issue injunctions, without a jury, to obtain compliance with their orders. On the other hand, in criminal cases involving noncompliance with a court order to permit Negro voting, trial could be with or without a jury. Although the provisions of this law fell far below the demands of the northern liberals, the Civil Rights Act, nevertheless, represented a major defeat for those southerners who had repeatedly refused to compromise their demands for white supremacy.

The American Negro made more substantial gains during Eisenhower's two terms as President than in any preceding administration. His progress reflected a slowly growing conviction that racial prejudice was a blatant and disgraceful violation of the American creed. Although Eisenhower did not take the lead in the campaign to provide equality for the Negro, the relative success of that campaign was undoubtedly one of the major accomplishments during his Administration.

The Frustrations of the Cold War

The Eisenhower Administration inherited from its predecessor a shooting war in Korea and a cold war throughout the rest of the world. Although the new government achieved great popularity when it helped to end the Korean War, it had little or no success in its efforts to end or win the cold war. The facts of international life did not change with a change of administration in Washington, and the Republicans, like the Democrats before them, had to learn how to live with the enemies as well as the friends of the United States. World events had progressively narrowed the possibilities open to the makers of American foreign policy until there were few choices. World peace offered the only hope for survival, but both Republicans and Democrats argued that it could only be maintained by building the military strength of the United States and its allies and in undermining the appeals of Communism in the free world.

When Eisenhower was inaugurated President in January, 1953, the war in Korea was two and one half years old. Eighteen months of truce negotiations had produced no tangible results other than an agreement on an armistice line between North and South Korea in the unlikely event that an armistice could be achieved. Neither side, however, could agree on any formula for the repatriation of prisoners of war. The United Nations' forces held approximately 173,000 prisoners, a large number of whom when polled flatly refused to return to North Korea or China, and the United Nations' negotiators were unwilling to accept any plan calling for their forced repatriation. The Communist negotiators were equally adamant in refusing a truce which did not provide for the return of all prisoners. There appeared to be no middle ground between these extremes.

Following his election in November, 1952, Eisenhower kept his campaign pledge to go to Korea. But his visit had no visible effect on the course of events, for the stalemate on the battle field and at Panmunjom, site of the truce negotiations, remained. Soon after entering office, however, Eisenhower launched a diplomatic offensive. In the first months of 1953, the United States removed the naval patrol that shut off the Chinese nationalists on Formosa from the mainland. The new Administration also made it clear to Peiping that it was prepared to widen the scope of the war rather than let the deadlock in Korea continue indefinitely. At the same time, Henry Cabot Lodge, the head of the American delegation, bluntly told the United Nations General Assembly: "The rulers of the Soviet Union can stop the war whenever they want to." And apparently for the first time since the war started, the Russians wished to end it.

In the spring of 1953 Stalin, the all-powerful Soviet leader, died under mysterious circumstances. The struggle within the Soviet high command following Stalin's death and the increasing strain of the war on the Chinese were presumably major influences behind the Communist decision in the spring of 1953 to agree on a truce. In April, the Chinese Communist foreign minister informed the United Nations that his country was prepared to abandon its stand on the question of the repatriation of prisoners. As evidence of his good faith, he proposed

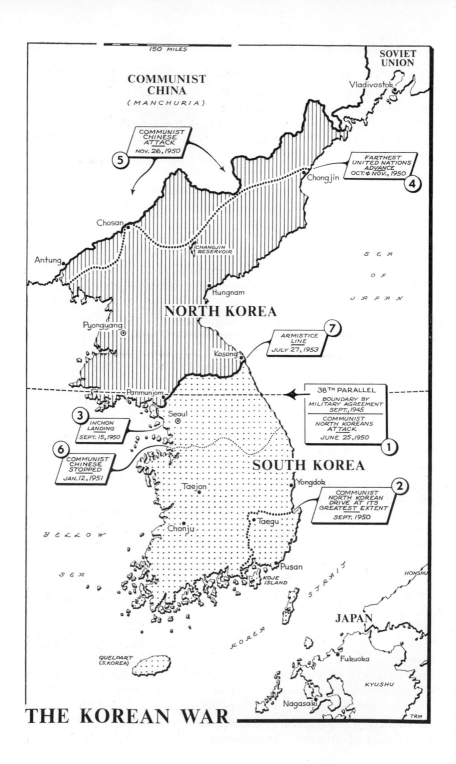

150 MILES

SOVIET
UNION

Vladivostok

COMMUNIST
CHINA
(MANCHURIA)

COMMUNIST
CHINESE
ATTACK
NOV. 26, 1950

⑤

FARTHEST
UNITED NATIONS
ADVANCE
OCT. ≠ NOV., 1950

④

Chongjin

Chosan

CHANGJIN
RESERVOIR

Antung

Hungnam

SEA

OF

JAPAN

NORTH KOREA

Pyongyang

ARMISTICE
LINE
JULY 27, 1953

⑦

Kosong

Panmunjom

38TH PARALLEL
BOUNDARY BY
MILITARY AGREEMENT
SEPT., 1945

③ INCHON
LANDING
SEPT. 15, 1950

Seoul

COMMUNIST
NORTH KOREANS
ATTACK
JUNE 25, 1950

⑥ COMMUNIST
CHINESE
STOPPED
JAN. 12, 1951

①

SOUTH KOREA

Taejon

Yongdok

② COMMUNIST
NORTH KOREAN
DRIVE AT ITS
GREATEST EXTENT
SEPT. 1950

Chonju

Taegu

YELLOW

SEA

Pusan

KOJE
ISLAND

HONSHU

KOREA STRAIT

JAPAN

Fukuoka

QUELPART
(S.KOREA)

KYUSHU

Nagasaki

THE KOREAN WAR

TRM

that "both parties repatriate immediately after cessation of hostilities all those prisoners of war in their custody who insist upon repatriation, and hand over the remaining prisoners of war to a neutral state so as to ensure a just solution." With this proposal as a working basis, the talks at Panmunjon were resumed; and, despite some exorbitant demands of the Communists and the recalcitrance of President Syngman Rhee of South Korea (who wanted a unified Korea), an armistice was concluded on July 27, 1953.

Under the terms of the truce, a small no-man's zone was established between the front lines of the two contending forces, complicated machinery was set up for the repatriation of prisoners, and a conference was to be held to settle the political problems arising from the Korean War. Repatriation of prisoners was entrusted to a commission consisting of delegates from Czechoslovakia, India, Poland, Sweden, and Switzerland. Under the Commission's direction, the exchange of the voluntary repatriates proceeded without major incidents. The problems posed by some 48,000 Chinese and North Korean prisoners who refused to return to their own countries presented a far more difficult problem. While some of these prisoners eventually agreed to return home, the majority of the North Koreans remained in South Korea, and many of the Chinese prisoners joined the Chinese Nationalist army on Formosa. Of the prisoners held by the Communists, twenty-two Americans who refused to return to the United States remained in China.

The political conference provided for by the Korean armistice agreement was postponed indefinitely, for the United States and the Communist countries were unable to agree on which nations should be permitted to attend. The United States thus had to settle for a truce in Korea rather than peace solemnized by a treaty. It had, moreover, to accept the fact that it had not won the Korean War, although more than 25,000 Americans had died in action and more than 100,000 Americans had been wounded. The Korean War, however, was neither a mistake nor a defeat. It upheld the power of the United Nations, checked Communist aggression, and prevented all of Asia from going Communist by default.

While seeking to check the Communist advance in the Far East, the Eisenhower Administration steadfastly refused to grant diplomatic recognition to China or to vote for that country's admission to the United Nations. In addition, in 1955, when China massed its forces to threaten the Tachens, Formosa, and other islands off the mainland of Asia, President Eisenhower asked and received from Congress the power to use armed force to safeguard Formosa. War was averted when the Chinese failed to carry out their offensive, but the threat of war remained. Both China and the United States continued to view each other with undisguised distrust. Only the threat of reprisals by the United States and its allies deterred China from aggression and preserved the uneasy peace in the Orient.

In Europe, as in the Far East, American foreign policy was based on the so-called "containment" hypothesis that armed strength and a system of alliances provided the only means for checking Communist aggression and preserving world peace until Communists, in frustration, sincerely changed their aims. This policy had been inherited from the Truman Administration, and the Republicans changed only its details and emphasis. The Soviet Union, rather than American plans and proposals, continued to set the conditions for United States foreign policy in Europe, and there was no diminution in the Soviet threat to American security during Eisenhower's presidency.

Several changes in the Kremlin, after Stalin's death, offered ample opportunity for American ingenuity, but these were not exploited. After the victory in 1955 of Nikita Khrushchev in the drawn-out and bloody power struggle in Russia, the Soviets talked of "peaceful coexistence" with capitalism and gave the veiled implication that a mad Stalin had been responsible for the intransigence that Khrushchev's Russia might be willing to abandon. Nearly forty years of Soviet duplicity had prepared some Western leaders for such sudden changes in Soviet talk, but the fear of a war fought with hydrogen bombs made panicky Westerners eager to grasp at any sign of a softer Soviet line. The sincere yearning for peace—indeed, its necessity if mankind was not to be annihilated or mutilated beyond recognition—strengthened Khrushchev's hand in the West and in the new nations of Africa and Asia which had come into being after World War II.

Certain events rather than softer talk disclosed the continuing real nature of the Soviet system and made non-Communists throughout the world more sober about the so-called "new look" in Soviet foreign policy. Bloody revolts in East Germany in 1953 and in Hungary in 1956 showed both the opposition within the Communist system and also the continued determination of the Soviet Union to wage all out war on its own subject peoples. The brutality of the Communist social revolution in China and the seizure of peaceful Tibet by Chinese forces made many Asians take a second look at Communism in action.

Despite the opportunities which these events provided the West— and American leaders particularly—the fundamental relations between East and West remained unchanged. The West seemed to have nothing except protests and moral censure to throw against direct Communist aggression, for it feared that anything stronger might precipitate a cata-

Sensing the Results at Geneva, 1955: Eisenhower with Bulganin

[BROWN BROTHERS]

clysmic hot war. But a hydrogen war was as unthinkable for the Kremlin as for the West. Knowing this, the Communists seemed willing to
take political risks, calculating, correctly, that the United States and its
allies would not be prepared to answer with war in peripheral areas.
The Soviet Union continued to exploit any situation in which it
thought it could make advances: if the West became too militant, Russia could pull back; if the West took no dangerous countersteps, the
Soviets advanced.

The "new look" in Soviet foreign policy, in other words, was designed to throw the West off guard while Russia continued to exploit
revolutionary situations throughout the world. Without making any
sacrifice of a major objective in 1954 and 1955, the Soviet Union took a
number of limited steps to give substance to its peaceful professions and
to make public opinion in the West less suspicious of Russia. The conclusion of a peace treaty with Austria, after ten years of Allied and Soviet occupation, was accepted by America as an important enough
token of sincerity to heed the urging of frightened Westerners to try
Khrushchev's intentions, at least. With much fanfare, a long sought
"meeting at the Summit" took place at Geneva in July, 1955. Attended
by all the principal Western and Soviet leaders, peaceful intentions
were proclaimed on all sides, but no substantial change followed on the

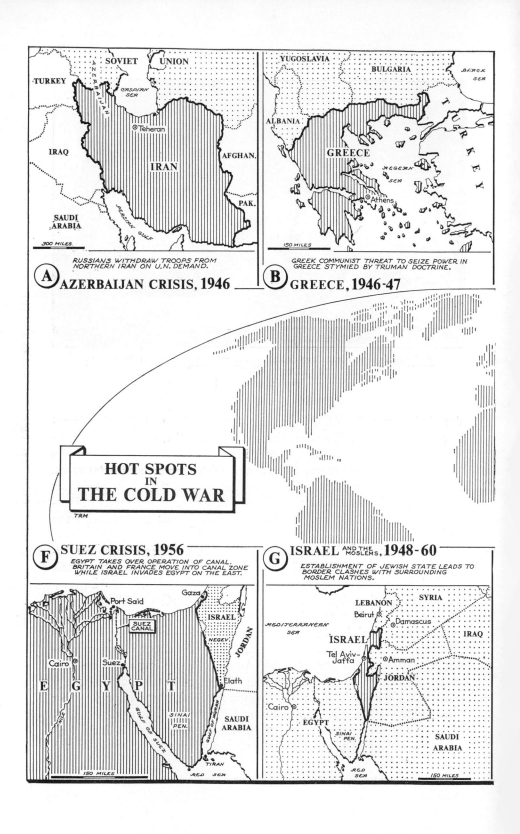

A AZERBAIJAN CRISIS, 1946

RUSSIANS WITHDRAW TROOPS FROM
NORTHERN IRAN ON U.N. DEMAND.

300 MILES

SOVIET UNION
TURKEY
AZERBAIJAN
CASPIAN SEA
Teheran
IRAQ
IRAN
AFGHAN.
PAK.
SAUDI ARABIA
PERSIAN GULF

B GREECE, 1946-47

GREEK COMMUNIST THREAT TO SEIZE POWER IN
GREECE STYMIED BY TRUMAN DOCTRINE.

150 MILES

YUGOSLAVIA
BULGARIA
BLACK SEA
ALBANIA
GREECE
TURKEY
AEGEAN SEA
Athens

HOT SPOTS
IN
THE COLD WAR

TRM

F SUEZ CRISIS, 1956

EGYPT TAKES OVER OPERATION OF CANAL.
BRITAIN AND FRANCE MOVE INTO CANAL ZONE
WHILE ISRAEL INVADES EGYPT ON THE EAST.

Port Said
Gaza
SUEZ CANAL
ISRAEL
NEGEV
JORDAN
Cairo
Suez
Elath
E G Y P T
NILE
SINAI PEN.
GULF OF SUEZ
GULF OF AQABA
TIRAN
SAUDI ARABIA
RED SEA
150 MILES

G ISRAEL AND THE MOSLEMS, 1948-60

ESTABLISHMENT OF JEWISH STATE LEADS TO
BORDER CLASHES WITH SURROUNDING
MOSLEM NATIONS.

SYRIA
LEBANON
Beirut
Damascus
MEDITERRANEAN SEA
ISRAEL
IRAQ
Tel Aviv-Jaffa
Amman
Cairo
JORDAN
EGYPT
SINAI PEN.
SAUDI ARABIA
RED SEA
150 MILES

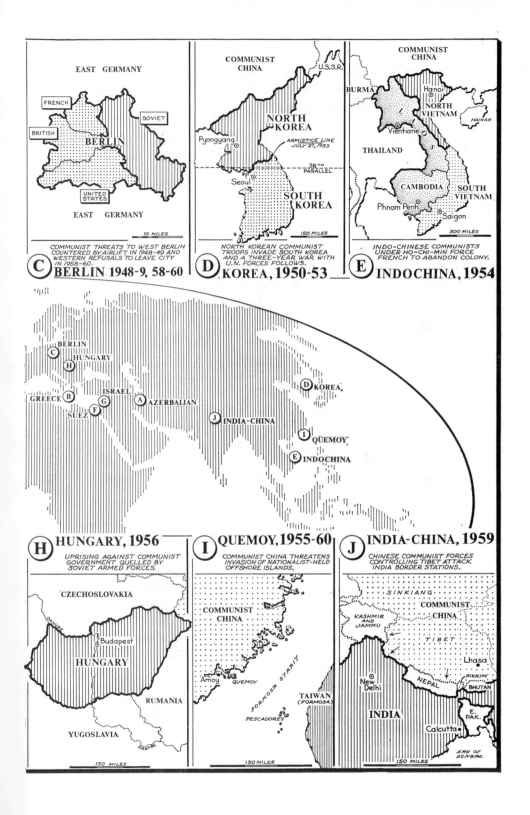

C **BERLIN, 1948-9, 58-60**

COMMUNIST THREATS TO WEST BERLIN COUNTERED BY AIRLIFT IN 1948-49 AND WESTERN REFUSALS TO LEAVE CITY IN 1958-60.

EAST GERMANY

FRENCH
SOVIET
BRITISH
BERLIN
UNITED STATES

EAST GERMANY

10 MILES

D **KOREA, 1950-53**

NORTH KOREAN COMMUNIST TROOPS INVADE SOUTH KOREA AND A THREE-YEAR WAR WITH U.N. FORCES FOLLOWS.

COMMUNIST CHINA

U.S.S.R.

NORTH KOREA

Pyongyang

ARMISTICE LINE JULY 27, 1953

38TH PARALLEL

Seoul

SOUTH KOREA

150 MILES

E **INDOCHINA, 1954**

INDO-CHINESE COMMUNISTS UNDER HO-CHI-MIN FORCE FRENCH TO ABANDON COLONY.

COMMUNIST CHINA

BURMA
Hanoi
NORTH VIETNAM
HAINAN
Vientiane

THAILAND

CAMBODIA
SOUTH VIETNAM
Phnom Penh
Saigon

300 MILES

BERLIN
HUNGARY
GREECE
ISRAEL
SUEZ
AZERBAIJAN
INDIA-CHINA
KOREA
QUEMOY
INDOCHINA

H **HUNGARY, 1956**

UPRISING AGAINST COMMUNIST GOVERNMENT QUELLED BY SOVIET ARMED FORCES.

CZECHOSLOVAKIA

Budapest

HUNGARY

RUMANIA

YUGOSLAVIA

150 MILES

I **QUEMOY, 1955-60**

COMMUNIST CHINA THREATENS INVASION OF NATIONALIST-HELD OFFSHORE ISLANDS.

COMMUNIST CHINA

Amoy
QUEMOY

FORMOSA STRAIT

TAIWAN (FORMOSA)

PESCADORES

150 MILES

J **INDIA-CHINA, 1959**

CHINESE COMMUNIST FORCES CONTROLLING TIBET ATTACK INDIA BORDER STATIONS.

SINKIANG

COMMUNIST CHINA

KASHMIR AND JAMMU

TIBET

Lhasa

New Delhi

NEPAL

SIKKIM

BHUTAN

INDIA

E. PAK.

Calcutta

BAY OF BENGAL

150 MILES

basic questions of Germany, disarmament, Communist China or world-wide Communist subversion. The "spirit of Geneva," although constantly invoked after the meeting ended, soon had to be tested against the facts of further Soviet penetration in Africa and Asia. By December, 1955, Secretary of State John Foster Dulles told a NATO meeting, "The Soviet Union has started a new cold war in the Middle East and Asia." Subsequent conferences between spokesmen of the two major power blocs produced either platitudes or recrimination, but they did nothing to narrow the chasm that divided the world's two armed camps. As the struggle with the Soviet Union shifted increasingly to Asia and Africa, the United States found that it could not control the major influences transforming the world. All that seemed possible was to try to contain Soviet force while hoping that friendly technical and economic aid would prevent so-called "uncommitted" and underdeveloped countries from falling under the constant threat of Communist control or influence.

To win new friends in these areas, leading American citizens called for giant funds to underwrite what was hoped would be pro-Western democratic regimes from Morocco to Manila. Congress, following a public resentful about high taxes, refused to provide such sums, but it did appropriate several billions yearly for foreign economic and military aid. Those who were enthusiastic about the possibilities of assistance to "backward areas" consistently ignored the warnings of international economists about the rate at which awakening nations could absorb capital and the extent to which their lack of expert industrial and financial technicians seriously interfered with their ability to use what capital they had or were likely to get. Those who thought that if America put money behind "awakening nationalist revolutions" the world would be won for democracy also failed to remember that nationalist regimes like Nasser's in Egypt, even if not Communist-dominated, could be dangerous to peace. Many new nations, furthermore, while accepting Western aid, still hated the West, which, rightly or wrongly, they distrusted because of its previous racist, imperialist, and capitalist exploitation. What new community of interest would emerge to tie the West and the new nations together would only become clear as suspicions subsided and the new peoples consolidated their revolutionary gains.

As for those European nations with which America had shared common ideals in peace and war, defense and diplomatic measures retained top priority. In 1952, plans were drawn up for a European Defense Community of six European nations, including West Germany, that was to form the basis for a European army counterweighing Russia's armed strength in Europe. But the E.D.C. treaty, which had the wholehearted support of the United States, revived France's traditional fears of a rearmed Germany. Although France had been the principal sponsor of the European Defense Community, in 1954, the French National Assembly voted down the E.D.C. treaty. Eisenhower considered the treaty's rejection a "major setback" to American policy, but a substitute plan was soon devised and approved. After a vigorous campaign by Anthony Eden of England, representatives of nine nations meeting in London in October, 1954, agreed to a proposal for a Western European Union that would fill the void left by the failure of E.D.C. Despite Soviet warnings, arrangements were also made for the admission of a sovereign and rearmed West Germany into the North Atlantic Treaty Organization.

The ultimate success of American foreign policy in Europe depended in large part on keeping close and friendly relations with Great Britain and France. But this was not always an easy task. In both countries, significant resentment against what was considered the domineering attitude of the United States continued, but in the Khrushchev era there was also a widespread fear that the undisguised hostility of the United States toward the Soviet Union would precipitate a third World War. Both countries, moreover, found it difficult to accept the fact that they were no longer major powers. Great Britain's prestige and power in the Mediterranean and the Near East declined steadily during Eisenhower's presidency, while France was compelled to give up its colony of Indo-China and to fight a protracted and expensive war against the opponents of French rule in Algeria.

The decline of British and French power posed a difficult problem for the United States. On the one hand, it had to maintain its alliance with Great Britain and France, while, on the other, it did not wish to endorse colonial policies that might eventually force the new nations of Asia and Africa into the camp of the Communists.

A major crisis between the United States and its European allies occurred in 1956 when Great Britain and France joined with Israel in an attack on Egypt after the revolutionary Nasser regime had seized the Suez Canal. Neither Great Britain nor France had informed the United States of intentions to attack Egypt, and on October 31, when the war was two days old, President Eisenhower stated: "We do not accept the use of force as an instrument for the settlement of international disputes." The following day, the United Nations, in a sixty-four-to-five vote, demanded an immediate cease-fire. By November 7, Great

Britain and France accepted the cease-fire, and the war was over. The United States' opposition to the war created an unprecedented degree of anti-American feeling among the leaders of France and Great Britain, although in England many liberal and labor spokesmen welcomed the American stand against aggression. The alliance between the United States and its principal European allies was strained almost to the breaking point. But it did not break. Despite recriminations and injured feelings on both sides of the Atlantic, the leaders of the three most powerful nations in the West fully realized that there was no alternative to continued cooperation.

The American people, however, were not prepared to fight Communist aggression on every front or even when their European allies were involved directly. In 1954, when French troops were waging a losing war against the Communists in Indo-China, the Eisenhower Administration at least hinted at the possibility of using American forces to aid France. Secretary of State John Foster Dulles stated that "united action" might be needed to save Indo-China, Vice-President Nixon thought that there was a good chance the United States would send troops to reinforce the French, and President Eisenhower said that Indo-China was of "transcendent interest" to the United States. But Americans, with the memory of Korea's bloody fighting fresh in their minds and bothered by their distrust of French colonialism, seemed strongly opposed to intervention in Indo-China. The Eisenhower Administration, after time for second thoughts on the strategic implications of military involvement on the Asiatic mainland, abandoned any plans it may have had for fighting Communists in Indo-China.

In April, 1954, a conference of nineteen regimes was held at Geneva to settle Far Eastern problems. It succeeded only in giving formal recognition to the French defeat and withdrawal from Indo-China. The United States regarded the conference as a defeat for the West. The French lost their largest colonial possession in Asia. The Communists were recognized as the undisputed rulers of North Vietnam, which was divided, on the Korean model, from a southern independent republic. The French loss convinced Administration leaders of the need for shoring up the free world's defenses in southeast Asia. As it was deemed impossible for the United States to rush troops to every spot in the Far East threatened by Communists, Secretary of State Dulles decided to enlist the aid of other interested nations in a defensive organization comparable to NATO. The result was the formation of the Southeast Asia Treaty Organization (SEATO) in 1954. Consisting of the United States, two European powers, (Great Britain and France) and five nations from the Far East (Australia, New Zealand, the Philippine Republic, Thailand, and Pakistan), SEATO was established to check Communist aggression and propaganda and to improve living conditions in the non-Communist countries of the Far East. A similar "Baghdad Pact," but lacking full formal American membership, was set up in 1956 to help stabilize the revolutionary situation in the Middle East that constantly invited Communist machinations.

The Prospect of Annihilation

The most dangerous feature of the cold war was the arms race in which each side sought to outdo the other in the development of new and more deadly weapons. Atom bomb tests were conducted regularly after 1945 by the United States and the Soviet Union; the United States launched the world's first atomic-powered submarine; and both countries, in addition to their work on conventional weapons, undertook large-scale programs for the development of military missiles. In 1954, the United States announced the explosion of a hydrogen bomb, and the Russians countered with the news that they already possessed such a bomb. The new bomb, which was the equivalent of at least ten million tons of T.N.T. could destroy everything within an area of fifty square miles. Such a bomb, moreover, produced a radioactive fallout that was carried around the world by winds. A Japanese fishing boat well outside the range of the American hydrogen bomb exploded at Bikini returned to Japan with twenty of its crew severely burned from radioactive ash particles. One of the crew members died, and fish caught in the Pacific Ocean had to be destroyed because of their radioactivity. This poisoning of the atmosphere increased demands in the West for an accommodation with the Soviet Union.

The real and potential dangers of the arms race were ignored by many Americans who comforted themselves with the belief that the technological superiority of the United States in deadly weapons would either provide a deterrent to Soviet aggression or insure an American victory in a nuclear war. But American complacency was shattered on October 4, 1957, when Soviet scientists launched the first man-made earth satellite, a sphere about 22 inches in diameter and weighing approximately 184 pounds, which circled the globe about every $1\frac{1}{2}$ hours and was known as "Sputnik." A month later, on November 3, the Russians launched a much larger (weighing 1,120 pounds) moon, called "Sputnik II," which carried a live dog as a passenger.

The American reaction to the Soviet invasion of space bordered on panic and hysteria. Newspaper readers were told that the Soviet

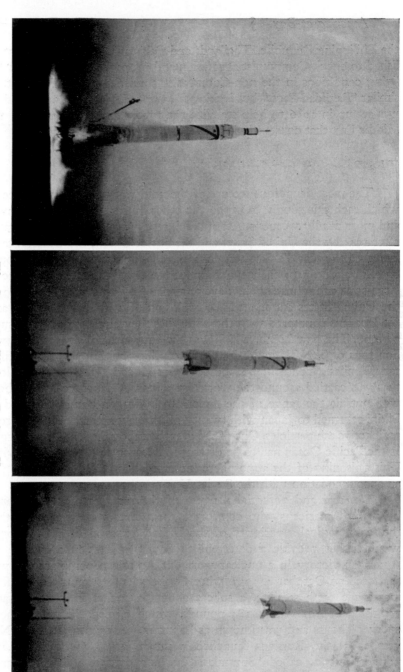

The Successful Flight of Explorer V

[WIDE WORLD]

Union was now in a position to destroy the United States with missiles and that it was only a matter of days or weeks before the Russians either reached the moon or established a space platform from which they could dominate the world.

Politicians demanded more appropriations for missile research, the reorganization of the nation's military administration, larger subsidies for scientists, overhauling the nation's educational system, and virtually any other proposal that would attract headlines. Overnight everyone became an authority on the nation's schools and colleges, which were held responsible for the United States' inability to launch a satellite before the Russians; and *Life* magazine stated: "It goes without saying nowadays that the outcome of the arms race will depend eventually on our schools and those of the Russians."

The United States became a full-fledged competitor in the satellite race on January 31, 1958, when the Army placed in orbit a 31-pound moon called Explorer I. In the following March, the Navy launched Vanguard I, which weighed less than Explorer I. Americans were chagrined that their satellites weighed less than those of the Russians, but they gained some consolation from the fact that the altitude achieved by Explorer I and Vanguard I was much higher than that attained by either of the Soviet's Sputniks. Within a year after the first Soviet triumph, the launchings of space rockets of various types and destinations became regular news items.

The advent of the satellite age marked a new—and perhaps final—stage in the history of man's warfare. Scientists in the Soviet Union and the United States were competing in the heavens for prestige, knowledge, and military advantage. The diplomats were not the principal actors in this grimmest of dramas, and the mass of mankind could play no part. The one hope was that with every scientific advance the threat of a war without victory became greater. But, despite shots at the stars, the Soviet Union and the West were still primarily in a political and economic race to win the loyalties and friendship of tens of millions on Earth.

FOR SUPPLEMENTARY READING

Many of the books cited for Chapter 20 carry over into the Eisenhower years. Whatever caution must be used with them because of closeness to the subject should be doubled for books published even more recently. E. Goldman has a short general essay, *The Crucial Decade: America, 1945–1955* (1956) that is, for example, essentially attractive journalism. On political alignments use S. Lubell, *The Future of American Politics* (1952) (Pb) and *Revolt of the Moderates* (1956). Many issues are analyzed as they occurred in R. Rovere, *Affairs of State: The Eisenhower Years* (1956). M. J. Pusey, *Eisenhower the President* (1956), has merit for all its topicality and contrasts in bias with M. Childs, *Captive Hero* (1958). On the later phases of the Korean venture use C. Berger, *The Korea Knot* (1957). N. Graebner, *The New Isolationism* (1956), gets into an underdiscussed subject. The debate about defense in the nuclear age had a notable analysis in H. A. Kissinger, *Nuclear Weapons and Foreign Policy* (1957). (Pb) No greater sense on foreign aid programs can be found than in G. Myrdal, *An International Economy: Problems and Prospects* (1956). Civil liberties after McCarthy are surveyed in J. W. Caughey, *In Clear and Present Danger* (1956). M. R. Konvitz's *Bill of Rights Reader* (1954) has assorted documents on a range of issues from the Communist trials to the desegregation decision.

22

-»»-»»-»»-»»-»»-»»-»»-»»

A New
American Culture

N THE 1950's, many Americans wondered whether the United States
had the stamina and fortitude to wage a long, frustrating cold war.
Politicians like Adlai Stevenson and respected students of international affairs like George Kennan and Hans Morgenthau complained
that the American public was not being prepared for the discipline and
sacrifices that were needed to win the deadly struggle with an ever
militant and growingly confident Soviet Union. Instead, these critics
noted that the American people seemed comfortably confirmed in a
new-found ease and sense of luxury that grew out of the spectacular increases in American productivity. Those who agreed with the critics
contrasted the implications of the nationalist revolutions in Asia and
Africa with the image of a hedonistic, lax, and frivolous American public more interested in do-it-yourself gadgets, home improvements, or
foreign sports cars than in trying to lead new nations to the political
stability and abundance that would halt future inroads by Communists.
A number of writers maintained that a momentous change had taken
place in the national character; although Americans had become more
easygoing and more wealthy, they were losing their capacity for independent judgment. Cooperativeness, or "togetherness" as it came to be
called, while making people easier to get along with, was, in the opinion
of a famous sociologist, David Riesman, transforming Americans into
so many "faces in a crowd," taking their cues for thought and action

not so much from any firm personal sense of right or wrong as from
what any situation or group happened to demand as a condition of "belonging." Whatever the truth in such assertions, it was clear that the
Americans of the 1950's were much different than the people who had
listened two generations earlier to Woodrow Wilson's or Theodore
Roosevelt's calls to duty.

The Passing of the Old American

The Progressive movements before the first World War were in
many ways inspired by the fear that the newly emerging way of life
in an urban, industrial, and multinational America was incompatible
with traditional American ideals of "character" and "faith." By the
1920's, the rewards of the machine and factory most familiar to the
average American—more money, more leisure, and greater ease—
were quickly blunting the force of the older rules of life in the Jacksonian and evangelical traditions. The growing power of factory and
machine and the rapidity and simplification of communication by
movie, radio, airplane, and automobile brought greater uniformity to
national culture. Although the twenties did not create all the forces
transforming national life, they tended to make dominant and irreversible what were previously scattered tendencies.

The twenties made the advertising agency, national press service,
newspaper chains, and the movies powerful influences on American
ideas and expectations. Increasingly, the ideals and style of the nation
were urban rather than rural. Press and screen invitations to luxury
and comfort were increasingly accepted in many middle-class families
as a radio and automobile were purchased, or as the celluloid collar,
high shoes, and heavier woolens gave way in summer to "sports
clothes." A new familiarity between the sexes lowered the prestige of
older lofty ideals of chastity. The "outdoor girl," the "bachelor girl,"
and the "career woman" became attractive models of behavior for
young ladies. Emily Post noted in later editions of her famous work
Etiquette that her section "Should a Young Woman Go Alone to a
Young Man's Apartment?" did not have a place in earlier editions;
times had changed.

For the young man as well as young woman the third stage of
the American educational revolution that was under way in the 1920's
had special significance. By 1860, a basic elementary education had become a normal expectation for most American children. After 1880,
the high-school revolution started to extend this birthright, and by
1929, a college education for the children was increasingly a norm in

many American homes. This change, coming together with the slow decline or outlawing of child labor, meant that American culture was continuing to extend the years during which a child remained dependent on his family; but, at the same time, it was gradually lowering the age at which children were permitted to be seen, to be heard, to enjoy privileges, and to learn the lore traditionally reserved for adults. All sorts of worries about what young America was coming to were implied in the famous descriptive phrase of the time—"flaming youth." Even in the home without a "flapper" daughter or raccoon-coated son, "Dad," "Mom," and other words denoting a new openness and familiarity in family life rapidly replaced the older American rhetoric.

The assessment of the extent and significance of such diverse cultural changes is always difficult to make, but on the eve of the Great Depression it seems clear that the roots of a new American culture were deeply planted. Most of the changes of the 1920's, however, had touched the more comfortable urban groups—often of native stock. But the Great Depression and the New Deal brought millions of Americans in all classes and backgrounds into closer touch with each other and started a massive redistribution of wealth that wartime and "cold war" taxes continued. New Deal benefits of shorter hours, higher wages, and basic social security helped prepare the great majority of the people for the benefits of prosperity when it reappeared with the explosion of American productive potential during and after World War II. By 1945, millions of Americans were ready to demand access to the possibilities for leisure and pleasure that had been paraded before their eyes by movies and picture magazines for years.

The Debate about "Mass Culture"

The great mass of Americans in the Eisenhower Era seemed to accept without question the uniform styles of taste and thought brought by a machine civilization; but some intellectuals protested that the United States was being transformed into a nation of mechanized "status seekers" who were manipulated by "hidden persuaders" and debased by an unending flow of trash on the television and movie screens.

Mass production, however, required both basic uniformity of style and mass consumption. Large-scale manufacturers were thus compelled to persuade every American consumer to buy their products. As more Americans came to buy similar goods, the people of one section might retain traditional attitudes and prejudices, but their daily rounds of of work and play were increasingly the same as those in every other section of the country. Tens of millions tuned to the same television and radio programs, kept their food in an electric refrigerator or deep freezer, cleaned their rugs with a vacuum cleaner, went to the same movies, and wore clothes of the latest style. Style no longer depended upon where one lived but on the ability to pay for nationally advertised products. Few American women did not prefer the easily prepared brand-name products and "instant mixes" in the supermarket to the time-consuming recipes that had been the pride of their grandmothers. In an earlier day, a woman's background and social status would often be revealed by her dress as well as by the food she served, but with the mass production of dresses at relatively low prices, the old correlation between style and rank disappeared. Expensive designers still set the mode, but their fashions were easily imitated by manufacturers who sold to a national market. The shop girl, stenographer, or farmer's daughter often wore clothes that to the untutored, masculine eye were the same as those imported from Paris for women of wealth and leisure.

The national advertising campaign helped make possible the standardization of customs and attitudes, as well as of consuming habits. Men and women in advertisements wore their good looks like uniforms, were interested in things rather than ideas, and wished only to improve their status. Readers, listeners, and viewers were told that if they made a small down payment, hurried to their nearest department store, or filled out the enclosed blank, they could look like the smiling, happy, handsome models that had been created by the account executives, copywriters, and commercial artists of the advertising agencies. Advertising helped move goods and kept production going, but by its very nature it was compelled to accentuate uniformity rather than individual differences.

The trend to uniformity of taste had parallels in the standardization of public information. The decline in the independent newspaper and the rise of newspaper chains made it possible for news, like groceries, to be distributed by A & P methods. With the development of the newspaper chain, a single publisher was able to formulate the editorial policy of papers throughout the country. Columnists often had their material syndicated in as many as 100 different papers. Press associations distributed the same news and what were accurately called "canned editorials" to papers read by readers who might be southern sharecroppers, Dakota wheat farmers, or New York tenement dwellers. In magazine publishing, older periodicals such as *Harper's* and the *Atlantic Monthly* had only a small percentage of the total magazine circulation. Magazines like the *Saturday Evening Post* and *Ladies' Home Journal*, which were read by millions, were crammed with the same advertisements, the same human-interest articles, and the same love, adventure, and success stories.

Among both the mass-circulation papers and magazines, journals appeared to fit the needs of people living at an accelerated tempo. The tabloid paper, an urban phenomenon, was small enough to be handled by passengers on crowded subway trains, simple enough in format, and packed with enough scandal and sensation to appeal to the lowest and largest type of curiosity. Businessmen so absorbed in their work and recreation that they had neither time nor inclination to keep abreast of current events were provided with *Time, Newsweek,* and other weekly summaries of recent developments in politics, business, medicine, science, education, and foreign affairs. The *Reader's Digest,* a monthly that compressed articles that had first appeared in national magazines, had enormous popularity and stimulated the establishment of similar digests publishing monthly condensations of articles on practically every subject. The advent of picture magazines in the 1930's brought the movement to simplify reading matter to its logical conclusion. *Life, Look,* and countless imitations made few demands on what they called their readers; Americans could perhaps look forward to the day when their magazines would be entirely free of the printed word.

In the nation's entertainment the same movies were exhibited in every community, and radio and television programs were carried simultaneously by chains of stations on national networks strung across the nation. The spectacular rise of television, however, took away much of the appeal of radio and the movies. But, with less pressure on them, radio stations and movie makers seemed freer to experiment. In major cities radio stations and "art movie" houses began to give the public some relief from a steady diet of pap. Here and there, radio devoted more of its time to classical music, serious dramas, and informed discussions. Some motion picture producers increasingly recognized both the educational and artistic potentials of their medium, although most movie scripts were still devoted to boy-meets-girl themes, adventure stories, and humor directed at the lowest intelligence in the audience. Television's much heralded "classrooms" and lectures by university scholars were scheduled for sunrise hours, least attractive to advertisers and used more for sleeping than for studying. As for the daily run of TV programs, if a student of American civilization in the 1950's were compelled to view only programs between 9 a.m. and 9 p.m. he might well conclude that all Americans except criminals lived and worked in pleasant surroundings and were primarily interested in killing Indians and gangsters.

It was difficult, however, to assess the actual effects of advertising and the mass media on the public. Exposure to similar ideas and low taste did not necessarily mean uniformity or vulgarity of response.

Critics of the new mass culture implied that the American audience was hopelessly manipulatable and had no resistance to what it saw or read. It was claimed that "subliminal" advertising appeals to unconscious wishes influenced the public more than it realized. Some studies, however, seemed to indicate that Americans had developed selective techniques of reading, viewing, or listening. What did not impress them went past their eye or ear. Psychiatrists maintained that although programs emphasizing violence might appeal to the least attractive parts of the personality, vicarious participation in violent acts might be helpful in discharging hostilities harmlessly. Although such contentions were not meant as positive defenses of the fare served in the mass media, they did imply more cautious judgments about its effects. Similarly, there was evidence to indicate that the public could learn to differentiate among products that seemed to be essentially the same. Producers did introduce various "price lines," and some buyers seemed to learn the true differences between the mass produced house at $20,000 and that costing twice as much.

What was most overlooked by those foreseeing only the continued standardization and degradation of American taste was the remarkable growth of interest throughout the nation in what the old-fashioned called "the finer things." In the years after World War II, many communities sponsored successful museums, symphony orchestras, and opera companies or welcomed major music and dramatic groups touring the country. With the introduction of inexpensive long-playing records the national sales of recorded classical music boomed, and Americans who had never taken the interest before debated the relative merits of a Toscanini or Bruno Walter interpretation. The sales of "hi-fidelity" and "stereophonic" record players in some ways reflected a need to keep up with Joneses, but it was again difficult to deduce from behavior —i.e., a purchase—the motive of and effect on the consumer. The growth of book clubs, dramatic and "great book" study groups, and singing societies and the phenomenal annual sales of hundreds of millions of new paperback books with the most serious and worthwhile titles all pointed to a greater compatability between mass culture and the refinement of interests and improvement of taste.

What made evaluation of these more hopeful trends especially difficult was the fact that "culture" had become chic and saleable. In the nineteenth century, the avant-garde artist had difficulty in finding an audience, and the refusal to accept him could be taken as a sincere—if philistine—expression of taste. But by the middle of the twentieth century, the rapid acceptance of much new serious work in the arts was no real test of public enlightenment. On the one hand, greater wealth and leisure gave the public the time for instruction and reflection, but the fear of appearing anti-intellectual was becoming a powerful influence in choosing a Picasso print or a Stravinsky recording for one's home. Some purchasers of "culture" refused to act on their true feelings, but, instead, bought what they did not really like in order not to seem philistine. A great deal that was meretricious, tricky, or fake thus received unmerited acceptance. "Culture" furthermore, became excessively serious work for the public, and "answers" to "the problems of our time," rather than spontaneous pleasure and enjoyment, were sought in the pages of James Joyce or Henry James.

Three popular words used to classify the new developments in American taste were "highbrow," "lowbrow," and "middlebrow." These broad categories were derived from a notable essay published in 1915 by the literary historian Van Wyck Brooks and called *America's Coming of Age.* Brooks believed that, historically, American culture had been divided between highbrows, typified by intellectual and philosophic writers and their audiences, from Jonathan Edwards to Henry James, and lowbrows who liked the common-sense, realistic, and colloquial writers like the Benjamin Franklin of *Poor Richard's Almanac.* Brooks wanted a middle position developed that would end the split between realism and intellectualism in American culture, make the artist less "alienated" from his society, and open up the possibilities of unconfused enlightenment and invigoration of the nation's cultural life as an "organic" whole.

By the 1950's, Americans seem to have oversubscribed Brooks's appeal for a middlebrow culture—but at the price of discounting the value to society of strong contrasts of opinions, such as divided Franklin and Edwards. Comfortable middlebrow standards had become norms behind which there lurked hostility to the genuine and important moral and intellectual distinctions that interested highbrows. Middlebrows also preferred ideas that were readily accessible. Those middlebrow ideas that seemed "challenging" were often safe moralisms, homilies, and higher clichés that both a Jonathan Edwards and a Mark Twain, although from radically different standards, would have delighted to expose.

Middlebrow culture thus tended to enervate mind and taste in a dangerous way, for it presented its standards with an aura of intellectual respectability. Middlebrowism was often smug, even arrogant, in its implication that the standards of the comfortable, rational, liberal middle classes were indefinitely extendable and beyond debate. The middlebrow versions of "difficult" thinkers like Freud or Kierkegaard that were printed in magazines and taken as authentic enlightenment strengthened the fallacious assumption that any system of thought or method of criticism could be adequately encompassed or mastered in a four- or six-page "spread" (with pictures) in *Time* or *Look*. Intellectual work or improving the mind seemed easy; supposedly anyone could learn enough about the most demanding ideas to speak authoritatively about them.

Critics of popularization warned that it was less dangerous for the specific misinformation it gave than for the demand it produced for quick and cheap ideas. Those who were opposed to the "popular versions" for the mass public were often regarded as snobs or undemocratic elitists who wanted to deny the public access to the best that had been thought or said in the world. In fact, most of the critics of what middlebrowism had become were only insisting that a little knowledge was a dangerous thing and that the popular version often drew the sting and complexity out of what was meant to be critical and difficult. The public's desire was for what all men could understand or agree on, rather than for what kept men and ideas different. Most Americans, however eager for knowledge, did not have the time, skill, or discipline to learn enough about psychoanalysis or the nature of Communism to have their opinions weigh equally with those of the specialist or professional. Middlebrowism, however, had tended to intensify the democratic notion that even on the gravest questions one man's opinion was as worthy as another's; it prepared people for facile, "human," and trite opinions rather than for a questioning, biting intellectual analysis.

Pluralism and Uniformity in American Life

The preponderant influences at work in American society by the 1950's were making the tendency to uniformity of behavior—if less clearly of inner response—stronger than the traditional distinctions that had set Americans off from one another. There seemed to be so serious a decline in contrasts and alternatives in American society and so great a store set by agreement, conformity, and likeness that many critics worried that the nation was headed toward a "soft totalitarianism" in which the amiable and cooperative were taking precedence over the solitary and heroic, and students of this tendency feared that the nation would lose its vitality and moral stamina.

The national debate over "conformity" and "togetherness" was, however, excessively abstract. The new virtues had their attractive features, for they made Americans less moralistic and more friendly. Too often the conformity to basic ideals essential to the nation's confidence in itself was not distinguished from conformity for its own sake or conformity to the passing fancy. Very often, too, what critics had in mind when they attacked conformity was not the alternative of true independent judgment, but the equally ritualistic acceptance of the opinion or view of a minority group convinced that it, rather than the majority, was right. For years, for example, many Americans had bemoaned the absence of a clear-cut distinction in American politics between conservatives and liberals; yet when a group of so-called neo-conservatives, led by men like Russell Kirk and Peter Viereck, did appear after World War II, they were greeted by some liberals not as intellectually thin and historically irrelevant moralists, but (partly because of the affinity of some of the newcomers for McCarthy or because of their irresponsible attacks on the liberal community) as genuine threats to the freedom of the republic and the liberal way of life.

One of the most important notions used to criticize conformity and standardization was that of a "pluralistic society." According to philosophers like John Dewey, Horace Kallen, and Sidney Hook, American society was to be conceived as one in which individuals and groups with the widest differences of opinion and interest competed with each other under the rule of law. The conflict among them would provide valuable alternatives in public policy, offer the citizen a range of choices in belief and action, and assure many chances for organizing opposition to unjust or unwise decisions of the majority or of the government. The only public "truth" in American society was that implied in the acceptance of peaceful democratic experiment and change. The ideal of pluralism, however, had important limitations. A common social life tended to create conceptions of right and wrong, of acceptable or unacceptable mores that became a basic faith or "consensus" with priority over other beliefs and customs. However inarticulate or laxly enforced these were, they were essential to the continuity and cohesion, identity, and self-confidence of any culture. Although the pluralists recognized such criticisms, they were intent on maintaining the possibilities of criticism and change against even the most attractive or seemingly unsurrenderable beliefs. They wanted most to be sure that the state did not adopt any belief as a dogma for its citizens and that it protected the dissenter or unorthodox citizen in his guaranteed constitutional rights.

Until the first World War, the pluralism of American society was evident in a wide variety of ethnic, regional, religious, and political affiliations and loyalties. But within that diversity there were certain ideals that had pre-eminent power and prestige and that were upheld by public opinion and often by laws. These ideals were that the "true" American was an Anglo-Saxon in national origin, white by race, middle-class in his income and habits, some variety of Protestant in his religion, and a small entrepreneur in business. These characteristics tended to be the norm against which the newly arrived immigrant, the Negro freedman, or the Mormon or Catholic or Socialist minority were measured, and usually found wanting.

In the late nineteenth century, however, Americans went through two dramatic changes in national life that broke up the old pluralistic organization of American society and challenged the prestige of the old American norm of national character. The industrial-urban revolution in America produced a variety of problems common to other countries undergoing industrialization. But, unlike England, France, or Germany, Americans also underwent an ethnic revolution stimulated by the arrival of millions of immigrants whose history and traditions were radically at variance with dominant older American ideals. The habits and ideals introduced by the immigrant were painful for those already here to accept. Until 1914, Americans actively debated several attitudes toward what was called the "new immigration" from southern and eastern Europe. One policy—restriction and exclusion—was gradually enacted into law after 1880. For the immigrant already here, however, the predominant attitude was to Americanize him, to make him drop as quickly as possible all signs of loyalty to or affiliation with his country of origin. In the picturesque phrase of Theodore Roosevelt, Americans did not propose having their nation turned into a "polyglot boardinghouse."

There was, of course, a paradox in the programs to Americanize the immigrant. The Americanizers insisted that the immigrant abandon his foreign language and habits and join the ranks of the "real Americans," but wherever the immigrant turned he found closed ranks in jobs, professions, schools, churches, and clubs in which Americanism was practiced. Even if he picked up an American style, his immigrant background was held against him. With advances closed to him by those safely behind the Anglo-Saxon curtain, the immigrant started a long hard climb toward his place in the sun. Only the slow painful erosion of cultures in conflict with each other and the votes delivered to his friends and denied to his enemies brought the immigrant the rewards that Americanization had seemed to promise.

The most famous answer to the implication of Americanization programs that there was a definite national style which the immigrant had to accept was the image of the melting-pot. The melting-pot was both a theory of American history and the basis for an immigration policy. According to the melting-pot ideal, America had been made by people of diverse religious and national origins rather than by one dominant group. The national stock and style were actually rich amalgams that would lose their strength and attractiveness unless new ingredients were constantly added. Any significant restriction on immigration would thus deprive the nation of future contributions to American life as significant as those already made by the different people who had come to America.

Although the melting-pot ideal was based on hopes for a generous immigration policy, in its own way it also projected a single American style—albeit made from different "elements"—and it ignored the extent to which the immigrant refused—even felt it wrong—to give up old ways, although jumping into the melting-pot might offer him many advantages. Throughout the nation there were enclaves of former immigrants like the Amish of Pennsylvania, the German Lutherans in the Middle West, and the Creoles of Louisiana who, although living in America for many generations, had not completely adopted any dominant variety of Americanism. Why, then, argued the newer immigrant, should he?

During World War I, tens of thousands of recent immigrants left this country to fight the Allies, and later America, on the side of the Central powers. Their departure increased the claims and strength of the immigration exclusionists and nativists. In their view, wartime disloyalty showed that both the Americanization and melting-pot ideals were mistakes. The immigrants had supposedly demonstrated that they would not be Americanized, or even contribute to creating a new melting-pot American. The "melting-pot mistake" became a repeated theme in the 1920's. Racists and nativists claimed that impure elements added to the "pure American stock" would debase, not strengthen it. The small group of cultural pluralists and believers in what Randolph Bourne had called a "trans-national America," also agreed that the melting-pot had not worked and that the nation would have to resign itself to a far more diverse and unstable national character than it had been content with before World War I. America, they claimed, now meant differences; diversity was both unavoidable and desirable.

Since the 1920's, however, cultural pluralists and melting-pot enthusiasts have not been able to modify significantly the nation's restrictive and quasi-racist immigrant policies. Occasionally, special allowances have been made for victims of religious persecution, for refugees from Communism, and for stateless Europeans after World War II. Asians were eventually assigned regular quotas and were no longer excluded completely from the United States. The basic policy of the 1920's, however, has endured.

798

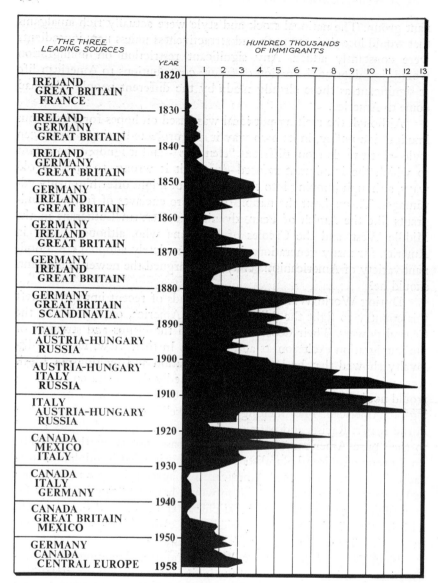

THE THREE LEADING SOURCES	YEAR	HUNDRED THOUSANDS OF IMMIGRANTS
IRELAND GREAT BRITAIN FRANCE	1820	
IRELAND GERMANY GREAT BRITAIN	1830	
IRELAND GERMANY GREAT BRITAIN	1840	
GERMANY IRELAND GREAT BRITAIN	1850	
GERMANY IRELAND GREAT BRITAIN	1860	
GERMANY IRELAND GREAT BRITAIN	1870	
GERMANY GREAT BRITAIN SCANDINAVIA	1880	
ITALY AUSTRIA-HUNGARY RUSSIA	1890	
AUSTRIA-HUNGARY ITALY RUSSIA	1900	
ITALY AUSTRIA-HUNGARY RUSSIA	1910	
CANADA MEXICO ITALY	1920	
CANADA ITALY GERMANY	1930	
CANADA GREAT BRITAIN MEXICO	1940	
GERMANY CANADA CENTRAL EUROPE	1950 1958	

Pattern of Migration to the United States, 1820–1958

The Emergency Quota Act of 1921 restricted the number of immigrants to 3 per cent of the number from each nationality that had been living in the United States in 1910. The Immigration Quota Act of 1924 made 1890 (when American stock was presumably even "purer") the base year and lowered the ratio from 3 to 2 per cent. A committee

The Klan Again—New Jersey, 1948

[NATIONAL ARCHIVES]

was established to propose individual immigration quotas for each foreign nation; in 1929, Congress put these quota requirements into law. As a result of the various immigration bills, the earlier flood of new arrivals was reduced to a trickle of between 200,000 and 300,000 a year. The American labor movement had traditionally demanded the restriction of immigration, and with notable success, but the new laws were enacted in response not only to labor's pressure but also to the demands of superpatriots who frequently confused Americanism with homogeneity. From the humanitarian point of view, the end of unrestricted immigration was a tacit admission that the United States was no longer a haven for the world's downtrodden and oppressed. For years, Americans had argued about the virtues of the national melting-pot; but now their argument would become academic, for in a generation or two there would be practically nothing left to melt. As for those immigrants already here, throughout the twenties and sporadically ever since, vigilante societies and hate groups have tried to terrorize individuals into conformity. The Ku Klux Klan has been revived in many states—and not exclusively in the South—to preach and practice its gospel of hate against Negroes, Jews, Roman Catholics and the foreign-born.

Other than the restriction of immigration and the work of groups like the Klan, the greatest threats to America's cultural pluralism and social diversity have been previously noted tendencies—the growth of mass standardized production, of rapid mass communication of standardized news, and of the cooperative habits necessary to keep production going and to maintain peace among people living in ever closer touch with each other. Although the growing needs of industrial society created new jobs, professions, and roles for the individual, the greater closeness of American life and the standardized styles of consumption of goods and ideas made available to citizens worked against the diversity of beliefs and interests that one might expect with a more extensive and complex division of labor.

Pluralists made much of the fact that the number of voluntary groups Americans joined for one purpose or another had continued to grow in number and in range of interests; this seemed to argue that citizens were still vigorous and alert about protecting or pursuing their interests and ideals despite tendencies toward uniformity and complacency. These groups certainly did provide alternatives and options, and they kept alive debate and social criticism. But, from another point of view, politically these groups formed a vast dense network which, while preventing the easy victory of an unwise or unfair program and working against what Tocqueville had called "the tyranny of the majority," tended also to make more difficult the passing of good laws or enactment of reforms that the majority desired. Free voluntary associations often turned out to be skillfully organized interest groups with a disproportionate veto power over proposed changes in domestic and foreign policy.

One continuing effect of the growing size of industry on American older groups was to diminish further the numbers and influence of the nation's small independent businessmen. A widely discussed analysis of this change was the book *White Collar*, by C. Wright Mills, a sociologist. Mills observed that the growth of big business had made it increasingly difficult for the small producer or shopkeeper to stay in business. The former independent small store, for example, was giving way to the local supermarket, and the local supermarket, in turn, was being absorbed by the coast-to-coast chain. Although the store owner who had been fortunate enough to find a good job as a manager in the chain might have greater security than in his former independence, he resented, Mills maintained, his loss of status and "identity" in becoming a cog in a machine. He might find temporary or substitute satisfactions in his new job as time passed, but in many cases his frustrations led to social resentment and hatred against "the system" that more money and leisure did not lessen. Any major economic crisis or a skillful demagogue might arouse the hunger for power and status of the former economically independent citizen. The larger white collar class would then show that it had accepted its new role only reluctantly, out of necessity rather than relief in losing the burdens of a competitive independence.

Very different in mood was the assessment by William H. Whyte, Jr., of America's managers and executives in the business bureaucracy. Whyte's *The Organization Man* did not isolate the formerly independent corporation employees from the younger group that had grown up in the culture of the corporation. But, given the growing size of the junior group and that it seemed to be setting the pace, the contrast with Mills's work was inevitable and striking. Equally impressive were affinities with Riesman's work. Whyte observed what he called the "decline of the Protestant ethic," the lessening in business life of strong individual drive and ambitiousness, and the growing prestige of team spirit and of modest, security conscious, career goals. Whether the evidence supported Whyte or Mills (and it seemed to strengthen Whyte's case) both books suggested disquieting possibilities under the surface of the smooth running, ever bigger, seemingly ever more benign world of the American corporation.

The Triumph of the City

Although the city had established itself in a dominating position in American life during the 1920's, there still remained important pockets of resistance to urban ideals and styles before the crash of 1929. Rural and small-town America still had national spokesmen like Bryan and La Follette with considerable, if waning, prestige. When Carol Kennicott, the heroine of Sinclair Lewis' *Main Street*, came to Gopher Prairie in the 1920's and tried to convert her neighbors to the new exciting ideas she had learned in a more cosmopolitan world, doors were closed against her until she learned that her city ways were not welcome. An automobile trip across the country, thirty years later, would have revealed thousands of main streets almost indistinguishable from each other, as they had been; but instead of rutted roads and dingy shop fronts, one would have found the same films playing in similar movie houses, national chain stores with uniformly large window fronts, and other shops competing actively with each other in selling big city chic and national American versions of Dior styles for women and the new "Italian cut" for men. The big city had conquered the small town.

In simplest terms, the triumph of the city is indicated by the growth in urban population. According to the census of 1900, more than 60 per cent of the population still lived in rural areas, and not until 1920 did city dwellers outnumber rural inhabitants. By 1930, almost 70,000,000 people in a population of more than 138,000,000 were city dwellers, and by 1960, a nation of 180,000,000 was overwhelmingly urbanized. The census, however, fails to include in its statistics on urban population many who live in the suburbs and are city people in all but name. Working in the city, reading city newspapers, and obtaining their recreation either in or not far from the city, the suburbanite resembles the inhabitant of the city in all but the small patch of grass that surrounds his home.

The city brought rootlessness, anonymity, and a mechanized sterile round of life, but it also meant money, power, success, excitement, and freedom. Many moved to the city to get or hold a job; but others went because they felt that they were misunderstood by their parents, because they had fought with their friends, or because they thought that their talent was being wasted in a small town. The city was able to absorb the ever-increasing flood of new arrivals because of technological advances made after the Civil War. The expansion of the railroad system, the refrigeration of meat, and the canning of fruits and vegetables made it possible to crowd together in a relatively small area vast numbers of people who were not able to produce their own food. The elevator and structural steel permitted cities to grow skyward, while the subway, elevated railroad, trolley, and automobile enabled them to expand horizontally. Each of these innovations might have relieved urban congestion, but each aggravated rather than eliminated problems. Every effort to make the life of the city dweller more bearable made it possible for the city to handle more people. Urbanization became the history of congestion, and the modern American city demonstrated beyond all doubt that congestion fed on congestion. By the mid-1950's, there were few major American cities that were not faced with a transportation problem of momentous proportion.

The constant pressure of population made it difficult, if not impossible, to find adequate space in which city dwellers could work, sleep, and play. Skyscrapers built in the city's most congested sections provided additional office space, but they contributed to the crowding that had made them necessary. Since industrial production could not be organized along the vertical lines of the skyscrapers, most factories were located on the cheaper land in the city's outskirts. Sites that had not been pre-empted by either factory or office structures went on default to the city's residents. Poorer citizens still lived in slums or buildings that had been abandoned fifty or more years before by the well-to-do. The "housing project" replaced the worst of these slums after the 1930's; but, as many critics complained, it increased the density of population per acre and made the city one unrelieved mass of red bricks. Gradually, however, builders were learning how to vary design and colors to prevent monotony, but little was done to relieve population density by locating the "project" in the suburbs where land was cheaper and greenery and fresh air more abundant.

By the 1920's, most of the urban middle and upper classes had abandoned private houses for apartments. Less crowded, cleaner, costlier, and better equipped than slum dwellings, the apartments of the rich were still cells in a hive. In fact, rich and poor alike lived in cells, the rich merely occupying bigger and better cells. After business firms and their employees had been housed, little room was left in cities for recreation facilities. Parks and playgrounds, most needed in congested areas, could seldom be placed there because overcrowding had made the cost of land so high. Some cities refused to face this problem, and others sought to solve it by establishing large play areas, such as New York City's Central Park, but no city was able to provide all its residents with enough space to ensure them a healthy existence.

The pre-Civil War city had been essentially a market place where goods from the immediate hinterland and abroad had been bought and sold. With factories, transport, communication and the nation's financiers all located in the city, its economic power was made virtually absolute. All lines of economic authority emanated from the city to the rest of the country, and decisions reached by small groups of businessmen in New York, Chicago, Los Angeles, and other cities affected the lives of countless Americans in every part of the United States. The radio and television, motion picture, newspaper, and magazine industries brought the urban style of life to the entire nation. The books that Americans read and the advertisements that helped to shape their habits of consumption were urban products that were distributed to a national audience. By 1960, no American was able to escape the city's influence. In the words of one student, "America is the city."

Science, Religion, and Education

Since the first English settlement in the New World, Americans have believed that religion, education, and gadgets could cure the ills of mankind. Until the twentieth century, however, there were strong influences at work in the schools and churches opposing the American tendency to prefer money and success to intellect and God. But in the last fifty years, despite impressive increases in the size of the nation's educational establishment, and especially after World War II, a prodigious growth in church membership, it was obvious that most educators and leading churchmen had made peace with the claims of the world. They had, in effect, tailored the Bible and school curriculum to the needs of a comfort-conscious, secular, and progressive society.

Even the long-waged battle of religion and science seemed finished. By the 1950's, few people cared to challenge the assumption that science and religion complemented each other, a belief easier than ever to maintain since religion had become increasingly a system of humane ethics and little else. Even the freshest phase of the battle—that between the psychoanalysts and ministers—had subsided; some Roman Catholics, as well as many pastors and rabbis, increasingly had good things to say about the so-called revisionist psychoanalysts, who gave greater autonomy than Freud had to man's conscious mind. One book after another asserted that religion need not be neurotic, that it represented a respectable satisfaction of a genuine aspiration, and that religion and psychiatry complemented each other in curing sick souls. One of the nation's most popular revisionist analysts, Erich Fromm, gave increasing importance to religion in his works and helped pull the sting from Freud's more pessimistic claims and ironic observations about man's nature. If more in popular theory than in private clinical practice, psychoanalysis thus became reconciled with the increasingly prestigeful human assumptions cherished by the nation's educated classes.

The invention of the atom and hydrogen bombs, however, did temper the previous American enthusiasm about the essential beneficence and inevitably progressive nature of scientific research. In the years after World War I, many Americans believed that natural science provided mankind with the possibility of unlimited progress. To most Americans, however, a scientist was a tinkerer who discovered new products and devised new machines that made life easier for all; everywhere they looked Americans could see the beneficent results of the scientist's labors. Plastics and "miracle fibers," color television and jet airplanes, "wonder" drugs and vitamin therapy, great advances against tuberculosis, poliomyelitis, and cancer—these were only a few of the many developments that helped strengthen the prestige of scientists. The popular view of the role of science in American life was reinforced by newspapers that publicized applied rather than pure science, by industrial firms that spent millions annually on research programs, and by universities that spent increasingly more on scientific research than on traditional scholarship in arts and letters.

Although laymen revered the scientist for his accuracy and certainty, scientists themselves had become increasingly aware of the tentative nature of their findings and conclusions. Both in the logic of scientific method and in the predictability of results, scientists were confronted with many difficulties and imponderables as they searched for basic "laws" governing the behavior of matter. Most physicists, for example, were attracted by the implications of the so-called indeterminacy principle according to which investigation of the smallest and largest scale phenomena did not disclose complete regularity and law but only statistically probable recurrences. Many laymen interested in the implications of indeterminacy mistakenly took it to mean that all certainty had been banished in the study of nature, although, in fact, indeterminacy governed only special cases and, with new techniques of observation or new concepts of matter, might itself turn out to be inadequate. The discovery, for example, of more than thirty subatomic particles disturbed some scientists, for these made study of the basic constitution of matter intellectually unwieldy and aesthetically unattractive. There was increasing conjecture that a Newton was needed to undercut the basic suppositions that had led to postulating so many particles. A radically different conception of matter could simplify and unify seemingly disparate observations and claims. Whatever the future status of scientific knowledge, it was clear to the interested public that there were deep and lively disagreements among scientists and that they were increasingly at pains to stress that many of their current ideas were provisional and hypothetical.

In trying to understand what the scientists were after, however, the intelligent layman was increasingly at a disadvantage. Common sense and his tendency to conceive of the actions of matter pictorially were not helpful in understanding what scientists were thinking. Scientific language and concepts were increasingly abstract, and the layman's curiosity could only be satisfied by developing an intellectual discipline beyond the time, talent, and work-a-day sensibility of the merely intelligent bystander. Some critics accused scientists of deliberately cultivating an unwarranted mystique and distasteful jargon and obscurantism, but the scientists answered that research and fact, not their desire to seem a secret elite, had made their work so highly specialized. Furthermore, as the physical scientists pointed out, the same tendency to close off knowledge from the common understanding could be found in other disciplines. As research pushed on, the study of the mind and emotions, of heredity, of economic behavior—to mention only a few

Albert Einstein: His Theories Changed History

subjects—became so complex, abstract, and specialized that the older tradition of a humanely educated lay intelligence was at a disadvantage if relied on to penetrate what seemed irritatingly and unnecessarily remote studies. Occasionally, a book like C. P. Snow's *The Two Cultures* would grant the scientists their claims but warn that the growing separation of the newer scientific and the older humanistic culture had great dangers, implying as it did that the scientific knowledge the moralist and politician needed to deal effectively with the problems of mankind was, by its very nature, almost beyond comprehension, let alone mastery. The two groups in the community who had the greatest power over man's fate were no longer speaking the same language and were too often at loggerheads.

In the two generations after World War I, American scientists made increasing contributions to basic research and theoretical knowledge. In recognition of their achievements, Nobel prizes in physics, chemistry, biology, and medicine went to many Americans. But it was none the less true that most of the fundamental conceptual knowledge used by American researchers was European in origin. The American contribution to the development of atomic energy, for example, was in many respects built on theories supplied by Europeans. Refugees from Hitler's persecutions had been especially helpful to their new American colleagues after the 1930's, and it was the greatest of these refugee scientists, Albert Einstein, who had carried the first news to President Roosevelt that started work on the atomic bomb. Students of American culture for more than a century had been pointing to the nation's penchant for practical and immediately available ideas rather than theoretical knowledge. A noteworthy effect of the nuclear and space age was to make clear that both for its own sake and for its eventual usefulness theoretical research would no longer be neglected in favor of developing better bombs or snag-proof nylon stockings. Yet, despite the signs of growing care for the state of theoretical studies, university, government, and research-foundation funds still went overwhelmingly to "projects" that promised quick and tangible results.

As it became clear that science had brought the human race the power to destroy itself as well as to further its liberation, many Americans became convinced that they had overinvested in faith in science. The possibility of the total destruction of civilization and the awareness that totalitarians as well as liberals could use science helped widen the appeal of existential and religious philosophies of life that had previously interested only a few isolated intellectuals. By the 1950's, many magazine and newspaper writers were trying to assess what seemed like a revival of religion in America. Universities and colleges reported resurgent interest in courses in religion. Suddenly orthodox theologians and moralists who attacked liberal culture for its allegedly naïve optimism and who criticized rationalists and secularists for shallow views of human nature had growing prestige among intellectuals as well as educated laymen.

The "religious revival," however, had conflicting tendencies. Although it involved dramatic increases in church and synagogue membership, in the building of houses of worship, and in the popularity of certain churchmen and religious writers, these provided no evidence of any widespread return to Calvinism or other orthodoxies. There was, it was true, a simultaneous invigoration of theology at the seminaries and in university departments of religion; but, as one of the foremost American theologians, Reinhold Niebuhr, noted, Americans were generally unaffected by or not eager to adopt neo-orthodoxy's challenge to the comfortable and progressive sermons preached in the many new churches and temples. For all its vitality, the religious revival was still based on the social gospel rather than Niebuhr's or Paul Tillich's criticisms of liberal religion and of religion as humane ethics. The predominant American rhetoric was that Catholics, Protestants, and Jews were really worshipping the same God and that His service was essentially the practice of brotherhood and the advance of democracy. What Americans, furthermore, seemed to want from religion was much less painful truths of God than a quick peace of mind and peace of soul.

Study of recent church history also tends to throw doubt on the extent to which greater church membership and expanded church programs constituted a religious revival. Between 1919 and 1939, church membership had at best kept pace with population growth. The depression, however, severely impaired church finances and cut down on the rate of growth in membership. The marked pick-up in church strength and influence came during the war years. Fifty-five million church goers in 1930 had grown to more than 70,000,000 by the early 1940's.

Despite the growth in church membership, many Protestants were no longer concerned with the strict observance of the Sabbath; Sunday movies, despite the opposition of some church groups, had become commonplace; and ministers repeatedly complained from their pulpits that the automobile and the golf course provided Sunday diversions more attractive to many parishioners than church. Religious controversies occurred less frequently and with less vehemence than in former years. Agnosticism was common enough to go largely unnoticed. Even those Americans who attended church regularly seemed to lack much of the enthusiasm and intensity that had once been considered essential to religious experience.

It was in order to check the declining influence of the churches that many religious leaders, especially of the older "institutional churches," made special efforts to appeal to the more mundane tastes of church members and thus helped spark what was called the revival of religion. Practically all urban—as well as many rural—churches undertook ambitious social and recreational programs that covered almost every social activity. Some churches provided their members with psychiatric assistance; others conducted classes in subjects that ranged from dancing to manual training; and still others conducted extensive athletic programs. C. Luther Fry, writing in *Recent Social Trends* in 1933, caught the spirit of religious changes that had been underway for nearly fifty years, and that continued to dominate American religious life in the 1950's.

> Church social life has been greatly elaborated. . . . Cultural activities incidental to educational aims have taken such new forms as dramatics and forums for discussions of public questions. . . . The vogue of athletics has brought about changes

in church plant and staff. Increasingly the modern church includes a gymnasium, baths, and game room, while athletic
directors and recreational specialists have appeared with increasing frequency among the church's paid workers.*

Although theology became less important to Americans than it
once had been, there is ample evidence that there was still widespread
interest in religious matters. The Bible continued to be the nation's best
seller. Novels with religious themes, religious magazines, popular sermons on the lives of religious figures, religious book-club selections and
guidebooks to religious understanding sold millions of copies. New
sects and cults, and evangelists like Oral Roberts and Billy Graham kept
up lively crusades to save souls. Jehovah's Witnesses warned against
the impending Last Judgment. George Baker, who was called Father
Divine, adopted as his slogan "Peace, it's wonderful!" and won many
adherents in New York's Harlem and in the Negro sections of other
cities. Radio and T.V. religious hours had listeners and viewers from
coast to coast. Billy Graham's nation-wide meetings for "decisions for
Christ" led to triumphal foreign tours for the popular young minister
who used what many complained were slick Madison Avenue methods.

The phenomenon of Billy Graham did remind the nation that the
comforts and gadgets of its benign culture were not satisfying completely the spiritual hunger of many citizens. A diminished, defensive,
but still powerful, fundamentalism pervaded many rural areas, and, as
the Graham crusades showed, still had considerable appeal in major
cities. Latter-day American fundamentalists, however, supported few
social or political ideas that had national prestige or respectability.
Once fundamentalists had comprised the shock troops of the national
Prohibition movement and had formed the last remaining stronghold of
opposition to Darwinism. In the South, a resurgent fundamentalism
in the 1920's had resulted in the trial of John T. Scopes, a young school
teacher in Dayton, Tennessee, for violating the state law against teaching evolution. Thirty years later, with revivalists like Billy Graham,
fundamentalists had taken to using techniques developed by the very
modern urban and scientific world that they had once so pathetically
attacked.

The same type of debate about the "revival of religion" in America took place in the 1950's on the subject of American education. Many
of those connected with the schools pridefully pointed to the expan-

* *Recent Social Trends in the United States; Report of the President's Research Committee on Social Trends* (New York: McGraw-Hill Book Company,
1933), Vol. II, p. 1058.

sion in their number and variety, the diversity and extensiveness of their curricula, and the growing size of their budgets, of teachers' salaries, and of pupil enrollments. Between 1920 and 1960, almost every American community had added to its school plant and proclaimed reverence for schools and respect for the teacher's calling. Critics, however, made the same charge about the bustle and busyness in education as others made about the expansion of the churches: quantity was being confused with quality. Despite more money, more time, and more praise for the schools, there were indications that the nation was not as well educated as it ought to be.

Even before the Soviet Union's space missiles stimulated a revaluation of what the extensive new educational machinery was, in fact, producing, there were many telling complaints about what were called the nation's "educational wastelands." When all allowances were made for mere cranks and special interests, the indictment of American education came down to the charge that the schools were geared to produce intellectually average docile citizens trained for a job, rather than men and women capable of informed individual judgment and of resistance to the comforts of an uncritical conformism. Between 1920 and the 1950's, American education acquired a very large group of professional administrators, and it was primarily this group that defended the American school system. Statistics, charts, and graphs were produced to show that the nation was in fact better educated than ever before. The "educationists" insisted that with most American children headed for a practical rather than intellectual life, the inclusion of such subjects as home economics, driver training, and "marriage and family living" in the curriculum was necessary and realistic.

The critics were on firmest ground when they claimed that more room had to be found in the precollege years for the intellectually gifted child who needed, wanted, and deserved more attention than he was getting in the admittedly democratic attempt to establish school standards tailored to the practical needs of most future citizens. "Progressive education," was accused of putting a premium on "group living" and peripheral subjects rather than on so-called basic disciplines and intellectual independence. One of the most hotly debated books of the 1950's, Rudolph Flesch's *Why Johnny Can't Read*, maintained that the widely used technique of teaching children to recognize whole words at a glance rather than to analyze the individual letters and sounds of the parts of words was leading the nation to slovenliness and semi-literacy. Progressive education, its most competent students contended, was intended to release the child's powers of judgment and stimulate his awareness by abandoning dull, rote, formalistic knowledge and mere training. The founders of progressive education in the early twentieth century wanted the schools to appeal to the child's imagination and to emphasize what was immediate and concrete instead of what was abstract and remote from his experience. Its critics in the 1950's, however, argued that progressive education had developed anti-intellectual tendencies, that it had decreased demands on the child, and that it had increasingly adopted an ideal of the good citizen as one who worked with his neighbors rather than pursued his own allegedly selfish interests. According to these critics, a pseudo-democratic ideal had thus been used in some communities to cut out special classes for gifted children or to justify promoting all children to the next grade, regardless of performance, for fear of the psychological harm that being "left back" would bring to the child.

The great debate about education was so clamorous that it was difficult to separate fact from mere allegation and to arrive at any reliable standards of evaluation and judgment. When, for example, college and university teachers complained that their students did not know how to read and write well, and blamed the high schools, principals and guidance counselors either pointed to the higher scores than ever before obtained on college entrance tests or blamed the elementary schools. College teachers answered that entrance examinations were easier than they had been or that they were tailored to fit the kind of minds that the high schools were producing. The debate went on, but as university and high school groups began to cooperate in devising new curricula for talented students and in setting up special high-school courses to prepare pupils for "advanced placement" when they entered college, a new pattern of American education began to emerge. Very little of what had been called into question by the critics of the schools would probably be dropped, but greater opportunity for the gifted child might be provided. The test of the worth of the new programs lay, however, in the future.

By 1960, the nation was on the verge of what was foreseen as a revolutionary increase in the number of students seeking admission to colleges. The "war babies" of World War II would then begin to reach college age and look beyond secondary school to higher education. The anticipated pressure of millions of new students aggravated existing problems of space, curriculum, and staffing for those schools, particularly the state universities, whose more liberal admission policies, wide variety of programs of study, or lower fees would tend to make them the first choice of the majority of students. Critics of American higher education were concerned that once again mere physical and budgetary expansion would be taken as a sign of health and vitality.

The steady growth in the size, wealth, and variety of American colleges and universities since the 1920's had already weakened the university's traditional role as what one educator called "the house of intellect." Many colleges and universities had added so many new subjects to their curricula that they resembled educational cafeterias where the customer could purchase whatever suited his fancy. The catalogues of some institutions listed classes in ceramics, fly-casting, hotel management, millinery, salesmanship, ice-cream manufacture, and a host of other "applied" subjects. Increasing attention was given to the arts, as new courses were offered in painting, sculpture, music, drama, and the dance. Colleges expanded their already extensive athletic programs and often bid for promising high-school athletes by offering what in effect were salaries while in school and guarantees of good jobs after graduation. Stadiums and field houses became important parts of the academic landscape. Football games between major college teams, more often than not manned by players with "athletic scholarships," attracted huge throngs of spectators and were accompanied by the same type of ballyhoo that attended any other large commercial undertaking in twentieth-century America.

The desire of alumni for winning teams was one continuous source of pressure to make the college or university compromise on its intellectual and scholarly standards. Threats to cut legislative appropriations or to withhold alumni funds for a new gymnasium or for faculty salary raises were sometimes successfully used to influence university policy-makers. On balance, American universities were probably more free from outside pressure than ever before; but the trustees and important alumni of the schools were largely drawn from America's upper income brackets, and many schools were dominated by men drawn from the ranks of business and the professional classes. Although these men generally respected education and were devoted to their tasks, they were frequently conservatives. Commenting on this situation, one prominent academic stated "Men are so used to confusing their own desires with fine principles that most men seeking to control the schools in order to protect their business probably have really convinced themselves that this is an act of pure public service." *

Although privately supported institutions were directly dependent on the successful businessman for most of their funds, business control of the collegiate purse strings seldom produced an easily discernible academic subservience. On the other hand, few college administrations,

* Howard K. Beale: *Are American Teachers Free?* (New York: Charles Scribner's Sons, 1936), pp. 545–546. Copyright 1936, and reprinted with the permission of Charles Scribner's Sons.

whatever the iconoclasm in their classrooms, pursued policies openly at variance with the ideals of their principal benefactors. Furthermore, college and university presidents, who were primarily concerned with raising endowment funds, frequently shared the economic and social views of their business-dominated boards of trustees. The indirect effect of business domination of higher education was partly revealed by the popularity of business schools in the large universities and the growing number of "practical," or "service," courses offered by various institutions. Business occupied a particularly strong position in many college science departments. Industrial firms increasingly contributed money to various educational institutions for scientific research. These business-financed projects were, however, usually confined to experiments that would produce commercially exploitable results, and the professor of physics or chemistry interested in pure science occasionally found himself without adequate research funds, while his more practical colleague was supplied with ample money by a large industrial corporation. In general, the growth of philanthropic foundations that supported even less commercial "projects" created serious problems for university administrators. Specialized research and frequent leaves of absence for "surveys" or "field trips" contributed as much as did increasing administrative duties to the lesser number of hours leading scholars gave to teaching in general and to basic courses in particular.

The Writers' Rediscovery of America

Despite the desolation most of America's leading writers sensed around them in the 1920's, the paradoxical effect of their alienation was to stimulate a notable group of novelists, poets, and essayists. In 1929, a leading critic, Joseph Wood Krutch, complained that "the modern temper" had given intellectuals nothing to believe in except perhaps their own talent. In fact, the death of many old gods at the hands of the Babbitts and of slashing sceptics like H. L. Mencken had left American writers potentially free from illusions and partisan affiliations than they had ever been.

Although the Great Depression increased the artists' sense of alienation from a capitalist-run mechanized American culture, it also gave the alienated and expatriate writers hope that something new could, after all, arise from the ash heaps. Edmund Wilson, the greatest of the critics to come out of the 1920's, raised the new possibilities in *An Appeal to Progressives* published early in 1931. Noting the quickening collapse of a world that Americans thought had banished depressions, he warned that the old liberalism of reformers like Herbert Croly was dead and that it had died because it had bet on capitalism. The crash had destroyed old faiths, but the Soviet Union had, at the same time, emerged from the back pages of the newspapers to rally other hopes for new social ideals that men and women could believe in. What was wanted, said Wilson, was an American reformism that would, in effect, take socialism away from the Communists.

Two years later a young American writer, John Dos Passos, completed a trilogy entitled *U.S.A.*, which was a summary indictment of American culture in what then seemed to be its capitalist death throes. In literary technique, it attempted to combine the widely used traditions of naturalism that dated back in America to the 1890's with that exploration of private states of consciousness and mental images that had formed so important an aspect of the symbolist movement in modern European and American letters.

Dos Passos' three novels *1919*, *The 42nd Parallel*, and *The Big Money* traced the careers of a host of modern American types through the first thirty years of the twentieth century. Short biographies of famous Americans—some idolatrous, others ironic and sardonic—and chapters labeled "Newsreel" tried to create a composite naturalistic exposé of the conflicting tendencies of an American society in which salesmen and chorus girls, millionaires and Wobblies lived only for frustration or failure. Other sections entitled "Camera Eye" explored the succession of thoughts and symbols that passed through the minds of the characters. Dos Passos' judgment was more devastating than Wilson's: America had gambled on capitalism, had lost everything, and would find nothing. The homeless boy in his final chapter is bumming rides on a highway and waiting ". . . with swimming head, needs knot the belly, idle hands numb, beside the speeding traffic. A hundred miles down the road."

In the 1930's, much of American literature was a response to appeals like Wilson's and to observations like Dos Passos'. Many writers sought to depict what capitalism in America had done to the lives of ordinary men and women. The more radical novelists were hopeful that they could help create a new socialist culture or planned society that would realize the wishes and dreams of the common man. However, there were notable exceptions to this. F. Scott Fitzgerald, in his later works, and Nathanael West had no "answers" or "programs." Their works, nevertheless, portrayed the continuing sense of futility or the hideous potentialities for violence and spiritual death that lingered on in American life in the 1930's despite the activism and optimism of Communists or New Dealers. Fitzgerald's two major novels in the 1930's were *Tender is the Night* (1934) and the posthumously published *The Last Tycoon* (1941). Although both novels took for granted the temptations and decadence of the American world of money and power, they were primarily concerned with individuals who seemed more destined by character than by economic circumstance to disaster and defeat. West's two principal works, *Miss Lonelyhearts* (1933) and *The Day of the Locust* (1939), were terrifying portraits of the private hell and public inferno in the lives of a newspaper columnist and a Hollywood designer trying to beat their way out of the modern urban horror to sanity and love.

By and large, however, writers like Fitzgerald and West did not set the tone of the literature of the 1930's. So-called proletarian novelists with explicit Communist biases urged their colleagues to abandon "bourgeois defeatism" or "right-wing sentimentality." Art was a weapon to arouse revolutionary consciousness. In comparison with men like West and Fitzgerald, the radical novelists were grossly deficient craftsmen, but their failings were due more to weakness of talent than to their Marxist ideology. Their stories and poems about grubby, commonplace, beaten, "little people," powerless to do anything except to endure the blows of capitalist culture and await deliverance by the Communist party, had a large vogue. Most of these stories, however, were so far from suggesting any complexity of character or any capacity of men to be more than social types that as years passed they became mere data for the student of American radical taste and lost any claim to be anything more than material for a chapter on the culture they tried to depict.

Evidence, however, of the prestige of the ideal of art as a weapon in the class war is abundant. William Faulkner was denounced for neglecting the farmers' problems. Edmund Wilson, on a notable occasion, felt called upon to take special note of the Marxist Michael Gold's denunciation of the works of Thornton Wilder for their remoteness from the class struggle. Although Wilson claimed that art had greater autonomy than Gold's vulgarized Marxist theory of literature granted it, he asked writers to take a better look at the influence of social class on art. Those writers who already shared the proletarian novelist's point of view strengthened the tendency of American writers since the 1890's to depict reality in America as hard, sordid, and hidden behind a façade of middle class sentiment. What was wanted was fresh air and the real truth: that America had made men little more than animals, that they were victims rather than masters of fate and that their destiny was to be born to futility, to fight or fall into violence or corruption and to suffer and die.

Drawing on the naturalistic *genre* established much earlier by

Theodore Dreiser, a young Chicago Irish-American James T. Farrell published one of the most sensational novels of the thirties. His *Studs Lonigan* trilogy used as much "real life" and profanity and as many sordid facts as could pass the censors or what remained of the author's restraint. Despite Farrell's serious intention to depict the destructive effect of the slums of Chicago on his young hero, many of his readers gobbled up the completed and suggested four-letter words or prided themselves on having read so tough and true a novel.

What Farrell tried to reveal about the modern American city, other novelists tried to show about American rural life. Books like Erskine Caldwell's *God's little Acre* and *Tobacco Road* were ribald best-selling tales of the degradation and hardships of southern poor whites, and John Steinbeck's *Grapes of Wrath* was an immensely popular account of the inhumanity and violence in the lives of impoverished migratory workers moving steadily westward from the dust bowl of Oklahoma in search of jobs and decency.

Most ages of reform in American history have activated a national tendency to contrast the present with a golden age that was past and a new golden age that was still to be made. In the 1930's, this tendency was often given populistic and working-class twists. Although a few novelists, like Willa Cather and Ellen Glasgow, wrote sadly of remnants of the past in small towns and nostalgically of older days in places like Virginia or the Middle West, most others searched the American past to glorify the "little people" and to demonstrate their continuous victimization by "the system." Such works were often drearily sentimental and overlooked the harsher aspects of the American populist tradition—its hostility to intellect or its recurrent nativism. An older poet, Robert Frost, however, continued to show that regional themes and dislike of modern urban America could be used by a major talent to create an image of another America that was not sentimental— and Frost's art transcended the poet's own ideology.

Two lasting effects of preoccupation in the thirties with "the people" were the revival of American folk songs and dances and the placing, however questionably, of writers like Whitman and Emerson in a populistic democratic tradition. The growing interest in the past also made for the wide popularity of historical novels like Margaret Mitchell's *Gone With the Wind*, Marjorie K. Rawling's *The Yearling*, and Stark Young's *So Red the Rose*. Perhaps the most notable attempt to glorify the folk came in 1939 with the completion of Carl Sandburg's four volumes on Abraham Lincoln as President, *The War Years*.

The interest in America's past had particular importance for southern writers. Often taking their lead from the twelve "Agrarians" who published their angry protest against the modern South in *I'll Take My Stand* (1930), a generation of excellent southern scholars, novelists, and poets stimulated a far-reaching national interest in southern history and cultural themes that continued on into the 1950's. Leading figures among the older members of the group were Robert Penn Warren, Allen Tate, and Cleanth Brooks, and among the younger, Carson McCullers, C. Vann Woodward, and Tennessee Williams. Concurrently, there arose a significant group of Negro writers and intellectuals, including Richard Wright and John Hope Franklin and, more recently, Ralph Ellison and Rayford Logan.

One notable effect of the southern revival was to increase the hold on the nation's imagination of the "plantation legend" whose origin dated back to before the Civil War. Whether the new southern writer strengthened the fantasy that his region's civilized and aristocratic way of life had been destroyed after 1865 by industrial capitalism, science, and liberalism or whether he tried to free fellow southerners from this crippling illusion, he had found a subject that was immensely fruitful and one that in William Faulkner found it most famous and eloquent expositor.

By 1960, Faulkner had become so widely regarded in America and Europe as the nation's greatest living novelist that it was difficult to remind students of the very uneven quality of his work. Although he had started to publish in the 1920's, his best novels did not appear until the next decade. Of these, *The Sound and the Fury* (1929), *Light in August* (1932), and *Absalom! Absalom!* (1936) had extraordinary power but had to wait years for an appreciative audience. Faulkner's complex style and portrait of the violence and disruption of southern life and traditions probably put readers off less than his deep misgivings about the modern enlightened culture that so many liberals and reformers stood for in the 1930's. In 1940 Faulkner published *The Hamlet,* the first volume of a trilogy about the last century of southern history which used many of the themes of Faulkner's earlier novels and superb short stories. Together with *The Town* (1957) and *The Mansion* (1959), *The Hamlet* told of the careers of various individuals and families in a fictional Yoknapatawpha County in Mississippi, starting in the nineteenth century. These books are the fullest expression of Faulkner's view of the world, though they are not his best works.

Unlike more sentimental southerners, Faulkner did understand that before the Civil War slavery and an impious violation of land and forest had already set the stage for the saga of decay and social disruption that followed the war. In outline, his version of southern history after the Civil War had familiar elements: the enervation and debase-

The Chronicler of Yoknapatawpha County, William Faulkner

[BROWN BROTHERS]

ment of the region's best tradition and families and the rise and eventual triumph of a poor-white clan, the Snopses, who bring with them incredible violence, degradation, coarseness, and a ruthless corrupting mindless energy.

But by the end of the saga in the 1950's, even some of the Snopses have become tame and their horror less shocking. At no time, as critics have pointed out, do the possibilities of modern enlightenment and rationality take hold in Faulkner's South. It is, in fact, a region where "the Enlightenment" simply never occurs. The South dooms itself in the distant past and merely proceeds from one form of savagery and barbarism to another. Faulkner has on several notable occasions put himself on record as a believer in the eventual triumph of human dignity (and thus at variance with those critics who envision him writing a Christian epic of the fall and damnation of man). But the few saintly and just figures in his epic, the wise Negroes, Indians, and white aristocrats, draw their strength not from reason or science or any of the other conventional modern faiths and nostrums but from refusal to violate intuitively perceived harmonies of nature and the peace of a pastoral life. The South's and man's liberation could perhaps come by returning to a premodern traditionalism which will bring peace and respect between the races and an end to the rape and dishonor that mark southern and modern life in general.

About the same time that *The Hamlet* appeared, it was clear that some American writers were abandoning the barricades of reformism and their old banners proclaiming hostility to American culture. The slowly growing realization of the hideousness of Stalinism, to which many of them had long closed their eyes, and the acclaimed entry of America into a just war against Nazism made native grounds seem far more attractive than they did in the dark years after World War I and the Crash of 1929. One by one, the older radicals, progressives, and reformers started a trend toward a literature of exhortation and affirmation that by 1960 often seemed as one-sidely praiseful of America as their alienated writing had once been excessively condemnatory. F. Scott Fitzgerald, however, died in 1940; Thomas Wolfe, who between 1929 and 1938 had written four huge sprawling pseudo-Whitmanesque lyrical novels about coming to terms with himself and America, had also died. Sherwood Anderson, revered celebrant of the small American village and its isolated and crushed little people, died in 1941.

Among the still active writers, Van Wyck Brooks, who in 1916 had scorned America's intellectual history as a "universe of talent and thwarted personality evaporating in stale culture," had already been at work since the midthirties glorifying New England's literary past in *The Flowering of New England* and *New England Indian Summer*. In 1940, in *The Irresponsibles*, Archibald MacLeish, a one-time exponent of the "new poetry," castigated intellectuals for their withdrawal from the life about them and their failure to defend the "rule of moral law, the rule of spiritual authority, the rule of intellectual truth" against the Fascist "revolution of gangs." Theodore Dreiser in 1941 told his readers that *America Is Worth Saving.* John Dos Passos in the same year published *The Ground We Stand On*, a sustained eulogy of an American tradition, which he thought the "grandest and most nearly realized . . . pictures in all history." Equally significant was Ernest Hemingway's transformation from faith in personal friendships and the craftsman's mastery of a style, to faith in the political cause of democracy. *For Whom the Bell Tolls*, which was also published in 1940, revealed Hemingway's old interest in the man of action; but, unlike Hemingway's earlier heroes, Robert Jordan as a member of the Loyalist forces in Spain knew why he was fighting.

Throughout most of the generation after 1940, very few writers promised any real breakthrough beyond the traditions of naturalism and symbolism that had long dominated American writing. Ernest Hemingway in *The Old Man and the Sea* (1952) perfected his unique genre in a story about an old fisherman who makes his greatest catch only to lose the fish to sharks in a magnificent fight that in essence represents a victory. Another Hemingway work, however, *Across the River and into the Trees* (1950), despite scattered fine passages, fell into the sentimentality that the author had often been guilty of before. Sinclair Lewis's and Theodore Dreiser's last works were literary disasters. After an excellent start in the 1930's John O'Hara failed to carry through to anything beyond "early promise." Two novelists after 1940 did use the novel well for its classic purpose of analyzing the manners and morals of characters whose personal sense of the world was in conflict with what their culture and class demanded of them: John P. Marquand's special concern was the lives of latter-day, well-to-do New Englanders, and James Gould Cozzens published *Guard of Honor* (about the military calling in modern America) and the much-acclaimed, if badly written, *By Love Possessed*, a story of a day in the life of a leading lawyer in a contemporary American town who must make a decision that requires revaluation of his sense of himself and of his way of life.

The works of Marquand and Cozzens continued to provide something that was increasingly absent in the American novel despite its avowed naturalism—a sense of the society of the protagonists, of their habits and customs and the complexity and concreteness of their reasons for doing what they did. None of the naturalistic war novels produced in the 1940's, on the other hand, gave readers anything like the feeling of military and wartime life that Hemingway, Dos Passos, or E. E. Cummings had provided after World War I. Furthermore, books like Norman Mailer's *The Naked and the Dead* and James Jones' *From Here to Eternity*, the two most important of the World War II novels, were written with considerably less craftsmanship than earlier war stories. The subsequent works of the two young authors further revealed an incapacity to write well about artistically imagined rather than direct personal experiences.

At the same time that older American traditions of the novel seemed to be running into the ground, writers and critics became increasingly enthusiastic about earlier American and certain recent European novelists. Although the revival of interest in Hawthorne, Melville, and Henry James started in the 1920's or 1930's, it did not assume major proportions until after 1945. Admiration of these men, as well as of Dostoevsky, Proust, and Kafka, seemed principally to be for their analysis of men and women in extreme conditions of life. These writers' stress on the irony and ambiguity of life, and their sense of disaster suited well the mood of readers who had known the horrors of totalitarianism and the defeats and betrayals of liberalism in their time.

Much of the critical revaluation of the older Americans and the modern Europeans came from the nation's academies. Increasingly, between 1940 and 1960, American critics and writers found posts in University departments of literature. Indeed, as American novelists began losing power in their traditional genres, there was a great burst of activity in American literary criticism and poetry. By the 1950's, professors of literature had come to dominate American criticism, and they brought the art of criticism to such fine achievements that many European observers became active, if sometimes grudging, admirers of American letters. Among Americans themselves, one heard increasingly that the 1950's were an age of criticism and that the most brilliant work was being done by the critics of the novelists rather than the novelists themselves.

Two principal trends have dominated the recent preoccupation with literary criticism. Both owe a great debt to T. S. Eliot, who, although not initiating either movement, had exemplified in his essays during and after World War I the conflicting tendencies that developed among American critics after the 1930's. In 1917, Eliot published his essay *Tradition and the Individual Talent*, which foreshadowed the debate between those who insisted that the work of art was not autonomous and required an understanding of the artist's biography and cultural milieu and those of the so-called "new" criticism, who, however much in disagreement with each other, on the whole, concentrated on the "individual talent," that is, the poem rather than the poet. The most notable practitioners of the older, so-called humanistic, criticism that Eliot had inherited from its nineteenth-century originators were Edmund Wilson and Lionel Trilling. Cleanth Brooks of Yale University was a leading spokesman for the "new critics." His work *Understanding Poetry* (with Robert Penn Warren) went through an unprecedented eighty-five printings and caught the imagination of the younger generation of academic critics. Some sense of the furor the war among the critics had aroused became apparent to the lay public when the new critics were charged with being fundamentally hostile to liberalism and democracy by Robert Gorham Davis in a widely discussed article published in 1950. By 1957, however, there had appeared Northrop Frye's *Anatomy of Criticism*, which admirably summed up and seemed to settle many of the issues fought over for a generation, for Frye tried to demonstrate the proper scope and use of both the historical and analytic methods.

The fecundity of American criticism after 1940 was matched by equally impressive work by a large number of poets seeking to work in or break away from the modern idioms first made available by elder statesmen in poetry like T. S. Eliot and Wallace Stevens. By 1960, poets like Theodore Roethke, W. S. Merwin, and Robert Lowell had absorbed most of what was valuable in the exciting work of the previous generation and turned, as the younger critics had, to preoccupation with more formal work, moving away from both Whitmanesque hortatory cadences and Eliot-like rhythmic sermons.

The work of the newest poets, together with Frye's criticism and some recent novels, seemed to herald the long-awaited departure from the older styles in American letters. Newer novels anchored the fantastic and symbolic in work-a-day naturalistic fact while trying to create mythic anti-heroes or so-called outsiders radically alienated from society and often incapable of commitment to any traditional or rational energetic vision of life.

This new departure had been predicted by George Orwell in an earlier essay *Inside the Whale*, and by Henry Miller, who had laughed at Hemingway's hero Robert Jordan for his involvement in the Spanish Civil War. In many cases, the new heroes lacked the capacity for engagement of the traditional hero in Western literature. The new hero was, as one title suggested, *On the Road*. He did not wish to conquer society, but to escape it entirely or pass through it untouched. His culture seemed to have lost absolutely all claim on him. The picaresque sense of life that the new characters brought with them was, however, in one respect reminiscent of the emergence of the classic modern hero in the eighteenth century. The bums, aesthetes, and "beatniks" in today's American novels sense that an old or corrupt culture that is dying forces them to make their own new destiny. But the old heroes had the strength of natural geniuses and forced society to accept them. The new "anti-hero" often seeks to escape the need to use his will at all. Often he is pathetically deficient in will and real genius and is understandably attracted to cults like Zen Buddhism. What he seems to want is release from the risks and pains of choice that rebellious "young men from the provinces" two centuries earlier had accepted eagerly; deliverance from and transcendence of society has become an ideal.

Forms, Functions, and Formulae in the Arts

The conflict between inherited and experimental forms is a constant theme in the history of art and has continued throughout the last forty years. A venerable tradition of portraying the natural world as recognizable objects or as common-sense thoughts and images has been on the defensive against newer attempts to break up traditional realistic forms in order to express some intensely personal image of life or to get at essential ideal forms from which everything else seems derived. This conflict has been as apparent in American art, architecture, and music as in American fiction and poetry. As in the case of the writers, changes in style, taste, and theory have been deeply affected by foreign as well as native ideas and have provoked wild charges and counter-charges about responsibility and irresponsibility, or rationality and barbarism. By the 1950's, however, the old image of the avant-garde became increasingly inadequate to express the relation between the radical innovator and his audience. Increasing leisure, wealth, and a combination of genuine appreciation and the neo-philistine fear of seeming philistine provided a larger and friendlier audience for the novel and *outré* works.

In the 1920's, American artists could draw upon the earlier experiments of men like Louis Sullivan in architecture and on the painters and sculptors of the Armory Show of 1913. Travelers and expatriates also had a special opportunity to study directly the various achievements of the modern movements in European art that had started about 1890 and that by 1920 had already entered a second or third round of experiment. In the postwar decade in America, the arts often reflected the traditional gulf between experimental artists and the mass of Americans. Although many artists continued to produce work that was wholly acceptable to the conventional-minded, others adopted techniques and forms of expression that made their art largely incomprehensible to all but a handful of professionals.

There was no lack of traditional art in America in the 1920's. Portraits were painted in the flattering style that their subjects had always demanded and to which artists had often been forced to conform. Murals in public buildings exalted the American past; those on the walls of business establishments glorified the exploits of industry, commerce, and finance. Popular art remained almost exclusively descriptive. Illustrations in advertisements and the slick magazines and on calendars and posters depicted American faces and scenes in idealized and unimaginative camera-like fashion. In sculpture, military and patriotic studies provided major themes. World War I, like earlier American wars, produced its quota of military monuments, and within a few years after Versailles, every American community of any size had at least one statue of a determined-looking doughboy advancing into battle. The taste for the monumentally heroic as well as the heroic monument was satisfied by Daniel C. French's figure of the Great Emancipator in the Lincoln Memorial in Washington and Gutzon Borglum's enormous heads of Washington, Jefferson, Lincoln, and Theodore Roosevelt, hacked out of the stone of a mountainside in the Black Hills of South Dakota; these were merely the most famous examples of the continued popularity of the grandiose in American sculpture in the postwar years.

Many modern sculptors and painters, however, found these styles either vulgar or prosaic. Rejecting pictorial art, they employed novel techniques and new materials to gain striking effects. Much of their work was characterized by a degree of distortion that made their subjects all but unrecognizable to the layman. Whether surrealists, cubists, or abstractionists, the modernists were united in finding means that would best enable them to express highly individualized responses and emotions. To the modern artist, a work of art was not a method of common-sense communication but a form of self-revelation. As such, it would seem to most eyes only introspective. The modernists were accused of insanity, degeneracy, or fraud by contemporaries, but close study of their work would have shown the genuine artist's control of his purposes. Their pictures might seem sick or nonsensical, but unprejudiced viewers eventually saw the rational attempt to create a new way of conceiving of the world that underlay the initially shocking world of limpid watches, violent colors, and shattered or highly formalized and abstracted geometric forms. It was indicative of the way that new visions eventually became conventional and popular that by the 1950's clever American advertisements sometimes showed characters drawn in Picassoesque style, with two eyes on one side of a nose, just as in music the seeming violence and cacophony of a piece like Stravinsky's *Rite of Spring*, which had caused a riot at its premiere in Paris before World War I, was respectfully or even enthusiastically received by audiences in Cleveland, Ohio, and Houston, Texas.

From the standpoint of the social historian, one of the most notable features of the history of realistic art in the 1920's was the growing preoccupation of American painters and sculptors with native themes. Little-known figures from the American past were resurrected, and the Indian, Negro, and immigrant were either less romanticized or no longer stripped of their dignity. Such painters as Thomas Hart Benton, John S. Curry, and Grant Wood used their native Middle West and "old American" types for realistic canvases, demonstrating Benton's dictum that "no American art can come to those who do not live an American life, who do not have an American psychology, and who cannot find in America justification of their lives." This emphasis, running alongside the contradictory anti-realism of other artists, was reflected in the patronage of art as well as in its creation. Private collectors displayed an increasing interest in the work of American artists; folk art and so-called American primitives achieved considerable vogue; and in 1930, the Whitney Museum in New York became the first institution to purchase and show only native art.

It also, however, became increasingly fashionable for wealthy patrons to collect modern works rather than old masters. The Whitney Museum placed its greatest emphasis on contemporary art, and the Museum of Modern Art, founded in New York in 1929, consistently lived up to its name. As Oliver W. Larkin in *Art and Life in America* has written:

> At the Museum of Modern Art in 1936 one could see . . . the nervous patterns and insistent flat colors of Miro's *Person Throwing a Stone at a Bird*, the alarming empty spaces of Tanguy's *Mama, Papa is Wounded!* the paradoxical objects which Pierre Roy assembled in *Daylight Saving Time* . . . ; a woman by Max Ernst whose head became a fan and through whose perforated torso one saw a distant shoreline; Mason's *Battle of Fishes* with scribbled shapes of brush and pencil on canvas and sandpaper; the flaccid watches of Dali with bugs swarming over them in *The Persistence of Memory*.*

During the 1930's, the depression and the New Deal's art program both broadened and redirected the more realistic trends in American art. Under the impact of hard times and the reform spirit, many artists, who, like the writers in the boom years, had ignored the masses, now sought to depict their plight. The Federal Arts Project provided sculptors and painters with work and encouragement and gave them a degree of freedom that had not always been possible under a system of private patronage. Murals, etchings, water colors, and statues of the depression decade recorded America's failures as well as its achievements and the aspirations of the poor as well as the accomplishments of the well-to-do. The dust bowl and the picket line were considered suitable subjects for the serious artist, and the tribulations of the sharecropper, wage earner, and unemployed received much of the attention that had once been accorded the triumphs of industrialist, politician, and soldier. Judged however even by the highest standards of realism, these creations were often as deficient in talent and imagination as were their counterparts in the proletarian novel.

By the beginning of the 1940's, however, both conventional real-

* Oliver W. Larkin: *Art and Life in America* (New York: Rinehart & Company, Inc., 1949), p. 410.

ism and the older modernism began to be challenged by a young group of artists who on a notable occasion picketed the Museum of Modern Art for not recognizing their work. Coming at their tasks from various directions and drawing heavily again on European experimenters or refugees like Hans Hoffman, within a decade the "abstract expression- ists," as they were called, had created a wide variety of works which at their best were exciting combinations of colors and forms which had completely abjured recognizable subjects or themes. Leading figures in the new group, like Jackson Pollock and Mark Rothko, had also made history in another way, for when their paintings were exhibited in Europe, for the first time in history younger European painters looked to the pictures of American artists as a point of departure for their own works. By 1960, abstract-expressionist canvases were in the museums and in homes (either as originals or as reproductions) from coast to coast, and again picket lines formed outside the Museum of Modern Art in New York—but this time to protest its allegedly unfair choice of so many abstract expressionists works over those of more objective painters. Among some critics there was also the sentiment that the new style had carried modern subjectivism to its furthest pos- sible development, and, as in the novel and poem, one could anticipate a new generation that would consolidate what was valid in a half- century of experimental work with a renewed interest in an objectively depicted world.

Modern American architecture developed in ways closely similar to those followed by the painters and sculptors. Native experiments initiated at the end of the nineteenth century by men like Louis Sulli- van were carried forward and then drew on or came into conflict with European innovations studied abroad or brought to America by immi- grant and refugee architects. At first America's modern architects, who depended on a mass market for their livelihood, were furnished with little opportunity for experimentation, and in their efforts to redesign the American home they met with almost universal opposition. The average American's taste was conventional; furthermore, a house, un- like a print or a recording, was a major investment, and few prospec- tive home owners had either the courage or inclination to sink their savings in a house that defied tradition. Though the ability and prestige of Frank Lloyd Wright enabled him to obtain commissions, his work did not represent the main trends in modern American architecture. Still, from California to New York, Wright and his small group of de- vout disciples created a wide variety of extraordinary buildings that continually provoked stormy debate.

Wright's "organic architecture" was based on the presumption that a building, including all its furnishings, should be conceived primarily with attention to its natural setting or as a problem of the relation between space and solids. His famous home and school, Taliesin West, in Arizona was designed to take advantage of the colors, flatness, and cycle of seasons of desert country. The "Falling Water" house incorporated into the building itself the waterfall and rock formation on the property. The Guggenheim Museum, in New York City, on the other hand, ignored both the natural and architectural setting in order to show the possibilities of pure architectural forms and of moulding a building as though it were a sculptured spiral.

More influential than Wright's was the American work of European émigrés Ludwig Mies van der Rohe, Marcel Breuer, and Walter Gropius. These men had come from the German Bauhaus architects of the 1920's and the Dutch painters and architects who were called the De Stijl group. They, more than Wright, seemed attentive to Louis Sullivan's and Le Corbusier's dictum that form must follow function. They constructed simple, austere buildings with geometric, mostly cubic, forms emphasizing flat undecorated surfaces. Because of their simplicity, these designs could be cheaply and inexpensively realized, and in Europe they were used in low-cost housing developments. The Bauhaus school building itself, in Dessau, Germany, also introduced the extensive use of outer glass surfaces without visible heavy supporting piers.

In America, the Bauhaus men became affiliated with several universities, and Chicago and Cambridge, Massachusetts, became important centers for their buildings. Their American work, however, was primarily industrial and institutional. They progressed so far beyond their original German creations that they evolved what has become a distinctive American architecture with influences throughout the world. The many recent buildings of the Skidmore, Owings and Merrill firm represent the most familiar and commercially successful use of their ideas. By 1960, New York and other cities had many skyscrapers that could be traced to the influence of Bauhaus ideas. Between the extremes of Wright's romantic organic architecture and the rationalism of Bauhaus-derived styles, there were also other types of architects, chief among them perhaps the Saarinens (father and son) and the distinctive group of San Francisco architects who have based their "Bay Area Style" on an architectural style indigenous to their part of the country.

In the main, however, despite the growing influence of these new ideas, American residential and business architecture has stayed close to older traditions. Home architects have been largely supplanted by building contractors who erect from a single set of plans houses indis-

Frank Lloyd Wright's Taliesin East, Madison, Wisconsin

tinguishable from one another in all but a few external features. Arranged row on row in real-estate developments, builders' houses are generally occuped by families of moderate income. Tudor, Colonial, Spanish, and French, and recently, the American ranch and split-level house styles have all had their vogue. They have been used without any attention to the terrain, seasons, traditions, or cultural life of the area in which they were built. Aside from their mechanical gadgets, the homes of the rich, like those of the poor, provided few indications that they had been built to fulfill the architectural possibilities of twentieth-century American life.

Businessmen were quicker to perceive the advantages of economic use of space, simplification of design, and cheaply maintained building materials. Rationally planned factories and office buildings with maximum light and air for workers were good business as well as good architecture. It was Frank Lloyd Wright who showed the way to his less imaginative colleagues. His pioneering designs for the Johnson Wax Company and the Larkin buildings demonstrated that modern architecture in the hands of a dedicated genius could be both profitable and aesthetically pleasing. On the other hand, the large number of government buildings erected in Washington and elsewhere since the 1920's were almost entirely traditional. Lewis Mumford thought they comprised

> a monument of irregional and irrational planning. Closed courts
> that trap the summer sun without taking advantage of summer

*The Seagram Building in New York City, designed by
Mies van der Rohe*

[© EZRA STOLLER]

breezes, window area sacrificed to classic massiveness, grotesque waste of money on tedious stone columns that further diminish light and air. Nowhere a clear indication of the purpose of the building, or the location of departments. This unified building project might have set a masterly precedent for rational building in every city: unfortunately, it was organized esthetically for an obsolete baroque picture, characteristic of a despotic order.*

Although the public-housing projects instituted by the New Deal represented a significant departure in urban housing, the same government's conservatism, justified as a need to hold down costs, left little room for the introduction of architectural innovation. Some impetus was given to community planning with the government's establishment of Greenbelt towns, but this type of planning never got beyond the experimental stage. Despite the models provided by Radburn, New Jersey, and the numerous planned communities in Europe, town planning remained an art that serious modern architects enjoyed discussing but were unable to practice.

Despite recent efforts to vary color and arrangement of space in the new "projects," billions of dollars had already been spent on masses of red-brick urban hives. The newer designs, if anything, increased the density of population in the center of the cities, where it was least desirable. Despite notable achievements by leading figures, by 1960 American architecture came closest to demonstrating the truth of the claims of the critics of mass culture about the tendencies to a mechanized drab uniformity in American society.

From the Jazz Age to a Lyric Theatre

After World War I, more Americans than ever before became interested in concert and operatic music, but at first it was Europe's classics rather than contemporary American pieces that attracted the largest audiences. Although the radio and the Federal Arts Project gave millions of Americans their first opportunity to listen to serious music, the works they heard were more often than not foreign rather than native compositions. Following World War II, President Truman urged Americans to patronize native composers, and in January, 1947, Douglas Moore wrote in *The Saturday Review of Literature*:

> American music is played and sung of course but more often than not as a gesture thought to involve sacrifice on the part of the artist, the manager, and the audience. . . . Even in New York, where there is a small public for new music and programs are somewhat more venturesome, a survey of . . . concerts given . . . at Carnegie, Town Hall, and New York Times Hall shows that, of seventy-three programs presented,

* Lewis Mumford: *The Culture of Cities* (New York: Harcourt, Brace and Company, Inc., 1938), p. 357.

fifty contained not a single American item. Of 739 compositions, forty-five (less than seven percent) were by American
composers of this age or any other.

Perhaps the most significant development in American music in
the last twenty years has been the emergence of a group of serious composers whose work was experimental. Roy Harris, Aaron Copland, and
Virgil Thomson, among the older men, and Samuel Barber, Gian
Carlo Menotti, and Leonard Bernstein, among the younger, sought a
new "musical language" that would "speak to the men and women of
the artist's own time with a directness and immediacy of communica-
tive power that no previous art expression [could] give." The modernists frequently dealt with American themes, but to traditionalists, who
had long associated "good music" with such names as Bach, Mozart,
Beethoven, and Chopin, modern composers seemed capable of producing only what Copland has called "cacophonous harmonies, . . . tune-
less melodies, . . . head-splitting sonorities . . . , confusing rhythms
and cerebral forms."

In the 1940's, American composers began to come into their own.
Most orchestras included American works in their season's offerings. In
1958, the New York City Center Opera company presented a successful season of American operas, some of which were then sent on an
enthusiastically greeted national tour. Younger conductors and instrumentalists born and trained in America under the sympathetic tutelage
of émigré musicians like Serge Koussevitzky, Paul Hindemith, and
Leopold Stokowski were warmly received by European critics and
audiences. In 1958, Van Cliburn, a youthful, Texas-born pianist trained
at the Juilliard School in New York won first prize at the international
piano competition at Moscow and was given an enthusiastic reception
on his return to the United States. His example together with the unprecedented sales of microgroove and hi-fidelity recordings of European as well as American compositions had by 1960 radically altered
the status of serious music across the nation.

In contrast to serious American music, jazz was an indigenous
product. Although few experts have been able to agree on a definition
of jazz, H. O. Osgood seems to have reached the only satisfactory conclusion when he wrote that it was the "spirit of the music, not the
mechanics of its fame . . . that determines whether or not it is jazz."
Flowering in the early years of the twentieth century among Negro
musicians extemporizing in honky-tonks in and around New Orleans,
jazz moved on to Chicago and then to the rest of the nation. By the
1920's, it had become both big business and a familiar part of the coun-

try's culture. Jazz was a generic term and might be "sweet," "hot," "swing," "blues," or "progressive" jazz. Whatever its name, it was immensely popular and made millionaires and national idols of singers, instrumentalists, and orchestra leaders.

In the 1920's, growing out of the popular musical theatre and paralleling the birth of serious American drama, the musical comedy also began to attract millions of fans. Gradually elements of the older operettas of men like Victor Herbert and of the revue, "scandals," and "follies" were absorbed into the Broadway and Hollywood "musical." The thinnest and most bizarre plots were used as the basis for a string of songs that the nation loved. George Gershwin, Irving Berlin, Jerome Kern, and Cole Porter were only four of a dozen or so popular composers who never had any problem of communicating with their audiences. In 1943 one of the greatest American hits of all time, *Oklahoma!* introduced a new possibility to American composers. Composers hoped for an American lyric theatre that would create a form of music that would have popular as well as highbrow appeal. Although there remained by 1960 an obvious split between sentimental but successful musical plays of men like Rodgers and Hammerstein and the operas of composers like Douglas Moore and Samuel Barber, there was a good chance that these two genres might be combined in the near future by the newer generation of composers. Leonard Bernstein, for example, was simultaneously conductor of the New York Philharmonic and the composer of *West Side Story,* an exciting Broadway musical rendition of a Romeo and Juliet theme that used the Puerto Rican colony in New York for its background. Overseas, the new American musical comedies from *Oklahoma!* to *My Fair Lady,* like jazz and American orchestral and chamber works, gained ever greater acclaim.

By 1960, American music, like the nation's criticism, poetry, architecture, and painting, had shown and expanded the truth of Henry James' prediction generations earlier that in a half-century after his time Europeans could not afford to refuse to take American letters seriously.

FOR SUPPLEMENTARY READING

On some implications of the new prosperity read J. K. Galbraith, *The Affluent Society* (1958). Two contrasting views of contemporary American culture can be found in B. Rosenberg and D. M. White, *Mass*

Culture (1958), and R. Chase, *The Democratic Vista* (1958). R. Lynes, *The Tastemakers* (1954), catalogues American styles. On the movies the best study is N. Leites and M. Wolfenstein, *Movies* (1950). On the big city and smaller city use *The Exploding Metropolis* (1958), by the editors of *Fortune*, and W. L. Warner and associates, *Democracy in Jonesville* (1949). On the church and religion start with H. W. Schneider, *Religion in Twentieth Century America* (1952), and W. Herberg, *Protestant, Catholic, Jew* (1955). A brilliant exposition of the suppositions of the modern physical scientist is J. R. Oppenheimer, *Science and the Common Understanding* (1954). Two books are especially recommended on the great debate about education: J. Barzun, *The House of Intellect* (1959), on the universities, and P. Woodring, *A Fourth of a Nation* (1957), on the public schools. Contrasting views of the effect of corporate life on American character are W. H. Whyte, Jr., *The Organization Man* (1956) (Pb), and C. W. Mills, *White Collar* (1951). On writers of the 1930's and after read M. Cowley, *Exile's Return* (1951); J. W. Beach, *American Fiction, 1920–1940* (1941); W. B. Rideout, *The Radical Novel in the United States, 1900–1954* (1956); R. Chase, *The American Novel and Its Tradition* (Pb, 1957); and E. Wilson, *The American Earthquake* (1958) and *Classics and Commercials* (1950).

Epilogue

THE FLOWERING of the American arts and a gross national product of half a trillion dollars a year were the two most impressive aspects of American life on the centenary of the Civil War. What had threatened to be the nation's most severe economic recession since 1937 was successfully avoided in 1958, and the nation looked forward again to the four-day, thirty-hour week that had been sighted on the horizon.

An affable and humane President Eisenhower had an understandable appeal for a comfortable public that was generally confident about the sufficiency of his good intentions and faith in calm discussion. Still, sweeping Democratic victories in the "off-year" elections of 1958 indicated widespread national discontents with public policies that the advertising images of a happy and harmonious America ignored. Indeed, as Eisenhower neared the end of his eight years in the White House, the nation faced problems of exacerbated race relations, of chronically depressed areas, of the thinness of social security, of corruption and autocracy in leading trade-unions, and of the inadequacy of the nation's schools and of its culture for the young. These were all reminders of how far the world's wealthiest nation had yet to go to make good on its promise of liberty and justice for all citizens.

Writing in the *New Leader* at the end of the 1950's one of America's foremost students of Soviet affairs, George Kennan, stated:

> If you ask me . . . whether a country in the state this country is in today: with no highly developed sense of national purpose, with the overwhelming accent of life on personal comfort and amusement, with a dearth of public services

and a surfeit of privately sold gadgetry, with a chaotic transportation system, with its great urban areas being gradually
disintegrated by the headlong switch to motor transportation,
with an educational system where quality has been extensively
sacrificed to quantity, and with insufficient social discipline
even to keep its major industries functioning without grievous
interruptions—if you ask me whether such a country has, over
the long run, good chances of competing with a purposeful,
serious and disciplined society such as that of the Soviet Union,
I must say that the answer is "no." In one of his recent columns
Walter Lippmann asked us to stop worrying whether Khrushchev will seduce us, "to stop huddling together for fear of his
witchery, and to become again the confident and purposeful
people, which, except when we have doped ourselves, we really
are."

Kennan's observations were as close as any national figure had come
to grasping the ironic position of the United States in world affairs.
The very comforts and lack of militancy we seemed to esteem were
looked upon by poorer peoples elsewhere as disqualifying us for moral
and political leadership. Regardless of what American capitalism and
liberalism were—and intellectuals of the 1950's debated them endlessly—
in many areas of the world they were declared passé, spiritually bankrupt, or simply inapplicable.

In the developing global struggle between the northern and southern nations of the world—between the wealthy, industrialized societies
of western Europe, North America, and the Soviet Union and the nations of Latin America, Africa, and southern Asia—new leaders seemed
ever more intent on winning for their people in one generation all the
possibilities of life that had taken so long and cost so much for the tech-
nologically-advanced nations to achieve. The continued conflict in the
United States over the race question pointed to the ominous racial aspects of this struggle between the northern and southern parts of the
world. The old imperialism was dead, but it had left behind an ugly
heritage of suspicion and hatred among the southern peoples, many of
them colored, for their former white governors and owners.

In the Cold War itself, despite fine or harsh words "at the summit" and during diplomatic follow-ups, no significant break came on
major issues such as a divided Germany or on Soviet threats to West
Berlin. On an agreement to ban nuclear testing, as men and women
waited fearfully and impatiently, progress was achingly slow. The
West demanded piecemeal steps and thorough inspection, and the Rus-

sians made sweeping disarmament proposals to a world longing for peace, while showing during actual negotiations that they regarded controls over inspection with deep suspicion. The Soviets, of course, continued to advertise themselves as serious partisans of peace and disarmament, while claiming that American "warmongers" and "imperialists" were still too powerful in Western circles. Since Russia overwhelmingly outnumbered the West in conventional land forces and armaments, the United States believed that it would throw away its greatest defense if, without guarantees, it abandoned nuclear testing or undertook nuclear disarmament without sizable reductions in conventional Soviet strength. Evidence, however, indicated that the West and the Soviet Union already had enough nuclear knowledge and all the bombs that might be necessary for the few hours of a World War III that scattered remainders of mankind might remember.

Yet, unthinkable as nuclear war seemed, while Khrushchev spoke of "peaceful coexistence," with an occasional Russian proverb to warn the West not to start anything, the Chinese Communists openly refused to abandon the possibility of a nuclear war to destroy capitalist imperialism. Such a war, they believed, would usher in the new era for mankind implicit in Marxist theory and Communist ideology.

However softer Khrushchev's talk, around the edges of the Western world and in allied areas the Communists continued widespread infiltration and subversion. Their propaganda depicted the building of a Soviet-financed steel mill in India as friendly and brotherly aid but denounced substantial American technical and financial help to India and other nations as a new disguise of Western imperialism. In countries like Cuba, Indonesia, the United Arab Republic (Egypt and Syria) and many others, Soviet agents and missions were busily at work trying to turn nationalist revolutions to their advantage, hoping ultimately, to bring these new countries under Soviet hegemony. Occasionally, therefore, the United States and its major allies had to risk reviving memories of imperialism and were forced to intervene in nations like Guatemala, Lebanon, and Jordan to forestall the victories of native Communists and their friends.

Within the Western community itself, minor quarrels among the allies over bomber and missile bases, the control of national contributions to NATO forces, and, increasingly, over trade encouraged the Soviet Union to try to split the West. Premier Khrushchev and President Eisenhower went on extensive visits all over the world seeking new friends and refreshing older ties. These visits, supplemented by trips by Adenauer of a resurgent West Germany, by De Gaulle of a reformed and more stable Fifth French Republic, and by Macmillan of

England, reached a climax in the visit in 1959 of Khrushchev to the United States. The contemplated return visit by Eisenhower to the U.S.S.R. was canceled, however, at the abortive but explosive Summit Meeting at Paris in May, 1960.

In speaking of his continued hopes for peace, despite the collapse of the Paris Conference, the President told the West that it would have to "tighten its belt." Given realistic and determined leadership, the United States had great resources of wealth and intelligence to do what was needed to contain Soviet imperialism. Only a generation earlier, several American observers, overimpressed by Hitler's militancy, had been ready to declare democracy bankrupt. Yet Hitler had been beaten by the "soft" nations he had derided. In 1960, the United States was immeasurably stronger than it was when it defeated Hitler. Left to themselves, uninformed about the perils they faced, the American people would almost inevitably prefer private pleasures and a "fun culture" to sacrifice and seriousness of purpose. As in the dark days of 1941, the Civil War, and the Revolution, what was thus needed was a leadership that would counter the usual drift to complacency in a prosperous democracy with a clear image of the national purpose and with policies that evoked the best energies and talents of the nation.

Appendix

✵

Bibliography

✵

Index

APPENDIX

APPENDIX

I

The Constitution of
The United States of America*

WE THE PEOPLE of the United States, in Order to form a more perfect Union, establish Justice, insure domestic Tranquility, provide for the common defence, promote the general Welfare, and secure the Blessings of Liberty to ourselves and our Posterity, do ordain and establish this CONSTITUTION for the United States of America.

Article 1.

SECTION 1. All legislative Powers herein granted shall be vested in a Congress of the United States, which shall consist of a Senate and House of Representatives.

SECTION 2. The House of Representatives shall be composed of Members chosen every second Year by the People of the several States, and the Electors in each State shall have the Qualifications requisite for Electors of the most numerous Branch of the State Legislature.

No Person shall be a Representative who shall not have attained to the Age of twenty-five Years, and been seven Years a Citizen of the United States, and who shall not, when elected, be an Inhabitant of that State in which he shall be chosen.

[Representatives and direct Taxes † shall be apportioned among the several States which may be included within this Union, according to their respective Numbers, which shall be determined by adding to the whole Number of free Persons, including those bound to Service for a Term of Years, and excluding Indians not taxed, three fifths of all

* This version of the Constitution is that published by the Office of Education, United States Department of the Interior, 1935, and follows the original document in spelling and capitalization.
† Modified as to income taxes by the 16th Amendment.

other Persons.] * The actual Enumeration shall be made within three Years after the first Meeting of the Congress of the United States, and within every subsequent Term of ten Years, in such Manner as they shall by Law direct. The Number of Representatives shall not exceed one for every thirty Thousand, but each State shall have at Least one Representative; and until such enumeration shall be made, the State of New Hampshire shall be entitled to chuse three, Massachusetts eight, Rhode-Island and Providence Plantations one, Connecticut five, New-York six, New Jersey four, Pennsylvania eight, Delaware one, Maryland six, Virginia ten, North Carolina five, South Carolina five, and Georgia three.

When vacancies happen in the Representation from any State, the Executive Authority thereof shall issue Writs of Election to fill such Vacancies.

The House of Representatives shall chuse their Speaker and other Officers; and shall have the sole Power of Impeachment.

SECTION 3. [The Senate of the United States shall be composed of two Senators from each State, chosen by the Legislature thereof, for six Years; and each Senator shall have one Vote.] †

Immediately after they shall be assembled in Consequence of the first Election, they shall be divided as equally as may be into three Classes. The Seats of the Senators of the first Class shall be vacated at the Expiration of the second Year, of the second Class at the Expiration of the fourth Year, and of the third Class at the Expiration of the sixth Year, so that one-third may be chosen every second Year; [and if Vacancies happen by Resignation, or otherwise, during the Recess of the Legislature of any State, the Executive thereof may make temporary Appointments until the next Meeting of the Legislature, which shall then fill such Vacancies.] ‡

No Person shall be a Senator who shall not have attained to the Age of thirty Years, and been nine Years a Citizen of the United States, and who shall not, when elected, be an Inhabitant of that State for which he shall be chosen.

The Vice President of the United States shall be President of the Senate, but shall have no vote, unless they be equally divided.

The Senate shall chuse their other Officers, and also a President pro tempore, in the absence of the Vice President, or when he shall exercise the Office of President of the United States.

The Senate shall have the sole Power to try all Impeachments.

* Replaced by the 14th Amendment.
† Superseded by the 17th Amendment.
‡ Modified by the 17th Amendment.

When sitting for that purpose, they shall be on Oath or Affirmation. When the President of the United States is tried, the Chief Justice shall preside: And no person shall be convicted without the Concurrence of two thirds of the Members present.

Judgment in Cases of Impeachment shall not extend further than to removal from Office, and disqualification to hold and enjoy any Office of honor, Trust, or Profit under the United States: but the Party convicted shall nevertheless be liable and subject to Indictment, Trial, Judgment, and Punishment, according to Law.

SECTION 4. The Times, Places and Manner of holding Elections for Senators and Representatives, shall be prescribed in each State by the Legislature thereof; but the Congress may at any time by Law make or alter such Regulations, except as to the Places of Chusing Senators.

[The Congress shall assemble at least once in every Year, and such Meeting shall be on the first Monday in December, unless they shall by Law appoint a different Day.] *

SECTION 5. Each House shall be the Judge of the Elections, Returns and Qualifications of its own Members, and a Majority of each shall constitute a Quorum to do Business; but a smaller number may adjourn from day to day, and may be authorized to compel the Attendance of absent Members, in such Manner, and under such Penalties, as each House may provide.

Each House may determine the Rules of its Proceedings, punish its Members for disorderly Behavior, and, with the Concurrence of two thirds, expel a Member.

Each House shall keep a Journal of its Proceedings, and from time to time publish the same, excepting such Parts as may in their Judgment require Secrecy; and the Yeas and Nays of the Members of either House on any question shall, at the Desire of one fifth of those Present, be entered on the Journal.

Neither House, during the Session of Congress, shall, without the Consent of the other, adjourn for more than three days, nor to any other Place than that in which the two Houses shall be sitting.

SECTION 6. The Senators and Representatives shall receive a Compensation for their Services, to be ascertained by Law, and paid out of the Treasury of the United States. They shall in all Cases, except Treason, Felony, and Breach of the Peace, be privileged from Arrest during their Attendance at the Session of their respective Houses, and in going to and returning from the same; and for any Speech or Debate in either House, they shall not be questioned in any other Place.

* Superseded by the 20th Amendment.

No Senator or Representative shall, during the Time for which he was elected, be appointed to any civil Office under the Authority of the United States, which shall have been created, or the Emoluments whereof shall have been increased, during such time; and no Person holding any Office under the United States shall be a Member of either House during his continuance in Office.

Section 7. All Bills for raising Revenue shall originate in the House of Representatives; but the Senate may propose or concur with Amendments as on other bills.

Every Bill which shall have passed the House of Representatives and the Senate, shall, before it become a Law, be presented to the President of the United States; If he approve he shall sign it, but if not he shall return it, with his Objections, to that House in which it shall have originated, who shall enter the Objections at large on their Journal, and proceed to reconsider it. If after such Reconsideration two thirds of that House shall agree to pass the bill, it shall be sent, together with the objections, to the other House, by which it shall likewise be reconsidered, and if approved by two thirds of that House, it shall become a Law. But in all such Cases the Votes of both Houses shall be determined by Yeas and Nays, and the Names of the Persons voting for and against the Bill shall be entered on the Journal of each House respectively. If any Bill shall not be returned by the President within ten Days (Sundays excepted) after it shall have been presented to him, the Same shall be a Law, in like Manner as if he had signed it, unless the Congress by their Adjournment prevent its Return, in which Case it shall not be a Law.

Every Order, Resolution, or Vote to which the Concurrence of the Senate and House of Representatives may be necessary (except on a question of Adjournment) shall be presented to the President of the United States; and before the Same shall take Effect, shall be approved by him, or being disapproved by him, shall be repassed by two thirds of the Senate and House of Representatives, according to the Rules and Limitations prescribed in the Case of a Bill.

Section 8. The Congress shall have Power To lay and collect Taxes, Duties, Imposts and Excises, to pay the Debts and provide for the common Defence and general Welfare of the United States; but all Duties, Imposts and Excises shall be uniform throughout the United States;

To borrow money on the credit of the United States;

To regulate Commerce with foreign Nations, and among the several States, and with the Indian Tribes;

To establish an uniform Rule of Naturalization, and uniform Laws on the subject of Bankruptcies throughout the United States;

To coin Money, regulate the Value thereof, and of foreign Coin, and fix the Standard of Weights and Measures;

To provide for the Punishment of counterfeiting the Securities and current Coin of the United States;

To establish Post Offices and post Roads;

To promote the Progress of Science and useful Arts, by securing for limited Times to Authors and Inventors the exclusive Right to their respective Writings and Discoveries;

To constitute Tribunals inferior to the Supreme Court;

To define and punish Piracies and Felonies committed on the high Seas, and Offenses against the Law of Nations;

To declare War, grant Letters of Marque and Reprisal, and make Rules concerning Captures on Land and Water;

To raise and support Armies, but no Appropriation of Money to that Use shall be for a longer Term than two Years;

To provide and maintain a Navy;

To make Rules for the Government and Regulation of the land and naval forces;

To provide for calling forth the Militia to execute the Laws of the Union, suppress Insurrections and repel Invasions;

To provide for organizing, arming, and disciplining the Militia, and for governing such Part of them as may be employed in the Service of the United States, reserving to the States respectively, the Appointment of the Officers, and the Authority of training the Militia according to the discipline prescribed by Congress;

To exercise exclusive Legislation in all Cases whatsoever, over such District (not exceeding ten Miles square) as may, by Cession of particular States, and the acceptance of Congress, become the Seat of the Government of the United States, and to exercise like Authority over all Places purchased by the Consent of the Legislature of the State in which the Same shall be, for the Erection of Forts, Magazines, Arsenals, dock-Yards, and other needful Buildings;—And

To make all Laws which shall be necessary and proper for carrying into Execution the foregoing Powers, and all other Powers vested by this Constitution in the Government of the United States, or in any Department or Officer thereof.

SECTION 9. The Migration or Importation of such Persons as any of the States now existing shall think proper to admit, shall not be prohibited by the Congress prior to the Year one thousand eight hundred and eight, but a tax or duty may be imposed on such Importation, not exceeding ten dollars for each Person.

The privilege of the Writ of Habeas Corpus shall not be suspended, unless when in Cases of Rebellion or Invasion the public Safety may require it.

No Bill of Attainder or ex post facto Law shall be passed.

No capitation, or other direct, Tax shall be laid unless in Proportion to the Census or Enumeration herein before directed to be taken.

No Tax or Duty shall be laid on Articles exported from any State.

No Preference shall be given by any Regulation of Commerce or Revenue to the Ports of one State over those of another: nor shall Vessels bound to, or from, one State, be obliged to enter, clear, or pay Duties in another.

No Money shall be drawn from the Treasury, but in Consequence of Appropriations made by Law; and a regular Statement and Account of the Receipts and Expenditures of all public Money shall be published from time to time.

No Title of Nobility shall be granted by the United States: And no Person holding any Office of Profit or Trust under them, shall, without the Consent of the Congress, accept of any present, Emolument, Office, or Title, of any kind whatever, from any King, Prince, or foreign State.

SECTION 10. No State shall enter into any Treaty, Alliance, or Confederation; grant Letters of Marque and Reprisal; coin Money; emit Bills of Credit; make any Thing but gold and silver Coin a Tender in Payment of Debts; pass any Bill of Attainder, ex post facto Law, or Law impairing the Obligation of Contracts, or grant any Title of Nobility.

No State shall, without the Consent of the Congress, lay any Imposts or Duties on Imports or Exports, except what may be absolutely necessary for executing its inspection Laws: and the net Produce of all Duties and Imposts, laid by any State on Imports or Exports, shall be for the Use of the Treasury of the United States; and all such Laws shall be subject to the Revision and Control of the Congress.

No State shall, without the Consent of Congress, lay any duty of Tonnage, keep Troops, or Ships of War in time of Peace, enter into any Agreement or Compact with another State, or with a foreign Power, or engage in War, unless actually invaded, or in such imminent Danger as will not admit of delay.

Article 2.

SECTION 1. The executive Power shall be vested in a President of the United States of America. He shall hold his Office during the Term of four years, and, together with the Vice-President, chosen for the same Term, be elected, as follows:

Each State shall appoint, in such Manner as the Legislature thereof may direct, a Number of Electors, equal to the whole Number of Senators and Representatives to which the State may be entitled in the Congress: but no Senator or Representative, or Person holding an Office of Trust or Profit under the United States, shall be appointed an Elector.

[The Electors shall meet in their respective States, and vote by Ballot for two persons, of whom one at least shall not be an Inhabitant of the same State with themselves. And they shall make a List of all the Persons voted for, and of the Number of Votes for each; which List they shall sign and certify, and transmit sealed to the Seat of the Government of the United States, directed to the President of the Senate. The President of the Senate shall, in the Presence of the Senate and House of Representatives, open all the Certificates, and the Votes shall then be counted. The Person having the greatest Number of Votes shall be the President, if such Number be a Majority of the whole Number of Electors appointed; and if there be more than one who have such Majority, and have an equal Number of Votes, then the House of Representatives shall immediately chuse by Ballot one of them for President; and if no Person have a Majority, then from the five highest on the List the said House shall in like Manner chuse the President. But in chusing the President, the Votes shall be taken by States, the Representation from each State having one Vote; a quorum for this Purpose shall consist of a Member or Members from two-thirds of the States, and a Majority of all the States shall be necessary to a Choice. In every Case, after the Choice of the President, the Person having the greatest Number of Votes of the Electors shall be the Vice-President. But if there should remain two or more who have equal votes, the Senate shall chuse from them by Ballot the Vice-President.] *

The Congress may determine the Time of chusing the Electors, and the Day on which they shall give their Votes; which Day shall be the same throughout the United States.

No person except a natural-born Citizen, or a Citizen of the United States, at the time of the Adoption of this Constitution, shall be eligible to the Office of President; neither shall any Person be eligible to that

* Superseded by 12th Amendment.

Office who shall not have attained to the Age of thirty-five years, and been fourteen Years a Resident within the United States.

In Case of the Removal of the President from Office, or of his Death, Resignation, or Inability to discharge the Powers and Duties of the said Office, the same shall devolve on the Vice President, and the Congress may by Law provide for the Case of Removal, Death, Resignation, or Inability, both of the President and Vice President, declaring what Officer shall then act as President, and such Officer shall act accordingly, until the disability be removed, or a President shall be elected.

The President shall, at stated Times, receive for his Services a Compensation, which shall neither be increased nor diminished during the Period for which he shall have been elected, and he shall not receive within that Period any other Emolument from the United States, or any of them.

Before he enter on the execution of his Office, he shall take the following Oath or Affirmation:—"I do solemnly swear (or affirm) that I will faithfully execute the Office of President of the United States, and will, to the best of my Ability, preserve, protect, and defend the Constitution of the United States."

SECTION 2. The President shall be Commander in Chief of the Army and Navy of the United States, and of the Militia of the several States, when called into the actual Service of the United States; he may require the Opinion, in writing, of the principal Officer in each of the executive Departments, upon any subject relating to the Duties of their respective Offices, and he shall have Power to Grant Reprieves and Pardons for Offenses against the United States, except in Cases of Impeachment.

He shall have Power, by and with the Advice and Consent of the Senate, to make Treaties, provided two thirds of the Senators present concur; and he shall nominate, and by and with the Advice and Consent of the Senate, shall appoint Ambassadors, other public Ministers and Consuls, Judges of the supreme Court, and all other Officers of the United States, whose Appointments are not herein otherwise provided for, and which shall be established by Law: but the Congress may by Law vest the Appointment of such inferior Officers, as they think proper, in the President alone, in the Courts of Law, or in the Heads of Departments.

The President shall have Power to fill up all Vacancies that may happen during the Recess of the Senate, by granting Commissions which shall expire at the End of their next Session.

SECTION 3. He shall from time to time give to the Congress Information of the State of the Union, and recommend to their Consideration such Measures as he shall judge necessary and expedient; he may, on extraordinary occasions, convene both Houses, or either of them, and in Case of Disagreement between them, with respect to the Time of Adjournment, he may adjourn them to such Time as he shall think proper; he shall receive Ambassadors and other public Ministers; he shall take Care that the Laws be faithfully executed, and shall Commission all the Officers of the United States.

SECTION 4. The President, Vice President and all civil Officers of the United States, shall be removed from Office on Impeachment for, and Conviction of, Treason, Bribery, or other high Crimes and Misdemeanors.

Article 3.

SECTION 1. The judicial Power of the United States, shall be vested in one supreme Court, and in such inferior Courts as the Congress may from time to time ordain and establish. The Judges, both of the supreme and inferior Courts, shall hold their Offices during good Behaviour, and shall, at stated Times, receive for their Services, a Compensation, which shall not be diminished during their Continuance in Office.

SECTION 2. The judicial Power shall extend to all Cases, in Law and Equity, arising under this Constitution, the Laws of the United States, and Treaties made, or which shall be made, under their Authority;— to all Cases affecting ambassadors, other public ministers and consuls;— to all cases of admiralty and maritime Jurisdiction;—to Controversies to which the United States shall be a Party;—to Controversies between two or more States;—between a State and Citizens of another State; *— between Citizens of different States,—between Citizens of the same State claiming Lands under Grants of different States, and between a State, or the Citizens thereof, and foreign States, Citizens or Subjects.

In all Cases affecting Ambassadors, other public Ministers and Consuls, and those in which a State shall be Party, the supreme Court shall have original Jurisdiction. In all the other Cases before mentioned, the supreme Court shall have appellate Jurisdiction, both as to Law and Fact, with such Exceptions, and under such Regulations as the Congress shall make.

The trial of all Crimes, except in Cases of Impeachment, shall be by Jury; and such Trial shall be held in the State where the said Crimes shall have been committed; but when not committed within any State, the Trial shall be at such Place or Places as the Congress may by Law have directed.

* Restricted by the 11th Amendment.

SECTION 3. Treason against the United States, shall consist only in levying War against them, or in adhering to their Enemies, giving them Aid and Comfort. No Person shall be convicted of Treason unless on the Testimony of two Witnesses to the same overt Act, or on Confession in open Court.

The Congress shall have power to declare the Punishment of Treason, but no Attainder of Treason shall work Corruption of Blood, or Forfeiture except during the Life of the Person attainted.

Article 4.

SECTION 1. Full Faith and Credit shall be given in each State to the public Acts, Records, and judicial Proceedings of every other State. And the Congress may by general Laws prescribe the Manner in which such Acts, Records and Proceedings shall be proved, and the Effect thereof.

SECTION 2. The Citizens of each State shall be entitled to all Privileges and Immunities of Citizens in the several States.

A Person charged in any State with Treason, Felony, or other Crime, who shall flee from Justice, and be found in another State, shall on demand of the executive Authority of the State from which he fled, be delivered up, to be removed to the State having Jurisdiction of the crime.

No Person held to Service or Labour in one State, under the Laws thereof, escaping into another, shall, in Consequence of any Law or Regulation therein, be discharged from such Service or Labour, but shall be delivered up on Claim of the Party to whom such Service or Labour may be due.

SECTION 3. New States may be admitted by the Congress into this Union; but no new State shall be formed or erected within the Jurisdiction of any other State; nor any State be formed by the Junction of two or more States, or parts of States, without the Consent of the Legislatures of the States concerned as well as of the Congress.

The Congress shall have Power to dispose of and make all needful Rules and Regulations respecting the Territory or other Property belonging to the United States; and nothing in this Constitution shall be so construed as to Prejudice any Claims of the United States, or of any particular State.

SECTION 4. The United States shall guarantee to every State in this Union a Republican Form of Government, and shall protect each of them against Invasion; and on Application of the Legislature, or of the Executive (when the Legislature cannot be convened) against domestic Violence.

Article 5.

The Congress, whenever two-thirds of both Houses shall deem it necessary, shall propose Amendments to this Constitution, or, on the Application of the Legislatures of two-thirds of the several States, shall call a Convention for proposing Amendments, which, in either Case, shall be valid to all Intents and Purposes, as part of this Constitution, when ratified by the Legislatures of three-fourth of the several States, or by Conventions in three-fourths thereof, as the one or the other Mode of Ratification may be proposed by the Congress; Provided that no Amendment which may be made prior to the Year One thousand eight hundred and eight shall in any Manner affect the first and fourth Clauses in the Ninth Section of the first Article; and that no State, without its Consent, shall be deprived of its equal Suffrage in the Senate.

Article 6.

All Debts contracted and Engagements entered into, before the Adoption of this Constitution, shall be as valid against the United States under this Constitution, as under the Confederation.

This Constitution, and the Laws of the United States which shall be made in Pursuance thereof; and all Treaties made, or which shall be made, under the Authority of the United States, shall be the supreme Law of the Land; and the Judges in every State shall be bound thereby, any Thing in the Constitution or Laws of any State to the Contrary notwithstanding.

The Senators and Representatives before mentioned, and the Members of the several State Legislatures, and all executive and judicial Officers, both of the United States and of the several States, shall be bound by Oath or Affirmation to support this Constitution; but no religious Test shall ever be required as a qualification to any Office or public Trust under the United States.

Article 7.

The Ratification of the Conventions of nine States shall be sufficient for the Establishment of this Constitution between the States so ratifying the same.

Done in Convention by the Unanimous Consent of the States present the Seventeenth Day of September in the Year of our Lord one thousand seven hundred and Eighty seven, and of the Independence of the United States of America the Twelfth. In Witness whereof We have hereunto subscribed our Names.*

George Washington
President and deputy from Virginia

NEW HAMPSHIRE
John Langdon
Nicholas Gilman

MASSACHUSETTS
Nathaniel Gorham
Rufus King

PENNSYLVANIA
Benjamin Franklin
Thomas Mifflin
Robert Morris
George Clymer
Thomas FitzSimons
Jared Ingersoll
James Wilson
Gouverneur Morris

DELAWARE
George Read
Gunning Bedford, Jr.
John Dickinson
Richard Bassett
Jacob Broom

MARYLAND
James McHenry
Daniel of St. Thomas Jenifer
Daniel Carroll

CONNECTICUT
William Samuel Johnson
Roger Sherman

NEW YORK
Alexander Hamilton

NEW JERSEY
William Livingston
David Brearley
William Paterson
Jonathan Dayton

VIRGINIA
John Blair
James Madison, Jr.

NORTH CAROLINA
William Blount
Richard Dobbs Spaight
Hugh Williamson

SOUTH CAROLINA
John Rutledge
Charles Cotesworth Pinckney
Charles Pinckney
Pierce Butler

GEORGIA
William Few
Abraham Baldwin

ARTICLES IN ADDITION TO, AND AMENDMENT OF, THE CONSTITUTION OF THE UNITED STATES OF AMERICA, PROPOSED BY CONGRESS, AND RATIFIED BY THE LEGISLATURES OF THE SEVERAL STATES, PURSUANT TO THE FIFTH ARTICLE OF THE ORIGINAL CONSTITUTION.†

* The full names of the signers follow, not the signatures as they appear on the document.

† This heading appears only in the joint resolution submitting the first ten amendments.

[*Article I.*] *

Congress shall make no law respecting an establishment of religion, or prohibiting the free exercise thereof; or abridging the freedom of speech, or of the press; or the right of the people peaceably to assemble, and to petition the Government for a redress of grievances.

[*Article II.*]

A well regulated Militia, being necessary to the security of a free State, the right of the people to keep and bear Arms shall not be infringed.

[*Article III.*]

No Soldier shall, in time of peace, be quartered in any house, without the consent of the Owner, nor in time of war, but in a manner to be prescribed by law.

[*Article IV.*]

The right of the people to be secure in their persons, houses, papers, and effects, against unreasonable searches and seizures, shall not be violated, and no Warrants shall issue, but upon probable cause, supported by Oath or affirmation, and particularly describing the place to be searched, and the persons or things to be seized.

[*Article V.*]

No person shall be held to answer for a capital or otherwise infamous crime, unless on a presentment or indictment of a Grand Jury, except in cases arising in the land or naval forces, or in the Militia, when in actual service in time of War or public danger; nor shall any person be subject for the same offence to be twice put in jeopardy of life or limb; nor shall be compelled in any criminal case to be a witness against himself, nor be deprived of life, liberty, or property, without due process of law; nor shall private property be taken for public use, without just compensation.

[*Article VI.*]

In all criminal prosecutions, the accused shall enjoy the right to a speedy and public trial, by an impartial jury of the State and district wherein the crime shall have been committed, which district shall have been previously ascertained by law, and to be informed of the nature

* In the original manuscripts the first twelve amendments have no numbers.

and cause of the accusation; to be confronted with the witnesses against him; to have compulsory process for obtaining witnesses in his favor, and to have the Assistance of Counsel for his defence.

[*Article VII.*]

In suits at common law, where the value in controversy shall exceed twenty dollars, the right of trial by jury shall be preserved, and no fact tried by a jury, shall be otherwise reexamined in any Court of the United States, than according to the rules of the common law.

[*Article VIII.*]

Excessive bail shall not be required, nor excessive fines imposed, nor cruel and unusual punishments inflicted.

[*Article IX.*]

The enumeration in the Constitution, of certain rights, shall not be construed to deny or disparage others retained by the people.

[*Article X.*]

The powers not delegated to the United States by the Constitution, nor prohibited by it to the States, are reserved to the States respectively, or to the people.

[Amendments I–X, in force 1791.]

[*Article XI.*] *

The Judicial power of the United States shall not be construed to extend to any suit in law or equity, commenced or prosecuted against one of the United States by Citizens of another State, or by Citizens or Subjects of any Foreign State.

[*Article XII.*] †

The Electors shall meet in their respective States and vote by ballot for President and Vice-President, one of whom, at least, shall not be an inhabitant of the same State with themselves; they shall name in their ballots the person voted for as President, and in distinct ballots the person voted for as Vice-President, and they shall make distinct lists of all persons voted for as President, and of all persons voted for as Vice-President, and of the number of votes for each, which lists they shall sign and certify, and transmit sealed to the seat of the government

* Adopted in 1798.
† Adopted in 1804.

of the United States, directed to the President of the Senate;—The
President of the Senate shall, in the presence of the Senate and House
of Representatives, open all the certificates and the votes shall then be
counted;—The person having the greatest number of votes for President, shall be the President, if such number be a majority of the whole
number of Electors appointed; and if no person have such majority,
then from the persons having the highest numbers not exceeding three
on the list of those voted for as President, the House of Representatives
shall choose immediately, by ballot, the President. But in choosing the
President, the votes shall be taken by states, the representation from
each state having one vote; a quorum for this purpose shall consist of
a member or members from two-thirds of the states, and a majority of
all the states shall be necessary to a choice. And if the House of Representatives shall not choose a President whenever the right of choice
shall devolve upon them, before the fourth day of March next following, then the Vice-President shall act as President, as in the case of the
death or other constitutional disability of the President.—The person
having the greatest number of votes as Vice-President, shall be the
Vice-President, if such number be a majority of the whole number of
Electors appointed, and if no person have a majority, then from the
two highest numbers on the list, the Senate shall choose the Vice-
President; a quorum for the purpose shall consist of two-thirds of the
whole number of Senators, and a majority of the whole number shall
be necessary to a choice. But no person constitutionally ineligible to
the office of President shall be eligible to that of Vice-President of the
United States.

[*Article XIII.*] *

SECTION 1. Neither slavery nor involuntary servitude, except as a
punishment for crime whereof the party shall have been duly convicted, shall exist within the United States, or any place subject to their
jurisdiction.

SECTION 2. Congress shall have power to enforce this article by appropriate legislation.

[*Article XIV.*] †

SECTION 1. All persons born or naturalized in the United States,
and subject to the jurisdiction thereof, are citizens of the United States
and of the State wherein they reside. No State shall make or enforce
any law which shall abridge the privileges or immunities of citizens of

* Adopted in 1865.
† Adopted in 1868, proclaimed July 28, 1868.

the United States; nor shall any State deprive any person of life, liberty, or property, without due process of law; nor deny to any person within its jurisdiction the equal protection of the laws.

SECTION 2. Representatives shall be apportioned among the several States according to their respective numbers, counting the whole number of persons in each State, excluding Indians not taxed. But when the right to vote at any election for the choice of electors for President and Vice-President of the United States, Representatives in Congress, the Executive and Judicial officers of a State, or the members of the Legislature thereof, is denied to any of the male inhabitants of such State, being twenty-one years of age, and citizens of the United States, or in any way abridged, except for participation in rebellion, or other crime, the basis of representation therein shall be reduced in the proportion which the number of such male citizens shall bear to the whole number of male citizens twenty-one years of age in such State.

SECTION 3. No person shall be a Senator or Representative in Congress, or elector of President and Vice-President, or hold any office, civil or military, under the United States, or under any State, who, having previously taken an oath, as a member of Congress, or as an officer of the United States, or as a member of any State legislature, or as an executive or judicial officer of any State, to support the Constitution of the United States, shall have engaged in insurrection or rebellion against the same, or given aid or comfort to the enemies thereof. But Congress may by a vote of two-thirds of each House, remove such disability.

SECTION 4. The validity of the public debt of the United States, authorized by law, including debts incurred for payment of pensions and bounties for services in suppressing insurrection or rebellion, shall not be questioned. But neither the United States nor any State shall assume or pay any debt or obligation incurred in aid of insurrection or rebellion against the United States, or any claim for the loss or emancipation of any slave; but all such debts, obligations, and claims shall be held illegal and void.

SECTION 5. The Congress shall have the power to enforce, by appropriate legislation, the provisions of this article.

[*Article XV.*] *

SECTION 1. The right of citizens of the United States to vote shall not be denied or abridged by the United States or by any State on account of race, color, or previous condition of servitude.

* Proclaimed March 30, 1870.

SECTION 2. The Congress shall have power to enforce this article by appropriate legislation.

[*Article XVI.*] *

The Congress shall have power to lay and collect taxes on incomes, from whatever source derived, without apportionment among the several States, and without regard to any census or enumeration.

[*Article XVII.*] †

The Senate of the United States shall be composed of two Senators from each State, elected by the people thereof, for six years; and each Senator shall have one vote. The electors in each State shall have the qualifications requisite for electors of the most numerous branch of the State legislatures.

When vacancies happen in the representation of any State in the Senate, the executive authority of such State shall issue writs of election to fill such vacancies: *Provided*, That the legislature of any State may empower the executive thereof to make temporary appointments until the people fill the vacancies by election as the legislature may direct.

This amendment shall not be so construed as to affect the election or term of any Senator chosen before it becomes valid as part of the Constitution.

[*Article XVIII.*] ‡

SECTION 1. After one year from the ratification of this article the manufacture, sale, or transportation of intoxicating liquors within, the importation thereof into, or the exportation thereof from the United States and all territory subject to the jurisdiction thereof for beverage purposes is hereby prohibited.

SECTION 2. The Congress and the several States shall have concurrent power to enforce this article by appropriate legislation.

SECTION 3. This article shall be inoperative unless it shall have been ratified as an amendment to the Constitution by the legislatures of the several States, as provided in the Constitution, within seven years from the date of the submission hereof to the States by the Congress.

---

* Passed July, 1909; proclaimed February 25, 1913.

† Passed May, 1912, in lieu of Article I, Section 3, clause 1, of the Constitution and so much of clause 2 of the same Section as relates to the filling of vacancies; proclaimed May 31, 1913.

‡ Passed December 3, 1917; proclaimed January 29, 1919. Repealed by the 21st Amendment.

[*Article XIX.*] *

The right of citizens of the United States to vote shall not be denied or abridged by the United States or by any State on account of sex.

Congress shall have power to enforce this article by appropriate legislation.

[*Article XX.*] †

SECTION 1. The terms of the President and Vice-President shall end at noon on the 20th day of January, and the terms of Senators and Representatives at noon on the 3d day of January, of the years in which such terms would have ended if this article had not been ratified; and the terms of their successors shall then begin.

SECTION 2. The Congress shall assemble at least once in every year, and such meeting shall begin at noon on the 3d day of January, unless they shall by law appoint a different day.

SECTION 3. If, at the time fixed for the beginning of the term of the President, the President elect shall have died, the Vice-President elect shall become President. If a President shall not have been chosen before the time fixed for the beginning of his term, or if the President elect shall have failed to qualify, then the Vice-President elect shall act as President until a President shall have qualified; and the Congress may by law provide for the case wherein neither a President elect nor a Vice-President elect shall have qualified, declaring who shall then act as President, or the manner in which one who is to act shall be selected, and such person shall act accordingly until a President or Vice-President shall have qualified.

SECTION 4. The Congress may by law provide for the case of the death of any of the persons from whom the House of Representatives may choose a President whenever the right of choice shall have devolved upon them, and for the case of the death of any of the persons from whom the Senate may choose a Vice-President whenever the right of choice shall have devolved upon them.

SECTION 5. Sections 1 and 2 shall take effect on the 15th day of October following the ratification of this article.

SECTION 6. This article shall be inoperative unless it shall have been ratified as an amendment to the Constitution by the legislatures of three-fourths of the several States within seven years from the date of its submission.

* Adopted in 1920.
† Adopted in 1933.

[*Article XXI.*] *

SECTION 1. The eighteenth article of amendment to the Constitution of the United States is hereby repealed.

SECTION 2. The transportation or importation into any State, Territory, or possession of the United States for delivery or use therein of intoxicating liquors, in violation of the laws thereof, is hereby prohibited.

SECTION 3. This article shall be inoperative unless it shall have been ratified as an amendment to the Constitution by conventions in the several States, as provided in the Constitution, within seven years from the date of the submission hereof to the States by the Congress.

[*Article XXII.*] †

No person shall be elected to the office of the President more than twice, and no person who has held the office of President, or acted as President, for more than two years of a term to which some other person was elected President shall be elected to the office of the President more than once.

But this Article shall not apply to any person holding the office of President when this Article was proposed by the Congress, and shall not prevent any person who may be holding the office of President, or acting as President, during the term within which this Article becomes operative from holding the office of President or acting as President during the remainder of such term.

* Adopted in 1933.
† Adopted in 1951.

II

Admission of States
to The Union

State	Entered Union	State	Entered Union
ALABAMA	1819	MONTANA	1889
ALASKA	1959	NEBRASKA	1867
ARIZONA	1912	NEVADA	1864
ARKANSAS	1836	NEW HAMPSHIRE	1788
CALIFORNIA	1850	NEW JERSEY	1787
COLORADO	1876	NEW MEXICO	1912
CONNECTICUT	1788	NEW YORK	1788
DELAWARE	1787	NORTH CAROLINA	1789
FLORIDA	1845	NORTH DAKOTA	1889
GEORGIA	1788	OHIO	1803
HAWAII	1959	OKLAHOMA	1907
IDAHO	1890	OREGON	1859
ILLINOIS	1818	PENNSYLVANIA	1787
INDIANA	1816	RHODE ISLAND	1790
IOWA	1846	SOUTH CAROLINA	1788
KANSAS	1861	SOUTH DAKOTA	1889
KENTUCKY	1792	TENNESSEE	1796
LOUISIANA	1812	TEXAS	1845
MAINE	1820	UTAH	1896
MARYLAND	1788	VERMONT	1791
MASSACHUSETTS	1788	VIRGINIA	1788
MICHIGAN	1837	WASHINGTON	1889
MINNESOTA	1858	WEST VIRGINIA	1863
MISSISSIPPI	1817	WISCONSIN	1848
MISSOURI	1821	WYOMING	1890

III

Presidential Elections, 1864-1956

Year	Number of States	Candidates	Party	Popular Vote	Electoral Vote
1864	36	ABRAHAM LINCOLN	Republican	2,213,665	212
		George B. McClellan	Democrat	1,805,237	21
		(Not voted)			81
1868	37	ULYSSES S. GRANT	Republican	3,012,833	214
		Horatio Seymour	Democrat	2,703,249	80
		(Not voted)			23
1872	37	ULYSSES S. GRANT	Republican	3,597,132	286
		Horace Greeley	Democrat & Liberal Republican	2,834,125	66
		Charles O'Conor	Straight Democrat	29,489	
		James Black	Temperance	5,608	
1876	38	RUTHERFORD B. HAYES	Republican	4,036,298	185
		Samuel J. Tilden	Democrat	4,300,590	184
		Peter Cooper	Greenback	81,737	
		Green Clay Smith	Prohibition	9,522	
		James B. Walker	American	2,636	
1880	38	JAMES A. GARFIELD	Republican	4,454,416	214
		Winfield S. Hancock	Democrat	4,444,952	155
		James B. Weaver	Greenback-Labor	308,578	
		Neal Dow	Prohibition	10,305	
		John W. Phelps	American	700	
1884	38	GROVER CLEVELAND	Democrat	4,874,986	219
		James G. Blaine	Republican	4,851,981	182
		John P. St. John	Prohibition	150,369	
		Benjamin F. Butler	Greenback-Labor	175,370	
1888	38	BENJAMIN HARRISON	Republican	5,439,853	233
		Grover Cleveland	Democrat	5,540,309	168
		Clinton B. Fisk	Prohibition	249,506	
		Anson J. Streeter	Union Labor	146,935	

Year	Number of States	Candidates	Party	Popular Vote	Electoral Vote
		Robert H. Cowdrey	United Labor	2,818	
		James Langdon Curtis	American	1,600	
1892	44	GROVER CLEVELAND	Democrat	5,556,918	277
		Benjamin Harrison	Republican	5,176,108	145
		James B. Weaver	People's	1,041,028	22
		John Bidwell	Prohibition	264,133	
		Simon Wing	Socialist-Labor	21,164	
1896	45	WILLIAM McKINLEY	Republican	7,104,779	271
		Wm. Jennings Bryan	Democrat & People's	6,502,925	176
		John M. Palmer	Nationalist Democrat	133,148	
		Joshua Levering	Prohibition	132,007	
		Charles H. Matchett	Socialist-Labor	36,274	
		Charles E. Bentley	Nationalist	13,969	
1900	45	WILLIAM McKINLEY	Republican	7,207,923	292
		Wm. Jennings Bryan	Democrat & Populist	6,358,133	155
		John C. Woolley	Prohibition	208,914	
		Eugene V. Debs	Socialist Democrat	87,814	
		Wharton Barker	People's	50,373	
		Joseph F. Malloney	Socialist-Labor	39,739	
		Seth H. Ellis	Union Reform	5,698	
		Jonah F. R. Leonard	United Christian	5,500	
1904	45	THEODORE ROOSEVELT	Republican	7,623,486	336
		Alton B. Parker	Democrat	5,077,911	140
		Eugene V. Debs	Socialist	402,283	
		Silas C. Swallow	Prohibition	258,536	
		Thomas E. Watson	People's	117,183	
		Charles H. Corregan	Socialist-Labor	31,249	
		Austin Holcomb	Continental	1,000	
1908	46	WILLIAM H. TAFT	Republican	7,678,908	321
		Wm. Jennings Bryan	Democrat	6,409,104	162
		Eugene V. Debs	Socialist	420,793	
		Eugene W. Chafin	Prohibition	253,840	
		Thomas L. Hisgen	Independence	82,872	
		Thomas E. Watson	People's	29,100	
		August Gillhaus	Socialist-Labor	14,021	
		Daniel B. Turney	United Christian	500	
1912	48	WOODROW WILSON	Democrat	6,293,454	435
		William H. Taft	Republican	3,484,980	8
		Theodore Roosevelt	Progressive	4,119,538	88
		Eugene V. Debs	Socialist	900,672	
		Eugene W. Chafin	Prohibition	206,275	
		Arthur E. Reimer	Socialist-Labor	28,750	
1916	48	WOODROW WILSON	Democrat	9,129,606	277
		Charles Evans Hughes	Republican	8,538,221	254
		A. L. Benson	Socialist	585,113	

Year	Num- ber of States	Candidates	Party	Pop- ular Vote	Elec- toral Vote
		J. Frank Hanly	Prohibition	220,506	
		Arthur E. Reimer	Socialist-Labor	13,403	
		(Various candidates)	Progressive	41,894	
1920	48	WARREN G. HARDING	Republican	16,152,200	404
		James M. Cox	Democrat	9,147,353	127
		Eugene V. Debs	Socialist	919,799	
		P. P. Christensen	Farmer-Labor	265,411	
		Aaron S. Watkins	Prohibition	189,408	
		W. W. Cox	Socialist-Labor	31,715	
		Robert C. Macauley	Single Tax	5,837	
		James E. Ferguson	American	48,000	
1924	48	CALVIN COOLIDGE	Republican	15,725,016	382
		John W. Davis	Democrat	8,386,503	136
		Robert LaFollette	Progressive	4,822,856	13
		Herman P. Faris	Prohibition	57,520	
		Frank T. Johns	Socialist-Labor	36,428	
		William Z. Foster	Workers	36,386	
		Gilbert O. Nations	American	23,967	
		William J. Wallace	Commonwealth Land	1,532	
1928	48	HERBERT HOOVER	Republican	21,391,381	444
		Alfred E. Smith	Democrat	15,016,443	87
		Norman Thomas	Socialist	267,835	
		William Z. Foster	Workers	21,181	
		Verne L. Reynolds	Socialist-Labor	21,603	
		William F. Varney	Prohibition	20,106	
		Frank E. Webb	Farmer-Labor	6,390	
1932	48	FRANKLIN D. ROOSEVELT	Democrat	22,821,857	472
		Herbert Hoover	Republican	15,761,841	59
		Norman Thomas	Socialist	881,951	
		William Z. Foster	Communist	102,785	
		Verne L. Reynolds	Socialist-Labor	33,276	
		William D. Upshaw	Prohibition	81,869	
		William H. Harvey	Liberty	53,425	
		Jacob S. Coxey, Sr.	Farmer-Labor	7,309	
1936	48	FRANKLIN D. ROOSEVELT	Democrat & Amer. Labor	27,751,597	523
		Alfred M. Landon	Republican	16,679,583	8
		William Lemke	Union, Royal Oak; Nat'l Union for Social Justice, 3d Party; Independent	882,479	
		Norman Thomas	Socialist	187,720	
		Earl Browder	Communist	80,159	
		D. Leigh Colvin	Prohibition & Commonwealth	37,847	
		John W. Aiken	Socialist-Labor & Industrial Labor	12,777	

Year	Number of States	Candidates	Party	Popular Vote	Electoral Vote
1940	48	FRANKLIN D. ROOSEVELT	Democrat & Amer. Labor	27,244,160	449
		Wendell L. Willkie	Republican	22,305,198	82
		Norman Thomas	Socialist & Progressive	99,557	
		Roger Q. Babson	Prohibition & National Prohibition	57,812	
		Earl Browder	Communist	46,251	
1944	48	FRANKLIN D. ROOSEVELT	Democrat Amer. Labor, & Liberal	25,602,504	432
		Thomas E. Dewey	Republican	22,006,285	99
		Norman Thomas	Socialist	80,518	
		Claude A. Watson	Prohibition	74,758	
		Edward A. Teichert	Socialist-Labor & Industrial Government	45,336	
		(Unpledged)	Texas Regulars	135,439	
1948	48	HARRY S. TRUMAN	Democrat & Liberal	24,105,695	303
		Thomas E. Dewey	Republican	21,969,170	189
		J. Strom Thurmond	States' Rights Democrat	1,169,021	39
		Henry A. Wallace	Progressive & American Labor	1,156,103	
		Norman Thomas	Socialist	139,009	
		Claude A. Watson	Prohibition	103,216	
		Edward A. Teichert	Socialist-Labor & Industrial Government	29,061	
		Farrell Dobbs	Socialist Workers & Militant Workers	13,613	
1952	48	DWIGHT D. EISENHOWER	Republican	33,824,351	442
		Adlai E. Stevenson	Democrat & Liberal	27,314,987	89
		Vincent Hallinan	Progressive & American Labor	132,608	
		Stuart Hamblen	Prohibition	72,768	
		Eric Hass	Socialist-Labor & Industrial Government	29,333	
		Darlington Hoopes	Socialist	20,203	
		Farrell Dobbs	Socialist Workers	10,312	
1956	48	DWIGHT D. EISENHOWER	Republican	35,585,316	457
		Adlai E. Stevenson	Democrat & Liberal	26,029,752	73

Year	Number of States	Candidates	Party	Popular Vote	Electoral Vote
		T. Coleman Andrews	Independent	175,679	
		Harry F. Byrd	Independent	134,132	
		Eric Hass	Socialist-Labor & Industrial Government	44,099	
		Enoch A. Holtwick	Prohibition	41,937	
		Farrell Dobbs	Socialist Workers	8,148	
		Darlington Hoopes	Socialist	2,126	
		Walter B. Jones *			1

* Received one of Alabama's electoral votes instead of Adlai E. Stevenson.

IV

Presidents and Their Cabinets
1865-1960

ANDREW JOHNSON 1865–9
  Secretary of State
  Secretary of Treasury
  Secretary of War

  Secretary of Navy
  Secretary of Interior

  Postmaster General

  Attorney General

    WILLIAM H. SEWARD, 1865–9
    HUGH MCCULLOCH, 1865–9
    EDWIN M. STANTON, 1865–7
    ULYSSES S. GRANT, 1867–8
    LORENZO THOMAS, 1868
    JOHN M. SCHOFIELD, 1868–9
    GIDEON WELLES, 1865–9
    JOHN P. USHER, 1865
    JAMES HARLAN, 1865–6
    ORVILLE H. BROWNING, 1866–9
    WILLIAM DENNISON, 1865–6
    ALEXANDER RANDALL, 1866–9
    JAMES SPEED, 1865–6
    HENRY STANBERY, 1866–8
    WILLIAM M. EVARTS, 1868–9

ULYSSES S. GRANT 1869–73
  SCHUYLER COLFAX
ULYSSES S. GRANT 1873–7
  HENRY WILSON
  Secretary of State

  Secretary of Treasury

  Secretary of War

    ELIHU B. WASHBURNE, 1869
    HAMILTON FISH, 1869–77
    GEORGE S. BOUTWELL, 1869–73
    WILLIAM A. RICHARDSON, 1873–4
    BENJAMIN H. BRISTOW, 1874–6
    LOT M. MORRILL, 1876–7
    JOHN A. RAWLINS, 1869
    WILLIAM T. SHERMAN, 1869
    WILLIAM W. BELKNAP, 1869–76
    ALPHONSO TAFT, 1876
    JAMES D. CAMERON, 1876–7

Secretary of Navy	ADOLPH E. BORIE, 1869
	GEORGE M. ROBESON, 1869–77
Secretary of Interior	JACOB D. COX, 1869–70
	COLUMBUS DELANO, 1870–5
	ZACHARY CHANDLER, 1875–7
Postmaster General	JOHN A. J. CRESWELL, 1869–74
	JAMES W. MARSHALL, 1874
	MARSHALL JEWELL, 1874–6
	JAMES N. TYNER, 1876–7
Attorney General	EBENEZER R. HOAR, 1869–70
	AMOS T. AKERMAN, 1870–1
	GEORGE H. WILLIAMS, 1871–5
	EDWARD PIERREPONT, 1875–6
	ALPHONSO TAFT, 1876–7

RUTHERFORD B. HAYES 1877–81
 WILLIAM A. WHEELER

Secretary of State	WILLIAM M. EVARTS, 1877–81
Secretary of Treasury	JOHN SHERMAN, 1877–81
Secretary of War	GEORGE W. McCRARY, 1877–9
	ALEXANDER RAMSEY, 1879–81
Secretary of Navy	RICHARD W. THOMPSON, 1877–81
	NATHAN GOFF, JR., 1881
Secretary of Interior	CARL SCHURZ, 1877–81
Postmaster General	DAVID M. KEY, 1877–80
	HORACE MAYNARD, 1880–1
Attorney General	CHARLES DEVENS, 1877–81

JAMES A. GARFIELD 1881
 CHESTER A. ARTHUR

Secretary of State	JAMES G. BLAINE, 1881
Secretary of Treasury	WILLIAM WINDOM, 1881
Secretary of War	ROBERT T. LINCOLN, 1881
Secretary of Navy	WILLIAM H. HUNT, 1881
Secretary of Interior	SAMUEL J. KIRKWOOD, 1881
Postmaster General	THOMAS L. JAMES, 1881
Attorney General	WAYNE MacVEAGH, 1881

CHESTER A. ARTHUR 1881–5

Secretary of State	FREDERICK T. FRELINGHUYSEN, 1881–5
Secretary of Treasury	CHARLES J. FOLGER, 1881–4
	WALTER Q. GRESHAM, 1884
	HUGH McCULLOCH, 1884–5

Secretary of War	ROBERT T. LINCOLN, 1881–5
Secretary of Navy	WILLIAM E. CHANDLER, 1881–5
Secretary of Interior	HENRY M. TELLER, 1881–5
Postmaster General	TIMOTHY O. HOWE, 1881–3
	WALTER Q. GRESHAM, 1883–4
	FRANK HATTON, 1884–5
Attorney General	BENJAMIN H. BREWSTER, 1881–5

GROVER CLEVELAND 1885–9
 T. A. HENDRICKS

Secretary of State	THOMAS F. BAYARD, 1885–9
Secretary of Treasury	DANIEL MANNING, 1885–7
	CHARLES S. FAIRCHILD, 1887–9
Secretary of War	WILLIAM C. ENDICOTT, 1885–9
Secretary of Navy	WILLIAM C. WHITNEY, 1885–9
Secretary of Interior	LUCIUS Q. C. LAMAR, 1885–8
	WILLIAM F. VILAS, 1888–9
Secretary of Agriculture	NORMAN J. COLMAN, 1889
Postmaster General	WILLIAM F. VILAS, 1885–8
	DON M. DICKINSON, 1888–9
Attorney General	AUGUSTUS H. GARLAND, 1885–9

BENJAMIN HARRISON 1889–93
 LEVI P. MORTON

Secretary of State	JAMES G. BLAINE, 1889–92
	JOHN W. FOSTER, 1892–3
Secretary of Treasury	WILLIAM WINDOM, 1889–91
	CHARLES FOSTER, 1891–3
Secretary of War	REDFIELD PROCTER, 1889–91
	STEPHEN B. ELKINS, 1891–3
Secretary of Navy	BENJAMIN F. TRACY, 1889–93
Secretary of Interior	JOHN W. NOBLE, 1889–93
Secretary of Agriculture	JEREMIAH M. RUSK, 1889–93
Postmaster General	JOHN WANAMAKER, 1889–93
Attorney General	WILLIAM H. H. MILLER, 1889–93

GROVER CLEVELAND 1893–7
 ADLAI E. STEVENSON

Secretary of State	WALTER Q. GRESHAM, 1893–5
	RICHARD OLNEY, 1895–7
Secretary of Treasury	JOHN G. CARLISLE, 1893–7
Secretary of War	DANIEL S. LAMONT, 1893–7

Secretary of Navy	HILARY A. HERBERT, 1893–7
Secretary of Interior	HOKE SMITH, 1893–6
	DAVID R. FRANCIS, 1896–7
Secretary of Agriculture	J. STERLING MORTON, 1893–7
Postmaster General	WILSON S. BISSEL, 1893–5
	WILLIAM L. WILSON, 1895–7
Attorney General	RICHARD OLNEY, 1893–5
	JUDSON HARMON, 1895–7

WILLIAM McKINLEY 1897–1901
  GARRET A. HOBART
WILLIAM McKINLEY 1901
  THEODORE ROOSEVELT 1901

Secretary of State	JOHN SHERMAN, 1897–8
	WILLIAM R. DAY, 1898
	JOHN HAY, 1898–1901
Secretary of Treasury	LYMAN J. GAGE, 1897–1901
Secretary of War	RUSSELL A. ALGER, 1897–9
	ELIHU ROOT, 1899–1901
Secretary of Navy	JOHN D. LONG, 1897–1901
Secretary of Interior	CORNELIUS N. BLISS, 1897–9
	ETHAN A. HITCHCOCK, 1899–1901
Secretary of Agriculture	JAMES WILSON, 1897–1901
Postmaster General	JAMES A. GARY, 1897–8
	CHARLES E. SMITH, 1898–1901
Attorney General	JOSEPH McKENNA, 1897
	JOHN W. GRIGGS, 1897–1901
	PHILANDER C. KNOX, 1901

THEODORE ROOSEVELT 1901–05
THEODORE ROOSEVELT 1905–09
  CHARLES FAIRBANKS

Secretary of State	JOHN HAY, 1901–05
	ELIHU ROOT, 1905–09
	ROBERT BACON, 1909
Secretary of Treasury	LYMAN J. GAGE, 1901–02
	LESLIE M. SHAW, 1902–07
	GEORGE B. CORTELYOU, 1907–09
Secretary of War	ELIHU ROOT, 1901–04
	WILLIAM H. TAFT, 1904–08
	LUKE E. WRIGHT, 1908–09

Secretary of Navy	JOHN D. LONG, 1901–02
	WILLIAM H. MOODY, 1902–04
	PAUL MORTON, 1904–05
	CHARLES J. BONAPARTE, 1905–07
	VICTOR H. METCALF, 1907–08
	TRUMAN H. NEWBERRY, 1908–09
Secretary of Interior	ETHAN A. HITCHCOCK, 1901–07
	JAMES R. GARFIELD, 1907–09
Secretary of Agriculture	JAMES WILSON, 1901–09
Secretary of Commerce	
and Labor	GEORGE B. CORTELYOU, 1903–04
	VICTOR H. METCALF, 1904–06
	OSCAR S. STRAUS, 1907–09
Postmaster General	CHARLES E. SMITH, 1901–02
	HENRY C. PAYNE, 1902–04
	ROBERT J. WYNNE, 1904–05
	GEORGE B. CORTELYOU, 1905–07
	GEORGE VON L. MEYER, 1907–09
Attorney General	PHILANDER C. KNOX, 1901–04
	WILLIAM H. MOODY, 1904–06
	CHARLES J. BONAPARTE, 1906–09

WILLIAM H. TAFT 1909–13
JAMES S. SHERMAN

Secretary of State	PHILANDER C. KNOX, 1909–13
Secretary of Treasury	FRANKLIN MACVEAGH, 1909–13
Secretary of War	JACOB M. DICKINSON, 1909–11
	HENRY L. STIMSON, 1911–13
Secretary of Navy	GEORGE VON L. MEYER, 1909–13
Secretary of Interior	RICHARD A. BALLINGER, 1909–11
	WALTER L. FISHER, 1911–13
Secretary of Agriculture	JAMES WILSON, 1909–13
Secretary of Commerce	
and Labor	CHARLES NAGEL, 1909–13
Postmaster General	FRANK H. HITCHCOCK, 1909–13
Attorney General	GEORGE W. WICKERSHAM, 1909–13

WOODROW WILSON 1913–21
THOMAS R. MARSHALL

Secretary of State	WILLIAM J. BRYAN, 1913–15
	ROBERT LANSING, 1915–20
	BAINBRIDGE COLBY, 1920–1

Secretary of Treasury	WILLIAM G. MCADOO, 1913–19
	CARTER GLASS, 1919–20
	DAVID F. HOUSTON, 1920–1
Secretary of War	LINDLEY M. GARRISON, 1913–16
	NEWTON D. BAKER, 1916–21
Secretary of Navy	JOSEPHUS DANIELS, 1913–21
Secretary of Interior	FRANKLIN K. LANE, 1913–20
	JOHN B. PAYNE, 1920–1
Secretary of Agriculture	DAVID F. HOUSTON, 1913–20
	EDWARD T. MEREDITH, 1920–1
Secretary of Commerce	WILLIAM C. REDFIELD, 1913–19
	JOSHUA W. ALEXANDER, 1919–21
Secretary of Labor	WILLIAM B. WILSON, 1913–21
Postmaster General	ALBERT S. BURLESON, 1913–21
Attorney General	JAMES C. MCREYNOLDS, 1913–14
	THOMAS W. GREGORY, 1914–19
	A. MITCHELL PALMER, 1919–21

WARREN G. HARDING 1921–3
  CALVIN COOLIDGE

Secretary of State	CHARLES E. HUGHES, 1921–3
Secretary of Treasury	ANDREW W. MELLON, 1921–3
Secretary of War	JOHN W. WEEKS, 1921–3
Secretary of Navy	EDWIN DENBY, 1921–3
Secretary of Interior	ALBERT B. FALL, 1921–3
	HUBERT WORK, 1923
Secretary of Agriculture	HENRY C. WALLACE, 1921–3
Secretary of Commerce	HERBERT C. HOOVER, 1921–3
Secretary of Labor	JAMES J. DAVIS, 1921–3
Postmaster General	WILL H. HAYS, 1921–2
	HUBERT WORK, 1922–3
	HARRY S. NEW, 1923
Attorney General	HARRY M. DAUGHERTY, 1921–3

CALVIN COOLIDGE 1923–5
CALVIN COOLIDGE 1925–9
  CHARLES G. DAWES

Secretary of State	CHARLES E. HUGHES, 1923–5
	FRANK B. KELLOGG, 1925–9
Secretary of Treasury	ANDREW W. MELLON, 1923–9
Secretary of War	JOHN W. WEEKS, 1923–5
	DWIGHT F. DAVIS, 1925–9

Secretary of Navy	EDWIN DENBY, 1923-4
	CURTIS D. WILBUR, 1924-9
Secretary of Interior	HUBERT WORK, 1923-8
	ROY O. WEST, 1928-9
Secretary of Agriculture	HENRY C. WALLACE, 1923-4
	HOWARD M. GORE, 1924-5
	WILLIAM M. JARDINE, 1925-9
Secretary of Commerce	HERBERT C. HOOVER, 1923-5
	WILLIAM F. WHITING, 1925-9
Secretary of Labor	JAMES J. DAVIS, 1923-9
Postmaster General	HARRY S. NEW, 1923-9
Attorney General	HARRY M. DAUGHERTY, 1923-4
	HARLAN F. STONE, 1924-5
	JOHN D. SARGENT, 1925-9

HERBERT C. HOOVER 1929-33
  CHARLES CURTIS

Secretary of State	HENRY L. STIMSON, 1929-33
Secretary of Treasury	ANDREW W. MELLON, 1929-32
	OGDEN L. MILLS, 1932-3
Secretary of War	JAMES W. GOOD, 1929
	PATRICK J. HURLEY, 1929-33
Secretary of Navy	CHARLES F. ADAMS, 1929-33
Secretary of Interior	RAY L. WILBUR, 1929-33
Secretary of Agriculture	ARTHUR M. HYDE, 1929-33
Secretary of Commerce	ROBERT P. LAMONT, 1929-32
	ROY D. CHAPIN, 1932-3
Secretary of Labor	WILLIAM N. DOAK, 1930-3
Postmaster General	WALTER F. BROWN, 1929-33
Attorney General	WILLIAM D. MITCHELL, 1929-33

FRANKLIN DELANO ROOSEVELT 1933-41
  JOHN NANCE GARNER
FRANKLIN DELANO ROOSEVELT 1941-5
  HENRY A. WALLACE
FRANKLIN DELANO ROOSEVELT 1945
  HARRY S. TRUMAN

Secretary of State	CORDELL HULL, 1933-44
	EDWARD R. STETTINIUS, JR., 1944-5
Secretary of Treasury	WILLIAM H. WOODIN, 1933-4
	HENRY MORGENTHAU, JR., 1934-45

Secretary of War	GEORGE H. DERN, 1933–6
	HARRY H. WOODRING, 1936–40
	HENRY L. STIMSON, 1940–5
Secretary of Navy	CLAUDE A. SWANSON, 1933–40
	CHARLES EDISON, 1940
	FRANK KNOX, 1940–4
	JAMES V. FORRESTAL, 1944–5
Secretary of Interior	HAROLD L. ICKES, 1933–45
Secretary of Agriculture	HENRY A. WALLACE, 1933–40
	CLAUDE R. WICKARD, 1940–5
Secretary of Commerce	DANIEL C. ROPER, 1933–9
	HARRY L. HOPKINS, 1939–40
	JESSE JONES, 1940–5
	HENRY A. WALLACE, 1945
Secretary of Labor	FRANCES PERKINS, 1933–45
Postmaster General	JAMES A. FARLEY, 1933–40
	FRANK C. WALKER, 1940–5
Attorney General	HOMER S. CUMMINGS, 1933–9
	FRANK MURPHY, 1939–40
	ROBERT JACKSON, 1940–1
	FRANCIS BIDDLE, 1941–5

HARRY S. TRUMAN 1945–9
HARRY S. TRUMAN 1949–53
ALBEN W. BARKLEY

Secretary of State	JAMES F. BYRNES, 1945–7
	GEORGE C. MARSHALL, 1947–9
	DEAN G. ACHESON, 1949–53
Secretary of Treasury	FRED M. VINSON, 1945–6
	JOHN W. SNYDER, 1946–53
Secretary of War	ROBERT P. PATTERSON, 1945–7
	KENNETH C. ROYALL, 1947
Secretary of Navy	JAMES V. FORRESTAL, 1945–7
Secretary of Defense	JAMES V. FORRESTAL, 1947–9
	LOUIS A. JOHNSON, 1949–50
	GEORGE C. MARSHALL, 1950–1
	ROBERT A. LOVETT, 1951–3
Secretary of Interior	HAROLD L. ICKES, 1945–6
	JULIUS A. KRUG, 1946–9
	OSCAR L. CHAPMAN, 1949–53
Secretary of Agriculture	CLINTON P. ANDERSON, 1945–8
	CHARLES F. BRANNAN, 1948–53

Secretary of Commerce	W. AVERELL HARRIMAN, 1946–8
	CHARLES W. SAWYER, 1948–53
Secretary of Labor	LEWIS B. SCHWELLENBACH, 1945–8
	MAURICE J. TOBIN, 1948–53
Postmaster General	ROBERT E. HANNEGAN, 1945–7
	JESSE L. DONALDSON, 1947–53
Attorney General	TOM C. CLARK, 1945–9
	J. HOWARD McGRATH, 1949–52
	J. P. McGRANERY, 1952–3

DWIGHT D. EISENHOWER 1953–61
  RICHARD M. NIXON

Secretary of State	JOHN FOSTER DULLES, 1953–9
	CHRISTIAN HERTER, 1959–
Secretary of Treasury	GEORGE M. HUMPHREY, 1953–7
	ROBERT B. ANDERSON, 1957–
Secretary of Defense	CHARLES E. WILSON, 1953–7
	NEIL H. McELROY, 1957–60
	THOMAS GATES, 1960–
Secretary of Interior	DOUGLAS McKAY, 1953–6
	FRED A. SEATON, 1956–
Secretary of Agriculture	EZRA TAFT BENSON, 1953–
Secretary of Commerce	SINCLAIR WEEKS, 1953–9
	FREDERICK H. MUELLER, 1959–
Secretary of Labor	MARTIN P. DURKIN, 1953
	JAMES P. MITCHELL, 1953–
Secretary of Health, Education, and Welfare	OVETA CULP HOBBY, 1953–5
	MARION B. FOLSOM, 1955–8
	ARTHUR S. FLEMMING, 1958–
Postmaster General	ARTHUR E. SUMMERFIELD, 1953–
Attorney General	HERBERT BROWNELL, JR., 1953–7
	WILLIAM P. ROGERS, 1957–

V

Justices of The United States Supreme Court
1860-1960

Name (Chief Justices in Italics)	Service Term	Years
John McLean, Ohio	1829–1861	32
James M. Wayne, Ga.	1835–1867	32
Roger B. Taney, Md.	1836–1864	28
John Catron, Tenn.	1837–1865	28
Peter V. Daniel, Va.	1841–1860	19
Samuel Nelson, N. Y.	1845–1872	27
Robert C. Grier, Pa.	1846–1870	24
John A. Campbell, Ala.	1853–1861	8
Nathan Clifford, Me.	1858–1881	23
Noah H. Swayne, Ohio	1862–1881	20
Samuel F. Miller, Iowa	1862–1890	28
David Davis, Ill.	1862–1877	15
Stephen J. Field, Cal.	1863–1897	34
Salmon P. Chase, Ohio	1864–1873	9
William Strong, Pa.	1870–1880	10
Joseph P. Bradley, N. J.	1870–1892	22
Ward Hunt, N. Y.	1872–1882	10
Morrison R. Waite, Ohio	1874–1888	14
John M. Harlan, Ky.	1877–1911	34
William B. Woods, Ga.	1880–1887	7
Stanley Matthews, Ohio	1881–1889	8
Horace Gray, Mass.	1881–1902	21
Samuel Blatchford, N. Y.	1882–1893	11

Name (Chief Justices in Italics)	Service Term	Years
Lucius Q. C. Lamar, Miss.	1888–1893	5
Melville W. Fuller, Ill.	1888–1910	22
David J. Brewer, Kan.	1889–1910	21
Henry B. Brown, Mich.	1890–1906	16
George Shiras, Jr., Pa.	1892–1903	11
Howell E. Jackson, Tenn.	1893–1895	2
Edward D. White, La.	1894–1910	16
Rufus W. Peckham, N. Y.	1895–1910	14
Joseph McKenna, Cal.	1898–1925	27
Oliver W. Holmes, Mass.	1902–1932	29
William R. Day, Ohio	1903–1922	19
William H. Moody, Mass.	1906–1910	4
Horace H. Lurton, Tenn.	1910–1914	5
Charles E. Hughes, N. Y.	1910–1916	6
Willis Van Devanter, Wyo.	1911–1937	26
Joseph R. Lamar, Ga.	1911–1916	6
Edward D. White, La.	1910–1921	11
Mahlon Pitney, N. J.	1912–1922	12
Jas. C. McReynolds, Tenn.	1914–1941	27
Louis D. Brandeis, Mass.	1916–1939	23
John H. Clark, Ohio	1916–1922	6
William H. Taft, Conn.	1921–1930	9
George Sutherland, Utah	1922–1938	16
Pierce Butler, Minn.	1922–1939	17
Edward T. Sanford, Tenn.	1923–1930	7
Harlan F. Stone, N. Y.	1925–1941	16
Charles E. Hughes, N. Y.	1930–1941	11
Owen J. Roberts, Pa.	1930–1945	15
Benjamin N. Cardozo, N. Y.	1932–1938	6
Hugo Black, Ala.	1937–	
Stanley Reed, Ky.	1938–1957	19
Felix Frankfurter, Mass.	1939–	
William O. Douglas, Conn.	1939–	
Frank Murphy, Mich.	1940–1949	9
Harlan F. Stone, N. Y.	1941–1946	5
James F. Byrnes, S. C.	1941–1942	2
Robert H. Jackson, N. Y.	1941–1954	13
Wiley B. Rutledge, Iowa	1943–1949	6
Harold H. Burton, Ohio	1945–1958	13

Fred M. Vinson, Ky.	1946–1953	7
Thomas C. Clark, Texas	1949–	
Sherman Minton, Ind.	1949–1956	7
Earl Warren, Cal.	1953–	
John Harlan, N. Y.	1955–	
William J. Brennan, Jr., N. J.	1956–	
Charles E. Whittaker, Md.	1957–	
Potter Stewart, Ohio	1958–	

VI

Statistical Tables

United States Population 1860-1950

DIVISION AND STATE	1860	1870	1880	1890	1900	1910	1920	1930	1940	1950
United States	31,443,321	39,818,449	50,155,783	62,947,714	75,994,575	91,972,266	105,710,620	122,775,046	131,669,275	150,697,361
New England	3,135,283	3,487,924	4,010,529	4,700,749	5,592,017	6,552,681	7,400,909	8,166,341	8,437,290	9,314,453
Maine	628,279	626,915	648,936	661,086	694,466	742,371	768,014	797,423	847,226	913,774
New Hampshire	326,073	318,300	346,991	376,530	411,588	430,572	443,083	465,293	491,524	533,242
Vermont	315,098	330,551	332,286	332,422	343,641	355,956	352,428	359,611	359,231	377,747
Massachusetts	1,231,066	1,457,351	1,783,085	2,238,947	2,805,346	3,366,416	3,852,356	4,249,614	4,316,721	4,690,514
Rhode Island	174,620	217,353	276,531	345,506	428,556	542,610	604,397	687,497	713,346	791,896
Connecticut	460,147	537,454	622,700	746,258	908,420	1,114,756	1,380,631	1,606,903	1,709,242	2,007,280
Middle Atlantic	7,458,985	8,810,806	10,496,878	12,706,220	15,454,678	19,315,892	22,261,144	26,260,750	27,539,487	30,163,533
New York	3,880,735	4,382,759	5,082,871	6,003,174	7,268,894	9,113,614	10,385,227	12,588,066	13,479,142	14,830,192
New Jersey	672,035	906,096	1,131,116	1,444,933	1,883,669	2,537,167	3,155,900	4,041,334	4,160,165	4,835,329
Pennsylvania	2,906,215	3,521,951	4,282,891	5,258,113	6,302,115	7,665,111	8,720,017	9,631,350	9,900,180	10,498,012
East North Central	6,926,884	9,124,517	11,206,668	13,478,305	15,985,581	18,250,621	21,475,543	25,297,185	26,626,342	30,399,368
Ohio	2,339,511	2,665,260	3,198,062	3,672,329	4,157,545	4,767,121	5,759,394	6,646,697	6,907,612	7,946,627
Indiana	1,350,428	1,680,637	1,978,301	2,192,404	2,516,462	2,700,876	2,930,390	3,238,503	3,427,796	3,934,224
Illinois	1,711,951	2,539,891	3,077,871	3,826,352	4,821,550	5,638,591	6,485,280	7,630,654	7,897,241	8,712,176
Michigan	749,113	1,184,059	1,636,937	2,093,890	2,420,982	2,810,173	3,668,412	4,842,325	5,256,106	6,371,766
Wisconsin	775,881	1,054,670	1,315,497	1,693,330	2,069,042	2,333,860	2,632,067	2,939,006	3,137,587	3,434,576
West North Central	2,169,832	3,856,594	6,157,443	8,932,112	10,347,423	11,637,921	12,544,249	13,296,915	13,516,990	14,061,394
Minnesota	172,023	439,706	780,773	1,310,283	1,751,394	2,075,708	2,387,125	2,563,953	2,792,300	2,982,483
Iowa	674,913	1,194,020	1,624,615	1,912,297	2,231,853	2,224,771	2,404,021	2,470,939	2,538,268	2,621,973
Missouri	1,182,012	1,721,295	2,168,380	2,679,185	3,106,665	3,293,335	3,404,055	3,629,367	3,784,664	3,954,653
North Dakota		2,405	36,909	190,983	319,146	577,056	646,872	680,845	641,935	619,636
South Dakota	4,837	11,776	98,268	348,600	401,570	583,888	636,547	692,849	642,961	652,740
Nebraska	28,841	122,993	452,402	1,062,656	1,066,300	1,192,214	1,296,372	1,377,963	1,315,834	1,325,510
Kansas	107,206	364,399	996,096	1,428,108	1,479,495	1,690,949	1,769,257	1,880,999	1,801,028	1,905,299

South Atlantic	**5,364,703**	**5,853,610**	**7,597,197**	**8,857,922**	**10,443,480**	**12,194,895**	**13,990,272**	**15,703,589**	**17,823,151**	**21,182,335**
Delaware	112,216	125,015	146,608	168,493	184,735	202,322	223,003	238,380	266,505	318,085
Maryland	687,049	780,894	934,943	1,042,390	1,188,044	1,295,346	1,449,661	1,631,526	1,821,244	2,343,001
Dist. of Columbia	75,080	131,700	177,624	230,392	278,718	331,069	437,571	486,869	663,091	802,178
Virginia	1,596,318	1,225,163	1,512,565	1,655,980	1,854,184	2,061,612	2,309,187	2,421,851	2,677,773	3,318,680
West Virginia		442,014	618,457	762,794	958,800	1,221,119	1,463,701	1,729,205	1,901,974	2,005,552
North Carolina	992,622	1,071,361	1,399,750	1,617,949	1,893,810	2,206,287	2,559,123	3,170,276	3,571,623	4,061,929
South Carolina	703,708	705,606	995,577	1,151,149	1,340,316	1,515,400	1,683,724	1,738,765	1,899,804	2,117,027
Georgia	1,057,286	1,184,109	1,542,180	1,837,353	2,216,331	2,609,121	2,895,832	2,908,506	3,123,723	3,444,578
Florida	140,424	187,748	269,493	391,422	528,542	752,619	968,470	1,468,211	1,897,414	2,771,305
East South Central	**4,020,991**	**4,404,445**	**5,585,151**	**6,429,154**	**7,547,757**	**8,409,901**	**8,893,307**	**9,887,214**	**10,778,225**	**11,477,181**
Kentucky	1,155,684	1,321,011	1,648,690	1,858,635	2,147,174	2,289,905	2,416,630	2,614,589	2,845,627	2,944,806
Tennessee	1,109,801	1,258,520	1,542,359	1,767,518	2,020,616	2,184,789	2,337,885	2,616,556	2,915,841	3,291,718
Alabama	964,201	996,992	1,262,505	1,513,401	1,828,697	2,138,093	2,348,174	2,646,248	2,832,961	3,061,743
Mississippi	791,305	827,922	1,131,597	1,289,600	1,551,270	1,797,114	1,790,618	2,009,821	2,183,796	2,178,914
West South Central	**1,747,667**	**2,029,965**	**3,334,220**	**4,740,983**	**6,532,290**	**8,784,534**	**10,242,224**	**12,176,830**	**13,064,525**	**14,537,572**
Arkansas	435,450	484,471	802,525	1,128,211	1,311,564	1,574,449	1,752,204	1,854,482	1,949,387	1,909,511
Louisiana	708,002	726,915	939,946	1,118,588	1,381,625	1,656,388	1,798,509	2,101,593	2,363,880	2,683,516
Oklahoma				258,657	790,391	1,657,155	2,028,283	2,396,040	2,336,434	2,233,351
Texas	604,215	818,579	1,591,749	2,235,527	3,048,710	3,896,542	4,663,228	5,824,715	6,414,824	7,711,194
Mountain	**174,923**	**315,385**	**653,119**	**1,213,935**	**1,674,657**	**2,633,517**	**3,336,101**	**3,701,789**	**4,150,003**	**5,074,998**
Montana		20,595	39,159	142,924	243,329	376,053	548,889	537,606	559,456	591,024
Idaho		14,999	32,610	88,548	161,772	325,594	431,866	445,032	524,873	588,637
Wyoming		9,118	20,789	62,555	92,531	145,965	194,402	225,565	250,742	290,529
Colorado	34,277	39,864	194,327	413,249	539,700	799,024	939,629	1,035,791	1,123,296	1,325,089
New Mexico	93,516	91,874	119,565	160,282	195,310	327,301	360,350	423,317	531,818	681,187
Arizona		9,658	40,440	88,243	122,931	204,354	334,162	435,573	499,261	749,587
Utah	40,273	86,786	143,963	210,779	276,749	373,351	449,396	507,847	550,310	688,862
Nevada	6,857	42,491	62,266	47,355	42,335	81,875	77,407	91,058	110,247	160,083
Pacific	**444,053**	**675,125**	**1,114,578**	**1,888,334**	**2,416,692**	**4,192,304**	**5,566,871**	**8,194,433**	**9,733,262**	**14,486,527**
Washington	11,594	23,955	75,116	357,232	518,103	1,141,990	1,356,621	1,563,396	1,736,191	2,378,963
Oregon	52,465	90,923	174,768	317,704	413,536	672,765	783,389	953,786	1,089,684	1,521,341
California	379,994	560,247	864,694	1,213,398	1,485,053	2,377,549	3,426,861	5,677,251	6,907,387	10,586,223

Immigration, by Country of Origin, (by decades) 1851-1950

COUNTRY	1851–60	1861–70	1871–80	1881–90	1891–1900	1901–10	1911–20	1921–30	1931–40	1941–50
All countries, total	2,598,214	2,314,824	2,812,191	5,246,613	3,687,564	8,795,386	5,735,811	4,107,209	528,431	1,035,039
Europe, total	2,452,660	2,065,270	2,272,262	4,737,046	3,558,978	8,136,016	4,376,564	2,477,853	348,289	621,704
Belgium	4,738	6,734	7,221	20,177	18,167	41,635	33,746	15,846	4,817	12,189
Bulgaria					160	39,280	22,533	2,945	938	375
Czechoslovakia							3,426	102,194	14,393	8,347
Denmark	3,749	17,094	31,771	88,132	50,231	65,285	41,983	32,430	2,559	5,393
Eire	914,119	435,778	436,871	655,482	388,416	339,065	146,181	220,591	10,973	27,503
Northern Ireland	(incl. above)								2,194	......
Finland							756	16,691	2,146	2,503
France	76,358	35,986	72,206	50,464	30,770	73,379	61,897	49,610	12,623	38,809
Germany	951,667	787,468	718,182	1,452,970	505,152	341,498	143,945	412,202	117,621	226,578
Austria		7,800	72,969	353,719	592,707	2,145,266	453,649	32,868		24,860
Hungary		(incl. Austria)					442,693	30,680	7,861	3,469
Great Britain:										
England	247,125	222,277	437,706	644,680	216,726	388,017	249,944	157,420	21,756	112,252
Scotland	38,331	38,769	87,564	149,869	44,188	120,469	78,357	159,781	6,887	16,131
Wales	6,319	4,313	6,631	12,640	10,557	17,464	13,107	13,012	735	3,209
United Kingdom not specified	132,199	341,537	16,142	168	67					
Greece	31	72	210	2,308	15,979	167,519	184,201	51,084	9,119	8,973

	1	2	3	4	5	6	7	8	9	10
Italy	9,231	11,725	55,759	307,309	651,893	2,045,877	1,109,524	455,315	68,028	57,661
Netherlands	10,789	9,102	16,541	53,701	26,758	48,262	43,718	26,948	7,150	14,860
Norway	20,931	71,631	95,323	176,586	95,015	190,505	66,395	68,531	4,740	10,100
Sweden		37,667	115,922	391,776	226,266	249,534	95,074	97,249	3,960	10,665
Poland	1,164	2,027	12,970	51,806	96,720	69,149	4,813	227,734	17,026	7,571
Portugal	1,055	2,658	14,082	16,978	27,508	53,008	89,732	29,994	3,329	7,423
Rumania			11	6,348	12,750		13,311	67,646	3,871	1,076
Soviet Union (Russia)	457	2,512	39,284	213,282	595,290	1,597,306	921,201	61,742	1,356	548
Spain	9,298	6,697	5,266	4,419	8,731	27,935	68,611	28,958	3,258	2,898
Switzerland	25,011	23,286	28,293	81,988	31,179	34,922	23,091	29,676	5,512	10,547
Turkey in Europe	83	129	337	1,562	3,626	79,976	54,677	14,659	737	580
Yugoslavia							1,888	49,064	5,835	1,576
Other Europe	5	8	1,001	682	122	665	8,111	22,983	8,865	5,668
Asia, total	**41,455**	**64,630**	**123,823**	**68,380**	**71,236**	**243,567**	**192,559**	**97,400**	**15,344**	**31,780**
China	41,397	64,301	123,201	61,711	14,799	20,605	21,278	29,907	4,928	16,709
Japan		186	149	2,270	25,942	129,797	83,837	33,462	1,948	1,555
Turkey in Asia	58	2	67	2,220	26,799	77,393	79,389	19,165	328	218
Other Asia		141	406	2,179	3,696	15,772	8,955	14,866	8,140	13,298
America, total	**74,720**	**166,607**	**404,044**	**426,967**	**38,972**	**361,888**	**1,143,671**	**1,516,716**	**160,037**	**354,804**
Canada and Newfoundland	59,309	153,878	383,640	393,304	3,311	179,226	742,185	924,515	108,527	171,698
Mexico	3,078	2,191	5,162	1,913	971	49,642	219,004	459,287	22,319	60,589
Central America	449	95	157	404	549	8,192	17,159	15,769	5,861	21,601
South America	1,224	1,397	1,128	2,304	1,075	17,280	41,899	42,215	7,803	21,831
West Indies	10,660	9,046	13,957	29,042	33,066	107,548	123,424	74,899	15,502	49,745
Other America								31	25	29,340
Africa	210	312	358	857	350	7,368	8,443	6,286	1,750	7,367
Australia, Tasmania, and New Zealand	36	36	9,886	7,017	2,740	11,975	12,348	8,299	2,231	13,805
Pacific Islands (not specified)			1,028	5,557	1,225	1,049	1,079	427	780	5,437
All other countries	29,169	17,969	790	789	14,063	33,523	1,147	228		142

Federal Expenditures and Gross Debt, 1861-1958
(yearly average)

PERIOD	EXPENDITURES (millions of dollars)							GROSS DEBT	
	Total	War Dept.	Navy	Indians	Veterans' Pensions	Interest on the Public Debt	All Other	Amount (millions of dollars)	Per Capita (dollars)
1861–65	684	548	65	3	5	35	28	2,678	75
1871–75	287	40	23	7	30	112	75	2,156	48
1881–85	258	43	16	7	58	64	70	1,579	28
1891–95	364	50	29	11	140	29	104	1,097	16
1901–05	536	133	86	12	140	28	136	1,132	13
1911–15	720	199	134	21	165	33	179	1,191	12
1921–25	3,579	540	428	42	245	974	1,350	20,516	177
1931–35	5,215	457	359	25	279	696	3,399	28,701	226
1941–45	64,243	32,144	17,673	30	515	2,081	11,800	258,682	1,853
		Army		Air Force					
1946–50	42,581	12,744	6,722		1,929	5,196	15,968	258,025	1,763
1951–55	63,216	13,222	9,798	13,274		6,146	20,777	265,206	1,660
1956*	66,540	9,274	9,744	16,750		6,787	23,986	272,751	1,622
1957	69,433	9,705	10,397	18,361		7,244	23,726	270,527	1,580
1958	71,936	9,776	10,913	18,437		7,607	25,203	276,343	1,588

* Year ending June 30.

Federal Receipts, and Surplus or Deficit, 1861-1958
(yearly average) (in millions of dollars)

PERIOD	Total		Customs	Internal Revenue		Sales of Public Lands†	Other Receipts	SURPLUS (+) or DEFICIT (−), Receipts Compared with Expenditures
	Net	Total		Income & Profits Taxes	Other			
1861-65	161	161	69	28	55	0.55	20	−523
1871-75	337	337	186	8	112	2	28	+50
1881-85	367	367	202	0.03	132	6	27	+109
1891-95	353	353	177	0.08	150	3	23	−11
1901-05	559	559	260		255	6	38	+23
1911-15	710	710	289	50	307	4	60	−10
1921-25	4,307	4,307	464	2,111	1,053	0.85	678	+728
1931-35	2,771	2,838	323	1,116	1,186	0.14	213	−2,444
1941-45	26,156	27,653	378	19,470	6,147	0.14	1,658	−38,087
1946-50	39,294	43,786	432	29,821	10,439		3,191	−3,287
1951-55	59,766	67,287	591	49,457	15,244		2,046	−3,450
1956*	68,165	78,820	705	56,633	18,476		3,006	+1,625
1957	71,029	83,675	754	60,560	19,612		2,749	+1,596
1958	69,117	83,974	800	59,102	20,877		3,196	−2,819

* Year ending June 30.
† Figures omitted after 1946.

Wholesale Price Indexes, by Major Commodity Groups, 1890-1958

Period	All Commodities	Farm Products	Foods	Hides and Leather Products	Textile Products	Fuel and Light	Metals and Metal Products	Building Materials	Chemicals and Allied Products	Home Furnishings	Misc.
					[Index: 1926 = 100]						
1890	56.2	50.4	55.5	47.5	57.8	38.1	105.3	46.5	73.2	49.9	97.9
1895	48.8	43.9	47.3	49.4	44.3	40.3	70.4	38.8	64.7	43.5	88.9
1900	56.1	50.5	50.8	49.4	53.3	46.3	98.0	46.2	82.1	48.9	102.0
1905	60.1	56.4	55.1	53.9	54.1	49.6	89.1	48.1	82.3	49.7	117.4
1910	70.4	74.3	64.9	60.2	58.4	47.6	85.2	55.3	82.0	54.0	152.7
1915	69.5	71.5	65.4	75.5	54.1	51.8	86.3	53.5	112.0	56.0	86.9
1920	154.4	150.7	137.4	171.3	164.8	163.7	149.4	150.1	164.7	141.8	167.5
1925	103.5	109.8	100.2	105.3	108.3	96.5	103.2	101.7	101.8	103.1	109.0
1929	95.3	104.9	99.9	109.1	90.4	83.0	100.5	95.4	94.0	94.3	82.6
1932	64.8	48.2	61.0	72.9	54.9	70.3	80.2	71.4	73.9	75.1	64.4
1935	80.0	78.8	83.7	89.6	70.9	73.5	86.4	85.3	79.0	80.6	68.3
1940	78.6	67.7	71.3	100.8	73.8	71.7	95.8	94.8	77.0	88.5	77.3
1945	105.8	128.2	106.2	118.1	100.1	84.0	104.7	117.8	95.2	104.5	94.7
					[Index: 1947-9 = 100]						
1950	103.1	97.5	98.5	104.6	99.2	103.0	110.3	109.5	96.3	105.3	96.6
1955	110.7	89.6	101.0	93.8	95.3	107.9	136.6	125.5	106.6	115.9	92.0
1958	119.2	94.9	109.5	100.6	93.5	112.7	150.4	130.5	110.4	123.2	94.2

Railroad Mileage 1870-1957

REGIONS	1870	1880	1890	1900	1910	1920	1930	1940	1948	1957
United States	**52,922**	**93,267**	**163,597**	**193,346**	**240,439**	**252,845**	**249,052**	**233,670**	**225,149**	**219,067**
New England	4,494	5,982	6,718	7,521	7,921	7,942	7,596	6,677	6,397	6,175
Middle Atlantic	9,709	13,832	18,161	20,709	21,980	22,293	21,752	20,175	19,291	17,892
South Atlantic	7,349	9,789	18,270	23,362	29,795	32,380	31,644	29,475	28,205	27,599
East North Central	14,701	25,109	36,924	41,007	44,928	44,904	43,770	41,281	39,946	39,154
West North Central	8,046	19,094	38,354	42,988	49,730	52,180	51,400	48,293	47,379	46,666
East South Central	4,656	6,343	11,144	13,343	17,074	17,754	17,452	16,179	15,602	15,368
West South Central	1,417	5,044	13,782	18,221	31,122	32,972	33,227	31,497	30,084	29,095
Mountain	1,466	5,082	12,676	15,808	22,956	25,170	24,973	23,518	22,286	21,412
Pacific	1,084	2,992	7,567	10,389	14,932	17,248	17,238	16,575	15,959	15,706
Alaska Territory					390	246	790	536	567	573
Hawaii Territory				22	175	243	232	192	25	25

Motor Vehicles: Factory Sales and Registrations 1900-58

YEAR	FACTORY SALES						REGISTRATION (*in thousands*)		
	Number (*in thousands*)			Wholesale Value (*millions of dollars*)			Total (excluding Publicly Owned)	Passenger Cars and Taxis	Motor Trucks and Buses
	Total	Passenger Cars	Motor Trucks	Total	Passenger Cars	Motor Trucks			
1900	4	4		4.9	4.9		8	8	
1905	25	24	1	40.0	38.7	1.3	79	77	1
1910	187	181	6	225.0	215.3	9.7	469	458	10
1915	970	896	74	701.8	576.0	125.8	2,491	2,332	159
1920	2,227	1,905	322	2,232.4	1,809.2	423.2	9,239	8,132	1,108
1925	4,266	3,735	531	2,916.8	2,458.4	458.4	19,941	17,440	2,501
1929	5,358	4,587	771	3,413.1	2,847.1	566.0	26,503	23,060	3,442
1930	3,356	2,785	571	2,034.8	1,645.4	389.4	26,532	22,973	3,559
1935	3,947	3,252	695	2,088.8	1,709.4	379.4	26,230	22,495	3,735
1940	4,472	3,717	755	2,938.5	2,370.7	567.8	32,035	27,372	4,663
1941	4,481	3,780	1,061	3,637.0	2,567.2	1,069.8	34,472	29,524	4,948
1944	738	1	738	1,701.4	0.5	1,700.9	30,086	25,466	4,620
1945	725	70	656	1,239.2	57.3	1,181.9	30,638	25,691	4,947
1946	3,090	2,149	941	3,023.0	1,979.8	1,043.2	33,946	28,100	5,846
1950	8,003	6666	1,337	10,176.0	8,468.0	1,708.0	49,162	40,334	8,828
1955	9,169	7,920	1,249	14,474.0	12,453.0	2,021.0	62,694	52,136	10,558
1958	5,135	4,258	877	9,729.0	8,010.0	1,719.0	68,299	56,871	11,428

The Labor Force 1870-1950

| YEAR | Population (millions) | All Occupations | | Non-Agricultural (millions) | Agricultural (millions) | WOMEN IN LABOR FORCE OR GAINFULLY OCCUPIED, 15 YEARS OLD AND OVER | | |
		Number (millions)	Percent of Population			Total Number (millions)	Married Number (millions)	Married Percent of Total
1870	29.1	12.9	44.4	6.1	6.8	3.7	0.5	13.9
1880	36.8	17.4	47.3	8.8	8.5	5.0	0.8	15.4
1890	47.4	23.3	49.2	13.4	9.9	7.6	1.9	24.7
1900	57.9	29.0	50.2	18.2	10.9	8.3	1.9	23.0
1910	71.6	37.3	52.2	25.8	11.6	10.6	3.1	28.9
1920	82.7	42.4	51.3	31.0	11.4	13.8	5.0	36.4
1930	98.7	48.8	49.5	38.3	10.5	17.7	9.3	52.5
1940	110.4	52.1	47.2	43.0	9.2			
1950	120.2	61.4	51.3	53.9	7.5			

Labor Union Membership 1931-56

YEAR	ALL UNIONS Membership (millions)	A.F.L. Number of Affiliated Unions	A.F.L. Total Membership (thousands)	C.I.O. Number of Affiliated Unions	C.I.O. Total Membership (thousands)	INDEPENDENT OR UNAFFILIATED UNIONS Membership (thousands)
1931	3.5	105	2890			636
1932	3.2	106	2532			694
1933	2.9	108	2127			730
1934	3.2	109	2608			641
1935	3.7	109	3045			683
1936	4.2	111	3422			742
1937	7.2	100	2861	32	3718	639
1938	8.3	102	3623	42	4038	604
1939	9.0	104	4006	45	4000	974
1940	8.9	105	4247	42	3625	1072
1941	10.5	106	4569	41	5000	920
1942	10.8	102	5483	39	4195	1084
1943	13.6	99	6564	40	5285	1793
1944	14.6	100	6807	41	5935	1879
1945	14.8	102	6931	40	6000	1865
1946	15.0	102	7152	40	6000	1822
1947	15.4	105	7578	41	6000	1836
1948	14.0–16.0	105	7221	40	5–6000*	18–2500
1949	14.0–16.0	107	7241	39	5–6000*	18–2500
1950	14.0–16.0	107	7143	30	5–6000*	24–2800
1951	16.5–17.0	108	7846	33	5000	20–2500
1952	16.5–17.0	109	8098	33	5000	20–2500
1953	17.9	110	10778	35	5252	1830
1954	18.0	109	10929	32	5200	1826
		A.F.L. — C.I.O.				
1955	17.7	139	16062			1688
1956	18.5	137	16904			1573

* Estimated.

BIBLIOGRAPHY

THE literature of American History is voluminous and constantly growing. This bibliography makes no pretense of being exhaustive and all-inclusive; only the most important and useful titles are cited. The list is intended for the convenience of students and others who desire wider knowledge of the topics discussed in the several chapters and sections of this book. To assist the reader further the list is preceded by citations of general works.

➤➤➤-➤➤➤-➤➤➤-➤➤➤-➤➤➤-➤➤➤-➤➤➤-➤➤➤

Bibliographical Guides

One of the most recent and valuable aids is H. P. Beers, *Bibliographies in American History: Guide to Materials for Research* (1942). Useful also are the annual volumes of bibliography sponsored by the American Historical Association and prepared by Grace G. Griffin and others under the title *Writings on American History* (1906-1938). W. H. Allison and others, *Guide to Historical Literature* (1931) is a general bibliography. Of the older bibliographies, the following are still authoritative: Edward Channing, A. B. Hart, and F. J. Turner, *Guide to the Study and Reading of American History* (1912) contains classified lists of books including general and special histories, geography, travel, biography, state and local history, literature, education, music, fine arts, and special topics relating to constitutional, diplomatic, economic, social and religious history. J. N. Larned (ed.), *Literature of American History* (1902) has signed evaluations or reviews of over 4,000 important books. A. P. C. Griffin, *Bibliography of American Historical Societies, The United States and the Dominion of Canada* (2nd ed., 1907) has tables of contents of all important historical societies in the United States from their foundation; it also has a subject index. It appeared as Volume II of the Annual Report of the American Historical Association in 1905. The most complete guide to American agricultural history is E. E. Edwards, *A Bibliography of the History of Agriculture in the United States* (1930).

The use of federal public documents published before 1881 is made laborious by the inadequacies of indexes. B. P. Poore, *A Descriptive Catalogue of the Government Publications of the United States, September 5, 1774–March 4, 1881* (1885) was published as Senate Miscellaneous Document No. 67, 48th Cong., 2 sess. Unfortunately, it is without subject entries. This difficulty was partially overcome when in 1902 there was published *Tables of and Annotated Index to Congressional Series of United States Public Documents*. J. G. Ames, *Comprehensive Index to the Publications of the United States Government, 1881–1893* (2 vols., 1905) appeared as *House Document* No. 754, 58 Cong. 2 sess. Since 1893, a separate index for each Congress has been published. For those interested in economic history, the most comprehensive guide to state documents is A. R. Hasse, *Index to Economic Material in Documents of the States of the United States* (13 vols., 1907-22). Also see Poole's *Index to Periodicals* (1893) and *Readers' Guide to Periodical Literature* (from 1901).

Dictionaries and Encyclopedias

Appleton's Cyclopedia of American Biography (1886–1922), though largely superseded by more recent works, is still useful. Allen Johnson and Dumas Malone (eds.), *Dictionary of American Biography* (20 vols., 1928–36), modeled after the *British Dictionary of National Biography*, contains 14,000 biographies of Americans with a bibliography at end of each biography and maintains high levels of scholarship and literary style. E. R. A. Seligman (ed.), *Encyclopaedia of the Social Sciences* (15 vols., 1930–5) should also be consulted by those interested in social and economic history. James T. Adams and R. V. Coleman (eds.), *Dictionary of American History* (6 vols., 1940) is a useful reference to anyone in search of specific facts, events, trends or policies relating to American history.

Periodicals

The American Historical Review (from 1895) is the organ of the American Historical Association founded in 1884. It reviews all new historical literature and in each of its quarterly issues prints important articles and documents. The following periodicals also include valuable book reviews as well as lists of current books and articles: *Annals* of the American Academy of Political and Social Science (from 1890), *Political Science Quarterly* (from 1886), *American Economic Review* (from 1911), *Journal of Economic History* (from 1941), and *Agricultural History* (from 1927). Of the many state, regional, or subject periodicals, the best are the *Mississippi Valley Historical Review* (from 1915), *The New England Quarterly* (from 1928), *New York History* (from 1919), *The William and Mary Quarterly* (from 1892), *The Pennsylvania Magazine of History and Biography* (from 1877), *Journal of Negro History* (from 1916), the *Proceedings and Collections of the Massachusetts Historical Society* (from 1791), the *Proceedings of the American Antiquarian Society* (from 1812), *Journal of Southern History* (from 1935), *Catholic Historical Review* (from 1915).

Geographical Background

R. H. Brown, *Historical Geography of the United States* (1948); E. C. Semple, *American History and Its Geographic Conditions* (revd. 1933); and A. P. Brigham, *Geographic Influences in American History* (1903) are pioneer works still standard. Isaiah Bowman, *Forest Physiography* (1911) and J. R. Smith, *North America* (1942) are the best descriptive accounts of the geography of the United States. Isaiah Bowman, *The New World* (1928) and N. S. Shaler (ed.), *The United States of America* (2 vols., 1894) stress the relation of geography to economics and history. A. B. Hulbert, *Soil* (1930) traces its influence on American history; his *Historic Highways of America* (16 vols., 1902–05) is a monographic collection on the great rivers and highways of the United States. Constance L. Skinner (ed.), *The Rivers of America* (1937–   ) interprets parts of our history against a geographical background. The three most usable historical atlases are D. R. Fox, *Harpers Atlas of American History* (1920); C. O. Paullin, *Atlas of the Historical Geography of the United States* (1932); and C. L. and E. H. Lord, *Historical Atlas of the United States* (1944). Those interested in maps should also consult E. M. Avery, *A History of the United States* (7 vols., 1904–10).

Comprehensive Histories of the United States

No individual work of a comprehensive nature covers the history of the United States from its beginning to the present; only cooperative undertakings have succeeded in this enterprise. The outstanding effort by an individual is Edward Channing *A History of the United States* (6 vols., 1905–25), which carries the story to 1865. Based on source materials and singularly free from inaccuracies, this work is most dependable. During the twentieth century, cooperative histories of the United States have increased in number. The first important series to appear was A. B. Hart (ed.), *The American Nation: A History* (28 vols., 1904–18). Volumes are uneven in content, but each contains excellent maps and bibliography; a new series of this work is now being prepared under the editorship of H. S. Commager. Another cooperative enterprise in historical writing is Allen Johnson and Allan Nevins (eds.), *Chronicles of America* (56 vols., 1918–51). These volumes though short and popular in literary style are, with some exceptions, scholarly and cover all phases of American history through the administration of Franklin D. Roosevelt; this series is uneven in merit. A. M. Schlesinger and D. R. Fox (eds.), *A History of American Life* (13 vols., 1927–48) with its emphasis upon social and intellectual rather than political history is unquestionably the most important work of its kind to date; it is especially valuable for bibliography. Henry David and others (eds.), *The Economic History of the United States* (9 vols., 1945–   ), now in progress, will be extremely useful for the history of the economic development of the United States. R. E. Spiller and others, *Literary History of the United States* (3 vols., 1948) is a major cooperative effort with a comprehensive bibliography constituting the third volume. R. H. Gabriel (ed.), *The Pageant of America* (15 vols., 1925–9) is a successful cooperative attempt to present the story of the United States through pictures and other graphic material. It should be supplemented by J. T. Adams (ed.), *Album of American History* (4 vols., 1944–8); Stefan Lorant, *The Presidency: A Pictorial History of Presidential Executives from Washington to Truman* (1951); and Marshall Davidson, *Life in America* (2 vols., 1951). The outstanding comprehensive interpretative work covering the entire period is C. A. and M. R. Beard, *The Rise of American Civilization: I, The Agricultural Era* (rev., 1933); *II, The Industrial Era* (rev., 1933); *III, America in Midpassage* (1939); *IV, The American Spirit* (1942). More factual but also interpretative is Joseph Dorfman, *The Economic Mind in American Civilization* (3 vols., 1946–9), which has detailed bibliography. In the field of biography, *The American Statesman* series (40 vols., 1898–1917), edited by John T. Morse, Jr., is comprehensive, but uneven; a new edition of this work is now being prepared under the editorship of Oscar Handlin.

Important for the colonial period are: H. L. Osgood, *The American Colonies in the Seventeenth Century* (3 vols., 1904–07) and *The American Colonies in the Eighteenth Century* (4 vols., 1924–5); C. M. Andrews, *The Colonial Period of American History* (4 vols., 1934–8); George Bancroft, *History of the United States* (10 vols., 1834–75). Bancroft catches the buoyant spirit of America, but his treatment is somewhat partisan and provincial. J. A. Doyle, *English Colonies in America* (5 vols., 1882–1907) best represents the English viewpoint. Osgood is excellent on the development of colonial political institutions. Another comprehensive work of great value is L. H. Gipson, *The British Empire before the American Revolution* (1936–   ). To date, seven volumes have been published.

Of the general histories of the United States during the period from the Revolution to 1865, the following should be consulted: James Schouler, *History of the United States of America, Under the Constitution* (7 vols., 1880–1913). Though biased and somewhat antiquated and peculiar in style, it contains much that is extremely valuable on political and constitutional matters. John B. McMaster, *A History of the People of the United States, from the Revolution to the Civil War* (8 vols., 1883–1913), which covers the years 1784–1861 is rich in social and economic facts and records obtained largely from newspapers and other contemporary sources; it is badly organized, however, and is difficult to read consecutively. It is supplemented by a ninth volume, *A History of the People of the United States during Lincoln's Administration* (1927). E. P. Oberholtzer, *A History of the*

United States Since the Civil War (5 vols., 1917–37) continues the work of McMaster and brings the story to 1901. Henry Adams, *History of the United States of America During the Administrations of Jefferson and Madison* (9 vols., 1889–91), covers the administrations of Jefferson and Madison. The first volume contains a valuable account of the state of society in 1800. Herbert Agar (ed.), *The Formative Years* (2 vols., 1947) is a convenient condensation of this famous work. See also Richard Hildreth, *The History of the United States of America* (6 vols., 1856–60), and Hermann von Holst, *Constitutional and Political History of the United States* (new ed., 8 vols., 1899). The first five volumes of J. R. Rhodes, *History of the United States from the Compromise of 1850* (9 vols., 1893–1919) give a detailed account of the causes and events of the Civil War. The same period is now being re-examined by Allan Nevins. To date, four volumes have been published: *Ordeal of the Union* (2 vols., 1947); *The Emergence of Lincoln* (2 vols., 1950). Admirable in almost every respect, these four volumes cover the years 1847 through 1861.

Source Materials

There is no lack of collections of source materials. The following are commended: H. S. Commager (ed.), *Documents of American History* (5th ed., 1949), excellent for political and constitutional sources; so also is William McDonald, *Documentary Source Book of American History, 1606–1926* (3rd ed., 1926). L. M. Hacker and H. S. Zahler, *The Shaping of the American Tradition* (2 vols., 1947) contains a voluminous amount of social, economic, and cultural material that is most illuminating; H. S. Commager and Allan Nevins (eds.), *The Heritage of America* (rev. ed., 1949) contains good materials on American social development; extremely useful are A. B. Hart (ed.), *American History Told by Contemporaries* (5 vols., 1897–1929) and Willard Thorp, M. E. Curti, and Carlos Baker (eds.), *American Issues* (2 vols., 1941). The principal source books on economic history are G. S. Callender, *Selections from the Economic History of the United States, 1765–1860* (1909), which has excellent introductory essays; E. L. Bogart and C. M. Thompson, *Readings in the Economic History of the United States* (1916); and F. Flügel and H. U. Faulkner, *Readings in the Economic and Social History of the United States* (1929). Those wishing source material on other special subjects should consult R. J. Bartlett, *The Record of American Diplomacy* (1947); I. F. Woestemeyer and J. M. Gambrill, *The Westward Movement* (1939); and L. B. Schmidt and E. D. Ross, *Readings in the Economic History of American Agriculture* (1925).

Special Phases of American Development

Useful on certain phases of American history are the following books:

1. ECONOMIC HISTORY. E. C. Kirkland, *A History of American Economic Life* (rev. ed., 1939); H. U. Faulkner, *American Economic History* (6th ed., 1949); E. L. Bogart and D. L. Kemmerer, *Economic History of the American People* (rev. ed., 1947); B. and L. M. Mitchell, *American Economic History* (1947); F. A. Shannon, *America's Economic Growth* (3rd ed., 1951) and C. W. Wright, *Economic History of the United States* (rev. ed., 1949) are the best of the one-volume economic histories. Several aspects of American economic history are treated in the volumes published by the Carnegie Institute of Washington. Though inadequate and uneven in merit, they are still very useful: E. R. Johnson et al., *History of Domestic and Foreign Commerce of the United States* (2 vols., 1915); B. H. Meyer et al., *History of Transportation in the United States Before 1860* (1917); F. W. Taussig, *The Tariff History of the United States* (8th ed., 1931); V. S.

Clark, *History of Manufactures in the United States* (new ed., 3 vols., 1929); P. W. Bidwell and J. A. Falconer, *History of Agriculture in the Northern United States, 1620–1860* (1925) and L. C. Gray, *History of Agriculture in the Southern United States to 1860* (2 vols., 1933). All of these works have extensive bibliographies.

2. FINANCIAL HISTORY. D. R. Dewey, *Financial History of the United States,* (12th ed., 1936) is the standard authority. It should be supplemented by W. J. Schultz and M. R. Caine, *Financial Development of the United States* (1937).

3. AGRICULTURE AND LAND POLICIES. The definitive history of American agriculture is yet to be written. Joseph Schafer, *The Social History of American Agriculture* (1936) is a brief outline. An older work is A. H. Sanford, *The Story of Agriculture in the United States* (1916). Far more satisfactory is E. E. Edwards, "American Agriculture—The First 300 Years," United States Department of Agriculture, *Yearbook* (1940). The newest treatise on public lands is R. M. Robbins, *Our Landed Heritage: The Public Domain, 1776–1936* (1942). An older work is B. H. Hibbard, *A History of the Public Land Policies* (1924). For a mass of undigested factual information, consult Thomas Donaldson, *The Public Domain* (1884).

4. IMMIGRATION. The best accounts are M. L. Hansen, *The Immigrant in American History* (1940) and *The Atlantic Migration, 1607–1860* (1940); J. R. Commons, *Races and Immigrants in America* (new ed., 1920); and G. M. Stephenson, *A History of American Immigration, 1820–1924* (1926). M. R. Davie, *World Immigration* (1936) gives valuable comparative material, a helpful list of immigrant biographies, and considerable literary material treating immigrants and immigration; Edith Abbott, *Historical Aspects of the Immigration Problem: Select Documents* (1926) also contains valuable source material. See also Carl Wittke, *We Who Built America* (1948) and Oscar Handlin's excellent *The Uprooted: The Epic Story of the Great Migrations that Made the American People* (1951).

5. CONSTITUTIONAL HISTORY. Consult A. C. McLaughlin, *A Constitutional History of the United States* (1935); C. B. Swisher, *American Constitutional Development* (1943); H. C. Hockett, *The Constitutional History of the United States, 1776–1876* (2 vols., 1939); B. F. Wright, *The Growth of American Constitutional Law* (1942); A. H. Kelly and W. A. Harbison, *The American Constitution, Its Origins and Development* (1948); and R. L. Schuyler, *The Constitution of the United States* (1923).

6. FOREIGN RELATIONS. T. A. Bailey, *A Diplomatic History of the American People* (4th ed., 1950) and S. F. Bemis, *The Diplomatic History of the United States* (rev. ed., 1948) are standard one-volume surveys. There is a wealth of material in S. F. Bemis (ed.), *The American Secretaries of State and Their Diplomacy* (10 vols., 1927–9). For our relations with Canada, see J. T. Shotwell (ed.), *The Relation of Canada with the United States* (14 vols., 1939). The best collection of treaties in convenient form is W. M. Malloy, *Treaties, Conventions, International Acts, Protocols, and Agreements between the United States and Other Powers 1776–1937* (4 vols., 1910–37). The documentary history of foreign relations is available in the following government compilations: *Diplomatic Correspondence of the United States, 1783–1789* (7 vols., 1833–4); American State Papers, *Foreign Relations 1789–1828* (6 vols., 1832–61); and since 1870, *Papers Relating to the Foreign Relations of the United States,* in one or more annual volumes. Between 1828 and 1860, the papers on foreign relations of the United States have not been collected and are to be found only in congressional documents. From 1860 to 1870, they were published annually under various titles. Students of foreign relations will find rich material in J. B. Moore, *History and Digest of the International Arbitrations to which the United States has been a Party* (6 vols., 1898), and *A Digest of International Law* (8 vols., 1906).

7. MILITARY AND NAVAL HISTORY. Few comprehensive accounts of these aspects of American history have as yet been written. Consult O. L. Spaulding, *The*

United States Army in War and Peace (1937); H. and M. Sprout, *The Rise of American Naval Power, 1776–1918* (1939); C. S. Alden and A. Westcott, *The United States Navy* (1943); D. W. Knox, *A History of the United States Navy* (1948); and C. H. Metcalf, *A History of the United States Marine Corps* (1939). Among the many works dealing with wars to which the United States has been a party the following may be cited: V. J. Esposito, *The West Point Atlas of American Wars* (2 vols., 1959), an exceedingly valuable general atlas of all our wars. On the War of Independence: C. F. Adams, *Studies Military and Diplomatic, 1775–1865* (1911); G. W. Allen, *A Naval History of the American Revolution* (2 vols., 1913); W. M. Wallace, *Appeal to Arms* (1951). The War of 1812: A. T. Mahan, *Sea Power in Its Relations to the War of 1812* (2 vols., 1905); C. P. Lucas, *The Canadian War of 1812* (1906). Mexican War; R. S. Henry, *The Story of the Mexican War* (1950); J. H. Smith, *The War with Mexico* (2 vols., 1919). Civil War: J. C. Ropes and W. R. Livermore, *The Story of the Civil War* (4 vols., 1894–1913); J. G. Randall, *Civil War and Reconstruction* (1937); F. A. Shannon, *The Organization and Administration of the Union Army* (2 vols., 1928); R. S. Henry, *Story of the Confederacy* (1931); D. S. Freeman, *R. E. Lee, A Biography* (4 vols., 1934–7) and by the same author, *Lee's Lieutenants* (3 vols., 1942–4) and *Lee's Dispatches to Davis* (1915); J. T. Scharf, *History of the Confederate States Navy* (1886); D. D. Porter, *The Naval History of the Civil War* (1887); J. P. Baxter, III, *The Introduction of the Ironclad Warship* (1933); H. S. Commager, *The Blue and the Gray* (2 vols., 1950).

8. TRAVEL AND TRAVELERS' DESCRIPTIONS. The best anthologies of travelers' accounts are H. S. Commager, *America in Perspective* (1947) and Oscar Handlin, *This Was America* (1949). Also consult J. L. Mesick, *The English Traveler in America, 1785–1835* (1922); Allan Nevins, *America Through British Eyes* (1948); H. T. Tuckerman, *America and Her Commentators* (1864); Frank Monaghan, *French Travelers in the United States, 1765–1832* (1933); R. G. Thwaites (ed.), *Early Western Travels* (32 vols., 1904–7) and S. J. Buck, *Travel and Description, 1765–1865* (1914). On conditions of travel, consult Seymour Dunbar, *A History of Travel in America* (4 vols., 1915).

9. EDUCATION. An older text is E. P. Cubberly, *Public Education in the United States* (1919). It should be supplemented by Paul Monroe (ed.), *A Cyclopedia of Education* (5 vols., 1911–13). Useful also are M. E. Curti, *The Social Ideas of American Educators* (1935); E. W. Knight, *Education in the United States* (rev. ed., 1941); E. G. Dexter, *A History of Education in the United States* (1922); C. F. Thwing, *A History of Higher Education in America* (1906); T. A. Woody, *A History of Women's Education in the United States* (2 vols., 1929); and C. G. Woodson, *The Education of the Negro Prior to 1861* (1915).

10. THE FINE ARTS AND MUSIC. For architecture, consult Sahdkichi Hartmann, *A History of American Art* (2 vols., 1902); C. H. Caffin, *The Story of American Painting* (1907); Eugen Neuhaus, *The History and Ideals of American Art* (1931); Alan Burroughs, *Limners and Likenesses: Three Centuries of American Painting* (1936); J. T. Flexner, *America's Old Masters* (1939); Samuel Isham and Royal Cortissoz, *The History of American Painting* (new ed., 1936); Jerome Mellquist, *The Emergence of an American Art* (1942); Homer St. Gaudens, *The American Artist and His Times* (1941); and Oliver W. Larkin, *Art and Life in America* (1949). The beginnings of American sculpture are appraised in Lorado Taft, *The History of American Sculpture* (rev. ed., 1924) and W. H. Downes, *The Life and Works of Winslow Homer* (1911). The most useful surveys of American music are L. C. Elson, *The History of American Music* (rev. ed., 1925) and J. T. Howard, *Our American Music* (1931). They may be supplemented by H. C. Lahee, *Annals of Music in America* (1922); T. F. Hamlin, *The American Spirit in Architecture* (1926); Lewis Mumford, *Sticks and Stones: A Study of American Architecture and Civilization* (1924); and H. B. Major, *The Domestic Architecture of the Early American Republic* (1926). The graphic arts are best covered by Frank

Weitenkampf, *American Graphic Art* (1912), and the drama by A. H. Quinn, *A History of the American Drama from the Beginning to the Civil War* (1923).

11. SCIENCE, RELIGION, AND PHILOSOPHY. On science, Max Meisel (comp.), *A Bibliography of American Natural History: The Pioneer Century 1769–1865* (3 vols., 1924–9) is for those who desire acquaintance with scientific progress in America before and during the Civil War. See also the excellent survey, W. M. and M. S. C. Smallwood, *Natural History and the American Mind* (1941). The following are also helpful: E. W. Bryn, *The Progress of Invention in the Nineteenth Century* (1900); Waldemar Kaempffert, *A Popular History of American Inventions* (2 vols., 1924); L. L. Woodruff (ed.), *The Development of the Sciences* (1923); John Fiske, *A Century of Science* (1899); E. S. Dana and others, *A Century of Science in America* (1918); D. J. Struik, *Yankee Science in the Making* (1948); Bernard Jaffe, *Men of Science in America* (1944); and F. R. Packard, *History of Medicine in the United States* (2 vols., 1931). The most usable books on religion are H. K. Rowe, *The History of Religion in the United States* (1924); W. W. Sweet, *The Story of Religions in America* (1930); and T. C. Hall, *Religious Background of American Culture* (1930). For more detailed accounts of leading denominations, consult Philip Schaff and others, *The American Church History Series* (13 vols., 1893–1901); J. G. Shea, *A History of the Catholic Church in the United States* (4 vols., 1886–92); H. E. Luccock and P. Hutchinson, *The Story of Methodism* (1926); W. S. Perry, *History of the American Episcopal Church* (2 vols., 1885); and Williston Walker, *A History of the Congregational Churches in the United States* (1894). E. B. Greene, *Religion and the State* (1941), examines a recurring theme in American history. Two older works on the history of American philosophy are still useful: Woodbridge Riley, *American Thought from Puritanism to Pragmatism and Beyond* (new ed., 1922) and H. G. Townsend, *Philosophical Ideas in the United States* (1934). More recent treatises are H. W. Schneider, *A History of American Philosophy* (1946) and W. H. Werkmeister, *A History of Philosophical Ideas in America* (1949).

12. INTELLECTUAL HISTORY. Among the major works are Harvey Wish, *Society and Thought in Early America* (1950); Alexis de Tocqueville, *Democracy in America* (new ed., 2 vols., 1945); V. L. Parrington, *Main Currents in American Thought* (3 vols., 1927–30); M. E. Curti, *The Growth of American Thought* (1951); R. H. Gabriel, *The Course of American Democratic Thought* (1940).

Historiography

For those desiring a critical estimate of American historiography the following will be useful: W. T. Hutchinson (ed.), *The Marcus W. Jernegan Essays in American Historiography* (1937); Michael Kraus, *A History of American History* (1937); H. E. Barnes, *A History of Historical Writing* (1937); Allan Nevins, *The Gateway to History* (1938); and Hermann Ausubel, *Historians and Their Craft; a Study of the Presidential Addresses of the American Historical Association* (1950).

➯➳➳➳➳➳➳➳➳➳➳➳➳➳➳➳➳➳

CHAPTER I

The Legacy of Civil War

GENERAL WORKS. The best single work covering the topics discussed in this chapter is the admirable volume by J. G. Randall, *The Civil War and Reconstruction* (1937), which contains a carefully selected bibliography. An even briefer and highly interpretative account is Volume II, Chapter I, of C. A. and M. R.

Beard, *The Rise of American Civilization* (4 vols., 1927–42). W. A. Dunning's older work, *Reconstruction, Political and Economic, 1865–1877* (1907), in the "American Nation" series, is still valuable, as is his *Essays on the Civil War and Reconstruction* (1904). J. F. Rhodes, *History of the United States from the Compromise of 1850* (9 vols., 1900–28), Volumes V–VII, is very useful for political (but neglects economic) history. It should be supplemented by Volumes I–III of E. P. Oberholtzer, *A History of the United States Since the Civil War* (5 vols., 1917–37); W. L. Fleming, *The Sequel of Appomattox* (1919), in the "Chronicles of America" series; Allan Nevins, *The Emergence of Modern America, 1865–1878* (1928), in the "History of American Life" series; and E. M. Coulter, *The South During Reconstruction, 1865–1877* (1947), in *The History of the South* series. C. G. Bowers, *The Tragic Era: The Revolution after Lincoln* (1929), is a well written but untrustworthy account. P. H. Buck, *The Road to Reunion, 1865–1900* (1937), is an excellent account of the efforts toward reconciliation of the North and South.

THE VICTORIOUS NORTH. The psychological atmosphere of the North after 1865 is evident in E. D. Fite's *Social and Industrial Conditions in the North during the Civil War* (1910). A contemporary account by S. M. Peto, *The Resources and Prospects of America, Ascertained During a Visit . . . in 1865* (1866), is also useful for the same purpose. For social, economic, and political changes in particular Northern states, see A. C. Cole, *The Era of the Civil War, 1848–1870* (1919); A. C. Flick (ed.), *History of the State of New York* (1933–7), Vol. III; C. M. Knapp, *New Jersey Politics during . . . the Civil War and Reconstruction* (1924); and Frederick Merk, *Economic History of Wisconsin During the Civil War Decade* (1916).

THE DEFEATED SOUTH. On the general aspects, see Volume I of E. P. Oberholtzer, *The United States Since the Civil War*, previously cited. Also consult F. B. Simkins, *The South, Old and New, 1820–1947* (1947); and W. B. Hesseltine, *The South In American History* (1943). Accounts of travelers to the South are very valuable. See especially Robert Somers, *The Southern States Since the War, 1870–1* (1871), good on the state of agriculture and industry; Sidney Andrews, *The South Since the War* (1866), observations of a newspaper correspondent; Whitelaw Reid, *After the War: A Southern Tour* (1866), observations by a future editor of the New York *Tribune;* and J. T. Trowbridge, *The South* (1866). Though biased and therefore not always completely reliable, reminiscences of Southerners afford insight into the psychology of the people of the defeated area. See Joseph LeConte, *The Autobiography of Joseph LeConte* (1903); M. B. Chesnut, *A Diary from Dixie* (1905); F. B. Leigh, *Ten Years on a Georgia Plantation since the War* (1883); Mrs. M. L. Avary, *Dixie after the War* (1906); E. C. Eggleston, *A Rebel's Recollections* (1875); Mrs. Roger Pryor, *Reminiscences of Peace and War* (1904); and E. W. Pringle, *Chronicles of Chicora Wood* (1922). For those who wish a more detailed Northern account of Southern conditions, see the report of Carl Schurz to President Johnson in the autumn of 1865, Senate Executive Documents, 39 Cong., 1 Sess., No. 2; and the report of B. D. Gruman, April, 1866, in Senate Executive Documents, 39 Cong., 1 Sess., No. 43.

LINCOLN AND JOHNSON AND THE RADICALS. The old work by J. W. Burgess, *Reconstruction and the Constitution, 1866–1876* (1902), is colored by the author's nationalistic bias. Much more readable and reliable are the accounts in W. A. Dunning, *Essays on the Civil War and Reconstruction;* and J. G. Randall, *The Civil War and Reconstruction*, already cited. See also H. K. Beale's illuminating articles "Reconstruction" in Volume XIII, *Encyclopaedia of the Social Sciences* (1934), edited by E. R. A. Seligman and Alvin Johnson, and "On Rewriting Reconstruction History," *American Historical Review*, Vol. XLV (July 1940), pp. 807–827. R. S. Henry, *The Story of Reconstruction* (1938), is valuable, but very detailed. On Lincoln's Reconstruction policy, see C. H. McCarthy, *Lincoln's Plan of Reconstruction* (1901); and J. G. Randall, *Constitutional Problems under*

Lincoln (1926). T. H. Williams, *Lincoln and the Radicals* (1941), is excellent. On President Johnson and the Radicals, the best treatment is H. K. Beale, *The Critical Year: A Study of Andrew Johnson and Reconstruction* (1930). See also C. E. Chadsey, *The Struggle Between President Johnson and Congress over Reconstruction* (1896); G. F. Milton, *The Age of Hate: Andrew Johnson and the Radicals* (1930), a scholarly account and superior to Chadsey; Edward Stanwood, *A History of the Presidency* (2 vols., 1916), a standard treatment; L. P. Stryker, *Andrew Johnson, A Study in Courage* (1929), prejudiced and at times dull; R. W. Winston, *Andrew Johnson, Plebeian and Patriot* (1928), which reads fairly well; and E. M. McPherson, *The Political History of the United States During Reconstruction* (1871), which contains source material. On the Fourteenth Amendment, see B. B. Kendrick, *The Journal of the Joint Committee of Fifteen on Reconstruction* (1914); C. A. Beard, *The Supreme Court and the Constitution* (1912); W. D. Guthrie, *Lectures on the Fourteenth Amendment* (1898); Jacobus Ten Broek, *The Antislavery Origins of the Fourteenth Amendment* (1951); and H. E. Flack, *The Adoption of the Fourteenth Amendment* (1908). On the Fifteenth Amendment, see J. M. Mathews, *Legislative and Judicial History of the Fifteenth Amendment* (1909). On the impeachment proceedings against President Johnson, consult D. M. DeWitt, *The Impeachment and Trial of Andrew Johnson* (1903), a skillful analysis; and the account on this topic in W. A. Dunning's *Essays on Civil War and Reconstruction*, cited earlier. There is rich material on the various aspects of Reconstruction and the conflict between the Administration and the Radical element in Congress in the biographical studies of the more outstanding personages of the period. Among the more important are J. A. Woodburn, *The Life of Thaddeus Stevens* (1913); A. B. Miller, *Thaddeus Stevens* (1939); R. N. Current, *Old Thad Stevens, A Story of Ambition* (1942), which is largely political; T. F. Woodley, *Great Leveler: The Life of Thaddeus Stevens* (1937), which presents new facts; J. T. Morse, Jr. (ed.), *The Diary of Gideon Welles* (3 vols., 1911); and H. K. Beale, "Is the Printed Diary of Gideon Welles Reliable?" *American Historical Review*, Vol. XXX (1925), pp. 547–52; T. C. Pease and J. G. Randall (eds.), *The Diary of Orville Hickman Browning* (2 vols., 1925–33); W. C. Harris, *Public Life of Zachariah Chandler, 1851–1875* (1917); D. V. Smith, *Chase and Civil War Politics* (1931); D. B. Chidsey, *The Gentleman from New York: A Life of Roscoe Conkling* (1935); B. C. Steiner, *Life of Henry Winter Davis* (1916); R. P. Ludlum, "Joshua Giddings, Radical," *Mississippi Valley Historical Review*, Vol. XXIII (1936), pp. 49–60; G. F. Hoar, *Autobiography of Seventy Years* (2 vols., 1903); G. W. Julian, *Political Recollections, 1840 to 1872* (1884); C. M. Fuess, *Carl Schurz, Reformer (1829–1906)* (1932); Frederic Bancroft, *The Life of William H. Seward* (2 vols., 1900); Moorfield Storey, *Charles Sumner* (1900); Horace White, *The Life of Lyman Trumbull* (1913); J. G. Blaine, *Twenty Years of Congress: From Lincoln to Garfield* (2 vols., 1884–6); C. R. Williams (ed.), *The Diary and Letters of Rutherford B. Hayes* (5 vols., 1922–6); W. D. Foulke, *Life of Oliver P. Morton, Including His Important Speeches* (2 vols., 1899); G. C. Gorham, *Life and Public Services of Edwin M. Stanton* (2 vols., 1899), which is not too satisfactory; C. L. Barrows, *William M. Evarts* (1941); Margaret Clapp, *Forgotten First Citizen: John Bigelow* (1947); Glyndon Van Deusen, *Thurlow Weed* (1947); Henry Adams, *The Education of Henry Adams: An Autobiography* (1918); Horace Greeley, *Recollections of a Busy Life* (1868); and C. F. Adams, Jr., *Charles Francis Adams* (1900). For the biographies of other political leaders, consult the *Dictionary of American Biography*, already cited.

RADICAL RULE IN THE SOUTH. The literature on this topic is considerable. In addition to the volumes cited in the above paragraphs, consult the monographs on each of the seceded states: W. L. Fleming, *Civil War and Reconstruction in Alabama* (1905); J. W. Garner, *Reconstruction in Mississippi* (1901); J. G. De R. Hamilton, *Reconstruction in North Carolina* (1914); Ella Lonn, *Reconstruction in Louisiana after 1868* (1918); W. M. Caskey, *Secession and Restoration of Louisiana* (1938); Garnie McGinty, *Louisiana Redeemed, The Overthrow of Carpet-Bag Rule, 1876–1880* (1941); J. R. Ficklen, *History of Reconstruction in Louisiana* (1910); J. P. Hollis, *The Early Reconstruction Period in South Carolina* (1905); J. S. Reynolds, *Reconstruction in South Carolina, 1865–77* (1905); F. B. Simkins and R. H. Woody, *South Carolina During Reconstruction* (1932); C. W. Ramsdell, *Reconstruction in Texas* (1910); E. M. Coulter, *The Civil War and Readjustment in Kentucky* (1926); H. J. Eckenrode, *The Political History of Virginia During the Reconstruction* (1904); W. W. Davis, *The Civil War and Reconstruction in Florida* (1913); J. W. Fertig, *The Secession and Reconstruction of Tennessee* (1898); J. W. Patton, *Unionism and Reconstruction in Tennessee, 1860–1869* (1934); T. S. Staples, *Reconstruction in Arkansas, 1862–1874* (1923); D. Y. Thomas, *Arkansas in War and Reconstruction, 1861–1874* (1926); John Wallace, *Carpetbag Rule in Florida* (1888); J. C. McGregor, *The Disruption of Virginia* (1922); E. C. Woolley, *The Reconstruction of Georgia* (1901); and C. M. Thompson, *Reconstruction in Georgia, Economic, Social, Political, 1865–1872* (1915). Treating the entire South during the decade after the Civil War are E. M. Coulter, *The South During Reconstruction, 1865–1877* (1947); W. E. B. DuBois, *Black Reconstruction* (1935), a detailed and challenging interpretation; W. A. Sinclair, *The Aftermath of Slavery* (1905); and W. L. Fleming's authoritative work, *Documentary History of Reconstruction* (2 vols., 1906–7). See also the essays dealing with Reconstruction in *Studies in Southern History* inscribed to W. A. Dunning. The following biographies contain valuable material on Reconstruction: E. M. Coulter, *W. G. Brownlow* (1937); C. H. Ambler, *Francis H. Pierpont* (1937); H. J. Pearce, Jr., *Benjamin H. Hill, Secession and Reconstruction* (1928); W. A. Cate, *Lucius Q. C. Lamar* (1935); and N. M. Blake, *William Mahone* (1935). On the freedmen during Reconstruction, consult W. E. B. DuBois, *Black Reconstruction*, cited above; and P. A. Bruce, *The Plantation Negro as a Freedman* (1889). G. T. Stephenson, *Race Distinctions in American Law* (1910), covers Black Codes and other legislation affecting freedmen. Paul Lewinson, *Race, Class, and Party* (1932), is also valuable. See also P. S. Peirce, *The Freedmen's Bureau* (1904); L. J. Webster, *The Operation of the Freedmen's Bureau in South Carolina* (1916), in the Smith College studies in history; V. L. Wharton, *The Negro in Mississippi, 1865–1890* (1948); and A. A. Taylor, *The Negro in South Carolina During the Reconstruction* (1924), and *The Negro in the Reconstruction of Virginia* (1926). Important, too, in connection with the freedmen is H. L. Swint, *The Northern Teacher in the South, 1862–1870* (1941). On Negro government and the restoration of white rule in the South, see the lively but unreliable volume by J. S. Pike, *The Prostrate State: South Carolina Under Negro Government* (1874); Charles Nordhoff, *The Cotton States in 1875* (1876); and R. F. Dibble, *Albion W. Tourgée* (1921). A satisfactory history of the Ku Klux Klan is yet to be written. J. C. Lester and D. L. Wilson, *Ku Klux Klan, Its Origin, Growth, and Disbandment* (new ed., 1905); and S. L. Davis, *Authentic History, Ku Klux Klan, 1865–1877* (1924), are both inferior to S. F. Horn, *Invisible Empire: The Story of the Ku Klux Klan, 1866–1871* (1939). The best brief account is to be found in W. G. Brown, *The Lower South in American History* (1902). On the restoration of white rule, see also Walter Allen, *Governor Chamberlain's Administration in South Carolina* (1888); and E. L. Wells, *Hampton and Reconstruction* (1907). Those who wish to view Reconstruction from the angle of race relations should consult B. G. Brawley, *A Social History of the American Negro* (1921); C. R. Johnson, *The Negro in American Civilization* (1930); G. W. Williams, *History of the Negro Race in America, 1619–1880* (2 vols., 1883); J. H. Franklin, *From Slavery to Freedom: A History of American Negroes* (1947); and most important of all, the brilliant study by Gunnar Myrdal, *An American Dilemma: The Negro Problem and Modern Democracy* (2 vols., 1944).

GRANTISM. For an understanding of Grant in public life, consult the following: Lloyd Lewis, *Captain Sam Grant* (1950), for his early life; Helen Todd, *A Man Named Grant* (1940), interesting, but not entirely reliable; L. A. Coolidge, *Ulysses S. Grant* (1917); W. B. Hesseltine, *Ulysses S. Grant, Politician* (1935), an excellent study; H. S. Garland, *Ulysses S. Grant: His Life and Character* (1898); Matthew Josephson, *The Politicos, 1865–1896* (1938), which is popular; and W. E. Woodward, *Meet General Grant* (1928), which is somewhat superficial. For Grant's elevation to the presidency, see C. H. Coleman, *The Election of 1868* (1933). The best single volume on Grant's administration is Allan Nevins, *Hamilton Fish: The Inner History of the Grant Administration* (1936). It may be supplemented with profit by the biographical accounts listed above; and Carl Schurz, *Reminiscences* (3 vols., 1907–08); Hugh McCulloch, *Men and Measures of a Half a Century* (1888); John Sherman, *Recollections of Forty Years* (2 vols., 1895); and A. D. White, *Autobiography of Andrew Dickson White* (2 vols., 1905). On financial questions and other domestic political matters, see W. C. Mitchell, *A History of the Greenbacks* (1903); D. C. Barrett, *The Greenback and Resumption of Specie Payments, 1862–1879* (1931); A. D. Noyes, *Forty Years of American Finance* (1909); A. B. Hepburn, *A History of Currency in the United States* (rev. ed., 1924); A. S. Bolles, *The Financial History of the United States* (3 vols., 1896), Vol. III; and D. R. Dewey, *Financial History of the United States* (new ed., 1936). For the Legal Tender cases, consult R. E. Cushman, *Leading Constitutional Decisions* (9th ed., 1950), Charles Warren, *The Supreme Court in United States History* (rev. ed., 2 vols., 1937); E. J. James, *Some Considerations on the Legal Tender Decisions* (1887); G. F. Hoar, *The Charge against President Grant of Packing the Supreme Court* (1896); and Sidney Ratner, "Was the Supreme Court Packed by President Grant?" *Political Science Quarterly*, Vol. L (1935). For Civil Service, see C. R. Fish, *The Civil Service and the Patronage* (1905). On the tariff, consult the standard works: F. W. Taussig, *The Tariff History of the United States* (8th ed., 1931) and Edward Stanwood, *American Tariff Controversies in the Nineteenth Century* (2 vols., 1903). Valuable for the subject covered is M. S. Wildman, *Money Inflation in the United States* (1905). The Panic of 1873 is treated adequately by E. R. McCartney, *The Crisis of 1873* (1935). Other helpful works are C. A. Collman, *Our Mysterious Panics, 1830–1930: A Story of Events and the Men Involved* (1931); H. M. Larson, *Jay Cooke, Private Banker* (1936); O. C. Lightner, *The History of Business Depressions* (1922); E. P. Oberholtzer, *Jay Cooke, Financier of the Civil War* (2 vols., 1907); W. C. Mitchell, *Business Cycles* (1913); and O. M. W. Sprague, *History of Crises Under the National Banking System* (1910), Senate Document, 61st Cong., 2nd Sess., No. 538. The literature on the corruption of the Grant Administrations is voluminous. The accounts in Rhodes and Oberholtzer may be supplemented by the following: S. P. Orth, *The Boss and the Machine* (1919), in the "Chronicles of America" series; C. F. Adams and Henry Adams, *Chapters of Erie, and Other Essays* (1871); J. B. Crawford, *The Credit Mobilier of America* (1880); D. C. Seitz, *The Dreadful Decade, 1869–1879* (1926), which is lively and exaggerated; R. H. Fuller, *Jubilee Jim: The Life of Colonel James Fiske, Jr.,* (1928), which is highly journalistic; D. T. Lynch, *"Boss" Tweed: The Story of a Grim Generation* (1927), the story of Tammany Hall at its worst, and *The Wild Seventies* (1941); R. I. Warshow, *Jay Gould* (1928); K. G. Crawford, *The Pressure Boys* (1939); M. R. Werner, *Tammany Hall* (1928), scholarly; Bouck White, *The Book of Daniel Drew* (1910); A. D. H. Smith, *Commodore Vanderbilt* (1927); A. B. Paine, *Thomas Nast, His Period and His Pictures* (1904); and F. C. Sharp and P. G. Fox, *Business Ethics, Studies in Fair Competition* (1937). E. D. Ross, *The Liberal Republican Movement* (1919) is definitive. Other works on this topic are T. S. Barclay, *The Liberal Republican Movement in Missouri, 1865–1871* (1926); Joseph Schafer, *Carl Schurz, Militant Liberal* (1930); and D. C. Seitz, *Horace Greeley, Founder of the New York Tribune* (1926). On foreign affairs see S. F. Bemis (ed.), *The American Secretaries of State and Their*

Diplomacy (10 vols., 1927–9), Vol. VII. On the Alaska purchase, consult J. M. Callahan, *The Alaska Purchase and Americo-Canadian Relations* (1908); J. P. Nichols, *Alaska* (1924); and S. R. Tompkins, *Alaska, Promyshlennik and Sourdough* (1945). B. P. Thomas, *Russo-America Relations, 1815–1867* (1930), gives the necessary background for the Alaska negotiations. F. E. Chadwick treats the *Virginius* affair in his *Relations of the United States and Spain, Diplomacy* (1909). H. M. Hyde, *Mexican Empire, The History of Maximilian and Carlota of Mexico* (1946), is a scholarly presentation. A companion account is Ralph Roeder, *Juarez and His Mexico* (2 vols., 1947). The Alabama claims and the Geneva arbitration are covered by J. B. Moore's *History and Digest of the International Arbitrations* (1898), Vol. I, chap. 14; J. C. B. Davis, *Mr. Fish and the Alabama Claims* (1893); and Volume III of *The Cambridge History of British Foreign Policy* (3 vols., 1922–3). On the Fenian raids, see J. M. Callahan, *American Foreign Policy in Canadian Relations* (1937); H. Keenleyside, *Canada and the United States* (1929); L. B. Shippee, *Canadian-American Relations, 1849–1874* (1939); and Goldwin Smith, *The Treaty of Washington, 1871: A Study in Imperial History* (1941). C. C. Tansill's *The Purchase of the Danish West Indies* (1932), and *The United States and Santo Domingo, 1798–1873* (1938), are definitive. J. M. Callahan, *Cuba and International Relations* (1899); and C. L. Jones, *Caribbean Interests of the United States* (1916), are masterly accounts.

THE COMPROMISE OF 1877. P. L. Haworth, *The Hayes-Tilden Election* (rev. ed., 1927), is the standard work on this event. See also W. W. Davis, *The Civil War and Reconstruction in Florida* (1913); Ella Lonn, *Reconstruction in Louisiana after 1868* (1918); and F. B. Simkins and R. H. Woody, *South Carolina During Reconstruction* (1932). The following biographies are indispensable: A. C. Flick, *Samuel Jones Tilden* (1939); L. B. Richardson, *William E. Chandler, Republican* (1940), a biography of the chairman of the Republican National Committee in 1876; Allan Nevins, *Abram S. Hewitt: with Some Account of Peter Cooper* (1935); H. J. Eckenrode, *Rutherford B. Hayes, Statesman of Reunion* (1930); and C. R. Williams, *The Life of Rutherford B. Hayes* (2 vols., 1914). C. Vann Woodward, *Reunion and Reaction* (1951), sheds much new light on the election.

CHAPTER 2

Creating an Industrial Republic

The history of this many-sided subject remains to be written. The factual material for such a history is available in the voluminous *Reports* of the Census Bureau and the comprehensive *Report of the Industrial Commission* (19 vols., 1902). Helpful also to the author of a history of industrial America would be *A Graphic Analysis of the Census of Manufactures of the United States, 1849–1919* (1923) prepared by the National Industrial Conference Board. V. S. Clark's *History of Manufactures in the United States 1860–1914* (1928) is highly factual and woefully lacking in interpretation. C. D. Wright, *The Industrial Evolution of the United States* (1897) is still useful but, like Clark, leans to the factual side. As a kind of antidote to these two volumes, the student should read L. M. Hacker, *The Triumph of American Capitalism* (1940); T. C. Cochran and William Miller, *The Age of Enterprise* (1942); Lewis Mumford, *Technics and Civilization* (1934); and Jerome Davis, *Capitalism and Its Culture* (1936). The several volumes of the History of American Life series covering the years since 1865, and especially Allan Nevins, *The Emergence of Modern America, 1865–1878* (1927); I. M. Tarbell, *The Nationalizing of Business, 1878–1898* (1936); and H. U. Faulkner, *The Quest for Social Justice, 1898–1914* (1931) contain both valuable material and bibliographical references on the several topics included in this chapter. B. J. Hendrick, *The Age of Big Business* (1921), in the Chronicles of America series is a popular survey; and Malcolm Keir, *Manufacturing Industries in America* (1920) is a scholarly account. All of the several texts on American economic history have chapters on the revolutionary changes that have transformed America economically, and culturally as well. See especially, Chapter 11 in E. C. Kirkland, *A History of American Economic Life* (rev. ed., 1947); H. U. Faulkner, *American Economic History* (rev. ed., 1937); F. A. Shannon, *America's Economic Growth* (1940); and Chester Wright, *Economic History of the United States* (2nd ed., 1949). There are also quantities of valuable material in Herbert Hoover and others, *Recent Economic Changes in the United States* (2 vols., 1929) evidencing the results of industrial transformation.

GOVERNMENT AID TO INDUSTRY. This aid has been both direct and indirect. Most important, perhaps, as far as industry is concerned, has been the protection of the home market. On the tariff, see P. Ashley, *Modern Tariff History* (3rd ed., 1920); Edward Stanwood, *American Tariff Controversies in the Nineteenth Century* (1903); F. W. Taussig, *Some Aspects of the Tariff Question* (3rd ed., 1931) and *Tariff History of the United States* (8th ed., 1931); W. S. Culbertson, "The Making of Tariffs," *Yale Review* (January, 1923), and "Tariff Problems of the United States" *Annals of the American Academy of Political and Social Science*, Vol. CXLI (January, 1929). There are rich storehouses of material on the tariff in Robert McElroy, *Grover Cleveland* (1923); Allan Nevins, *Grover Cleveland* (1932); J. A. Barnes, *John J. Carlisle* (1931); and C. S. Olcott, *The Life of William McKinley* (2 vols., 1916). Other government aids to industry include marketing facilities, improved roads, and other means of communications. On the postal system, see D. C. Roper, *The United States Post Office* (1917). On waterways, consult *Inland Water Transportation in the United States*, Department of Commerce, Bureau of Foreign and Domestic Commerce, Miscellaneous Series no. 119 (1923).

THE CONTINUING TRANSPORTATION REVOLUTION. Although the story of the development of a number of our railroads has been competently traced, a first-class history of American railroads is yet to be written. Two volumes in the Chronicles of America series can perhaps be recommended as an introduction to the subject. These are John Moody, *The Railroad Builders* (1919) and *The Masters of Capital* (1919). These should be followed by S. H. Holbrook, *The Story of American Railroads* (1947); A. C. Laut, *The Romance of the Rails* (2 vols., 1929); E. R. Johnson and T. W. Van Metre, *Principles of Railroad Transportation* (rev. ed., 1932). Other brief résumés are E. R. Johnson, *American Railway Transportation* (rev. ed., 1908); C. F. Adams, Jr., *Railroads: Their Origin and Problems* (rev. ed., 1887); A. T. Hadley, *Railroad Transportation* (1885); F. L. McVey, *Railway Transportation* (1921); I. L. Sharfman, *The American Railroad Problem* (1921); Eliot Jones, *Principles of Railway Transportation* (1924); Slason Thompson, *A Short History of American Railways* (1925); M. D. Stevers, *Steel Trails* (1933); and Lebert St. Clair, *Transportation* (1933). The last two are popular presentations. For contemporary information, consult the *American Railroad Journal* (1832–71); H. V. Poore, *Poore's Manual of the Railroads of the United States* (1868–1925), the *Commercial and Financial Chronicle* (1865–1925), *The Final Report of the Industrial Commission* (1902), and the *Annual Reports* of the Interstate Commerce Commission. The government documents of the utmost importance to anyone concerned with the history of American railroads are the famous Windom Report, entitled *Report of the Select Committee on Transportation-Routes to the Seaboard*, 43rd Cong., 1st Sess., Senate Report no. 307, parts 1–2 (1874); the Cullom Report, *Report of the Senate Select Committee on Interstate Commerce*, 49th Cong., 1st Sess., Senate Report no. 46, parts 1–2 (1886); and the Hepburn Committee, *Proceedings of the Select Committee on Railroads, New York Assembly* (5 vols., 1879). There is a wealth of biographic material that covers practically every part of the history of American railroads. See especially Thomas C. Cochran, *Railroad*

Leaders: The Business Mind in Action (1953), an important work, and the thoughtful study of J. Grodinsky, *Jay Gould: His Business Career* (1957). There are accounts of Daniel C. Drew, Jay Gould, and Cornelius Vanderbilt in the *Dictionary of American Biography.* J. G. Pyle, *The Life of James J. Hill* (2 vols., 1917) and George Kennan, *E. H. Harriman* (2 vols., 1922) are typically "authorized" treatments, and therefore sympathetic. H. J. Eckenrode and P. W. Edmunds, *E. H. Harriman: The Little Giant of Wall Street* (1933) is unfortunately not objective. A. D. H. Smith, *Commodore Vanderbilt* (1927) suffers likewise. Lewis Corey, *The House of Morgan* (1930) is authoritative and excellent on the part played by J. P. Morgan in railroad consolidation. J. B. Hedges, *Henry Villard and the Railways of the Northwest* (1930) is scholarly. Oscar Lewis, *The Big Four: The Story of Huntington, Stanford, Hopkins, and Crocker, and of the Building of the Central Pacific* (1938) is lively. G. T. Clark, *Leland Stanford* (1931) is an earlier work. E. P. Oberholtzer, *Jay Cooke, Financier of the Civil War* (2 vols., 1907) is first-rate, as is H. G. Larson, *Jay Cooke, Private Banker* (1936). H. G. Pearson, *An American Railroad Builder, John Murray Forbes* (1911) is excellent. Not to be overlooked is H. G. Prout, *A Life of George Westinghouse* (1921). A. D. Turnbull, *John Stevens, An American Record* (1928) is an interesting account of a pioneer in railroad building and equipment. M. W. Schlegel, *Franklin B. Gowan: Ruler of the Reading* (1948) sheds light on this anthracite carrier. N. C. Wilson and F. J. Taylor, *Southern Pacific: The Roaring Story of a Fighting Railroad* (1951) is a popular account but of interest to serious students.

CREATING THE ESSENTIAL INDUSTRIAL PLANT. The history of many industries is yet to be written. On the textile industry, consult T. M. Young, *The American Cotton Industry* (1902); P. H. Nystrom, *Textiles* (1916); B. F. Lemert, *The Cotton Textile Industry of the Southern Appalachian Piedmont* (1933); J. H. Burgy, *The New England Cotton Textile Industry: A Study in Industrial Geography* (1932); A. H. Cole, *The American Wool Manufacture* (2 vols., 1926); M. T. Copeland, *The Cotton Manufacturing Industry of the United States* (1912); and P. T. Cherington, *The Wool Industry* (1916). For the oil industry, the reader may profitably consult P. H. Giddens, *The Birth of the Oil Industry* (1938); G. W. Stocking, *The Oil Industry and the Competitive System* (1925); John Ise, *The United States Oil Policy* (1926); I. M. Tarbell, *The History of the Standard Oil Company* (2 vols., 1904), not entirely satisfactory; and C. C. Rister, *Oil: Titan of the Southwest* (1949), which is excellent. Allan Nevins, *John D. Rockefeller: The Heroic Age of American Enterprise* (2 vols., 1940) is a comprehensive study that opens many doors to the oil industry. See also the revision of this work, *Study in Power: John D. Rockefeller, Industrialist and Philanthropist* (1953), which contains modifications. Less favorable to Rockefeller is J. T. Flynn, *God's Gold: The Story of Rockefeller and His Times* (1932). *The Report of the Commissioner of Corporations on the Petroleum Industry*, parts 1 and 2 (1907) and *Report of the Federal Trade Commission on the Petroleum Industry: Prices, Profits and Competition* (1928) are of major importance. On lumbering, see John Ise, *The United States Forest Policy* (1920); S. H. Holbrook, *Holy Old Mackinaw: A Natural History of the American Lumberjack* (1938); and the *Report on the Lumber Industry* by the *Bureau of Corporations*, Department of Commerce and Labor (1913). Several works on the coal industry are worthwhile: W. H. Hamilton and H. R. Wright, *The Case of Bituminous Coal* (1925); *Report of the United States Coal Commission* (5 vols., 1925) and *What the Coal Commission Found* (1925) by the staff of the commission; and Eliot Jones, *The Anthracite Coal Combination* (1914). The story of iron and steel is incomplete, but the following are important: J. D. Swank, *History of the Manufacture of Iron and Steel in All Ages* (2nd ed., 1892); J. R. Smith, *The Story of Iron and Steel* (1908); O. A. Backert (ed.), *The A. B. C. of Iron and Steel* (5th ed., 1925); Abraham Berglund, *The United States Steel Corporation* (1907); J. H. Bridge, *The Inside History of the Carnegie Steel Company* (1903), an exposé; Arundel Cotter, *The Authentic History of the United States*

Steel Corporation (1916) and *United States Steel: A Corporation with a Soul* (1921), an apology to soften and, if possible, fend off an impending government investigation and labor trouble; H. B. Vanderblue and W. L. Crum, *The Iron Industry in Prosperity and Depression* (1927); B. J. Hendrick, *The Life of Andrew Carnegie* (2 vols., 1932), "official" and noncritical; Allan Nevins, *Abram S. Hewitt: With Some Account of Peter Cooper* (1935); I. M. Tarbell, *The Life of Elbert H. Gary: The Story of Steel* (1925), an apology; Andrew Carnegie, *The Autobiography of Andrew Carnegie* (1920), best foot always forward!; George Harvey, *Henry Clay Frick, The Man* (1928), one man's portrayal; J. K. Winkler, *Incredible Carnegie: The Life of Andrew Carnegie (1835–1919)* (1931), an eulogistic account; F. P. Wirth, *The Discovery and Exploitation of the Minnesota Iron Lands* (1937); Paul de Kruif, *Seven Iron Men* (1929), interesting but unreliable; and S. H. Holbrook, *Iron Brew: A Century of American Ore and Steel* (1939), written for popular consumption. On the automobile the best works to date are R. C. Epstein, *The Automobile Industry: Its Economic and Commercial Development* (1928); L. H. Seltzer, *A Financial History of the American Automobile Industry* (1928); Arthur Pound, *The Turning Wheel* (1934), the story of General Motors; Henry Ford, *My Life and Work* (1922) an autobiography; and E. P. Norwood, *Ford Men and Methods* (1931). The history of the electrical industry must yet be written. On Edison, see F. L. Dyer and T. C. Martin, *Edison, His Life and Inventions* (2 vols., 1929) and G. S. Bryan, *Edison, the Man and His Work* (1926). Studies of the meat industry are C. B. Kuhlmann, *The Development of the Flour-Milling Industry in the United States* (1929), excellent; R. A. Clemen, *The American Livestock and Meat Industry* (1923), which should be examined in connection with *Report of the Commissioner of Corporations on the Beef Industry* (1905) and the *Report of the Federal Trade Commission on the Meat Packing Industry*, parts 1–3 (1918–20); L. F. Swift, *The Yankee of the Yards: The Biography of Gustavus Franklin Swift* (1927), another eulogistic biography. On the leather industry, see F. J. Allen, *The Shoe Industry* (1916), and B. E. Hazard, *The Organization of the Boot and Shoe Industry in Massachusetts Before 1875* (1921). See also R. G. Blakey, *The United States Beet-Sugar Industry and the Tariff* (1912) and Alfred Lief, *Harvey Firestone: Free Man of Enterprise* (1952), a laudatory treatment.

TOWARD WESTERN AND SOUTHERN INDUSTRIALIZATION. *The Twelfth Census of the United States*, Vol. VII, on manufacturing, is indispensable for this topic. Also see C. Goodrich and others, *Migration and Economic Opportunity* (1936); F. B. Garver, F. M. Boddy, and A. J. Nixon, *The Location of Manufactures in the United States 1899–1929* (1933); G. E. McLaughlin, *Growth of American Manufacturing Areas: A Comparative Analysis with Special Emphasis on Trends in the Pittsburgh District* (1938); H. W. Odum, *Southern Regions of the United States* (1936); R. B. Vance, *Human Geography of the South* (1932); Broadus Mitchell and G. S. Mitchell, *The Industrial Revolution in the South* (1930); B. F. Lemert, *The Cotton Textile Industry of the Southern Appalachian Piedmont*, already cited; and M. H. Ross, *Machine Age in the Hills* (1933). Twentieth-century tendencies are discussed in Jonathan Daniels, *A Southerner Discovers the South* (1938).

CHAPTER 3

Business Regulation: Private or Public

THE COMING OF THE RAILROAD GIANTS. Most of the material on this topic is to be found in the following: L. H. Haney, *A Congressional History of Railways in the United States to 1850* (1908); C. R. Fish, *The Restoration of the Southern Railroads* (1919); W. F. Gephart, *Transportation and Industrial Development in the Middle West* (1909); E. H. Mott, *Between the Ocean and the Lakes: The*

Story of Erie (1899); C. F. Adams, Chapters of Erie (1871); H. D. Dozier, A History of the Atlantic Coast Line Railroad (1920); J. I. Bogen, The Anthracite Railroads (1927); S. M. Derrick, Centennial History of South Carolina Railroad (1930); Edward Hungerford, The Story of the Baltimore and Ohio Railroad, 1827–1927 (2 vols., 1928) and Men and Iron; the History of the New York Central (1938); F. W. Stevens, The Beginnings of the New York Central Railroad (1926); T. F. Joyce, The Boston and Maine Railroad (1925); H. W. Schotter, The Growth and Development of the Pennsylvania Railroad Company (1927); Paul Gates, The Illinois Central Railroad and Its Colonization Work (1934), and A Century of Progress: History of the Delaware and Hudson Company (1925). The more important material on the growth of the railroads in the West is to be found in L. H. Haney, A Congressional History of Railways in the United States, 1850–1887 (1910); R. E. Riegel, The Story of the Western Railroads (1926), the best single volume; J. P. Davis, The Union Pacific Railway (1896); G. M. Dodge, How We Built the Union Pacific Railway (1910); Stuart Daggett, Chapters on the History of the Southern Pacific (1922); G. D. Bradley, The Story of the Santa Fe (1920); A. M. Borak, "The Chicago, Milwaukee and St. Paul Railroad," Journal of Economic and Business History, Vol. III (November, 1930), pp. 81–117; H. G. Brownson, History of the Illinois Central Railroad to 1870 (1915); J. B. Hedges, Henry Villard and the Railways of the North West (1930); Oscar Lewis, The Big Four: The Story of Huntington, Stanford, Hopkins, and Crocker, and of the Building of the Central Pacific (1938); R. C. Overton, Burlington West: A Colonization History of the Burlington Railroad (1941), a lively account; E. L. Sabin, Building the Pacific Railway (1919); W. H. Stennett, Yesterday and Today: A History of the Chicago and Northwestern Railway System (1910); Montgomery Schuyler, Westward the Course of Empire (1906); and H. K. White, History of the Union Pacific Railway (1895).

THE SORRY TALE OF RAILROAD FINANCING. On this topic, consult W. Z. Ripley, Railroads: Finance and Organization (1915); F. A. Cleveland and F. W. Powell, Railroad Promotion and Capitalization in the United States (1909), which contains excellent biography. See also G. W. Julian, "Railway Influence in the Land Office," North American Review, Vol. CXXXVI, pp. 237 ff., which is invaluable; J. B. Sanborn, Congressional Grants of Land in Aid of Railways (1899); and J. W. Million, State Aid to Railways in Missouri (1896). The Report of the United States Pacific Railway Commission of 1887 (5 vols., 50th Cong. 1st Sess: Senate Executive Document no. 51); and, in addition, for the scandals in connection with the building of the Union Pacific, the Central Pacific and other roads, J. B. Crawford, The Credit Mobilier (1880) and Oscar Lewis, The Big Four, previously cited. Excellent studies of railroad financial malpractice are Max Lowenthal, The Investor Pays (1933) and E. G. Campbell, The Reorganization of the American Railroad System, 1893–1900 (1938). Valuable for the earlier period is F. C. Hicks (ed.), High Finance in the Sixties (1929). More journalistic and muckraking in quality are C. E. Russell, Stories of the Great Railroads (1912); Gustavus Myers, History of the Great American Fortunes (3 vols., 1910); and Matthew Josephson, The Robber Barons: The Great American Capitalists, 1861–1901 (1934). On the electric railroad, see the Proceedings of the Federal Electric Railway Commission (3 vols., 1920) and the much more usable treatment of this material by D. F. Wilcox, Analysis of the Electric Railway Problem: Report to the Federal Electric Railways Commission (1921). The conditions paving the way for government regulation are discussed in S. J. Buck, The Granger Movement (1913); C. S. Langstroth, Railway Cooperation . . . in the United States (1899), a story of early railroad pools; W. Larrabee, The Railroad Question (1893); and W. Z. Ripley, Railroads, Rates and Regulations (1912); A. T. Hadley, Railroad Transportation, Its History and Its Laws (1885); W. J. Cunningham, American Railroads: Government Control and Reconstruction Policies (1922); B. H. Meyer, Railroad Legislation in the United States (1903). R. E. Cushman, The Independent Regulatory

Commissions (1941) and Walter Thompson, *Federal Centralization: a Study and Criticism of the Expanding Scope of Congressional Legislation* (1923) cover the history of government regulation. The constitutional aspects are reviewed in E. S. Corwin, *The Commerce Power versus States Rights* (1936) and Felix Frankfurter, *The Commerce Clause under Marshall, Taney and Waite* (1937). For court decisions, see A. R. Ellingwood and W. Coombs (eds.), *The Government and Railroad Transportation* (1930) and I. L. Sharfman, *The Interstate Commerce Commission* (4 vols., 1931–7).

THE BUSINESSMAN REJECTS LAISSEZ FAIRE. John Moody, *The Masters of Capital* (1919) and B. J. Hendrick, *The Age of Big Business* (1919), both in the Chronicles of America series, are introductory surveys. They should be followed by two older but still useful volumes: John Moody, *The Truth About the Trusts* (1904) and R. T. Ely, *Monopolies and Trusts* (1900). The best general texts on the trust problem are Eliot Jones, *The Trust Problem in the United States* (1921); H. R. Seager and C. A. Gulick, Jr., *Trust and Corporation Problems* (1929); J. W. Jenks and W. E. Clark, *The Trust Problem* (4th ed., 1917); and L. H. Haney, *Business Organization and Combination* (rev. ed., 1914). W. Z. Ripley, *Trusts, Pools and Corporations* (rev. ed., 1916) is useful for source materials.

BEHEMOTH BUSINESS. See C. R. Van Hise, *Concentration and Control* (rev. ed., 1914) and H. W. Laidler, *Concentration of Control in American Industry* (1931). Important, too, are J. R. Commons, *Legal Foundations of American Capitalism* (1924), and O. F. Boucke, *Laissez Faire and After* (1932). Agitation against the ills of big business is best seen in Henry George, *Progress and Poverty*, already cited; Edward Bellamy, *Looking Backward, 2000–1887* (1888); H. D. Lloyd, *Wealth Against Commonwealth* (1894); and C. Lloyd, *Henry Demarest Lloyd* (2 vols., 1912). Henry George's beliefs are summarized in L. F. Post, *The Prophet of San Francisco* (1930) and G. R. Geiger, *The Philosophy of Henry George* (1933). C. C. Regier, *The Era of the Muckrakers* (1932); C. E. Russell, *Bare Hands and Stone Walls* (1933); Lincoln Steffens, *The Autobiography of Lincoln Steffens* (2 vols., 1931); and H. U. Faulkner, *The Quest for Social Justice, 1898–1914*, previously cited, are indispensable for those interested in the literature of protest. Evidence that George, Bellamy, Lloyd, and the others had cause to agitate for reform is to be found not only in the Windom, Cullom, and Hepburn *Reports*, cited in the previous chapter, but also in the *Preliminary Report of the Industrial Commission on Trusts and Industrial Combinations* (1900), in the Commission's Report, and the *Report of the Committee Pursuant to House Resolutions 429 and 504 to Investigate the Concentration of the Control of Money and Credit* (Pujo Committee) 62nd Cong. 3rd Sess., *House of Representatives Report*, no. 1593 (1913). Other valuable sources of information are H. R. Mussey, *Combination in the Mining Industry: A Study of Concentration in Lake Superior Iron Ore Production* (1905) and J. W. Stenman, *The Financial History of the American Telephone and Telegraph Industry* (1925).

THE BANKERS ENTER INDUSTRY. On this topic, consult Lewis Corey, *The House of Morgan*, already cited; Harvey O'Connor, *Mellon's Millions* (1933); J. W. Jenkins, *James B. Duke, Master Builder* (1927); Cyrus Adler, *Jacob H. Schiff: His Life and Letters* (2 vols., 1928); Robert McElroy, *Levi Parsons Morton* (1930); Henry Clews, *Fifty Years in Wall Street* (1908); T. W. Lawson, *Frenzied Finance* (1905), an overstated exposé; Arthur Pound and S. T. Moore (eds.), *They Told Barron* (1930); L. D. Brandeis, *Other People's Money, and How the Bankers Use It* (1914); W. Z. Ripley, *Main Street and Wall Street* (1927); M. G. Myers, *The New York Money Market* (1931); and F. C. James, *The Growth of Chicago Banks* (1938).

THE DEFENSE OF BUSINESS. The question of business ethics is discussed at length by the following: Werner Sombart, *The Quintessence of Capitalism* (1915); R. H. Tawney, *Religion and the Rise of Capitalism: A Historical Study* (1926); Chamber of Commerce of the United States, *Principles of Business Con-*

duct (1924); E. L. Herrmance, *The Ethics of Business* (1926); and C. F. Taeusch, *Professional and Business Ethics* (1926).

THE STATE VIOLATES THE "NATURAL ORDER." The history of government regulation is treated in M. W. Watkins, *Industrial Combinations and Public Policy* (1927); D. M. Keezer and Stacy May, *The Public Control of Business* (1930); J. D. Clark, *The Federal Trust Policy* (1931); A. H. Walker, *History of the Sherman Law of the United States of America* (1910), which is highly interpretative; O. W. Knauth, *The Policy of the United States Towards Industrial Monopoly* (1914), which is badly organized but contains much on the Sherman Anti-Trust Act. For the legislative background of the law, see *Bills and Debates in Congress Relating to Trusts, 57th Cong., 2nd Sess., Senate Document* no. 147 (1903). For legal aspects of the law, consult W. H. Taft, *The Anti-Trust Act and the Supreme Court* (1914). On the early history of the Federal Trade Commission, consult G. C. Henderson, *The Federal Trade Commission* (1924). Woodrow Wilson's attitude towards government regulation of business is summarized in his *The New Freedom* (1913).

CHAPTER 4

The Worker's World

The standard authority on the labor movement is J. R. Commons and others, *History of Labour in the United States* (4 vols., 1918–35). Unfortunately, his monumental *A Documentary History of American Industrial Society* (11 vols., 1910–11) stops at 1880. Since 1890, this gap has been partially filled by the *Bulletin of the Bureau of Labor*, which subsequently became the *Bulletin of the United States Bureau of Labor Statistics*, a veritable encyclopedia of information on wages, hours, prices, union standards and industrial accidents. *The Monthly Labor Review*, also a government publication, is useful. Very helpful, too, is the *Report of the Industrial Commission*, previously cited; Volumes VII, XII, XIV, and XVIII are especially important on labor. The biennial *Census on Manufactures* and *The Report of the Commission on Industrial Relations*, 64th Cong., 1st Sess., *Senate Document* no. 415 (11 vols., 1916) contain valuable material. P. H. Douglas, C. N. Hitchcock, and W. E. Atkins, *The Worker in Modern Economic Society* (1923) is a collection of readings. A very brief but suggestive treatise covering the entire period is Mary Beard, *A Short History of the American Labor Movement* (1920). Other one-volume summaries are: G. C. Groat, *An Introduction to the Study of Organized Labor in America* (1919); F. T. Carlton, *The History and Problems of Organized Labor* (rev. ed., 1920); G. S. Watkins, *An Introduction to the Study of Labor Problems* (1922); R. T. Ely, *The Labor Movement in the United States* (1905); and N. J. Ware, *The Labor Movement in America, 1860–1895* (1929). A more recent survey by C. R. Daugherty, *Labor Problems in American Industry* (1933), is excellent.

THE LABOR SUPPLY. Our principal sources of labor supply have been from increase of native-born population and from immigration. On the former, the reports of the United States Bureau of the Census are indispensable. See especially *A Century of Population Growth from the First Census of the United States to the Twelfth, 1790–1900* (1909) and *Negro Population 1790–1915* (1918). There is also valuable material in W. S. Thompson, *Population Problems* (1930); W. S. Rossiter, *Increase of Population in the United States, 1910–1920* (1922), Census Monograph I; Frank Lorimer and Frederick Osborn, *Dynamics of Population: Social and Biological Significance of Changing Birth Rates in the United States* (1934); and Committee on Recent Economic Changes, *Recent Economic Changes in the United States* (1929). The principal source of information about immigration is the *Report of the Immigration Commission* (42 vols., 1911) and the two-volume abstract thereof, 61st Cong., 3rd Sess., *Senate Document* no. 747 (1911); J. W. Jenks and W. J. Lanck, *The Immigration Problem* (4th ed., rev., 1917) is a one-volume synopsis of this report. Other worthwhile volumes are J. R. Commons, *Races and Immigrants in America* (1907); J. Higham, *Strangers in the Land: Patterns of American Nativism* (1955); I. A. Hourwich, *Immigration and Labor* (rev. ed., 1923); M. L. Hansen, *The Immigrant in American History* (1940); Maurice Davie, *World Immigration* (1936); A. B. Faust, *The German Element in the United States* (2 vols., 1909); H. J. Ford, *The Scotch-Irish in America* (1915); Theodore Blegen, *Norwegian Migration to America* (2 vols., 1931–40); F. E. Janson, *The Background of Swedish Immigration, 1840–1930* (1931); J. S. Lindberg, *The Background of Swedish Emigration to the United States* (1930); K. C. Babcock, *The Scandinavian Element in the United States* (1914); E. G. Balch, *Our Slavic Fellow Citizens* (1910); C. S. Bernheimer, *The Russian Jew in the United States* (1905); H. P. Fairchild, *Greek Immigration to the United States* (1911); Thomas Capek, *The Czechs in America* (1920); R. F. Foerster, *The Italian Emigration of Our Times* (1919); Samuel Joseph, *Jewish Immigration to the United States from 1881 to 1910* (1914); Jerome Davis, *The Russian Immigrant* (1922); William I. Thomas and Florian Znaniecki, *The Polish Peasant in Europe and America* (1927); M. Gamio, *Mexican Immigration to the United States* (1930); Harry Jerome, *Migration and Business Cycles* (1926); M. R. Coolidge, *Chinese Immigration* (1909); G. F. Seward, *Chinese Immigration, in Its Social and Economical Aspects* (1881); S. L. Gulick, *The American Japanese Problem* (1914); E. G. Mears, *Resident Orientals on the American Pacific Coast* (1927); E. S. Brunner, *Immigrant Farmers and Their Children* (1929); Grace Abbott, *The Immigrant and the Community* (1917); Herman Feldman, *Racial Factors in American Industry* (1931); Edith Abbott, *Historical Aspects of the Immigration Problem* (1926) and *Immigration: Select Documents and Case Records* (1924); E. L. Anderson, *We Americans* (1937); and Carl Wittke, *We Who Built America: The Saga of the Immigrant* (1939). Students will also profit from O. E. Rölvaag, *Giants in the Earth: A Saga of the Prairie* (1927) and *Peder Victorious* (1929); Edna Ferber, *American Beauty* (1931) and Gladys H. Carroll, *As the Earth Turns* (1933), both tales of immigrant life in rural New England; and Abraham Cahan, *The Rise of David Levinsky* (1917), a stirring account of a New York Jewish immigrant. Donald Peterson, *The Refugee Intellectual: The Americanization of the Immigrants* (1953), is a thoughtful study. On Negro labor, consult C. H. Wesley, *Negro Labor in the United States, 1850–1925* (1927); S. D. Spero and A. L. Harris, *The Black Worker* (1931), C. G. Woodson, *A Century of Negro Migration* (1918); and C. Goodrich and others, *Migration and Economic Opportunity, the Report of the Study of Population Redistribution* (1936). For the women and children workers, see the *Report on the Conditions of Women and Child Wage Earners in the United States*, 61st Cong., 2nd Sess., *Senate Report* no. 645 (19 vols., 1910–12) and the subsequent reports issued by the Women's and Children's Bureau of the Department of Labor. Certain volumes in the 1911 *Report* are most valuable; E. L. Otey, *The Beginnings of Child Labor Legislation in Certain States: A Comparative Study* (Vol. VI); H. L. Sumner, *History of Women in Industry in the United States* (Vol. IX); and J. B. Andrews and W. D. P. Bliss, *History of Women in Trade Unions* (Vol. X). Also consult A. M. Anderson, *Women in the Factory* (1922); John Spargo, *The Bitter Cry of the Children* (1906), old but still useful; and J. A. Hill, *Women in Gainful Occupations, 1870 to 1920* (1929), Census monograph no. 9.

THE GROWTH OF THE LABOR MOVEMENT. The literature on this topic is abundant, but the following are adequate: Herbert Harris, *American Labor* (1939); Selig Perlman, *A History of Trade Unionism in the United States* (1922); R. F. Hoxie, *Trade Unionism in the United States* (1917); S. P. Orth, *The Armies of Labor* (1919), in the Chronicles of America series; N. J. Ware, *The Labor Move-*

ment in the United States, 1860–1895 (1929); Leo Wolman, *The Growth of Trade Unions, 1880–1923* (1924); L. L. Lorwin, *The American Federation of Labor; History, Policies, and Prospects* (1933); T. S. Adams and H. L. Sumner, *Labor Problems* (1905); W. B. Catlin, *The Labor Problem in the United States and Great Britain* (rev. ed., 1935); M. C. Cahill, *Shorter Hours: A Study of the Movement since the Civil War* (1932); and D. D. Lescohier, *The Knights of St. Crispin, 1867–1874* (1910). On labor in particular industries, see L. L. Lorwin, *The Women's Garment Workers* (1924); Herbert Lahne, *The Cotton Mill Worker* (1944); A. E. Galster, *The Labor Movement in the Shoe Industry* (1924); Andrew Roy, *A History of the Coal Miners of the United States* (1907); A. E. Suffern, *The Coal Miner's Struggle for Industrial Status* (1926); Anna Rochester, *Labor and Coal* (1931), written from a left-wing point of view; H. L. Herring, *Welfare Work in Mill Villages: The Story of Extra-Mill Activities in North Carolina* (1929); J. A. Fitch, *The Steel Workers* (1910); C. A. Gulick, Jr., *Labor Policy of the United States Steel Corporation* (1924); R. W. Dunn, *Labor and Automobiles* (1929); Grace Hutchins, *Labor and Silk* (1929); and Charlotte Todes, *Labor and Lumber* (1931). There is a wealth of valuable material on the history of the labor movement in biographical sources: Samuel Gompers, *Seventy Years of Life and Labor* (2 vols., 1925); L. S. Reed, *The Labor Philosophy of Samuel Gompers* (1930); R. H. Harvey, *Samuel Gompers, Champion of the Toiling Masses* (1935); J. R. Buchanan, *The Story of a Labor Agitator* (1903); T. V. Powderly, *Thirty Years of Labor, 1859 to 1889* (1889); H. J. Carman, Henry David, and Paul Guthrie (eds.), *The Path I Trod: The Autobiography of Terrence V. Powderly* (1940); Elsie Glück, *John Mitchell, Miner* (1929); W. D. Haywood, *Bill Haywood's Book* (1929); Ray Ginger, *The Bending Cross* (1949), the story of Eugene V. Debs; Brand Whitlock, *Forty Years of It* (1914); and J. R. Commons, *Trade Unionism and Labor Problems* (1905).

THE THEORY AND PRACTICE OF CLASS CONSCIOUSNESS. P. W. Brissenden's *The I. W. W., A Study of American Syndicalism* (1919) is the standard authority but should be supplemented by J. S. Gambs, *The Decline of the I. W. W.* (1932). Also see J. G. Brooks, *American Syndicalism: The I. W. W.* (1913) and John Spargo, *Syndicalism, Industrial Unionism and Socialism* (1913). For other radical labor movements, consult C. H. Parker, *The Casual Laborer, and Other Essays* (1920); George Soule, *The New Unionism in the Clothing Industry* (1920); D. J. Saposs, *Left Wing Unionism* (1926); James O'Neal, *American Communism* (1927); Anthony Bimba, *The History of the American Working Class* (1927); Nathan Fine, *Labor and Farmer Parties in the United States, 1828–1928* (1928); J. A. Fitch, *The Causes of Industrial Unrest* (1924); Louis Adamic, *Dynamite, the Story of Class Violence in America* (rev. ed., 1934); Samuel Yellen, *American Labor Struggles* (1936); Henry David, *The History of the Haymarket Affair: A Study in the American Social-Revolutionary and Labor Movements* (1936), an admirable volume in every respect; Bureau of Labor, *Report on Strike of Textile Workers in Lawrence, Mass., in 1912*, 62nd Cong., 2nd Sess., *Senate Document* no. 870 (1912); J. W. Coleman, *The Molly Maguire Riots: Industrial Conflict in the Pennsylvania Coal Region* (1936); United States Strike Commission, *Report on the Chicago Strike of June–July, 1894* (1895); Carter Goodrich, *The Miner's Freedom* (1925); Winthrop Lane, *Civil War in West Virginia* (1921); A. F. Hinrichs, *The United Mine Workers of America, and the Non-Union Coal Fields* (1923); C. E. Bonnett, *Employers' Associations in the United States* (1922); Edward Levenson, *I Break Strikes! The Technique of Pearl L. Bergoff* (1935); Leo Huberman, *The Labor Spy Racket* (1937); Clinch Calkins, *Spy Overhead, the Story of Industrial Espionage* (1937); A. G. Taylor, *Labor Policies of the National Association of Manufacturers* (1928); Benjamin Rastall, *The Labor History of the Cripple Creek District* (1908); Almont Lindsey, *The Pullman Strike* (1942); Harry Barnard, *Eagle Forgotten* (1938); Tom Tippett, *When Southern Labor Stirs* (1931); and G. S. Mitchell, *Textile Unionism in the South* (1931).

STATE AND FEDERAL LABOR LEGISLATION. This topic may be prefaced by John Lombardi, *Labor's Voice in the Cabinet: A History of the Department of Labor from Its Origin to 1921* (1942); E. E. White, *The Government in Labor Disputes* (1932); A. T. Mason, *Organized Labor and the Law* (1925); Edward Berman, *Labor and the Sherman Act* (1930). On state labor legislation, consult A. M. Edwards, *The Labor Legislation of Connecticut* (1907); F. R. Fairchild, *The Factory Legislation of the State of New York* (1905); A. S. Field, *The Child Labor Policy of New Jersey* (1909); J. L. Barnard, *Factory Legislation in Pennsylvania* (1907); J. K. Towles, *Factory Legislation of Rhode Island* (1908); C. E. Persons et al., *Labor Laws and Their Enforcement, with Special Reference to Massachusetts* (1911); E. F. Baker, *Protective Labor Legislation, with Special Reference to Women in the State of New York* (1925); C. E. Beyer, *History of Labor Legislation for Women in Three States,* Department of Labor, Women's Bureau, Bulletin no. 66 (1929); and E. R. Beckner, *A History of Labor Legislation in Illinois* (1929). Also see J. R. Commons and J. B. Andrews, *Principles of Labor Legislation* (new ed., 1936); and H. L. Sumner, *The Working Children of Boston* (1922).

ORGANIZED LABOR AND THE COURTS. G. G. Groat, *Attitude of American Courts in Labor Cases* (1911) is excellent; so is Felix Frankfurter and Nathan Greene, *The Labor Injunction* (1930). These should be supplemented by *The Dissenting Opinions of Mr. Justice Holmes* (1929) and *The Social and Economic Views of Mr. Justice Brandeis* (1930), both edited by Alfred Lief. M. R. Carroll, *Labor and Politics: The Attitude of the American Federation of Labor Toward Legislation and Politics* (1923) and Edward Berman, *Labor Disputes and the President of the United States* (1924) are valuable. A. R. Ellingwood and W. Coombs, *The Government and Labor* (1926) and Carl Raushenbush and Emmanuel Stein, *Labor Cases and Materials* (1941) furnish collections of source materials and court decisions.

CHAPTER 5

The Last Frontier

The literature concerning the disappearance of frontier America is extensive. On this see F. J. Turner and Frederick Merk, *List of References on the History of the West* (rev. ed., 1922). R. A. Billington, *Westward Expansion* (1949) is an admirable text and contains a carefully selected bibliography covering all phases of the westward movement. But most important of all is W. P. Webb's excellent volume, *The Great Plains* (1931), which is indispensable for understanding the history of the Trans-Mississippi West. The last chapters of F. L. Paxson, *History of the American Frontier, 1763–1893* (1924) and his *The Last American Frontier* (1910) are helpful summaries. E. D. Branch, *Westward: The Romance of the American Frontier* (1930); D. E. Clark, *The West in American History* (1937); R. E. Riegel, *America Moves West* (rev. ed., 1947); Cardinal Goodwin, *The Trans-Mississippi West* (1922); and Emerson Hough, *The Passing of the Frontier* (1918), in the Chronicles of America series, are general accounts. E. P. Oberholtzer, *A History of the United States Since the Civil War* (5 vols., 1917–37) and Allan Nevins, *The Emergence of Modern America, 1865–1878* (1927), in the History of American Life series, are rich in material. The history of the several western states by H. H. Bancroft, *Works* (34 vols., 1882–90) are storehouses of valuable material; so are the regional histories, notably, H. E. Briggs, *Frontiers of the Northwest: A History of the Upper Missouri Valley* (1940); Everett Dick, *The Sod-House Frontier, 1854–1890* (1937), which is excellent on frontier life; S. L. Clemens (Mark Twain), *Roughing It* (2 vols., 1872); G. W. Fuller, *The Inland Empire of the Pacific Northwest* (3 vols., 1928); Oscar Winther, *The Great Northwest* (2nd ed., 1950); C. C. Rister, *The Southwestern Frontier—1865–1881* (1928); R. N. Richardson and C. C. Rister, *The Greater Southwest* (1934); J. C. Caughey, *History of The Pacific Coast* (1933); and C. C. Rister, *Land Hunger: David L. Payne and the Oklahoma Boomers* (1942). On the administration of western territories, see E. S. Pomeroy, *The Territories and the United States, 1861–1890* (1947). The best accounts of western land speculation are to be found in A. M. Sakolski, *The Great American Land Bubble* (1932) and A. N. Chandler, *Land Title Origins, A Tale of Force and Fraud* (1945).

THE LAST STAND OF THE FIRST AMERICANS. Much of the literature on the Indians consists of highly romanticized accounts. Among the historically trustworthy works that merit consideration are G. B. Grinnell, *The Story of the Indian* (1895); F. E. Leupp, *The Indian and his Problem* (1910); W. C. Macleod, *The American Indian Frontier* (1928); John Collier, *Indians of the Americas* (1947); Paul Radin, *The Story of the American Indian* (1934); Angie Debo, *And Still the Waters Run* (1940); G. D. Harmon, *Sixty Years of Indian Affairs* (1941); F. W. Seymour, *The Story of the Red Man* (1929), a well-written popular account; and P. E. Byrne, *Soldiers of the Plain* (1926), whch is highly sympathetic to the Indian. For particular tribes, see E. E. Dale, *Cherokee Cavaliers: Forty Years of Cherokee History* (1939) and his *The Indians of the Southwest: A Century of Development Under the United States* (1949); G. B. Grinnell, *The Fighting Cheyennes* (1915); F. C. Lockwood, *The Apache Indians* (1938); R. N. Richardson, *The Comanche Barrier to South Plains Settlement* (1933); Grant Foreman, *The Five Civilized Tribes* (1934); Angie Debo, *The Rise and Fall of the Choctaw Republic* (1934); and Woodworth Clum, *Apache Agent* (1936). On Indian warfare, consult Robert Gessner, *Massacre* (1931); P. I. Wellman, *Death on the Prairie* (1934) and *Death in the Desert* (1935); Stanley Vestal, *Sitting Bull* (1932) and *Warpath: The True Story of the Fighting Sioux* (1934); W. P. Webb, *The Texas Rangers* (1935); J. P. Dunn, *Massacres of the Mountains: A History of the Indian Wars of the Far West* (1886); C. T. Brady, *Northwest Fights and Fighters* (1907); and C. A. Fee, *Chief Joseph* (1936). The best accounts of the conflict between Indians and whites are Philip Sheridan, *Personal Memoirs* (2 vols., 1888); Marguerite Merington (ed.), *The Custer Story* (1950); Frederic Van de Water, *Glory Hunter: A Life of General Custer* (1934); N. A. Miles, *Serving the Republic* (1911); and F. C. Carrington, *My Army Life and the Fort Phil. Kearney Massacre* (1910). For Indian policy and the crusade for more humane treatment of the Indian, see Lewis Meriam and others, *The Problem of Indian Administration* (1928); G. D. Harmon, *Sixty Years of Indian Affairs* (1941); L. B. Priest, *Uncle Sam's Stepchildren, The Reformation of the United States Indian Policy, 1865–1887* (1942); and L. F. Schmeckebier, *The Office of Indian Affairs* (1927). See also H. H. Jackson, *A Century of Dishonor* (1887), a passionate plea for reform; G. W. Manypenny, *Our Indian Wards* (1880); Ethelbert Talbot, *My People of the Plains* (1906); James McLaughlin, *My Friend the Indian* (1910); and M. A. DeW. Howe, *Portrait of An Independent, Moorfield Storey, 1845–1929* (1932). J. P. Kinney's *A Continent Lost—A Civilization Won: Indian Land Tenure in America* (1937) and E. D. Branch, *The Hunting of the Buffalo* (1929) deal with special topics.

THE MINING FRONTIER. The best introduction to the history of the mining kingdom is T. A. Rickard, *A History of American Mining* (1932). It may be profitably supplemented with his more detailed account, *Man and Metals* (2 vols., 1932). H. H. Bancroft's *Histories of the Western States*, already cited, are rich sources of valuable material on this topic. See also G. C. Quiett, *Pay Dirt: A Panorama of American Gold Rushes* (1936), a popular account, as are C. B. Glasscock, *Gold in Them Hills* (1932) and *The War of the Copper Kings* (1935). Glasscock's, *Big Bonanza* (1931); C. H. Shinn, *The Story of the Mine* (1901); G. D. Lyman's *The Saga of the Comstock Lode* (1934); and E. Lord, *Comstock Mining and Miners* (monograph United States Geological Survey, no. 9, 1883) are concerned principally with the Comstock Lode. Oscar Lewis, *Silver Kings* (1947) is for popular consumption. S. E. White, *The Forty Niners* (1918), in the Chronicles of America series, and R. G. Cleland, *A History of California: The American Period* (1922) are lively accounts of the gold rush and its aftermath. W. J. Trimble, *The Mining Advance into the Inland Empire* (1914) is a scholarly presentation of an important development. Though not descriptive of the last frontier, W. B. Gates, Jr., *Michigan Copper and Boston Dollars: An Economic History of the Michigan Copper Mining Industry* (1951) sheds light on the mining industry of the period.

THE CATTLE KINGDOM. W. P. Webb's *The Great Plains*, previously cited, is unexcelled. Other excellent works are E. S. Osgood, *The Day of the Cattleman* (1929); E. E. Dale, *The Range Cattle Industry* (1930); Louis Pelzer, *The Cattlemen's Frontier* (1936); O. B. Peake, *The Colorado Range Cattle Industry* (1937); J. Evetts Haley, *The XIT Ranch of Texas* (1929), story of the X.I.T. ranch; and M. G. Burlingame, *The Montana Frontier* (1942), the last three being studies of special areas. Two other vivid portrayals of cattle areas are Struthers Burt, *Powder River* (1938) and Charles Lindsay, *The Big Horn Basin* (1932). The character and activities of the cowboy are best seen in Emerson Hough, *The Story of the Cowboy* (1897), P. A. Rollins, *The Cowboy* (rev. ed., 1936); E. D. Branch, *The Cowboy and His Interpreters* (1926); P. I. Wellman, *The Trampling Herd* (1939); R. M. Wright, *Dodge City, The Cowboy Capital* (1913); W. M. Raine and W. C. Barnes, *Cattle* (1930); Will James, *American Cowboy* (1942); Andy Adams, *The Log of a Cowboy* (1931); and Reed Anthony, *Cowman* (1907). For interesting contemporary accounts, see J. G. McCoy, *Historic Sketches of the Cattle Trade of the West and Southwest* (1940), written in 1874, and Stuart Henry, *Conquering Our Great American Plains* (1930). For an account of the trials, the cow towns, and the long drive, see, in addition to Webb's *The Great Plains*, G. R. Hebard and E. A. Brininstool, *The Bozeman Trail* (2 vols., 1922). The sheep frontier is treated in E. N. Wentworth's *America's Sheep Trails* (1948) and R. G. Cleland's *The Cattle on a Thousand Hills* (1941). On range balladry, consult J. A. Lomax, *Cowboy Songs* (1910) and *Songs of the Cattle Trail and Cow Camp* (1919), Badger Clark, *Sun and Saddle Leather* (1915), and E. F. Piper, *Barbed Wire and other Poems* (1917).

THE FARMER'S FRONTIER. The outstanding authority is F. A. Shannon, *The Farmer's Last Frontier, 1860–1897* (1945), in the Economic History of the United States series. On the public lands, consult G. I. Dubois and G. S. Matthews, *Galusha A. Grow, Father of the Homestead Act* (1917); R. M. Robbins, *Our Landed Heritage: The Public Domain, 1776–1936* (1942); B. H. Hibbard, *A History of the Public Land Policies* (1924); and Thomas Donaldson, *The Public Domain* (1884), which contains a mass of valuable undigested information. Also see P. W. Gates, "The Homestead Act in an Incongruous Land System," *American Historical Review*, Vol. XLI, no. 4 (July, 1946), pp. 652–81, and F. A. Shannon, "The Homestead Act and the Labor Surplus," *American Historical Review*, Vol. XLI, no. 4 (July, 1936), pp. 637–51. Willis Drummond, *Brief Description of the Public Lands of the United States of America, Prepared by the Commissioner of the General Land-Office for the Information of Foreigners Seeking a Home in the United States* (1873); H. N. Copp, *The American Settler's Guide: A Brief Exposition of the Public Land System of the United States of America* (2nd ed., 1882); and Henry George, *Our Land and Land Policy* (1902). On the settlement of the Trans-Mississippi West, see W. S. Thompson and P. K. Whelpton, *Population Trends in the United States* (1933); C. W. Thornthwaite and H. I. Slentz, *Internal Migration in the United States* (1934), excellent for maps; and C. L. Goodrich and others, *Migration and Economic Opportunity* (1936). The farmer's difficulties with the cattlemen are set forth in a number of federal government publications. Consult especially the 1880 *Report* of the Public Lands Commission; *Senate Executive Document* no. 127, 48th Cong., 1st Sess. (1883); *House Report*, no. 1809, 47th Cong. 1st Sess. (1881); and *House Miscellaneous Document* no. 45, 47th Cong., 2nd Sess. (1882), Vols. I–III. A number of works dealing with various vicissitudes of the frontier farmer should also be mentioned. For his troubles with the sheep rancher, see E. A. Carman, H. A. Heath, and John Minto, *The History and Present Condition of the Sheep Industry in the United States* (United States Dept. of Agr., Bureau of Animal Husbandry, Special Report, 1892); on adjustment to a new physical environment, J. C. Malin, "The Adaptation of the Agricultural System to Sub-Humid Environment" *Agricultural History*, Vol. X (July, 1936), pp. 118–42; and for water supply and fencing, W. P. Webb, *The Great Plains*, already cited, which is unequaled. On fencing, the last may be supplemented by E. W. Hayter, "Barbed Wire Fencing—a Prairie Invention," *Agricultural History*, Vol. XIII, (Oct., 1939), pp. 180–207 and "The Fencing of Western Railroads," *ibid.*, Vol. XIX, pp. 163–7. Information concerning the everyday life of the frontier farmer is dealt with by Everett Dick, *The Sod-House Frontier, 1854–1890* (1937) and *Vanguards of the Frontier* (1941); R. R. Wilson, *Out of the West* (1936); John Ise, *Sod and Stubble: The Story of A Kansas Homestead* (1936); A. F. Bentley, "The Condition of the Western Farmer as Illustrated by the Economic History of a Nebraska Township," Johns Hopkins University *Studies in Historical and Political Science*, Vol. XI (1893) pp. 285–370; H. E. Briggs, *Frontiers of the Northwest: A History of the Upper Missouri Valley* (1940); Ole Rolvaäg, *Giants in the Earth* (1929); Willa Cather, *O Pioneers!* (1913); E. J. Dies, *Titans of the Soil: Great Builders of Agriculture* (1949); Hamlin Garland, *Boy Life on the Prairie* (1899); Seth Humphrey, *Following the Prairie Frontier* (1931); and Joseph Schafer, *The Social History of American Agriculture* (1936).

CHAPTER 6

The Farming Business

Unfortunately, there is no history of American agriculture for the period after 1860 comparable to L. C. Gray, *History of Agriculture in the Southern United States to 1860* (2 vols., 1933) and P. W. Bidwell and J. I. Falconer, *History of Agriculture in the Northern United States, 1620–1860* (1925). Nevertheless, there is a great mass of monographic literature and an almost inexhaustible supply of official publications and other documentary material. The best bibliographies of this material are E. E. Edwards, *A Bibliography of the History of Agriculture in the United States*, Department of Agriculture, Miscellaneous Publication No. 84 (1930), and L. B. Schmidt, *Topical Studies and References on the History of American Agriculture* (4th ed., 1940). Exceedingly important, too, are the *Bulletins of the Department of Agriculture*, the *Bulletins of the Office of Experimental Stations*, the *Annual Reports of the Secretary of Agriculture*, and the *Yearbooks of the Department of Agriculture*. Certain of the *Yearbooks* are especially valuable. That for 1899, for example, devoted nearly 700 of its 880 pages to the history of different phases of agriculture; those for 1921–25 contain monographic material on farm crops and farm life; the *Yearbooks* for 1936 and 1937 are excellent handbooks on agricultural genetics; that for 1938 is one of the best accounts ever written on agricultural soils; the *Yearbook for 1940* is unsurpassed for its wealth of monographic material, including the admirable summary by E. E. Edwards, *American Agriculture—The First 300 Years* (1940). Volumes X and XI on agriculture of the *Report of the Industrial Commission*, already cited, are disappointing. The *Statistical Abstract* (1879-), the various decennial censuses, the *Yearbooks*, and the special *United States Census of Agriculture* (3 vols., 1925) are indispensable for statistical data. For maps, charts, and other graphic material, consult O. E. Baker (ed.), *Atlas of American Agriculture* (8 vols., 1917–35), published by United States Department of Agriculture. For the geographical basis, see J. R. Smith, *North America* (1925).

THE GROWTH OF AMERICAN AGRICULTURE. The best single volume carrying the period from 1860 to the end of the century is F. A. Shannon, *The Farmer's Last Frontier: Agriculture, 1860–1897* (1945), in the Economic History of the United States series. Brief accounts are A. H. Sanford, *The Story of Agriculture in the United States* (1916); E. L. Bogart, *Economic History of American Agriculture* (1923); and Joseph Schafer, *The Social History of American Agriculture* (1936). These volumes may be profitably supplemented by L. B. Schmidt and E. D. Ross (eds.), *Readings in the Economic History of American Agriculture* (1925). L. H. Bailey, *Cyclopedia of American Agriculture* (4 vols., 1907–09), especially Volume IV, contains much material that indicates the agricultural expansion of the nation. On irrigation and reclamation, see Elwood Mead, *Irrigation Institutions* (1903), an old work but still useful; R. P. Teele, *The Economics of Land Reclamation in the United States* (1927), first-rate; *The U. S. Reclamation Service: Its History, Activities and Organization*, Service Monograph of the United States Government, No. 2 (1919); and J. W. Haw and F. E. Schmidt, *Report on Federal Reclamation to the Secretary of the Interior* (1935), an excellent summary. On agricultural settlement, see bibliography, Chapter II above and R. T. Hill, *The Public Domain and Democracy* (1910); E. Van D. Robinson, *Early Economic Conditions and the Development of Agriculture in Minnesota* (1915); Rupert Vance, *Human Geography of the South* (1932); H. W. Odum, *Southern Regions of the United States* (1936); Joseph Schafer, *A History of Agriculture in Wisconsin* (1922); B. H. Hibbard, *The History of Agriculture in Dane County* (1904); J. G. Thompson, *The Rise and Decline of the Wheat Growing Industry in Wisconsin* (1909); U. P. Hedrick, *A History of Agriculture in the State of New York* (1933); H. F. Wilson, *The Hill Country of Northern New England, 1790–1930* (1936); and E. J. Wickson, *Rural California* (1923).

IMPROVED MACHINES AND TECHNIQUES. The best treatises on agricultural machinery are R. L. Ardrey, *American Agricultural Implements; A Review of Invention and Development in the Agricultural Implement Industry of the United States* (1894); E. H. Knight, *Agricultural Implements*, a report to the Commissioners of Agriculture on the Paris Exposition of 1878, 46th Cong., 3rd Sess., *House Executive Document* 42, part 5; E. W. Byrn, *The Progress of Invention in the Nineteenth Century* (1900); Waldemar Kaempffert (ed.), *A Popular History of American Invention* (2 vols., 1924), section of Volume II, pp. 1246–1309; R. M. La Follette (ed.) *The Making of America* (10 vols., 1905), especially Vol. V, pp. 332–42; H. N. Casson, *The Romance of the Reaper* (1908); W. MacDonald, *Makers of Modern Agriculture* (1913); and L. W. Ellis and E. A. Rumeley, *Power and the Plow* (1911). The second volume of W. T. Hutchinson's *Cyrus Hall McCormick* (2 vols., 1935) contains an exhaustive account of the development of post-Civil War harvesting machinery. Leo Rogin, *The Introduction of Farm Machinery in Its Relation to the Productivity of Labor in the Agriculture of the United States During the Nineteenth Century* (1931) deals primarily with the plow and with wheat production. For the influence of machinery since 1900, see O. E. Baker, "Changes in Production and Consumption of Our Farm Products and the Trend of Population," *Annals of the American Academy of Political and Social Science*, (March, 1929). The role played by the federal government in furthering agricultural expansion is described by W. L. Wanlass, *The United States Department of Agriculture, A Study in Administration* (1920) and A. C. True and V. A. Clark, *The Agricultural Experiment Stations in the United States* (1900). The Bureaus of the Department of Agriculture are elaborated by Milton Conover, *The Office of Experiment Stations* (1924); F. W. Powell, *The Bureau of Animal Industry* (1927); G. A. Weber, *The Bureau of Chemistry and Soils* (1928); Janks Cameron, *The Bureau of Dairy Industry* (1929); and G. A. Weber, *The Plant Quarantine and Control Administration* (1930). On agricultural education, the best work is A. C. True, *A History of Agricultural Extension Work in the United States, 1785–1923*, Department of Agriculture, Miscellaneous Publication No. 15 (1928).

and *A History of Agricultural Education in the United States, 1785-1925*, Department of Agriculture, Miscellaneous Publication No. 36 (1929). See, too, J. C. Bailey, *Seaman A. Knapp, Schoolmaster of American Agriculture* (1945); E. D. Ross *Democracy's College; The Land-Grant Movement in the Formative Stage* (1942); W. H. Shepardson, *Agricultural Education in the United States* (1929); and Eugene Davenport, *Education for Efficiency* (1909). On scientific agriculture, consult O. M. Kile, *The New Agriculture* (1932); A. C. True, *A History of Agricultural Experimentation and Research in the United States 1607-1925* (1937); Paul de Kruif, *Hunger Fighters* (1928); L. O. Howard, *A History of Applied Entomology*, Smithsonian Miscellaneous Collections, Vol. 84 (1930) and his *Fighting the Insects* (1933); D. G. Fairchild, *The World Was My Garden; Travels of a Plant Explorer* (1938); D. S. Jordan and V. Kellogg, *The Scientific Aspects of Luther Burbank's Work* (1909); H. S. Williams, *Luther Burbank, His Life and Work* (1915); and W. E. Smythe, *The Conquest of Arid America* (rev. ed., 1905). There are also many valuable articles on agricultural science in *Agricultural History*. Among the more important of these are: B. T. Galloway, "Plant Pathology; A Review of the Development of the Science in the United States," Vol. II, pp. 49-60; A. G. McCall, "The Development of Soil Science," Vol. V, pp. 43-56; K. A. Ryerson, "History and Significance of the Foreign Plant Introduction Work of the United States Development of Agriculture," Vol. VII, pp. 110-28; C. R. Ball, "The History of American Wheat Improvement," Vol. IV, pp. 48-71; and G. F. Johnson, "The Early History of Copper Fungicides," Vol. IX, pp. 67-9.

AGRICULTURAL SPECIALIZATION. On this topic the reader should consult F. I. Anderson, *The Farmer of Tomorrow* (1913); T. B. Gold, *Handbook of Connecticut Agriculture* (1901); C. H. Eckles, *Dairy Cattle and Milk Production* (rev. ed., 1939).

THE FARMER'S MARKET. There is much valuable material on this topic in three older works: "American Produce Exchange Markets," *Annals of the American Academy of Political and Social Science*, Vol. XXXVIII, No. 2 (1911); Volume VI of the *Report of the Industrial Commission*, already cited, on the "Distribution of Farm Products"; and H. C. Emery, *Speculation on the Stock and Produce Exchanges of the United States* (1896). More recent publications are H. M. Larson, *The Wheat Market and the Farmer in Minnesota, 1858-1900* (1926); C. H. Taylor, *History of the Board of Trade of the City of Chicago* (3 vols., 1917); *Report of the Federal Trade Commission on the Grain Trade* (7 vols., 1920-6), especially Vols. I-III; *Report of Federal Trade Commission on Methods and Operations of Grain Exporters* (2 vols., 1922-3); and W. H. Hubbard, *Cotton and the Cotton Market* (1923), which is very good.

THE FARMER AS BUSINESSMAN AND WORKER. The subject of farm cooperatives is best discussed by A. H. Hirsch, "Efforts of the Grange in the Middle West to Control the Price of Farm Machinery, 1870-1880," *Mississippi Valley Historical Review*, Vol. XV, pp. 473-96. O. N. Refsell, "The Farmer's Elevator Movement," *Journal of Political Economy*, Vol. XXII, pp. 872-95, 969-91; W. Gee and E. A. Terry, *The Cotton Coöperatives in the Southeast* (1933); and E. G. Nourse, *Fifty Years of Farmers' Elevators in Iowa*, Bulletin of Agriculture and Mechanic Arts No. 211 (1923). For later developments, see O. M. Kile, *The Farm Bureau Movement* (1921); R. H. Elsworth, *Agricultural Cooperative Associations, Marketing and Purchasing, 1925*, Department of Agriculture Technical Bulletin No. 40 (1928); and E. A. Stokdyk and C. H. West, *The Farm Board* (1930). On the marketing of livestock, see E. G. Nourse and J. G. Knapp, *The Cooperative Marketing of Livestock* (1931). The problems of the Pacific coast fruit-shippers are discussed by R. M. MacCurdy, *The History of the California Fruit Growers Exchange* (1925).

PATTERNS OF AGRARIAN DISCONTENT. The best brief volume on this topic is S. J. Buck, *The Agrarian Crusade* (1920), in the Chronicles of America series. The same author's *The Granger Movement* (1913) is the standard authority on this subject. Equally authoritative is J. D. Hicks' *The Populist Revolt* (1931). Unsympathetic is F. L. Mcvey, *The Populist Movement* (1896). Also see F. B. Simkins, *The Tillman Movement in South Carolina* (1926) and his *Pitchfork Ben Tillman, South Carolinian* (1944); C. Vann Woodward, *Tom Watson; Agrarian Rebel* (1938), and his *Origins of the New South* (1951), which contains an understanding account of southern Populism in addition to much new material on the South between the years 1876–1913; A. M. Arnett, *The Populist Movement in Georgia* (1922); W. D. Sheldon, *Populism in the Old Dominion; Virginia Farm Politics, 1885–1900* (1935); W. J. Bryan, *The First Battle* (1896); Elmer Ellis, *Henry Moore Teller, Defender of the West* (1941); F. E. Haynes, *James Baird Weaver* (1919) and *Third Party Movements Since the Civil War, with Special Reference to Iowa; A Study in Social Politics* (1916); Nathan Fine, *Labor and Farmer Parties in the United States, 1828–1928* (1928); and the following articles: J. D. Hicks, "The Political Career of Ignatius Donnelly," *Mississippi Valley Historical Review*, Vol. VIII, pp. 80–132; H. C. Nixon, "The Economic Basis of the Populist Movement in Iowa," *Iowa Journal of History and Politics*, Vol. XXI, pp. 373–96 and "The Populist Movement in Iowa," ibid., Vol. XXII, pp. 3–107; L. W. Fuller, "Colorado's Revolt Against Capitalism," *Mississippi Valley Historical Review*, Vol. XXI, pp. 343–60; D. M. Robinson, "Tennessee Politics and the Agrarian Revolt," ibid., Vol. XX, pp. 365–80; C. M. Destler, "Consummation of a Labor-Populist Alliance in Illinois," ibid., Vol. XXVII, pp. 589–602; Sidney Glazer, "Patrons of Industry in Michigan," ibid., Vol. XXIV, pp. 185–94; and Harvey Wish, "John P. Altgeld and the Backbone of the Campaign of 1896," ibid., Vol. XXIV, pp. 503–18. For a vicious attack on the Populist movement, read F. B. Tracy, "Rise and Doom of the Populist Party," *The Forum*, Vol. XVI, pp. 241–50. The principal grievances of the farmer, in addition to prices and marketing, were centered on credit and tenancy. On the former, see E. S. Sparks, *History and Theory of Agricultural Credit in the United States* (1932); J. B. Norman, *Farm Credits in the United States and Canada* (1924); and Clara Eliot, *The Farmers' Campaign for Credit* (1927). On tenancy, consult the 1923 *Agricultural Yearbook*; L. C. Gray "The Trend in Farm Ownership," *Annals of the American Academy of Political and Social Science* (March, 1929); *Farm Tenancy, Report of the President's Committee, Prepared Under the Auspices of the National Resources Committee* (1937); E. A. Goldenweiser and L. E. Truesdell, *Farm Tenancy in the United States*, Census Monographs No. 4, 1920 Census (1924); and J. D. Black and R. H. Allen, "The Growth of Farm Tenancy in the United States," *Quarterly Journal of Economics*, Vol. LI, pp. 393–425. Farm discontent is also reflected in such volumes as C. E. Russell, *Bare Hands and Stone Walls* (1933); J. W. Witham, *Fifty Years on the Firing Line* (1924); Herbert Quick, *One Man's Life* (1925), *Vandemark's Folly* (1922), and *The Hawkeye* (1923); Mari Sandoz, *Old Jules* (1935); Hamlin Garland, *A Son of the Middle Border* (1917); Willa Cather, *O Pioneers!* (1913) and *My Antonia* (1918); Ole Rolvaåg, *Giants in the Earth* (1927); Frank Norris, *The Octopus* (1901); W. A. White, *A Certain Rich Man* (1909); G. H. Carroll, *As The Earth Turns* (1933); Ellen Glasgow, *Barren Ground* (1925); Edward Howe, *The Story of a Country Town* (1884); Louis Bromfield, *The Farm* (1933); Ruth Suckow, *Iowa Interiors* (1926) and *The Folks* (1934); and Josephine Johnson, *Now in November* (1934).

CHAPTER 7

The Politics of Conformity and Revolt

A first-class political history covering the last two decades of the nineteenth century is yet to be written. Neither of the two general histories, J. F. Rhodes,

History of the United States from the Compromise of 1850 (9 vols., 1900–28) and E. P. Oberholtzer, *A History of the United States Since the Civil War* (5 vols., 1917–37) are satisfactory. E. E. Sparks, *National Development, 1877–1885* (1907) and D. R. Dewey, *National Problems, 1885–1897* (1907), in the American Nation series, need the benefit of more recent scholarship. Volume II of C. A. and M. R. Beard, *The Rise of American Civilization* (4 vols., rev. and enl., 1933) is excellent but suffers from brevity. H. T. Peck, *Twenty Years of the Republic, 1885–1905* (1906) is a popular, well-written account. On parties and politics, consult Edward Stanwood, *A History of the Presidency* (2 vols., 1928); E. E. Robinson, *The Evolution of American Political Parties* (1924); W. E. Binkley, *American Political Parties* (1943); C. E. Merriam, *The American Party System* (4th ed., 1949); M. Ostrogorski, *Democracy and the Organization of Political Parties* (2 vols., 1902); H. J. Ford, *The Rise and Growth of American Politics* (1898); and Nathan Fine, *Labor and Farmer Parties in the United States, 1828–1928* (1928). For institutional history, James Bryce, *The American Commonwealth* (new ed., 2 vols., rev. 1931–3); Herbert Agar, *The Price of Union* (1950); and L. D. White, *The Republican Era 1865–1900* (1958) are unsurpassed. Fortunately, the student delving into the political history of the years after Reconstruction has at his disposal a wealth of material in the form of memoirs, biographies, and autobiographies. For brief accounts of those who played a part on the political scene there is the *Dictionary of American Biography*. See also Matthew Josephson, *The Politicos, 1865–1896* (1938); W. A. White, *Masks in a Pageant* (1928); A. W. Dunn, *From Harrison to Harding* (2 vols., 1922); and Margaret Leech, *In the Days of McKinley* (1959), a delightful study. Also consult N. W. Stephenson, *Nelson W. Aldrich: A Leader in American Politics* (1930), which is very partisan; Harry Barnard, *Eagle Forgotten, The Life of John P. Altgeld* (1938); G. F. Howe, *Chester A. Arthur* (1934); S. H. Acheson, *Joe Bailey, The Last of the Democrats* (1932); Margaret Clapp, *Forgotten First Citizen: John Bigelow* (1947); D. S. Muzzey, *James G. Blaine, A Political Idol of Other Days* (1934), which is excellent; C. E. Russell, *Blaine of Maine: His Life and Times* (1931); Lew Wallace, *The Life of Gen. Ben Harrison* (1888), a campaign biography; J. G. Blaine, *Twenty Years in Congress* (2 vols., 1884–6); W. V. Byars, *An American Commoner: The Life and Times of Richard Parks Bland* (1900), the only full length biography of "Silver Dick"; L. W. Busbey, *Uncle Joe Cannon* (1927), which is overly sympathetic; J. A. Barnes, *John G. Carlisle, Financial Statesman* (1931), which is excellent, especially on money questions; L. B. Richardson, *William E. Chandler, Republican* (1940); Robert McElroy, *Grover Cleveland* (2 vols., 1923), which is too eulogistic; Allan Nevins, *Grover Cleveland: A Study in Courage* (1932), which is well balanced and may be supplemented by *Letters of Grover Cleveland, 1850–1908* (1933), edited by the same author; S. M. Cullom, *Fifty Years of Public Service* (1911); D. B. Chidsey, *The Gentleman from New York: A Life of Roscoe Conkling* (1935); A. R. Conkling, *Life and Letters of Roscoe Conkling* (1889); D. L. Alexander, *Four Famous New Yorkers: The Political Careers of Cleveland, Platt, Hill and Roosevelt* (1923); Ray Ginger, *The Bending Cross: Eugene V. Debs* (1949); T. C. Smith, *Life and Letters of James Abram Garfield* (2 vols., 1925); R. G. Caldwell, *James A. Garfield, Party Chieftain* (1931); Herbert Croly, *Marcus Alonzo Hanna* (1912); Thomas Beer, *Hanna* (1929); Paxton Hibben, *The Peerless Leader: William Jennings Bryan* (1929) and M. R. Werner, *Bryan* (1929), both satirical; J. C. Long, *Bryan, the Great Commoner* (1928); W. J. Bryan, *The First Battle: A Story of the Campaign of 1896* (1896); Tyler Dennett, *John Hay: From Poetry to Politics* (1933), which is excellent; W. R. Thayer, *John Hay* (2 vols., 1910); C. R. Williams, *The Life of Rutherford B. Hayes* (2 vols., 1914), an able presentation; H. J. Eckenrode, *Rutherford B. Hayes, Statesman of Reunion* (1930), a good study; C. R. Williams, *The Diary and Letters of Rutherford Birchard Hayes* (5 vols., 1922–6); Allan Nevins, *Abram S. Hewitt: With Some Account of Peter Cooper* (1935); F. H. Gillett, *George Frisbie Hoar* (1934); G. F. Hoar, *Autobiography of Seventy Years*

(2 vols., 1903); G. G. Clarke, *George W. Julian* (1923); W. A. Cate, *Lucius Q. C. Lamar, Secession and Reunion* (1935), which is first-rate; Robert McElroy, *Levi P. Morton: Banker, Diplomat, Statesman* (1930); R. D. Bowden, *Boise Penrose* (1937); H. F. Gosnell, *Boss Platt and His New York Machine* (1924); T. C. Platt, *Autobiography of Thomas Collier Platt* (1910); Rollo Ogden, *The Life and Letters of Edwin Lawrence Godkin* (2 vols., 1907); Edward Cary, *George William Curtis* (1894); W. A. Robinson, *Thomas B. Reed, Parliamentarian* (1930); S. W. McCall, *The Life of Thomas Brackett Reed* (1911), eulogistic; C. M. Fuess, *Carl Schurz, Reformer* (1932); Joseph Schafter, *Carl Schurz, Militant Liberal* (1930); Carl Schurz, *Reminiscences* (3 vols., 1907–08); John Sherman, *John Sherman's Recollections of Forty Years in the House, Senate and Cabinet* (2 vols., 1895), dull, as is T. E. Burton, *John Sherman* (1906); D. W. Grantham, *Hoke Smith and the Politics of the New South* (1958); Matilda Gresham, *Life of Walter Quinton Gresham, 1832–95* (2 vols., 1919); Royal Cortissoz, *The Life of Whitelaw Reid* (2 vols., 1921); Elmer Ellis, *Henry Moore Teller, Defender of the West* (1941); A. C. Flick, *Samuel Jones Tilden: A Study in Political Sagacity* (1939), which is definitive and displaces John Bigelow, *The Life of Samuel J. Tilden* (2 vols., 1895); J. F. Fall, *Henry Watterson, Reconstructed Rebel* (1956); F. E. Haynes, *James Baird Weaver* (1919), excellent; M. A. Hirsch, *William C. Whitney* (1948); Walter Johnson, *William Allen White's America* (1947); and C. S. Olcott, *The Life of William McKinley* (2 vols., 1916), which is somewhat uncritical.

HAYES, GARFIELD AND ARTHUR. On Hayes's Administration, see J. W. Burgess, *Administration of President Hayes* (1916), scholarly; F. E. Haynes, *Third Party Movements Since the Civil War, with Special Reference to Iowa*, previously cited, which discusses the Greenback movement; A. D. Noyes, *Forty Years of American Finance* (1898); W. C. Mitchell, *A History of the Greenbacks* (1903); J. L. Laughlin, *History of Bimetallism in the United States* (4th ed., 1897); E. B. Usher, *The Greenback Movement of 1875–1884 and Wisconsin's Part in It* (1911). For Garfield and Arthur, see Henry Adams, *The Education of Henry Adams* (1927); K. H. Porter, *National Party Platforms* (1924); C. R. Fish, *The Civil Service and the Patronage* (1905); A. B. Sageser, *The First Two Decades of the Pendelton Act* (1935), a thorough study; and F. M. Stewart, *The National Civil Service Reform League* (1929).

CLEVELAND AND HARRISON. See H. S. Merrill, *Bourbon Democracy of the Middle West* (1953), a recent good account, and H. C. Thomas, *The Return of the Democratic Party to Power in 1884* (1919). See also H. J. Ford, *The Cleveland Era* (1919), in the Chronicles of America series. On pensions, see W. H. Glasson, *Federal Military Pensions in the United States* (1918) and J. W. Oliver, *History of the Civil War Military Pensions* (1917). On the tariff controversy, consult P. W. C. Ashley, *Modern Tariff History* (1904); Edward Stanwood, *American Tariff Controversies in the Nineteenth Century* (2 vols., 1903); F. W. Taussig, *The Tariff History of the United States* (rev. ed., 1931); Hugh McCulloch, *Men and Measures of Half a Century* (1888); W. D. Orcutt, *Burrows of Michigan and the Republican Party* (2 vols., 1917), which gives arguments for high protection; and I. M. Tarbell, *The Tariff in Our Times* (1911), an unbiased account. For Cleveland's second election, the best account is G. H. Knoles, *The Presidential Campaign and Election of 1892* (1942).

THE CURRENCY ISSUE AND THE GOLD STANDARD. On monetary standards, see references cited under Hayes, Garfield, and Arthur above and D. R. Dewey, *Financial History of the United States* (12th ed., 1936); A. B. Hepburn, *A History of Coinage and Currency in the United States and the Perennial Contest for Sound Money* (1905); M. S. Wildman, *Money Inflation in the United States* (1905); Horace White, *Money and Banking* (rev. ed., 1914); W. H. Harvey, *Coin's Financial School* (1894), propaganda for cheap money; and Grover Cleveland, *Presidential Problems* (1904). On the Panic of 1893, the standard book is W. J. Lauck, *The Causes of the Panic of 1893* (1907), which emphasizes the monetary situation as principal cause; not definitive, but better is F. B. Weberg, *The Background of the Panic of 1893* (1929). On unemployment and industrial unrest, consult D. L. McMurry, *Coxeys Army* (1929). The Pullman strike and its aftermath are discussed in Harry Barnard, *Eagle Forgotten, the Life of John Peter Altgeld* (1938), cited earlier, which gives Altgeld's position in the Cleveland-Altgeld controversy; Edward Berman, *Labor Disputes and the President of the United States* (1924); Grover Cleveland, *The Government in the Chicago Strike of 1894* (1913); Henry James, *Richard Olney and His Public Service* (1923); Coleman McAlister, *Eugene V. Debs: A Man Unafraid* (1930), which discusses Debs' relation to the Pullman strike; Almont Lindsey, *The Pullman Strike* (1942); and *United States Strike Commission Report*, 53rd Cong., 3rd Sess., Senate Executive Document no. 7. For the Homestead strike, see George Harvey, *Henry Clay Frick*, cited earlier. On the income-tax decision, consult Sidney Ratner, *American Taxation* (1941); Charles Warren, *The Supreme Court in United States History* (3 vols., final rev., 1937), Vol. III; and L. Boudin, *Government by Judiciary* (1932). For relations with the Morgan interests on the bond issue, consult Lewis Corey, *The House of Morgan* (1930) and F. L. Allen, *The Great Pierpont Morgan* (1949).

THE AGRARIAN PROTEST. See the references under "Patterns of Agrarian Protest," Chapter 6, and B. B. Kendrick, "Agrarian Discontent in the South, 1880–1890," *American Historical Association Report* (1920), pp. 267–72 (1925); Hallie Farmer, "Economic Background of Frontier Populism," *Mississippi Valley Historical Review*, Vol. X, pp. 406–27 (March, 1924); C. R. Miller, "Background of Populism in Kansas," ibid., Vol. XI (March, 1925), pp. 469–89; C. McA. Destler, *American Radicalism, 1865–1901, Essays and Documents* (1946); and his "Western Radicalism 1865–1901," *Mississippi Valley Historical Review*, Vol. XXXI (December, 1944), pp. 335–68; and P. R. Fossum, *The Agrarian Movement in North Dakota* (1925).

THE CAMPAIGN OF 1896 AND ITS AFTERMATH. In addition to the biographic material listed at the beginning of this chapter, especially that dealing with Bryan and McKinley, consult H. T. Peck, *Twenty Years of the Republic, 1885–1905*, already cited; C. Vann Woodward, *Tom Watson, Agrarian Rebel* (1938); Walter Johnson, *William Allen White's America*, cited previously; and Harvey Wish, "John Peter Altgeld and the Background of the Campaign of 1896," *Mississippi Valley Historical Review*, Vol. XXIV, pp. 503–18 (March, 1938). For the gold Democrats and the split in the Democratic party, see Mark Hirsch, *William C. Whitney*, cited above, and J. C. Olson, *J. Sterling Morton* (1942). For source material, see W. J. Bryan, *The First Battle*, cited above, and H. S. Commager, *Documents of American History* (5th ed., 1950).

CHAPTER 8

Expansion Overseas

S. F. Bemis and G. G. Griffin, *Guide to the Diplomatic History of the United States* (1935) is indispensable for bibliography. See also S. F. Bemis (ed.), *The American Secretaries of State and Their Diplomacy* (10 vols., 1927–9); Vols. VI and VIII cover this chapter. The two most satisfactory texts are T. A. Bailey, *A Diplomatic History of the American People* (4th ed., 1950) and S. F. Bemis, *A Diplomatic History of the United States* (3rd ed., 1950). Other texts are R. G. Adams, *A History of the Foreign Policy of the United States* (1924); J. H. Latané and D. W. Wainhouse, *A History of American Foreign Policy* (rev. ed., 1940); L. M. Sears, *A History of American Foreign Relations* (rev. 3rd ed., 1936); and W. F. Johnson, *American Foreign Relations* (2 vols., 1916). On the psychology of imperialism, consult J. A. Hobson, *Imperialism* (rev. 3rd ed., 1938); P. T. Moon, *Imperialism and World Politics* (1926); and A. K. Weinberg, *Manifest Destiny: A*

Study of Nationalist Expansion in American History (1935). A. L. P. Dennis, *Adventures in American Diplomacy, 1896–1906* (1928) is valuable for the period covered. B. H. Williams, *Economic Foreign Policy of the United States* (1929) and Dexter Perkins, *Hands Off: A History of the Monroe Doctrine* (1941) are excellent.

IMPERIALIST WITHOUT A MANDATE. F. E. Chadwick, *The Relations of the United States and Spain, Diplomacy* (1909) discusses the *Virginius* affair. See also R. W. Logan, *The Diplomatic Relations of the United States with Haiti, 1776–1891* (1941). C. C. Tansill, *The Purchase of the Danish West Indies* (1932) treats Seward's designs, and his *The United States and Santo Domingo, 1789–1873* (1938) is excellent. Allan Nevins, *Hamilton Fish*, already cited, is indispensable on the diplomacy of the Grant Administration. Nor should A. F. Tyler's *The Foreign Policy of James G. Blaine* (1927) be overlooked. Sumner Welles, *Naboth's Vineyard* (1928) covers American imperialistic ambitions in the island of Santo Domingo.

THE WILL TO EXPAND. The Alabama Claims, Venezuelan crisis, and other matters are covered by W. A. Dunning, *The British Empire and the United States* (1914); R. W. Mowat, *The Diplomatic Relations of Great Britain and the United States* (1925); G. R. Dulebohn, *Principles of Foreign Policy Under the Cleveland Administration* (1941); Dexter Perkins, *The Monroe Doctrine, 1867–1907* (1937); and C. C. Tansill, *The Foreign Policy of Thomas F. Bayard, 1885–1897* (1940); valuable also in this connection are Henry James, *Richard Olney and His Public Service* (1923) and Allan Nevins, *Hamilton Fish* (1936). For Canadian-American relations, see the excellent volume by J. B. Brebner, *The North Atlantic Triangle: The Interplay of Canada, the United States, and Great Britain* (1945); L. B. Shippee, *Canadian American Relations, 1849–1874* (1939); Goldwin Smith, *The Treaty of Washington, 1871: A Study in Imperial History* (1941); P. E. Corbett, *The Settlement of Canadian-American Disputes* (1937); and Brainerd Dyer, *The Public Career of William M. Evarts* (1933). On the acquisition of Alaska, consult J. M. Callahan, *The Alaska Purchase and Americo-Canadian Relations* (1908); J. P. Nichols, *Alaska. . . . Under the Rule of the United States* (1924), a first-rate account; V. J. Farrar, *The Annexation of Russian America to the United States* (1937), containing new material; T. A. Bailey, "Why The United States Purchased Alaska," *Pacific Historical Review*, Vol. III, pp. 39–49 (1934); B. P. Thomas, *Russo-American Relations, 1815–1867* (1930); and S. R. Tompkins, *Alaska, Promyshlennik and Sourdough* (1945), which summarizes the Alaska purchase.

INTERVENTION IN SAMOA. The best accounts are R. L. Stevenson, *A Footnote to History: Eight Years of Trouble in Samoa* (1892); J. W. Foster, *American Diplomacy in the Orient* (1903); J. M. Callahan, *American Relations in the Pacific and in the Far East, 1784–1900* (1901); and G. H. Ryden, *The Foreign Policy of the United States in Relation of Samoa* (1933), which is excellent.

THE ANNEXATION OF HAWAII. The accounts in Rhodes and Oberholtzer are somewhat superficial. See S. K. Stevens, *American Expansion in Hawaii, 1842–1898* (1945); Charles Nordhoff, *Northern California, Oregon and the Sandwich Islands* (1874), which sheds light on American penetration; C. Whitney, *Hawaiian America* (1899); Katherine Coman, *The History of Contract Labor in the Hawaiian Islands* (1903); S. B. Dole, *Memoirs of the Hawaiian Revolution* (1936); J. E. Carpenter, *America in Hawaii* (1899); and Tyler Dennett, *Americans in Eastern Asia* (1922). G. F. Hoar, *Autobiography*, already cited, and R. F. Pettigrew, *The Course of Empire* (1920) are the reactions of anti-imperialist senators. J. W. Pratt, *Expansionists of 1898* (1936), presents new materials and fresh interpretation. See also H. W. Bradley, *The American Frontier in Hawaii: The Pioneers, 1789–1843* (1942) and "Hawaii and the American Penetration of the Northeastern Pacific, 1801–1845," *Pacific Historical Review*, Vol. XII, pp. 277–86 (1943). For the period of pre-American penetration, see R. S. Kuykendall, *The Hawaiian Kingdom, 1778–1854* (1938).

THE MARTIAL SPIRIT. On this topic, see C. A. Beard, *The Idea of National Interest* (1934); B. H. Williams, *Economic Foreign Policy of the United States*, previously cited; Scott Nearing and Joseph Freeman, *Dollar Diplomacy* (1925); J. F. Rhodes, *The McKinley and Roosevelt Administrations, 1897–1902* (1922); Joseph Wisan, *The Cuban Crisis as Reflected in the New York Press, (1895–1898)* (1934); Marcus Wilkerson, *Public Opinion and the Spanish-American War* (1932); and G. W. Anxier, "The Propaganda Activities of the Cuban *Junta* in Precipitating the Spanish-American War, 1895–1898," *Hispanic American Historical Review*, Vol. XIX (1939), pp. 286–305. J. W. Pratt, *Expansionists of 1898*, previously cited, is indispensable for the emotional and psychological background of imperialism. Illuminating, too, are J. B. Moore, *Four Phases of American Development: Federalism-Democracy-Imperialism-Expansion* (1912); A. T. Mahan, *From Sail to Steam: Recollections on Naval Life* (1907); and C. C. Taylor, *The Life of Admiral Mahan* (1920); W. D. Puleston, *Mahan* (1939). R. S. West, *Admirals of American Empire* (1948) tells the story of Dewey, Simpson, and other Great White Fleet Admirals. H. F. Pringle, *Theodore Roosevelt* (1931) and C. G. Bowers, *Beveridge and the Progressive Era* (1932) are accounts of two leading imperialists.

LIQUIDATING THE SPANISH EMPIRE. The leading authorities are F. E. Chadwick, *The Relations of the United States and Spain* (2 vols., 1909–11); Walter Millis, *The Martial Spirit: A Study of Our War with Spain* (1931); E. J. Benton, *International Law and Diplomacy of the Spanish-American War* (1908); Orestes Ferrara, *The Last Spanish War* (1937), which sheds new light on the basis of material from the Spanish archives; J. D. Long, *The New American Navy, 1897–1902* (1913), which argues for a bigger navy; A. T. Mahan, *Lessons of the War with Spain* (1899); R. A. Alger, *The Spanish American War* (1901), by the Secretary of War; T. R. Roosevelt, *The Rough Riders* (1899); George Dewey, *Autobiography* (1913); N. A. Miles, *Serving the Republic* (1911); J. W. Pratt, *Expansionists of 1898*, already cited; C. D. Sigsbee, *The "Maine": An Account of Her Destruction in Havana Harbor* (1899); H. H. Sargent, *The Campaign of Santiago de Cuba* (3 vols., 1907), which discusses the principal naval and military campaigns in Cuba; W. S. Schley, *Forty-Five Years Under the Flag* (1904); Joseph Wheeler, *The Santiago Campaign* (1898); John Bigelow, *Reminiscences of the Santiago Campaign* (1899); and Frederick Funston, *Memories of Two Wars* (1911). On foreign relations during the war, see R. A. Reuter, *Anglo-American Relations During the Spanish-American War* (1924); L. B. Shipee, "Germany and the Spanish-American War," *American Historical Review*, Vol. XX (July, 1925), pp. 754–77; and R. H. Heindel, *The American Impact on Britain, 1898–1914* (1940). Important, too, are Tyler Dennett, *John Hay: From Poetry to Politics*, already cited; P. C. Jessup, *Elihu Root* (2 vols., 1938); and Royal Cortissoz, *The Life of Whitelaw Reid* (2 vols., 1921). For the Treaty of Paris, see the volumes by Chadwick and Benton above and *Papers on the Treaty of Paris*, 55th Cong., 3rd Sess., Senate Document no. 62. The hue and cry against imperialistic expansion by the United States was loudly expressed in the writings of the anti-imperialists. See especially M. E. Curti, *Bryan and World Peace* (1931); Moorfield Storey and M. P. Lichauco, *The Conquest of the Philippines by the United States, 1898–1925* (1926); A. S. Pier, *American Apostles to the Philippines* (1950); M. A. DeW. Howe, *Portrait of an Independent, Moorfield Storey* (1932); G. F. Hoar, *Autobiography of Seventy Years*, cited earlier, and the *Autobiography of Andrew Carnegie* (1920); F. H. Harrington, "The Anti-Imperialist Movement in the United States, 1898–1900," *Mississippi Valley Historical Review*, Vol. XXII (September, 1935), pp. 211–23; and T. A. Bailey, "Was the Presidential Election of 1900 a Mandate on Imperialism?," ibid., Vol. XXIV (June, 1937), pp. 43–52.

CHAPTER 9
The American Empire

The acquisition of a colonial empire brought to the United States many vexing problems. By all odds the most valuable single volume is J. W. Pratt's admirable *America's Colonial Experiment: How the United States Gained, Governed, and in Part Gave Away a Colonial Empire* (1950). Also of great value is H. K. Beale, *Theodore Roosevelt and the Rise of America to World Power* (1956). On the constitutional status of these acquisitions, see W. F. Willoughby, *Territories and Dependencies of the United States* (1905); C. F. Randolph, *The Law and Policy of Annexation* (1901); and C. E. Magoon, *Report on the Legal Status of the Territory. . . . Acquired by the United States During the War with Spain* (1900).

PROBLEMS OF ADMINISTRATION. The best single volume is probably W. H. Haas, *The American Empire* (1940). See also W. D. Boyce, *United States Colonies and Dependencies* (1914); A. L. P. Dennis, *Adventures in American Diplomacy, 1896–1906* (1928); J. H. Latané, *America as a World Power, 1897–1907* (1907), in the American Nations series; J. F. Rippy, *Latin America in World Politics* (rev. ed., 1931); G. H. Stuart, *Latin America and the United States* (4th ed., 1943). J. E. Thomson, *Our Atlantic Possessions* (1928) and *Our Pacific Possessions* (1931) are both very readable. On Cuba, consult L. H. Jenks, *Our Cuban Colony, A Study in Sugar* (1928); Carleton Beals, *The Crime of Cuba* (1934), far from objective; H. F. Guggenheim, *The United States and Cuba* (1934), a defense of United States domination of the island; D. A. Lockmiller, *Magoon in Cuba: A History of the Second Intervention, 1906–1909* (1938), a defense of Magoon's regime; and C. L. Jones, *Caribbean Interests of the United States* (1916). See also A. G. Robinson, *Cuba and the Intervention* (1905); G. H. Stuart, *Cuba and Its International Relations* (1923); and C. E. Chapman, *A History of the Cuban Republic* (1927). Three works cover the essential material on Puerto Rico: B. W. and J. W. Diffie, *Porto Rico: A Broken Pledge* (1931), which is extremely critical of American occupation; Knowlton Mixer, *Porto Rico* (1926), which traces the history of American occupation, and V. S. Clark and others, *Porto Rico and Its Problems* (1930), an objective survey. On the Philippines, the literature is large. See D. C. Worcester, *The Philippines Past and Present* (2 vols., 1914), which discusses the administration of the islands to 1913; C. B. Elliot, *The Philippines* (1917); W. C. Forbes, *The Philippine Islands* (2 vols., 1928), a careful evaluation by an admirer of American achievement; J. H. Blount, *The American Occupation of the Philippines, 1898–1912* (1912); J. A. Le Roy, *The Americans in the Philippines* (2 vols., 1914); D. P. Barrows, *A History of the Philippines* (rev. ed., 1924); F. B. Harrison, *The Cornerstone of Philippine Independence* (1922), an account by an anti-imperialistic Governor General; Nicholas Roosevelt, *The Philippines, A Treasure and a Problem* (1926); J. S. Reyes, *Legislative History of America's Economic Policy Toward the Philippines* (1923); J. R. Hayden, *The Philippines, A Study in National Development* (1942), an able study; Grayson Kirk, *Philippine Independence* (1936), an able survey; and H. Hagedorn, *Leonard Wood* (2 vols., 1931), which defends an unpopular Governor.

POWER POLITICS IN THE FAR EAST. On this subject there is also abundant literature. See J. M. Callahan, *American Relations in the Pacific and in the Far East,* previously cited; Tyler Dennett, *Americans in Eastern Asia* (1922); T. F. Millard, *America and the Far Eastern Question* (1909); F. R. Dulles, *China and America . . . since 1784* (1946); J. W. Foster, *American Diplomacy in the Orient* (1903); A. W. Griswold, *The Far Eastern Policy of the United States* (1938); W. W. Willoughby, *Foreign Rights and Interests in China* (2 vols., rev., 1927), which covers the relations of the great powers to China; H. K. Norton, *China and the Powers* (1927); J. G. Reid, *The Manchu Abdication and the Powers, 1908–1912* (1935), which is excellent; J. V. A. MacMurray, *Treaties and Agreements With and Concerning China, 1894–1919* (2 vols., 1921); P. S. Rensch, *An American Diplomat in China* (1922); P. H. Clyde, *A History of the Modern and Contemporary Far East* (1937); G. H. Blakeslee, *Conflicts of Policy in the Far East* (1934); M. Pao, *The Open Door Doctrine in Relation to China* (1923); P. H. Clements, *The Boxer Rebellion* (1915), scholarly; H. Chung, *The Oriental Policy of the United States* (1919); P. J. Treat, *Japan and the United States, 1853–1921* (2nd ed., 1928), *The Diplomatic Relations Between the United States and Japan, 1853–1895* (1932), and the companion volume, *Diplomatic Relations Between the Uited States and Japan, 1895–1905* (1938); F. R. Dulles, *Forty Years of American-Japanese Relations* (1937); and J. A. Barnes (ed.), *Empire in the East* (1934), which is highly critical of American policy.

THE STRUGGLE FOR THE PANAMA CANAL. For historical background, see H. G. Miller, *The Isthmian Highway* (rev. ed., 1932); J. B. Bishop, *The Panama Gateway* (1913); and W. J. Abbott, *Panama and the Canal* (1914). For the creation of the Republic of Panama, consult Philippe Bunau-Varilla, *Panama, The Creation, Destruction, and Resurrection* (1914), by the leading conspirator; W. D. McCain, *The United States and the Republic of Panama* (1937); and H. F. Pringle, *Theodore Roosevelt* (1931), which is highly critical of Roosevelt's part in creating the new republic. On the actual selection and building of the canal, see D. C. Miner, *The Fight for the Panama Route* (1940), excellent; M. P. DuVal, *Cadiz to Cathay* (1940) and *And the Mountains Will Move; the Story of the Building of the Panama Canal* (1947); Gerstle Mack, *The Land Divided* (1944); J. B. and F. Bishop, *Goethals, Genius of the Panama Canal* (1930); C. I. Judson, *Soldier Doctor* (1942), the life of Gorgas; and B. J. Hendrick, *W. C. Gorgas, His Life and Work* (1924). Other works of value are: H. C. Hill, *Roosevelt and the Caribbean* (1927); E. R. Johnson, *The Panama Canal and Commerce* (1916); W. H. Callcott, *The Caribbean Policy of the United States, 1890–1920* (1942); J. F. Rippy, *The Capitalists and Colombia* (1931), which describes Panama's revolution; M. W. Williams, *Anglo-American Isthmian Diplomacy, 1815–1915* (1916), an able study; Scott Nearing and Joseph Freeman, *Dollar Diplomacy*, cited earlier, which is biased; J. B. Bishop, *Theodore Roosevelt and His Times* (2 vols., 1920); and the congressional investigations: *Diplomatic History of Panama*, 63rd Cong., 2nd Sess., Senate Document no. 474, and *Senate Committee on Interoceanic Canals*, 59th Cong., 2nd Sess., Senate Document no. 401.

BUSINESS AND IMPERIALISM. The best bibliographic sources are P. T. Moon, *Syllabus on International Relations* (1925) and the quarterly lists of books in *Foreign Affairs* (1922–). There is both textual and bibliographic material in R. L. Buell, *International Relations* (rev. ed., 1932); W. S. Culbertson, *International Economic Policies* (1925); P. T. Moon, *Imperialism and World Politics*, cited previously; and Achille Viallate, *Economic Imperialism and International Relations During the Last Fifty Years* (1923). For trade between continental United States and its colonial overseas empire, see E. R. Johnson and others, *History of Domestic and Foreign Commerce of the United States* (2 vols., 1915) and National Industrial Conference Board, *Trends in the Foreign Trade of the United States* (1930). On economic relations of the United States with various parts of its colonial empire, consult H. W. Clarke, *History of Alaska* and J. P. Nichols, *Alaska. . . . Under the Rule of the United States*, both cited earlier; C. Whitney, *Hawaiian America*, cited above; A. D. Gayer, E. K. James and others, *The Sugar Economy of Porto Rico* (1938); B. W. and J. W. Diffie, *Porto Rico: A Broken Pledge*, cited above; R. S. Tucker, "A Balance Sheet of the Philippines," *Harvard Business Review*, Vol. VIII, pp. 10–23; and C. A. Thompson, *Conditions in the Philippine Islands*, 69th Cong., 2nd Sess., Senate Document no. 180 (1926). "Philippine Independence," *Foreign Policy Association Information Service*, Vol. VI, nos. 3–4 contains admirable summaries of economic developments. For American trade relations in the Orient, see Tyler Dennett, *Americans in Eastern Asia*, cited above; Chong Su See, *The*

Foreign Trade of China (1919); C. F. Remer, *The Foreign Trade of China* (1926); Shü-lun Pan, *The Trade of the United States with China* (1924). On trade with the Caribbean islands, consult C. L. Jones, *Caribbean Backgrounds and Prospects* (1931); M. M. Knight, *The Americans in Santo Domingo* (1928); C. C. Tansill, *The United States and Santo Domingo, 1798–1873*, previously cited; A. C. Mills-paugh, *Haiti Under American Control, 1915–1930* (1931); and L. H. Jenks, *Our Cuban Colony*, cited above.

CHAPTER 10

Old Ideals and New Ideas

Though he did not live to complete it, V. L. Parrington's *Beginnings of Critical Realism in America, 1860–1920* (1930), the third volume of his provocative and pioneering *Main Currents in American Thought*, previously cited, contains some rewarding ideas on the various cultural patterns that developed in post-Civil War America. More recent works include H. S. Commager, *The American Mind* (1950); R. H. Gabriel, *The Course of American Democratic Thought* (1940); Elmer Ellis, *Mr. Dooley's America* (1941); Walter Johnson, *William Allen White's America* (1947); Joseph Dorfman, *Thorstein Veblen and His America* (1934); M. E. Curti, *Growth of American Thought* (1943); and Chapter 25 of Volume II of C. A. and M. R. Beard, *The Rise of American Civilization* (4 vols., 1927–42). The biographic and autobiographic material of leading spokesmen of the period constitutes an indispensable source of information. See Worthington C. Ford (ed.) *The Letters of Henry Adams* (2 vols., 1930–8); Henry James (ed.), *The Letters of William James* (2 vols., 1920); M. A. De Wolfe Howe, *John Jay Chapman and His Letters* (1937); N. S. Shaler, *Autobiography* (1909); Raphael Pumpelly, *My Reminiscences* (1918); W. D. Howells, *Literary Friends and Acquaintances* (1900); E. Bisland, *Life and Letters of Lafcadio Hearn* (2 vols., 1906); Rollo Ogden (ed.), *Life and Letters of E. L. Godkin* (2 vols., 1907); Van Wyck Brooks, *The Times of Melville and Whitman* (1947); Bernard DeVoto, *Mark Twain's America* (1932); J. S. Clark, *The Life and Letters of John Fiske* (2 vols., 1917); Henry Holt, *Garrulities of an Octogenarian Editor* (1923); Mildred Howells, *Life and Letters of William Dean Howells* (2 vols., 1928); Hamlin Garland, *A Son of the Middle Border* (1917); and *The Autobiography of William Allen White* (1946). The novels of Mark Twain, Edith Wharton, Henry James, W. D. Howells, Ellen Glasgow, and Booth Tarkington portray the character of the period.

THE EXPANSION OF EDUCATIONAL OPPORTUNITIES. For details, Paul Monroe (ed.), *Cyclopedia of American Education* (5 vols., 1911–13) is the standard work. Three widely used texts are E. P. Cubberly, *Public Education in the United States* (rev. ed., 1934); E. G. Dexter, *A History of Education in the United States* (1904); and R. G. Boone, *Education in the United States* (1909). Useful also are N. M. Butler (ed.), *Education in the United States* (2 vols., 1900); C. D. Aborn and others (eds.), *Pioneers of the Kindergarten in America* (1924); S. E. Parker, *History of Modern Elementary Education* (1912), a standard treatise for period covered; E. E. Brown, *The Making of Our Middle Schools* (1903); E. W. Knight, *Influence of Reconstruction on Education in the South* (1913) and *Public Education in the South* (1922); C. W. Dabney, *Universal Education in the South* (2 vols., 1936); J. A. Burns, *The Growth and Development of the Catholic School System in the United States* (1912); B. T. Washington, *Up From Slavery* (new ed., 1937) and *The Story of My Life and Work* (1900); J. L. M. Curry, *Education of the Negroes since 1860* (1894); W. E. B. DuBois, *The Negro Common School* (1901); and E. E. Slosson, *The American Spirit in Education* (1921), in the Chronicles of America series. Three works of prime significance are M. E. Curti, *The Social*

Ideas of American Educators (1935); H. K. Beale, *Are American Teachers Free?*
(1936) and J. L. M. Curry, *A Brief Sketch of George Peabody, and a History of
the Peabody Education Fund through Thirty Years* (1898). Another work of special importance is Thomas Woody, *A History of Women's Education in the
United States* (2 vols., 1929), which is scholarly and definitive. For later trends,
see I. L. Kandel (ed.), *Twenty-Five Years of American Education* (1924); John
Dewey, *The School and Society* (1899) and *Democracy and Education* (1916);
John and Evelyn Dewey, *Schools of Tomorrow* (1915); and Irving King, *Education for Social Efficiency* (1913). On country schools, see J. D. Eggleston and
R. W. Bruére, *The Work of the Rural School* (1913). Mabel Newcomer's *Financial Statistics of Public Education in the United States, 1910–1920* (1924) is excellent. On education for adults, see R. L. Lurie, *The Challenge of the Forum* (1930);
J. L. Hurlbut, *The Story of Chautauqua* (1921); H. A. Orchard, *Fifty Years of
Chautauqua* (1923); V. and R. O. Case, *We Called It Culture; The Story of Chautauqua* (1948); and A. E. Bestor, *Chautauqua Publications* (1934). The history of
the public library is best told by the following: S. H. Ditzion, *Arsenals of a Democratic Culture* (1947); S. S. Green, *The Public Library Movement in the United
States 1853–1893* (1913); A. E. Bostwick, *The American Public Library* (4th rev.,
1929); R. D. Leigh, *The Public Library in the United States* (1950); and W. I.
Fletcher, *Public Libraries in America* (1894).

UNIVERSITIES AND THE HIGHER LEARNING. On higher education, the standard
authority is C. F. Thwing, *The American College in American Life* (1897); *College
Administration* (1900); *A History of Higher Education in America* (1906); *A His-
tory of Education in the United States Since the Civil War* (1910), which emphasizes university education; and *The American and the German University* (1928).
College histories are appearing at an increasing tempo. Already the following have
appeared: D. C. Gilman, *The Launching of a University* (1906) and Fabian
Franklin, *The Life of Daniel Coit Gilman* (1910) tell the story of Johns Hopkins;
S. E. Morison, *The Founding of Harvard College* (1935), his *Three Centuries of
Harvard 1636–1936* (1936), and Henry James, III, *Charles W. Eliot* (2 vols., 1930)
give the story of Harvard; G. S. Hall, *Life and Confessions of a Psychologist*
(1923), recounts the story of the founding of Clark University; A. D. White,
Autobiography (2 vols., 1905) and C. L. Becker, *Cornell University: Founders and
Founding* (1943) tell the history of Cornell University. See Jonas Viles, *The Uni-
versity of Missouri* (1939); Walter Dyson, *Howard University* (1941); Thomas
LeDuc, *Piety and Intellect at Amherst College, 1865–1912* (1946); Robert Fletcher,
A History of Oberlin College . . . Through the Civil War (2 vols., 1943); Edwin
Mims, *History of Vanderbilt University* (1946); E. McBurns, *David Starr Jordan:
Prophet of Freedom* (1953), describing the energetic president of Stanford Uni-
versity; and M. E. Curti and Vernon Carstensen, *The University of Wisconsin*
(1949). E. E. Slosson, *Great American Universities* (1910) is a popular account,
while Abraham Flexner, *The American College* (1908) is detailed and scholarly.
Another careful study is that by L. V. Koos. *The Junior College* (1924). The ques-
tion of academic freedom is handled brilliantly by Thorstein Veblen, *The Higher
Learning in America* (1918), and R. Hofstadter and W. P. Metzger, *The Develop-
ment of Academic Freedom in the United States* (2 vols., 1954). Upton Sinclair,
The Goose-Step (1923) supplements Veblen by pointing out many infractions.
Two works on the education of adults at the university level are L. E. Reber,
University Extension in the United States (1914) and A. J. L. Klein, *Correspond-
ence Study in Universities and College* (1920), both being bulletins of the United
States Bureau of Education. Two volumes of some historical significance are H. D.
Sheldon, *Student Life and Customs* (1901) and W. T. Field, *Eight O'Clock Chapel*
(1927).

THE CHURCH IN RURAL AND URBAN AMERICA. During the decades between the
Civil War and the end of the nineteenth century, religion both in spirit and practice was challenged by the rise and spread of new scientific and philosophical

ideas. For these ideas, consult H. W. Schneider, *A History of American Philosophy* (1946), the best single volume survey; George Santayana, *Winds of Doctrine* (1913); Philip Wiener, *Evolution and the Founders of Pragmatism* (1949); Richard Hofstadter, *Social Darwinism in American Thought, 1860–1915* (1944), which is excellent; W. H. Werkmeister, *A History of Philosophical Ideas in America* (1949), a very helpful introduction to American philosophical spokesmen; G. P. Adams and W. P. Montague (eds.), *Contemporary American Philosophy* (2 vols., 1930); John Dewey, *The Influence of Darwin on Philosophy* (1910); S. Chugerman, *Lester F. Ward, the American Aristotle* (1939); H. S. Commager, *The American Mind*, previously cited, especially the chapters on William James and Lester Ward; R. B. Perry, *The Thought and Character of William James* (1948); and William James, *The Will to Believe* (1897), *The Varieties of Religious Experience* (1902), and *Pragmatism* (1907). For the impact of these ideas on religion, consult Willard Sperry, *Religion in America* (1946); W. E. Garrison, *The March of Faith* (1933); J. W. Draper, *History of the Conflict Between Religion and Science* (1875); John Fiske, *A Century of Science* (1899); J. Y. Simpson, *Landmarks in the Struggle Between Science and Religion* (1925); A. D. White, *History of the Warfare of Science with Theology in Christendom* (2 vols., 1896); B. J. Loewenberg, "Darwinism Comes to America, 1859–1900," *Mississippi Valley Historical Review*, Vol. XXVIII, pp. 309–65 (1941); A. P. Stokes, *Church and State in the United States* (3 vols., 1950); Paul A. Carter, *The Decline and Revival of the Social Gospel: Social and Political Liberalism in American Protestant Churches* (1956); C. H. Hopkins, *The Rise of the Social Gospel in American Protestantism, 1865–1915* (1940); H. F. May, *Protestant Churches and Industrial America* (1949); and George Harris, *A Century's Change in Religion* (1914). A. V. G. Allen, *Life and Letters of Phillips Brooks* (3 vols., 1901) is the story of a forceful and influential churchman who, outwardly at least, remained indifferent, though not antagonistic, to the forces that were remaking religion. On Christian socialism, the reader should consult Francis Peabody, *Jesus Christ and the Social Question* (1915); Walter Rauschenbusch, *Christianity and the Social Crisis* (1907) and *Christianizing the Social Order* (1912); W. J. Tucker, *My Generation* (1919); J. F. Clarke, *Autobiography, Diary and Correspondence* (1891); J. Dombrowski, *The Early Days of Christian Socialism in America* (1936); Lyman Abbott, *Christianity and Social Problems* (1896) and *Reminiscences* (1915); Washington Gladden, *Recollections* (1909); William Lawrence, *Memories of a Happy Life* (1926); Josiah Strong, *Religious Movements for Social Betterment* (1900); M. E. Chase, *A Goodly Heritage* (1932); G. B. Smith (ed.), *Religious Thought in the Last Quarter Century* (1927); and W. M. Tippy, *The Church a Community Force* (1914), which describes activities of a sociological church. The urban impact on religion is seen in A. I. Abell, *The Urban Impact on American Protestantism, 1865–1900* (1943). On this problem, also consult Theodore Maynard, *The Story of American Catholicism* (1941); Gerald Shaughnessy, *Has the Immigrant Kept the Faith?* (1925); N. Glazer, *American Judaism* (1957); and J. Leiser, *American Judaism* (1925). Of great importance for the student of Catholicism are A. S. Will, *Life of Cardinal Gibbons* (2 vols., 1922); F. J. Zwierlein, *The Life and Letters of Bishop McQuaid* (3 vols., 1925–7); J. Barry, *The Catholic Church and German Americans* (1953); D. Cross, *The Emergence of Liberal Catholicism in America* (1958), dealing with a revealing and neglected subject; J. T. Ellis, *American Catholicism* (1956); H. Moynihan, *The Life of Archbishop John Ireland* (1953); and T. McAvoy, *The Great Crisis in American Catholic History* (1958). The best treatment of anti-Catholic sentiment is H. J. Desmond, *The A.P.A. Movement* (1912). On revivalism, see F. G. Beardsley, *A History of American Revivals* (rev. ed., 1912); Gamaliel Bradford, *D. L. Moody* (1927); H. D. Farish, *The Circuit Rider Dismounts: A Social History of Southern Methodism, 1865–1900* (1938); and W. W. Sweet, *Revivalism in America, Its Origin, Growth and Decline* (1944). An interesting volume is S. G. Cole, *The History of Fundamentalism* (1931). For a sophisticated account of tendencies on the eve of the 1929 depression, see Gilbert Seldes, *The Stammering Century* (1928). On foreign missions, see J. S. Dennis, *Centennial Survey of Christian Missions* (1902). The Salvation Army, largely an urban organization, is described by three of its leaders: Maud Ballington Booth, *Beneath Two Flags* (1889); Ballington Booth, *From Ocean to Ocean* (1891); and F. de L. Booth-Tucker, *The Social Relief Work of the Salvation Army in the United States* (1900). No satisfactory historical account of Christian Science has yet appeared. The literature on its founder is contradictory. The official biography by Sibyl Wilbur, *The Life of Mary Baker Eddy* (rev. ed., 1913) has the approval of the Church, whereas Georgine Milmine, *The Life of Mary Baker G. Eddy and the History of Christian Science* (1909) and E. F. Dakin, *Mrs. Eddy, the Biography of a Virginal Mind* (1929) are both unacceptable to it. On the American Sunday School, see E. W. Rice, *The Sunday School Movement, 1780–1917* (1917). On the trend toward church consolidation, consult E. R. Hooker, *United Churches* (1926).

NEWSPAPERS FOR THE MASSES. The number and volume of newspapers published increased in almost geometric progression after 1870. Almost none was indexed, and with the exception of the metropolitan papers—and not all of them—their history is yet to be written. The best general accounts are F. L. Mott, *American Journalism: A History of Newspapers in the United States through 260 Years, 1690 to 1950* (rev. ed., 1950) and W. G. Bleyer, *Main Currents in the History of American Journalism* (1927). Particular newspapers have had their histories written: Elmer Davis, *History of the New York Times, 1851–1921* (1921); E. Francis Brown, *Raymond of the Times* (1951); Gerald Johnson, *An Honorable Titan, a Biographical Study of Adolph S. Ochs* (1946); Allan Nevins, *The Evening Post: A Century of Journalism* (1922); G. S. Merriam, *The Life and Times of Samuel Bowles* (2 vols., 1885), editor of the *Springfield* (Mass.) *Republican;* Richard Hooker, *The Story of an Independent Newspaper* (1924), the story of the *Springfield Republican;* J. E. Chamberlain, *The Boston Transcript* (1930); Horace Greeley, *Recollections of a Busy Life* (1868); D. C. Seitz, *Joseph Pulitzer, His Life and Letters* (1924) and *The James Gordon Bennetts* (1928); J. K. Winkler, *W. R. Hearst* (1928); E. S. Bates and O. Carlson, *Hearst, Lord of San Simeon* (1936); F. M. O'Brien, *The Story of the Sun* (1928); Harry Baehr, *The New York Tribune Since the War* (1936); and Gerald Johnson and others, *The Sunpapers of Baltimore* (1937). O. G. Villard, *Some Newspapers and Newspaper-Men* (rev. ed., 1926) contains brilliant pen portraits. Victor Rosewater, *History of Coöperative News-Gathering in the United States* (1930) traces the progress of cooperative journalism. See, too, Oliver Gramling, *AP; the Story of News* (1940), and Meyer Berger, *The Story of the New York Times* (1951).

THE DEVELOPMENT OF THE POPULAR MAGAZINE. For the historian, magazines are a real source of material on many aspects of life. Winifred Gregory (comp.), *Union List of Serials in Libraries of the United States and Canada* (rev. ed., 1943) contains the most complete list of magazines with date and place of issue. *Poole's Index to Periodical Literature* provides a subject guide to the contents of the more important magazines. F. L. Mott, *A History of American Magazines* (3 vols., 1938) is thorough; Volume III covers the period since 1865. Algernon Tassin, *The Magazine in America* (1916) is readable but highly opinionated. Few magazine histories have been published. See, however, M. A. DeW. Howe, *The Atlantic Monthly and Its Makers* (1919) and the following biographic references: L. F. Tooker, *The Joys and Tribulations of an Editor* (1924); R. U. Johnson, *Remembered Yesterdays* (1923); George Britt, *Forty Years—Forty Millions: The Career of Frank A. Munsey* (1935); Rollo Ogden, *Life and Letters of Edwin Lawrence Godkin* (2 vols., 1907); S. S. McClure, *My Autobiography* (1914); and Edward Bok, *The Americanization of Edward Bok* (1920), the editor's story of how the *Ladies' Home Journal* gained pre-eminence.

REGIONAL AND NATIONAL TRENDS IN LITERATURE. As indicated elsewhere in this volume, the two indispensable works on American literature are the *Cambridge*

History of American Literature, edited by W. P. Trent and others, and R. E. Spiller and others (eds.), *Literary History of the United States*. Rich also in bibliographic material is W. F. Taylor, *The History of American Letters* (1930). Other useful works are V. L. Parrington, *Main Currents in American Thought*, Vol. III; and F. L. Pattee, *A History of American Literature Since 1870* (1915) and *The New American Literature 1890–1930* (1930); Constance Rourke, *American Humor* (1931), which is unmatched; Bliss Perry, *The American Spirit in Literature* (1918), in the Chronicles of America series; and S. T. Williams, *The American Spirit in Letters* (1926), in The Pageant of America series. National in interest too are Alfred Kazin, *On Native Grounds* (1942) and W. F. Taylor, *The Economic Novel in America* (1942). Ludwig Lewisohn, *Expression in America* (1932) approaches American literature from a Freudian angle and is taken to task by H. S. Commager in *The American Mind*, previously cited. A regional study of prime importance in literary criticism is Van Wyck Brooks, *New England: Indian Summer, 1865–1915* (1940). See also his splendid survey *The Times of Melville and Whitman* (1947). Lucy Hazard, *The Frontier in American Literature* (1927) and D. A. Dondore, *The Prairie and the Making of Middle America* (1926) are first-class volumes. Other excellent studies of regional figures are A. H. Starke, *Sidney Lanier* (1933) and J. F. Harris, *The Life and Letters of Joel Chandler Harris* (1918). On Mark Twain and Walt Whitman, the reader has a considerable field from which to pick. For the former see Parrington's admirable essay in Volume III of *Main Currents in American Thought*; cited; A. B. Paine, *Mark Twain: A Biography* (3 vols., rev. ed., 1935) and *A Short Life of Mark Twain* (1920); W. D. Howells, *My Mark Twain* (1910); Van Wyck Brooks, *The Ordeal of Mark Twain* (1920), a frustrated-man theory with which Bernard DeVoto quarrels in his *Mark Twain's America* (1932). On Whitman, the best of the many biographies are Newton Arvin, *Whitman* (1938); Emory Holloway, *Whitman* (1926); and H. S. Canby, *Walt Whitman, an American* (1943). Similarly, the literature on William Dean Howells is voluminous, but the better accounts are those by Parrington in Volume III of his *Main Currents in American Thought*; D. G. Cooke, *William Dean Howells* (1922); and O. W. Firkins, *William Dean Howells* (1924). Best of all are Howells' own writings, for he gives us a picture of American middle-class life and thought that even his biographers fail to fathom completely. Probably the best of the many studies on Henry James is F. O. Matthiessen, *The James Family* (1947) and *Henry James: The Major Phase* (1944). Interesting also are Rebecca West, *Henry James* (1916) and Van Wyck Brooks, *The Pilgrimage of Henry James* (1925). F. O. Matthiessen's *Sarah Orne Jewett* (1929) is a masterpiece. Less charming but very competent is Genevieve Taggard's *Life and Mind of Emily Dickinson* (1930). David Henry, *William Vaughn Moody* (1934) and John Manly (ed.), *The Poems and Plays of William Vaughn Moody* (2 vols., 1912) do justice to this poet. C. H. Dennis, *Eugene Field's Creative Years* (1924); Thomas Beer, *Stephen Crane* (1926); John Berryman, *Stephen Crane* (1950); Ferris Greenslet, *The Life of Thomas Bailey Aldrich* (1908); G. M. Gould, *Life and Letters of Edmund Clarence Stedman* (2 vols., 1910); A. R. Burr, *Weir Mitchell* (1929); and Franklin Walker, *Frank Norris* (1932) are satisfactory portrayals. H. R. Mayes, *Alger: A Biography Without A Hero* (1928) and M. A. Roe, *E. P. Roe* (1899) are biographies of influential if not great literary personages. Edmund Pearson's *Dime Novels* (1929) describes juvenile thrillers. See also Richard Chase, *Emily Dickinson* (1951) in the American Men of Letters series.

THE ARTS IN A BUSINESS AGE. Perhaps the best over-all brief surveys are H. Cahill and A. Barr, *Art in America: A Complete Survey* (1935) and O. W. Larkin, *Art and Life in America* (1949). Other works of varying quality but all worthy of examination are C. H. Caffin, *The Story of American Painting* (1907); Alan Burroughs, *Limners and Likenesses: Three Centuries of American Painting* (1936); Samuel Isham, *The History of American Painting* (rev. ed., 1927); J. C. Van Dyke, *American Painting and Its Tradition* (1919); Homer St. Gaudens, *The*

American Artist and His Times (1941), beautifully illustrated; Cecilia Beaux, *Background with Figures* (1930), an autobiography; A. Young, *Art Young, His Life and Times* (1939), the autobiography of a great American cartoonist; George Biddle, *An American Artist's Story* (1939); T. H. Benton, *An Artist in America* (1937); E. H. Blashfield, *Mural Painting in America* (1913); Frank Weitenkampf, *American Graphic Art* (rev. ed., 1924); William Murrell, *A History of American Graphic Humor* (2 vols., 1933–8); and A. B. Maurice and F. T. Cooper, *The History of the Nineteenth Century in Caricature* (1904). Of the numerous biographies the following are recommended: Kenyon Cox, *Winslow Homer* (1914); Lloyd Goodrich, *Winslow Homer* (1944); W. H. Downes, *The Life and Works of Winslow Homer* (1911); George Inness, Jr., *Life, Art, and Letters of George Inness* (1917); Elizabeth McCausland, *George Inness* (1946); F. J. Mather, *Homer Martin* (1912); Henry C. White, *Life and Art of Dwight William Tryon* (1930); Royal Cortissoz, *John LaFarge* (1911); W. H. Downes, *John Sargent, His Life and Work* (1925); E. R. and J. Pennell, *The Life of James McNeill Whistler* (rev. ed., 1911); E. L. Cary, *The Works of James McNeill Whistler* (1907); C. D. Abbott, *Howard Pyle* (1925); J. W. McSpadden, *Famous Painters of America* (rev. ed., 1916); Royal Cortissoz, *American Artists* (1923); Wolfgang Born, *American Landscape Painting* (1948); Eugene Neuhaus, *The History and Ideals of American Art* (1931); and Fairfax Downey, *Portrait of an Era as Drawn by C. P. Gibson* (1936).

For sculpture, consult Lorado Taft, *The History of American Sculpture* (rev. ed., 1924); Adeline Adams, *The Spirit of American Sculpture* (rev. ed., 1929); and Joseph Hudnut, *Modern Sculpture* (1929). J. W. McSpadden, *Famous Sculptors of America* (1924) and Royal Cortissoz, *Augustus St. Gaudens* (1907) are highly instructive; on St. Gaudens, consult also Homer St. Gaudens (ed.), *The Reminiscences of Augustus Saint Gaudens* (2 vols., 1913).

Four comprehensive surveys on American music have been published on this period: L. C. Elson, *The History of American Music* (rev. ed., 1925); W. L. Hubbard (ed.), *The American History and Encyclopedia of Music* (12 vols., 1910); Arthur Farwell and W. D. Darby (eds.), *Music in America*, Vol. IV of *The Art of Music* (14 vols., 1915–17), edited by D. G. Mason; and J. T. Howard, *Our American Music* (1941), the best. For orchestral music, see C. E. Russell, *The American Orchestra and Theodore Thomas* (1927); M. A. DeW. Howe, *The Boston Symphony Orchestra* (rev. ed., 1931); F. A. Wister, *Twenty-Five Years of the Philadelphia Orchestra, 1900–1925* (1925). For grand opera, consult H. C. Lahee, *Grand Opera in America* (1902); E. E. Hipsher, *American Opera and Its Composers* (1934); and H. E. Krehbiel, *More Chapters of Opera* (1919). On Negro music, the best authorities are Dorothy Scarborough, *On the Trail of Negro Folk Songs* (1925); H. E. Krehbiel, *Afro-American Folksongs* (1914); J. W. Johnson, *Book of American Negro Spirituals* (1925); and R. H. Dett, *Religious Folk Songs of the Negro as Sung at Hampton Institute* (1927). For popular songs, see C. K. Harris, *After the Ball, Forty Years of Melody* (1926) and Sigmund Spaeth, *Read 'Em and Weep* (1926) and his *Weep Some More, My Lady* (1927). Julius Mattfeld (comp.), *The Folk Music of the Western Hemisphere* (1925) contains much material on the folk music of Negroes, cowboys, lumberjacks, mountaineers, sailors, miners, and so on.

FORM AND FUNCTION IN AMERICAN ARCHITECTURE. The standard works are T. E. Tallmadge, *The Story of Architecture in America* (1927); S. Fiske Kimball, *American Architecture* (1928); and G. H. Edgell, *The American Architecture of Today* (1928). T. F. Hamlin, *The American Spirit in Architecture* (1926), in the Pageant of America series, contains valuable illustrative material. Lewis Mumford, *Sticks and Stones* (1924) is a brilliant interpretative account; see also his *The Brown Decades* (1931). W. A. Starrett, *Skyscrapers and the Men Who Build Them* (1928) traces the origin of this distinctly American architectural form. The following biographies are most valuable: M. G. Van Rensselaer, *Henry Hobson Richardson, and His Works* (1888); Harriet Monroe, *John Wellborn Root* (1896);

Charles Moore, *Daniel H. Burnham, Architect, Planner of Cities* (2 vols., 1921) and *The Life and Times of Charles Follen McKim* (1929); Louis Sullivan, *Autobiography of An Idea* (1924); Frederick Gutheim (ed.), *Frank Lloyd Wright on Architecture* (1941); C. C. Baldwin, *Stanford White* (1931); and F. L. Wright, *An Autobiography* (1943).

CHAPTER 11
Progressive Movements

Though a mass of material on the subject has appeared, an adequate history of the Progressive movement is yet to be written. The best over-all interpretation is R. Hofstadter, *The Age of Reform: From Bryan to F. D. R.* (1955). Also important are A. Mann, *Yankee Reformers in the Urban Age* (1954) and John Chamberlain, *Farewell to Reform* (1932). These may be supplemented with *Autobiography of Lincoln Steffens* (2 vols., 1931); B. P. DeWitt, *The Progressive Movement* (1915); H. U. Faulkner, *The Quest for Social Justice, 1898–1914* (1931), in the History of American Life series, and C. M. Destler, *The Influence of Edward Kellogg upon American Radicalism, 1865–1901* (1932). In Volumes II and III Mark Sullivan, *Our Times: The United States, 1900–1925* (6 vols., 1926–35) presents in lively style the essential social background. For the philosophical basis, see Herbert Croly, *The Promise of American Life* (1909) and *Progressive Democracy* (1914); Walter Weyl, *The New Democracy* (rev. ed., 1920); Walter Lippmann, *Preface to Politics* (1913) and *Drift and Mastery* (1914); and T. N. Carver, *Essays in Social Justice* (1915). Extremely valuable in the same respect are Joseph Dorfman's *Thorstein Veblen and His America* (1934) and *The Economic Mind in American Civilization* (4 vols., 1946–50), Vol. III. For the political philosophy of the movement, consult C. E. Merriam, *American Political Ideas, 1865–1917* (1920); E. R. Lewis, *A History of American Political Thought from the Civil War to the World War* (1937); and V. L. Parrington, *Main Currents in American Thought*, Vol. III (*Beginning of Critical Realism in America*). For the influence of big business on the movement, see E. A. Ross, *Sin and Society* (1907); Matthew Josephson, *The Robber Barons* (1934); Gustavus Myers, *History of Great American Fortunes* (3 vols., 1910); C. B. Spahr, *An Essay on the Present Distribution of Wealth in the United States* (1896); J. A. Ryan, *A Living Wage* (1906); Robert Hunter, *Poverty* (1904); and F. L. Allen, *The Lords of Creation* (1935). Out of a voluminous biographic and autobiographic literature the following are highly recommended: G. R. Geiger, *The Philosophy of Henry George* (1931); A. E. Morgan, *The Philosophy of Edward Bellamy* (1945) and *Edward Bellamy* (1944); *La Follette's Autobiography* (1913); C. E. Russell, *Bare Hands and Stone Walls* (1933); F. C. Howe, *Confessions of a Reformer* (1925); Morris Hillquit, *Loose Leaves from a Busy Life* (1934); Ida Tarbell, *All in the Day's Work* (1939); W. A. White, *The Autobiography of William Allen White* (1946); Walter Johnson, *William Allen White's America* (1947) and *Selected Letters of William Allen White* (1947); S. S. McClure, *My Autobiography* (1914); Brand Whitlock, *Forty Years of It* (1913) and Allan Nevins (ed.), *The Letters of Brand Whitlock* (1936); R. G. Baker, *American Chronicle* (1945); Oscar Ameringer, *If You Don't Weaken* (1940); Mary Vorse, *A Footnote to Folly* (1935); Caroline Lloyd, *Life of Henry Demarest Lloyd* (2 vols., 1912); M. A. DeW. Howe, *Portrait of an Independent, Moorfield Storey* (1932); Tom Johnson, *My Story* (1911); Claude Bowers, *Beveridge and the Progressive Era* (1932); and H. F. Williamson, *Edward Atkinson* (1934).

THE PROGRESSIVE SPIRIT. In addition to the references already listed above, see Louis Filler, *Crusaders for American Liberalism* (1939), an admirable portrayal; Harold Howland, *Theodore Roosevelt and His Times* (1921), in the Chronicles of

America series; C. C. McCarthy, *The Wisconsin Idea* (1912), the movement explained by a supporter of La Follette; F. E. Haynes, *Social Politics in the United States* (1924); Edward Fitzpatrick, *McCarthy of Wisconsin* (1944), a biography of the author of *The Wisconsin Idea*, cited above, and not of the later, accusing Senator McCarthy from the same state; F. C. Howe, *Wisconsin, an Experiment in Democracy* (1912); and E. N. Doan, *The La Follettes and the Wisconsin Idea* (1947). B. C. La Follette and F. La Follette, *Robert M. La Follette, June 14, 1855–June 18, 1925* (2 vols., 1953) is a loving memoir. Two worthwhile studies of more radical dissent are D. A. Shannon, *The Socialist Party of America: A History* (1955) and D. D. Egbert and Stow Persons (ed.), *Socialism and American Life* (2 vols., 1952), a monumental work.

THE MUCKRAKERS. On this topic, consult C. C. Regier, *The Era of the Muckrakers* (1932). This volume should be supplemented by the above and Lincoln Steffens, *The Shame of the Cities* (1904) and *Upbuilders* (1909); D. G. Phillips, "The Treason of the Senate" in *Cosmopolitan* (1906); Thomas Lawson, *Frenzied Finance* (1905); Franklin Hichborn, "*The System*" *as Uncovered by the San Francisco Graft Prosecution* (1915); Fremont Older, *My Own Story* (1919); F. C. Howe, *The City, The Hope of Democracy* (1905); R. C. Brooks, *Corruption in American Politics and Life* (1910). Writers of contemporary literature also contributed to the cause of reform. In fact, some were labeled Muckrakers. Consult F. M. Crawford, *An American Politician* (1885); Brand Whitlock, *The Thirteenth District* (1902) and *The Turn of the Balance* (1924); Theodore Dreiser, *The Titan* (1914) and *The Financier* (1912); Winston Churchill, *Coniston* (1906) and *Mr. Crewe's Career* (1908); Booth Tarkington, *The Turmoil* (1915) and *The Midlanders* (1923); J. W. De Forest, *Honest John Vane* (1875) and *Playing the Mischief* (1875); D. G. Phillips, *The Plum Tree* (1905); and W. A. White, *In the Heart of a Fool* (1919) and *A Certain Rich Man* (1909).

THE STRUGGLE AGAINST BOSS RULE. Consult the above and A. O. Barton, *La Follette's Winning of Wisconsin, 1894–1904* (1922); K. W. Hechler, *Insurgency: Personalities and Policies of the Taft Era* (1940), which describes the revolt of the Progressives in Congress; F. E. Haynes, *Third Party Movements Since the Civil War* (1916); Carter Harrison, *Stormy Years* (1935); W. D. Foulke, *Fighting the Spoilsmen* (1919); C. W. Patton, *The Battle for Municipal Reform* (1940); A. H. Eaton, *The Oregon System* (1912); W. B. Munro, *The Initiative, Referendum and Recall* (1912) and J. A. Riis, *A Ten Years War* (1900); J. D. Barnett, *The Operation of the Initiative, Referendum and Recall in Oregon* (1915); C. A. Beard and B. E. Schultz, *Documents on the Statewide Initiative, Referendum and Recall* (1912); F. A. Ogg, *National Progress, 1907–1917* (1918), in the American Nation series; G. E. Mowry, *Theodore Roosevelt and the Progressive Movement* (1946), excellent; Tso-Shuen Chang, *History and Analysis of the Commission and City-Manager Plans of Municipal Government in the United States* (1918); C. D. Thompson, *Public Ownership* (1925); F. H. MacGregor, *City Government by Commission* (1911); and J. J. Hamilton, *The Dethronement of the City Boss* (1910).

AID FOR THE UNDERPRIVILEGED. In addition to Walter Rauschenbusch's *Christianity and the Social Crisis* (1907) and *Christianizing the Social Order* (1912), see, on housing, R. W. DeForest and Laurence Veiller, *The Tenement House Problem* (2 vols., 1903), which contains report of New York State Tenement House Commission of 1900. These volumes should be supplemented by E. E. Wood, *The Housing of the Unskilled Wage Earner* (1919). Edith Abbott, *The Tenements of Chicago 1908–1935* (1936) is a very scholarly study. But the classic work against overcrowded tenements as breeding places for vice, crime, and epidemics was Jacob Riis, *How the Other Half Lives* (1890). The history of social settlements to the date of its publication is summarized by R. A. Woods and A. J. Kennedy, *The Settlement Horizon* (1922). It should be supplemented by Jane Addams, *Forty Years at Hull House* (1935) and Lillian D. Wald, *The House on Henry Street*

(1915) and *Windows on Henry Street* (1934). See, too, J. W. Linn, *Jane Addams* (1935) and W. E. Wise, *Jane Addams of Hull House* (1935). On safeguarding children, see G. B. Margold, *Problems of Child Welfare* (1914); Jacob Riis, *The Battle with the Slums* (1902); Homer Folks, *The Care of Destitute, Neglected and Delinquent Children* (1902); H. H. Hart, *Selective Migration as a Factor in Child Welfare in the United States* (1915); John Spargo, *The Bitter Cry of the Children* (1906), which pictures child labor conditions; and H. L. Sumner and E. A. Merritt, *Child Labor Legislation in the United States* (1915), United States Department of Labor, Children's Bureau, Industrial Series no. 1. H. H. Lou, *Juvenile Courts in the United States* (1927) is a first-rate study. For improvement in the status of women, see C. C. Catt and N. R. Shuler, *Woman Suffrage and Politics* (1926); E. C. Stanton and others, *History of Woman Suffrage* (6 vols., 1881–1922), a detailed account; I. H. Irwin, *Angels and Amazons* (1933); J. L. Wilson, *The Legal and Political Status of Women in the United States* (1912); R. L. Dorr, *What Eight Million Women Want* (1910), the objectives of the "new woman"; T. S. McMahon, *Women and Economic Evolution* (1912); and Jessie Taft, *The Woman Movement from the Point of View of Social Consciousness* (1915). On civil rights for women, consult A. E. Hecker, *A Short History of Women's Rights from the Days of Augustus to the Present Time* (2nd ed., 1914). On living standards, consult C. B. Spahr, *The Present Distribution of Wealth in the United States* (1896); Robert Hunter, *Poverty* (1904); J. A. Ryan, *A Living Wage* (1906), cited above; P. H. Douglas, *Real Wages in the United States, 1890–1926* (1930), which is authoritative; Alice Henry, *The Trade Union Woman* (1915); and L. H. Gulick and L. P. Ayres, *Medical Inspection of Schools* (1908); F. H. Streightoff, *The Standard of Living among the Industrial People of America* (1911); and Whitney Coombs, *The Wages of Unskilled Labor in Manufacturing Industries in the United States 1890–1920* (1926). The need for better facilities for recreation during the period considered can be obtained from C. E. Rainwater, *The Play Movement in the United States* (1921) and H. S. Curtis, *The Play Movement and Its Significance* (1917). For charities, the best volumes are F. D. Watson, *The Charity Organization Movement in the United States* (1922) and A. G. Warner, *American Charities* (rev. ed., 1908). The problem of crime, especially as it relates to the underprivileged, is discussed by Sheldon Glueck, *Crime and Justice* (1936) and C. R. Henderson (ed.), *Correction and Prevention* (4 vols., 1910). The race question is ably handled by Booker T. Washington, *Up from Slavery* (1901); A. F. Raper, *The Tragedy of Lynching* (1933); R. S. Baker, *Following the Color Line* (1908); and Walter White, *Rope and Faggot* (1929). For Indian reform, consult Oliver Lafarge (ed.), *The Changing Indian* (1942) and M. A. DeW. Howe, *The Portrait of an Independent, Moorfield Storey* (1922). Associated with the underprivileged is the temperance movement. On this, see Mary Earhart, *Frances Willard: From Prayers to Politics* (1944); Ray Strachey, *Frances Willard: Her Life and Work* (1912); and F. E. Willard, *Glimpses of Fifty Years* (1889), reminiscences. See also P. H. Odegard, *Pressure Politics* (1928) and Justin Steuart, *Wayne Wheeler, Dry Boss* (1928).

CHAPTER 12

T. R., Taft, and Wilson

J. F. Rhodes, *The McKinley and Roosevelt Administrations* (1922) is disappointing principally for its failure to deal adequately with the underlying economic forces. F. A. Ogg, *National Progress, 1907–1917* (1918), in the American Nation series, is old and somewhat superficial. Mark Sullivan, *Our Times; the United States, 1900–1925*, cited previously, has much useful material presented in lively style.

D. L. Dumond, *Roosevelt to Roosevelt* (1937) is a useful survey. A. W. Dunn, *From Harrison to Harding* (2 vols., 1922) is a journalistic survey by a Washington newspaper correspondent. Harold Howland, *Theodore Roosevelt and His Times* (1921), in the Chronicles of America series, is also thin. Matthew Josephson, *The President Makers* (1940) is straight political narrative. H. H. Kohlsaat, *From McKinley to Harding* (1923) is little more than reminiscences. G. McConnell, *The Decline of Agrarian Democracy* (1953) is a recent study.

THE STRENUOUS LIFE. The two best volumes on Roosevelt are *Theodore Roosevelt; an Autobiography* (1913) and H. F. Pringle, *Theodore Roosevelt* (1931). J. B. Bishop, *Theodore Roosevelt and His Time Shown in His Own Letters* (2 vols., 1920) is an authorized version and, as so frequently happens in such cases, is disappointing. W. R. Thayer, *Theodore Roosevelt, An Intimate Biography* (1919), written by a friend and admirer, is far from objective. The most recent edition of Roosevelt's works, edited by E. E. Morison, as well as older editions, leave no doubt about either Roosevelt's dynamic qualities or his strenuous life. T. R. Roosevelt and H. C. Lodge, *Selections from the Correspondence of Theodore Roosevelt and Henry Cabot Lodge, 1884–1918* (2 vols., 1925) does little to enhance the reputation of either man. W. F. McCaleb, *Theodore Roosevelt* (1931) and Lewis Einstein, *Roosevelt, His Mind in Action* (1930) are both first rate; so is G. E. Mowry's *Theodore Roosevelt and the Progressive Movement* (1946). No one should overlook Albert Shaw, *A Cartoon History of Roosevelt's Career* (1910). Also valuable in understanding Roosevelt and his Administration are N. W. Stephenson, *Nelson W. Aldrich: A Leader in American Politics* (1930); Champ Clark, *My Quarter Century of American Politics* (1920); R. W. Leopold, *Elihu Root and the Conservative Tradition* (1954); *The Autobiography of Lincoln Steffens*, cited earlier; Tyler Dennett, *John Hay: From Poetry to Politics*, previously cited; and P. C. Jessup, *Elihu Root*, cited above.

THEODORE ROOSEVELT AND THE TRUSTS. See the references listed in the preceding sections of this chapter and H. R. Seager and C. A. Gulick, Jr., *Trust and Corporation Problems* (1929); Eliot Jones, *The Trust Problem in the United States* (1921); J. W. Jenks and W. E. Clark, *The Trust Problem* (rev. 5th ed., 1929); H. B. Therelli, *The Federal Anti-Trust Policy: Origination of an American Tradition* (1955); B. H. Meyer, *A History of the Northern Securities Case* (1906); J. G. Pyle, *The Life of James J. Hill* (2 vols., 1917), good for account of struggle between government and the railroads; W. Z. Ripley, *Railroads: Rates and Regulations* (1912) and *Railroads: Finance and Organization* (1915), useful on this topic; I. M. Tarbell, *The Life of Elbert H. Gary: The Story of Steel* (1925); A. H. Walker, *History of the Sherman Law of the United States of America* (1910); W. H. Taft, *The Anti-Trust Act and the Supreme Court* (1914); D. M. Keezer and Stacy May, *The Public Control of Business* (1930); F. B. Clark, *Constitutional Doctrines of Justice Harlan* (1915); and Lewis Corey, *The House of Morgan* (1930).

SAFEGUARDING THE PEOPLE'S INTERESTS. For the early beginnings of the conservation movement, see Gifford Pinchot, *Breaking New Ground* (1947). Roosevelt's part in conservation is admirably told in G. E. Mowry, *Theodore Roosevelt and the Progressive Movement*, cited above; Roosevelt's *Autobiography*, previously cited; and Gifford Pinchot, *The Fight for Conservation* (1910). Two general works of differing character are H. W. Fairbanks, *Conservation Reader* (1920) and C. R. Van Hise and L. Havemeyer, *Conservation of Natural Resources in the United States* (1930). On land reclamation and irrigation, see B. H. Hibbard, *A History of Public Land Policies* (1924); A. B. Darling (ed.), *The Public Papers of Francis G. Newlands* (2 vols., 1932); F. H. Newell, *Irrigation in the United States* (rev. ed., 1906); and W. E. Smythe, *The Conquest of Arid America* (1900). W. G. Van Name, *Vanishing Forest Reserves* (1929) takes the United States Forestry Service to task for its laxity and want of vision. Also see John Ise, *The United States Forest Policy* (1920). On pure food and drug legislation there is a good account in Mark Sullivan, *Our Times, The United States, 1900–1925*, Volumes I and II. See also C. G.

Bowers, *Beveridge and the Progressive Era,* cited earlier; and H. W. Wiley, *An Autobiography* (1930).

THE TAFT ADMINISTRATION. The best treatment of Taft's Administration is H. F. Pringle, *The Life and Times of William Howard Taft* (1939). Other works of lesser importance are A. W. Butt, *Taft and Roosevelt: The Intimate Letters of Archie Butt* (2 vols., 1930), impressions of a White House aide; C. E. Barker, *With President Taft in the White House: Memories of William Howard Taft* (1947), reminiscences; Mrs. W. H. Taft, *Recollections of Full Years* (1914), Taft's earlier activities; O. S. Straus, *Under Four Administrations: From Cleveland to Taft* (1922), by Roosevelt's Secretary of Commerce; M. A. DeW. Howe, *George von Lengerke Meyer, His Life and Public Service* (1920), a biographical account of Taft's Secretary of the Navy; L. W. Busbey, *Uncle Joe Cannon* (1927), a second-rate biography of a second-rate man; and Blair Bolles, *Tyrant from Illinois* (1951). On the tariff controversies R. M. La Follette's *Autobiography,* cited earlier, is excellent. See also F. W. Taussig, *The Tariff History of the United States* (rev. ed., 1931); N. W. Stephenson, *Nelson W. Aldrich,* already cited; U. S. Tariff Commission, *Reciprocity with Canada* (1920); and L. E. Ellis, *Reciprocity; 1911: A Study on Canadian-American Relations* (1939). On the Ballinger-Pinchot controversy, Pinchot presents his case in *The Fight for Conservation* (1910). But this should be supplemented by R. M. Stahl, *The Ballinger-Pinchot Controversy* (1926) and A. T. Mason, *Bureaucracy Convicts Itself: The Ballinger-Pinchot Controversy* (1941). K. W. Hechler, *Insurgency: Personalities and Policies of the Taft Era,* cited earlier, is an admirable study that sheds much light on this controversy.

THE SCHOLAR IN POLITICS. Anyone who desires to understand the political career of Taft's successor to the presidency should start with Arthur Link's splendid volumes *Wilson: The Road to the White House* (1947), which deals with Wilson's development to 1912, *Wilson: The New Freedom* (1956), and his succinct *Woodrow Wilson and the Progressive Era* (1954). By far the best biography is Arthur Walworth's *Woodrow Wilson: American Prophet and World Prophet* (2 vols., 1958). It may be followed with profit by James Kerney, *The Political Education of Woodrow Wilson* (1926), an excellent study of Wilson's connection with New Jersey politics. The best single volume account is H. C. F. Bell, *Woodrow Wilson and the People* (1945). For psychological interpretation, consult W. A. White, *Woodrow Wilson: The Man, His Times and His Task* (1924), and A. L. and J. L. George, *Woodrow Wilson and Colonel House: A Personality Study* (1956). J. P. Tumulty, *Woodrow Wilson as I Knew Him* (1921), by his private secretary; John M. Blum, *Joe Tumulty and the Wilson Era* (1951), and *Woodrow Wilson and the Politics of Morality* (1956); W. E. Dodd, *Woodrow Wilson and His Work* (rev., 1932); Ruth Cranston, *The Story of Woodrow Wilson, Twenty-Eighth President of the United States, Pioneer of World Democracy* (1945); Herbert Hoover, *The Ordeal of Woodrow Wilson* (1958); and Josephus Daniels, *The Wilson Era: Years of Peace, 1910–1917* (1944), by a member of Wilson's cabinet, are all sympathetic accounts. Eleanor W. McAdoo, *The Woodrow Wilsons* (1937), by a daughter, and Edith B. Wilson, *My Memoir* (1939), by his widow, are also laudatory but revealing. Those who desire a more comprehensive and detailed narrative should consult R. S. Baker, *Woodrow Wilson: Life and Letters* (8 vols., 1927–39), the authorized biography, and R. S. Baker and W. E. Dodd (eds.), *The Public Papers of Woodrow Wilson* (6 vols., 1925–7). The election of 1912 is best described by W. J. Bryan, *A Tale of Two Conventions* (1912); D. P. DeWitt, *The Progressive Movement;* G. E. Mowry, *Theodore Roosevelt and the Progressive Movement;* K. W. Hechler, *Insurgency: Personalities and Policies of the Taft Era,* and H. F. Pringle, *Theodore Roosevelt* and *The Life and Times of William Howard Taft,* all of which, with the exception of the Bryan volume, have been previously cited. Volume II of Mark Sullivan's *Our Times: The United States, 1900–1925* recaptures much of the color and excitement of the campaign. Other works, somewhat less reliable, that deal with the election are Victor Rosewater, *Back Stage in 1912* (1932), which defends the Republican National Committee; O. K. Davis, *Released for Publication: Some Inside Political History of Theodore Roosevelt and His Times* (1925); W. F. McCombs, *Making Woodrow Wilson President* (1921), which provides background; Champ Clark, *My Quarter Century of American Politics*, cited earlier; Donald Richberg, *Tents of the Mighty* (1930); and Wayne Williams, *William Jennings Bryan* (1936). The attitude of Wilson's opponent in the presidential campaign of 1916 is described admirably in M. J. Pusey, *Charles Evans Hughes* (2 vols., 1951).

THE NEW FREEDOM. Wilson's speeches delivered during the campaign of 1912 and brought together in book form, *The New Freedom* (1913) not only revealed his philosophy but pointed in the direction that he was to follow in matters of domestic policy. The best accounts, giving the reader opportunity to judge the degree to which Wilson was successful in putting his theories into practice, are F. L. Paxson, *American Democracy and the World War* (3 vols., 1936–48), Vol. I, *The Pre-War Years, 1913–1917*; R. S. Baker, *Woodrow Wilson, Life and Letters*, cited above, Vols. III, IV; and William Diamond, *Economic Thought of Woodrow Wilson* (1943). These may be supplemented by Charles Seymour (ed.), *The Intimate Papers of Colonel House* (4 vols., 1926–8) and G. S. Viereck, *The Strangest Friendship in History* (1932), on the relations between Wilson and House; W. J. and M. B. Bryan, *The Memoirs of William Jennings Bryan* (1925); D. F. Houston, *Eight Years with Wilson's Cabinet, 1913–1920* (2 vols., 1926); W. C. Redfield, *With Congress and Cabinet* (1924); A. W. Lane and L. H. Wall, *The Letters of Franklin K. Lane, Personal and Political* (1922); W. G. McAdoo, *Crowded Years* (1931); T. R. Marshall, *Recollections* (1925); and B. J. Hendrick, *Life and Letters of Walter H. Page* (3 vols., 1922–5). On particular domestic policies, the following are recommended. On taxation reforms, Sidney Ratner, *American Taxation* (1942); on the tariff, F. W. Taussig, *Tariff History of the United States* (rev. ed., 1931) and *Some Aspects of the Tariff Question* (rev. ed., 1931); and H. P. Willis, "The Tariff of 1913," *Journal of Political Economy*, Vol. XXII, pp. 1–40. For the Federal Reserve system, consult E. W. Kemmerer, *The A.B.C. of the Federal Reserve System* (11th ed., 1938); H. P. Willis, *The Federal Reserve System* (1923); P. M. Warburg, *The Federal Reserve System* (2 vols., 1930), on its beginnings, with a criticism; W. P. G. Harding, *Formative Period of the Federal Reserve System* (1925); S. E. Harris, *Twenty Years of the Federal Reserve Policy, Including an Extended Discussion of the Monetary Crisis 1927–1933* (2 vols., 1933), an exhaustive treatment; J. L. Laughlin, *The Federal Reserve Act, Its Origin and Problems* (1933), an excellent history of the act; and A. D. Noyes, *War Period of American Finance, 1908–1925* (1926). On financial concentration, see the *Report* of the Pujo committee, 2nd Cong., 3rd Sess., House Report no. 1593, cited earlier, which is summarized in understandable language by L. D. Brandeis, *Other People's Money, and How the Bankers Use It*, also previously cited. The *Report* of the Industrial Commission of 1915, 64th Cong., 1st Sess., Senate Document no. 415, already cited, is digested in A. A. Berle, Jr. and G. C. Means, *The Modern Corporation and Private Property* (1932). On this topic there is also valuable material in Lewis Corey, *The House of Morgan*, cited earlier; T. W. Lamont, *Henry P. Davison* (1933); and Cyrus Adler, *Jacob Henry Schiff, His Life and Letters* (2 vols., 1921). On trusts and business regulation, see Edward Berman, *Labor and the Sherman Act* (1930); G. C. Henderson, *The Federal Trade Commission* (1924); T. C. Blaisdell, *The Federal Trade Commission: An Experiment in the Control of Business* (1932); O. W. Knauth, *The Policy of the United States Toward Industrial Monopoly* (1913); F. A. Fetter, *The Masquerade of Monopoly* (1931), critical of trust legislation; M. W. Watkins, *Industrial Combinations and Public Policy* (1927); and J. D. Clark, *The Federal Trust Policy* (1931). On labor and the farmer, see E. C. Robbins, "The Trainmen's Eight Hour Day," *Political Science Quarterly*, Vol. XXXI (Dec., 1916), pp. 541–57, and Vol. XXXII (September, 1917), pp. 412–28;

R. Fuller, *Child Labor and the Constitution* (1923); W. S. Holt, *The Federal Farm Loan Bureau* (1924); and O. R. Agresti, *David Lubin* (1922).

CHAPTER 13
The Profits and Price of Peace

The literature on America's part in World War I is already very extensive. That part of it concerned with the reasons for the participation of the United States is mostly controversial. Indispensable for bibliographic and reference purposes is W. G. Leland and N. D. Mereness, *Introduction to the American Official Sources for the Economic and Social History of the World War* (1926). Prepared primarily for the studies in the economic and social history of the war, edited by J. T. Shotwell, it is especially useful to the student who wishes to understand the relations of the various branches of the federal government to the individual citizen—for example, the Food Administration and the Council of National Defense. It also includes a great mass of statistical material gathered in many offices of the government. These compilations bear upon all phases of economic life and activity.

THE UNITED STATES, ENGLAND, AND GERMANY, 1870–1914. The best book on the European background is H. E. Barnes, *World Politics in Modern Civilization* (1930). Two other general accounts should also be read: F. L. Paxson, *American Democracy and the World War* (1936) cited earlier, especially Vol. I, and C. C. Tansill, *America Goes to War* (1938), anti-Wilson in spirit. H. E. Barnes, *Genesis of the World War* (rev. ed., 1929) is a forthright revisionist's point of view. S. B. Fay, *The Origins of the World War* (2 vols., rev. ed., 1930) and B. E. Schmitt, *The Coming of the War* (2 vols., 1930), though differing markedly in emphasis and interpretation, are indispensable for background. These secondary works may be supplemented by important documentary materials: the annual *Foreign Relations of the United States;* R. S. Baker and W. E. Dodd (eds.), *The Public Papers of Woodrow Wilson*, cited earlier; J. B. Scott (ed.), *A Survey of International Relations between the United States and Germany, August 1, 1914–April 6, 1917* (1917); J. B. Scott, *Diplomatic Correspondence between the United States and Germany, August, 1914–April, 1917* (1917); Carleton Savage (ed.), *Policy of the United States toward Maritime Commerce in War* (1934); David Lloyd George, *War Memoirs* (6 vols., 1933–7); Charles Seymour, *The Intimate Papers of Colonel House*, already cited; H. H. Asquith, *Moments of Memory* (1937); Stephen Gwynn, *Letters and Friendships of Sir Cecil Spring Rice* (1929) and C. E. Schieber, *The Transformation of American Sentiment toward Germany 1870–1914* (1921).

THE WAR OF WORDS. See H. C. Peterson, *Propaganda for War: The Campaign against American Neutrality 1914–1917* (1939); T. A. Bailey, *The Man in the Street: Impact of American Public Opinion on Foreign Policy* (1948); H. D. Lasswell, *Propaganda Technique in the World War* (1927); C. H. Grattan, *Why We Fought* (1929); J. D. Squires, *British Propaganda at Home and in the United States 1914–1917* (1935); H. Lavine and J. Wachsler, *War Propaganda and the United States* (1940); Walter Millis, *Road to War* (1935), a popular account; J. Heinrich von Bernstorff, *My Three Years in America* (1920) and *Memoirs* (1936); C. J. Child, *The German-Americans in Politics 1914–1917* (1939), first rate; J. P. Jones and P. M. Hollister, *German Secret Service in America* (1918); G. S. Viereck, *Spreading Seeds of Hate* (1930); A. Ponsonby, *Falsehood in War Time* (1928); R. H. Heindel, *The American Impact on Britain, 1898–1914* (1940); and L. M. Gelber, *The Rise of Anglo-American Friendship* (1938).

WAR TRADE AND LOANS. On this topic, consult Herbert Feis, *Europe, The World's Banker, 1870–1914* (1930); C. K. Hobson, *The Export of Capital* (1914);

C A. Beard, *The Idea of National Interest* (1934); R. W. Dunn, *American Foreign Investments* (1926); A. D. Noyes, *War Period of American Finance, 1908–1925* (1926). Also consult J. S. Bassett, *Our War with Germany* (1919) and J. B. McMaster, *The United States in the World War* (2 vols., 1918–20).

THE DIPLOMACY OF NEUTRALITY. In addition to the books already cited in this chapter, see the official state papers published in the United States Department of State, *Papers Relating to the Foreign Relations of the United States: 1914, 1915, 1916, 1917 War Supplements* (1928–31). Also consult M. E. Curti, *Bryan and World Peace* (1931); Arthur S. Link, *Wilson the Diplomat* (1957); J. Kenworthy Strabolgi and G. Young, *Freedom of the Seas* (1928), good on British blockade; A. M. McDiarmid, *The American Defense of Neutral Rights, 1914–1917* (1939), excellent; Edwin Borchard and W. P. Lage, *Neutrality for the United States* (1937), which questions whether the United States was entirely neutral; T. A. Bailey, *The Policy of the United States Toward Neutrals* (1942); Edgar Turlington, *Neutrality* (4 vols., 1935–6), especially Volume III; A. M. Arnett, *Claude Kitchin and the Wilson War Policies* (1937), which is critical of Wilson; Charles Seymour, *American Diplomacy During the World War* (1934), excellent in content and presentation; J. W. Garner, *International Law and the World War* (1937), a legalistic approach; N. D. Baker, "Why We Went to War," *Foreign Affairs*, Vol. XV, pp. 1–86; T. A. Bailey "The Sinking of the Lusitania," *American Historical Review*, Vol. XLI, pp. 54–73; Harley Notter, *The Origins of the Foreign Policy of Woodrow Wilson* (1937), an able study; and H. C. Syrett, "The Business Press and American Neutrality, 1914–1917," *Mississippi Valley Historical Review*, Vol. XXXII, pp. 215–30 (September, 1945), which exonerates the business press from war mongering prior to 1917.

THE END OF NEUTRALITY. With the declaration of war, neutrality quickly gave way to preparedness. One of the best works on this aspect of the Wilson Administration is Benedict Crowell and R. F. Wilson, *How America Went to War* (6 vols., 1921). On military organization and build-up, consult W. F. Willoughby, *Government Organization in War Time and After* (1919); Arthur Bullard, *Mobilizing America* (1917); B. M. Baruch, *American Industry in the War: A Report of the War Industries Board* (1921); W. G. McAdoo, *Crowded Years*, already cited; W. D. Hines, *War History of American Railroads* (1928); and E. N. Hurley, *The New Merchant Marine* (1920).

CHAPTER 14

"Over There"

The best statistical summary of America's military and naval contribution to World War I was prepared by L. P. Ayres in *The War with Germany* (2nd ed., 1919) at the direction of the War Department. On the military campaigns, see J. J. Pershing, *Final Report* (1919) and *My Experiences in the World War* (2 vols., 1931), a good account; and the unfinished 17-volume documentary history now being prepared by the Historical Branch of the United States Army under the title *The United States Army in the World War, 1917–1919*. T. G. Frothingham, *American Reinforcement in the World War* (1927) is well organized. There are also a number of interesting and informative volumes by commanding officers and others. Among these are Thomas Shipley, *The History of the A.E.F.* (1920); W. J. Wilgus, *Transporting the A.E.F. in Western Europe, 1917–1919* (1931), a description of the transport service; R. L. Bullard, *Personalities and Reminiscences of the War* (1925); J. G. Harbord, *The American Army in France, 1917–1918* (1936); H. Liggett, *Commanding an American Army* (1925); Johnson Hagood, *The Services of Supply: A Memoir of the Great War* (1927); E. N. Hurley, *The Bridge to*

France (1927); A. W. Page, *Our 110 Day's Fighting* (1920); F. V. Greene, *Our First Year in the Great War* (1918); Edouard Réquin, *America's Race to Victory* (1919); Frederick Palmer, *America in France* (1918) and *Our Greatest Battle* (1919); R. J. Beamish and F. A. March, *America's Part in the World War* (1919); Dale Van Every, *The A.E.F. in Battle* (1928); and J. C. Wise, *The Turn of the Tide* (1920). On the naval history of the war, consult T. G. Frothingham, *The Naval History of the World War* (3 vols., 1924–6); Josephus Daniels, *Our Navy at War* (1922), by the Secretary of the Navy; Louis Guichard, *The Naval Blockade, 1914–1918* (1930); H. J. James, *German Subs in Yankee Waters* (1940); W. S. Sims and B. J. Hendrick, *The Victory at Sea* (1920); Albert Gleaves, *A History of the Transport Service* (1921); E. E. Morison, *Admiral Sims and the Modern American Navy* (1942); and R. H. Gibson and M. Prendergast, *The German Submarine War, 1914–1918* (1931). Excellent brief histories of the entire struggle are B. H. L. Hart, *The Real War, 1914–1918* (1930) and C. J. H. Hayes, *Brief History of the Great War* (1920).

THE HOME FRONT. The most informative and most readable volumes are E. A. Powell, *The Army Behind the Army* (1919); Frederick Palmer, *Newton D. Baker: America at War* (2 vols., 1931); E. H. Crowder, *The Spirit of Selective Service* (1920); G. B. Clarkson, *Industrial America in the World War* (1923); Norman Thomas, *The Conscientious Objector in America* (1923); C. M. Case, *Non Violent Coercion* (1923); Zechariah Chafee, Jr., *Freedom of Speech* (1920); George Creel, *How We Advertised America* (1920); J. R. Mock and Cedric Larson, *Words that Won the War: The Story of the Committee on Public Information, 1917–1919* (1939); Samuel Gompers, *American Labor and the War* (1919); Alexander Bing, *War-Time Strikes and Their Adjustment* (1921); H. S. Hanna, and W. J. Lauck, *Wages and the War* (1918); G. S. Watkins, *Labor Problems and Labor Administration in the United States during the World War* (1920); E. L. Bogart, *Direct and Indirect Costs of the Great World War* (rev. ed., 1920); J. M. Clark, *The Costs of the World War to the American People* (1931); J. A. Emery and N. B. Williams, *Governmental War Agencies Affecting Business* (1918); W. S. Culbertson, *Commercial Policy in War Time and After* (1919); F. H. Dixon, *Railroads and Government: Their Relations in the United States, 1910–1921* (1922); C. R. Van Hise, *Conservation and Regulation in the United States during the World War* (1917); F. M. Surface, *The Grain Trade during the World War* (1928); "Mobilizing America's Resources for the War," *Annals of the American Academy of Political and Social Science*, Vol. LXXVIII (1918); H. P. Davison, *The American Red Cross in the Great War* (1919); P. R. Kolbe, *The Colleges in War Times and After* (1919); I. C. Clarke, *American Women and the World War* (1918); and J. A. B. Scherer, *The Nation at War* (1918), which describes state councils of defense and the varying local enthusiasm, indifference, or undercover hostility to the war. P. W. Slosson, *The Great Crusade and After, 1914–1928* (1930), in the History of American Life series, is excellent for its description of American social life in wartime. Valuable, too, for the same reasons, is Mark Sullivan's *Our Times: The United States, 1900–1925*, Vol. V. J. B. McMaster, *The United States in the World War* and J. S. Bassett, *Our War with Germany*, both cited earlier, though not easy reading, contain a mass of valuable detail.

THE FIGHT FOR A JUST PEACE. For termination of actual warfare, see H. R. Rudin, *Armistice, 1918* (1944), a scholarly study buttressed by documents. The standard authority on the peace conference is H. W. V. Temperley and others, *A History of the Peace Conference of Paris* (6 vols., 1920–4). This lengthy work may well be preceded by R. C. Binkley, "Ten Years of Peace Conference History," *Journal of Modern History*, Vol. I, pp. 607–30, and the same author's "New Light on the Paris Peace Conference," *Political Science Quarterly*, Vol. XLVI, pp. 335–61; 509–47. It may well be followed by a good brief summary to be found in either F. L. Benns, *Europe Since 1914* (rev. ed., 1935) or W. C. Langsam, *The World Since 1914* (rev. ed., 1933). Wilson's role at the Paris conference is the subject of dispute. Laudatory of him and his work are R. S. Baker, *Woodrow Wilson and World Settlement* (3 vols., 1922) and *What Wilson Did at Paris* (1919); E. M. House and Charles Seymour (ed.), *What Really Happened at Paris* (1921); D. H. Miller, *The Drafting of the Covenant* (2 vols., 1928), by one of the participants; Paul Birdsall, *Versailles Twenty Years After* (1941); and J. T. Shotwell, *At the Paris Peace Conference* (1937), the observations of a trained and highly objective historian. Critical of Wilson is T. A. Bailey, *Woodrow Wilson and the Lost Peace* (1944), and *Woodrow Wilson and the Great Betrayal* (1945). Critical of both Wilson and the peace treaty itself is J. M. Keynes, *Economic Consequences of the Peace* (1920). By some the Keynes volume is regarded as "brilliant," by others as "superficial and misleading," especially as far as Wilson is concerned. The truth lies between these extremes. Other valuable works on the Paris conference are Robert Lansing, *Peace Negotiations, A Personal Narrative* (1921) and *The Big Four and others of the Peace Conference* (1921). Allan Nevins, *Henry White: Thirty Years of American Diplomacy* (1930) and Frederick Palmer, *Bliss, Peacemaker: The Life and Letters of General Tasker Howard Bliss* (1934) are biographies of two of the peacemakers. Harold Nicolson, *Peace Making, 1919* (1939) and Stephen Bonsal, *Unfinished Business* (1944) are careful studies. B. M. Baruch, *The Making of the Reparation and Economic Sections of the Treaty* (1920) sheds light on that vexing subject. C. H. Haskins and R. H. Lord, *Some Problems of the Peace Conference* (1920) is illuminating. A Tardieu, *The Truth About the Treaty* (1921) presents the case for France, while K. F. Nowak, *Versailles* (1928) presents a German interpretation extremely critical of Wilson. For source materials other than those already cited, see J. B. Scott (ed.), *Official Statements of War Aims and Peace Proposals* (1921).

THE LOST PEACE. On this topic, too, some of the literature is controversial. On the League of Nations and American rejection of the treaty, see J. S. Bassett, *The League of Nations* (1928); J. H. Latané, *Development of the League of Nations Idea: Documents and Correspondence of Theodore Marburg* (2 vols., 1932); D. F. Fleming, *The United States and the League of Nations, 1918–1920* (1932) and *The United States and World Organization, 1920–1933* (1938); W. S. Holt, *Treaties Defeated by the Senate* (1933), which includes the Treaty of Versailles; J. A. Garraty, *Henry Cabot Lodge: A Biography* (1953); and H. C. Lodge, *The Senate and the League of Nations* (1925), a defense of the Senate's action in refusing to approve the treaty. Allan Cranston, *The Killing of the Peace* (1945) is an excellent analysis of the causes for the wrecking of this particular effort to achieve world peace. Other volumes of value are Kenneth Colegrove, *The American Senate and World Peace* (1944); J. T. Shotwell, *The Origins of International Labor Organization* (2 vols., 1934); D. H. Miller, *The Peace Pact of Paris* (1928), which deals with Kellogg Pact; M. O. Hudson, *The Permanent Court of International Justice, and the Question of American Participation* (1925); D. F. Fleming, *The United States and the World Court* (1945); and Frank Simonds, *How Europe Made Peace Without America* (1927) and *Can America Stay at Home?* (1932). Robert E. Osgood, *Ideals and Self-Interest in America's Foreign Relations: The Great Transformation of the Twentieth Century* (1953) is a major work that provokes thought.

CHAPTER 15

America During Normalcy

For the decade of the 1920's, the following works can be recommended: D. L. Dumond, *Roosevelt to Roosevelt: The United States in the Twentieth Century* (1937) and *America in Our Time, 1896–1946* (1947); C. A. and M. R. Beard, *The Rise of American Civilization*, Vols. II (*The Industrial Era*) and III (*America in*

Midpassage); Harvey Wish, *Contemporary America* (1945); H. B. Parkes, *Recent America* (1941); and F. R. Dulles, *Twentieth Century America* (1945). For the political history of the period, see J. C. Malin, *The United States After the World War* (1930). On social and economic development, there is rich material in Mark Sullivan, *Our Times: The United States, 1900–1925*, Vol. VI; P. W. Slosson, *The Great Crusade and After, 1914–1928* (1930); and H. U. Faulkner, *From Versailles to the New Deal* (1950), in the Chronicles of America series. S. H. Adams, *Incredible Era: The Life and Times of Warren Gamaliel Harding* (1939) covers the campaign of 1920 and gives much information about Harding. It should be supplemented by the article on Harding in the *Dictionary of American Biography* by Allan Nevins. J. T. Adams, *Our Business Civilization: Some Aspects of American Culture* (1929) is a suggestive interpretation, and F. L. Allen, *Only Yesterday* (1931) gives journalistic color and atmosphere. By far the best analysis of a cross-section of American culture in the twenties is R. S. and H. M. Lynd, *Middletown* (1929), a brilliant study of a small midwestern city (Muncie, Indiana). The real factual backbone for this chapter, however, is to be found, not in texts or journalistic accounts, but in government documents and reports and in books built upon or around such materials. Three of these works are indispensable to anyone who would understand the golden age of American business: The President's Conference on Unemployment, *Recent Economic Changes in the United States* (2 vols., 1929); F. C. Mills, *Economic Tendencies in the United States* (1932); and the President's Research Committee on Social Trends, *Recent Social Trends in the United States* (2 vols., 1933). To these may be added E. G. Nourse and associates, *America's Capacity to Produce* (1934) and the Report of the Subcommittee on Technology to the National Resources Committee, *Technological Trends and National Policy* (1937). Lewis Mumford's *Technics and Civilization* (1934) is highly stimulating.

FROM DEPRESSION TO PROSPERITY. As in all immediate postwar periods, demobilization and a downward turn of the business cycle followed World War I. On demobilization, see Volume VI of B. Crowell and R. F. Wilson, *How America Went to War*, cited previously; Roger Burlingame, *Peace Veterans* (1932); H. U. Faulkner, *From Versailles to the New Deal*, already cited; Dixon Wecter, *When Johnny Comes Marching Home* (1944); Rogers MacVeagh, *The Transportation Act, 1920: Its Sources, History and Text* (1923), the story of return of railroads to private control; Katherine Mayo, *Soldiers What Next!* (1934), on the problems of the veteran; National Industrial Conference Board, *The World War Veterans and the Federal Treasury* (1932), which discusses the veterans' bonus, and *The American Merchant Marine Problem* (1929); and P. W. Slosson, *The Great Crusade and After, 1914–1928*, cited above. On the brief depression, see P. L. Haworth, *The United States in Our Own Times, 1865–1935* (1935); E. A. Filene, *The Way Out: A Forecast of Coming Changes in American Business and Industry* (1924); E. R. A. Seligman, *The Economics of Farm Relief* (1929); and George Soule, *Prosperity Decade; From War to Depression: 1917–1929* (1947).

AMERICAN INDUSTRY DURING THE BOOM. At the head of the list stands *Recent Economic Changes in the United States*, cited above, with its numerous special articles and statistical estimates. It may be supplemented by the monthly *Bulletins* of the Federal Department of Labor; the *Report* of the Federal Trade Commission on *National Wealth and Income* (1926), 69th Cong. 1st Sess., Senate Document no. 126; the *Report* of the Census Bureau on *Wealth, Debt, and Taxation, 1922* (1924); the report of the National Industrial Conference Board on *Wages in the United States 1914–1929* (1930); and the report of the National Bureau of Economic Research, *Income in the United States* (2 vols., 1921–3). Several general treatments should be noted: R. G. Tugwell, *Industry's Coming of Age* (1927); T. N. Carver, *Present Economic Revolution in the United States* (1925); L. M. Hacker, *The Triumph of American Capitalism* (1940); T. C. Cochran and William Miller, *The Age of Enterprise* (1942); H. T. Warshow, *Representative In-*

dustries in the United States (1938); and Garet Garrett, *The American Omen* (1928). Other valuable works are W. I. King, *Wealth and Income of the People of the United States* (1915); H. G. Moulton, *Income and Economic Progress* (1935); A. L. Bernheim (ed.), *Big Business, Its Growth and Its Place* (1939); Carter Goodrich and others, *Migration and Economic Opportunity* (1936); F. B. Garver, F. M. Boddy, and A. J. Nixon, *The Location of Manufacturers in the United States, 1899-1929* (1933), G. E. McLaughlin, *Growth of American Manufacturing Areas: A Comparative Analysis with Special Emphasis on Trends in the Pittsburgh District* (1938); B. F. Lemert, *The Cotton Textile Industry of the Southern Appalachian Piedmont*, cited previously; Allan Nevins, *Ford: The Times, the Man, the Company* and *Ford: Expansion and Challenge* (2 vols., 1954-57), a valuable account of the industrial symbol of the age; J. W. Jenkins, *James B. Duke, Master Builder* (1927) on the tobacco industry; Anton Mohr, *The Oil War* (1926); E. H. Davenport and S. R. Cooke, *The Oil Trusts and Anglo-American Relations* (1924); Ludwell Denny, *We Fight for Oil* (1928); Harry Jerome, *Mechanization in Industry* (1934); W. N. Polakov, *The Power Age: Its Quest and Challenge* (1933); Alexander Findlay, *Chemistry in the Service of Man* (5th ed., 1939); C. L. Mantell, *Sparks from the Electrode* (1933); William Haynes, *Men, Money and Molecules* (1936), Paul Schubert, *The Electric Word: The Rise of Radio* (1928); and A. E. Krows, *The Talkies* (1930); A. F. Harlow, *Old Wires and New Waves* (1936). On business organization, see A. R. Burns, *The Decline of Competition: A Study of the Evolution of American Industry* (1936) and A. A. Berle and G. C. Means, *The Modern Corporation and Private Property*, already cited. Of the other books on this subject, Stuart Chase, *Men and Machines* (1929) criticizes existing economic arrangements; and his *Prosperity: Fact or Myth* (1929) is also critical. Stuart Chase and F. J. Schlink, *Your Money's Worth* (1927) is an attack on high-pressure advertising. On mass production, consult the Taylor Society, *Scientific Management in American Industry* (1929); Stuart Chase, *The Tragedy of Waste* (1928); C. A. Beard (ed.), *Whither Mankind?* (1928); and E. L. Bogart and C. E. Landon, *Modern Industry* (1927). Valuable also are P. M. Mazur, *American Prosperity* (1928), F. W. Wile (ed.), *A Century of Industrial Progress* (1928); Herbert Hoover, *American Individualism* (1922), a statement of Republican party creed; and his *The New Day* (1928), more of the same; W. Z. Ripley, *Main Street and Wall Street* (1927), on methods of high finance; and Lewis Corey, *Decline of American Capitalism* (1934), a Marxist interpretation. Opinions of foreign students about American prosperity are J. E. Barker, *America's Secret: The Causes of Her Economic Success* (1927); George Peel, *The Economic Impact of America* (1928); G. K. Simonds and J. G. Thompson, *The American Way to Prosperity* (1928); Albert Demangeon, *America and the Race for World Dominion* (1921), a French view; and Julius Hirsch, *Das Amerikanische Wirtschaftwunder* (1926). That American prosperity and continued economic well-being depends on the welfare of other parts of the world is the thesis of W. C. Redfield, *Dependent America* (1926).

CONTROL OF BUSINESS. Though business enjoyed a comparatively free rein during the Golden Age, government control was not entirely absent. As an introduction to this topic, see D. M. Keezer and Stacy May, *The Public Control of Business* (1930). On transportation, see Rogers MacVeagh, *The Transportation Act of 1920: Its Sources, History and Text*, cited above; D. P. Locklin, *Railroad Regulation since 1920* (1928); H. G. Moulton and associates, *The American Transportation Problem* (1933); The Interstate Commerce Commission, *Regulation of Transportation Agencies: Report of Federal Coordination of Transportation on the Regulation of Transportation Agencies other than Railroads and on Proposed Changes in Railroad Regulation* (1934), 73rd Cong., 2nd Sess. Senate Document no. 152; and A. R. Ellington and W. Coombs, *The Government and Railroad Transportation*, cited earlier. Water power and utilities concentration is best discussed by J. C. Bonbright and G. C. Means, *The Holding Company, Its Public Significance and*

Its Regulation (1932); J. H. Stehman, *The Financial History of the American Telephone and Telegraph Company* (1925); Federal Trade Commission, *Electric-Power Industry* (2 vols., 1927–8); J. G. Kerwin, *Federal Water Power Legislation* (1926); H. S. Raushenbush, *The Power Fight* (1932); and C. O. Hardy, *Recent Growth of the Electric Light and Power Industry* (1929). On the public debt and taxation, consult Sidney Ratner, *American Taxation*, already cited; C. L. King, *Public Finance* (1935); and Twentieth Century Fund, *Facing the Tax Problem* (1937).

On trusts and mergers in general, see, in addition to the references listed above, H. W. Laidler, *Concentration of Control in American Industry* (1931); W. J. A. Donald, *Trade Associations* (1933); F. A. Fetter, *Masquerade of Monopoly* (1931); National Industrial Conference Board, *Mergers and the Law* (1929); J. T. Flynn, *Security Speculation* (1934); H. G. Moulton, *The Financial Organization of Society* (1920), and his *Financial Organization and the Economic System* (1938); Anna Rochester, *Rulers of America* (1936), a left-of-center interpretation; Ferdinand Lundberg, *America's Sixty Families* (1937); and Twentieth Century Fund, *Big Business, Its Growth and Its Place* (1937) and *How Profitable is Big Business?* (1937). For concentration in particular industries, consult Reavis Cox, *Competition in the American Tobacco Industry, 1911–1932* (1933) and J. W. Jenkins, *James B. Duke, Master Builder*, previously cited; D. H. Wallace, *Market Control in the Aluminum Industry* (1937); M. W. Watkins, *Oil: Stabilization or Conservation* (1937). The chain-store development is another excellent example of business concentration. See "A and P and the Hartfords," *Fortune* (March, 1933); "Case History of a Chain Store," *Fortune* (November, 1934), the story of W. T. Grant; and "Woolworth's $250,000,000 Trick," *Fortune* (November, 1933). See also the account of the DuPonts in *Fortune* (November, 1934) and (December, 1934). For America's participation in the cartel movement, consult Robert Liefmann, *International Cartels, Combines and Trusts* (1927); Alfred Plummer, *International Combines in Modern Industry* (1934); and W. F. Notz, *Representative International Cartels, Combines and Trusts* (1929).

EXPORTING AMERICAN CAPITAL. For background, see C. K. Hobson, *The Export of Capital* (1914) and Herbert Feis, *Europe, The World's Banker, 1870–1914* (1930). The activity of America in overseas investment is described by R. W. Dunn, *American Foreign Investments* (1926); P. M. Mazur, *America Looks Abroad* (1930); Hiram Motherwell, *Imperial Dollar* (1929); B. H. Williams, *Economic Foreign Policy of the United States* (1929); C. A. Beard, *The Idea of National Interest* (1934) and *The Open Door at Home* (1934), Scott Nearing and Joseph Freeman, *Dollar Diplomacy* (1925); Scott Nearing, *The Twilight of Empire* (1930); Nicholas Roosevelt, *America and England?* (1930); C. Lewis and K. T. Schlotterbeck, *America's Stake in International Investments* (1938). America's postwar investments in Germany are discussed by R. R. Kuczynski, *American Loans to Germany* (1927); Max Winkler, *Foreign Bonds, An Autopsy* (1933); J. T. Madden, Marcus Nadler and H. C. Sauvain, *America's Experience as a Creditor Nation* (1937); and R. A. Young, *Handbook on American Underwriting of Foreign Securities* (1930) and *The International Financial Position of the United States* (1929). On particular countries or regions, see, for the Far East, C. F. Remer, *American Investments in China* (1929), a good description of American penetration to that date; P. H. Clyde, *International Rivalries in Manchuria, 1689–1922* (rev., 1928), a pro-Japanese point of view; Herbert Croly, *Willard Straight* (1924), which describes, among other things, the efforts of a member of the House of Morgan to increase American investments in China and especially in Manchuria; F. V. Field, *American Participation in the China Consortiums* (1931); G. Odate, *Japan's Financial Relations with the United States* (1922). On Latin America, consult F. M. Halsey, *Investments in Latin America* (1925); M. A. Marsh, *The Bankers in Bolivia* (1928); J. F. Rippy, *The Capitalists and Colombia* (1931); D. M. Phelps, *Migration of Industry to South America* (1936); A. D. Gayer, P. T.

Homan, and E. K. James, *The Sugar Economy of Porto Rico* (1938); C. L. Jones, *Mexico and Its Reconstruction* (1921); F. W. Powell, *The Railroads of Mexico* (1921); C. W. Hackett, *The Mexican Revolution and the United States, 1910–1926* (1926); Edgar Turlington, *Mexico and Her Foreign Creditors* (1930); F. S. Dunn, *The Diplomatic Protection of Americans in Mexico* (1933). There is also valuable material on American investments in Mexico. The best books on the United States and Mexico are: Ernest H. Gruening, *Mexico and Its Heritage* (1928); J. F. Rippy, *The United States and Mexico* (1926); and the two volumes of the *Investigation of Mexican Affairs by the Committee on Foreign Relations of the United States* (1920), 66th Cong., 2nd Sess. Sen. Doc. No. 285. For Canada, see the admirable volume by H. L. Keenleyside, *Canada and the United States* (1929) It may be supplemented by two special volumes which are part of a larger detailed study on the relationship of Canada and the United States sponsored by the Carnegie Endowment for International Peace. These are W. J. Wilgus, *The Railway Interrelations of the United States and Canada* (1937) and H. Marshall, F. A. Southard, Jr., and K. W. Taylor, *Canadian-American Industry; A Study in International Investment* (1936).

EXPORTING AMERICAN GOODS. In addition to the references listed above, especially in the last paragraph, see *The Commerce Year Book* which was published annually between 1922 and 1932, with the exception of 1927, by the Federal Department of Commerce. Other publications by the Department of great value to the student of foreign trade are *Special Agents Series, Miscellaneous Series, Special Consular Reports, Trade Information Bulletin* and *Trade Promotion Series.* The Department's annual *Foreign Commerce and Navigation of the United States* is likewise valuable. For a detailed description of each of these publications, see L. F. Schmeckebier and G. A. Weber, *The Bureau of Foreign and Domestic Commerce; Its History, Activities, and Organization* (1924). Useful also for the period covered by this chapter is National Industrial Conference Board, *Trends in the Foreign Trade of the United States* (1930). The best discussions of imports are to be found in B. B. Wallace and L. R. Edminster, *International Control of Raw Materials* (1930) and W. C. Redfield, *Dependent America*, already cited. For particular commodities, countries, or regions, see E. G. Nourse, *American Agriculture and the European Market* (1924). For trade with the Far East, consult "The New Pacific," *Survey of American Foreign Relations for 1930*; A. W. Griswold, *The Far Eastern Policy of the United States* (1938); C. F. Remer, *The Foreign Trade of China* (1926); Carl Crow, *Four Hundred Million Customers* (1937); Shü-Lun Pan, *The Trade of the United States with China*, already cited; S. Uyehara, *The Industry and Trade of Japan* (rev. ed., 1936). On Latin America, there is much material on foreign trade in C. L. Jones, *Caribbean Backgrounds and Prospects* (1931); "The Caribbean," *Survey of American Foreign Relations for 1929*; C. D. Kepner and J. H. Soothill, *The Banana Empire: A Case Study of Economic Imperialism* (1935) and C. D. Kepner, *Social Aspects of the Banana Industry* (1936). On the merchant marine, see W. P. Elderton, *Shipping Problems, 1916–1921* (1927); J. C. Malin, *The United States After the World War*, previously cited; Brookings Institution, *United States Shipping Board* (1931); and L. W. Maxwell, *Discriminating Duties and the American Merchant Marine* (1926). The influence of tariffs on foreign trade may be seen in F. W. Taussig, *Tariff History of the United States* and *Some Aspects of the Tariff Question*, both cited earlier. See also Abraham Berglund and P. G. Wright, *The Tariff on Iron and Steel* (1929); L. R. Edminster, *The Cattle Industry and the Tariff* (1926); M. A. Smith, *The Tariff on Wool* (1926); P. G. Wright, *Sugar in Relation to the Tariff* (1924) and *The Tariff on Animal and Vegetable Oils* (1928); and B. B. Wallace and L. R. Edminster, *International Control of Raw Materials*, already cited.

THE CULT OF BUSINESS. That business was in the saddle and riding hard during the decade following World War I is evident when one looks at the state of both the commercial farmer and organized labor and realizes the role played by the business man in American life. On this, consult, J. T. Adams, *Our Business Civilization: Some Aspects of American Culture*, and *Recent Social Trends*, both cited above. The business ethics of the Golden Age of the twenties also came under scrutiny. For background, read Werner Sombart, *The Quintessence of Capitalism* (1915) and R. H. Tawney, *Religion and the Rise of Capitalism: A Historical Study* (1926). These should be followed by the Chamber of Commerce of the United States, *Principles of Business Conduct* (1924); E. L. Heermance, *The Ethics of Business, A Study of Current Standards* (1926); and C. F. Taeusch, *Professional and Business Ethics* (1926). All these should be supplemented by James W. Prothro, *The Dollar Decade: Business Ideas in the 1920's* (1954).

BUSINESS IN THE WHITE HOUSE. Consult Nathan Fine, *Labor and Farmer Parties in the United States*, cited earlier; W. A. White, *Masks in a Pageant*, also cited before, and his *A Puritan in Babylon, The Story of Calvin Coolidge* (1938), excellent; Calvin Coolidge, *The Autobiography of Calvin Coolidge* (1929); C. M. Fuess, *Calvin Coolidge, The Man from Vermont* (1940), inferior to White's volume; Alfred Lief, *Democracy's Norris* (1939); G. W. Norris, *Fighting Liberal* (1945); C. O. Johnson, *Borah of Idaho* (1936); J. M. Cox, *Through My Years* (1946); H. F. Pringle, *Alfred E. Smith: A Critical Study* (1927); A. E. Smith, *Up To Now: An Autobiography* (1929); W. H. Allen, *Al Smith, Tammany Hall* (1928), a critical account; William T. Hutchinson, *Lowden of Illinois: The Life of Frank O. Lowden* (2 vols., 1957); Arthur Mann, *La Guardia: A Fighter Against His Times, 1882–1933* (1959); Harvey O'Connor, *Mellon's Millions* (1933), sharply critical; Will Irwin, *Herbert Hoover, A Reminiscent Biography* (1928); Herbert Hoover, *Memoirs of Herbert Hoover: Years of Adventure, 1874–1920* (1951), an autobiography, and his *American Individualism* (1922), *The Challenge to Liberty* (1934), and *The New Day* (1928), the last containing campaign speeches and his political creed; K. C. McKay, *The Progressive Movement of 1924* (1947), a full-length study of election campaign of that year; R. V. Peel and T. C. Donnelly, *The Campaign of 1928* (1931), a good analysis; W. S. Myers and W. H. Newton, *The Hoover Administration* (1936); R. L. Wilbur and A. M. Hyde, *The Hoover Policies* (1937); W. S. Myers, *The Foreign Policies of Herbert Hoover, 1929–1933* (1940)—the last three are highly partisan—and R. S. Allen, *Washington Merry-Go-Round* (1931).

THE ADVENT OF NORMALCY. Three items stand out in connection with the defeat of Wilson and the return of the Republicans to power: political and economic reaction; spiritual and intellectual repression; and betrayals of public trust. On repression and intolerance the best works are Zechariah Chafee, Jr., *Freedom of Speech* (1920) and *Free Speech in the United States* (1941); J. M. Mecklin, *The Ku Klux Klan: a Study of the American Mind* (1924); E. S. Bates, *This Land of Liberty* (1930); Walter Lippmann, *American Inquisitors* (1928); Robert K. Murray, *Red Scare: A Study in National Hysteria* (1955); B. L. Pierce, *Public Opinion and the Teaching of History in the United States* (1926); A. G. Hays, *Let Freedom Ring* (rev. ed., 1937), an account of the activities of the American Civil Liberties Union, and *Trial by Prejudice* (1933); Will Irwin, *How Red Is America?* (1927); H. K. Beale, *Are American Teachers Free?* (1936); W. E. Garrison, *Intolerance* (1934); M. L. Ernst, *The First Freedom* (1946); Francis Biddle, *The Fear of Freedom* (1951), which discusses historically the effect of anxiety and fear upon national security and free institutions; O. K. Fraenkel, *Our Civil Liberties* (1944); George Seldes, *Freedom of the Press* (1935); E. M. Borchard, *Convicting the Innocent* (1932); and Maynard Shipley, *The War on Modern Science* (1927). On intolerance toward the Negro, see Gunnar Myrdal, *An American Dilemma* (1944); R. B. Vance, *All These People* (1946); R. R. Moton, *What the Negro Thinks* (1929); and B. H. Nelson, *The Fourteenth Amendment and the Negro since 1920* (1946). On the Mooney-Billings and Sacco-Vanzetti cases, consult, for the first, the report of the Wickersham Committee, 71st Cong., 2nd Sess., House Document no. 252 and H. T. Hunt, *The Case of Thomas J. Mooney and War-*

ren K. Billings (1929); for the second, Jeannette Marks, *Thirteen Days* (1929), the story of the efforts to stay the execution; Felix Frankfurter, *The Case of Sacco and Vanzetti* (1927), a legal analysis by an outstanding authority; O. K. Fraenkel (ed.), *The Sacco-Vanzetti Case* (1931), extremely valuable for source material; and Louis Joughin and Edmund Morgan, *The Legacy of Sacco and Vanzetti* (1948). For the hysteria about undesirable aliens, consult Jane Clark, *Deportation of Aliens from the United States to Europe* (1931) and F. C. Howe, *The Confessions of a Reformer*, cited earlier. For the student interested in repression and intolerance there is much of value in O. G. Villard, *Fighting Years* (1939), the autobiography of a distinguished editor of the *Nation;* André Siegfried, *America Comes of Age*, previously cited; and Harvey Wish, *Contemporary America* (1945). For the betrayal of public trust, consult C. A. Beard, *The Rise of American Civilization*, Vol. III (*America in Midpassage*); M. R. Werner, *Privileged Characters* (1935); M. E. Ravage, *The Story of Teapot Dome* (1924); W. B. and J. B. Northrop, *The Insolvence of Office* (1932); Norman Thomas and Paul Blanshard, *What's the Matter with New York?* (1932); Lloyd Lewis and H. J. Smith, *Chicago, The History of Its Reputation* (1929); and C. E. Merriam, *Chicago* (1929).

COOLIDGE AND HOOVER. See the works listed above for this chapter and in addition the following on special topics that were of concern during the decade of the twenties: On immigration and Americanization, see J. W. Jenks and W. J. Lauck, *The Immigration Problem* (6th ed., 1926); G. M. Stephenson, *A History of American Immigration, 1820–1924* (1926); R. L. Garis, *Immigration Restriction* (1927); R. E. Park, *The Immigrant Press and Its Control* (1922); E. deS. Brunner, *Immigrant Farmers and Their Children* (1929); E. A. Steiner, *The Making of a Great Race: Racial and Religious Cross-Currents in the United States* (1929); T. L. Stoddard, *Re-forging America* (1927) and William MacDougall, *Is America Safe for Democracy?* (1921), which are anti-alien; M. R. Davie, *World Immigration, With Special Reference to the United States* (1936); Manuel Gamio, *Mexican Immigration to the United States* (1930); and R. W. Paul, *The Abrogation of the Gentlemen's Agreement* (1936), which discusses the Immigration Act of 1924. On prohibition, the most satisfactory works are E. H. Cherrington, *The Evolution of Prohibition in the United States of America* (1920), good for background; Peter Odegard, *Pressure Politics, The Story of the Anti-Saloon League* (1928); Justin Steuart, *Wayne Wheeler, Dry Boss* (1928); D. L. Colvin, *Prohibition in the United States* (1926); Charles Merz, *Dry Decade* (1931); M. B. Bruère, *Does Prohibition Work?* (1927); Mary Earhart, *Frances Willard: From Prayers to Politics* (1945); Herman Feldman, *Prohibition: Its Economic and Industrial Aspects* (1927); H. Asbury, *The Great Illusion* (1950); V. Dabney, *Dry Messiah: The Life of Bishop Cannon* (1949), which is excellent; National Commission on Law Enforcement, *Report on the Enforcement of the Prohibition Laws of the United States* (1931), 71st Cong., 3rd Sess., House Document no. 722; and L. V. Harrison and Elizabeth Laine, *After Repeal* (1936). On the peace movement, see J. S. Bassett, *The League of Nations* (1928), factual but dull; David Bryn-Jones, *Frank B. Kellogg* (1937); D. F. Fleming, *The United States and the World Court* (1945) and *The United States and World Organization, 1920–33* (1938); D. H. Miller, *The Peace Pact of Paris* (1928), which treats the Kellogg Pact; J. T. Shotwell, *War as an Instrument of National Policy* (1929); W. E. Rappard, *The Quest for Peace Since the World War* (1940); and M. O. Hudson, *The World Court, 1921–1938* (5th ed., 1938). The subject of inter-Allied debts and reparation payments is handled adequately by C. Bergmann, *The History of Reparations* (1927); C. G. Dawes, *A Journal of Reparations* (1939), the story of the Dawes Plan; National Industrial Conference Board, *The Inter-Ally Debts and the United States* (1925); H. G. Moulton and Leo Pasvolsky, *World War Debt Settlements* (1926) and *War Debts and World Prosperity* (1932); and Allan Nevins, *The United States in a Chaotic World* (1950), in the Chronicles of America series, which is good on war debts. On naval limitation, see the general treatments by S. F. Bemis, *Diplomatic History of the United States* (rev. ed., 1950); C. P. Howland (ed.), *Survey of American Foreign Relations 1928–1931* (4 vols., 1928–31); and W. S. Myers, *The Foreign Policies of Herbert Hoover, 1929–33* (1940). More particularly, consult R. L. Buell, *The Washington Conference* (1922); C. G. Dawes, *Journal as Ambassador to Great Britain,* cited above, for material on the abortive London Naval Conference; Yomato Ichihashi, *The Washington Conference and After* (1928); Harold and Margaret Sprout, *Toward a New Order of Sea Power* (1940); B. H. Williams, *The United States and Disarmament* (1931); Mark Sullivan, *The Great Adventure at Washington* (1922), a journalistic account; and C. L. Hoag, *Preface to Preparedness* (1941), an excellent study of public opinion on Washington Conference. On the United States and Latin America there is abundant material in J. F. Rippy, *Latin America in World Politics* (3rd ed., 1938); Carleton Beals, *Mexican Maze* (1931); Ernest Gruening, *Mexico and Its Heritage,* cited earlier; M. M. Knight, *The Americans in Santo Domingo,* cited above; A. C. Millspaugh, *Haiti Under American Control, 1915–30,* cited previously; L. L. Montague, *Haiti and the United States, 1719–1938* (1940); Harold Nicolson, *Dwight Morrow* (1935); H. L. Stimson, *American Policy in Nicaragua* (1927); and A. Alvarez, *The Monroe Doctrine* (1924). On relations with Russia, consult W. S. Graves, *America's Siberian Adventure, 1918–1920* (1931) and F. L. Schuman, *American Policy Toward Russia since 1917* (1928).

THE GOVERNMENT AND BUSINESS ENTERPRISE. See the references listed under "Control of Business" in Chapter 14 and the following on the courts, business enterprise, and property: J. R. Commons, *Legal Foundations of Capitalism* (1924); Louis Boudin, *Government by Judiciary* (2 vols., 1932); Charles Warren, *The Supreme Court in United States History,* Vol. III, already cited; E. S. Corwin, *Twilight of the Supreme Court* (1934); Felix Frankfurter (ed.), *Mr. Justice Holmes and the Constitution* (1927); Max Lerner, *The Mind and Faith of Justice Holmes* (1943); J. P. Pollard, *Mr. Justice Cardozo* (1935); M. R. Cohen, *Law and the Social Order* (1933); S. J. Konefsky, *Chief Justice Stone and the Supreme Court* (1945); and A. T. Mason, *Brandeis: A Free Man's Life* (1946).

THE GOVERNMENT AND THE FARMER. On this topic, see B. H. Hibbard, *Effects of the Great War Upon Agriculture in the United States and Great Britain* (1919); W. Gee, *The Place of Agriculture in American Life* (1930); U. S. Chamber of Commerce, *Large Scale Farming* (1929); J. D. Black, *Agricultural Reform in the United States* (1929); Bernhard Ostrolenk, *The Surplus Farmer* (1932); L. M. Hacker, "The Farmer is Doomed," John Day Pamphlets (1933); Clara Eliot, *The Farmer's Campaign for Credit,* cited earlier; J. E. Boyle, *Farm Relief: A Brief on the McNary-Haugen Plan* (1928); A. A. Bruce, *Non-Partisan League* (1921), adversely critical; H. E. Gaston, *The Nonpartisan League* (1920) friendly; B. H. Hibbard, *Marketing Agricultural Products* (1921), which sheds light on the postwar situation; E. G. Nourse, *American Agriculture and the European Market* (1924); Arthur Capper, *The Agricultural Bloc* (1922), which explains the reasons for its existence; and Edward Wiest, *Agricultural Organization in the United States* (1923), a study of the Farm Bureau. On farm cooperatives, see H. H. Bakken and M. A. Schaars, *The Economics of Cooperative Marketing* (1937); F. E. Clark and L. D. H. Weld, *Marketing Agricultural Products in the United States* (1932), a text; R. H. Elsworth, *Agricultural Cooperative Associations, Marketing and Purchasing, 1925* (1928), Department of Agriculture Technical Bulletin no. 40 and his *Cooperative Marketing and Purchasing, 1920–1930* (1930), Department of Agriculture Circular no. 121; C. L. Christensen, *Farmer's Cooperative Associations in the United States* (1929), Department of Agriculture Circular no. 94; and Federal Trade Commission, *Cooperative Marketing* (1928), 70th Cong., 1st Sess., Senate Document no. 93, an exhaustive study. E. H. Wiecking, *The Farm Real Estate Situation* (1927), Department of Agriculture Circular no. 377; Macy Campbell, *Rural Life at the Crossroads* (1927); R. C. Engberg, *Industrial Prosperity and the Farmer* (1927); a symposium "The Agricultural Situation in the United States,"

Annals of the American Academy of Political and Social Science, Vols. CXVII (1925) and CXLIX (1929); and E. R. Eastman, *These Changing Times* (1927). On technical changes, consult the Agriculture Yearbooks for 1936 and 1937 for plant and animal breeding, and that for 1938 for soil conservation. See also H. S. Person, *Little Waters: A Study of Headwater Streams and Other Little Waters, Their Use and Relations to the Land* (1936); Russell Lord, *To Hold This Soil* (1938), Department of Agriculture, Miscellaneous Publication no. 321; and Stuart Chase, *Rich Land, Poor Land* (1936), an excellent popularization. On farm tenancy, consult E. A. Goldenweise and L. E. Truesdell, *Farm Tenancy in the United States*, cited previously.

THE DECLINE OF ORGANIZED LABOR. Good introductions to this topic are Herbert Harris, *American Labor* (1939) and V. W. Lanfear, *Business Fluctuations and the American Labor Movement, 1915–1922* (1924). Equally good is Selig Perlman, *A History of Trade Unionism in the United States* (rev. ed., 1950); and Leo Wolman, *Ebb and Flow in American Trade Unionism* (1936) is indispensable for this period. See also C. R. Daugherty, *Labor Problems in American Industry* (rev. ed., 1938); L. L. Lorwin, *The American Federation of Labor: History, Policies and Prospects* (1933); Herman Feldman, *Racial Factors in American Industry*, cited previously; and R. W. Dunn, *The Americanization of Labor* (1927). On the steel strike of 1919, consult Abraham Epstein, *The Challenge of the Aged* (1928). Interchurch World Movement, *Report on the Steel Strike of 1919* (1920) is sympathetic to strikers and based on insufficient evidence; Marshall Olds, *Analysis of the Interchurch World Movement Report on the Steel Strike* (1922) suffers from same deficiencies as the document he analyzes; W. Z. Foster, *The Great Steel Strike and Its Lessons* (1920) justifies the strikers. More objective are C. A. Gulick, Jr., *Labor Policy of the United States Steel Corporation* (1924) and C. R. Daugherty, M. G. De Chazeau, and S. S. Stratton, *The Economics of the Iron and Steel Industry* (2 vols., 1937). See also H. B. Davis, *Labor and Steel* (1933) and Harvey O'Connor, *Steel-Dictator* (1935). On textile unrest, which also characterized the decade of the twenties, see G. S. Mitchell, *Textile Unionism in the South* (1931); Samuel Yellen, *American Labor Struggles* (1936); and A. Berglund, G. T. Starnes and F. T. De Vyver, *Labor in the Industrial South* (1930). For radical unionism, see J. S. Gambs, *The Decline of the I. W. W.* (1932). L. V. Kennedy, *The Negro Peasant Turns Cityward* (1930) outlines reasons. On the influx of women into industry, consult Grace Hutchins, *Women Who Work* (1934); S. P. Breckenridge, *Women in the Twentieth Century, A Study of Their Political, Social and Economic Activities* (1933); and N. E. Pidgeon, *Women in the Economy of the United States* (1937), Department of Labor, Women's Bureau Bulletin no. 155, an excellent summary. On child labor, see K. D. Lumpkin and D. S. Douglas, *Child Workers in America* (1937). The offensive against labor is treated by Savel Zimand, *The Open Shop Drive* (1921); J. I. Seidman, *The Yellow Dog Contract* (1932); and Leo Huberman, *The Labor Spy Racket* (1937). On welfare capitalism, see B. M. Selekman and Mary Van Kleeck, *Employes' Representation in Coal Mines* (1924), which describes the Colorado Fuel and Iron industrial representation plan; B. M. Selekman, *Employes' Representation in Steel Works* (1924); R. F. Foerster and E. H. Dietel, *Employee Stock Ownership in the United States* (1926); National Industrial Conference Board, *Employee Stock Purchase Plans in the United States* (1928); and M. W. Latimer, *Industrial Pension Systems in the United States and Canada* (2 vols., 1932). The attitude of the government in labor disputes during the Golden Age is obtainable in E. E. Witte, *The Government in Labor Disputes* (1932). It may be supplemented with Felix Frankfurter and Nathan Greene, *The Labor Injunction* (1930).

WRITERS OF THE LOST GENERATION. Those interested in this topic and the age that follows would profit by consulting R. E. Spiller and others (eds.), *Literary History of the United States* (3 vols., 1943) and H. S. Commager, *The American Mind*, cited earlier; both have excellent bibliographies. Interpretive accounts are given in V. L. Parrington's *Main Currents in American Thought* (1930); M. Cowley, *Exile's Return* (rev., 1951); Alfred Kazin's *On Native Grounds* (1942); Oscar Cargill, *Intellectual America* (1941); J. W. Krutch, *The Modern Temper* (1929); and Harry Hartwick, *The Foreground of American Literature* (1934). See also P. H. Boynton, *Some Contemporary Americans* (1924), *More Contemporary Americans* (1927), and *America in Contemporary Fiction* (1940); S. P. Sherman, *On Contemporary Literature* (rev. ed., 1931) and *Points of View* (1924); H. L. Mencken, *A Book of Prefaces* (1917); Carl and Mark Van Doren, *American and British Literature since 1890* (rev. ed., 1939). A. H. Quinn, *American Fiction* (1936) and F. L. Pattee, *The New American Literature, 1890–1930* (1930) are lightweight in content and interpretation. For biographical and critical studies, see Norman Foerster (ed.), *The Reinterpretation of American Literature* (1928); Burton Rascoe, *Theodore Dreiser* (1925); J. L. Jessup, *The Faith of our Feminists* (1950); F. O. Matthiessen, *Theodore Dreiser* (1951); Dorothy Dudley, *Forgotten Frontiers: Dreiser and the Land of the Free* (1932); B. R. Redman, *Edwin Arlington Robinson* (1926); Herman Hagedorn, *Edwin Arlington Robinson* (1938); Emory Neff, *Edward Arlington Robinson* (1948); F. O. Matthiessen, *The Achievement of T. S. Eliot* (1935); D. D. Paige (ed.), *The Letters of Ezra Pound, 1907–1941* (1950); R. M. Lovett, *Edith Wharton* (1925); and Percy Lubbock, *A Portrait of Edith Wharton* (1947); W. Manchester, *Disturber of the Peace* (1950); A. Mizener, *The Far Side of Paradise* (1951). The best authorities on poetry are Alfred Kreymborg, *A History of American Poetry* (1934); Conrad Aiken, *Scepticisms* (1919); Louis Untermeyer, *The New Era in American Poetry* (1919); Amy Lowell, *Tendencies in Modern American Poetry* (1917); Harriet Monroe, *Poets and Their Art* (1926); and Babette Deutsch, *This Modern Poetry* (1935). Two works do justice to the drama: A. H. Quinn, *A History of the American Drama from the Civil War to the Present* (rev. ed., 1936) and J. W. Krutch, *The American Drama Since 1918* (1939).

CHAPTER 16

American Capitalism in Crisis

The Brookings Institution, *The Recovery Problem in the United States* (1936) analyzes the causes of the depression. It should be supplemented by E. L. Dulles, *Depression and Reconstruction: A Study of Causes and Controls* (1936); A. M. Bernheim and M. G. Schneider (eds.), *Security Markets* (1935); F. W. Hirst, *Wall Street and Lombard Street* (1931); Maurice Levin and others, *America's Capacity to Consume* (1934); Lionel Robbins, *The Great Depression* (1934); Lewis Corey, *The Crises of the Middle Class* (1935); Irving Fisher, *The Stock Market Crash and After* (1930); J. K. Galbraith, *The Great Crash* (1954); W. B. Donham, *Business Adrift* (1931) and J. M. Clark, *Strategic Factors in Business Cycles* (1934). Other important works on this topic are F. C. Mills, *Economic Tendencies in the United States*, previously cited; National Industrial Conference Board, *Major Forces in World Business Depression* (1931); Broadus Mitchell, *Depression Decade* (1947); W. C. Schluter, *Economic Cycles and Crises* (1933); E. M. Patterson, *The World's Economic Dilemma* (1930); F. T. Pecora, *Wall Street Under Oath* (1939), the revelations by the attorney for the Senate Committee on Banking about activities of Wall Street during the twenties; G. V. Seldes, *The Years of the Locust* (*America, 1929–1932*) (1933); Norman Thomas, *The Plight of the Sharecropper* (1934); C. S. Johnson and others, *The Collapse of Cotton Tenancy* (1935), a statistical summary; Max Winkler, *Foreign Bonds, an Autopsy* (1933); and Dixon Wecter, *The Age of the Great Depression, 1929–1941* (1948), in the History of American Life series, first chapter of which is entitled "From Riches to Rags."

THE GOVERNMENT AND THE DEPRESSION. Mr. Hoover's methods of dealing with the depression are discussed at length by W. S. Myers and W. H. Newton, *The Hoover Administration: A Documented Narrative* and R. L. Wilbur and A. M. Hyde, *The Hoover Policies*, both previously cited. These may be supplemented by W. S. Myers, (ed.), *The State Papers and Other Public Writings of Herbert Hoover*, cited earlier, and Harris G. Warren, *Herbert Hoover and the Great Depression* (1959). Also consult T. G. Joslin, *Hoover Off the Record* (1934), by a former secretary; R. G. Tugwell, *Mr. Hoover's Economic Policy* (1932), critical and valuable; and W. W. Waters, *B. E. F.: The Whole Story of the Bonus Army* (1933), the story of veterans' bonus demands. On the campaign of 1932 and Hoover's defeat, the best account is R. V. Peel and T. C. Donnelly, *The 1932 Campaign*, cited above. F. D. Roosevelt, *Looking Forward* (1933) includes Roosevelt's more important campaign speeches. For election statistics, see E. E. Robinson, *The Presidential Vote, 1896–1932* (1934).

The literature on the New Deal is already immense and with each passing year becomes larger. Perhaps the best introductory survey is D. W. Brogan, *The Era of Franklin D. Roosevelt: A Chronicle of the New Deal and Global War* (1950), in the Chronicles of America series. D. L. Dumond, *From Roosevelt to Roosevelt*, cited earlier, is extremely good on the shift from Hoover to Roosevelt. Basil Rauch, *History of the New Deal 1933–38* (1944) is a first-rate appraisal. Other valuable works are C. A. Beard and G. H. E. Smith, *The Old Deal and the New* (1940); C. A. Beard, *The Future Comes: A Study of the New Deal* (1933); E. K. Lindley, *Half Way With Roosevelt* (rev. ed., 1937) and *The Roosevelt Revolution, First Phase* (1933); L. M. Hacker, *A Short History of the New Deal* (1934), which covers first year only, and his *Shaping of the American Tradition* (1947), sec. XI; Columbia University Commission, *Economic Reconstruction: Report of the Columbia University Commission* (1934); Broadus Mitchell, *Depression Decade: From New Era Through New Deal, 1929–1941* (1947); Leo Gurko, *The Angry Decade* (1947); F. D. Roosevelt, *On Our Way*, cited above; S. C. Wallace, *The New Deal in Action* (1934); C. A. and M. R. Beard, *America in Midpassage* (1939), Volume III of *The Rise of American Civilization*; B. L. Landis, *The Third American Revolution: An Interpretation* (1933); A. M. Schlesinger, *The New Deal in Action, 1933–1939* (1940); Stuart Chase, *A New Deal* (1932); George Soule, *A Planned Society* (1934) and *The Coming American Revolution* (1934), and *The Future of Liberty* (1936); and L. P. Ayres, *Economics of Recovery* (1934), which discusses the early stages of New Deal. On Roosevelt and his Administrations *The Public Papers and Addresses of Franklin D. Roosevelt* (9 vols., 1938–41), edited by Roosevelt himself and S. I. Rosenman, are basic. Roosevelt's early speeches and comments appear in *Looking Forward* and *On Our Way*, cited above; later ones can be found in *Rendezvous with History* (1944) and *Nothing to Fear* (1946). Useful in understanding the New Deal and its chief protagonist are the following personal accounts, biographies, and memoirs: Eleanor Roosevelt, *This Is My Story* (1939), which is autobiographical; E. K. Lindley, *Franklin D. Roosevelt: A Career in Progressive Democracy* (1931), a campaign biography; Emil Ludwig, *Roosevelt: A Study in Fortune and Power* (1938); Gerald Johnson, *Roosevelt: Dictator or Democrat?* (1941); Rexford G. Tugwell, *The Democratic Roosevelt: A Biography of Franklin D. Roosevelt* (1957); R. E. Sherwood, *Roosevelt and Hopkins: An Intimate History* (1948); Frances Perkins, *The Roosevelt I Knew* (1946), full of approbation; H. L. Ickes, *Back to Work: The Story of P. W. A.* (1935) and *The Autobiography of a Curmudgeon* (1943), which is pungent; D. C. Roper, *Fifty Years of Public Life* (1941), colorless; J. A. Farley, *Jim Farley's Story: The Roosevelt Years* (1948); Raymond Moley, *After Seven Years* (1939), which reflects disenchantment; Cordell Hull, *Memoirs* (2 vols., 1948); I. H. Hoover, *Forty-Two Years in the White House*, cited earlier; E. W. Starling and Thomas Sugrue, *Starling of the White House* (1946); R. T. McIntire, *White House Physician* (1946); Huey Long, *Every Man a King* (1933); F. E. Townshend, *New Horizons* (1943); H. L. Stimson, *On Active Service in Peace and War* (1948); and J. F. Byrnes, *Speaking Frankly* (1947); Karl Schriftgiesser, *The Amazing Roosevelt Family, 1613–1942* (1942); and John Gunther, *Roosevelt in Retrospect* (1950), an excellent character analysis. A recent series of Roosevelt studies are superior: Frank Freidel, *Franklin D. Roosevelt* (3 vols., 1950–56); Arthur Schlesinger, Jr., *The Age of Roosevelt* (2 vols., 1957–59); and James MacGregor Burns, *Roosevelt: The Lion and the Fox* (1956). Very critical are J. P. Warburg, *Hell Bent for Election* (1936); J. T. Flynn, *Country Squire in the White House* (1940); Edgar E. Robinson, *The Roosevelt Leadership, 1933–1945* (1955); William MacDonald, *The Menace of Recovery* (1934); Norman Thomas, *After the New Deal What?* (1936); Herbert Hoover, *The Challenge to Liberty,* cited above, and *Addresses upon the American Road, 1933–1938* (1938); Benjamin Stolberg and W. J. Vinton, *The Economic Consequences of the New Deal* (1935); D. R. Richberg, *Rainbow* (1936), a study in disillusionment; Eli Ginzberg, *Illusion of Economic Stability* (1939); F. A. Von Hayek, *Collectivist Economic Planning* (1935); M. A. Hallgren, *The Gay Reformer* (1935); and Lewis Corey, *The Decline of American Capitalism* (1934).

THE NATURE OF THE NEW DEAL. In addition to the above works the following will be found helpful: Mordecai Ezekiel, *$2500 a Year: From Scarcity to Abundance* (1936); H. A. Wallace, *America Must Choose* (1934) and *New Frontiers* (1934); R. G. Tugwell, *The Industrial Discipline and the Governmental Arts* (1933) and *The Battle for Democracy* (1935); H. W. Laidler, *A Program for Modern America* (1936); Walter Lippmann, *The Method of Freedom* (1934), critical; A. B. Adams, *National Economic Security* (1936); Brookings Institution, *Recovery Problem in the United States* (1937); and "The New Deal: An Analysis and An Appraisal," *London Economist,* October 5, 1936, a balanced viewpoint from an English source.

THE POLITICS OF THE NEW DEAL. See the works already listed for this chapter, especially the personal material; and J. T. Salter (ed.), *American Politician* (1938); A. M. Landon, *America at the Crossroads,* cited previously, which gives the views of the Republican candidate in the presidential campaign of 1936; Wendell Willkie, *This is Wendell Willkie* (1940), a collection of campaign speeches; J. McG. Burns, *Congress on Trial* (1949), which analyzes the work of World War II and postwar Congresses; W. B. Hesseltine, *The Rise and Fall of Third Parties from Anti-Masonry to Wallace* (1948); and C. A. M. Ewing's *Presidential Elections from Abraham Lincoln to Franklin D. Roosevelt* (1940) and *Congressional Elections, 1896–1944* (1947), both of which are highly statistical, as is E. E. Robinson, *They Voted for Roosevelt: The Presidential Vote, 1932–44* (1947). On third and fourth terms, consult C. W. Stein, *The Third Term Tradition* (1943). J. A. Farley, *Behind the Ballots: The Personal History of a Politician* (1938) is informative on the 1936 election. On expansion of government, see G. C. S. Benson, *The New Centralization* (1941); K. G. Crawford, *The Pressure Boys* (1939); E. P. Herring, *Public Administration and the Public Interest* (1936); A. N. Holcombe, *The New Party Politics* (1933); F. R. Kent, *Without Grease* (1936); J. L. McCamy, *Government Publicity: Its Practice in Federal Administration* (1939); John McDiarmid, *Government Corporations and Federal Funds* (1939); M. N. McGreary, *Development of Congressional Investigative Power* (1940); Stuart Chase, *Government in Business* (1935); A. C. Millspaugh, *Democracy, Efficiency, Stability: An Appraisal of American Government* (1942); and Thorsten Sellen and Donald Young, "Pressure Groups and Propaganda," *Annals of the American Academy of Political and Social Science,* Vol. CLXXIX (May, 1935). On governmental reorganization, see Lewis Meriam and L. F. Schmeckebier, *Reorganization of the National Government,* cited earlier. On expanding government costs, see Twentieth Century Fund, *Facing the Tax Problem* (1937) and Lucius Wilmerding, *The Spending Power* (1943). On the Supreme Court fight, consult E. S. Corwin, *Court Over Constitution* (1938), *The Twilight of the Supreme Court* (4th ed., 1935) and *Constitutional Revolution* (1941); E. M. Eriksson, *The Supreme Court and the New Deal* (1941), which has a good bibliography; R. H. Jackson, *The Struggle for Judicial Supremacy: A Study of a Crisis of American Power Politics* (1941); Alpheus T. Mason, *Harlan Fiske Stone: Pillar of the Law* (1956); and Joseph Alsop and Turner Catledge, *The 168 Days* (1938), a popular treatment. See also M. L. Ernst, *The Ultimate Power* (1937); Irving Brant, *Storm over the Constitution* (1936); C. P. Curtis, *Lions under the Throne* (1947); B. H. Levy, *Our Constitution: Tool or Testament?* (1941); and Wesley McCune, *The Nine Young Men* (1947). C. H. Pritchett, *The Roosevelt Court* (1948) deals with cases and decisions during the Roosevelt period.

BANKING AND CURRENCY LEGISLATION. A good summary of the crisis is to be found in J. I. Bogen and Marcus Nadler, *The Banking Crisis* (1933). Also consult C. C. Chapman, *The Development of American Business and Banking Thought, 1913–1936* (rev. ed., 1936); E. D. Kennedy, *Dividends to Pay* (1939); B. H. Beckhart, *The New York Money Market* (4 vols., 1932); W. R. Burgess, *The Reserve Banks and the Money Market* (1936); N. H. Jacoby and R. J. Saulnier, *Business, Finance and Banking* (1948); H. G. Moulton, *The Financial Organization of Society* (1931); F. T. Pecora, *Wall Street Under Oath*, cited before; Emanuel Stein, *Government and the Investor* (1941); R. L. Weissman, *The New Federal Reserve System* (1936) and *The New Wall Street* (1939); and E. R. Taus, *Central Banking Functions of the United States Treasury, 1789–1941* (1943). For government and the banking business, see Reconstruction Finance Corporation, *Seven Year Report to the President and the Congress of the United States* (1939) and Jesse H. Jones with Edward Angly, *Fifty Billion Dollars: My Thirteen Years with the RFC (1932–1945)* (1951). Also consult H. J. Bittermann, *State and Federal Grants-in-Aid* (1938). Critical of the practices of the stock exchanges are J. T. Flynn, *Security Speculation, Its Economic Effects* (1934) and B. J. Reis, *False Security, The Betrayal of the American Investor* (1937). On guaranty of bank deposits, see Guy Emerson, "Guaranty of Deposits under the Banking Act of 1933," *Quarterly Journal of Economics*, Vol. XLVIII, pp. 229–44; A. D. Gayer, "The Banking Act of 1935," *Journal of Political Economy*, Vol. XLIII, pp. 743–62.

MONEY AND ITS CONTROL. Consult *National Industrial Conference Board, The New Monetary System of the United States* (1934); Leo Pasvolsky, *Current Monetary Issues* (1933); Twentieth Century Fund, *Debts and Recovery, 1929–1937* (1938); A. W. Crawford, *Monetary Management Under the New Deal* (1940); and J. D. Paris, *Monetary Policies of the United States, 1932–1938* (1938), a detailed but very hostile treatment. A. Nussbaum, *Money in the Law, National and International* (1950) and G. G. Johnson, *The Treasury and Monetary Policy, 1933–1938* (1939) are useful for monetary policy and the history of fiscal developments. On special features, see R. B. Westerfield, *Our Silver Debacle* (1936); G. F. Warren and F. A. Pearson, *Prices* (1933); R. Cassady, Jr. and A. R. Lipgren, "International Trade and Devaluation of the Dollar, 1932–1934," *Quarterly Journal of Economics*, Vol. L, pp. 415–35; A. R. Lipgren, "Devaluation of the Dollar in Relation to Exports and Imports," *Journal of Political Economy*, Vol. XLIV, pp. 70–83; A. E. Harris, "British and American Exchange Policies: The American Experience," *Quarterly Journal of Economics*, Vol. XLVIII, pp. 686–726; and N. L. Silverstein, "Effects of the American Devaluation on Prices and Export Trade," *American Economic Review*, Vol. XXVII, pp. 279–93.

CURBING COMPETITION AND MONOPOLY. A. R. Burns, *The Decline of Competition* already cited, is useful on this topic. See also J. M. Clark, *The Social Control of Business*, cited earlier; L. S. Lyon and Victor Abramson, *Government and Economic Life* (2 vols., 1939–40); Merle Fainsod and Lincoln Gordon, *Government and the American Economy* (1941); L. S. Lyon and others, *The National Recovery Administration* (1935); M. F. Gallagher, *Government Rules Industry* (1934); C. F. Roos, *NRA Economic Planning* (1937); G. B. Galloway, *Industrial Planning under Codes* (1935); President's Committee of Industrial Analysis, *National Recovery Administration* (1937), a critical appraisal; E. T. Grether, *Price Control under Fair Trade Legislation* (1939); and H. S. Johnson, *The Blue Eagle from Egg to*

Earth (1935), an account of the N.R.A. by its administrator. For the reaction of private enterprise to regulation, see S. H. Walker and Paul Sklar, *The Regulations of Collective Bargaining under the National Industrial Recovery Act.*

CHAPTER 17

Creating a National Welfare State

LABOR LEGISLATION. The best material on this subject is to be found in Emanuel Stein and others, *Labor and the New Deal* (1934) and C. R. Daugherty, *Labor under the NRA* (1934). Also see R. R. R. Brooks, *Unions of Their Own Choosing* (1939), which gives the background of Wagner Act; L. L. Lorwin and Arthur Wubnig, *Labor Relations Boards* (1935); S. H. Walker and Paul Sklar, *Business Finds Its Voice* (1938); Joseph Rosenfarb, *The National Labor Policy and How It Works* (1940); and Twentieth Century Fund, *Labor and the Government, An Investigation of the Role of the Government in Labor Relations* (1935) and, in briefer compass, *Governmental Protection of Labor's Right to Organize.* Trade practices under the N.R.A. and in other forms since its invalidation by the Supreme Court are best discussed in B. A. Zorn and C. J. Feldman, *Business under the New Price Laws* (1937); B. Werne (ed.), *Business and the Robinson-Patman Law* (1938); and Wright Patman, *The Robinson-Patman Act* (1938).

THE GROWTH OF INDUSTRIAL UNIONISM. This topic is covered adequately by Herbert Harris, *American Labor* (1939) and *Labor's Civil War* (1940); M. R. Clark and S. F. Simon, *The Labor Movement in America* (1938); J. R. Walsh, *C.I.O.: Industrial Unionism in Action* (1937); Edward Levinson, *Labor on the March* (1938), violently anti-A.F. of L.; Benjamin Stolberg, *The Story of the CIO* (1938), which reaches conclusions based on incomplete evidence; Mary Vorse, *Labor's New Millions* (1938); H. R. Clayton and G. S. Mitchell, *Black Workers and the New Unions* (1939); Sterling Spero and A. H. Harris, *The Black Worker* (1931); Twentieth Century Fund, *Trends in Collective Bargaining* (1945); and H. R. Northrup, *Organized Labor and the Negro* (1944). Harold Seidman, *Labor Czars* (1938), discusses racketeering; Clinch Calkins, *Spy Overhead* (1937), describes industrial espionage. C. R. Walker, *American City, A Rank-and-File History* (1937) is a case history. The growth of unionism in an unorganized industry is traced by H. J. Lahne, *The Cotton Mill Worker* (1944). For the rising demands of military production, see Twentieth Century Fund, *Labor and National Defense* (1941).

SUBSIDIZING THE COMMERCIAL FARMER. See references under "The Government and the Farmer" in Chapter 15. To these should be added E. G. Nourse and others, *Three Years of the Agricultural Adjustment Administration* (1937); U. S. Department of Agriculture, *Yearbook of Agriculture, 1940* (1940), which gives briefly the background of New Deal legislation; H. I. Richards, *Cotton and the A.A.A.* (1936); J. S. Davis, *Wheat and the A.A.A.* (1935); H. B. Rowe, *Tobacco Under the A.A.A.* (1935); Harold Barger and H. H. Landsberg, *American Agriculture, 1899-1939* (1942); H. A. Wallace, *New Frontiers* (1934); C. T. Schmidt, *American Farmers in the World Crisis* (1941); E. G. Nourse, *Marketing Agreements Under the A.A.A.* (1935); Jules Backman, *Government Price Fixing* (1938); and O. E. Baker, Ralph Borsodi and M. L. Wilson, *Agriculture in Modern Life* (1939).

AIDING THE MARGINAL FARMER. For the "little" farmer, consult E. deS. Brunner and J. H. Kolb, *Rural Social Trends* (1933); E. deS. Brunner and Irving Lorge, *Rural Trends in Depression Years . . . 1930-36* (1937); E. D. Sanderson, *Research Memorandum on Rural Life in the Depression* (1937); C. E. Lively and Conrad Taeuber, *Rural Migration in the United States* (1939); Stuart Chase, *Rich Land, Poor Land* (1936); F. M. Vreeland and E. J. Fitzgerald, *Farm-City Migration and Industry's Labor Reserve* (1939); J. N. Webb, *The Migratory-*

Casual Worker (1937); U. S. Department of Labor, *Migration of Workers* (2 vols., 1938); Carey McWilliams, *Factories in the Field* (1939) and *Ill Fares the Land* (1942); C. C. Taylor, H. W. Wheeler and E. L. Kirkpatrick, *Disadvantaged Classes in American Agriculture* (1938); C. C. Zimmerman and N. L. Whetten, *Rural Families on Relief* (1938), C. S. Johnson, W. W. Alexander, and E. R. Embree, *The Collapse of Cotton Tenancy* (1935); A. F. Raper, *Preface to Peasantry* (1936); I. deA. Reid, *Share-croppers All* (1941); T. J. Woofter, Jr. and Ellen Winston, *Seven Lean Years* (1939); Waller Wynne, Jr., *Five Years of Rural Relief* (1938); Jonathan Daniels, *A Southerner Discovers the South* (1938); and R. G. Tugwell, *Stricken Land* (1947). John Steinbeck's *Grapes of Wrath* also sheds light on the problem of the rural migratory worker.

RELIEF GRANTS AND JOBS FOR THE UNEMPLOYED. Dixon Wecter, *The Age of the Great Depression, 1929–1941*, cited earlier, gives the over-all picture. It may be supplemented by A. D. Gayer, *Public Works in Prosperity and Depression* (1935); H. L. Hopkins, *Spending to Save, The Complete Story of Relief* (1936); H. L. Ickes, *Back to Work: The Story of P.W.A.* (1935); L. V. Armstrong, *We Too, Are the People* (1938), the story of relief in a Michigan village; Eli Ginzberg and associates, *Unemployed* (1943); J. N. Leonard, *Three Years Down* (1939); J. C. Brown, *Public Relief, 1929–1939* (1940); A. E. Burns and E. A. Williams, *A Survey of Relief and Security Programs* (1938) and *Federal Work, Security and Relief Programs* (1941); National Resources Planning Board, *Security, Work, and Relief Policies* (1942) and *Development of Resources and Stabilization of Employment in the United States* (1942); A. W. Macmahon, J. D. Millett, and Gladys Ogden, *The Administration of Federal Work Relief* (1941); J. F. Isakoff, *The Public Works Administration* (1938); F. S. Chapin and S. A. Queen, *Social Work in the Depression* (1937); R. C. and M. K. White, *Research Memorandum on Social Aspects of Relief Policies in the Depression* (1937); Jacob Baker, *Concerning Government Benefits* (1936); George Biddle, *American Artist's Story* (1939); Wilson Whitman, *Bread and Circuses* (1937), on the W.P.A. theater project; Grace Overmyer, *Government and the Arts* (1939); Hallie Flanagan, *Arena* (1940); Kenneth Holland and T. E. Hill, *Youth in the CCC Camps* (1942); L. L. Lorwin, *Youth Work Programs* (1941); D. G. Howard, *WPA and Federal Relief Policy* (1943), excellent; and D. S. Campbell, F. H. Bair, and O. L. Harvey, *Educational Activities of the Works Progress Administration* (1939). For the human side, see E. W. Bakke, *The Unemployed Worker* (1940) and *Citizens Without Work* (1940); J. M. Williams, *Human Aspects of Unemployment and Relief* (1933); and M. D. Lane and Francis Steegmuller, *America on Relief* (1938). On the subject of the usefulness of relief and pump-priming, consult H. L. Ickes, *Back to Work: The Story of P.W.A.* (1936) and J. K. Galbraith and C. G. Johnson, Jr., *Economic Effects of the Federal Public Works Expenditures, 1933–1938* (1940).

SOCIAL SECURITY AND HOUSING PROGRAM. The basic problem of social security is discussed by Abraham Epstein, *Insecurity, A Challenge to America* (rev. ed., 1938). See also Social Security Board, *Security in America* (1937); P. H. Douglas, *Social Security in the United States* (rev. ed., 1939); I. G. Carter (ed.), "Appraising the Social Security Program," *Annals of the American Academy of Political and Social Science*, Vol. CCII, (1939); I. M. Rubinow, *The Quest for Security* (1934); E. M. Burns, *Toward Social Security* (1936); Lewis Meriam, *Relief and Social Security* (1946); James Parker, *Social Security Reserves* (1942); and Marietta Stevenson and Ralph Spear, *The Social Security Program* (1936). For valuable material on social security given for the most part by experts at congressional hearings, see *Social Security in America, the Factual Background of the Social Security Act, as Summarized from Staff Reports to the Committee on Economic Security* (1937). Pressure for old-age assistance is described in Twentieth Century Fund, *The Townsend Crusade* (1936).

Housing, as far as the New Deal was concerned, was part of the larger concept of planning, which in turn was thought of in terms of city and region. Although a definitive work on cities has yet to be written, see E. C. Ridley and O. F. Nolting (eds.), *What the Depression Has Done to Cities* (1935), which discusses, among other items, municipal finance, health, housing, hospitals, schools, and public libraries; National Resources Committee, *Status of City and County Planning in the United States* (1937) and *Our Cities* (1937); W. F. Ogburn, *Social Characteristics of Cities* (1937); G. R. Leighton, *Five Cities* (1939); and Lewis Mumford, *The Culture of Cities* (1938), which presents a brilliant case for planning.

The best works on housing are M. W. Straus and Talbot Wegg, *Housing Comes of Age* (1938), mainly about P.W.A. construction; E. E. Wood, *Recent Trends in American Housing* (1931) and *Slums and Blighted Areas in the United States* (1935), both illuminating; Carol Aronovici, *Housing the Masses* (1939), which has good bibliography; James Ford and others, *Slums and Housing, With Special Reference to New York City* (2 vols., 1936), which is detailed and good for historical perspective; James and K. M. Ford, *The Modern House in America* (1940), which discusses mostly new trends; L. W. Post, *The Challenge of Housing* (1938); T. R. Carskadon, *Houses for Tomorrow* (rev. ed., 1945); Nathan Straus, *The Seven Myths of Housing* (1944); and L. H. Pink, *The New Day in Housing* (1928). For an account of restrictions in the building trades, see the report of The Temporary National Economic Committee, *Toward More Housing* (1940).

On the region, see National Resources Committee, *Regional Factors in National Planning and Development* (1935). Other official agencies have also sponsored important reports. In the period between 1936 and 1943, for example, the National Resources Planning Board was responsible for thirteen *Regional Planning Reports*, beginning with the Pacific Northwest and closing with Puerto Rico. From the same source came in 1937, no less than twenty-two *Drainage Basin Reports*. Of nonofficial publications H. W. Odum and H. E. Moore, *American Regionalism: A Cultural Historical Approach to National Integration* (1938) is the most important. The principal experiment in regional planning is, to date, the TVA. On this, consult the authoritative volume by David Lilienthal, *TVA: Democracy on the March* (1945), which has a complete bibliography. Valuable also are C. L. Hodge, *The Tennessee Valley Authority* (1938), a scholarly presentation; Willson Whitman, *God's Valley* (1939), which stresses human angle; C. H. Pritchett, *TVA: A Study in Public Administration* (1943); R. L. Duffus and others, *The Valley and Its People* (1944); Russell R. Lord, *Behold Our Land* (1938); J. F. Carter, *The Future is Ours* (1939); Philip Selznick, *TVA and the Grass Roots* (1949), a sociological study; and Julian Huxley, *TVA: Adventure in Planning* (1943), an English view. R. L. Neuberger and S. B. Kahn, *Integrity: The Life of George W. Norris* (1937) is a second-rate biography of the person who perhaps more than anyone else was responsible for TVA. On TVA and the power utilities, see J. C. Bonbright, *Public Utilities and the National Power Policies* (1940) and Twentieth Century Fund, *The Power Industry and the Public Interest*, already cited. On conservation, see Carter Goodrich and others, *Migration and Economic Opportunity*, previously cited, which stresses depressed and overpopulated areas; Resettlement Administration, *The Resettlement Administration* (1935); H. H. Bennett, *Conservation Farming Practices and Flood Control* (1936); Stuart Chase, *Rich Land, Poor Land*, cited above, and P. B. Sears, *Deserts on the March* (1935), both popular treatments; and A. E. Parkins and J. R. Whitaker (eds.), *Our National Resources and Their Conservation* (1936).

That the movement for conservation as well as other features of the New Deal was slowing down even before the coming World War II was evident to many. On this, see Harold Barger, *Outlay and Income in the United States, 1921–38* (1942); R. C. Epstein, *Industrial Profits in the United States* (1934); Solomon Fabricant, *Employment in Manufacturing, 1899–1939* (1942) and *Labor Savings in American Industry, 1899–1939* (1945); Simon Kuznets, *Commodity Flow and Capital Formation* (1938) and *National Income and Its Composition, 1919–1938* (2 vols., 1941); F. C. Mills, *Prices in Recession and Recovery, A Survey of Recent Changes*

(1936); National Resources Committee, *Technological Trends and National Policy* (1937); and A. H. Hansen, *Full Recovery or Stagnation?* (1938), on the recession of 1937-8.

CHAPTER 18
From Isolation to Intervention

For background, read Allan Nevins, *The New Deal and World Affairs* (1950), in the Chronicles of America series; C. G. Haines and R. J. S. Hoffman, *The Origins and Background of the Second World War* (2nd ed., 1947); J. W. Gantenbein, *Documentary Background of World War II, 1931-1941* (1943); Kenneth Ingram, *Years of Crisis, 1919-1945* (1947); D. E. Lee, *Ten Years: The World on the Way to War, 1930-1940* (1942); F. L. Schuman, *Design for Power* (1942); S. H. Roberts, *The House that Hitler Built* (1937); J. W. Wheeler-Bennett, *Pipe Dream of Peace: The Story of the Collapse of Disarmament* (1935); and J. T. Shotwell, *On the Rim of the Abyss* (1936). Other useful works are J. H. Borgese, *Goliath: The March of Fascism* (1937); V. M. Dean, *Europe in Retreat* (1941); Merze Tate, *The Disarmament Illusion* (1942); Gaetano Salvemini, *Under the Axe of Fascism* (1936) and *The Fascist Dictatorship in Italy* (1927); C. T. Schmidt, *The Corporate State in Action: Italy under Fascism* (1939); R. A. Brady, *The Spirit and Structure of German Fascism* (1937); F. L. Neumann, *Behemoth, The Structure and Practice of National Socialism* (1944); Gustav Stolper, *German Economy, 1870-1940* (1940); Herman Rauschning, *The Revolution of Nihilism: Warning to the West* (1939), and *Voice of Destruction* (1940); Otto Tolischus, *They Wanted War* (1940); W. L. Shirer, *Berlin Diary* (1934-1941) (1941); and G. E. R. Gedye, *Betrayal in Central Europe; Austria and Czechoslovakia: The Fallen Bastions* (1939). The best account of what official England was observing and thinking about the European scene is set forth in W. S. Churchill's war history, *The Gathering Storm* (1948). For Russia, consult F. L. Schuman, *Soviet Politics at Home and Abroad* (1946); Rudolph Schlesinger, *The Spirit of Post-War Russia: Soviet Ideology, 1917-1946* (1947); Julian Towster, *Political Power in the USSR, 1917-1947* (1948); and Isaac Deutscher, *Stalin: A Political Biography* (1949).

PEACE AT BARGAIN RATES. C. A. Beard, *American Foreign Policy in the Making, 1932-1940* (1946) is severely critical of Roosevelt policies. See N. J. Spykman, *America's Strategy in World Politics* (1942); F. H. Simonds, *American Foreign Policy in the Post-War Years* (1935); P. C. Jessup, *International Security: The American Role in Collective Action for Peace* (1935); Dexter Perkins, *America and Two World Wars* (1944); Cordell Hull, *Memoirs of Cordell Hull* (1948); and J. F. Rippy, *America and the Strife of Europe* (1938).

MARINE DIPLOMACY. Consult the references in the preceding paragraph and, in addition, Volume X of S. F. Bemis (ed.), *The American Secretaries of State*, cited previously; Allan Nevins, *The United States in a Chaotic World* (1950), in the Chronicles of America series; W. A. Myers, *The Foreign Policies of Herbert Hoover, 1929-1933;* R. L. Buell, *The Washington Conference* and Ichihashi Yamato, *The Washington Conference and After*, all previously cited; and Allan Nevins, *America in World Affairs* (1941).

THE GOOD NEIGHBOR POLICY. The most authoritative accounts are S. F. Bemis, *The Latin American Policy of the United States* (1943); J. F. Rippy, *Latin America in World Politics* (rev. ed., 1938) and *The Caribbean Danger Zone* (1940); H. C. Herring, *Good Neighbors* (1941); Carnegie Endowment for International Peace, *The International Conferences of American States* (2 vols., 1931-40); C. L. Jones, *The Caribbean Since 1900* (1936); C. A. Beard, *The Open Door at Home* (1934); Sumner Welles, *The Time for Decision* (1944); A. P. Whitaker, *Americas to the*

South (1939) and *The United States and South America, The Northern Republics* (1948); L. D. Baldwin, *The Story of the Americas* (1943); Lawrence Duggan, *The Americas: The Search for Hemispheric Security* (1949); Dexter Perkins, *Hands Off: A History of the Monroe Doctrine* (1941); M. W. Williams, *The Peoples and Politics of Latin America* (rev. ed., 1945); Duncan Aikman, *The All-American Front* (1940); Virginia Prewett, *The Americas and Tomorrow* (1944); Charles Wertenbaker, *A New Doctrine for the Americas* (1941); Frank Tannenbaum, *Mexico* (1950); Carleton Beals, *The Coming Struggle for Latin America* (1938); W. A. M. Burden, *The Struggle for Airways in Latin America* (1943); C. G. Fenwick, *The Inter-American Regional System* (1949); Ray Josephs, *Latin America: Continent in Crisis* (1948); G. H. Stuart, *Latin America and the United States* (4th ed., 1943); and T. R. Ybarra, *America Faces South* (1939). The *Survey of American Foreign Relations*, issued annually by the Council on Foreign Relations, and the Foreign Policy Reports for the decade of the thirties are especially valuable.

RETREAT IN THE FAR EAST. The best works on this topic are T. A. Bisson, *America's Far Eastern Policy* (1945); J. C. Grew, *Ten Years in Japan* (1944); W. W. Willoughby, *Japan's Case Examined* (1940); W. C. Johnstone, *The United States and Japan's New Order* (1941); Hugo Byas, *Government by Assassination* (1942); Otto Tolischus, *Tokyo Record* (1943); S. K. Hornbeck, *The United States and the Far East* (1942); H. S. Quigley, *Far Eastern War, 1937–1941* (1942); H. S. Quigley and G. H. Blakeslee, *The Far East: An International Survey* (1938); J. K. Fairbank, *The United States and China* (1948); F. R. Dulles, *China and America . . . since 1784* (1946) and *Forty Years of American-Japanese Relations* (1937); A. W. Griswold, *The Far Eastern Policy of the United States* (1938); E. A. Falk, *From Perry to Pearl Harbor* (1943); S. E. Morison, *The Rising Sun in the Pacific, 1931–1942* (1948); Owen Lattimore, *Manchuria, Cradle of Conflict* (1932); Nathaniel Peffer, *Prerequisites to Peace in the Far East* (1940); and H. L. Stimson, *The Far Eastern Crisis* (1936).

THE QUEST FOR NEUTRALITY. See the general works listed at the beginning of this chapter and C. G. Fenwick, *American Neutrality, Trial and Failure* (1940); W. E. Rappard, *The Quest for Peace Since the World War* (1940); Herbert Feis, *The Road to Pearl Harbor* (1950); United States, Department of State, *Peace and War, United States Foreign Policy, 1931–1941* (1943); J. R. Carlson, *Undercover* (1943); E. M. Earle, *Against This Torrent* (1941); R. L. Buell, *Isolated America* (1940); H. F. Armstrong, *When There is No Peace* (1939); Edwin Borchard and W. P. Page, *Neutrality for the United States* (rev. ed., 1940); Joseph Alsop and Robert Kintner, *American White Paper: The Story of American Diplomacy and the Second World War* (1940); and A. W. Dulles and H. F. Armstrong, *Can America Stay Neutral?* (1939).

ISOLATIONISTS AND INTERVENTIONISTS. See the works listed above and Selig Adler, *The Isolationist Impulse: Its Twentieth Century Reaction* (1957); C. A. Beard, *A Foreign Policy for America* (1940); H. W. Baldwin and Sheppard Stone (eds.), *We Saw It Happen* (1938); W. E. Dodd, Jr. and Martha Dodd (eds.), *Ambassador Dodd's Diary, 1933–1938* (1941); Meno Lovenstein, *American Opinion of Soviet Russia* (1941), based on current literature from 1917 to 1939; E. Tupper and G. E. McReynolds, *Japan in American Public Opinion* (1937); Walter Johnson, *The Battle Against Isolation* (1944); T. A. Bailey, *The Man in the Street* (1948); W. W. Willoughby, *Japan's Case Examined* (1940); Sumner Welles, *The Time for Decision* (1944); and W. H. Shephardson, *The Interests of the United States as a World Power* (1942); W. O. Scroggs, *The United States in World Affairs, 1939* (1940); Lewis Mumford, *Men Must Act* (1939); Harold Lavine and J. A. Wechsler, *War Propaganda and the United States* (1940); and Michael Sayers and A. E. Kahn, *Sabotage: The Secret War Against America* (1942). Also see W. L. Langer and S. E. Gleason, *The Challenge to Isolation, 1937–1940* (1952), and *The Undeclared War: The World Crisis and American Foreign Policy* (1953).

PEARL HARBOR: AMERICA GOES TO WAR. The best accounts to date on this topic are Forest Davis and E. K. Lindley, *How War Came* (1942); Basil Rauch, *Roosevelt, From Munich to Pearl Harbor* (1950); Winston Churchill, *The Second World War: Their Finest Hour* (1949); H. S. Commager, *The Story of the Second World War* (1945); Walter Millis, *This Is Pearl Harbor! The United States and Japan— 1941* (1947); G. Morgenstern, *Pearl Harbor; The Story of the Secret War* (1947); and M. Grodzins, *Americans Betrayed, Politics and the Japanese Evacuation* (1949).

CHAPTER 19

World War II: Triumph and Tragedy

The best introductory accounts are C. G. Haines and R. J. S. Hoffman, *Origins and Background of the Second World War,* cited earlier; W. S. Churchill, *The Second World War: The Gathering Storm, 1919–1939* (1948); Allan Nevins and L. M. Hacker, *The United States and Its Place in World Affairs, 1918–1943* (1943); R. W. Shugg and H. A. DeWeerd, *World War II, A Concise History* (1946); H. S. Commager, *The Story of the Second World War* (1945); and R. C. K. Ensor, *A Miniature History of the War* (2nd ed., 1946), an English view; Fletcher Pratt, *War for the World* (1950), in the Chronicles of America series; Floyd Cave and others, *Origins and Consequences of World War II* (1948); F. T. Miller, *History of World War II* (1946); W. P. Hall, *Iron out of Cavalry* (1946); Cyril Falls, *The Second World War* (1948), excellent; and J. F. C. Fuller, *The Second World War* (1939–45), far from objective. For longer accounts, see Edgar McInnis, *The War* (6 vols., 1940–6) and Sir Ronald Storrs and Philip Graves (eds.) *A Record of the War* (1940–47). This may be supplemented profitably by Winston Churchill's *The Second World War* (1948–53), in six volumes, and his six volumes of wartime speeches: *While England Slept* (1938); *Blood, Sweat, and Tears* (1941); *The Unrelenting Struggle* (1942); *The End of the Beginning* (1943); *Onward to Victory* (1944); and *The Dawn of Liberation* (1945). *The Public Papers and Addresses of Franklin D. Roosevelt,* cited previously, will also prove to be helpful in adding light to these several-volume histories of the war. See also Walter Millis (ed.), *The Forrestal Diaries* (1951). Waverley Root, *The Secret History of the War* (3 vols., 1945–6) is rich in details, but anti-Department of State. American preparation for war in terms of man power and other resources is best described by H. J. Tobin and P. W. Bidwell, *Mobilizing Civilian America* (1940); United States Office of Facts and Figures, *The American Preparation for War* (1942); Pendleton Herring, *The Impact of War* (1941); W. F. Ogburn and others, *American Society in Wartime* (1943); L. B. Hershey, *Selective Service in Peacetime* (1941) and *Selective Service in Wartime* (1942, 1944, 1945); S. Menefee, *Assignment: U. S. A.* (1943); M. Rosebery, *This Day's Madness* (1944); D. M. Nelson, *Arsenal of Democracy, The Story of American War Production* (1946); S. E. Harris, *The Economics of America at War* (1943) and *Price and Related Controls in the United States* (1945); Emanuel Stein, J. D. Magee, and W. J. Ronan, *Our War Economy: Government, Production, Finance* (1943); S. H. Slichter, *The American Economy* (1948); Emanuel Stein and Jules Backman, *War Economics* (1942); G. H. Moore, *Production of Industrial Materials in World War I and II* (1944); War Production Board, *War Production in 1945* (1946); F. A. Howard, *Buna Rubber: The Birth of an Industry* (1947); Smaller War Plants Corporation, *Economic Concentration and World War II* (1946); E. Stettinius, *Lend Lease, Weapon for Victory* (1944); and Eliot Janeway, *The Struggle for Survival: A Chronicle of Economic Mobilization in World War II* (1951), Chronicles of America series.

GLOBAL WAR. Of the enormous literature dealing with the military and naval aspects of World War II, one must of necessity be selective. For the careful student, official sources are indispensable. The history of army operations is now being officially prepared under the title *The United States Army in World War II*. When completed, this set will probably run to a hundred volumes; eight have already been published under the competent editorship of K. R. Greenfield. The activities of the Air Force will be described in a series entitled *Army Air Forces in World War II*. Four volumes have appeared under the editorship of W. F. Craven and J. L. Cate. This work should be supplemented with the official *United States Strategic Bombing Survey*. A semiofficial *History of United States Naval Operations in World War II* is being published under the guidance of S. E. Morison. Fifteen volumes have already appeared. For maps, see the American Forces in Action series prepared by the War Department Historical Division. Useful in this respect is Francis Brown (ed.), *The War in Maps* (1944), based on maps that appeared in the *New York Times*. See Fletcher Pratt, *War for the World: A Chronicle of Our Fighting Forces in World War II* (1951), Chronicles of America series.

On sea power and the fight for control of the Atlantic, consult Bernard Brodie, *Sea Power in the Machine Age* (1941) and *A Guide to Naval Strategy* (1944); Fletcher Pratt, *The Navy's War* (1944); W. D. Puleston, *The Influence of Sea Power in World War II* (1948); and Gilbert Cant, *America's Navy in World War II* (1943). For the battle of the Atlantic the authoritative work is S. E. Morison, *The Battle for the Atlantic, 1939–1943* (1947), Vol. I of the History of the United States Naval Operations series. Other works of importance are Gilbert Cant, *The War at Sea* (1942); D. S. Ballantine, *U. S. Naval Logistics in the Second World War* (1947); and Robert Carse, *There Go the Ships* (1942), the story of naval convoys to the Arctic, and his *Lifeline* (1943), which describes the work of the merchant marine.

For the war in the Pacific, see, in addition to the volumes of S. E. Morison's History of United States Naval Operations series, Gilbert Cant, *The Great Pacific Victory from the Solomons to Tokyo* (1946); W. F. Halsey and J. Bryan, *Admiral Halsey's Story* (1947); Clive Howard and Joe Whitley, *One Damned Island After Another* (1946), an account of Seventh Air Force; Frazier Hunt, *MacArthur and the War Against Japan* (1944); Foster Hailey, *Pacific Battle Line* (1944), which terminates with end of 1943; Walter Karig and Wellbourne Kelley, *Battle Report* (5 vols., 1944–9); L. H. Brereton, *The Brereton Diaries* (1946); John Hersey, *Men on Bataan* (1942) and *Into the Valley* (1943); C. P. Romulo, *I Saw the Fall of the Philippines* (1942); E. B. Miller, *Bataan Uncensored* (1949); Allison Ind, *Bataan, The Judgment Seat* (1944); and Richard Tregaskis, *Guadalcanal Diary* (1943). The fight for New Guinea is described by Pat Robinson, *The Fight for New Guinea* (1943) and G. H. Johnston, *The Toughest Fighting in the World* (1943). On Leyte Gulf, see J. A. Field, *The Japanese at Leyte Gulf: The Shō Operation* (1947); and C. Vann Woodward, *The Battle for Leyte Gulf* (1947). Roy Appleman and others, *Okinawa: The Last Battle* (1948) is informative. For China, consult Robert Hotz, *With General Chennault* (1943); C. L. Chennault, *Way of a Fighter* (1949); T. H. White (ed.), *The Stilwell Papers* (1948); and Jack Belden, *Retreat with Stilwell* (1944). On Burma, see C. J. Rolo, *Wingate's Raiders* (1944). For the atom bomb and Hiroshima, see H. D. Smyth, *Atomic Energy for Military Purposes* (1945); Bernard Brodie (ed.), *The Absolute Weapon: Atomic Power and World Order* (1946); John Hersey, *Hiroshima* (1946); Cyril Falls, *The Nature of Modern Warfare* (1941); and Oliver Jensen, *Carrier War* (1945), important. The Pacific war from the angle of a Japanese can be obtained in Masuo Kato, *The Lost War* (1946).

On the war in the Mediterranean, see Philip Guedalla, *The Middle East, 1940–1942* (1944). W. L. Langer, *Our Vichy Gamble* (1947) is a first-rate summary. On the relation of Spain to the war, see C. J. H. Hayes, *Wartime Mission in Spain, 1942–45*, (1946); and T. J. Hamilton, *Appeasement's Child* (1943). On the African campaign the best accounts are A. C. Clifford, *The Conquest of North Africa, 1940–43* (1943); Alan Moorehead, *The Mediterranean Front* (1942), and *Montgomery, a Biography* (1946). The official account by Sir B. L. Montgomery, *El*

Alamein to the River Sangro (1948) should be read in connection with Strategicus, *From Dunkirk to Benghazi* (1941), by an anonymous British military critic, and Sir Francis de Guingand, *Operation Victory* (1947). The Italian campaign is handled adequately by Christopher Buckley, *The Road to Rome* (1945) and Alan Moorehead, *Eclipse* (1945). See also the four volumes prepared by the Historical Division of the War Department as part of its American Forces in Action series: *Anzio Beachhead* (1948), *Salerno* (1944), *From the Volturno to the Winter Line* (1944), and *The Winter Line* (1945). The best description of the fighting from the soldiers' point of view can be found in Ernie Pyle's *Brave Men* (1945). Other valuable accounts are R. M. Ingersoll, *The Battle is the Pay-Off* (1943); Wesley Gallagher, *Back Door to Berlin* (1943) and Richard Tregaskis, *Invasion Diary* (1944). The story of the landing of troops and supplies is told by S. E. Morison, *Operations in North African Waters* (1947-8); D. D. Eisenhower, *Crusade in Europe* (1948); and H. C. Butcher, *Three Years with Eisenhower* (1946).

For the war in the main European theater, see on planning the invasion D. D. Eisenhower, *Crusade in Europe*, cited above; Sir B. L. Montgomery, *Normandy to the Baltic* (1948); Sir Francis de Guingand, *Operation Victory*, cited above; Sir Gifford Martel, *Our Armoured Forces* (1945); Alan Melville, *First Tide* (1945); and Sir Frederick Morgan, *Overture to Overlord* (1950). The invasion itself is described by John Gunther, *D Day* (1944); C. C. Wertenbaker, *Invasion* (1944); J. M. Brown, *Many a Watchful Night* (1944); W. W. Chaplin, *The Fifty-two Days* (1944); Everett Holles, *Unconditional Surrender* (1945); and Ralph Ingersoll, *Top Secret* (1946). Battles and campaigns are described by those in command in official reports and in personal accounts. Of the latter, see in addition to those of Eisenhower, Montgomery, Halsey, Stilwell and Chennault, already mentioned, the following: B. G. Wallace, *Patton and His Third Army* (1946); H. H. Arnold, *Global Mission* (1949); W. D. Leahy, *I Was There* (1950); Oliver LaFarge, *The Eagle in the Egg* (1949), the story of the Air Force Command; Stewart Alsop and Thomas Braden, *Sub Rosa* (1946), the history of the O.S.S.; G. S. Patton, *War As I Knew It* (1947); Robert Payne, *The Marshall Story: A Biography of General George C. Marshall* (1951); and Omar N. Bradley, *A Soldier's Story* (1951).

On the Battle of the Bulge, see R. E. Merriam, *Dark December* (1947) and S. L. A. Marshall, *Rendezvous with Destiny; Bastogne* (1948). For the Russian part in the struggle, see J. R. Deane, *The Strange Alliance* (1947); J. E. Davies, *Mission to Moscow* (1941) and W. E. D. Allen and Paul Misatoff, *The Russian Campaign of 1941-43* (1948) and *The Russian Campaigns of 1944-45* (1949). Germany's defeat is admirably described by B. H. L. Hart, *The German Generals Talk* (1948); Milton Shulman, *Defeat in the West* (1947); and H. R. Trevor-Roper, *The Last Days of Hitler* (1947).

THE CIVILIAN AND THE WAR. W. F. Ogburn (ed.), *American Society in Wartime* (1943); John Dos Passos, *State of the Nation* (1944); Carey McWilliams, *Prejudice; Japanese Americans: Symbol of Racial Intolerance* (1944); H. L. Childs and J. Whitton, *Propaganda by Shortwave* (1943); M. E. Curti, "The American Mind in Three Wars," *Journal of the History of Ideas*, Vol. III (June 1942); C. C. Pratt, *Psychology: The Third Dimension of War* (1942); G. B. Watson (ed.), *Civilian Morale* (1942); J. Goodman (ed.), *While You Were Gone: A Report on Wartime Life in the United States* (1946). On wartime government and administration, consult W. H. Nichols and J. A. Vieg, *Wartime Government in Operation* (1943); W. J. Wilson and others, *The Beginnings of OPA* (1947); H. C. Mansfield and others, *A Short History of OPA* (1948); L. D. White (ed.), *Civil Service in Wartime* (1945); Luther Gulick, *Administrative Reflections from World War II* (1948); and Pendleton Herring, *Impact of War* (1941). On mobilizing science, see E. C. Andrus, D. W. Brouk, and others, *Advances in Military Medicine* (2 vols., 1948); J. P. Baxter, *Scientists Against Time* (1946); and H. D. Smyth, *Atomic Energy for Military Purposes* (1945).

On the economics of the war, see, in addition to the works cited above, K. C.

Stokes, *Regional Shifts in Population, Production and Markets, 1939–43* (1943); C. O. Hardy, *Wartime Control of Prices* (1941); Meyer Jacobstein and H. G. Moulton, *Effects of the Defense Program on Prices, Wages and Profits* (1941); F. C. Mills, *Prices in a War Economy* (1942); *National Product: War and Prewar* (1944) and *National Product in Wartime* (1945); W. L. Crum, J. H. Fennelly, and L. H. Seltzer, *Fiscal Planning for Total War* (1942). On economic warfare, consult Antonin Basch, *The New Economic Warfare* (1941); R. W. B. Clarke, *Britain's Blockade* (1940); Paul Emzig, *Economic Warfare, 1939–40* (1940); D. L. Gordon and Royden Dangerfield, *Hidden Weapon* (1947); C. L. Leith, J. W. Furness, and Cleona Lewis, *World Minerals and World Peace* (1943); and T. Reveille, *Spoil of Europe: The Nazi Technique in Political and Economic Conquest* (1941). On American labor and agriculture in wartime the best works are Aaron Levenstein, *Labor Today and Tomorrow* (1945); S. T. Willmans and Herbert Harris, *Trends in Collective Bargaining* (1945); W. W. Wilcox, *The Farmer in the Second World War* (1947).

CHAPTER 20

The Truman Legacy

The literature of American history after 1945 is often too close to journalism. Reliable bibliography is difficult to compile and students should thus proceed with caution in using the materials cited hereafter.

For estimates of the Truman administration see M. B. Schnapper (ed.), *The Truman Program* (1949), a collection of Truman's speeches; Jonathan Daniels, *The Man of Independence* (1950), the most perceptive of the biographies of Truman to date; R. S. Allen and W. V. Shannon, *The Truman Merry-Go-Round* (1950) and G. E. Allen, *Presidents Who Have Known Me* (1950), both of which emphasize the sensational; A. M. Smith, *Thank You, Mr. President* (1946), good on the early Truman. Two aspects of the 1948 election are treated in V. O. Key, Jr., *Southern Politics in State and Nation* (1949) and Lindsay Rogers, *The Pollsters* (1949). Eric Goldman, *The Crucial Decade* (1956) is a general account from a liberal point of view. *Truman Speaks* (1960) is the President's own view of his office. Truman's *Memoirs* (2 vols., 1955) are invaluable.

On labor, see Alcine Austin, *The Labor Story, A Popular History of American Labor, 1786–1949* (1949), thin; Henry Millis and E. C. Brown, *From the Wagner Act to Taft-Hartley: A Study of National Labor Policy and Labor Relations* (1950); C. O. Gregory, *Labor and the Law* (rev. ed., 1949); C. E. Warne, K. W. Lumpkin and others, *Labor in Post-War America* (1949); Harold Metz, *Labor Policy of the Federal Government* (1945); F. H. Harrison and R. Dubin, *Patterns of Union Management Relations* (1947); L. Howe and A. Widick, *The U.A.W. and Walter Reuther* (1949); D. I. Ash and George Rifkin, *The Taft-Hartley Law* (1947); and C. A. Madison, *American Labor Leaders: The Personalities and Forces in the Labor Movement* (1950), pen portraits of sixteen labor leaders. On the veteran, consult C. G. Botte, *The New Veteran* (1946); R. S. Martin, *The Best Is None Too Good* (1948); J. H. Miller and J. S. Allen, *Veterans Challenge the Colleges* (1947); G. K. Pratt, *Soldier to Civilian* (1944); and H. A. Wallace, *Sixty Million Jobs* (1945). On civil rights, read *To Secure These Rights: Report of the President's Committee on Civil Rights* (1949); Ellis Arnall, *The Shore Dimly Seen* (1946); Hodding Carter, *Southern Legacy* (1950); Milton Konvitz, *The Constitution and Civil Rights* (1947). On debt and inflation there is a constantly growing literature. Much of the writing on these problems is to be found in the files of the *New York Times*, the *Nation*, *Fortune*, *Harpers*, and the

Atlantic. See also Freda Utley, *The High Cost of Vengeance: How Our German Policy Is Leading Us to Bankruptcy and War* (1949); B. M. Anderson, *Economics and the Public Welfare: Financial and Economic History of the United States, 1914–1946* (1949); Seymour Harris (ed.), *Economic Reconstruction* (1945); C. C. Abbott, *Financing Business During......the Transition* (1946); B. M. Baruch and J. M. Hancock, *Report on War and Post War Adjustment Policies;* Board of Governors of Federal Reserve System, *Public Finance and Full Employment* (1945); J. M. Clark, *Demobilization of Wartime Economic Controls* (1944); M. G. de Chazeau, A. G. Hart, G. C. Means, and others, *Jobs and Markets* (1946); H. M. Groves, *Postwar Taxation and Economic Progress* (1946); C. B. Hoover, *International Trade and Domestic Employment* (1945); C. O. Hardy, *Prices, Wages, and Unemployment* (1946); A. D. H. Kaplan, *Liquidation of War Production* (1945); H. G. Moulton and K. T. Schlotterbeck, *Collapse or Boom at the End of the War* (1942); T. W. Schultz, *Agriculture in an Unstable Economy* (1945); J. H. Williams, *Postwar Monetary Plans and Other Essays* (1945); Twentieth Century Fund, *America's Needs and Resources* (1947); B. M. Anderson, J. M. Clark, and others, *Financing American Prosperity* (1946); Simon Kuznets, *National Income* (1946); and H. C. Murphy, *The National Debt in War and Transition* (1950). On Communism, see N. Weyl, *The Story of Disloyalty and Betrayal in American History* (1950); G. Marion, *The Communist Trials* (1949); I. Howe and L. Coser, *The American Communist Party* (1957).

THE UNITED STATES AND THE UNITED NATIONS. For a brief survey, read Arne Sigrid, *United Nations Primer* (1945). The case for world organization is ably presented by Crane Brinton, *From Many One: The Process of Political Integration and the Problem of World Government* (1948). F. A. Cave and others, *The Origins and Consequences of World War II* (1948) is rich in material on the United Nations. For background, see W. L. Willkie, *One World* (1943); H. A. Wallace, *The Century of the Common Man* (1943); J. C. Campbell and others, *The United States in World Affairs, 1945–1947* (1947); K. W. Colgrove, *The American Senate and World Peace* (1944); Emery Reves, *Anatomy of Peace* (1946); United States Department of State, Publications no. 2353, *The Charter of the United Nations* (1945) and no. 2774, *The Making of the Peace Treaties* (1947); E. S. Corwin, *The Constitution and World Organization* (1944); Norman Cousins, *Modern Man Is Obsolete* (1945); R. J. S. Hoffman, *Durable Peace: A Study in American National Policy* (1944); and J. B. Whitton (ed.), *The Second Chance: America and the Peace* (1944). There is also valuable material in Cordell Hull, *The Memoirs of Cordell Hull*, cited earlier. On the structure and operation of the United Nations, consult L. M. Goodrich, and Edvard Hambro, *Charter of the United Nations, Commentary and Documents* (1946); Tom Galt, *How the United Nations Works* (1947); Louis Dolevit, *The United Nations, A Handbook of the New World Organization* (1946); *The United Nations at Work; Basic Documents* (1947); Julian Huxley, *UNESCO: Its Purpose and Philosophy* (1948); Herman Finer, *The United Nations Economic and Social Council* (1946); Clair Wilcox, *A Charter for World Trade* (1949); V. M. Dean, *The Four Cornerstones of Peace* (1946); and P. W. Bidwell, *The United States and the United Nations* (1943).

THE UNITED STATES AND A DIVIDED WORLD. Dexter Perkins, *The Evolution of Domestic Foreign Policy* (1948) is an excellent survey, and Norman A. Graebner, *The New Isolationism: A Study in Politics and Foreign Policy Since 1950* (1956) is of interest. See also G. A. Almond, *The American People and Foreign Policy* (1950); J. C. Campbell and others, *The United States in World Affairs, 1945–1947* (1947) and *The United States in World Affairs, 1948–1949* (1949); E. A. Speiser, *The United States and the Near East* (1947); J. K. Fairbanks, *The United States and China* (1948); Crane Brinton, *The United States and Britain* (rev. ed., 1948); A. P. Whitaker, *The United States and South America, The Northern Republics* (1948); Carlos Davila, *We of the Americas* (1949); L. M. Goodrich and M. J. Carroll, *Documents on American Foreign Relations* (1945); K. S. Latourette, *The*

United States Moves Across the Pacific (1946); H. J. Van Mook, *The Stakes of Democracy in Southeast Asia* (1950); William Reitzel, *The Mediterranean: Its Role in American Foreign Policy* (1948); W. B. Wilcox and R. B. Hall, *The United States in the Postwar World* (1947); H. J. Morgenthau, *Politics among Nations, the Struggle for Power and Peace* (1948); and Leland Stowe, *While Time Remains* (1946).

On the wartime trials and the occupation of Germany, consult R. H. Jackson, *The Case Against the Nazi War Criminals* (1946) and *The Nuremberg Case* (1947); Sheldon Glueck, *The Nuremberg Trials and Aggressive War* (1946); and Alexander Mitrokerich and Fred Miceke, *Doctors of Infamy, the Story of the Nazi Medical Crimes* (1949). On military occupation, see W. Friedmann, *The Allied Military Government of Germany* (1947); Harold Zink, *American Military Government in Germany* (1947); and C. J. Friedrich and others, *American Experiences in Military Government in World War II* (1948). The literature on atomic energy in a divided world grows larger. A few of the more important nontechnical works are D. V. Bradley, *No Place to Hide* (1948), on the Bikini experiments; P. W. S. Blackett, *Fear, War and the Bomb; Military and Political Consequences of Atomic Energy* (1949), a criticism of American policy by a British scientist; Sir Gerald Dickens, *Bombing and Strategy: The Fallacy of Total War* (1947); Bernard Brodie (ed.), *The Absolute Weapon: Atomic Power and World Order* (1946); J. E. Johnsen, *The Atomic Bomb* (1946); Dexter Masters and Katherine Way (eds.), *One World or None* (1946); Norman Cousins, *Modern Man Is Obsolete* (1945); J. W. Campbell, *The Atomic Story* (1947); John Hersey, *Hiroshima* (1946); and W. L. Laurence, *Dawn Over Zero* (1946).

On Russia and the cold war, consult E. D. Carman, *Soviet Imperialism: Russia's Drive Toward World Dominion* (1950); Robert Stransz-Hupe and S. T. Possomy, *International Relations in the Age of Conflict between Democracy and Dictatorship* (1950); J. R. Deane, *The Strange Alliance* (1946); Barbara Ward, *The West at Bay* (1948); V. M. Dean, *The United States and Russia* (1947); W. H. Chamberlain, *The European Cockpit* (1947); J. F. Dulles, *War or Peace* (1950); Walter Lippmann, *The Cold War* (1947); Max Lerner, *World of the Great Powers* (1947); Lester Markel and others, *Public Opinion and Foreign Policy* (1948); E. A. Mourer, *The Nightmare of American Foreign Policy* (1948), highly critical; G. H. Stuart, *The Department of State* (1949), an able study; J. R. Deane and others, *Negotiating with the Russians* (1951); Felix Morley, *The Foreign Policy of the United States* (1951); G. F. Kennan, *American Diplomacy, 1900–1950* (1951); E. M. Zacharias, *Behind Closed Doors: The Secret History of the Cold War* (1950); W. B. Ziff, *Two Worlds* (1946); H. S. Commager (ed.), *America in Perspective: The United States through Foreign Eyes* (1947); Martin Ebon, *World Communism Today* (1948); and W. C. Bullitt, *The Great Globe Itself* (1946), very critical of Russia. For post-Yalta, see J. F. Byrnes, *Speaking Frankly* (1947), which contains information on both Yalta and Potsdam; W. B. Smith, *My Three Years in Moscow* (1949); and Lucius Clay, *Decision in Germany* (1950); Sumner Welles, *Where Are We Heading?* (1946) and B. G. Ivanyi and A. Bell, *Route to Potsdam* (1945) cover the Potsdam agreement. Marina Salvin, *The North Atlantic Pact* (1950) and H. L. Hoskins, *Atlantic Pact* (1949) describe briefly an agency of the expanding policy of containment.

KOREA AND THE DOMESTIC SCENE. The best general account of the country is McCune, *Korea Today* (1950) and an appraisal of the conflict without benefit of perspective is E. J. Kahn, Jr., *The Peculiar War* (1951). The recall of General MacArthur provoked a rash of books of which the best are John Gunther, *The Riddle of MacArthur* (1950) and R. H. Rovere and A. M. Schlesinger, Jr., *The General and the President* (1951).

A well-reasoned criticism of the methods employed by some officials in their attack on Communism is revealed in Francis Biddle, *The Fear of Freedom* (1951). A less reliable account is Owen Lattimore, *Ordeal by Slander* (1950). See also

Alistair Cooke, *A Generation on Trial* (1950), an excellent study of the Chambers-Hiss affair by an Englishman. Read too Earl Jowett, *The Strange Case of Alger Hiss* (1953), a controversial study of the controversial case by a British Labourite jurist. Counter with R. de Toledano and V. Lasky, *Seeds of Treason* (1950). Chambers' own account can be found in *Witness* (1952), and Hiss' reply in *In the Court of Public Opinion* (1957). The literature by former Communists is very large. The most welcomed assessment was Granville Hicks, *Where We Came Out* (1954).

CHAPTER 21
America at Bay

There are no extensive general studies of American life after 1950. Two short essays, however, are Herbert Agar, *The Price of Power: America Since 1945* (1957) and Eric Goldman, *The Crucial Decade* (1956). Consult also: Richard Rovere, *Affairs of State, The Eisenhower Years* (1956); R. J. Donovan, *Eisenhower, The Inside Story* (1956); and M. J. Pusey, *Eisenhower the President* (1956). William Reitzel and others, *United States Foreign Policy, 1945-1955* (1956) concentrates on international politics.

Important figures in American politics after 1950 are discussed in several works. Kevin McCann, *The Man From Abilene* (1952), a campaign biography, and Marquis Childs, *Captive Hero* (1958) are on Eisenhower. Adlai Stevenson is glamorized in N. F. Busch, *Adlai Stevenson of Illinois* (1952); his 1952 campaign speeches can be found in *Major Campaign Speeches* (1952). Senator Robert A. Taft wrote *A Foreign Policy for Americans* (1951) and is the subject of W. S. White, *The Taft Story* (1954). There are several works on Senator Joseph R. McCarthy: J. Anderson and R. W. May, *McCarthy: The Man, The Senator, the "Ism"* (1952); J. Rorty and M. Decter, *McCarthy and the Communists* (1954); and Richard Rovere, *Senator Joe McCarthy* (1959) can be consulted, along with McCarthy's *McCarthyism* (1952).

Party politics can be found in all the above books, but also see: Samuel Lubell, *The Future of American Politics* (1952; rev. 1956) and *Revolt of the Moderates* (1956); L. Harris, *Is There a Republican Majority?* (1954); A. Larson, *A Republican Looks at His Party* (1956); Dean Acheson, *A Democrat Looks at His Party* (1955); and D. Bell, ed., *The New American Right* (1955). See also L. W. Koenig, ed., *The Truman Administration* (1956), a post-mortem.

Recent, and varied, reappraisals of the period of World War II include: R. Young, *Congressional Politics in the Second World War* (1955); W. L. Langer and S. E. Gleason, *The Challenge to Isolation, 1937-1940* (1952) and *The Undeclared War* (1953); W. S. Cole, *America First* (1953); J. K. Galbraith, *Theory of Price Control* (1952); S. E. Morison, *Strategy and Compromise* (1958), an essay on wartime strategy; Chester Wilmot, *Struggle For Europe* (1952); H. Feis, *Churchill, Roosevelt, Stalin* (1957); Arthur Vandenberg, Jr., *The Private Papers of Senator Vandenberg* (1952); C. C. Tansill, *Backdoor to War* (1952); W. H. McNeil, *America, Britain and Russia, 1941-1946* (1953); J. Snell, ed., *The Meaning of Yalta* (1956); and R. F. Fenno, Jr., ed., *The Yalta Conference* (1955).

Domestic problems at the end of the Truman era and under Eisenhower are the subject of many works. General economic tendencies are covered in G. Colm, *The American Economy in 1960* (1952); J. F. Dewhurst and associates, *America's Needs and Resources* (rev. ed., 1955); Rockefeller Bros. Fund, *The Challenge to America* (1958); T. C. Cochran, *The American Business System, A Historical Perspective, 1900-1955* (1957); A. F. Burns, *Prosperity Without Inflation* (1957); *Economic Reports of the President* (1947 to date); W. N. Peach and W. Krause,

Basic Data of the American Economy (1955); P. F. Drucker, *America's Next Twenty Years* (1957); J. K. Galbraith, *American Capitalism* (1952) and *The Affluent Society* (1958); and G. A. Steiner, *The Government's Role in Economic Life* (1953). Crime and corruption are dealt with in B. Bolles, *How to Get Rich in Washington* (1952); E. Kefauver, *Crime in America* (1951); P. H. Douglas, *Ethics in Government* (1952); and G. A. Graham, *Morality in American Politics* (1952). E. R. Bartley, *The Tidelands Oil Controversy* (1953) covers a much debated issue. Recent labor history is the subject of J. Seidman, *American Labor from Defense to Reconversion* (1953). The steady flow of literature on civil rights and civil liberties includes: A. Barth, *The Loyalty of Free Men* (1951); C. Wilcox, ed., *Civil Liberties Under Attack* (1951); C. H. Pritchett, *Civil Liberties and the Vinson Court* (1954); S. Hook, *Heresy, Yes—Conspiracy, No* (1953); N. Weyl, *The Battle Against Disloyalty* (1951); W. Gellhorn, *The States and Subversion* (1952); R. K. Carr, *The House Committee on Un-American Activities* (1952); J. W. Caughey, *In Clear and Present Danger* (1958); M. Straight, *Trial by Television* (1954), on the McCarthy-Army dispute; J. L. O'Brian, *National Security and Individual Freedom* (1955); C. P. Curtis, *The Oppenheimer Case* (1955); M. R. Konvitz, *Bill of Rights Reader* (1954); M. Berger, *Equality by Statute* (1952); and J. B. Martin, *The Deep South Says "Never"* (1958).

Korean and Far Eastern policies have been argued in E. O. Reischauer, *Wanted: An Asian Policy* (1955) and *The United States and Japan* (rev. ed., 1957); H. Feis, *The China Tangle* (1953); J. C. Caldwell and L. Frost, *The Korea Story* (1952); C. Berger, *The Korea Knot, A Military-Political History* (1957); Department of the Army, *Korea—1950* (1952); M. W. Cagle and F. A. Manson, *The Sea War in Korea* (1957); C. Whitney, *MacArthur: His Rendezvous With History* (1955); McGeorge Bundy, ed., *Pattern of Responsibility* (1952), an analysis of Acheson's policies; and G. Fitch, *Formosa Beachhead* (1953), a rare defense of Chiang Kai-shek.

Middle and Near Eastern Affairs have recent students in: J. C. Hurewitz, *Middle East Dilemmas* (1953); R. N. Frye, *The Near East and the Great Powers* (1951); G. Lenczowski, *The Middle East in World Affairs* (1952); L. V. Thomas and R. N. Frye, *The United States and Turkey and Iran* (1951); and W. Z. Laqueur, *Communism and Nationalism in the Middle East* (1957). Russo-American relations enter the above books but are central in the following: Council on Foreign Relations, *The United States in World Affairs* (a series of surveys); H. A. Kissinger, *Nuclear Weapons and Foreign Policy* (1957), essential to the major issue of balanced armaments; and H. L. Roberts, *Russia and America: Dangers and Prospects* (1956).

CHAPTER 22

A New American Culture

During the last quarter of a century several attempts have been made to take inventory of American culture in the machine age. As a consequence there is a considerable body of literature that merits serious consideration. For background, see Crane Brinton, *Ideas and Men: The Story of Western Thought* (1950); Van Wyck Brooks, *The Confident Years: 1885–1915* (1952), which recreates a generation of vigor, vitality, and variety; H. S. Commager, *The American Mind* (1950), which is concerned with American character and deals with such items as literature, journalism, philosophy, religion, sociology, economics, history, politics, law and architecture; Denis Brogan, *The American Character* (1944), a penetrating analysis of American life and institutions by an Englishman; H. J. Laski, *The American Democracy* (1948), by an Englishman well acquainted with America, who condemns its materialism and intolerance; Lloyd Morris, *Postscript to Yesterday; America: The Last Fifty Years* (1947), excellent on society, literature, and philosophy of the last half-century, and his *Not So Long Ago* (1949), which describes social changes with emphasis on the role of automobile, radio, and movies; John Gunther, *Inside U. S. A.* (rev., 1951), a detailed, journalistic account that emphasizes the war years; Max Lerner, *America as a Civilization* (1957) is sprawling and Pollyanna-ish. For a social anthropologist's ideas of what is fundamentally American, see Margaret Mead, *Male and Female* (1949) and *And Keep Your Power Dry* (1943). Other works are C. A. and M. R. Beard, *America in Midpassage*, cited earlier; Mark Sullivan, *Our Times: The United States, 1900–1925*, Vol. VI; P. W. Slosson, *The Great Crusade and After, 1914–1928*, and Dixon Wecter, *The Age of the Great Depression, 1929–1941*, volumes in The History of American Life series, previously cited; H. B. Parkes, *The American Experience: An Interpretation of the History and Civilization of the American People* (1947), scholarly; D. L. Cohn, *Combustion on Wheels, An Informal History of the Automobile Age* (1944), for popular consumption; J. W. Chase (ed.), *Years of the Modern: An American Appraisal* (1949), a symposium contrasting the security of average American of the midtwentieth century with that of average American of 1900; R. Chase, *The Democratic Vista* (1958), a sober assessment in dialogue form.

THE STANDARDIZATION OF AMERICAN LIFE. Much of the material bearing on this topic is to be found in the works listed above. Others that will be of outstanding value are R. S. and H. M. Lynd, *Middletown* (1929) and *Middletown in Transition* (1937); E. H. Gruening (ed.), *These United States* (2 vols., 1923–4); H. E. Stearns (ed.), *Civilization in the United States, An Inquiry by Thirty Americans* (1922), and *America Now* (1938); J. T. Adams, *Our Business Civilization*, cited earlier; Walter Johnson, *William Allen White's America* (1947); C. B. Davis, *The Age of Indiscretion* (1950); Laurence Greene, *The Era of Wonderful Nonsense* (1939); President's Research Committee on Social Trends, *Recent Social Trends in the United States*, cited previously; J. C. Ransom, F. L. Owsley and others, *I'll Take My Stand* (1930); Caroline Ware, *Greenwich Village, 1920–30* (1935); F. L. Allen, *Only Yesterday* and *Since Yesterday*, cited before; Anna de Koven, *Women in Cycles of Culture* (1941); Alfred Bingham, *Insurgent America* (1935); Franz Alexander, *Our Age of Unreason* (rev. ed., 1951); T. H. Greer, *American Social Reform Movements: Their Patterns Since 1865* (1949); Ernie Pyle, *Home Country* (1947); and a series of articles "Recent Social Trends," *American Journal of Sociology*, Vol. LXVII (May, 1942). As contributions to the standardization of American life the automobile, airplane, movie, radio and television are important. On the automobile, see R. C. Epstein, *The Automobile Industry* (1928); E. D. Kennedy, *The Automobile Industry: The Coming of Age of Capitalism's Favorite Child* (1941), which is very good; C. B. Glasscock, *The Gasoline Age, the Story of the Men Who Made It* (1937); H. L. Barber, *Story of the Automobile* (1917); and C. L. Dearing, *American Highway Policy* (1941). On aviation, see "Fleet Birds of a Feather," *Fortune* (May, 1933), pp. 23 ff.; Henry A. Bruno, *Wings over America* (1942); W. F. Ogburn, *Social Effects of Aviation* (1946). There is also material in J. H. Frederick, *Commercial Air Transportation* (rev. ed., 1951). On communications, consult Paul Schubert, *The Electric Word: The Rise of Radio* (1928); A. E. Krows, *The Talkies* (1930); A. F. Harlow, *Old Wires and New Waves* (1936); Hadley Cantril and G. W. Allport, *The Psychology of Radio* (1935); H. S. Hettinger, "New Horizons in Radio," *Annals of the American Academy of Political and Social Science*, Vol. CCXIII (1941); Llewellyn White, *The American Radio* (1947); A. N. Goldsmith and H. A. Lescarboura, *This Thing Called Broadcasting* (1930); K. S. Tyler, *Modern Radio* (1944); P. F. Lazarsfeld, *People Look at Radio* (1946) and *Radio and the Printed Page* (1940); and Hadley Cantril, *The Invasion from Mars* (1940), which deals with radio-generated mass hysteria. On the movies the best works are M. D. Haettig, *Economic Control of the Motion Picture Industry* (1944); Deems Taylor, M. Peterson, and B. Hale, *A*

Pictorial History of the Movies (1943); Margaret Thorp, *America at the Movies* (1939); W. M. Seabury, *The Public and the Motion Picture Industry* (1926); L. C. Rosten, *Hollywood: The Movie Colony, The Movie Makers* (1941) amusing; Lewis Jacobs, *The Rise of the American Film* (1939); Gilbert Seldes, *The Seven Lively Arts* (1924), *The Great Audience* (1950), and *The Public Arts* (1956); N. Leites and M. Wolfenstein, *Movies* (1950); H. Powdermaker, *Hollywood: The Dream Factory* (1950); R. A. Inglis, *Freedom of the Movies* (1947); and Edgar Dale, *The Content of Motion Pictures* (1935). For movie censorship, see R. G. Moley, *The Hays Office* (1945). Another valuable work on standardization of American life is Roger Burlingame, *Engines of Democracy: Inventions and Society in Mature America* (1940). Newspapers, periodicals, and books are another medium of standardization. See Commission on Freedom of the Press, *A Free and Responsible Press: A General Report on Mass Communication: Newspapers, Radio, Motion Pictures, Magazines, and Books* (1947); R. W. Jones, *Journalism in the United States* (1947), which stresses the social-economic background of press; and F. L. Mott, *American Journalism: A History of Newspapers in the United States through 260 years: 1690 to 1950* (rev. ed., 1950), a good survey. Mott is also the authority on magazine literature; see his *A History of American Magazines*, Vols. III–IV. It may be supplemented by Coulton Waugh, *The Comics* (1947). On books, see R. L. Duffus, *Our Starving Libraries* (1933), which discusses the impact of hard times; O. H. Cheney, *Economic Survey of the Book Industry, 1930–1931* (1931); Jacob Loft, *The Printing Trades* (1944), which emphasizes labor; Douglas Waples and R. W. Tyler, *What People Want to Read About* (1931); and A. P. Hackett, *Fifty Years of Best Sellers, 1895–1945* (1945).

Literature of Protest and Affirmation. In addition to the references listed for this chapter the following are most important: H. E. Luccock, *American Mirror: Social, Ethical and Religious Aspects of American Literature, 1930–1940* (1940); Granville Hicks, *The Great Tradition* (rev. ed., 1935); Maxwell Geismar, *Writers in Crisis* (1942) and *The Last of the Provincials* (1947); J. W. Beach, *American Fiction, 1920–1940* (1941); and W. M. Frohock, *The Novel of Violence in America, 1920–1950* (1950). The character of the literature of protest and affirmation can perhaps be best understood by reading it, rather than reading about it. Recommended in this respect are writings of F. Scott Fitzgerald, *Tender is the Night* (1934), *The Last Tycoon* (1941), and *The Crack Up* (1945). More outspoken are Theodore Dreiser, *Tragic America* (1931), *The Bulwark* (1946), and *The Stoic* (1947); James T. Farrell, *Studs Lonigan* (1935); John Dos Passos, *U. S. A.* (1937); Thomas Wolfe, *Of Time and the River* (1935) and *The Web and the Rock* (1939); John Steinbeck, *The Grapes of Wrath* (1939); and Erskine Caldwell, *Tobacco Road* (1932). See also J. W. Aldridge, *After the Lost Generation* (1951).

The Arts. O. W. Larkin, *Art and Life in America* (1949) has an excellent bibliography. Good for background is F. P. Keppel and R. L. Duffus, *The Arts in American Life* (1933). Jacob Baker, *Government Aid During the Depression to Professional, Technical and Other Service Workers* (1936) and Grace Overmyer, *Government and the Arts* (1939) are informative. See also Martha Cheney, *Modern Art in America* (1939); H. Cahill and A. H. Barr (eds.), *Art in America in Modern Times* (1935); and Augustus St. Gaudens, *The American Artist and His Times* (1941). On painting and sculpture, see Sheldon Cheney, *The Story of Modern Art* (1941); Peyton Boswell, Jr., *Modern American Painting* (1940), an excellent text; C. B. Ely, *The Modern Tendency in American Painting* (1925); Frederick Wight, *Milestones of American Painting in our Century* (1949); Samuel Kootz, *Modern American Painters* (1930); Robert Henri, *The Art Spirit* (1923); The Museum of Modern Art Catalogue, *New Horizons in American Art* (1936), which shows the best work done under the W.P.A.; Lorado Taft, *The History of American Sculpture* (rev. ed., 1924); A. V. Adams, *The Spirit of American Sculpture* (1923); and most important of all Joseph Hudnut, *Modern Sculpture* (1929).

There is much valuable material in George Biddle, *An American Artist's Story* (1939), autobiography of the father of federal art program; T. H. Benton, *An Artist in America* (1937); Rockwell Kent, *This Is My Own* (1940); H. A. Read, *Robert Henri* (1931); Elisabeth Cary, *George Luks* (1931); G. P. DuBois, *William J. Glackens* (1931); Royal Cortissoz, *Guy Pène DuBois* (1931); and Constance Rourke, *Charles Sheeler* (1938). On music, see C. Reis, *Composers in America* (1938); J. T. Howard's detailed and authoritative *Our American Music* (3rd ed., 1946); Aaron Copland, *Our New Music* (1941); Isaac Goldberg, *Tin Pan Alley* (1930); Herbert Graf, *The Opera and Its Future in America* (1941); Lazare Saminsky, *Music of Our Day* (rev. ed., 1939); and D. G. Mason, *The Dilemma of American Music* (1928). For popular music, consult S. W. Finkelstein, *Jazz: A People's Music* (1948); H. O. Osgood, *So This is Jazz* (1926); W. Sargeant, *Jazz Hot and Hybrid* (1939); and Gilbert Seldes, *The Seven Lively Arts*, cited above. For biographic material, see J. T. Howard, *Our Contemporary Composers* (1941). On architecture, see John McAndrew, *Guide to Modern Architecture, Northeast States* (1940) and Elizabeth Mock (ed.), *Built in U. S. A., 1932–1944* (1944); Talbot Hamlin, *Architecture, An Art for All Men* (1947); F. L. Wright, *Modern Architecture* (1931); T. E. Tallmadge, *The Story of Architecture in America* (1927); S. Fiske Kimball, *American Architecture* (1928); G. H. Edgell, *The American Architecture of Today* (1928); and W. A. Starrett, *Skyscrapers and the Men Who Build Them* (1928). Extremely useful also are R. A. Cram, *My Life in Architecture* (1936), by an exponent of Gothic; F. L. Wright, *An Autobiography* (1932), by a champion of the modern; and L. H. Sullivan, *The Autobiography of An Idea* (1924), which emphasizes the relation of architecture to society.

SCIENCE, RELIGION AND EDUCATION. For general introductions to physical science in the machine age, read S. M. and L. F. Rosen, *Technology and Society* (1941) and Lewis Mumford, *Technics and Civilization* (1934). These may well be followed by Bernard Jaffe's useful study, *Men of Science in America: the Role of Science in the Growth of Our Country* (1944); James Stokley, *Science Remakes Our World* (1946); Harold Ward (ed.), *New Worlds in Science* (1941); J. E. Thornton, *Science and Social Change* (1939); National Resources Committee, *Technological Trends and National Policy* (1937) and *Energy Resources and National Policy* (1939); and Bernard Jaffe, *Outposts of Science* (1935). On particular subjects, see R. T. Young, *Biology in America* (1922); G. W. Gray, *New World Pictures* (1936), an introduction to physics and astronomy; E. P. Hubble, *The Observational Approach to Cosmology* (1937); H. B. Lemon, *From Galileo to Cosmic Rays* (1934); G. R. Harrison, *Atoms in Action* (1939); A. K. Solomon, *Why Smash Atoms?* (1940); R. A. Millikan, *Electrons (+ and −), Protons, Photons, Neutrons, Mesotrons and Cosmic Rays* (rev. ed., 1947), somewhat technical, and his *Autobiography* (1950); Richard Goldschmidt, *Ascaris* (1937), a summary of basic knowledge in biology; T. H. Morgan, *The Scientific Basis of Evolution* (2nd ed., 1935); W. B. Cannon, *The Wisdom of the Body* (rev. ed., 1939), physiologic advances; E. E. Freudenthal, *Flight into History: The Wright Brothers and the Air Age* (1949); Henry Borsook, *Vitamins* (1940); William S. Haynes, *Men, Money and Molecules* (1936); Wheeler McMillen, *New Riches from the Soil* (1946); and L. I. Dublin, "Science in Modern Industry," *Annals of the American Academy of Political and Social Science*, Vol. CXIX (1925). For the advances in medicine, see Paul de Kruif, *The Fight for Life* (1938), which is somewhat emotional; Harold Ward (ed.), *New Worlds in Medicine* (1946); B. J. Stern, *Society and Medical Progress* (1941) and *American Medical Practice in the Perspectives of a Century* (1945), both concerned with social implications; M. M. Davis, *America Organizes Medicine* (1941); H. E. Sigerest, *Medicine and Human Welfare* (1941); G. W. Gray, *The Advancing Front of Medicine* (1941); R. H. Shryock, *The Development of Modern Medicine* (1947); and James Rorty, *American Medicine Mobilizes* (1939), which describes clash between American Medical Association and sponsors of the Wagner health bill of 1938. Biographic material of importance is to be found in Helen Clapesattle, *The Doctors Mayo* (1941) and S. R. and F. T. Flexner, *William Henry Welch and the Heroic Age of American Medicine* (1941). On medical care, see Hugh Cabot, *The Doctor's Bill* (1935).

The social sciences await a comprehensive study. H. S. Commager's *The American Mind*, already cited, will prove most helpful. See also H. E. Barnes, *The New History and the Social Studies* (1925) and, M. G. White, *Social Thought in America* (1949). For economic thought, consult P. T. Homan, *Contemporary Economic Thought* (1928); Joseph Dorfman, *The Economic Mind in American Civilization*, Vols. III and IV, cited above; H. W. Odum (ed.), *American Masters of Social Science* (1927); W. T. Hutchinson (ed.), *Essays in American Historiography* (1937); G. A. Lundberg and others, *Trends in American Sociology* (1929); H. E. Barnes and Howard Becker, *Social Thought from Lore to Science* (1938); C. H. Page, *Class and American Sociology* (1940); and F. N. House, *The Development of Sociology* (1936). Three autobiographic accounts will also prove helpful: E. A. Ross, *Seventy Years of It* (1936); R. T. Ely, *Ground Under Our Feet* (1938); and J. R. Commons, *Myself* (1934). The religious situation in the machine age is discussed by H. S. Commager, *The American Mind*, cited earlier. See also H. K. Rowe, *The History of Religion in the United States* (1924), the concluding chapter; T. C. Hall, *The Religious Background of American Culture* (1930); A. B. Bass, *Protestantism in the United States* (1929), an inventory; W. A. Brown, *The Church in America; A Study of the Present Condition and Future Prospects of American Protestantism* (1922); H. P. Douglass, *The Church in the Changing City* (1927); H. P. Douglass and E. deS. Brunner, *The Protestant Church as a Social Institution* (1935); H. W. Schneider, *Religion in Twentieth Century America* (1952); W. Herberg, *Protestant, Catholic, Jew* (1955); J. A. Ryan, *Seven Troubled Years, 1930-1936* (1937), the situation as seen by a liberal Catholic; and Marcus Bach, *They Have Found a Faith* (1946), which describes the cultists. Some of the religious spokesmen as well as others expressed concern about the weakening of family ties and the changing mores of youth. On this topic there is helpful material in E. R. Groves and W. F. Ogburn, *American Marriage and Family Relationships* (1928); A. G. Spencer, *The Family and Its Members* (1923); Elizabeth Benson, *The Younger Generation* (1927); Miriam Van Waters, *Parents on Probation* (1927) and *Our Changing Morality* (1928); and B. B. Lindsey, *The Revolt of Modern Youth* (1925). Of the extensive literature on education the following can be recommended: I. L. Kandel (ed.), *Twenty-Five Years of American Education* (1924) and E. W. Knight, *Education in the United States* (rev. ed., 1941); and A. E. Meyer, *The Development of Education in the Twentieth Century* (1939). Sanford Winston, *Illiteracy in the United States* (1930) is illuminating. It may be supplemented with John Dewey, *Democracy and Education* (1916); M. E. Curti, *The Social Ideas of American Educators* (1935); R. B. Raup, *Education and Organized Interests* (1936); W. S. Deffenbaugh, *Recent Movements in City School Systems* (1927); T. H. Briggs, *The Junior High School* (1920); H. B. Bruner, *The Junior High School at Work* (1925); and National Education Association, *Education and Economic Well-being in American Democracy* (1940). On higher education, consult D. A. Robertson and E. R. Holme (eds.), *American Universities and Colleges* (1928). Thorstein Veblen, *The Higher Learning in America* (1918); R. M. Hutchins, *The Higher Learning in America* (1936); M. Smith, *The Diminished Mind* (1954); A. Bestor, *Academic Wastelands* (1953) and *The Restoration of American Learning* (1954); and J. E. Kirkpatrick, *The American College and Its Rulers* (1926) are all highly critical. Specific reforms in curricula may be reviewed in R. F. Butts, *The College Charts Its Course* (1939); Alexander Meiklejohn, *Freedom and the College* (1923); R. C. Brooks, *Reading for Honors at Swarthmore* (1927); Frank Aydelotte, *Honors Courses in American Colleges and Universities* (1924); Jacques Barzun and H. R. Steeves (eds.), *A College Program in Action* (1944), a description of educational programs in Columbia College; *Edu-*

cation in a Free Society (1945) the famous Harvard Report; C. H. Faust (ed.), *The College at Chicago* (1949); and the Report of the President's Commission. Upton Sinclair, *The Goose Step* (1923) deals with academic freedom. See also R. H. Edwards, J. M. Artman, and G. M. Fisher, *Undergraduates: A Study of Morale in Twenty-three American Colleges and Universities* (1928); F. P. Keppel, *The Undergraduate and His College* (1917), sound advice by a great dean of an undergraduate college; Percy Marks, *Which Way Parnassus* (1926); J. A. Benn, *Columbus Undergraduate* (1928); R. L. Duffus, *Democracy Enters College* (1936); J. A. Hawes, *Twenty Years Among the Twenty Year Olds* (1929); R. S. Lynd, *Knowledge for What? The Place of the Social Science in American Culture* (1939); J. U. Nef, *The United States and Civilization* (1942); and E. V. Hollis, *Philanthropic Foundations and Higher Education* (1938) discuss important items. On education for adults there is valuable material in L. E. Reber, *University Extension in the United States* (1914); Dorothy Rowden, *Two Handbooks on Adult Education* (1934, 1936); M. A. Cartwright, *Ten Years of Adult Education* (1935); and R. A. Beals and Leon Brody (comp.), *The Literature of Adult Education* (1941). There is a useful, brief account of education in the three volumes of the History of American Life series that spans the greater part of the first half of the twentieth century: H. U. Faulkner, *The Quest for Social Justice, 1898–1914*; P. W. Slosson, *The Great Crusade and After, 1914–1928* and Dixon Wecter, *The Age of the Great Depression, 1929–1941*, all previously cited.

LEISURE AND RECREATION. The best historical treatment is F. R. Dulles, *America Learns to Play; A History of Popular Recreation, 1607–1940* (1940). Valuable also are J. F. Steiner, *Americans at Play* (1933); B. Rosenberg and D. M. White, *Mass Culture* (1958); Gove Hambidge, *Time to Live* (1933); on the use of leisure time; R. B. Weaver, *Amusements and Sports in American Life* (1939); M. M. Willey and S. A. Rice, *Communication Agencies and Social Life* (1933), on touring, pleasure travel, and related matters; R. Cummings (ed.), *Dictionary of Sports* (1949); D. Houlgate, *The Football Thesaurus* (1946); R. M. Smith, *Baseball: A Historical Narrative* (1947); E. A. Rice, *A Brief History of Physical Education* (1926); A. M. Weyand, *American Football* (1926), historical; L. F. Harmer, *Public Recreation: A Study of Parks, Playgrounds and Other Outdoor Recreation Facilities* (1928); L. H. Weir (ed.), *Parks, A Manual of Municipal and County Parks* (2 vols., 1928); and National Recreation Association, *Park Recreation Areas in the United States: 1940* (1940).

INDEX

A Note on the Type

THE TEXT of this book was set on the Linotype in Janson, a recutting made direct from the type cast from matrices long thought to have been made by Anton Janson, a Dutchman who was a practising type-founder in Leipzig during the years 1668–1687. However, it has been conclusively demonstrated that these types are actually the work of Nicholas Kis (1650–1702), a Hungarian who learned his trade most probably from the master Dutch type-founder Dirk Voskens.

The type is an excellent example of the influential and sturdy Dutch types that prevailed in England prior to the development by William Caslon (1692–1766) of his own incomparable designs, which he evolved from these Dutch faces. The Dutch in their turn had been influenced by Claude Garamond (1510–1561) in France. The general tone of the Janson, however, is darker than Garamond and has a sturdiness and substance quite different from its predecessors. It is a highly legible type, and its individual letters have a pleasing variety of design. Its heavy and light strokes make it sharp and clear, and the full-page effect is characterful and harmonious.

Composed, printed, and bound by THE PLIMPTON PRESS, Norwood, Massachusetts. Paper manufactured by S. D. WARREN COMPANY, Boston. Typography and binding design by VINCENT TORRE.

THE DIVIDED

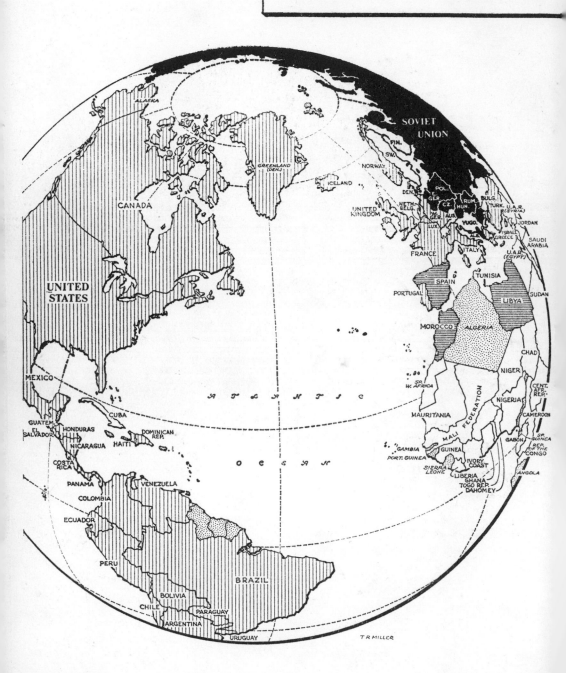

ALASKA

GREENLAND
(DEN.)

CANADA

ICELAND

UNITED
KINGDOM

NORWAY

SOVIET
UNION

FIN.

SW.

DEN.
NETH.
BELG.
W.
GER.
LUX.

E.
GER.

POL.
CZ.
AUS.
HUN.

RUM.
YUGO.

BULG.
TURK.

U.A.R.
(SYRIA)

JORDAN

ISRAEL
GREECE

SAUDI
ARABIA

UNITED
STATES

FRANCE

ITALY

PORTUGAL

SPAIN

TUNISIA

U.A.R.
(EGYPT)

MOROCCO

ALGERIA

LIBYA

SUDAN

MEXICO

CUBA

GUATEM.
EL
SALVADOR

HONDURAS

NICARAGUA

HAITI

DOMINICAN
REP.

SP.
W. AFRICA

MAURITANIA

MALI FEDERATION

NIGER

CHAD

NIGERIA

CENT.
AFR.
REP.

CAMEROON

COSTA
RICA

PANAMA

COLOMBIA

VENEZUELA

GAMBIA

PORT. GUINEA

GUINEA

SIERRA
LEONE

IVORY
COAST

LIBERIA

GHANA
TOGO REP.
DAHOMEY

GABON

SP. GUINEA

REP.
OF THE
CONGO

ANGOLA

ECUADOR

PERU

BOLIVIA

BRAZIL

CHILE

PARAGUAY

ARGENTINA

URUGUAY

A T L A N T I C

O C E A N

T.R. MILLER